7|19

Passio Christi ab Alberto Durer Nu

renbergensi effigiata cũ varij generis carmi
nibus Fratris Beñedicti Chelidonij
Musophili.

O mihi tantorum. iusto mihi causa dolorum
O crucis O mortis causa cruenta mihi.
O homo sat fuerit. tibi me semel ista tulisse.
O cessa culpis me cruciare nouis.

Cum priuilegio.

The Faith

A HISTORY OF CHRISTIANITY

BRIAN MOYNAHAN

DOUBLEDAY

New York   London   Toronto   Sydney   Auckland

For

Con and Katie

PUBLISHED BY DOUBLEDAY
a division of Random House, Inc.
1540 Broadway, New York, New York 10036

DOUBLEDAY and the portrayal of an anchor with a dolphin are registered trademarks
of Doubleday, a division of Random House, Inc.

Book design by Donna Sinisgalli
Photo research by Deirdre O'Day

Library of Congress Cataloging-in-Publication Data
Moynahan, Brian, 1941–
    The faith: a history of Christianity / Brian Moynahan.—1st ed.
        p. cm.
    Includes bibliographical references and index.
    1. Church history.   I. Title
    BR145.2 .M69 2002
    270—dc21   2001037242

ISBN 0-385-49114-X
Copyright © 2002 Brian Moynahan
All Rights Reserved

PRINTED IN THE UNITED STATES OF AMERICA

April 2002
First Edition

10   9   8   7   6   5   4   3   2   1

CONTENTS

Introduction   *vii*

I   The Cross   1

II   The Master Builder: Paul   22

III   The Third Race: Early Writing and Worship   44

IV   The Blood of Martyrs   69

V   "Conquer by this": Constantine   89

VI   Heretics   110

VII   "Through them the world is kept in being": Monks   129

VIII   The Transpierced Heart: Augustine   144

IX   Lost Atlantis: The Islamic Invasions   156

X   "A slave in Christ for foreign people":
The Pagan Conversions   191

XI   "A carnage of pagans": Crusades   222

XII   "Act with a kindly harshness": The Laws of War   240

XIII   "O fire of love": Manifestations of the Spirit   265

XIV   "If golde ruste, what should iren do?": Early Reformers   295

XV   "Something that appeals to the eye": Papal Attitudes   324

XVI   "By faith alone": Printing and Protestants   340

XVII   The Word of God: The Bible as Lethal Weapon   354

XVIII   "Keep watch over the lives of everyone . . .": Calvin and the
Puritans   370

XIX   "The prince's wrath means death": English Speakers   398

XX   Roman Soldiers: Counter-Reformation   415

XXI   "Art thou become quite other than thyself, so cruel?": The
        Spanish Inquisition   432

XXII   "Rather a country ruined than a country damned . . .":
        The Wars of Religion   455

XXIII   God's Charnel House: The Witch-Finders   479

XXIV   "I the voice of Christ in the desert of this island":
        The Americas   504

XXV   "A desert-dweller in pursuit of wild beasts":
        The Jesuits in Paraguay   525

XXVI   "The attractive African meteor": The Slave Trade   537

XXVII   "Rock, rock, oh when will thou open, rock?":
        Eastern Missions   553

XXVIII "The Lord make it like New England":
        Protestant America   568

XXIX   "The melancholy wastes of woe": Revolutions   593

XXX   "American Zion": Mormons   610

XXXI   "Drawing the eye-tooth of the tiger": Missions   629

XXXII   The Descent of Man: Darwin   651

XXXIII "The godless rulers of darkness": Totalitarians   663

XXXIV   "I have a dream": Liberation Theology   694

XXXV   Charisma   712

        Notes   731
        Select Bibliography   761
        Picture Credits   768
        Index   769

INTRODUCTION

Over the past two thousand years, a handful of vulnerable and persecuted Christians—"they were crucified or set on fire," the historian Tacitus wrote of them in Nero's Rome, "so that when darkness came they burned like torches in the night"—has grown to become the world's greatest congregation, embracing almost two billion souls.

This book is an attempt to trace the outlines of the extraordinary journey that Christianity has made since the Cross.

It is a story of fierce and incomparable scope. Christianity has inspired the noblest and most searching minds. It has produced martyrs whose sufferings have emulated Christ's own Passion. It created the first orders of men and women devoted to the sick and vulnerable, the first hospitals and lazar houses. The cathedrals, paintings, music, and sculpture produced by its believers are among the most sublime artifacts on earth. The great universities, of the New World and the Old, are Christian foundations.

It has also given succor to the censor, the inquisitor, the slaver, and the witchfinder. It was used to underpin conquest and empire. The burning alive of heretics was for several centuries another characteristic.

There is something of the wolf to the religion that adores the Lamb, and the characters to be found in these pages mirror every condition of humanity. There are crusaders and pacifists, mystics, hermits, jolly friars and joyless puritans, polygamists, flagellants, missionaries both sensitive and crass, misogynists, heroines, bigots, popes, emperors, and the frankly deranged.

They appear on every continent. Christianity has been a global enterprise since St. Paul insisted that it must evangelize the Gentiles. Long before the Puritans sailed to settle in the Americas, there were Christians in India and China and at the court of the Mongol Khan.

The faith has survived many catastrophes, the loss of old heartlands to Islam, self-inflicted wars of religion, and, more recently, assaults by Soviet and Maoist

The mocking of Christ from a sixteenth-century Calvary in Brittany in France. Jesus had predicted that he would be "mocked, and shamefully entreated, and spat upon" in Jerusalem. This fulfilled the prophecy in Isaiah of a Messiah who was "despised, and rejected of men." He was "a man of sorrows . . . wounded for our transgressions . . . bruised for our iniquities" who at his death bore "the sins of many, and made intercession for the transgressors . . ."

Communists. "Christianity is like a nail," Yemelian Yaroslavsky, chairman of Stalin's League of the Militant Godless, complained. "The harder you strike it, the deeper it goes." Islamic fundamentalists would do well to reflect on that.

It is expanding briskly in Asia and Africa. Converts in China number in the scores of millions, proof that, as Tertullian observed eighteen hundred years ago, "the blood of martyrs is the seed of the church." Seven in ten Americans continue to believe that Jesus is the Son of God. Only in Europe and in the surviving Christian pockets in the Middle East does the faith seem to be in decline.

It is, of course, impossible to do justice to a subject so immense in sweep and so subtle in detail. I hope, however, to have caught some essence of the faith, its restlessness and experimentation, its cruelties and kindnesses, and the way in which—by citing the inspiration of grace or the Holy Spirit—individuals have so often claimed it for their own.

the FAITH

❖

CHAPTER I

The cross

li, Eli, lama sabachthani?" cried the dying man. "My God, my God, why hast thou forsaken me?" (Matt. 27:46). This forlorn reproach was delivered from a hillside on the periphery of the Roman Empire, in a strange tongue unknown to the vast majority of its subjects, by a condemned man of profound obscurity who had an alien belief in a single God. A darkening sky; a claim that the veil in the Temple of Solomon, far down the slope from the execution ground, was "rent in twain" at the moment of death; a strange earthquake, mentioned only in Matthew's gospel, that split open rocks and opened tombs but did no damage to buildings—the Father's response to the crucifixion of the Son was modest even in the Gospels that proclaimed it.

Human reaction was as muted. The Roman governor who had authorized the execution—with such extreme reluctance that some Christians later honored his memory with a feast day—marveled only that Jesus had died so swiftly, in little more than three hours. To the soldiers who carried it out, the crucifixion was mere routine, a standard punishment for slaves and non-Romans, that ended in the traditional perk of sharing out the victim's clothes. The priests who had demanded the death noted with sarcastic satisfaction: "he saved others, himself he cannot save" (Matt. 27:42). No disciple or relative was bold enough to claim the body for burial. He had been almost recklessly brave at his trial; they had expected miracles at his death, and none had occurred. They hid their ebbing belief behind barred doors in the steep streets of Jerusalem.

The painters and sculptors who were to fill the world with his image worked from imagination alone. No physical description of Jesus was left by any who knew him; no hint existed of the color of the eyes, the timbre of the voice, the carriage of the head. His age, and the year of his birth and death, is not accurately recorded. The abbot Dionysius Exiguus, who created our system of dating years from the conception of Christ, as anno Domini, the year of the Lord, made his calculations five hundred years later. The abbot estimated that Jesus was born in the year 753 A.U.C. of the Roman system of dating *ab urbe condita,* "from the founding of the city" of Rome. He set this as A.D. 1, with previous years in receding order as "before Christ," B.C. or A.C. for *ante Christum* in Latin. But Matthew's gospel says that Jesus was "born in Bethlehem . . . in the days of Herod the King." Herod is known to have died in 4 B.C., and most modern scholars date Jesus' birth to 6 or 5 B.C.* The dates of his brief ministry—John's gospel supports a ministry of two or three years, the others of a single year—and his final journey to Jerusalem are also uncertain. The crucifixion may have been as early as A.D. 27, instead of the traditional date of A.D. 33; it is certain only that he died on a Friday in the Jewish lunar month of Nisan, which straddles March and April.

A single incident is known of his childhood; as a twelve-year-old, he went missing on a visit from his native town of Nazareth to Jerusalem until his parents found him in the temple, "sitting in the midst of the doctors both hearing them and asking questions" (Luke 2:46). He may—or may not—have worked as a carpenter in his youth. His public ministry probably lasted little more than two years at most and seemed fragile and incomplete. His teaching was informal, often in the open air; his message was literally hearsay, for no contemporary notes were written down. It demanded an absolute morality and selflessness never expressed before; it lacked the familiar comfort of an established rite, and he had taught only a single prayer, the brief formula beginning "Our Father, which art in heaven . . ."

He never formally stated that he was the "Son of God," an imperial title claimed in Latin as *divi filius* by the Roman emperor. He described himself as "the Son" indirectly and in John's gospel alone: "Say ye of him, whom the Father sanctified and sent into the world, Thou blasphemest; because I said, I am the Son of God?" (John 10:36). The Hebrew title of Messiah, or Christos in Greek, was equally regal; it meant "anointed" and was used of kings whose investiture was marked by anointing with oil. Jesus refused to directly claim divinity as Christ when he was asked during his trial: "Tell us whether thou be the Christ, the Son of God." "Thou hast said," he replied (Matt. 26:63–64). His miraculous birth— the impregnation of his virgin mother by God's Holy Spirit—is mentioned in only two Gospels. He himself made no specific reference to it.

---

*Luke's gospel, however, refers to the birth taking place at the time of the census "made when Quirinius was governor of Syria" (Luke 2:2), which is thought to have taken place in A.D. 7. Most scholars discount this. A crucifixion date of Friday, April 7, A.D. 30, is perhaps the strongest contender. Dates at the time of Jesus were normally given in terms of the reign of a ruler; thus Jesus was baptized "in the fifteenth year of the reign of Tiberius Caesar." Other systems of dating included the four-year cycle of Greek olympiads from 776 B.C.; or, as used by Jews until the fifteenth century A.D., from the occupation of Babylon by the Seleucids in 312 B.C. The use of A.D. did not become widespread until the eighth century. The Spanish and Portuguese continued to date by the Era of the Caesars until the fifteenth century.

At the moment of its extinction, it was inconceivable that his brief life—and terrible but commonplace death—would inspire a faith of immense power and complexity; that his simple prayer would be repeated in the very crannies of the earth; that his name and the cross itself, the ancient instrument of his suffering, would become universal symbols, of love and redemption and, at times, of bigotry and terror.

The faith did not begin to flow until the third day after death, until the Resurrection.

❖ JESUS HAD SET out from Galilee on his final journey in the late winter, meandering southwards toward Jerusalem. His reputation as a miracle worker—healing the sick, paralytics, and the blind, raising the dead, exorcising demons, turning water into wine, transforming a few loaves and fishes into food for a multitude—was growing but still largely confined to the towns and fishing villages round the Sea of Galilee. His life was centered in this backward area, the northernmost region of ancient Israel, its lake set deep beneath mountains in a great rift running to Africa, seven hundred feet below sea level. It was a turbulent place, known for its extremists and their apocalyptic visions. "Can any good thing come out of Nazareth?" a potential follower said doubtfully when he was told where Jesus had grown up (John 1:46). He had few convinced followers, with a core of only a dozen apostles; they were men of little apparent distinction, and he himself was the son of a carpenter.

The message of gentleness and humility he brought—"love thine enemies and pray for them that persecute thee"—was at odds with the cruel and imperial spirit of the age. Herod the Great, king of Judea, had ordered the massacre of all male infants in Bethlehem shortly after Jesus was born in the city. Whether this claim in Matthew's gospel was true or not, it was said with reason to be "better to be Herod's pig than Herod's son"; from his deathbed, having already murdered two of his sons, the king had commanded a third to be put to death. Herod ruled by the grace and favor of Roman masters, at the height of their power and majesty. Their empire embraced the Mediterranean world; its frontiers ran for ten thousand miles, enclosing eighty million people. To the north and west, it traversed Europe to the coasts of the Atlantic and the North Sea. In the east, it lapped as far as the Syrian and Arabian deserts; a century before, the great soldier Pompey had entered Rome in triumph after his conquest of Jerusalem and the Jews.

To the south, in Egypt, a quarter of a millennium of rule by the Hellenistic Ptolemies had ended within living memory with the suicide of Cleopatra. The rich granaries of the Nile and the great city of Alexandria had fallen to Rome; the empire continued westward along the African coastal strip past Carthage until, after a gap for the Mauritanian desert, it again reached the Atlantic at the edge of the known world. The first Roman emperor, Augustus, had been deified on his death and the eighth month was named for him. His spirit was seen to ascend to heaven from the flames of his funeral pyre, or so it was said; the Roman Senate had declared him immortal and appointed priests to conduct the sacred rites of his cult. Jesus had been born in the reign of Augustus; he was now the subject of Tiberius, the second emperor, the son of a god.

This insignificant young Jew was nevertheless proclaimed by his followers as the *Masiah,* Hebrew for the "Lord's anointed." As Messiah, he was seen in the light of generations of Jewish expectation and prophecy, which applied to the nature of his imminent death as well as to his life. The Jews dated their special relationship with God from the days of Abraham, some two thousand years before, when the Lord had told the patriarch that he would "multiply thy seed as the stars of heaven and . . . in thy seed shall all the nations of the earth be blessed, because thou has obeyed my voice" (Gen. 22:17–18). Prophecies of the coming of a Messiah went back for more than a millennium, when God had promised King David that he would "establish the throne of his kingdom for ever" (2 Sam. 7:13) under his descendants. Messianic writings were a constant theme in the Psalms and the Prophets; the "Coming One" was expected to be "of the line of David" and would be granted "dominion, and glory, and a kingdom that all the peoples, nations and languages should serve him" (Dan. 7:14). The vision was often martial, of a leader who would defeat the enemies of Israel; hopes of such divine intervention, to expel the Romans, ran high as Jesus neared Jerusalem.

He was not the figure of the unwritten New Testament; he was seen by the eager crowds as the culmination of the Old, a living Messiah fulfilling ancient expectations. "Behold, we go up to Jerusalem," he told his disciples, "and all the things that are written by the prophets shall be accomplished unto the Son of Man" (Luke 18:31). Those things were far from glorious or martial; he predicted that he would die violently in the city, having first been publicly whipped and mocked. A purely spiritual Messiah who mirrored this death had been prophesied by Isaiah in about 735 B.C. This redeemer was to be a suffering servant of humanity, atoning for their sins. His birth would be miraculous, for "a virgin shall conceive, and bear a son, and shall call his name Immanuel" (Isaiah 7:14).* His life would be short and his end violent. "He was despised, and rejected of men; a man of sorrows," the book of Isaiah says of him. "He was wounded for our transgres-

---

*Jesus is referred to as Immanuel, meaning "God with us," in the Gospels; the name Jesus comes from *yesua,* a Hebrew derivative of "God saves." The parallel of the Virgin Birth is particularly stressed in Matthew, where it is stated that it occurred with Jesus that "it might be fulfilled which was spoken by the Lord through the prophet" (Matt. 1:22). Matthew also works its way through forty-two generations to prove that Jesus was indeed "the son of David, the son of Abraham."

sions, he was bruised for our iniquities: . . . and with his stripes we are healed. . . . He was oppressed, yet he humbled himself and opened not his mouth, as a lamb that is led to the slaughter. . . . By oppression and judgement he was taken away . . . and they made his grave with the wicked although he had done no violence, neither was there any deceit in his mouth" (Isaiah 53:3–9). As he died, he bore "the sins of many, and made intercession for the transgressors. . . ."

❖ WARNINGS OF SUCH a fate were clear throughout the final journey. A group of Pharisees, strict Orthodox Jews, approached Jesus and told him that Herod Antipas "would fain kill thee" (Luke 13:31). It was a real threat; Herod Antipas, a surviving son of Herod the Great, was a known killer of prophets. He had recently disposed of John the Baptist, a troublesome man in a homemade shift of camel hair strapped by a leather belt, who had preached the coming of the Messiah and had described the political establishment of Pharisees and Sadducee priests and aristocrats as a "brood of vipers." He lived on locusts and wild honey, the food of the deprived; he described himself as "the voice of one crying in the wilderness," but the poor had listened to his unsettling message. John had baptized Jesus in the river Jordan; as he did so, he saw the Holy Spirit descend on Jesus in the form of a dove, and declared Jesus to be "the Lamb of God, which taketh away the sins of the world" (John 1:29). He had also denounced Herod's marriage to his niece Herodias, for which Herod had him decapitated in the fortress of Machaerus near the Dead Sea, and presented his head on a salver to Salome, the daughter of his new wife.

Jesus asked the Pharisees to tell "that fox," Herod, that the threat of death would not deflect him. He also revealed the place where he would die. "I must go on my way today and tomorrow and the day following," he said. "For it cannot be that a prophet perish out of Jerusalem. O Jerusalem, Jerusalem, which killeth the prophets, and stoneth them that are sent unto her!" (Luke 13:33–34). He cured a man of dropsy on the Sabbath, a provocation to orthodox Pharisees for whom it was strictly a day of rest. He preached to all—"he who hath ears to hear, let him hear"—and the Pharisees murmured angrily that the crowds who pressed close to hear him were full of "all the publicans and sinners"; marginals, the discontented, the "publicans," tax collectors who sat in roadside stalls to levy tolls from travelers for Herod and the Romans.

His message was inflammatory and disturbing for those in power: the exalted were humbled, the humble exalted; the mark of the blessed was to share with the "poor, the maimed, the lame, the blind"; the beggar Lazarus lay in life at the gate of the rich man, fed with crumbs, dogs licking his sores, but in heaven he nestled in the bosom of Abraham while the rich man pleaded with him from hell to "dip the tip of his fingers in water, and cool my tongue, for I am in anguish in this flame" (Luke 16:19–24). In Jericho, Jesus lodged in the house of a chief tax collector, Zacchaeus, a man so despised in the town that he was obliged to quieten a grumbling mob by promising to repay fourfold any he had defrauded. By now the travelers were accompanied by "great multitudes," so thick that Zacchaeus had been obliged to climb a tree to watch them arrive; the miraculous cure of a blind man added to the fervor of the onlookers. Jesus, however, predicted no triumph when they reached Jerusalem; instead he had hinted at how he would die. "Whosoever doth not bear his own cross, and come after me," he preached, "cannot be my disciple" (Luke 14:27).

❖ THE DISCIPLES "PERCEIVED not the things that were said." They were exhilarated to arrive at the Mount of Olives, the moist and fertile ridge that overlooked Jerusalem across the Kidron Valley. Jesus bade them go to a nearby village, where "ye shall find a colt tied, whereon no man ever yet sat: loose him, and bring him" (Luke 19:30). They found the animal; it fulfilled another prophecy, that of Zechariah, who had lived 550 years before. "Shout, O daughter of Jerusalem," the book of Zechariah foretold. "Behold, thy king cometh unto thee; he is just, and having salvation; lowly, and riding upon an ass, even upon a colt the foal of an ass." The prophet had predicted, too, the nature of this new king and the spread of his power; "he shall speak peace unto the nations, and his dominion shall be from sea to sea, and from the River to the ends of the earth" (Zech. 9:9–10).

They were thus in a state of high excitement as Jesus rode down the Mount of Olives and across the stony valley and the brook at its foot, spreading their clothes in front of the ass. He was greeted with cries of *"Hosanna,"* the Hebrew cry for divine mercy, "Save us, we pray." Pharisees, mingling with the crowds of well-wishers, bade Jesus rebuke them for this near blasphemy. "I tell you," he replied, "that if these shall hold their peace, the stones will cry out."

The city was dominated from this approach by the gleaming stone of the temple complex built recently by Herod the Great. Solomon had built the first Jerusalem temple almost a thousand years before. A courtyard where sacrifices were made surrounded a vestibule and a "holy place" where priestly rites took place before an altar made of gold and a table bearing the Bread of the Presence offered to the Lord, twelve loaves freshly baked each Sabbath. At the heart of the temple was the "holy of holies," protected by the temple veil, a multicolored curtain of fine linen. It could be entered only by the high priest and only on the Day of Atonement, Yom Kippur, a day of solemn fast and sacrifice. This sanctuary housed the ark of the covenant, the symbol of the presence of God, a chest of acacia wood overlaid with gold and decorative cherubims, and covered by the mercy seat, a rectangular slab of pure gold. Rings of gold were fastened to each foot of the ark, so that it could be carried away in flight like a litter.

The temple was a reminder of the precariousness of the Jews, their exiles and enslavements, their sense of apocalypse. It had been burned to the ground in 586 B.C., when Jerusalem fell to Nebuchadnezzar and the Jews suffered their Babylonian exile; the sacred treasures were looted and the Bible makes no further mention of the ark. A second temple was built some sixty years later. It weathered fresh conquerors—Alexander the Great, the Seleucid and Ptolemaic empires, Parthians, Romans—until its ambitious reconstruction by Herod. The Temple Mount on which it stood was built up with excavated earth retained by high walls of hewn stone. The perimeter was lined with colonnades. Inside were a series of courts. The largest was the Court of the Gentiles, into which non-Jews could enter, though an inscription warned them that the penalty for proceeding further was death. This gave on to the Court of Women and the Court of Israelites, the limits of entry for Jewish women and laymen. The Court of Priests surrounded the temple proper, a massive and ornate building of white stone.

Jesus arrived a few days before Passover, the spring festival celebrating the delivery of the Israelites from Egyptian bondage at the time of Moses. The crush of pilgrims in the city had transformed the Court of the Gentiles into a thriving marketplace. Stallholders sold wine and oil, and doves, lambs, and cattle to be sacrificed on the altar. Relatives of Caiaphas, the reigning high priest, held the lucrative dove-selling concession. Money changers exchanged coins from different mints into the Tyrian coinage accepted by the temple treasury as offerings and for the annual half-shekel temple tax.

At once, in a public display of contempt, Jesus "began to cast out them that sold and them that bought . . . and overthrew the tables of the money changers, and the seats of them that sold doves" (Mark 11:15). His action extended beyond the tradesmen to those entrusted as guardians of the temple, the Sadducee priests, allies of the Herodian and Roman rulers. "It is written, And my house shall be a house of prayer," Jesus said, "but ye have made it a den of robbers" (Luke 19:45–46). The insult directly challenged the Sadducee claim to be spiritual stewards of Israel. The establishment, the "chief priests and the scribes and the principle men," were alarmed as well as aggrieved by the Galilean. Public sympathy was running dangerously in his favor, for "all the people hung upon him, listening" (Luke 19:47–48). Evidence was needed before a charge of sedition could be brought against him in front of the Roman authorities. He was watched carefully and spies were infiltrated into the crowds "that they might take hold of his speech, so as to deliver him up to the rule and to the authority of the governor" (Luke 20:20).

"Tell us, by what authority doest thou these things?" he was asked by the Sadducees. "Or who is he that gave thee this authority?" To claim power from God could be construed as blasphemy, so Jesus used the rabbinical device of replying with another question. "The baptism of John," he asked, "was it from heaven, or from men?" Since John the Baptist had included the Sadducees in his "brood of vipers," they could hardly credit his baptism to God. But neither could they ascribe the baptism to ordinary mortals; if they did so, they realized, "all the people will stone us, for they be persuaded that John was a prophet" (John 20:6).

A similar attempt was made to tempt him into treason. "Is it lawful for us to give tribute unto Caesar, or not?" they asked. Luke, in his Gospel, says that Jesus "perceived their craftiness"; any Roman subject was aware that a negative reply would prompt an instant death sentence. Jesus asked for a "penny," a denarius, a coin of three to four grams of silver, inscribed "Tiberius Caesar son of the divine Augustus" and bearing his profile. "Whose image and superscription hath it?" Jesus asked. "Caesar's," they replied. "Then render unto Caesar the things that are Caesar's, and unto God the things that are God's," he said (Luke 20:22–25). It was a political statement of great significance, permitting rulers, including future Caesars themselves, to declare faith in Jesus to be the official religion of their states, without compromising their own political supremacy. For the moment it showed that Jesus was not subverting imperial government.

He was, however, openly seditious in his attacks on the religious establishment. He urged his disciples—"and in the hearing of all the people"—to beware of the Sadducees, hypocrites who "desire to walk in long robes, and love salutations in the marketplaces and chief seats in the synagogue," and who "devour widows' houses" in their greed and their exploitation of the poor. "For a pretence" they might "make long prayers," but in the next life they would suffer the "greater condemnation" (Luke 20:46–47). He stressed that his mission was for the poor and humble. He pointed to a woman who followed some rich men to make a donation to the temple treasury, offering a two-mite piece, one of the smallest copper coins in circulation. "This poor widow cast in more than they all," he said. "For all these did of their superfluity cast in unto the gifts, but she of her want did cast in all the living that she had" (Luke 21:3–4).

❖ AN INNOCENT REMARK from one of his listeners on the splendor of the temple—"how it was adorned with goodly stones and offerings"—drew a response. "The days will come," Jesus replied, "in which there shall not be left here one stone upon another that shall not be thrown down." He predicted war, earthquake, famine, and plague amid "terrors and great signs from heaven." He told his followers that they faced persecution and prison; "ye shall be hated of all men for my sake," he said, reassuring them that "in your patience ye shall win your souls." Jerusalem itself faced days of vengeance, he said, when it would be surrounded by armies and be "trodden down of the Gentiles," its people put to the sword and "let captive unto all the nations"; men would faint for fear before looking up to "see the Son of man coming in a cloud with power and great glory" as their redemption drew close. "Heaven and earth shall pass away," Jesus said of his ministry on earth, "but my words shall not pass away" (Luke 21:5–33 passim).

The Sadducees, naturally unaware of the virtual annihilation they would suffer when these events indeed took place forty years later, seized on the prediction of the destruction of the temple, the house of God, as legal evidence of Jesus' blasphemy. "The chief priests and the scribes sought how they might put him to death," Luke stated, "for they feared the people" (Luke 22:2).

It was difficult to arrest him without inciting riots. Each day he taught publicly in the temple, withdrawing at night to lodge in safety on the Mount of Olives; "and all the people came early in the morning to hear him" (Luke 21:37–38). In order to seize him "in the absence of the multitude," it would be necessary for his private program to be betrayed. Judas Iscariot was the treasurer of the group, who carried the bag of money used to buy supplies and provide donations for the poor. He was, according to John's gospel, a thief who "having the bag took away what was put therein" (John 12:6). Judas now slipped away and "communed with the chief priests and captains" on terms of betrayal. He agreed to deliver Jesus to them for thirty pieces of silver, probably Tyrian shekels, the coins used in the temple treasury. A shekel was worth four drachma; a drachma contained about 0.1 ounces of silver and was equivalent to a laborer's daily wage. Thus, Judas sold Jesus for the equivalent of four months' pay for a workingman.

That evening, Jesus ate a last supper with his disciples in the city. He did not reveal where it was to be; a man carrying a pitcher of water led them to a house belonging to a sympathizer, where a large upper room had been set aside for the meal. "With desire I have desired," Jesus said, "to eat this Passover with you before I suffer." In the traditional meal, a year-old male lamb without blemish was slaughtered at dusk and its blood smeared on the doorposts and lintel of the house; it was roasted without breaking its bones, and eaten with unleavened bread and bitter herbs. The Gospels make only a passing reference to Jesus "sitting at meat" with the twelve disciples. They speak of the bread and wine, in words now armored by time and faith but used soon enough to condemn Christians for cannibalism. Jesus took the unleavened Passover bread and broke it, and gave it to the disciples, saying: "Take, eat, this is my body, which is given for you: do this in remembrance of me." Then he took a cup of wine and gave it to them: "Drink ye all of it, for this is my blood of the covenant, which is shed for many unto a remission of sins" (Matt. 26:27–28). After the meal, all except Judas crossed the valley below the city to the foot of the Mount of Olives. Jesus prayed in a garden called Gethsemane, after the Aramaic word for the oil press located there, perhaps in a small grotto whose cool temperature was suited to pressing olives. "My soul is exceeding sorrowful, even unto death," he said. His ministry was about to end, in apparent failure; one of his few disciples had betrayed him and another, Peter, the rock on whom he had talked of building his church, would deny him three times before the dawn cock crowed.

Judas crossed the valley with the chief priests' men, lighting their way with lanterns and armed with swords and staves. "Behold, the hour is at hand, and the Son of man is betrayed into the hands of sinners," Jesus said. He spoke to Judas as he came up to him: "Friend," he said, "do that for which thou art come." Judas kissed him to identify him to the guards. There was a brief skirmish, during which one of the disciples—Peter, according to John's gospel—drew his sword and cut off the right ear of one of the guards. "Put up again thy sword into its place," Jesus told him. "For all they that take the sword shall perish with the sword" (Matt. 26–52). Jesus was bound and led off in the predawn to the house of Caiaphas, an experienced administrator appointed high priest by the Romans in A.D. 18. Peter followed at a distance.

The Kiss of Judas, caught by a medieval stonemason decorating the church at St. Gilles du Gard in Provence, France. Heretics were often compared to Judas, since their doctrines were said to be equivalent to a betrayal of Christ, and this was reflected in the terrible punishments later inflicted on them.

A session of the Sanhedrin, the central judicial authority for the Jews, was convened to meet in the house at Friday daybreak. Before then, Peter sat at a fire in the courtyard of the house; three different people asked him if he knew the accused. As he denied it for the third time, a cock crowed and he went away in tears. The guards amused themselves by blindfolding Jesus, hitting him, and asking, "Prophesy, who is he that struck thee?" (Luke 22:64. Matthew says that this happened at the end of the trial). The members of the Sanhedrin were drawn from leading Sadducees and Pharisees; seventy of them assembled with Caiaphas presiding. A number of witnesses gave evidence, the most damning coming from the last two, who referred to Jesus' speech on the temple. They quoted him as saying: "I am able to destroy the temple of God, and to build it in three days" (Matt. 26:61).

"Answereth thou nothing?" Caiaphas asked. Jesus remained silent.

Caiaphas pressed on with the charge of blasphemy. "I adjure thee by the living God," he demanded, "that thou tell us whether thou be the Christ, the Son of God."

"If I tell you, ye will not believe; and if I ask you, ye will not answer," Jesus replied, but he added: "From henceforth shall the Son of man be seated at the right hand of the power of God." It was enough. Caiaphas tore his own robes, a traditional sign of grief at proof of the guilt of an accused. "He hath spoken blasphemy," he told the court. "What further need have we of witnesses?" (Matt. 26:65). He asked what sentence should be passed. "He is worthy of death" was the reply.

Under Roman rule, the Sanhedrin could impose a death penalty only with the agreement of the Roman governor, who was able to halt proceedings at any time on his own initiative, and only soldiers under his command could carry out the sentence. Jesus was thus taken in front of Pontius Pilate, the fifth Roman to govern Judea since its conquest by Pompey. Pilate was a hard-minded man; Judea was an important posting, for it acted as a buffer between marauding Parthians and the granaries of Egypt, and its governor was expected to deal ruthlessly with any signs of rebellion by its turbulent people. The Romans allowed the Jews considerable religious freedom, accepting their refusal to worship the emperor, a capital offense elsewhere, and allowing the Sanhedrin to arbitrate on Jewish religious affairs in Judea; but Pilate had offended their sensibilities by bringing into the city military insignia and shields with the name and image of the emperor Tiberius on them, thus defiling the temple in orthodox eyes. He had also financed the building of an aqueduct with money confiscated from the temple treasury, and had set troops in plain clothes to stab and club demonstrators in the protests that followed. He was little loved. Luke's gospel speaks of "the Galileans whose blood Pilate had mingled with their sacrifice" (Luke 13:1), probably during such a melee; Pilate's contemporary, Philo, a Jewish philosopher from Alexandria, wrote of his "venality, his violence, his thefts, his abusive behavior, his frequent executions of untried prisoners and his endless savage ferocity."[1]

He proved, however, unwilling to have Jesus put to death. The prisoner was led to his palace; the chief priests and other accusers remained outside, lest they defile themselves by entering a place with images of the pagan emperor. From here, they told Pilate that Jesus was "perverting our nation, and forbidding to give tribute to Caesar, and saying that he himself is Christ, a king." There was no evidence of revolt to justify the first claim; that Pilate ignored the second charge, the most serious in Roman eyes, suggests that he knew it to be false. The third seems merely to have amused him.

"Art thou the King of the Jews?" he asked. Jesus responded with his own question: "Sayest thou this of thyself, or did others tell it thee concerning me?"

"Am I a Jew?" the Roman responded. "Thine own nation and the chief priests delivered thee unto me. What hast thou done?"

Jesus replied that, if his kingdom had been of this world, his followers would have fought to prevent his trial; "but now is my kingdom not from hence." Pilate again asked him if he were a king. "To this end have I been born, and to this end am I come into the world," Jesus explained of his mission, "that I should bear witness unto the truth."

"What is truth?" Pilate said to him (John 18:33–38).

The remark was ironic, not accusatory. Pilate followed it by going outside to tell the Sanhedrin members that: "I find no fault in this man" (Luke 23:4). This made the accusers "the more urgent"; they said that Jesus was stirring up the people throughout all Judea, "beginning from Galilee." Luke's gospel claims that Pilate seized on the mention of Galilee to refer the case to Herod. As a Galilean, Jesus came under the jurisdiction of Herod, who was in Jerusalem for the Passover. Herod had faced serious unrest after the beheading of John the Baptist, and he had no desire to become involved in the Jesus affair. When the prisoner was sent to him, he and his soldiers "mocked him, and arraying him in gorgeous apparel sent him back to Pilate" (Luke 23:11). The other Gospels make no mention of Herod, but they detail a further attempt by Pilate to spare Jesus.

It was a custom for the governor to release a prisoner in celebration of the Passover. "Will ye that I release unto you the king of the Jews?" he asked. The crowd shouted for him to release a "notorious prisoner" named Barabbas. As to Jesus, they "cried out exceedingly, 'Let him be crucified'" (Matt. 27:22). Those words are important; they are identical in Matthew (Matt. 27:22) and Mark (Mark 15:14); in Luke they are "they shouted, saying, 'Crucify, crucify him'" (Luke 23:21) and in John: "they cried out, saying 'Crucify him, crucify him'" (John 19:6). In Matthew, Pilate then washed his hands—a Jewish ritual of purification, not a Roman custom—and then said, "I am innocent of the blood of this righteous man: see ye to it" (Matt. 27:24). At this, "all the people answered and said, his blood be on us, and on our children" (Matt. 27:25). The cries of "crucify him" and the supposed admission of blood guilt were to echo down the centuries in Christian violence against Jews.

Pilate then had Jesus scourged with whips; the soldiers plaited a crown from the leaves and thorns of the *akanthos* plant and placed it on his head in mocking imitation of the victory crowns awarded Roman emperors. They dressed him a purple robe, the mark of royalty, colored with an expensive dye made from the Mediterranean snail. "Hail, King of the Jews!" they said, slapping him.

Pilate returned to the crowd. "I bring him out to you," he said, "that ye may know that I find no crime in him." Jesus was led out of the palace, in crown and robe. *"Ecce homo!"* Pilate said. "Behold the man!" The crowd was not appeased by the flogging and humiliation of its victim. The chant resumed: "Crucify him, crucify him." Pilate again refused. He may have done so through dislike of the priests; Philo believed that he had brought the imperial shields into the city "with the intention of annoying the Jews rather than of honoring Tiberius." But he may also have been genuinely sympathetic to Jesus. Matthew's gospel says that his wife urged him not to judge Jesus, and that he "took water, and washed his hands before the multitude, saying, I am innocent of the blood of this righteous man." He was shown as such in early Christian tradition, described as "a Christian before his own conscience";[2] Pilate was to be honored with a feast day by the Ethiopian Church and his wife by the Greek Orthodox.

A decisive point was now reached. The crowds outside the palace shouted a warning to the governor: "If thou release this man, thou art not Caesar's friend; everyone that maketh himself a king speaketh against Caesar" (John 19:12). It was a shrewd blow. Pilate was vulnerable to any charge of disloyalty to the emperor. His patron Lucius Sejanus, an ambitious prefect of the Praetorian Guard, had secured his appointment. Sejanus had later been strangled on suspicion of plotting to overthrow the emperor. His body had been thrown to the Roman mob, who vented their spite on it for three days before hurling it into the Tiber; since it was a nicety of Roman custom not to execute a virgin, his little daughter Junilla had been raped before she was killed. These were brutal times; if word of the case reached Rome, with its reference to "not Caesar's friend," Pilate's life as well as career might be at stake. As soon as Pilate "therefore heard these words," he had Jesus brought out and sat down on the judgment seat in the Gabbatha, the paved courtyard outside the palace.

"Shall I crucify your king?" he asked the priests.

"We have no king but Caesar," they replied. Jesus was delivered to them to be crucified. It was by now "about the sixth hour," or midday.

✤ BLASPHEMERS AND REBELS in ancient Israel were typically put to death by stoning—"and all the men of his city shall stone him with stones, that he die" (Deut. 21:21)—and their bodies were sometimes hanged from a tree as a warning. Crucifixion had come with the Greeks. It was one of Alexander the Great's preferred methods of execution, and the Seleucid emperors who followed him had crucified Jews who resisted Hellenistic culture. It had remained in constant use. Alexander Jannaeus, the warlike high priest who had ruled Judea a century before Jesus, had crucified eight hundred Pharisaic rebels from the single town of Bethome.³ The Romans adopted it for general crimes by slaves and non-Romans—Spartacus and the remnants of his army of rebel slaves and gladiators had been crucified—and occasionally for citizens found guilty of treason. They refined it from the original simple stake on which the victim was impaled, adding a horizontal beam, placed at the top of the upright, or slightly below it in the form of the traditional Latin cross.*

Spared no humiliation, the condemned man was usually flogged and then forced to carry the crossbeam to the place of execution, where it was hoisted onto the waiting shaft. A single nail was used to pierce the victim's feet.† This nail was then driven, not into the upright shaft itself, but into a small board of olive wood that served to keep the feet together. The forearms—not the hands, which would tear free—were nailed into the crossbar. A small horizontal board was often attached to the cross below the hips to support the body and prolong the death agony.

The victim died of suffocation, a process that could take several days; executioners sometimes broke the victim's rib cage and legs to cut short his suffering. The onset of suffocation produced intense thirst, while the weight of the body in its arched position caused excruciating pain. A high fever and convulsions, which wracked the whole body, accompanied the thirst of the final stages.

Roman custom and Jewish law demanded that the execution take place outside the city, at a place called Calvaria in Latin, or, in Greek, Golgotha, "the place

---

*There are scores of variants of the Latin cross. The X-shaped St. Andrew's cross is a later Roman variant. The beam in the Greek cross is the same length as the upright, joined in the center in the form of the + sign; St. Peter's cross is similar but with a longer upright. The Cardinal's cross, or Cross of Lorraine, has two beams, the Papal cross and the Triple cross have three. The Orthodox cross has two beams and an angled bar for the feet; the cross of the Crusades has a large Greek cross with four smaller crosses, one in each quadrant. The Templar's cross is shaped like a disc; the Celtic cross has a circle representing the sunset in it. The Teutonic or Iron Cross is familiar from German aircraft and tanks; the Anchor cross is shaped with the flukes of an anchor. Maltese, Germanic, Jerusalem, George, Gamma, Alpha, Omega, and Heart crosses—the symbol retains its power in many shapes and forms.

†This is shown by the first-century remains of a victim found in a tomb at Jerusalem.⁴

of the skull." It probably took its name from a rocky outcrop in the shape of a skull. The ruin and rebuilding of Jerusalem were to make it difficult to identify the site with accuracy. The Church of the Holy Sepulchre was built three hundred years later over a rock pile at what had become the traditional place of Golgotha, now in the west part of the Old City.*

John says that Jesus carried his own cross to Calvary, but in the other Gospels his guards forced a visiting Jew from North Africa, Simon of Cyrene, to carry it. Jesus was nailed to it, between two other condemned men, with a board above his head that read: THIS IS THE KING OF THE JEWS. The crowd waited for him to die, encouraged by his helplessness to mock him as the pseudo-Messiah. His mother Mary watched, with the "disciple . . . whom he loved," who may have been John himself; Jesus said to Mary, "Woman, behold, thy son!" (John 19:26). The soldiers on execution duty shared out his clothes; this was to be claimed as evidence that the prophecy in Psalms was fulfilled:

"The assembly of the evil-doers have enclosed me;
They pierced my hands and my feet . . .
They part my garments among them,
And upon my vesture do they cast lots."
(Psalms 22:16–18)

Sometime after noon "a darkness came over the whole land until the ninth hour," about 3 P.M. At about this time, Jesus cried out, *Eli, Eli, lama sabachthani?*" In response to his thirst, the soldiers brought him "a sponge full of vinegar upon hyssop," hyssop being the marjoram plant, fragrant and aromatic with a volatile oil sometimes used to flavor wine. They put it to his mouth.

"When Jesus had received the vinegar, he said, 'It is finished,'" John wrote, "and he bowed his head and gave up his spirit." The two other men were still alive. Because a body could not remain on the cross on the Sabbath, the soldiers broke their legs to finish them off. They found Jesus to be dead; such treatment was thus unnecessary and, like the Passover lamb and the righteous of the Psalms, he kept "all his bones, not one of them is broken" (Psalms 35:20). A soldier pierced his side with a spear to make sure.

---

*The British general Charles Gordon suggested in 1885 that the true site was further north, near the present Damascus Gate, in an area of gardens, with a number of simple graves and a rock formation that, in certain light, resembles a human skull. This is known as the "Garden Tomb" or "Gordon's Calvary." But the traditional site is probably correct. The church built on it in 336 was destroyed by the Arabs, rebuilt by crusaders in 1130, and destroyed by fire in 1808. It is still not fully restored.

✤ THE ACCOUNTS OF the crucifixion make no attempt to exaggerate the event. Men died often enough on the cross and Jesus went more easily than many. He died in little more than three hours; Pilate did not believe he could have gone so swiftly, and "marvelled if he were already dead" (Mark 15:44). His disciples, fearing their own arrest, were not with him. Instead, his agony was watched "from afar" by Mary Magdalene, a devoted follower from whom he had cast out devils (Mark 16:9), and by other women who had followed him on the journey from Galilee.

Since early times Jewish custom had demanded that a body be buried on the day of death. This applied even to those "accursed of God" who had been hanged on trees after execution; "his body shall not remain all night upon the tree," the ancient book of Deuteronomy demanded, "but thou shalt surely bury him the same day" (Deut. 21:23). A burial was normally a public event during which the body was washed and anointed with spices, and family and friends, together with professional mourners who were "skilful of lamentation," accompanied it to the grave "wailing in all the broad streets . . . Alas! alas!" (Amos 5:16).

No disciple or relative was brave enough to bury Jesus. His body was saved from a common grave for criminals by Joseph of Arimathea, a devout Jew and se-cret follower of Jesus. He was a wealthy man with the social self-confidence to go boldly to Pilate and ask him for the body. The governor granted it to him. Helped by Nicodemus, another high-ranking sympathizer, Joseph took the body down from the cross and carried it to a garden. Here he had hewn out a rock to make a tomb for his own eventual use. He anointed the body with aloes and myrrh, wrapped it in a linen cloth, and placed it in the tomb. He was watched by Mary Magdalene and "the other Mary," the mother of James. Then he "rolled a great stone to the door of the tomb, and departed" (Matt 27:60).

✤ THE PHYSICAL JESUS was dead and buried; the affair seemed closed. No written accounts of his life appeared for at least thirty years. When they did, the biographical detail was fragmentary and sometimes contradictory. At his birth, for example, only Matthew's gospel mentions the wise men who came from the east to worship the infant. The shepherds who came to the Bethlehem manger af-ter an angel brought them "good things of great joy" appear only in Luke. Jesus made nothing of his mother's virginity, while John treats it in purely metaphysi-cal terms—"born not of blood, nor of the will of the flesh, nor of the will of man, but of God" (John 1:13)—and Mark does not mention the birth at all.

What emerged of his life was set deeply into Old Testament prophecies fa-miliar only to Jews. There were communities of Jews in the major cities of the eastern empire, and in Rome itself, but they were a race apart, hostile to inter-marriage, clinging to their own culture and sacred writings, and to a single god, Yahweh.* This belief in one god and their expectation of a Messiah were shared by no others in the empire.

The Romans were tolerant of cults and deities among their subjects and had adopted many themselves, particularly from the Greeks. They worshiped great celestial gods whose names survive in the planets—Jupiter, god of the sky, Mars, god of war, Venus, goddess of love and beauty—and the humbler local spirits of the tree groves and springs. So many gods did the Romans accept, indeed, that their success in war was sometimes attributed to their ability to draw upon them all. Their human manipulation, however, was obvious; auguries were tailored to fit the wishes of the powerful, and priesthoods were exploited for social and political ends. The apotheosis of emperors, eventually extended to empresses, added fresh cynicism. The process was supposedly posthumous; the dying Vespasian remarked that he felt himself becoming a god, whilst Caracalla, as he ordered centurions to murder his brother, remarked brutally that the victim would have the consolation of divinity. Cautious subjects, however, often referred to the *aeternitas* of their rulers while they were still living. Religion had little moral content; it was more a matter of insurance than conviction. It was, too, an entertainment. In a world without weekends, cult festivals were great local events, eagerly anticipated; new robes were worn, noble families mingled with the poor in procession, girls of marriageable age showed themselves off, bands struck up dances, hymns were sung. The blood sacrifice of an animal—an ox, a piglet—provided a moment of solemnity and then, when it had been roasted, a meal for the participants.

Christ demanded absolute belief in a single God, and he was himself the sacrifice. Such concepts were alien to the Gentile world, or so it seemed. Only the Jews were equipped by custom and culture to comprehend him and only they could enable his word to survive. They had responded to him on his last journey to Jerusalem. As a rule, they now rejected him. It was from among the few exceptions that the new religion was born.

✤ ON THE THIRD day after the crucifixion, Mary Magdalene and the other Mary came to the tomb with the aromatic spices used to hide the smell of putrefaction. The stone guarding the entrance had been rolled away and the tomb was

---

*The word appeared in Hebrew as the four letters YHWH; because of its sanctity, Jews avoided uttering it whilst reading scriptures and substituted the word "Adonai," the Hebrew word for "Lord." The word "Jehovah" is a sixteenth-century construction in which the consonants of YHWH were mistakenly mixed with the vowels of "Adonai."

empty. The women saw a dazzling vision which asked, "Why seek ye the living among the dead?" The angel said that Jesus was risen from the dead, and as they went back to the city, Jesus appeared to them. "Fear not," he said. "Go tell my brethren that they depart into Galilee, and there shall they see me" (Matt. 28:9–10). They ran in fear and joy to tell the eleven surviving apostles; Judas had committed suicide in remorse for his betrayal, or was about to do so.*

The men were cowering in a house "for fear of the Jews" (John 20:19), unnerved by the execution. They were in no mood to hear hysterical reports of a resurrection, which they dismissed as "idle talk" (Luke 24:11). Women alone had shown the courage and faith to watch Jesus die; they were the first witnesses of the risen Christ. The men now went to Galilee; there, for forty days after his Passion, the living Jesus presented himself to them—spoke with them, ate with them—before he was "carried up into heaven" (Luke 24:51).

It was, for them, absolute evidence that he was Christ. "Reach hither thy finger, and see my hands," he said to doubting Thomas of the wounds of his crucifixion. "Reach hither thy hand, and put it into my side; and be not faithless, but believing." Thomas replied simply and without compromise: "My Lord and my God."

❖ THE DEATH ON the cross was the end of a prophet. The Resurrection was the beginning of a new religion, for it was the evidence of Christ's divinity; but the event that gave the faith its defining human essence—that enabled men to call upon Christ's authority in its interpretation and structure—was still some days off. The period of the apostles' contact with the resurrected Christ before his ascension into heaven was brief. He "showed himself alive after his passion by many proofs appearing unto them by the space of forty days," according to Acts; he was then "taken up, and a cloud received him out of their sight" (Acts 1:3 and 9). His reappearance, and the establishment of his Kingdom on earth, was imminently expected, but it did not occur.

His followers were left only with a memory and an inspiration. They inherited his extraordinary message, of the terrestrial passage of the divine, of redemption, the forgiveness of sins, deliverance from the power of darkness, eternal life. They had the example of his Passion; within a few years, several among them had followed him to their own executions. They had his admonition to future generations: "If any man would come after me, let him deny himself, and take up his

---

*In Matthew, Judas flung the thirty pieces of silver into the temple sanctuary before hanging himself; the priests took it and used it to buy a potter's field as a burial ground for strangers (Matt. 27:3–7). In Acts, he bought the field himself before apparently eviscerating himself, like a shamed samurai: "falling headlong, he burst asunder in the midst, and all his bowels gushed out" (Acts 1:18). The field was called Akeldama, the "field of blood," and tradition locates it on the southern slope of the Valley of Hinnom.

cross, and follow me. For whosoever should save his life shall lose it; and whosoever shall lose his life for my sake shall find it" (Matt. 16:24–25). But those words themselves, so harsh and compelling, were not written down for more than half a century; and then, not by the apostle Matthew, to whom the Gospel in which they appeared was attributed, but by an anonymous Greek speaker probably living in Syria.

On the first Ascension Day, Christians had no book of their own, only the Old Testament of Judaism. They had no laws other than the ancient Mosaic Laws. The commandments revealed to Moses were said to have been engraved upon tablets of stone; Muhammad was to leave his believers a formal framework of faith in the Koran, most or all of which was written down during his lifetime. Christians had no such certainties. They had no defined creed, no forms of worship, no liturgy. They lacked a priesthood and hierarchy. "Feed my lambs . . . tend my sheep" (John 21:15–16) was Christ's only reported instruction on the immense task of creating a church; "thou art Peter, and upon this rock I will build my church" (Matt. 16:18) was the only indication of hierarchy. They had no buildings, no funds, and unlike Muhammad, Christ left no political testament and had levied no taxes. Their infant faith had no name. They called it simply "the Way," and themselves saints, brothers, or disciples. Indeed, when the word "Christian" was coined, by pagans, it was as a term of abuse. They had no firm guidance on questions that at times would come to obsess them, on the celibacy of priests, the use of icons and images, the adoration of the Virgin, the predestination of souls. Christ had made no mention of the authority of the pope or the Church of Rome, for neither existed. Fundamental issues of belief—the nature of Christ himself, whether it be human, or divine, or both; the relationship of the Son to the Father—were unresolved. The Trinity was to become a core of Christian doctrine, though the term appears nowhere in the New Testament.

Believers had, perforce, to fill these great voids, and they did so with a will. Where there had been no texts, they wrote with such vigor that more than two dozen gospels appeared in the next two centuries. They then defined which were orthodox—Matthew, Mark, Luke, and John—and which were apocryphal; it was not until 382 that the complete text of the canonical books of the Old and New Testaments were authorized. Some refused to accept the canon as closed; Joseph Smith founded the Church of the Latter Day Saints in 1830 upon the new Book of Mormon, as revealed to him in upstate New York. Liturgies were created, laws framed, hierarchies designated. Men adjudicated on what was true to the faith, and what merited excommunication from it. Ultimately, they would burn alive those whom they judged to be deviants.

But on what grounds could mere men and women, subject to every manner of sin, prey to vanity, greed, and arrogance, to lunacy itself, thus interpret the di-

With a sound like the "rushing of a mighty wind," and "tongues . . . as of fire," the Holy Spirit poured down at Pentecost to sit upon the apostles and the Virgin. This was a key moment in the faith, for it established the belief that individual Christians could be touched by divine inspiration. Pentecostal churches and the modern charismatic movement are based on the first Pentecost, seen here in Titian's *Effusion of the Holy Spirit.*

vine purpose? "Tell us, by what authority doest thou these things?" the Sadducees had asked of Christ. "Or who is he that gave thee this authority?" Christ had his authority from God, so Christians believed; but what of themselves?

On the fiftieth day after the Last Supper, and ten days after the Ascension, an apparent answer to this profoundly troubling dilemma was received. The apostles were gathered at Jerusalem for the Jewish feast of Pentecost, so Acts record, when "suddenly there came from heaven a sound as of the rushing of a mighty wind." This marked the arrival of the Holy Spirit, the divine force which had conceived Christ, which had descended on him at his baptism in the form of the dove, and which had directed his life. It was accompanied now by tongues of fire. "It sat upon each one of them," Acts continues. "And they were all filled with the Holy Spirit, and began to speak with other tongues, as the Spirit gave them utterance." They spoke in the language of "every nation under heaven." Some onlookers mocked them, and said that they were filled with new wine. Peter responded that they were not drunk—"it is but the third hour of the day"—but were fulfilling the words of the prophet Joel. "And it shall be in the last days, saith God," he quoted, "I will pour forth of my Spirit upon all flesh. And your sons and your daughters shall prophesy, and your young men shall see visions, and your old men shall dream dreams. . . ." (Acts 2:1 passim).

To the Jews, the Holy Spirit had been *ruah,* the "breath" or "wind" of God. To Christians, it was to become the Third Person of the Trinity, with the Father and the Son; it was the alter ego of Christ, its presence equivalent to his own. At Pentecost it descended upon the infant church and the apostles; it was the fulfillment of Christ's promise that his followers would "be clothed with power from on high" (Luke 24:49). They were so powerfully endowed with it that they could convey it to others through the laying on of hands. It was a continuing force, the Godhead's permanent representative on earth, the means through which authority descends from the Lord to the faithful.

Thus was created the fateful human link with the divine. "If any man is in Christ, he is a new creature," the apostle Paul wrote some two decades later. "The old things are passed away; behold, they are become new" (2 Cor. 6:17). The Christian was indeed a new creature, whom Paul was actively molding as he wrote, and he was one who, by calling upon the unverifiable inspiration of the Spirit, was thereby able to redefine himself and his faith at will. Paul had done so, transforming himself from a rigorous and orthodox Jew into a prime founder of the faith he had persecuted as a young man. He had not known the living Jesus, but this did not inhibit him, for, as he wrote, "the law of the Spirit of life in Christ Jesus made me free from the law of sin and of death" (Rom. 8:2). He had, too, a further power that was believed to emanate from the deity, that of God's grace, which impelled those who received it to righteousness. Paul said that he felt set apart at "the good pleasure of God, who separated me, even from my mother's womb, and called me through his grace."

Others, throughout the lengthening history of the faith, would claim that same grace or Spirit as the source of their ideas and strivings. They might do so at the peril of their lives, for they were seen to be tampering with God himself; or they might invoke it in order to take the lives of others, who failed to share their interpretation of its desires, for Christ had said: "whosoever shall speak against the Holy Spirit, it shall not be forgiven him, neither in this world, nor in that which is to come" (Matt. 12:32). They were propelled by certainty for they believed that their actions reflected the will of God. The individual who was brushed by grace was justified, in his own eyes at least; and this human claim to direct intimacy with the divine, behind which both noble and vile causes have found shelter, was established by the apostles within a few days of Christ's withdrawal.

This essence of the faith—a cause of its perpetual restlessness, of its energy, curiosity, experimentations, schisms, and heresies, of its countless sects, of the vengeful orthodoxies and wild idealisms to which it remains so uniquely prone—was present at birth. From the moment of the first Pentecost, Christianity was vulnerable to mortal man.

CHAPTER II

ThE MASTER BUILDER:

Paul

"Yea, the hour cometh, that whosoever killeth you shall think that he offereth service unto God" (John 16:2). With these words Jesus had warned his disciples of coming danger, yet fresh idealism sustained them after Pentecost. They sold their possessions to give to the poor, urged their listeners to accept the "Prince of life" who had been delivered up to Pilate, and performed "many wonders and signs" (Acts 2:43). Peter healed a lame man in front of a Jerusalem crowd, telling them that the miracle was not of his doing, but came from faith in Jesus. He appealed to them to accept the "Prince of life" whom they had delivered up to Pilate. Repent, he said, "that your sins may be blotted out" (Acts 3:19). The divine power made its deepest impression, however, when it killed rather than cured. A man named Ananias and his wife Sapphira sold a plot of land as a gift for the needy, but they held some of the money back; in thus betraying the Holy Spirit, according to Acts, they were both struck dead.

A "great fear came upon all that heard it" (Acts 6:5); in a fever of preaching and expectation of the imminent Second Coming of Christ, five thousand converts were claimed, but such popularity, or notoriety, alarmed the guardians of the temple. The apostles were arrested, ordered "not to speak in the name of Jesus" (Acts 5:40), and publicly flogged; they were freed from prison, or so it was said, only when an angel opened the gates. Stephen, a Greek-speaking Jew with a fiery temper, was the first disciple to die. Orthodox Jews were worried that "the Way," as the movement remained known, was spreading from native-born Hebrews to Stephen's Hellenists, who came from the Greek cities to the north. Informers reported that Stephen had prophesied that Jesus would return and destroy the Temple, thus repeating part of the blasphemy that had led three or four years before to the crucifixion.

Stephen was wildly unrepentant when he was tried in front of the San-hedrin. He said that the temple was of no account, since God does not dwell in buildings made by man. "Ye stiffnecked and uncircumcised in heart and ears," he told his judges, "ye do always resist the Holy Ghost; as your fathers did, so do ye." He called them "the betrayers and murderers" of Christ (Acts 7:52). As they "gnashed on him with their teeth" in their fury, he looked up and said that the heavens had opened to him, and that he could see Christ standing on the right hand of God. At this further blasphemy, the members of the Sanhedrin "stopped their ears and rushed upon him." He was taken out of the city to be stoned to death as the Law of Moses demanded. He knelt as the missiles struck him; dying, he cried, "Lord, lay not this sin to their charge" (Acts 7:51–60). The cloaks of the stone-throwers, taken off to free their arms, were guarded by a young man named Saul.

The stoning was a watershed, perhaps a godsend, for it drove the small and strange new sect out of the land of its birth and into the wider world at a moment when its beliefs were still unformed. It provided it with its protomartyr, too, an emblem of endurance to death; and Stephen's judicial execution as a blasphemer confirmed the fracture with Judaism. Making progress among the Jews in the city was slow and perilous. If Stephen was prepared to die for his faith, Orthodox Jews like Saul were ready to kill to protect theirs. A wave of persecution broke over Jerusalem, and Christians fled to the more tolerant cities to the north in their diaspora. They took the message of the risen Christ with them—"they that were scattered abroad went about preaching the word" (Acts 8:4)—and they introduced it to the Gentile world which, over time, it would transform.

❖   THE CATALYST WAS the young zealot Saul. Like Stephen, Saul was a Hellenist Jew whose two names—he was Paul in Greek—reflected the mixed cultures in which he was raised. He was born at Tarsus, "no mean city" as he described it (Acts 21:39), the capital of the Roman province of Cilicia, a lively and cosmopolitan place known for linen weaving and intellectual debate. Once visited by Cleopatra in a burnished royal barge, it lay on a river a few miles inland from the southeastern coast of Asia Minor. Saul's parents were strict Orthodox Jews who spoke Hebrew in the house. His father, most likely a tent maker, was prominent enough to be a Roman citizen. Saul was fully at ease in Greek, writing it with style and vigor, but he was devoted to his Jewish inheritance and may have studied at the synagogue in Tarsus before moving to Jerusalem for the final stage of his education. Here, "zealous for

St. Paul is felled from his horse and spreads his arms with wonder and pleading in Caravaggio's painting of his conversion on the road to Damascus. Paul both shaped the theology of the faith and ensured its survival by taking it into the Gentile world. He found himself "in perils from my countrymen, in perils from the Gentiles, in perils in the city, in perils in the wilderness"; he was beaten, snakebitten, and shipwrecked, but before he was martyred, he had inspired and browbeaten a Church into existence.

God" (Acts 22:3), he was tutored by Rabbi Gamaliel,* the leading rabbinical teacher of the day. A strict and devoted Pharisee, Saul breathed "threatening and slaughter" (Acts 9:1) against Christianity and its followers, tricking secret sympathizers into blasphemies, giving evidence at trials, and leading house-to-house searches for suspects.

Not satisfied with his work in Jerusalem, he volunteered to go to Damascus to track down Christians who had fled there; "if he found any that were of the Way, whether men or women," he was to bring them back in chains for sentence. On the road to Damascus, a miracle took place. A light shone from heaven, and a voice asked him, "Saul, Saul, why persecuteth thou me?" It identified itself: "I am Jesus whom thou persecutest" (Acts 9:4–5). Blinded, Saul was led by the hand to Damascus. The disciple Ananias restored his sight by laying hands on him, and he was baptized. He became, as he was later to write of converts in general, a "new creature." He changed his name to Paul, and transformed his Pharisaic ferocity into a burning commitment to Christ.

---

*The rabbi was considerably more liberal to Christians than his pupil. According to Acts, he advised the Sanhedrin to "refrain from these men [Christian leaders] and let them alone: for if this counsel or this work [Christianity] be of men, it will be overthrown. But if it is of God, ye will not be able to overthrow them" (Acts 5:38–39).

Paul's temporary blindness and the recovery of his sight could be taken as symbols of his spiritual rebirth, and of revelation or enlightenment, but he wrote of them as physical events, and the consequences are a matter of record. Paul was the colossus of the Church, the most striking and powerful human being in its history. Physical descriptions—"bow-legged, strongly built, full of grace," with a large nose and deep-set eyes beneath a bald pate—date from after his death, and cannot be verified;* but his writing is awash with his personality: incisive, unflagging, practical, tetchy, humane, humorous, wishing that stubborn supporters of circumcision "would even cut themselves off" (Gal. 5:12), a master builder. He made the largest single contribution to the New Testament; his letters, written before the appearance of the Gospels, shaped the ideology of the faith. His concept of the Church as the mystical body of Christ was later used to justify its authority, while the individual churches he planted became the basis for its administration. He badgered and harried against the splits and conflicts that all too soon broke the surface. He saw himself first and foremost, however, as the "Apostle of the Gentiles."

After his call, he spent some time in contemplation in the Syrian desert. He preached at Damascus, to obvious effect, for the governor ordered his arrest and he escaped by being lowered down the city wall in a basket. He later went back to his native Tarsus and from there he was brought by the disciple Barnabas to help with the church at Antioch. This was the third most important city of the empire, after Rome and Alexandria, a handsome place with the Paradise of Daphne to the south, a stretch of pools and groves where worshipers met at the Temple of Apollo. The city lay on the main route from Jerusalem to Rome; it was traversed by colonnades of marble pillars, through which ran a central road for heavy carts flanked by others for pedestrians and horses and carriages. The Antioch church attracted Gentiles as well as Jews. It was the first place where the word "Christian" was used, and it was wealthy enough for Paul and Barnabas to raise the money to send supplies to the Christians still in Jerusalem in about A.D. 44.

The two men soon set out on a missionary journey, sailing first to Cyprus and then moving through Asia Minor. Paul was proud of his ancestry—"I am Paul," he introduced himself, "a Jew of Tarsus"—and local synagogues were his first stopping place in a new city. They provided an ideal base. Jewish traders had been welcomed into Greek cities by Alexander the Great and, over the intervening 350 years, they had settled in every large town in the Roman Empire. But Paul felt himself to be "entrusted with the gospel of the uncircumcision," that is,

---

*The apocryphal Acts of Paul, which Tertullian said was written by a presbyter of Asia Minor, described him as "little in stature, with a bald head and crooked legs . . . with eyebrows meeting and a nose somewhat hooked."[1]

with the conversion of non-Jews. This led to a fundamental clash with the church at Jerusalem, which taught that all Christians must obey the Law of Moses.

✤ RIGOROUS JERUSALEM CHRISTIANS insisted that Gentile converts must accept the law in its entirety. This included complex and, to Gentiles, bizarre regulations on what was clean and unclean. Jewish dietary laws forbade the eating of pigs and other animals which did not chew the cud and had uncloven feet, fish without fins or scales, creatures which crawl on their bellies, and "birds of abomination." A clean animal could not be eaten if it had died a natural death, or been torn by beasts, or had not been drained of blood. Other rules applied to people. A Jewish woman who gave birth to a son was unclean for seven days, for example, and underwent purification for a further thirty-three days. During this time she could not touch holy objects or enter a holy place; the timescale was doubled if she delivered a daughter. To purify herself she had to offer a year-old lamb and a dove. A person who touched a dead body was purified with running water poured on the ashes of a sacrificial heifer.

To the Jews these measures were commands ordained by God, but to uncomprehending Gentiles they were a senseless barrier, which Paul was determined to remove. Jesus himself had considered that what a man said was more important than what he ate. "Hear, and understand," he had told the multitude. "Not that which entereth into the mouth defileth the man; but that which cometh out of the mouth, this defileth the man" (Matt. 15:11). He had opened himself to uncleanness by touching the dead and lepers. "Christ redeemed us from the curse of the law," Paul argued (Gal. 3:13); he had freed man of impurity by taking it upon himself. Christian Pharisees in particular would have no truck with laxity in cleanliness and diet, but the pivotal argument surrounded circumcision.

"Except ye be circumcised after the customs of Moses," the Jerusalemites ruled, "ye cannot be saved" (Acts 5:11). They had biblical backing. The prophet Ezekiel had warned of God's displeasure at Israel "in that ye have brought in aliens, uncircumcised in heart and uncircumcised in flesh, to be in my sanctuary, to profane it" (Ezek. 44:7), and God had commanded Abraham that every male throughout the generations should have the foreskin of his penis cut away when he was eight days old. The operation was considered a privilege, and it was offered to non-Jews who wished to take part in public worship. The custom was common to the region. The ancient Egyptians and Phoenicians had practiced it, and the Arabs still do. Hellenized Gentiles, however, facing the operation as adults rather than as infants, found it barbaric.

A council was held at Jerusalem to debate the issue. Peter made the decisive speech against the hard-liners. He said that Gentiles as well as Jews had been given the Holy Spirit. God "made no distinction between us and them, cleansing our heart by faith. Now wherefore tempt ye God, that ye should put a yoke upon the neck of the disciples? . . . We believe that we shall be saved through the grace of the Lord Jesus, in like manner as they." This was accepted, the council ruling that "we trouble not them which from among the Gentiles turn to God." The only requirement to be made of Gentiles was that they "abstain from the pollution of idols, and from fornication, and from what is strangled, and from blood" (Acts 15:20). The first two were intrinsic to Christian ethics; the dietary rules were minor concessions that most Gentiles ignored.

Peter had misgivings. When he visited Antioch he refused to eat with the uncircumcised. "I resisted him to the face," Paul wrote after one encounter with him, "because he stood condemned" (Gal. 2:11). The poor ex-fisherman, with his strong Galilean accent,* had been born Simon; the title of Peter—the Greek translation of the Aramaic *kepa,* or Cephas, meaning "stone" or "rock"—had been given to him by Jesus. This honor may have rankled with Paul, the educated Roman citizen. That the two men, and others, did not see eye to eye is revealed in Paul's complaint that unity was already being undermined by each Christian claiming that "I am of Paul; and I of Apollos; and I of Cephas; and I of Christ" (1 Cor. 1:12). Such factions were to make Christianity the most sectarian of religions, for any Christian could repeat the claim of divine insight—"and I of Christ"—to justify founding a new sect.

Paul's approach to circumcision was practical. He carried out the operation himself where it might help gain converts. When traveling with his fellow missionary Timothy, whose mixed parentage was illegal in Jewish eyes, he "took and circumcised him because of the Jews that were in those parts" (Acts 16:3). Otherwise, he was opposed to it, and his stress on baptism as the sign of entry into the new faith—he called it a "circumcision not made with hands" (Col. 2:11)—effectively ended the debate. The origins of Christianity might still be almost wholly Jewish, but without the Mosaic Law it was no longer a Jewish religion.

❖ THE ACCEPTANCE OF Gentiles as equals proved to be a means of survival. Christianity largely failed to win Jews away from Judaism, and Christians who remained observant Jews died out entirely. The last survivors were the Ebionites,[2] who were probably driven from Jerusalem during its destruction in A.D. 70 to live in harsh frugality on the east bank of the Jordan. They clung to the law and de-

---

*A maid had recognized him as a follower of Jesus the Galilean during the trial. He denied this with an oath, saying, "I know not the man." Others in the crowd then said: "Of a truth thou also art one of them; for thy speech betrayeth thee" (Matt. 26:73).

nied the Virgin Birth, believing that Jesus was an ordinary Jew upon whom the Holy Spirit had descended in the form of the dove during his baptism. Other Christians thought them heretics. They flourished briefly in the second century, but by the fourth they had disappeared.

Opening the faith to non-Jews did more than immeasurably increase its potential membership; it also adjusted its nature. The Jewish roots were not abandoned. Attempts were made to scrap all Judaic influence, including the Old Testament, by the second-century Marcionites and others, but they failed. What would come to be the Christian Bible alone ensured that it remained profoundly attached to the ancient traditions of Israel. Paul himself remained loyal to his origins. "Are they Hebrew?" he said. "So am I. Are they Israelites? So am I. . . ." The infant religion was, however, now exposed to an external culture of far greater variety and scope, the Greco-Roman.

The Gentile, or pagan, world* was not the hostile place that its multitude of gods and superstitions made it seem. The Roman historian Tacitus might regard Christianity as a "new and evil superstition," but neither did he defend the merits of the Roman tangle of deities and oracles. Pagans had no profound attachment to their traditional gods, and they were open-minded to imports. The ancient cults satisfied neither spiritual nor intellectual needs; the sophisticated dismissed them as puerile myths, while those with a desire to worship experimented restlessly with exotic imports from the East.

Eastern transplants—a category into which Christianity fell—could flourish in Rome. Seamen and merchants carried the cult of Isis, principal goddess of Egypt, daughter of Earth and Sky, from her home on the Nile to Rome and as far as the Rhine. Worship of Cybele, the Great Mother, had spread from Asia Minor to the temple built for her on the summit of Palatine Hill in Rome, where priests flagellated themselves with whips decorated with knucklebones. At about the time of the crucifixion, the Persian cult of the sun god Mithras was brought to Rome by army officers attracted by the moral zeal and belligerence attached to the bull-slaying deity. Mithras was shown in sculptures in a Phrygian cap, sacrificing a charging bull with his sword beneath the figure of the sun, the *Sol Invictus,* the "unconquered sun" whom devotees believed to be the only element that remains absolute and undefeated. The god's birth was celebrated on December 25, with initiates bathing themselves in bulls' blood. Emperors practiced the cult.

---

*The word Gentile was used originally of all non-Hebrews, but it came to apply to the Christian converts among them. Those who remained nonbelievers were known as "pagans" from about A.D. 300 on, a word derived from the Latin *paganus;* its common meaning was "rustic," but Christians, conscious that they were soldiers of Christ, used it in its subsidiary meaning of "civilian." The word was not used in the East, where non-Christians were called "Hellenes."

More than 250 years after the death of Christ, Diocletian, the scourge of Christians, personally consecrated a temple to Mithras and hailed the god as "Protector of the Empire."

At a deeper level, Christian thought was to be profoundly influenced by Greek concepts of ethics and logic. Four centuries before Jesus was condemned for outraging orthodox opinion in Jerusalem, Socrates had been ordered to drink a lethal draft of hemlock after his penetrating moral questions had alienated the Athenian establishment. Among his successors, the insights of Plato and Aristotle into ethics, wisdom, and the soul became the basis of schools of Christian thinking. Common ground was identified between Christians and the Stoic school of Greco-Roman philosophy. Stoics stressed human brotherhood. They strove for virtue and practiced civic responsibility, summarizing it in lists of duties later copied by Christians. Some came close to belief in a single god.* Stoics believed the universe to be permeated by a Logos, a Word, an active principle that, like the Holy Spirit of the Christians, lives in the world and determines it. Humans are a particle of this Logos, deriving from it knowledge of matters human and divine in their search for harmony with nature. The opening lines of John's gospel—"in the beginning was the Word, and the Word was with God, and the Word was God" (John 1:1)—shows a familiarity with Stoicism that Paul also shared. Stoics saw, too, a nobility and purpose in suffering. The great philosopher and tragedian Seneca wrote of all outward calamity as a divine instrument that, far from damaging the true self, trained a man to exercise his spirit in indifference to worldly setbacks. Despite man's weakness and misery in his struggle with evil, Seneca recognized the human soul as an emanation of the divine spirit, which preserved in it an essential dignity and freedom. It was only with the death of the body that the true life of the soul began. "The body is not a permanent dwelling," he wrote, "but a sort of inn (with a brief sojourn at that) which is to be left behind when one perceives that one is a burden to the host."[3]

Two of Christianity's most powerful elements—morality and immortality—were present in Seneca's Stoicism. So was the sense of deity. "Live among men as if God beheld you," he memorably wrote. "Speak to God as if men were listening" (Epistles). As to Seneca himself, the early Christian theologian Tertullian remarked that he "often speaks like a Christian." Another Stoic moralist, the Greek Epictetus, was expressing his own gospel of self-abnegation and submission to

---

*In his "Hymn to Zeus," Cleanthes, the Greek who succeeded Zeno as head of the Stoa in 262 B.C., addressed the god as: "almighty and everlasting, sovereign of nature, directing all in accordance with law. . . . No work upon earth is wrought without thee, lord, nor through the divine ethereal sphere, nor upon the sea; save only whatsoever deeds wicked men do in their own foolishness. . . . Deliver men from fell ignorance. Banish it, father, and grant to them to obtain wisdom, whereon relying thou rulest all things with justice."[4]

providence while the Christian Gospels were being written. An ex-slave, he taught that love and forbearance must be extended even to enemies; human weakness was redeemed by man's need for God, while—echoing Paul—Epictetus wrote that whoever would be good must first realize that he is evil.

These pagan philosophies did not allow, of course, for the divinity of Christ or the resurrection of the flesh. Nonetheless, if Paul preserved the Jewish gifts of spiritual insight and emphasis on the divine within the new faith, he also opened it to the Greek world, and to its humanism, artistic genius, and spirit of rational inquiry.* The Old Testament tradition could produce fits of apocalyptic fury in Christianity, while Greek influence could lead it into sterile intellectual disputes. Combined, the two elements inspired the Christian search for knowledge and beauty, seen in the religious foundation of schools and universities and in devotional works of sublime brilliance.

❖ THIS FUSION BEGAN with Paul's first missions abroad. The strength of the Roman Empire was immensely beneficial to him. It was still expanding; Britannia, Thrace, and Mauretania were added during his travels. The *limes,* the frontier line, was continuous, marked by wooden palings, by forts and fortified farming villages in North Africa, by the stone of Hadrian's Wall in Britain. Barbarians were obliged to pay a tax and accept the authority of the emperor as the price of entry. The only internal borders were provincial and easily crossed. The army numbered almost half a million men; native Italians rarely served, but a flow of volunteers from the conquered provinces was maintained by granting them immediate Roman citizenship, and a pension on retirement. Skirmishes sometimes broke out on the *limes,* and political turbulences might disturb the interior. The imperial peoples enjoyed general peace and security, however, and to this was added ease of movement.

All roads were said to lead to Rome, but they also linked the provincial cities in which the initial Christian gains were made. The Romans built some 50,000 miles of first-class roads, secure from brigands, from fifteen feet to twenty feet wide, paved with stone or basaltic lava where traffic was heavy, their tunnels and bridges attesting to the genius of Roman engineers. These were fed by perhaps 200,000 miles of narrower secondary roads. The sea-lanes were generally free of pirates; evangelists could roam as far as the Arabian Sea and India. Greek had been the common language of the East since Alexander the Great, providing a unifying culture and language in the cities.

*A Christian emperor, Justinian, was to close Plato's academy and the other schools of Athens in A.D. 529; this act of ingratitude was too late to have any lasting impact.

Paul's great journeyings would have been impossible without the stability of the Pax Romana. Within the space of about a dozen years, up to A.D. 57, he traveled for some eight thousand miles by road and by sea through Asia Minor and Greece. On his second journey, around A.D. 51, he visited a dozen cities with Timothy and Silas in a great circuit that took him from Antioch through the provinces of Cilicia, Galatia, and Asia to sail to Philippi on the European mainland. Passing through Thessalonica and Athens, he sailed from Corinth to Ephesus in Asia, taking another ship to Jerusalem before returning by road to Antioch. He preached in the synagogues until he was driven out; the first converts provided the base for a congregation or church, meeting in a house or hired room. He was frequently denounced by Jews and pagans, but the Romans generally protected him. He counted "certain chief officers of Asia" (Acts 19:31) among his friends. The proconsul of Cyprus listened politely to his preaching; at Ephesus, the center of the cult of Artemis,* the town clerk braved a mob to dismiss charges of blasphemy against Paul; at Corinth, the proconsul dismissed accusations on the grounds that an internal Jewish dispute was of no concern to the empire; and at Philippi, though the praetors had him whipped and imprisoned, they apologized upon learning that he was a Roman citizen after a miraculous earthquake had—like the Jerusalem angel—burst open the prison gates.

His travels were preserved in his writings. Those of the other apostles are impossible to confirm. Thaddeus is said to have evangelized Edesssa. Christians on the Malabar coast of India claim that the gospel was brought to them by doubting Thomas; he was said to have been killed by a spear at Mylapore near Madras, and when Portuguese navigators arrived in 1522, they found his supposed tomb there. Jude, the patron of lost causes, was believed to have been clubbed to death in Persia. In another persistent tradition, the Coptic Church in Egypt claims Mark as its founder. Though there was fierce competition between rival churches to claim the grandest pedigree, none of these claims is necessarily invalid. There was a flourishing spice trade in the first century between India and the Middle East, for example, and it is feasible that Thomas did sail to Malabar.

Despite benign officials, planting the faith was dangerous. Paul was beaten with rods, stoned, and shipwrecked. He found himself "in perils of rivers, in perils of robbers, in perils from my countrymen, in perils from the Gentiles, in perils in the city, in perils in the wilderness, in perils in the sea, in perils among false

---

*The Greek goddess of hunting, Diana to the Romans. The cult had spread to Spain in the West and Palestine in the East; her temple at Ephesus was one of the seven wonders of the world, built of 127 marble columns each sixty feet high. Sacked by Gothic invaders in the third century, it fell into final ruins after Christianity became the established imperial religion.

brethren; in labour and travail, in watchings often, in hunger and thirst, in fastings often, in cold and nakedness" (2 Cor. 11:24–28). The Christian message was dangerous; the Romans had crucified the Christ to whom it was devoted, and those who believed in him were as vulnerable. Toleration was withdrawn as soon as the authorities realized that Christianity was distinct from Judaism. It became a *religio illicita,* an unlicensed cult without recognized status; it was illegal for the Church to own buildings, and Christian worship was clandestine and under the fear of betrayal.

Besides these external pressures, the "things that are without," Paul wrote of an internal hazard that "presseth on me daily; anxiety for all the churches . . ." (2 Cor. 11:28). He identified "factions, divisions, heresies, envyings" (Gal. 5:19–21) as enemies as dangerous as idolatry and sorcery. This was the inevitable result of the creation of individual Christian communities at a time when the religion was still largely formless. Paul was not the only charismatic figure who was attempting to shape it. The word "church" itself revealed the tensions. In its original meaning, the Greek *ekklesia* stood for an assembly of people holding a political or religious meeting. In that sense the church was a scattering of individual congregations, often at loggerheads; in another sense it defined the Christian community as a whole. The word "church" is used only twice in the—still unwritten—Gospels, once in the narrow sense of congregation, and once in Jesus' broader remark about Peter that "on this rock I will build my church" (Matt. 16:18).

Paul stressed the Church as the entirety of believers rather than as individual units; he called it "the body of Christ," the "household of God," the "bride of Christ," even the "commonwealth of Israel." It was not until about A.D. 100, however, that the phrase "catholic church" with its unequivocal meaning of "universal" was first used (by Ignatius of Antioch). Paul was well aware that his drive for orthodoxy was resented by many Christians as meddling in the affairs of their local congregation. He begged them to "speak the same thing . . . that ye be perfected together in the same mind and judgment."

This theological orthodoxy was easier to call for than to achieve. The arrogant preachers of Corinth, "them which are puffed up" to Paul (1 Cor. 4:19), with their claims to special insight, were a foretaste of a time when the unity of the church would be destroyed by internal factions and disputes. Corinth was an important crossroads, lying between two busy harbors on a Greek isthmus, a provincial capital made prosperous by sailors and traders. Many banqueting halls were attached to its temples, and its sexual license was so notorious that *korinthiazomai* was a Greek word for fornication. Paul was shocked at the immorality of the congregation—"it is actually reported that . . . one of you hath his father's wife" (1 Cor. 5:1–2)—and at its indulgence in ecstatic prophecies.

The Corinthians took a particular pride in "speaking with tongues,"* and their meetings were marked by shrieks and strange sounds that were claimed to echo the outpourings of the Holy Spirit at Pentecost. Paul dismissed this as a "sounding brass, or a clanging cymbal"; it might be suited to private devotion, but its public manifestation was equivalent to "speaking into the air," and he advised them that it held a lowly place in the hierarchy of supernatural gifts. Apostles were most blessed, he said, followed by prophets, teachers, miracle workers, healers, helpers, and administrators; speakers of "divers kinds of tongues" came last (1 Cor. 12:28). The warning was ineffective. The gift of tongues was embedded; it would be present in many future Christian revivals, and a hallmark of the great Pentecostalist and charismatic movements that flourish almost two thousand years later.

Paul was concerned by the Corinthians' belief that the gift of the Spirit freed them to do as they pleased and ignore his drive for unity and orthodoxy. "Conscience, I say, not for thy own, but the other's," he wrote to them, "for why is my liberty judged by another conscience?" (1 Cor. 10:29). His antidote was love. "Knowledge puffeth up," he wrote, "but love edifieth." Any man who "thinketh he knoweth anything, he knoweth not yet as he ought to know" (1 Cor. 8:1–2); but if he loved God, he would gain knowledge. This argument has a danger, of course, in that those who use it may claim that they themselves have acquired this special knowledge that is denied to others. Paul claimed this knowledge for himself, and he used a violence of language in attacking those who lacked it—"false apostles, deceitful workers, fashioning themselves into apostles of Christ [as] Satan fashioned himself into an angel of light" (2 Cor. 11:13–14)—that was to echo in Christian disputes down the centuries. The "love of God" that he urged was perilously close to love of Paul, or at least of his ideas, for he believed his mission to be divine. "Be ye imitators of me," Paul instructed the Corinthians, "even as I also am of Christ" (1 Cor. 11:1). But he could not fully imitate a Christ whom he had met only in his roadside vision, and whose words were not yet recorded[†] in any Gospel. Paul projected his doctrines into a void; he pronounced on issues on which his Lord had remained silent.

---

*The technical term is glossolalia (from the Greek *laleín hetérais glóssais,* meaning "to speak in other tongues"). It was found among the Israelites; in modern times its revival by the American Holiness Churches spread to large Pentecostal congregations such as the Assemblies of God and the Church of God in Christ, and to Africa, Indonesia, and Latin America in particular.

†A collection of the sayings of Jesus may have existed during Paul's missions; it is referred to as "Q," *Quelle,* or "source," in German, since German scholars first held that it was an earlier source for the Gospels of Matthew and Luke. No written document, or reference to it, survives.

He was the first to explore the nature of Christ, and of the union in him of the human and the divine, a study later known as Christology. Jesus, Paul wrote to the Philippians, possessed "the form of God," but since he "counted it not a prize to be on an equality with God," he emptied himself to take "the form of a servant" who was made in the likeness of a man. He had humbled himself by being obedient even to death. At that, God exalted him so that "every knee should bow" at his name, and "every tongue should confess that Jesus Christ is Lord." All Christians must work out their own salvation in fear and trembling, for "it is God which worketh in you" (Phil. 2:6–13).

Central to Paul's thought was his insistence that faith is in itself the basis of salvation. He traced this back to Abraham, whose righteousness stemmed from his belief in God. Faith alone justified a man in the sight of God; faith in Christ "delivered us out of the power of darkness, and translated us into the kingdom of the Son of his love, in whom we have our redemption, the forgiveness of our sins" (Col. 1:13). Through faith in Christ, an individual could receive *charisma,* the "free gift" of God's grace, through which insight, powers of healing, and miracles could flow. Parallel to this was the concept of the Elect of God, an idea that was to develop extraordinary power, a cause of future burnings and theologies of predestination. Paul wrote that the elect are "called according to his purpose" by God; they are those whom God has "foreordained to be conformed in the image of his Son, that [they] might be the firstborn among the many brethren" (Rom. 8:28–30). The Church, too, had inherited this divine power as the mystical Body of Christ.

If mankind could aspire to grace, it could also fall from it. Paul dwelt on Original Sin, the concept that sin and death originated with Adam. "Through one man sin entered into the world," he wrote, so that "by the trespass of the one the many died" (Rom. 5:12–21). Through Christ, man was redeemed from sin and death; for "as in Adam all die, so also in Christ shall all be made alive" (1 Cor. 15:22).

Paul held the resurrection of the dead to be an absolute truth in which every Christian must have faith. Corrupt flesh becomes incorruptible, and mortals put on immortality: "Death is swallowed up in victory" (1 Cor. 15:42–54 passim). If that now seems a belief indissoluble from Christianity, it is partly because Paul made it so. Pagans who were attracted by the morality and sincerity of Christians nonetheless often balked at the apparent impossibility of resurrection. Some early Christians, while accepting that the divine Christ could rise from the dead, also felt that God's generosity did not necessarily extend to ordinary mortals. Paul wrote to members of the Corinth congregation who held his view that, if there were no resurrection of the dead, then Christ could not have been raised; and "if Christ hath not been raised, then is our preaching vain, your faith also is in vain"

(1 Cor. 15:12–20). Worship and baptism were futile without resurrection; "if the dead are not raised, let us eat and drink, for tomorrow we die."

The Christian insistence that believers were equal was revolutionary in principle, though much less so in practice. "There can be neither Jew nor Greek," Paul wrote to the Galatians, "there can be neither bond nor free; there can be no male and female; for ye are all one man in Christ Jesus" (Gal. 3:28). The new faith was open to all comers. Many of Paul's converts were slaves, while others were Roman citizens rich enough to give to charity and provide meeting places in their houses. The equality granted to women was as striking as that of slaves. Jewish women were segregated in worship, uneducated, veiled in public, and forbidden to speak with strangers. If they were raped, they were given to the rapist in marriage; if they were found to have had sex before marriage, they could be stoned to death. The respect Jesus had shown them—teaching and ministering to them, admitting them to his inner circle—was continued. Women were significant in every aspect of early Christianity. They preached and prophesied, they served as church ministers, they were, as Paul put it, "my fellow-workers in Christ."

Christian communities often failed to live up to these ideals, however. Christian sects were to become quite as patriarchal as Judaism. They drew justification from Paul, correctly when they quoted Corinthians, less so when the wrongly attributed epistles to Timothy and Titus were cited, for these were written not by Paul but by his followers. "The man is not of the woman," Paul wrote to the Corinthians, "but the woman of the man: neither was the man created for the woman, but the woman for the man" (1 Cor. 11 passim). The harsher edict that women were not to speak in church was made in the espistles to Timothy; each was to pray with a veil over her head, on pain of having her head shaved; and if they wished to learn, they were to do so "in quietness with all subjection." They were to wear modest clothes; they should shine through good works, not "with braided hair and gold or pearls" (1 Tim. 2:9–13). Roman women worked as lawyers, merchants, physicians, midwives, artists, teachers, prostitutes, laborers, and "professionals of all sorts";[5] Paul stayed at Philippi with Lydia, a woman who had her own business as a seller of purple. Women usually outlived men and were the focus of family life. Yet, in a command that had dire consequences for the status of women, Paul was quoted in Timothy as saying: "I permit not a woman to teach, nor to have dominion over a man, but to be in quietness. For Adam was formed first, then Eve. . . ." (1 Tim. 2:9–13).

His ambiguity on the sexual relationship between men and women was also to persist. Jesus had condoned those who "made themselves eunuchs for the kingdom of heaven's sake" (Matt. 19:12), which would lead seventeen hundred years later to a sect of *skoptsy* self-castrates in Russia, but he accepted that God had joined husband and wife and that they should not be "put asunder." Christians from Paul onwards, however, also condemned the "bondage of the flesh." Paul claimed that "to be carnally minded is death," and he saw an evil law in his own body "warring against the law of my mind, and bringing me into activity under the law of sin which is in my members." With his mind he served the law of God, he wrote to the Romans, "but with the flesh the law of sin" (Rom. 7:25).

Chastity had never before been promoted as a broad ideal. The vestal virgins in Rome practiced it in solitary state and on pain of death; in Israel it was equally rare, followed only by a few sects such as the Essenes at Qumran on the Dead Sea. Together with the Christian acceptance of martyrdom, celibacy was suicidally dangerous for a small group. Taken literally, it would rapidly have led to extinction, a certainty that only those who believed in the imminent arrival of apocalypse and the Kingdom of Heaven could ignore. In the ancient world, life expectancy was no more than twenty-five years. Infant mortality and childhood disease made it necessary for each woman to undergo five pregnancies simply to maintain stable numbers in a community.

An ambivalence was thus planted in the faith. At a practical level, it accepted God's command in Genesis to "be fruitful and multiply" (Gen. 1:28). It was leery of the pleasures of sex—Paul's condemnation of "fornication . . . lasciviousness . . . revellings and suchlike" (Gal. 5:19–21) was a constant if often disregarded theme—but it accepted sex as a necessity for procreation. "If they have not continency, let them marry," Paul wrote grudgingly, "for it is better to marry than to burn" (1 Cor. 7 passim).

At a spiritual level, however, Paul's praise of chastity has had a profound and lasting effect. Within a few years the author of the Book of Revelation was writing of male virgins singing to harps amid the 144,000 female virgins of heaven. The virgin birth of Christ, not mentioned in two of the Gospels, was widely proclaimed. The four brothers of Jesus, who were named in the Gospels, were wished away as half-brothers or stepbrothers; the perpetual virginity of Mary was first asserted in the apocryphal Book of James in the mid-second century. To an early Christian apologist, Athenagoras, marriage was merely a "respectable form of adultery," while rigorists described it as a "defilement and fornication." Virginity, the scholar Jerome wrote later, "makes itself equal to the angels; it exalts the angels, because it must struggle against the flesh to master a nature which the angels do not possess. . . ." A harsh edge of misogyny was brewing—by the 190s, the Church father Tertullian was describing women as "the gateway to hell"—which the growing cult of the Virgin Mary, with its emphasis on her unique perfection, did nothing to dispel. Though Peter had been a married man, it was soon the custom and then the demand of the Roman Church for bishops, then presbyters and eventually deacons, to be celibate. The first formal insistence on an unmarried clergy was made at the Council of Elvira in Spain in about A.D. 306.

The same council had Paul's authority, too, for proclaiming anathema as the punishment for adultery, apostasy, and heresy. Anathema banished the sinful from the body of the faithful and condemned them to Satan and eternal hell. Paul used the ancient Hebrew curse* for crimes of the mind as well as of deed; in a savage passage, he said that even if "an angel from heaven should preach unto you any gospel other than that which we preached unto you, let him be anathema" (Gal. 1:8). Through grace and the Spirit, Paul had arrogated true doctrine to himself; those who preached otherwise were accursed. It had the whiff of the stake to it.

❖   OF COURSE, MUCH in Paul was not vengeful, but followed and reinforced Christ's teaching of kindness and humanity. Where pagans saw no merit in the poor, Jesus had sought them out and blessed them. Christians had an ideal of humility and *ptocheia,* abject poverty. "We toil, working with our own hands," Paul wrote, "being reviled, we bless; being persecuted, we endure. Being defamed, we entreat: we are made as the filth of the world, the offscouring of all things, even until now" (1 Cor. 4:10–13). He held charity to be voluntary; it was not a commandment, but a proof of the sincerity of a Christian's love and a recognition that, through the poverty of Jesus, man had been made spiritually rich. Paul organized collections to be sent to the poor of Jerusalem and he ensured that the sick were visited.

This morality and generosity contrasted, to Christian advantage, with the squalid intrigues and violence of Roman emperors. The reign of Tiberius had descended into the purges and poisonings of which Pontius Pilate had been so pointedly reminded during the trial of Jesus. Abandoning Rome for the lascivious pleasures of Capri and the pursuit of family feuds, Tiberius may have ordered the mysterious death of his adopted son Germanicus, whose wife Agrippina he had exiled to die of starvation on the island of Pandataria. Two of Agrippina's sons were murdered; it was perhaps natural for the surviving orphan, Caligula, to show signs of madness when he succeeded Tiberius as emperor in A.D. 37. Caligula made his horse a consul and himself a god; bald but hairy of body, he

---

*The Hebrew term was *herem;* it could be used of an object offered to a deity to be either consecrated or cursed, but it had become used for a person given to God for destruction.[6] Excommunication, in which the guilty were excluded from taking Holy Communion, was a milder form of censure. The distinction between anathema and excommunication later disappeared.

imposed the death sentence for the mention of goats in public. He banished or murdered his relatives apart from his sister Drusilla, with whom he was said to commit incest, and his uncle Claudius. Caligula was murdered by a tribune of the guard in A.D. 41. Claudius suffered marital problems in turn. His third wife, Messalina, fourteen when he married her, gained a reputation for greed and cruelty. Overcome by a third vice, lust, she went through a public display of marriage with a young lover, giving Claudius grounds for her execution. He then married his niece, Agrippina's daughter, and became stepfather to her son Nero. Agrippina the Younger persuaded Claudius to adopt Nero as his heir, and then set about poisoning her son's rivals. Claudius died from toadstools sliced into a mushroom sauce.

Nero continued the family traditions. He stabbed his mother to death, after an attempt to drown her failed; he poisoned an aunt with a laxative, executed his first wife on a false adultery charge, and kicked his pregnant second wife to death. Not content with "seducing freeborn boys and married women"—sleeping with

Nero, whose bust is seen here, was emperor when two-thirds of Rome was destroyed by fire in July, A.D. 64. Rumor spread that he was himself the arsonist. To deflect suspicion, Tacitus wrote, Nero "charged and tortured some people hated for their evil practices, the group known as 'Christians.' In their deaths they were made a mockery. They were covered in the skins of wild animals, torn to death by dogs, crucified or set on fire." Nero opened his own gardens for the spectacle. Peter and Paul were almost certainly among his victims.

a slave boy was socially quite acceptable—the biographer Suetonius claimed that he also raped a vestal virgin. He went through a wedding ceremony—"dowry, veil and all"—with a boy named Sporius, whom he had castrated to make more girl-like, and lived with him as man and wife. "The world would have been a happier place had Nero's father . . . married the same sort of wife," Suetonius wrote acidly.

Against this, Christians offered an example of moral stability. Debauchery was replaced by chastity, so the apologist Justin Martyr later claimed, and the love of wealth gave way to sharing with the needy. Amid the imperial bloodletting, Justin wrote, "we who hated one another, and murdered one another, we who would not even throw our hearths open to those who differed from us in blood or custom, now, since the manifestation of Christ, live together, pray for our enemies, and seek to win over those who unjustly hate us."[7]

A pattern of devotion was emerging. Sunday was the Christian day of worship, meeting, and sermonizing, for it had been in the early hours of Sunday that Jesus was resurrected. The Jewish Sabbath was held on the last day of the week,* but Acts observes that "upon the first day of the week, when we were gathered to break bread, Paul discoursed with them . . . and prolonged his speech until midnight" (Acts 20:7). The celebration of the Lord's Supper was the high point of the Sunday meeting. At Corinth, at least, the meal seems to have involved heavy eating and drinking. People brought their own food and drink with them, which led to tensions between the well-supplied rich and the meager fare of the poor, so that, as Paul complained, "one is hungry and another is drunken" (1 Cor. 11:21). He stressed that the meal was a symbol of unity in the salvation bought with the body and blood of Christ. Were not the cup and the bread, he asked, a "communion in the blood [and] body of Christ?" (1 Cor. 10:16). He reminded them of the simplicity Jesus had shown on the night of his betrayal. When he had taken bread, "he brake it, and said, This is my body, which is for you: this do in remembrance of me. In like manner also he took the cup, saying: This is the new covenant in my blood: this do, as oft as ye drink it, in remembrance of me." As often as they ate the bread and drank the cup, Paul told them, "ye proclaim the Lord's death till he come" (1 Cor. 11:23–26).

The celebration came to be known by other names, the Eucharist, Holy Communion, and the Mass, and it was to create schisms. It was, nevertheless, the sacramental core of the faith. The apostles celebrated it daily—"and day

---

*Or, more accurately, for twenty-four hours from sunset on Friday. The Jews, unlike the Romans, counted a new day as starting with the setting of the sun on the old day. In the nineteenth century, the Seventh Day Adventists reverted to strict observance of the Sabbath from sunset on Friday, on the grounds that, although Christians, they were obliged to obey Old Testament demands.

by day, continuing steadfastly . . . and breaking bread at home" (Acts 2:46)—and it appears that, for at least the first two centuries, the members of local churches all communicated at the Sunday Eucharist. The Ten Commandments were recited during service, together with the Lord's Prayer—the "Our Father," the Paternoster in Latin, though without its concluding doxology, "For thine is the kingdom and the power and the glory," in its earliest Greek form—and the singing of a psalm or hymn. The bread was so powerful a symbol of fellowship that fragments were taken to those unable to attend the service, through illness or imprisonment; those guilty of a serious moral lapse were excluded from communion until the fault was purged, but were allowed to attend the first part of the service.

Baptism was both dangerous and liberating. The rite involved formal entry into an illegal cult, but it offered freedom from past sins, for the act of being "buried with Christ," as Paul put it, implied a total renunciation of evil. In the early church, baptism followed immediately upon a person's declaration of belief in Christ. No examination was made of a candidate's knowledge of the faith, for there was as yet little doctrine to be examined; indeed, dead friends and relatives were sometimes retrospectively included in a baptism. Changes came in the second century—lengthy periods of preparation, deathbed and infant baptisms—but the first Christians had no inhibitions about the instant baptism of adults. Ritual bathing was familiar to pagans and Jews alike; it was practiced in the Greco-Roman cults of healing divinities such as Asklepius, while the Jews purified themselves with water after having sex or touching a corpse. John the Baptist had immersed followers in the river Jordan while they were "confessing their sins" (Matt. 3:6), and had preached "the baptism of repentance unto remission of sins" (Mark 1:4) as the Christians now did. Early baptisms were often carried out during the Mass. No instructions were laid down over whether the whole body should be immersed, or whether a mere sprinkling of water sufficed.*

Most early Christian communities met in rooms in the houses of well-to-do believers. At Corinth, Paul remarked that the house of Stephenas was set up "to minister unto the saints" and urged the brethren "also be in subjection unto such, and to every one that helpeth in the work and laboureth" (1 Cor. 16:15–17). A

---

*Baptisteries were built as a later compromise; although they did not have the running water of a river like the Jordan, they contained stone pools into which the candidates could step. Like so much else, this lack of clarity led to controversy; in the East, infant baptism was followed at once by Holy Communion, whereas in the West this awaited Confirmation at a more mature age; Baptists, among the most powerful of Protestant sects, were to believe in adult baptism by immersion alone.

husband and wife, Aquila and Priscia, had "a church in their house" at Corinth and then at Rome. A hierarchy began to develop within two decades or so of the crucifixion. The mother church at Jerusalem had a single head in James, the Lord's brother. In Gentile cities there were bishops, presbyters, and deacons. The ordination of clergy was mentioned by Paul, writing to Timothy of the "gift of God which is in thee through the laying on of my hands" (2 Tim. 1:6). Paul laid down the moral requirements for a bishop; the candidate must be "without reproach, the husband of one wife, temperate, sober minded, orderly, given to hospitality, apt to teach, no brawler, but gentle, not contentious, no lover of money" (1 Tim. 3:2–3). Quietly, modestly, so it seemed, the faith was making its way through the Roman world. Then came apocalypse.

Paul was attacked by an angry mob in Jerusalem in about A.D. 58, and Roman troops were forced to arrest him to prevent a lynching. He was transferred for this own protection to Caesarea, which was heavily guarded as the residence of the Roman governor, and held for two years before successfully pleading to be tried at Rome. He was shipped under escort on a small coastal vessel to Myra in southern Asia Minor, where he and other prisoners were transferred to a large grain carrier plying between Alexandria and Italy. The ship was caught by violent October gales and driven west from Crete for two weeks. The crew threw the cargo overboard; an angel told Paul that he would be spared to stand in front of Caesar. Running ashore on the coast of Malta, the ship struck a reef and the stern broke up. The soldiers aboard wished to kill the prisoners, but a centurion restrained them, and all on board were washed safely onto the beach. They lit a fire; as Paul tossed a bundle of sticks on it, a viper bit his hand.

He survived the snake; Caesar, in the form of Nero, he did not. He spent two years in rented rooms in Rome, preaching "with all boldness, none forbidding him" (Acts 28:31). By tradition, Peter was also in the city. The papacy was to claim that Peter was the first bishop of the church at Rome, and that his preeminence among the apostles—Jesus had given him "the keys of the kingdom of heaven," promising him that "whatsoever thou shall bind on earth shall be bound in heaven" (Matt. 16:19)—transferred to itself. No proof exists; concrete sighting of Peter in the New Testament vanish after the circumcision debate. A mysterious passage in John's gospel—in which the resurrected Jesus says that, when Peter is old, he will stretch out his hands, and be tied and carried "whither thou wouldest not" (John 21:18)—hints at crucifixion.

It is likely that both Peter and Paul were at Rome when, in A.D. 64, Nero turned on the Christians in the city, burning them "like candles in the night." The tradition that they were martyred at Rome is ancient and was accepted without question by early writers. The certainty is that both disappeared with no trace beyond the traditional sites of their burials, Peter in a necropolis on the Vatican Hill, Paul on the road to Ostia.*

In Jerusalem the Jews were close to rebellion. A new Roman prefect of Judea, Gessius Florus, arrested a number of zealots at Caesarea in A.D. 66. Tensions grew worse when the prefect attempted to appropriate funds from the temple. A group of youngsters carried a basket round Jerusalem, asking people to toss loose change into it for Florus, as if he were a beggar. The satire did not pass unnoticed. "Far from being ashamed of his greed," the Jewish historian Josephus wrote, the prefect "became further enraged and was provoked to . . . drain the city dry." Even though Jewish leaders apologized for the insult, many were arrested and brought in front of Florus, who had them first whipped and then crucified.

An uprising began. The rebels captured the Antonia fortress on the third day. They burnt the archives where notes of debts were kept in order to encourage the poor to join the uprising. Nero ordered the inevitable Roman counterattack under Vespasian, a veteran who had commanded legions in Britain and Germany. "Those who believed in Christ migrated from Jerusalem," Eusebius, the first historian of the church, wrote, "and it was as if holy men had abandoned the royal capital of the Jews and the entire Jewish land; and the judgment of God at last overtook them for the hateful crimes against Christ. . . ."[8] By the end of A.D. 67 the Romans had retaken all of Galilee. Nero committed suicide on June 9, A.D. 68, murmuring *"qualis artifiex pereo,"* "what an artist perishes in me." Vespasian departed for Rome in the summer of A.D. 70 to replace him as emperor, leaving his son Titus to direct the final siege of Jerusalem.

It took fifteen days for the Roman battering rams to breach the first wall. Five days later Titus broke through the second wall with a thousand legionaries into a maze of alleys housing braziers' smithies and wool shops. Josephus claims that Titus offered safe conduct to anyone who wished to leave the city, but the "militants mistook his humanity for weakness," counterattacking and using their knowledge of the narrow streets to ambush the enemy. Titus was forced to retreat. The Romans toiled for seventeen days to raise immense earthworks opposite the Antonia, a marble-encrusted fortress adjoining the northern portico of the temple. In darkness, a small Roman assault group penetrated into the Antonia and cut down the sleeping sentries. Fighting continued around the temple gates for ten

---

*Cities competed fiercely to be recognized as the sites of martydoms; Rome's claims for Peter and Paul were not contested. Shrines to the two were recorded in 200. A cemetery on the slope of the Vatican Hill was discovered during building work on the crypt of St. Peter's in 1939. A small shrine dating from around A.D. 165 was uncovered at a spot to which the basilica had been oriented. Fragments of bone found within it were declared to be relics of St. Peter in 1965. Executed criminals were habitually thrown into mass graves, however, so the assignation is controversial. A letter written in A.D. 96 from the church at Rome to Christians in Corinth refers to Peter and Paul as "our apostles" who had achieved glory "having borne testimony before the rulers."[9]

hours; at length, "Jewish fury prevailing over Roman skill," the legionaries wavered and fell back. The Romans spent a week razing the Antonia and then built further embankments. The conflict around the temple "raged incessantly, and fights between small parties sallying out upon each other were continuous."[10] Siege engines were dragged up the embankments to batter the western wall of the temple, but had no effect on the massive Herodian masonry. Attempts to scale the walls with ladders failed.

Two days later Titus attacked at dawn with his whole force. As they broke into the courtyards, one of his soldiers seized a burning brand of timber and, hoisted on the shoulders of a comrade, flung it through a low golden door that led to the rooms surrounding the temple sanctuary. "As the flame shot up, a cry, as poignant as the tragedy, arose from the Jews," Josephus recounted, "who flocked to the rescue, lost to all thought of self-preservation, all husbanding of strength, now that the object of all their past vigilance was vanishing." A pile of bodies accumulated around the altar outside the building, down whose steps "flowed a stream of blood, and the bodies of those killed above went sliding to the bottom." The rebels retreated into the upper part of the city. The legionaries so glutted themselves with plunder from the treasury chambers that the value of gold throughout the region was depreciated by half.

The Romans took the lower part of the city the next day, setting it on fire as far as the pool of Siloam. The rebels were in an apocalyptic mood; watching from the upper city, "they declared with beaming faces that they cheerfully awaited the end, seeing that, with the people slaughtered, the temple in ashes, and the town in flames, they were leaving nothing to their foes. . . ." It took the legions eighteen days to build the embankments necessary to break into the upper city; the trees for several miles around had already been cut down and timber had to be hauled for many miles. A portion of the wall was broken by battering rams, and the Romans planted their standards on the towers "with clapping of hands and jubilation"; then, "pouring into the alleys, sword in hand, they massacred indiscriminately all whom they met, and burnt the houses of all who had taken refuge within. . . ."[11] They ceased killing in the evening, but the city burnt through the night. Thus, on September 26, A.D. 70, ended the siege of Jerusalem. The bulk of the city was razed to the ground, to "leave future visitors to the spot no ground for believing that it had ever been inhabited."

The Third Race:

Early Writing and Worship

The Gospels, and more settled and formal patterns of worship, were beginning to emerge as Jerusalem burned. The city was to maintain a dazzling grip on the Christian imagination, often under its alternative name of Zion, but by A.D. 70 the religion was gaining strength and coherence in the Gentile world. The Gospels provided the essential written core of belief, impervious to time and place. They were written anonymously, in capital letters with no spaces between the words, and in Greek. Provided they remained in being, the seed of the faith could not be extinguished by onslaughts against the faithful, who were reviled in a popular insult as the "third race," distinct from Jews and pagans. Roman officials recognized the importance of the Gospel texts, singling them out for burning and confiscation.

The origins of the Gospels lie in the memories and evocations passed on by those who had known Jesus. The Gospel writers molded this into narratives of his life and Passion—the earliest description refers to "the memoirs called the Gospels"*—to which the frequent use of direct speech gives great power and cadence. They did their work well. Together with Paul, what the Gospel writers wrote made up nine-tenths of the New Testament (in its normally accepted form of twenty-seven books; the Ethiopic Church includes eight additional texts). Over time their words have been translated as a whole into more than 1,000 languages, and in part into another 900,[†1] progressing from papyrus and parchment

---

*In about A.D. 150 the Christian teacher and writer Justin Martyr wrote of the Eucharist that "the apostles, in the memoirs called the Gospels composed by them, have thus delivered unto us what was enjoined upon them."[2] The word "gospel" comes from the old Anglo-Saxon "god-spell," meaning "good news." The original Greek word for "evangelist" meant a person carrying good news.

†In 1999, Wycliffe Bible Translators calculated that the world has 6,701 languages and that the Bible had been translated in part or whole into 2,197 of them.[3]

to paper and the printing press, divided into chapters in the thirteenth century and numbered verses in the sixteenth. Their message remains the wellspring of the faith; the way in which they wrote it, blending oratory, parable, mystery, and miracle, indelibly marks the Christian imagination.

Who they were, and when they wrote, are not certain. The tradition of Matthew, Mark, Luke, and John, supposedly writing in that order, was already ancient when the church historian Eusebius noted it in the fourth century and declared it to be "undoubtedly true."[4] In fact, Mark was probably the first Gospel to be completed, shortly after the deaths of Peter and Paul in A.D. 64 or 65. The Gospel was attributed to "Mark the interpreter of Peter"[5] by Papias, the bishop of Hierapolis in about A.D. 130, and this was taken to be the John Mark mentioned in Acts.* Matthew and Luke draw heavily on Mark;† and their accurate descriptions of how Titus used earthworks and demolition to deal with Jerusalem— Luke refers to Jesus weeping over the city and prophesying that "thine enemies shall cast up a bank about thee" (Luke 19:43), and Matthew includes a warning that "there shall not be left one stone upon another" (Matt. 24:2)—suggest that they wrote after the destruction of the temple in A.D. 70. Luke, a Gentile and the "beloved physician" to whom the writer of Colossians refers (Col. 4:14), wrote both his own Gospel and the Acts of the Apostles, which includes firsthand accounts of his journeys with Paul, at a probable date around A.D. 80. The disciple Matthew was credited with his Gospel by Papias, who said that "Matthew compiled the Sayings in the Aramaic language, and everyone translated them as well as he could."[6] In fact, the Gospel seems to have been written in Greek between A.D. 85 and 90 by an unknown Christian living in Antioch.

The order of the first Gospels is thus most likely to have been Mark, Luke, and then Matthew, with Luke the only actual author. Many of the details of Jesus' life broadly overlap, though Mark makes no mention of the Nativity, and the everyday observations that they make give their wondrous story an earthy reality. John's gospel is a sharp contrast, philosophical, probing the identity of Jesus and his relationship with God more closely than the Synoptic Gospels, speaking of him in the abstract, as the Word, the Light, the Way. It is less biographical and less anecdotal. The Gospel mentions only seven miracles, though the raising of Lazarus appears only in John; it makes no use of parables and says nothing of the exorcisms and casting out of devils that pepper the other Gospels. A special blessing is reserved for future believers, for "they that have not seen, and yet have be-

---

*John Mark was associated in Acts with Paul rather than Peter, however.

†The passages in Matthew and Luke that are not included in Mark are often so similar that many scholars believe that they come from the same source, a lost gospel or collection of the sayings of Jesus. This hypothetical text is referred to as Q, from the German word *Quelle*, or "source."

lieved" (John 20:26). The strongest statement of Christ's divinity is made in John, when Jesus replies directly to the Samaritan woman who says that she knows that Christ is coming: "I that speak unto thee am he" (John 4:26). Like Paul, John stresses rebirth and faith as the prerequisites of salvation: "Except a man be born of water and the Spirit, he cannot enter into the kingdom of God" (John 3:5). It was claimed by the second half of the second century that the Gospel was written by the apostle John, who, having read and approved the earlier Gospels, felt that they left gaps and so wrote his own at Ephesus in his old age. In its finished form, at least, it is unlikely to have appeared before A.D. 125, well after his death; but references within the Gospel suggest that original material was written in about A.D. 85, and the work may have been completed at a later date by followers from the church John founded at Ephesus.

The Epistles—the great body of letters ascribed to Paul, and the brief contributions of James, Peter, John, and Jude—combined with Acts to chart the spread of the faith after the Resurrection. It is uncertain how many of Paul's epistles were written by the apostle himself. The early Church credited him with all thirteen, as well as Hebrews, though the scholar Origen said early in the third century "who wrote that epistle, in truth, God alone knows." The English divine Edward Evanson questioned the authorship of Ephesians for the first time in 1792. Since then only four epistles have survived as indisputably Paul's work, with a further three most likely to be his, and the remainder most likely not.*

To this core of Gospels and Epistles was added the Book of Revelation. With it, the expectation of apocalypse was transferred from Jews to Christians. Revelation mirrors in its tone and content the Book of Daniel, which portrays the sufferings of the Jews from the Babylonian conquests to the desecration of the Jerusalem Temple and the building on its site of a Greek altar, the "abomination that makes desolate," by the Seleucid king Antiochus IV in 167 B.C. The book, with Daniel's visions of devastation and ultimate resurrection, was written around that date. The Babylonians, Medes, Persians, and Greeks, the four powers which had tormented the Jews, become the four beasts of Daniel, a lion with eagle's wings and a man's heart, a slavering bear with ribs in its mouth, a leopard

---

*Paul is accepted as the author of Galatians, Romans, and 1 and 2 Corinthians by almost all scholars, and of 1 Thessalonians, Colossians, and Philippians by most. Of the other New Testament books, it is possible that James draws on the sermons and sayings of Jesus' brother James, who became leader of the church at Jerusalem before being martyred at the urging of the high priest Ananus in A.D. 61. 1 Peter is written in an educated Greek that the fisherman is unlikely to have used himself; it may have been written at his prompting by a follower, but seems more likely to be pseudonymous. 2 Peter refers to a situation after the deaths of the apostles—"from the day that the fathers fell asleep, all things continue. . . ." (2 Pet. 3:4)—and was almost certainly written in his name sometime after his death. John's letters may be the work of the gospel writer or of the congregation he led. The same uncertainty applies to Jude, whose letter is traditionally ascribed to Judas, the brother of Jesus; the shortened name Jude is used to avoid any link to Judas Iscariot.

with four heads and the wings of a fowl, and, most terrible of all, a beast with ten horns and iron teeth. *Apokalypsis* means no more than "revelation" in Greek, but the word was pregnant with trauma, with empires and kingdoms emerging from the sea in the guise of Daniel's foul hybrids to savage the faithful before they are destroyed in turn by the wrath of God.

The power of apocalyptic belief was shown in the Jerusalem uprising of A.D. 70, where the Roman Empire was seen as the fifth Beast, and where Josephus had described rebels with "beaming faces" rejoicing as the city burnt about their ears. Survivors held out after A.D. 70 in the wilderness fortress of Masada. Here, near the western shore of the Dead Sea, cliffs rose 820 feet from scrub and sand to a flat-topped summit where Herod the Great had built a palace on three stony terraces, equipped with bathhouses, grain stores, and cisterns hewn from the living rock. A double wall with thirty towers guarded the steep path leading up the eastern face. The legions surrounded it after they had destroyed Jerusalem. Forced labor was drafted to build a prodigious earthwork, a ramp that slowly grew from a col on the western flank to reach the walls. The final assault came in April of A.D. 73 or 74. When the legionaries broke in, they found only seven of the 960 Jews alive. The rest had committed mass suicide; perhaps they had expected a Messiah other than Christ to save them.

If the military apocalypse was over, Jewish writers continued with apocalyptic literature, much of which—the apocalypses of Enoch, Esdras, Baruch, Abraham—entered the Christian tradition. The Book of Revelation ensured that the concept passed directly into the Christian Testament with its power and intensity refreshed. The work was attributed to John the apostle, but it was probably written in about A.D. 95 by a Christian prophet of the same name in response to his own exile and a wave of Roman persecution under the emperor Domitian. Through it, a reworked apocalypse—unspeakable suffering now inflicted upon Christians by the horned beasts of empire; then pitiless vengeance from heaven, the triumphant Second Coming of Christ, and the creation of the messianic Kingdom on earth—entered the New Testament. It was a strange and restless addition; haunting in its imagery, violent, troubled, a prophecy of blood and fire.

✤ SCORES OF OTHER works—gospels, epistles, acts, apocalypses—were rejected from the formal canon of biblical texts. Some two dozen gospels alone appeared in the early centuries, intended to fill gaps, or to defend heresies, or written for the sheer joy of fable-making. Their writers ascribed their inventions to the apostles, to Mary Magdalene and the Virgin Mary, even to Judas Iscariot and Pontius Pilate. The most obvious gap was the childhood of Jesus, to which only Luke had referred, and then with the single anecdote that he had briefly strayed from his parents as a twelve-year-old. Several "infancy gospels" soon provided embroidery. Supposedly authentic accounts by the apostle Thomas and by James, Jesus' brother, were among the earliest. Miracles were said to flow from feeling the child Jesus' clothes or sipping the water he bathed in. Vipers "burst apart" in his presence, and the severed foot of a woodcutter was instantly healed at his touch. The fictional Jesus emerged as an otherwise unlovable lad, however. As a five-year-old he was so wise that none could instruct him. He told his teachers that "I existed when you were born . . . listen to me and I'll teach you a wisdom that no one else knows except for me and the one who sent me to you"; he "fashioned twelve sparrows with mud" and when his father rebuked him for playing on the Sabbath, clapped his hands in temper and shouted to the birds to "be off, fly away, and remember me"; he had the power to kill as well as cure, warning another child who angered him that "you won't continue your journey," whereupon "all of a sudden he fell down and died."[7]

Mary is rarely sighted in the Gospels after the Nativity; her appearance at the marriage feast at Cana, and at the crucifixion, is mentioned only in John's gospel. At her son's death, the disciple "whom he loved"—John, perhaps—"took her into his own house" (John 19:26). After Pentecost there is silence. No mention is made of her perpetual virginity; the Gospels list four brothers of Jesus by name—"is not his mother called Mary? and his brethren, James, and Joseph, and Simon, and Judas?" (Matt. 13:55. Mark uses Joses for Joseph)—and refer to "sisters" as well (Mark 6:3). Neither is there evidence that she considered her son to be the Son of God while he was alive. Far from that, Mark wrote that the family tried to restrain Jesus from preaching on the grounds that he was "beside himself" (Mark 3:21). Only with the Resurrection, and not before, is mention made that Mary and her surviving sons were convinced of his divinity; they were members of the group that "continued stedfastly in prayer" after Pentecost (Acts 1:14). James became the leader of the Jerusalem church, but accounts of Mary's last years, her death, and her assumption into heaven were manufactured later.

The first signs of the coming cult of the Virgin appear in about A.D. 150 in the infancy gospel or Protevangelium of James. The writer stresses Mary's special holiness for the first time. An angel appears to her mother as well as to herself, and she believes in the divinity of her son from his birth. She remains a lifelong virgin; a midwife who doubts this, and examines her, cries: "I have put the living God on trial. Look! My hand is disappearing! It's being consumed by the flames. . . ."[8] The problem of the "sisters" and "brothers" of Jesus is solved by making Joseph an elderly widower who already has children when he marries Mary. Apocryphal gospels of Mary were written from the end of the second century onwards. The Assumption of the Virgin, a gospel in which the risen Christ tells her of her imminent death and transformation to heaven, and where she performs her own miraculous healings, was written in the fourth century. It was denounced as a heresy in the fifth century, but some still considered it to be authentic a millennium later. Mary was also awarded her own apocalypse, the Revelation of Mary, in which she intercedes for the damned, who are cast into the pit for such sins as lying late in bed on Sundays and not rising when a priest enters the room.

Joseph himself vanishes from the Gospels of Matthew and Luke after Jesus' childhood; John makes only two passing references to him, and Mark none at all. This did not inhibit later writers, who fashioned a history of Joseph the Carpenter, and made of him a pious saint who died at the age of 111 after a life so ascetic and free from lust that Jesus' siblings regress further, from half-brothers and half-sisters to cousins.

Not all the inventions were harmless. Pontius Pilate is known to have been recalled to Rome from Palestine in A.D. 36. This followed his overreaction to a crowd that had gathered at the urging of a Samaritan prophet in the unfulfilled hope of witnessing the miraculous rediscovery of buried temple treasures. The crowd was bloodily attacked by Roman troops and Pilate authorized several executions. No official trace is left of Pilate after this, but Christian legend filled the silence. The emperor Caligula was said to have ordered him to commit suicide in one account,[9] while in another, Nero had him beheaded,[10] so that he joined Peter and Paul as a Christian martyr. As hostility between Jews and Christians increased, the African church father Tertullian described him as "Christian before his own conscience."[11] An apocryphal Acts of Pilate has Pilate vigorously defending Jesus against the Jews. Not content with crucifying Jesus and seeing him buried by Joseph of Arimathea, the Jews then imprison Joseph until he makes a miraculous escape. Some versions included a letter from Pilate to the emperor Claudius blaming the Jews for Christ's death and testifying to the truth of the Resurrection. Pilate is described as a Gentile Christian, "uncircumcised in the flesh, but circumcised in the heart" (Acts Pil. 12:1). The Acts of Pilate was very popular, appearing in Syriac, Coptic, and Armenian as well as Latin and Greek. It inspired the Egyptian Copts to venerate Pilate as a saint and martyr, and the Greek Orthodox to canonize his wife; less happily, its legends were used in mystery plays that stirred medieval hatreds against the Jews.

The Gospel of Peter, written about A.D. 150, also defended Pilate in order to heighten the guilt of the Jews. It was ultimately condemned, not for this, but because its claim that the crucified Jesus "remained silent, as if in no pain"[12] smacked of the heresy that Christ was immune from human suffering. Peter had his apocalypses, too. The first Revelation of Peter, written around A.D. 130, contrasted the torments of hell with the pleasures of paradise; it was popular and still being read in Palestinian churches in the fifth century. The second* was a heretical attack on the orthodox church, in which the "living Jesus" stands laughing by the cross as his physical form is crucified. Peter's later life was a frustrating shadow, not mentioned in Acts. Legend gave it substance: miracles, of a speaking dog and a dried fish restored to life; a struggle with the magician Simon Magus, who attempts and fails to fly to heaven from the Roman forum; and Peter's eventual crucifixion under Nero, after Christ persuades him to return to Rome after he had made his escape.

Curiosity also demanded that the nameless characters in the Gospels be identified. The wise men of the Nativity appeared only in Matthew, who left their number and names blank. In one tradition, in Europe, it was held that there were three of them, because they had offered the three gifts of gold, frankincense, and myrrh. Their names were filled in as Balthasar, Melchior, and Gaspar; in a later English elaboration, each was said to have come from one of the three known continents, Asia, Africa, and Europe. Armenian and Syrian texts insisted that they were a dozen strong, and named each one, and his father for good measure. The rich man who spurned Lazarus became Dives or Nineveh. The robbers crucified on each side of Jesus were named as Zoatham and Camma in the West; the Acts of Pilate called them Dysmas and Gestas, and identified the Roman soldier who pierced Jesus with his spear as Longinus. Pilate's wife, unnamed in the Gospels, became sanctified as Procla.

It was not until 382 that Pope Damasus authorized a complete text of the canonical books of the Bible; disputed works† were definitively excluded by a council held eighteen years later at Carthage, which fixed the New Testament canon in its present form. The core works, however—the four Gospels, Acts, and Paul's letters—were established very early. Bishop Polycarp spoke of New Testament books being read in church at Smyrna in about A.D. 107. The Gospels began to circulate as a single collection at this time, with Acts separated from Luke's gospel and soon used as the hinge between the Gospels and Paul's letters. The

---

*It was among a large collection of Gnostic texts found near Nag Hammadi in Egypt in 1946. The significance of the Gnostic heresy—the dualism of the supreme God of love and the evil of the material world—is covered in a later chapter.

†They included several widely read texts: Peter's Acts and Revelation; the apocalyptic Shepherd of Hermas; the Gospel of the Hebrews, in which the Holy Spirit carried Jesus away from temptation by one of the hairs of his head; the Epistle of Barnabas, supposedly the work of Paul's fellow missionary but probably written by a Gentile from Alexandria; and the Epistle of the Apostles, with its fanciful claim to have been written by eleven of the apostles.

Muratorian Canon,* the oldest surviving list of recognized texts, is believed to date from later in the second century. With a few minor exceptions, it lists all the New Testament books. The Greek for books is *biblia;* a century after the crucifixion, the Christians had their Bible.

✤   BY THE LAST third of the first century, local authorities were taking notice of the Church and had identified a distinct form of worship. Pliny the Younger, the Roman governor of Bithynia in today's northern Turkey, was as perplexed by Christianity as Pilate had been by Christ. He was an observant man, the adopted son of the great natural historian Pliny, and he carefully investigated the new cult in about A.D. 112 and wrote to the emperor Trajan for advice in dealing with it.

Informers had come to Pliny with tales of Christian cannibalism, incest, and treason, and with lists of suspects. The charge of cannibalism resulted from pagan misunderstanding of the Communion, and the taking of the "blood" and "body" of Christ. Incest was evoked by the Christians' proclamation of "love" for their "sisters and brothers," and treason by their refusal to worship the emperor. Pliny used a triple test on the accused. He obliged them to invoke the gods, to worship a specially set up statue of Trajan with offerings of wine and incense, and to revile Christ; "things," he explained to the emperor, "which it is said that no real Christian will do under any compulsion." Some denied that they had ever been Christians; others admitted it but said that they had ceased believing, and cursed Christ as evidence. The sum of their "crime or error"—Pliny was not sure which—had been to "meet together on a fixed day before daybreak, to repeat in turn a hymn to Christ as to a god and to bind themselves by an oath, not to commit adultery, not to break their word, and not to deny a loan when demanded." They later ate together, not the human flesh and blood that the informers had misinterpreted from the Mass, but "food of an ordinary and harmless kind." Pliny was reluctant to believe that Christianity was as innocent as this, and he determined to find out the truth "by the examination—even with torture—of two maids who were called deaconesses." He drew a blank: "I found nothing but a perverse and extravagant superstition."[13]

Pliny supervised the trials of those who persisted in their belief, asking them three times if they were Christians. After the third affirmation, he wrote, "I ordered them to be led to execution," a fate he thought they deserved if only for

---

*The canon was discovered by Ludovico Muratori, an eighteenth-century Italian historian and theological scholar, in an eighth-century manuscript. The list mentions all the New Testament books except Hebrews, James, and 1 and 2 Peter.

their "inflexible obstinacy." Pliny was a humane and polished man, however, the author of charming love letters to his wife, and he was concerned at both the morality and the practical results of executions. He asked Trajan whether those of tender age should be treated as adults, if the penitent should be pardoned, if the "mere name of Christian" was enough in itself for punishment. Persecution had some effect in reviving paganism; deserted temples refilled, and trade resumed in the fodder for the animals sacrificed in pagan rites. But Pliny also noted that prosecuting Christians produced "the usual result of spreading the crime." He reported that "many persons of every age, of every rank, of both sexes even, are daily involved," and that the contagion was spreading from the cities to villages and the countryside. Trajan was sympathetic to the new religion in his reply. No universal formula could be applied, he wrote; Christians were "not to be sought out" and, though they should be punished if reported and convicted, even the most suspect should be pardoned if they proved their disbelief in Christ "by worshiping our gods." The emperor was scathing about the anonymous pamphlets being circulated against Christians; he said they were "unworthy of our age" and should not be used as a basis for prosecution.

Pliny's analysis of Christian strengths was shrewd. A generation that was now remote from the living Christ remained willing to die for him. Ignatius, bishop of Antioch, was transported to Rome to be slain by animals in the Colosseum in about A.D. 107. "I will entice them to devour me quickly," the bishop wrote on his last journey. "Let come on me fire and cross and conflicts with wild beasts, wrenching of bones, mangling of limbs . . . only let me reach Jesus Christ." Ignatius was widely respected, and Pliny was correct in observing that persecuting people of devotion served merely to spread curiosity about the faith for which they had died. Open-air preaching was easily observed by enemies and had become dangerous since Nero's persecution. Jewish hostility mounted after the destruction of Jerusalem; from A.D. 70 it was rare for Christians to be allowed to preach in synagogues. Worship retreated into private houses. Services were generally split into two parts, one open to all and the other only to the baptized. In times of tolerance, interested pagans would watch the first half of the service and thus be tempted to become baptized. Pliny was right, too, to note the Christians' strong moral code. Paul's letters to the Corinthians showed that they did not always live up to it—members of the flock were living in sin, warring with one another, disturbing worship by screeching in tongues, preaching false doctrines—but they were obliged to try. No pagan cult made such moral demands on its members.

Charity was an important part of the belief. Pliny mentioned that Christians never refused a request for a loan, and he could have added that they cared for the sick and vulnerable, that they visited their brethren who were imprisoned or sent to the mines, and that they helped others in times of catastrophe, plague, famine, and earthquake. Regular collections for the poor were made on Sundays. Acts of individual generosity were recorded very early, like those of the centurion Cornelius who "gave much alms to the people" (Acts 10:2) at Caesarea. "We, who loved . . . wealth and possession," the Christian apologist Justin wrote in about A.D. 155, "now put together even what we have and share it with all who are in need." By 251 the church at Rome was supporting fifteen hundred widows and poor people; the following year, when Carthage was struck by plague, Bishop Cyprian sent his deacons to tend the sick. "Jews do not allow any of their own people to become beggars," a later pagan emperor, Julian, complained, "and the Christians support not only their own but also our poor." Any Christian traveler would be lodged and fed for three days with no questions asked, a custom that led to mendicant friars and medieval holy wanderers.

Even the poorest Christians were decently buried in cemeteries or catacombs. The latter took their name from the web of tunnels dug in the soft tufa-stone two miles from Rome near the Appian Way in an area called Catacumbas. At Rome they eventually extended for many miles in thirty distinct catacombs; the earliest tombs include that of Flavia Domitilla, exiled widow of the consul of A.D. 95. The catacombs at Syracuse made up an underground city, with layers of streets and squares cut out of the rock, and large bottle-shaped halls lit by air shafts. They were popular meeting places, and services and festivals were held in them. The largest complex, built by the ex-slave, Pope St. Callistus, in A.D. 217–22, includes a papal chamber. At first there was no expressly Christian art other than the cross, since the second commandment forbade graven images, but by the end of the second century this restriction was ignored.

Walls were painted with doves, anchors, olive branches, dolphin fishermen, and portraits of the Good Shepherd and Jonah escaping from the whale. Signs of the cross and the fish were common; one of the earliest wooden crosses to survive was found in a small room in a villa at Herculaneum, overwhelmed in the same volcanic apocalypse of A.D. 79 that destroyed Pompeii. The fish was a secret sign; the first letters of the Greek words *Iesous CHristos THeou Uios Soter,* "Jesus Christ God's Son and Savior," spell *Ichthus,* Greek for fish. "Fill me with the fish," ran an early epitaph in Gaul. "Remember thy Pectorius in the peace of the fish." By A.D. 200, Peter and Paul were widely understood to have been the founders of the Roman Church. Peter was already thought to be the gatekeeper of heaven. Graffiti and sketches in catacombs show a square-jawed face and a short beard below a bald or cropped head, with a set of keys, and sometimes a fishing boat or a cock in memory of his denial of Christ. Opponents scratched their graffiti on walls,

A silver plaque with the monogram of Chi-Rho, the first two letters of "Christ" in Greek. It was used on Christian standards and on priests' vestments. This example is Romano-British. The outline of a fish was a more secret sign. The first letters of the Greek words *Iesous CHristos THeou Uios Soter*, "Jesus Christ God's Son and Savior," spell *Ichthus*, Greek for fish. "Fill me with the fish," ran an early epitaph in Gaul. "Remember thy Pectorius in the peace of the fish."

too. In one, a boy raises his arm in worship to a crucified figure with the head of an ass, with the title: "Alexamenos worships his god."

Christians were persistent, a virtue that the illegality of their faith demanded of them. Pliny chose to torture deaconesses, but they had proved no easier to break down than the men. They looked for converts even among those who persecuted and abused them. As pagans they had spurned those who differed from them in blood and custom, Justin wrote in about A.D. 150, but as Christians "we now . . . live together, pray for our enemies, and seek to win over those who unjustly hate us."[14] Pliny found that they were making inroads at all levels of society, rural and urban. He could find no reason for condemning them as treasonable. Christians were clean-living and politically docile. It was only their "obstinacy" in clinging to their illegal faith that gave Pliny grounds to punish them.

The basics of that faith were outlined by the Christian philosopher Aristides of Athens. He wrote an "apology"—the word meant a defense or vindication—that was presented to the emperor, perhaps to Hadrian in about A.D. 124, or to Antoninus Pius some twenty years later. "As for Christians," Aristides informed the emperor, "they trace their origins to the Lord Jesus Christ. He is confessed to be the Son of the most high God, who came down from heaven by the Holy Spirit and was born of a virgin and took flesh, and in a daughter of man there lived the Son of God. . . . This Jesus . . . was pierced by the Jews, and he died and was buried; and they say that after three days he rose and ascended into heaven. . . . They believe God to be the creator and Maker of all things, in whom are all things and from whom are all things."[15] It was an effective encapsulation, if lacking detail on the Last Judgment. It took a further two centuries for a formal creed to be agreed upon, but a Rule of Truth—also known simply as "the faith" or "the tradition"—was recorded by Irenaeus, the bishop of Lyons, in about A.D. 180. This included the belief that Christ would reappear to judge and "raise up anew all flesh of the whole human race."

❖ IN WORSHIP, A distinction arose between the Lord's Supper and the full meal that the Corinthians had eaten. The Communion service was held early in the morning. The agape, or love feast, took place later in the day. It was a communal meal, which provided members of the small and vulnerable cult with a sense of fellowship and the poor and widows and orphans with a decent spread of food. Although pagans described gluttony and drunkenness, the meal was considered an act of worship in which "vileness and immodesty" played no part. "The participants, before sitting, first taste prayer of God," Tertullian wrote in about A.D. 197. "As much is eaten as satisfies the cravings of hunger; as much is drunk as befits the chaste." It was essential to remain sober, he added, because after the meal "each is asked to stand forth and sing, as he can, a hymn to God, either one from the Holy Scripture or one of his own composing—a proof of the measure of our drinking."[16]

Only the baptized, who had been reborn and washed with the remission of sins, were allowed to take Communion in the early morning service of *eucharistia*, or "thanksgiving." Even among them, Justin wrote in 155, the honor was conditional on moral behavior and was restricted to "he or she who . . . is living as Christ commanded." The service began with a reading from the apostles or the Old Testament prophets. After a sermon from the bishop or senior priest, all stood for solemn prayer and the kiss of peace. The bishop was then brought a cup of wine mixed with water and the bread. He took the sacraments and offered "praise and glory to the Father of the universe, through the name of the Son and the Holy Spirit." After his prayers, the congregation "express their joyful assent by saying 'Amen,'" the Hebrew word for "So be it." Justin wrote of the sacraments that "we do not receive them as common bread and common drink; but as Jesus Christ our Savior. . . . [W]e have been taught that the food which is blessed by the word of prayer transmitted from him, and by which our blood and flesh are changed and nourished, is the flesh and blood of that Jesus who was made flesh."[17] The sacraments were presented to each communicant by a deacon.

The early Eucharist prayer, recorded by Hippolytus, a presbyter at Rome who died in exile on Sardinia in about A.D. 236, remains utterly familiar:

> *Bishop:* The Lord be with you.
> *People:* And with your spirit.
> *Bishop:* Lift up your hearts.
> *People:* We lift them up to the Lord.
> *Bishop:* Let us give thanks to the Lord.
> *People:* It is right and meet.
> *Bishop:* We give thanks, O God, through your beloved Son Jesus Christ . . . whom by your good pleasure you sent from heaven to a Virgin's womb . . . who stretched out his hands when he suffered that he might free from suffering those who have believed in you . . . who when he was betrayed . . . took bread and gave thanks to you and said: "Take, eat, this is my body which is broken for you. Likewise also the cup, saying: this is my blood which is shed for you. When you do this, do it in remembrance of me. . . ."[18]

Great care was taken not to drop the bread, for it represented Christ's body; communicants received it in their hollowed palms, the left hand supporting the right. After the service, deacons carried pieces to the sick and those in prison, and communicants often took bread home to take privately during the week. Hippolytus warned against leaving it lying about the house, lest an unbaptized person—or even a mouse—should eat it.

Candidates for baptism were now given lengthy instruction in the new Gospels and doctrine. They were called catechumens, from the Greek word *katachizein,* to "din into the ears" or learn by rote, a process that could last for three years, and more in the East. A famous catechetical school was flourishing at Alexandria from about A.D. 180, attracting students from across the empire; Clement and his pupil Origen, who headed it between 190 and 215, were two of the greatest of the early Christian writers, sophisticated thinkers deeply read in the Greek philosophers and vulnerable both to pagan emperors and Christian bishops who scorned their originality.* Such schools were the basis of Christian education. Their teachers were often laymen who encouraged curious pagans as

---

*Both men had to flee Alexandria. Origen went to Palestine and was deposed from the priesthood, but founded a school at Caesarea before being tortured under the emperor Decius. Clement's name was removed from the martyrology, the official record of Christian martyrs, by Pope Clement VIII some thirteen hundred years after his death because some of his writings were considered unorthodox.

well as converts to attend their lectures. Brave souls held public debates or "apologetics" with pagan philosophers.

A catechumen was expected to lead a blameless life during the long period of teaching. Baptism normally took place at Easter. It was preceded by an intense period of fasting, and the confession of sins and exorcism, that became formalized in Lent. Careful preparation was essential because baptism addressed a person's past sins, but not his or her future faults. Since baptism was held to be the only moment apart from martyrdom when existing sin was washed away—"there are two things which give remission of sins," Melito of Sardis wrote in the 170s, "baptism and suffering for the sake of Christ"—it was sometimes delayed to the deathbed so that the departing Christian would enter the next life as free from sin as possible. No mention is made of infant baptism until the early third century, but the Pauline doctrine of Original Sin was to encourage it; by the fifth century the great theologian Augustine saw the whole of humanity as a *massa damnata,* a doomed race in which even the newborn, being infected with the sin of Adam, were in need of the purification of baptism.

During the baptism service, Hippolytus wrote in the early 200s, the candidate was asked three questions: "Do you believe in God, the Father Almighty . . . in Jesus Christ, the Son of God, who was born of the Holy Spirit and the Virgin Mary . . . in the Holy Spirit, in the holy church, and the resurrection of the body?" At each answer of "I believe," he or she was dipped in water before being anointed with oil as a symbol of the gift of the Spirit. In North Africa, milk and honey were given to the newly baptized to represent their entry into the promised land.

The catechumens kept a candidate vigil on the Saturday night after Easter Friday, and were baptized and received their first Communion early on Easter Day. The festival celebrating the Resurrection became increasingly important.* The date was fixed by the paschal full moon, with extreme limits of March 21 and April 25. The Jews celebrated Passover on the fourteenth day of the lunar month of Nisan. Early Christians followed this until those in Alexandria began to celebrate Easter on the following Sunday. When the church at Rome began to observe a regular Easter in about A.D. 170, it used the Alexandrian fashion. In 190, Bishop Victor of Rome demanded that all the Asian churches do likewise. He claimed that Peter and Paul had ordained this—although no mention is made in the New Testament—and declared that no Catholic Christian could do otherwise.† Some

---

*It was called *pascha* by the Greeks, from the Hebrew word for the Passover; the English Easter comes from the Anglo-Saxon goddess Oestre.

†Easter Day was fixed as the first Sunday after the full moon following the vernal equinox at the Council of Nicaea in 325. Despite this supposedly binding decision, Easter was celebrated in A.D. 387 on March 21 in Gaul, April 18 in Italy, and April 25 in Egypt.

Christians, known as Quartodecimans, continued to celebrate on the fourteenth day for another four centuries; Eastern Orthodox churches use a different dating system, and, although using Sunday, observed the festival Sunday four or five weeks later than in the West.

Fasting was demanded of Jews only on the Day of Atonement. Jesus himself had fasted for forty days before the start of his ministry, although he had criticized Pharisees who made a display of their rigor and starvation. Christians since Paul had fasted before their baptism, and some fasted on Wednesdays and Fridays. A fast day was called a "station," a military term for a day spent on watch; abstinence was required from desires and lusts as well as meat. The pre-Easter fast was not extended in the West to cover the forty-day preparation for baptism until the fourth century, with the Easterners eventually shamed into prolonging their weeklong fast. Holy Week ceremonies began to develop at the same time, at first with Maundy Thursday to commemorate the inauguration of the Eucharist, and later with Palm Sunday. Pentecost was adapted from the Jewish festival fifty days after the Passover. Christmas, Christ's Mass, was not celebrated in the West until about 336. December 25 may have been chosen to counter the pagan feast of *Natalis Solis Invicti,* the "Birth of the unconquered sun," on the same day; in the East it was held on January 6, the date already established for the celebration of Jesus' baptism at Epiphany.

Singing and chanting followed the Jewish traditions. The refrain "Alleluia"— "praise God"—was used without translation from the Hebrew. A pagan philosopher, Celsus, resented Christian singing because it had a soft beauty and comfort that dulled his critical senses. An early baptismal hymn has words from Paul's letter to the Ephesians:

> Awake thou that sleepeth
> and arise from the dead
> and Christ shall shine upon thee.
>   (Eph. 5:14)

Church music was to become sophisticated—as choirs grew, two sets of singers would chant alternately in the antiphonal singing that spread from Mesopotamia and Syria—but its origins were simple enough for families to gather and sing at the lighting of the evening lamp:

> Now we are come to the sun's hour of rest,
> The lights of evening round us shine,
> We hymn the Father, Son and Holy Spirit divine.[19]

As well as at Sunday Eucharist, many prayed privately at home each day. Hippolytus wrote that Christians should pray seven times daily: on rising, at the lighting of the evening lamp, at bedtime, at midnight, and at the third, sixth, and ninth hours of the day.

❖ CELSUS, WHO WROTE the first detailed criticism of Christianity in about A.D. 178, praised Christians' morality as well as their hymn-singing, but ridiculed their doctrine and their lowly social status. The majority of converts were found among the freeborn poor. "We see wooldressers, cobblers and fullers, the more uneducated and common individuals, not daring to say a word in the presence of their masters who are older and wiser," Celsus remarked with patrician disdain in his *True Discourse.* But he was impressed by their solidarity—"their agreement is quite amazing," he wrote, "the more so as it may be shown to rest on no trustworthy foundations"[20]—and their preaching skills. "When they get hold of children in private, and silly women with them, they are wonderfully eloquent," he allowed; but he stressed that it was the eloquence of "frogs holding a discourse round a swamp or worms in a conventicle in a corner of the mud." He mocked their claim for the "whole universe and the course of the heavenly spheres to dwell in us alone." If Jesus had divine power, Celsus thought, he would have appeared as the Son of God to those who reviled him; the miracles were the inventions of disciples as lowborn and poverty-stricken as their Lord, and their philosophy struck him as a botched misrepresentation of Plato's concept of the transmigration of souls.

A contemporary, the Christian apologist Athenagoras, confirmed the humble standing of most early Christians. "With us," he wrote, "you will find unlettered people, tradesmen and old women, who though they are unable to express in words the advantages of our teaching, demonstrate by acts the value of their principles." Inscriptions record a Christian butcher in Phrygia, a woodcarver in Ithnyia, a boat owner in Ostia. Christians rarely served in the army, the favorite career for ambitious young men. They avoided the administration and magistrature, lest they come in contact with idolatry or compromise Christian hostility to executions by condemning criminals to death. There were few converts among the great Roman families, whose members served as civic priests and gave generously to the pagan gods. Rich and powerful sympathizers did exist, however, if not in great numbers. Paul had preached to the governor of Cyprus, Sergius Paulus, who "believed"; a steward at Corinth was among other converts. The emperor Domitian arrested his cousin Flavius Clemens, his wife Domitilla, and the consul Acilius Glabrio on charges of atheism. They had "slipped into Jewish customs"—which probably meant Christianity and a refusal to worship Domitian as *Dominus et Deus,* Lord and God—and the two men were executed while Domitilla was exiled. The mistress of the emperor Commodus at the end of the second century intervened to prevent Christians from being sent to the mines.

The faith appealed strongly to women. Widows were particularly numerous, since girls as young as thirteen or fourteen were often married to much older men, and they were probably a majority in many congregations. A catalog of goods confiscated from church members at Cirta in North Africa lists 38 women's veils, 82 ladies' tunics, and 47 pairs of women's slippers, but only 16 men's tunics.[21] Women were important figures in the early Church. Paul praised the deaconess Phoebe, who "hath been a succourer of many, and of mine own self" (Rom. 16:2), the Philippians Euodia and Syntyche who "laboured with me in the gospel" (Phil. 4:2), and the missionary couple Prisca and Aquila who were "my fellow workers in Christ" (Rom. 16:3). Women such as Mary, the mother of John Mark, ran house churches where "many were gathered together and praying" (Acts 12:12).

Soon enough, however, men worried that women were becoming too influential. The Church encouraged their charity and their role in good works, and protected the dignity of vulnerable widows and the unmarried; but it blocked any aspirations to leadership. Writing in about A.D. 110, Polycarp, the bishop of Smyrna, allowed them no role beyond virgin, widow, or faithful wife. From the second century they were forbidden to minister to men and could serve women only as deaconesses. The powerful positions of presbyter and bishop were reserved for men. Women deacons were usually at least fifty years old; they administered to sick and poor women, assisted at the baptism of women, and were present as chaperones when women met bishops and male priests. "It is not permitted for a woman to speak in church," wrote the misogynist Tertullian in his treatise *On the Veiling of Women* in about A.D. 200. That was reaffirming Paul; but Tertullian added: "neither is it permitted her to teach, nor to baptize, nor to offer, nor to claim to herself a lot in any manly functions, not to say in any sacerdotal office."[22] The slow-growing cult of the Virgin Mary also tended to undermine the independence of women; Mary's blend of the motherly, the chaste, and the devout set an unattainable benchmark of perfection.

Slaves, too, were offered a spiritual equality that bore little trace of earthly emancipation. To pagan astonishment, masters and slaves were brethren while in church. Outside it, the social order was unchallenged. Slavery was a social and economic pillar of the ancient world. Prehistoric graves in Lower Egypt show that in about 8000 B.C. a Libyan people enslaved a bushman tribe;[23] the first recorded code of laws, the Babylonian Code of Hammurabi of about 1750 B.C., made specific provisions for slaves. Slaves had toiled to build the pyramids and the

Parthenon, and made up perhaps a third of the population of the Roman Empire; the huge slave market at Ephesus maintained the city's prosperity. They were taken captive in wars—Julius Caesar sold off 53,000 Gallic prisoners taken in one campaign—or captured in manhunts. Some were exchanged for goods; the trade in Italian wine to Gaul was valued at 15,000 slaves a year. They worked in mines and on building sites in gangs, and individually on farms, in trade, and in houses and palaces; a prefect might have 400 slaves in his household, and some slaves practiced as lawyers, physicians, and confidential secretaries.

Christians accepted slavery as an eternal condition of man, although their attitude reflected the humane concern of the Jews rather than the indifference and scorn of Greeks and Romans. The nation of Israel had itself been enslaved and was admonished by God to "remember that thou wast a bondman in Egypt, and the Lord thy God redeemed thee" (Deut. 15:15). Slaves celebrated the Sabbath with the free and could leave a master who beat them. The Jews recognized, too, that God would "pour out [his] spirit" (Joel 2:29) on slaves as well as the free. Paul reminded Christians that Jesus had taken the "form of a servant" (Phil. 2:7), and Paul had described himself as a slave of Christ (Rom. 1:1). Masters were told to treat their slaves well. Paul sent the runaway slave Onesimus back to his master Philemon, but he told Philemon to welcome the slave as a "brother beloved . . . both in the flesh and the Lord."[24]

No question of undermining the institution of slavery arose, however. The faith was a spiritual revolution, but it was meek and intensely conservative in the face of temporal authority and the social order. "Render to all their dues," Paul wrote: "tribute to whom tribute is due; custom to whom custom; fear to whom fear; honour to whom honour" (Rom. 13:7). He applied this directly to slavery. "Servants, be obedient unto them that according to the flesh are your masters," Paul warned them, "with fear and trembling, in singleness of your heart. . . ." (Eph. 6:5). He acknowledged that it was wrong that a man should own another, but the blame lay with Adam and the Fall for bringing sin and death into the world. He called for slaves to be resigned to their fate while rejoicing that in God's eyes they were free: "he that was called in the Lord, being a bondservant, is the Lord's freedman" (1 Cor. 7:22).

The Pauline view remained largely unchallenged for seventeen hundred years. In the fourth century, St. John Chrysostom advised the slave to prefer the security of captivity to the erratic tensions of freedom. His fellow saint, Augustine, thought that slavery "had not been done without the will of God, who knows no injustice." Augustine believed in equality—"whoever is born anywhere as a human being . . . however strange . . . in bodily form, or color, or motion, or utterance . . . let no true believer have any doubt that such an individual is descended from the one man who first existed"—but some were more equal than others, and he remembered the curse on Ham.* The Church encouraged manumission; funds were used to free slaves from cruel households and to liberate prisoners of war. A convert named Hermes is said to have freed 1,250 slaves at Easter in about A.D. 135;[25] three centuries later, Melania, a rich Roman matron who later founded a monastery on the Mount of Olives, was said to have earned canonization by liberating 8,000 slaves. Under Roman law a slave could not marry at all, but the Church regarded marriages between slaves and the free as indissoluble. In the early centuries several emancipated slaves became bishops; one, Callistus, was bishop of Rome before his death in about 222. As the Church itself became a major landowner, however, its outlook hardened. A general council of the Church at Gangra in Paphlagonia in about 345 condemned those who used their faith as a pretext to teach slaves to hate their masters; a council at Carthage in 419 refused slaves the right to appear as witnesses in court, and in 443, Pope Leo the Great proclaimed that no slave could become a priest.

✦ ALTHOUGH TRAVELING MISSIONARIES remained, a static priesthood of bishops, presbyters, and deacons was established in the cities. A career pattern slowly evolved. A boy or adolescent might start as a reader, moving on to become an acolyte serving at the altar, and then a subdeacon and deacon by the age of thirty. The deacon organized the community's charitable efforts, visited the sick and prisoners, and helped administer church funds. Hippolytus noted in about 210 that the deacon "is not ordained for priesthood but for the service of the bishop."[26] In practice, deacons sometimes celebrated the Eucharist until this was specifically banned in the early fourth century. By then even small congregations had their own presbyter or priest. A deacon of five years' standing could aspire to become a presbyter or priest; an archdeacon, a senior deacon with large administrative and financial responsibilities, might become a bishop without the intervening period as a presbyter. A bishop was typically elected when he was in his mid-forties; there were no hard-and-fast rules, however, and laymen were sometimes elected at the popular demand of a congregation.

Members of the early clergy maintained themselves with the financial offerings of their flocks. The flow of funds was encouraged by reminders that contributions were aids to the remission of sins. Fixed clerical salaries were at first considered an "outrage,"[27] but they became a regular practice. A system of tithes evolved, based on the one used by the Jews to support their landless Levite priests,

---

*Ham saw his father Noah lying drunken and naked in his tent, according to Genesis, and failed to cover him. When Noah awoke, he condemned Ham's son Canaan to slavery. Some of Ham's descendants were Nubians; the "curse on Ham" was later used by white masters in an attempt to justify the enslavement of blacks.

in which a tenth of livestock, food produce, or income from trade was given each year. In A.D. 251 the church at Rome was providing from its common purse for its bishop, 46 presbyters, 7 deacons and 7 subdeacons, 42 acolytes, and 52 exorcists, readers, and doorkeepers. At Rome, funds were split in four between the bishop, the remaining clergy, the maintenance of buildings, and widows, paupers, and virgins.

Each individual church was financially independent—although contributions were sometimes made to other congregations that had fallen on hard times—and the level of income varied greatly. Pagans lodged valuables in temples for safekeeping, and Christian clergy also acted as bankers. The Old Testament had forbidden Jews from charging interest on loans to fellow Jews. The Church disapproved of usury in principle; but the clergy lent money to Christian merchants and others, and a limit of 12 percent interest was later imposed on such loans.* Some were attracted into the Church by the prospect of rich pickings. The satirist Lucian of Samosata wrote in about 170 of a famous charlatan called Peregrinus Proteus who, inspired by Christians' generosity to their leaders, became a bishop before being arrested by the governor of Syria for fraud.

Bishops had forged well ahead of their fellow presbyters by the end of the second century. They baptized, led the Eucharist, imposed penance and excommunication, and acted as the father—*Papa* or *Pope* in Latin, *Pappas* in Greek—of their flock. At first they were elected by their congregation, clergy and people together, who were urged to appoint "men that are not lovers of money, true and reliable."[28] Sometimes an apparent sign from heaven clinched the matter; a dove alighting on the head of the presbyter Fabian in 236 was taken as proof that the Holy Spirit had chosen him to become bishop of Rome. Neighboring bishops had to consent to appointments, however, and at least three had to be present to lay on their hands at the consecration. Celibacy was expected first of bishops; at the Council of Elvira in 306, it was extended to all clergy in the West, although it was not strictly enforced for many centuries. In the East it applied to bishops, but priests and deacons were free to marry provided they did so before they were ordained.

The special status of bishops was increased by their supposed links with the apostles. "Obedience is due to those presbyters who are in the succession after the apostles," Irenaeus, the bishop of Lyons, wrote in about 180, "and who with their episcopal succession have received according to the will of the Lord the charisma of truth." In fact, few churches existed in apostolic times, and the succession lists that were drawn up were notoriously unreliable. Even at Rome, although St. Pe-

---

*By the Council of Nicaea in 325. The market rate for commercial loans, particularly when maritime risk was involved, was considerably higher.

ter may have led the congregation before his execution, little was known of his successor bishops until Clement, who was martyred at some time after A.D. 96.

Rome was the center of imperial rule and administration, and this glory was exploited in favor of its bishop. The martyred bishop of Antioch, Ignatius, had recognized the Roman Church as "she who is pre-eminent in the territory of the Romans . . . foremost in love . . . purified from every alien and discoloring stain." Irenaeus acknowledged Rome as "the greatest and most ancient of churches"; he argued that the "faithful from all other parts ought to be harmonized with it" by virtue of its apostolic origins with Peter and Paul. It was not until 190, however, that a strong bishop of Rome began imposing his views on other churches, when Victor threatened to excommunicate the Asian churches in the argument over the date of Easter. Stephen was the first bishop of Rome to claim to have inherited the unique authority Jesus gave to Peter—"thou art Peter, and upon this rock I will build my church" (Matt. 16:19)—and he did so almost two centuries after Peter's death.

Bishops had no thrones or high pulpits until the fourth century, and still sat with their presbyters at floor level. Priests had no distinctive dress at first; they were instructed only that their clothes should be "wholly clean." By the third century it was becoming common for them to wear either white or penitential black, sometimes in sackcloth; the elaborate robes of bishops, based on those worn by Roman aristocrats, developed later. But their claims to divine authority were already awesome. The Pauline power of anathema—Paul had "delivered unto Satan" two men who had "made shipwreck concerning the faith" so that they would be "taught not to blaspheme" (1 Tim. 20)—enabled them to separate sinners from God and pursue them beyond the grave to the pits of hell. "We terrify people," the Alexandrine theologian Origen wrote in the 240s. "To people who come and ask us to do something for them, we behave as no tyrant even would: we are more savage to pensioners than any civil rulers are. You can see this happening in many recognized churches, especially in the bigger cities."[29]

For all its joyful message of redemption, Christianity did not always seem a happy religion. Penance was its pride. "Christian sinners spend the day sorrowing and the night in vigils and tears," Tertullian wrote, "lying on the ground among clinging ashes, tossing in rough sackcloth and dirt, fasting and praying." Adulterers atoned for their sins through humiliation; they were led among the congregation to prostrate themselves in sackcloth and ashes and to become "a compound of disgrace and horror, before the widows, the elders, suing for everyone's tears, licking their footprints, clasping their knees." The devout shunned the spectacles in the amphitheaters and any entertainments involving magic or the erotic. Pagans were seen by many Christians as morally depraved, inferior creatures enslaved by unnatural vice. The Christian writer Tatian wrote that

Romans held pederasty to be a particular privilege, describing how they "try to round up herds of boys like herds of grazing mares." Christians, like the Jews, condemned incest and fornication, and thought homosexuality to be a cause of the wrath of God, while rigorists like Tatian held marriage itself to be a "defilement and fornication."

This early puritanism spilled into a bitter debate between "spiritualists" and "sensualists" over the "digamists" who entered second marriages. Tertullian said proudly that the former "admit but one marriage, just as we recognize but one God," while the sensualists took no pleasure in the things of the spirit but "find their joy in things of the flesh."[30] He maintained that the bishops of the earthly Church had no power to pardon sexual sins; the sovereign right of forgiveness "belongs to God himself," he said, "not to a priest." The guilty were to be cast out of the Church. "We excommunicate digamists as persons who bring disgrace on the Holy Spirit . . . [and] adulterers and fornicators also," he wrote. "They will shed tears barren of peace and receive from the Church nothing more than the publication of their shame." Tertullian's solution to the large numbers of widows was for well-to-do men to take them into their houses as "spiritual spouses." Some groups of ascetics, men and women, showed off the power of their chastity by living together in strict abstinence; the hierarchy disapproved of such displays, but Irish men and women continued so to cohabit into the sixth century.

❖ BY THE 150S there were churches in almost all the provinces between Syria and Rome, extending through Alexandria to Carthage in North Africa and beyond to Mauritania, modern Algeria, and eastward beyond the fringes of empire to Persia and India. Seven men and five women were condemned to death by the Roman prefect Saturninus at Scillium near Carthage in 180 for refusing to renounce Christianity. The community was almost certainly well established; reports around A.D. 200 speak of churches throughout Carthage and Africa Proconsularis in Tunisia. "We are but of yesterday and we have filled all you have," Tertullian wrote triumphantly to the pagans from Carthage; "cities, islands, forts, towns, assembly halls, even military camps, tribes, town councils, the palace, senate and forum. We have left you nothing but the temples."[31] By 202 the emperor Septimius Severus was so alarmed by the size of the Christian community in Egypt that he issued an edict forbidding conversion and closing the catechetical school of Alexandria. Scholars such as Clement, who became its head in 190, were attracting educated pagans of high Greek culture.

The Christians of the eastern and African shores of the Mediterranean dominated the early faith. It may seem a mirage now. Copts make up a tenth of the once almost entirely Christian population of Egypt. The columns of the basilica of Carthage stand empty in the coastal sands of modern Tunisia; a Turkish township squats in the ruins of Antioch; the harbor at Ephesus has silted up, and its fine church is reduced to marble stumps. Yet six churches that survive—Greek Orthodox, Maronite, Melchite, Nestorian, Armenian, and Georgian—were intimately linked with Antioch alone. These were the nurseries of Christian ideas, and of a vital intensity. It was from here that great heresies and dogmas were derived and the rolls of martyrs were filled; here that Christian scholarship was born; here that Origen castrated himself, or so Eusebius claimed, rather than be tempted by the charms of Alexandrine women.

The Copts* dated their contact with Christianity from the infancy of Jesus and the flight into Egypt. An angel warned that Herod sought to destroy the infant, according to Matthew's gospel, and Joseph "took the young child and his mother by night, and departed into Egypt" (Matt. 2:13–14); this fulfilled the claim in Hosea that God would "call my son out of Egypt" (Hos. 11:1). An elaborate journey was described by Coptic writers, crossing the Sinai by the caravan route along the northern shore of the Mediterranean, and then heading deep into Upper Egypt to a cave at a point 150 miles south of modern Cairo. A monastery was built here;† a sycamore tree and a grotto, with a niche where the infant was said to have slept, became other places of pilgrimage where the holy family was said to have taken shelter.

Alexandrines claimed that their city, the second greatest in the empire, was evangelized by St. Mark. On entering the city, at a date before A.D. 61, the apostle was said to have stumbled and broken a strap on his sandal. A cobbler named Ananius was mending it when he pierced his hand with the awl and cried *"Heis ho Theos,"* "God is One." Mark rejoiced to hear this; he healed the hand and converted Ananius to such effect that the cobbler replaced him as patriarch of Alexandria when Mark left for Rome. When the apostle returned, some time after the martyrdom of Peter and Paul, he found that Ananius and other converts had built a church at Baucalis, a suburb where cattle grazed by the shore. As the Christians in the city multiplied, so did rumors that they were defiling and overthrowing pagan deities. A mob descended on them while they were celebrating Easter in 68. Mark was dragged around the streets on a rope to be bled and bruised to death; a violent storm saved his body from being burnt by his tor-

---

*The words Copt and Egyptian are interchangeable; both derive from the Greek *Aigyptos,* which the Hellenes used for Egypt and the Nile.

†The Monastery of Our Lady, known as the Dair al-Muharraq. The sycamore tree, in the village of Matariya, has been preserved through transplanting to the present. The Copts built the church of Abu Sarga, or St. Sergius, at the site of the grotto in the fourth century.

mentors, and the Christians secretly buried it in a tomb carved beneath the altar of their church.*"

By 211 there were twenty Coptic bishops. Fragments of papyrus show that the new faith had moved far up the Nile Valley within a century; it then slowly penetrated south of the first cataract at Syene, modern Aswan, to the Nubian kingdoms and Ethiopia. Coptic monks from Egypt were consecrated as heads of the Ethiopian Church in a tradition that lasted until 1948. It is known that a bishopric existed at Beth Katraye, in the country of the Qatars opposite the islands of Bahrain in southeastern Arabia, by 225. Eastern missionaries were to reach to India and China; the Phrygian bishop Abercius founded congregations beyond the Euphrates, and the king of Edessa, Abgar II, was claimed as a Christian.

Easterners illuminated, too, the pagan darkness of the West. The first bishop of Lyons, the martyr Pothinus, was a native of Asia Minor; his successor Irenaeus, the first great Catholic theologian, came from Smyrna. From North Africa, Cyprian, former pagan rhetorician, bishop of Carthage, and eventual martyr, wrote letters of encouragement to fellow Christians in Spain, southern Gaul, and Rome. A persistent legend has it that Coptic soldiers serving with the Theban Legion evangelized Switzerland in 287. The Theban Legion was raised exclusively in Egypt and posted to Martigny near the lake of Geneva to deal with rebellious Gauls. Here the emperor Maximian ordered the whole army to sacrifice to pagan gods for success in combat. The *primerius* or senior officer of the legion was a Copt named Maurice. The soldier/saint refused to sacrifice and was executed; three companions are said to have fled to Lake Zurich, where they baptized many converts until they were arrested and beheaded before, at the command of an angel, taking up their heads and soaring to paradise. The modern ski resort of St. Moritz is named for the commander, while the city arms of Zurich include his companions, their heads nestling beneath their arms; whether or not the legend has a basis in truth, Coptic and other Christian troops serving with the Roman army may well have tried to plant their faith on distant frontiers.[†] At Rome itself,

---

*His relics had a bizarre future. His vestments and head were stolen after the city was conquered by the Arabs in 642. The body was smuggled from the harbor by Venetian merchants in 828, hidden in a tub of pickled pork to prevent inspection by Moslem customs officers. Thus Venice became the Republic of St. Mark, proudly displaying the lion, the symbol of the apostle's evangelism; his relics are still in the basilica of San Marco. Alexandrines exacted their revenge on idolaters by smashing idols with particular gusto after Christianity triumphed in the fourth century. Accounts record the destruction of twenty camel-loads of pagan artifacts at a time, "idols of all kinds, especially dogs, cats, apes, crocodiles and reptiles, because in former times Egyptians also venerated animals."

†Another legend suggests that the Irish Church is the "child of the Egyptian Church" and was influenced by Coptic missionaries.

all the early popes were Greek speakers; although the Bible had been translated into variants of Old Latin by the end of the second century, it was not until 382 that the Western scholar Jerome began to translate the definitive Latin or Vulgate version of the Testaments from the Greek and Hebrew originals. To learn Hebrew he had to travel east, to Syria.

The earliest building known to be specifically Christian, showing the self-confidence to move worship out into the open from the secrecy of private places, is at Dura-Europos on the Euphrates, close to the present Syrian-Iraqi border. The interior walls of a house built round a courtyard in about 232 were knocked through to provide a large hall which could hold about sixty worshipers. Its walls had paintings of Adam and Eve, the Good Shepherd, David and Goliath, and a procession of women carrying candles.[32] The bishop presided from a small platform, and a smaller room was fitted out as a baptistery with a bath covered by a canopy. The street door was marked with a red cross. Two hundred years after the crucifixion, Christians had their first surviving Church.

The Blood of Martyrs

"Do not then wish to die on bridal beds, or in miscarriages, or from gentle fevers," Tertullian urged the women of Carthage early in the third century. "Rather, seek to die a martyr that he may be glorified who suffered for you."[1]

In this, Tertullian went beyond Christ. Jesus had anticipated Christian persecution. "Ye shall be hated of all men for my name's sake," he said; he promised that martyrdom brought salvation, saying that "he that endureth to the end, the same shall be saved"; but he had not demanded it. He said that he was sending his disciples into the world "as sheep in the midst of wolves," and warned them to be as wise as serpents and harmless as doves in their dealings with men. "When they persecute you in this city, flee into the next," he advised them (Matt. 10:16–23). The wolves were now active; as Tertullian spoke, an edict of the emperor Severus forbidding conversion to Christianity was being enforced in Carthage in 203 with grisly vigor. Tertullian did not, however, offer Christ's option of flight. He claimed the authority of the Holy Spirit to state that "almost all are advised to offer themselves for martyrdom, never to flee from it."[2]

He did so as a matter of policy. Martyrdom was a legally sanctioned hazard for Christians for almost three hundred years. It was a fate usually easily avoided; if conscience allowed it, a Christian could recant by burning a stick of incense on a pagan altar or tasting a sacrificial offering of wine or flesh. To Tertullian, however, the blood of martyrs, shed so piteously and publicly in crowded amphitheaters, was the "seed of the church." It enabled martyrs to escape the eternal damnation reserved for *traditores* who denied Christ under pressure, and it gave the religion an impact far in excess of its numbers. He observed the respectful pagan curiosity that mingled with sadism at mass executions: "See how these Christians love one another!" they murmured. The death of women had a particular resonance, as Tertullian knew well. Two members of his congregation, a well-bred mother named Perpetua and her slave Felicitas, had followed his instructions in the arena at Carthage in 202. It is possible that Tertullian edited the account of their martyrdom.[3] They were brought out stripped naked and trapped in nets; at the sight—"one a delicate young woman, the other fresh from childbirth with dripping breasts"—the account noted that "the cruelty of the crowd gave way."[4] They were called back and dressed in tunics; after they had been gored by wild animals, the women went among the spectators and gave each other the kiss of peace before their throats were cut by trainee gladiators.

The devotion of individual martyrs has a beauty that, still remembered in the canon of the Mass, is impervious to time. They believed that, in leading their lives in imitation of Christ, they performed their noblest act in dying like him. In truth, their courage was at least equal to that of their Savior, for many of their deaths were more prolonged and agonizing than his. Even when they were crucified, Eusebius wrote in his great *Ecclesiastical History,* they were often "with still greater cruelty nailed the other way up, head down, and kept alive until they starved to death on the very cross." He listed other torments in detail and with regional variations. In Arabia, Christians were killed with axes; in Macedonia they

The torturers of Christians, the fourth-century historian Eusebius wrote, were "constantly inventing new outrages, as if they were taking part in a prize competition." Marcus, the bishop of Arethusa, was rubbed with honey and then hung up in a basket to be stung to death by wasps.

were hung by the feet above a fire and slowly asphyxiated; at Alexandria, noses, ears, and hands were severed; at Antioch they were roasted over braziers; in the Thebais they were "torn to bits from head to foot with potsherds like claws," while women were tied by one foot and "hoisted high in the air, their bodies completely naked." The torturers of Pontus on the Black Sea were "constantly inventing new outrages, as if they were taking part in a prize competition"; they drove pointed reeds under fingernails, poured molten lead over backs, and inflicted "shameful, merciless and unmentionable" sufferings on private parts and bowels. The "lightest of punishments" was to hack out the right eye with a sword, to cripple the left foot by applying branding irons to the joint, and to condemn the half-blind victim to toil in the copper mines.[5]

To endure such a fate showed an extraordinary tenacity of belief. The martyrs, hailed as the "snow white number of the elect"[6] who were linked "by a bond to the whole of eternity," created a continuity with Calvary and Christ's own Passion. The clergy who died increased the authority of the Church; Eusebius listed the "church leaders who by their blood proved the religion they preached genuine,"[7] the bishops of Nicomedia, Emesa, Antioch, and Gaza, for example, respectively beheaded, thrown to wild beasts, drowned, and beheaded in the mines. Future bishops of Rome drew strength from four martyr popes; it was said that a *traditor* pope, Marcellinus, who sacrificed incense to the gods at Rome in 303 and meekly surrendered his vestments and scriptures to be burnt, had died of shame.

There was, however, a dangerous edge to the exploitation of martyrs. They became, as it were, the sacrifice in a human Eucharist. Before he himself joined their number in the arena at the Colosseum in Rome, Ignatius, bishop of Antioch, declared the martyrs' blood to be the wine of Christ and their crushed bodies to be his bread. Persecutions were shaped into the battle honors of the Church. Those who died at pagan hands were transformed from Christ's sheep into triumphant soldiers who were awarded spiritual decorations; the saint at the summit, but also "spiritual nursling of Christ," "glory of the community," "palm of wonder," or, simply, "fulfilled." Martyrs were said to undergo "second baptisms" or to win the "crown" of Christ, which guaranteed them remission of sins. The anniversaries of their deaths, which formed the basis of the first church calendars, were called their "birthdays." Believers in Numidia, present-day Algeria, greeted each other daily with the remark: "May you gain your crown."

The faith was stamped with a sense that it was legitimized by blood. Martyrdom was claimed to be "unmistakable proof of our Savior's truly divine and ineffable powers."[8] The divine demand for death invoked by Tertullian in response to pagan repression did not change when the persecutors became Christians. Two hundred years later, it was repeated by another great North African churchman in the face of Arian heretics. "In our charity towards God's sheep, who must all die some day, some way," St. Augustine wrote, "we should be more afraid of a butchery of their minds by the sword of spiritual evil than of their bodies by a sword of steel."[9]

The unbearable was sanctified. During the Great Persecution that began in 303, a small town in Phrygia in Asia Minor was encircled by Roman legions enforcing an imperial edict to sacrifice to the gods. When the demand was refused, the Romans set the town on fire, killing everyone within it, including women and children. "And why?" Eusebius asked a few years later. Why indeed should parents overcome the most powerful of instincts, and condemn their children as well as themselves? "Because," Eusebius wrote, as if it were the most natural thing in the world, "all the inhabitants of the town without exception—the mayor himself and the magistrates, with all the officials and the whole populace—declared themselves Christians and absolutely refused to obey the command to commit idolatry."[10]

Despite their vulnerability, Christians foresaw a time of vengeance when they, the righteous, would triumph and their torturers would be cast into the eternal pit. The sense of apocalypse was fed by the Book of Revelation. Its author, John, had been persecuted. He wrote it, either on the island of Patmos where he had been imprisoned, or at Ephesus after his release, around A.D. 95; his wounds are fresh, and his feelings of suffering and revenge are raw. The Antichrist* who leads the forces of evil resembles Nero; after his suicide—he stabbed himself in the throat—legends grew that Nero would return from the dead at the head of an army from the east to massacre once more. In his visions, John saw Death mounted upon a pale horse while men were killed, as Christians were, by the sword and by wild beasts; then, "I saw underneath the altar the souls of them that had been slain for the word of God . . . and they cried out with a great voice, saying, 'How long, O Master, the holy and true, dost thou not judge and avenge our blood on them that dwell on the earth?'" (Rev. 6:9–10).

As martyrdom was slowly elevated into a cult, the relics of martyrs were indeed placed beneath altars, as predicted in Revelation, and elements of apocalypse and vengeance entered the faith.

THE WORD MARTYR, in the sense of suffering for a belief, is specifically Christian. During the lifetime of Jesus, *martys* merely signified "witness" in Greek; the apostles are often described in Acts as "witnesses" of the resurrected

---

*The term Antichrist, as the enemy of Christ, appears only in 1 and 2 John: "Who is the liar but he that denieth that Jesus is the Christ? This is the antichrist, even he that denieth the Father and the Son" (1 John). The concept goes back at least as far as the Book of Daniel, probably written in about 165 B.C.

Christ. The word, however, already carried the implication that they should be willing to suffer for their testimony. The first to suffer death was Stephen—"when the blood of Stephen thy witness was shed" (Acts 22:20)—and *martyrés* gradually came to apply only to those who died for the faith.

Both the concept and practice of so doing were well established in Judaism. The Seleucid king Antiochus IV had issued an edict in 168 B.C. requiring the Jews to "abandon their ancestral customs and live no longer by the laws of God" (2 Macc. 6:1). Many Jewish women preferred to die rather than obey the order to leave their sons uncircumcised; seven brothers and their mother were killed for refusing "to partake of unlawful swine's flesh" (2 Macc. 7). The persecution, however, failed; Antiochus, having provoked a furious Jewish response in the Maccabean wars, died insane, his title of Epiphanes or "illustrious" mockingly changed to Epimanes, "madman."

Nero, an emperor whose sanity was also questioned, carried out the first major persecution of Christians. In July of A.D. 64, nearly two-thirds of Rome was destroyed by a fire of suspect origin. The emperor himself was rumored to be the arsonist, and to have admired the glowing embers of his handiwork while reciting verses on the burning of Troy. Christians, fragile, few, misunderstood, and mistrusted, were ideal scapegoats. To scotch the loose talk, the historian Tacitus wrote, Nero "charged and tortured some people hated for their evil practices, the group known as 'Christians.'" Tacitus explained that the leader of this sect was named Christ, and that he had been put to death by Pontius Pilate, but the "evil superstition" of belief in him had reached Rome itself, where it was attracting "all manner of sordid and shameful activities." Those who confessed to being Christians were arrested first, he reported; the names of others were then extracted from them.

The suffering of Christians was established as a blood sport popular among Romans. Nero opened his own gardens for the spectacle and had them slain in the arena, where he mingled with the crowds, dressed as a charioteer. "In their deaths they were made a mockery," Tacitus continued. "They were covered in the skins of wild animals, torn to death by dogs, crucified or set on fire—so that when darkness fell they burned like torches in the night." He wrote of an "immense number" being killed, although the Christian community in Rome was still small enough for a figure of several hundred to be the most likely.

The terror of Nero's reign failed to diminish the faith. Those who fled from Rome carried their belief with them, and those who died left a trace of idealism upon a brutal age. Christians were noted for their high principles, at least among those who observed them; and even Tacitus, with his well-bred scorn for their "superstitions," noted that Nero's victims were innocents. He thought that they were convicted "more for their hatred of the human race than for fire-raising,"

A lion kills a Christian during Roman games in the first century. Believers were useful scapegoats. "If the Tiber reaches the walls," the Church father Tertullian wrote, "if the Nile does not rise to the fields, if the sky does not move or the earth does, if there is a famine, if there is plague, the cry is at once 'Christians to the lion!'" He noted that curiosity mingled with the bloodlust of the pagan audience: "See how these Christians love one another," they murmured. The Colosseum at Rome was the deathplace of many Christians, killed by beasts and gladiators. Tertullian noted that the blood of martyrs, shed so piteously and publicly in crowded amphitheaters, was "the seed of the Church." The spectacle of men and women dying for their faith often impressed the pagans who watched it. The Colosseum at Rome held an audience of 87,000 in seating that rose almost 160 feet, sheltered from the sun by awnings hung from masts of pine.

and he acknowledged that their suffering earned them much sympathy. "Although they were guilty of being Christians and deserved death," he wrote, "people began to feel sorry for them. For they realized that they were being massacred not for the public good but to satisfy one man's madness."[11] Mobs took advantage of a persecution at Edessa to loot Christian properties; nevertheless, "some of the Jews and pagans took part in shrouding and burying [the body of a victim] with the Christian brethren."[12] The moral certainty of Christians impressed those who witnessed or heard of it. "That there is no one who can reduce us to panic or enslave us—we who all over the earth have believed in Jesus—is manifest," Justin wrote before his own martyrdom. "We are beheaded, we are crucified, thrown to wild beasts, burned and put to every kind of torture. Everyone sees it. But, the more all this happens, the more numerous become those who believe through the name of Jesus."[13]

Christian usefulness in deflecting public unrest over the fire at Rome was easily applied to other catastrophes, man-made or natural. "If the Tiber reaches the walls," Tertullian wrote, "if the Nile does not rise to the fields, if the sky does not move or the earth does, if there is a famine, if there is plague, the cry is at once 'Christians to the lion!'" For at least two centuries some respectable pagans refused to speak or have social contact with Christians on the grounds that they were cannibals. Blasphemy was another popular charge. Christian zealots hissed in disapproval as they walked past temples, and pagans regarded this as a dangerous insult to the gods.

The persecutions were furious while they raged, but they were restricted to single reigns and therefore brief. After Nero, only four emperors, Domitian, Decius, Valerian, and Diocletian, launched full-scale pogroms, although a total of thirty-nine emperors were proclaimed during this period of less than 240 years, the high turnover reflecting the incidence of army mutiny, intrigue, and assassination. Domitian was provoked into his outburst of terror by the revolt of the army commander in upper Germany in A.D. 89. His victims included members of his own family as well as Christians; he was stabbed to death in 96, perhaps on the orders of his niece after he had put her husband to death.

The millennium celebrations in A.D. 248 of the founding of Rome in 753 B.C. precipitated the next concentrated campaign.* Christians disapproved of the festivities and the honors shown to the city's ancestral gods, and pagans feared that the angry deities would favor the barbarian invaders on the imperial frontiers. Anti-Christian rioting broke out in the city. Decius, an experienced soldier born at Pannonia in Hungary, was proclaimed emperor while fighting against the Goths on the Danube at the end of the year. In his attempt to revive the religion and institutions of ancient Rome, and to placate the gods at the millennium, he issued an edict in 249 ordering sacrifices to the gods to be made by all his subjects except the Jews, who retained their traditional exemption. A fierce attack on the Church centered on the bishops, whom Decius accurately identified as the main source of Christian discipline and coherence. The pope, Fabian, was among the first of the leading churchmen to be arrested, dying of ill-treatment in prison in 250. Decius was killed the following year when the Goths at Dobruja snared his

*The foundation of the city, which the Romans used as zero year, was originally set at the equivalent of 750 B.C. This was modified in the first century B.C. by the scholar Marcus Terentius Varro, who set the date at the equivalent of 753 B.C.

army in swampy ground. After the murder of his successor Gallus in 253, the new emperor Valerian continued to attack the senior clergy. Another pope was martyred, Sixtus II, who was taken while addressing a congregation and decapitated. "Valerian has sent an order to the senate to the effect that bishops, priests and deacons should forthwith die," Cyprian, the bishop of Carthage, reported from Rome in 258. "Sixtus suffered in a cemetery on the 6th day of August, and with him four deacons." Valerian was taken prisoner in battle against the Persians in 259 and died in captivity the same year.

The final wave was the most devastating, and came to be known as the Great Persecution. Diocletian, a soldier from Illyricum, modern Dalmatia, was declared emperor by the legions at Chalcedon in 284. A ruthless man who killed the Praetorian prefect with his own hand, he reorganized the empire and restored it to health, securing the frontiers against barbarians and Persians. His wife Prisca and her daughter Valeria were thought to be Christian sympathizers, and the Church prospered during his first two decades. He was concerned, however, at the decline of paganism and the growing Christian influence at court, among governors' wives, and in the army. The last was a direct threat to discipline, as cases of men refusing to serve proved. In 295, Maximilian, the twenty-one-year-old son of a veteran of the third Augustan Legion based at Tebessa in North Africa, refused to join his unit. "You may cut off my head," he told his commander, "but I will not be a soldier of this world because I am a soldier of God." In another case, in 298, the centurion first-class Marcellus was martyred after throwing off his belt during a parade in honor of Diocletian's birthday. "I am a soldier of Jesus Christ," he said. "From now on I cease to serve your emperors and I despise the worship of your gods of wood and stone, for they are deaf and dumb images." The oracle of Apollo at Didyma recommended that Christian impertinence be punished. Diocletian issued a decree on February 23, 303. Services were banned, places of worship destroyed, and scriptures burnt. All privileges were ended, including Roman citizenship and the right to be executed by the sword. A further edict in 304 ordered all Christians to sacrifice to pagan gods. There were no martyrs in Britain and Gaul, where the future emperor Constantine's father Constantius Chlorus ruled and largely ignored the edict; the full fury broke in Syria, Palestine, Egypt, and North Africa.

✤ CHRISTIANS WERE TAUGHT by the Church to respect authority and the law. They could rarely be punished for rebellion or resistance, for they offered little. Justin stressed that they were ideal citizens who posed no threat to the state; they embraced chastity in place of debauchery, and charity rather than greed, prayed for their enemies, and sought to win over those who despised them.

"Everywhere we try to be the first to pay tribute and taxes," he added. "God alone do we adore, but for the rest we gladly obey yourselves, recognizing you as kings and governors of mankind. . . ."[14] To confess to the "name" of Christ thus became sufficient grounds for a conviction; belief itself was a crime, rather than any specific act. The prime cause for arrest was the refusal to acknowledge respect to the gods, including the "genius" or tutelary spirit of the emperor; as a result, these most devout of souls were charged with "atheism."

The authorities seldom had accurate lists of Christians and relied on torture and denunciation to identify them. The motive could be jealousy—Justin was accused by a spiteful Cynic philosopher named Crescens, a "lover of display rather than wisdom,"[15] whom he had beaten in debate—or greed. Informers and magistrates could claim part of a martyr's possessions. In peaceful years people tempted to identify Christians had to exercise caution; the emperor Hadrian had confirmed in a letter to the proconsul of Asia in 124 that Christians falsely accused of crimes could sue their accusers for damages. No such legal niceties applied during pogroms, and the catchall nature of imperial edicts exposed all but Jews to compulsory sacrifice. "The Roman officers are very keen on this persecution," Cyprian noted under Valerian. "The people brought before them are certain to suffer and forfeit their estates."

Christian defendants were released if they agreed to sacrifice to Roman gods, or if they produced a certificate confirming that they had done so. This was called a *libelli,* and one that presumably saved the life of a Christian woman during the Decian persecution of A.D. 250 survives. "It has ever been my practice to sacrifice to the gods," it reads. "Now in your presence, in accordance with the Command, I have sacrificed, poured libation, and tasted the offering. I beg you to certify my statement. . . . I Aurelia Demos have presented this declaration. I Aurelius Ireneus [her husband] wrote for her as she is illiterate. I Aurelius Sabinus the commissioner saw you sacrificing."[16] So many asked for certificates that the officials supervising the sacrifices complained of overwork. The external gesture was enough, without the need to display any sincerity; forged *libelli* could be bought from corrupt administrators.

Flight and going underground in the cities were alternatives. Bishop Gregory Thaumaturgus, the "Wonderworker," advised his entire flock at Neo-Caesarea in Pontus to flee rather than risk apostasy; he himself hid in the desert. This was not necessarily a safe option. Eusebius wrote of a "vast number who wandered over deserts and mountains till hunger, thirst, cold, sickness or wild beasts destroyed them."[17] The elderly bishop of Nilopolis in Egypt fled with his wife into the mountains of Arabia, and search parties found no trace of him. Others were enslaved by Arabs, a few being ransomed and recovered. Blood from sacrifices was sprinkled on food stalls in the marketplaces, in order to defile the food in Christian eyes and thus starve out those who had remained hidden in the cities.

The zealous, particularly in North Africa, made no attempt to conceal themselves. They continued to hold services, refusing to part with their vestments and scriptures until they were taken. The formalities that preceded their martyrdom were brief. An account of Justin's trial, held before the prefect Rustinus between 163 and 167, has survived. The accused made a statement confirming his belief "in the God of the Christians, whom alone we believe to have been the maker and creator of the entire world from the beginning, also the Lord Jesus Christ, the child of God. . . ." He inculpated himself further by adding that he had spread the faith, since "anyone who wished could come to my house and I would impart to him the words of truth." Rustinus asked him whether he was a Christian. "Yes, I am," he replied. He said that he, and his six coaccused, "are confident that if we suffer the [death] penalty for the sake of our Lord Jesus Christ we shall be saved, for this is the confidence and salvation we shall have at the terrible tribunal of our Savior and Master sitting in judgement over the whole world." The prefect gave them a last opportunity to acknowledge the gods. "Do what you will," they told him. "We are Christians and we do not offer sacrifice to idols." Sentencing was immediate. "Those who have refused to sacrifice to the gods," Rustinus said without further ado, "are to be led away to be scourged and beheaded in accordance with the laws."[18]

There were occasional variations to this simple process. Christians often repeated the phrase "Jesus is Lord" (1 Cor. 12:3), and some magistrates required them to curse Christ and say: "Caesar is Lord." Most martyrs appear to have been defiant only in the sense that they declined to sacrifice, and continued to extol their faith; North Africans, less deferential to Roman power, were again an exception. When twelve men and women from Scillium were charged with refusing to worship the emperor in 180, one of them snapped at the proconsul Saturninus: "I do not believe in the empire of this world." "We too are a religious people, and our religion is a simple one," Saturninus replied. "We swear by the genius of our lord the emperor and we offer prayers for his health—as you also ought to do." He ordered their execution. "Thanks be to God!" they replied.[19] Another, asked for his place of residence, replied: "Heavenly Jerusalem." The standard trial was quickly over, for the only relevant issue was the response to the questions "Are you a Christian?" and "Do you refuse to sacrifice?" The accused were permitted, however, to make public confessions. These speeches by the condemned, with their impassioned pleas for their faith and their warnings of the hellfire that awaited those who did not heed them, drew the vivid attention of any city in which a trial was held.

The death sentence was not inevitable. The fortunate were exiled or imprisoned. Others were sent to the galleys, to the mines, or to cut timber in the forests of Corsica. They might still be executed, however, like the bishop of Gaza, or St. Clement, the third bishop of Rome after St. Peter, who was said to have been thrown into the Black Sea with an anchor round his neck while serving his sentence in the Crimean copper mines in about A.D. 100. In North Africa, forced labor involved humiliation; senior clerics such as Bishop Marcellus II were made to work as keepers of the imperial camels and horses.

❖ IT WAS PARTICULARLY dangerous to be a Christian at times of games and festivals. Mortal combat had been a staple of the *ludi* since three pairs of slaves had fought to the death in the first recorded games in Rome in 246 B.C. They had become immensely popular.

"The people who conquered the world now have only two interests—bread and circuses," observed the brilliant satirist Juvenal, writing in about A.D. 120, a Stoic whose anger at vice, poverty, and the spendthrift immorality of the ruling classes matched that of any Christian. The entertainments were held in cities throughout the empire; in the capital, the Circus Maximus and the Colosseum ran almost continuous shows. Chariot racing had a large following, with six teams of four horses apiece racing seven times around the arena. The drivers were idols of the rich as well as the mob, and Seneca mourned: "The art of conversation is dead! Can no one talk of anything else than charioteers?" The prize money made them rich men if they survived the frequent, limb-breaking collisions; but the core attraction was the planned violence of human combat.

Gladiators were trained in professional schools whose particular style of fighting they reflected. They entered the arena in procession through the *porta sanavivaria,* the Gate of the Living, hailing the imperial podium with the traditional and elegantly concise cry of *"Ave, Caesar, morituri salutamus!"*—"Hail, Caesar, we who are about to die salute thee!"—before attending to their business. Some pairs were matched like for like, according to height of gladiator and type of weapon used; for connoisseurs, small *retiarii* were pitted against taller *secutores* armed with heavy swords and shields, the shorter men making up for their lack of reach through their agility and adept use of a net and trident. Combatants were listed much like horses in a modern racing form. The entry T v Pugnax Ner III, for example, indicated that the gladiator Pugnax was from the Ner(onian) training school in Capua, that he was equipped with T(hracian) arms of a small shield and curved sword, and that he had three (III) previous victories.[20] The "v" indicated his emergence from his most recent contest as a still living *v(ictor);* had he lost, a "p" would indicate that he was *p(eritus),* dead, dragged from the arena through the Gate of Death on a meat hook. To add variety, teams of gladiators were sometimes loosed on groups of prisoners of war or barbarians; arenas were flooded for battles between the crews of ships. In *venationes,* wild beasts fought humans or each other.

Christians were used for such sport from Nero's time onward for some 250 years. They were easier to acquire for the entertainment than barbarians because, as they spread, their communities could be found in the lowliest of provincial cities; they were more easily disposed of, too, for where onlookers expected captured barbarians to be given at least some means of self-defense, Christians could be massacred with impunity. Special enjoyment was derived from watching them being thrown to the beasts in *venationes.* As the mauling produced a flow of blood, the crowd amused itself by taunting them with cries of *"salvum lotum, salve lotum!"*—a greeting used in bathhouses, "Well bathed, well bathed!" Eusebius listed "panthers, bears of different kinds, wild boars and bulls goaded with red-hot irons" as standard provincial fare. Lions were rare enough for it to be an offense to kill one in the wild, and they were expensive to capture and ship from Africa. Roman promoters could afford to use them regularly, but elsewhere they appeared only in gala events.

The larger the scale of the games, the more publicity was gained from Christian deaths. The Colosseum at Rome, for example, held an audience of 87,000 in seating that rose almost 160 feet, sheltered from the sun by awnings hung from masts of pine. News of an upcoming spectacle must have reached the majority of the population in any city where one was held. Spectators appear to have relished the prospect of Christian victims and sometimes took it upon themselves to provide them, as in the case of Polycarp, bishop of Smyrna in Asia Minor. He had been born about A.D. 70, in the days of the apostles, and some of those who knew him lived on until the end of the second century. He visited Rome in 155 and had the misfortune to return to Smyrna at the time of a great festival attended by the proconsul Statius Quadratus. His fate was documented in a circular letter sent out by the church at Smyrna, and is the first detailed account of a martyrdom.[21] Eleven Christians had been put to death in the arena by lions, but the bloodlust continued to run high and the crowd wanted a fresh kill. A cry was raised: "Let us search for Polycarp." The bishop was found hiding on a farm and brought before Statius. A chant—"Away with the atheists"—arose from the arena. Polycarp stared at the "lawless heathens" and waved his hand at them in disdain. "Away with the godless," he replied. A memorable exchange with the proconsul followed.

"Swear and I will set you free," Statius urged. "Curse Christ."

"Eighty and six years have I served him, and he has done me no wrong," Polycarp replied. "How then can I blaspheme my king who has saved me?" At this the onlookers demanded that the lions he loosed on him then and there.

"Swear by the Fortune of Caesar," Statius said.

"If you vainly imagine that I will swear by Caesar, and pretend that you do not know who I am, listen plainly," Polycarp replied. "I am a Christian. . . ."

"I have wild beasts," the proconsul warned. "If you do not repent, I will have you thrown to them."

"Send for them."

"If you do not despise the wild beasts, I will order you to be burned alive."

"You threaten the fire that burns for an hour and in a little while will be quenched," the old man replied. "But you are unaware of the fire of the judgment to come, and the fire of the eternal punishment which is kept for the wicked. Why do you delay? Bring on what you will."

Timber and scraps of wood were collected. Polycarp was bound and placed on top of the pyre. "This is the teacher of Asia," the crowd shouted. "This is the father of the Christians, this is the destroyer of our gods, this is the man who has taught so many no longer to sacrifice and no longer to pray to the gods." He looked, the writer of the letter said, like "a splendid ram taken out of a great flock for a . . . burnt sacrifice acceptable to God."

The victim looked to heaven and said: "I bless thee that thou hast deemed me worthy of this day and hour, that I should share in the number of martyrs in the cup of thy Christ, to the resurrection of life eternal of soul and body in the incorruption of the Holy Ghost. . . ." At that, the wood was set on fire. The flames were said to be shaped like the sail of a ship driven by the wind; they arched away from Polycarp so that he was "not like burning flesh, but like bread being baked, or gold and silver being refined in the furnace. . . ." A slaughterer was dispatched to finish him off with a dagger. The first eleven martyrs were apparently soon forgotten, but Polycarp "is generally remembered, even being spoken of by the heathen in every phrase."

There was a grim sequel to the Smyrna persecution. Some of the Christians who fled settled at Lyons in Gaul, where a great public games was held on August 1, 177. The notables who organized the entertainments were concerned at the high cost of professional fighters, and the Christian immigrants from Asia Minor provided a cheap substitute. They were charged with belief in the "name" of Christ and sent to the arena; the bishop of Lyons was included to give local interest. First, they were clawed with iron scrapers so that "the bowels themselves were exposed to view," Eusebius recorded. "Then they were laid on conch shells from the sea, and on sharp heads and points of spears on the ground and . . . were at last thrown as food to the wild beasts."[22] Several onlookers, inspired by the martyrs' refusal to give up their faith, joined them in the arena. The Christian community at Lyons, and at Vienne where similar killings took place, appears to have been strengthened by the experience.

A martyr is broken on the wheel, in a carving on the south portal of Chartres Cathedral in France. Many methods were used. In Macedonia, Christians were slowly asphyxiated over fires; at Alexandria, noses, ears, and hands were severed; at Antioch, they were roasted over braziers. Yet it was often easy to avoid such fates by burning a stick of incense on a pagan altar or sipping a sacrificial offering of wine.

❖ ACCOUNTS OF MARTYRDOM, or "hagiographies," from the Greek for holy, *hagios,* were often embellished with miraculous details. The Smyrna letter, for instance, claimed that the flow of Polycarp's blood was so copious that it extinguished the flames. His last words, his joy in death and the unshakable belief that underpinned it, are common to other accounts. While victims were being beaten to death during the Diocletian persecution in Egypt, one "would announce at the top of his voice his determination never to sacrifice, another would shout that he was a Christian, exulting in the confession of his Savior's name. . . ."[23] Saturninus, who was one of those martyred at Carthage in 203, demanded to be thrown to all the beasts in turn, "so that he might wear a more glorious crown."

Roman officials were often reluctant to condemn such otherwise law-abiding and unremarkable people. Pliny gave the accused three opportunities to recant; even with a crowd baying at his back, Hilarian, the procurator who condemned Perpetua, urged her to "spare your father's white hairs." A governor in Smyrna, a century after Polycarp, suggested plaintively to the accused that, if he would not pay homage to the emperor, he should "sacrifice to the air instead." The man refused on the grounds that he paid attention only to "him who made the air." Another magistrate remarked on the "beauty of this pleasant weather" to his prisoner, pointing out that, in order to live to enjoy it, he had merely to obey the law. "The death which is coming to me is more pleasant than the life which you would give me," he replied.[24]

This was, of course, the fundamental belief that helped martyrs accept their fate. In the visions she recorded before her execution, Perpetua saw herself climbing a ladder that reached up into heaven. It was guarded by a dragon which, when she hailed it in Christ's name, "gently lowered his head . . . and I trod his head as if I were treading on the first step. And I went up and saw an immense garden, and sitting in the midst of it a tall white-haired man, in the dress of a shepherd, milking sheep . . . [who] raised his head and looked at me, and said, 'You are welcome my child.'" Her fellow victim, Saturus, also dreamt of heaven. He saw Perpetua and himself, after their suffering, being carried up by angels into a green park that had rose trees and flowers and leaves that sang; then they came to a place "whose walls were such as if they were built of light" with a man "with hair white as snow but a youthful face." Perpetua was happy. "Thanks be to God, that as I was merry in the flesh, I am still merrier here."

Perhaps the visions were the result of preexecution emotions, exhaustion, dread, the intense feeling of comradeship among the condemned; perhaps, as they thought, they were comforts from God himself. They were not induced, however; they did not starve or ill-treat themselves into ecstasy in the fashion of later mystics. They focused on practical issues, paying to be transferred into a less-crowded part of the Carthage prison and for better food. Perpetua used her breeding to shame the senior army officer present into ordering more humane treatment for them; when her infant son was taken from her after sentencing, she noted with relief that "he no longer wished for my breasts, nor did they become inflamed." They were aware, too, of the impression they made on onlookers. After he had been mauled by a leopard, Saturus asked the prison adjutant for a ring from his finger, dipped it in his wound, and calmly gave it back to him as "a memorial of his endurance unto blood."

It was not simply courage that drove Christian martyrs, however, but also a kind of fear beyond the comprehension of pagans—the fear of hell.* Christians were divided over whether the *lapsi,* the "fallen" who denied their faith under threat of death, had damned themselves for eternity. The Scriptures justified either side of the debate. Moderates felt that Paul's epistles, and the parables of the

---

*The Romans had no devil, no great divinity of the underworld. At the moment of death the soul was thought to be led to the afterworld by two groups of genii or divinities, one malevolent and one benevolent, who struggled with one another for the soul. The Infernal Region was believed to be in the center of the earth, reached by caves, lakes, and marshes. The ghosts of the dead could return as mischievous spirits, Lemures, against whose spite a strange ritual was performed each May. The head of the family arose at midnight, snapping his fingers to drive the spirits away. He then washed his hands three times. Filling his mouth with black beans, he tossed them over his shoulder, chanting nine times: "I throw away these beans and with them I redeem myself and mine."

lost sheep and the prodigal son, showed that no sin was unpardonable. The rigorist Phileas, bishop of Thmuis in Lower Egypt, went to his death quoting Exodus: "He that sacrificeth to any god, save unto the Lord only, shall be destroyed utterly" (Exod. 22:20). He was offered a reprieve if he touched the pagan sacrifice, but this was "the freedom that brought a curse with it" made by a Roman magistrate he considered to be an agent of the devil. Papylus, a deacon at Pergamum, was equally confident that he was avoiding hell by being burnt on earth. "Here the fire burns briefly, but there it burns for ever, and by it, God will judge the world," he said. Papylus told his torturers that he had no pain: "one whom you do not see suffers with me." His sister Agathonice, however, cried out as she was hanged over the fire: "Lord Jesus Christ, help me because I am enduring this for your sake."[25]

That cry goes beyond visible motive, beyond the expectation of an imminent transfer to paradise, or fear of damnation, or hope of heavenly reward, or obedience to the Church. It rings with another quality of the faith, obscure to nonbelievers, rare and often falsely claimed: the love of Christ. Perhaps the English poet Wordsworth, writing fifteen hundred years later, captured the essence of its manifestation at Pergamum:

> There is a comfort in the strength of love;
> 'Twill make a thing endurable, which else
> Would overset the brain, or break the heart.[26]

✤ THE GREAT PERSECUTION came too late and was too unevenly enforced to destroy the Church. Weary, Diocletian retired to his native Dalmatia in 305 "to grow cabbages" as a country gentleman. His successor Galerius issued an edict of toleration on his deathbed in 311. With Constantine, the pogroms ceased. The games continued, although now Christians were in the audience rather than in the arena, as pagan gladiators killed each other.

A final, strange martyrdom was needed before mortal combat was banned in the now Christian empire. It involved a monk named Telemachus, from an Egyptian monastery in the desert between Alexandria and the Sodium Lakes. Telemachus was told by an official named Valerian, who was returning from Rome, that gladiatorial shows continued in Rome in front of spectators who were largely—if nominally—Christians. Deeply shocked, Telemachus persuaded Valerian to set out with him on a corn-ship bound from Alexandria for Ostia, the port of Rome. They visited the Colosseum together at a date variously put at January 391 or 400, in the reign of Honorius. The games, organized by the emperor's father-in-law, were in their tenth day when Telemachus attended them, his monk's habit covered with a white cloak. Gladiators were fighting with their heads encased in helmets without eyepieces so that they hacked blindly at each other. The monk took off his cloak, jumped down into the arena, and placed himself between two gladiators. "I demand it, not in my own name, but in His name who shed His blood in order that we might not wantonly shed the blood of another," he said. An absolute silence was broken by Alypius, the prefect of Rome, who told the gladiators: "Do your duty; he deserves to die." Telemachus was slain on the spot, and the revulsion caused by his death led to the ban.

Interest in martyrdom did not evaporate, however, as Christians and the Church became established and secure. It intensified. The pagans at Smyrna had been reluctant to give up Polycarp's bones to the Christians for burial on the grounds that "the Christians will now forsake the Crucified and worship Polycarp." The pagans were right to be suspicious. Reliquiae, "remains" or relics, were retrieved, and Polycarp was elevated to the status of a saint. Martyrs were proclaimed saints—the word comes from *sanctus,* Latin for "holy"—by local bishops without any formal rules.* Cults grew up around them, and the relics—pieces of skin and bone, locks of hair, shreds of clothing, or ashes—were taken from their places of execution. Critics argued that Christianity, with its reverence for the three beings of the Trinity and now dozens of saints, had become pantheistic. A distinction was drawn between the worship or adoration of God, *adorare,* and *venerari,* the veneration of saints. The cult of Polycarp was so intense that clarification was needed. "We worship Christ, as the Son of God," the Smyrna elders explained. "As to the martyrs, we love them as the disciples and imitators of the Lord."[27]

Believers prayed to the saints to intercede with God on their behalf, and their relics were held to have miraculous powers. "We do not worship relics," the papal secretary Jerome was obliged to make clear, "but we venerate the relics of martyrs in order better to adore Him whose martyrs they are." Nevertheless, a Church council in 340 had decreed the excommunication of those who did not believe wholeheartedly in relics, and churches were no longer content to commemorate local saints and relics. New congregations sought relics of their own. These were placed in shrines that attracted so many believers that a town's prosperity might come to depend on the pilgrim trade, giving these holy scraps such value that they were bought and sold for huge sums, and stolen and faked. They were cate-

*Bishops continued to declare saints in the Roman Church for many centuries; in the Orthodox churches they still do. The first saint to be officially canonized by the pope was Ulrich, bishop of Augsburg, by Pope John XV in 993. It was only in 1170 that Pope Alexander III declared that no saint could be venerated without papal authority. Many local saints have been suppressed, usually on the grounds that there was no evidence of their existence. Pope Paul VI in 1968 abolished forty saints' feast days from the calendar of the Church, including St. Christopher, the universally popular patron of travelers.

gorized; first-class for corporeal parts of a saint—hair, bones, teeth, "incorrupt-ible" flesh, blood, and heart; second-class for clothing and household artifacts; third-class for objects that had touched a relic of higher status. At Rome in the 370s, Pope Damasus collected the bones of saints and reburied them in shrines. The epitaphs he wrote for them claimed that they hailed from Rome, which irri-tated the Eastern churches. "The East sent the disciples—that we readily admit," Damasus wrote for the joint shrine of Peter and Paul as San Sebastiano. "But on account of the merit of their blood . . . Rome has gained the superior right to claim them as citizens."[28] Before his death in 397, Ambrose, bishop of Milan, ob-tained relics for the new churches he had built around the city in order to give "the church of Milan, hitherto barren of martyrs, the ability to rejoice in its own sufferings."[29]

Other forms of holiness—virginity, the life of solitude, extreme self-denial—were incorporated into new forms of martyrdom and sainthood. A powerful cult of self-imposed suffering was created. "Many who bear the attacks of the adver-sary and resist the desires of the flesh are martyrs, even in time of peace, in virtue of this self-immolation to God in their heart," Isidore of Seville explained, adding with nostalgia, "They would have been martyrs in the time of persecution."[30]

A NEW FORM of martyrdom flowed from the old. The first Christians had been burned by pagans at Rome "like torches in the night." In 386, at Trier in modern France, Christians set fire to a group of their own for the first time. The accused were charged with heresy, and their fellow Christians imposed the same penalty on them as had Nero. The incident was seen as an aberration. It was bit-terly criticized by a leading bishop; after the sentence had been carried out, the Church recoiled from the use of the stake as a punishment for heresy and did not return to it for more than six centuries. Nonetheless, a precedent had been set.

The first heretic to die at the stake was Priscillian, bishop of Avila, a Chris-tian mystic who believed that life should be a journey towards perfection. All earthly honor and luxury were to be renounced in "a total abandonment of the foul darkness of secular activities."* This included marriage; citing Peter, Priscil-lian urged his followers to "make your souls chaste for the obedience of faith." His sympathizers were organized into bands of *spiritales* and *abstinentes* who re-fused to touch meat or wine. He made no distinction between the lay and cleri-cal members of his community, nor between men and the many women who joined him.

*It was long thought that all the writings of the "heretic" had been destroyed, but eleven genuine tracts were dis-covered at Wurzburg in 1885.

They gathered in the distant isolation of farms and mountains. "After we had cast off the filthy darkness of worldly acts," Priscillian wrote, "we gave ourselves wholly to God, for we read that whoever loves anyone more than God cannot be his disciple." They shunned local churches, which they thought were impure; they fasted, prayed, had lengthy Bible readings—"for to us learning is scripture and to know the power of the living word"[31]—and "laboured with our lives so that we would be chosen."[32] Priscillian added that "we pursued the quiet of catholic peace," but the silence was broken by angry churchmen. They resented the Priscillian egality between laymen and clerics, and his call for the Church to strip itself of worldly vanity. They were also scandalized that women, particularly young women, mixed freely with the men; there were rumors of sorcery and orgies.

A synod was held at Saragossa in October 380 to condemn the movement. It dealt first with the mingling of the sexes. "All women who are of the Catholic Church and faithful," the synod laid down, "are to be separated from the meetings with strange men."[33] A lengthy list of Priscillian practices was also proscribed—fasting on Sundays and Christmas Day, "lurking in the hiding places of cells and mountains," not attending church, laymen assuming the title of "teacher" without ecclesiastical authority, going about in bare feet. Particular venom was reserved for clerics who left their offices to join the Priscillians "on account of the presumed luxury and vanity" of the Church; they were to be "driven away from the church" unless they made amends by "beseeching and begging many times . . ." The synod excommunicated the leaders of the movement in absentia. Priscillian was banished to Italy but returned to Spain. He was rearrested in 386 and charged at Trier in Gaul with sorcery, sexual immorality, and heresy.

The case was tried by the prefect Evodius, "a man of passionate severity." Priscillian appears to have been fatalistic; he did not deny charges of teaching obscene doctrines, nor even that he had led "night-time gatherings of infamous women, that he had the habit of praying naked."[34] His views on the Trinity were unorthodox. He did not believe Christ to be the Son; he held him to be God and man, writing that: "Our God assumes flesh taking to himself the form of God and man, that is of divine soul and earthly flesh."[35] The chronicler Sulpicius Severus found "as much fault with the accusers as with the accused," for the prosecutors were "fired by an excessive eagerness for victory." He thought one of them, Bishop Ithacius, to be a man "without principle or scruple; he was audacious, excessively talkative, impudent, a spendthrift who bestowed most of his attention on his gullet and his belly."[36]

Guilty verdicts were returned. Since it was illegal for churchmen to take life, the death sentences were pronounced by the prefect. The verdict led to furious argument between Gallic Christians. Bishop Martin of Tours, who had founded the first monastery in Gaul a few years before, sensed that an evil precedent had been set. "It was enough and more," he declared, "that these men should be declared heretics by the judgement of the bishops and dismissed from their sees." He thought it "a monstrosity and an unheard-of impiety for an ecclesiastical case to be tried by a secular judge."[37]

Priscillian and six followers were burnt alive, the first heretics, and, in antiquity, the only heretics to die in this manner. Martin of Tours, however, was prescient. The impiety of which he complained—the capital punishment of religious deviants by the secular authority at the insistence of the Church—was to become commonplace.

"CONQUER BY THIS":

Constantine

I n an army camp a few miles north of Rome on or about October 28, 312, the emperor Constantine saw a "heavenly sign of God." The result was unimaginable. "Render unto Caesar the things that are Caesar's," Jesus had said three centuries before, "and unto God the things that are God's" (Matt. 22:21). A Caesar now rendered honor to the Christian God, and respect and legality to the faithful. The beast nestled with the lamb; the wounds of persecution were bandaged in imperial purple; the empire became the comforter of the Church.

The conversion of Constantine appeared, then as now, as miraculous as that of Paul. It, too, shifted the course of world history. At the moment of the emperor's vision, tax exemptions were being offered to cities in the East that uncovered Christians in their midst. Copies of a fraudulent "Memoranda of Pilate," "full of every kind of blasphemy against Christ,"[1] were being circulated by officials to whip up hatred against Christians; and an army officer at Damascus— who later committed suicide, gleeful Christians noted, and so "paid the penalty of his malignity"[2]—was rounding up prostitutes on the city square and forcing them to fabricate confessions of vile Christian perversions. Rome was without a bishop for four years after Pope Marcellinus had shamed himself by sacrificing to the gods. At Carthage, one group of schismatic Christians was said to have posted armed guards outside prisons to prevent food and drink from being taken to their imprisoned rivals. Bishop Peter of Alexandria and his colleague Melitius of Lycopolis may have been reconciled in heaven, for both were martyred; but on earth, Peter had excommunicated Melitius and hung a barrier of a cloak, a blanket, and a shirt in his prison cell so that he did not have to look at his rival's supporters. Christians were fearful, lacking settled doctrine and leadership. Their brotherly love was threadbare.

Of a sudden, against any expectation, they were offered a prize beyond compare. The emperor, a sacred being to his pagan subjects whose palace rather than any church was held to be *domus divina,* the seat of the divine, opened the Roman world to Christ. In personal terms, at least, Constantine's vision was more startling than the one Paul had on the road to Damascus. It did not redirect an existing religious fervor, as Paul's had; its recipient was a career despot and political survivalist—a sniffer of plots, a strategist of factions, a builder of monuments to himself—whose commanders and advisers were pagan almost to a man and whose morals were so steeped in Roman tradition that his victims included his second wife and his firstborn son. He was lean-faced as shown in a contemporary bronze, with a taut and thin-lipped mouth, a predatory nose, and alert and wary eyes. Yet he granted Christians freedom to worship. He built their first great churches; he gave generously to their cause and made it legal for others to do so; he made Sunday, their day of worship, a public holiday; and, on his deathbed, he was baptized. He was not the first ruler to become a Christian—that distinction, also attributed to a vision, belonged to the Armenian king Tiridates—but he was the first Christian layman of undisputed grandeur. The Western Church beatified his mother and other rulers of comparatively trifling significance; but, as if the debt owed to him was too naked in its association of Church and State, it left Constantine unhonored. Only in the East is he venerated as a saint.

✤   HE WAS BORN in Naissus, or Nish, in modern Serbia. It is not known when; scholars place it anywhere from 274 to 288. His father, Constantius Chlorus, was a Roman officer with imperial connections; his mother Helena was said to be the daughter of an innkeeper. His parents divorced in 292 as his father rose in power; although Helena became a devout Christian and was much honored by her son, there are no signs that she introduced him to the faith during his formative years. The age was ill-omened. Tax revenues were falling, the coinage debased, and barbarians were terrorizing the frontiers; waves of plague—a "malignant pustule that . . . spread over the entire body but the eyes were the chief target for attack"[3]—combined with famines that left people "shrunken like ghosts. . . . some became food for dogs."[4] To these evils was added the growing fragmentation of the empire. Retaining the East for himself, Diocletian proclaimed Galerius the Caesar of the Danube Valley and Illyricum; Italy and Africa were ruled by Maximian, "savage in his manners, countenance and temper," while Constantius became Caesar of Britain, Gaul, and Spain. The boy Constantine was sent to the Eastern court more or less as a hostage to ensure the good conduct of his father.

As a young man Constantine served Diocletian in Egypt and fought under Galerius, who was as hostile to Christians as Diocletian, on the Danube. He was

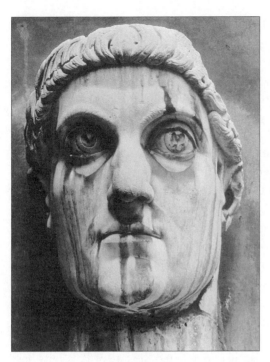

A monumental head of the emperor Constantine, the career soldier whose conversion in October A.D. 312 appeared as miraculous as that of St. Paul. He was said to have seen a Cross of light with the inscription "Conquer by this" in a vision before the battle that gave him control of Rome. His adoption of Christianity transformed the faith from an illegal cult into a rich and powerful institution, and his founding of the city of Constantinople gave it a new base in the East.

in the East at the height of the Great Persecution before leaving the court of Galerius—escaping, at least in legend, by taking all the post-horses with him to deny their use to his pursuers—and joining his father at Bononia, modern Boulogne. They sailed to Britain together to fight the Picts and Scots in the summer of 305. Constantine was at York when his father died in July 306. The army declared him his father's successor as Caesar of the West. It was an uneasy honor; by 308, six emperors* were vying jealously with each other, three in the East, and Maximian, his son Maxentius, and Constantine in the West. Maximian was driven from Rome by his son and committed suicide in 309.

Constantine's instincts were imperial. He lusted for grandeur, the consolidation of power, and the destruction of opponents; and he demanded from his subjects the servilities of the *adoratio purpurae,* the adoration of the purple, far removed from the Christian ideal of humility. He was greeted with traditional pagan honors—parades filled with images of the gods, music, flattering panegyrics comparing him to Apollo—when he toured cities in Gaul in 310 and 311. In the spring of the following year Maxentius threatened to invade Gaul and rid himself of his rival. Constantine crossed the Alps by the Mont Cenis Pass to forestall him.

*The senior bore the title of Augustus and the junior that of Caesar.

Maxentius remained in Rome, warned by an oracle that he would die if he ventured beyond the city gates. In October 312, Constantine moved his army through Turin and Verona and set up camp near the Milvian Bridge north of Rome.

This was the site of his vision. Lactantius,* who was then the tutor of Constantine's son, wrote that Constantine was "admonished in a dream to inscribe on the shields [of his men] the heavenly sign of God and thus to commit himself to battle. He obeyed and inscribed the sign of Christ on the shields: the letter X intersected by the letter I, bent at the top."[5] Armed with this sign, his army took up their swords as Maxentius's soldiers crossed a bridge of boats and advanced to meet them. As battle was joined, Maxentius was presiding over celebrations in the Circus. There was a sudden cry that Constantine could not be defeated. Disturbed, Maxentius ordered the Sibylline oracles to be consulted. It was divined that on that day, October 28, an enemy of the Romans would perish. "Misled by this oracle in the hope of victory," Lactantius wrote, "Maxentius went out and engaged in battle." The bridge was destroyed behind him, the fighting intensified, and "the hand of God passed over the battlefield." As his army began to retreat in panic, Maxentius "hurried to the bridge; pushed along by the multitude of those fleeing, he was driven into the Tiber." His armor dragged him beneath the waters. Eusebius, the contemporary Christian historian, cited the fate of Pharaoh's host in the Red Sea with glee; quoting Exodus, he wrote that Maxentius and his bodyguard of infantry and pikemen "went down into the depths like a stone."[6]

Other versions of the apparent miracle followed. Constantine told Eusebius[†] that he had seen a cross of light above the sun, but added that it bore an inscription—"Conquer by this"—and that his "whole army" witnessed it. As the emperor fell into a fitful sleep later in the day, it was followed by a second apparition in which "the Christ of God appeared to him with the same sign . . . and commanded him to make a likeness of it and to use it as a safeguard in all his engagements with his enemies." Constantine obeyed and constructed the labarum, the military standard of the cross. It was made from a spear with a transverse bar to give it the shape of the cross; the Greek letters X and P intersected within a golden wreath on the point of the spear to form the monogram of Chi-Rho, the first two letters of "Christ" in Greek. A cloth hung from the crossbar, in the traditional style of Roman standards, bearing "a golden half-length portrait of the pious em-

---

*Born in the province of Africa around A.D. 250, Lactantius was tutor to Constantine's son Crispus from 313. He witnessed the Diocletian persecution in Bithynia, and may have been converted by witnessing the courage of the Christian martyrs. His work *On the Deaths of the Persecutors* includes the first reference made to the vision at the Milvian Bridge.

†Or so Eusebius claimed, adding that the emperor "confirmed his statement by an oath." Eusebius certainly had lengthy conversations with Constantine.

peror and his children. . . ." Eusebius also claimed that Constantine had time before the battle to send for Christians to inquire "who that God was" that he had seen, to make "the priests of God his counselors," and to receive instruction in the incarnation and immortality of Christ.

❧ IT WAS NATURAL that the vision should attract legend, for it was a watershed in Christian fortunes. In 313, Constantine met the Eastern emperor Licinius at Milan. They jointly issued an edict granting "both to Christians and to all men" the unrestricted right to "follow the form of worship each desired." The edict was not a statement of faith, but a form of divine insurance policy. The two emperors, hedging their bets on the nature of the Almighty, attributed their tolerance "to the end that whatever divinity there may be on the heavenly seat may be favorably disposed and propitious to us and all those placed under our authority." All cults were now protected, and it was not until 391 that Christians enjoyed a definitive monopoly as the state religion.

Imperial ordinances to provincial governors nonetheless made it clear that Christians were especially privileged. The "complete cancellation" of persecution was stressed; Christians were to be given "free and absolute permission to practice their own form of worship"; all property and goods seized from them must be "restored without payment and without any demand for compensation"; the governors were to ensure that the property "be handed over to the Christian body immediately, by energetic action on your part, without any delay." This did not merely cover individuals whose houses had been seized as "places where it was their habit to meet"; it was known that other places existed, "belonging not to individuals but to the legal estate of the whole body." These, too, were to be returned "without any argument whatsoever." Thus, for the first time, the legal identity of the Church, and its right to own its place of worship, was established.[7]

Freedom from civic duties—on town councils, public ceremony committees, road and public building maintenance boards, and so forth—followed. In 314, Constantine wrote to Anulinus, the proconsul of Africa, ordering that those "who with due holiness and constant attention to the law give their services to the conduct of divine worship shall receive the rewards of their own labors"; he desired that the "people commonly known as clergymen . . . once and for all be kept entirely free from all public duties." He suggested that this was in the interests of the state since, in rendering service to God, "they will be making an immense contribution to the welfare of the community."[8] It also had the happy result, from Constantine's viewpoint, of making the Christian priesthood beholden to the emperor for this valuable concession. Public service was expensive and time-consuming. So many rich pagans claimed to be Christian priests in order to avoid it that Constantine had to legislate against the abuse.

He also made direct grants of cash to "named ministers of the lawful and most holy Catholic Religion." In a letter to Caecilian, bishop of Carthage, whom he addressed respectfully as "Your Steadfastness," he wrote that he had arranged with the imperial finance officer to transfer the sum of 3,000 *folles* to defray the expenses of the clergy in the African provinces. A *follis* was a bag of gold equivalent to 12,500 denarii. A denarius had originally represented a day's pay for a laborer; inflation had eaten away its value to the point where a legionary now drew some 7,500 denarii a year. Even at this rate the gift was generous; it represented the annual pay of some five thousand soldiers, and the emperor added that Caecilian was to ask for further funds if this was not enough.

Other favors followed. On March 7, 321, the first day of the week was proclaimed to be a day of rest, in the cities at least, if not in the villages that toiled to feed them. "All judges, cityfolk and craftsmen shall rest on the venerable day of the Sun," the imperial edict stated, still describing it in pagan terms. "But country people may attend to farming without hindrance, since it is often the best day for planting vines or sowing grain." This link of a holiday with the Christian day of worship enhanced the prestige of the Church; popular pagan festivals and feasts were slowly absorbed into the Christian calendar, with "holy days" in memory of local martyrs providing other welcome breaks from drudgery. Pagans had paraded through the fields in early summer to pray that the crops would ripen; Christians held Rogation Days of prayer and fasting to achieve the same goal. Christmas Day is first referred to in a Roman calendar of 336. The date of December 25 was probably chosen to replace the pagan feast celebrating the birth of the Unconquered Sun on the same day. A law of 321 made it legal for people to leave land, money, and other bequests to the Church in their wills, a change that greatly helped Church finances.

These benefits were offered only in the provinces controlled by Constantine. In the East, Licinius abandoned the joint edict of toleration he had agreed on at Milan. He reverted to traditional vices—"the besotted old dotard used countless married women and unwedded girls"[9]—and to the murder of bishops and the demolition of churches. "God intervened in the darkness," Eusebius wrote, "kindling a great beacon light" and leading Constantine and his son Crispus, also "most dear to God," into battle against the tyrant at Chrysopolis. Here, on September 18, 324, God threw the "madman" prone at their feet. Constantine had the defeated Licinius strangled and was soon to execute the beloved Crispus; but Christian celebration was justifiable enough. "Men have witnessed battles and watched a war in which God's providence granted victory to this host," Constantine told them in a Good Friday oration at Antioch. The "worthless usurper"

Licinius had been destroyed; "does not this in every way prove the Providence of God and his loving care for the interests of men?"[10]

It indeed seemed as if God had intervened on Constantine's behalf. The empire was reunited under a sole Christian ruler whose writ extended over some 2.5 million square miles, from the sweltering headwaters of the Red Sea to the Atlantic and the foggy shoals at the mouth of the Rhine on the North Sea. Christian prisoners forced to work in the mines under Licinius were released and chanted psalms as they journeyed back to their homes. "Light was everywhere, and men who once dared not look up greeted each other with smiling faces and shining eyes," Eusebius wrote. "They danced and sang in city and country alike, giving honor first to God our Sovereign Lord and then to the pious emperor with his sons, dear to God. . . ."[11]

Constantine raised a great new capital city in the East. The motivation behind moving his capital had much to do with dislike of Rome. The Eternal City was an affront to his imperial personage, a reminder of the distant republican days when its people and its senate had been the rulers of the Roman world. It remained a stronghold of paganism, and its senators, though politically long since emasculated, resented the absolutism of emperors as fervently as they clung to the old religion. The transfer of government to Constantinople was in part strategic—the Eastern Empire was of growing economic importance and was dangerously exposed to barbarian and Persian attack—and also symbolic. Rome was no longer master of the empire that bore its name; it was ruled by the *gens Flavia,* the dynasty of Constantine, from a new city that bore the unmistakable imprint of its founder, and his name. He christened it Constantinople.

His New Rome was built on the hilly site of the small town of Byzantium, which lay on the western shores of the Bosporus, commanding the narrow channel that divided Europe from Asia Minor and that provided a waterway between the Mediterranean and the Black Sea. He laid the first stone of the western walls on November 4, 326. A pagan philosopher, Sopater, cast spells to ensure the city's good fortune; a palladium, a sacred talisman of protection dating back to ancient Troy, was said to have been buried beneath the giant statue of Constantine that towered atop a ninety-foot porphyry column in the forum, created by mounting the emperor's head on an old Colossus of Apollo.[12] The city had its own pagan guardians, the goddesses Rhea, mother of the Olympian gods, and Tyche, daughter of Oceanus and bringer of fortune and abundance; but a cross was welded to Tyche's forehead, and the pagan Sopater was executed before the city was dedicated to the Blessed Virgin and inaugurated as the new seat of government in prayer and torchlight processions on May 11, 330.

This was a Christian place, insofar as the despot who founded it was Christian. A fresh vision was credited for Constantine's choice of the spot. He was said to have walked the line of the walls himself; when a surveyor asked him how much farther he would go, he replied: "Until He who walks before me stops walking." Here, protected by sea and a land wall stretching from the Golden Horn to the Sea of Marmara, Constantine created a court of oriental pomp, with a new aristocracy to replace the senatorial class of pagan Rome. The surrounding provinces were beggared to provide colonists for the city; it was watered by underground aqueducts driven from forest springs and streams, and the grain shipments of Egypt and Syria were diverted to feed the city. Its seven hills were covered with buildings designed to match those of Rome, and decorated with the requisitioned statuary of old Greece. New taxes on real estate and the profits of trade flowed into the coffers of the "count of the sacred bounties," the imperial treasurer, to fund the gigantic construction site. The municipal officials who levied taxes were forbidden to evade their responsibilities by joining the Christian clergy. Within eighty years Constantinople had 4,388 residences grand enough to be individually listed as being of architectural merit,[13] a forum and acropolis, scores of baths, two theaters overlooking the brilliant waters of Marmara, harbors, barracks, reservoirs and covered cisterns, and, as if to demonstrate an equality between power and faith, fourteen palaces and fourteen churches.

PAGANS DID NOT think that the emperor's Christianity was real, much less that it came from genuine religious conviction. Some ascribed it to greed, thinking that he had converted only so that he could plunder their temples. Others thought he professed Christianity from guilt over the murder of his son and wife. Still others believed it was the result of disease, saying that he suffered secretly from leprosy and that Christians alone would not shun him. It is true that he continued to proclaim himself Pontifex Maximus, the pagan title for chief priest, and that he felt this conferred on him a general overlordship of religion. Gold coins portrayed him receiving a symbol of victory from the Unconquered Sun, a flattering and wholly pagan reference, and others immodestly described him as the Emperor of the Whole World. Pagan priests attended his ceremonials, and he was not baptized until he was on his deathbed; his tomb was placed in the center of the circular mausoleum he built for himself in Constantinople, with twelve sepulchres placed around it, as though the apostles lay at his feet.

His speeches and letters, however, reveal a mind of clearly Christian persuasion. He linked his career to his faith. "Surely all men know that the holy service in which these hands have been busied," he asked during an oration, "has begun in pure truth and faith towards God?"[14] He gave generously to the poor, whether Christian or pagan; "even for the beggars in the forum, miserable and shiftless, he provided, not with money only, or necessary food, but also decent clothing."

The virtues that Eusebius rained on him—caring for orphans like a father, relieving the destitution of widows, providing poor virgins with dowries so they could marry wealthy men—were no doubt exaggerated but are confirmed by legal acts.

The branding of slaves on the face was forbidden; celibates, childless couples, and widows who did not remarry were freed from a special tax; the law of debt was made less fearsome. Grants were made to support poor children, discouraging the practice of leaving unwanted babies to die on hillsides. Crucifixion was banned; in 325, Constantine legislated against gladiatorial games and withdrew imperial patronage. His distastes for paganism was real—he called it an "error" and described sacrifices as "foul pollution"[15]—and he sought out Christian ministers, admitting them to his table despite their poor clothing and modest appearance. If he took the title of Pontifex Maximus, so too did popes from the fifteenth century onward; and he had practical reasons for maintaining heathen traditions, for the majority of his subjects were still pagans. His delayed baptism was equally a matter of sensible insurance. Rulers dealt in war and coercion, and Constantine in family murder, and the Church taught that sins can be washed clean but once. For a powerful man like Constantine, baptism came better at the end of a lifetime than in its middle.

In the realm of high politics, Constantine was not the pupil of the Church but its instructor. To many Christians, the state was a pit of eternal wickedness that corrupted the souls of those who governed; few Christians had sought or held public office, and those who did risked expulsion from the Church if they attended pagan functions as part of their duties. Constantine introduced the Church to worldly power and wealth, and here his motives were perhaps more cynical than spiritual. As head of state it made sound sense to favor Christians. They were politically docile. Their faith admonished them to civil obedience, to "render to all their dues; tribute to whom tribute is due; custom to whom custom; fear to whom fear; honour to whom honour" (Rom. 13:7); Paul's comparison of the ruler to "a minister of God to thee for good . . . an avenger for wrath to him that doeth evil" (Rom. 13:4) was used from the sixteenth century as evidence to support the divine right of kings. Submission was a matter of faith as well as of fear; "ye must needs be in subjection," Paul had added, "not only because of the wrath, but also for conscience sake" (Ibid). Christians might have an ideal of liberty, but it had an otherworldly quality—"the Jerusalem that is above is free, which is our mother" (Gal. 4:26)—that did not disturb the general deference to the powers on earth. The Church had as yet few temporal ambitions; by offering spiritual unity it offered useful underpinning to the political unity of empire.

The largesse that Constantine proffered—a "stream of personal letters from the emperor reached the bishops," Eusebius rejoiced, "accompanied by honors and gifts and money" (Eus x.2)—came at a price. Jesus had said that "my kingdom is not of this world" and spurned any involvement in it. With imperial patronage, God mingled with Caesar and faith fused with the politics of absolutism. Fracture and dissent are mortal foes of empire, and Constantine was no more inclined to accept them in matters spiritual than temporal. He added a rider to his letter showering Bishop Caecilian with gold. He warned the bishop that he had learned that "certain persons of unstable character desire to lead astray the laity of the Catholic Church by disreputable enticements." The emperor said he had instructed his proconsul, and Patricius, vicar of Africa, not to overlook such incidents on any account; the bishop was instructed to refer anyone persisting in "insane conduct" immediately to the authorities for judgment.[16]

Priests were intimately aware of individual failings among their flock. They were appointed as "penitentiaries" to act for bishops in hearing confessions. An elaborate system of public penance was imposed on sinners; they wore sackcloth, made their beds in ashes and ate the plainest food when not fasting, and were barred from sharing in the Eucharist, sometimes for many years. To the sins that most concerned the Church—idolatry, adultery or fornication, and murder—the emperor now added "insane conduct," a catchall that went beyond moral lapses to include political dissent. A network of *agentes in rebus,* inspectors of the imperial post and messenger service, already acted as spies in the farthest outposts of the empire. The clergy was an unrivaled intelligence resource that Constantine, in requiring the bishop to inform on members of his flock, determined to tap.

His view of the theological disputes that plagued the Church was equally proprietorial. Caecilian had been consecrated as bishop of Carthage by a *traditor* in the Great Persecution. Rigorists were outraged and consecrated Donatus as a rival to Caecilian. Constantine threatened to go to Africa himself to deal with the Donatist schismatics and to "make plain what kind of worship is to be offered to God." He saw himself as the defender of the faith; he thought that an emperor had no higher duty than to "destroy error and repress rash indiscretions" in the cause of "true religion, honest concord and due worship."[17] He worried, too, lest the Christian God who had shown him such favor might be angered by such squabbles; the "Supreme Being," he wrote "may perhaps be roused not only against the human race but against myself, to whose care he has by his celestial will committed the government of all earthly things." In the event, he did not sail for Carthage; instead he summoned a synod to Arles in 316 to "cut short such quarrels" and to expose the "base and perverted motives" and "private enmities" that had caused them. Constantine's personal interest is shown in the instructions he gave to Chrestus, bishop of Syracuse, one of the large number of prelates ordered to assemble at Arles. The emperor outlined Chrestus's travel arrangements; the governor of Sicily would provide a public carriage, the bishop was to bring two presbyters with him, and he was permitted to take three servants to "look after your comforts on the journey."[18] The emperor did not enter into the theological disputes, but he left no doubt of his disapproval of schismatics. They were "distasteful if not positively sickening; and to people whose minds are strangers to this most holy religion they give a pretext for mockery"; their troublesome ideas were to be "terminated once and for all," and Chrestus had a duty to transform their disputes into "genuine religious feeling, faith, and brotherly concord."[19]

A precedent was set. Soon after, Constantine was irritated by a fresh controversy surrounding Arius, a priest at Alexandria who denied the full divinity of Christ and held that the Son was subordinate to the Father. He was excommunicated in 321, but a large following of Arians remained convinced of his beliefs. The emperor sent Hosius of Cordoba, the bishop who advised him on Church matters, to Egypt to reach a compromise. The mission failed. A few months after his conquest of the East, Constantine called leading churchmen to a meeting to resolve the dispute in May 325. This first Ecumenical, or world-wide council of the Church, was summoned and funded by the state; the emperor paid the piper, and if he did not write the tune, theological intricacy being beyond him, it was understood that the one played should be pleasing to him.*

He chose the venue, the handsome city of Nicaea, Izmir in modern Turkey; he dictated its principal topic, the Arian heresy; he permitted the bishops to travel free with the imperial post, where he planted spies who might disclose the views expressed during the journey; he lodged and fed them; he gave each delegate a present and invited them to a feast to celebrate the twentieth anniversary of his declaration as emperor by the army at York. He attended the council in person, arriving, Eusebius recalled in his biography of Constantine, like "some heavenly messenger of God, clothed in a shining raiment, which flashed with glittering rays of light." Those who saw him were "stunned and amazed at the sight, like children who have seen a frightening apparition." Units of the bodyguard and other troops surrounded the palace with drawn swords, and "through them the men of God proceeded without fear into the innermost rooms of the emperor, in which some were his companions at table, while others reclined on couches at either side." It was, the impressed churchman wrote, "like a dream" of the promised Kingdom of Christ.[20] When an anti-Arian creed was agreed upon, imperial notaries led by Constantine's "master of the offices" took it to each delegate for signature.[21] The emperor himself imposed sentences of exile on the Arian bishops who refused to sign. Little more than a decade after his vision, the Christian emperor had made Christian dissent a criminal offense.

---

*For the debate at the council, and the battles over heresy and orthodoxy, see the following chapter.

❖ AT FIRST CHURCH leaders were enraptured at the way the state appeared to have changed from worst enemy to closest ally.* Eusebius declared that a united Christian empire was the divine goal of history, and that the emperor heralded the prophesied time when the knowledge of God will fill the earth as water fills the seas. He came close to comparing Constantine with Christ. "Speech and reason are mute," he wrote in his biography, "when I gaze in spirit upon this thrice-blessed soul, united with God, free of all mortal dross, in robes gleaming like lightning, and in ever radiant diadem."[22] He believed that Constantine had been blessed with "a transcript of the divine sovereignty" to direct "the administration of this world's affairs"[23] in "imitation of God himself."

This flattery had much to do with money. Constantine's law of 321 permitting bequests and deathbed legacies to be made to the Church entangled the faith with Mammon. Priests were readily able to exploit the new law; they had moral authority over the living, and they were present at the bedside as the dying contemplated their departure to the next world. Women were the most lucrative targets. They well outnumbered men in most congregations. They were entitled to their own wealth, and widows to a share of a dead husband's estate. Second marriages, which had the side effect of diluting their fortune, were frowned on by many and thought sinful by some priests. The Church's encouragement of virginity, though doctrinal, also had a happy effect on its funds. Virgins shared in the estates of their parents but had no dependents of their own; it was natural for them to leave their possessions to those who had inspired and praised their chastity. The clergy did not let such opportunities slip by and soon earned itself a reputation as "a force without equal in the race for inheritance."[25] Fifty years after the law on legacies was enacted, the emperor Valentinian was forced to instruct Pope Damasus to forbid clerics from loitering outside the houses of spinsters and widows in the hope of picking up a bequest for themselves or their church.

A particular scandal involved four future saints: the fiery scholar Jerome, translator of the Scriptures into Latin; two rich, holy widows, Marcella and Paula; and the latter's virgin daughter Eustochium. They met with other devoted and well-born widows and virgins at the palace of Marcella in Rome. Jerome taught them Hebrew and the virtues of celibacy, explaining that "Christ and Mary were both virgins and thus consecrated the pattern of virginity for both sexes." He

---

*The notion of a mutual interest between them had occasionally been explored. A century before, Origen suggested that Augustus had served God's purpose as the first emperor because he had "reduced to a single uniformity the many kingdoms on earth so that he had a single empire";[24] it was easier for the apostles to obey Jesus' instruction to "Go and teach all nations" in one state rather than in a number of warring kingdoms. It was also, of course, the ambition of the Church to reduce its own factions to a similar uniformity in a spiritual empire. But such explorations were tentative and rare.

urged them to renounce their riches and lead lives of hermitlike poverty and chastity, as if they were in the Egyptian deserts and not amid Roman high society. Paula "surpassed all other Roman ladies in wealth," or so legend has it; she now "abstained from all meat, fish, eggs, honey and wine . . . lay on a stone floor covered in sackcloth . . . and laid aside all costly garments."[26] She devoted her fortune to the poor and to the faith; she gave her children nothing, explaining that she could do no better than "to secure for them by alms the blessings of heaven." Relatives were alarmed at Jerome's ability to separate the ladies from their money and at his intense discussions of virginity with Eustochium; the Roman clergy also resented its failure to tap these funds. Jerome left for Palestine in 385, shortly after the death of Pope Damasus, his protector. He was joined there by Paula and Eustochium. Paula, who was once "carried about by eunuchs in litters," now sat on the back of an ass and "distributed immense alms."[27] She built a monastery for Jerome at Bethlehem, as well as three convents which she directed with her daughter.

Jerome was deeply ascetic and hardly a fortune-hunter; but others had fewer scruples, and there were such numbers of them that Valentinian's ruling against "despoilers of the weaker sex" proved unenforceable and was abandoned. By the end of the century it was commonplace for Christians in Asia Minor and Syria to bequest as much as a third of their estate to the Church. In the West, legators often gave the same amount that they would have left to an additional child had they had one. Priests may not have directly linked miserliness with hellfire, but they hinted strongly at it. Rich pagans had given money to temples as a matter of honor and civic pride; the Church offered spiritual rewards in return for donations. Salvian, a presbyter of Marseilles, claimed that to leave even the smallest part of one's estate to family and friends instead of the Church was "to prejudice one's eternal interest."

Bishops were the great beneficiaries. "Make me bishop of Rome and I will become a Christian tomorrow," the pagan senator Praetextatus said in tribute to the wealth that now went with the office. A rich see like Rome was a prize for which clerics now fought. Two presbyters, Damasus and Ursinus, each declared himself to be pope in 366. Damasus hired tough Roman *fossores,* catacomb diggers, to pursue his rival's supporters in bloody street battles that ended in a massacre in a newly built church. "They engaged in actual battle, in which men were killed and wounded," the pagan historian Ammianus Marcellinus wrote. "The prefect of the city, being unable to end these disorders, was compelled to withdraw to the suburbs. . . . One day 137 dead bodies were found in the Basilica of Sicininus and the populace, raised to a state of ferocity, were with great difficulty restored to order. . . ." Men strove to become pope with every sinew, or so Marcellinus observed, because the winners "will be secure for the future, enriched by offerings from matrons, riding in carriages, dressing splendidly and feasting luxuriously, so that their entertainments surpass even royal banquets . . ."[28]

Damasus won the battle, but Ursinus continued the war from the suburbs. "To disturb peaceful affairs still delights some persons and repeated uproar is incited at meetings outside the city walls," an imperial decree noted in 368. It instructed the prefect to forbid the "mad group" from worshiping or congregating within twenty miles of Rome, so that "at last, after all disturbances have been removed to a great distance, settled peace will be granted to the people for all time."[29] It was a vain hope. In 381, a Church council begged "the most clement Emperors and Christian Princes" to exile the tenacious Ursinus—"an excommunicated individual, the standard-bearer of his madness, he sows confusion and tries to excite even heathens and abandoned characters"—in order to "restore peace to us bishops and to the Roman people."[30] Damasus died in 384, succeeded by Siricius. Ursinus persisted with his claim, prompting the first imperial confirmation of a papal election. The people of Rome, the emperor Valentinian II wrote to the vicar of Rome in February 385, "have not only expressed their wishes that the religious and holy Bishop Siricius should thus provide over the clergy, but by their acclamations have rejected Ursinus as a wrongdoer, let the aforesaid bishop . . . continue in office with our hearty approval. . . ."[31]

✦ DESPITE SUCH SQUABBLING among the personnel, Christianity's new status was cast in stone for every pagan eye to see and admire. The huge church-building program launched by Constantine was on a scale unmatched since Alexander the Great's lavish projects almost seven centuries before.[32] It was an incurious soul who did not at least step inside to examine the strange places where Christians worshiped. Constantine made endowments for upkeep, granting the Church vast estates in Numidia, Egypt, the Adriatic islands, and Gozo, farms in Tyre, Tarsus, and Antioch, and houses, gardens, and bakeries in Rome. The most significant of his foundations were in the Eternal City, where he provided the pope with a cathedral, baptistery, and residence at the Lateran. Part of the site had been the barracks of the imperial cavalry that had fought against him at the Milvian Bridge; another section had been the palace of the Laterani family, part of his wife Fausta's dowry. The potential influence of the bishops of Rome was greatly increased by the transfer of government to Constantinople; now distant from the imperial eye and bureaucracy, they were able to develop their own power base from the grand Lateran palace that remained the official papal residence for almost a thousand years.

Modest churches, such as the meeting hall at Dura-Europos, already existed; Alexandria is thought to have had ten of them in A.D. 300.[33] St. John Lateran at

Rome was a model of the great buildings of the new era. It was a basilica—a name drawn from the Roman law courts and trade exchanges on which it was based—with a rectangular space opening into a semicircular apse. The apse was decorated with beaten gold at a cost of 36,000 *solidi,* calculated at ninety million dollars in modern money[34]; a further 22,000 *solidi* was spent on silver candelabra and other lights, and the mosaics were made of gold, silver, and precious stones set within glass. The interior was divided by rows of columns into a broad central nave reserved for the lesser clergy and choir, and two narrower aisles in which the laity was segregated by sex. Catechumens under instruction and penitents under discipline stood in the porch at the rear of the nave. The intimacy between clergy and congregation, so strong in the cramped conditions of the old house churches and catacomb chapels, was now lost; the senior clergy was seated in the apse, with the bishop installed on a throne in the center.

The ordinary wooden table once used for the Lord's Supper became a fixed altar on a raised platform at the front of the apse. The only light came through the doors and from windows pierced in the "clear story," or clerestory, the walls of the nave above the columns. Darkness heightened the sense of mystery; it was softened by candles and garlands of flowers, and the sweet odor of incense, pagan devices now adopted by the Church. The apse and altar were placed at the western end so that the rays of the rising sun fell on the bishop as he faced eastward toward the congregation; from pagan habit, worshipers often bowed to the sun before entering the basilica. Churches became centers of local life where people met for conversation as well as worship; several thousand people could assemble in St. John Lateran. At Antioch, at least, the sexes also ogled each other; they were separated by a wooden partition, but the young priest John Chrysostom told the men that they needed "a wall to keep you apart from the women. . . . the women have learned the manners of the brothel, and the men are no better than maddened stallions."

The fashion of building a church around the shrine or tomb of a martyr began with Constantine. He started construction of the great Basilica of St. Peter at the spot on Vatican Hill where the apostle was said to have been crucified; he ordered another to be built over the shrine to St. Paul on the Ostian Way outside the city walls. The Basilica of Santa Maria Maggiore rose on the Esquiline Hill, on a spot which the Blessed Virgin was later said to have indicated by leaving her footprints in the snow during a miraculous August snowfall. Domes were developed for churches that had a martyr's tomb as their focal point. In the East these centralized churches became the general rule as architects perfected the erection of a cupola above a square base.

Services became longer and more elaborate during the fourth century, for there was no longer need of secrecy, and an air of pomp was acquired from court ceremonial. The rules against paintings and sculptures—a meeting of bishops at the beginning of the century had barred pictures from church "so that what is worshiped and adored may not be depicted on walls"—were relaxed as wealth flowed in. The rites were more awesome; in the East the altar became a place of "terror and trembling," silvered beneath a rich canopy, screened off from the body of the church by an embroidered curtain or an iconostasis, an elaborate screen decorated with icons. Benefactors donated finely wrought chalices and candelabra. Bishops dressed in the exquisite vestments typical of the nobility, the alb and chasuble corresponding to the tunic and cloak worn by the highborn. As laymen slowly abandoned them, these robes became a distinctive ecclesiastical dress. The lesser clergy remained humble figures—"the most rigid abstinence in eating and drinking, and plainness of apparel, and eyes always cast on the ground. . . ."[35]— and the gap between them and their episcopal masters grew wider.

With the new shrines and churches came pilgrimages. Christians did not invent this practice; Jews had been commanded to appear before the Lord three times a year, and they sang psalms—"I will lift up mine eyes unto the mountains: from whence shall my help come? . . ." (Ps. 121:1)—as they journeyed toward the hills of Jerusalem. Pious souls already visited the Roman catacombs, and some had traveled as far as the Holy City, but its destruction had left it with no Christian site beyond the Cenaculum, a house in whose upper room the Last Supper was supposedly celebrated and which served as the only church in the city. A century before, Origen had seen the wells of Abraham at Ascalon, and the cliff at Gergesa over which he was told the Gadarene swine had rushed; the writer Julius Africanus had traveled to the alleged site of Noah's ark. A whole complex of holy places was now created, and relics were installed under altars or displayed within them. As pagan cities had their local gods, so Christian cities and congregations acquired patron saints to protect them and intercede on their behalf. A pilgrimage might be no more than a few miles to the tomb of a local martyr, or an expedition to the grand and distant shrine of an apostle. In the Holy Land the cave in which Joseph of Arimathea had supposedly laid the body of Jesus was discovered after Constantine ordered a mound of rubbish to be removed from the site. The Church of the Holy Sepulchre was built above it on the Hill of the Crucifixion; the emperor also founded a shrine at Mambree, where Abraham was believed to have lived with Isaac among the great oak trees, and had it decorated with gold and jewels.

Constantine's mother Helena made her own pilgrimage to Palestine in 326–27, the pagan writer Zosimus suggesting that she did so as penance for having helped drown her daughter-in-law Fausta in her bath. The excavators she employed to dig on Calvary found three crosses beneath it, or so it was claimed. Helena touched a sick woman with each of them in turn. When one of them produced a miraculous recovery, Helena knew it to be the True Cross. "She adored not the wood, but the King, Him who hung on the wood," Ambrose of Milan wrote later. "She burned with an earnest desire of touching the remedy of immortality."[36] Part of the cross was covered in a rich silver case and placed in the Church of the Holy Sepulchre as a relic; another part she sent to her son, while she threw one of the nails into the Adriatic to calm the waters during a storm at sea. She also built churches on the Mount of Olives and at Bethlehem, and a convent, in which she appeared "amidst the women at prayer in a most humble garment," so Eusebius wrote, and waited at table for visitors.

Her journey encouraged further pilgrims, with women notable among them. Melania, a wealthy Roman widow, visited Palestine in about 374 and founded a double monastery for nuns and monks on the Mount of Olives. Pamphlets giving directions to Jerusalem from places as distant as Bordeaux were now being produced; one of these guides may have been used by Egeria, a nun or abbess who probably set out from Gaul for Jerusalem in 381. The bishop of Edessa was already well used to giving such visitors a guided tour; "we shall, if you desire it, show you all the places here which Christians like to see," he told her. A little later, Paula and Eustochium left Rome to tour the Holy Land and the hermitages of the Egyptian desert with Jerome. Paula was shown the tower of Elijah at Sarepta and the grave of the four virgins at Caesarea; at Bethlehem she saw the grave of Rachel. In Hebron the swaddling clothes of Isaac were displayed in the hut of Sarah. The locals had become adept at satisfying the new pilgrim-tourists; they were "ready to show everything for which the foreigners inquired, and the pilgrim was eager to credit everything."[37]

❖ CONSTANTINE WAS WARY of alienating his pagan subjects by seizing their sites and temples. Few antiheathen incidents took place during his lifetime; a prophet of Apollo was tortured at Antioch, another at Didyma was forced to confess to "fraud," and a shrine of Aphrodite was razed at the site of the crucifixion at Jerusalem. The pace quickened in the decades after his death in 337. The first demands for pagans to be routed out in their entirety came in the 340s; it took little enough time for Christians to turn from persecuted to persecutors. In 356, Constantine's son Constantius decreed that all pagan temples should close and he prohibited sacrifices to the gods on pain of death. He removed the Altar of Victory from the Senate House at Rome, on which senators had offered incense since the reign of Augustus more than three centuries before. The cults were ailing, but they survived.

One last effort to revive the ancient gods was made by Julian, Constantine's nephew. He was a worthy adversary of Christianity, possessing many of the ancient qualities of Rome and Greece. Hardy self-reliance and self-control, tenacity, and a sense of duty and martial spirit mingled with his lively interest in literature and philosophy. His childhood was deeply scarred; to him, Christians were not victims but persecutors. Upon his uncle's death, his father, brother, and cousins were all murdered by soldiers to ensure the undisputed succession of Constantine's sons. Julian was then six years old; he and his half-brother Gallus survived only because they were thought too young to be dangerous. He was left in the care of Bishop Eusebius of Nicomedia until he was about ten, when he and Gallus were banished to a remote fortress in Cappadocia, where Christianity was again force-fed to them. Julian was released when his half-brother was made Caesar in 351; three years later Gallus was executed for misgovernment. Julian spent some months in 355 studying Greek philosophy at the schools in Athens; he was heavily influenced by Maximus of Smyrna, a practitioner of magical science and devotee of miracle-working spirits, and a follower of Iamblichus, who blended Neoplatonism with oriental mysticism.

Intelligent and able, Julian was twenty-four when he was made Caesar of Gaul at the end of 355. The Alemanni and other Frankish tribes had crossed the Rhine and were pillaging and burning cities deep into Gaul. Julian pushed them back, stabilizing the frontier defenses and rebuilding cities and the administration. His popularity earned him the jealous mistrust of his cousin Constantius, the emperor, who ordered him to send his best troops to fight against the Persians. Julian's army halted at Paris on the way east and proclaimed him emperor; he marched on rapidly for Constantinople, traversing the Black Forest and continuing down the Danube. He had been a pagan for several years in secret; he now openly proclaimed that he was not Christian. Civil war was avoided by Constantius's death in 361. The sole Roman emperor was once more a pagan.

Christians called Julian "the Apostate," or religious turncoat, and he called them "Galileans," insulting them as obscure provincials. Having been raised in their faith, he had an insight into their ways of thinking that was rare among pagans as well as advantageous. He knew that the pagan cults, now scattered and lacking mutual support, were vulnerable to Christian unity of purpose and organization. To compensate, he created a new religion from the mythologies of the old, which he called "Hellenism," and attempted to launch it throughout the empire. This new invention wove the many strands of traditional paganism into a distinct whole; above the old gods and rituals stood Plato's Supreme Being, made visible in the life-giving Sun. The emperor aped the Christian hierarchy; he appointed metropolitans in the provinces who presided over the district priesthood in much the same way that bishops did, except that they directly served Julian as Pontifex Maximus.

He tried to reproduce the virtues of the Christians. He noted that it was "their kindness to strangers, their care for the graves of the dead and the pretended holiness of their lives" that brought them fresh recruits. He admonished Arsacius, the high priest of Galatia, to be certain that his conduct matched that of Christian priests and to make sure that no pagan priest should "enter into a theater or drink in a tavern or control any craft or trade that is base . . ." He instructed the high priest to set up hostels for strangers and for the needy; the "impious Galileans" supported the pagan poor as well as their own, while "all people see that our people lack aid from us."[38] He had, too, an eye for Christian weakness, writing an extensive attack on them in his polemic *Adversus Christianos.* He encouraged disputes by allowing exiled bishops to return to their sees, where they clashed with the new incumbents. He stripped the clergy of their legal and financial privileges. Pagans were favored in the civil service. Christian laymen who had been tempted to convert because of special concessions now found their progress blocked. Julian ordered that all instruction in imperial schools should revert to pagan practice, and Christians were forbidden to teach literature. He was careful, however, to stop short of open persecution; he thought Christianity was better degraded by the deprivation of funds, education, and status than by crucifixion.

The method was shrewd enough. Alarmed Christians drew up plans to circumvent the ruling on literature by rewriting the Old Testament as Greek epic and tragedy and the New in the guise of Platonic dialogue. It was unnecessary. Hellenism was too artificial, and its creator too short-lived, to restore fresh heart to pagan worship. "Be of good courage," Athanasius, the patriarch of Alexandria, told his weeping flock when heathens forced him to flee to the deserts in 362. "It is but a cloud that will quickly pass." Julian set out on campaign against the Persians that year. He sailed down the Euphrates with a fleet, advancing through Mesopotamia and Assyria as far as Ctesiphon. He defeated a Persian army after crossing the Tigris, but was lured into a long march through barren country. He was wounded by an arrow in a skirmish on June 26, 363; the same night, as he lay dying in his tent, Christians claimed that he murmured *"Vicisti Galilaee,"* "Thou hast conquered, Galilean." The words are legend, but the sentiment was true. The last great pagan emperor was dead at thirty-two; his mentor, Maximus of Smyrna, was put to death.

❖ THE COUP DE GRÂCE was administered by Theodosius, a pious and intolerant Christian and heretic-hunter who became emperor in 379. He definitively banned all pagan cults in 391. Like the Church before them, they were denied the legal right to own property. Clerics helped mobs of laymen smash statues and idols; the biblical prophecy of the end of idolatry—"all her graven images shall be beaten to pieces . . . and all her idols will I lay desolate" (Mic. 1:7)—seemed fulfilled. In Rome, the sites of the temples of Minerva, Venus, and Romulus were

requisitioned for churches, as were senators' mansions and the audience hall of
the city prefect. In Athens, the Parthenon escaped only because it became the
Church of St. Mary. In Egypt, churches were built in the mortuary temple of the
pharaoh Ramses III and in the temples of Luxor. At Alexandria, the patriarch personally led the rioters who destroyed the temple of Serapis; the major part of the
city's ancient library, the Museion, was taken by storm and largely destroyed. The
temple of the city's presiding deity, its Genius, became a tavern. Armies of monks
descended from the desert to the city to rout out the last vestiges of paganism, intercepting Hypatia, last of the great Neoplatonist philosophers, while she was
driving back from the Museion, and stoning her to death.

Violence broke out against Jews as well as pagans, inspired by the same conviction that Christianity was now all-conquering, with riots in Alexandria and
Minorca. The empire had previously protected Judaism; the Jewish patriarchs enjoyed the high social rank of "Illustrious." Constantine had described them as a
"deadly sect," the murderers of the Son of God, but restrained from attacking
them. When Christian zealots at Callinicum on the Euphrates burnt down a synagogue in 388, Theodosius ordered the local bishop to make restitution in full
from Church funds. Ambrose, bishop of Milan, insisted that he revoke the order
on the grounds that it was a sin for a Christian emperor to help the Jews. Christians
were forbidden to marry Jews; Church councils legislated against social contact
with them, and the greatest of Christian orators, John Chrysostom, the "golden-
mouthed," delivered a passionate series of homilies against them in 388 at Antioch.

Judaism survived, of course, and paganism did not entirely disappear;
amulets were still worn and spirits summoned, particularly in country districts,
and the witch-hunters of the sixteenth century saw their victims as part of a chain
stretching back unbroken to pre-Constantinian days. Many pagans did not understand the new religion and submitted questions and requests to the Christian
God on pieces of papyrus, as though he were an old oracle. But Christianity was
now the state religion, and it offered the only means to social advancement and
power. The civic gymnasiums, where well-educated young pagans had met for exercise and companionship, were now closed. The nobility competed in endowing
monasteries and shrines, with women leading the way. Christians had once
shunned civil office, for fear the Church would expel them if they attended pagan
festivities; now they rose to the highest reaches of the administration.

Some churchmen came to rue their dependence on the state. Constantius
banished Hosius, his father's old adviser, and the bishop railed angrily from exile.
"Do not intrude yourself into church matters, nor give commands to us concerning them," he wrote. "God has put into your hands the kingdom; to us he
has entrusted the affairs of the Church." Another who had accepted the imperial
right to intervene in disputes, the Alexandrian patriarch Anastasius, also changed

his outlook. "When did a judgment of the Church receive its validity from the emperor?" he asked in 358. "There have been many councils held until the present and many judgments passed by the Church; but the Church leaders never sought the consent of the emperor for them, and neither did the emperor busy himself with the affairs of the Church. . . ." Jerome, as he toiled to translate the Bible into Latin, was shocked by the Church's new wealth. "Parchments are dyed purple," he wrote, "gold is melted into lettering, manuscripts are dressed up in jewels, while Christ lies at the door naked and dying."

A brave soul could still resist the emperor. In 390 a circus mob lynched the governor of Thessalonica; he had arrested a very popular charioteer for the attempted rape of an officer and refused to release him to take part in an important series of races. Theodosius tricked the rioters into returning to the circus and had seven thousand of them massacred. "Sin is not to be removed except by tears and penance," Ambrose of Milan wrote sternly to the emperor. "I urge, I ask, I beg, I warn, for my grief is that you, who were a model of unheard-of piety, who had reached the apex of clemency . . . are now not mourning that so many guiltless have perished . . . I dare not offer the Holy Sacrifice if you intend to be present. Can that which is not allowable, after the blood of one man is shed, be allowable when many persons' blood was shed? I think not."[39] With that, Ambrose excommunicated the emperor until he had completed eight months of public penance.

Ambrose was, however, a personal friend of Theodosius, and it was rare to find God's will thus imposed on a Caesar. "Roman and barbarian are as distinct one from the other," the Spanish Christian poet Prudentius wrote proudly in about 390, "as are four-footed beasts from humans." Christianity was no longer a religion of dissenters; it had become the client of the great whore of Babylon, the partner of empire.

ḣeretics

nswereth thou nothing? Behold how many things are said against thee. But Jesus no more answered anything: insomuch that Pilate marvelled" (Mark 15:4–5). Heresy thrives in those many mysteries—in his own nature, whether human or divine, in the nature of the sacraments, whether Body and Blood or symbolic bread and wine, in the imminence or otherwise of the Second Coming, in the Trinity, the Immaculate Conception, the elect, the predestination of souls, and much else—which Jesus left to silence. "What is truth?" Pilate had asked. The purpose of Constantine's great council at Nicaea was to provide it in the form of a true creed; and to deny that creed was made a mark of heresy. To the heretic, however, the beliefs for which the orthodox condemn him are also truth. They are the objects of his devotion; no less than with the orthodox, they are divine revelations that he cannot betray. Heresy is, and ever has been, the hardy and often courageous companion of the faith.

In its original sense the word did not mean blasphemy. It came from the Greek for "choice," and it meant no more than a sect or faction whose membership involved a choice of belief, whether good or bad. It was applied to the Jewish sects; the Church was once described by Eusebius as "the most sacred heresy."[1] By the early second century, however, the word already implied falsehood and evil, and was beginning the journey that made it perhaps the most ominous expression in the Christian vocabulary.*

---

*"Sect" can be used in a malevolent sense by members of an established church to describe a dissenting minority; but it remains technically neutral and distinct from heresy. Two types of heresy have also emerged. A formal heresy, involving excommunication, is the grave sin committed by a baptized Catholic who obstinately denies or doubts a truth that is a formal part of the orthodox faith. A material heretic is one who has been brought up amid heresy, and who accepts false doctrines in good faith; since orthodox beliefs have not been put to him, no sin has been committed. A clear gap also opened up between schism and heresy. In this, schism is the formal and voluntary withdrawal of a congregation or sect from the unity of the Church. The separation is offensive to Christian charity and love but it is not doctrinal, and schismatic bishops and priests can continue to ordain and celebrate the Eucharist.

Heresy naturally breeds orthodoxy. In seeking to combat false doctrine, the Church was obliged to elaborate its own dogma; to make this dogma binding, it also had to establish itself as the sole judge and guardian of true faith. After Paul, the early outlines of orthodoxy were most vividly sketched in the letters written by Ignatius, bishop of Antioch, as he traveled under an escort of ten soldiers from Antioch to his martyrdom in the Colosseum at Rome in about 107. It was he who first used the phrase "catholic church";*² he did so to express its universality and its claim to have authority over the whole body of the faithful. This authority, he said, lay wholly with the leadership of the Church. "Do nothing," he wrote to the church at Magnesia, "without the bishops and presbyters. . . ." The bishop was supreme because he was "as the Lord," Ignatius insisted; to celebrate baptism or the Eucharist "is not lawful apart from the bishop." The Church was to make three other claims—that it was "one, holy, and apostolic"—but Ignatius's assertion of its catholicity was the basis of orthodoxy. The Church alone could declare truths "which must be believed with divine and catholic faith";³ to deny or doubt such a truth was to commit a grave sin for which the punishment—"and if he refuse to hear the Church," Jesus had said, "let him be unto thee as the Gentile and the publican" (Matt. 18:17)—was excommunication.

A particular target for Ignatius, and the first widespread heresy, was the belief that Christ was a spirit in a phantom body.† Ignatius wrote that Christ "was truly born and ate and drank, was truly persecuted under Pontius Pilate [and] was truly raised from the dead."⁴ He said that: "I know that he was in the flesh even after the resurrection, and when he came to Peter and his company, he said to them 'Lay hold and handle me, and see that I am not an incorporeal spirit.'"⁵ If Christ was not truly human, the sacraments would be mere symbols, but Ignatius described them as "the flesh of Jesus Christ. . . . the medicine of immortality and the antidote against death." His belief in the Virgin Birth was strong enough for him to compare it with the crucifixion. "Hidden from the prince of this world," he wrote, "were the virginity of Mary and her childbearing and likewise the death of the Lord, three mysteries to be cried aloud, which were wrought in the silence of God." He confirmed the rupture of the faith from Judaism. "It is monstrous to

---

*From *katholikos,* Greek for "universal" and the name retained by the Western Church. In its original sense, "orthodox" meant true or upright doctrine; its meaning as conventional or generally accepted—and with a capital, Orthodox, as the Greek or Eastern Church—came later.

†It was current while the apostles were still living. John had been at pains to affirm Christ's humanity in his gospel, saying that "the Word became flesh, and dwelt among us" (John 1:14). In a variant, a preacher named Cerinthus believed that the Christ-spirit had descended on the man Jesus at his baptism and had departed from him before the crucifixion; John was said to have run from the public baths at Ephesus on seeing him, saying: "Let us flee, before the baths cave in, for Cerinthus the enemy of truth is inside!"

talk of Jesus Christ and to practice Judaism," he protested, "for Christianity did not believe in Judaism but Judaism in Christianity."[6] He added that the incarnate Christ was supreme over the "archives" of the faith, by which he meant the Old Testament, for the New was still uncollected. "As for me, my archives—my inviolable archives—are Jesus Christ, his cross, his death, his resurrection and faith through him," he wrote to the church at Philadelphia.[7]

These concepts survived as true doctrine, which would prove to be a rare achievement. The parameters of orthodoxy were constantly shifting, and the early Church fathers often held beliefs that at least overlapped with some that were later condemned. In one respect, though, Ignatius was identical to the heretics he decried during his last journey. He believed himself able to understand heavenly things, and to see "the arrays of angels and the musterings of principalities."[8]

✤ THAT BELIEF—AND little else—was shared by Marcion, a wealthy shipowner who in about 140 arrived at Rome. Marcion's appeal lay in his attempt to reconcile the loving and all-powerful Christian God with the existence of earthly pain and evil. Had he and others like him succeeded—and they had the advantage of preaching before orthodox battle lines were drawn up—the faith would have changed utterly.

Marcion held that Christianity is a gospel of love to which the Jewish God of Law is wholly hostile. He said that mankind was created by the cruel, vindictive, and fickle Demiurge* revealed in the Old Testament as the God of Moses. This creator-God subjects man to laws too strict for human nature to abide; the Demiurge is a "committed barbarian" who exposes women to the pains and dangers of childbearing.[9] The result is sin and suffering. But a supreme and loving God, not known before and hidden even from the Demiurge, pitied humanity and sent his Son to earth for its redemption. Clothed in a visionary body, the Son descended to earth in the likeness of a man of thirty. It was his mission to reveal the loving God and overthrow the Demiurge.

He preached, but the Jews failed to understand him; even the apostles mistook him for the Messiah promised by the Demiurge through the Old Testament prophets. The Demiurge did not suspect the true identity of the Son. He was enraged by the Son's compassion, and, even though the Son did not break the Law, caused him to be nailed to the cross. In doing so, the Demiurge doomed himself, for he had broken his own code of justice; he was forced to deliver up to the higher God the souls of those redeemed through the death of Christ. Paul was the

---

*The word comes from the Greek for "craftsman" and was used by Plato to describe the creator of the visible world.

true apostle chosen by Christ to bring this knowledge to the living. It was Paul alone who, recognizing the distinction between Jehovah's Law and the Grace of the true God, opposed the Judaism of the original apostles and founded communities of true Christians. But the faith was now mired in alien influences, Marcion warned; false Christians had corrupted the Gospels and the writings of Paul.

The faith, he believed, was in mortal need of reformation. To Marcion, salvation lay in an edited version of Luke's gospel and the ten Pauline Epistles, which he rewrote to restore what he claimed were Paul's actual words. This slim body of texts was the core of his reformed and de-Judaized faith; he rejected the other gospels and letters, and damned the Hebrew Bible in its entirety as the work of the Demiurge.

Marcion was excommunicated in about 144. Unabashed and with his shipping fortune to support him, he founded his own community at Rome and traveled widely to found his own churches and win over Christians as a whole. The Marcionites were practical, generous, and clean living; they welcomed all no matter what their sex, social class, or culture, and women sometimes presided over their worship. They did not use wine at communion—they thought the sacraments no more than magic symbols—and they shunned the sensual and pleasurable. In theory they were free to live as they pleased since they rejected the Demiurge and his Law, but in practice they were moral and austere, regarding the body as a "nest of guilt." The martyr Polycarp might call Marcion "the firstborn child of Satan," but nonetheless Marcion's message was reassuring and attractive. All who renounced the Demiurge, putting their trust in the good God and the crucified Son, and who showed charity and love, would be saved. Those who lacked this insight, including other Christians, were predestined for annihilation. By 250 the Marcionites had an entrenched heartland around Damascus, with communities spreading from Arabia, Armenia, and Egypt to Italy.

The "gnostics" were other early heretics, although their beliefs were so varied that they were a loose tendency and not a movement. They drew on magic, the occult, and pagan myth. They adapted the Platonic concept of the soul as a divine spark captured in a material body from which it yearned to escape; like the ancient Persian Zoroaster, they perceived a dualism in which the Wise Lord of goodness and light is pitted against the Evil Spirit of darkness and his demons. Christ became the catalyst in this cosmic struggle; he was the divine bringer of "gnosis," the special knowledge of God through which the few who imbibe his secret message are saved. Not all gnostics claimed to be Christians, but those who did usually denied Christ's incarnation.* As the Son of goodness, Christ could

---

*The conviction that the incarnation was illusory acquired its own status as the heresy of Docetism, drawn from the Greek *dokéō*, meaning "seem."

not defile himself by becoming a part of the corrupt material world. Since he had no material body, the sacraments were irrelevant; "the heretics abstain from eucharist," Ignatius had complained, "because they do not allow that the eucharist is the flesh of Christ."[10] Gnostics believed that the crucifixion was likewise more apparent than real; some said that Christ stood by laughing as his illusory body underwent its Passion, others that Judas Iscariot had miraculously replaced him on the cross.

These ideas made some progress. Valentinus, an Egyptian who lived at Rome for thirty years from about 136, was a prominent figure who had hopes of being elected bishop of Rome. When he failed, he seceded from the Church and followed Marcion in setting up his own sect. Valentinus taught that the visible world owed its origins to the fall of Sophia, one of the "aeons" or powers emanating from the supreme divinity. Sophia created the Demiurge, whom Valentinus identified with the God of the Old Testament. Redemption was achieved through Christ, a similar aeon who united himself at conception or baptism with the man Jesus to bring mankind the saving gnosis.

Only the spiritually aware—Valentinus and his followers—possess this knowledge; it reveals "who we were, what we have become, where we were, whither we have sunk, whither we hasten, whence we are redeemed, what is birth and what rebirth."[11] With it, the aware enter into the highest spiritual world, the *pleroma;* other Christians can only reach the middle realm, through faith and good works; the rest of humanity is doomed to eternal perdition. A strong mysticism lay within the Valentinians; in their sacraments they awaited a union with the angels of heaven "as a bride who awaits her bridegroom. . . . Let the seed of light descend into thy bridal chamber; receive the bridegroom and give place to him, and open thine arms to embrace him. Behold, grace has descended upon thee."[12]

Though Marcion and Valentinus were identified as heretics, their sects were persistent and caused deep alarm. Irenaeus, the orthodox bishop of Lyons from about 178, attacked them in his antiheretical work *Adversus Omnes Haeresis.* He emphasized Christ's full humanity and the traditional teaching of the apostles; they had deposited the truth in the Church, he claimed, and in particular in the Church of Rome and its bishops, who alone should teach, for "all the rest are thieves and robbers." The gnostic sects declined in the West during the third century, but as late as 447, Pope Leo the Great was complaining of heretics who fasted on Christmas Day because "they do not truly believe that Christ was born in true man's nature, but maintain that by a sort of illusion there was an appearance of what was not a reality, following the views of Marcion. . . ."[13]

Gnostics survived for much longer in the East. In the seventh century a Paulician community was founded by Constantine of Mananali in Armenia.

They denied the reality of Christ's body and of the redemption of sins; like Marcion, they rejected the Old Testament and centered their beliefs on Luke's gospel and the Pauline Epistles. Constantine was stoned to death in about 684. Survivors who fled westward brought the heresy with them to flourish in the Balkans. One gnostic sect, the Mandaeans, still exists in southern Iraq and Iran. Its roots may go back to the second century; missionaries who contacted them in the sixteenth century called them "Christians of St. John." Its members practice repeated baptisms and rites to help the souls of the dead reach the World of Light.

❖ EVERY CHRISTIAN WHO says the Lord's Prayer—"Thy kingdom come"—confirms his or her belief in God's eventual reign on earth. "And then shall they see the Son of man coming in clouds with great power and glory. . . ." (Mark 13:26); thus Mark's gospel wrote of the Second Coming of Christ. He would return to judge all mankind, gathering "his elect from the four winds, from the uttermost part of the earth to the uttermost part of heaven" (Mark 13:27) and "rendering vengeance to them that know not God" (2 Thess. 1:8); his Kingdom of peace and love would appear in "new heavens and a new earth, wherein dwelleth righteousness" (2 Pet. 3:13). Jesus had not predicted when this would happen, saying that "of that day or that hour knoweth no one . . . but the Father" (Mark 13:32). He had warned, however, that it would be preceded by an "abomination of desolation" and by suffering and tribulation on a scale not seen since the beginning of creation.

The earliest Christians had readied themselves for the Second Coming during their lifetimes; Jesus had said that there were some of his disciples "which shall in no wise taste of death, till they see the Son of man coming in his kingdom" (Matt. 16:28). When this did not happen, the Second Epistle of Peter, written in about 150, suggested that Christ's compassion for sinners meant that he would delay his coming "until all should have come to repentance." The Church reserved the right to proclaim the end of the world for itself; but it was natural that, in times of trouble, preachers should declare that the period of desolation had begun. The Book of Daniel, Mark's gospel, and Revelation gave them ammunition in plenty.

A preacher named Montanus headed an apocalyptic movement in Phrygia, in west Asia Minor, in about 156. Two prophetesses, Prisca and Maximilla, joined him. The trio had no false modesty. The women claimed to be mouthpieces for the Paraclete, the Greek word used in John's gospel for the Holy Spirit or "comforter"; Maximilla assured her listeners that: "After me, there will no longer be a prophet, but the end. . . . Hear not me, but hear Christ!" Montanus denied that he was a mere envoy of the divinity, declaring that: "I am the Lord God, the

Almighty dwelling in man."[14] He fell into trances so ecstatic that he "became frenzied and began to babble and utter strange sounds."[15] The orthodox thought his powerful hold over his audience to be the work of the devil, who "secretly stirred and enflamed minds,"[16] while the two women "chattered in a frenzied, inopportune and unnatural fashion . . ." to excite the audience.

Montanus prophesied that heavenly Jerusalem would soon appear on the plain outside the Phrygian town of Pepuza. It was a time of plague, war, and poverty, and his listeners were eager to hear that their squalid and unhappy province would soon play host to the Savior. Strict austerity and self-induced starvation induced a sense of frenzy. At first the members of the cult fasted almost continuously, for they expected the arrival of Christ at any moment. When this did not happen, they existed on a diet of dried fruit eaten only after dark. Montanus denounced any form of marriage; he said that it attached men and women too strongly to the world. The two prophetesses stopped living with their husbands, though Prisca said that Christ had slept with her to pass on his secrets. "Having assumed the form of a woman," she said, "Christ came to me in a bright robe and put wisdom in me, and revealed to me that this place is holy, and that it is here that Jerusalem will descend from heaven."[17]

The death of the three founders in the 170s had little impact on the movement. It spread rapidly to Syria, gaining many converts at Antioch, and was soon rife in Thrace. Irenaeus pointed out that it was pure blasphemy for Montanus to compare himself to God and for Maximilla to say that Christ spoke through her. Rome at first paid little attention; Pope Zephyrinus sent sympathetic letters to cult leaders in the early 200s. In North Africa it won over the Church father Tertullian at Carthage, for it corresponded to his own rigorist outlook. "She converses with angels, and sometimes even with the Lord," he wrote of a Montanist prophetess who claimed to experience the Holy Spirit during church services. "She both sees and hears mysterious communications. . . . A spirit appeared to her, not a void and empty illusion, but such as would suffer itself to be even grasped by the hand, soft and transparent and of an ethereal colour."[18] Her witness, Tertullian thought, was God himself; he wrote that a walled city had been seen in the sky over Judea early every morning for forty days, fading away as the sun rose, a sure sign that the heavenly Jerusalem was about to descend.

The Roman presbyter Hippolytus mounted an effective counteroffensive in the 230s. He labeled the prophetesses "those wretched women" whom the heretics had placed above the apostles "so that some of them presume to assert that there is in them something superior to Christ." He ridiculed the cult's "novelties or fasts . . . and meals of parched food and repasts of radishes," and exposed the blasphemy that some Montanists "affirm that the Father Himself is the Son" and thus believed that God was exposed to conception, suffering, and death.[19] By

250 the Church was thoroughly alarmed by the heresy; the cult acquired formal doctrines—second marriages and flight from persecution were banned—and reached as far as Spain and Gaul before declining. Other apocalyptic movements would replace it.

✤ THE PURITAN FLAME in Montanism was not in itself a mark of heresy. To lead an austere life of self-denial was recognized by all as a Christian virtue. Puritan sects, rigorist and exclusive but doctrinally orthodox, could nevertheless be branded as heresies; in time, the tension between extremists and easier-going majorities would help populate North America. Hippolytus was himself an early example. He condemned Montanism for its doctrines but shared its compulsion for spiritual cleanliness. He set himself up as the first antipope in 217, declaring that the election of Callistus was made invalid by the latter's moral laxity in readmitting adulterers and fornicators to Communion. "The imposter invented the device of conniving with men for their indulgence in sensual pleasures," Hippolytus wrote of his rival. "Bishops, priests and deacons who had been twice married and thrice married began to retain their places among the clergy. . . . He permitted females . . . that they might have whomsoever they would choose as a bedfellow, whether a slave or free. . . ."[20]

Hippolytus died in exile in Sardinia in 236, probably while laboring in the mines. The papal schisms he initiated continued, in farce or bloodshed, until 1439. Another rigorist presbyter, Novatian, declared that those who had apostatized during the Decian persecution were eternally damned. The pope elected in 251, Cornelius, was willing to readmit them to Communion; Novatian apparently declared himself pope and formed his own congregation of "those who, in their pride of mind, styled themselves Puritans . . . with brother-hating and most inhuman opinion."[21] Another bishop, Novatus, was set up in Carthage. "A heretic and a traitor, a flatterer to deceive," was how Cyprian, orthodox bishop of Carthage, described his rival with the ferocity characteristic of Christian infighting, "never faithful to love, a torch and a fire to kindle the flames of sedition, a whirlwind and tempest to make shipwrecks of faith, an enemy of quiet, an adversary of tranquillity, a foe of peace. . . ."[22]

Although Novatian achieved his desire of martyrdom in about 258, the movement continued. The bishop of Arles in France was a sympathizer; it also grew rapidly in the East, with congregations who called themselves "Cathari"— "pure spirits"—and despised others for their weakness and leniency. Those who joined the sect were rebaptized to show that they were joining the only true church; no penance was possible, they believed, for any major sin committed after this ceremony. They were excommunicated in ringing terms—"lament and shed tears and groan day and night," Cyprian advised them, "but, after these things, you will die outside the Church!"—to little effect. By the fourth century they had communities in Spain and Egypt. Because they were orthodox in doctrine, they were gradually reabsorbed into the mainstream Church. The concept of the puritan Cathari merely lay dormant, however, and would burst out again a thousand years later.

✤ GNOSTIC PROCLAMATIONS OF an elect proved to be equally enduring. They were revived among the Manichaeans. The movement was founded by a Persian, Mani, a figure in blue cloak and red and green trousers, with staff in one hand and book in the other, who proclaimed himself the "ambassador of Light" of a new and universal religion in about 240. He, too, taught of a primeval conflict between Light, the spirit of love and goodness, and Darkness, the contrary spirit of evil from which Satan was born. The devil ruled in the evil domain of matter, while the spirit belonged to God. Mani taught that these two kingdoms had existed in perfect separation before Satan emerged from the Darkness to rob man of part of his light and replace it with darkness. The object of worship was to restore and purify those particles of light that Satan had imprisoned; when this was achieved, the God of Light would appear, and the world would be consumed with fire as the separation of the kingdoms was restored. Buddha, Noah, Abraham, Jesus, and Mani himself had been sent to help in the task of purification; like Muhammad after him, Mani claimed to be the last and greatest of the prophets.

To restore the Light, he demanded the most severe austerity of the white-robed *electi,* the priesthood of the Elect. As well as outlawing idolatry and fornication, Mani's ten commandments forbade them from killing any living thing. They withdrew into a strict monastic regime of celibacy, vegetarianism, and abstention from alcohol and—perhaps more welcome—manual labor. Earthly perfection ensured that they would be gathered to the blessedness of the Light when they died. Less was expected of the *auditores,* or "hearers." They led more normal lives, supplying the *electi* with daily gifts of fruit, cucumbers, and melons, which were thought to be rich with Light. Their more pleasant life on earth was paid for by a period of pain after death.

Mani was flayed alive in 276 when he fell out of favor with the Persian court. But he had made long missionary journeys, west into Christian territory and south and east as far as India and western China; a vivid painter, he illustrated picture books to reach to the illiterate. Disciples also traveled with his message. It spread rapidly in the Roman Empire about fifty years after Mani's death. It offered a simple explanation for good and evil, and the struggle between them; like

Marcion, it promoted itself in the West as a Christianity freed of the wild-seeming claims of the Old Testament, honoring Jesus and Paul, and drawing on familiar passages such as the Sermon on the Mount. In North Africa, St. Augustine himself was an *auditor* for nine years before his conversion.

Leo the Great railed at the "fount of Manichaean wickedness" in 447; it still had a large following among scholars and teachers. The pope condemned their belief that the devil was not a fallen angel who had once been good, but an independent power that had emerged from darkness. "God, who is Maker of the Universe," Leo said in defense of orthodox belief, "made nothing that was not good." Despite his vigorous assaults, and the punishments of death or exile imposed by emperors, Christianized versions of Mani's teachings persisted into the great heresies of medieval Europe.

✤   THE MOST COMPLEX of heresies revolved around the doctrine of the Trinity. Although this became central to Christian dogma, Jesus and the apostles never used the word. The Gospels established the presence of three divine "persons"*—Jesus had commanded the disciples to baptize "in the name of the Father and of the Son and of the Holy Spirit" (Matt. 28:19), though the Gospels never used "persons" to describe them—while also affirming that there was but one God. The question of the relationship between the three was largely begged; it was unclear whether the Son and Spirit were inferior or equal to the Father, whether the Son's divinity coexisted with his humanity or excelled it, how God was three and yet one. Early confessions of faith were often twofold, excluding the Holy Spirit: "We know truly of one God, we know of Christ, we know of the Son. . . ." The word Trinity itself did not appear until about 180, as the Greek word *Triad* in the writings of the Christian apologist Theophilus of Antioch. In one of the first trinitarian confessions, Irenaeus wrote at the same date of faith "in one God, the Father, the Almighty . . . in one Christ Jesus, the Son of God, who became flesh for our salvation . . . and in the Holy Spirit."[23] The expression "three persons, one essence" was first coined by Tertullian more than a century after that. Lacking guidance from the apostles, and from the Savior himself, it was accepted that the Trinity was a mystery in the formal sense; it was a truth divinely revealed, unknowable to reason but compatible with it.

Mystery invites the religious mind to speculation; a fresh area of heresy was opened that spilled over into Christology, the debate on the nature of Christ. The so-called Monarchians were strict monotheists who defended the unity or monarchy of God. The theologian Sabellius claimed that Father, Son, and Spirit were

---

*"Persons," from the Latin *personae* was used in the sense of "faces" or "masks."

The concept of the Holy Trinity was the cause of early heresy and argument. In this fifteenth-century triptych by Colijn de Coter from St. Omer in France, a bearded God wears a mitre like a pope while the Holy Spirit perches as a dove on Christ's shoulder. The word "Trinity" itself was not mentioned until about A.D. 180. It raised the question of how God was three and yet one, and of the relationship between Father, Son, and Holy Spirit. Unitarians reject all doctrines of the Trinity.

not separate entities; they were—like water, steam, and ice—manifestations of the same God. This meant that God himself had been crucified, so that Sabellius's followers were known as "Patripassians," from "the Father suffers." Paul of Samosata, bishop of Antioch from about 260, taught that Jesus was a complete human being to whom the word or spirit joined himself. He said that the God-head, the fount of divinity, was a Trinity of Father, Wisdom, and Word in which Jesus played no part. This Trinity had descended on to Jesus' human person to a unique degree, Paul said, but this alone distinguished Jesus from the prophets. Paul showed other signs of heresy—he allowed his listeners to take part in sermons, he had women singers in his choir and encouraged their involvement in pastoral work—and he was deposed from his see in 268 after accusations of bribe-taking. The Paulianist heresy nevertheless outlived him; Leo the Great wrote 150 years later of those who "drink the poison of Paul of Samosata . . . who said that our Lord Jesus Christ did not exist until he was born of the Virgin Mary . . ."[24] The rejection of the Trinity in favor of the single personality of God was revived thirteen hundred years later in Poland and created the great Unitarian churches of England and America.

Arius, a priest in Alexandria, evolved the major heresy of denying the true divinity of Christ. He was the senior presbyter in one of the dozen parishes in the city. He was a fine preacher, who put his ideas into verses and popular hymns sung by the longshoremen on the docks and wharfs of the great grain port. He argued that the Son of God did not share the full divinity of the Father. The Son was not eternal, but was created from nothingness as an instrument for the salvation of the world. The Son was not God by nature, and, having no communion with God, could not be called either creator or redeemer. His dignity was no more than a gift from the Father. Arius cited John's gospel as evidence. "This is life eternal, that they should know thee the only true God, and him whom thou didst send, even Jesus Christ" (John 17:3): did this not make it clear that there was only one true God, and that Christ is no more than the mediator who reveals him?

Arius was excommunicated by a Church council at Alexandria in about 320 and exiled to the province of Illyria on the Danube frontier. His followers multiplied, however; the concept of a son subordinate to his father was readily understood by rank-and-file Christians as a practical and sensible explanation of their relationship. Many other debates were festering—on the doctrine of grace, on atonement and the readmission of the lapsed, on the nature of the sacraments— but the bitter arguments over the Trinity persuaded Constantine to call the first general council of the Church at Nicaea in 325 in order to impose some discipline on the newly imperial faith. The council's major task was to agree on a creed, a concise and formal statement of belief. It met in an imperial palace under imperial auspices, and Constantine presided over its opening session. Its delegates—traditionally 318 in number but probably no more than 250—were dominated by anti-Arian Alexandrines. The pope, Sylvester I, did not attend, and the two legates representing Rome had little influence on the outcome; the bishops of Cordoba and Lyons were among a mere handful of Western bishops. Like much else, it was dominated by Easterners.

The writings of Athanasius, then secretary to the bishop of Alexandria, were used in support of Christ's divinity. In his work *De Incarnatione*, Athanasius wrote that "the Word was made human that we might be made divine"; through his union with mankind, Christ had given back to man the image of God that had been lost at the Fall; and through his Passion and Resurrection, he had defeated death. If Christ was the Savior, Athanasius argued against the Arians, he could not be less than God; for only God could restore humanity to communion with himself. A proposed Arian creed was rejected by the council. The basis for an acceptable formulation of the faith was found in a confession used at Jerusalem by candidates for baptism. The Jerusalem formula confirmed the coeternity and coequality of the Father and the Son. To this was added the Greek word *homoousios,* meaning "of one substance," which expressed their consubstantiality. Christ was thus defended against the Arian charge that he was manufactured as God's messenger; he was confirmed as belonging to the realm of the eternal and uncreated, a "true God from true God."

Three hundred years after the death of its Lord, the faith received its first universal creed:

> We believe in one God, the Father Almighty
> Maker of all things both visible and invisible;
> And in one Lord Jesus Christ, the Son of God,
> Begotten of the Father, Only-begotten,
> That is, of one substance with the Father;
> By whom all things both in heaven and earth were made;
> Who for us men and our salvation
> Came down and was incarnate, became man,
> Suffered and rose again the third day;
> Ascended into the heavens;
> Cometh to judge the quick and the dead;
> And in the Holy Spirit.

For good measure, the creed placed under the curse of the Church all those who said that Christ came into being from nothing, or was "created" or "alterable," or was of another substance than the Father.

Only two bishops objected to the formula, but the debate was far from finished. Constantine wavered in his support for the Nicene faith. Arius was recalled from exile in 334, and collapsed and died while walking the streets of Constantinople two years later. He had sown his beliefs deeply in Illyria during his banishment, however; from there they were adopted by invading Visigoths to enjoy fresh life among the Teutonic tribes as they overran the Western Empire and North Africa. Athanasius was himself expelled from Alexandria five times, hiding in Egypt, living in Gaul, Rome, and with desert monks; to its human combatants, exile was a paltry price to pay in the struggle for eternal truth.

Antagonisms erupted between West and East, and between pro-Nicene and Arian-leaning churches in the same cities. Supporters of Nicaea were exiled on trumped up charges of insulting Constantine's mother; Marcellus of Ancyra was condemned as a heretic—a Monarchian, he maintained that the Son and the Spirit emerge only to achieve the Creation and Redemption, and will contract back into Divine Unity once their work is completed—and Easterners were scandalized when a council at Rome undid his excommunication. Constantine's son Constantius summoned the bishops of the West to Ariminum, modern Rimini, in 359 and pressured them into abandoning the Nicene creed; the Eastern bishops also recanted at Seleucia later in the year. In the new creed the Son was merely *homoios*, "like," the Father; "the whole world groaned in astonishment at finding itself Arian," the biblical scholar Jerome wrote later. Further councils were held at Antioch and at Serdica, modern Sofia in Bulgaria; the two sides hurled anathemas at each other.

Christians at Antioch fractured into three congregations; the Arians themselves split. Hard-line Anomoeans insisted on the total distinction between Father and Son; more moderate Homoeans allowed that the Son was similar to the Father "according to the scriptures"; while semi-Arians softened their stance by using *homoiousios*, "of like substance," in place of the Nicene *homoousios*, "of one substance," thus providing for both the similarity and the distinction between Father and Son. The Church, so Basil the Great thought, had been reduced to a "tattered old coat" by the constant accusations of heresy; he worked on a compromise with his brother Gregory of Nyssa and his friend Gregory of Nazianzus. They argued that it was possible to accept both the Nicene concept of the single substance of *homoousios* and the three distinct *hypostaseis*, or persons, of Father, Son, and Spirit. It needed fresh imperial pressure, from the pro-Nicene emperor Theodosius, to force the issue through. In a decree of 380, he declared Christianity in its Nicene version to be the official faith of the empire. A council was summoned at Constantinople in 381.

Dispute was a popular pastime, a game of doctrinal chess. The debates tumbled into the streets. "If you ask someone to give you change, he philosophizes about the Begotten and the Unbegotten," Gregory of Nyssa complained while attending the council. "If you say to the attendant 'Is my bath ready?' he tells you that the Son was made out of nothing." The factions who taunted each other at the Hippodrome, the Blues and Greens, championed their favorite points of Christology. The council reaffirmed the Nicene creed and added further orthodox armor to it. (The "Nicene creed" in use today is the longer Niceno-Constantinopolitan version.) The Virgin Mary was now included; Christ was "incarnate by the Holy Spirit of the Virgin Mary." The Spirit became the equal of the other two persons in the Trinity; it "proceedeth from the Father, and with the Father and Son together is worshipped and glorified."

The status of the Church was also made a formal part of doctrine. "And we believe in one holy catholic and apostolic Church," the lengthened creed proclaimed. "We acknowledge one baptism for the remission of sins. . . ."* The one-ness implied that the Church had the same right to exercise power over nations and peoples in spiritual matters that the empire enjoyed in secular terms. Holiness was implied to reside in the Church itself rather than in its members. Catholicity allowed the Church to claim all Christians for its own, and apostolicity enshrined the claim of its bishops to derive their authority from their succession to the original apostles. Laymen were no longer allowed to address congregations when the Spirit moved them, as once they had; sermonizing was restricted to the clergy. The "teaching church" of the priesthood was separated from the humble "listening church" of the laity. The creed compelled all Christians to acknowledge the authority of the Church as an article of faith; as the sole repository of eternal truth, it had potentially vast powers of coercion.

❖ FURTHER HERESIES OPENED as the emphasis shifted to the person of Christ. If Christ is true God, as the creed now affirmed, how fully is he also human; and, if he is both God and human, how can he be one? This was a further mystery, as unverifiable as the Trinity. Christ could be primarily divine or primarily human, or separately or jointly both; that is to put matters crudely, for infinite and subtle variations were and still are argued, but each faction tended toward one of these propositions. The orthodox view that he was both human and God had been established outside the Scriptures by Ignatius long before; "there is one physician, of flesh and spirit, generate and ingenerate, God in man, true life in death, son of Mary and son of God," he had written (Eph. 7). Tertullian had written of two *substantiae* in one *persona*, of two natures in a single person; but the concept continued to be challenged.

Apollinaris, bishop of Laodicea in Syria from about 360, was in most respects an orthodox and pro-Nicene theologian. He denied that Christ was fully human, however, arguing that he was the "one enfleshed nature of the divine Word" which could not share in human corruption. The Constantinople Council denounced Apollinaris; "what is not assumed is not healed," Gregory of Nazianzus argued, saying that only a Christ with a fully human nature could fully redeem humanity.

---

*The orthodox definition of the Trinity still had a sting left. Does the Spirit proceed from the Father, as the sole source of divinity, and hence through the Son? Or does it proceed in the so-called "double procession" from the Father and the Son? By 598, Rome and the Western Church had added the word *filioque* to the creed so that the Spirit proceeded from the Father "and the Son." Constantinople and the Eastern Church insisted on *per Filium,* "through the Son." The dispute appeared to be settled when the Greek Church sought the help of the West to repel the Turks at the Council of Florence in 1438; the Greeks reluctantly accepted *filioque* and a decree of union was signed. The loss of Constantinople to the Turks made it less important for the Greeks to woo the West; the union was soon null and void and the matter remained unresolved.

The growing veneration of the Virgin Mary, seen in the profusion of icons devoted to her, produced its own heresy. In the Greek East, which dominated the first seven centuries of theology, she was known as "Theokotos," the "God-bearer." Followers of the Antioch preacher Nestorius declared this to be false, "for Mary was a human being, and that God should be born of a human being is impossible." Arius, a priest from Alexandria, evolved the major heresy of denying the true divinity of Christ. Theology had mass popularity, and Arian ideas were set into hymns sung by Alexandrine longshoremen.

The growing veneration of the Virgin Mary provoked a contrary heresy. In popular devotion she had become "Theotokos," the "God-bearer" or "Mother of God." Nestorius, an eloquent preacher at Antioch who was appointed bishop of Constantinople in 428, thought himself a fierce defender of orthodoxy; the Arians nicknamed him "the incendiary" after their meetinghouse was gutted by fire during his persecutions. He strayed into heresy, however, by attacking the concept of Theotokos as incompatible with the humanity of Christ; he denied that a divine being could be born to a woman and that it could exist as an infant.* His presbyter Anastasius outraged devotees of the Virgin by declaring from the pulpit: "Let no one call Mary the mother of God, for Mary was a human being, and that God should be born of a human being is impossible." Nestorius argued that there were two separate natures in Christ, human and divine; although he allowed that the two could merge, he denied that they shared the same essence. "I hold the natures apart," he wrote, "but unite the worship."

This dualism earned him the enmity of Cyril, patriarch of Alexandria, who insisted that Christ had "one incarnate nature." Cyril was a brilliant theologian

---

*The undiluted integrity of Christ's humanity had been emphasized by Theodore, bishop of Mopsuestia from 392, and was a hallmark of the Christology of Antioch.

and a ruthless hunter of heretics. He defended the use of Theotokos in his paschal letter; he roused his own clergy, and Nestorius's opponents in Constantinople, and sent the most inflammatory of his antagonist's sermons to Pope Celestine at Rome. Celestine summoned a Roman synod, which affirmed the use of Theotokos, and ordered Nestorius to renounce his views on pain of instant excommunication. Cyril was given the task of ensuring that this was obeyed; he demanded that Nestorius agree to twelve anathemas condemning his Christology. The emperor Theodosius called a council at Ephesus in 431. It was held in the newly built Church of the Mother of God, the first known church to be dedicated to Mary; as her cult gathered pace, the great Church of St. Mary Major with its mosaics of the Annunciation was built in 440.

Cyril mustered fifty bishops; Nestorius attended with sixteen bishops and a posse of armed men, but his Syrian supporters were late in arriving and Cyril had Nestorius deposed. When the Syrians reached the city, they condemned Cyril in turn. Fresh legates appeared from Rome; Cyril used his majority to excommunicate the Syrian bishops. Nestorius retired to his monastery; from there he was banished first to Petra in modern Jordan, and then to the deserts of Upper Egypt where he was persecuted by Egyptian monks and taken prisoner by hostile nomads. The affair was as much political as theological—the Romans and Alexandrines were jealous of his influence as patriarch of Constantinople—but it led to permanent schisms. After the Council of Ephesus the Eastern bishops who supported him gradually formed a separate church, centered in the Persian Empire with a patriarchal see in the trading city of Seleucia-Ctesiphon on the Tigris. They called it the "Church of the East"; Westerners called them Assyrians, Chaldeans, or Nestorians and thought them heretics and Christ-splitters who divided him in two, though their insistence that his full humanity was not diluted by his divinity was but a nuance away from Orthodoxy.

An elderly monastic superior at Constantinople named Eutyches caused a fresh crisis. He taught that Christ had "two natures before, but only one after" the incarnation, his humanity being absorbed by his divinity like a drop of wine in the sea. This doctrine, that the Person of Christ has a single and divine nature, was called monophysitism; the orthodox dyophysite doctrine affirmed that Christ had a double nature, divine and human, after he was made flesh. Eutyches was condemned, but he had influence at court and was supported by Dioscorus, patriarch of Alexandria. Emperor Theodosius summoned another council at Ephesus in 449. Leo the Great sent a *Tome,* a statement of doctrine, supporting the dual position; it was one of the few Western interventions in the great Eastern disputes. Dioscorus packed the meeting; Leo called it the *Latrocinium,* the "robber council." It rehabilitated Eutyches and excommunicated the dyophysites.

Theodosius was killed in a fall from his horse the following year. He was succeeded by his sister Pulcheria, reigning jointly with her husband Marcian. They were sympathetic to Leo and the dyophysites. A further council was held in 451 at Chalcedon, across the straits from Constantinople. More than four hundred Greek bishops attended, and legates were sent from Rome. The acts of the *Latrocinium* were blamed on fraud and violence, and were undone; Eutyches and Dioscorus and their followers were deposed and banished. A confession was compiled affirming the orthodox Christiology: "We all with a single voice confess our Lord Jesus Christ one and the same Son, at once complete in Godhead and complete in manhood, truly God and truly man . . . of one substance with the Father as regards his Godhead, of one substance with us as regards his manhood, like us in all things, apart from sin, begotten of the Father before the ages as regards his Godhead . . . born of the Virgin Mary, the God-bearer; one and the same Christ, Son, Lord, Only-begotten, to be acknowledged in two natures, unconfusedly, unchangeable, indivisibly and inseparably. . . ."

The orthodox emerged from Chalcedon with a settled Christology to add to the Trinity, but the swirl of political and doctrinal cross-hatreds mocked Christian unity. Romans were angered that, while their legates were absent, a canon had been ratified that granted Constantinople equal privileges to Rome and elevated it to second rank above Alexandria and Antioch. Leo the Great rejected the canon. The dissident churches of the East were bitterly hostile to Chalcedon; the fact that the rulings were imposed by imperial edict heightened political tensions in provinces already hostile to rule from distant Constantinople. Coptic-speaking Egyptians referred to Greek-speaking Chalcedonians as "the emperor's men." In Syria, too, the monophysites were a majority. In Persia, whose rulers saw the Orthodox Church as the agent of an alien power, the Nestorians were glad to use the rift to further their religious independence.

Imperial governments alternately persecuted the dissidents and attempted to reach compromises with them. A council at Constantinople in 553 appealed to the non-Chalcedonians by accepting that Christ had "one incarnate nature"; but the council still insisted that Christ was "in two natures" where its members would admit no more than that he was "from two natures." Monothelitism, which asserted that Christ had two natures but only one "energy" or "will," was an ingenious effort almost two centuries after Chalcedon at finding a formula acceptable to both. It failed. The monophysites settled into three great churches: the Copts and Abyssinians; the Syrian Jacobites, who took their name from Jacob Baradeus, bishop of Edessa, through whose work they became the national church of Syria; and the Armenians. The Nestorians, isolated from the West, channeled their energy into an extraordinary missionary drive to the East, planting bishoprics in Tashkent, Samarkand, India, and China as well as Persia and Arabia.

A terrible price was paid for doctrines that few understood or were even aware of; the creed was not recited in public worship in the West for a further four hundred years. Christians had taken the descent of the Holy Spirit among them at the first Pentecost—the rushing wind, the ability to speak in tongues—as a sign of God's grace. As they fractured their faith beyond repair, as each church claimed its own right to reach to heaven, they were heedless of an earlier and grimmer miracle. "Behold, they are one people, and they all have one language," God had said as he looked down on the tower-builders of Babel. "And this is what they begin to do. . . . Let us go down, and there confound their language, that they may not understand one another's speech. So the Lord scattered them abroad from thence upon the face of all the earth" (Gen. 11:6–9).

❖

❖

❖

"Through Them The World Is Kept In Being":

Monks

A s well as creeds and heresies, the streak of spiritual intensity and adventure among the Easterners produced the first monks and hermits, and stranger beings who dwelt on the tops of pillars and in trees. Martyrs had thought themselves blessed to die like Jesus; ascetics now competed to outdo him in the mortification of their living flesh. Jesus had gone "into the wilderness to be tempted of the devil, and . . . had fasted forty days and forty nights" (Matt. 4:1–2). Hermits withdrew to the deserts* for decades on end. Early Christians believed the desert to be infested with devils and demons. In resisting these and in enduring meager food and caves and cells of ferocious discomfort, the hermits believed that they could echo Jesus and fight for the sake of humanity in cosmic warfare against the forces of evil.

The origins of monasticism lay in the Egyptian wilderness. "I buffet my body and bring it into bondage," Paul had written, "lest I myself should be rejected" (1 Cor. 9:27); following his advice, hermits "wandered over deserts and mountains, in caves and ravines of the earth." The first Christian hermit was said to be Paul of Thebes on the bend of the upper Nile, a young man who fled to a cave during the Decian persecution in about 250. He remained there for almost a century before dying at the age of 113 in 340. Shortly before his death, Paul of Thebes met a marginally younger hermit, Antony of Egypt, who had been guiding him across the burning sands by a revelation. As they met, legend has it, a crow flew softly down and dropped a loaf of bread before them. "Behold," said Paul. "God hath sent us our dinner . . . I have had each day a half loaf of bread: but at thy coming, Christ hath doubled the soldiers' rations. . . ."[1]

---

*Hermit derives from the Greek word for "desert," and asceticism from the Greek for "exercise" or "training."

St. Antony founded the first monastery near Memphis in Egypt in 305. Seen here attacked by monsters in an engraving by Cranach, Antony lived as a hermit for twenty years, believing that he "who sits in solitude and quiet hath escaped from three wars: hearing, speaking, seeing." He was then persuaded to organize a community of his followers. Humility and discipline were imposed on all. Novices were told to "be continent of thy tongue and belly."

Whether Paul of Thebes existed or not is debatable—the Bible translator St. Jerome is the only writer to mention him, and he makes the further claim that a pair of lions scraped out Paul's grave with their paws—but Antony certainly did. He was born in Egypt in about 250 and came into an inheritance as a teenager. "If thou wouldest be perfect," Jesus had told a young man in the Gospels, "Sell that thou hast, and give to the poor, and thou shalt have treasure in heaven: and come, follow me" (Matt. 19:21). Inspired by reading this, Antony at once "gave to the townspeople the possessions he had from his forebears."[2] He then retired into the desert to live in self-denial and contemplation. He ate once daily, bread and salt taken after sunset and washed down with a little water, and he slept on the bare ground. Antony wore an animal skin with the hair on the inside, and Jerome says that he later adopted Paul of Thebes's yet more uncomfortable tunic of woven palm fronds.

Word of Antony's holiness spread. The loneliness of his faith and his purging of bodily passions was held to give him miraculous powers. He was said to wrestle demons in the form of desert beasts; his presence in the desolation of scrub and gravel gave comfort to those in distant towns, healing their spirits, and he was called "a physician to all Egypt." A growing number of followers sought him out. In about 305 he came out of his isolation to organize them into a loose community of hermits. He permitted them no bedding beyond rush mats; the use of oil to soften skin weathered by sun and wind was forbidden; like Antony himself, frequently they took food only every fourth day. "The soul's intensity is strong," he told them, "when the pleasures of the body are weakened."[3] Their mortification would bring them eternal reward, Antony said, for Christ "glorifies those who glorify him, and leads those who serve him into the Kingdom of Heaven."[4]

His hermits had little communal life—"who sits in solitude and quiet hath escaped from three wars: hearing, speaking, seeing," he said[5]—but he expected humility and discipline. He instructed them not to feel self-righteous and to "be continent of thy tongue and of thy belly"; he warned that those who exaggerated their austerity and wore out their bodies with abstinence were far from God "because they have no discretion."[6] Within five years several dozen hermits were installed near to each other, their cells "like tents filled with divine choirs—people chanting, studying, fasting, praying, rejoicing in the hope of future boons, distributing alms. . . ."[7] Antony returned to solitude, to what he called his "inner mountain" near the Red Sea. Early hermits were able to leave and rejoin their retirement at will; only later did they vow to remain permanently within the walls of their cells.

An ex-soldier converted Antony's concept of clusters of hermits' cells into the first communal or coenobitic monasteries. Pachomius was born a pagan in Upper Egypt in about 290. He served in the Roman army and was converted through the kindness of Christians who bathed and fed the troops stationed in their villages. After his discharge in 313 he became the disciple of a famous hermit, Palaeomon. He felt that the virtues of prayer and self-denial were better practiced in a group than in solitary confinement. He dreamt that he was commanded by the Lord to "struggle, dwell in this place and build a monastery"[8] near an abandoned village called Tabennesi in the Thebais, the upper part of the Nile around Thebes. Pachomius settled in this remote spot and, like Antony, attracted followers by his rigor; he lived on bread and salt, wore a hair shirt, and mortified himself during all-night prayer vigils, moving neither his feet nor his hands, which he kept stretched out lest he fall asleep. He had visions; an angel told him that it was God's will that he serve men.

Pachomius's first three recruits—"we want to become monks in your company and to serve Christ"[9]—swiftly grew to several hundred. They were drawn at first from among the hermits living in caves in the hills that flanked the floodplain of the Nile, but they were joined by others who came from towns across Egypt. Pachomius did not abandon the world, as the hermits did; he re-created it within the monastery, a world of discipline, security, and hard work, a self-contained community supplying its own food and clothing and other wants, governed by military rules and imbued with comradeship and loyalty. It was independent, too, of the Church and its factions and quarrels; Pachomius refused to allow any clerics to enter since he felt them to be overproud and to suffer from "jealousy and vainglory." For many, the appeal of this new life was immense and immediate. At his death in 346 the former legionary was abbot-general of nine monasteries for men and two for women.

The buildings themselves were self-sufficient bastions of faith, able to withstand prolonged siege, fortified in the Roman manner familiar to Pachomius from his army days. High walls with a well-protected gatehouse surrounded an outer court with a guest house for visitors. The inner court, reserved for monks, was built round a fortified tower. It had chapels, a scriptorium or library, a hospital, kitchens, a flour mill, and bakery. The court had a kitchen garden and well. The monks slept three to a room in cells. If attacked, they could flee from the outer walls to the central tower by drawbridges which could be raised behind them. Most of Pachomius's monasteries were situated in the desert or along the edges of valleys. Where three or four were close together, they came under a superior-general, the head of the largest monastery, and a president elected from the abbots; they met together at Easter and in August, to discuss finances and administration and to pronounce a mutual forgiveness of sins.

A novice presenting himself at the monastery was kept outside the gates for a few days. He was taught the Lord's Prayer and some psalms if he did not know them—fresh ex-pagans were welcomed—and interrogated on his motives and fortitude. "Has he done something wrong and, troubled by fear, suddenly run away?" was a standard question. "Can he renounce his parents and spurn his own possessions?" Once inside, he was stripped of his ordinary clothes—which were put in a storeroom for safekeeping should he change his mind—and issued with three sleeveless shifts for working and sleeping, a long scarf, a goatskin worn hanging from the shoulders, two hoods for protection against the sun, a linen belt, and shoes and a staff for going on journeys. The novice was not allowed to stand by the evening fire to ward off the cold of the desert night. Instead, he was given a task to perform to keep warm: "with a quick hand you shall prepare ropes for the warps of mats."[10] If he spoke or laughed during prayer or reading, "he shall unfasten his belt immediately and with neck bowed he shall stand before the altar and be rebuked by the superior of the monastery." If he was late for prayers after the dawn trumpet blast, he had to remain standing during meals like a naughty child. Penance was required for falling asleep during services, for standing on the rushes used to weave mats, for lighting a fire without permission, for drinking wine or broth except when in the infirmary, for being late for a meal, or for speaking during one: "if anything is needed at table, no one shall dare to speak, but he shall make a sign."

It took up to three years for the novice to become a monk. He had to master the virtues of monastic life—"fasting, purity, silence, humility, self-effacement, love," Pachomius wrote, "virginity not only of the body, but the virginity that is an armor against every sin"[11]—and memorize twenty psalms and two New Testament epistles. The unlettered were obliged to learn to read and write, forging a link between monks and learning that deeply impressed the largely illiterate laity.

Each hour of the day and night was allotted to work, prayer, meals, or sleep; Pachomius's Rules were shot through with a military sense of order. Every monk was expected to work, a few as copyists and scholars, most as laborers or tradesmen; while they did so, they "shall talk of no worldly matter, but either recite holy things or else keep silent." Baskets and ropes were woven for sale on the open market. A visitor to a Pachomian monastery at Panopolis found thirty tailors and fullers making cloth and robes, and a dozen camel drivers as well as carriage makers, smiths, linen weavers, and carpenters. "They work at every handicraft," he wrote, "and from their surplus they provide for the monasteries of women and for the prison."[12] Boatmen and bakers, who sweated hard from the effort of rowing or the heat of ovens, were excluded from the general rule that laundry could be washed only on Sundays; harvesters of date palms were permitted to eat one or two dates, but those in the fruit orchards were forbidden to eat even windfalls. The practitioners of each trade were gathered into a house under a master. Each house had some forty members, and a monastery had thirty to forty houses, making a large community of well over a thousand men.

Brothers were chosen by their individual character to cook and tend the sick, or to greet visitors at the gate. Pachomius recognized the danger of fraud, and used men of noted piety to transact sales and make purchases. Harmony was cherished, and Pachomius drew up special instructions for the "spiteful monk." "A thought? Come to terms with it in patience, waiting for God to give you calm," he wrote. "Fasting? Put up with it in perseverance. Prayer? Without let-up, in your room between you and God. One single heart with your brother. Virginity in all your members; virginity in your thoughts, purity of body, purity of heart. Head bowed, and a humble heart; gentleness in the hour of anger . . ."[13] Seniority was based on length of service, not on age. The sick were "sustained with wonderful care and a great abundance of food."[14] The healthy fasted on Wednesdays and Fridays. They ate together at noon on other days, although an evening meal was also served for the "tired, the old, and the boys, and on account of the very severe heat." Those who wished to remain in their cells received only bread with salt and water.

Visitors were welcomed by having their feet washed, "according to the Gospel precept," before being brought to the guest house. "Weaker vessels," as women were called, were cared for with special honor. If they came in the evening, it was thought wicked to turn them away. They were lodged in special quarters away from the men "so that there may be no occasion for slander." Pachomius was equally anxious to avoid any hint of homosexuality; he ruled that no one "may clasp the hand or anything else of his companion"; they were to maintain a forearm's distance from each other and "shall not sit together on a bare backed donkey or on a wagon shaft"; and when sitting, all were to arrange their tunics modestly so that their knees were covered. Even gift parcels from parents and relatives were regulated; Rule 53 laid down that the recipient could eat fruit and sweets, but anything else was to be taken to the infirmary. Nobody could go outside the monastery without the permission of his housemaster; those who traveled were forbidden to make any mention of what they had seen in the outside world.

MARY, THE SISTER of Pachomius, founded the first women's monastery. She had lived as a hermit in a cave near to him and gathered a group of women into a "monastery of the virgins." It was run under similar rules, except that no man could visit unless he had a mother, sister, or daughter there; he was obliged to be accompanied by a monk "of proven age and life" and was not to talk of worldly matters.[15] Earlier, on leaving for the desert, Antony had been able to entrust his younger sister to a parthenon, a house for virgins. Here young women were protected and taught to read, write, and paint; if the house were Christian, they would have prayed together and done good works.

The convent thus predates the male monastery, at least in an informal sense, and women took to monasticism with zeal. They produced illuminated manuscripts as well as sketches used by architects in laying mosaics in new basilicas; they wove tapestries and exquisite robes for the clergy; it is likely that they decorated silver Communion ware and candelabra, and certain that they taught reading and writing and art. Whether they conducted services themselves is unclear; an epistle by Pope Gelasius at the end of the fifth century complains that women were officiating at the altar, and references to *presbytera* confirm that some bishops at least were still ordaining women to holy office.[16]

An elder sister had a crucial influence on Basil the Great, one of the most influential of the Greek fathers, who stressed that monks should devote themselves to charity as well as prayer. The monastic Rule that Basil wrote between 358 and 364 is still followed by monks of the Greek and Slavonic churches. He was born about A.D. 330 into a wealthy and cultured family in Cappadocia and educated in pagan and Christian thought at Constantinople and Athens. As a student he was "puffed up beyond measure with the pride of oratory" and was set on a career as a lawyer. Basil's sister Macrina persuaded him to search out a spiritual life; the dazzling and privileged young man changed into a humble soul whose "wealth was to have nothing . . . he was poor and unkempt . . . he had only one tunic and one threadbare cloak, the ground was his bed, and he went unwashed."[17] He visited Egypt and found that he preferred the monastic life to the hermitage. "Whose feet will they wash?" he asked of the solitaries, finding that a man who was altogether alone "will not recognize his defeats, not having anyone to reprove and set him right."

Basil found a site in Pontus, close to the family estate where his sister had her own flourishing community, and began a lasting tradition for building monasteries in solitary places of great natural beauty. "A lofty, densely wooded mountain, watered on the north by cold, transparent streams," he wrote with joy. "A forest of trees of every color has become almost an enclosing wall . . . apt for the production of every kind of fruits; it nourishes the sweetest of all fruits to me—solitude."[18] His Rule stressed calm and moderation; his monks were to betray no sign of anger, envy, unforgiveness, or argument. The Seven Hours were recited daily*; the early desert monks had sometimes prayed ceaselessly, with different groups taking over from each other to read long parts of the Psalter, and Basil helped formulate this into the regular recital at fixed hours that developed into the Divine Office. Basil allowed no excessive fasting, holding that hard work served God better than agonies of self-denial. His foundations were often dual, one for men and one for women under the same abbot; the women wove and made clothes and bedcoverings for sale while the men were builders and carpenters and did the heavy fieldwork. Drink was served at meals; "wine should not be held in abomination," he said, a concession that was to be of importance in later years when monks paid their way through winemaking and distilling liqueurs. Pachomius, gruff and practical, had dwelt little on spiritual questions. Basil wrote widely on the Holy Spirit; he played an important part in refuting the Arian heresy, and his *Asceticon* set out the moral rules of monasticism in the form of questions and answers based on queries put to him by curious laypeople on his travels.

To withdraw from the world was close to abandoning it, and Jesus had done so for no more than a few weeks; the line between selflessness and selfishness in a monk could become thin, and his choice of earthly existence reflected at least in part the greedy hope of earning a permanent billet in heaven at its end. Basil saw *philanthropia,* love of mankind, as a justification for the religious life and as a means of avoiding self-absorption. He insisted that his monks care for the poor and sick of the region; hospitals, orphanages, and hostels for the poor were part of his great buildings in Caesarea. He took in lepers, feared outcasts from society;

---

*The standard Hours have become Matins at dawn, Prime at 6 A.M., Terce at 9 A.M., Sext at midday, None at 3 P.M., Vespers at sunset, Compline on retiring at night.

he greeted them "like brothers," saying that to despise a leper was to dishonor Christ. "Others had their cooks and rich tables and enchanting refinements of cuisine," it was noted; "Basil had his sick, and the dressing of their wounds, and the imitation of Christ, cleaning leprosy not by word but in deed."[19]

TWO OF THE three great coenobitic Rules were now in place, that of Pachomius, written in the Coptic of Upper Egypt, and Basil in the Greek of Asia Minor. Monasticism was an Eastern creation. Not until about 415 were two Western monasteries built near Marseilles, by John Cassian, a monk who had spent seven years learning the system in the Nitrean Desert west of the Nile Delta in modern Libya. The Latin Rule of Benedict was not written until about 540, almost two centuries after Basil; in drawing it up for his small community on the crags of Monte Cassino, midway between Rome and Naples, Benedict drew heavily on the Eastern pioneers.* He placed great stress on learning and culture, and the survival in the West of the literary and philosophical glories of antiquity owed much to him. His Rule required monks to read and study for two hours a day. During Lent they were to "receive a book apiece from the library and read it straight through."[20] Every Benedictine monastery had its library. "A monastery without a library is like a castle without an armory," a monk wrote. "Our library is our armory. Thence it is that we bring forth the sentences of the Divine Law like sharp arrows to attack the enemy. . . ." Books were lent to monasteries and to educated laymen. To make sure that borrowers returned a book, the name of the monastery that owned it was written on the title page, with the threat that "whosoever shall steal it, or sell it, or in any way alienate it from this house, or mutilate it, let him be forever accursed. Amen." In the monastery's scriptorium, monks copied and illuminated manuscripts, of the Scriptures, the writings of the Church fathers, and the Greek and Latin classics, thus adding to the West's slender cultural reservoir.

By the beginning of the fifth century there was "no town or village in Egypt or the Thebais that is not surrounded by hermitages as if by walls, and the people depend on their prayers as if on God himself," a contemporary wrote. "Through them the world is kept in being."[21] Only through the constant intercession of prayer, it was believed, did mankind survive. Jesus was held to have commanded it—"he spake a parable unto them to the end that they ought always to pray and not to faint" (Matt. 18:1)—and the prayers that issued from individual hermitages were thought to offer particular protection for nearby villages.

---

*He also used the *Regula Magistri,* written in Latin by the unnamed master of a small monastery southeast of Rome at some date between 500 and 525.

✤ PILGRIMS CAME TO the Egyptian monasteries from across the Christian world: Greeks, Romans, Gauls, Spaniards, Cappadocians, Libyans, Syrians, Ethiopians. The monk and historian Rufinus, writing around A.D. 390, described meeting 10,000 monks at Arsinoe, south of the pyramids. The poet Palladius, who spent several years with the Egyptian monks, gave the same figure, adding that there were also a dozen convents for women at Arsinoe. The bishop of Bahnasa estimated that 10,000 monks and 20,000 nuns lived in Middle Egypt alone, in forty monasteries and convents. Archaeologists have found a huge monastic settlement at the remote Kharja oasis in the Western Desert, dating from the fourth century; its necropolis has more than two hundred chapels. Wadi al-Natrun once had fifty monasteries and more than 5,000 monks. To the east of Wadi al-Natrun, at Kelya, are more than 750 abandoned hermitages dating from the fifth century. A biography of the sixth-century saint Macrufius reported that the village of Ishnin al-Nasarah had "as many churches as there are days in the year"; that was an exaggeration typical of much religious writing, but it also had a more feasible description of 2,000 youths wearing cowls, half of them girls, as well as old men and women who had renounced the world.

Monasteries spread throughout the Christian East. Some were elaborate, built by emperors and nobles, and held a thousand and more monks or nuns; others had no more than three or four individuals and were founded by villagers anxious for prayers to be said for them. Each was a self-governing unit under its abbot or abbess. There were to be three hundred monasteries in Constantinople alone; others were located in the most remote places, on volcanic crags in Thessaly, the rocks of Cappadocia, the flanks of Mount Sinai, beyond the forests that isolated Mount Athos amid the waters of the Aegean. At Decra Damo in Ethiopia, great wooden beams were hauled to the mountaintop to create a church, which craftsmen decorated with exquisite panels of animals; when the work was finished, the steps cut in the rock face were demolished and the monastery could be reached only by rope. Hilarion, a pagan convert from Alexandria, founded the anchorite life at Gaza in Palestine. Silence, prayer, and mortification were followed within the strict confines of a cell. *Lavras,* large colonies of anchorites, were founded around 450 by the Armenian monk Euthymius near Jerusalem; at his death "an immense crowd of monks and laypeople were brought together . . . and from all parts assembled the anchorites of the desert."[22] Jordan had the renowned monasteries of the Towers and of the Baptism.

As monasteries spread and multiplied, the ideal of contemplation was refined. The Nitrean monk Evragius Pontus linked it to the Stoic concept of *apatheia,* dispassion, in which the emotions that disturb the soul are progressively dimmed until a state of purely spiritual love is attained. Monks were expected to care for the sick and give alms to the poor; the word "alms" itself derived from *elos,* Greek for compassion. John Chrysostom, patriarch of Constantinople and former hermit, spoke powerfully of the "two altars" of the faith. "You honour the altar in church, because the Body of Christ rests upon it; but those who are themselves the very Body of Christ you treat with contempt, and you remain indifferent when you see them perishing," he said of the needy. "This living altar you can see everywhere, lying in the streets and market places, and at any time you can offer sacrifice upon it."[23] The charter of a community of eight monks in Constantinople later laid down that each day they should give six destitutes a meal—"meat, fish, cheese, cooked vegetables, dried or green, or whatever else God shall send"[24]—and that the gates of the monastery and the hearts of those within it should be open to all who were poor.

Syrian monasteries were known for their intellectual and ascetic rigor. Theodoret, bishop of Cyrrhus, described hero-monks who have "broken the body in sweat and toil, who have not experienced the passion of laughter but spent all their life in mourning and tears, who have deemed fasting a Sybaritic nourishment, laborious vigil a most pleasant sleep, the hard resistance of the ground a soft couch. . . ."[25] Much time was devoted to logic and dogma. In these "pious wrestling-schools" of the mind, "athletes of virtue" were trained to deal with the "assaults of heretics" a thousand years before the Jesuits.

❖ SUCH PIETY AND self-denial reached extremes of obsession. In these Olympics of the soul, devotees competed against each other to set records of abstinence and mortification; like Theodoret, their admirers used the language of the games—"spiritual athlete," "wrestler for Christ"—to describe them, and named them "champion" and "unbeaten."

Ceaseless prayer of this record-breaking and ostentatious type was the mark of the wandering beggars of the Messalian sect. Led by monks, this strange movement spread from Mesopotamia to Syria and Egypt in the mid-fourth century. They shunned all work as "iniquitous," an evil that interfered with the muttering of prayers that filled their waking hours, and begged for a living. They believed that Adam's sin had attached a demon to mankind that clung so ferociously to its prey that neither baptism nor divine grace could shake it off. "It is only by earnest prayer that the in-dwelling demon is driven out," a Messalian explained to Church interrogators at Antioch, "for every one born into the world derives from his first father [Adam] slavery to the demons."[26] Through unending prayer, he went on, there "comes the Holy Spirit . . . and not only is the recipient liberated from the wanton motions of the body, but also clearly foresees things to come, and with the eyes beholds the Holy Trinity."[27]

The orthodox were not impressed by these claims to moral perfection and divine visions. "Giving themselves over to sloth," Theodoret wrote, "they call the imaginations of their dreams prophecies . . . attacking with their peculiar poison all with whom they come in contact." The sect was condemned at synods in 390 and 426, but it was difficult to eradicate since Messalians accused of heresy "shamelessly deny it even after conviction" and happily condemned other heretics whose sentiments they secretly shared.[28] The bishop of Mytilene burnt down monasteries—"or, shall I rather say, brigands' caves," Theodoret wrote icily—in which the belief flourished. Many laypeople were impressed, however, by these ragged men whose lips perpetually fluttered with holy patter, and they did not die out until the seventh century.

Ascetics vied to achieve the smallest intake of food and water, the least sleep, the most discomfort. Their acknowledged champion was Simeon the Stylite, one of Christianity's supreme eccentrics. He was known as the "great wonder of the world" and his fame was said to have reached the Persians, Medes, and Ethiopians as well as "all the subjects of the Roman empire"; his life was recorded directly from "his sacred tongue" by Theodoret, who admired him as deeply as he loathed the prayer-mutterers. Simeon's career started in about 402, when he was a fifteen-year-old shepherd boy in Syria. A heavy snowfall marooned his flock indoors, and he spent his free time in church. Much moved on hearing a beatitude—"blessed are they that mourn; blessed are the clean of heart"—he was told by one of the congregation that a solitary life of prayer and fasting was the surest path to virtue. He hastened to a nearby martyrs' shrine. Here a "sweet sleep" fell upon him, and he underwent the mystic's rite of passage. He had a vision in which he was digging a trench; someone standing by him urged him to work harder, until the trench was deep enough, and he found that he was able to build without effort.

A little later the boy entered a monastery above the village of Tell 'Ada, between Antioch and Edessa. Its elderly superior, Heliodorus, was himself an eccentric figure; he had been immured within its walls from the age of three and boasted that he was so ignorant of the outside world that he did not know "the shape of pigs or cocks or other animals." The eighty monks prided themselves on their self-denial, but young Simeon, "this all-round contestant in piety," spent ten years contending with them and "outshot all of them." The others took food every other day, but Simeon fasted for a week at a time. His irritated superiors mocked him for self-conceit in vain. He took a rough cord made from palm fronds and tied it so tightly about him that it lacerated his stomach; after ten days his brother monks saw blood seeping through his clothing and forced him to remove it. He was finally expelled from the monastery, on the reasonable grounds that any weaker soul who tried to emulate him would die in the attempt.

His antics—they could be taken as zeal for God or exhibitionism—caused further trouble when he moved to the village of Telanissos and set himself up as a hermit in a tiny hillside cottage. He announced that he would fast for forty days, like Moses and Elijah; he asked the senior priest in the region, Bassus, to verify that there was nothing in the cottage and to seal the door with mud. Bassus thought this tantamount to suicide and refused. Simeon agreed that ten rolls of bread and a jar of water should be placed inside before the door was sealed. When Bassus broke into the cottage after forty days, he found the bread uneaten; Theodoret also claims that the water was untouched, a medical impossibility. Simeon was found stretched out, unable to speak or move. Bassus gave him a sponge to wet his mouth, and Simeon took a little lettuce and chicory. Bassus went to give the news of this "great miracle" to his own followers, two hundred of them; he ordered them to sell their mules, to refuse to accept money, and never to venture outdoors for any reason, living on whatever scraps of food charity might bring them. Many years later, Theodoret recorded, they were still obeying this rule.

Fasting for forty days ceased to be a challenge for Simeon, for he found that "time and practice have allayed most of the effort." So he devised a fresh spectacular. He moved from his cottage to the hilltop and made a circular enclosure amid the rocks. He fixed one end of a thirty-foot-long iron chain to a large boulder and fastened the other around his right ankle. Church officials were uneasy at the public display of a self-chained and half-starved man, and a cleric from Antioch argued that it would be nobler for him to confine himself through an effort of willpower alone, without recourse to artificial aids. Simeon reluctantly agreed; when a smith removed the chain, many large bugs were found feasting on his festering ankle.

Whatever the misgivings of the clergy, ordinary Christians saw the self-mortifier as a living saint. They flocked to him to beg him for cures; the paralyzed, the sick, the impotent "asking to become fathers." Theodoret is vague on the details of the miracles performed; he says merely that those who were healed proclaimed the benefits they had gained and sent others, so that the hilltop became "a sea of men" fed by "rivers from every side." The pilgrims included "Ishmaelites" from northern Arabia, Persians, Armenians, and even "many inhabitants of the extreme west, Spaniards, Britons and the Gauls who live between them." Though this seems to smack of wishful thinking, it may be partly true; certainly Theodoret's grasp of geography was accurate.

All clamored to touch him, and to fondle the animal skins he wore, but eventually he could not "abide the wearisomeness of it." He thus "devised the standing on a pillar," as Theodoret put it, becoming the first Stylite. The word comes from the Greek *stylos,* meaning pillar. The first pillar raised on the hilltop in 423 was nine feet high; by the time of Simeon's death thirty-six years later it had been

Simeon Stylites spent thirty-six years atop a fifty-four-foot pillar near Antioch until his death in 459. Supplies, as seen in this relief from Damascus Museum, were taken up to him by ladder. He harangued the crowds below twice a day on the virtues of fearing hell, despising riches, and avoiding usury. The last pillar-dweller was recorded in the Caucasus in 1848.

raised in stages to reach fifty-four feet, reflecting his yearning "to fly up to heaven . . ." The stump of the pillar remains and suggests that each side of the square platform at its top was six feet long.

Although he must have descended during the brief periods of building work, he otherwise remained atop his pillar throughout three and a half decades, standing for as long as his body could bear it, and then bending repeatedly to pray. On onlooker noted 1,244 such continuous acts of worship before himself "slackening and giving up the count." At Easter and other festivals Simeon stood from sunset until dawn, his arms outstretched. He shouted down exhortations to the crowds twice a day. His eyrie did not soften his temper, nor make him modest; he sent vengeful instructions to the emperor and, "rousing the governors to divine zeal," demanded that they fight pagans, scatter heretics, and defeat "the insolence of the Jews." The emperor Marcian is said to have visited the lofty celebrity in disguise; the patriarch of Antioch brought him Holy Communion up the ladder that was occasionally placed against the pillar so meager food supplies could be taken to the platform.

The spectacle was bizarre; an emaciated and filthy figure in skins, pus oozing from an ulcer on his left foot, motionless when not bending in prayer, exposed to and beaten by sun and storms, haranguing on the virtues of fearing hell, despising earthly riches, and avoiding usury. Charges of "extravagance" were brought against him. Theodoret asked "fault-finders to hold their tongues." He pointed out that God had asked Isaiah to walk naked and barefoot (Isa. 20:2), and said that the Lord had ordained this new and spectacular performance to "draw all men to look"; in the absence of fresh martyrs, the fiery pillar-dweller brought the Church welcome publicity. Theodoret claimed that Ishmaelites, "two or three hundred at the same time," smashed their idols at the base of the pillar and that these Arabs then accepted the divine mysteries of Christianity; and that envoys from the king of Persia, and their muleteers, servants, and soldiers, became convinced that Simeon was a man of God. When the "universal decoration and ornament of piety" died—reaching the then advanced age of sixty-nine despite his cramped and meager existence—his body was said to have remained standing on the pillar "like an unbeaten athlete," a feat as miraculous as the untouched water.

Other Stylites followed, prominent among them Simeon's disciple Daniel. Several froze to death in winter; Daniel was found unconscious after a violent storm blew off his animal-skin tunic. His followers revived him and he consented to sleep in a small shelter on the platform. The Eucharist was either carried up the ladder by a priest or hauled up in a basket; sometimes, like Daniel, the stylite was ordained a priest on his column so that he could conduct his own services. Permission was not always granted. When some stylites appealed to Alexandria in about 535 for a bishop to ordain them from the ground while they remained pillar-bound, they received the ratty response that "such a thing has never been done." A stylite was supposed to remain on his post until death; they sometimes descended temporarily, however, in times of invasion or to harangue a bishop or official. Daniel's pillar was only four miles from Constantinople, and he came down once to rebuke the emperor Basiliscus for ungodliness. There was generally no shortage of admirers to keep a stylite supplied with a modicum of food. Paul of Latros, however, climbed up a natural rock spire in remote mountains without revealing his whereabouts. He was close to death when a traveler spotted him and brought him foodstuffs, an oil lamp, and a flint and tinder; Paul claimed that his discovery was an act of God.

Others, the "dendrites," lived in trees. "There are several who make their refuge in a tree with thick foliage," wrote George, an eighth-century bishop to the Arabs. "They feed on its fruits and its leaves, and they spend all their lives there, battered from side to side in gales."[29] An Ethiopian king, Yasai, was recorded as "ending his days at the top of a tree."[30] A monk from a monastery near Apamea recorded a dendrite who lived in a large cypress tree. "The devil never ceased struggling with him and several times hurled him out of the tree," he wrote. "He chained himself to the tree by his foot, and the next time Satan shook him out of the tree he remained suspended in the air until the villagers helped him back into it." Like Simeon, however, he became irritated by the number of sightseers who interrupted his prayers. One night he climbed out of his tree and took himself to the distant desert; his zeal deserted him until "God took pity on him and he entered a monastery."

It was more uncomfortable to live in a tree than on a pillar. The monk David of Thessalonica lasted three years in an almond tree; he could, like a stylite, endure the rigors of the climate, but the violent buffetings he suffered during gales persuaded him to beg his brother monks to prepare a solitary cell for him at ground level. After David's death, another monk, named Adolas, found a solution to the problem of perpetual motion; he lay inside the trunk of the tree, communicating with the outside world through a small window.[31] By the eleventh century, despite occasional revivals, the fashion was passing; though a traveler, Brosset, recorded a recluse living in a tiny cell atop a column at Djondidi in the Caucasus in 1848.

The Transpierced Heart:

Augustine

The greatest of the Latin fathers, the "glory of the Roman Church" whose ardor and insights molded the religious spirit of the West, was a Berber from North Africa, one of the fierce people who had lived on the Mediterranean coast between Egypt and the Atlantic since prehistoric times. Augustine of Hippo was born in 354 on a small farmstead in the hills of what is now Souk Ahras in Algeria. It was then Thagaste in the Roman province of Numidia. His writings have an influence on Christianity surpassed only by Paul; he himself listed 93 of his works written in 232 books or sections, his *City of God* alone being divided into 22 books, but this total omits his many hundreds of letters and sermons.

Augustine wrote on divine grace, the Fall and Original Sin, free will and predestination; he explored the morality of war and suicide and divorce; the texts that make up his monastic Rule were adopted centuries later by the Augustinian Canons and Friars, and by Dominican monks and Ursuline nuns. His autobiographical *Confessions* is a masterpiece of lyrical candor that catches the reckless heat of his youth—"all around me hissed a cauldron of illicit loves . . . I sought an object for my love; I was in love with love, and I hated safety and a path free of snares"[1]—with timeless force. Painters drew him with a transpierced or flaming heart, a symbol of the "ardent devotion and poignant repentance"[2] that marked his life.

His parents were Romanized Berbers, his father a hard-drinking man of violent temper and his mother Monica a patient and devout Christian who had overcome her own problems with drink. Their son was boisterous and brilliant; he loved games, he went on scrumping expeditions to steal pears from orchards, and he was frequently whipped at school. He developed a loathing for Greek, complaining that Homer had been hammered into him "from the canes of schoolmasters," but, significantly in view of his preference for the Roman above the Greek world, loved Latin, which he learned as a young child from the "caresses" of his nurses. As a student of rhetoric on the coast at Carthage he was top of his class, but joined a gang called the Wreckers who mocked "shy and unknown freshmen" for amusement, and adored the theater. He took a lowborn local girl as a mistress when he was seventeen.

The following year she bore him a son, Adeodatus, and the young father began to take an interest in philosophy. He read Cicero's dialogue *Hortensius;* the "book changed my feelings . . . it gave me different values and priorities." It taught him that happiness did not lie in the vain pleasures of the body. Cicero urged his readers to "love and seek and pursue . . . wisdom itself, wherever found."[3] The book had been written in 45 B.C. and naturally made no mention of Christ. This disappointed Augustine; although he had abandoned what faith he had, "my infant heart had piously drunk in my Savior's name . . . with my mother's milk,"[4] and he turned to the Scriptures to see what wisdom they contained. Jerome had yet to write his elegant Latin Vulgate. Augustine was obliged to read the Old Latin Bible, crudely translated by African missionaries some 150 years before; he thought it rough and unworthy in comparison with the dignity of Cicero and he set it aside with contempt.

He turned now, at twenty, to the Manichees and the theology of light and darkness. The African devotees of Mani thought themselves greatly superior to orthodox Christians. Augustine found them eloquent and proud; their "many huge tomes," finely bound and illustrated, and written with panache and style, impressed him. Their mouths were filled with "devil's traps and a birdlime compounded of the syllables of [God's] name and that of the Lord Jesus Christ, and that of . . . the Holy Spirit," he wrote in his *Confessions;* he was captivated by them. To provide for his baby and concubine—"she was the only girl for me, and I was faithful to her"—he taught the arts of rhetoric at Thagaste and then Carthage, "selling the eloquence that would overcome an opponent." His Carthage students were "foul and uncontrolled" and mobbed into his lectures without paying for them. Friends told him that pupils in Rome were less hot-blooded and that the fees were higher, so he sailed for Italy. The Roman students were quieter but they had a trick of their own; when they were due to pay their annual fee, they would desert their tutor and transfer to another.

A post as professor of rhetoric at Milan fell vacant, which brought with it access to powerful administrators at the court of the Western emperor, Valentinian II, a boy of thirteen. Augustine was appointed through the influence of his Manichaean friends; they convinced the pagan prefect of Rome that he was untainted by Catholic Christianity, though his relations with the Manichees were in fact beginning to founder. He found many of their beliefs to be fantastical; they said that eclipses were caused by the sun and moon veiling human eyes from the cosmic battle of light and dark, a notion that Augustine, who had a lively interest in astronomy, knew to be absurd. He was depressed at Milan. Though he had progressed far from the Numidian hills, he thought of himself as a mere "salesman of words" who crafted flattering panegyrics to order for the emperor. Brilliant orators could reach high office, and some became governors of provinces; but to do so they needed wives more suitable than Augustine's lowly Carthaginian concubine. His mother found a girl of suitable class and fortune for him to marry; she was only ten, and he had to wait for two years until she reached the minimum legal age for marriage. He sent his mistress back to Carthage and procured another—"Grant me chastity and continence, but not yet"—but his heart was wounded by his cynicism, and "left a trail of blood." He delved deep into Platonism and the mystic writings of the philosopher Plotinus, from whom he derived his own quest for the union of the soul with God in a moment of dazzling insight, in the "flash of a trembling glance." He also listened to the sermons of Ambrose, the tough-minded bishop of Milan, at first with a rhetorician's professional interest in their style and then, increasingly, in their content.

A crisis seized him as he lay under a fig tree in the garden of his lodgings at Milan in the July heat in 386. "I probed the hidden depths of my soul and wrung its pitiful secrets from it," he wrote, "and when I gathered them all before the eyes of my heart, a great storm broke within me, bringing with it a deluge of tears." In his misery, he kept crying: "How long shall I go on saying 'Tomorrow, tomorrow'? Why not now? Why not make an end of my ugly sins at this moment?" Just

The Devil holds the Book of Vices in front of St. Augustine, as seen by the painter and wood-carver Michael Pacher. "I probed the hidden depths of my soul and wrung its pitiful secrets from it," Augustine wrote of his forsaking of the vices of his youth, "and when I gathered them all before the eyes of my heart, a great storm broke within me . . . How long shall I go on saying 'Tomorrow, tomorrow'? Why not make an end of my ugly sins at this moment?" His sharp sense of sin was inherited by the Western Church.

then, he heard the singsong voice of a child in a nearby house repeating again and again *"Tolle lege, tolle lege"* . . . "Take it and read, take it and read. . . ." He felt that this was God's command for him to open his Bible. His eye fell on a passage from Paul: "Let us walk honestly, as in the day; not in revelling and drunkenness, not in cambering [recklessness] and wantonness, not in strife and jealousy; but put ye on the Lord Jesus Christ, and make not provision for the flesh, to fulfil the lusts thereof" (Rom. 13:13–14). He had no need to read on; in an instant, as he came to the end of the sentence, the "light of faith flooded into my heart and all the darkness of doubt was dispelled."[5] He was freed from the cares of place-seeking, from desire for money and the itch of lust; he was converted. . . .

He was baptized the following Easter Eve by Ambrose. Asthma attacks, and his disillusion with rhetoric, persuaded Augustine to resign his professorship at Milan. He moved to Rome and then to Ostia, at the mouth of the Tiber, to prepare for the sea journey back to Africa. He was in Ostia with his mother when they shared a vision while leaning from the window overlooking a garden. By "internal reflection and dialogue," mother and son lifted their minds beyond all physical objects and beyond heaven itself to a "region of inexhaustible abundance." Here they heard God, not through the voice of an angel or tongues of flesh, or thunder, but through himself; for "we extended our reach and in a flash of mental energy attained the eternal wisdom which abides beyond all things."[6] His mother was taken seriously ill with a fever a few days later; she had wanted to see her son a Catholic Christian before she died, she said, and now that God had granted this she found no further pleasure in life. "On the ninth day of her illness, when she was aged 56, and I was 33, this religious and devout soul was released from her body," Augustine wrote in words that were used as an epitaph on her tomb at Ostia; it was much visited by medieval pilgrims before being neglected and rediscovered in 1945 by boys digging a hole for a basketball post.[7] Adeodatus wept for his grandmother, but Augustine checked his tears, for "my mother's dying meant neither that her state was miserable nor that she was suffering extinction."

Augustine was able to summon this ferocious self-control when his son, Adeodatus, died at age seventeen a short time later. God, his father wrote, had "made him a fine person. . . . His intelligence left me awestruck. . . . I recall him with no anxiety; there was nothing to fear in his boyhood or adolescence. . . ." His companionship and conversation gave his father much pleasure; they were baptized together, but Augustine said of God without complaint that "early you took him away from life on earth." The intensity of his love of Christ bred in his mind indifference or even contempt for human frailty and emotion. Augustine shared his life for fifteen years with his concubine before discarding her to an unknown fate at Carthage; he never wrote of her by name, but only as "the woman with whom I shared my bed," and referred to their child as "my natural son begotten of my sin." Neither did he marry the girl his mother had found for him, though he was free to do so until he was ordained at thirty-seven. "If God had wanted Adam to have a partner in scintillating conversation he would have created another man," he wrote later; "the fact that God created a woman showed that he had in mind the survival of the human race."

The dismissal of half of humanity as mere breeding stock is at odds with the sensitivity and sensual beauty that he lavished on his faith and the divine. "Late have I loved you, beauty so old and so new, late have I loved you," he wrote after he had returned from Ostia to Africa. "And see, you were within and I was in the external world and sought you there. . . . You were with me, and I was not with you. The lovely things kept me far from you. . . . You called and cried out loud and shattered my deafness. You were radiant and resplendent, you put flight to my blindness. You were fragrant, and I drew in my breath and now pant after you. I tasted you, and I feel but hunger and thirst for you. You touched me, and I am set on fire to attain the peace which is yours. . . ."[8] Such mysticism may ring with poetry and the sublime, but it sits oddly with his indifference to the mother of his child.

✤ ON HIS RETURN to Thagaste in the late summer of 388, Augustine set up a monastery with like-minded friends. The monks were trained to oppose "the African heresies and especially the Donatists, the Manichaeans and the pagans," it was recorded. "As divine truth made headway, those who had been serving God in the monastery of the holy Augustine, and under his rule, began to be ordained as clergy for the church at Hippo. . . . In fact, by God's good gift, the Catholic Church in Africa began to lift its head again. . . ."[9] From Augustine's point of view, he was too successful; when visiting Hippo on the coast to the west of Carthage, he was seized by the people and ordained a priest against his will, later becoming their bishop.

The tensions in the Church in Africa forced him to think beyond existing doctrines. A schism had arisen during the Diocletian persecution, when so-called Donatists refused to accept a bishop of Carthage because his consecrator was a *traditor* who had avoided martyrdom by sacrificing to the gods. The wound was still unhealed eighty-five years later. Bands of violent Donatist peasants roamed Numidia from bases at *cellae,* or martyrs' shrines. They were fanatical and at times suicidal in their adoration of martyrdom. Officials dubbed them Circumcellions, since they lived around, or "circum," the *cellae,* but they called themselves "Agonistici," soldiers of Christ, and they entered battle with troops and raids against Catholic landlords with cries of "*laudes Deo,*" "praises be to God."

Augustine stressed the authority of the Catholic Church during this crisis. "I would not have believed the gospel unless the universal Church had constrained me to do so," he wrote; the Church was "one" through the mutual charity of its members, but it was "holy" because of its purposes, and not because of its members, who included both the evil and the good. The Pelagian controversy took him deep into the concepts of divine grace and Original Sin. Pelagius was a British theologian who, at the start of the fifth century, was much in vogue among aristocrats on the great estates of Sicily. He taught that man can take steps to achieve his salvation through his own efforts, unaided by God's grace. This led to the denial of Adam's transmission of Original Sin and Paul's claim that "by the trespass of the one the many died"; Pelagius did not see evil as inherent in the newborn child but as a later acquisition. Augustine maintained that Adam's guilt was passed on like some inherited moral disease to his descendants through sexual appetite, making humanity a *massa damnata* whose freedom of will was much enfeebled though not destroyed. So corrupt and self-seeking was this mass of the damned that it could not be saved except through grace; faith and escape from evil could not exist without this divine intervention. Since sin was present from birth, Augustine held that even infants who died unbaptized were damned. The faith or character of the priest who carried out the ceremony was irrelevant; the act of baptism itself has a *character regius,* a royal character that stamps the soul as God's.

It was natural for every sect, heretical or orthodox, to believe that its members would make up the elect who would be gathered "from the uttermost parts of the earth" for salvation on the Last Day, and that its opponents would be among the damned. Jesus had said that some people would be led to salvation infallibly and irretrievably; "and no one," he had told the Jews in the temple, "is able to snatch them out of the Father's hand" (John 10:29). He did not, however, explain why such souls should be predestined to enter heaven; it was the privilege of the Father to grant it, not the Son. "To sit on my right hand, and on my left hand, is not mine to give," he told the apostles, "but it is for them for whom it hath been prepared of my Father" (Matt. 20:23). Paul had confirmed the principle of God's elect—"for whom he foreknew, he also foreordained to be conformed to the image of his Son, that he might be the firstborn among many brethren" (Rom. 8:28–30)—but he, too, gave no guidance on the Almighty's selection procedures other than to say that the foreordained are called "not according to our works, but according to His own purpose and grace" (2 Tim. 1:9). Augustine accepted predestination as a gratuitous act of God; the divine choice of who is elect and who is not is a mystery beyond the reckoning of the human mind, but the choice is an infallible result of perfect justice. God grants the elect the call to be baptized and enter the Christian faith, he believed, and also bestows on them *donum perseverantiae,* the gift of perseverance that enables them to remain true to their faith with steady persistence.

His own life was shot through with individual will and scorn for society and its failings. Yet his view of the human condition was passive and resigned, and his attitude to the Church was passive. *Salus extra ecclesiam non est,* he wrote; "There is no salvation outside the Church"; *Roma locuta est; causa finita;* "Rome has spoken, the case is closed." The papacy had good reason to look back on him with favor. He praised affection and freedom—*dilige et quod vis fac,* "love and do what you wish"—but some sense of servility ran alongside the lyricism in his praise of God. "Man is one of your creatures, Lord, and his instinct is to praise you," he wrote. "He bears about him the mark of death, the sign of his own sin, to remind him that you thwart the proud. But still, since he is part of your creation, he wishes to praise you. The thought of you stirs him so deeply that he cannot be content unless he praises you, because you made us for yourself and our hearts find no peace unless they rest in you. . . ."

AS AUGUSTINE GREW older and the fifth century dawned, the age grew darker and more troubling. Distant events in Asia had shifted peoples bodily westward and the frontiers of the Roman Empire were collapsing. The Chinese had destroyed the empire of the Huns, whom they knew as the Xiongu, shortly before the birth of Christ, driving the Hunnish horde and their cattle into Turkestan. In the second century the Huns had moved north of the Caspian, putting pressure on the Germanic Goths. By 375 the Huns had penetrated into the Ukraine, forcing the Ostrogoths and the neighboring Visigoths westward into the empire. In 378 the Ostrogoths, spearheaded by heavy cavalry with powerful horses and long lances, had routed the Roman legions at Hardianopolis and killed the emperor Valens.

The Visigoth king Alaric, an Arian Christian whose men had once served as imperial auxiliaries, invaded Greece in 395 and seized temporary control of Athens. Legions were transferred from Gaul to defend Constantinople, leaving a tempting vacuum behind them. On New Year's Eve in 406, a mass of barbarians—Germanic Vandals and Suevi, and Alans, a once Iranian-speaking people from the Caspian—crossed the frozen Rhine near Coblenz and rampaged across Gaul. They crossed the Pyrenees in 409. The Suevi established a kingdom in Galicia in northern Spain, and the Alans another in the valley of the Tagus in Portugal; the Vandals had a predatory eye on Augustine's Africa.

Rome, inviolate for more than a millennium, fell to Alaric in 410. His troops pillaged the city for six days, though Alaric forbade rape and the desecration of Christian buildings. The Western Empire was traumatized; refugees flooded into

Augustine died in 430 shortly before Vandal barbarians broke into Hippo. Across the Mediterranean, Attila the Hun, the "scourge of God," portrayed here by Ulpiano Checa y Sauz, invaded northern Italy in 452, sacking Turin and Padua, whose ruins "the succeeding generations could scarcely find." Pope Leo bribed him not to take Rome, but the escape was temporary. A Vandal fleet sailed up the Tiber and sacked the city for fourteen days in 455. All the Western Empire was eventually overrun by successive waves of barbarian invasions.

Africa and the safer Greek East. The great historian Gibbon equated the collapse of Rome with the "triumph of barbarism and religion." Pious Christians despised government and the administration as worldly evils and refused to serve in them; Augustine himself wrote that to accept baptism meant a "total abandonment of the foul darkness of secular activities." Powerful minds that might have reversed the moral decay of the empire were lost to the Church; the religious chose to cloister themselves in monasteries and hermitages, and ignored the brutality and decadence of the secular world. Christianity had done little to improve political or social habits. Valentinian II, the boy emperor whom Augustine had served at Milan, barely reached twenty before the commander of his army murdered him. The bureaucracy was venal and bloated; chariot racing, wild beast hunts, and erotic theater replaced Christian martyrs as public spectacles.

"When we used to sacrifice to our gods, Rome was flourishing," a pagan complained to Augustine. "But now when people sacrifice to your God everywhere, and our sacrifices are forbidden, see what is happening to Rome." Peter and Paul, its patron saints, had abandoned the city to its fate; the gods of old, no longer nourished by sacrifice, their temples torn down, had exacted their revenge.

For fourteen years, from 413 to 427, Augustine wrote his reply to the accusation that Christianity had ruined Rome in the twenty-two books that make up *The City of God*. It explored the contrast between Christianity and the world; the City of God, existing in faith, was the truly eternal city, while the earthly cities of empires were subject to constant flux and violence. Man's fallen state exposed him to war, slavery, and injustice. There had been no happiness when Rome was pagan, and its beliefs were squalid and petty. The Church brought forgiveness and concern for justice under a Christian emperor, or so he claimed, but the perfection that the City of God reaches is not attainable in this life.

If, as he believed, the Church was the *totus Christi,* the totality of Christ, and salvation was impossible outside it, then it followed that compelling a person into it was an act of mercy. Augustine wrote of the "kindly harshness" that the Church should use to make unwilling souls yield. "We have to consider their welfare rather than their inclination," he explained. "For when we are stripping a man of the lawlessness of sin, it is good for him to be vanquished since nothing is more hopeless than the happiness of sinners. . . ." What is to be feared "is not temporal death, which must come some time or other, but eternal death."

Repression and violence were the day-to-day tools of a flawed world to Augustine, and he condoned their use provided that the intention was just. This was new ground. Tertullian had encouraged Christian martyrdom, for example, but he denied that violence should be used against pagans. "God has not hangmen for priests," he wrote. "Christ teaches us to bear wrong, not to avenge it." Athanasius linked force with the devil; Satan bursts in with axe and sword, but the Savior knocks and speaks gently to the soul: "Open to me, my sister." The French prelate Hilary complained bitterly that the Church, once the victim of prison and exile, was now its sponsor; Augustine's contemporary Chrysostom said heresy should be treated with "persuasion, instruction and love."

Augustine at first agreed. "If we are dragged to Christ, we believe against our will," he wrote in his commentary on St. John's gospel; "violence therefore is applied, the will is not kindled. . . ." In his struggle with the Donatists, however, he came to approve of the punishments—exile, property confiscations, and imprisonment—imposed on them by the emperor Honorius after 412. Augustine claimed a justification in Christ; had not Jesus said: "Compel them to come in"? He wrote that "certain wars that must be waged against the violence of those resisting are commanded by God or by a legitimate ruler and are undertaken by the good."

THAT AUGUSTINE'S HARSHNESS was real, and not academic, was shown by his reaction when the barbarians engulfed Africa. In 429, Vandals and Alans under their king Gaiseric "poured into Africa from across the sea in ships from Spain . . . a huge host of savage enemies armed with every kind of weapon and trained in war."[10] The Vandals' urge for destruction was so great that their name became a synonym for it; these "subverters of Romanity"* spared "neither sex nor age, nor the very priests and ministers of God, nor the ornaments and vessels of the churches, nor the buildings."[11] Families fled to mountain forests, caves, and rocky dens, or choked the few cities that held out.

As Arians, the invaders had no scruples against attacking the native Catholics. "They gave vent to their wicked ferocity with great strength against the churches and basilicas of the saints, cemeteries, and monasteries," a chronicler recorded, "so that they burned houses of prayer with fires greater than those they used against the cities. . . ."[12]

Augustine was besieged by the Arians at Hippo early in 430. He wrote from there to the bishop of Thiabe, a small town south of Hippo, urging him to remain with his congregation. "While those who wished to withdraw while they could to fortified centers should not be prevented," he said, "at the same time we have no right to throw off the fetters of our ministry, with which the love of Christ has bound us, and desert the Churches that we have the duty of serving."[13] He took a hard line against those who quoted Jesus' recommendation to flee from persecution. "Who supposes that Our Lord meant by this that the flocks that He bought with His own blood were to be left without the ministrations necessary to their very life?" he wrote.[14] He conceded that Paul had escaped from the clutches of the governor of Damascus by being let down the walls in a basket, but he insisted that others had remained in the city to continue the ministry. If someone was specially sought by the invaders, Augustine permitted him to "fly from city to city" only if others stayed behind to supply life-giving spiritual nourishment.

If the laity "are not being hunted to death themselves, they can hide their bishops and clergy," he wrote. "The case when laymen and clergy are in the same danger cannot be compared with one of those storms when merchants and seamen are in the same danger on a ship. God forbid that this ship of ours should be valued at so little that it could be right for the sailors, and even for the pilot, to abandon it in its dangers, just because they can escape by jumping into the ship's boat or even by swimming."[15] The priest who abandoned his flock was "the hireling who sees the wolf coming and who flees because he is not concerned for the sheep."[16]

And what of the sheep? "In our charity towards God's sheep, who must all die some day, some way," Augustine wrote in another instruction that has acted as an

---

*In Latin "Romania," a new word coined to describe the civilized life of the Roman world as distinct from the savage barbarism that now threatened it.

apologia for inquisitors down the centuries, "we should be more afraid of a butchery of their minds by the sword of spiritual evil than of their bodies by a sword of steel."[17] A woman should fear loss of the purity of faith more than rape; "for violence cannot violate chastity if the mind preserves it. Even the chastity of the body is not violated when she who suffers is not voluntarily abusing her body but is enduring, without consenting, what another is perpetrating."[18] A rape victim, in short, remained as chaste as a virgin provided she kept to her faith; spiritual deprivation was a greater calamity than torture.

On August 28, 430, as Gaiseric prepared to break into Hippo, Augustine died. The city was sacked; Catholics were driven into the southern deserts, and priests were shipped to Corsica to cut timber for Gaiseric's fleet. At Vita and Usurita the bishops were tortured to death. Maddened by resistance at Carthage, the Vandals slew so many when the city fell in 439 that the dead were dumped in mass graves without funeral rites. The main churches were given to the Arian clergy while others were turned into barracks for the Vandals. Bishop Quodvult-deus, who blamed the fall on his flock's preference for the pleasures of the circus over the example of their early martyrs, was expelled on an unseaworthy ship that limped into Naples; other clergy and senators fled as far as Syria.

A brilliant general, Flavius Aetius, staved off the barbarians for twenty years in Europe, defeating Goths, Burgundians, rebellious Gauls, and Franks. The legions had already departed from Britain, leaving it open to sea raiders, Jutes, Angles, and Saxons; contact between Romanized Britons and the empire was severed after a last and unanswered appeal to Aetius for help in 446. By now Attila the Hun, the "scourge of God," had erupted from his tented capital on the *tisza* or plains of Hungary. In 447 he devastated the territories between the Black Sea and the Mediterranean, the "grass never growing where his horse had trod." He turned his attention to Gaul in 451 before Aetius and his Visigoth allies defeated him in a fearful battle near Châlons-sur-Marne. It was the last victory in the name of the Western emperor. Three years later that emperor, Valentinian III, jealous of his great commander, had Aetius stabbed to death. Attila broke into Italy and sacked Turin, Padua, and Aquileia, whose ruins "the succeeding generations could scarcely find." Pope Leo bribed him not to take Rome; the Hun retired to the *tisza* to die on his nuptial night of a burst artery, "suffocated by a torrent of blood . . . which regurgitated into his stomach and lungs."

Valentinian was murdered in his turn by Aetius's bodyguards in 455. In revenge, Valentinian's widow, Eudoxia, invited Gaiseric to Rome. The Vandal fleet sailed up the Tiber in 455 and sacked the city for fourteen days. Leo was forced to surrender Church vessels and gold; Gaiseric carried off Eudoxia and her two daughters, one of whom he married to his elder son Huneric. Gaiseric defeated imperial fleets sent against him from Constantinople; the succession of Huneric in 477 spelled the final humiliation of Catholic Africa. All who did not convert to Arianism were declared heretics; all Catholic churches were closed, all masses, baptisms, and ordinations banned, all liturgical books destroyed. Priests were put to work in the mines. In 483, five thousand clergy and laity were deported to the Moorish frontier district of Byzacena; their journey through the desert was a death march.

Victor of Vita prayed to the angels to "look upon all Africa, formerly supported by companies of great churches, now deprived of them all; then adorned with great ranks of priests, now sitting as a downcast widow. . . ."[19] In the West, the terrors already suffered in the *Volkerwanderung,* the eruptions of peoples, were merely a frontispiece to the coming Dark Ages.

CHAPTER IX

Lost atLantis:

The Islamic Invasions

In the year 20 of the Moslem era, an Arab soldier fighting in a small Egyptian village close to Alexandria witnessed in miniature the catastrophe that was overwhelming the ancient Christian heartlands. Ziyad ibn Jaz al-Zubaydi was part of a small force of horsemen, ragged and dusty, in thin woolen cloaks, some riding their agile ponies barefoot, that was closing on Alexandria, the last significant place in Egypt still in Christian hands. The Byzantine troops had fled in panic; it was easy fighting. "We advanced on the villages one after another," the soldier said, "until we ended up in Balhib, one of those rural villages."

The village was swiftly overrun. The Arabs assembled all their fresh captives and their families. "Then we began to bring forward every single man from among them and we gave them the choice between Islam and Christianity," Ziyad ibn Jaz reported.[1] Those who apostatized had only to repeat a simple profession of faith—"there is no God but Allah, and Muhammad is his Prophet"—to be accepted as Moslems and as equals of their conquerors. Those who refused did so at a price; a special poll tax, the *jizya,* was levied on them.

Each captive was dealt with personally. "We all shouted 'God is great' even louder than we had done when the village was conquered," Ziyad ibn Jaz said of those who chose Islam, "and we gathered him within our ranks." When a captive refused, the Christians "would snort and pull him back into their midst, while we imposed the *jizya* on him." Families split on the spot. The parents of a certain Abu Maryam had already opted for Christianity when their son stepped forward; he chose Islam, and the Moslem soldiers made him step into their ranks. Distraught, "his father, mother and brothers pounced on him, struggling with us for control of him, until they tore the clothes from his body." There was no going back; the son was now a Moslem.

It was the year 641 of the Christian era.

Thus, by the million, across a vast and expanding arc already stretching from Persia to the borders of the Libyan desert, individuals were required to choose between the religion of Christ and that of Muhammad, a prophet who had died less than ten years before in an obscure trading town in Arabia. Of the faith's five great patriarchates,* two had already fallen to Islam. The Christians of Antioch were left to survive as best they could *in partibus infidelium;* as he had surrendered Jerusalem, its weeping patriarch had softly repeated Christ's words: "Behold the abomination of desolation, which was spoken of by Daniel the prophet, standing in the holy place" (Matt. 24:15). A third would follow in a few months. After noting how Abu Maryam's decision served to earn him high rank in the forces of his adopted Islam, Ziyad ibn Jaz added with the perfunctory self-confidence of the victor: "Then God conquered Alexandria for us and we could enter the city." To the west, the faith for which Perpetua had been thrown to the beasts 450 years before would soon be obliterated from North Africa. Christianity would be engulfed for many centuries in Spain; the first Islamic siege of Constantinople would start in twenty-five years and continue intermittently for eight centuries, until that great patriarchate also fell to Islam. Rome would be—is—the only ancient patriarchate left under Christian control.

❖ THE CATACLYSM SHAPED history. It created the Arab and Moslem world; it severed the Mediterranean world, destroying forever its ancient Roman integrity, as Arabic replaced Greek and Latin as the language of the rulers of the eastern and southern shores. It consigned the Eastern churches, the glory of Christendom, to isolated and dwindling pockets, and for centuries it reduced the physical links with China, India, and Africa to the ethereal legend of Prester John's kingdom of Christians. Above all, like some gigantic earthwork, it diverted the mainstream of the faith westward to the dark recesses of barbarian Europe.

It was entirely unexpected; a shock wave rolling out of the deserts of Arabia, a place on the periphery of Christian consciousness, carried by men so equally exotic to the civilized mind that at first they were called not Arabs but "Ishmaelites," the biblical name for the camel-riding nomads who had bought Joseph after his brothers had stripped him of the coat of many colors.

Moslems were—the fact is pitiful, but a commonplace—welcomed by many of those who were conquered. The immense and rapid Christian losses were in part the price exacted for the schisms, the fatal fascination with Christology, the eagerness with which Christians savaged each other. The Copts, Syrians, and Armenians were harried by the empire for their belief in the single divine nature of

*The grandest provinces, ruled by bishops ranking above primates and metropolitans.

the incarnate Christ, the Nestorians for their insistence on his two distinct natures or hypostases. Condemned as heretics, they saw the Moslem armies as a release from persecution. "And the hearts of the Christians rejoiced at the
domination of the Arabs (may God strengthen it and prosper it)," wrote a Nestorian chronicler;[2] while Syrians felt that "the God of vengeance" had "raised from
the region of the south the Children of Ishmael to deliver us by them from the
hands of the Romans. . . ."[3]

The barbarian hordes of Goths and Huns flooding into Europe were pagans
who in time adopted the faith of their new subjects. The Arabs, coming out of
Arabia like their prophet Muhammad, with "the sword in one hand, the Koran in
the other,"[4] had a proselytising religion of their own that exposed Christianity for
the first time to a universal rival. The Church was the inclusive Body of Christ
only in the imagination. Fractiousness remained in its bloodstream. Its mind did
not respond to the Moslem crisis by shutting down its feckless quarrels, and its
heart did not pump fraternal love.

Instead, the pope was martyred. Martin I was elected as the Arabs made their
first raids to the west of Alexandria in 649. He was known for his intelligence and
humanity; he had done much charitable work as a deacon at Rome, and had
served as a papal nuncio at Constantinople. It served him little when he fell foul
of an edict issued by the emperor, Constans II, which supported the denial that
Christ had a human will. Martin held a council at Rome, which condemned this
as an error. The bishops of Africa and Spain, who would soon enough be overrun
by the urgent simplicity of Islam, supported him. Constans commanded that
Martin be deposed and arrested. The pope was taken from his palace at midnight
and thrown aboard a boat on the Tiber to be shipped to Constantinople. He arrived there in September 654. Although weakened by dysentery on the long voyage, he was kept in a dungeon for almost three months. "It is now forty seven
days since I have been permitted to wash myself in either warm or cold water,"
Martin wrote. "I am quite wasted and chilled, and have had no respite either
upon sea or land from the flux from which I suffer. My body is broken and
spent. . . ."[5] He was condemned for treason in the presence of the Senate and
taken out onto a terrace so that Constans could watch the first stage of his humiliation. The guards took away his papal pallium, the white woolen vestment in
the shape of a double Y; they then stripped him of all his clothes except a tunic,
which they tore from top to bottom to expose his naked body. An iron collar was
put around Martin's neck and he was dragged through the city by a jailer, with
an executioner carrying a sword in front of him to show that he was condemned
to die.

After three months of being chained to a bench in the notorious Diomedes
prison he was exiled to the Crimea. This merely prolonged the pope's agony;

famine was rife—"bread is talked of here," he wrote, "but never seen"⁶—and he found that the local pagans had not "even that natural compassion which is to be found among barbarians." His fellow Christians were worse. "I wonder still more at those who belong to the church of St. Peter," he wrote, "for the little concern they show for one of their body. . . ." They sent him no money, corn, or oil; he prayed for the preservation of their faith, and begged God that "He will not prolong my course." His appeal was answered; he died of famine and neglect on April 13, 655. In time the papacy was to become the focal point of a Christendom blown northwestwards by Islam; Martin was the last pope whom an emperor dared to martyr.

The Arabs did not kill Christian priests, however, as Christians themselves often did. As they advanced, they released heretics from prison and restored fugitive bishops to their sees. Neither did they at first destroy churches. The Basilica of St. John was divided in two during the taking of Damascus, with one sanctuary for Moslems and the other for Christians, and the two congregations worshiped alongside each other, as they did at first in the great church at Cordoba in Spain. Such conduct was a key to the early Moslem success. Their victories came from deep insight as much as military brilliance. Dirt-poor and outnumbered, they used toleration and taxation as weapons, the first to secure easy surrender, the second to finance further conquest and swell their numbers by stimulating conversation. They knew their Christians well.

✤ THEY CAME FROM the towns and desert camps of central Arabia and Yemen, where their prophet had been born about 570. Muhammad was the son of a poor and sickly merchant in the city of Mecca. Orphaned at six and reared in the traders' arts, accompanying caravans as a camel-driver, he was a religious boy with a strong urge for the mystical. It was likely that he would express this through Christianity, for it was to this religion that pagan Arabia was then converting. Jews were gaining some Arab converts in the cities, and Zoroastrians in Persian-controlled areas; but Christians spread south and east from the monasteries of the Sinai Desert and Petra in modern Jordan to the Arabian Sea and the Persian Gulf.

Arab caravans frequently visited the great Christian cities of Syria, Egypt, and Iraq; important tribes on the periphery of the desert, the Banu Ghassan and the Banu Taghlib, were almost wholly Christian, and the faith had traveled the desert and sea routes to Yemen and the Hadramaut. The heartland, Arabia Felix to the ancient world, lay on the route to the Mediterranean taken by camel trains freighted with frankincense, gold, gems, sweet cane, and spices from Africa, India, and the East. The queen of Sheba who visited King Solomon with her displays of trade goods came from the region of southern Arabia around Ma'rib; in the fourth century, the ruler of Ma'rib had converted to Christianity. To the south lay Sana'a, captured in the mid-sixth century by the armies of King Caleb, Christian ruler of Aksum in Ethiopia on the African side of the Red Sea. "I have built you a temple in Sana'a, the like of which Arabs nor non-Arabs have constructed," the governor, Abraha, wrote to the bishop of Aksum. "I shall not desist until I divert the pilgrims of the Arabs to it, and they abandon the pilgrimage to their own temple."[7] Other churches were built in Aden, Zafar, and Najran; stone reliefs of saints and hands clasped in prayer have been found in houses in Zafar, and columns and reliefs of doves and rosettes in the great mosque of Sana'a may come from Abraha's cathedral.

The Arab pilgrims Abraha referred to went to Mecca, where members of Muhammad's Quaraysh tribe were guardians of the Ka'ba, the shrine whose black stone was believed to have been given to Abraham by the archangel Gabriel. As a youth the prophet went with caravans to Syria and Yemen and perhaps to Egypt and Mesopotamia; he learned the ways of the desert and the Bedouin nomads. At about twenty-five he married a wealthy widow some fifteen years his senior and thus was able to leave the harsh caravanner's trade for a life of religious preparation. He may have had Christian instruction from a Syrian monk named Sergius Bahira;[8] certainly, he claimed that his revelation confirmed the Jewish and Christian Scriptures; he accepted monotheism if not monogamy with vigor, and he queried neither the miracles of Jesus nor the validity of the Mosaic Law. His divine mission was to act as God's mouthpiece; he delivered these revelations in a trance, preparing himself by wrapping in a blanket to produce the heavy perspiration that preceded their delivery. They were related orally to a few trusted followers; Muhammad was probably semiliterate, and the definitive text of his revelations, the Koran or "reading," was not completed until after his death.

Though a mystic, he was intensely practical and active. Of middle height, according to tradition, he had "a large head, large eyes, heavy eyelashes, reddish tint in the eyes, thick-bearded, broad-shouldered, with thick hands and feet"[9] He was in his mid-forties, with an established core of disciples, when he began his public preaching in about 616. The elite in Mecca took no more kindly to the Prophet of God than their predecessors in Jerusalem had to Jesus; he demanded that the many idols at the profitable shrine should be destroyed, and that the rich should give to the poor. Several of his followers were forced to flee the city; he is said to have advised them to go to the court of the Christian king of Aksum, "under whom no man is persecuted" and where "God will bring you rest from your afflictions."[10] Mecca was a sacred city where bloodshed was forbidden by custom, so the Meccans instead attempted to starve the troublesome prophet to death, blockading the district in which he and his remaining believers lived. The people of Yathrib, a farming town to the north, invited him to come as a leader to heal an outbreak of feuding. He exiled himself from Mecca; a group of assassins, chosen from all tribes but his own in order to share the guilt of breaking the bloodshed code, found his cousin Ali in his bed when they burst into his house to murder him. His flight, or *hijira,* marked the start of the Moslem era on July 16, 622.

He reached Yathrib in September; the town was afterwards known as al-Medina, "the City," of the Prophet. There were Jews in Medina; but despite the common bond of Abraham—who appears in twenty-five suras, or chapters, of the Koran as "Ibrahim"—no accommodation was reached with them; the direction of Moslem prayer had been to Jerusalem, but after a year's residence in the town Muhammad turned it southward, to the still pagan temple at Mecca. He bound his followers to himself and to each other by the closest possible ties; he himself had a harem of nine wives, becoming the elderly son-in-law of Abu Bakr and Omar, the first two Moslem caliphs who succeeded him as God's supreme commanders on earth; he was both father-in-law and cousin to the fourth, Ali.

The new faith had need of funds and converts, and Muhammad had no inhibitions about using the sword to acquire them. He sent a force to ransack a Meccan caravan during the sacred month of Rajab, a season when Arab raiding was unknown. Some months later, in December 623, a band of three hundred men attacked a force of a thousand Meccans at a place called Badr. The Koran refers to it as the "Day of Deliverance." The victory enabled him to gain control of the Red Sea shoreline from Jeddah to Yanbo. The Meccans counterattacked successfully a year later at Ohod, northwest of Medina; Muhammad was himself badly wounded, but the victors left the battlefield when they had killed as many of his men as they had lost themselves at Badr. It was a miscalculation; Muhammad continued his raids and beat off an attempt to crush Medina by an alliance of tribes. Mecca itself fell to him in 629; he conducted the pilgrimage there himself the following year, and it became the religious center of Islam, while political power remained in Medina. He now gave all Arabs four months' grace to convert to Islam before force would be used against them. At his death, in the house of his favorite wife Aishah in 632, he controlled Arabia, and his successor Abu Bakr, Aishah's father, was embarking on campaigns against the Persians and Romans. Muhammad had also declared to the Arabs that God had completed their new religion.

Islam was less complex and very much less prone to schism than its older rival; its only major enduring division, between Sunnis and Shiites,* was as much

---

*The Sunnis held that Moslems were obliged to appoint a leader in succession to Muhammad. The Shiites argued that the appointment lies with God, and that, though the appointment may not be known or accepted, God always makes one.

dynastic as theological. The Christian convert, at least in theory, underwent a period of instruction and trial before baptism. He faced a host of conflicting claims—on the primacy of different churches and patriarchs, the nature of Christ, the Virgin Birth, the use of icons, the celibacy of the priesthood, the celebration of Communion, the readmission of apostates—with the sole certainty that his response would be judged heresy by at least some of his fellow Christians. Islam had no such inhibitions at its birth, and it acquired few as it matured. It had one God, whose unity suffered none of the confusion of the Christians' Trinity; its Koran was the product of a single mind, Muhammad's, and a single era, undisturbed by the diversity and contradictions of the many writers of the Christians' Bible; it was expressed in a single language, Arabic, for no translation of the Koran was allowed.

The "five pillars of Islam" were sturdy and immediately comprehensible. The first is a confession of faith of utter simplicity. To become a Moslem, the convert had merely to confirm his belief in Allah, and Muhammad's status as His Prophet, in front of witnesses. The second obligation is to pray four times a day—at daybreak, midday, sunset, and evening—and touch the forehead to the ground while facing Mecca. The third is to give alms to the poor; the fourth, to fast from dawn to dusk throughout the holy month of Ramadan; the last is to make the hajj pilgrimage to Mecca at least once in a lifetime. The 114 suras or chapters of the Koran provide a handbook of law, philosophy, and morality.

Like Christianity its appeal was global; but it was also a religion of conquest. "God is the Commander in the past and in the future," the Koran specifies. "He helps to victory whom He wills." It must indeed have seemed that God favored the Arabs. The Roman eastern frontier had stood for six hundred years against more formidable foes, Parthians and Persians, and the Arabs would not have breached it but for a combination of circumstances.

THE ARABS HAD made no earlier impact on the empire. Their energies dissipated by tribal and family feuds, they were capable of mounting no more than *razzias,* swift Bedouin raids. Muhammad and his new creed united them into a disciplined force. He had led public prayers, sat as supreme judge, and controlled the army; he had absolute command of the faithful, and so did the caliphs or "successors" who followed him. They operated from a secure base, made immune from pursuit by distance and desert. The early campaigns were aimed at winning complete control of Arabia and dominance over the nomadic tribes on its Iraqi and Syrian borders. "The land of the Arabs is different from the land of non-Arabs in that the Arabs are only fought over to make them accept Islam," the chronicler Abu Yusuf explained. "*Jizya* was not demanded of them, and nothing but the acceptance of Islam was accepted of them. . . ."[11] There was no truck with pagans; for the "idolators among the Arabs . . . it was only acceptance of Islam or death." Jews and Christian Arabs were rapidly expelled from the central Arabian heartland. The infant Moslem forces were cohesive, and memories of their prophet were fresh and often personal; his relatives led them.

They profited, too, from the extreme debilitation of their enemies. Conditions by 632, though only the Moslem year 10, were uniquely favorable. Twenty years before, the Byzantine Empire had sunk into near anarchy under the vice and tyranny of the usurper Phocas. The general of African armies, Heraclius, had sailed to Constantinople to murder and replace Phocas. Persian armies under the Sassanid Shah, Chosroes Parviz, feasting on the chaos and intrigue, crashed through Syria, Palestine, and Egypt. Chosroes, referring to himself as "greatest of Gods, and master of the earth," warned Heraclius, his "vile and insensate slave," that he should not console himself with "vain hope in that Christ, who was not able to save himself from the Jews"; even if Heraclius took refuge in the depths of the sea, he said, "I will stretch out my hand and take you. . . ."[12] In 613 the Persians took Damascus. The following year they closed on Jerusalem. It was a prosperous place of pilgrimage; a mosaic laid recently by the bishop of Madaba in Transjordan on the floor of his transept showed the grandeur of its columned streets and the magnificence of its domed churches: Constantine's Holy Sepulchre, the cathedral on Mount Sion, the huge Nea or New Church of Justinian. "We make offering to Thee also, O Lord, for the Holy places," its worshipers repeated proudly each day, "especially for the glorious Sion, the Mother of all the Churches. . . ."[13]

The siege began on April 15, 614. After three weeks the Persians breached the city walls. The defenders hid in caverns and cisterns and the people fled into the churches, but "the enemy entered in mighty wrath, gnashing their teeth in violent fury; like evil beasts they roared, bellowed like lions, hissed like ferocious serpents, and slew all whom they found."[14] The Persians "tore with their teeth the flesh of the faithful, and respected none at all, . . . neither child nor baby, neither priest nor monk, neither virgin nor widow. . . ." The patriarch Zachariah was captured; he was led out of the city "like a brigand, pinioned with cords" to the Mount of Olives, and here "as for a widowed bride, so he wept for the holy church." Debris drifted across from the burning city; "some smote themselves upon the face, others strewed ashes upon their heads, others rubbed their faces in the dust, and some tore their hair, when they beheld the holy [church of the] Anastasis afire, Sion in smoke and flames, and Jerusalem devastated."[15] Many of the survivors were held in a reservoir near the city; "as of old they bought the Lord with silver," it was said of the Jews, "so they purchased Christians out of the reservoir; for they gave the Persians silver." Chosroes carried off the city's most treasured relics, the True Cross and the instruments of the Passion. Zachariah was among the many Christians taken captive to Persia. At Mar Saba, the great *lavra* founded by St. Sabas in the wild country between Bethlehem and the Dead Sea, the Persians tossed the anchorites down the sheer face of the canyon into whose rock they had cut their cells; some three hundred of their skulls remain to this day in a cabinet by the altar of the *lavra*'s cave-chapel.

The empire was brought almost to its knees. Egypt was invaded to little resistance in 619; with the Persians moving toward the Bosporus, Heraclius considered abandoning Constantinople and fleeing to Carthage. In desperation, the patriarch of Constantinople, Sergius, gave the emperor the treasure of the Church to pay for fresh auxiliaries, thus financing what has been called the "first war of the Cross"; in a series of daring expeditions, crossing the Mediterranean and the Black Sea, at a time when Muhammad was struggling for control of two insignificant desert towns, Heraclius recovered the lost territories. He pursued Chosroes into Persia, defeating him at Nineveh in 627. The shah was deposed and executed by his son; Heraclius triumphantly restored the True Cross to Jerusalem.

Both giants were, as the Arabs advanced out of Arabia, now prostrate. A fourteen-year-old boy, elected in the throes of defeat and civil war, ruled Persia. Heraclius was more than sixty, worn out by continuous warfare, suffering from dropsy, a "lion in winter"; the Roman Empire was bankrupt, the army a motley of barbarian auxiliaries, the ravaged provinces familiar with foreign occupation.

It was the last that brought into play the third factor that so favored infant Islam: its toleration. The conduct of the fire-worshiping Persian troops set a benchmark for Christian terror that the Moslems were able to exploit to formidable effect. Muhammad respected Christians and Jews as "people of the Book," the Bible. Provided they paid the *jizya* poll tax and a *kharaj* land tax, they were not to be forcibly converted, but would enjoy protection, or *dhimma*. As *dhimmis,* they "shall have the patronage of God and the protection of Muhammad, the Prophet, the Apostle of God, for their goods and their lives, their lands and their religion, their absent ones, their present ones, and their relatives, their churches, and all that is in their hands, whether great or small," the chronicler Abu Yusuf recorded. "A bishop shall not be moved from his bishopric; nor a monk from his monastic life, nor a priest from his priesthood."[16] The Koran made it clear that Christians were closer to Moslems than other infidels. "Thou wilt certainly find nearest in affection to them that believe, those who say 'We are Christians'," it stated. "This is because some of them are priests and monks, and because they are free from pride."[17] Moslems had no interest in Christology or in persecuting schismatics; they insisted only on the *jizya,* and a Christian who apostatized was free even of that.

JIHAD

Arab columns moved swiftly on their light horses, their minimal impedimenta—dates, bread, oil, and water—carried on camels that were themselves eaten in crisis. Their invasions were carefully planned. Actions of small, separate forces were coordinated from Medina, with contact maintained by couriers on camelback who were expected to ride 400 miles in a week and 700 in a fortnight. The tribesmen were willing to attack in the early afternoon, the hottest part of the day. The desert frontiers of the empire and Persia were undefended because no invaders had come from there before. Khalid ibn al-Walid, the key commander in Iraq and Syria, marched for six days across the waterless country between them. Short of water-skins, he forced twenty camels to drink great quantities of water; then their mouths were tied to stop them from chewing cud that would spoil the water in their stomachs. Each night some of the camels were slaughtered, and the water extracted from their stomachs was enough for the column to reach a spring.

Justification was provided by jihad, the religious duty of "striving" against enemies of Islam practiced by the Prophet and enjoined in the Koran.[18] Iraq, with its Christian Nestorians, was rapidly overrun. In making peace with them, Khalid made it clear that they were not "to raise opposition, nor assist an unbeliever against a Moslem, whether Arab or non-Arab, nor disclose to them the vulnerable places of the Moslems. . . ."[19] All were given the choice of converting; when the people of Hira refused, he was meticulously fair in imposing the *jizya*. He made a head count of seven thousand men; on examination, he found a thousand of them to have chronic diseases. "I subtracted them from the total, so the number on whom the *jizya* fell was six thousand," he said. "And they made peace with me on the basis of 60,000 pieces of silver."

At the fall of Edessa, the Moslem commander, Iyad ibn Ghanm, "stood at its gate riding a brown horse; and the inhabitants made terms . . . that they should keep their cathedral and the buildings around it, and agreeing not to start a new church, to give succor to the Moslems against their enemy, and to forfeit their right of protection in case they failed to keep any of these conditions." The terms in the rest of Mesopotamia and Armenia were similar. In return for protection, the Christians (and Jews) paid the *jizya*. As a result, they could "enter no intrigue"; they could build no new churches; they could not "publicly strike clappers [the wooden boards used as church bells], or openly celebrate Easter Monday, or show the cross in public."[20] Christians were also obliged to guide Moslems who had lost their way, and to repair road and bridges.

But they were alive. A Nestorian chronicler speaks of the "uninterrupted evils and continual trials" that preceded the establishment of Arab rule. "And they demanded the *jizya* of the subject people, and they paid it," he continued with relief. "And they [the Arabs] treated them well. And affairs prospered by the grace of God most high." The longer-term effects, however, sprawled across a vast canvas stretching from the Indus to the Atlantic, were not so favorable to Christianity. Protected by the mountains of northern Iraq, the Nestorians remained strong enough to continue to send missions to China; the patriarch Ishu'yab III was able to write shortly after the conquest that the Arabs "have not attacked the Christian religion, but rather they commended our faith, honoured our priests and the saints of the Lord, and conferred benefits on churches and monasteries."[21]

In Mesopotamia, in the south, however, the fall in receipts of the *jizya* revealed a flood of apostasy. Under Omar, the second caliph who ruled from 634 to 644, the *jizya* was bringing in some 120 million dirhams a year; by the time of Abd al-Malik in 685, the amount had dwindled to 40 million. Thus about two-thirds of the population converted to Islam during the first fifty years of the conquest; Baghdad and Basra ceased to be Christian cities. Many of the remainder apostatized in the early eighth century. Although this coincided with the reign of the pious Omar II, taxation rather than coercion remained the root cause. Those who "have rushed headlong into the pit of faithlessness," an Iraqi Christian lamented, had not been threatened by "sword, nor fire, nor torture"; they were "captivated only by love for a moiety of their goods."[22] The long tradition of accepting death rather than apostasy was broken; "out of the many thousands who have the name of Christians," the chronicler continued, "not one single victim was consecrated unto God by the shedding of blood for the true faith."

Christian Arab tribesmen, whose knowledge of desert and oasis life gave them insight into Moslem tactics, suffered similar erosion. Muhammad had tolerated them; he was less favorable to the Jews after their rejection of his claim to supreme power in Medina, but a flourishing settlement of Jews in nearby Khaibar was allowed to retain its land on payment of tax. A few years after his death, however, the caliph Omar claimed that the prophet had wished to cleanse Arabia itself of nonbelievers. Omar "investigated until he found it certain and assured that the Prophet had said, 'There can be no two religions at the same time in the Arabian peninsula,'" the chronicler Abu Yusuf wrote. "Accordingly he expelled the Jews of Khaibar."[23] The Christians of the Banu Taghlib were proud of their Arab blood; they refused to pay the *jizya* like non-Arabs, but agreed to pay double the poor tax that Moslems paid. "And Omar made peace with them on the condition that they should not plunge into water [baptize] any of their children into Christianity," Abu Yusuf recorded, "and that their poor tax should be doubled . . . and that the *jizya* should not be charged to them."[24] It was an unusual concession, even if an eventual death sentence on their faith, and Moslem commanders did not like it. The prophet's cousin Ali complained that the tribesmen had broken their protection by illicit baptisms. "I would have my own way with them," he said. "Their fighters I would surely put to death, and their children I would take as captives, because by making their children Christians they violated the covenant and are no longer in our *dhimma*."

Other Christians left Arabia. Omar gave the leader of the Banu Ghassan, Jabalah ibn al-Aiham, three choices: Islam, *jizya*, or "going where thou willest." He opted for the last; "accordingly Jabalah left with 30,000 men to the land of the Greeks." He was apparently welcomed with honor by the Byzantines; the emperor Nicephorus I claimed nearly two centuries later than he was a lineal descendant of this Jabalah. Omar also expelled the Christians of Najran, granting them new lands in Iraq; they were "so numerous as to be considered by him a menace to Islam." Their bishop appealed to Omar's successor Uthman against their annual tax of two thousand robes; fine cloth could be substituted for cash. The caliph investigated, told the governor of Iraq that "they are included among the people entitled to our protection," and lowered their taxation by two hundred robes. Later they complained: "now we have still more decreased and become weaker"; they blamed "their dispersion, the death of some of them, and the conversion to Islam of others." The tax was reduced by a further two hundred robes. A new and tyrannical governor of Iraq, al-Hajjaj, raised the tribute back to eighteen hundred robes. In 717 they complained to the caliph that they were "in danger of extinction, that they were decreasing in number, that the continual raids of the Arabs overburdened them with heavy taxes for revictualling them, and that they suffered from the unjust treatment of al-Hajjaj." A census was taken and they were found to be reduced to one-tenth of their original numbers. Their tax was cut to two hundred robes; the Christian Arabs of Najran had been reduced from forty thousand to about four thousand in the space of some eighty years.

Christianity was not eradicated, however. It probably survived even in Yemen for some centuries, the Spanish traveler Ordeno de Cenaltos meeting Arabs in Morocco in the sixteenth century who told him that they were descended from Christians expelled from Arabia. Armenians and a minority of Iraqis cling to their faith today. Christians played a major part in Arab culture; they were the leading scholars at Dar al-Hikmah, the "house of wisdom" founded at Baghdad in 830, translating the great scientific and philosophical works of the Greeks into Arabic. The Nestorian Hunayn ibn Ishaq is said to have translated one hundred works before his death in 873; the caliph al-Mamun paid him a retainer of five hundred gold dinars a month. He was succeeded by his son and nephew; it was "through these and others that the miracle of the Greek mind was transplanted into Arabic literature. . . ."[25] In the tenth century an Arab writer[26] recorded fifty-three monasteries in Iraq; a geographer of the thirteenth century referred to a thousand monks living in the monastery of St. Matthew near Nineveh, a few miles from Mosul. But they were at the mercy of others; under the constant attrition of the *jizya*, punctuated by massacre, by Tamerlane's Mongols, by Kurds, and Ottoman Turks.

THE FALL OF JERUSALEM

As the Persian Empire collapsed, the Arabs turned on Byzantine Syria and Palestine in 633. They had only twenty-four thousand lightly armed men operating in four distinct forces. The imperial armies, weakened by the campaigns against the Persians, were concentrated on the coast and in the cities; the Arabs were largely undisturbed as they mopped up the tribes on the desert borders. One force, under the tough campaigner 'Amr ibn al-As, penetrated the Negev as far as Gaza in southern Palestine; a second column subdued the Quda'a tribes in Jordan, another advanced around the Dead Sea, while the fourth moved on the Golan south of Damascus.

The main Christian cities—Antioch, Damascus, Jerusalem, Gaza, Pella or Fahl, Philadelphia or modern Amman—were not at first touched. It took time for the Byzantines to recognize the threat; when they did, at Ajnadayn, eighteen miles southwest of Jerusalem, 'Amr's forces had been reinforced by fresh converts from Arabia. The Roman troops broke and fled in disorder to Fahl on the east bank of the Jordan. The Arabs were not skilled at siege warfare and it took them four months to take Fahl as the Romans fell back on Damascus. A relief column sent by Heraclius was destroyed before it could reach the city; the valley where the battle took place "was filled with fallen Byzantines, the ground was stinking with them."[27] The Arabs combined their forces outside Damascus. One general was said to have been negotiating a surrender at the Paradise Gate while another broke through the East Gate. In any event there was little bloodshed as the Moslems burst through to the covered market in the center of the city.

Heraclius, watching from Antioch with alarm, raised a force said to number 100,000, of whom 12,000 were Syrian Arabs of dubious loyalty. Commanded by a eunuch called al-Saqallar by the Arabs, and a Persian Christian general called Bahan, they marched south from Antioch. The Moslems, outnumbered by about four to one, abandoned Damascus and withdrew to the Golan. They were skillful riders and devoted to their horses—referring to them by color, marking, temperament, and name—but the Byzantine cavalry was heavier. When the Arabs were obliged to fight pitched battles, they chose positions which favored infantry and archers. A deep ravine scoured the ground in front of them at Yarmuk, where a decisive battle was fought in August or September 636. It started badly for them. Some of the few women who marched with the columns to tend to the wounded joined the fighting; this resolve—and a southerly wind that whipped up dust clouds in the face of the enemy—helped eventually to win the day. The Byzantines were broken, many of them dying in the ravine while trying to escape at night.

A laborious siege now took place at Hims. Heraclius was encouraged to learn that the Arabs lived on camel meat and camel milk, a diet he thought so poor that he hoped they would not survive the winter. "Do not fight them except on cold days," he ordered his troops, or so it was claimed.[28] Though the besieged Christians took comfort that the enemy was often barefoot, their own hunger and disease became so bad that "the feet of some fell off in their shoes."[29] Winter failed to lift the siege, and morale in the city broke when an earthquake shattered several buildings. It was taken as a divine punishment; they promptly "looked and called out: 'Peace, peace.'" They could opt either to pay a flat *jizya* of one dinar "forever, whether they were prosperous or not"; or payment according to ability, the tax rising or falling in line with their wealth. The city surrendered.

Islam had a moral force that served it well. "They are horsemen during the day and monks at night," an admiring ex-prisoner of the Moslems told Heraclius. He claimed that they paid for their meals and never entered a Christian house without a greeting of peace, though "they stand up to those who fight them until they destroy them." At Antioch, the next target, such behavior was contrasted by Michael the Syrian, a later Jacobite patriarch of the city, with that of Heraclius. The emperor had ordered that "anyone who would adhere to the Council of Chalcedon was to have his nose and ears cut off and his house pillaged. . . . It was no light advantage for us to be delivered from the cruelty of the Romans, from their wickedness, from their anger, from their cruel zeal towards us, and to find ourselves at rest."[30] As Antioch, too, surrendered, Heraclius left with the lament: "Peace be upon you, O Syria! This is a farewell that will have no reunion."

The Moslems were camped round Bethlehem by 637, cutting it off from Jerusalem and preventing the faithful from celebrating the Christmas Eve liturgy in the town of Jesus' birth. Patriarch Sophronius gave a Christmas Eve sermon, telling his congregation that "countless sins and serious faults" had made them unworthy to see the holy places of Bethlehem. "We are required to stay at home, not bound closely by bodily bonds, but bound by fear of Saracens,"* he said; "the slime of the godless Saracens" would evaporate in the face of Christian repentance, "their blood-loving blade will enter their hearts, their bows will be shattered. . . ." Soon, he promised, the Christians would embrace God-bearing Bethlehem, "dancing with lambs, shouting with the Magi, giving glory with the angels. . . ."[31] It was wishful thinking.

The fortifications had been repaired after the Persians had been driven off; the Arabs had no siege equipment beyond a few requisitioned ladders, their formidable horsemen were dismounted and made little impression, and their archers found few targets. But because the Moslems held the countryside and all the towns of Palestine and Syria except Caesarea, which was protected by the impe-

---

*Saracen, which comes from the Greek *Sarakenos,* was not generally used of Arabs—and then of all Moslems—until later.

rial navy, the city was beginning to go hungry. The nearest imperial army was in Egypt, where it was actively persecuting the Copts, its fellow Christians. There was no prospect of a relief column reaching Jerusalem. Thus Patriarch Sophronius, the chief magistrate, decided to surrender rather than risk an eventual massacre. No doubt he hoped that the occupation would be brief; the Persians' had lasted little more than a decade, and Caliph Omar's desert Arabs and their new religion cannot have seemed harbingers of permanent change.

The patriarch negotiated with Omar in person, riding out on his ass to the Mount of Olives to meet him. It was symbolic that the Christian should ride a humble ass, as Jesus had when he entered the city six centuries before; but when Muhammad had ridden into Mecca only a decade back, he had done so on his war camel at the head of ten thousand armed men. The advance of Islam was based on militancy, not humility. Christianity in its own distant infancy had been the martyred recipient of the sword, and it retained a submissive element; those facing the Persian butchers at Jerusalem had "rejoiced because they were being slain for Christ's sake . . . and took on themselves death for His death . . ."[32]

The entry of Caliph Omar into Jerusalem in 638. His conquests were greatly helped by bitter differences between the eastern churches, and by the generous Moslem treatment of the defeated Christians. As he surrendered the city, the weeping patriarch softly repeated Christ's words: "Behold the abomination of desolation, which was spoken of by Daniel the prophet, standing in the holy place." In five years, three of the five great Christian patriarchies—Antioch, Jerusalem, and Alexandria—were lost to Islam. The fourth, Constantinople, succumbed eight hundred years later. Only Rome remains under Christian control.

Christian heroes were for the most part passive victims of torture and execution; Moslem martyrdom involved active participation in battle. Muhammad had led the faithful in war; Moslems sensed a divine purpose in combat that Christian armies came eventually to emulate, but which was quite lacking among the demoralized imperial troops upon whom the first fury of the Islamic onslaught was breaking.

Omar's experience of Islam was immediate and intimate. Looking across the valley to the besieged city, he could see the site of Solomon's Temple and remember that the prophet had himself told him of his night journey there astride his magical mare al-Burak. He remembered, too, the prophet's instructions that *dhimmis* were entitled to protection. The surrender terms the caliph negotiated with the patriarch were later known as the Convention of Omar, and developed into the basis of the Moslem treatment of conquered Christians. "In the name of God, the Compassionate, the Merciful. This is a writing of Omar ibn al-Khattab to the inhabitants of the Holy House," a chronicler recorded.[33] "You are guaranteed your life, your goods, and your churches, which will neither be occupied nor destroyed, as long as you do not initiate anything blameworthy."

Christians could keep their churches and continue to worship in them, but they became inferior subjects, and visibly so. They paid the *jizya*. They were not allowed to ride horses, a social humiliation and a military precaution, for it was folly for a horseless people to contemplate revolt. Their church bells were tolled softly, if at all, lest they offend Moslem ears. No cross could be displayed in public; neither could a pig nor a glass of wine. No Christian building could be higher than those of Moslems, no pomp could accompany a Christian funeral. A Christian was required to respect the Koran and never speak ill of Islam or Muhammad; he was forbidden to marry or be intimate with a Moslem woman, or to try to apostatize a Moslem, or to help an enemy of Islam. Provided he kept to these ground rules, detailed by the writer al-Mawardi in the eleventh century but in force if not always respected from Omar onwards, the Christian enjoyed the protection offered to *dhimmis*. It was less generous than it might seem, of course. The *jizya* provided the money for further conquests, and for building mosques. The Dome of the Rock, for instance, the shimmering mosque soon built on the site of Solomon's Temple in Jerusalem, was said to have cost seven years' revenue from conquered Christian Egypt. Marriage supplied fresh Moslems. Few women accompanied the armies, and the men were encouraged to take local wives. A Moslem man might marry a Christian girl but not vice versa, and all children from such mixed marriages were brought up as Moslems.

But Sophronius could have expected no better terms; the Persians had massacred sixty thousand and sold half that number into slavery when they sacked the city in 614. The surrender was agreed upon; Omar kept his word that there

The Islamic invasions were a cataclysm. They created the Arab and Moslem world, severing the Mediterranean and destroying its historic Roman and Christian integrity. The eastern churches, the glory of Christendom, were isolated, and the mainstream of the faith was diverted westwards to the dark backwaters of barbarian Europe. Moslem domination of Jerusalem was symbolized by the mosque of the Dome of the Rock, seen here. Built on the site of Solomon's Temple, it was said to have cost seven years' tax revenue from the conquered Christians of Egypt.

would be no slaughter. Like Muhammad at Mecca, he rode into the city on his favorite white camel and went at once to the site of the temple. Sophronius watched and wept at the "abomination of desolation. . . ." (Matt. 24:15). The conqueror went next to the Church of the Holy Sepulchre. The time came for him to pray towards Mecca, and the nervous patriarch begged him to lay his prayer rug in the church, but Omar feared that his ardent troops would claim the church for Islam. He prayed in the porch, which indeed became a Moslem place. The church remained a Christian sanctuary.

The fate of cities that resisted the Arabs left little doubt that Sophronius was right to surrender. When Caesarea fell the following year, the Moslems put the defenders and thousands of civilians to the sword and "took the women and children captive and divided them amongst themselves, and made that city a desolation."[24] For well over two hundred years Christians remained a majority in Syria and Palestine; eight in ten Lebanese were Christian well into the twentieth century. The coastal cities retained their ecclesiastical and trading links with Constantinople and returned briefly to Christian rule under the Western crusaders. But the Christian cities of the plains of northern Syria, stretching eastward from Antioch toward Edessa and north to the edge of the Taurus Mountains, fell rapidly into decay as the great trade routes from East Asia, India, and Mesopotamia to Byzantium and Europe were cut by the new Arab empire. These cities' churches, ancient and magnificent, were silent and unrepaired, sagging amid "half-ruined walls, towers, arches, vaults, stone pavements, pillars, forums . . ."[35]

Constantinople itself barely survived the first onslaught; although an Arab blockage of the city was broken in 674, the remnants of the empire had to absorb continuous pressure. The Moslems had a dual view of the world. In their own lands, *dar al-Islam,* the non-Moslem People of the Book—Christians and Jews— enjoyed *dhimma.* Infidel territory, *dar al-harb,* was a region of war or potential war. Muhammad had ventured against the infidels at least once a year; campaigns against the Byzantines became a duty for which a schedule was laid down. "The spring expedition should take place after the horses have been given pasture, from 10 May to 10 June, when grass in enemy country is most plentiful," the chronicler Qaduma wrote. "The second or summer expedition begins on 10 July, when the horses have regained their strength and lasts sixty days. . . . The winter expedition . . . lasts only twenty days from the end of February into March. . . . the horses must carry provisions for themselves and their riders, but [it] has the advantage of catching the enemy at a weak moment."[36] Like tectonic plates, Christendom and Islam were to grind against each other ceaselessly, with wars erupting on their margins like seismic shocks on a fault line; the loss of Jerusalem was the symbolic opening to a process that continues. It broke Sophronius's heart; he died within a few weeks of surrendering the city.

THE CONQUEST OF THE COPTS

Egypt was next to fall. The Arab general 'Amr ibn al-As had seen its riches while leading trade caravans to the Nile Valley. Omar reluctantly gave him permission to invade it after the fall of Jerusalem. The caliph changed his mind after he had returned to Medina, and sent 'Amr a letter instructing him to turn back if he had not yet crossed into Byzantine territory. If the letter were late he could proceed, but the enterprise was so risky that the caliph assured his general that all Moslems would pray for divine intervention. 'Amr crossed the northern Sinai and reached the Egyptian frontier in December 639.

It was again Christian schism that helped 'Amr and his initial handful of four thousand horsemen subjugate the fairest province of Byzantium. Since Chalcedon, the bishopric of Alexandria had been split into two patriarchates; one Melchite, supported by the empire, and the other native Coptic, rejecting Greek suzerainty and Chalcedon. Heraclius created a compromise, monothelitism, to gloss over the bitter question of the single and dual natures of Jesus; it dwelt on the oneness of Christ's human and divine wills, identical, unchanging, harmonious. It was hoped that this would be acceptable to the monophysites, while not conflicting with the doctrine of the two natures held by the supporters of Chalcedon. It failed. The Copts were immediately hostile.

The man Heraclius chose to impose the new doctrine inflamed tensions in a land still devastated by the Persian invasion. Cyrus was plucked from an obscure bishopric in the Caucasus to become both the Melchite patriarch of Alexandria and the imperial prefect of Egypt. The powers of Church and state were combined in a cruel and devious personality. He arrived in Alexandria early in 631, using "the Cross as an iron mace to club native resistance"[37] to the new doctrine. Coptic prelates were pursued until they paid lip service to the imperial faith, fled, or were killed. The Coptic patriarch, Benjamin I, became a fugitive in obscure monasteries in the wild Thebaid. Cyrus martyred the patriarch's brother Menas; he "caused lighted torches to be held to his sides until the fat of his body oozed forth and flowed upon the ground, and knocked out his teeth because he confessed the faith, and finally commanded that a sack should be filled with sand, and the Holy Menas placed in it, and drowned in the sea."[38] Through the delta and the Nile Valley, sacred vessels were seized from Coptic churches. Samuel, an ascetic at the monastery of Qalamon in the wilderness of Arsinoe, was dragged from his hermitage in chains with a criminal's iron collar around his neck and taken to the city of Piom (modern Faiyum) to be scourged until devotees rescued his "mutilated body still wavering between life and death." Some bishops gave way to Cyrus. Most Copts retained their faith, however, and nourished their hatred of the empire.

When he reached the frontier town of al-Arish, 'Amr read the caliph's letter and rode on. By early 640 he had reached Pelusium, set in winegrowing country a mile from the Mediterranean at the northeast extremity of the Nile Delta. It was an important military town, the historic guardian of the eastern entry into Egypt. It had been known to the prophet Ezekiel twelve hundred years before as Sin; he had written of its role in God's vengeance upon Egypt at the hand of the "terrible of the nations" under the Babylonian king Nebuchadnezzar. "And I will pour my fury upon Sin, the stronghold of Egypt," he wrote of God's words. "And I will set a fire in Egypt; Sin shall be in great anguish . . . I shall break the yokes of Egypt, and the pride of her power shall cease in her!" (Ezek. 30:15–16). It took 'Amr two months to capture the frontier fortress. Egypt then lay open to the Arabs.

A month later the Byzantine garrison at Bilbais, east of the delta, surrendered with the loss of a thousand dead and three thousand captives. The major fortress of Babylon* or Old Cairo, built by Trajan more than five hundred years before and close to the site where 'Amr would soon start building a new Cairo, was beyond the Arabs. The countryside far to the south was soon subdued. The Chris-

---

*This had no connection with Assyrian Babylon, but was the Arabic corruption of Per-hapi-n-On, the "Nile City of On."[43]

tian chronicler of the fall of Egypt, John, bishop of Nikiu, makes clear that the Copts despised the "Romans," as they called the bickering Byzantines, to the point of betraying them to the "Ishmaelites," the term for desert-dwelling Arabs.* The "weakness of the Romans and the hostility of the people to the emperor Heraclius" caused by Cyrus's persecution was soon obvious to 'Amr; it made him, the bishop wrote, "bolder and stronger in the war."[39] Local levies frequently refused to fight the Moslems, and the Byzantine forces were slow-moving and prone to ambush. The bishop describes how the Arabs simply took to the desert when a force of horsemen and archers was sent against them. Waiting until the enemy was pinned on the banks of the Nile, "these Ishmaelites came and slew without mercy the commander of the troops and all his companions."[40]

The city of Bahnasa, about one hundred miles south of the Babylon fortress, was nearby. The Byzantine general John, duke of Barca, hid his horses and men in the date plantations and fields, but the Copts "informed the Moslem troops of the Roman troops who were hidden, and so these took them and put them to death."[41] A general named Leontius, who was "obese in person, quite without energy and unacquainted with warlike affairs," commanded the relief force sent south from Babylon.[42] He needed to act swiftly before the sowing season deprived him of local levies, who had to return to their fields lest famine be added to their woes. Time was squandered searching the Nile for the body of the drowned Duke John, which was eventually recovered in a net and returned to Constantinople. Leontius and many of the Byzantines returned to seek refuge in the Babylon fortress, while relations between the army commanders and the local governors deteriorated amid "great indignation."

By contrast, the bishop wrote, 'Amr showed "great vigilance and strenuous thought";[44] still grossly outnumbered, he pleaded with Omar for reinforcements and was sent several thousand fresh troops. Their morale was high. The Byzantine commanders never disclosed strategy or the imperial orders they received to their troops. 'Amr was open with his men. "Our leaders never kept secret from us the letters they wrote," the soldier Ziyad ibn Jaz reported;[45] he added that 'Amr discussed his own tactics and possible enemy reactions with them. He then divided his forces into three corps, which succeeded in trapping a Byzantine force between them. He seized Tendunias, or Umm Dunain, a town slightly south of Babylon; the garrison withdrew into the town fortress; witnessing a "great slaughter . . . they were seized with panic and fled by ship in great grief and sorrow."[46]

---

*The biblical Ishmaelites had lived in the northern Arabian deserts, from Lower Egypt to the Euphrates, and traced their ancestry through Abraham's son Ishmael. They are linked with the Midianites to whom Joseph was sold by his brothers.

The Byzantine garrison at Heliopolis, slightly to the north of Babylon, was routed, and a column reached south to Memphis.

Unnerved, Cyrus negotiated the handover of the Babylon fortress. In the peace treaty, 'Amr guaranteed not to interfere with the Christians' "religion, their possessions, churches, crucifixes, as well as their land and their waterways."[47] In return for this protection, they were to pay a *jizya** in three annual installments; the tax would be reduced in years when the Nile failed, but they were held responsible for any "robbers from among them." As a sweetener to Byzantines thinking of quitting the country, those who rejected the terms were given safe passage on their journey out of Moslem territory. The treaty was accepted; "then the horses were rounded up," for the Arabs were acutely sensitive to the risk of allowing any mobility to subject peoples.

The fortress surrendered on Good Friday, April 6, 641. A number of Copts had been imprisoned in the fortress by Cyrus; 'Amr released them. The Moslems had no interest in Christology. Omar was shrewd and realistic. Though the Arabs could replenish their ranks with converted Christians, they were outnumbered and had no experience of administering societies vastly greater and more complex than their own. "Take the interest of the Copts to heart," he directed in an order read out to Ziyad ibn Jaz and his fellow soldiers, "for the Messenger of God enjoined their best interests upon us, because they have ties of kinship with us and are therefore entitled to our protection."[48] It was debatable whether such blood ties existed—"it is truly a distant relationship," a Copt priest responded, although he did allow that the Arabians might be the descendants of a people once expelled from Memphis to "embark on a vagrant life"—but the Copts were reassured by the promise of peace.

Numbers of them were now converting; Bishop John was naturally less pleased about this than Ziyad ibn Jaz. "Many of the Egyptians who had been false Christians denied the holy faith and lifegiving baptism," he lamented, "and embraced the religion of the Moslem, the enemies of God, and accepted the detestable doctrine of the beast, that is, Mohammed. . . ."[49] Some of the apostates "took arms in their hands and fought against the Christians." The bishop gave the example of John, a monk from St. Catherine's Monastery in Sinai, who embraced Islam, and "quitting his monk's habit, took up the sword," persecuting those who remained faithful to Christ.[50]

Most retained their faith and paid tribute, and passive resignation often gave way to active collaboration. "People began to help the Moslem," the bishop noted;[51] they labored on a bridge that cut off river traffic and allowed the Arabs to cross their horses from bank to bank, and "so they effected the submission of the

---

*Put by the Arab chronicler Al-Tabari at an exaggerated figure of fifty million dirhams a year.

province." The Byzantine magistrates were put in irons. The following month the fortress at Niku was taken by storm and the garrison slaughtered as a warning of the futility of resistance. As the Arabs rode southward toward Alexandria in 642, the Byzantine prefect Domentianus abandoned his army and fled by boat down the Nile; his men threw themselves into the river, where they were slaughtered in the shallows. "A panic fell on all the cities of Egypt," the bishop noted, "and all their inhabitants took to flight, and made their way to Alexandria, abandoning all their possessions and wealth and cattle."[52] A "great strife" broke out between factions; some wanted to fight the Arabs, but the others who wished to join them benefited little, for "the Moslem distrusted them." 'Amr's horsemen reached Karium on the outskirts of Alexandria almost unopposed.

The great Mediterranean city could have resisted indefinitely. Its walls were stout and fortified with towers, and its garrison of 50,000 outnumbered the besiegers. It had open access to the sea; the Arabs had as yet no naval forces, and the city could be resupplied from Constantinople. Its population was 600,000, Greeks, Copts, Jews. It was said to have four hundred theaters, four thousand palaces, and as many public baths; its civilizing influence dated back almost a thousand years, and its Christianity for more than five hundred. The initial Arab assault failed before it reached the gates, for "stones were hurled against them from the top of the walls, and they were driven far from the city."[53]

To surrender lightly such a prize would be an act close to treachery. Nonetheless the city was split between "Blues," a faction loyal to the disgraced governor Domentianus, and "Greens" who supported the military commander. Fighting broke out between them in the besieged city; houses were burnt, property pillaged, and many were wounded. Cyrus provided the treachery. Heraclius had recalled him to Constantinople on suspicion of treason in his dealings with 'Amr. The emperor died in 641, however, of a fever said to have been brought on by the shame of Arab conquest and the guilt of his incestuous marriage to his sister's daughter. His son Constantine began vomiting blood and succumbed to his malady three months later. A weak and unpopular regime followed under the niece-widow, the empress-regent Martina, who was more concerned with avoiding assassination than the recovery of Egypt. Cyrus was ordered to return to Alexandria with the authority to sue for peace.

He left amid a fury of intrigue. A powerful group in Constantinople, backed by the clergy, rejected Martina and her children as "reprobate seed." Envoys were sent to Rhodes, where Cyrus's ship put in, to tell the troops sailing with him not to take sides with him. A message was sent to Alexandria—"and likewise to Africa, and to every province under the sway of Rome"—telling officials: "Do not hearken to the voice of Martina, and do not obey her sons."[54] The Copts and Jews were already hostile to the empire. Now, Bishop John recorded, some of the Romans themselves "gave over warring against the Moslem, and turned their hostilities against their own countrymen . . ."[55] The city was in no military danger when Cyrus arrived, though morally it was feverish for settlement. As the patriarch made his way to the great Church of the Caesarion, carpets were strewn in front of him and hymns chanted in his honor, the crowds swelling until "the people trod each other down." A few noticed that the wrong psalm was chanted at the service, and thought it an evil augury.

The first indication that the city was ready to capitulate came in a letter from "the ruler of Alexandria," presumably Cyrus; Ziyad was an eyewitness when 'Amr read it out to the troops. "If you want me to pay you the *jizya,* I am agreeable," it read, "on condition that you return to me all those people . . . whom you have captured."[56] Captive Christians had been sent to Medina, Mecca, and Yemen. 'Amr wrote to Caliph Omar for advice. "Upon my life," the caliph wrote, "a fixed *jizya* that comes to us, and will be coming to those Moslems who live after us, is in my view preferable to booty, which seems never to have existed once it is divided out." All those conquered were to be offered "the choice between Islam and the religion of their own people. Should anyone of them opt for Islam, then he belongs to the Moslems, with the same privileges and obligations as they. And he who opts for the religion of his own people has to pay the same *jizya* as his fellows." As for the captives who had been "scattered over Arabia," they would remain slaves.

Cyrus traveled to al-Fustat, 'Amr's camp on the edge of the desert near the Babylon fortress that became the basis of modern Cairo. "God has delivered this land into your hands," he told 'Amr. "Let there be no enmity from henceforth between you and Rome. Heretofore there has been no persistent strife with you."[57] By Rome, of course, Cyrus meant the empire and Constantinople; if there had been no drawn-out warfare, it was only because the Christians had succumbed so swiftly. The terms he agreed upon amounted to abject surrender; the city was sacrificed to guarantee the safety of its imperial masters. The Romans in Alexandria were to "carry off their possessions and their treasures and proceed home by sea," but no other Roman army was to return. As a guarantee of this, the Moslems were given 150 soldiers and 50 civilians as hostages. For their part, the Moslems were to "desist from seizing Christian churches and . . . were not to intermeddle with any concerns of the Christians." They also agreed to leave the city to its own devices for eleven months, an undertaking that was swiftly broken.

The troops and generals in the city were pleased enough to escape with their lives and their treasures, and paid homage to the patriarch on his return. The Alexandrines, however, were another matter. Cyrus had failed to tell them that he had agreed that they would pay a heavy poll tax of two gold dinars per adult and a large sum in gold to the Arabs. When 'Amr sent men to collect the tribute, the citizens prepared to attack them and sought to stone Cyrus. Army support settled the issue; Alexandria was surrendered on September 17, 642, and "the Moslems took possession of all the land of Egypt, southern and northern, and trebled their taxes."

❖ IT WAS AN extraordinary victory, but it was not yet definitive. 'Amr and his army seemed invincible on the march, the starkness of their message—"our Prophet informed us that we would conquer your lands"[58]—concealing their small numbers, and the dust and horses hiding their rags. They were much less impressive when static, and the Copts began to lose their awe. "How worn out these Arabs look, how little they take care of themselves," 'Amr was told they were saying; "people like us should not be obedient to people like them."[59] He responded with the guile and psychological insight that were essential to survive in an advanced position far beyond the natural limits of Arab power.

'Amr had several camels slaughtered and cooked in water and salt. He assembled his men, dressed in their shabby woolen cloaks and unarmed, and invited local Christians to join them for the meal. His troops ate "in typical Arab fashion, tearing at the meat with their teeth and slurping the broth,"[60] a sight so pitiful and uncivilized to the educated Christians that they "dispersed with their ambitions and courage boosted." The next day 'Amr ordered his men to dress in Egyptian clothes and again invited the Copts to eat with them. Instead of shabby wolves, the Christians saw "erect figures dressed in Egyptian colours, the Arabs eating Egyptian food, behaving in an Egyptian manner." They muttered that they had been made fools of.

A roll call of soldiers armed and in battle order was held on the third day. 'Amr explained his purpose to the Christians. He had wanted them to see how his Arabs "lived in their own country, then what they have come to in yours, and then how ready they are for war." He said that in their rough Arabian homeland they had determined to take Egypt, and how, when they had done so, they were willing to appropriate its customs. They were now committed to Egyptian customs and would not abandon them, "nor will they resume the lifestyle you saw depicted on the first day." This promise of assimilation was offset by the parade on the third day. "They have defeated you," 'Amr warned the Christians. "Warfare is their life." The moral went home; "the Arabs have smitten us," they acknowledged, "with this hero of theirs." When news of this perceptive ploy reached Omar, the caliph was delighted. "By God, 'Amr's campaign has become truly easy, no more attacks or assaults," he exclaimed. "He is indeed a crafty fellow!"

The Arabs were still spread thin and vulnerable to counterattack, the more so when 'Amr was recalled to Medina in 644. By then the Arab yoke on the *dhimmis* was said to be harsher than that of the Pharaohs. Former imperial prefects had been appointed to maximize revenue. These men "loved the heathens but hated the Christians." The Copts, living "under the constraint of an unceasing fear,"[61] were put to forced labor digging canals and taxed in foodstuffs, milk, honey, fruit, and leeks as well as gold and silver.

A new and more vigorous regime in Constantinople had deposed Martina. Cyrus, who had remained patriarch in Alexandria as part of his agreement with 'Amr, was "excessively grieved" to hear of the fate of his patroness; Bishop John claimed that her nose was cut off and that her son was castrated to prevent him from continuing the dynasty. The boy died under the knife, and the bishop thought that this was the punishment of a righteous God. An army was embarked at Constantinople aboard a fleet of three hundred sail to retake Alexandria. This was achieved with ease; the Arabs had too few men to garrison it, but it prompted the return of 'Amr. He intercepted and defeated the imperial army as it moved south toward Babylon. The survivors abandoned the city and sailed for Cyprus, and "thereupon 'Amr the chief of the Moslems made his entry without effort into the city of Alexandria."

This time the Arab occupation was permanent. The walls of the city were torn down to ensure that any seaborne troops who retook it would find themselves defenseless. Many of the Greeks fled with the fleet. 'Amr punished the Christians who remained by increasing the taxes from 22,000 to 32,057 gold dinars; amid mourning and lamentation, many hid themselves and some "even gave their children [into slavery] in exchange for the great sums which they had to pay monthly."[62] 'Amr himself claimed that no *dhimma* applied. "I am bound to none of the Egyptian Copts by covenant and contract," the chronicler Al-Baladhuri quotes him as saying "from the pulpit." He continued: "If I want I can kill; if I want I can take one fifth of the possessions; if I want I can sell captives." He said he could not do this with the people of Pentapolis because they "have a covenant which must be kept."[63]

✤ THE LOSS WAS a catastrophe. The number of monks in Egypt may have peaked at more than 100,000, in a population of 7.5 million. The Wadi al-Natrun region alone had over one hundred monasteries, the single diocese of Nikiu in the delta had seven hundred hermits. All missionary effort ceased; the Nubians and Ethiopians were left to their isolation. In the West, Christians converted their barbarian invaders; there was no prospect of this in the Arab empire, for to evangelize a Moslem was a crime punishable by death. The traffic in conversion was strictly one-way.

None of this was immediately apparent. The Copts were free to worship and their churches remained open. The Coptic patriarch Benjamin, a hunted fugitive for ten years under the Byzantines, was given safe conduct by 'Amr to resume his duties in peace. Thousands of monks, each carrying his staff, are said to have come out of their monasteries to welcome 'Amr as he passed on his way back from Alexandria. There was, indeed, something of a Coptic revival; they replaced Greeks in the administration as scribes and magistrates, and flourished as jewelers, smiths, engineers, and builders. Christian architects designed great mosques, using brick columns to avoid the usual practice of dismembering churches for their marble columns. A Christian was even to serve as viceroy of Syria.

But their numbers dwindled. Individual rulers could be brutal. Four centuries later, the caliph al-Hakim made Christians wear a five-pound cross around their necks, encouraged mobs to burn churches, and forbade women to appear on the streets, walling up the entrances to womens' bathhouses, entombing them alive. But al-Hakim was half-mad, and usually Copts "were preserved as a fine source of revenue."[64] The *jizya* was again an engine of conversion; where 'Amr raised twelve million gold dinars, this had dwindled to three million by the ninth century, and provincial governors sometimes intervened to slow the rate of conversion in order to protect their revenues.

Language also played a part in boosting Islam. Arabic became the official state language in 705, which, since it was also the language of the Koran, helped expose Egyptians to Islam. Coptic was slowly extinguished as a spoken tongue, surviving only in Church liturgy. The decline was slow; by 1075 the Nitrean wilderness still supported 737 monks, down from five thousand before the conquest, but still a significant number. The great festivals of the Church were celebrated by large crowds in medieval times: the caliph and his harem attended the torchlit Epiphany on the Nile, with its gaily decorated boats from which Copts took their annual dip in the river; the Nauruz, the Coptic New Year, was a general public holiday marked by banquets and new clothes; lanterns hung over many Cairo doors at Christmas, while families feasted on fish and sweetmeats; at the Feast of St. George the Martyr, the saint's remaining relic, his finger, was still dipped into the Nile at a service to ensure that the river's life-giving flood would take place. The chain of patriarchs remains unbroken from St. Mark to the present day, but the number of Nitreal monks had fallen to 201 by 1924, and today only a remnant of the hundred thousand remains.

The Copts had no doubts in identifying the guilty. Patriarch Benjamin toured the churches of Alexandria shortly after 'Amr's triumphant entry. "And everyone said," Bishop John wrote, "'This expulsion of the Romans and victory of the Moslem is due to the wickedness of the emperor Heraclius and his persecution of the Orthodox through the patriarch Cyrus. This was the cause of the ruin of Egypt and the subjugation of Egypt by the Moslem.'" Christology was identified as the reason for God's vengeance. "All these things fell out," the bishop continued, "because they divided Christ into two natures . . . they divided the indivisible." The great Coptic Church was left to its indivisibility and monophysitism. A sizable community remained on an axis from Luxor to Alexandria, but it enjoyed its faith by the sufferance of Islam and in isolation from Western Christendom.

AFRICAN AND IBERIAN CATACLYSM

The empire still held the territories of ancient Proconsular Africa, stretching along the southern Mediterranean shore to the Atlantic. The population is put by modern demographers at two million, and of these the large majority, about 1.5 million, were Christians.[65] The eastern section of modern Libya, Barca to Christians, the Arabs called Barqa; the lands beyond, arcing out from Carthage, they knew as Ifriqiya. From here St. Victor had sailed for Rome to become the first pope to write in Latin rather than Greek. At his death in 198, Tertullian was writing his *Apologeticum* in Carthage and laboring to build the African Church. At Carthage, St. Cyprian had backed his stand against apostate Christians with his own martyrdom in 258; and here, at Hippo, St. Augustine had written his *City of God* after the sack of Rome more than two centuries before.

In what is now Tunisia, Algeria, and Morocco, an ancient bastion of the faith had been softened up by schism and heresy. No remnant was to survive. Augustine's ferocious resolve against apostasy had prevailed against the Vandal Arian heretics, but it did not withstand the Moslems.

Vandal power had gradually decayed. The emperor Justinian dispatched a Byzantine force under the great general Belisarius that restored the North African provinces to the empire in 535; the last Vandal king, Gelimer, was exhibited in the triumphal procession at Constantinople. The Arians and Donatists were now persecuted in their turn, together with the Jews; their churches were closed, gatherings and cultic acts forbidden. The pope congratulated Justinian for his ardor. A further bout of Christological strife followed, this time over the "Three Chapters";* Justinian had Pope Vigilius brought to Constantinople in 548 to personally sign a condemnation of Theodore of Mopsuestia as a heretic. Theodore had

---

*Three subjects were condemned by Justinian in an edict of 543–44: the person and work of Theodore of Mopsuestia, the writings of Theodoret against Cyril of Alexandria, and a letter from Ibas of Edessa to Maris. Theodoret had written a polemic in which he maintained a duality in Christ and accepted the title Theotokos, or "God-bearer," for the Virgin Mary only in a figurative sense. Ibas was the mid-fifth-century bishop of Edessa who had tried to create a Christological compromise which Justinian rejected. The letter of Ibas was 110 years old; and Theodoret had abandoned the stance taken in his polemic 95 years before. Antiquity, however, did not dull the passions of Christology.

been dead for 115 years; his offense had been to deny that Old Testament prophecies and psalms about the Messiah were predictions of Christ, and to maintain that the Song of Songs was a love poem rather than a forecast of the union between Christ and Church. Justinian's edict aroused strong opposition in North Africa. The pope was in no position to resist; two years before, Goths had broken into Rome, smashing the aqueducts and deporting the citizens, and for forty days the city had been "given up to the wolf and the owl." In 550 the Synod of Carthage withdrew its Communion from Pope Vigilius and formally protested to Justinian. The emperor responded by banishing the bishop of Carthage.

Some progress was made in converting the pagan tribes on the frontiers. The Moorish tribes of southern Tripolitania and those in the Fezzan area of southwest Libya were converted. Missionaries worked tribes of the Girba Oasis and those in the slopes of the Aurès Mountains in the south of Byzacena. Bishops from the extreme west of Mauretania, close to the Atlantic, traveled to Carthage for synods. But the spiritual and cultural ties between North Africa and the empire, broken by the Vandals, had lost their old intimacy. Arianism persisted among the peasants and Berber nomads as an alternative to imperial Catholicism because it was simpler and easier to grasp. Vandal inscriptions made no reference to the Trinity; Jesus was not bafflingly coequal or coeternal with the Father, but was identified as a "great tribal leader, healer, commander, and historical figure, a man manifested as the Son of God."[66] Islam did not shatter the fundamentals of Arian faith. In Muhammad, it superimposed on a human Jesus its own newer and more potent prophet.

The Moslems began to push westward from Alexandria in 647. At first they were content to raid and withdraw after levying tribute. But Byzantine rule was weak, plagued by rebellious governors; stiffer resistance came from the Berber tribes who themselves were formidable raiders, but their Christianity was an imperial imposition and often shallow, and they had a natural affinity to the Arabs as fellow nomads and desert dwellers. Despite his small column—four hundred cavalrymen and a supply train of the same number of camels carrying two large water bags apiece—the commander Uqba ibn Nafi al-Fihra often found it unnecessary to fight. The Arabs' reputation had preceded them, and he had a unique way of reinforcing it.

Agreeing to a peace treaty at a settlement called Waddan, the chronicler Ibn 'Abd al Hakam reported that Uqba sent for the local leader and cut off his ear. The latter asked why he had been so treated when he was on the point of making peace. "It will be a lesson to you," responded Uqba. "Every time you go to touch your ear, you will remember that it is useless to try to fight Arabs."[67] North Africa was slaving country, and he exacted 360 slaves as tribute. He repeated the process at Fazzan. He camped six miles outside the town. The town governor rode out to surrender; Uqba sent an escort to force him to dismount. The man was exhausted and sickly, perhaps tubercular for he was spitting blood. He complained that, since the town had submitted, the loss of his ear was misplaced. "It is a lesson," came the stock reply, "and when you remember it, you will not be tempted to fight Arabs." After extracting a tribute of slaves, Uqba continued his drive westward.

The Arabs knew little of the lands into which they were moving. The speed of their advance obliged them to get information on what lay ahead from those they had just conquered. At Fazzan, Uqba asked the locals simply: "Is there still anything out there?" They replied: "Yes, the people of Khawar."[68] This was the main town of the Kuwwar region, a large fortified area on a mountain at the entry to the desert. Uqba reached it after a fourteen-night march. He blockaded it unsuccessfully for a month, and then turned to raiding fortified farms. At each, he taught his familiar lesson to whomever appeared to be the leader by cutting off his finger. When the Fazzan guides reached the limit of their familiarity with the terrain, he retraced his steps. He passed close by Khawar and continued back for three days. The inhabitants, thinking that they were now safe from him, opened the gates. Uqba had exhausted his water supply; his horse fell to its knees. In one of those miracles attributed to both Christian and Muslim commanders, the chronicler says that he struck a rock and water flowed from it. The place was named Ma' Faras, the Water of the Horse. Uqba turned back for Khawar by a different route, moving stealthily. He stormed the town in a surprise night attack, "carrying off all the children and riches." The young Berber slave girls, the poet Nucaib said, were so beautiful that "some are certainly worth a thousand dinars." Uqba laid out a town at Qayrawn, choosing a spot, the chronicler wrote, of thickets with "beasts of prey and snakes . . . God, Almighty and Great, summoned them . . . they all fled and the beasts of prey carried off their cubs."[69] Uqba built a mosque so that it could serve as a religious center to convert tribesmen as well as a military camp.

As mobile as the Arabs, and knowing the terrain well, the Berbers could be a formidable foe. Uqba was rash; it was said that he would "enter Paradise in the saddle and fully armed,"[70] and that Arab warriors would go "anywhere where there was water."[71] Pushing too far, he was ambushed in 682 and killed with all his men. Another commander, Hassan ibn an-Numan, led a column ten years later against a formidable Berber queen, Kahina, who controlled a large area of Ifriqiya. The Moslems were routed at a battle on the Nahr (river) al-Bala; although Hassan escaped, many were killed and eighty were taken prisoner. The queen freed all of them—or so the chronicler claims—except a young Arab called Khalid ibn Yazid, whom she kept as an adopted son. He was able to smuggle notes on Berber deployments to Hassan concealed in loaves of bread and a saddle. As Hassan closed on her encampment with a fresh force, she asked her men what they saw on the horizon. "Some red clouds," they said. "No, by God, it is the dust kicked up by Arab horses," she said, adding to Khalid: "I am going to die."[72] The battle took place at the foot of a mountain, the chronicler wrote: "Kahina perished, with all her men, and the place was called Bi'r al-Kahina."[73] Hassan then imposed taxes on the "foreigners living in Ifriqiya, and on the Berbers who, like them, professed Christianity."

The Byzantines did little to hold the cities. It was only when Carthage was about to fall in 697 that the emperor Leontius sent a fleet under the *patricius* Johannes. He "forced open the harbour's chain, routed his opponents, and drove them away," the chronicler Theophanes recorded.[74] The Arabs returned in 698. The city surrendered and Johannes sailed for Constantinople to plead with the emperor for reinforcements. He had got no further than Crete, however, when the army was "suborned by its officers"; "afraid and disgraced," they tried to deflect from their failure with "a wicked plot" to overthrow their commander.[75] The leading Christians in the city fled to Spain, Sicily, Italy, and Constantinople. Resistance west of Carthage through to the Atlantic was swiftly broken. By 709 all the North African provinces of the empire—Cyrenaica and the Pentapolis, Tripolitana, Byzacena, Africa Proconsularis, Numidia, and Mauretania, embracing modern Libya, Tunisia, Algeria, and Morocco—had fallen. Islam was also becoming a sea power and winning control of the western Mediterranean.

As nomads, the Berbers were a particular target for conversion. They were offered allegiance status, which allowed them to retain their own leaders. Groups of Moslem teachers were sent from Egypt to instruct them in their new faith. Apparently they did their work well, for the bulk of the Moslems who now swept on to Spain were Berber converts. They arrived in the Visigothic kingdom by Christian invitation. The monarchy was weak and unstable, and opponents of King Roderick sought help from the Arab leader Tarik. He crossed the straits from North Africa in 711, landing with twelve thousand men at a place from then on known as the Gebel-Tarik, the Rock of Tarik, Gilbraltar.* He was followed a year later by another large force under Musa, the Moslem governor of Mauretania. The Spaniards called the Berbers *moros,* Moors. They were "dressed with silk and black wool that had been forcibly acquired; their black faces were like pitch . . . their horses fast as leopards and their knights more cruel than a wolf in the midst of a herd of lambs at night . . ."[76]

The tactics were familiar. Musa dealt ruthlessly with resistance; "he ruined beautiful cities with fire; he condemned lords and powerful men to the cross. . . ."[77] But for those who accepted his "evil and fraudulent peace"—pay-

---

*Tarik is said to have burned the ships provided to him by the Spanish rebels after arriving at Gibraltar. "Whither can you fly?" he told his men. "The enemy is before you and the sea behind you."

ment of the *jizya* and acceptance of inferior status—he "granted their requests without delay." He rapidly took Toledo, the royal capital, where the widow of King Roderick became one of his wives, and by 720 the Moslems had crossed the Pyrenees into Gaul. A force under 'Abd ar-Rahman defeated the duke of Aquitaine on the banks of the Garonne and seized Bordeaux; the campaigning was brutal, and "the unbelieving Saracen people . . . burnt down the churches and slew the inhabitants."[78] Poitiers held out against them, though they burnt the basilica of St. Hilary* outside the walls. Advancing toward Tours in October 732, they were met at the confluence of the Chair and Vienne Rivers by an army hastily raised by Charles, ruler of the Franks. "With Christ's help he overran their tents," a chronicler recorded, "following hard after them in the battle to grind them small . . . scattering them like stubble before the fury of his onslaught."[79] 'Abd ar-Rahman was killed; "in the power of Christ Charles utterly destroyed them."

Poitiers decisively checked the Islamic advance into Western Europe. It took place one hundred years after the death of Muhammad. Charles was to be known as "Martellus," "the Hammer." He drove the Moslems out of Burgundy and Languedoc, and his grandson Charlemagne was to become Christian emperor of the West. Resistance in Spain was rekindled; despite harsh punishment—crucifixion, the public display of corpses, denial of burial—some accepted martyrdom and others "fled to the mountains where they risked hunger and various forms of death." The first stirrings of the *reconquista* were soon evident.

In North Africa, however, the old faith was extinguished. The remnants of the "Rum," as the Arabs called the Byzantine officials, traders, and craftsmen in the cities, and the *frarij,* the Romanized peasants, were slowly converted. Carthage was still sending a bishop to Rome to be consecrated in 990; the last letter written by a pope to the bishop of Carthage was in 1076. But the Norman conquest of Sicily, and the killing of many Moslems during the campaign from 1072 to 1091, led to reprisals in North Africa. The final devastation took place under ibn Tumart, a self proclaimed Mahdi-Messiah, who overran the Maghreb in the mid-twelfth century; fiercely Islamic, he razed the see of Carthage and forced the remaining believers into exile or apostasy.

Christians disappear from recorded history in Libya in 1049, in Tunisia in 1091, in Algeria in 1150, in Morocco in 1300.[80]

❖   NUBIANS HELD OUT much longer. Their three kingdoms, Nuba, Maqurra, and Alwa, ran along the Nile from the first cataract at Syene, or Aswan, to the con-

---

*A fourth-century bishop of Poitiers, noted for his attacks on Arianism; his feast day is January 13, and the Oxford term and English law sittings that begin then each year still bear his name.

fluence of the White Nile and Blue Nile at Khartoum and beyond. The first Arab assault in 651 imposed an annual tribute of 360 slaves on the Nuba kingdom, but it was paid only intermittently and the Nubians often made sorties into southern Egypt. An embassy sent by the caliphate to George, the king of Nubia, in 969, invited him to accept Islam and resume the tribute; his refusal passed unpunished. The Crusaders dreamed of linking with the Nubian Christians against Islam; although Saladin's brother invaded in 1173, the kingdoms survived. By then, Maqurra was said to have seven bishoprics, while Alwa had four hundred churches.

A refusal by King David of Nuba to pay tribute to the Mamluk sultan Baybars in 1272 led to more serious problems, as the sultan's troops imposed a treaty extracting one gold dinar for every adult male Christian. The sultan's successor Qalaun occupied the important Nile town of Dongola in 1298; his son al-Nasr Muhammed campaigned in Nubia in 1315 and 1316, putting a nephew of King David on the throne. The puppet king, Abdallah ibn Sanbu, apostatised to Islam.

Most Nubians remained Christian, but a Moslem principality established at Aswan in Nubia was opened to Arab settlers. The Moslem inroads in the north were matched by Fung blacks who attacked the southern Nubian kingdom of Alwa from the upper reaches of the Nile. By 1390, Nubians were pinned between the Fung kingdom of Sennar on the Blue Nile and Arabs moving downstream from Dongola. The last reports of the Christians of Nubia came from Portuguese sailors on the Red Sea in the sixteenth century. Francisco Alvares, a priest who reached the court of the Ethiopian emperor Lebna Dengel in 1520, witnessed the last emissaries of Christian Nubia vainly plead with the emperor to send them priests to sustain their dying faith.

Further to the south, isolated among its mountains and escarpments, the Ethiopian Church disappeared from contact with Western Christendom until the fifteenth century. Its devotion during the long silence is shown by the churches built by the pious King Lalibela in the twelfth century, hewn from the living rock, with rows of columns and capitals, apses and domes, and colossal crosses in bas-relief and haute. Persistent rumors of its survival were confirmed by the arrival of Ethiopian delegates to a Catholic council at Ferrara in 1438, to the curious astonishment of Europe. Fifty years later, Portuguese sailors landed on the coast of the Red Sea to report on Ethiopia's ancient rites: girls with the cross tattooed on their forehead; its annual 250 days of fasting, when no food could be taken until the third hour of the afternoon; the dabtera chanters at services; the Jewish practices of circumcision and a Saturday Sabbath; the beauty of its miniatures and icons, painted in reds, azures, deep browns, and gold.

A Moslem attempt to eradicate Christianity from Ethiopia began in 1528 under an emir and imam known as Grãn, "the Left-Handed." His armies destroyed almost every church—as they sacked the church of Makana-Selassie, or

Holy Trinity, in Wollo, its nave full of gold and silver plaques set with pearls, he remarked that nowhere else were there "such figures and works of art"[81]—and massacred or forcibly converted much of the population.

Four hundred Portuguese volunteers from an Indian Ocean expedition set out on a crusade to the Ethiopian highlands in 1541. The Portuguese, under Christofe da Gama, at first did well, forcing Grān's troops down towards the Red Sea. Moslem reinforcements then tipped the balance. Grān had da Gama martyred, stripped, whipped, beheaded, and quartered before Portuguese survivors linked up with the Ethiopians to avenge da Gama by killing Grān and finally expelling the last Moslems from the mountainous empire.

Portuguese navigators found another exotic survivor from Islam, the Christians of the island of Socotra. Far offshore in the Indian Ocean, almost six hundred miles east of Aden, Socotra was known to the ancients as the Island of Bliss, renowned for its rare plants and aromatic trees. It had valleys of frankincense trees with clusters of bloodred flowers and myrrhs and tamarinds. Dragon's blood trees perched like giant umbrellas on its mountain slopes, from which was extracted the cinnabar resin used as a lacquer for musical instruments. Its native birds included the *rukh,* which was said to carry Sinbad in the *Arabian Nights.* It is possible that St. Thomas visited the island on his way to Malabar and left Christians behind him, and certain that Christian Aksumites from Ethiopia seized the island in 525. Nestorians fleeing Byzantine persecution settled on the island, and by 600 it supported a bishop who was subordinate to the Nestorian patriarch. It survived the initial surge of Islam, although Moslems from the Euphrates valley emigrated there in the ninth century. Marco Polo may have visited the island in about 1294. "All the people, both male and female, go nearly naked, having only a scanty covering before and behind," he wrote. "Their religion is Christian, and they are duly baptized, and they are under the government, as well temporal as spiritual, of an archbishop, who is not in subjection to the pope of Rome, but to a patriarch who resides in the city of Baghdad. . . ." This indicated that the Socotrans remained Nestorian. Marco Polo said that they "deal more in sorcery and witchcraft than any other people"; the archbishop excommunicated those caught practicing magic, but they took little account of this.

Moslems from Yemen did not take the island until 1480. The Portuguese captured it in 1507, and though they remained for only three years, Christian missionaries were allowed to practice there for a further sixty years. A curious mixture of Christianity, Islam, and a moon cult survived well into the nineteenth century. "The people still maintained a perfect jumble of rites and ceremonies, sacrificing to the moon, circumcising, and abominating wine and pork," Padre Vicenzo, a Carmelite, wrote. Each day they anointed the altars in their dark and dirty churches with butter. Their priests were called *Odambo;* they carried a cross and a candle in processions and held services three times a night as well as by day. The dead were deposited in family caves. All the women were named Maria. The sorcery remarked on by Marco Polo had developed a darker side. "If the rain failed," Vicenzo reported, "they selected a victim by lot and prayed round him to the moon, and if this failed they cut off his hands." Early in the twentieth century, islanders still prayed with their backs to Mecca, and in their native Socotri rather than in Arabic; but orthodox Islam slowly eradicated the last traces of the moon cult and Christianity.

Other reports of Christians evangelized by Nestorians deep in Central Asia and China filtered back to medieval Europe to feed the legends of Prester John. The chronicler John of Marga wrote that the Nestorian patriarch Timothy sent eighty monks to Turkestan in the eighth century, including a metropolitan who based himself at Samarkand, and bishops at Bukhara and Tashkent. The Nestorians pushed on toward Lake Baikal in Siberia and preached to Tartar tribes, Keraits, Uighurs, Naimans. In 1077 the patriarch was told of the miraculous conversion of a king of the Keraits with two hundred thousand of his people. Marco Polo, on his great journey two hundred years later, reported finding a church in the Kerait capital of Karakorum. Christian cemeteries have been found in the province of Semiryechensk in southern Siberia; inscriptions in Syriac mention bishops and their wives, priests, and generals, and show an ethnic mix—"Terim the Chinese," "Tatta the Mongol," "Banus the Uigurian."[82] The last recorded date is 1345. Within fifty years Tamerlane had overrun Transoxiana and Central Asia, and Nestorian Christianity was obliterated.

The first Nestorian mission to China arrived in 635. A millennium later Jesuit missionaries found a great stone monument at Tsinan in Middle China commemorating the "propagation of the Luminous Religion," as Christianity was called; it said that the "polished Emperor," Tsai-tsung, had received a "Persian monk of high virtue who carried the true Scriptures." In an edict of 638 the emperor stated that: "We find this religion excellent and separate from the world, and acknowledge that it is quickening for mankind and is indispensable. It succors living beings, is beneficial to the human race and is worthy of being spread all over the Celestial Empire."[83] A monastery was built for the monk Alopen and for twenty monks; within fifty years they had spread the faith in ten provinces. A diocese was later established at Cathay in North China; a Nestorian in Kublai Khan's household, Mar Sergius, ruled over the province of Kansu and built seven monasteries in 1281. Christians were much in demand as physicians, scribes, and craftsmen at the Mongol court. Rabban Sauma, the metropolitan of Khan Baliq, was sent on a diplomatic mission to Europe by the khan in 1287, visiting Constantinople, Rome, Paris, and Bordeaux, and meeting the pope and the kings of England and France. When a Roman cardinal said that it was strange for a Christian to act as ambassador for the Mongol khan, Sauma replied that Nestorians had taught the gospel to Mongols, Turks, and Chinese, and that "many of the sons of the Mongol kings and queens have been baptized and confess Christ."[84] He was allowed to celebrate Mass at St. Peter's in Rome on Passion Sunday in 1288. A large congregation gathered to see the exotic Mongol envoy, and people cried: "The language is different but the rite is the same."[85]

The Church had a last flowering under Kublai Khan's successors. Sauma's appearance in Rome spurred the pope to send out a lone missionary in 1289. John of Monte Corvino arrived in China three years later, the first Catholic priest to set foot there. He was allowed to build a church in the imperial city of Peking. The emperor was so enraptured by the chanting of the choir that he permitted another to be built by the gates of his palace. By 1305, John reported that he had baptized six thousand people and would have had many more but for Nestorian jealousy. He said that the Nestorians claimed that "I was a spy, magician and deceiver of men,"[86] and that they bribed officials to turn against him. "If I had but two or three comrades to aid me, it is possible that Emperor Cham would have been baptised by now," he wrote to the pope in January 1305. "I ask then for such brethren to come, if any are willing. . . ."[87] Clement V commanded the minister-general of the Franciscans to choose seven brothers, who were to be made bishops and to go to China to consecrate Friar John as archbishop and patriarch of the East. Three survived the journey, arriving in Peking in 1308 and consecrating John as archbishop. They were given money by the emperor to build churches and monasteries; at John's death in 1328, his Franciscan companions claimed that only the Nestorians had prevented him from converting the whole country. No doubt that was exaggerated—most of the converts were drawn from the foreign mercenaries who had flooded into China after the Mongol invasions—but the archbishop was buried in Peking "with great honour, after the manner of faithful Christians."

The success was short-lived. A time of troubles and rebellion swept over China; churches were destroyed and priests and bishops killed. Persecution was pitiless after 1356, when the rebel Chu Yuan-chang seized power and founded the Ming dynasty. By 1400 the Christian community in China had ceased to exist.

"a slave in christ for foreign people":

The Pagan Conversions

espite Pope Martin's lonely and humiliating death in the Crimea, the papacy was key to the future of the faith in the West. In the troubled years before the Islamic conquests, Gregory the Great had set about defining its authority and purpose, defiant and cajoling, converting papal pretension into fact. At his death in 604 the papacy was still vulnerable; but it had acquired the aura of a great power in the making, and missions had begun to the violent and pagan backwaters of Europe that would in part compensate the faith for its grievous losses to the Moslems.

Gregory had inherited a wounded office in a collapsing city. The Byzantine effort to recover Italy from its Gothic masters took much longer than the lightning campaigns against the Vandals in North Africa. War and plague carried off a third of the population. The survivors were hounded by the "scissor-man," the chief Byzantine tax collector, to pay for the doubtful privilege of their liberation. Floods, bitter winters, and failed harvests brought hunger, and venal officials from Constantinople scooped up the plum posts in the imperial administration. The political capital remained at Ravenna, as it had under the Goths; in the basilica of San Vitale the icons of Justinian and his empress Theodora, the actress daughter of a circus bear trainer, bore witness to the spiritual majesty of the emperor and the irrelevance of the pope.

Papal prestige had collapsed during the miserable affair of Vigilius. Silverius, the candidate of the Gothic king, had become pope in 536. Belisarius, the Byzantine general, retook Rome at the end of the year. Prompted by Theodora, he arrested Silverius on false charges of plotting to open the gates of the city to the Goths. Vigilius, a papal envoy who had insinuated himself into Theodora's confidence while in Constantinople, was elected in his place. Silverius was banished to the island of Palmaria where he died of neglect and starvation, in effect murdered by his successor. Vigilius himself was kidnapped by Justinian in 545; he was seized while presiding over the festival of St. Cecilia and put aboard a ship for Constantinople, the Roman crowd jeering and throwing stones from the dockside. Once in the imperial capital, Vigilius was pressured into accepting imperial Christology. When this caused fury in the West, Justinian allowed him to withdraw his judgment but extracted a secret promise from him that he would resume his opposition if the climate improved. It did not, and Vigilius tried to curry Western favor by excommunicating the patriarch of Constantinople. Seeking sanctuary from Justinian's wrath in the church of the imperial palace, the pope clung pitifully to the altar as palace guards tried to drag him away by his robe and beard. Onlookers rescued him as the altar collapsed. Justinian revealed the secret assurances that Vigilius had made on the Three Chapters. The pope's reputation for treachery was confirmed and he was put under house arrest; his subordinates were imprisoned or sent to the mines, and the emperor wrung further shameful concessions from him before he was allowed to return to Rome. He died of gallstones on the journey.

Memories of Vigilius, however, lingered. Thirteen hundred years later his example was raised at the First Vatican Council by opponents of the new doctrine of papal infallibility, who argued in vain that he proved that a pope could be driven less by wisdom than by caprice and perfidy. To his contemporaries, the disgrace Vigilius brought to the Holy See was mirrored by the state of Rome itself. Its population, 800,000 in A.D. 400, had shrunk with the early barbarian onslaughts to 500,000 by the year 500; after the Goths broke into the city in 546, smashing the arches of the aqueducts that fed its cisterns and fountains, only 30,000 remained in the ruins. The Tiber rose in the winter of 589; foul waters coursed round the Capitol and spoiled the grain stores, and the surrounding plain was reduced to malarial swamps. Gregory's predecessor Pelagius died in the resulting plague and famine.

Gregory was born in about 540 to a devout and patrician Roman family. His great-grandfather had been pope, his widowed mother became a nun, and two of his aunts claimed to have had visions of their papal forebear. Gregory's own faith, revealed in his *Dialogues,* with their stories of the lives and miracles of Italian saints, was open to mystery and marvels. He stamped Catholicism with its cults of saints and relics, its fear of demons, and its respect for austere monastic virtue. As a young man he served as the Roman *praefectus urbi,* the senior civic official; he resigned when in his early thirties and sold off his estates. Some of the money went to the poor; with the rest he founded six monasteries in Sicily and converted the family palace on the Caelian Hill into a seventh, which he entered as a monk.

The Church needed his administrative genius, however, and he left the ob-

"The world grows old and hoary," Gregory the Great wrote after he became pope in 590, "and hastens to approaching death." He inherited a wounded office in a collapsing city, but he restored dignity to both with courage and administrative genius. His writing—he is seen in his scriptorium in this ivory carving—encompassed the dogmatic system of the modern Church. He completed Church ritual and systematized the Gregorian chant. He sent missions to convert England and the Arian Gothic kingdom of Spain.

scurity of the cloister to work as one of the seven deacons of Rome, and then as papal envoy to the imperial court at Constantinople. An agile diplomat, he stood as godfather to the son of the new Emperor Maurice but remained unmistakably Roman. He refused to learn Greek and mistrusted Eastern theology and rites. "How anyone can be seduced by Constantinople and how anyone can forget Rome," he wrote, "I do not know."[1] Constantinople was patently superior, in wealth, security, achievement, and sophistication, but Gregory did not falter in his devotion to the faded glories of his impoverished birthplace. Neither did he succumb to the pleasures of the imperial court. He maintained a monastic rigor in his legation, writing the *Moralia,* a commentary on the Book of Job shot through with moral zeal. Returning to his monastery in Rome, he reluctantly accepted to become pope in 590. To the ravages of the Gothic war was now added the greater menace of the Arian Lombards, the *langobardi* or "longbeards" who had swept from the Danube lands into northern Italy, capturing Milan in 569 and establishing themselves at Pavia.

❖ "THE WORLD GROWS old and hoary," Gregory wrote, "and hastens to approaching death."[2] He nursed his part of it with courage, pragmatic skill, and an immense energy that belied his failing health, the result of excessive fasting and a ruined stomach. More than 850 of his letters survive and they have an extraordinary range, darting from discussion of Church-owned livestock in Sicily and the diet of the poor to the praise of relics and practical advice for individual missionaries. His *Regulae Pastoralis* became a classic handbook for bishops, stressing humility and the care of souls, urging the bishop to subdue himself rather than his flock, and to act as "a minister, not a master." He was musical, collecting some three thousand melodies, and he helped develop the Latin plainsong used for the unaccompanied singing of psalms, hymns, and antiphons. He also organized the Schola Cantorum at Rome, the "school of singers" from which the Gregorian chant spread throughout the West.

He consolidated the papal hold on Rome. An imperial governor housed in the palace on the Capitol was the nominal ruler of the city, but Gregory took a personal hand in the administration. Twelve paupers ate with him each day; he kept a register of the names and details of all the city's poor and ensured that they were sent a weekly ration of corn, wine, cheese, and oil. Papal finances were overhauled. The pope was the leading landowner in the West, with particularly rich holdings in fertile Sicily, but his estates were spread haphazardly from North Africa to Gaul and Dalmatia. Much revenue was pilfered by corrupt officials or squandered by slovenly bishops. Gregory replaced them with Roman clergy and laymen selected for their honesty and diligence, and secured a cash flow that underpinned the growing aspirations of his office. Part was used for charity, but Gregory also used funds to strengthen papal patronage within the Church and to develop his own defense and diplomatic policies independently from the exarch at Ravenna, the emperor's Italian representative.

The pope found the Lombards "abominable,"[3] complaining that he had to watch "Romans tied by the neck like dogs, to be taken to Gaul for sale";[4] but he dealt with them nonetheless. He raised bribes to buy off their raids, negotiated treaties, and arranged ransoms. When the Lombard king Agilulf married a Frankish Catholic princess, Theodelinda, Gregory swallowed his distaste for the Arian court and sent her lavish presents. His policy was successful; her son was baptized a Catholic and the Lombards ultimately renounced their Arianism.

It was irritating enough to the emperor that Gregory should negotiate directly with imperial enemies and insist on the primacy of Rome with prickly tenacity; Gregory also lectured him on the morality of government. He reminded Maurice that the distinction between barbarian kings and the Roman emperor was that the subjects of the first were slaves, and of the second free men, and that, in all imperial acts, "your first object should be the maintenance of justice, your second to preserve a perfect liberty." This hectoring clashed with the semidivine status that the emperor enjoyed in the East; there he ruled as *Kosmocrator,* the master of his world, demanding obedience from laymen and clergy alike. Yet the meddlesome Roman bishop condemned the patriarch of Constantinople for using the title "ecumenical patriarch," on the grounds that it was the pope alone to whom "the care and principate of the whole Church was committed."[5] This was not a matter of vanity—Gregory himself used the title *Servus servorum dei,* servant of the servants of God, but to reinforce the papal claim to universal authority in spiritual affairs.

In reality that power carried little weight in the East and was tenuous enough in the West. Arianism survived among the Lombards. In Spain the Visigoth king Reccared, son of an Arian father and a Catholic mother, had accepted Catholicism in 589; Gregory wrote to congratulate him, but papal influence was marginal. Isidore of Seville, an archbishop thought to be the most learned man of his age, recognized that Rome had special rights, but stressed that all Christian societies were *membra Christi,* limbs of Christ, and thus equal. A canon of the Spanish Church gave priority to "the strength of our kingdom and the stability of the Gothic race."[6]

The Franks in Gaul had been Catholic since Clovis, their first great ruler, had converted a century before. The circumstances were similar to those of Constantine, so much so that they hint of fabrication; but the basics—marriage to a Christian princess, visions, a famous victory attributed to Christ followed by mass baptisms—were to be repeated in future conversions of rulers across Europe. Clovis was a pagan when he overthrew the last Roman governor of Gaul in 486 and took the land between the Loire and the Somme. He married a Burgundian princess, Clotilda, a pious and saintly Catholic, but remained pagan until hard pressed in battle against the rival Alemanni at Cologne in 496. Here he called upon "Jesus Christ . . . Thou that art said to grant victory to those that hope in Thee,"[7] promising to undergo baptism if victorious. The battle won, he and two thousand of his men accepted mass baptism on Christmas Day. Clovis proved as generous to his new faith as Constantine; he established a new capital, at Paris, gave valuable land and buildings to the Church, and presided over its councils. His defeat of the Arian Visigoths near Poitiers in 507 opened the country as far as Bordeaux and Toulouse for the Church.

These were important Catholic victories, but Gaul was no haven of virtue in Gregory's day. Queen Brunhilde, the regent, was the power in the land, but her eventual end, dragged to death behind a wild horse on the orders of her nephew, reflected the brutalities of Frankish power play. The Church was used as a dynastic instrument; simony was rife, and bishoprics were sold off to the highest bidder or given to laymen in return for political favors. Brunhilde was devout and pious, however, and Gregory cultivated her with care. He sent her books, and relics of St. Peter and St. Paul. At her request he granted the bishop of Autun the exceptional honor of the pallium, the circular band with black crosses spun from the wool of lambs blessed on St. Agnes' Day, worn on the shoulders by the pope himself. He tried, as best he could, to improve the morality of the Gallic Church and extend papal influence over it, and he used Gaul as a base for the mission of restoring the faith to England.

❖ HADRIAN'S WALL, RUNNING for seventy miles across the island from the Tyne to the Solway, had marked the northern extremity of the Roman Empire. Christianity had been planted in imperial times, at least among the elite. Britain had a protomartyr, Alban, a Roman officer said to have been executed for sheltering a priest during a persecution in the third century; the Church was vigorous enough by 314 to send three bishops to the Council of Arles. The legions had left Britain in 403 to defend Italy, however, and heavy raids by Saxons were followed by the withdrawal of the Roman administration in 410. The defenseless country was preyed on by the Irish from the west; by the Picts from the north, modern Scotland; and by Germanic barbarians sailing from the North Sea coasts between the mouth of the Rhine and Jutland. These Anglo-Saxons came from well beyond the old imperial frontiers and were untouched by Roman influence; they worshiped the gods Thor and Woden and saw sacred powers in springs and groves of trees. Place-names suggest that some Christian pockets survived for a time, but the faith was slowly eradicated from all but the western Celtic fringes. England was a patchwork of small pagan kingdoms, ruled by Anglo-Saxon dynasties and their illiterate warriors.

Gregory's interest in these heathens is said to stem from seeing fair-haired youths for sale in the Roman slave market. He was told that they were Angli, Angles, and he replied: *"Non Angli sed angeli."* They were not Angles but angels. Whatever the truth of the papal pun, Gregory was certainly aware that, of all the barbarian successors to the Roman Empire, only the English kingdoms remained pagan. He wrote to the rector of the papal states in southern Gaul in 595, instructing him to buy "English boys of seventeen or eighteen years of age that they may, dedicated to God, make progress in monasteries." A priest was to accompany the boys on their way to Rome, so that "he may baptise those whom he sees to be at the point of death."[8] Gregory may have wanted them to use as slaves in his monastery, or he may have planned to train them as missionaries. In any event, the following year he sent out a mission to England.

He entrusted the task to Augustine, the prior of his monastery at Rome. A major expedition of some forty missionaries was prepared, equipped with vestments, altar cloths, relics, books, and church plate. The party landed at Thanet in Kent, southeast of London, in the spring or early summer of 597. A Christian wife was again a decisive factor. Kent was probably chosen because its king, Ethelbert, was married to Bertha, the Catholic daughter of the Frankish king. A bishop named Liudhard had come to Kent with the young bride as her private chaplain; Bede, who wrote his great *History of the English Church and People* a century later, recorded that her husband gave her "a church built in ancient times while the Romans were still in Britain, next to the city of Canterbury on its eastern side."[9] Ethelbert was quickly won over by the missionaries; he gave them food and a house in Canterbury, and allowed them to preach in Bertha's church. Gregory wrote in 598 that "at Christmas last more than 10,000 Englishmen had been baptised."

The pope had strong and pragmatic views on missionary work. He was not obsessed with dogma. His friend Leander, the archbishop of Seville, who was weaning the Spanish Visigoths from their Arianism, asked what method of baptism should be used; Gregory replied that "where there is one faith, a diversity of usage does no harm to the Church."[10] He preferred to adapt heathen practices to Christianity rather than destroy them. It could be a simple matter of changing the venue. The peasants at Javols in France, for example, made offerings to the spirits of a local lake. They feasted for three days on its shores, throwing linen cloths, pelts of wool, and models of cheese and wax into its waters. The bishop of Javols built a church near the lake and suggested they should worship there; a chronicler recorded that they left the lake and "brought everything they usually threw into it into the church instead."[11]

Pagan habits—visiting soothsayers, burning candles at sacred spots, placing offerings in springs—persisted alongside Christianity for many centuries. Gregory acknowledged their existence, telling Augustine that he must "on no account" raze pagan temples to the ground or forbid feasts. "They are no longer to sacrifice beasts to the Devil, but they may kill them for food to the praise of God," he wrote. "If the people are allowed some worldly pleasures . . . they will come more readily to desire the joys of the spirit." He said that it was fruitless to expect all errors to vanish from obstinate minds at a stroke; "whoever wishes to climb to a mountain top climbs step by step. . . ."[12] Augustine was permitted to destroy pagan idols, but he was urged to set up altars and relics in the temples after sprinkling them with holy water.

Gregory handled the royal convert with tact. In his letters, the pope assured Ethelbert that he was among the "good men raised up by almighty God to be a ruler over nations," and that God would make his name glorious for all time; he urged the king to be as zealous as Constantine, and said that

Bertha was another Helena. It was, of course, immensely flattering for a rough barbarian to find himself compared to the great Roman, and his wife to the emperor's mother. It was also pleasing to have it confirmed that the Christian God was a monarchist. Ethelbert responded by granting Augustine land to build a monastery outside the walls of the Roman Church, which was restored as the cathedral of the new see of Canterbury. He encouraged his nephew, the king of the East Saxons, to follow his example, and a bishopric was founded at London in 604. The ruler of the East Angles, the next kingdom to the north, was more difficult to convince; he compromised by erecting a Christian altar in his pagan temple.

The pattern of a Christian wife, and victory at war, was repeated in the northern kingdom of Northumbria. Its ruler, King Edwin, married Ethelbert's daughter, Ethelburga; she took a priest from Canterbury called Paulinus with her to York as her chaplain. In 626, Ethelburga gave birth to a daughter. Paulinus claimed that mother and child owed their health to the Christian God. Edwin pledged to accept the faith if God granted him success in his coming campaign against the king of the West Saxons, and he allowed his daughter to be baptized as evidence of his oath. The West Saxons were duly routed, and Edwin returned to the north with his plunder. He was baptized in a wooden chapel at York on Easter Day, A.D. 627, after Paulinus had instructed him in the mysteries of the new religion. The ceremony was followed by the mass baptisms of hundreds of Northumbrians in the waters of the river Glen.

No doubt Ethelbert and Edwin were sincere in their conversions.* Some of their subjects, Bede admitted, chose baptism "through fear of the king or to win his favour"; after Edwin was killed in battle against the pagan Penda of Mercia, Northumbrian Christianity stopped dead in its tracks for a time. Gregory for his part made no bones about the throne being the primary target for a mission. He backed up his flattering correspondence to royalty with papal gifts of mirrors, combs, and costly garments.

It was a two-way exchange. The pope gathered new believers, and Anglo-Saxon illiterates were exposed to the civilizing influence of Roman culture from the distant Mediterranean. Bede noted that life and sophistication were breathed back into Canterbury; it became "a metropolis" once more. With Augustine's help, Ethelbert produced the first written Anglo-Saxon code of law. It lacked the elegance of the classical jurists—"If a man strike another on the nose with his fist, 3 shillings"[13]—but Bede nonetheless said that the king did it "following models of

---

*The word *conversio* was rarely used. Contemporaries wrote of "accepting" or "submitting" to the faith, or of "bowing to Christ."

the Romans . . . with the advice of his wise men." It reflected a deep respect for things Roman, and the "wise men" who advised the monarch were all churchmen. English priests, and kings, made the pilgrimage to Rome; they acquired a love for Latin learning, building, and liturgy, and for the pope. Gregory thought England was "on the edge of the world," but he won a reservoir of goodwill for the papacy in the barbarian north and a source of future missionaries who would penetrate beyond the Rhine.

Pining for his monastery, Gregory found no pleasure in his dealings with power and politics. But he accepted that, as pope, "by reason of my pastoral care, I have to bear with secular business and . . . am fouled with worldly dust." He left the papacy toughened, a point of certainty amid what he called the "changeable and decaying things" of the world, and he led the effort to drive Christendom into Europe's heathen recesses.

✤ INDIVIDUALS ALSO CREATED their own missions from a spontaneous urge to evangelize. Patrick, the "apostle of the Irish," was born in Britain in the early or mid-fifth century; the year, and the site of his home village of Bannavem Taburniae, has not been identified. His father was a deacon in the local church.

St. Patrick was not the first Irish evangelist, an honor that belongs to the obscure St. Palladius. He did not banish snakes from Ireland, the Roman geographer Solinus having already remarked on their absence. But he did survive the hostility of the druids, tribal priests whose penchant for human entrails the Romans had also noted, and he established a see at Armagh from which a notably vigorous and cultured Christianity was carried through Ireland and then as far as Germany.

When he was sixteen he was captured by Irish raiders and shipped off as a slave, probably to County Mayo. Here Patrick worked as a herdsman for six years. His captivity turned him toward God, his autobiographical *Confession* says, and he received a divine message that he should escape. He made his way to the southeast coast of Ireland and persuaded some sailors to take him back to Britain.

Patrick's family thought his escape was miracle enough; "they asked me earnestly not to go off anywhere and leave them this time," he wrote. As he slept, however, he heard the voices of his old companions from Ireland: "We beg you, holy boy, to come and walk again among us." He awoke with joy and saw God "praying within me and I was, as it were, inside my own body and I heard Him above me . . ." The missionary impulse Patrick described is a Christian constant; the majority who feel no such call may find it difficult to comprehend, but a proportion of every generation has felt compelled to follow this urge. It overwhelmed St. Paul and it continues today to drive men and women to transplant the faith to the most diseased and dangerous crannies of the earth. Patrick felt himself touched by a divine favor—"He granted me such grace as through me many peoples should be reborn in God"—that required him "to fish well and diligently . . . so that a vast multitude and throng might be caught for God." He saw himself as "a slave in Christ for foreign people," obeying Christ's order: "Go now, teach all nations, baptising them . . ."[14] He trained as a priest and was probably consecrated as a bishop in Gaul before returning to spend the rest of his life in Ireland.

Many of Patrick's exploits are legend. He was not the first Irish evangelist, an honor that belongs to the more obscure St. Palladius; he did not expel the snakes from Ireland, the Roman geographer Solinus having already remarked on their absence; the hymn "St. Patrick's Breastplate" was written long after his death; and there is no contemporary evidence that he used a three-leafed shamrock to explain the Trinity. He did, however, survive the hostility of the druids, tribal priests whose penchant for using human entrails to consult the gods had been noted by Roman writers; he converted a large if unverifiable number of people, influenced chieftains, ordained priests, and established a see at Armagh from which the faith was carried through the island.

He also left the Irish Church with a tradition of mission and learning. Ireland had not been part of the Roman Empire; it had no cities or civic roots to which the Church could graft itself, and Latin was a wholly alien language that Irish Christians had to learn from scratch. Monasteries filled these voids. They were places of education, where manuscripts of exquisite design and illumination were produced; they offered safety within their dry stone walls, for livestock as well as people; and they were engines for the faith. Like the desert fathers of Egypt,* some Irish monks abandoned themselves to the wilderness, clinging to craggy islets in the Atlantic swells off the coast of county Kerry; other monasteries were large enough to serve the functions of the towns that Ireland otherwise lacked.

Columba, the most notable monastic founder and missionary, was born into the warrior aristocracy in Donegal in 521; Irish monks were generally of noble birth, and their abbots greeted them, "Now you become a ploughman."[15] He had an excellent monastic schooling, becoming "refined in speech, holy in work,"[16] and was said to have copied three hundred books in his own hand. Despite his accomplishments, however, he retained a toughness and pugnacity that earned him a livid scar in battle. The Rule for his monasteries was rigorous and austere. As monks "will have abundance in the world to come," he wrote, they should have no more in this one than the minimum to stave off extreme want, for "covetousness proved to be a leprosy to monks. . . ."[17] In 563, after involvement in a clan war, he sailed for exile to the island of Iona off the west coast of Scotland with twelve companions, "wishing to be a pilgrim for Christ." The monastery he built served as a frontier mission station for evangelizing the Scots and Picts, whose king he visited near Inverness. Many miracles were attributed to him, of the sort that would appeal to illiterate and superstitious clansmen; he repulsed demons and "the raging fury of wild beasts," he "restored to life the dead son of a believing layman," he blessed a white stone so that it floated in a river like an apple, and changed water into wine.[19]

Significantly, the Constantinian link between Christianity and success on the battlefield was maintained. The warrior King Oswald was said to have had a vision in 634 of the dead Columba, who appeared "in the midst of the camp in his shining raiment." Oswald had fled from Northumbria to Scotland and was baptized by the Ionian monks. His vision came to him as he was preparing to fight the pagan Cadwallon, "mighty king of the Britons"; in it, the saint repeated to him God's words to Joshua—"Be strong and act manfully; behold I will be with you"—and assured him that Cadwallon "shall be delivered into your hands." Oswald related his vision to his men, all but twelve of whom were pagans, and "the whole people promised that after returning from the battle they would believe, and accept baptism." Cadwallon was slaughtered, and Oswald was "ordained by God as the emperor of the whole of Britain."[20] This was an exaggeration; Oswald was soon killed in battle against the same obstinate pagan, Penda of Mercia, who had slain Edwin. It does, however, show the importance of the Irish monks; where

---

*It is conceivable that desert monks visited Ireland. An eighth-century Irish Litany of Saints includes an invocation of "seven monks of Egypt in Diseart Uilaig," and St. Antony of Egypt figures prominently in carvings on Irish High Crosses.[18]

Edwin had been converted through the southern Roman mission of Augustine, Oswald learned the Celtic faith from the north.* He sent for monks from Iona to establish a church and see on the island of Lindisfarne. Its first bishop was Aidan. His life, Bede wrote, was "in great contrast to our modern slothfulness"; he seldom rode, for it was easier to fall into conversations with pagans on foot; he used what money he was given to redeem slaves, training and ordaining some as priests; his simplicity and abstinence impressed the rich and endeared him to the poor.

The Irish were formidable wanderers. "Our first duty is to love nothing here," the missionary-monk Columbanus wrote, "for our fatherland is where our Father is. Thus we have no home on earth."[21] Columbanus left the monastery at Bangor in northern Ireland in about 585 to sail for Gaul; he spoke later of "my vow to make my way to the heathen to preach the gospel to them." He founded three monasteries on the edge of the Vosges not far from modern Mulhouse, and went on to Bregenz on Lake Constance. It was here that he converted the local heathen, or so it was claimed, by blowing on a barrel of ale they were preparing to sacrifice to their god Woden, whereupon it burst with a great crack, unmasking the devil concealed inside. He then crossed the Alps to found his last monastery at Bobbio inland from Genoa in the Apennines, dying there in 615. Individuals like Columbanus had a multiplier effect on the faith; Bobbio was to become a center of learning, while the hermitage of a disciple whom he left at Constance was transformed into a monastery that bore his name, St. Gallen, boasting a scriptorium where some of the finest manuscripts in Europe were copied.

English missionaries, mirroring the Irish, were crucial in evangelizing Germany and the Low Countries. The pioneer, Wilfrid of York, preached in Friesland in 679; his follower, the Northumbrian Willibrord, founded the monastery of Echternach in Luxembourg. Wynfrith, or Boniface of Crediton, became a monk at Exeter and the scholarly writer of a Latin grammar before sailing from England for Frisia in 716. He then turned south into German Hesse and Thuringia. At Geismar he felled the great Oak of Thor in front of the heathens who worshipped it, an act so recklessly courageous that "the heathens who had been cursing ceased and began . . . to believe and bless the Lord."[22] He used planks from the oak to build a chapel at Fritzlar, which grew into a monastery. He founded the great monastery of Fulda and others further south, and became arch-

---

*The Roman and Celtic Churches were torn by a dispute that was, as so often, arcane but bitter. It arose from differences in dating Easter, and came to a head when the Northumbrian king's Celtic Easter clashed with his queen's Roman observance. A synod was held at Whitby in 664; Roman practices were adopted and an organized and united Church evolved. The derivation of the English word Easter is pagan, coming from the Teutonic goddess Eostre.

bishop of Mainz. As an Anglo-Saxon he had a special calling to convert the German Frisians and Saxons; he spoke their tongue, for they were "sprung from the race and stock of the English." It was a dangerous vocation. Saxons burned churches on their raids to the west and killed the bishop of Cologne. "My priests near the frontier with the pagans have a poor livelihood," Boniface noted. "They can get bread to eat, but cannot obtain clothing . . . unless they have a supporter." In 753 he returned to the coastal marshes of Frisia, church building, baptizing, and destroying shrines. The following summer, while waiting to confirm his converts at Dokkum, well beyond the Christian frontier, he was set upon by sea raiders and murdered. Two brothers and a sister, possibly related to Boniface, and canonized all, maintained the mission to the south; Willibald, the first known English pilgrim to the Holy Land, and bishop of Eichstätt, Wynnebald, and Walburga, abbess of Heidenheim.

THESE WERE PEACEFUL persuaders. The Franks preferred coercion. Their ruler, from 768, earned the honorific of Charlemagne, Charles the Great. He reversed the long disintegration of the Roman legacy into a fresh Western empire that, at his death in 814, stretched from the Atlantic to the Danube, from Barcelona to Lombardy and on to the borders of Croatia, and northward through Bavaria and Saxony to the North Sea. He was crowned as universal Roman emperor during Christmas Mass at St. Peter's in 800; though his title ignored the existence of the rival Christian emperor in Constantinople, Charlemagne was acclaimed as "Caesar" and "Augustus," and the pope knelt in homage before him.*

The link between the Church and learning was revived. A statute ordered the founding of "schools for reading-boys; let them learn psalms, notes, chants, the computus and grammar, in every monastery and bishop's house."[23] A palace school was founded to teach the seven liberal arts, the basic *trivium* of grammar, rhetoric and dialectic, and the *quadrivium* of music, arithmetic, geometry, and astronomy. The school was open to the sons of the nobility and commoners, and it was probably the first of any scale to give laymen a formal education. The Northumbrian monk Alcuin founded a school at Tours that served as a model for others attached to monasteries and cathedrals. "Writing books is better than planting vines," Alcuin wrote of the scribes who copied out texts, "for he who plants a vine serves his belly, but he who writes a book serves his soul." The Romans had written only in capital letters. Alcuin perfected lower case or small let-

---

*The title was to survive for almost a millennium, until its abolition by Napoleon in 1806. It would acquire an additional adjective in the twelfth century, to create the Holy Roman emperor; but this flattered to deceive, for the emperors were not Roman but Germanic, and their holiness was seldom striking.

ters at his school of calligraphy in Tours, and the "Roman" alphabet that we use today is in fact Alcuin's Carolingian minuscule. Charlemagne encouraged bishops to supervise the work of counts, who administered the three hundred *comitates* or counties into which the empire was divided; bishops and counts sat jointly on special clerical courts. The death penalty was applied to the murder of priests, eating meat in Lent, pagan cremations of the dead, damaging church buildings, and refusal of baptism. The naked Christian bias in Carolingian law reflected Charlemagne's view of the Church as a part of his realm. "Our Lord Jesus Christ has set you up as the ruler of the Christian people, in power more excellent than the pope or the Emperor of Constantinople," his priests flattered him. "On you alone depends the whole safety of the churches of Christ."[24]

He used the faith as a battering ram for conquest. Prisoners taken in his invasions of Saxony bought their lives with conversion. Defeated ex-pagans had to provide land, buildings, and slaves for new churches; they could marry only in Christian ceremonies, and they had to present infants for baptism within a year of birth. Sacred groves of trees where they worshipped were axed. Reprisals for backsliding were ferocious. After a rebellion in 782, Charlemagne ordered forty-five hundred Saxons to be beheaded in the massacre of Verdun and others were sold into slavery. The policy was effective, and imperial troops had reached the Elbe by 785; but the thousands of pagans who were baptized with their families in Saxon rivers were paying homage to Charlemagne as much as Christ. "They promised that they would be Christians," a royal annalist noted, "and bound themselves to the lordship of King Charles."[25]

This glimpse of a united Western Christendom did not outlive its founder. His heirs dissipated their legacy in family spite and slaughter. At the Treaty of Verdun in 843 the empire was split in three; the western and eastern wings, the cores of modern France and Germany, were separated by the "Middle Kingdom," an uneasy buffer state extending from Burgundy into Italy. By then Vikings had sailed up the Seine to plunder Rouen, and a new pagan menace was loose. These Teutonic Northmen spilled out of their overpopulated Scandinavian lairs to slice south through modern Russia to the Black Sea, raiding and settling the coasts of the British Isles and northern France, and cruising to Spain and into the Mediterranean. They returned to burn Paris in 854 while Charlemagne's grandson Charles the Bald cowered in his stronghold in Montmartre.

Monasteries and churches were particularly vulnerable. The Vikings were drawn to them by treasure rather than pagan devilment. Coastal British monasteries bore the early brunt. Lindisfarne was ransacked in 793 and Iona two years later. The raiders found rich plate, jeweled crosses, embroidered vestments, and gold and silver coinage; there were monks to be ransomed, and books, too, for devout Christians paid to recover the Scriptures from heathen hands. A target

The European coastline was vulnerable to the Vikings, who raided as far as Spain and the Mediterranean. Monasteries were often plundered for their riches. The Vikings adopted the native Christianity when they settled in Britain, Ireland, and France, although some hedged their bets. "He was baptized and professed faith in Christ," it was said of one Viking chieftain, "but he vowed to Thor for sea journeys and difficult undertakings."

was often given time to recover and then raided again. Iona suffered its worst raid in 806, when the abbot and sixty-eight monks were killed. Lindisfarne was abandoned altogether. Monks retreated inland; a community at the mouth of the Loire moved farther and farther from the long ships and the sea until they arrived in Burgundy, where, pitifully, they fell prey to a new horseborne scourge, the Magyars.

All the Christian shoreline was vulnerable, for the Vikings had the skills to sail beyond the known world, to Greenland and probably on to North America. The restless ferocity of their raiding was mirrored in their religion. The Teutons believed that the phantoms of dead warriors galloped on stormy nights on a "savage hunt," a wild chase through the skies under the command of the god of fury, Woden to Germans and Odin to Scandinavians, mounted on an eight-legged horse. Odin held court at Valhalla, a vast hall with a roof of shining shields, where he feasted with warriors chosen by the spear-wielding Valkyries, graceful warrior goddesses with the power to turn themselves into swans, who decided who should be victorious on the battlefield and who should die. It was at Odin's command that the Vikings burned dead warriors on funeral pyres, or buried them with their ships and weapons and fineries so that they could retrieve them when they reached Valhalla. In Norway, Thor, the red-bearded and hard-drinking god of thunder, prevailed over other gods, slaying his enemies with a miraculous stone hammer called Mjolnir, "the destroyer." The Northmen expected that the world would end in catastrophe when Thor abandoned it; at the "twilight of the gods," the Götterdämmerung to the Germans and *ragna rök* to Scandinavians, the gods would slaughter each other, the heavens would fracture asunder, and the earth would burn and disappear beneath the sea. Nature was thought to be full of spirits; giant *trolls* were glimpsed in the black storm clouds and manifested themselves in snowstorms, gales, and earthquakes while gentler elves and dwarfs amused themselves in games and dancing.

These myths were already ancient when the Roman historian Tacitus described them among the West Teutons in his *Germania* early in the second century. Apart from a faint echo of Christian apocalypse in the Götterdämmerung, Christianity was wholly alien to Viking beliefs and it made slow progress in Scandinavia itself. Where the Vikings settled among Christians, however, they swiftly proved amenable to the faith. In England, where the Anglo-Saxons struggled against them, they had a permanent presence from 866. Huge camps were maintained at the mouth of the Seine to aid the plunder of northern France; a fleet of seven hundred long ships disgorged forty thousand raiders on the left bank of the Seine, on the site of the Champs de Mars, in the siege of Paris in 885. These base areas were consolidated as Normandy, the territory of the Northmen, by the early 900s. The newcomers intermarried with the natives, adopting their religion and much of their culture. They often hedged their bets, carving Christian crosses and symbols of Thor on the same runic stones; "he was baptised and professed faith in Christ," it was said of one Northman, "but he vowed to Thor for sea journeys and difficult undertakings."[26] The Danish leader Guthrun agreed to accept Christianity as part of a treaty with the English king Alfred in 878; he came with thirty of his men to Alfred, who "raised him from the holy font of baptism, and received him as his adoptive son."[27] Such baptisms might be more a matter of convenience than faith; nonetheless, all the emigrant communities acquired the religion of their adopted countries. It took only a generation for the Danish ruler of Dublin to become a Christian sincere enough to end his days as a penitent at Iona.

THERE WERE OTHERS in the restless swill of peoples in Europe. The Slavs had begun to migrate from a starting point north of Kiev in about 550. Some went westward into Poland and Bohemia, others crossed the Danube into the Balkans and Greece, and a third group moved northeast into Russia. They had no formal hierarchy of gods or rites; their beliefs were rustic, in the spirits of sky, wind, forests, and *mati-syra-zemlya,* "moist mother earth." An early attempt to convert them was made by Amandus, the apostle of Flanders. At some time in the

660s, hearing that "the Slavs were caught in the devil's snares," he crossed the Danube to preach to them but returned after "a very few were reborn in Christ."[28]* As a people they lent their name to slavery; a thriving Christian trade lay in the capture of Slavs, who were driven to Venice or Arles for sale to Moslems and shipment to Cairo or Algiers.

An Irishman, Virgilius, a scholar and mathematician, preached among the Alpine Slavs of Carinthia and in 774 dedicated the first cathedral at Salzburg. Almost a century later the "apostles of the Slavs," the Greek brothers Cyril and Methodius, with the rare backing of both Rome and Constantinople, evangelized Moravia and translated the Bible and the liturgy into Slavonic. The Cyrillic alphabet of the Slavs is named for Cyril, although it differs somewhat from the one he devised; Czechs, Croats, Serbs, and Bulgars revered the brothers. The bishopric of Prague was founded in 967. There was rivalry between Catholic and Orthodox for control in Bohemia. Prague was subordinate to the Catholic metropolitan of Mainz, but the Slavonic rite was used alongside the Latin for a century.

A Moroccan Jew, Ibrahim ibn Jakub, was sent on an embassy by the caliph of Cordova to the Polish Slavs in about 965. He found himself in a land so cold that "when people breathe, icicles form on their beards, as if made of glass"; he remarked on the saunas, huts with a heated stone stove on which they poured water, wafting the steam round so that their pores opened, and "all excess matter escapes from their bodies." The people were "violent and inclined to aggression. If not for the disharmony among them . . . no people could match their strength. They wage war with the Byzantines, with the Franks and Langobards, and with other peoples. . . ."[29] In 966 the prince of Poland, Mieszko, made a strategic marriage with a Czech princess and was baptized a Catholic. A metropolitan see was founded at Gniezno in 1000, and Benedictine monasteries were built; Mieszko's son Boleslaw the Brave was awarded a royal crown by the pope before his death in 1025. A major pagan revolt in 1037 proved to be its own death rattle; under the powerful Piast dynasty with its royal capital at Cracow, Poland became an east European fortress of Catholicism.

Fear of Magyar invaders—"worse, far worse, than the Huns"—drove believers to compare them to Gog and Magog, the Antichrists of the Apocalypse. They were the last nomads to migrate into Central Europe. Their origins were in Siberia, and they crossed the Carpathians into the Pannonian plain east of the

---

*This remarkable man confirms that distance did not inhibit the determined missionary of the Dark Ages. Amandus also ventured to the Pyrenees to work with the pagan Basques, and he founded monasteries from Flanders to the Cévennes; in his will in 674 he wrote that "my body is worn out . . . having travelled far and wide through all the provinces and nations for the love of Christ."

Danube in about 895, separating the Balkan Slavs from their Polish brothers in the north. The Magyars numbered up to half a million, with perhaps twenty thousand warriors, formidable archers whose horses gave them speed and range. They were as rapacious as Vikings, with yearly raiding parties that had swept through Moravia, Bavaria, and Saxony by 922, and then struck deep into France, Italy, and Macedonia. A Magyar delegation arrived at Constantinople in the 940s. One of their chiefs, Bultsu, was baptized and given the imperial title of *patricius.* He reverted to paganism on his return and joined the summer expedition of 955, whose target was once more Bavaria. A German force under Otto of Saxony met them on the river Lech on August 10. After three days of slaughter the Germans broke them. Otto's soldiers raised him on their shields and acclaimed him emperor; Bultsu was captured and hanged as an apostate. The Magyar wanderings were over. They made peace with their German neighbors, who pressed their religion on them. The Magyar prince Géza was baptized into the Latin rite in 975. His son István, St. Stephen, married the Bavarian princess Gisella and was presented with a "holy crown" from the pope for his coronation in the new see of Esztergom on Christmas Day, 1000. Catholic monks and scholars were invited to his court. Rome, not Constantinople, had won the allegiance of the new kingdom on the Danube.

THE FIRST STIRRINGS of Rus, the Kiev-based prototype of the immense and Christian Russian empire that would stretch to the Pacific, were felt at this time. Vladimir, who ruled Kiev from 980, began his career as a polygamist, a fratricide, and a heathen; at his death thirty-five years later his realm, stretching from the Ukraine to the Baltic, had earned him the title of *Ravnoapóstolny,* "ranking with the apostles." Rus lay on the trading route to Byzantium and the Islamic caliphates, along which silks, ivory, incense, and pepper flowed north in exchange for furs, slaves, and amber. It was open to Christian influence. While regent, Vladimir's grandmother Olga had made a state visit to Constantinople, where she was baptized by the patriarch. She had a church built in Kiev on her return, and, as a balance to Orthodoxy, she received a German Catholic mission. Her son remained a pagan, allegedly rejecting baptism with the remark, "My retainers will laugh at me."[30]

It is natural that Vladimir should have become a saint, for nations were Christianized from the top downward, and his conversion was of historic consequence. He confirms the pattern of marriage as a catalyst for the initial royal baptism, followed by the mass conversion of subjects and the bestowment of generous gifts to the fledgling Church. His sincerity, however, can be no better judged than that of the English or Magyar kings.* The events may be purely cynical; the marriage may be a matter of dynastic alliance, the mass baptisms the by-product of a regal instinct for uniformity and coercion, and the largesse a means of placing the new institution in the debt of the crown. If true piety is involved, the picture can be as easily reversed. The ruler is baptized through his belief in Christian salvation; his extension of God's grace to his people is his Christian duty; and his generosity to the Church reflects his gratitude to it, and his wish to emulate the much-mentioned Constantine.

Vladimir can be seen in either light. In 988 he married Anna, sister of the Byzantine emperor Basil II. This was an extraordinary honor for a polygamous Slav, a reward for his help in suppressing a Byzantine revolt, and an incentive for him to hire out six thousand of his warriors for the imperial Varangian Guard. It was inconceivable for the groom to remain a pagan, and mission priests accompanied the bride from Constantinople to Kiev. Vladimir's own baptism was followed by those of nobles and commoners on the banks of the Dnieper. Greek craftsmen were brought in to build a great dynastic church at Kiev. Missionaries traveled the villages preaching the Bulgarian variant of Orthodoxy. The Cyrillic alphabet was adopted, and loyalty to the patriarch of Constantinople was proclaimed; a code of law was written which, as in the West, linked justice with the Church. Vladimir took to Christianity with personal vigor, although his end—killed in a battle against his son by one of his pagan ex-wives—was more martial than saintly. He preached and evangelized in villages, using compulsion where persuasion failed. Rus was a firm part of Orthodox Christendom within a few decades of his conversion; the Church of the Holy Wisdom, whose icons and frescoes still retain their sense of wonder, graced Kiev, and three of Vladimir's granddaughters were married to Christian kings.

Rome made the running with the Scandinavian monarchs. A missionary bishopric aimed at the Vikings had been established at Bremen in the 780s. St. Anskar, a monk from Picardy and the "apostle of the North," set up a school at Schleswig in Denmark in about 829, but was soon expelled by local heathens; he built the first church in Sweden and returned to Denmark to convert Erik, the king of Jutland, and to ease the horrors of the slave trade. At his death in 865, however, Scandinavia slid entirely back to paganism. It was a century before further gains were made. Harald Bluetooth of Denmark converted in 960 after a Christian priest had carried a hot iron in an ordeal without burning his hand, or so it was said. His grandson Canute, who ruled England and Norway as well as Denmark, made a pilgrimage to Rome in 1027—he wrote that he went "because I heard from wise

---

*Vladimir is said to have considered adopting Judaism, Islam, or Christianity, sending out envoys to glean intelligence on each; his choice of the latter, in one Russian legend, was because it allowed the use of alcohol.

men that St. Peter the Apostle has received from the Lord a great power of loosing and binding"—and had his moneyers strike coins with the sign of the cross.

Olaf Haraldsson, a Norwegian sea raider who roamed as far as Spain, became a Christian while fighting as a mercenary in England. He returned to Norway in 1016, ousted the Danes, and ruled as king until Canute drove him into Russia in 1028. Olaf was killed in battle near Trondheim when he tried to win back his throne. He was revered as a martyr even though he was killed by fellow Christians; miracles were attributed to him, and a cult of St. Olaf spread rapidly, linking the Norwegian Church and throne. In Sweden, Olaf Skötkonung was baptized by the English missionary St. Sigfrid in about 1008; he struck Christian coinage at Sigtuna, north of modern Stockholm,[31] but paganism persisted. When King Inge tried to end a pagan cult in Uppsala in the 1080s, he was expelled and replaced by his more amenable brother-in-law, who became known as "Sweyn the Sacrificer." Inge later raised an army and killed Sweyn, imposing Christianity once more and earning himself a laudatory letter from Pope Gregory VII in Rome. The Swedes, too, acquired a royal saint and martyr, Erik, killed in a drunken dispute in 1160. Sweden was finally honored with an archbishopric, at Sigtuna, in 1164.

GREGORY THE GREAT'S missionary vision had paid handsome dividends. Catholicism dominated all of Western Europe and the north; in Central Europe it had snatched Hungary and Poland from under the patriarch's nose. Only in Russia and the Balkans did the richer and more stable Orthodox Church advance.

Relations between pope and patriarch had long since turned sour. A bitter dispute over icons had followed the election of an army commander, Leo III, "the Isaurian," as Byzantine emperor in 717. He was a fine administrator and an able military strategist; Constantinople withstood a long Moslem siege at the start of his reign, its large fleet of biremes more than a match for the Arab navies, and Leo won a crushing victory over Arab armies in 740. His religious policies were less happy. He held the veneration of icons to be idolatry and published a decree ordering their destruction. Crucifixes were replaced by plain crosses; the images of the saints, and particularly of the Virgin, were burnt or whitewashed. Army officers supported this, since icons were a hindrance to the conversion of Moslem prisoners instilled with the Islamic ban on representational art.

An *iconomachia*, a war of the icons, was sparked off, sapping the energies of the Eastern Church and fouling its dealings with the West. The inconostasis, an elaborate screen traditionally made up of four rows of icons, separated the congregation from the sanctuary in churches. The double doors in the center, the "gates of beauty" to the Greeks, had further panels of Gabriel, the Virgin, and the evangelists, painted in pure egg tempera on a white or gilded surface. The Virgin was usually prominent, portrayed in three classic poses, the *eleus,* with the Child held to her face; the *odititria,* with the Child on her outstretched arm; and the *orakta,* with her arms raised and the Child in her womb.

Those who venerated these images were mocked as *iconodules,* slaves of the icons. They had two champions. St. John of Damascus, a theologian and a monk at Mar Saba, argued that, since Christ had become Man and Man was made in the image of God, icons were true images of the Godhead and the saints. They were not to be adored in themselves, but serene and patient contemplation of them would lead to a deeper reflection of God. John also taught the divine maternity of Mary, her freedom from sin, and her bodily Assumption into heaven; he foreshadowed the doctrine of the Immaculate Conception, eventually to be included in Catholic dogma in 1854 when the bull *Ineffabilis Deus* stated that, from the moment of her conception, Mary was "kept free from all stain of original sin."[32] John was supported by the patriarch of Constantinople, Germanus I, a eunuch who had been castrated after his father had been executed in a court intrigue. Both men regarded the Virgin as a symbol of incomparable purity and her icons to be a part of the faith; the Virgin's robe was the most treasured relic in the empire.

Germanus was dismissed as patriarch and replaced by an iconoclast. Monks led riots in Constantinople. In Rome the pope held two synods to defend icons and to condemn the emperor's assaults on them; Leo retaliated by annexing the papal patrimonies in southern Italy. Leo's son Constantine Copronymus, known as the "hammer of the monks," confiscated monastic land and martyred monks in reprisal for their fierce resistance. He held a synod at Hieria in 753 to confirm that all images, the Virgin's included, were idols; the pope and the patriarchs of Antioch, Jerusalem, and Alexandria boycotted the meeting. Monks and nuns who refused to submit were given the choice of instant marriage or exile to Cyprus.

Empress Irena, an *iconodule,* restored the images in 780. A Church council held at Nicaea reversed the declarations made at Hieria; it anathematized those who despised relics and ruled that no church should be consecrated without them, stimulating the already brisk trade in the remains of saints. The Eastern practice of dismembering bodies to maximize the number of available parts, previously banned by Roman civil law, spread to the West. Iconoclasm resumed under Leo V, "the Armenian," another general elected emperor by the military, until it met its end under Michael III. He had the body of Constantine Copronymus dug up and burnt. At his appointment of the *inconodule* monk Methodius as patriarch in 843, a great celebration was held in honor of the icons. It remains the Feast of Orthodoxy.

The issue was far from over—seven hundred years later, Protestants were to burn relics and whitewash images with as much relish as Leo's soldiers—and Orthodox and Catholic soon found other reasons to be at one another's throat. In 858 the patriarch refused Michael III Communion because of his alleged incest. The emperor dismissed the patriarch and replaced him with Photius, a brilliant soldier and courtier, but a layman who was elevated through the necessary ranks of the clergy in less than a week. The pope, Nicholas the Great, a stern moralist, refused to accept the appointment, and deposed and excommunicated Photius. Nicholas countered Michael's anger with gusto; Michael spoke only Greek, and the pope questioned the authority of a Roman emperor who had no Latin, adding that "the privileges of this see existed before your empire, and will remain when it has long gone."[33] Nicholas also sent Latin missionaries to Bulgaria, a clear challenge to the Greek Church. Photius responded by listing Catholic "heresies," which included the celibate priesthood, the use of unleavened bread in the Mass, and the creed; where the Orthodox creed stated that the Holy Spirit "proceeds from the Father," Catholics added *Filioque,* "and the Son." In 867, Photius assembled a council at Constantinople that excommunicated Nicholas and withdrew from communion with Rome. Nicholas was dead before the news reached Rome.

Michael was murdered the same year by Basil the Macedonian, an ex-horsebreaker whose dynasty ruled in Constantinople for the next two centuries. The schism with Rome was patched up, in the technical sense of restored relations, until 1054. That year, after the patriarch Michael Cerularius denounced Roman practices and closed all the Latin churches in Constantinople, the pope sent a legation to demand confirmation of papal supremacy. Cerularius refused, and the legates excommunicated him with a bull (decree), which they placed on the altar of St. Sophia. The insult was unforgivable, and the pope was himself excommunicated by a Greek synod.

Each Church had gone its own way well before the formal fracture. Byzantium still grieved for the limbs lopped off by Islam, but Anatolia had replaced Egypt as its breadbasket, and it slowly recovered its balance and wealth. Its ceremonials were cadent and exquisitely mannered, its music sonorous and poignant; the university at Constantinople bred scholars and churchmen of meticulous mind. At Mount Athos, recognized by Basil the Macedonian in 885 as the "holy mountain," the most wondrous monastic complex in Christendom was created. Here, cut off from the mainland by forests, rocky promontories rise sheer in an azure haze from the sea to a peak of sixty-five hundred feet in a landscape reserved for monks and hermits, and ruled by a *protos,* or primate, with a council of abbots; no laymen or female, human or animal, was permitted to set foot on its 140 square miles. Its monasteries were divided into the coenobitic, in which life is communal, and the idiorhythmic, where monks eat and work alone. Each was linked to farms, chapels, and anchorite cells; the hermits of Karoulia traveled from their huts at the plunging end of the peninsula by cliff paths and chain ladders.

The East was steeped in devotion; what stuck in the Western craw was its focus on the emperor, and not pope or patriarch, as the earthly representative of the divine. Its people included Slavs, Armenians, Syrians, Macedonians, and Bulgars. They were held together by Greek culture, and by their common faith and subordination to the *autokrator;* Church and state were fused in his single personality. The phenomenon of "Caesaropapism" was not unique to Byzantium; the Russian Czars adopted its principles, and it survived in loosely modified form until 1917. The imperial aura of holiness—in icons, the emperors were depicted as being crowned by Christ—was natural anathema to the pope, and it encouraged a prodigious bureaucracy in which matters both temporal and spiritual were centralized, servile, secretive, prey to plots and poisonings. The principal figures of the court were, like Germanus, eunuchs; by castrating them, the emperors sought to restrict hereditary power in the palace to themselves. The Byzantine ideal was *taxis,* a changeless and intricately structured response to life in which every nuance of status and behavior was preordained by custom. Byzantine society was delicately cultured in comparison to the crudities of the West; its architecture and artifacts were magnificent, its coinage universally recognized, its religion pervasive. But it lived off its inheritance. Its purpose was *agalma,* or "statuesque calm,"[34] and it lacked the restless dynamic that stamped the Western faith.

❖ IF PATRIARCHS WERE servile, a string of pontiffs were degenerates. Nicholas the Great was the last pope to be canonized for almost two hundred years. The period of the first millennium was a time of papal depravity and fear of apocalypse. John VIII, elected in 872, was beaten to death by his own attendants; of the forty-one popes and antipopes who followed him, a third had unnatural deaths, by strangulation, suffocation, or mutilation. Stephen VIII had his ears and nose cut off, and was never again seen in public; the Greek antipope John XVI lost his eyes, nose, lips, tongue, and hands. Another, Benedict IX, was a teenager when he was enthroned, a "mere urchin."

These popes, the cardinal-historian Cesare Baronius wrote later, were *non apostolicos sed apostaticos,* "not apostles but apostates," "vainglorious Messalinas filled with fleshly lusts and cunning in all forms of wickedness . . ." He did not exaggerate. Lacking the protection of a great power, the papacy became the plaything of leading Roman families. The counts Alberic of Tusculum, warlords from the Alban Hills fifteen miles outside the city, installed seven family members on the throne of St. Peter, including young Benedict; the Crescenti family countered with the murder of Tusculan candidates and the election of their own; and a third family, the Theophlyacts, appointed John X and, when he ceased to be amenable, had him deposed and killed in the Castel Sant' Angelo.

Stephen VI,* elected in 896, was insane. He dug up the corpse of his predecessor Formosus, dressed it in full pontificals, placed it on the Lateran throne, and personally interrogated it at the so-called Cadaveric Synod. Stephen charged Formosus with fraud in being elected pope while still holding another bishopric; a teenage deacon, chattering with fear, replied on behalf of the deceased. The corpse was duly found guilty. Stripped of all but a hair shirt, the two fingers with which it had administered apostolic blessings lopped off, it was flung into the Tiber. The body was recovered from the river by admirers and quietly reburied. Stephen was deposed by a Roman mob and strangled in prison in 897. There were six popes in the next eight years. The last of them, Sergius III, having murdered his immediate predecessor, had the unfortunate Formosus exhumed again. This time the corpse was beheaded and three more fingers were removed. Fishermen caught it in their nets, and it was finally laid to rest in St. Peter's.

Theodora, the Theophylact courtesan and mistress of the unfortunate John X, and her daughter Marozia, helped create eight popes in a decade; Gibbon dubbed them the "she-popes" in his *Decline and Fall,* and suggested that the legend of Pope Joan[†] arose from them. Theodora's lover was bishop of Bologna when they first met. She became uneasy when he was elevated to Ravenna. "Fearing she would have fewer opportunities of bedding her sweetheart," Liutprand, the bishop of Cremona, wrote, "she forced him to abandon his bishopric and take for himself—oh, monstrous crime—the papacy of Rome."[35] After her mother's death in 928, Marozia had John imprisoned and suffocated. She herself was the mistress of Pope Sergius III; she had their illegitimate son installed as John XI, and her grandson Octavian became John XII.

John XII was a teenager when he was elected, although his vices were adult.

---

*Stephen VII to some. A presbyter called Stephen was elected pope in 752, but died before he was ordained bishop. Those who hold that a pope is created at the moment of election, regardless of whether he survives to take up the office, thus count an additional Stephen in the list of popes.

†Legends of a female pope, a distinguished scholar disguised as a man, first appeared in the mid-thirteenth century. In one version she gave birth during a procession to the Lateran and died soon afterward; in another she revealed her sex while mounting a horse. The dates of her supposed election vary from 855 to 1100. The fiction was widely believed, although there is not a scrap of evidence to support it, and it was shown by the great nineteenth-century Church historian Johann Döllinger to stem from an ancient Roman folktale.

He was accused of incessant copulation, ordaining a deacon in a stable, saying Mass without communicating, and castrating a cardinal. Otto I of Germany, the victor over the Magyars, revived Carolingian tradition by having himself crowned Holy Roman Emperor; he was unimpressed by the young man who anointed him in Rome in 962, ironically on the Feast of the Purification. "Everyone, clergy as well as laity, accuses you, Holiness," Otto wrote to John, "of homicide, perjury, sacrilege, incest with your relatives, including two of your sisters, and with having, like a pagan, invoked Jupiter, Venus and other demons."[36] John was found dead in bed two years later, allegedly murdered by a cuckolded husband. He was twenty-seven. John's nine immediate successors were respectively exiled, imprisoned, murdered, banished, exiled, murdered, forced to flee, exiled, and deposed.

The devil seemed loose in Rome, and the millennium closed with feelings of dread. "Surely, if he is empty of charity and filled with vain knowledge," Bishop Arnulf said of Pope John XV at the Synod of Rheims in 991, "he is Antichrist sitting in God's temple." In Paris, the abbot of Fleury told of sermons preached on the end of the world in the cathedral in 995. "As soon as the number of a thousand years is completed, the Antichrist will come and the Last Judgment will follow in a brief time," he reported.

A letter written by Adso, a reforming monk and later abbot of Montier-en-Der, was eagerly read and translated into vernaculars. He predicted that the Antichrist would soon be born in Babylon. Skilled in wizardry, the Antichrist would go to Jerusalem, rebuild the temple, and "circumcise himself and pretend that he is the son of almighty God." He would enslave the faithful by "terror, gifts and prodigies," imitating Christ by raising the dead. His reign would last forty-two days, during which the days would shorten into perpetual darkness, before being slain by Christ on the Mount of Olives. The chronicler Adhemer identified a group of heretics found in France in 1020 as "ambassadors of Antichrist," a view shared by the bishop of Chartres; a large French pilgrimage set off for the Holy Land in 1028 to warn of the "coming of the Lost One, the Antichrist."

The Irish shared the millenary fever. In one popular prophecy a phoenix builds its nest, fire comes from heaven and burns the nest into ashes, and then rain from Africa puts out the fire. "From the ash and the rain will be born the girl from whom the Antichrist will come," the writer continues. The Antichrist is suckled by two virgins for five years before beginning to reign, growing nine cubits, or fifteen feet, tall, with black hair like iron chains and no upper lip. He dries up the seas and darkens the sun and the moon, and "the stars fall from heaven." In another Irish version the Antichrist is born of a harlot of the tribe of Dan; he has no knees and cannot genuflect, and has wheels on the soles of his feet.

✤ THE ABILITY OF the papacy to survive such popes and prophecies struck some as a miracle. The nadir was reached in 1046. Benedict IX, squalid and lecherous, so shamed the office that the Roman populace had deposed him in favor of Silvester III two years before. Benedict had become pope through his father's bribery; he now used the family's hired thugs in street riots to force Silvester to resign and to reclaim his throne. He then negotiated to abdicate in favor of his godfather in return for a large cash sum and an inflated pension. The godfather was elected as Gregory VI in 1045, an honest man of whom reformers had high hopes, after the Roman mob had been placated with bribes.

This clerical stew passed for normality in Rome but it was intolerable to Henry III, the pious and powerful German king. He came to Italy the following year to be crowned Holy Roman Emperor. He refused to deal with any pope sullied by simony, the sin of buying spiritual office for money, and he insisted that the three rival popes be formally deposed. For good measure he forced Gregory VI to read a humiliating declaration: "I, Gregory, bishop, Servant of the servants of God, on account of simony, which, by the cunning of the devil, entered into my election, decide that I must be deposed from the Roman bishopric."[37] Gregory was exiled to Germany; with him went his chaplain, the young Cluniac monk Hildebrand, son of a Tuscan carpenter.

The popes whom Henry appointed were Germans and reformers devoted to the ideals of the great monastery of Cluny. The monarchy had been founded by Duke William of Aquitaine, who had encouraged it to be independent of secular pressures, decreeing that its monks "shall be wholly freed from our power . . . and from the jurisdiction of royal greatness." Cluniacs were renowned for the spirituality that Rome so lacked as well as for their rigid discipline, their hostility to simony and clerical marriage, and the beauty and solemnity of their architecture and worship. There were several hundred Cluniac houses across Europe, and they provided a reservoir of reforming influence. It was tapped by Leo IX, elected pope at Henry's urging in 1048.

Leo brooked no delay in reversing the long decay. The first startled victim of the papal attack on the trade in Church appointments was the bishop of Langres, who found himself deposed and excommunicated for simony. Leo asked bishops and abbots to their face if they had paid for their office, traveling to Germany and France to do so. None were invulnerable; the archbishop of Rheims was summoned to explain himself. Celibacy was imposed on all clergy from the rank of deacon upwards at the Easter Synod of 1049. Leo dismissed the Roman placemen in the Curia and began to transform it into a body of highly qualified advisers and specialists, Hildebrand among them. Less happily, his delving into suspect doctrines and drive for orthodoxy helped to create the final schism with Constantinople.

His successors maintained the momentum. In 1059, Nicholas II decreed that popes should be elected by the college of cardinals. The new system was not perfect. Cardinals remained a local breed, drawn from the senior Roman clergy and deacons, and from adjacent bishoprics. Even after leading foreign churchmen were included in the college, infighting between them could result in scandalous delays; meeting in Viterbo in 1268, they wrangled for three years, until the town authorities locked the doors of their residence, removed the roof, and put them on a starvation diet. Thereafter, the cardinals were obliged to meet in Rome within fifteen days of the death of a pope and vote twice a day until the necessary majority of two-thirds plus one was reached; since non-Italian cardinals were often unable to keep the deadline, this gave an artificial weighting to Italians. Nonetheless, it did away with the much-abused tradition of acclaim "by the people and clergy of Rome."

This had a final outing when a Roman congregation—"Hildebrand is Pope, Saint Peter has chosen him!"—spontaneously acclaimed the most decisive medieval pope in 1073. Hildebrand was so small that he was known as *homuncio,* the midget, but he was a midget as hard as steel. A friend remarked that one dare not lean on him for fear of impaling oneself. He had been adviser to four popes over a period of eighteen years, and he had never forgotten Gregory VI's humiliation at imperial hands. He was intent on breaking the power of emperors, princes, and prelates over the pontiff for good; he chose to call himself Gregory VII.

His ambition was revealed by the *dictatus,* the list of twenty-seven theses he drew up to outline his powers as Vicar of Christ and St. Peter's successor. It stated that the pope can be judged by no one on earth; that the Roman Church has never erred, nor can it err until the end of time; that the pope alone can depose bishops; that a rightly elected pope is a saint, made so by the merits of Peter; that all princes are obliged to kiss the pope's feet, and that the pope can absolve their subjects from allegiance to them. Thesis 12 stated that the pope is permitted to depose emperors; thesis 20 that no one can condemn a decision of the Holy See.

These were dangerous doctrines, and Gregory was playing for high stakes. It cannot be told whether he realized that many of his claims were based on forged documents. The Greeks had long called Rome the "home of forgeries." The most important was the Donation of Constantine, which purported to show that the emperor had given the pope primacy over Church and rulers. The pseudo-Isidorian Decretals, 115 documents allegedly written by early bishops of Rome, banned all commerce and trade with an excommunicated person, a doctrine that

Gregory extended to emperors and kings and their realms. The Decretals were, in fact, of much later French invention.

Gregory was ruthless in Church reform. His insistence on clerical celibacy saw thousands of wives turned out on the street, "driven blasted, heart-broken and helpless, not a few of them shortened their agony by suicide."[38] A group of Italian bishops met at Pavia in 1076 and excommunicated the pope for preferring clerical immorality to honorable marriage; German clergy asked where he would find angels to replace them. Gregory ignored them. He obliged all bishops to take an oath of loyalty to himself, a new departure that made them formally dependent upon the "favour of the Apostolic See."

Finally, he made the challenge that he had been storing up for thirty years. He accused Emperor Henry IV, son of his namesake's tormentor, of simony and interference in the affairs of the Church. Piqued and astonished, Henry called a council at Worms and declared that Gregory's election was void on the grounds that he had not been consulted in advance. The *homuncio* published his furious response. "On the part of God the omnipotent," he declared, "I forbid Henry to govern the kingdom of Italy and Germany. I absolve all his subjects from every oath they have taken or may take, and I excommunicate every person who shall serve him as king."[39] Never before had a pope dared to depose an emperor.

Henry's mother, Empress Agnes, sided with the pope; so did the powerful Matilda of Tuscany, and the German barons chose the duke of Swabia as their "Anticaesar." German merchants feared that other nations would cease trading with them. Henry, only twenty-one years old, capitulated. He crossed the Alps in midwinter on an ox-hide sled and toiled on to Canossa, Matilda's triple-walled fortress on a crag in the Apennines southeast of Parma where Gregory awaited him. As the emperor approached the gates alone, the pope stood high on the walls dressed in full pontificals. Henry was stripped of his clothes and thrown the hair shirt of beggary; he clutched a broom and a pair of shears, tokens of his willingness to be whipped and shorn. The Holy Roman Emperor, heir to Charlemagne, stood for three days with bare head ankle-deep in the snow, praying to God and the pope for forgiveness while on the battlements his relatives wept. On the fourth day the pope came down and the emperor flung himself at his feet: "Holy Father, spare me!" The price was swearing to submit to the pope's judgment; as Machiavelli wrote four centuries later, "Henry was the first prince to have the honor of feeling the sharp thrust of spiritual weapons."

The promises extracted at Canossa were not kept. Henry was excommunicated again in 1080; this time the emperor set up the archbishop of Ravenna as an antipope and marched on Rome. The city fell to him in 1084. Gregory was rescued by Norman troops, who plundered the city with the relish of their pagan Viking forebears; the ravaged Roman populace turned on Gregory for calling the

Normans in. He fled, tired and abandoned by his cardinals, and died in Salerno in 1085. His last words are said to have been: "I have loved justice and hated iniquity, therefore I die in exile." An aide, conscious of the old man's achievement, queried him. "How in exile, Holiness," he asked, "when the whole world is thine?" Over the next century, popes were to excommunicate eight emperors; Gregory had fashioned a new power.

❖ HE DIED WHILE there were still European pagans in the lands south and east of the Baltic. They were reduced to isolated pockets by the conversion of their neighbors and finished off by crusaders with colonial ambitions.* Their cults were elaborate. The Wendish Slavs beyond the eastern border of Germany had a finely carved wooden temple in the forests near Stettin, decorated with images of gods in helmets and chain mail, tended by priests who held sacrifices and sought auguries from the paces of horses led through a slalom of spears placed in the ground. On the Baltic island of Rügen, a twelfth-century Danish chronicler described the cult of the god Svantovit, a "huge image bigger than any man, astonishing for its four heads and four necks . . . clean shaven and crop headed . . . the wonder increased by a gigantic sword, of which the scabbard and hilt were not only painted with exquisite skill, but enhanced with silver."[40] Each year the Slavs sacrificed a Christian to Svantovit; a third of the spoils of war were given for the maintenance of the god, and, a parallel that the Church might not wish to draw, the cult priest had in his keeping "a huge quantity of public and private gifts, contributed with the anxious prayers of those who sought advantage from it."[41]

The pagans linked Christianity with foreign domination, and they defended their beliefs ferociously. Gottshchalk, the ruler of the western Wends near Lübeck in the 1060s, was a Christian who brought in German clerics and monks. In 1066 the eastern Wends rebelled and killed him; they stoned the monks to death and tortured and decapitated the bishop of Mecklenburg, offering his head to their god on the point of a lance. A few years later the Wends attacked and burned Hamburg. Those who fought them were promised earthly and spiritual rewards. The writer of the Mecklenburg Appeal in the early twelfth century pointed out that the "wicked" Wends had land "rich in meat, honey, corn and birds"; he promised that Christian warriors who defeated them would have the chance "to save your souls and, if you wish, to acquire the best land." In the bull *Divina dispensatione,* the pope promised Christians who took part in the Wendish crusade of 1147 the same remission of sins as those who fought in the

*The Crusades in the Holy Land are covered in subsequent chapters.

Holy Land; St. Bernard of Clairvaux, guardian of Christian conscience, urged that there should be no truce "until such time as, with God's help, either their religion or their nation be destroyed."[42] It took almost forty years for Saxon, Danish, and Polish crusaders to reduce the Wends to Catholic obedience. The archbishop of Bremen launched a "continuous crusade" in Livonia in 1198. Armed German monks of the Brothers of the Sword, based at Riga, campaigned in Livonia.

Papal encouragement to the Scandinavian kings to destroy "the Estonians and other pagans of those parts" was successful. Estonia was overrun by the Danes in 1219, a victory attributed to divine intervention. The Estonians had tricked the Danes into believing that they were about to submit to baptism. At night they broke into the Danish camp, killing the bishop; as they drove the crusaders into the sea, a red banner with a white cross fell from the heavens and a voice commanded the Danes to rally round it. The Danish king, Valdemar the Victorious, duly triumphed; the city of Tallin, or "Danish Castle," was founded, and Denmark adopted the Dannebrog or "red rag" as the national flag. Swedes brought the faith to Finland.

The Prussians had murdered Adalbert, the first Slav bishop of Prague, who had carried the gospel to the Hungarians and the Poles, in 997. They remained obstinately pagan, raiding Polish Christians, and a crusade was mounted against them in 1230. A Polish prince, Conrad of Masovia, invited the Teutonic Knights to help him subdue them. The Teutonic Order had been founded as a hospital order of German knights and priests in Palestine. It later converted into a military order and switched its efforts to the pagan borderlands of Europe, obtaining charters of permanent crusading rights from both the pope and the German emperor. The knights, in white surcoats with black crosses, rode eastward from the Vistula in 1231. The blockhouses they built as they progressed made their intentions clear; they did not come to minister to the heathen but to master them. Paganism was not destroyed, of course, by the mere act of mass baptism that followed subjugation. When the Order suffered a defeat on the Dvina, the resentful people of Ösel took it as a sign that they could "live free and oppose the knights of God . . . young and old, [they] broke away and left not a single Christian alive in all their territories."[43] Later, inevitably, "many of them were destroyed for doing this." Christian retribution was pitiless. The knights "yearn for battle like a hungry falcon," an anonymous author who was probably a knight wrote in 1290; it was God's purpose that "we should expand our dominion," and massacre was justified since "to break a stubborn stone one has to strike hard." In the last analysis, as the knights put it, "The sword is our pope."[44] By 1295, after a final pagan revolt, Prussia had become an *Ordenstaat,* a state belonging to the Teutonic Order.

Lithuania remained pagan. Its grand dukes married their daughters to Christian princes, and a Catholic church stood in Vilnius to cater to the many Christian merchants in the city. Missionaries who tried to make pagan converts were executed, however; a grand duke who had accepted Christianity under pressure in 1251 apostatized soon after, and replaced a cathedral he had built in Vilnius with a pagan temple; and the country declared itself in its diplomatic dealings to be officially pagan. At his death in 1382, Grand Duke Kestutis was cremated in heathen splendor with his horses, hounds, and hawks.[45] The end was swift, and to the familiar pattern. The dynastic merger of Lithuania and Poland was arranged. Jogaila, successor to Kestutis, was to marry Jadwiga, the ten-year-old girl who had inherited the Polish throne. His reward was to become king of Poland; the price was Christianity. Three days before his marriage, Jogalia was baptized in Cracow and given the Christian name of Ladislas. Mass baptisms followed at once.

The faith, thirteen centuries old, had penetrated all Europe, or almost so, for, at the icy northern extremity above the Arctic Circle, the Lapps alone were still unevangelized.

CHAPTER XI

"A CARNAGE OF PAGANS":

Crusades

"R eligion," an ancient Arab saying went, "is a falcon with which to hunt." Christians also learned to use their faith as an instrument of war, finding the fierce bird to be immensely adaptable. They flew it against German emperors, French heretics, and Greek schismatics as well as nonbelievers in the Mediterranean and the Baltic; it was to cross the Atlantic and the Pacific to add religious zeal to the expansion of empires. It was difficult to control once set loose, however; and, as mastery of the Church slipped in time from clerical hands, it became the creature of kings and parliaments. It was used in the first instance by the pope, and Moslems were its prey.

A crowd too large to fit into the cathedral gathered in a sloping field outside Clermont in the high plateau of central France on November 17, 1095. Clerics, knights, and commoners jostled to hear Pope Urban II tell them that Alexius Comnenus, the Byzantine emperor, was pleading for help to enable their brothers in the East to fight the Seljuk Turks. The pope gave his audience news of Turkish atrocities. Christians were being forcibly circumcised, he claimed, and the resulting blood was spread on altars or poured into baptismal fonts; the Turks "cut open the navels of those whom they choose to torment with a loathsome death . . . tie them to a stake, drag them around and flog them"; they tied some to posts and used them for archery practice; others they attacked with drawn swords "to see whether they can cut off their heads with a single stroke."* He said that it would be a disgrace "if a race so despicable, degenerate and enslaved by demons" should overcome a Christian people.[1]

*There are five accounts of Urban's historic speech by chroniclers, by Fulcher of Chartres, Baldric of Bourgueil, Guibert of Nogent, and William of Malmesbury as well as by Robert the Monk. The versions are substantially different; Robert's makes most of the alleged Moslem atrocities. He did, however, claim to be present to listen to the address. Guibert mentioned that Urban introduced the concept of the "just war" into the sermon. "Until now you have fought unjust wars," he told his audience. "You have savagely branded your spears at each other

Pope Urban preaching the sacred violence of the First Crusade at Clermont in central France in November 1095. All those who fought the Turks—"ferocious blood drinking beasts . . . the instruments of God's anger against the Christians"—were promised remission of sins. "I, not I, but God exhorts you!" Urban said in a speech that tapped the new vigor and martial pride of Latin Christendom.

Although the Byzantine empire had stabilized after the huge losses of the seventh century, regaining Antioch and parts of Syria, nomadic Turkish horsemen from the arid grasslands beyond the Oxus were now driving westward to the Mediterranean in a fresh Moslem wave. They had overrun Persia and Baghdad. Armenia, a chronicler lamented, had been smothered by these "ferocious blood-drinking beasts . . . the instruments of God's anger against the Christians,"[3] and they were raiding deep into imperial territory in Anatolia. A large Byzantine army was decimated at Manzikert in August 1071; the first survivor arrived at Constantinople a few days later, "then there was another, then a third and fourth, having nothing precise to announce except the catastrophe itself."[4] Almost all of Asia Minor was lost by the time Alexius Comnenus appealed to Rome.

The Turks had cut the land route to Jerusalem, and Urban prayed for a pil-

---

in mutual carnage only out of greed and pride. . . . Now we are proposing that you should fight wars which contain the glorious reward of martyrdom, in which you can gain present and eternal glory. . . ." The pope said that "in particular cases it is good to brandish the sword against the Saracens," Baldric related, "because it is love to lay down one's life for one's brothers . . ."[2]

grimage that would reopen it by force of arms. He begged his listeners—"I, not I, but God exhorts you!"—to urge men of all ranks, knights and foot soldiers, rich and poor, to "hasten to exterminate this vile race from our lands." His voice was frequently drowned by tremendous cries of *"Deus le volt!,"* "God wills it!" Any who fought the pagans would enjoy remission of sins; "this I grant to all who go," he said, "through the power vested in me by God."

He had no illusions about where to find the sinners whose depravities would be wiped clean with Moslem blood by enlisting in the holy cause; his appeal was directed to feuding barons, brigands, and mercenaries. "Let those who . . . wantonly wage private war against the faithful march upon the infidels," he said. "Let those who have long been robbers now be soldiers of Christ. . . . Let those who have been hirelings for a few pieces of silver now attain an eternal reward."[5] He had no doubts, either, of the perils of the enterprise, promising them "wretchedness, poverty, nakedness, persecution, need, sickness, hunger, thirst and other things of this kind." But he offered, too, a glimpse of the divine, for had not Christ himself said to his disciples: "You must suffer many things in my name"? Those who died for the Cross would be freed from past sin. Many of those who found their way to heaven by this means, a Dominican preacher remarked, would never reach it by another road. Survivors would be liberated from penance; "Christ commands it," the pope affirmed. Conquest was a further motivation. The West "is shut in by sea and mountains," he added, and "is overcrowded by your numbers . . . This is why you devour and fight one another." Take the road to Jerusalem, he urged, "rescue that land from a dreadful race and rule over it yourselves." Speed was essential if the Eastern Christians were to be rescued. "Let nothing delay those who are going to go," Urban concluded. "Let them settle their affairs, collect money, and when winter has ended and spring has come, zealously undertake the journey under the guidance of the Lord."[6]

On the spot, men declared themselves to have joined the armed pilgrimage. The word "crusade," which comes from the Latin *crux* for "cross" via the French *croisade,* was not yet used. A cardinal fell to his knees and, shivering with emotion, recited the Confiteor, the confession of sins. Across France, men vowed to follow in the footsteps of Christ. In Italy, the Norman warrior Bohemond of Taranto heard that a great army of Christians was assembling while he was besieging Amalfi. He asked what arms and sign they were to bear on Christ's journey, and what cry they would make in battle. "They carry weapons suited for war," he was told, "they bear the cross of Christ on their right shoulder or between the two shoulders; and with one voice they cry out the words 'God wills it!' . . ."[7] He began to prepare himself for the journey to the Holy Sepulchre.

✦ THE POPE HIMSELF had, as it were, claimed an authority bolder and more ancient than that of St. Peter; he was now the successor to Moses, able to command his flock to war. No Christian doctrine of holy war existed before Clermont.* To find a detailed Christian exposition on the morality of war, Church theorists had to go back almost seven centuries to the writings of St. Augustine. Urban's sermon at Clermont was the definitive moment when the Church "preached the cross," taking the initiative in calling for war, defining its scope and purpose, and offering those who took part the rewards of heaven. The concept was romantic, brave, spiritual, and flawed. The Crusades were not Christian in any general sense, but specifically Catholic and European. Within a few years, the killing—"coercion" was the technical term used—of non-Catholic heretics as well as nonbelieving Moslems was enshrined in the canon law of the Western Church.

Those who answered Urban's appeal did not do so from any love for Byzantine Christians, whom they found, in the words of a bishop of Cremona, to be "soft, effeminate, long-sleeved, bejewelled and begowned liars, eunuchs and idlers."[8] Rifts continued over divorce, the celibacy of the clergy, the rules of fasting, the use of unleavened bread, the creed. A visit in 1054 by a papal legate to Constantinople to improve relations with the Orthodox patriarch had ended in farce. Cardinal Humbert accused his host, the patriarch Michael Cerularius, of preaching the "tares of false doctrine" and complained that the Byzantines "castrate their guests . . . they would deny baptism to babies dying within eight days of birth . . . they refuse communion to those who shave, cut their hair, or have a Roman tonsure." Claiming the authority of "the Holy and Undivided Trinity"—itself an intentional insult to the Orthodox for the omission of the *Filioque*—Humbert declared Michael and all his successors to be excommunicated.

Michael returned the compliment. "They accept people who eat unleavened bread," he wrote of the Latins. "They prohibit the marriage of priests. . . . Bishops wear rings on their fingers, as though they take the church as wives. . . . They go into battle and pollute their hands with blood: because of this, they destroy lives and are destroyed. . . ."[10] With that, he excommunicated the pope. At a political level, the Byzantines resented papal intervention in imperial policy

---

*A first appeal to arms was said to have been made by Pope Sergius IV in about 1010. This was in response to the insane Egyptian caliph Al-Hakim, who destroyed the Church of the Holy Sepulchre and forced Christians to carry heavy wooden crosses round their necks. Jews were ordered to wear bells around their necks. In an encyclical, Sergius allegedly urged the faithful to "kill all these enemies and to restore the Redeemer's Holy Sepulchre. . . . Nor, my sons, are you to fear the sea's turbulence, nor dread the fury of war, for God has promised that whoever loses the present life for the sake of Christ will gain another life which he will never lose. . . ."[9] It was nicely put, but the encyclical was forged by the monks of an abbey in southern France a century later.

and Rome's strictures against the profitable tolls levied on Western pilgrims and their horses. They feared that crusading was sinful, since St. Basil's canon in the Eastern Church banned those who "commit murder at war" from taking Communion for three years. The emperor's daughter, Anna Comnena, described the Crusaders as "barbarians," uncivilized and brutal, and when they arrived found them "more terrible than rumour suggested."[11] The Christian allies, in short, despised and mistrusted each other. The mutual anathemas of 1054 were not revoked until 1965.

Urban's words nevertheless caught the mass imagination of the West. Fusing power and violence with penitence, they were vivid with the spirits of the age. High among these was the eagerness of the papacy itself to establish its claims to temporal supremacy. Urban was tall and impressive, "courteously mannered and persuasive in his speech."[12] Like Gregory, he was a product of Cluny, and he owed his air of handsome authority to the angry zeal of the midget *homuncio* who had preceded him. The demand for a crusade was an extension of Gregory's *Dictatus Papae* and Henry's humiliation in the snows of Canossa. The Church no longer restricted itself to the spiritual welfare of its flock. Gregory had placed it at the heart of the political agenda, and had buttressed its authority with divine sanction. The *Dictatus* had established that the Church of Rome "can never err," that any individual who opposed its wishes "cannot be considered Catholic," and that the pope had the power to "release the vassals of unjust men from their oath of loyalty." To criticize a papally ordained crusade was to risk excommunication.

Urban reflected, too, the new vigor of Latin Christendom. It was no longer washed in the migratory fury of invading peoples. The tremors and sudden shocks that marked the borderlands between Christianity and Islam had turned beneficial in the western segment. The Cordoba caliphate in southern Spain had collapsed into a welter of *taifas,* petty Moslem kingdoms upon which Ferdinand, king of the northern Christian kingdom of Castile and Leon, imposed his own *jizya,* levying tribute in return for peace and protection. Toledo had fallen to the Christians in 1085.* Five months before the pope spoke at Clermont, the Christian warrior Rodrigo Diaz de Vivar, whom the Moors knew as Al-Sayyid, "the Lord," and the Spaniards as El Cid, had taken Valencia. The Moslems still encircled the city, "howling and shouting many different war-cries." El Cid "offered ceaseless prayers for divine assistance to the Lord Jesus Christ" and held them off for the moment. Further east, the Norman Robert Guiscard was driving the Moslems from Sicily, which they had held since the ninth century. He had dis-

---

*The loss was so severe that the Moslem emir of Seville sought aid from the Almoravid dynasty of Morocco and Algeria; the ferocity of the Almoravid's North African soldiers and Christian countercruelties became hallmarks of the *Reconquista,* the four hundred-year Christian reconquest of Iberia.

patched his brother Roger to the island with a slender force of sixty knights. "Our trust in God is worth more than mere numbers," he reassured them. "Fear not, the Lord Jesus Christ is with us. . . ."[13] By 1072 they had taken Palermo, the Sicilian capital. Roger's first act was to rededicate the cathedral of Santa Maria, which had been used as a mosque.

To this feeling of Christian expansion, Urban added a strong appeal to conscience. Penance was embedded in Western life. It offered the only defense against sin, an ever-present and mortal enemy whose consequences—the pits of hell, places of starvation, roasting furnaces and freezing icecaps, snakebites and dismemberment, nakedness and misery—were graphically carved and painted in churches. The fraction of humanity that would escape this fate was calculated in terms of the survival of Noah and his family in the Flood; it was put at one in a thousand, sometimes at one in ten thousand.[14] Besides the standard forty days of Lent and abstinence from meat on Fridays, many made individual penance by regular fasting to the point of collapse. "Forbidden days," when it was sinful for husband and wife to have sex, took up more than half the year. Children were urged to enter local abbeys and priories, so that the family could "benefit directly from the stream of intercessory prayer that flowed upwards to God from within the walls."[15] The proliferating riches of the Church, in estates and buildings, were physical evidence of the sense of guilt among the laity who donated them in the hope of remission of sins.

Pilgrimage was a powerful form of penance. The more arduous the journey, the more sins it washed away. The difficulties of reaching Jerusalem had placed it at the apex of penance even before the arrival of the Turks. A large group of German pilgrims had set off in 1064 under the leadership of the archbishops of Mainz and Trier, the bishop of Regensburg, and Gunther, the remarkable bishop of Bamberg.* They reached Constantinople, Gunther wrote, despite "those devious bandits the Bulgars . . . [and] the Romanians, whose raging was beyond the fury of man or beast." In Palestine the archbishop of Trier was robbed by bandits and left naked and half-dead. Arabs, one of whom lassoed Gunther round the neck with his headdress, surrounded the pilgrims. The bishop "gave his assailant a hefty blow in the face and . . . shouted that he would pay him back for his impiety in having the audacity to raise his unclean, idolatrous hands against a priest of Christ."[16] The man was bound and the bishop threatened to use his head as a shield if the Arabs continued to attack. The Arabs dispersed and Gunther reached Jerusalem, dying in Hungary on his return journey the following year.

The prospect of war added immensely to the existing risks of the journey, but

*This percursor of the Crusaders was mourned as "a man of high moral and spiritual standing";[17] six centuries later, Johann von Dorheim, his successor as bishop of Bamberg, led a crusade against witches of peerless infamy.

also to its sacred nature and to its rewards. In freeing Jerusalem of the infidel, the armed pilgrims would free themselves of sin. Other factors worked on them, of course; their boisterous and aggressive temperament, and the free range now given it by papal blessing; curiosity to see Eastern cities, so elegant compared to their own wattle and daub drabness; the shame of nonparticipation; tales of chivalry and miracles, such as the rescue of Roger's outnumbered men on Sicily by a heavenly knight "mounted on a white horse and carrying on the point of his spear a white banner bearing a splendid cross";[18] the prospect of booty. The prime motivator, however, was their faith. The Moslems were to be left in no doubt of that. "He told me that he was an only son and that his mother had sold her house to buy his equipment," a Moslem said of a young crusader captured by Saladin. "The religious motivation of the Franks was so strong. . . ."[19]

❖ THE POOR AND destitute were the first to set out after the Clermont address, at Easter in 1096. As the warlike classes busied themselves in preparations for a long campaign, peasants listened to the wandering preachers who spoke of the crusade at fairs and markets. Urban, aware that overenthusiasm could create social chaos, had decreed that no layman should depart for the Holy Land without the permission of his parish priest and the consent of his wife. The freelance preachers ignored such constraints.

A former solitary named Peter the Hermit was the most charismatic of these pious agitators. A simple figure from Amiens in northern France, he dressed in a homespun cloak, arms and feet bare, his energetic preaching fueled by a diet of wine and fish. He gave away the money that was pressed on him, providing prostitutes with dowries so they could marry. The simple folk among whom he preached thought that Little Peter was possessed "of something divine . . . so that they pulled out hairs from his mule to keep them as relics."[20] The numbers of ragged souls who followed him swelled into an army; the astonishing idea spread that the humble should themselves set out at once for Jerusalem. The departure of the barons and knights had been set for August 1096. The peasants were too eager to wait. "The poor were soon inflamed with so burning a zeal," the monk Guibert of Nogent recorded, "that none stopped to consider the slenderness of his means . . ."[21] They were in such haste to realize their few assets that the price of farm goods collapsed; "you saw such things as seven sheep being sold for five derniers," where the average price of a single animal had been some ten derniers. The rich saw "truly astonishing things" which provoked their laughter, "peasants shoeing their oxen as though they were horses, harnessing them to two-wheeled wagons on which they piled their scanty possessions and their small children . . ."[22]

Their inspiration came from the belief that life was a pilgrimage towards God, in which Christ's city of Jerusalem—"the navel of the world, illuminated by his coming, graced by his living there, made holy by his suffering, redeemed by his death, distinguished by his burial"[23]—was the most sacred earthly way station. Perhaps this mingled with a folk memory of the epic migrations of their tribal ancestors. Most people's knowledge of the world was confined to a few villages and a market town within a radius of thirty miles from their homes at best; yet they left it in raptured abandon for a city which shimmered in their imagination but whose physical location was a mystery beyond their compass. As each town or castle came into sight as they trekked southeast, they "eagerly asked if that was the Jerusalem towards which they were journeying." Though the French predominated, there was "hardly a people living according to the law of Christ that did not . . . make every effort to join them." Guibert told of men arriving in French seaports who spoke a language so unknown that they laid their fingers on one another in the form of the cross to show by signs, in default of words, that they wanted to set out "for the cause of the faith." Scots were among them, "barelegged, wearing cloaks of shaggy skins . . . hastening in crowds from their mist-shrouded lands."[24]

They took the traditional pilgrim route across Germany. Peter arrived at Cologne on Easter Saturday in 1096. He rested for a week, preaching to increase the numbers of his horde; a group of Franks led by Walter Sans-Avoir, Walter the Penniless, pressed on at once for Hungary. Peter followed, scavengers leaving a trail of atrocity in his wake. A petty lord of the Rhineland, Count Emich of Leisingen, let word out that a cross had miraculously burned itself into his flesh, and acquired his own band of pilgrims and brigands. In May he arrived at Worms and claimed that the Jews had drowned a Christian, using the water in which they kept his decomposing body to poison the city wells.

Jews were better protected than heretics—the Church forbade their forcible conversion or killing—but this modicum of safety was being undermined both by the act of crusade against nonbelievers and by a more vivid and personal perception of the crucifixion. It was once seen as a remote and austere cataclysm. Painters were now portraying Christ in the reality of his suffering, his robe cast aside and naked to the waist, his head no longer upright but lolling in his agony, blood coursing from his wounds, his eyes clamped in resignation. The distant Moslems had played no part in his Passion. It was easy to stigmatize the Jews as the descendants of those who had. They were close at hand; they were renowned for trading and moneylending, stealing from them was passed off as fund-gathering or punishment for their usury. On May 20, Emich sacked the Jewish quarter of the city. The bishop of Worms tried to protect those who fled to his palace, but

Emich and the mob broke the gates and massacred some five hundred Jews. By May 25 he had moved on to Mainz.

The gates of the city were closed to him on the orders of the archbishop, but a sympathizer opened them the next day. Emich accepted six gold pounds to spare the Jews of the city, but killed those who would not abjure their faith. "They laid hold of Mose Isak just as he was leaving his house, and took him to a church," a Jewish chronicler recorded. "But he spat upon them and reviled them, so they put him to death. . . ."[25] The killings went on for two days; one Jew burned down the synagogue to save it from desecration before killing himself and his family. About a thousand perished in Mainz. Emich found fewer victims when he backtracked north to Cologne. Christian households hid many Jews over Whitsunday, June 1, when he entered the city. The synagogue was burned and a Jewish man and woman killed, but the archbishop prevented worse outrages. Emich set off for Hungary while a splinter group broke off and persecuted the Jews in Trier and Metz.

Other wandering pilgrims imitated Emich. On June 30 a German group began to murder the Jews in Prague, where, as generally, the bishop did his best to protect them. From Prague they marched south, but the Hungarian king Coloman attacked them and broke them up before they could carry out fresh massacres. Another group that moved into Hungary, after killing Jews in Ratisbon (Regensburg), met a similar fate. They ransacked the countryside for wine, meat, and corn, impaling a local boy on a lance, until Coloman's troops disarmed and killed them. Peter was unable to control his followers, for "each lived by his wits, murdering and plundering, and all boasted with inconceivable effrontery that they would behave in the same way with the Turks." Some were killed or drowned in rivers; others straggled back to France "worn out with fatigue, penniless, in the most terrible state of want and, worse still, overcome with shame . . ."[26] Emich's army was large enough to force its way into Hungary by building a bridge over a tributary of the Danube. His men laid siege to the fortress of Wiesselburg, but a panic set in when it was rumored that Coloman was advancing, and the garrison was able to make a sortie and rout them. Only the mounted knights were able to escape; Emich himself fled back to Germany.

The inhabitants of Belgrade abandoned their city as the ferocious cavalcade shuffled towards it. The Bulgarian forests were the lair of bandits "wearing cloaks, naked beneath them, with crested headdresses and enormous boots,"[27] and a quarter of those who set out from Belgrade were dead or sold into slavery before they reached Sofia. The survivors arrived in Constantinople on August 1. The Byzantines were shocked by their numbers, by the exhausted women and children peering from the ox wagons, and by the crude instruments—clubs, pitchforks, meat choppers—wielded by the men. They outnumbered the stars in the sky, the emperor's shocked daughter Anna Comnena recorded; "like tributaries joining a river, from all directions they streamed toward us in full force," their shoulders adorned with red crosses, flocking about Little Peter "as though aflame with divine fire."[28]

For the moment their faces were "full of good humour and zeal," but only small parties were allowed into Constantinople for sightseeing. It was a wise precaution. The brief glimpse the unwashed Westerners had of the city aroused their wonder, for its scale and magnificence were unimaginable. London and Paris each had 25,000 or so inhabitants; once-mighty Rome had dwindled to 30,000, but the double walls of Constantinople protected more than 300,000 people. Alexius ruled from a new palace complex, the Blachernae, whose gardens contained a menagerie of exotic beasts. At the Hippodrome, crowds of 100,000 urged on their chariot teams. The holy relics included the Crown of Thorns, the seamless garment, a cloth with Christ's face, the hair of John the Baptist.

At first the emperor advised them not to cross the Sound of St. George, the Bosporus. It was clear that the Turks would make short shrift of them if they did not await the arrival of the barons and their experienced soldiers. After five days they began to amuse themselves, setting suburban villas alight and stripping the lead from church roofs, and Alexius had a change of heart. He ordered them to be ferried across without delay. On the Asian shore, a group was soon surrounded by Turks in an abandoned and waterless castle at Xerigordon. "Our men suffered so much from thirst that they opened the veins of their horses and donkeys to drink their blood," a chronicler recorded; "others threw belts and rags into the latrines and squeezed the liquid into their mouths . . . others dug up the damp earth and then lay down and spread it over their chests. . . ."[29]

The main body camped at Civetot on the Sea of Marmara. The Turkish leader, Kilij Arslan, played on their greed and naiveté. Peter left them to return to Constantinople, probably to ask for supplies. While he was gone, Kilij Arslan sent spies into the camp to spread false rumor that other crusaders had captured nearby Nicaea and were keeping the loot for themselves. A mass of twenty thousand men swarmed from the safety of their camp, leaving their women and children behind, to march in a slovenly column for Nicaea. They were ambushed and overrun three miles down the road. It took the Turks five hours to eliminate the People's Crusade. A year later the chronicler Fulcher of Chartres, marching to Nicaea with the baronial army, found the fields full of the severed heads and bones of his countrymen. "When they gathered up the remains of the fallen," Anna Comnena wrote, "they heaped up, I will not say a mighty hill or peak, but a mountain of considerable height and depth and width, so huge was the mass of bones."[30] Her father sent ships to bring back the survivors.

❖ THE PROFESSIONALS WHO arrived in Constantinople in the first months of 1097 were a more menacing force. They had been delayed by the need to raise funds for armor, horses, and the hire of squires and men-at-arms. The Church was often the only source of credit, and it required collateral despite the spiritual motivation of its supplicants. Thus the brothers Gaufredus and Guiogo sold an estate to the abbey of St. Victor at Marseilles to equip themselves for the expedition "to quench the accursed madness of the pagans, who rushed out at innumerable Christian people, oppressing, capturing and killing them with a barbarous furor."[31] The knight Achard of Montmerle agreed with Abbot Hugh of Cluny to pledge his possessions against an advance of the two thousand sous* and four she-mules he needed to get to Jerusalem. He achieved his heart's desire. He reached the Holy City in the summer of 1099 but was killed during its siege, and his estate passed to the Cluny monastery.

The physical presence of these Western nobles, the strangely fair hair and eyes, the robes emblazoned with the cross, the air of reckless violence, was intimidating. Bohemond kept the promise he had made while besieging Amalfi. "The sight of him caused astonishment," Anna Comnena wrote of his arrival, "the mention of his name occasioned panic." The taller Germans often mocked the Normans as dwarfs, but both were larger than the Easterners, and Bohemond "towered almost a full cubit over the tallest man. He was slender of waist and flanks, with broad shoulders and chest, strong in the arms . . . His hair was light-ish brown and not as long as that of the other barbarians (that is, it did not hang on his shoulders); he cut his short, to the ears. . . . His eyes were light blue and gave some hint of the man's spirit and dignity." He had a certain charm, but it was dimmed by the alarm he inspired; "there was a hard savage quality to his whole aspect . . . even his laugh sounded like a threat to others. Such was his constitution, mental and physical, that in him both courage and love were armed, both ready for combat."[33]

Moslems shared this view. They called the Crusaders the *Franj*, the Franks, to distinguish them from the *Nazara*, the familiar Nazarenes or Eastern Christians. "All those who were well-informed about the Franj saw them as beasts superior in courage and fighting ardour but in nothing else," wrote the chronicler Usamah

---

*Variations in local coinage make values difficult to estimate in the Middle Ages, but this was a very considerable sum, enough to buy some seven hundred head of sheep, and an indication of the financial strain a knight faced in journeying to fight at such a distance. A few Crusaders might turn a profit from this investment in booty and ransom; Count Stephen of Blois was to write enthusiastically to his wife after a year of campaigning that "now I have twice the amount of gold, silver and many other riches as your loving heart would have given me when I departed from you."[32] Most of the early Crusaders gained little or nothing, and the families of those who died were often impoverished.

ibn Munqidh, "just as animals are superior in strength and aggression."[34] Some sixty thousand of them assembled in Constantinople, accompanied by clerics, camp followers, unarmed pilgrims, some of them old and sick, and survivors from Peter's hordes. The emperor was eager to be rid of them. They were reluctant to make an oath of fealty to him and muttered when he remained seated in their presence. "I am a pure Frank," one of them told him. "At a cross-roads in the country where I was born, there is a sanctuary founded long ago, where anyone who wishes to fight a duel takes up his position. . . . I stayed for a long time at this cross-roads doing nothing and waiting for an antagonist; but a bold enough man never came." If he had been looking for an occasion to fight, the emperor assured him, "you are now going to have your fill."[35] He had them ferried over the Bosporus in April 1097.

At first they were more than a match for the Turks. They rode sturdy stallions, each bred for power and weight with a broad flat back to act as a secure fulcrum for a rider protected by a heavy mail shirt and a thick jerkin. They charged as a solid block, their lances lodged firmly beneath their arms, immovably shoulder to shoulder in tight formation. "A Frank on horseback could knock a hole in the walls of Babylon," Anna Comnena commented. The Turks were more agile on their long-legged mares, lightly armored, harrying with arrows from their short bows before wheeling away. They were merciless with stragglers, but unable to deal a severe blow to a Crusader force unless it became misshapen through indiscipline or difficult terrain. The Crusaders defeated the Seljuk sultan outside Nicaea but found the city hard to take. Their light siege artillery made little im-

Mistrusting native Christians as much as Moslems, the Crusaders held the Holy Land from great castles, here Krak des Chevaliers. A theology of war was written into canon law, drawing heavily on St. Augustine, which justified the use of force "to coerce bad people and sustain the good."

pression on the walls as it hurled small rocks, severed heads, and even beehives against the Turks. After six fruitless weeks, on June 19, 1097, they awoke to find the imperial flag flying over Nicaea. Alexius had negotiated a secret deal with the Turks, confirming the mutual distrust of Crusaders and Byzantines.

As they toiled southward beneath the Taurus Mountains, women gave birth at the roadside, and packhorses and fine Spanish warhorses were killed and eaten as supplies ran out. Carts were pulled by dogs and goats while some knights rode oxen and others dragged their armor in sacks behind them. Amid the screeching of hawks and falcons, "knights and sergeants, fair young girls alike" rent their clothes and cried out: "God who died on the cross for us, come to our aid!"[36] A group of eighty knights under Baldwin of Boulogne set off eastward across the Euphrates in February 1098. In the Armenian towns, his companion Fulcher of Chartres recorded, the Christians saw them as their saviors from the Turks and "humbly came out to meet us with crosses and standards and kissed our feet and cloaks for the love of God." Baldwin was welcomed as a liberator by the Armenian prince Thoros when he reached Edessa. On March 7 a mob encouraged by the Crusaders ransacked the palace and trapped Thoros in a tower. He pleaded with Baldwin to spare his life, offering him treasure—"in purple, in vessels of gold and silver, in golden bezants"—that merely inflamed the Frank's greed. The prince was shot down as he tried to flee the tower. Baldwin was proclaimed ruler of Edessa; the first Crusader principality was established as the decapitated corpse of its Christian prince was dragged through the streets.

The main Crusader body reached the gates of Antioch on October 20, 1097. The city had long lost the Roman grandeur that St. Paul had known; after more than three hundred years under Islam, the Byzantines had retaken it in 960 before it had again fallen to the Moslems in 1085. It remained a formidable objective, however, whose six-mile wall was studded with more than four hundred towers. The Turks inside its great citadel thought it impregnable and taunted the Christians by dangling the patriarch of Antioch in a cage from the walls. The winter was harsh and rainsodden, and the besiegers had to forage for fifty miles for scraps. It took nine months and an act of treachery for them to break into the city. In June 1098 a defender—an Armenian apostate who feared punishment for hoarding grain in one account, a breastplate maker seduced with silver in another—opened a gate and they flooded in to kill every Turk they found.

A Turkish relief force arrived a few days later. The Crusaders were now besieged and famished in their turn. At first they had cut up Moslem bodies to see if the victims had swallowed gold coins before being killed; now they "cut off the flesh in pieces and cooked it in order to eat them." "Not only did our troops not shrink from eating dead Turks and Saracens," recorded Albert of Aix, "they also ate dogs." The head of a horse without its tongue and the innards of a goat sold

The Crusaders break into Antioch in June 1098. The city had held out for nine months, and the Turks inside its citadel had taunted the Christians by dangling the patriarch of Antioch in a cage from the walls. When the Crusaders were themselves besieged in Antioch, their morale was restored by discovery of what they held to be the Holy Lance that had pierced Christ's side at the crucifixion.

for a small fortune; the leaves of fig trees and the dried skins of camels were eaten. Knights opened the veins of their living horses to drink their blood. "We endured this anxiety, and torments so varied that I cannot recall them," a chronicler wrote, "for the sake of Christ, and to open the route to the Holy Sepulchre. . . ."[37]

Their desolation was in need of a miracle, and one was duly provided. Peter Bartholomew, a shabby young cleric from Provence, claimed that St. Andrew had appeared to him in a vision and had told him that the Holy Lance with which the Romans had pierced Christ's side was buried in the cathedral at Antioch. A trench was dug in the floor of the cathedral, into which Peter jumped with a mattock. Iron was heard to strike iron and the cleric emerged with a rusty lance. The lance had a sad sequel. Miracles were frequently claimed; at times of crisis they brought comfort, like whistling in the dark, but it did not mean that they were believed. The Normans saw Peter as a cheap Provencal trickster, and Bohemond thought him a liar who "seems born to be hanged at the crossroads." Peter insisted on proving his good faith by the ordeal of fire. He walked through a pyre of blazing logs. Though he died a few days later, his supporters claimed that he had emerged unscathed but was pressed back into the flames by the crush of onlookers. For the moment, however, the lance gave heart to most, and other visions were reported, of deserters climbing down ropes over the walls to be turned back by the spirits of dead comrades, of fiery meteors.

On June 24, the bishop of Le Puy, the pope's legate, ordered a three-day fast; a technicality in a city already starving, but a sign of penance. At dawn on June 28 the Crusaders attended mass in the cathedral, their cries and tears creating the effect of a "flagellation of voices"[38] as they prayed for deliverance. They marched out of the gates behind the Holy Lance, led by priests and monks in white robes, "singing and calling on the help of God." Attempts to break them up into vulnerable pockets by setting the hay fields on fire failed. Urged on by the barefoot priests, they forced the Turks to flee. Antioch became the second Crusader state, with Bohemond as its prince.

Flemish survivors of Peter's ragged bands insisted on pressing on at once for Jerusalem. Inflamed with boils and ingrained with dirt, they believed that destitution was a necessity for salvation and that a pure spirit was found only in a filthy body. The Arabs called them *Tafurs,* "the penniless," as they carried cudgels in place of swords and hatchets. The Tafurs "always marched barefoot, bore no arms, themselves had absolutely no money but, entirely filthy in their nakedness and want," Guibert of Nogent recorded, "marched in advance of all the others, and lived on the roots of plants."[39] They spread panic among the Moslems, who had heard that the Franks feasted on Saracen corpses. To encourage this fear, the Tafurs roasted the body of a Turk over a fire in sight of his companions. They were led by a Norman knight who, seeing the Tafurs wandering about without a lord, laid down his own weapons and clothes and became King Tafur. When they marched through a narrow pass the king searched them one by one. If he found so much as a sou, the man was dismissed and told to join the corps of armed men. The savagery of the Tafurs was puritanical indeed.

In part to satisfy their restlessness, Bohemond assaulted the town of Maarat An-Numan in the olive and fig-growing country south of Antioch. It was taken on December 12, 1098 after a siege in which the ill-supplied Crusaders were again so frenzied by hunger that they "tore flesh from the buttocks of the Saracens who had died which they cooked and chewed with savage mouths."[40] Bohemond told the Saracen leaders to bring their wives and children, with their goods, to a palace by the gate. He promised to spare them; the rest were slaughtered. The Tafurs destroyed the food supplies to force the knights to press on to Jerusalem.

Led by Raymond, count of Toulouse, barefoot and in a penitential shirt, the Crusaders set out from Maarat to march the final three hundred miles to Jerusalem in January 1099. They moved into territory that the Egyptian Fatimids had recently recovered from the Turks; Jerusalem itself was again under Egyptian rule and open access to all Christians had been restored. The Egyptian vizier, happy enough to see the Turks expelled from the former Byzantine territories to the north, was alarmed at the Crusaders' continuing advance. He sent a message to Alexius in Constantinople; the emperor reaffirmed his alliance with Cairo and regretted that he had no influence over the Franks. Neither, since Urban's legate, the bishop of Le Puy, had died in an epidemic at Antioch, did Rome. The crusade moved south along the coast at its own whim. It turned inland from Jaffa on June 2.

On June 7, "mad with joy," from a hill they called Montjoie, the Crusaders saw the ochre stones of the Holy City against the early sun. By evening they were camped under its walls. The Egyptian governor, Ifrikhar al-Duala, had taken the city from the Turks a year before. The walls had been repaired and strengthened. The civilian population was small—the Turks had slaughtered many Moslems, and Ifrikhar had expelled the Christians for fear of treachery—and the food stocks were large enough to withstand a prolonged siege. Ifrikhar had a large force of Arab cavalry and Sudanese archers, and the vizier had promised to send a relief force from Egypt by the end of July. The wells around the city had been poisoned, and the besiegers had to haul vile-smelling water for six miles in ox hides. Disease and privation had reduced their numbers to about twelve thousand, a fifth of those who had been shipped across the Bosporus two years before.

The first assault on the walls was made after a day of fasting, on June 13. This was easily driven off, and it was clear that the attack would fail unless timber was found to make siege towers and scaling ladders. Its discovery was attributed to a miracle. Bohemond's nephew Tancred was scouring the hills for wood when he was overcome by a bout of dysentery. Modestly seeking to avoid the gaze of his companions, he slithered into a deep recess beneath a hollow rock. He found himself facing a cave in which lay four hundred timbers. "God has given us more than we sought," he told his foragers.[41] A "singing as if in litany" was heard from the Frankish tents. A more prosaic reason for the exultation was the arrival of Genoese and English ships at Jaffa. These brought provisions and carpenters, who dismantled two of the ships and began building siege towers with the timbers. Children from both sides met and skirmished in no man's land. Families had set out on the crusade together, and even when the parents died, the children continued on the journey. They formed a small battalion of their own. They elected princes among them who were given the titles of the adult leaders—Count of Normandy, Hugh the Great, Bohemond of Taranto—and who sought out their namesakes when they were short of supplies to beg for food.

On July 8, priests led the Crusaders in barefoot procession around the city as a sign of penance and in imitation of the circling of Jericho by the ancient Israelites. As they gathered on the Mount of Olives to hear sermons, the defenders mocked them from the walls. A completed siege tower, topped by a golden cross, was wheeled forward against the northern wall on the morning of Friday, July 15.

"If you want to know what was done to the enemies we found in the city, know this," Raymond of Toulouse wrote to the pope when Jerusalem fell in July 1099, "that in the portico of Solomon and in his Temple, our men rode in the blood of the Saracens up to the knees of their horses." It was, so the Crusaders believed, a divine slaughter. Before the assault they had been led by priests in barefoot procession around the city walls as a sign of penance.

The Moslems attempted to destroy it with Greek fire, a mixture of oil and sulphur placed in jugs that were set alight and hurled by catapult against its frame. The Franks protected the timbers with freshly flayed animal skins soaked in vinegar. At noon the men in the tower succeeded in flinging a bridge onto the wall. Two Flemish brothers, Litold and Gilbert of Tournai, scrambled across. The Moslems fell back to the temple area to seek safety in the Dome of the Rock and the al-Aqsa Mosque as Bohemond's nephew Tancred and his men burst through from the north wall. He trapped the Moslems in the mosque and on its roof, giving them a banner to fly as a sign of protection. Raymond crossed the southern wall. Ifrikhar and the garrison surrendered the Tower of David; Raymond guaranteed the governor and his men safe conduct out of the city, the only Christian pledge that was kept.

"Soon the crusaders were running all over town," a Frankish chronicle recorded,[42] "carrying off gold, silver, horses and mules, and plundering the houses, which were crammed with riches." This was no ordinary slaughter—"It was impossible to see without horror that mass of the dead," William of Tyre wrote, "and even the sight of the victors covered with blood from head to foot was also a ghastly sight"—and it was God himself who seemed to inspire the Crusaders to rid the city of all trace of its 461 years of Moslem domination. "Oh day so ardently desired!" Fulcher continued. "Oh time of times the most memorable! Oh deed before all other deeds! . . . They desired that this place, so long contaminated by the superstition of the pagan inhabitants, should be cleansed from their contagion." That evening, "full of happiness and weeping for joy," the Crusaders went to worship Christ in the church of his Holy Sepulchre.

At daybreak the slaughter continued. Ignoring Tancred's banner, a group climbed up on the roof of a mosque and decapitated those Moslems, men, women and children, who did not first fling themselves to the ground. The synagogue in which the city's Jews were sheltering was set on fire to burn them alive. The few living Moslems were ordered to dump the bodies of the dead outside the walls because they filled the streets with their stench. They "made piles of them almost as high as the houses before the gates. No one had ever seen, no one had even heard of such a carnage of pagans; funeral pyres were set up like milestones and none but God knows their number."[43]

The victors wrote to the pope with pride. "If you want to know what was done to the enemies we found in the city, know this," Raymond and the bishop of Pisa advised the pope in a letter, "that in the portico of Solomon and in his Temple, our men rode in the blood of the Saracens up to the knees of their horses."[44] Urban died shortly before this evidence of the handiwork he had instigated at Clermont reached him.

"ACT WITH A KINDLY HARSHNESS":

The Laws of War

oslems had been familiar with Christianity for more than four hundred years; many were, of course, descendants of Christians. Without turban, his head shaved as a sign of mourning, the venerable *Qadi,* or judge of Damascus, Abu Sa'ad Al-Harani, burst into the court of the caliph in Baghdad in late July 1099 to warn of a Western mutation they had not seen before, an unnerving blend of ferocity and devotion that allowed Moslems no dwelling place save the saddles of camels and the bellies of vultures, carried into Jerusalem by "fair-haired and heavily armed warriors spilling through the streets, swords in hand, slaughtering. . . ."[1]

The old ambivalence at the heart of the Christian faith—the ability of men of conscience to construct ideologies that are in startling contradiction to the common raw material of the Testaments—was laid bare by the massacre. Apologists said that the God of Exodus ordained it. "The Lord is a man of war," they quoted. "Pharaoh's chariots and his host he hath cast into the sea. . . . The deep covers them" (Exod. 15:3–4). A smaller number stressed the Son and his warning that those who take up the sword shall perish by the sword. "Christ did not shed his blood for the acquisition of Jerusalem," Abbot Adam of Perseigne said with revulsion, "but rather to win and save souls."[2]

Between the meekness of Christ and the cruelty of the Christian soldier lay a gulf so wide and obvious that it required an explanation.* The Western Church looked to St. Augustine to provide it. His thoughts dated back to the Vandal invasion of North Africa; they were not systematic, for they were scattered through-

---

*All-Christian armies had been in the field since 416, when the Roman army was purged—at least in theory—of pagan troops, but they had not been used as an arm of Church policy. Roman law justified war on the basis of *vim vi repellere,* "force to repel force."

out his letters and writings, but they remained the only significant examination, and a number of works had drawn attention to them shortly before the Clermont sermon.* Soldiering was not inimical to the faith, Augustine stated. Soldiers who asked John the Baptist how to attain salvation were not told to throw away their arms, merely to "be content with your pay" (Luke 3:14). It was, moreover, a Christian duty to fight in a "just war," provided that it reflected the will of God and not the desires and rashness of men. "Then no one will wonder or be aghast at the wars waged under Moses," Augustine wrote. "The reason is that, as Moses was following divine commands, he was not savage but obedient, and God, in ordering such things, was not savage but was . . . striking with awe those who deserved it." Revenge, lust for domination, revolt, and desire to harm—these things were unjust. But why should war itself be blamed? "This is the complaint of the timid mind, not of the religious," he said. "Certain wars that must be waged against the violence of those resisting are commanded by God or by a legitimate ruler and are undertaken by the good."[3]

He denied that Christ was a pacifist. "If anyone supposes that God could not have commanded anyone to wage war because in later times the Lord Jesus Christ said, 'I say unto you, do not resist evil, but if anyone should strike you on the right cheek, offer him the left as well' (Matt. 5:39), he should understand that this does not refer to a disposition of the body but of the heart."[4] The key to this distinction was Christ's response to Pilate when he was asked what he had done to protect himself. "My kingdom is not of this world," Jesus replied. "If my kingdom were of this world, then would my servants fight, that I should not be delivered to the Jews: but now is my kingdom not from hence" (John 18:36). Augustine saw Jesus as transferring physical combat into the spiritual warfare described in Ephesians; a wrestling "not against flesh and blood, but against the principalities, against the powers of . . . darkness, against the spiritual hosts of wickedness in the heavenly places" (Eph. 6:12–13). Had Jesus not considered war to be as natural as famine and earthquake? "And ye shall hear of war and rumours of wars," he had said on the Mount of Olives. "See that ye be not troubled for these things must needs come to pass" (Matt. 24:6). Was there not steel in his meekness: "Think not that I came to send peace on the earth; I came not to send peace, but a sword . . ."? (Matt. 10:34).

True, Augustine argued that the concept of holy war was wrong because no one has a monopoly on divine truth. "Because thy truth, O Lord, does not belong to me, to this man or that man, but to us all, Thou hast called us to it with a terrible warning not to claim it exclusively for ourselves," he wrote, "for if we do, we

---

*Notably Anselm of Lucca's *Collection canonum* in c. 1083, and the *Decretum* and *Panormia* of Ivo of Chartres in c. 1094.

shall lose it."[5] It was difficult to justify the slaying of Moslems and Jews in that light; in another passage, however, Augustine suggested that "unwilling souls"— a category into which nonbelievers could easily be made to fit—brought coercion on themselves. "We often have to act with a sort of kindly harshness, when we are trying to make unwilling souls yield, because we have to consider their welfare rather than their inclination," he wrote.[6] "For when we are stripping a man of the lawlessness of sin, it is good for him to be vanquished since nothing is more hopeless than the happiness of sinners. . . ." Indeed, whole groups could be exposed to such "kindly harshness." A man who deserted the true God and yielded himself to impure demons lost all claim to justice; "and if there is no justice in such an individual," the saint continued, "certainly there can be none in a community composed of such persons."[7] Though all should acknowledge that war is misery, victory in a just cause is a gift of God. "Do not imagine that no one can please God while he is engaged in military service," Augustine had written to the warrior Count Boniface. "Among such was holy David to whom the Lord gave such high testimony. Among such were many just men of the time. . . ."

❖   MUCH OF AUGUSTINE'S thought was incorporated verbatim by the Bolognese monk and jurist Gratian into the *Decretum Gratiani* in c. 1140. This was the basic text of the *Corpus Iuris Canonici,* the chief collection of canon law, which laid down ecclesiastical rules on matters of faith, morals, and discipline in the Catholic Church for the next nine centuries.

Religious warfare became an act of peace in Gratian's concise and unyielding Latin: *pacata sunt bella, que geruntur, ut mali coherceantur et boni subleuentur,* "peaceful are wars which are waged to coerce bad people and sustain the good."[8] Direct provision was made for both heretics and Moslems: *ecclesiasticae religionis inimici etiam bellis sunt cohercendi,* "the enemies of the Church and religion are coerced by war."[9] The heavenly reward for Crusaders was confirmed: "certainly, whoever dies, when waging war against the infidels, merits the celestial kingdom."[10] The Roman concept of patriotic death was reintroduced: "full of justice is he who protects his fatherland by war from barbarians."[11] The papal right to exhort the faithful to war was legitimized and backdated to Leo IV and the Saracen attack on Rome in 846: "It is even allowed with Leo to urge whomever to defend themselves against the enemies of the faith and to rouse them to force to keep away the infidels."[12] A chilling license was given to the actions of soldiers: *quod militare non est peccatum, et quod precepta patienciae in preparatione cordis, non ostentatione corporis seruanda sunt,* "soldiering is not a sin, and the precept of patience operates in the workings of the heart, not in the actions of the body."[13] A soldier was judged good or evil by his intentions, not by his acts.

Priests were to refrain from violence themselves but were free to encourage it in others: "Priests themselves ought not seize arms in their hands, but it is allowed for them to encourage others to do so for defence against oppressors and to fight the enemies of God."[14] The sermon at Clermont was now a matter of law, and the Church formally reserved to itself the right to initiate religious war and heretic hunts.*

❖ THESE IDEAS PROFOUNDLY influenced the Crusaders. As a body they professed their love of Christ and Church, and individual actions often reflected this. Raymond of Saint-Gilles would not accept the offer of a king's golden crown in the city where Jesus had worn the crown of thorns. Dying in Syria, Guy of Bré gathered his friends to witness his final mortal act, the gift of his last possessions to monasteries in their distant homeland of the Limousin in France. Crusaders did not share this love with the native Christians, however, and neither did they proclaim it to the Moslems in the hope of winning their souls.

The sacred violence of Clermont was not evangelical but sectarian, and it entombed the Catholic invaders in a spiritual isolation that added to the perils of malaria, dysentery, plague, and Moslem vengeance. The climate was alien to their own fogs and rain; "water is never cool," a chronicler noted, "intense heat, like a furnace, scorches relentlessly . . . here one finds no shaded corner for a siesta, one breathes in oppressive gasps."[15] They were outnumbered by more than seven to one in the small slivers of territory they controlled; at first only three hundred knights remained in the wreckage of Jerusalem. The original Islamic conquests had thrived on Christian disunity, and the Crusaders owed much of their own success to Moslem tensions, which pitted Seljuk Turk against Danishmend, Shia against Sunni, the caliph of Baghdad against his rival in Cairo. The lesson was ignored.

When the priests of the Orthodox Greeks, Armenians, Georgians, Jacobites, and Copts returned to Jerusalem, they were banished from the Church of the Holy Sepulchre. The ecclesiastical hierarchy became entirely Latin; "in the great shrines of their faith the native Christians [were] made to attend ceremonies whose language and ritual were alien to them."[16] The new patriarch, Arnulf of Rhodes, had non-Catholics tortured to reveal where they had hidden fragments

---

*The concept of the just war was refined by St. Thomas Aquinas in the mid-thirteenth century. He laid down three conditions: the war must be on the authority of the sovereign, who, Aquinas quoted St. Paul, "is God's minister, an avenger to execute wrath upon him that doeth evil" (Rom. 13:4); the cause must be just; and the belligerent must have rightful intentions. This left, of course, much latitude in defining what was just and rightful. To this, the Spanish Dominican Francisco de Vitoria added that war must be waged by "proper means"; this might have ruled out the atrocities of Jerusalem, but Vitoria wrote in the sixteenth century.

from the True Cross.* Urban had wished the Holy Land to become an ecclesiastical kingdom ruled by a papal legate in the name of the pope. The control of a crusade, however, was a very different matter to preaching it. The barons had no intention of ceding political power to Rome. On Christmas Day, 1100, in the Basilica of the Blessed Mary at Bethlehem, Baldwin, a landless younger son from the windy dampness of the French Channel coast, whose men were borrowed from his brothers for he had no vassals of his own, was proclaimed king of Jerusalem.

Expeditions were sent to flush potential rebels from the caves where they had fled. "We lit great fires at the mouths of these lairs," the chronicler Fulcher of Chartres recorded, "and soon an unbearable heat and smoke forced them to come out and surrender to us." Among the fugitives were some Syrians. It was a matter of indifference that these were fellow Christians, and "we cut off their heads as soon as they set foot outside the caves." Moving on to the Dead Sea, Fulcher came across wretches blacker than soot, whom "we left there like the most worthless seaweed."[18] The new state was dangerously small, and Baldwin expanded it. Tripoli was taken, its famous Dar al-Ilm library sacked and its books burned. A three-month siege of Beirut ended in another massacre. "I do not know whether it is pasture for wild animals, or my house, my birthplace," a survivor said in shock. "I turn to it, my voice full of tears, my heart torn with suffering and love, and ask: House, why did destiny pronounce such an unjust sentence on us?"[19] Sidon surrendered. Within eighteen months, four of the most renowned cities of the Moslem world had fallen.

"We who were Occidentals have now become Orientals," Fulcher was claiming by 1125. "He who was a Roman or a Frank has in this land been made into a Galilean or a Palestinian. . . . He who was born an alien has become as a native."[20] Some wore turbans and kept unofficial harems. They ate apricots, drank sherbet, and bathed regularly, all things unknown in the unwashed West. They called their small empire Outremer, however, "the land across the sea," a name evocative of exile and longing for home. Little assimilation took place with local Christians; the Moslem ban on them carrying arms remained, and they continued to pay their new masters poll taxes that differed from the *jizya* only in being set higher. The Armenians of Edessa, who at first had welcomed the Latins, found their yoke intolerable; in a repetition of the first Islamic conquests, native Chris-

---

*Such a fragment was sent to the canons of Notre Dame in Paris by Anseau, the Latin preceptor of the Church of the Holy Sepulchre in Jerusalem, in 1108. Accompanying letters explained that fragments from the True Cross had been cut up and distributed for safekeeping when the Arabs had taken Jerusalem in 638; this fragment "belonged to David, King of Georgia, who holds the mouths of the Caspian . . ." At his death, David's widow took the veil and entered a congregation of Georgian nuns at Jerusalem, presenting them with the fragment. It was flushed out by the Crusaders and sold to Anseau. "Thus it was that for mere money was brought this wood without price," he wrote to Paris, "that I now send to you."[17]

tians often preferred Moslem rule. The Latins made some distinctions—they favored Syrian Christians over the Orthodox, for example, because of the Greeks' allegiance to Byzantium—but only with the Maronites, high in the mountains above Tripoli and Beirut, did they find warmth. A union of the Maronite and Roman Churches was achieved. It brought the Latins skilled archers and loyal allies, but it was late—in 1182—and proved to be merely the exception to the general rule of Christian alienation.

❖ ONLY WESTERN-BORN CATHOLICS were fighting men, therefore, and the shortage of them was acute. For security against Moslem raiders, the kingdom of Jerusalem had to push its borders south toward Egypt and east into Transjordan. The deepwater port at Acre had to be taken; Jaffa's port was too shallow for seagoing ships, and a thousand pilgrims had drowned there in 1102 when the wind got up as lighters were transferring them. A solution was found in the creation of military orders, which, marrying the martial instinct with the monastic, created a new breed of warrior-monk. In 1118 a knight of Champagne in northern France, Hugh de Payens, bound himself and eight companions to a solemn vow to defend pilgrims on the dangerous roads of the Holy Land. They were known as the "Poor Knights of Christ and of the Temple of Solomon," or Templars, after the site in Jerusalem where they were given quarters.* They seized the intense and mystic imagination of St. Bernard of Clairvaux, the Cistercian abbot of Clairvaux. He won recognition for the Rule of their order in 1128, which imposed Cistercian discipline and simplicity on them.

The saddlery and weapons of the Templars were plain, without trace of gold or silver. They slept in dormitories in shirts and breeches, wore beards and cropped hair, and were chaste, forbidden to embrace even a mother or sister. Martial sports—hawking and hunting for anything but lion—were banned. They ate in silence. They prayed; when campaigning, they said thirteen Paternosters in place of matins, seven for each canonical hour and nine for vespers.[21] The master of the order was both their general and their abbot. St. Bernard, who preached a fresh crusade with driving force of personality and eloquence, had no doubt that it was the purpose and duty of the Templars to slaughter the infidel. Urging them to action in 1130, he told them that it was better that Moslems "be killed than to let them remain a rod of sinners over the fate of the just, lest perhaps the just extend their hands toward iniquity."[22]

They drew inspiration directly from the Old Testament, with frequent read-

*The other great order in the East was that of the Hospital of St. John. The Hospitallers maintained a hospital at Jerusalem that offered both shelter and nursing for sick and poor pilgrims.

ings from the Books of Joshua and Maccabees on the heroic combats of Judas Maccabeus against the Seleucids. Warfare in ancient Israel had blended with religion. Prophets foretold God's will before the start of campaigns, and lambs were sacrificed to ensure divine favor. To achieve the same end, Crusaders walked barefoot in processions, and their womenfolk shaved their heads and bathed in cold water when battle was imminent. The Jews believed that they met victory or defeat at God's pleasure; the Hebrews escaped from Egypt through his grace, but, when they sinned, God condemned them to wander in the wilderness. Christians likewise blamed sin for their defeats. One papal bull, for instance, referred to the concern for "costly garments, external appearances, dogs, hawks or other signs of licentiousness . . ."[23] Gambling, the wearing of furs of vair* or gris, gilt stirrups and spurs, and dinners of more than two courses were sacrificed to appease God. "So do I give up joy and delight and furs and sable," a depressed knight from Poitou complained. This fear of God's wrath was tangible even to the enemy. "Now you have been brought so low by your sins that we take you in the fields like cattle," a triumphant Moslem told Christian prisoners.[24]

The sense of sin was not attached to the morality of warfare itself. The knights drew strength from the Book of Deuteronomy, and its guidelines on the treatment of besieged cities. Those which "are far off from thee" were to be offered terms of surrender by which the vanquished would serve as forced labor for the victors, but could keep their property and their lives. If this was refused, the men should all be killed; the "women and the little ones, and the cattle and all that is in the city, even all the spoil thereof, shalt thou take for a prey for thyself." But in cities "which the Lord thy God giveth thee for an inheritance," the order was precise. "Thou shalt save nothing alive that breatheth, but thou shalt utterly destroy them," Deuteronomy instructed, "that they teach you not to do after all their abominations . . ." (Deut. 20:16–18). St. Bernard's words—kill the infidel "lest perhaps the just extend their hands towards iniquity . . ."—are identical in meaning. The Holy Land was far from northern Europe; but the Crusaders and their priests frequently referred to it as "Christ's patrimony," a place that was theirs by virtue of their Christian inheritance. The slaying at Jerusalem thus acquired its biblical blessing.

The martial spirit was accepted by the gentlest souls. Francis of Assisi showed rare compassion for the Moslems when he visited Crusaders in Egypt. He bravely crossed the lines armed with no more than "the shield of faith" to preach the gospel to the Egyptian sultan, telling the Arabs who intercepted him: "I am a Christian, take me to your master."[25] When he was brought to the sultan, "the fierce beast . . . was turned to gentleness" and listened attentively to his sermon.

*Vair is a type of squirrel fur, bluish gray and white, and then much popular; gris is a gray fur.

Francis returned safely, if without converts. This much-loved man, the second most rapidly canonized saint of the Church,* nevertheless considered Christian warriors to be "strong men mighty in battle, pursuing the infidel with much sweat and toil even unto death . . . holy martyrs [who] died in battle for the faith of Christ."[26]

Another man noted for his humanity, Jacques of Vitry, the crusader-bishop of Acre, who concerned himself with the Moslems in his see, educating their children and preventing them from being sold into slavery, preached a sermon at Acre that was a masterly précis of Augustine and the emerging philosophy of Christian violence. "When people falsely assert that you are not allowed to take up the physical sword or fight bodily against the enemies of the Church," he told his Templar audience, "it is the devil trying to attack the fabric of your Order and by means of these people to destroy it utterly. . . . The precepts of forebearance should be observed not so much in a false show of action as in circumspection of heart. That is why the Lord, when struck on the cheek, was not seen to offer the other, but patiently bore it and exposed his whole body to death. . . . [E]nemies need to be bent with benign harshness, because if you take away the license to sin from a man you give him the reward of serving God. . . . If we were not resisting the Church's enemies, the Saracens and heretics would have destroyed the whole Church." He spoke of the ideal Christian, a "certain soldier who on seeing a host of Saracens began to say to his horse with rejoicing in his heart: 'Oh, Morel, my good companion, I have done many a good day's work mounted and riding on you, but this day's work will be better than the others, because today you will take me to eternal life.' And then, after killing many Saracens, he himself died, crowned in war by blessed martyrdom."[28] The glory of the early martyrs had been their passive acceptance of death. As Stephen had been stoned a millennium before, he had knelt and cried: "Lord, lay not this sin to their charge" (Acts 7:60). Jacques of Vitry's crusader was changed utterly. He sought his salvation in the death of others, cutting them off like "poisonous limbs . . . and decayed flesh."

A MINORITY IN the West joined Abbot Adam in condemning the policy of killing rather than converting. "Solely by the word of God," the Dominican William of Tripoli wrote, "without philosophical arguments, without military weapons, [the Moslems] will seek, like simple sheep, the baptism of Christ and will enter into the flock of God."[29] The English courtier Walter Map concurred.

---

*The Franciscan friar Antony of Padua, renowned as a worker of miracles, was canonized a year after his death in 1231; Francis was canonized after two years. The wait for Thomas à Becket, the murdered archbishop of Canterbury, was three years.[27]

He despised the Templars in Jerusalem who "take up in defence of Christianity the sword that had been denied Peter in the defence of Christ . . . I do not know who taught them to overcome force by violence. . . . With the word of the Lord, not with the edge of the sword, had the Apostles conquered Damascus, Alexandria and a great part of the world, which the sword did lose. . . ."[30] Isaac, an English Cistercian philosopher and abbot, thought the Templars were a *monstrum novum,* a new monstrosity which "despoils licitly and murders religiously," running counter to "Christ's clemency, patience and manner of preaching."[31]

For their part, Orthodox Christians encouraged Moslem apostates. Anna Comnena noted that her father was "eager to convert to Christ . . . the whole of Persia and all the barbarians who dwell in Egypt and Libya and worship Muhammad."[32] Refugees from the caliphates were warmly welcomed, and Moslem prisoners were given incentives to settle in the empire. Each convert received six silver coins at baptism, along with fifty-four measures of grain for seed-corn and a contribution toward the cost of plowing oxen. Christian parents who married their daughters to converts were rewarded with a three-year exemption from the hearth tax. The offspring of one such union, Tacitus, was the army general appointed to liaise with the Latins in the First Crusade. Orthodox priests had a specific ritual for the abjuration of Islam, in which the convert anathematized "the God of Muhammad about whom he says: 'He is God alone, a god of hammer-beaten metal.' "*

The drive to convert Moslems in Iberia and the western Mediterranean† was as implacable as the title given to its great exponent in Majorca and Ibiza, the Dominican Raymond of Penyaforte, *zelator fidei propagandae inter Sarracenos,* "zealot of the faith among the Saracens." Moslem serfs in Aragon and Castile who apostatized were accorded free status and full property rights; while he besieged Valencia, Jaime I of Aragon proudly baptized Moslems beneath the city walls. The chronicler of the siege of Moslem Lisbon in 1147 prayed that its starving people be spared their suffering and be brought to the faith. "Spare now, Lord, spare the work of your hands," he wrote. "But rather, if it be possible, let the sorrow be turned into joy, 'in order that they may know You, the only living and true God, and Jesus Christ, whom You had sent' (John 17:3). . . ."[33] The work of Is-

---

*The emperor Manuel Comnenus (1143–80) objected to this formula on the grounds that potential converts might take it to be a damnation of God, as he himself did. Converts were instructed to direct their anathema "to Muhammad, to all his teaching and all his inheritance."

†The first Latin European conversions followed the kidnapping of the abbot of Cluny in 972; as he was crossing the Alps on his return from Rome, the abbot was seized by a group of Moslem marauders who maintained a base on the French coast near Marseilles. The monks of Cluny had to ransom him, causing such outrage among the barons of Burgundy and Provence that they pursued the kidnappers deep into the mountains of the Alpes Maritimes and captured them. The abbot himself had already "pierced these enemies of Christ with the spear of God's word"[35] and the brigands renounced Islam.

lamic scholars was studied, and the vibrant swirls of Moorish architecture mingled with Romanesque and Gothic. In time, the *conversos,* or "new Christians," attained high rank in the Church as well as in government

In Sicily, too, the Norman conqueror Roger stood as godfather to two distinguished Moslem converts, one of whom served as chamberlain and another as an admiral. A few were spontaneously attracted to their new faith. Constantine the African, a remarkable physician and merchant from Tunis who died a few months before the Clermont address, had sailed to Italy of his own free will and joined the monastery of Monte Cassino, where he translated Arabic medical tracts into Latin. Most converts were the result of pressures familiar from the Islamic conquests: greater opportunity and lesser taxation, improved social status, coercion. The Moslem pilgrim Ibn Djubayr, boarding a ship in Sicily on his way from Granada to Mecca, saw a father trying to marry his young daughter to a Moslem passenger to spare her the temptation of apostasy.[34] He rightly feared that all Sicilian Moslems would convert. A contemporary list of the Christians of Corleone, a town later notorious as the center of the Sicilian mafia, revealed the great majority to have Arabic family names prefaced by a "Christian name," the first name given them on baptism into the faith.

The process was crude—Christian preachers branded Muhammad's paradise a brothel and spoke of his putrid corpse being eaten by dogs, while apostates recaptured by Moslems were tortured to death—and reopened a debate on forced conversion. Gregory I had declared in 602 that Christians should strive to lead infidels to the faith by "blandishments, not asperities." The Council of Toledo in 633 had confirmed the ban on force; it added, however, that a convert was obliged to remain a Christian whether his baptism was voluntary or not. Gratian included both statements in his Decretals, and Pope Innocent III attempted to clarify the issue in 1202. He ruled that if an infidel was physically forced to undergo baptism, but maintained his unwillingness as it was taking place, then the act of baptism was invalid. But if he agreed to baptism—even when in pain and terror and with the motive of avoiding further torture—then the baptism had binding force. The ruling had savage consequences for Jews and Moslems in the lands of the *Reconquista.*

❖   IT MATTERED LITTLE in Outremer. The Crusaders had no intention of creating a Catholic population and were under no pressure to do so. None of the scores of papal summonses to crusade in the Holy Land mentioned Moslem conversion as a goal. Three popes* called on successive archbishops of Toledo to

*Urban II, Paschal II, and Hadrian IV.

bring infidels to Christ; no papal letter to the prelates of Outremer dictated conversion. It was a Rule of the Spanish military Order of Santiago to lead Saracens to Christianity, but not of any order in the East. Almost the only reference is from the chaplain accompanying Louis VII of France in 1147, who remarked that the Crusader leaders wished "to visit the Holy Sepulchre and, by the command of the Supreme Pontiff, wipe out our sins with the blood or conversion of the pagans."[36]

In practice, voluntary requests for baptism were regularly refused. Jacques of Vitry railed from his pulpit against Crusader masters who refused their Saracen slaves baptism "although these earnestly and tearfully requested it." The masters retorted that if the Moslems converted, they could no longer be coerced. Gregory IX wrote to the patriarch of Jerusalem and the masters of the military orders in 1237 to complain that, although some slaves might accept baptism only to be freed and then revert to Islam, others who asked for baptism with truth and humility were denied. He found this intolerable, but recognized that masters would thwart any generosity. Gregory therefore ruled that baptized slaves would maintain their servile status while being free to attend church and receive the sacraments. No notice was taken. He wrote again, accusing the masters of loving "possessions more than souls," to no effect.

A few conversions did take place. Ibn Jubayr, passing through Galilee on his return from Mecca, remarked on a Moslem who had mixed with Christians in Damascus and Acre and "had been baptised and become unclean, and had put on the girdle of a monk, thereby hastening for himself the flames of hell."[37] A captured Turkish messenger asked for baptism, the chronicler Albert of Aachen recorded, though "more out of fear than love for the Catholic faith"; another Turk fell in love with a nun and begged to be allowed to convert.[38] Legend made much of a seductive Moslem princess who falls in love with a captured Christian knight, helps to free him, and accepts baptism for his sake; the tale was first told to Bohemond, prince of Antioch.

Reality was less romantic. Death in combat, and the shortage of men, was a more common cause for alliances across the religious divide. A Christian who killed a Saracen could marry the widow if she converted, Pope Celestine II informed the bishop of Acre. A Saracen who killed a Christian and converted was equally free to take the widow. Polygamy, however, was denied to converts, who were obliged to return to the first wife they had taken as a Moslem. But it was rare for captured soldiers on either side to convert even on pain of death. Baldwin of Bourg offered baptism to a noble Saracen captured during the siege of Jerusalem; he refused, and Baldwin's esquire decapitated the Saracen in front of the city walls. Six knights sent to the governor of Damascus to demand that he surrender the city were given a similar choice. One apostatized while the other five were executed. The only Moslems to convert in some numbers were Turkopoles, light cavalrymen perhaps overawed by the heavier Christian knights, recognizable in lists of troops by the common surname of Baptizatus.

The Crusaders had equally little interest in Eastern culture. An accurate account of Islam, and its rites and tenets, was written by the Spanish Jew Pedro Alfonsi in his *Musulmilitica Religio* after his conversion to Christianity in 1106. Yet the notion that Moslems worshiped "gods, goddesses and demons" persisted. After a century of Outremer, the patriarch of Jerusalem was still claiming that "the Saracens adore their god Magometh,* just as Christians worship Christ in their churches."[39] To the mystic Joachim of Fiore, Moslems were "the Beast of the Sea of the Apocalypse and the Fourth Beast of Daniel," and Muhammad was "the Fourth Head of the Seven-Headed Dragon." Peter the Venerable, the studious abbot of Cluny, had the Koran translated into Latin in about 1145. "I approach you," he addressed the Arabs in the preface to his own work on Islam, "not, as men often do, with arms, but with words; not with force, but with reason, not in hatred, but in love . . . I love you; loving you, I write you; writing you I invite you to salvation."[40] He earned his "Venerable" title for his "moderation and gentleness," but he titled his work *Against the Abominable Heresy or Sect of the Saracens,* and he wrote to the crusading Louis VII urging him to destroy the Arabs "as Moses and Joshua destroyed the Amonites and Canaanites."

The Moslems, like the Byzantines, found the Westerners barbarous. Usamah ibn Munqidh, who visited Jerusalem in 1140 on a diplomatic mission, was repelled by their invocation of the "judgment of God" in trial by ordeal. Arab justice was a formal procedure in which a respected *Qadis,* or judge, listened carefully to pleas and testimony. Usamah watched the Christian method when an aged farmer of Nablus, accused of pillage, was forced to fight a young smith chosen by the viscount of Nablus. Each was given a lance and a shield. As the viscount shouted "Faster!" the exchange of blows was so violent that it "seemed to form a single column of blood . . . The smith rose and finished off his opponent with a thrust of his lance. A rope was wound around the neck of the corpse, which was dragged to a gallows and hanged. . . . You may see what justice is among the Franj!"[41] Usamah was also struck by Crusader contempt for more learned Eastern Christians. He recorded that a Christian Arab doctor was treating a Crusader who had a leg abscess with a poultice, and a consumptive woman with a special diet, when a Frankish physician intervened. The Frank ordered the leg to be severed with a battle-ax, and, announcing that the woman had been en-

---

*Many names were used for Muhammad. The emperor's daughter Anna Comnena used Moamet, but she could equally have chosen Mahamet, Muameth, Machmoth, Mathomus, Mahumet, Mahometus, or Magometh. The Byzantines were well aware that Moslems did not worship Muhammad, of course; there were mosques in Constantinople, as there were churches in every major Moslem city.

tered by the devil, cut an incision in the shape of the Holy Cross in her head with a razor. Both patients died.

The ways in which Catholic men treated women, so unlike their own, was another source of wonder. Moslem women were seldom seen in public and forbidden to make the pilgrimage to Mecca, but it was fashionable for Christian women to visit Jerusalem; others served the armies as laundresses, hair-washers and louse-pickers, serving women, and prostitutes. Usamah saw a Crusader walking in a Jerusalem street with his wife when they met another man, who took the wife's hand and chatted with her "while her husband stands waiting for them to finish their conversation." He was astounded. "Imagine this contradiction!" he wrote. "These people possess neither jealousy nor honour, whereas they are so courageous. Courage, however, comes only from one's sense of honour and from contempt for that which is evil!"

Courage was a quality that the Catholics needed in abundance. A Moslem countercrusade, a jihad, or holy war, gathered pace in raids and ambuscades. Its heroes had names that remain familiar: the *fida'i,* or fedayeen, fighters whose title meant "one who sacrifices himself," and the *mujahid,* or mujahedin, from the same root as jihad. It became dangerous for Christians to leave the cities or the network of great castles that they built. In the countryside the chronicler Fulcher wrote of the "Great Fear Which Then Possessed Everyone." He quoted Matthew: "In many fields the ripened harvest withered, and no one went into the fields to gather it," adding: "For none dared to do so."

Edessa (Urfa in present-day Turkey), isolated, its count absent, and its archbishop Hugo a miser, was the first Frankish city to fall. On Christmas Eve, 1144, its walls collapsed due to a sap dug beneath them by Imad ed-Din Zengi, a tough and ambitious Turk. He killed the Franks, including the archbishop, sold their women into slavery, and destroyed the Latin churches. Significantly, he spared the Armenian, Jacobite, and Greek churches and their congregations. The city was recovered only to be again besieged and taken by the Turk's son Nur ed-Din, as a helpless mass of the old and sick, women and babies at the breast, were trampled by each other and Turkish horses as they fled.

It was not a massacre to compare with Jerusalem, but the shock raced to Europe. Bernard of Clairvaux preached a new crusade in 1146 with theatrical brilliance; when he ran out of crosses to hand to his audience, he tore his robe into strips to make more. "I opened my mouth," he wrote to the pope Eugenius III, "I spoke, and at once the crusaders multiplied to infinity. Villages and towns are now deserted. You will scarcely find one man for every seven women. Everywhere you will see widows whose husbands are still alive."[42] A large German army under Conrad III set out for the East, followed by the French host of Louis VII. The Germans crossed the Bosporus in the summer of 1147 after the traditional rites

of passage—looting, the killing of Jews, mutual hostility with the Byzantines—
and were led by their Byzantine guide into "the great wilderness and . . . their
souls gradually failed." They were ambushed near Dorylaeum. "Nothing could be
heard except the depths of grief and the groans and crashes of the dying," a German chronicler wrote; "on the other side nothing except the awful shout: 'Death
to the pilgrims!' as the Saracens urged each other on with mouths . . . All that
night . . . the Christians were struck down and captured as they wandered like
sheep among the pathless places."[43] After a failed attack on Damascus, the great
monarchs returned to Europe.

Bernard thought that the collapse of the Second Crusade pointed to "an end
almost to existence itself." The worst, however, was yet to come. Nur ed-Din's
successor Saladin, small, delicate, chivalrous, and formidable, proclaimed himself
sultan of Egypt and Syria and consolidated his power in Mesopotamia. Raising
an army of perhaps 30,000 men supported by many volunteers, he crossed the
Jordan River on July 1, 1187, and marched into Tiberias. The Crusaders moved
onto the plateau above the Sea of Galilee on July 3. They numbered some
20,000, every fit man the Franks could muster. They camped beneath a waterless
double hill called the Horns of Hattin, licking at dry wells and sipping "even the
source of their tears as they teetered on the brink of calamity."[44] They remained in
their armor all night. After dawn the dehydrated Franks were cut down by archers
and choked by flame and smoke as Saladin set the dry grasslands alight. Raymond, the count of Tripoli, led a cavalry charge; the Moslems opened their ranks
to let him through, and he rode on for two hundred miles to Tripoli while the carnage continued behind him. The Crusaders rallied behind the great cross carried
by the bishop of Acre, in which a piece of the True Cross was said to be embedded, until he fell. By midafternoon it was over. "They, the people of the Trinity,
were consumed by a worldly fire of three types, each invincible and obliterating,"
Saladin's secretary wrote acidly. "The fire of flames, the fire of thirst, and the fire
of arrows."[45]

The pope, Gregory VIII, collapsed and died after hearing news of the battle.
Acre surrendered at the beginning of August; Beirut fell, Jaffa resisted and its
people were enslaved. Refugees fell back on Jerusalem, where a "terrified and
craven mob" begged the patriarch to begin immediate negotiations with Saladin.
Terms for ransom were agreed at twelve sovereigns for a man, five for a woman,
and one for a child. They would be free to travel to Antioch or sail to Alexandria
under safe conduct; those who could not pay were enslaved. The patriarch took
with him carloads of treasure. Saladin released the elderly and all captive husbands of freed wives, while his brother asked for a gift of a thousand captives, and
freed them all. There was no massacre when the city was surrendered at noon on
October 2, 1187. A Christian chronicler claimed that a muezzin climbed the

high mount of Calvary, and, "where Christ on his cross put an end to the law of death, the proclamation of a bastard law rang out."[46] Saladin's secretary recalled only that his master's "expression shone, giving off a sweet perfume," while on the walls "pennants were raised and unfurled, as pens inscribing the news" of the triumph of Islam.

Christians looked to their own sins for explanation. "So the Lord 'gave his people over also unto the sword' (Ps. 78:62), as the sins of mankind demanded," one wrote. "What more is there to say?"[47]

In 1179 the Third Lateran Council gave limited indulgence to all who fought against heretics. It was a modest start to what would become a terrifying enterprise; a small expedition under the command of a papal legate was sent against the Cathars of the Languedoc in France, achieving little beyond the capture of a minor fortress.* A Third Crusade, called to reconquer Jerusalem in 1189, ended in stalemate. Frederick Barbarossa, the Holy Roman emperor, drowned in a swift-flowing river in Cilicia. His son Henry VI pickled his body so that his mortal remains could keep his vow of reaching the Holy City, but the vinegar in the barrel failed and the rotting corpse of Germany's greatest monarch was buried at Antioch. Richard the Lionheart, the English king, retook Acre; though he got close enough to glimpse Jerusalem, Richard covered his face with his shield lest he break his vow to see it only as its conqueror. A truce was agreed with Saladin.

❖   THE CRUSADING IDEAL was disintegrating in cynicism and disgust with the Church. A German monk at Wurzburg condemned it as the work of the devil. "God allowed the Western Church on account of its sins to be cast down," he wrote. "Thereupon there arose certain pseudo-prophets, sons of Belial and witnesses of Antichrist, who seduced Christians with empty words. . . . They were so influential that the inhabitants of nearly every region by common vows offered themselves up to common destruction."[48] In Italy, people said that Muhammad was more powerful than Christ; friars who preached the cross were publicly insulted and mass apostasy was feared in Italian cities. "Ah, God, why did you bring this misfortune?" the troubadour Austorc d'Aurillac lamented. "It is with good reason that we cease to believe in God and worship Muhammad . . . because God and the blessed Virgin Mary desire that we shall be conquered against all justice and that evil ones shall receive all the honour."[49]

Income tax was a by-product of the fighting for which the Church was equally blamed. The first royal crusading tax was levied by Louis VII in 1146 to

*For the escalation of the campaign against the Cathars, see the next chapter.

finance the Second Crusade. The king of England raised the first income tax in 1166, set a tuppence in the pound for the first year, and a penny for each of the four succeeding years. Both clergy and laity were eligible. In 1188 a "Saladin tithe" of a tenth of income was extracted from clerks and laymen who had not taken up the cross. Collectors were appointed in each parish to investigate dishonesty amid fierce talk of crusades being "financed by the spoliation of the poor."[50]

Papal levies were bitterly resented by northern Europeans convinced that the money would merely line pockets in Rome. "How the pope now laughs," railed the German poet Walther von der Vogelweide, "when he says to his Italians 'All that [the Germans] have belongs to me, their German silver is flowing into my Italian casket. You priests eat chicken and drink wine and let the Germans hunger and fast.'" Like many laymen, Walther was convinced that "little of the silver will come to help God's land, for priests seldom share great treasures."[51] In England, Henry III's counselors begged him not to part with money for the pope. "Why do you permit England," the English chronicler Matthew Paris quoted them as saying, "to become the booty and spoil of those coming across it like a vineyard without a wall, open to every traveller and subject to destruction by wild beasts?" Matthew's own monastery was deep in debt through the taxes, and he wrote angrily of the greed of the "sulphurous fountain of Rome."[52]

Other ways were used to raise money. Innocent III licensed dispensators to redeem Crusader vows for cash. The scheme was intended for the aged and sick, but a Cistercian in Germany reported that fit men were buying themselves out of military service, paying dispensators with forged papal credentials five marks each. One of them sat in a tavern and scoffed at his fellow drinkers. "You fools will cross the seas and waste your substance and expose your lives to many dangers," he told them, "while I shall sit at home, with my wife and children, and get a similar reward to yours through the 5 marks with which I redeemed my cross."[53] The defeats in the East were blamed on the pope for allowing the able-bodied to escape their vows, and spending the cash on his own pleasures. "I will tell you how those who once distributed the cross behave," the troubadour Raimon Gaucelm de Beziers wrote. "For a sum of money they permit most to rid themselves of it."[54]

     LUST FOR MONEY brought calamity in the Fourth Crusade. Its mission, approved by Pope Innocent III, was the recapture of Jerusalem. The Venetians agreed to ship a host of almost 35,000 men and 5,000 horses to the Holy Land for the colossal sum of 85,000 silver marks. Less than a third of the expected

The supplies for Crusaders, here being loaded aboard ship, were paid for with much-hated taxes. The "divine fire" of the early period gave way to apathy and discontent. The soldiers of the Fourth Crusade abandoned their goal of recapturing Jerusalem from the Moslems in favor of plundering the Orthodox Christians of Constantinople. "So much booty had never been gained since the creation of the world," a chronicler wrote of the sack of the city in 1204, an event that poisoned relations between the Orthodox and Catholic Churches for centuries.

number of Crusader's assembled over the summer of 1202. The doge of Venice insisted that the original contract be honored, and offered to forgo the shortfall in return for Crusader help in recovering the Adriatic city of Zara, which the king of Hungary had seized from the Venetians. Old and blind though he was, the doge vowed to accompany them. "I shall go to live or die with the pilgrims," he said; then he knelt before the altar of the Church of San Marco while a cross was sewn on the front of his cotton cap.

The fleet sailed for Zara in November. In the name of the pope, the abbot of Vaux forbade the Crusaders to attack the city, "for the people in it are Christians, and you wear the sign of the cross." The doge reminded the barons of their agreement. Zara surrendered after five days of bombardment. A richer prize now offered itself. Byzantine affairs—that "monotonous story of the intrigues of priests, eunuchs, and women, of poisonings, of conspiracies, of uniform ingratitude, of perpetual fraticide . . ."[55]—were running true to form. The former emperor, Isaac Angelus, had ransomed his brother Alexius from the Turks. In return, Alexius usurped the throne and had Isaac blinded and thrown into prison. Isaac's son, also named Alexius, had escaped to Germany and now sent word to the Crusaders that he would pay them two hundred thousand silver marks if they attacked Constantinople and restored his father to the throne. As a religious sop, he offered to bring the empire under the authority of Rome, and to maintain five hundred knights in the Holy Land at his own expense. Such favorable conditions had "never before been offered to anyone," his envoys pointed out, and "the man who could refuse to accept them can have little wish to conquer anything at all."[56]

Greed outmatched the vows to fight for Jerusalem. Like Peter the Hermit's ragged band, the northerners shuddered in admiration when they arrived at Constantinople and saw its "high walls and lofty towers . . . rich palaces and tall churches, of which there were so many that no one would have believed it true if he had not seen it with his own eyes . . ."[57] The domes and crosses gave it an unmistakably Christian silhouette. The same cross appeared on the banners and pennants hoisted on the castles of the invaders' ships and on the shields lashed to the bulwarks. The Venetians broke into the city from the sea, led by the agile old doge who leaped ashore behind the banner of St. Mark, and the usurper Alexius fled through the land wall to Thrace, taking his favorite daughter and a bag of jewels with him. Blind Isaac was taken from his prison cell, clothed in the imperial robes, and carried to the throne. The Crusaders and Venetians kept their armor on and their weapons close to hand—for "none of them put much trust in the Greeks"—and told the restored emperor of the covenant they had signed with his son. Isaac complained that the conditions were so hard that "I do not really see how we can put them into effect." He agreed to step down in favor of his son; Alexius IV was duly crowned in St. Sophia on August 1, 1203.

The covenant was indeed difficult to keep. The Orthodox clergy morosely evaded recognition of papal supremacy and Latin rites. Though he whetted Crusader appetites with early gifts, Alexius was unable to pay them off despite melting down ecclesiastical plate. The atmosphere in the city thickened through the autumn and winter. Brawling broke out between Greeks and Latins. Some Franks set fire to a mosque built for visiting Moslems. The fire spread and burned for a week, threatening the Basilica of St. Sophia, the Crusaders watching from their encampment across the harbor. In February 1204, Alexius was deposed and strangled, his father dying of "grief and judicious ill-treatment"[58] a few days later. The new emperor, Alexius Murzuphlus, refused any payments. All thoughts of fighting Moslems were discarded.* "Thus the war began," the Crusader chronicler Villehardouin reported; "and each side did its utmost to harm the other, both by sea and by land."[59]

A Crusader attack on April 12 had been underway for some hours when a

---

*Villehardouin mocked other French Crusaders who, having wintered in Marseilles, had set sail for the Holy Land. One group of eighty knights was ambushed by Turks and all were killed or captured. As to the others, "the unhealthy climate of Syria proved fatal to some; others went back to their own country." Villehardouin made the remarkable claim that they would have served Christianity better by fighting the Greeks, "but because of their sins God would not allow it."

stiff breeze, which the Crusaders attributed to divine intervention, drove the scaling ships *Pilgrim* and *Paradise* onto a tower. A Venetian and a French knight forced their way over *Pilgrim*'s scaling ladder and took the tower. The knights aboard the transports scrambled ashore with ladders and took four more towers. Three of the gates were broken down. Horses were brought ashore and the knights mounted and charged the camp of Murzuphlus; the emperor fled.

The Franks and Venetians broke into the city in "a scene of massacre and pillage," Villehardouin wrote. "On every hand Greeks were cut down, their horses, palfreys, mules, and other possessions snatched as booty. So great was the number of killed and wounded that no man could count them. . . ." The doge and the barons moved into the Great Palace, and the troops were told that they could spend the next three days in pillage. That night a fire began to take hold of the city, burning until the next evening. It was, as Villehardouin noted, the third fire in the city since the French and Venetians had arrived, and "more houses had been burnt in that city than there are in any three of the greatest cities in the kingdom of France."

He added that "so much booty had never been gained in any city since the creation of the world."[60] For most of its nine centuries the city had been the greatest center of Christian civilization. To the treasures of ancient Greece it had added the fruits of its own artistic genius. The Venetians appreciated the exquisite beauty of its treasures and shipped them home for their own palaces; they took the four horses from the Hippodrome, the magnificent sixth-century Quadriga, that still rear from the Church of San Marco. The Franks and Flemings had no such taste. They had a perverse pride in their own barbarism; some went round the city pretending to write, laughing that literacy had not saved the Byzantines. They looted not works of art, but "gold and silver, table-services and precious stones, mantles of squirrel fur, ermine and miniver, and every choicest thing to be found on this earth," and they smashed what they could not carry. They broke into wine cellars and went on drunken sprees of rape and murder; they ravished Christian nuns in Christian convents; in St. Sophia they tore down the silken hangings, broke up the iconostasis for its silver, and drank from the altar vessels while a prostitute sat on the patriarch's throne and sang obscene songs. Men kept booty back from the common pool, though they risked excommunication by the pope or, of more pressing concern, execution by their superiors. The Conte de Saint-Pol hanged one of his own knights, with his shield at his neck, for not declaring his spoils. Nevertheless, apart from what was stolen or paid to the Venetians, some four hundred thousand silver marks were left for distribution among the Crusaders as well as ten thousand horses.

The priests were little better as they committed *furta sacra*, "sacred thefts," of the valuable relics of saints. Abbot Martin of Paris, who "out of piety robbed only churches," tortured an elderly Greek priest to reveal the relics at the Church of the Pantocrator. He and his chaplain plunged their hands into the iron chest where the relics were stored, and, "briskly tucking up their skirts, filled the folds with holy sacrilege . . ."[61] As he hurried to the ships, the abbot was asked what he had found. "We have done well," he replied, smiling. The looters spent Palm Sunday praying with "hearts full of joy for the benefits our Lord and Saviour had bestowed on them."

A general rejoicing swept the West. Hymns were sung to celebrate the fall of *Constantinopolitana profana,* "the profane city," and the stolen relics were carried in proud procession when they arrived in Venetian and French churches. The Venetians took Crete, Corfu, and three-eighths of Constantinople, where they installed a patriarch without reference to the pope. The Crusaders declared a new Latin empire of Romania and crowned one of their number, Baldwin, count of Hainault and Flanders, as its emperor. Their rewards did not endure. Within a year Baldwin had died as a prisoner in a Balkan castle; his nephew Baldwin II was driven from Constantinople when the Greeks retook the city in 1261 and died a fugitive.

For their pieces of silver, the Crusaders had savaged an empire that had defended Europe against the infidel East; that had, though often sorely pressed, resisted the pressure of Islam and absorbed and evangelized waves of barbarians. Its near ruin was an act of infamy. It broke the integrity of the Byzantine world and planted the seeds of Islamic expansion into Europe. Its unforgotten and unforgiven cruelties split Eastern Christians irrevocably from the Western Catholics.

"How can we call upon the other Western peoples for aid to the Holy Land," Pope Innocent lamented, "when those who plundered the . . . empire turn back and return with their spoils, free of guilt?"[62]

❖ WHERE GROWN MEN had failed, children now tried in a tragic sequel that began at Easter and Pentecost in 1212. "Prompted by I know not what spirit," a chronicler wrote, "many thousands of boys, ranging in age from six years to full maturity, left the ploughs or carts which they were driving, the flocks which they were pasturing, and anything else they were doing. . . . Suddenly one ran after another to take the Cross. Thus, by groups of twenty, or fifty, or a hundred, they put up banners and began to journey to Jerusalem."[63]

The ideal of living in imitation of Christ was transformed by these innocents into an imitation of the adult world. They reflected its fervor and longings, and its sudden descents—or elevations, for the religious found the children's action to be "an outstanding thing . . . unheard of throughout the ages"—into frenzy. The children were prey to the obsessive nature of the age; "neither bars nor bolts could hold them back; nor could the commands of fathers and mothers, soft words or inducements recall them."[64] Observers, however, credited them with a clearer sense of mission than their elders of the Fourth Crusade. They knew that "many kings, a great many dukes and innumerable people in powerful companies . . . had returned with the business unfinished."[65] They said that they intended to put this right by taking Jerusalem, telling adults who scolded them that they were "equal to the Divine Will . . . and that, whatever God might wish to do with them, they would accept it willingly and with humble spirit."[66] When they were asked where they were going, a monk noted that they had a single reply: "to God."

Two children were identified as the leaders of the crusade; a boy named Nicholas in the Cologne region of western Germany, and Stephen, a shepherd boy from the village of Cloyes in northern France, who said that Christ had appeared before him in a vision dressed as a poor pilgrim.

As the German boys marched south, monks who tried to turn them back were alarmed at the sympathy they aroused. "Many thought that all this arose not from any foolishness but rather through Divine inspiration and a kind of piety," the chronicler of the monastery at Marbach on the Upper Rhine recorded, "and helped them with food and other necessities." Local people resented Church opposition to the young crusaders; they "said the clergy were unbelievers and that their opposition sprang more from envy than from any love of truth and justice."[67] Crossing the Alps, equipped with pilgrim staves and crosses, they reached Piacenza in Italy on August 20, "a great and innumerable multitude of German children, babes at the breast, women and girls."[68] Five days later Nicholas led them to Genoa, but shipowners refused to carry them to the Holy Land. They trudged on to Rome, where Innocent III is said to have remarked that: "These children put us to shame, they rush to recover the Holy Land whilst we sleep."[69] No ships were available at Brindisi. The crusade collapsed; Nicholas is thought to have died in Italy, and the survivors toiled back over the Alps, "footsore and ridiculed."

Stephen, revered as *sanctus puer,* the "holy boy," led his band through Provence to the Mediterranean, chanting: "Lord God, exalt Christianity! Lord God, restore to us the True Cross."[70] The chronicler Aubrey of Trois-Fontaines claimed that thirty thousand reached Marseilles, where they were betrayed by two merchants, Hugh Ferreus and William Porcus, who promised to give them free passage across the Mediterranean to Jerusalem in seven large ships. The convoy ran into a storm off the island of St. Peter, near Sardinia, and Aubrey said that two ships were lost before the survivors arrived at Bougie and Alexandria. He claimed that four hundred were sold to the caliph al-Nas, while others were sent on to Baghdad. Ferreus and Porcus next plotted with a Saracen, Prince Mirabel of

Sicily, against the Emperor Frederick, but the emperor discovered the plot and "hanged Mirabel, his two sons, and those two betrayers, all from one gallows." Though the numbers are doubtless exaggerated, there may be truth to this sad tale. Hugh Ferreus certainly existed, holding an administrative post at Marseilles, and William Porcus, though not a merchant, was a well-known Genoese ship's captain. It is known that the Moslem pirate ibn-Abs, known as Mirabel to the French, was hanged by the emperor at Palermo in 1222. Aubrey added a post-script to his account; eighteen years after the unhappy crusade, seven hundred of the participants were still in slavery in Alexandria, "no longer children but grown men."[71]

JERUSALEM WAS BRIEFLY restored to Christian control in 1229. Frederick II, the Holy Roman Emperor, negotiated its return with the Egyptian sultan. He spent only two nights in the city, for fear that the Templars would fulfill papal orders and kill him. The golden crown of the king of Jerusalem was placed on the high altar of the choir of the Holy Sepulchre; Frederick walked to it and put it on his head. "No priest or prelate or any cleric said or sang anything whatever" at this extraordinary scene; the new king then "suddenly left the town without letting anyone know where he was going."[72] To his admirers he was *stupor mundi,* "the wonder of the world," whose curiosity and breadth of interests, mathematical, philosophical, zoological, legal, and poetic, helped reilluminate the Western spirit. To Pope Gregory IX, who had preached a crusade against him, the savior of Jerusalem was an excommunicate and Antichrist.

The long campaign waged against Frederick and his heirs by successive popes marked the transfer of crusading from an external ideal into a European affair of high politics and heresy. When Gregory ordered in 1239 that vows to go to the Holy Land should be commuted to a crusade against Frederick in Lombardy and Germany, supporters of the emperor were so incensed that, at Regensburg, they put to death anyone found wearing a cross. "Treacherous Rome, avarice leads you astray, so that you shear too much wool from your sheep," the poet Guilhelm Figueira lamented. "May the Holy Spirit who takes on human flesh hear my prayers and break your beak. . . . Rome, you do little harm to the Saracens, but you massacre Greeks and Latins. In hellfire and perdition you have your home, Rome."[73]

The Crusader kingdoms of Outremer degenerated apace. Jerusalem was taken by the Turks in 1244; no Christian general would enter it again until the British drove out the Turks in 1917. The Crusaders in the field did not have the heroism of their ancestors, or so thought their nemesis, Sultan Baybars, a former Mamluk soldier-slave who had murdered his masters to win command of Egypt and Syria. He reduced the great fortresses of Jaffa and Beaufort, battering them with siege engines that hurled quarter-ton rocks. In 1268 he took Antioch. "Ah!" he wrote to the count of Tripoli. "If you had seen your treasures distributed by the hundredweights, your ladies sold at the rate of a gold piece for four! If you had seen the churches and crosses overthrown, the leaves of the sacred Gospels scattered. . . . If you had seen your enemy the Moslem walking on the tabernacle . . ."[74]

His death in 1277 gave the Franks a brief respite. They used it for final pleasures. At Acre they celebrated the coronation of the king of Cyprus with the finest festival for a hundred years, where knights dressed as ladies jousted together, and others dressed as Lancelot and Tristan in a pastiche of chivalry. In 1289, Baybars's successor Qalawun captured Tripoli. Acre itself was safe until a group of Italian Crusaders broke a truce with the sultan, and the city was besieged. The King's Tower, crucial to the town's defense, was taken by the Moslems on May 16, 1291. It was clear that the city would fall, and women and children were hastily put aboard ships, but a gale blew up and many disembarked. The defenders heard the "loud and terrible sound" of a kettledrum before dawn two days later, the signal for a general assault. The Saracens broke in through the Accursed Tower, a salient on the walls. "They came on foot, in countless numbers," a Christian chronicler wrote. "First came those who carried great tall shields, then those who threw Greek fire, and after those who shot darts and feathered arrows so thickly that it seemed as though rain was falling. . . . That day was appalling, for nobles and citizens, women and girls were frantic with terror; they went running through the streets, their children in their arms, weeping and desperate; they fled to the sea-shore to escape death, and when the Saracens caught them one would take the mother and the other the child, they would drag from place to place and pull them apart."[75] The sultan singled out the Templars for decapitation. Tyre was abandoned in May, Sidon and Beirut shortly afterward.

"Thus were the Franj, who had once nearly conquered Damascus, Egypt and many other lands, expelled from all of Syria and the coast," the Moslem writer Abdul Fida concluded. "God grant that they never set foot there again!"[76]

❖ CHRISTIAN RULE IN the East was not extinguished, nor the last forlorn appeal to crusade against Islam yet made. On May 22, 1453, at the first hour of night, a miraculous sign appeared in a cloudless sky above the Bosporus. When the moon rose, it should have been full, but very little of it could be made out until it regained its roundness in the sixth hour of night. The Byzantines had a prophecy that Constantinople would never be lost unless the full moon showed a sign. "It filled their people with fear," a Venetian ship's doctor reported, while the Ottoman Turks who were besieging the city rejoiced greatly.[77]

The great city had survived periodic Moslem blockades for 779 years. Half a century before, the Ottomans had overrun Christian Bulgaria, along with parts of Serbia, Macedonia, and Thessaly, and had reached the Danube. Constantinople had seemed certain to fall until the Ottomans were diverted by Tamerlane's Mongol hordes. The Turks had now returned. Constantine XI Paleologus, the emperor, offered to pay tribute if they withdrew. "Either I take the City or the City takes me dead or alive" was Sultan Mehmed's reply.[78] His gunners fired triangular patterns of stone shot against the walls, collapsing them in parts, while a floating bridge made of wine casks was readied for the assault. On May 26, Mehmed affirmed to his troops that he would take only the buildings and walls of Constantinople for his own. As for the treasures and captives, he declared: "Let those be your reward." The men, enraptured at the promise of booty, began to "chant and shout in their foul and impious tongue." They lit torches that lit the islands and the surface of the water. As the Christians saw the Turks dancing and heard their joy, they "foresaw the future" and paraded their icons along the walls while the Kyrie Elison was chanted in tears. The emperor went to pray in St. Sophia; afterward the chronicler George Sphrantzes recorded, "He returned to the palace for a while and asked to be forgiven by all. Who can describe the wailing and tears that arose in the palace at that hour? No man, even if he were made of wood or stone, could have held back his tears."[79]

At daybreak on the Feast of All Saints, Sunday, May 27, the assault began with skirmishing at the walls while heavily laden ships with scaling ladders landed their equipment. On Monday the defenders saw Mehmed on horseback with a large cavalry force while thousands of other troops were aboard the ships or crossing the bridge of wine barrels. In the late afternoon the enemy sounded their drums and horns and attacked. The fighting continued throughout the night. At dawn the Christians thought themselves victorious. A dark cloud of smoke from cannon and burning Greek fire drifted across the sky. Mehmed's police and court officials beat their men with iron clubs and whips to prevent them from falling back. The emperor toured his troops on horseback, noting that the Turks were no longer attacking in formation. "God is fighting on our side and cowardice is invading the multitude of the impious," he told his men, promising them a heavenly crown if they held firm. As he did so, Giovanni Giustinianni, the giant-bodied Christian general, was wounded. He was pierced through the arm by a lead shot in one account, and by an arrow in his right calf in another. Both accounts agreed that he left his post and that the Christians at once lost heart. Some deserted from a portion of collapsed wall; the Turks pursued them and broke through the St. Romanos Gate.

The tocsin sounded in the doomed city; "everyone was crying 'Almighty God have mercy!', men, women and nuns and young girls." The Turks sought out the convents, so the Italian Niccolo Barbaro claimed, and took the nuns out to ships in the harbor to dishonor them before selling them as slaves to Turkey. The bodies of Christians and Turks alike were thrown into the Hellespont, where "they were carried along in the current like melons." At the ninth hour of Tuesday, May 29, 1453, the city of Constantine became Moslem, and St. Sophia, once the finest church of Christendom, became a mosque.

Pope Pius II preached the final crusade in 1459 as the Turks advanced in the Balkans. They could be halted, the pope said, "if only God himself will bless our enterprise." No king or emperor accepted his challenge. In June 1464 he took the cross himself at St. Peter's in Rome and, vowing to lead the crusade in person, set off for Ancona. There he died of plague. The East was abandoned.

"O FIRE OF LOVE":

Manifestations of the Spirit

he titanic, crusading energy of the medieval faith infused its architecture. Gothic perspectives created brilliants of stone in midair, burning an imprint in the dazzled eye. From below, a medieval church sprang like a fountain at the stars, so the writer G. K. Chesterton found; to a watcher from its tower or steeple, it poured to the ground in a cataract. Details of stone, made monstrous by foreshortening, turned surrounding houses and fields into distant pygmies; a carved bird or beast at a corner appeared as some vast dragon wasting the villages and pastures below it. The atmosphere was dizzy and dangerous, yearning for heaven but freighted with warnings of hell, with misshapen gargoyles, grinning devils, and skeletal sinners; panels of stained glass made exquisite rainbows against the gloomy billows of the nave, and the whole edifice seemed "to sit upon the sunlit country like a cloudburst."[1]

Between 1050 and 1350, eighty cathedrals, five hundred large churches, and tens of thousands of smaller ones were built in France alone. More stone was excavated in these three centuries than at any time since ancient Egypt, although the volume of the Great Pyramid is 2.5 million cubic meters. The foundations of cathedrals are laid as deep as 35 feet; in some cases, there is as much stone below ground as can be seen above it. The vault of Notre Dame reached a height of 114 feet in 1163; this record was constantly broken, by Chartres, then Rheims, and Amiens at 138 feet, until the ceiling of possibility was exceeded at Beauvais and its 157-foot vault collapsed in 1284. The spire at Strasbourg, began in 1270 but not completed for more than 150 years, topped 450 feet. No buildings on earth had been built to such a scale.

Prosperous towns had a church or chapel for every 200 or so inhabitants, so that the places of the faith were visible from every street and angle. Norwich, Lincoln, and York, cities with populations between 5,000 and 10,000, had 50, 49, and 31 churches and chapels respectively. The cathedral at Amiens was large enough for the 10,000-strong population to attend the same service. Before it became fashionable for the rich to build exclusive private chapels, all attended Sunday services—nobles, peasants, merchants, and tradesmen. Large numbers of feast days were celebrated, twenty-nine a year in medieval England, and congregations used churches as public meeting places on weekdays. They brought dogs and sparrowhawks into the nave and side aisles, ate, argued, gossiped, and thrashed out business deals. The crypt was always open to shelter strangers, pilgrims, and the sick; plays were performed on the steps, and magistrates and municipal officers held meetings in the nave. Clothiers, stonecutters, and carpenters sometimes advertised their wares in the stained glass windows.

The earlier cathedrals were built in the Romanesque style. Wooden roofs were a fire hazard, and they were replaced by thick half-cylinders of stone in barrel vaulting. The massive weight required uniform and heavy walls. These could only be pierced by a few small windows, and the dark and restful interiors, their lines leading horizontally to the altar, were enlivened by vivid tapestries and painted or gilded freestanding sculptures. Gothic architecture was first used on a

The sweat and devotion poured into church-building—seen here at Beauvais in France in the thirteenth century—reflected the titanic energy of the medieval faith. Eighty cathedrals were built in France alone, exquisite in their detail, prodigious in their size. The vault of Notre Dame in Paris reached a height of 114 feet in 1163, a record that was constantly broken. The spire at Strasbourg topped 450 feet. No buildings on earth had been built to such a scale.

major scale at St. Denis in Paris in 1137. It was light and delicate; the stonework lost its weightiness, leading the eye upwards, and stained glass windows fashioned in exquisite tracery created luminous walls of color. The flying buttress was invented to support the structure from the outside, while crossvaulting in the nave transferred the weight of the roof onto posts and pilasters, creating an airy spaciousness. The roof ridges were often finely decorated, and mosaic patterns were made by the differing reflections of the slates, while gargoyles carved in fantastical shapes spewed rainwater well away from the walls. Though only the few who climbed the steep and coiling stairways could see the affection lavished on the vertiginous heights, these were God's houses, and, if the roof effects were hidden from men looking up, God could most certainly see them in looking down. Details of the faith, the Trinity, the Passion, the Last Judgment, were picked out in stained glass and sculpture. Notre Dame had twelve hundred statues, and Rheims three thousand. The grandest buildings were equipped with mechanical clocks; the canon Étienne Musique spent twenty years building the musical clock at Beauvais, and an astronomical clock with seven dials was constructed at Padua.

Chalices, plate, and altars matched the magnificence of the stonework. Suger, the abbot of St. Denis, commissioned porphyry vases, a chalice made from one huge piece of sardonyx, and a twenty-four-foot-high cross decorated with amethysts, sapphires, rubies, and emeralds. Five goldsmiths worked on the site, illustrating its pedestal and enameling the column. Not all approved of ornamentation. Bernard of Clairvaux, whose austerity ran to a diet of barley bread and boiled beech leaves, wrote that some cloisters had such a wealth of boisterous carvings—"here a quadruped with the tail of a serpent, there a fish with the head of a goat"—that it became "more delightful to read the marble" than the Scriptures. No such distractions tempted his new order of Cistercians. Their architecture was severe, if serenely beautiful, and built to such a constant plan that it was said that a blind monk moving into any of the 742 Cistercian monasteries that came to be scattered through Europe would instantly know where he was. Suger was unmoved. "Should we dispose of the golden vases and precious stones and all that creation holds most valuable?" he retorted. "Those who criticize us claim that celebration needs only a holy soul, a pure mind and a faithful intention. We are certainly in complete agreement. But we believe that outward ornament and sacred chalices should serve nowhere so much as in our worship. . . ."[2]

These tensions would eventually lead sixteenth- and seventeenth-century puritans to destroy Church ornaments, and the same whiff of reformation lingered in the means of financing them. "This ever present passion for building is a sickness," a cathedral dignitary in Paris wrote in 1180. "Monastic churches and cathedrals are being built by usury and avarice, by cunning and lies, and by the deceptions of preachers."[3] The clergymen were indeed adept at raising money.

Large donations were counted as "cathedral crusades," in which the donors were granted indulgences; sermons made much of the sins of usury to shame money changers and merchants into giving, and relics were taken on fund-raising tours. "Beautiful and gentle people," said a preacher introducing an indulgence at Amiens, "you can be 27 days nearer to Paradise than you were yesterday. . . ."[4] Canons and laymen from Laon toured northern France in 1112 with fragments of the Virgin's gown, a part of the sponge of the Passion, and a piece of the True Cross. The money they raised was quickly spent, and the following year they sailed to England. They were robbed by Flemish cloth merchants and attacked by pirates, but persevered to reach Canterbury and the English West Country, returning with enough money to complete their building.

Civic pride was the most common inspiration, however, and the poorest made gifts of cheese, grain, and animal skins. The works were colossal and expensive. Monks might help in the construction of their monasteries, but cathedral builders were well-paid professionals. The masons—the "hard hewers" of stone blocks, and the "freestone masons"* who worked with more fragile stone to create sculptures and ornaments—were a traveling elite who guarded their secrets and hired themselves to the highest bidder. Westminster Abbey in London had 428 workers on-site in 1253—masons, smiths, carpenters, plasterers, tilers, scaffolders, and stone fitters. It cost as much to transport stone for ten miles as it did to buy it in the quarry, and a cathedral could consume several hundred thousand cartloads.

The effort was a spur to technology. The development of waterpower was in large part pioneered by monks. As St. Bernard's monastery at Clairvaux was built, a Cistercian recorded, the monks "divided the river, set it in new channels and lifted the leaping waters to the mill-wheels; fullers and bakers and tanners and smiths and other artificers prepared suitable machines for the task, that the river might do good wherever it was needed in every building, flowing freely in underground conduits. . . ."[5] Water drove hammer-forges, milled wheat, sieved flour, powdered oak bark for tanning, and crushed olives; it powered the great wooden hammers of the cloth-fullers, produced the beer from the monastic brewery, helped to make paper, and flushed the latrines.

Horses were in huge demand for hauling stone to cathedral sites. Their full strength was exploited for the first time, through the improved grip of horseshoes and a rigid shoulder collar that placed the strain on the body rather than the neck. The invention of the mechanical clock made the church a town's most consulted building. Smiths improved the quality of steel to make tools strong enough to cut

---

*The workshops in which the freestone masons worked were known as lodges. From these, "freemason" and the Masonic lodge are derived.

harder stone, which allowed for slender columns and walls. "Iron is more useful to man than gold," a Franciscan observed in 1260; every site had a forge to make claws for lifting stone, nails, horseshoes, tie rods, and iron chains, which were run inside the walls for reinforcement.

The men who poured their devotion into these masterpieces were also alive with curiosity and intelligence. The master builder Villard de Honnecourt left a sketchbook that shows his skills in mechanics, geometry, carpentry, ornamental design, and hydraulics as well as construction and architecture. He traveled widely, making notes on elevations at Rheims, rose windows in Chartres and Lausanne, and towers at Laon to help in his own designs in France and Hungary. He sketched wildlife, cicadas, dragonflies, hedgehogs, horses, and a lion cub, and drew a crucifixion and the descent from the Cross as references for statuary. He invented screws and levers for lifting weights and a machine for cutting keyholes, and designed a waterpowered saw and a clockwork angel that kept its finger pointing perpetually at the sun.

After 1350 the building fervor abated, a victim of economic collapse, the Black Death, and the Hundred Years' War in France. Its monuments, among the most durable structures made by man, remain as witnesses to the power of faith. As his great cathedral of St. Denis was finished, Suger reflected on his emotions. "I seemed to find myself, as it were, in some strange part of the universe which was neither wholly of the baseness of earth, nor wholly of the serenity of heaven," he wrote, "but by the grace of God I seemed lifted in a mystic manner from this lower towards the upper sphere."

MYSTICISM—THE SEARCH for *unio mystica,* "personal union with God"— was part of the spirituality of the age. Bernard might not approve of Suger's ornaments, but his complex character as man-of-action, crusade preacher, administrator, and politician had space for the mystic.

He believed that through abstraction from earthly things, or through a sudden and ecstatic insight of the sort experienced by Paul, the mind is able to rise to *contemplatio,* or the "vision of the divine." These rewards are given to those who blot out the body and the world, and whose self-love is so enveloped by the love of God that it exists only in serving God. "As the little water-drop poured into a large measure of wine seems to lose its own nature entirely and to take on both the taste and the colour of the wine," Bernard wrote, "or as iron heated red-hot loses its own appearance and glows like fire; or as air filled with sunlight is transformed into the same brightness so that it does not so much appear to be illuminated as to be itself light—so must all human feeling towards the Holy One be self-dissolved in unspeakable wise, and wholly transformed into the will of God. For how shall God be all in all if anything of man remains in man?"[6]

Early writings on mystical theology were attributed to Dionysius the Areopagite, who according to legend was converted by Paul at Athens in the first century. In fact, these works were written around A.D. 500 and became important only after the Irishman John Scotus Erigena translated them into Latin in the ninth century. The pseudo-Dionysius described the ascent of the soul through purification and illumination to a state of perfection of union with God. To achieve this, the soul must lose the inhibitions of the senses and of reason. God is beyond the intellect, beyond goodness itself, and it is through unknowing, and the discarding of human concepts, that the soul returns to God and is united with the "ray of divine darkness."

The Carthusians, founded by St. Bruno at Chartreuse near Grenoble in 1084, confined their monks in silence in closed cells to hone their contemplation. At monasteries such as La Verne in Provence, isolated in forests on a rocky headland, they came together only for divine service in the chapel. Otherwise, each monk prayed, worked, slept, and ate in his cell of solitude; this private hermitage had a set of small rooms of stone plastered with lime, a *cubiculum* with a plank bed and a straw mattress set in a recess, an Ave Maria with a statue of the Virgin, a dining room with a table and a stall for prayer and meditation, and a workroom with a privy. The small garden attached to each cell was blocked off with a high wall. New terms were coined to describe mystic intuition; in his *Itinerarium mentis ad Deum,* Bonaventura used *apex mentis* and *scintilla* as way points on the mind's journey to God.

Bernard added an intensity of love to mystic contemplation. God is love—*Deus caritas est* (1 John 4:8)—and it is only through love that he can be glimpsed; "I love because I love," Bernard wrote, "I love that I may love." In a remarkable series of sermons on the Song of Songs, still unfinished at his death in 1153, Bernard explored the mystic union between Christ and the believer, the moment at which the believer is kissed "with the kisses of his mouth," finding perfection in the love of the Virgin for her son: "With what a tranquil face, with what an unclouded expression, with what joyous embraces was she taken up by her son!"

This nuptial moment remains at the heart of the consecration of nuns. "My beloved spake and said unto me, 'Rise up, my love, my fair one and come away,'" the priest says. The woman takes the veil, and the ring that binds her as the bride of Christ. In ancient ceremony, the symbolism of marriage was stronger still. "Receive this sign of Christ on your head," the priest said as he garlanded the nun, "that you may be his wife, and if you remain in that state, be crowned for all eternity"; after a honeymoon of three days' retreat, the nun's veil was lifted and her face revealed, and she joined her companions to celebrate a wedding feast.[7]

Women, denied the sacrament and the freedom to teach the word, matched Bernard's ardor in their visions of Christ. Secular and divine love become indistinguishable in the writing of St. Agnes; though enjoying Christ's caresses, she remains a virgin:

And takyn of his mouth many a kys have I,
Swettere then eythir mylk or hony:
And full oftyn in armys he halsyd hath me
Wyth-out blemyssyng of myn virgynyte.

The anchoress Julian of Norwich saw Christ as love in her visions—"Love was his mening. Who shewid it thee? Love. What shewid he thee? Love. Wherefore shewid it he? For Love"—and described that love as maternal. "The moder may geven hir child soken hir mylke," she wrote, "but our precious moder Iesus, he may feden us with himself. . . ."

Hildegard of Bingen, playwright, poet, composer, and mystic, adviser to popes and emperors, described herself as "a feather on the breath of God." She was born to noble parents in Rheinhessen in 1098. In her third year she saw so great a brightness that her soul trembled; at eight she entered a community of nuns at Bingen and, at forty-three, having become abbess, the light returned to her as tongues of flame descending from the heavens. A great pressure of pains, she said, forced her to manifest what she had seen and heard. Her creativity was astounding. She wrote and illustrated three books of her visions, *Scivias,* a musical morality play, and acutely observed works of natural history and medicine. Her *Liber vitae meritorum* devotes six books to a disputation of virtues and vices; another major work, *Liber divinorum operum* contains visions of the cosmos, and the earth and its creations.

Her collection of poetry and music, the *Symphony of the Harmony of Celestial Revelations,* echoes her devotional life. "I brought forth songs within their melody," she wrote of her visions, "and I sang them too, even though I had never learned either musical notation or any kind of singing." Her music is rich and cadent, its emotions both intense and tranquil, running to Christ "as the clouds course in the purest air like sapphire." She spoke of "writing, seeing, hearing and knowing all in one manner," and she described the Pentecostal fire which settled upon her in *O ignis spiritus,* her melodic apostrophe to her Muse:

O fire of the comforting Spirit,
life of the life of all Creation,
you are holy in quickening all Kind. . . .
O breath of holiness,

O fire of love
O sweet draught in the breast
and flooding of the heart . . .[8]

The passionate embrace of the divine remains a hallmark of mysticism,
reaching fresh heights with Teresa of Ávila almost four hundred years later, but alternatives were sometimes stressed. Abstraction was the highest virtue for the Dominican mystic Meister Eckhart. "I praise detachment more than all love," he
wrote. "The best thing about love is that it forces me to love God. On the other
hand, detachment forces God to love me. Now it is much nobler that I should
force God to love myself than that I should force myself to God. . . . Love forces
me to suffer all things for the sake of God, but detachment makes me receptive
of nothing but God. . . ."[9] Union could be reached, he said, only if "all the limbs
of man and his powers, his eyes, ears, mouth, heart and all his mind be directed
to it."[10]

❖ COMPASSION AND CRUELTY are twins of the faith, and Francis of Assisi
and Dominic de Guzman exemplify this fact. They were born of the same devotion and led by it to the opposite poles. In the early 1200s, each created a new and
surviving order of *fraters,* or friars, known by the colors of the coarse cloth they
wore, the Franciscans as Gray Friars, the Dominicans as Black. Each believed
in absolute poverty. Their friars were denied the contemplative solace of the
monastery; they became mendicants, begging for alms and living and working in
the squalid places of the world. Neither man spared himself; they died within five
years of each other, and both were swiftly canonized. There the common character ends.

"To the world a Sun is born," Dante wrote of Francis, the lightest and most
loved of saints, friend of lepers and outcasts, barefoot and cheerful in his scare-
crow cloak, seeing God's love in all created things, and able, so it was said, to
charm the lark from the sky and the wolf from the forest. He enjoyed a carefree
youth as the son of a rich cloth merchant from Assisi, until he was held prisoner
for a year in Perugia during an intercity conflict and suffered a serious illness. By
1205, and his return to Assisi, he was converted, in the sense that an already baptized and practicing believer becomes, as it were, flooded by his faith. In a vision,
the crucifix in the ruined chapel of San Damiano ordered him to restore its home,
and he sold a horse-load of cloth from his father's warehouse to buy materials to
repair it. He gave his fine clothes to a decayed old gentleman he met on the road,
and wore a country laborer's cloak that he marked with a cross in chalk. His father, outraged, disinherited him. In 1208 a voice repeated to him Jesus' com-

St. Francis of Assisi, painted here by Zurbaran, refreshed the Christian ideal of charity. He comforted lepers, outcasts, and the desperate, and wrote of the natural world and its creatures as brothers and sisters. The friars of the order he founded in 1209 worked in slums and dirt-poor villages where the faith had seldom penetrated. The prayers he wrote ring with a tender humility and joy that restored virtue to a religion that was in danger of forgetting the Sermon on the Mount.

mand to the disciples, to preach to the world, to heal the sick and cleanse the lepers, and to possess nothing, "neither two coats, neither shoes, nor yet staves" (Matt. 10:10).

He worked among the lepers and the marginals who lived in huts in the woods of Monte Subasio. Leprosy was a disease of ancient terror, in itself and in the rituals that surrounded it. A chapter in Leviticus is devoted to God's meticulous instructions to Moses on identifying the symptoms. Skin diseases—itch, ringworm, scabies, eczema, and ulceration—were common, and the consequences of leprosy were so pitiable that it was essential for a proper diagnosis to be made. Moses was told to ignore spots that did not spread, or that were dark in color, and inflammations that remained on the surface; he was to look for telltale signs of "white hair and quick raw flesh," or for a "white rising, or a bright spot, white and somewhat reddish." The Old Testament leper was condemned by a priest. His clothes were rent and his head bared; "he shall dwell alone, without the camp shall his habitation be," and he had to cry "Unclean, unclean" if others approached him (Lev. 13 passim).

Christian lepers were bound by the Old Testament regulations; they made the same warning cry, or sounded a bell or horn as they walked, and wore cloaks marked with the letter L. They were forbidden to talk to anyone unless they were downwind. Those suspected of having the disease were examined by magistrates, and, if found to be infected, were banished from the community by a ceremony of ritual burial dating from the Third Lateran Council in 1179. The penitent leper stood by an open grave with a black cloth on his head. "Be dead to the world, be reborn in God," the priest intoned. "Jesus, my Redeemer," the leper responded, "may I be reborn in Thee." The priest then read out a proscription: "I forbid you to enter church, monastery, fair, mill, marketplace or tavern. . . . I forbid you ever to leave your house without your leper's costume . . . to live with any woman other than your own . . . to touch a well, or well cord, without your gloves . . . to touch children, or to give them anything . . . to eat or drink, except with lepers."[11]

Some cities built a leprosarium or lazar-house outside the city walls, but most lepers lived as beggars in hovels, and the love that Francis brought to them in their wretchedness refreshed the Christian ideal of charity. He gathered a band of followers who elected him their superior. In 1210 he sought approval for his friars from Innocent III at Rome. Shocked by his ragged appearance at their first meeting, or so the chronicler Matthew Paris claimed, Innocent told Francis to go and play where he belonged, in a pigsty; the young man took the pope at his word, and appeared at the Lateran palace the next day covered in pig dung. Innocent had the little group tonsured, their bald pates affording them the protection due to clerics, and gave them permission to preach. A wellborn young nun of Assisi, Clare, joined the Franciscan fellowship in 1212 and founded the order of Poor Ladies of San Damiano, the "Poor Clares."* Within seven years the Franciscans were five thousand strong, "husbands of Lady Poverty" whose barefoot simplicity and devotion comforted the sick and the slum dwellers among whom they worked. Their purity was thought by the rich to be a defense against the devil; on their deathbeds, knights and noble ladies clad themselves in Franciscan habits patched with sackcloth, believing that they could not go to hell if they were so buried.

Francis knew that his ideal might be corrupted. "When you have a psalter," he told a novice who asked for one, "you will wish to have a breviary. And when you have a breviary, you will sit in a chair like a great prelate and say to your brother, 'Brother, bring me my breviary.'"[12] Elias of Cortona, a less generous-minded man, was appointed vicar-general of the order while Francis was in Egypt on a brave but fruitless mission to convert Moslems. A new Rule was introduced that allowed for the growth of an elaborate hierarchy. Francis withdrew from the leadership and retired to a hermitage on Monte Alverno. Over time, his insistence that "the brothers shall possess nothing, neither a house, nor a place, nor any-

---

*At Christmas in 1252, shortly before her death, Clare was said to have "seen and heard" a service being held in the church of St. Francis in Assisi from her cell at San Damiano. She was thus chosen to become the patron saint of television in 1958.

thing" was reinterpreted to allow corporate ownership of fine buildings and estates. Friars lived well by selling pardons that enabled sinners to draw on the "treasury of merit" supposedly stored up by Francis in heaven, expensive scraps of parchment that the English reformer John Wycliffe described as good only "to cover mustard pottis."[13] The order split and resplit as the laxer and property-owning Conventuals were challenged by a string of poverty-minded reformers—Spirituals, Fraticelli, Observants, Recollects, Capuchins in pointed cowls, and barefoot Discalced. These schisms, typical of the fundamentalist urges to which the faith is so open, were not healed until 1897.

Yet an enduring inspiration flowed from Francis. A monastery could become a mere prayer-engine; however, his friars, and the other mendicants who followed—Dominicans, Carmelites or White Friars, Augustinians, Trinitarians or Red Friars, Crutched Friars with crosses sewn on the front of their habits—worked in dark slums where the faith seldom penetrated. They spread rapidly across Europe, preaching in plain churches or in the open air, bringing evangelical fervor to the humble and care to the sick and poor. They tapped a rich religious vein. "Many people of both sexes—rich people of the world—having left all for Christ, were fleeing from the world, who were called friars minor," the crusader-bishop Jacques de Vitry wrote in 1216. "These people gave no heed to the temporal things, but with fervent desire and impetuous energy labour every day to withdraw perishing souls from the world. . . . They receive nothing, but live by the work of their hands."[14] Friars were exempt from episcopal jurisdiction, and their freedom to preach and hear confessions where they pleased was resented by bishops and the secular clergy;* popes, too, discouraged extreme displays of poverty among friars, uneasily aware of the contrast with their own opulence. The laity, however, saw a fresh idealism in friars that reflected to the credit of the Church in general, and in Francis himself they found a gaiety and simplicity that lit the somber recesses of the faith.

Though ill and half blind in his hermitage, he composed his joyous "Canticle to the Sun" and wrote of the natural world and its creatures as brothers and sisters. His biographer St. Bonaventure claimed that, while praying in an ecstasy of pain and joy, Francis became the first person to receive the *stigmata,* the reproduction on his body of the wounds of Christ's Passion, hard and black flesh appearing like nails on the palms of his hands and the upper instep of his feet, and a bleeding wound on the right side. Francis is credited with making the first

---

*This somewhat confusing term, used from the twelfth century, means priests living in the world such as parish clergy, as opposed to the "regular clergy" who are members of religious orders and live in communities following a Rule, such as monks and friars. The secular clergy are not bound by vows, are allowed to own property, and are subject to the authority of their bishop.

Christmas crib, a manger with a model of the Christ child in it, to decorate his church on Christmas Eve in 1223; the Franciscans also made popular the Stations of the Cross.* He wrote hymns and prayers that ring with the tender humility and virtue of the Sermon on the Mount:

> Lord, make me an instrument of thy peace.
> Where there is hatred, let me sow love;
> Where there is injury, pardon;
> Where there is doubt, faith;
> Where there is despair, hope;
> Where there is darkness, light;
> Where there is sadness, joy.[15]

He prayed that "I may never possess under heaven anything of my own"; on his deathbed he stripped himself naked to leave the world as he had entered it. His was the selfless faith that seeks to console, to understand, and to love; and his prayer contains one line that separates the quiet decencies at the heart of his Christian ethic from that of Dominic de Guzman: "It is in pardoning that we are pardoned."

DOMINIC ATTENDED TO heretics, the lepers of the soul, and he pursued them with pious and pitiless rigor. During her pregnancy in 1170, his aristocratic Castilian mother dreamed that she "brought forth a whelp which carried in its mouth a burning torch, with which it set the world on fire,"[16] and she hurried to have him baptized. Her fears that he would be godless were misplaced.

As a child he often rose to pray during the night and began a lifelong habit of sleeping on bare boards. Once a priest, he had no small talk, speaking "only of God and heavenly things." Where others fasted gently, Dominic mortified his flesh with a brutality that made his body a "perpetual victim of penance." He

---

*Pilgrims in Jerusalem had long followed Christ's final journey from Pilate's house to Calvary, pausing to pray at the site, or Station, of each incident of the Passion. The Franciscans devised a devotion based on pictures or carvings of the incidents, which, arranged on the walls of churches, enabled congregations to reflect and pray at each Station. This has been followed during Lent and Passiontide from medieval times, although the final choice of fourteen Stations was not made until the nineteenth century. They are: Christ's condemnation to death; his weighing down with the cross; his first fall; his meeting with his mother; the bearing of the cross by Simon of Cyrene; the mopping of Christ's face by Veronica; his second fall; his meeting with the women of Jerusalem; his third fall; the stripping of his garments; the nailing to the cross; his death on the cross; the taking down of his body from the cross; and the laying of his body in the tomb.

walked barefoot on the roughest roads, rejoicing in his sores and bruises; he urged his companions to go ahead of him, so that he might "think on our Redeemer" and have "a freer scope for his sighs and tears." His devotion to poverty was equally fierce; when a rich merchant of Bologna donated an estate to his new order, Dominic ripped the deed of gift to shreds in front of the benefactor. He was, in short, "perfectly dead to himself and the world."[17] This extreme alienation from his own feelings and from his fellow men was admired as a mark of sanctity; his self-humiliation—he flung himself to the ground when he approached a new town, begging God to forgive his unworthy presence—was imagined to reflect a purity of soul that rendered him impervious to the wiles of hardened heretics.

His order grew out of his early failure to eradicate the Cathar heresy, which was spreading through southern France and parts of northern Italy. In 1204, Dominic was sent from Spain to preach against it in the region around Toulouse and Albi, from which its French devotees drew their alternative name of Albigensians. The heresy had roots in the nobility and indeed the local Church, as well as among merchants and peasants. It ran too deep to be touched by individual effort, though Dominic journeyed from village to village on bleeding feet, St. Paul's Epistles in hand. "I have preached to you, I begged you with tears," he warned the Cathars. "Now we shall arouse priests and prelates against you." He founded his order in Toulouse in 1214 with sixteen disciples, and a mission to eradicate heresy; of the nineteen priories Dominic established over the following four years, ten were in Cathar regions.

Dominic was impressed by the Cathars' organization and commitment, and he realized that learning was needed to challenge them. Semimonastic universities had existed in the East since the Nestorian school at Nisibis in the fifth century, where lay students were obliged to follow a rule of celibacy, residence, and scholarship. The West was slow to adapt Charlemagne's schools into universities pursuing the *Studium Generale,* with faculties for theology, law, medicine, music, and philosophy. Bologna and Paris were the oldest Western universities, dating from 1088 and 1150. Dominic sent his friars to study at them—the clerical demand for education resulted in a score of universities being founded in Italy, France, England, and Spain by 1300—and acquired minds trained in canon law and theology to break heretics.

A new instrument, the Inquisition, was also at the Church's disposal. Dominic enjoyed close relations with the papacy; the position of *Magister sacri palatii,* "master of the sacred palace," was created for him as the pope's personal theological adviser. His Dominicans, austere, dressed in rough cloth, hardened by wandering and begging, had the moral zeal and dialectic force of the natural born inquisitor.

✤ THE CONCEPT OF the professional inquisitor was first outlined by Pope Alexander III in 1163. Unmasking heretics had been a haphazard affair, dependent on reports by lay and clerical informers. Alexander suggested that specialists should be appointed as investigators. His successor, Lucius III, established a bishops' inquisition, dependent on local sees, and opened the way for the execution of heretics by fire. Being burned alive was a punishment for criminals under late Roman law, and it was included in the penal codes of most medieval European states; under English law, for example, it was applied to women convicted of high treason, and to counterfeiters. The first recorded burning of medieval heretics took place at Orléans in France in 1022. The Church itself disapproved of such executions, however, until Lucius decreed in 1184 that unrepentant heretics should be handed over to the civil secular authorities for punishment. This was to preserve the principle of *Ecclesia non novit sanguinem*, "the Church does not shed blood." This provided some form of theological fig leaf, since laymen carried out the actual execution, but it was, of course, the grossest hypocrisy. No churchmen exonerated the Jews on the grounds that they had merely handed Jesus to Pilate for sentencing, and that Roman soldiers had performed the crucifixion

Heresy was declared to be "treason against God" by Innocent III in 1199. This hugely increased the dangers to the unorthodox, since treason was universally subject to the death penalty in civil law. In 1209, Innocent upgraded the struggle against the Cathars to a full crusade, granting combatants the same blanket remission of sins and heavenly rewards as those fighting Moslems and pagans. Within a few years, trained Dominican interrogators were being used to distinguish recalcitrants among apparent penitents. Burning by the secular arm received its formal papal blessing from Gregory IX in the bull *Excommunicanus* in 1231. The definition of heresy was extended to include opposition to any papal pronouncement as well as to sacrilege, blasphemy, sorcery, sodomy, and the refusal to pay papal taxes; it was made "the duty of every Catholic to persecute heretics."

A final touch was added by Innocent IV in his bull *Ad Extirpanda* in 1252, which recognized past papal statements on the Inquisition and condoned the use of torture. It was said that "bodily torture has ever been found the most salutary and efficient means of leading to spiritual repentance." The choice of "the most befitting mode of torture" was left to the Inquisitor. He was to take the age, sex, and health of the victim into account; pregnant women were only excluded until they had given birth. Those who persisted in denying their guilt merited "no compassion from the servants of God" and were "to perish among the damned."[18] A ruling that a torture session could not be "repeated" was negated by the fact that the session could be "continued" at any time. Witnesses could also be tortured, with exemptions for boys under age fourteen and girls under twelve.

The Inquisition matured into a special court with the power to judge intentions as well as actions. The inquisitor's staff included delegates who carried out preliminary investigations and formalities, a *socius* who acted as his adviser and companion, familiars who were both bodyguards and denouncers, and notaries to file information and keep records. An inquisitor opened his business in a town with a sermon. He called for the congregation to report suspects to his court, and appealed to those who felt they harbored heresy within themselves to confess within a period of grace, normally a week in towns and a month in country districts. Those who did so were promised leniency, and they were typically required to hear a number of masses or make a pilgrimage to a shrine. From this "light" sentence punishments escalated, from wearing a distinctive robe marked with crosses along with a fine and confiscation of property to a spell in an inquisitorial prison, or—for the "unreconciled" who were insubordinate, impenitent, or relapsed—death at the stake.

It was dangerous and usually futile to claim innocence. No witness could be called for the defense. The accused had the right to be represented by a lawyer, but this was a rarity since the lawyer was liable to be charged himself if he lost the case. Prosecution witnesses were guaranteed anonymity, so that the defendant could not challenge their evidence on grounds of personal malice. If he refused to confess voluntarily, he was taken to a dungeon that was normally equipped with a rack or a *strappado,* a system of pulleys that hoisted the victim off the ground. As each bout of torture began, the inquisitor intoned: "Tell the truth, for the love of God."

❖ THIS ENGINE OF repression—the great Catholic historian Lord Acton called it "religious assassination" by which the pope "made murder a legal basis of the Christian Church"[19]—was let loose on several sects. *Humiliati,* extreme Italian penitentials who cared for the sick, were condemned for their cavalier attitude to Church discipline. Arnoldists believed that the immorality of the priesthood destroyed the value of sacraments administered by the clergy, and made confession to one another and not to a priest; Arnold of Brescia, their leader, had been hanged in 1154 and his ashes thrown into the Tiber, but his followers continued with their antipapal insistence that no spiritual person should possess worldly goods or enjoy secular power.

Waldensians were also devoted to poverty. They were disciples of Peter Valdes (or Waldo), a rich Lyons merchant who gave his property to the poor in 1173 and became an itinerant preacher. His faith was orthodox, but his popularity and his message of the blessings of poverty were an affront to clerical wealth and privilege. "They go about in twos, barefoot, in woollen garments, owning nothing," an observer noted of the Waldensians in Rome in 1179, "holding all things in common like the apostles."[20] The line between saint and heretic can be thin, and Valdes, in other respects a precursor of St. Francis, crossed it when he refused to accept a papal command that banned him from preaching without the consent of the local clergy. This was effectively a gagging order, since the clergy had a vested interest in keeping him silent, and he and his followers were excommunicated for ignoring it. The movement spread in northern Italy, Germany, Provence, and Spain. It suffered savage persecution under Innocent III and seemed to be obliterated; but it was hardy, and survived underground to reemerge more than two hundred years later in the Reformation. Despite further repression, it still clings to life as the *Chiesa evangelica Valdese* in modern Piedmont.

The persistence of certain heresies, and the ability of ideas to be engulfed in one place only to emerge emboldened in another, suggests that the desires and responses they reflect are so natural that they are not repetitions, in the sense that an ancient heresy is consciously revived, but may arise spontaneously. This applies to the Inquisition's great foe, the Cathars, and to their belief that evil weighs too heavily on the world to allow for the existence of a unique and benign creator. This denies monotheism, for it follows that good and evil must be the result of distinct creators.

Past concepts that we have already met echo in Cathar thought. Zoroaster had preached the dualism of existence and the struggle between the good spirit Ormuzd and the evil Ahriman more than five hundred years before Christ. Another Persian, Mani, added in the third century A.D. the caste of *electi,* the priesthood of the Elect, whose austere regime of celibacy and vegetarianism resembled that of the Cathar *Perfecti,* as the Manichaean *auditores,* leading lesser and more normal lives, were similar to the Cathar *credentes,* or believers. Within Christianity, Marcion distinguished between the cruel Jehovah and the loving Christian God and saw Christ's body as a mere vision, ideas that had led to his excommunication in A.D. 144 and would now, a millennium later, see the Cathars suffer the same fate. Paulician followers of Constantine of Mananali in Armenia continued to deny the reality of Christ's body in the seventh century; like Marcion, they believed only in the Gospels and the letters of Paul, and rejected the Old Testament and the material world as the work of the evil deity. The Orthodox Church wounded the Paulicians, and the empress Theodora had many thousands executed in the ninth century, but they were not killed off. In 975 the Byzantine emperor John Tzimisces exiled a surviving community of Armenian Paulicians to Bulgarian Thrace.

A Bulgarian priest called Bogomil—the name was Bulgarian for Theophilus, "beloved of God"—recreated the heresy among a large following of resentful Slav peasants. He taught that God's firstborn son was Satanael. This devil spirit was expelled from heaven because of his overweening pride, and created the earth and Adam and Eve. Satanael coupled with Eve to produce Cain, the originator of the evil in mankind. Moses and John the Baptist were servants of Satanael. God then sent Jesus, his second son and the embodiment of the word, to heal humanity. Jesus entered the Virgin through her ear and took the semblance of flesh; he lived and taught, and by seeming to be crucified by Satanael, was able to descend into hell and there bind his elder brother. The Bogomils rejected Orthodox liturgy and symbols, and nourished a special hatred of the cross as the instrument of Christ's murder; their only prayer was the "Our Father," which they recited 120 times a day. They fasted and discouraged marriage, and honored an elite of the Elect. An extreme sect, followers of Cyril the Barefoot, were nudists, who hoped that their nakedness would restore them to the innocence of the Garden of Eden.

Bogomilism was eradicated in Byzantium and Bulgaria during the thirteenth century, but it was transplanted under the name of Patarene to Bosnia and Hum, modern Herzegovina. The Bosnian court declared itself Patarene in 1199, separating itself from its Catholic Hungarian and Orthodox Serb neighbors, and remained so until the Ottoman conquest 250 years later, when the Bosnian aristocracy largely apostatized to Islam. Several dualist sects of the Bogomil style flickered briefly in Europe, German Runkelers, Serb Babuni, Macedonian Kudugers, and Poplicani in northern France. The Albigensians and Cathars of Languedoc were the most significant and sophisticated; they were strong in the weaving towns of Albi, Agen, Pamiers, Carcassonne, and Toulouse, where they were protected by local counts.

Cathars believed that the material world was created by an evil God, the source of corruption and death, who had imprisoned the human soul in its earthly body, thrusting it into a "tunic of flesh"; the Church and the pope were his creatures together with their relics, liturgy, images, and the cross itself. The world of the spirit was the domain of the separate God of goodness. He had sent Christ to reveal the way of salvation to those who would listen; Christ had come to earth as the Spirit, a purity whose body was but a phantom—for flesh would else have corrupted him—and who thus could not suffer or rise again. Cathars held that the Eucharist, as a celebration of the body and blood of Christ, was a particularly evil fiction; they sought to alienate themselves from the physical and all that smacked of bodily evil. Sex and marriage were condemned as gross bodily functions, although women were regarded as the equals of men. The most devout would not eat meat, for they believed that at death the souls of the unsaved migrate to other bodies, human or animal.

The Cathars' name was derived from *katharos,* "purity" in Greek. Those who could withstand temptation and the rigors of mortifying the flesh were described as *Perfecti,* or *parfaits,* or were loosely called *bonshommes,* "goodmen," or *héré-*

tiques. They received the Cathar baptism or *consolamentum* during their active lives. This "consolation" was the only Cathar sacrament, performed by another *parfait* through the laying on of hands. It was held to be the true baptism initiated by Christ, which, in giving the Holy Spirit to the faithful, enabled the soul to be united with the good God at the death of the corrupt body. "Baptism of water profits nothing," Cathars said, and indeed they believed John the Baptist to be the servant of evil. A *parfait* had to abstain from women and from meat, cheese, and eggs; he was austere, chaste, lean, a vegetarian or fish eater, a moral paragon to the humble *credentes,* the unbaptized "believers" who greeted him with a ritual adoration, the *melioramentum,* in recognition of his virtue. The *credentes,* feeling themselves too weak to submit to the rigors of attaining perfection, followed normal lives until they sensed that the end was near. As death approached, a *parfait* would offer them the *consolamentum;* on receiving it, they had to embark upon the *endura,* a fasting unto death that confirmed their salvation.

POPE INNOCENT III was at a moral disadvantage in dealing with the Cathars. The Catholic clergy in Languedoc was famously dissolute. Innocent complained of monks and canons who "have cast aside their habits, taken wives or mistresses and are living on usury"; he attributed this evil to the archbishop of Narbonne, a man who "knows no God but money and keeps a purse where his heart should be."

The *parfaits*—black-clad, pale, longhaired—were a shaming contrast. "They are the only ones to walk in the ways of justice and truth that the apostles followed," a Cathar told his inquisitor. "They do not lie. They do not take what belongs to others. . . . Salvation is better achieved in the faith of these men called heretics than in any other faith."[21] They had a vigorous contempt for wealth and possessions, and for the pope and priests "who devour the blood and sweat of the poor." A starveling shepherd said that, though ruined, he was wealthier than he ever had been. "I am rich," he explained, "because our custom, thus ordered by God, is as follows: if we have but one farthing, we must share it with our poor brothers."[22]

Innocent needed a pretext to launch his crusade against such virtue. It was provided by the murder of his legate, the Cistercian Peter of Castelnau, who was sent to Languedoc in 1208 after Dominic's failure to make progress. Raymond IV, the count of Toulouse, was sympathetic to the many Cathars among his subjects. When he refused to suppress them, the legate excommunicated him, warning him that "he who strikes you dead will earn a blessing from God." One of Raymond's seigneurs, infuriated by papal interference, ran Peter through with a lance on the banks of the Rhone. Innocent canonized him as a martyr and delivered a bull of anathema against the Cathars, ordering that the dead man's blood-stained white habit should be shown in churches throughout Languedoc.

Crusaders were offered a special indulgence and the promise of land and booty. A force of twenty thousand cavalry was raised under the legate Arnald-Amalric, with perhaps four times that number of foot soldiers. It marched from Montpellier to the Albigensian stronghold at Béziers, whose defenders refused to hand over some two hundred known heretics. The crusaders rushed the gates after a group of young Cathars came out to taunt them, and the townspeople fled for sanctuary into the churches of St. Jude and St. Mary Magdalene. "Kill them all," Arnald ordered his men. "The Lord will look after his own." The invaders sang "Veni Sancte Spiritus" as they broke into the churches. Women and suckling infants were massacred in the stone confines; priests, considered guilty for remaining with their heretical flocks, were slaughtered on the altars. "Today, Your Holiness," Arnald informed the pope of his handiwork, "twenty thousand citizens were put to the sword, regardless of age or sex."

When it was over, the legate ordered his crusaders to hand over their booty in order to finance the campaign; in a fury of dashed expectations, they set the town on fire. Carcassonne was taken next. It escaped the flames, for it was needed as a base; instead, Arnald expelled its citizens, driving them out, as he put it, "naked but for the sins they wore." The Norman knight Simon de Montfort, a veteran of the Fourth Crusade, took control of the campaign. When the castle of Bram fell in 1210, de Montfort had the eyes of the prisoners gouged out and their noses lopped off; one prisoner had an eye spared so that he could lead the others to the nearest Cathar village. When he took Minerve later in the year, de Montfort had 140 *parfaits* taken to a meadow where a vast pyre was lit. "There was no need for our men to cast them in," the Cistercian chronicler Vaux de Cernay recorded. "Nay, all were so obstinate in their wickedness as to cast themselves in of their own free will."[23] At Lavaur, the Cathar count, Roger, was hanged, and his sister, loved throughout the district for her charity, was thrown alive into a well and buried beneath stones. Here, only a single *parfait* renounced his faith; some four hundred others were burned. *"Cum ingenti gaudio combusserunt,"* Vaux de Cernay notified Innocent; "they set them alight with immense joy." The pope was kept fully abreast of events. He gloried in them, starting one letter to de Montfort with: "Praise and thanks to the Lord for that which He hath mercifully wrought through thee . . . against His most penitential enemies."[24]

The king of France, seizing the chance to annex Languedoc in 1229, sent his armies to the south. Village by village, the Cathars were slowly overwhelmed. Montségur, the holy place of the *parfaits,* was overrun in 1244. Two hundred prisoners who refused to abjure their faith were burned, but public recantations were growing. Some ten thousand people took advantage of a period of grace offered by the Inquisition in Toulouse in 1245; the flood of voluntary confessions was so great that extra notaries had to be hired to cope with the paperwork. The castle of Queribus fell in 1255, ending armed resistance.

Inquisitors now scoured the countryside for the surviving traces of the heresy, a task that took more than seventy years. Jacques Fournier, the bishop and inquisitor of Pamiers, west of Toulouse on the road to Spain, was a heretic hunter of particular distinction. He was equipped with messengers, jailers, informers, fifteen or so notaries and scribes, a prison, a court, and canons and monks as assessors. The meticulous notes of the 578 interrogations he carried out between 1318 and 1325 leave no doubt that, from a Catholic viewpoint, he was dealing with a highly developed heresy that was dangerous both to the Church and to his own person.

The *parfait* Bernard Bélibaste, who came from the village of Montaillou in the foothills of the Pyrenees, said that the world was ruled by four great devils: "The lord Pope, the major devil whom I call Satan; the lord King of France . . . the bishop of Pamiers . . . and the lord Inquisitor of Carcassonne."[25] Fournier was already bishop and inquisitor; in 1334, when he was elected pope as Benedict XII, he became a triple devil in Cathar eyes.

Prelates, cardinals, and the pope figured prominently in the Cathar vision of the Last Judgment, when *parfaits* would trample them underfoot "as the lambs dance on the grass in the meadows." The incarnation and the sacraments were condemned as part of the corrupt world of matter; Mary was not the mother of God, but "the vessel of flesh in which Jesus Christ was shadowed forth." The Church was tagged as the whore of Babylon, enslaved by riches ill gotten from the toil of the poor. The true Church of God lay in the heart of man, which had no need of priests and liturgy. "We can absolve anyone of his sins," a *parfait* claimed. "Our power of absolution is equal to that of the apostles Peter and Paul, whereas the Catholic Church does not possess this power, because it is a bawd and a whore."[26]

A single prayer, the Paternoster, sufficed for *parfaits;* one of them rose six times a night to repeat it, and those who shared his bed in crowded inns made him sleep on the outside so they would not be disturbed. Ordinary *credentes* were forbidden to recite it for fear that their mouths would soil its words. "No one should say the Paternoster except our lords the goodmen who are in the path of truth," a believer said. "The rest of us, when we say the Lord's Prayer, sin mortally because we are not in the path of truth, for we eat meat and sleep with women."

The cross was held to be a sign of evil. "If I could, I'd chop them down with an axe," a *parfait* said. "I'd use them as wood to boil the pots." Cathars pretended to cross themselves in public; while they did so, they thought of flapping flies away, one from the forehead, one from the beard, the others from the ears. They had an armory of similar deceptions to allay suspicions. They said little, lest they be "caught by the jaw"; they visited other Cathars at night, whistling softly or throwing pebbles against the shutters to alert them. They took Communion when necessary, on the grounds that "to eat a little biscuit never did anyone any harm." Since they believed that all who had been hereticated and had received the *consolamentum* were saved, the mourning they displayed at funerals was mere insurance lest an Inquisition informer be present. "When my mother-in-law died, I went to the funeral and uttered loud laments," a woman from Montaillou told Fournier. "But my eyes were dry, for I knew that she had been hereticated before her death."[27]

Elements of ancient witchcraft persisted; Cathars believed that cats, owls, wolves, and reptiles were the creatures of the evil God. There was, too, a strong sense of injustice and a belief that society would be turned on its head after death, a common theme in peasant movements; those who have possessions on earth—"kings, princes, prelates"—will find nothing but evil in the next world, where the oppressed will find only good.

FOURNIER WAS RELATIVELY restrained in his punishments. He was sincere, and patient; he spent a fortnight convincing a Jew of the mystery of the Trinity, and a further week persuading him to accept the dual nature of Christ. He resorted to torture only when agents of the French crown made false charges against lepers, who had been forced to confess to poisoning wells with powdered toads. Of the 114 people he convicted, five went to the stake. Forty-eight suffered imprisonment of varying degrees of severity, the worst cases being fettered in small cells on a diet of black bread and water. Twenty-five were humiliated by having the heretics' yellow cross sewn on their cloaks, and the remainder were obliged to make a pilgrimage or had possessions confiscated.

Some inquisitors, however, displayed naked sadism. The Dominican Robert le Bougre, investigating allegations that Bishop Moranis of Champagne harbored heretics, put a whole town on trial in 1239 and dispatched 180 people to the stake, including the bishop, on a single day. Conrad of Marburg, a secular priest from the small German town of that name, was equally notorious. In 1228 he became confessor to Elizabeth of Hungary, the young widow of the landgrave (landed count) of Thuringia and the daughter of the king of Hungary. She was known for her exceptional charity, founding hospitals and providing for helpless children; after her husband died of plague while crusading, she was expelled from court on the pretext that her almsgiving had exhausted the treasury. She settled in a modest house at Marburg, where she built a hospital and labored for the relief of the sick and poor, cleaning their homes and spinning and carding wool for their clothes. Conrad separated her from her children and replaced her ladies-in-waiting with harsh companions who slapped her and beat her with rods; austerities and humiliations undermined her health. "If I fear a man like this," she said of Conrad, "what must God be like?" She died in 1231, aged twenty-four.*

With no visible misgivings, Gregory personally appointed her tormentor as papal inquisitor in Germany, with instructions to investigate an alleged cult of Lucifer. Conrad believed that salvation was attainable only through pain, a conclusion he seems to have reached after witnessing a Cistercian being burned for heresy. He had eighty men, women, and children burned in Strasbourg, the supposed seat of the Luciferians. The state of terror he created was ended by his murder in 1233. The assassination of inquisitors was, in fact, remarkably rare. Peter of Verona, a Dominican friar appointed inquisitor for Milan a year after Conrad's murder, had his head split open with an axe as he traveled from Como to Milan in 1252. The Church did not, of course, admit that such men had gained their just desserts. The number of Dominican inquisitors in Lombardy was promptly doubled; Peter was awarded the title of "martyr," and the legend was spread that he had written "I believe in God"—*Credo in Deus*—in his own blood before dying.

Abuse was endemic; accusations were often fueled by spite, vendetta, and greed. The Knights Templars, whose wealth attracted the piratical interest of the French throne, were suppressed on trumped-up charges of sodomy, heresy, and witchcraft with the collaboration of Pope Clement V at the beginning of the fourteenth century. Knights confessed under torture—"I would gladly admit that I killed God," one knight cried out—that they worshiped a vast idol in the shape of a goat called Baphomet, that the devil appeared to them as a black tomcat, and that they fornicated with demons disguised as women. In one session, fifty-nine Knights Templars were burned.

Yet the theology and apparatus of the Inquisition passed unchallenged by successive popes. How could this be? How could the faith allow its Church to do to the living what the ancients had done to Christ: condemning him as a heretic in a show trial and sentencing him to a death of deliberate agony?

The Inquisition flew in the face of Christian tradition. A synod in Rome in 384 had denounced the use of torture; Gregory the Great had said that testimony given under duress should be ignored, and Nicholas I had condemned torture as a violation of divine law in the ninth century. It was a modern invention, and seemingly perverse. Some regions—Bohemia, Venice, Christian Spain, and, most notably, England—all but ignored it. English common law held a defendant to

---

*She was canonized by Gregory IX four years later. Her relics, translated to the Church of St. Elizabeth at Marburg, were a major point of pilgrimage until Protestants removed them three hundred years later.

be innocent until proved guilty in a public trial. "The inquisitors are the greatest heretics of all, since, against the doctrine and example of Christ, they condemn heretics to the fire," a German parish priest, Balthasar Hübmaier, was to write. "For Christ did not come to butcher, destroy and burn but that those who live might live more abundantly." Hübmaier was himself to be burned as a heretic, in Vienna on March 10, 1528, and his wife was thrown into the Danube with a stone tied around her neck a few days later.

Popes and inquisitors were, in a sense, at war with the nature of Christianity itself, with its tendency to spawn individuals and sects who consider their wildly varying beliefs to be blessed by Pauline grace and the Holy Spirit of Pentecost. The Church had a vested interest in claiming heresy to be the worst of all crimes. "It's vileness renders pure even Sodom and Gomorrah," Bishop Lucas of Tuy said. "Its pollution cleanses the filthy madness of Mahomet. . . ." Thomas Aquinas demonstrated, to his own satisfaction at least, that heresy separates man from God more than any other sin. As an actual and physical emissary of Satan, the heretic merited the fiercest punishment; Gregory the Great had said, cruelly, that the bliss of the elect in heaven would not be perfect unless they could look across the abyss and see the torment of those in eternal fire.[28] The death penalty was divinely sanctioned. "Thou shalt smite them," God had said of the infidel Hittites and Canaanites; "then thou shalt utterly destroy them; thou shalt make no covenant with them, nor show mercy unto them. . . ." (Deut. 7:2). The inquisitor saw himself as the "righteous Branch" who "shall execute judgement and justice in the land" (Jer. 23:5).

In defending its orthodoxy in so terrible a manner, however, the Church helped to heighten religious intensity to the point of madness. The continuous preaching of crusade had a ferocious effect on those who heard it. "Around this time naked women ran through the towns and cities, saying nothing," a chronicler recorded of 1212.[29] It was an age when simpletons, the "holy fools," whipped up bands of followers to fulfill their strange visions. One such had been Eon de l'Etoile, who—hearing the chant *per Eum qui venturus est judiciare. . . .* and believing that *per Eum* meant "through Eon" and not "through Christ"—declared that he had been appointed to judge the quick and the dead. He called those who flocked to him his apostles and angels; they armed themselves and preyed on churches and monasteries, spending their booty on high living. Eon amused his judges when he was captured; he appeared before them with a forked branch, explaining that when the fork pointed upward to heaven, God had two-thirds of the world to his own one-third, the ratio reversing when the stick pointed downwards. They burst out laughing, and he was merely imprisoned, but his three principal apostles, called Wisdom, Knowledge, and Judgment, were burned.

An obscure French carpenter, Durand of Le Puy, was a similar mystic-brigand.

He claimed to have had a vision in which the Virgin ordered him to exhort people to peace, giving him a scrap of paper with the words "Lamb of God, who taketh away the sins of the world, give us peace" scrawled on it. A company grew up around him. At first, Durand led them against the mercenaries and scavengers, the *routiers* and *ribaldi,* who scourged the land; but they themselves soon degenerated into a mob of outcasts that showed "no fear, no reverence of their superiors . . ." In 1251 a leader called the "master of Hungary" preached a crusade to French peasants to venture to the Holy Land to free Louis IX, then a Moslem captive. The "master" kept an *epistola caelestis,* a "heavenly letter," in his closed hand. He said that it was a command from the Virgin to preach the crusade to lowly shepherds, whom he gathered in numbers from Picardy, Flanders, Brabant, and Hainault. At first they had the approval of the queen, Blanche of Castile. At Rouen, however, they ejected the archbishop and his clergy from the cathedral; they killed or threw twenty-five theology students into the Loire at Orleans, and profaned churches and invaded a convent at Tours. The "Master" met his nemesis at Bourges, where, Matthew Paris recorded, "an executioner with a two-edged sword sent him headless to hell." His body was left at a crossroads to be eaten by animals, while his followers were "everywhere cut down like mad dogs."[30]

A string of impostors claimed to be the resurrected Emperor Frederick II after his death in 1250. One, driven from Cologne as a lunatic, set up a court in Neuss. Claiming that God had sent him to chastize the clergy and rule the world, his followers continued to believe in him even after he was burned in 1284; it was said that no bones had been found among the ashes and that he had a magic ring that enabled him to disappear. Another pseudo-Frederick promptly appeared in the Low Countries, claiming that he had risen from the dead three days after being burned in Germany, a fate he now shared in Utrecht; a third lived on the slopes of Mount Etna, from whose fiery bowels he claimed to have emerged, attracting numerous devotees.

❖ MASS SICKNESS MIGHT also be expected to induce psychosis, and so it proved. "In January of the year 1348," the Flemish chronicler De Smet wrote, "three galleys put in at Genoa, driven by a fierce wind from the East, horribly infected. . . . They were driven forth from that port by burning arrows and divers engines of war, for no man dared touch them. . . . Thus they were scattered from port to port."[31] They spread bubonic plague, an evil more ferocious and mobile than the Mongol hordes; in its wake, flagellation, another manifestation of spiritual intensity or hysteria, reached its peak.

Christ's suffering and the sense of sin suffuse the faith. Flagellation, often inspired by catastrophe, is a means of expressing penance and sharing in the Passion. It survives to this day, most notably in the Philippines; a chronicler caught its essence in the fourteenth century. He described how a friar stripped himself naked in his cell on a winter's night and set about hitting himself with a scourge tipped with crooked spikes. These tore his flesh with such force that the scourge broke into pieces and the metal tips embedded themselves in the wall. As he gazed at his wounds, the friar "was reminded in many ways of the beloved Christ, when he was fearfully beaten." The friar knelt, naked and bloody in the frosty air, and "prayed to God to wipe out his sins from before his gentle eyes . . ."[32]

The practice was first recorded in Europe among eleventh-century hermits in Italy. The earliest organized processions appeared in Italian cities in 1260, inspired by a hermit of Perugia and the ravages of civil war; large numbers of men and youths with banners and burning candles stood in front of churches and flogged themselves. "Holy Virgin, take pity on us!" they cried. "Beg Jesus Christ to spare us!" The movement spread two years later to the towns of southern

Flagellants in procession in the Netherlands in 1349. The practice had begun among hermits in Italy in the eleventh century, escalating at times of plague, war, and other disasters. The flagellants toured towns and villages, flogging themselves with metal-tipped leather scourges, praying, and sobbing. They said that Christ's blood mingled with their own, and that they were an army of saints whose suffering would absolve others. Some claimed to raise the dead.

Germany and the Rhine. Its leaders claimed that God had written a heavenly letter, on a marble tablet ablaze with light, in which he threatened to destroy sinful humanity. The Virgin Mary interceded on man's behalf to save those who joined a flagellant procession, whose duration was commonly set at thirty-three and one-third days, corresponding to the number of years Jesus had spent on earth.

A ruinous deterioration in the weather preceded the Black Death* that accompanied the Genoese galleys. Heavy rains and cold, so intense that the Alpine glaciers advanced and vines no longer grew in England, ruined harvests across Europe. Some places suffered multiple crop failures. The lack of sun made it difficult to produce salt by evaporation, and unsalted meat soon rotted. "These pestilences were for pure sin," the English chronicler Langland wrote. Ill omens— columns of fire, drops of blood on freshly baked bread, church bells that tolled without human intervention—abounded in superstitious minds. The plague seemed to confirm God's anger.

Other Genoese galleys brought the epidemic to the port of Messina in Sicily, the crews with "sickness clinging to their very bones." The disease gripped the city within a few days. Panic-stricken, the Messinese fled into the countryside, taking it with them. The people in the nearby city of Catania were sympathetic at first, but as they too succumbed, they "refused even to speak to any from Messina, but quickly fled at their approach." The Messinese appealed to the archbishop to send them relics of St. Agatha, in the hope of obtaining a miraculous cure. The Catanians tore the keys from the sacristy to prevent this. The archbishop dipped the relics in water and bravely agreed to take this holy water to Messina. Many were already dead, their unburied bodies eaten by dogs. The archbishop organized the survivors into a procession, which he led around the city reciting litanies. A Franciscan chronicler, writing ten years later, claimed that "a black dog, bearing a drawn sword in his paws, appeared among them, gnashing his teeth and rushing upon them and breaking all the silver vessels and lamps and candlesticks. . . ."[33] The pestilence was so violent that "one man could not succour another"; the archbishop and perhaps half the population died.

Sicily was an ideal entry point for the poisoning of the western Mediterranean and Europe. The plague spread along the trade routes from Messina, Genoa, and Venice. By the summer of 1348 it had crossed the Alps and was raging in Germany, and in less than a year most of Western Christendom was infected. The onset of the disease was marked by "certain tumours in the groin or armpits," Boccaccio recorded, some of these buboes being as large as an apple or egg; from here it "soon began to propagate and spread itself in all directions indifferently . . . black spots making their approach as . . . an infallible token of ap-

*The term is not contemporary; it was first used in Swedish, as *Swarta Döden,* in 1555.

A priest blesses those with the telltale mark of bubonic plague, buboes or swellings in the groin or armpits, after its arrival in Europe in 1348. About a third of the European population died. Only Poland and Bohemia, which had time to seal their frontiers, escaped. It was a cataclysm beyond medieval understanding, and many saw it as divine punishment.

proaching death."[34] The buboes might discharge and the patient recover, but this was rare, and most died amid "unbearable stench, sweat, excrement, spittle, breath so foetid as to be overpowering; urine turbid, thick, black or red."[35]

A flea harbored in the fur of *rattus rattus,* the vagabond black rat, carried the disease; but it was thought to be caused by a corruption in the air itself, and indeed in its pulmonary variant it attacked the lungs, so that the victim sprayed out the plague bacilli during coughing fits. Proper hygiene, a rarity in medieval Europe, was the best protective. At Avignon, the new seat of the papacy, Pope Clement VI and eight in ten members of his *curia* survived. The pope was isolated in his palace, he bathed frequently, and his airy rooms were scrubbed with vinegar. But in the city outside, a canon wrote, half of the inhabitants died, 62,000 in the first three months, and 7,000 houses were empty and abandoned. About a third of the European population died; only Bohemia and Poland, which had time to seal their frontiers, escaped. It was a cataclysm beyond medieval understanding. The medical faculty of the University of Paris was reduced to astrology as an explanation. In a report prepared at royal command in 1348, it found that a conjunction of Saturn, Jupiter, and Mars had taken place in the house of Aquarius on March 20, 1345. The conjunction of the first two planets was believed to cause death and destruction; the pestilence in the air was explained by humid Jupiter drawing evil vapors from the earth that arid Mars kindled into an infectious fire.[36]

Many saw it as divine punishment, however, and sought pardon in flagellation. Processions began in Hungary late in 1348 and spread through the towns of Germany to the Low Countries and France. A band of flagellants might have fifty members or more than five hundred; a new band arrived at Strasbourg each week for six months, and some fifty-three hundred flagellants were recorded visiting Tournai in a ten-week period. They gave themselves collective names—Cross-Bearers, or Brethren of the Cross—and wore uniforms, white robes with a red cross on front and back, and hats or hoods. Each band had a lay "master," who heard confessions and granted absolution. Discipline was strict. Flagellants were forbidden to shave, bathe, change their clothes, or have dealings with women. They formed a circle outside the church when they arrived in a town. One by one they threw themselves to the ground with arms outstretched like crucifixes. They then rose and flogged themselves with metal-tipped leather scourges, singing hymns and praying and sobbing while the master walked among them and read out the heavenly letter. The ceremony was invalidated if a woman or priest entered the circle. It was repeated twice a day in public, and each night in the privacy of bedrooms.

The scourgings, prayers, and hymns made a compelling spectacle. Flagellants said that Christ's blood mingled with their own, and that they were an army of saints whose suffering would absolve others; some claimed that they could raise the dead and cast out devils, or that they spoke with the Virgin Mary. Townspeople lodged and sheltered them, seeing them as men of God and cursing the clergy; they dipped cloths in their blood to keep as sacred relics and brought out the sick to be cured. As they marched, the flagellants sang the haunting words of the *Stabat Mater* to the Virgin:

Wound me with his wounds
Let me drink his cross
For the love of thy son

The cult of the Mater Dolorosa, the Virgin of the Sorrows, was greatly strengthened by the horrors of the plague; where the surfeit of death made Christ appear more awesome, the Virgin, mourning her son, became a companion in grief. But the obsession with death, the skulls on rosary beads, the wall paintings of dancing skeletons, and the fervent reminders of the crucifixion, spilled easily into the persecution of Jews.

Jews were a convenient scapegoat for desperate souls, and for those who sensed a chance for plunder. As pawnbrokers and moneylenders, they were widely despised by Christians, who conveniently overlooked the fact that they were forbidden to work in most crafts and trades. Their reputation as "Christ-killers" went back to the start of the Crusades and before. Jews were now charged with poisoning wells, so as to "kill and destroy the whole of Christendom and have lordship over all the world."[37] The conspiracy was said to be based in Toledo, from where messengers carried poison in stitched leather bags with instructions from rabbis to spinkle it in wells and springs. The first formal trials were held in Savoy in September 1348. Confessions were extracted by torture, and eleven Jews were burned alive; the survivors were forced to pay a tax of 160 florins a month for permission to remain in Savoy. In Carinthia, a chronicler recorded that earthquakes and pogroms followed the flagellants:

> Plague ruled the common people and overthrew many,
> The earth quaked. The people of the Jews is burnt,
> A strange multitude of half-naked men beat themselves.[38]

When flagellants entered Frankfurt in July 1349 the locals helped them destroy the Jewish quarter; at Mainz, a crowd watching a ceremony went wild and annihilated the largest Jewish community in Germany, with six thousand "poisoners of wells" said to have been killed; hundreds more were burned to death in a specially built wooden house on an island in the Rhine at Basle, and in Brussels all six hundred Jews were killed despite the attempts of the duke of Brabant to save them.

When the plague arrived in Avignon in March 1348, Clement VI approved flagellant processions in the city, with up to two thousand men and women taking part, in sackcloth and ashes, "wailing as they walked, tearing their hair, and lashing themselves with scourges . . ."[39] In October the following year, aware of the perils, he issued a bull condemning flagellants, saying that their "masters of error" should be burned if necessary; he complained that, beneath the cloak of piety, they "set their hands to cruel and impious works, shedding the blood of Jews, whom Christian piety accepts and sustains."[40] The pope stressed that "by a mysterious decree of God," none were spared the plague; Jews were as much victims as Christians, and the charge that they spread it was "without plausibility." King Philip V of France forbade the practice on pain of death; although a boatload of flagellants sailed to London and performed in front of St. Paul's, they made no English converts. After a series of executions in Westphalia, a chronicler wrote of them "vanishing as suddenly as they had come, like night phantoms or mocking ghosts."

It took the Inquisition more than a century to mop up the remnants. A flagellant pseudo-Frederick appeared in central Germany in the 1360s. Konrad Schmid claimed to have a miraculous birthmark, a gold cross between his shoulder blades, that confirmed him to be the resurrected emperor who would lead his people in the Last Days. He styled himself the king of Thuringia. After he had flogged them, his subjects were obliged to make their confession to him and take an oath of absolute obedience. They addressed him as "Our Father" and were baptized with blood. In 1368 he announced that the millennium would start the following year; before it was reached the Thuringian inquisitor had arrested many of his followers, and Schmid himself was probably included in a group of seven who were burned at Nordhausen. A large group of flagellants was discovered at Sangerhausen in 1414; although the inquisitor had only the leader and two disciples burned as impenitents, the local princes seized those who had recanted and burned several hundred of them. The last covert flagellants were executed in the 1480s.

❖

❖

❖

CHAPTER XIV

"IF GOLDE RUSTE,
WHAT SHOULD IREN DO?":

Early Reformers

Ominous warnings of an idea that had the force to fracture Western Christendom came first from England. Scripture, John Wycliffe asserted in 1378, was "the highest authority for every Christian and the standard of faith and of all human perfection." For Wycliffe, a Yorkshireman of sour temper and restless mind, what was not in the Bible was mere invention or superstition. He taught that the word of God was the greatest authority to which a Christian was bound; since "the truth of God standeth not in one language more than in another," he added that the Bible must be translated into English so that "it may edify the lewd people as it doth clerks in Latin." No institution that God had not sanctioned—be it the papacy or Catholic doctrine—was to be trusted. Wycliffe was born in about 1329. A fine scholar, he was master of Balliol College at Oxford at thirty-one; the Church then hounded him from the university, charged him with heresy, burned his writings, and ultimately exhumed his corpse and cast it into a river. By then, the perils that the Church rightly sensed lay beneath his simple proposition had been loosed. Poor preachers, dressed in modest russet cloth, were spreading his beliefs at impromptu gatherings in churchyards and at markets. The bishop of Chichester, vexed by this new breed of unlicensed sermonizers, dubbed them "Bible men."

The term was contemptuous, but accurate. Wycliffe broke new ground by looking back to the Scriptures and the era of the early fathers, before the Church had established its rituals and its wealth. He gave a series of lectures at Oxford that covered the whole of the Bible, a sweeping commentary that—remarkably—had never been attempted before. He stressed the importance of personal faith in Christ. "As belief is the first virtue and the ground of all others," he preached, "so unbelief is the first sin of all others."[1] This belief was not gained from the intercession of the Church; it flowed from the individual, and the decadence of churchmen was an obstacle to it.

Christ had been the "poorest man of alle," thus true priests should be "moost pore men and moost meke in spirit," for they were made not by bishops but "by power that Crist gyveth."[2] No cleric had the right to be wealthy, and Wycliffe singled out the orders of monks and friars for special attention. He said that it was better to dwell among Saracens and pagans than amid "sects of these newe religiouse," for they preferred to drink "podel water of ye canal"[3] than the pure wisdom of Christ. He noted that the Bible made no mention of any pope. "What good doeth his gabbling that the Pope would be called 'Most Holy Father'?" he asked. The dignities and privileges that Rome bestowed were "not worth a fly's foot"; men should "shake awey al ye lawe that ye Pope hath maad,"[4] and return to the laws of God.

THE CLERGY, THE precious metal of the Church, was indeed frequently so debased that Wycliffe's contemporary, the poet Geoffrey Chaucer, feared for the souls of common folk:

If golde ruste, what should iren do?
For if a preest be foul, on whom we truste
No wonder is a lewed man to ruste![5]

The primary aim of many Christian shepherds was the fleecing of their flock; they billeted themselves upon the faithful with the rapacity of an occupying army. Chaucer included three such men among the group of pilgrims he sent on an imaginary but lifelike journey from London to the shrine of St. Thomas Becket in his great work of verse, the *Canterbury Tales*.

Chaucer's clerical characters show all too clearly the frailties of the Church and the reason why it was ripe for reform even at the most humble level. His pardoner, who prospered by selling the remission of sins, scavenged among the guilty and gullible with a silver tongue. His trade was advertised on his cap, to which he had sewn a vernicle, a small replica of the handkerchief St. Veronica gave to Jesus to wipe the sweat and blood from his face on his way to Calvary; this was itself a fraud, for St. Veronica was a recent French invention who enabled pardoners to add scraps of linen to their line of goods. He carried his stock with him: a wallet brimful with pardons "comen from Rome all hot"; a pillowcase in which he kept a piece of "the sail that Sainte Peter had whan he wente upon the see"; and a glass case full of "pigges bones" that he claimed to be relics of the saints. He was a skilled preacher; "my theme is one and ever was," he said, *"radix malorum est cupiditas."* Having thus established that "money is the root of all evil" (1 Tim. 6:10), he parted his audience from their sinful savings, selling them pardons "which were me given by the Popes hand" and promising absolution to any purchaser "who hath done sinne horrible." By his trickery, he confessed, "have I wonne, yeer by yeer, an hundred mark since I was pardoner . . ." He claimed that he was raising funds for the hospital of Our Lady of Rouncivalle near Charing Cross in London; in fact, he used the money to "drinke licour of the vine and have a jolly wench in every town."[6]

Also living high on the wages of the remission of sins was the "frere" or friar; he was an "esy man to give penaunce," believing that "instede of weeping and prayeres," the penitent was best advised to give "silver to the poure freres." He wheedled the last farthing from shoeless widows; he spurned lepers and the sick and the destitute, but crawled anywhere "as profit sholde aryse." His flesh was as white as a fleur-de-lys and he was dressed as well as "a maister or a pope" in double-worsted cloth; like the pardoner, he "knew the taverns well in every town" and doled out rich gifts to the "faire wives" he seduced. The monk in the party spared no cost in edging the sleeves of his habit with rich furs and fastened his hood with a gold pin twined in a love-knot. His boots were supple, his horse in fine condition, his body "ful fat and in good poynte." Prayer bothered him little, and he held monastic rules to be "nat worth an oyster"; he enjoyed the pleasures of the hunt, keeping greyhounds "as fast as any fowl in flight," and of the table, where "a fat swan loved he best of any roast."[7]

Avarice in the Church had been criticized since Constantine. Chaucer accepted its abuses with good humor and acknowledged happily enough that it also contained those who "Cristes Gospel trewly wolde preche." The parish priest was the most intimate point of contact between the ordinary Christian and the Church, and the parson Chaucer sketched on the pilgrimage was poor in money but rich in "holy thought and werk." He had not abandoned his flock to go to London to say prayers for the dead in a wealthy chantry, as many did, leaving a curate to run the parish for a pittance; instead he was the good shepherd who "dwelt at home and kept well his folde," visiting the sick with patient diligence. The clerk of Oxford, preparing himself for the priesthood, preferred to have "twenty books, clad in black and red, of Aristotle and his philosophye" than rich robes and gay music. The pilgrim prioress, Madame Eglantine, was "so charitable and so pitous" that she wept if she saw a mouse caught in a trap. Such gentle souls—"al concience and tendre herte"—redeemed the venality of the Church for Chaucer, and for the mass of the laity. They did not yet question it as an institution.

✤ WYCLIFFE DID, AND it made him dangerous. He went beyond ridicule of Church riches, simony,* and indulgences to damn its doctrines and the way in which it "stuffs the people only too effectually with garbage."[8] His concern was the gulf between the nature of the faith as seen in the Scriptures and its practice by the Church in general and by the pope in particular. In 1376 he argued in his book *De Civili Dominio* that all authority, spiritual and secular, is founded in grace. The dominion of the Church rests wholly upon this gift. If it is not in a state of grace and fails to discharge its spiritual obligation, the civil power has the right to deprive it of its endowments and property. Wycliffe was in no doubt that this stage had been reached. He described the pope as a thief, the "most cursed of dippers and purse-heavers," who "vilified, nullified and utterly defaced" the commandments of God. The papacy had no right to intervene in English affairs, since it was led by the *potissimus Antichristi*.

The abandoning of Rome by its bishops added weight to Wycliffe's assaults. Clement V had transferred the papacy to Avignon in southern France at the beginning of the century. Rome and nothern Italy were so beset by anarchy and disastrous wars that "the bark of Peter is in danger of sinking,"[9] Clement's cardinals complained, begging him to leave for the safety of France; "ah, Italy, abode of sorrow," Dante wept, "vessel without a helmsman amidst a dreadful storm, no longer art thou mistress of thy peoples, but a place of prostitution. . . ."[10] The French desire to coerce the pope was an equal reason, however; and one that enabled papal critics to speak of a "Babylonian captivity." Clement was former archbishop of Bordeaux and member of a noted French family; his loyalty, and the subservience of his court to the French crown, was enhanced by prising him from Rome. The move to Avignon was formalized by John XXII, another Frenchman, and the former bishop of the city who was elected pope at French behest in 1316. John declared Avignon to be his seat on the imperial principal of *ubi papa, ibi Roma*, "where the pope is, there is Rome"; but French influence was never in doubt and, of the cardinals created between 1316 and 1375, ninety were Frenchmen as against fourteen Italians, five Spaniards, and an Englishman.

In time, Avignon was bought by the papacy from its owner, Joanna of Naples; a great palace was built, fit for a pope and his five hundred household staff, with masters of the kitchen, food, drink, and stables, and chapels, audience

---

*The sale of positions in the Church was known as simony after Simon Magus, the sorcerer in Acts who offered money to receive the Holy Spirit. "Thy silver perish with thee," Peter rebuked him, "because thou has thought to obtain the gift of God with money" (Acts 8:20). The practice was common enough in the period after Constantine for the purchase of ordination to have been forbidden by the Council of Chalcedon in 451. Frequent later bans were largely ignored.

halls, libraries, a vaulted treasury whose cargo of precious metals and stones was cunningly concealed beneath the flagstones, and a banqueting hall supplied by a vast kitchen with an octagonal chimney piece. Papal summer residences were created at Pont-Sorgue and Châteauneuf-du-Pape. A giant bureaucracy dealt with Church business; the apostolic chancery employed eight layers of lawyers, clerks, registrars, copyists, and correctors. A petition was first submitted to a *referendari* or the pope for initial approval; it then entered a slow round of rough drafts and fair copies, fee assessment, seal-placing, posting in the *registrum* of bulls, and the appointment of executors. If a difficulty arose in filling a benefice, which often occurred due to an applicant's age, bodily defects, or his tenure of other benefices without proper dispensation, the suit had to be presented to the *auditores sacri palatii* before the process was repeated. Each obstacle involved fees, perquisites, and gratuities. Hundreds of thousands of these documents survive in the Vatican archives, sixty-five thousand from John XXII's reign alone.[11]

The machine was voracious. As well as the constant drain of Italian wars, the popes spent heavily to gather artists, craftsmen, and scholars to glorify Avignon. Money for the *camera apostolica* was raised from across Western Christendom by *collectores*. Bishoprics and monasteries had to pay a *servitium* on new appointments. Clement V introduced "annates," demanding a year's income from all benefices, vacant or to be vacated, in the British isles; this was later extended to benefices with incomes above twenty-four gold florins in much of Europe, but it rankled particularly with Wycliffe and the English. Crusade tithes were levied whether the crusade took place or not. A *subsidium* was collected in specific regions. *Spolia,* the seizure of the estates of cardinals and prelates who died at the Curia, was an old practice; it was extended by Urban V to the estates of all bishops, abbots, and deans. Benefices were often deliberately left vacant in order to allow revenue to flow directly to Avignon. Fines and censures were imposed for late payments; in July 1328, five archbishops, 30 bishops, and 46 abbots incurred suspension and excommunication for nonpayment of *servitia*.

Money was spent as the Curia and pope saw fit. At the end of his reign, Clement V had one million gold florins at his disposal. He gave 800,000 florins to his nephew, the viscount of Lomagne; when John XXII succeeded Clement, only 70,000 florins remained in the papal coffers, and the new pope was obliged to sue Clement's heirs, recovering only a fraction of his treasure.[12] Avignon itself became a gigantic honey pot, or, as the poet Petrarch thought, a "sewer where all the filth of the universe has gathered." Pining for his Italian homeland, Petrarch described the booming city on the Rhône as a place where "no piety dwells, no charity, no faith . . . where whoever is the worst is promoted, God is despised, money worshipped, the laws trodden underfoot, and good men ridiculed."[13] He wrote of two cardinals surrounded by suppliants as they left the papal palace.

One cardinal cajoled money from them with false promises; when the other remonstrated with him, he retorted, with the unblushing gaze of a harlot, "Rather, you should be ashamed to be so slow-witted that you haven't learnt the arts of the court in all this time. . . ."[14] The city swarmed with "troupes of the most debased hangers-on," flatterers, purveyors of jewels, furs, and velvets, bankers earning fat commissions, musicians and painters seeking patronage. St. Bridget, scarcely less shocked than Petrarch or Wycliffe, thought the papal court to be "a field full of tares, that must be rooted out with a sharp steel, then purified with fire, and finally levelled with the plough."[15]

The return to Rome, after seventy years at Avignon, was made by Gregory XI. He did so despite the protests of the French king and a majority of cardinals to try to restore some stability to the city and the papal states. "I say to you from Christ crucified, to come and overthrow our enemies," the mystic Catherine of Siena appealed to him. "Show the manliness I expect from you, no more cowardice! Take possession of the place of the glorious shepherd St. Peter, whose vicar you still are. . . ."[16] He entered Rome in January 1377. Riots and bloodshed continued in the city. Gregory planned to return to Avignon, but first he dealt with the troublesome Wycliffe.

✤ THE REFORMER'S SCORN for the papacy and its financial demands interested the English government. Retained as a government pamphleteer and propagandist, Wycliffe was sent to Bruges to discuss clerical abuses with papal ambassadors. His call to confiscate Church estates and wealth on the grounds of dereliction of spiritual duty was intriguing to noblemen and landowners, and deeply alarming to the English bishops. They summoned him to explain himself in front of the archbishop at St. Paul's in London in 1377. Wycliffe was protected by John of Gaunt, anticlerical and the most influential man in the kingdom, obliging Rome to enter the fray directly. Gregory XI banned Wycliffe in May and sent bulls to the king and the bishops ordering them to imprison him for the heresies which he "vomit[s] forth from the poisonous confines of his breast."[17] The pope also wrote to the chancellor of Oxford University complaining that "through some idleness and sloth [you have] permitted cockle to spring up among the clean grain on the campus of your illustrious school. . . ."[18]

Gregory died in March 1378, however, and Wycliffe was greatly helped by the moral squalor into which the papacy now sank. The conclave to choose a successor was besieged by a Roman mob demanding a Roman pope. They piled firewood in the room above the conclave and banged on the floor with pikes and halberds, lest the cardinals elect a Frenchman who would return papal spending power to Avignon. A decrepit Roman cardinal, Tebaldeschi, was dressed in papal robes and displayed as a sop to the crowds. In fact, the cardinals elected Bartolo-meo Prignano, the absentee archbishop of Bari, who took the name of Urban VI. He had served as an efficient regent of the papal chancery at Avignon, but his elevation unhinged him. Urban was violent, drank heavily, and told a cardinal who remonstrated with him that: "I can do anything, absolutely anything I like." After six months a group of cardinals fled from Rome to Anagni and declared Urban's election invalid because it had been held under duress due to the mob. In his place they elected Robert, the cardinal-bishop of Geneva, who took the name Clement VII. The existing Curia followed Clement to Avignon, but Urban defiantly appointed twenty-nine new cardinals to recreate a Curia of his own.

There had been two popes, two administrations, and two courts before; but never had there been two popes elected by the same group of cardinals. A Great Schism was born. The loyalties of nations, universities, and religious orders were divided as France, Burgundy, Savoy, Naples, the Spanish kingdoms, and Scotland declared for Clement in Avignon, while England, Germany, Poland, Hungary, and Scandinavia remained with Urban in Rome. Future saints where themselves divided. Catherine of Siena was faithful to Urban, although the schism so tormented her that it was blamed for her premature death at age thirty-three. The Spaniard Vincent Ferrer, leading processions of flagellants and praying for an end to disunity, opted for Clement.

The two popes at once excommunicated each other. They placed rival supporters and countries under interdict, where the normal sacraments and services ceased, although priests not personally responsible for the dispute could continue to perform rites in a low voice and in private behind closed doors. Both sides naturally ignored the other's censures; Urban's manias ran unchecked. He excommunicated Queen Joanna of Naples for supporting Clement, but soon fell out with her replacement, Charles of Durazzo, accusing him of treason. When the new king besieged him in his fortress at Nocera near Naples, Urban climbed the battlements four times a day and, "serenely, with bell, book and candle,"[19] excommunicated the army below. Five cardinals consulted a jurist to see whether insanity could be used as grounds for removing him, but Urban had them arrested and tortured, ignoring their screams while he walked in a nearby garden reciting his breviary. They were not seen again.

✤   IT WAS GRIST for Wycliffe's antipapal mill. "I always knew that the pope had cloven feet," he mocked. "Now he has a cloven head." He wrote that Christ had taught that holiness should be "hid in men's hearts and not shown to the people in outward signs," but the "fiend" in Rome had turned true religion on its head in his desire for riches. Wycliffe justified the power and trappings of secular

The books written by the pioneer reformer John Wycliffe were burned, as seen here, but he escaped that fate during his lifetime. A brilliant scholar at Oxford, he taught that the Bible was the only authority to which a Christian is bound. All that was not in it was human invention. This included the pope, whom he described as a thief, the "most cursed of dippers and purse-heavers." He died in 1384, having been protected by powerful laymen in England. It was not until 1428 that the Church had its vengeance, exhuming his body and burning it.

princes and lords, a concession that many would later find tempting, as it was necessary for them to "teach the fear of God by harshness and wordly fear."[20] He ruled it blasphemous, however, for popes and prelates to confound worldly and spiritual glory. No pope who was personally evil merited power over faithful Christians, and no prelate who was "foul" in the sight of God should ordain, consecrate, or baptize.

Wycliffe found no biblical justification either for the dogma of transubstantiation that supported the Eucharist, the central act of worship in the Church. This held that the whole substance of bread and wine in the sacraments is converted into the Body and Blood of Christ, with the mere appearance of bread and wine remaining as "accidents." The doctrine was first elaborated by the theologian Paschasius Radbertus in about 831 in his work *De Corpore et Sanguine Domini*. He wrote that "from the substance of bread and wine that same body and blood is miraculously consecrated."[21] As God had implanted Christ in the Virgin Mary, he also created the real Presence of the flesh born of Mary in the Eucharist. By consuming the Host, the faithful enter into Christ's mystical body, the Church. The mystery of this transubstantiation was confirmed at the Lateran council of 1215.

The Host had always been treated with reverence. Hippolytus had warned against leftovers being consumed by mice a thousand years before. It was now an object of awe, it was "Goddys' flessh," "Cristes own bodi . . . as hale as he toke it of that blessed maiden."[22] Bells were rung and candles lit as it was elevated at Mass amid whorls of incense, the faithful looking up in devotion to the divine evidence of Christ's sacrifice and their own redemption. It was taken to the sick and dying in a pyx, a flat gold or silver-gilt box, and it was paraded in processions at the Feast of Corpus Christi, the holy day to commemorate the gift of the Eucharist which had been proposed by the Blessed Juliana, a visionary from Liege, and commanded by papal bull in 1264. The Eucharist bound the faithful to the Church and to reverence for it, for only a priest could celebrate its mysteries, and only he could receive the wine. Since the doctrine of concomitance allowed for the flesh and blood to be present in both bread and wine, the laity was denied the chalice.

"The consecrated Host which we see on the altar is neither Christ nor any part of him," Wycliffe insisted in 1381, "but the efficacious sign of him."[23] This denial of transubstantiation struck at the heart of Catholic dogma and grandeur. Archbishop Courtenay convoked a council at Blackfriars in London on May 17, 1382. It condemned twenty-four of Wycliffe's propositions as "heretical and erroneous." Wycliffe's first and gravest heresy was his statement that "the substance of the material bread and wine remains in the sacrament of the altar after consecration."[24]

This was the point of spiritual schism. A powerful earthquake shook the city as the council was sitting. Courtenay saw the tremors as a portent of the purging of noxious heresies from the bowels of the earth, but to Wycliffe, they were a sign of God's anger with the Church. He was forced to give up his teaching at Oxford and retired to his rectory at Lutterworth in the Midlands. From here he continued to rail against the clergy. In an appeal to Parliament in 1383, he demanded that the poor should no longer be forced to furnish a worldly priest with the means to satisfy his ostentation and gluttony, his "showy horse, costly saddles, bridles with dangling bells, rich garments and soft furs," while they "see the wives and children of their neighbours dying with hunger."[25]

His sense of nationalism was early and strong. "Already a third and more of England is in the hands of the Pope," he thundered. "There cannot be two temporal sovereigns in one country; either Edward is King or Urban is king. We make our choice. We accept Edward of England and refute Urban of Rome."[26]

Writing almost entirely in English now, he spurned Latin as the language of ecclesiastical privilege. He thought the Paternoster to be the best of all prayers, and said that all men should know and understand it. The same held true for the Bible. It had already existed in Syriac, Coptic, Armenian, Ethiopic, Gothic, and Georgian and Arabic for the better part of a millennium, and in Arabic and

Slavonic for more than five centuries as well as in Greek and Latin. Tatian's *Diatessaron,* a "harmony" of the four Gospels compiled in about A.D. 150, had been translated into Dutch in the twelfth century. "Why may we not write in English the gospel and other things declaring the gospel," Wycliffe asked, "to the edification of Christian men's souls?"[27]

Wycliffe died of a stroke at Lutterworth on New Year's Eve, 1384, some eight years before the translation of the Vulgate into the English dialect of the Midlands was completed. Although it was largely the work of his followers, he was its inspiration, and its rendering from dusty Latin into vivid prose—"If I speke with tungis of men and aungels, sothli I haue not charite. . . ." and "Forsothe God so louede the world that he gaf his oon bigetun sone, that ech man that bileueth in to him perische not, but haue euerlastinge lyf"—gave the English their first direct contact* with the word of God in their own language.

❖　　THE IMPACT OF the translated Scripture was strong and immediate. It was said that a man would give a cartload of hay for a few handwritten pages of St. Paul, and the Church took vigorous steps to suppress both the English Bible and Wycliffe's following. "This wicked kindred," Wycliffe had said of the priesthood, "wulde that the gospel slept." He was correct. The Church had no desire to share the secrets of its trade. Its monopoly of faith was bolstered by its near monopoly of Latin. The common people were dependent on the clergy to interpret the gospel for them, and the Church feared that an English version would reduce its prestige and open its dogmas to question.

Fresh translations, and the use of any made "in the times of John Wyclif or since," were forbidden in 1407. Wycliffe's translation made the Scriptures the "property of the masses," noted Knighton, a leading observer of the day, and the Bible was now "more open to the laity, and even to women who were able to read, than formerly it had been even to the scholarly and most learned of the clergy." Knighton did not find this admirable. To him it meant that "the Gospel pearl is thrown before swine and trodden underfoot . . . and become a joke, and this precious gem of the clergy has been turned into the sport of the laity. . . ."[28]

Injunctions were issued against Wycliffe's followers. The word "Lollard"† was

---

*Parts of the Bible had been translated into Anglo-Saxon before: passages from Exodus and the first fifty psalms in the ninth century, possibly the work of the pious King Alfred; a section of Genesis by the grammarian Abbot Aelfric in the tenth century; metrical versions of Genesis, Exodus, and the Psalter in Middle English from the mid-thirteenth century. Nothing resembling a complete version, however, was attempted before Wycliffe.

†It seems to have derived from the Dutch word "lollen," to mumble, and was applied in English to religious eccentrics and wandering vagabonds.

used to describe a large and well-educated band of sympathizers. They produced a large compilation known as the *Floretum*, a collection of biblical and patristic authorities on moral and ecclesiastical subjects, well spiced with lengthy passages from Wycliffe. A bitter opponent, Thomas Netter, railed at "so many of this sect of Wyclif, standing in the line of battle, provoking the Church to war; fearlessly they preach, they publish their doctrines, they boast of their strength. . . ."[29] Unlicensed preachers roamed from diocese to diocese, evading every summons to stop. Lollards kept schools, wrote books, and held disputations and Bible readings. They attracted some gentry and merchants, but most were skilled craftsmen and artisans, weavers, millers, thatchers, butchers, and the like; many were women, for it seems that some Lollards accepted that they could be ordained and even celebrate the Eucharist.[30]

The "Bible men" disdained all practices that were nonbiblical. They ate meat on fast days; two Lollard chaplains in Leicester so disapproved of relics and images that they used a wooden statue of St. Katherine as fuel to cook a meal. They did not consider Sunday to be a special day. They did not confess and did not raise their eyes when the Host was elevated. Some went even further. Eleanor Higges of Burford was accused of putting the sacrament in her oven and eating it.[31]

A LIST OF the teachings in their secret conventicles was drawn up for Thomas Arundel, archbishop of Canterbury, a political prelate who was twice chancellor of England, and a leading Lollard persecutor. They were accused of mocking confession, indulgences, pilgrimage, and the use of images. They held the pope, the Church hierarchy, and the "private religions" of monks and friars to be against the Scriptures. Only God could beatify, they said; no pope had the power to make a saint.

The sacraments were said to be "but dead signs of no value . . . a mouthful of bread with no life." Virginity and a celibate priesthood were "not states approved by God," and wedlock was superior; the Church was "nothing but a synagogue of Satan"; none should be baptized by priests, and purgatory was an invention. Forgiveness of sins flowed from belief, "because, as they say, whatever is stands in faith, as Christ said to Mary Magdalene, 'Thy faith hath made thee whole'."[32] They declared many Church rituals to be magic and the craft of the devil. "Exorcisms and hallowings, made in the Church, of wine, bread and wax, water, salt and oil and incense, the stone of the altar, upon vestments, mitre, cross and pilgrims' staves, be the very practice of necromancy, not of holy theology. . . ."[33]

These thoughts would echo across Europe in time. For the moment they were thought so serious a threat to civil peace in England that a Suppressions of Heresy Act was passed by Parliament in 1401. At the urging of Convocation, the assembly of the clergy in England, the act empowered bishops to arrest Lollards and try them by canon law. If found guilty of heresy, the prisoners were to be given to a secular court which would "cause [them] to be burnt that such punishment may strike fear to the minds of others."[34] Even before the legislation was completed, special parliamentary sanction was granted in March 1401 for the execution of the Lollard William Sawtrey, a priest from Lynn in Norfolk. There had been no recorded burning of a heretic in England since that of a deacon convicted of converting to Judaism nearly two hundred years before.[35] Sawtrey was unrepentant. "I, sent by God, tell thee that thou and thy whole clergy, and the King also," he told Archbishop Arundel during his trial, "will shortly die an evil death. . . ."[36]

His burning at Smithfield in London caused some to recant, but the Lollards then found a leader in a remarkable knight from Herefordshire. Sir John Oldcastle was rich, a soldier and intimate of the king, devoted to Wycliffe's ideas and recklessly brave. As a young man of action he was close enough to the future Henry V for Shakespeare to dub him Prince Hal's "boon companion" and to base the character of Falstaff on him; he served on the Welsh marches and commanded an English army in France with success and panache, raising a siege of Paris; he married a great heiress. Yet he abandoned a brilliant career for rebellion and heresy, using his wife's fortune to have Wycliffe's works copied and distributed, fostering conspiracy against Church and state, surviving for four years as the most wanted fugitive in the kingdom. He did so, a contemporary ballad claimed, under the influence of the Lollards' translation of the Bible:

> Hit is unkyndly for a knight,
> That shuld a Kynges castel kepe,
> To babble the Bibel day and night
> In restyng tyme when he shuld slepe.[37]

Soon after his marriage, in 1409, aged about thirty, Oldcastle presented a remonstrance to Parliament on the corruptions of the Church. He sent a number of chaplains to preach without license in several counties. The "tares and heresies" they sowed came to the notice of the watchful Arundel. Sightings of Oldcastle from up and down the country were reported to Convocation in 1413. He was described as the principal protector of Lollards; he had particularly infected the dioceses of Hereford and Rochester in Kent, but his influence elsewhere was such that it had become "almost impossible to repair the rent in the seamless garment of our Lord unless certain great men of the kingdom who were authors, favourers, defenders and receivers of these heretics were . . . if necessary revoked from their waywardness by the invocation of the secular arm."[38] This direct threat of burning was underlined when Lollard treatises belonging to Oldcastle were found with a book illuminator at Paternoster Row in London. Arundel had them thrown on a bonfire in St. Paul's churchyard.

As a familiar of Henry V, the man himself was more difficult to deal with. Arundel consulted with the young king, and Oldcastle was summoned to Windsor in August 1413 to see if he would recant. He did not. "Full of the devil," he quit Windsor without royal leave and withdrew to his own castle at Cooling in Kent. He was brought before the Church court in London on September 23, 1413. He declared that he would not seek the Church's absolution, but only that of God. He described the pope as the skull of the Antichrist, the archbishops and prelates as its limbs, and friars as its tail. No obedience was due to any priest, high or low, except insofar as they were imitators of Christ in their lives and morals. "Those who judge and mean to condemn me will seduce you all and themselves also," he told onlookers, "and will lead you to hell. Therefore beware of them!"[39] The court duly declared him a "most pernicious and detestable heretic . . . against the faith and religion of the holy and universal church of Rome" and committed him to the secular power for execution.[40] "Though ye judge my body, which is but a wretched thing," he retorted, "yet am I certain that ye can do no harm to my soul, no more than could Satan upon the soul of Job. He that created that, will of his infinite mercy and promise save it. . . ."

In fact, he saved himself. The death sentence being postponed for forty days to allow him time to repent, he escaped from the Tower of London before the time expired. From hiding, using secret emissaries, Oldcastle now planned an uprising. Informers disclosed a plot to a stage a mumming, a play for the entertainment of the court at the royal palace at Eltham near London, and "under colour of this mumming to destroy the king and the Holy Church." A number of conspirators were seized at the Axe, an inn outside London's Bishopsgate. The prisoners confessed that Oldcastle had arranged for a great muster of Lollards to take place at night in St. Giles' Fields in London on January 9, 1414. The king ordered the gates of the city to be shut that night and closely guarded. He led armed men to the Fields shortly after midnight and fell upon the rebels. Henry pardoned some of them on the grounds that the absent Oldcastle had deluded them. A brewer from Dunstable said that Oldcastle had promised him a knighthood; the wretch was found with a pair of gilt spurs and two warhorses with gold trappings ready for the ceremony. He was spared, but thirty-eight prisoners were taken back to the Fields and hanged or burned.

Oldcastle remained a fugitive, charged with conspiracy to kill the king and bishops. Once in power, it was alleged, he intended to abolish religious orders, drive monks into secular occupations, destroy the houses of the clergy, seize Church property, and plunder cathedrals and monasteries and level them to the ground. A text detailed the partition of the clerical riches; they were to be used to fund 15 earls, 1,500 knights, and 6,200 squires to protect the new regime, with enough left over to maintain 100 almshouses, 15 universities, and 15,000 Lollard priests.[41] Much of this program would be put into effect a century later, and at the command of the king. For the moment it was fantasy. Although documents mentioned adherents "to the number of 20 thousand men,"[42] the Lollards were far from achieving a critical mass of support.

A reward of one thousand marks was posted for Oldcastle's capture, and freedom from taxation was offered to the city or borough that discovered him. Judges, justices of the peace, sheriffs, and mayors were required to take an oath to put down "heresies and errors commonly called Lollardies." Oldcastle was blamed for violent outbreaks of arson and poaching in chases and parks in 1417, and he was also believed to have offered the Scots three thousand pounds to invade England. When one of his houses was raided, books were found in which he had erased the heads of saints from the illuminations and deleted their names from litanies. An example of these maltreated books was sent to the king, and Arundel exhibited one when he preached as evidence of Lollard irreverence.

Oldcastle was tracked down in Wales and taken to London at the end of 1417. He was laid on a hurdle and dragged to St. Giles' Fields on December 14, and then suspended in a stout chair from a gallows while a blazing fire was lit beneath him. As he was hanged for his treason, he was simultaneously burned for his heresy. The movement did not die with him. It persisted in several cities, Bristol, Coventry, Leicester, and in the country districts of Kent and East Anglia and the Berkshire Downs. It reached as far as Scotland, where an English priest was burned at Perth. Texts were still copied and eventually printed. Looking back 150 years after his death, Elizabethan Protestants saw Oldcastle as their spiritual forefather, a "blessed martyr" killed by the popish clergy for "calling upon a Christian Reformation in that Romish church of theirs."[43]

FROM THE VILLAGES of England, Wycliffe's ideas were carried to Bohemia and the reformer John Hus. Born into a family of Czech peasants about 1372, he became a brilliant scholar at Prague and was elected dean of the Charles University philosophy faculty there in 1401, where he had a large student audience. He preached at the Bethlehem Chapel, an austere building founded by pious citizens, whose central room, plain and unadorned, was more lecture hall than place of worship.

Hus's attack on the Church's thriving pilgrim trade at Wilsnack near Wittenberg was the first sign of his Wycliffite radicalism. After a fire in the Wilsnack village church in 1383, three consecrated Hosts were found unharmed there but sprinkled with drops of blood. As believers flocked to see the wondrous pieces of Communion bread, which eager promoters claimed had the power to answer prayers, Wilsnack grew from a rough village into a prosperous pilgrim town. The pilgrimage was highly profitable to the Church and for local innkeepers and tradesmen, and successive popes encouraged it*; Hus denounced the "miracle" as a fraud.

He translated and adapted Wycliffe's writings, and drew on Lollard tracts sent to Prague by a Scot, Quentin Folkhyrd. He thought of the Church as the "congregation of the faithful to be saved . . . the totality of the predestinate,"[44] as distinct from the "church of the reprobate" headed by the devil. "Know that many popes were heretics or otherwise evil," he preached. "As for the argument that the pope is the most holy father who cannot sin, I deny it; for it is our Father most holy, the Lord God, who alone cannot sin. . . . Be it known to you that papal power is limited by God's law."[45] He mocked the sale of indulgences. "What a strange thing!" he said. "They cannot rid themselves of fleas and flies, and yet want to rid others of the torments of hell . . . !"[46] He criticized the Church for its "miserable worldly possession" that "blocked the way of Christ" and exposed it to simony, avarice, and quarrels. His appeal to the Czech nation won him support from nobles as well as merchants and peasants, and Prague University seethed with Wycliffe's doctrines.

Papal counterblasts were weakened by the emergence of a third pope. A group of cardinals, despairing of reaching any negotiated settlement to the Great Schism, summoned a council to meet in the marbled black-and-white splendor of the Duomo at Pisa in 1409. They deposed both Gregory XII and Benedict XIII, respectively the Roman and Avignon popes, and elected as a single replacement the pious, learned, and decrepit archbishop of Milan. Bells were rung as he rode through the city on a white mule to accept the name of Alexander V.

The joy was premature. Gregory and Benedict refused to abdicate, so instead of two popes, the Church now had three. Benedict called a synod at Perpignan to refute the Pisa council. He endured a siege and then imprisonment in the papal castle at Avignon rather than submit, until, abandoned by his adherents and immured in his own castle near Valencia in his native Spain, still pope in his own eyes and still excommunicating his enemies, he died in 1423. Gregory, although nearing ninety, also clung to his office, pawning his papal tiara to clear his gambling debts. Alexander was dead within ten months of his election. He was succeeded by Baldassare Cossa, an impoverished Neapolitan aristocrat who had repaired his fortunes by piracy before turning to an equally lucrative but less

*When Wilsnack turned Protestant in 1552, the Hosts were burned by its preacher and the pilgrimage trade disappeared.

stressful career in religion. He was said never to have confessed, nor to have taken the sacraments; previously a cardinal-deacon, he was not ordained a priest until the day before his coronation as John XXIII. Wags put about a new version of the creed, intoning "I believe in three holy Catholic churches."[47] They called the Roman pope Benefictus, or "fake," and the Avignon Gregorious became Errorius, or "error."

Fear of Wycliffe and Hus was one factor that the warring pontiffs had in common. In 1410, Alexander V complained that many in Bohemia and Moravia "hold Wyclif's articles contrary to the faith and the hearts of many are infected by heresy." He ordered the archbishop of Prague to burn Wycliffe's books and forbid Hus from preaching. Hus was defiant. He asked his audience at the Bethlehem Chapel to support him. The following year John XXIII sentenced him to "lesser" excommunication, depriving him of the right to receive the sacrament and to hold Church office. Hus responded by copying Wycliffe almost verbatim in much of his new work, *De Ecclesia*. John now imposed "greater" excommunication on him, depriving him of all intercourse in public or in private with his fellow Christians, and for good measure his followers were placed under interdict. In his *Responsio finalis* of June 1413, Hus complained that Wycliffites were called "infidels, perfidious, insane and scurrilous clergy. All such slanders I would have ignored, had they not strengthened the Antichrist in his wrath. I hope, however, with God's grace to oppose them until I am consumed by fire. . . ."[48]

THE FLAMES WERE not far distant. John convoked a council in 1414 at Constance, the lakeside city on the southern German border with Switzerland. He did so at the insistence of the emperor Sigismund for the purpose of reform and to "reduce the number of popes consistent with the Gospel." A further motive, the chronicler Ulrich Richental wrote, was "to condemn unbelief and extirpate heresy in Bohemia."[49] It was the largest council yet held in the West, attended by more than six hundred bishops and theologians; John preached at its opening session on All Saints' Day.

Papal farce, a reason for Hus's disillusionment with the Church, loomed like a ship of fools through the dark mists of his final days. Commanded to defend himself in front of the council, his misgivings were overcome by a formal safe conduct which bore Sigismund's seal and guaranteed his "coming and return." The emperor also provided him with an escort of thirty horsemen and two wagons under the command of Lord Henry Latzenborck. Hus arrived at Constance on November 3, 1414, lodging in a house on St. Paul's Street. After he had rested for a day or two, he said mass in his bedchamber. Curious locals crowded into the house, spilling from the bedroom into the living room; Richental, the city's public notary, noted with some surprise that the supposed heretic "said mass there like our own clergy."[50] The bishop of Constance, Otto, demanded that Hus desist at once. Hus replied that he would "perform mass as often as he had grace."

Such defiance was dangerous. A papal legate who had interrogated Hus in Prague assured the council that "since the birth of Christ no more dangerous heretic has arisen, save Wyclif!"[51] Oldcastle's adversary Thomas Netter had been sent to Constance as an observer by Henry V, and he drew a direct link between Hus and the Lollards. The council condemned two hundred of Wycliffe's propositions and ordered that his body be removed from consecrated ground. In due course, Wycliffe's remains were exhumed from the churchyard at Lutterworth and scattered into the waters of the nearby river Swift.* On November 28 the papal notary Jacob Cerretano wrote, "John Hus, the Wycliffite, . . . was taken into custody to prevent his further teaching of that doctrine. This was done by order of our Lord Pope. . . ."[53] A knight who had escorted him to Constance protested loudly that Hus had a safe conduct. The pope denied this, but because of the complaint Hus was kept under house arrest rather than in prison.

He tried to flee the city on March 3, 1415. He hid in one of Latzenborck's wagons, which was due to go out after dinner to bring back hay and fodder from a nearby village. He took a loaf of bread and a bottle of wine with him, presumably so he could continue to celebrate Mass. When he failed to appear for dinner, his guards raised the alarm and Latzenborck ran to the city mayor to have the gates shut and pursuit parties made ready. Hus was soon discovered, and Latzenborck took him on a horse to the palace of Pope John. Hus leaped from the horse and tried to run into a crowd of sympathetic Bohemians who had heard that he had been taken prisoner. Papal guards beat their way into the crowd with their silver staves and put him under lock and key in the palace. Sigismund thought it a great disgrace that his safe conduct was thus dishonored. Church lawyers told him that there was no law that could offer a heretic safe passage, and "when he heard their severity, he let it be."[54] The next morning Hus was transferred to a cell in the Dominican monastery. He was interrogated daily by "the most learned theologians" who pleaded with him to "turn from his wicked beliefs."

On the night of March 20, Pope John himself fled Constance disguised as a groom; Hus's was not the only life at peril of the council. John had assumed that he would control the council through the overall majority enjoyed by the Italian

---

*His followers took solace from the fact that his ashes would eventually find their way to the ocean "so the whole world became his sepulchre as the whole of Christendom would become his convert." Relics were overlooked— a fragment of his cope, the pulpit itself from which he preached his "poison"—and survive at Lutterworth.[52] Ironically, the Reformers were to hold relics as mere superstition, and the cult of Protestant relics that the Roman Church so feared never developed.

bishops. Voting was not by individuals, however, but by nations. The English, French, and Germans were set on using their superiority over the Italians to be rid of all three popes in favor of a schism-free fourth. Allegations of John's sins—blackmails, fornications, simonies, poisonings, and cuckoldings—were circulated. The English in particular wanted to have him burned. Frightened, John offered to abdicate provided Gregory and Benedict followed suit; as insurance, he then ran off thirty miles to Schaffhausen. The council was without its papal convenor.

A placard was found in the city on April 1 declaring that Hus taught and preached the truth, and that the charges against him were false. It was the work of Jerome of Prague, a friend of the accused who fled the city for the Bohemian forests immediately after he had nailed up his poster. Jerome was also a man of learning; encouraged by Hus, he had studied Wycliffe's writings at Oxford. His piety had taken him on the dangerous pilgrimage to Jerusalem, but his scathing attacks on Church abuses and his violent denunciation of Pope John's sale of indulgences led to accusations of heresy. Jerome's undoing, Richental noted, was that he was "very talkative." While lying low in Bohemia he was asked to dine by a parish priest. He told his host that he had been to Constance, adding that the council was "a school of Satan . . . and a synagogue of all iniquity." The priest informed on him, and Jerome was taken in chains to Constance on April 21.

Pope John was still in hiding. To give itself judicial legitimacy in his absence, the council enacted the decree *Haec Sancta* at its fifth session on April 15. This unanimous declaration of faith stated that the "holy Council of Constance holds its power direct from Christ; everyone, no matter what his rank or office, even if it be Papal, is bound to obey it in whatever pertains to faith, to the extirpation of the . . . schism, as well as to the reform of the Church in its head and its members."[55] This statement, with its specific reference to authority over the pope, still haunts the Catholic Church. In its immediate aftermath it gave the council the power to do what it willed with both Pope John and John Hus. It dealt with the pontiff first. He was brought back from Schaffhausen by an imperial guard. Fifty-four allegations had been laid against him, but these were reduced to five. "The most scandalous charges were suppressed," the great historian Edward Gibbon noted; "the Vicar of Christ was only accused of piracy, murder, rape, sodomy and incest."[56] On May 29, 1415, John XXIII's seals of office were formally smashed with a hammer and he became a nonpope.* He was held prisoner for three years in Germany, but made cardinal-bishop of Tusculum on his release.

---

*There was another John XXIII still to come; the name was adopted by Angelo Roncalli when he was elected pope in 1963. Earlier there had been a second Benedict XIII, for Pietro Orsini chose the name of the old Avignon pope on his election in 1724. The Church denies that either of the originals has a valid place in the papal succession; of the many questions this begs, that of the authority of general council over pontiff remains the most significant.

Thus the Church dealt with the wicked and corrupt. Against the chaste and pious Hus it brought forty-seven charges. When they were read out, the prosecutor emphasized the six most serious: the "accused not does believe in the transubstantiation . . . despises the belief in the infallibility of the Pope . . . disputes the power of absolution by a vicious priest and confession to him . . . rejects the absolute obedience to worldly superiors . . . rejects the prohibition of marriage for priests . . . calls the indulgence a simony, sinning against the Holy Spirit."[57] For these and "many other godless reasons and talks" he was accused of arch-heresy.

He was unrepentant. He said that the doctrine of the transubstantiation of the sacraments into the body and blood of Christ "seems repulsive to me . . . just as nobody can really create blood out of water and wine, so nobody can create flesh out of a dough made of flour." He thought the doctrine sinful and ungodly, and added that the Bible provided no foundation for it. He agreed that he did not believe in papal infallibility, and found "little or no solace" in the worship of the saints. No one had been given the power to sanctify any man, no matter how pure and godly. As to the pope, Hus said with heroic understatement,* "his shortcomings are the same as those of other men, from their birth on, and to err is his and everybody's main sin. . . ." Hus admitted that he thought confession and absolution were worthless. "It is written in the holy scriptures," he insisted. "'Nobody may forgive sins but God!'" He was condemned and shunned, he said, because he refused to acknowledge absolute obedience to earthly authority. "I admit this accusation also," he said. "That human laws are to be obeyed unquestioned is a senseless demand and humiliates man. . . . Even the Christians of the earliest times argued against their superior thus: 'One must obey God more than man!'. . . ." He described his stand against simony and indulgences as "truly apostolic and evangelical . . . Nothing appears more godless to me than to commercialise the forgiveness of sins, to deceive the poor and miserable people that heaven might be bought with a few farthings." He said that his preaching against the celibacy of the clergy was based on common sense. "Has not God himself instituted marriage," he asked his accusers, "as a means to satisfy the craving for love in all men, even in all animals? Is not he, who becomes a priest, also made of flesh and blood?"[58]

All these things, he said, "I am courageous enough to repeat here." The clerical lords could not contain their "maniacal ire." Ignoring the presence of the emperor, and refusing to be called to order, they screamed: "Hus, the Satan, is an heretic! an archheretic! such as none has come out of hell to this day. Cast him out

---

*He was less circumspect in a letter written from his cell on June 21, 1415. Hus described the prelates of the Church adoring John on bended knee, "kissing his feet, and calling him most holy, although they knew that he was a base murderer, a sodomite, a simoniac and a heretic."

into the darkness, to his lot of wailing and gnashing of teeth! so that he may pay all his dues and perish in the fire. Burn him, burn him, for he is a monster such as hell has never before cast out, to be despised by all Christians. . . ."[59]

On July 4, Gregory XII abdicated. There was now no pope other than Benedict XIII, deposed at Pisa, but still clutching grimly to the wreckage of his claim. The emperor sent a small party of noblemen and bishops to see Hus on July 5 to beg him to recant. He said that he would be most willing to do so if the council would "instruct me by better and more relevant Scripture." The bishops railed at him for his "obstinacy" and ordered him to be returned to his cell.[60]

The fifteenth session of the council met in the Constance cathedral at 6 A.M. on July 6, 1415.* As an excommunicate, Hus had to wait at the entrance to the cathedral while mass was celebrated before being led in by the archbishop of Riga. A sermon was preached by the bishop of Lodi on the text in Romans that "the body of sin might be done away" (Rom. 6:6). The bishop stressed how heresies tore the Church asunder, and remarked pointedly—the emperor was present—that it was the duty of kings and princes to destroy them. The papal auditor then stood up in the pulpit and read the proceedings of the trial. Hus was forbidden to reply. On the evidence of a "certain doctor," Hus was accused of claiming himself to be the fourth person of the Godhead; he cried: "Name that doctor who testified that against me! . . . for that has never entered my heart." The cardinal of Florence, Francesco Zabarella, shouted at him to be silent. With exquisite black humor, Hus was further charged with "error" in appealing to God for justice. "I continue to declare," he said loudly, "that there is no safer appeal than to the Lord Jesus Christ, who will not be suborned by a perverse bribe, nor deceived by a false testimony. . . ." The definitive sentence of guilt was read by Antony, the old and bald bishop of Concordia. All books written by Hus, "either in Latin written by him or translated into whatever language," were to be destroyed. Hus protested that his accusers had failed to find any biblical evidence that discredited a word he had written. "Indeed," he added, "how can you condemn the books written in vernacular Czech or translated into another language when you have never even seen them?" Antony then declared Hus "to have been and still to be a veritable and manifest heretic . . ." At this, Hus knelt and said: "Lord Jesus Christ, I implore thee, forgive all mine enemies for thy great mercy's sake. . . ." The senior clergy jeered as he prayed for their souls.

As an ordained priest, Hus had to be stripped of his consecration before being handed to the civil power. A table was placed in the middle of the cathedral;

---

*Richental's account differs from that of Peter Mladoňovice. Although he was an eyewitness, Richental gives an inaccurate date, July 8, and says that the sermon was preached by the rector of divinity at Paris, John Dacherty.

on it were laid out the vestments and the chasuble for the mass and the priestly garments to be used in his defrocking. Seven bishops helped dress him as if he were about to celebrate mass; he was made to stand on the table so that all could witness his humiliation. They called on him again to abjure. "I fear to do so," he said, "lest I be a liar in the sight of the Lord, and also lest I offend against my own conscience and the truth of God." He was ordered off the table and the bishops began defrocking him. They first took the cup from his hands, pronouncing a solemn curse: "O cursed Judas, because you have abandoned the counsel of peace and have counselled with the Jews, we take away from you this cup of redemption." Curses were pronounced as the other vestments, the stole and chasuble, were taken from him. The bishops had finally to obliterate his tonsure. They argued among themselves over the best method. Some thought a pair of scissors would do, while the others wanted to take a razor to shave his head bald. "Look," he said, "these bishops so far do not know how to agree in this vilification!" They settled on cutting his tonsure with scissors into four parts, right, left, front and back. They placed a paper crown on his head—"my Lord Jesus Christ on account of me, a miserable wretch," Hus reminded them, "bore a much heavier and harsher crown of thorns"—which had three devils crudely drawn on it, and the scrawled inscription *Heresiarch,* arch-heretic. With that, they told him, "We commit your soul to the devil!" The bishops then followed the ritual that ensured that the Church would not be stained with his blood; having deprived him of all ecclesiastical rights, they called out: "We turn him over to the secular court."[61]

The emperor acknowledged that "I am the one who wields the temporal sword," but avoided the embarrassment of his safe conduct to Hus by asking Duke Louis of Bavaria-Heidelberg, his uncle and imperial elector of the region, to "deal with him as a heretic, in our stead."[62] Duke Louis called to the advocate of Constance, who was also an imperial prosecutor: "Advocate, take him, under the joint sentence of us both and burn him as a heretic." The legal niceties now settled, the advocate summoned the soldiers of the town council and the city executioner. He forbade them to remove the condemned man's clothes and possessions lest they become relics. Hus was wearing two black coats of good cloth and a girdle with small ornaments on it.

He was led out of the cathedral. His books were already being burned in the cemetery, and he smiled as he passed. More than a thousand armed men surrounded him to discourage any Bohemian rescue attempt. He walked between two servants of Duke Louis and the notary-chronicler Richental, for "they called me to go with them." The crowds were so dense that they were forced to take to a meadow instead of the street, and the bridge over the Rhine at the city's western limits was cleared of onlookers for fear it would collapse. On his way, Hus "uttered only the prayer; *Jesu Christe, fili Dei Vivi, miserere mei,'*"[63] "Jesus Christ, Son of the Living God, have mercy upon me!" When he was led into the field where he was to be burned, he fell on his knees three times and cried the same prayer, adding the words *"qui passus est pro nobis,"* "Jesus Christ . . . who suffered for us."

Laymen in the crowd were impressed by his courage. They muttered that "we see and hear that he prays and speaks with holy words." A local priest, bizarrely dressed in a green suit with a red silk lining, was sitting on a horse nearby, and the crowd asked him to hear Hus's confession. "He should not be heard, nor a confessor be given him," the priest said, "for he is a heretic."[64] Richental says that Hus replied: "I do not need it. I am no mortal sinner." The executioners tied his hands behind his back and bound him to the stake with ropes and a sooty chain that went around his neck. At first he faced to the east, as at prayer, but bystanders said that this was not right for a heretic, and he was turned toward the west. Two wagonloads of wood, interspersed with straw, were piled up around him until they reached his chin. The imperial marshal and Duke Louis asked him to recant. "In that truth of the Gospel that I wrote, taught, and preached," he said, "I am willing gladly to die today."[65] At that, the marshal and the duke clapped their hands and retreated. The executioners poured pitch over the pyre and set it alight. Hus "began to cry out terribly but soon was burned," according to Richental. How-

Hæc fuit effigies quondam uenerabilis Hufsi,
Dum fua pro Chrifto membra cremanda dedit.

Na Obraʒ Miʃtra Jana Huʃy/
Mucedlnyka Boʒyho.

A devil's cap identifies the reformer Jan Hus as a heretic and Antichrist at his burning at Constance on the German border with Switzerland in July 1415. Hus, deeply influenced by Wycliffe, preached violent sermons in Prague denouncing the papacy and clerical immorality. He was promised a safe-conduct if he attended the church council of Constance, but he was arrested and tried for heresy. "Burn him, burn him," the assembled bishops and cardinals cried, "for he is a monster such as hell has never before cast out, to be despised by all Christians . . ."

ever, Peter of Mladoňovice, a sympathizer, said that he sang in a loud voice: "Christ, thou son of the living God, have mercy upon us. . . . Christ, thou son of the living God, have mercy upon me. . . . Thou who art born of Mary the Virgin . . . ," before the wind blew the flames into his face and he was gone.

Jerome of Prague remained in prison. He was pliable, or at least appeared so to his captors. Lauds were rung when he recanted and agreed to read a document condemning the teaching of Wycliffe and Hus, but his sincerity was doubted. His interrogators found him "far more expert and artful" than Hus, and he refused to sign an open letter to the people of Bohemia saying that his preaching was false. On September 8, 1416, a Sunday, after the Solemn Mass of the Holy Trinity had been sung, Jerome was condemned by the council for heresy and handed to Duke Louis for sentencing. As he was led out of the city to his death, Jerome recited the creed; when he had crossed the bridge, he sang the litany. He was burned at the same spot as his friend, and none heard his confession. "He lived much longer in the fire than Hus and shrieked terribly," Richental reported, "for he was a stouter, stronger man, with a broad, thick, black beard."[66]

After that, the council "continued in good peace, and there was no dispute between anyone." Delegates could ride or stroll a mile beyond Constance, through woods and villages, without fear. Many went into the Aichorn Woods, where taverns sold all manner of wines and roast fowls, sausages, and broiled fish, finding "whatever they wanted . . . and gay women who belonged to the establishments." The spiritual lords, the cardinals and bishops, "wandered in any gardens they chose, and no one opposed them, and they did no harm."

❧ WHEN HE PUT on the alb during his defrocking, Hus had said: "My Lord Jesus Christ, when he was led from Herod to Pilate, was mocked in a white garment." The parallels between Jesus and Hus, Sanhedrin and the Constance council, Caiaphas the high priest and Pope John, Pilate and Duke Louis, were raw and piercing. The Church knew the darkness of its act. It knew, intimately, the power of the martyr and his relics that it was releasing. The first had been its own seed, as Tertullian had reminded it twelve hundred years before, and it had created a thriving industry around the second.

Not a scrap of Hus or an ash of the fire remained to bear witness to what had been done to him. After the ropes and wood had burnt, the remains of the body still stood hanging by the chains round the neck. The executioners pulled the body and the stake onto the ground and burned them further by adding wood from a third wagon to the fire. As they worked, Richental noted that the "worst stench arose that one could smell," for an old mule belonging to a cardinal had recently been buried at the spot, and when the heat went into the earth, the smell of its putrefaction was released. The bones were smashed into shards so that they would be incinerated more quickly. Finding the head, the executioners "broke it to pieces with the clubs and again threw it into the fire." When they found the heart, they sharpened a club like a spit, impaled it, and "took particular care to roast and consume it, piercing it with spears until finally the whole mass was turned into ashes." Duke Louis promised them extra money to burn all of Hus's clothing, "so that the Czechs would not regard it as relics."[67] This was done, and then all the ashes were loaded into a cart and thrown into the Rhine.

✤ THE WRATH OF the Church had special qualities. It pursued the dead; having failed to burn Wycliffe while he was alive, it took its vengeance on his corpse. It damned its living victims twice. The *poena sensus,* the punishment of the senses, was achieved by the earthly fire, but it also imposed the *poena damni,* the absolute separation from God that doomed the guilty to an eternity in hell. Diocletian had condemned the early Christians to death. That was an end to the matter. For the Constance council, however, the burning of Hus was merely the last way station in this world on his journey to the limitless tortures of the next. Paul provided the justification for the first penalty: "The fire itself shall prove each man's work of what sort it is" (1 Cor. 3:13). Christ himself was invoked for the second: "Depart from me, ye cursed, into the eternal fire which is prepared for the devil and his angels" (Matt. 25:41).

Hell was not an abstract. The place to which Hus was consigned was vivid to the Christian mind, particularly in the West, where the doctrine of purgatory had been added to the existing states of heaven and hell in the thirteenth century. In this halfway house, Thomas Aquinas taught, the unforgiven *culpa,* or guilt, of venial sins is expiated. The smallest pain in purgatory is greater than the greatest on earth, but the certainty of eventual salvation gives the soul great peace despite its suffering. Purgatory was financially rewarding for the Church, since the sinner spent less time there if he purchased indulgences in advance, or if he had a priest say expensive posthumous prayers for his soul. Wycliffe and Hus rejected purgatory as nonbiblical invention, and the Eastern Church also declined to include it in formal doctrine.

Writings on the other world were hugely popular. The sophisticated looked back a century to Dante and *The Divine Comedy,** though not, perhaps, the cardinals of Constance, for the author had unkindly included several of their predecessors among the denizens of hell. In his poem, Dante travels in the company of Virgil through the three realms of Inferno, Purgatorio, and Paradiso on a spiritual

---

*Dante called his work *La Commedia*; admirers of its vivacity prefaced it as *Divina.*

pilgrimage from sin to salvation. They descend from a black forest to the naked sinners in the Pit of Hell— *"lasciate ogni speranza voi ch'entrate"*, "abandon hope all ye who enter here"[68]—where Love is lost in the icy wastes that surround the frozen soul of Judas. Here they find Muhammad, and Pope Boniface VIII, the "prince of the Pharisees," greedy promoter of the great Jubilee indulgence of 1300, whose condemnation Dante attributes to St. Peter himself:

> He who on earth usurps my see,
>> my see, my see, which now stands vacant
>> before the Son of God
> Has made a sewer from my sepulchre
>> full of blood and pus—at which the Perverse One,
>> who fell from here, takes pleasure down below . . ."[69]

There is a sweet irony in Boniface's presence in the pit, for it was he who had issued the bull *Unam Sanctam* in 1302, declaring that there was "neither salvation nor remission of sins" outside the Church, of which he—as the successor to St. Peter—was supreme head. Dante locates Boniface's soul in the Eighth Circle of Hell, facedown in a fissure in the rock. In the Fourth Circle, naked squads of cardinals heave boulders for eternity as a punishment for their avarice. After his journey through hell, Dante emerges onto the beach of the island mountain of Purgatory. He ascends its seven terraces, passing repentant sinners as they are purged of past faults, to the Earthly Paradise at the summit where Adam and Eve were created. Virgil leaves him, and Dante is escorted through the nine planetary and stellar spheres of Paradise by Beatrice, until St. Bernard presents him to the Virgin. He glimpses the Beatific Vision, the very essence of God, and in the ecstasy of the Rose of Light he finds "the Love that moves the Sun and the other stars."

The popular view of Hus's destination was less elegant. The *Vision of Tundale,* written by an Irish monk in about 1149, had been translated into at least thirteen languages and still retained enormous appeal. Tundale was an Irish knight who was guided by an angel on a tour of hell, where he sees there "many associates, acquaintances and friends" who had been his friends on earth. He meets the Prince of Shadows, a "horrible stooping spectacle" as black as a raven, with a great beak and a long tail with sharp points, and a thousand hands with iron claws eager to savage souls. Tundale sees murderers descending into a valley covered by the fog of death and filled with burning coal; they are burned over a grate "as broth cooked down in a frying pan is totally liquefied,"[70] until they are restored to be burned again in an eternal process of melting and remelting. Spies and traitors are condemned to a mountainside enveloped in fumes of "putrid, sulphurous and shadowy fire," before torturers with flaming iron pitchforks hurl them onto a slope of snow and ice, tossing them back into the fire when they are frozen. The proud fall endlessly from a bridge a thousand feet long and a foot wide into a sea of sulphur from which arises a "great howling in the depths of endurance." The greedy are dragged by parasites into the belly of a beast with eyes like burning hills and a mouth great enough to hold nine thousand men, into which the river Jordan flows. Robbers cross a lake by a bridge perforated with iron nails that slash their feet, while bellowing beasts below wait for their food. Fornicators are confined in a house as high as a mountain and as round as a bread oven, where executioners with "axes and knives and sticks and double needles with pick-axes and bores and very sharp sickles" chop them in pieces, and beasts torture their genitals which become "putrid and corrupt, seeming to gush with worms." This happens not only with laymen and women, the writer notes, "but also—which I cannot say without grave sorrow—the fearful beasts twisted under the habits of the clergy . . ."

The most awful fate awaits those "who add sin to sin," heathens and heretics. They suffer "the torture which is called Vulcan" in a valley filled with iron foundries. As they approach the valley, the victims are seized by torturers who toss them into the forge with forceps and place them on a forging stone to be struck with hammers until thirty or a hundred souls are reduced into one mass. "This is enough, isn't it?" the torturers say, but others reply: "Throw them to us and let us see if it is enough!" So the souls are tossed again into the forge. There, like Hus and Jerome, "they suffered and burned until their skin and their flesh, their nerves and bones were reduced to the ash and flame of the fire. . . ."

❖ RELIGIOUS REFORM WAS not, like political rebellion, a game that is dangerous but that is played out in this life. Failure pursued players beyond the grave. The stakes were eternal and divine, and reform engaged every fear and sinew of a religious people. It made adversaries of the word of Christ and the body of Christ, of his Bible and his Church, the two most powerful elements in the faith. "In His will is our peace,"[71] Dante had written of paradise. The burning of Hus and his condemnation to hell revealed the fragility of peace on earth.

The destruction of Hus's remains was to little avail. A careful note of the disposal of the body was made by Peter of Mladoňovice precisely so that the memory of "the eminent preacher of the evangelical truth . . . might be vividly recollected."[72] As Pliny had noted thirteen centuries before, such persecution merely served to "spread the crime." Bohemia seethed with national repugnance. King Wenceslas, brother of the emperor Sigismund, was forced to make concessions. Although there was no formal break with Rome, the Church hierarchy fell largely under the patronage of the nobility. *Utraquism,* Communion of bread and wine for the laity in place of bread alone, was introduced. Under pressure from his brother and the pope, Wenceslas then reneged on his promises to the Hussites. In July 1419, when he tried to replace Hussite counselors in Prague, the citizens stormed the town hall and threw the new counselors out the windows.

Wenceslas died in August, and in November, Sigismund began a furious persecution of the rebels. Some priests took their parishioners with them to mountaintops in southern Bohemia. They were called Taborites. Jesus had said that, before his Second Coming, "Let them that are in Judea flee unto the mountains" (Matt. 13:14). Tradition had long claimed that this would take place at Mount Tabor, the spot mentioned by the prophetess Deborah (Judg. 4:6). Dreams of a Bohemian millennium were fed by *Pikarti,* refugees from Picardy who claimed to be vessels of the Holy Spirit and who denounced the Church as the Whore of Babylon. It was prophesied that every town and village would be consumed by fire like Sodom between February 10 and 14, 1420. Only those who fled to the mountains and joined the Taborites would be saved. The vision was violent. John Capek, a Prague University graduate, wrote a tract "fuller of blood than a pond is of water" saying that it was the duty of believers to kill in Christ's name. Sins punishable by death included *avaritia* and *luxuria,* a catchall that covered the rich, be they churchmen or not, and all who "opposed the men of the Divine Law."

The apocalyptics were led by John Zizka, a one-eyed nobleman brought up as a page to King Wenceslas. A veteran soldier who had fought for the Teutonic Knights against the Poles, for Austria in the Turkish wars, and for the English at Agincourt, he organized a brilliant resistance to the Catholic army that Sigismund sent into Bohemia in 1420. Taborites were the backbone of Zizka's forces. Driven by divine zeal and certain that they lived in "the consummation of time, the extermination of all evils," they awaited the descent of Christ into their midst to banquet with them in their holy mountains and to rule a realm in which the saints would "shine like the sun in the Kingdom of the Father . . . living, radiant, quite without stain."

A program of violent communalism was established. All taxes, dues, obligations, rents, and private property were to be abolished. The supporters of Dives, the rich man of Luke's gospel, would be butchered as the allies of the Antichrist; "all lords, nobles and knights shall be cut down and exterminated in the forests like outlaws." Prague, the stronghold of Sigismund, was seen as the doomed replica of Babylon. "How much she hath glorified herself, and lived deliciously, so much torment and sorrow give her," the Taborites exalted. "Therefore shall her plague come in one day, death, and mourning, and famine; and she shall be utterly burned with fire: for strong is the Lord God who judgeth her. And the kings of the earth, who have committed fornication and lived deliciously with her, shall bewail her, and lament for her, when they shall see the smoke of her burning. . . . And the merchants of the earth shall weep and mourn over her, for no man buyeth their merchandise any more. . . ."[73]

Plans were made to conquer surrounding regions, "for this is what the Romans did, and in this way they came to dominate the whole world." To finance this global ambition, thousands of peasants and artisans sold all that they had and put the money into communal chests. Some burned down their own homesteads to make an irrevocable break with their past. The first community was set up at Pisek in southern Bohemia. Though disappointed by the nonappearance of Christ in February 1420, they seized the town of Usti later in the year and established a fortress that they called Tabor on a river promontory. Zizka proclaimed a society in which owning private property was a mortal sin, and "mine and thine" was abolished. They had no churches or altars and kept no feast days; their priests wore ordinary clothes; they rejected oaths and law courts, and took Communion in both kinds from a plain table. The more radical also rejected work; Zizka led robber bands that ravaged the countryside for provisions. Moderate Utraquists complained that they treated even the poor "in quite inhuman fashion, oppress them like tyrants and pagans, and extort rent pitilessly . . ."[74]

Demented even by the standards of their hosts, a small group of Adamites was expelled from Tabor in 1421. They believed that God dwells among the Saints of the Last Days. Since they included themselves in this elect, they felt themselves superior to Jesus, whose death showed him to be a mere human. They scorned the Bible, having as their prayer: "Our Father, who art in us, illumine us, Thy will be done . . ." They had antecedents, at least of a sort, among the Adamites of Augustine's days, a sect that believed they would regain the innocence of Paradise by practicing the nudity and promiscuity of the Garden of Eden before the Fall. Zizka captured seventy-five of them within a few months and burned them and their leader, a priest named Peter Kanis.

The survivors found themselves a new leader, a blacksmith who called himself Adam-Moses. His woman companion styled herself the Virgin Mary. The group went naked despite the Bohemian cold and damp, holding ritual dances around a fire, waiting for Adam-Moses to grant them permission to have sex: "Go, be fruitful and multiply and replenish the earth." Taking refuge from Zizka on an island in the river Nezarka, they emerged at night for plunder and massacre. They called this "holy war" and found justification in Matthew's gospel: "At midnight there is a cry, Behold, the bridegroom!" (Matt. 25:6). On October 21, 1421, Zizka overran the island with four hundred Taborites and killed all but one on the spot. Zizka extracted an account of the Adamites from the survivor before having him burned and his ashes thrown into the river.

Zizka lost his remaining eye during a siege the same year. He still led his men to a string of victories, compelling Sigismund to offer religious toleration until Zizka died of plague in 1424. His death split the movement between the Utraquist moderates, who eventually merged with the Catholics, and the Taborite wing. The extremists were decimated at the Battle of Lipan in 1434, and their decline was sealed by the loss of Tabor in 1452. Reform, however, and the phenomena that accompanied it—nationalism, burnings, revolts, anarchy, and religious dementia—were merely quiescent.

"something that appeals to the eye":

Papal Attitudes

s he lay dying in March 1455, Nicholas V summoned his cardinals to his bedside and spoke to them about the crisis in Christendom. Fear of advancing Turkish armies had briefly achieved the old dream of reconciliation between the Greek and Roman Churches. A delegation of seven hundred Byzantines had wrangled for months at Ferrara and Florence over the doctrinal concessions needed to win Catholic support. Wounds that had festered for centuries—the Western use of leavened bread in the Eucharist, a cause of the Great Schism four hundred years before; the 1,007-year-old dispute over the Latin addition of the *Filioque* to the creed; above all, the Western claim to the primacy of Rome—seemed healed. On July 6, 1438 the papal bull *Laetentur Coeli*, "Let the heavens rejoice," had announced a decree of union in which the Greek bishops accepted the Roman position.

The celebration was premature. The bishops met with fierce popular resistance when they returned to Constantinople, and many of them recanted. Even in extremis the devout instinctively clung to doctrinal purity. Two years before Nicholas addressed his cardinals, the city had fallen to the Turks. The union was dead; the Turkish sultan invested a new patriarch, with his crosier and mantle, a symbol of the dependence of the Greek Church on the Moslem power.*

Nicholas salvaged what learning he could from the wreckage of Byzantium, striving for a *translatio imperii,* a "transfer of dominion," in which the Latins would preserve the heritage of the Greeks. As a poor priest in Florence he had

---

*The concordat agreed to between the patriarch George Scholarius and Sultan Muhammad II was to govern relations between the two until 1923. The Treaty of Lausanne of that year obliged the new Turkish republic to protect the Greek Christians in Istanbul, as the conquerors renamed the city, but stipulated that the patriarch must have Turkish nationality.

spent any extra money he earned for bell-ringing on books. As pope, he employed a team of scholars to make Latin copies of works previously known only to Greek and Arabic speakers. He drove them hard and purposefully—the brilliant translator Trapezuntius complained that Nicholas "would not allow us to relax or take our ease"[1]—and his collection of three thousand volumes became the basis of the magnificent Vatican Library. The Eastern catastrophe was irreversible, however, and further humiliations were close. A union had also been proclaimed with the Armenian Church in 1439. That, too, ceased when the Turks overran Caffa; Moslem armies soon annexed Bosnia and Serbia, whose Christians they had already driven from Kosovo. Before the end of the century the grand dukes of Moscow were to declare their city to be the "third Rome" in succession to Constantinople, and themselves to be the czars, or "Caesars," who inherited the guardianship of the Orthodox Church; but they were isolated by distance and ignorance, and the Orthodox East, where it escaped Moslem servitude, was severed from the vigors and tensions that were setting the West on edge.

The unity of Catholic Christendom itself was about to be tested to the breaking point by the successors to Wycliffe and Hus. Western cultures that would dominate much of the world were being incubated. As Nicholas spoke, the first printed edition of the Bible was appearing at Mainz. Lay literacy and education, Renaissance humanism with its stress on independence of thought and scientific curiosity, the decline of Latin in favor of vernacular tongues, had begun to make inroads into the Church's near-monopoly of European thought and civilization. The rulers of nation-states and the merchants of trading cities resented papal influence and cast covetous eyes on Church land and treasure.

Amid this flux, Nicholas told his cardinals, the loyalty of the "uncultured masses" was best secured by giving them "something that appeals to the eye." Argument and ideas, the troublesome progeny of the reformers, served only to weaken the convictions of ordinary people. Display and grandeur made the deepest impression on them. "A popular faith, sustained only on doctrines, will never be anything but feeble and vacillating," he continued. "But if the Holy See were visible, displayed in majestic buildings, imperishable memorials and witnesses seemingly planted by the hand of God himself, belief could grow and strengthen like a tradition from one generation to another, and all the world would accept and revere it. . . ."[2]

❖ THIS SIMPLE, DEATHBED vision had deep significance. It defined the battle lines of the coming struggle. To Nicholas, the real business of religion was not doctrine, nor even the Church itself, for the pope was the only legitimate source

The Sistine Chapel is alive with human genius, and with the sense of papal majesty. In the *Challenge to Christ bearer of the Law* by Pietro Perugino, St. Peter kneels as Christ gives him the golden key of spirituality, from which hangs the iron key of temporal power. The painting is a reminder that popes, as successors to St. Peter, claim both spiritual and temporal dominion.

of the first and the master of the second. Its true purpose lay in the strengthening of tradition, of custom and habit, *consuetudo* in Latin, and it rested on the visible majesty of the pontiff and his see. New buildings inspired an awe and reverence that new doctrines might undermine; sermons in stone were better than babblings from the pulpit. Nicholas had practiced this ideology himself, striving to restore Rome to splendor. Ruined by schism and the Avignon captivity, the city had been reduced to squalid settlements "surrounded by grassy wooded mounds from which the wreckage of the pagan past stood out."[3] Beggars squatted amid the ruined marble of windowless churches while cattle foraged in the Forum and sheep roamed on four of the seven hills. Nicholas abandoned the peeling Lateran palace, transferring the main papal residence to the Vatican on the site of Nero's old Circus, adding a new wing made radiant with the frescoes of Fra Angelico. Derelict churches were brought back to life. He planned to reconstruct St. Peter's, which had stood since Constantine and was now so dilapidated that it was in danger of collapsing.

Papal prestige was rebuilt. Nicholas dispatched special legates to bear down on clerical abuses and promote personal piety. He put a final end to the humiliation of schism, accepting the submission of the last antipope, Felix V, in 1449.

The restoration of Catholic unity was celebrated by a Jubilee* in which sins were purged for penitents who made the pilgrimage to Rome. Nicholas inaugurated the Jubilee on Christmas Day, 1449. It was hugely popular. Tens of thousands of pilgrims camped out in fields and vineyards, militiamen prodding them with staves to keep traffic moving in the streets. Food ran short, and Nicholas cut the required length of stay in the city from eight days to three. The great relics of Rome, the enshrined heads of Peter and Paul, the cloth with which Veronica had wiped Jesus' face, were displayed each weekend. It had its tragedies—during its last week, in December 1450, a kicking mule panicked the pilgrims streaming across the Pont Sant' Angelo and two hundred were crushed to death or drowned in the Tiber—but money nonetheless poured into Rome. Nicholas was said to have lodged one hundred thousand gold florins in the Medici bank alone.

Money was essential to Nicholas's concept of dignity, but papal demand for cash became a trigger of discontent. So, too, did his censorious view of learning. The benchmark for the scholarship he commissioned was that it should be "worthy of the dignity of the Pope and the Vatican See." He was happy to rescue works that were ancient and respectable. The modern was another matter. Trapezuntius translated Ptolemy's *Almagest*, the great second-century compendium of mathematical astronomy, on Nicholas's direct orders. Ptolemy was doctrinally acceptable—his geocentric view of the heavens corresponded with the passage in Psalms that "the world also is established, that it cannot be moved" (Ps. 93:1), and indeed with Nicholas's own papocentric view of the theological universe—but Trapezuntius added his own fresh commentary on the text. Nicholas refused to accept it.[†] He maintained the ban on translation of the Bible into modern languages. New concepts—even if drawn from old scriptures—were disquieting.

---

*The origins of Jubilee and Sabbatical years date back to Moses. One year in seven was observed as a Sabbatical year under Mosaic Law, with a Jubilee taking place every seven Sabbatical years. "In the seventh year shall be a sabbath of solemn rest for the Lord," God told Moses on Mount Sinai, "thou shalt neither sow they field, nor prune thy vineyard." Sabbaticals, as a rest from normal duties, survive to the present day through their adoption by university teaching staff, the vast majority of whom were originally clerics. Every fifty years, at least in theory, Jewish slaves were freed to meet God's command that "ye shall return every man unto his family" (Lev. 25:10). Boniface VIII, whom Dante had sent to hell for his pains, had proclaimed 1300 to be a Jubilee year in which the sins of penitents who made the pilgrimage to Rome were wiped clean.

---

†Aggrieved, Trapezuntius later dedicated the work to the Turkish sultan Mehmed. Indeed, he pleaded with Mehmed to unite Islam and Christendom. "The Christian peoples are many and great, they have great influence, and are wise and good," he wrote. "The Islamic people are very great and admirable. If someone were to bring together the Christians and Moslems, in one single faith and confession, he would be, I swear by heaven and earth, glorified by all mankind. . . . This work, O admirable Sovereign, none other than you can accomplish."[4]

❖ SUCCESSIVE POPES REMAINED faithful to his formula. They dazzled the eye with the accoutrements of power, with lovers, goldsmiths, scholars, armies, palacies, intrigues, and poisonings. They muzzled new doctrine, but patronized artists, composers, and architects, whose exquisite creations possessed that hint of God's handiwork on which Nicholas set such store.

No memorial is more imperishable than the Sistine Chapel, built a few years after his death, and none more perfectly displays the reasons for the coming storm. The chapel was alive with human genius—and with the sense of papal majesty. It used matched frescoes of Moses and Christ, and portraits of the popes of the early centuries, to make of this place—built for the worship of the two hundred clerics who with the pope made up the *capella papale*—a symbol of an authority that it traced back for three thousand years through the first Christians to Jesus and the patriarch of ancient Israel. Botticelli's *Punishment of Korah* shows Moses as a pope of his people, stern, with a rod uplifted in his hand, while the disobedient cower on the ground. Lest any mistake the moral, the picture bore the legend: "Challenge to Moses bearer of the written Law." Opposite, Pietro Perugino painted the *Challenge to Christ bearer of the Law*. Peter kneels as Christ gives him the golden key of spirituality, from which hangs the iron key of temporal power, a reminder of the papal claim to dominion in both spheres.

If some came to find an austere and truer beauty in the plain, white chapel and black dress of the Protestant pastor, the majority continued to find greater comfort and stability in the familiar cadence of the Latin Mass and in the rich tumult of Catholic ornament. The reformers were to decapitate statues and whitewash paintings as feckless vanities, but the popes shared the artistic genius of the age, and the feeling that heaven could wait while man pursued his own ambitions on earth. "It may be only glory that we seek here, but I persuade myself that, as long as we remain here, that is right," the poet Petrarch had written. "This is the natural order, that among mortals the care of things mortal should come first; to the transitory will then succeed the eternal. . . ."[5]

The master of political realism, Machiavelli, acknowledged that such display was effective. He wrote that "leaders disposed to make trouble" were held in check by "the greatness of the Church, which overawed them."[6] He added that "men in general judge by their eyes . . . the common people are always impressed by appearances and results."[7]

Northern reformers were to care little about Moslem encroachment through the Balkans. Rome was acutely aware that it was competing with a faith that exploited grandeur with equal brilliance and purpose. Mehmed II, the Turkish sultan, reconsecrated Constantinople's sublime St. Sophia as a mosque in 1453 almost immediately after the conquest. "He zealously directed operations on the buildings he was erecting on his own account—that is the mosque and the palace," a contemporary reported. "For he was constructing great edifices which were to be worth seeing and should in every respect vie with the greatest and best of the past."[8] The Venetian painter Gentile Bellini and other Christian architects and artists were commissioned by the Turks to adorn the city as the symbol of Moslem domination of Eastern Christendom. In a Christian tit for tat, Ferdinand and Isabella in Spain reconsecrated the Royal Mosque in Granada for Christian worship when they entered the city in 1492. Their grandson Charles V built a lavish palace that towered above the Alhambra to celebrate the Christian reconquest of the Moslem West. The Turks were feared and admired by many as the "new wonder of the world." It was essential for the papacy to emphasize its own majesty.

A troubling shape nonetheless lingered in the Sistine brilliance. Its claim to the primacy of the Holy See was naked, exposing each individual incumbent to the harshest moral scrutiny. Was he fit to be Christ's keyholder? Was he a worthy successor to St. Peter? Nicholas himself, gentle, pious, striving for reconciliation with the Hussites, might pass muster. Others did not.

The Sistine chapel was built by and named for Sixtus IV. His artistic virtues were matched by personal vice. He squandered one hundred thousand ducats on his coronation tiara; he made cardinals of nine of his relatives, connived in conspiracies to murder, and refreshed papal funds by licensing Roman brothels and inventing indulgences for the souls of the dead. At his death, during a rare break in papally inspired wars, a wag suggested that he had been "slain by peace." His nephew Julius II commissioned Michelangelo to paint the Sistine ceiling with stupefying tenderness and force, and sought out the genius in Raphael and Bramante. Julius also fathered three daughters, contracted syphilis, and led papal armies on campaigns of butchery dressed in silver armor.

Such popes were indisputably great Renaissance princes but they were equally seen to be in urgent need of reformation. As landed magnates struggling to maintain their papal estates, they were exposed to secular stress. As Christ's vicars on earth, they were open to spiritual assault. Nicholas's vision exposed them to a dual vulnerability, and placed their office in peril of moral and strategic overload.

❖ CONTEMPT FOR WORLDLY wealth had been a running sore in the Church at least since the early hermits and monks of Egypt. It had, more recently, split the Franciscans. A group of Spirituals (or Zealots) held that Christ and the apostles had lived in absolute poverty, and condemned fellow Franciscans who lived high off alms and bequests. Inspired by the visions of the twelfth-century mystic Joachim of Fiore, who prophesied that the world was about to enter an age of the spirit, they practiced an unyielding austerity and renounced all possessions. Pope John XXII had responded to this challenge to his own riches by burning four Spirituals in 1318. Papal decretals declared doctrines of the poverty of Christ and the rejection of property to be heretical.[9] The Beguines, an equally pious and ascetic group of women, were condemned as an "abominable sect." They were among the first to write religious poetry in the vernacular, another habit that did not endear them to the orthodox; Margaret Porette, a Beguine who wrote the popular Mirror of Simple Souls encouraging liberty of the spirit, was burned at the stake in Paris.

The mystic Meister Eckhart, who preached with deep effect to nuns and Beguines, wrote of the soul being "weaned from the physical hindrances of temporal things and made apt for spiritual things." He accepted that naked want could persuade a Christian to say: "Ah, Lord, I am not aware of any great things in myself except poverty. How then could I dare to go to thee?" But to change that poverty to wealth, it was necessary only to go to Christ, to the "abundant treasure of inexhaustible riches." "Therefore say: 'I will go to thee,'" Eckhart urged, "'that Thy riches may fill my poverty and Thy infinite capacity may fill my emptiness. . . .'"[10] Eckhart's praise of "abstractedness," in which the soul was united with God by piercing the particulars of earthly living, was at odds with the pomp of churchmen. He was condemned by the court of archbishop of Cologne for heretical teaching in 1326 and died soon afterwards.

Another challenge came from the Brethren of the Common Life. The movement was founded by Gert Groote, a Dutchman of fame and fortune who abandoned a life of pleasure in 1374 and gathered a community of devout women in his house at Deventer to practice poverty, chastity, and devotion. Laymen and clergy joined them, and their drive for moral rebirth became known as *Devotio Moderna,* the "modern devotion." They did not beg for alms and took no formal vows. They met their modest needs through the book industry, writing, copying, and binding manuscripts. They also taught in local schools or opened their own as the movement spread to Germany and Switzerland.

Private prayer and contemplation of Christ were seen as superior to the public rituals of the Church. The search for a fresh intimacy with the Savior echoes still in the Jesus Movement; it won immense popular appeal with *De Imitatione Christi,* the *Imitation of Christ,* a devotional book written about 1418 by the German Thomas à Kempis. He saw Jesus as a friend as well as the model of perfection. "What can the world offer you, without Jesus?" he asked. "To be without Jesus is hell most grievous; to be with Jesus is to know the sweetness of heaven." Jesus was the good above every good; to lose him was to lose everything. "It is Jesus whom you must love and keep to be your friend; when all else fades away, he will not leave you, nor let you perish at the end."

Display and status were empty. "It is vanity to seek riches which shall perish," Kempis wrote. "It is vanity to pursue office and climb to high rank . . . vanity to follow the desires of the flesh . . . vanity to love what passeth away so quickly . . ."[11] The object of life is to seek God's will, and to approach Jesus, blessing him in times of anguish as well as joy. Many share the feast with Jesus, but few his fasting; "many admire his miracles, but few follow him to the humiliation of his cross." The devotion which Kempis described with elegant simplicity—the phrases *sic transit gloria mundi,* and "man proposes, but God disposes" are his—has a melancholy, a sense that the closer a man draws to Christ, the deeper he drowns in his own imperfections. Kempis had entered the Brethren's house near Zwolle in Holland as a teenager in 1399, and he was still there when he died seventy-two years later; but he felt this handsome life span to be more hazard than good fortune. "Of what use to us is a long life, if we change so little?" he asked. "Alas, a long life often adds to our sins rather than to our virtue! Would to God that we might spend a single day well!" God gave him so many days, and he felt that he failed in all of them.

Kempis was morally embarrassing to the Church. If this pious man, so clearly sin-free by its own rickety standards, could declare that he was a failure in the eyes of God, what would his readers make of the pope? A more dangerous aspect touched on basic doctrine. Popes and priests were not intermediaries in Kempis's faith. He appealed directly to Christ. "Grant me, Lord, to know all that I should know," he prayed, "to love what I should love, to esteem what most pleases you, and to reject all that is evil in your sight." The Church played no part in transmitting truth and understanding; these qualities were granted to the individual by the Almighty. The implications were disturbing. Faith bypassed the clergy; it needed no outside intervention. The impact of this was offset, at least for the present, by the emphasis that Kempis placed on the next world at the expense of this. His ideal lay in heaven, and not—to the considerable relief of the Church—on earth. Life was but a preparation for death. "Blessed is the man who keeps the hour of his death always in his mind," Kempis wrote, "and daily prepares himself to die." That may be a noble sadness, or a pitiable sense of shame, but it was not a call to revolt and reform.

STRANGE OBSESSIONS, DREAMS, and popular fantasies drifted into the valley of the Tauber in the years after Pope Nicholas's death in 1455, and settled in the village of Niklashausen. Germany was collapsing into a patchwork of principalities, and this region of Bavaria was ruled by the prince-bishops of Würzburg, noted for their high taxation. "Oh Lord our God, hear our plea," the mastersinger of Augsburg prayed. "Why do Your servants have to suffer whilst these greedy bishops get more arrogant? I beg You, O Lord, bend their stiff and proud heads, turn their minds from pride . . ."[12]

In mid-Lent 1476 a young shepherd named Hans Böhm had a vision of the Virgin Mary. He sang in the inns on market days and was known affectionately as the "drummer of Niklashausen." The Virgin bade him to stop urging the people to dance and instead to preach them the word of God. He burned his drum in front of the parish church and announced that the statue of the Virgin in the church had become the salvation of the world. God was set on punishing mankind, he said, until the Virgin interceded. Those who made the pilgrimage to her statue would be absolved from sin, for divine grace was to be found on the banks of the Tauber and not in Rome. He was eloquent, attractive, and adored, and he slowly filled with that sense of exaltation that some find to be the mark of grace and others to be lunacy.

A great tented camp of pilgrims sprang up round the village. Chroniclers spoke of thirty and even seventy thousand people; no doubt they exaggerated, but the archbishop of Mainz, the primate of Germany, was deeply alarmed and sent his spies to mingle with the pilgrims. At first, Böhm urged his followers to repent and cast off their vanities and baubles. He went on to claim miraculous powers for himself; he could, he said, lead souls by the hand from hell. As the Lollards had broken into English parks and chases, so "the drummer" said that woods, pastures, hunting, and water would be free to all in the coming kingdom of the millennium. Ranks and taxes would be abolished and none would work harder than another. "The emperor is a scoundrel and the pope is useless," he said. "The time will come when princes and lords will work for their daily bread. . . ." He turned on the clergy. It was easier to make a good Christian out of a Jew than a priest, he preached; to kill a cleric was not a sin, and none should pay them taxes. They should give up their benefices and live from meal to meal on charity.

"What would the layman like better than to see the clergy and priesthood robbed of all their privileges and rights, their tithes and revenues?" observed the abbot of Spondheim in the spring of 1476. "For the common people is by nature hungry for novelties and ever eager to shake off its master's yoke." The explanation is revealing. To the abbot, Church income and privilege were rights which laymen wished to steal, but to the peasants and the drummer, of course, the clergymen themselves were the thieves. The abbot spoke, too, of the clergy as the "master," and in Würzburg, with its prince-bishop, he was right to do so. A German prince-bishop was the sovereign of his petty state, governing it with his chapter in the interests of his own caste of aristocratic churchmen. Taxes at Würzburg were so heavy that peasants compared themselves to a horse that would collapse if as much as an egg were added to its load; the equally beggared people of Mainz supported four monasteries, seven convents, and ten churches as well as the archbishop's palace and cathedral. The bishops were little loved, though to lose one was a catastrophe, for a large sum had to be paid to the Roman Curia at each new election. Rebellion was as much economic as religious protest.

Yet, as the abbot noted, there was also a desire for "novelty." A cathedral with its naves, aisles, choirs, chancels, chantries, shrines, tombs, fonts, organs, spires, and stained glass was immovable and seemingly immortal, buttressed in stone. The Church itself was an equally magnificent edifice, undeniably immense, intimately involved in almost every aspect of human affairs. Perhaps it had done its work too well. It filled the minds of men and women with religion, and, for all the rigid splendor of the Church, the Christian religion remained as mutable as ever. The pursuit of novelty, ascribed by the abbot to the "common people" with lofty disdain, was open to any Christian who felt himself impelled by the Holy Spirit, be he drummer boy or Wycliffe or Hus; it was a quality of the faith itself, and, in a deeply religious age, the worldly motivations of rebels—liberty, money, jealousy—were readily subsumed into an act of faith.

A fever spread from the Alps to the Rhineland in the early summer of 1476. Peasants and artisans abandoned their labors and marched with banners to the promised land of Niklashausen, as the poor had followed Peter the Hermit for Jerusalem four centuries before. The threats they chanted were aimed not at Moslems, but at the clergy:

> To God in heaven we complain
> Kyrie eleison
> That the priests cannot be slain
> Kyrie eleison.[13]

The drummer was now known as the "holy youth"; the pilgrims fell to their knees when they glimpsed him, murmuring: "O Man of God sent from Heaven, take pity on us!" Cloth was ripped from his garments and divided into relics that were guarded "as though it were hay from the manger of Bethlehem." He was said to cure the blind, to make water gush from a rock, to raise the dead. By July the Church saw the holy youth as an apostle of anarchy. Würzburg closed its gates against the pilgrim tide and its prince-bishop determined to arrest him.

Informers claimed that Böhm preached a sermon on Monday, July 7, 1474, in which he asked his followers to come armed and without their women and children the following Sunday, for the Virgin had serious matters for him to tell them. On the night of Saturday, July 12, a troop of horsemen sent by the prince-bishop rode into Niklashausen, seized Böhm, and took him as a prisoner to the castle at Würzburg. On Sunday morning a peasant said that the Holy Trinity had appeared to him and told him that the pilgrims should march on the castle; the walls would tumble like those of Jericho at their approach and the holy youth would be reunited with them. They walked by candlelight through the night to Würzburg. The castle walls remained intact, and they were greeted with cannon fire and cavalry. Some forty were killed and the others fled. Böhm, found guilty of heresy and sorcery by an ecclesiastical court, sang hymns to the Virgin as he was burned. The church at Niklashausen was destroyed on orders of the archbishop of Mainz, but the drummer's disciples visited the site in the secrecy of darkness for many years.

❖   TO THE SOUTH, a few years later, the friar Girolamo Savonarola sounded a more sophisticated alarm. He had a vision of apocalypse as a young Dominican in 1484—"It revealed many reasons showing that some scourge of the Church was at hand," he was to say at his trial, "and from that moment I fell to thinking much on these things"[14]—and it left a mark of wild rapture on him. In 1491 he became prior of the monastery of San Marco at Florence; the city was the heartland of the Renaissance, the profits of banking, silk, and commerce making it incomparable in its arts and frivolous in its habits. Savonarola was pungent with

Savonarola preaches against luxuries in this painting by Langenmantel, while rich vestments, silver, and goblets are thrown to his feet to be ready for the Bonfire of Vanities. A Dominican prior, Savonarola proclaimed Florence to be a City of God in 1494, a theocratic republic of which he was master. His puritanical crusade was popular at first, as a reaction to clerical and lay decadence, but Florentines wearied of it. In 1498 they hanged and burned him.

charisma, in its modern sense of spellbinding personality, and also, so his follow-ers claimed, in its old Greek meaning of divine grace. A burning spirituality emerged from his cowled visage, with its great hooked nose and thin, unsmiling lips. Like Wycliffe, he stressed the importance of biblical studies, and he made San Marco a center for the study of oriental languages and for meetings of hu-manist scholars. He was a hero to artists, to Pico della Mirandola and to Sandro Botticelli, whose style changed under his influence from the sensuality of the *Birth of Venus* to the haunting tenderness of the *Madonna of the Annunciation*.

Savonarola was orthodox in doctrine, ruthless in morality, and reckless and ambitious in politics. Florence, nominally a republic, was effectively ruled by Lorenzo de' Medici, "the Magnificent." Theoretically a mere citizen, Lorenzo's personal control was such that foreign ambassadors lived with him at his palace; he settled the city's internal crises and held at bay its many enemies—the pope, the Milanese, the king of Naples. He died in 1492. His son Pietro was weak and nicknamed "the Unfortunate." Savonarola commanded congregations of fifteen thousand in the Duomo, who heard him predict a coming disaster in which Flor-ence, abandoning its vices, would save the faith. His prophecies seemed to come true when the French king Charles VIII invaded Italy in 1494. Pietro de' Medici capitulated, and Savonarola proclaimed Florence to be a "city of God," a theo-cratic republic to be administered by a great council, of which Savonarola was master.

An apocalyptic puritanism was let loose. Most forms of public entertainment were banned. Married women left their husbands and entered convents, and the number of monks quintupled. Gaming houses and brothels were closed, and fashionable tailors and jewelers ruined. As he scourged Florentines of their vice and excesses, Savonarola turned on the Church and pope. "I saw in a vision a black cross above the Babylon that is Rome, upon which was written Ira Domini, the wrath of the Lord," he preached. "I say to you, the Church of God must be renewed, and it will be soon."

At the Vatican, the pope recognized that he was confronted by a fury of Pentecostal self-belief. "You predict the future and affirm that all that you say comes from eternal hand as an inspiration of the Holy Spirit," Alexander VI re-torted in October 1495, "whereby you lead simple men away from the road of salvation and from obedience to the Holy Roman Church." He ordered Savonarola not to make "prophecies and divinations."[15]

The pope was at a moral disadvantage to the friar. Alexander was born Ro-drigo Borgia, a Spaniard whose uncle Callistus III had made him a cardinal when he was twenty-five, and whose loose living was notorious. "We have heard that the dance was indulged in with much wantonness," Pope Pius II had written to him after a party he threw in Siena. "None of the allurements of love were lacking. . . . In order that your lust might be all the more unrestrained, the husbands, fathers, brothers and kinsmen of the young women and girls were not invited to be present. Shame forbids mention of all that took place. . . ." The scandal spread far beyond Siena, and Pius complained that "nothing is talked of . . . but your vanity which is the subject of universal ridicule."[16] The cardinal was a glutton for sardines and sex. He fathered eight children by at least three women, including the infamous Cesare and Lucrezia Borgia by the Roman beauty Rosa Vanozza.

This "vain and showy young man" was nonetheless created pope as Alexander VI in the early morning of August 11, 1492. The Sienese ambassador wrote of his "God-like virtues and gifts . . . he seemed to have been chosen and preordained by Divine Providence." He was not. He was chosen through buying votes. "Immediately," the chronicler Burchard wrote ironically, "he distributed his goods and gave them to the poor."[17] This was not charity. Instead, it meant that he paid off the cardinals for their support. Scores of benefices, bishoprics, abbeys, fortified towns, and castles had been allocated in advance. Pinturicchio painted Alexander kneeling in the fresco of the Resurrection in the Borgia apartments at the Vatican, portly and fat-handed, with gray jowls and a look of simplistic piety. "Now we are in the jaws of a ravening wolf," Lorenzo de' Medici's nephew, a cardinal, wrote with more accuracy, "and if we do not flee he will devour us."[18] The pope flaunted a new young mistress at the Vatican and used his office to promote his children. Cesare became archbishop of Valencia at sixteen and a cardinal at seventeen; at twenty-three he was captain-general of the papal army, succeeding his brother Juan, whom he was widely suspected of murdering. Alexander married off Lucrezia Borgia to a Sforza warlord when she was thirteen, but he then annulled the marriage to seek advantage by bethrothing her to the nephew of the king of Naples. This marriage ended when Cesare murdered the bridegroom.

A chronicler allowed that Alexander was intelligent and eloquent, and that "there was nothing small about him." He rebuilt the Castel Sant' Angelo at Rome; he patronized artists of the quality of Bramante, and the much maligned Lucrezia, unfairly accused of committing incest with both her father and brother, encouraged Titian at her brilliant court. He was practical, taking pains to pay his soldiers on time to ensure their loyalty. He was broad-minded and took little notice of satire at his expense. "There is liberty of speech in Rome," he said, "and we care nothing for libels against ourselves. If they are witty and well-written, they are amusing, if not, we take no interest." His son Cesare was less tolerant; tracing the authorship of a scandalous tract to a Neapolitan writer, Girolamo Manciano, he had his right hand cut off and his tongue pierced with a hot iron.[19] The chronicler felt safe in saying that Alexander's "splendid qualities were matched by equally great vices," but he declined to detail this immorality, mentioning only his "overwhelming desire to secure a great position for his bastard children . . ."[20]

Savonarola would not acquiesce to such a man. Alexander summoned him to Rome and banned him from preaching. Savonarola retorted that such orders were against the commandments of God and the Church. At the Florence carnival in 1496 he had a great bonfire prepared on the Piazza de' Signori. Lutes, women's wigs, perfumes, mirrors, lewd books and pictures, playing cards, dice, gaming tables, and immodest dresses were flung on it. Then, to the sound of church bells, trumpets, fifes, and hymn-singing children, it was set ablaze. He redoubled his assault on Rome. "You harlot Church, you used to be ashamed of pride and lasciviousness," he thundered. "Now you are ashamed no longer. See how once the priests called their children nephews; now they are called sons, not nephews; sons everywhere." This impertinence was to cost him his life. It was no secret to whom he referred. "I am an honest man," Alexander had boasted. "I frankly admit that my children are not my nephews. I love them dearly."[21]

The pope reluctantly excommunicated Savonarola as a heretic and schismatic on May 13, 1497. In response, the friar wrote *Triumphus Crucis,* a powerful apologia of his beliefs that—although it confirmed the pope's view that Savonarola was so prickly that he would "cause discord even if perfect peace were reigning"— contained not a hint of heresy. He also sent startling letters to the Christian princes asking them to convene a council to overthrow Alexander, who, he said, far from being a legitimate pope, was not even a Christian. Alexander retaliated by threatening to place Florence under interdiction. This was a serious matter for a trading city, for if the pope had pursued the interdiction, all good Catholics would have been barred from doing business with the city. The Florentines, grown weary of his moral fevers, and manipulated by the *Arrabbiati,* his "enraged" enemies, turned against Savonarola.

Machiavelli noted the perils that await reformers. They make enemies of those who prospered under the old order, while what support they have is lukewarm because "men are generally incredulous, never really trusting new things until they have tested them by experience." He observed that "all armed prophets have conquered, and unarmed prophets have come to grief," and that "the most dangerous time for them is when they are still striving"; Savonarola had reached that stage where the "crowd started to lose faith in him" and he had no armed force to fall back on.[22] He was arrested and tried. Torture failed to produce a recantation, though his last testament, the *Miserere,* compared his own frailty to St. Peter's denial of Christ. Another bonfire was made ready on the Piazza de' Signori on May 23, 1498. Savonarola was first hanged and then burned at the stake. Two disciples were at his side, loyalists noted, like the robbers at Calvary. His ashes were thrown into the Arno.

✤ IT WAS NOT necessary to break with the Church in order to reform it. Savonarola died an Orthodox Catholic. His demands for morality and his fearless attack on the Borgia pope—Alexander died in 1503, perhaps of a fever, but so reviled that tradition held that he was accidentally poisoned by a beverage he had intended should be drunk by Cardinal da Corneto, his host—won him many Catholic admirers. The English martyr, Bishop John Fisher, who went to the scaffold in the defense of papal authority, blessed his memory. St. Catherine de Ricci, a Dominican nun famous fifty years later for her mystical unions with Christ's Passion, was convinced that he was a saint.*

The great Catholic scholar Erasmus was as hostile to Church abuses as any Lollard or Hussite. "I see some merchant or soldier or judge laying down one small coin from his extensive booty," he wrote of indulgences in *The Praise of Folly* in 1509, "and expecting that the whole cesspool of his life will be at once purified." Erasmus ridiculed the supposed powers of the saints to ease toothache and labor pains, to cure epilepsy and the dancing mania, to guard against theft and shipwreck. "Some of them are good for a number of purposes," he noted, "particularly the Virgin Mother, to whom the common people tend to attribute more than to the Son."[23]

Erasmus also mocked monks, who brayed psalms they had learned by rote and begged so universally that not an inn or even a ship was free of them; yet, by their dirtiness, ignorance, and bad manners they claimed to be leading the lives of the apostles. As to popes, cardinals, and bishops, they had copied the pomp and circumstance of princes and "come near to beating them at their own game." The word "bishop" was supposed to mean labor, vigilance, and solicitude. They practiced none of these virtues, he said, save vigilance when "raking in moneys . . . overseeing everything—and overlooking nothing." Erasmus then turned his savage wit on Rome. "What disasters would befall if ever the supreme pontiffs, the Vicars of Christ, should attempt to imitate His life of poverty and toil?" he asked. The answer was that "thousands of scribes, sycophants . . . muleteers . . . and pimps" would become unemployed.

Like Wycliffe, he wanted the Scriptures to be translated into all languages, so that the Turk and the Saracen might understand them, and the laborer might sing them as he followed the plow, and the weaver hum them at his shuttle. His *Adagia* of 1500 collected earthy proverbs and phrases that still survive—"flogging a dead horse . . . cutting the throat of a corpse . . . milking a billy goat . . . in the land of the blind, the one-eyed man is king . . . wise as far as the beard . . ." No

---

*Dominicans continue to revere Savonarola as a martyr to this day, their proposal to beatify him being opposed in 1999 by Jesuits on the grounds that he was a "rebel . . . who inspired contradictory passions."[24]

less than any Lollard, Erasmus had to defend his new Greek text of the New Testament against churchmen who saw it as a breach of their monopoly. "None bark louder than those who have never seen the cover of one of my books," he wrote to a friend. "Whenever you meet someone like this, let him rant on about my New Testament and when he has made himself hoarse ask if he has read any of it. If he can say he has (without blushing) then ask him to show you one passage he dislikes. You will not find any one of them who can do it." He compared his Catholic critics to Swiss peasants; as soon as one of them pointed a finger at someone, they all did the same and then started throwing stones at him. Erasmus quoted Psalms against them: "They have sharpened their tongues like a serpent; adder's poison is under their lips. . . ."[25]

Holding these views, Erasmus had no thought of rebellion. He rejected any rupture on the grounds of solace and tradition that Nicholas had sketched from his deathbed. "I was among the first to see that there was danger that this matter might end in uproar," he wrote of a young ex-monk, Martin Luther, who broke with the Church, "and no one has ever hated uproar more than I."[26] Erasmus might say in 1502 that it was an unpardonable insult to call a layman a cleric; the bishop of London might comment that any jury that laid its hands on a clergyman would condemn him, even if he were as innocent as Abel. Neither had any difficulty in remaining a Catholic.

The Church had survived peasant uprisings, messianic visionaries, puritan firebrands, troublesome rulers, and unhappy taxpayers in past centuries. The age was pious. Popular use of the rosary was spreading. Many churches commissioned statues of the Pièta, the Virgin of Pity with her dead son; the prayer of the Virgin was joined to the tolling of a bell to create the Angelus. There was every prospect that Catholicism would cope with the Renaissance shift from a God to a man-centered universe through its own internal reformation.

It was the Church's profound misfortune that a period of intense religious revival should coincide with a Borgia-induced moral nadir and its merciless exposure by the greatest advance in human communication for four thousand years, the printing press.

"BY FAITH ALONE":

Printing and Protestants

rinting spread doubt and heresy at a gallop. The hand-copied book had been an exquisite rarity, usually commissioned as a single volume from a team of scribes and illuminators. The humble religious tract of the Lollard was an individual labor of love, not of profit and mass circulation. The press transformed supply and cost. A collector who wished to have a volume hand-illustrated paid eight times as much for this traditional work as for the plain printed text. A skilled artisan at Venice could buy four printed volumes with a week's salary by the end of the fifteenth century.[1] Books were already being promoted at the annual fair at Frankfurt,* and pirate editions were appearing. The more controversial the subject, the more eager was the demand. A Paris printer was soon running off twenty-four thousand copies of Erasmus's *Colloquies,* and the author's *Praise of Folly,* which was so wounding to the papacy, ran to forty-three separate editions in his lifetime. Humble readers were snapping up copies of religious tracts and sermons. The major constraint, in an age of rapidly growing literacy, was the high price of paper, which made up two-thirds of production costs.

The first documents printed with movable type in the West* were letters of indulgence, produced by Johannes Gutenberg at Mainz in 1445. A goldsmith by

---

*The Frankfurt Book Fair, remains the world's most famous publishing exhibition.

†Printing with movable type was first achieved in China in about 1041; because of the large numbers of characters in Chinese script, the method failed to become established. Block prints made from engraved wooden blocks had been produced in Japan at least as early as 770. The simplicity of Western alphabets was ideally suited to printing, however, and enabled the new medium to revolutionize the flow of information in Europe. Gutenberg's invention is thought by some to have been predated by Laurens Janszoon, a sacristan at Haarlem in Holland, between 1420 and 1426.

training, Gutenberg raised loans from the banker Johann Fust to finance the printing of the Latin Vulgate Bible between 1453 and 1455. Separate letters were cast in a metal typeface designed by the professional scribe Peter Schoeffer and made up into pages and printed on six presses in a production run of some three hundred copies. From the outset, the technical quality was excellent. The pages were beautifully illuminated in color to give the appearance of a traditional hand-copied manuscript, for the partners wished their invention to remain secret. The first dated book was a fine Psalter produced in 1457, which already experimented with color printing.

The Mainz monopoly was brief. Fust ran his own presses after falling out with Gutenberg, and print workers fleeing from the city after it was sacked in 1462 took the new art with them. These wandering German pioneers arrived at Rome in 1464; five years later they were at Venice where lower case type in Roman and italic was added to the original Roman capital letters. A year later they set up a press in the Sorbonne at Paris. Others were established at Utrecht and Valencia by 1475. William Caxton founded a press in England at Westminster the following year after learning the new art at Cologne. Where the others printed in Latin, he used only English, and much of his material was in translation.

Bankers and merchants invested heavily in the new print shops. More than two dozen universities had been founded across Europe during the fifteenth century, and their graduates provided consumers as well as typesetters, editors, proofreaders, and authors. Erasmus soon established the popularity of religious satire and controversy, apologizing to a friend that he could not send him a new work because his publisher "sold out entirely at Frankfurt in three hours."[2] Indulgence printing was profitable, highly so if the printer ran off extra copies and sold them himself. This fraud was investigated at Seville, where one printer also held stocks of more than eighty thousand sheets of prayers, rhymes, and devotional woodcuts. Pamphlets and cartoons mocking clerical abuses could now be run off by the thousand.

THE PAPACY PROVIDED material in plenty. Giuliano della Rovere, nephew of Sixtus IV, became pope as Julius II in 1503, the year of Alexander's death. He loathed his predecessor—he had spent long periods hiding in northern Italy due to fear of a Borgia assassination attempt—but he breathed the same secular energy and the same ferocity, land hunger, license, and splendor. Machiavelli thought him a paragon of princely guile, courage, and ruthlessness. Raphael painted his portrait in old age, fierce if now toothless, with a grim set to his mouth and a long yellow-gray beard; as Julius Caesar had stopped shaving as a vow of vengeance against the Gauls, so his namesake pledged the hair of his chin

Raphael's portrait of Julius II, pope for ten years from 1503. Julius was more Renaissance prince than bishop. He brought Raphael to Rome to decorate his private apartments, and commissioned Michelangelo to paint the Sistine ceiling. He also fathered three daughters, contracted syphilis, and, dressed in silver armor, led papal armies on campaigns of butchery.

against his many enemies, French, Venetian, Perugian, Bolognese. He was a violent man, known as *il terribile,* and beat those who displeased him with his papal staff. "It is far better to be feared than loved," Machiavelli noted approvingly, "for . . . fear is strengthened by a dread of punishment which is always effective."[3]

Julius was recklessly brave. He led his troops in his silver armor across frozen ditches to breach the walls of Mirandola and overwhelm its French defenders. His alliances shifted restlessly. He fought with the French against the Venetians; then he turned on them, forming the Holy League with England, Spain, and Venice against them. "Julius was impetuous in everything," Machiavelli wrote, "and he found the time and circumstances so favourable to his way of proceeding that he always met with success."[4] He drove first Cesare Borgia and then the French from Italy. His extension of the papal states to include Parma, Piacenza, and Reggio Emilia gave future popes a territorial base and—combined with the fortuitous discovery of an alum mine near Rome which was a monopoly supplier to the textile and tanning trades—a secure income.

Refusing to live in the Borgia apartments at the Vatican, Julius decorated his own rooms with fresh artistic miracles, some celebrating the mind, as with Raphael's *School of Athens,* and others reflecting his own bellicosity, the *Repulse of Attila* and the *Expulsion of Heliodorus.* On April 18, 1506, he laid the foundation stone of the new St. Peter's at Rome. Grander by far than the plans of Nicholas, the work begun by Julius was the largest church in Christendom when it was consecrated 120 years later. He planned an immense tomb for himself in the choir and summoned Michelangelo to Rome to sculpt it. A magnificent statue of Moses is the finest remnant of the unfinished monument. In 1508, Michelangelo recorded that "I have received 500 ducats on account . . . for painting the vault of the Sistine Chapel." He toiled on his back beneath a concave ceiling sixty feet high to depict the progress of man through the Old Testament. On All Saints' Day in 1512, Julius celebrated mass at the altar beneath perhaps the most glorious work of art this earth has seen.

Michelangelo recorded his unsentimental views of popes in a poem:

Of chalices they make helmet and sword
And sell by the bucket the blood of the Lord.
His cross, his thorns are blades in poisoned dipped
And even Christ himself is of all patience stripped.[5]

Julius was a product of nepotism; his uncle had made him archbishop of Avignon, and of Bologna, and bishop of Lausanne, Constance, Viviers, Mende, Ostia, and Velletri. He had fathered three daughters as a cardinal. He suffered from syphilis; his master of ceremonies reported that he could not allow his foot to be kissed, since it was "completely ulcerated with the French disease." Erasmus, who was in Italy between 1506 and 1509, mocked his worldliness and his high-handed treatment of the Fifth Lateran Council, the last held before the breakup of Western Christendom. "I told it what to say," Julius thundered in Erasmus's satire. "We had two Masses to show that we were acting under Divine Inspiration, and there was a speech in honour of myself. At the next session I cursed the schismatic cardinals. At the 3rd I laid France under interdict. . . ."[6] At his death in 1513 the council had passed only minor reforms.

His successor was crowned in a pavilion in front of the facade of St. Peter's, the only part of the old building left standing. Giovanni de' Medici was the second son of Lorenzo the Magnificent. As a youth, his family expelled from Florence, he had wandered through northern Europe. He became pope at thirty-seven, taking the name Leo X, plump and self-indulgent. He squandered the hard-won treasure left by Julius in two years. He was attended by almost seven hundred courtiers, an orchestra, a midget friar, a theater company, and a menagerie; his processions were graced by Persian horses, a panther, two leopards, and Hanno the white elephant, whose portrait he had painted by Raphael. A concordat concluded with Francis I of France restored much-needed annates to Rome, but gave the French king the right to appoint to bishoprics, abbeys, and major benefices in his lands, and effectively made the king master of a national church. Leo was firmer with the Sacred College. Cardinal Petrucci of Siena, then twenty-seven years old, offended by Leo's failure to keep the electoral promises he had made in the conclave, plotted with the papal doctor Battista de Vercelli to have him poisoned during treatment for piles. The conspiracy was uncovered. Vercelli was hung, drawn, and quartered. It was improper for a Christian to execute a prince of the Church, and Cardinal Petrucci was strangled by a Moor in the Marocco, the foulest dungeon in the Castel Sant' Angelo. Leo created thirty-one new cardinals in a day in 1517, crushing dissent, and, since cardinals were paid from a fixed pool of revenue, reducing their incomes and thus their independence.

The Lateran council ended in 1517 with papal superiority over general councils confirmed. Cardinals were now supreme only in conclave, when they were locked into airless wooden cells in the Vatican, cut off from the world; Pius II recalled endless plotting in the lavatory block, a "fit place for such elections."[7] Far from electing God's candidate, conclaves reflected the jealousies between Spain and France and the intrigues of Italian families; with the single exception of the Dutchman Hadrian VI, who lived little more than a year after his election in 1522, every pope until 1978 was an Italian. In consolidating his power, Leo less happily exposed himself to deeper scrutiny. "He would have been a perfect pope," wrote the theologian and historian Fra Paolo Sarpi, "if to these accomplishments he had added even the slightest knowledge of religion."

It worried Leo little that there had been no reforms, nor that at the obscure new University of Wittenberg a German professor of theology named Martin Luther was demanding a debate on indulgences. Luther was particularly incensed by the great indulgence to fund the building of St. Peter's, started by Julius and now continued by Leo. To Luther the Holy See was more corrupt than Babylon or Sodom; as to the pope, "in him who calls himself most holy and most spiritual, there is more worldliness than in the world itself."

Solemn warning had been given at the Council of Basle more than eighty years before. "From now on," delegates had resolved, "all simony shall cease. . . . All priests shall put away their concubines [or] shall be deprived of his office, though he be the Bishop of Rome. . . . The abuse of ban and anathema by the popes shall cease. . . . The Roman Curia, that is, the popes shall neither demand nor receive any fees for ecclesiastical offices. From now on, a pope should think not of this world's treasures but only of those of the world to come."[8] For their pains they had been denounced as "apostates, blaspheming rebels, men guilty of sacrilege, gaolbirds," and ignored.

Nepotism flourished. Leo had been made an abbot at age seven, a canon at eight, and a cardinal at thirteen. Simony accelerated as investors bought positions for cash, exploiting them to recoup their capital and turn a profit. New posts were

Gloria in Excelsis.

Indulgence plenière.

König des Carneval.

An anti-Catholic satire engraved in Germany, in which a monk, swilling from a bottle, is made the "King of the Carnival." The sign on his chest for "full indulgence" shows that he makes his living selling the remission of sins to the gullible. The new art of printing was immensely helpful to reformers, and propaganda sheets like this were run off in the tens of thousands.

invented to pay for wars and buildings. Innocent VIII created fifty-two *pulembatores,* officials who put lead seals on documents. Each paid twenty-five hundred ducats for his post, about a hundred times the annual salary of a country priest, and charged extortionate fees to those who needed papal paperwork. The sale of offices made it difficult for the lowborn but able to win a suitable post, so that the Curia became "soft billets for idle drones."[9] Sixtus IV traded in some 650 offices. By the time of Leo X the number had swollen to 2,150 with a value of three million ducats.

Relics were a further cause of scandal. They had some—slight—justification in the Bible. Paul's clothes were said to have miraculous powers in Acts, "insomuch that unto the sick were carried away from his body handkerchiefs or aprons, and the diseases departed from them, and the evil spirits went out" (Acts 19:12). Some were genuine. It was found by radiocarbon dating and DNA profiling in 2000—that remains in an ornate lead coffin in the Basilica of Santa Giustina in Padua, Italy, venerated since 1172 as the relic of St. Luke, could indeed be those of the author of the third Gospel and of Acts. The coffin was brought to Padua from Constantinople during the Crusades.

All new churches and religious houses were required to have them, however. Demand far outstripped supply, and forgery was rampant as private collectors vied with clerics for trophies. A bishop of Lincoln, frustrated at his cathedral's lack of world-class objects, bit off a piece of the finger of St. Mary Magdalene displayed at Fécamp. At the abbey of St. Denis outside Paris, parts of the bodies of five saints and the head of another were carried in solemn procession while the monks sang canticles. Then, the abbey chronicler recorded, came "the chin of St. Mary Magdalene and the finger of St. Louis . . . and the hand of the apostle Thomas; finally came the reverend Abbots with . . . the insignia of the passion of our Lord, that is to say, the Crown of Thorns, the Holy Nail and a [piece] of the Cross of our Lord."[10] As Erasmus pointed out to his growing readership, there was enough wood of the True Cross to build a battleship; he might have added that some saints had more arms than an octopus and more feet than a centipede.

THE FUNDING OF the new St. Peter's caused the immediate crisis. Indulgences—"the holy trade" in which sinners purchased remission of sins—dated back to the first crusades. Theological justification, approved in the bull *Unigenitus* of 1343, rested on the claim that the pope was able to dispense the "accumulated merit" of the Church to individuals in return for cash. The proceeds of Leo's great indulgence of 1517 in central Germany were to be divided between the pope, who would supposedly use them for the building work, and Prince Albert of Brandenburg, the young archbishop of Magdeburg and Mainz. The papal dispensation for permission to hold the two archbishoprics was hugely expensive. Albert had borrowed heavily from the Fugger bankers, and he was anxious to pay off the loans.

Johann Tetzel, a German Dominican who served as an inquisitor as well as a fund-raiser, led a special team of indulgence preachers. The rates for the indulgences were relatively modest—Albert fixed them at just over 1 percent of total income, or three gold florins for a merchant with a turnover of two hundred florins, and those without money were able to supply their contribution with prayer—but Tetzel aimed higher. He prepared sample sermons for parish priests bidding them to point out that every mortal sin required seven years of penance even after confession and contrition. They were then to ask their parishioners how many sins they committed each day, each week, month, year, how many in a lifetime. The total would be infinite, and infinite would be the penance that must be suffered. The sales pitch followed. "Won't you part with even a farthing to buy this letter? It won't bring you money but rather a divine and immortal soul, whole and secure in the Kingdom of Heaven. . . ." Great play was made for the living to redeem the souls of dead family and friends. "Listen to the cries of your parents and the pleading of the lost," the priest was to say. "'Have mercy, have mercy on me. . . . We are in great pain and torment. You have the power to ease our anguish a little and yet you do nothing.' Open your ears. A father cries out to his son, a mother to her daughter: 'Why is the Lord tormenting me?' . . ."[11]

When Tetzel visited the silver-mining town of St. Annaberg, the official letter confirming the indulgence, stamped with a red cross and the papal coat of arms, was carried on a satin pillow in front of him. He was greeted with banners, candles, songs, and a parade; all the town's priests, monks, counselors, scholars, and womenfolk flocked to see him. The bells rang out and the organ boomed as he was led into the church, which was decorated with the papal flag. "Basically, even God Himself could not have got a better reception," an eyewitness reported.[12] He told them that if they gave "happily," buying grace and pardon, the surrounding hills would turn to solid silver. He said that the indulgence was so powerful that "even if someone had slept with Christ's dear Mother, the Pope had power in heaven and on earth to forgive as long as money was put into the indulgence coffer."[13]

Tetzel was forbidden from preaching the indulgence in Saxony by its ruler, the elector Frederick the Wise. Frederick disliked Albert and wished to protect his own income from relics. He had 17,443 fragments of holy bones and other relics in his castle church at Wittenberg. An inventory included a twig from the burning bush and a straw from the Bethlehem manger, a piece of the seamless robe of Christ and a hair from his beard, three pieces of the holy cross, eight complete thorns from the crown of thorns. His collection was said to have a total 1,902,202 years and 270 days of remission of sins available for visiting pilgrims. Saxons crossed the border to hear Tetzel preach, however, and word of the indulgence angered the professor of biblical studies at the recently founded University of Wittenberg, Martin Luther.

❖ MARTIN LUTHER WAS in his mid-thirties, the son of a prosperous and godly copper miner from Eisleben. He was stocky and tough, vigorous, coarse, and lusty, proudly calling himself "the son of a peasant" and writing for preference in an earthy German, though his Latin was also powerful. His shoulders were heavy with obstinacy, his eyes deep-set and confident. He had graduated from Erfurt with a degree in liberal arts in 1505. Later that year he was caught in the open during a severe thunderstorm and terrified by a flash of lightning. "Help me, St. Anne," he cried, "and I will become a monk." He did so, entering a monastery of the Augustinian friars. His friends, he recalled, "escorted me with tears in their eyes. My father was also very angry about my vow, but I persisted. I never thought that I would leave the cloister. I had died unto the world."[14] In fact, by 1510 he was visiting Rome. Like a "frantic saint," he wrote later, "I ran through all the churches and catacombs, and believed everything, their lies and falsehood." He was shocked by the city's godlessness and evil, and the speed with which priests raced through the mass; he "shuddered" to hear that some reviled the sacrament—"bread thou art and bread thou wilt remain"—before elevating it.

He was appointed professor of biblical studies at Wittenberg on his return and suffered a spiritual crisis. His life was earnest; he prayed, he fasted, he carried out penances and made lists of his sins. "And yet my conscience kept nagging," he wrote. "It kept telling me: 'You fell short there. . . . You were not sorry enough. . . . You left that sin off your list.'" He felt that he would never be redeemed, and it terrified him. He was trying to cure the pains of his soul with "human remedies, the traditions of men," and the harder he tried, the more troubled he became. He read Augustine and Paul continuously, and six words of Paul—"the righteous shall live by faith"—struck into his conscience "as flashes of lightning, frightening me each time I heard them . . ." As he meditated on them, the thought suddenly came into his mind that "if we as righteous are to live by faith, and if the righteousness of faith is to be for salvation to everyone who believes, then it is not our merit, but the mercy of God."[15] Man was too corrupt and vicious to save himself, Luther wrote, echoing Paul's claim that "all have sinned and fall short of the glory of the Lord" (Rom. 3:23). No penance, good works, fasting, pilgrimage, almsgiving, or indulgence-buying could redeem him. The grace of Christ was bestowed upon the soul through faith. Righteousness was not a function of behavior, but a gift promised by Christ to all who had faith in him. A Christian was justified *per solam fidem,* by faith alone. As he pondered this insight, Luther "felt as though I had been reborn altogether and had entered Paradise." In the same moment, he wrote, "The face of the whole of Scripture became apparent to me."

To Luther, Christian righteousness—"whatsoever things are true, whatsoever things are honourable . . . just . . . pure . . . lovely . . . of good report," Paul had described it to the Philippians; "if there be any virtue, and if there be any praise, think on these things" (Phil. 4:8)—flowed directly from God, without the priestly or institutional intercession of the Church. Paul had directly denied that the righteous were those who kept to the Mosaic Law. "By the works of the law shall no flesh be justified in his sight" (Rom. 3:20), he wrote; "I do not make void the grace of God: for if righteousness is through the law, then Christ died for nought" (Gal. 2:21). Salvation did not lie in being circumcised or eating the right food; it was attained through God's gift of Christ and the Cross. Luther was "quite sure" that the Church would never be reformed "unless we get rid of canon law . . ."

Luther did not think his ideology to be a giant departure, for he traced it

Martin Luther is seen here by Dürer in his room in the Wartburg as St. Jerome, the translator of the original Latin Vulgate Bible. The publication of Luther's German New Testament in September 1522 helped to embed the Reformation in Germany and inspired the translation of the Bible into English and other languages. Luther drew many ideas from Wycliffe, but the key dogma of justification by faith was his own.

back to the apostles and Augustine, and nor was it. In its religious essence, Luther's thought was orthodox enough when seen against the great radical heresies of the past. His mortal assault was on the Church itself. He rejected its "human remedies"; to him, the "traditions of men" that Nicholas had so praised were a thickening carapace that blocked out faith. He held that its inventions, greed, and immortality, its shameless abuse of papal authority through "the threat of the stake, and the shame of heresy," the "loose blabber" of its priests (*Resolutiones disputationum de indulgentiarum virtute*) all impeded the faithful from comprehending the visible and manifest things of God.

Many shared his contempt. "For some years before Luther," Roberto Bellarmine, a cardinal and a future saint, confessed, "there was in the Church almost no religion left." Erasmus mocked Church teaching that sins were washed away by a scrap of paper, a gift of money, a pilgrimage, a relic, or a wax image. He said that those who believed it were "utterly deceived." But devout Catholics were leery of anarchy—"no one has ever hated uproar more than I," Erasmus reassured Pope Leo—and stopped short of questioning the majesty of Rome.

❖ INDULGENCES WERE LUTHER'S first target. On October 31, 1517, he nailed ninety-five theses attacking the Tetzel indulgence to the door of the castle church at Wittenberg. He wrote that it was to "preach human doctrines" to claim that a soul flew from purgatory at the moment a coin fell into the coffer. Any

Christian, living or dead, participated in Christ's works; this was granted by God, not through a papal indulgence. He stressed that penance was not a sacrament that could be "administered by the ministry of priests" and that "the Pope cannot remit any guilt, except by stating and confirming that it has been remitted by God."

The theses caused a public sensation. "Nobody," Luther boasted, "will go to hear a lecture unless the lecturer is teaching my theology, which is the theology of the Bible, of St. Augustine, and of all true theologians of the Church." Many Germans resented the demands of distant Rome, and his arguments were taken as a direct attack on papal authority. Luther worried that this went too far—"the song was pitched in too high a key for my voice"—but he could do little to control it. Tetzel was threatened by angry mobs, and kept off the streets. If Archbishop Albert cared little for theological debate, he complained to the pope at the slump in sales of indulgences. Leo did no more than ask the Augustinian friars to rein in their meddlesome colleague.

It was a vain hope. Luther was a brilliant pampleteer—"I am hot-blooded by temperament," he wrote, "and my pen gets irritated easily"—and he had an eager audience. In April 1518 he defended himself at a disputation in Heidelberg; in the summer he was convicted of heresy in absentia at Rome. By October, Leo was alarmed enough to order Cardinal Cajetan, a Dominican theologian, to "prevent such a pest from growing strong and infecting the minds of the simple." Luther was summoned to appear before the cardinal at Augsburg. Luther noted that Cajetan was gracious—he was "in all respects different from those extremely harsh bloodhounds who track down monks among us"[16]—but he refused point blank to "come to my senses and retract my errors . . . and abstain from doing anything which might disturb the Church." Friends hurried him out of Augsburg to the safety of Wittenberg on the night of October 14. He published an account of his interview with the cardinal, adding a commentary that savaged the doctrinal basis of the Roman see and papal claims to divine primacy and infallibility. Another envoy, the nobleman Charles von Miltitz, was dispatched to see how the ground lay. Miltitz expected to find an aged divine mumbling to himself in a cozy corner; instead he was alarmed to find a man who was "young, strong and original," and so popular among the Germans that a papal army of twenty-five thousand would have found it difficult to remove him to Rome by force.

Luther was driven further into heresy over three weeks of public disputation at Leipzig with Johann Eck, a professor of theology and the most gifted controversialist of the day. The antagonists faced each other in pulpits in June 1519. Eck skillfully goaded Luther for many hours and then snared him; the works of Wycliffe and Hus served as the noose. "Among the condemned articles of John Hus and the Bohemians," Luther admitted, "there are many which are truly

Christian and evangelical and which the Catholic Church cannot condemn." There was uproar in the crowded hall. Leipzig was close to the Bohemian border, and "Hussite" was a local insult; Duke George of Saxony, the main notable present, roared: "A plague upon it!" Eck was gleeful. Luther had already denied the infallibility of the pope, and he now denied the judgment of the council that had condemned a heretic. Was nothing sacred to him? Eck wrote much of the inevitable papal bull that followed in June 1520. Titled *Exsurge Domine,* it condemned forty-one of Luther's propositions as heretical and ordered the faithful to burn all of his books and pamphlets. He was given two months to recant or be excommunicated. Eck found it difficult to publish the bull in Germany, so strong was popular support for Luther.

His defiance was public and well staged. At 9 A.M. on December 10, 1520, Luther ceremoniously burned the books of canon law, papal decretals, and a copy of the papal bull on a bonfire in the meadow that ran to the river Elbe from the walls of Wittenberg. He watched them turn to ashes and walked back into the town. A large crowd of students remained at the fire, staging a mock funeral for the bull. They marched through the streets with a brass band, collecting books by Eck, returning to the bonfire to burn them with a Te Deum. On January 3, 1521, Luther's excommunication became absolute. His "retraction" was savage theater. "I said [at Leipzig] that the Council of Constance condemned some propositions of Hus that were truly Christian," he wrote. "I retract. All his propositions were Christian, and in condemning them the Pope has condemned the Gospel."

Christendom was cracking. "All Germany is in revolution," a papal legate wrote. "Nine tenths shout 'Luther!' as their war-cry, and the other tenth cares nothing about Luther, and cries: 'Death to the court of Rome!'"[17] When peasants met a traveler on Saxon roads, they asked: "Are you for Martin?" If he was not, they beat him.

Barely three weeks later the young emperor Charles V opened his first imperial diet at Worms. Luther enjoyed the protection of the elector Frederick, who disliked Italian meddling in Germany and was proud of his new university and its professor; but the safe conduct the emperor promised him had not protected Hus at Constance. Charles had little admiration for Leo. He thought the pope shallow and vain, but his realms were flung across Europe—Naples and Spain, as well as Germany—and he could not sever relations with Rome. Luther refused to retract his assaults on the pope. "To go against the conscience is neither safe nor right," he said. "God help me. Amen."* He had expected the emperor to collect fifty doctors of divinity to confute him. "But all they said," he wrote to the artist

---

*Tradition has it that he added: "Here I stand. I can do no other." These words do not appear in contemporary accounts.

Cranach, "was: 'Are these books yours?' 'Yes.' 'Will you recant?' 'No.' 'Then get out!'"[18] Twenty days later, on May 14, 1521, the diet declared him outlawed as a "limb cut off from the Church of God."

Imperial subjects were commanded to safely take him prisoner, though they were free to attack his supporters and strip them of their property. The elector Frederick neither wished to see Luther burned nor himself accused of harboring a heretic. He thus stage-managed a fake kidnapping. Five horsemen surrounded Luther's cart as it passed through woods on its return from Worms; they seized him, books still in his arms, and spirited him off to the safety of the elector's Wartburg castle. "Some say I captured him, some say the archbishop of Mainz," the papal legate wrote. "I wish it were true!" A rumor was spread that Luther's mutilated body had been found down a mine shaft.

In fact, he was concealed in Wartburg, dressed as a country gentleman and addressed as Squire George. He suffered deep depressions; he imagined the cawing of the crows and rooks that gathered beyond his window to be the echoes of his soul; he was sleepless, hearing a devil crack walnuts on his ceiling in the darkness. Venturing out of the castle, he saw the hunt for hare and partridge as priests trapping the souls of the poor. He slowly recovered. He wrote a stream of pamphlets, an account of the relationship between grace and faith, and worked on a hymnal and a new liturgy. He condemned clerical celibacy and Communion in one kind. At Wittenberg, rioting students smashed an altar in the Franciscan church. On Christmas Day, 1521, Luther's colleague Carlstadt celebrated the Eucharist in German, the first reformer to do so. He wore no vestments but ordinary layman's clothes, abandoned the canon of the mass, and gave the congregation Communion in wine as well as bread. Side altars were removed and some statues and pictures were desecrated.

A Swiss printer, Johann Froben, wrote to Luther reporting heavy demand for his books from France, Spain, and Italy; he said this was because readers who studied the Scriptures had not before found "the same freedom that you show." "We have sold out all your books except ten copies," he reported, "and never remember to have sold any more quickly." Pamphlets and cartoons sold in huge numbers. The papal nuncio at Worms, Girolamo Aleander, complained in 1521 that people kissed a picture showing Luther, book in hand, with Ulrich von Hutten, the humanist and poet and ardent champion of Luther, in armor with sword in hand and the caption "Champions of Christian Liberty." The nuncio said that "such a quantity have been sold that I was not able to obtain one." Other cartoons showed Luther with Hus, "whom Luther has recently proclaimed his saint," and the pope and the cardinals being pinioned by soldiers.

The "Passional of Christ and Antichrist" of the same year showed Christ with a crown of thorns and the Antichrist Leo X in an emperor's crown; Christ washing his disciples' feet while the pope demands that his minions kiss his; Christ driving the money changers from the temple where the pope sells favors; Christ ascending to heaven while the pope tumbles to hell like a plump pigeon as demonic birds of prey feast on him. Aleander, a humanist scholar, had no illusions of the popularity of Luther and the contempt for the pope. "I cannot go out onto the streets but the Germans put their hands to their swords and gnash their teeth at me," he added fearfully. "I hope that the pope will give me a plenary indulgence and look after my brothers and sisters if anything happens to me."* At Nuremberg, Fra Ziana lamented that "in these parts the sincere faith of Christ is utterly canceled. No respect is paid either ot the Virgin Mary or the saints. On the contrary, it is said that those who employ their aid sin mortally. They deny the papal rights and call the relics of the saints bones of those who have been hanged. In Lent they eat meat openly. Confession is neglected, as they say it should be made to God. . . . They make a laughing-stock of the pope and the cardinals in pictures. . . . In short, they consider Martin their inspiration." He added grimly, and correctly, that "doubtless . . . as the princes and part of the nobility remain staunch Catholics, whilst the people persist in their errors, they will some day cut each other to pieces." At Magdeburg an old weaver came through the city gate offering printed hymns for sale and singing them. The burgomaster saw him when he returned from early mass; asking why there was a crowd of people, he was told that "an old scamp is singing and selling the hymns of the heretic Luther." He had the man arrested and thrown into prison, but a crowd of two hundred citizens demanded and got his release.

There was worse to follow. While Luther was in the Wartburg, he began to translate the New Testament into German. A new and individual faith was in the making, founded on belief in personal justification, and reached through the private reading of gospels laid bare in living languages.

*He survived to become a cardinal.

CHAPTER XVII

ThE WORÒ OF GOÒ:

The Bible as Lethal Weapon

ow excellent, perhaps, if the Bible had remained as it was, a priestly text submerged beneath centuries of tradition, lore, and law; if the Christian religion, which had come to mean the Church, had continued to be so; or if the heretic Marcion had succeeded fourteen hundred years before in restricting the Scriptures to the Gospel of Luke and the letters of Paul, purging them of Old Testament cruelties and grotesqueries that were now exhumed once more. As the Renaissance drew its inspiration and dynamic from the glories of the ancient world, however, the Reformation rediscovered the Bible.

Vernacular translations of the Bible were profoundly dangerous weapons. Read as it had never been before—by a mass audience, in their mother tongues, line by line, in its totality—its 774,746 words and 41,773 verses* could reveal all things to all men. The contradictions it contained had emerged long ago, of course. Matthew's gospel had been used by Augustine to sanction war, as we have seen, and by William of Tripoli to defend pacifism. But from the 1520s it passed beyond the realm of the scholar and the divine, and the implications of what was not in it—in particular the Church practices and privileges that were found to be blessed by custom but not directly by God—were as important as what was. "Luther's New Testament has been so widely spread by the book printers," the Catholic controversialist Johannes Cochlaeus complained, "that even the tailors

---

*As calculated by the nineteenth-century bibliographer Thomas Horne of the 1611 King James Version of the Bible[1] The Anglican Bible contained sixty-six books; many Protestant versions were shorter. The Roman Catholic version accepted at the Council of Trent in 1546 retains the Apocrypha and has seventy-three books, including Tobit, Judith, Sirach, Baruch, the letter of Jeremiah, and 1 and 2 Maccabees and the Wisdom of Solomon. The Greek Orthodox Bible has 1 Esdras, the Prayer of Manasseh, Psalm 151, and 3 Maccabees. The Ethiopic Church has the largest Bible, with thirty-five books in the New Testament instead of the normal twenty-seven, and a total of eighty-one books.

and shoemakers, and indeed women and simple idiots . . . read it as eagerly as if it were the fountain of all truth. . . ." That, indeed, was the rub. Ordinary men—worse, even "despicable women . . . proudly rejecting the supposed ignorance of men"—were looking to the Bible, and not to the Church, for evidence of God's purpose. "Some carried it in their bosoms and learnt it by heart," Cochlaeus reported with distaste. "Thus they claimed within a few months such skill and experience that without timidity they debated not only with Catholic laymen, but also with priests and monks."

They did so at great personal risk. A sad horror attached itself to the Bible, quoted by defendants and prosecutors alike with trusting self-assurance. A young Dutchman, Jan Claesz, and his fellow sectarian Lucas Lamberts, a man of eighty-seven, greeted each other with a cheerful kiss when they appeared in court at Amsterdam. They were Anabaptists, members of a new Bible-based sect accused of

A BOOKSELLER Burnt at AVIGNON, for selling Bibles in the French-Tongue, with some of them tied round his Neck.

A bookseller is burned at Avignon for selling Bibles in French, one of which is tied to his back as the flames engulf him. The Church feared that it would lose its monopoly of the Scriptures if they became available to the laity. All translations into living languages were therefore banned on pain of death. The problem for the Church was as much from the many things readers found not to be in the Bible—the papacy, the Church hierarchy, purgatory, indulgences, and much else—as from what did appear.

the heresy of adult rebaptism. "My dear brother, how do you feel?" Claesz asked the old man. "Quite well, my dear brother," he replied. Claesz said: "Fear neither fire nor the sword. Oh, what a joyful feat will be prepared for us before the clock strikes twelve!"

The court bailiff accused them: "You have been rebaptized."

Claesz answered: "I was baptized upon my faith, as all Christians ought to be, according to the Scriptures. Read this." He pointed to Matthew's gospel: "Go ye therefore, and make disciples of all the nations, baptizing them into the name of the Father and of the Son and of the Holy Spirit" (Matt. 28:19).

"You belong to the accursed Anabaptists," the bailiff responded, "who originate strange sects, opinions and errors and contention among the people." The official referred to two passages in Acts: "These men, being Jews, do exceedingly trouble our city, and set forth customs which it is not lawful for us to receive. . . ." (Acts 16:20–21) and "These that have turned the world upside down are come hither. . . ." (Acts 17:6).

Claesz and old Lamberts defended themselves with the Bible, but were convicted by the same Bible, to "be executed with the sword, the body to be placed on the wheel, and the head upon a stake . . ."

It may seem that such dreadful events are devalued by repetition, and that it is malevolent in itself to dwell on the atrocities to which Western believers now subjected each other. But they are part of the essence of the Reformation. "You citizens bear witness," Jan Claesz said as he was led from court, "that we die for no other reason than for the true Word of God." The victims believed in the Resurrection and in Pentecost. Like the early martyrs, they believed that eternal life lay beyond their premature deaths, and that the Holy Spirit had touched them with truth. So did those who condemned them.

✢   "WHAT ARE THESE new doctrines? The gospel?" remarked the Lutheran moderate Philip Melanchthon. "Why, that is 1,522 years old." But the Bible was ancient only in a technical sense. Its impact now, particularly in vernacular translation, was almost wholly new; troubling, a cause of spiritual collapse and ecstasy, a divider of families, a breaker of kingdoms. "We will try everything by the touchstone of the gospel," Melanchthon added, "and the fire of Paul"; in that light, the Bible became a force with the power of Revelation, and serving Catholic priests lost their faith simply by reading it.

Menno Simons was a twenty-eight-year-old priest in his home village of Pingjum in Holland in 1524. His pastor, an educated older man, had read the Scriptures "a little," and Simons himself claimed "I had never touched them." After three years handling the bread and wine in the Mass, Simons had the troubling notion that they were not the flesh and blood of Christ. He attributed this to the devil trying to separate him from his faith. "I confessed it often, sighed, and prayed," he wrote, "yet I could not come clear of the ideas."[2] He spent his time drinking, playing cards, and brooding. "Finally, I got the idea to examine the New Testament diligently," he said. "I had not gone very far when I discovered that we were deceived. . . ."

He was "quickly relieved" to find that his doubts over the bread and wine were justified, finding no evidence that they were anything but mere symbols of Christ's passion. He heard that an Anabaptist, rejecting infant baptism, had been beheaded at Leeuwarden for being rebaptized as an adult. "I examined the scriptures diligently and pondered them earnestly," Simons wrote, "but could find no report of infant baptism." He realized that his new beliefs on baptism and the sacraments now made him a heretic in the eyes of his Church. He had become so, he wrote, "through the illumination of the Holy Spirit, through much reading and pondering of the scriptures, and by the gracious favour and gift of God. . . ." The experience was as overwhelming as Augustine's eleven hundred years before. Simons abandoned the lusts of his youth and his search for "gain, ease, fame and the favour of men"; he was a hunted fugitive until his death. He thought it a bargain, for "if I should gain the whole world and live a thousand years, and at last have to endure the wrath of God, what would I have gained?"*

Clerical conservatives like Cochlaeus tried to staunch the flow of Scripture. When the English reformer William Tyndale discussed a fresh Bible translation in 1522, to be taken directly from the original Hebrew and Greek rather than the Vulgate, the bishop of London† banned the project. Tyndale was a determined man. "I defy the pope and all his laws," he said in dispute with a fellow scholar. "If God spare my life, ere many years I will cause a boy that driveth a plough shall know more of the Scripture than thou dost." Tyndale fled England for Germany in 1524, never to return. He quickly completed his translation of the New Testament and arranged for it to be printed at Cologne. Cochlaeus and others pres-

---

*Menno Simons's followers, Mennonites, survive. Almost 450 years later, communities of more than 850,000 Mennonites[3] are scattered from the United States, Canada, and Mexico to Germany, the Netherlands, the former Soviet Union, and Zaire, India, and Indonesia.

†Cuthbert Tunstall. His own career shows the violent strains that the Reformation placed on churchmen. A Catholic sympathizer, Henry VIII nevertheless made him bishop of Durham in 1530. Despite this, and his opposition to Tyndale, he submitted to royal supremacy and helped in the preparation of the English-language Great Bible of 1538. He voted against the act permitting the marriage of priests in 1541, however, and was imprisoned in London. In 1552 he was tried for high treason and deprived of his bishopric; he was reinstated by the Catholic Queen Mary in 1554, but refused to take the Oath of Supremacy under the Protestant Queen Elizabeth in 1559, and died a prisoner a few months later.

The Four Horsemen of the Apocalypse portrayed by Dürer. German peasants began a series of apocalyptic risings in 1524, butchering those in authority as "God's jailers and hangmen." After seeming to support them, Luther turned against them and urged the princes to "stab, smite and slay all you can." Near Frankenhausen, a peasant army sang, "Now we pray the Holy Spirit" as artillery and cavalry ravaged them. They neither resisted nor fled, but stood still in a divine coma "as if they were insane."

sured local magistrates to prevent a full production run, but Tyndale transferred the printing contract to Worms. The first printed copies reached London in March 1526 but they were banned, and the copies that were seized were burned at St. Paul's Cross in October on the orders of the bishop of London. Tyndale was hunted in Germany and the Low Countries for the rest of his life.

It was impossible to destroy his work. The vigor of his English prose gave it living warmth and appeal, and fed a sense of a national and English Christianity far removed from Latin and Rome. Luther, too, was keen to make the Bible as German as possible, visiting an abattoir to get German terms from the slaughterers and rummaging through the elector Frederick's jewel boxes for the same purpose. "I aimed to make Moses so German that no one would suspect that he was a Jew," his friend Albrecht Dürer said of the woodcuts used to illustrate the new Bibles.

Copies of Tyndale's Bibles were concealed under ships' cargoes and smuggled into England.* Betrayed in Antwerp, he was first strangled and then burned at the stake near Brussels on October 16, 1536. Two years after his death the tide

---

*Tyndale's translation remained the basis of the English Bible through to the Revised Version of 1881 and the American Standard Version of 1901.

turned. Henry VIII determined that his subjects should be able to "perceive the great and ineffable Omnipotent Power" in their own tongue. A royal proclamation ordered Bibles to be placed in parish churches.

An account survives of the immense impression this novelty made on a young Englishman, and the shock to the older generation. At Chelmsford in Essex, a lad of fifteen listened spellbound to the "sweet and glad tidings of the Gospel" being read aloud in English until his father forbade it and told him to restrict himself to the Latin Mass. He rebelled and became determined to learn to read English for himself. "When he had by diligence effected this," a chronicler recorded, "he and his father's apprentice bought the New Testament, joining their stocks together, and to conceal it laid it under the bedstraw, and read it at convenient times." He discussed what he had found in it with his mother one evening when his father was asleep. He mocked the reverence that his elders displayed to the cross, kneeling before it in church, raising hands towards it when it passed in procession. This was "plain idolatry," he claimed, "and against the commandment of God, when he saith, 'Thou shalt not make any graven image, nor bow down to it, nor worship it.'" His mother was enraged, crying: "Wilt thou not worship his cross, which was about thee when thou wast christened, and must be laid on thee when thou art dead?" She awoke her husband, who, "boiling in fury against his son for denying worship due to the cross," at once burst into his son's room and whipped him unmercifully. The young man related that he bore the beating "with a kind of joy, considering it was for Christ's sake, and shed not a tear." This maddened his father yet more. He raced downstairs and fetched a halter, putting it round his son's neck and saying he would hang him. At length, "with much entreaty of the mother and brother," he left him almost dead.[4]

❧ THE TRADITION OF preaching a sermon on a text gave the single biblical verse, or part of a verse, an extraordinary power. Christians were used to lengthy diatribes being hung on the briefest piece of Scripture. One phrase—"the righteous shall live by faith" (Gal. 3:11)—is at the heart of Lutheranism; another—"there was the true light, even the light which lighteth every man, coming into the world" (John 1:9)—among the Quakers. A line could acquire an intense ferocity. Ten words from Exodus—"Who made thee a prince and a judge over us?" (Exod. 2:14)—were used to justify rejection of the papacy, the massacres of German noblemen, and peasant uprisings.

At first, protagonists used chapter references to bludgeon each other. The German reformer Thomas Müntzer wrote to the princes on the eve of battle that "God spoke of you and yours in . . . Micah 3,"[5] leaving it to them to work out that they were "rulers . . . who hate the good, and love the evil . . . who eat the flesh of my people; and they flay their skin from off them, and break their bones . . . therefore it shall be night unto you, that ye shall have no vision. . . ." (Mic. 3:1–6). Later, after the introduction of numbered verses by the printer Robert Stephanus at Geneva in 1551, the process was refined so that a specific verse could be used as ammunition.

Each copy of the Bible offered a baffling array of wildly conflicting truths on issues both grand and intimate. Extreme Anabaptists declared that the Bible justifies polygamy. In Genesis, the childless Sara "took Hagar the Egyptian, her handmaid . . . and gave her to Abram her husband to be his wife" (Gen. 15:3), an arrangement that so pleased God that he sent an angel to tell Hagar that "I will greatly multiply thy seed" (Gen. 15:10). As those who burned Anabaptists hastened to point out, however, it also condemns polygamy; in Mark's gospel, Jesus said "a man . . . shall cleave to his wife" (Mark 10:6). Divorce is permitted in Deuteronomy: "When a man taketh a wife, and marrieth her," Deuteronomy states, "then it shall be, if she find no favour in his eyes, because he hath found some unseemly thing in her, that he shall write her a bill of divorcement . . . and send her out of his house" (Deut. 24:1). Matthew's gospel forbids it: "What therefore God has put together," Matthew's gospel says, "let no man put asunder" (Matt. 19:6).

Clarity was also lacking in the lethal areas of social order, liberty, and authority. Paul's letter to the Galatians promised the Christian freedom from serfdom and oppression: "So that thou art no longer a bondservant, but a son; and if a son, then an heir through God" (Gal. 4:7). His letter to the Colossians insists upon servile obedience: "Servants, obey in all things them that are your masters" (Col. 3:22). The book of Kings encourages nonpayment of taxes: "Then king Rehoboam sent Adoram, who was over the levy; and all Israel stoned him with stones, that he died. And king Rehoboam made speed to get him up to his chariot, to flee. . . ." (1 Kings 12:18). Matthew's gospel says that they must be paid: "Render therefore unto Caesar the things that are Caesar's" (Matt. 22:21). Bloody rebellion against unjust rulers is incited in Kings: "Thou shalt smite the house of Ahab thy master, that I may avenge the blood of my servants the prophets, and the blood of all the servants of the Lord . . . for the whole house of Ahab shall perish" (2 Kings 9:7–8). Romans preached submission to them: "Let every soul be in subjection to the higher powers; for there is no power but of God; and the powers that be are ordained of God" (Rom. 13:1). Most unsettling of all, at a time of flux when many fevered souls felt close to the Holy Spirit, was the catchall freedom in Acts to do as one's conscience dictated: "Peter and the apostles answered and said, We must obey God rather than man" (Acts 5:29).

Tensions were thrown up by biblical voids. Many traditions were so hallowed by time—papal authority, celibate priests, transubstantiation, infant baptism,

Masses for the dead, the canonization of saints, the impossibility of salvation outside the Roman Church—that it was assumed that they were in the Scriptures. Readers like Menno Simons were deeply shocked to find that they were not. The Englishman Simon Fish, writing in 1529, pointed out of purgatory: "There is not one word spoken of it in all holy Scripture, and also if the pope with his pardons may for money deliver one soul hence, he may deliver him as well without money: if he may deliver one, he may deliver a thousand: if he may deliver a thousand, he may deliver them all; and so destroy purgatory: and then he is a cruel tyrant, without all charity, if he keep them there in prison and in pain, till men will give him money."[6]

Luther was meticulous in stripping Rome of biblical pretensions and in claiming that his own thought was based wholly on the Scriptures. "My conscience is captive to the word of God," he claimed. "I only wrote, preached and used God's word, and nothing else. I did nothing but only let the Word act." But he, too, played with the Bible. He added a vital word to Paul—"alone"—to claim that "The just shall be saved by faith alone." Furthermore, Paul was directly contradicted in the Epistle of James: "What doth it profit, my brethren, if a man say he hath faith, but have not works? can that faith save him? If a brother or sister be naked, and in lack of daily food, And one of you say unto them, Go in peace, be ye warmed and filled; and yet ye give them not the things needful to the body; what doth it profit? Even so faith, if it hath not works, is dead in itself." (James 2:14–17). Luther disposed of this embarrassment by attacking the letter of James as being an "epistle of straw"[7] which was "Jewish" in its reliance on good deeds and the fulfillment of the Mosaic Law.

❖ ONE LINE WAS inconvenient to reformers and loyalists alike: "Thou shalt not kill" (Matt. 5:21). Many found a verse from Daniel more appealing than the pacifism of the Sermon on the Mount: "if ye worship not," it said, which they took to include not worshipping in the correct way, "ye shall be cast the same hour into the midst of a burning fiery furnace" (Dan. 3:15).

Politics was inseparable from the spiritual. Luther's attack on the papacy had immense temporal as well as moral and biblical implications. In 1518 he had opened a letter to Leo X with traditional subservience: "I prostrate myself before your Holiness and dedicate myself to you." Four years later, describing Leo as "that man of sin and perdition," he warned the pope that the Roman see "is more scandalous and shameful than any Sodom or Babylon . . . its wickedness is beyond all counsel and help . . . under your name the poor people in the world are cheated and injured."

His political ideology stirred rebellion, but its basis was deeply conservative.

It centered on the right of the "worldly ruler" to demand obedience and the duty of the Christian to obey. "You must render obedience to the powers that be, and sustain the authority of His Imperial Majesty with all your might," he wrote to the elector Frederick in 1522, "and not oppose the authorities in the event of their imprisoning or slaying me. For no one must oppose the authorities except He who has instituted them; for it is rebellion against God." He warned that "turbulence has never had a good end," and that to seize the riches of a ruler, no matter how unjust he might be, was "nothing but theft and highway robbery."[8]

The radical departure was the denial that the pope and the Church were in any sense a part of worldly rule. Much of the spadework had already been done for Luther. The Donation of Constantine, a basis for the papacy's temporal claims supposedly dating back to March 315, had been shown to be a forgery eighty years before.* It described how Constantine, suffering from acute leprosy, was healed when Pope Sylvester baptized him. "When I was at the bottom of the font," the document cited Constantine, "I saw a hand from heaven touching me." In gratitude, the emperor wrote that "the sacred See of Blessed Peter shall be exalted even above our Empire and earthly throne," granting the pope rule over the sees of Antioch, Alexandria, Constantinople, and Jerusalem." This had become somewhat of a technicality after their fall to Islam, but Constantine also granted the pope power "over all the churches of God in the world," and commanded that he should enjoy "all the prerogatives of our supreme imperial position and the glory of our authority." The classical scholar Lorenzo Valla demolished the story of the Donation in 1440. He pointed out that Constantinople did not exist in 315, but was still the insignificant town of Byzantium, and that the document was written in the bastardized Latin of the eighth century, not the eloquent language of the fourth. Valla added that the forged claims of worldly power had a ruinous effect on popes. "So far from giving food and bread to the household of God," he wrote, "they have devoured us as food . . . the

---

*It was concocted in about 754, when the papal lands around Rome were threatened by the Lombard incursions from northern Italy. Pope Stephen II traveled to Gaul to seek the help of Pepin the Short, the king of the Franks and father of Charlemagne; dressed in black, ashes in his hair, the pope begged the king in January 754 to defend the papacy in return for recognition as the "patrician of the Romans" and a solemn religious vow binding the Franks to his dynasty. Pepin marched into Italy, crushed the Lombards, and handed the exarchate of Ravenna, Emilia Province, and the duchies of the Pentapolis and Rome to the pope. Pepin's donation created a papal state that survived for more than a millennium. It had a flaw, however; Pepin had seized the territories by force of arms and without reference to the emperor at Constantinople. The papacy thus predated its legitimacy as landlord and as supreme Church authority by fabricating a donation from Constantine himself and dating it March 30, 315. It elaborated that pagan priests told Constantine that he would be cured by bathing in a pool filled with the blood of small children. The emperor refused out of pity for the young. In a vision, Peter and Paul told him to find Pope Sylvester, then hiding in the mountains, who would reveal to him the true "pool of piety"; in return, the emperor must restore the Church and worship God.

Pope himself makes war on peaceable people, and sows discord among states and princes."⁹

Luther's proclamation of the power of kings and princes to rule without the trammel of clerical competition had been anticipated two centuries before. Marsiglio of Padua, a scholar and medical practitioner who became rector of the University of Paris, had argued against the temporal power of the clergy and the pope in his work *Defensor Pacis*. Marsiglio believed that the state was the great unifying engine of society and that the Church was inferior to it. The authority of the state was drawn from the people, who had the right to depose an unjust ruler. The Church had no such authority, whether spiritual or temporal, and whatever rights and property it enjoyed could be withdrawn by the state. The hierarchy of the Church was not divinely sanctioned but was a human invention, and the pope should be elected and deposed at the pleasure of the emperor. Clerics should have no special privileges over laymen, Marsiglio wrote, for "all Christ's faithful are churchmen." He believed that the papacy should be subordinate to general councils, which should include laymen as well as priests.* Marsiglio was excommunicated for his pains in 1327, and so was the English philosopher William of Ockham, who maintained that Christ was the sole head of the Church and that the papacy had no legitimate civil authority.

A king had reason to pause before breaking with Rome. The fiscal advantages had to be weighed against the dangers of unrest. In terms of political power, the French had already won major concessions from Leo X. The petty rulers of Germany—princes, bishops, nobility, city magistrates—had fewer constraints. Princes of independent mind, like Luther's protector Frederick, were immediately attracted by his preaching. It prevented the outflow of money to Rome, and it confirmed that they were masters of all matters temporal in their own house, feeding their subjects' prejudices against a grasping clergy controlled by a foreign pope.

No ruler, however, and few others with a stake in society would have supported Luther had he been shown to share the anarchic seed of the drummer of Niklashausen. Irrespective of the forgery, Constantine had indeed donated land

---

*An attempt to put Marsiglio's ideas into practice by his protector, Louis of Bavaria, failed. Louis seized Rome in 1328 and was crowned Roman emperor; with Pope John XXII absent in Avignon, Louis appointed an antipope, Nicholas V, and made Marsiglio his imperial vicar. Marsiglio was excommunicated, and his book anathematized by Pope John XXII in 1327; but Nicholas V soon submitted to John, and Marsiglio retreated to spend the rest of his life at Louis's court at Munich. William of Ockham, an Oxford philosopher, was also excommunicated by John XXII after upholding apostolic poverty in the Franciscan debate, and sought protection with Louis. He wrote several bitter polemics against papal claims to secular authority; he was expelled from the Franciscan order and sentenced to perpetual imprisonment in absentia. His use of "Ockham's Razor," the principle that entities must not be multiplied beyond necessity, did much to advance formal logic in theology. Luther acknowledged Ockham's influence; he may not have read Marsiglio.

and buildings to the Church. He did so—at least partly, or so it seems safe to assume—because Christianity provided social stability. The critical issue for Luther was whether he would render unto the modern Caesars the powers they regarded as their own. Had he not, his variant of the faith would not have entered the mainstream.

His wilder contemporaries were destroyed. Among them were the peasants of southern Germany. Deprived, bitter at those who taxed them, whether lord or cleric, led by disbanded soldiers and ruined knights, they began a series of apocalyptic risings in 1524. Their emblem was a shoe; their demands, like those of the drummer, included justice, freedom from oppressive landlords, and the right to hunt and fish where they wished and to choose their own pastors. They aped Luther's attacks on the pope—now Clement VII, nephew of Leo X and bastard son of Giuliano de' Medici, pious and hardworking enough, but softly complacent—and his pamphleteering skills. A tract addressed to the "Common Peasantry" printed at Nuremberg showed the pope bound to a spinning wheel, with an infantry formation of peasants on the left and a cavalry unit of princes and prelates on the right. "Now is the hour and time of the wheel of fortune," the caption ran. "God knows who will remain on top." It echoed Luther in saying that, without authority, the "hairy worm" of unrestrained human nature would tear itself to pieces like a mad dog. "Thus both great need and divine commandment compel us to be obedient to authorities," it said. "In truth, disobedience is hated by God to the highest degree." But it went on to argue that the lords had forfeited their right to rule, for utter obedience was nothing but "a disguised straw doll, with which the lords have long played their carnival games." Its anonymous author had read his Bible well. He used Paul to attack serfdom—"Here is neither lord nor servant. . . . We are all one in Christ" (Gal. 3:28)—and to put the rebels above the law. "Law is not made for a righteous man," he quoted Paul again, "but for the lawless and ungodly" (1 Tim. 1:9). A sweeping claim followed: "True Christian faith needs no human authority. . . ."

This was religious anarchy, and Luther was at first ambivalent. He dismissed "these drunken and mad princes" as being no more than "God's gaolers and hangmen," and savaged "you blind bishops and mad priests and monks, whose hearts are hardened . . . you do nothing but flay and rob your subjects." He warned them that it was not the peasants who were rebelling; "it is God Himself who is resisting you in order to visit your raging upon you. . . ." At the same time he advised the peasants that vengeance was the prerogative of God, not man. In a pamphlet addressed to both rulers and peasants, he told them to make peace, "because both of you are wrong . . . and God will use one knave to flog another." He went round country districts, at huge risk since he was an outlaw, preaching: "I do not want to struggle for the Gospel by violence and murder." Germany, he said, "will be laid waste; and if this bloodshed once starts, it will scarcely cease until everything is destroyed . . ."[10]

❖ ON APRIL 17, 1525, to the sound of pipes, peasants speared eighteen knights to death at Weinsberg, and the count of Helfenstein was slain in front of his wife and child. Luther swung irrevocably and pitilessly in favor of the social status quo. In a tract "Against the Murdering Thieving Hordes of Peasants," he urged the princes to spare innocents, "but the wicked, stab, smite and slay all you can. These times are so extraordinary that a prince can win heaven more easily by bloodshed than by prayer."

They needed little prompting. The Bavarian chancellor reported on May 27 that Duke Anthony of Lorraine alone had already killed 20,000 peasants in Alsace; the figure of dead for Germany as a whole was put at 100,000. The ferocity of repression was tempered only by the realization that wholesale slaughter would leave nobody to work the fields. "If all the peasants are killed," the margrave George wrote to his brother Casimir, "where shall we get other peasants to make provisions for us?"[11] Casimir nonetheless put out the eyes of fifty-nine townsfolk at Kutzingen near Würzburg and threatened any who helped them with the same fate.

Some held that Luther had incited the violence. If their motivation was their own, the rebels certainly traded on his popularity and the fervid spirit he had aroused. He denied it. "Some of you are beginning to blame this affair on the Gospel and say it is the fruit of my teaching," he wrote. "Well, well! Slander away, dear lords. . . . I have taught with all quietness, have diligently exhorted subjects to obedience and reverence. . . . This rebellion cannot be coming from me."[12]

He took great pains to establish that Lutheran "quietness." A Christian must "suffer wrong and endure evil," he said. "There is no other way." Rebellion was contrary not only to Christian law and the gospel, but also to natural law and equity. His detailed examination of peasant claims was deeply reassuring to the powers that be. The notion that a community should have the power to choose its pastor was correct "only in a Christian sense." The ruler should first be "humbly" asked to supply a pastor, and only if he was unwilling could the community choose its own, and at its own expense. Luther ruled that the demand for tithes to be shared between the pastor and the poor "is nothing but theft and highway robbery."

Equality had no part in his faith. He mocked the demand that "There shall be no serfs, for Christ made all men free." He retorted that this made Christian liberty "an utterly carnal thing. Did not Abraham and other patriarchs and prophets have slaves? Read what St. Paul teaches about servants, who, at that time, were all slaves. Therefore this article is dead against the gospel. It is a piece of robbery by which every man takes from his lord the body, which has become the lord's property." A slave can be a Christian and have Christian liberty, in the same way that prisoners or the sick are Christian and yet are not free. To make all men equal would turn Christ's spiritual kingdom into a worldly kingdom, and that is impossible. "For a worldly kingdom cannot stand unless there is in it an inequality of persons," he continued, "so that some are free, some imprisoned, some lords, some subjects, etc; and St. Paul says in Gal. 5, that in Christ master and servants are one thing." As to the other peasant articles—on freedom of game, birds, fish, wood, forests, on services, tithes, imposts, excises—"these I leave to the lawyers, for it is not fitting that I, an evangelist, should judge or decide them."[13]

Others did not share this deference. Luther, however earthy and at home in country inns, was deeply shocked when peasant followers of his colleague Andreas Carlstadt at Orlamünde addressed him in the familiar "Du."

A starker warning of the Reformation's capacity to loose the explosive elements of the faith—martyrdom and salvation through suffering, miracles, the gift of the Holy Spirit and the superiority of the elect, new sects and heresies, apocalypse from Revelation in the New Testament, bloodlust from Kings in the Old—came from another of Luther's ex-associates. Thomas Müntzer was born five or six years after Luther. He studied at Frankfurt an der Oder, learning Greek and Hebrew, reading Eusebius and the medieval mystics. He served as a chantry priest at Brunswick before attending lectures at Wittenberg and falling under Luther's influence. Probably on Luther's recommendation, he became preacher in 1520 at Zwickau, a silver-mining town close to the Bohemian border. Here he was exposed to the Taborite views of a weaver named Niklas Storch, who claimed that God was again in direct touch with his elect and that the Last Days were imminent. The Turks would conquer the world and the Antichrist would reign before the elect initiated the Second Coming by slaughtering the godless.

Müntzer was expelled from Zwickau in 1521 for denouncing local Franciscans and burghers, and moved to Prague. He elaborated his concept of the elect as those who received the Holy Spirit in the form of what he called "the living Christ," the spiritual Savior who is born in the soul of the individual through sufferings of mind and body. These "elect friends of God's Word," he said, would learn to prophesy as Paul had taught. God would talk to them in a "friendly, indeed intimate way" and enable them to do "marvellous things." He claimed that this would happen in Prague, for "here the new Church will arise and [the elect] will be a reflection of the entire world."[14] This new church, made up of the elect and in direct contact with God, would destroy the "priests and monkeys" of the old. "Harvest time is here, so God himself has hired me for his harvest," Müntzer said with joyful anticipation. "I have sharpened my scythe, for my thoughts are most strongly fixed on the truth, and my lips, hands, skin, hair, soul, body, life curse the unbelievers."[15]

He was thrown out of Prague and roamed through Germany, in poverty and obscurity, signing himself "God's messenger." Müntzer rejoiced in his hardships, believing that "the living God is sharpening his scythe in me, so that later I can cut down the red poppies and the blue cornflowers." A pamphlet mocking him said that he thought piety to mean that "the body must be castigated and martyred with fasting and poor clothing." It added a classic description of a puritan—"one should talk little, look sour, and not cut off one's beard."[16] At Easter, 1523 he became the pastor of Allstedt, a small Saxon town. He composed the first liturgies in German and translated Latin hymns into the vernacular, and his reputation spread through central Germany. Copper miners from Mansfeld and the poor of Allstadt became the nucleus of a bund, or covenant of the elect, based on the Old Testament: "and the king stood by the pillar, and made a covenant before the Lord, to walk after the Lord, and to keep his commandments, with all his heart, and all his soul . . . and all the people stood to the covenant" (2 Kings 23:3). He started a pamphlet war against Luther, describing his former mentor as "the Pope of Wittenberg . . . the unspiritual soft-living flesh at Wittenberg . . . Dr Sit-on-the-Fence." Luther returned the compliment, calling Müntzer the "Satan of Allstedt."

The duke visited Allstedt in July 1524 and ordered Müntzer to preach a sermon to him. The pastor chose the Book of Daniel as his text, warning of apocalypse and calling on the Saxon princes to decide whether to serve God or the devil, for priests and monks and godless rulers would all perish; "the sword is necessary to exterminate them . . . for the ungodly have no right to live, save what the Elect choose to allow them. . . ."[17] Duke John and the princes were unmoved. At the end of July, Müntzer announced that the time of the destruction of tyrants and the messianic kingdom had come. He was summoned to Weimar to explain himself, but instead sent a pamphlet accusing the princes of "bestial eating and drinking . . . the powerful, self-willed unbelievers must be put down from their seats." In his turn, Luther advised the rulers that Satan himself had set up a "nest" at Allstedt. In August, feeling vulnerable at Allstedt, Müntzer slipped over the town walls at night and made his way to the free imperial city of Mühlhausen.

A red crucifix and a naked sword were carried in front of him when he strode round the city with a band of armed supporters. His talk was openly populist now; he spoke of lords stealing all creatures as their property; "the fish in the water, the birds in the air, the plants on the ground have all got to be theirs . . . they oppress all people, and shear and shave the poor ploughman and everything that lives." He mined the Old Testament for justification, casting himself as Jehu, the triumphant leader of revolt who had seized the throne of Israel, trampling Jezebel herself, the queen-whore and worshiper of Baal, beneath the hooves of his horse, so that when they went to bury her, "they found no more of her than the skull, and the feet, and the palms of her hand" (2 Kings 9:35).

Müntzer was duly expelled from Mühlhausen and wandered through southern Germany, but he was back in the city when revolt broke out in March 1525. The rising had secular motives; German taxes were rising as the princes consolidated their principalities, Roman law was replacing traditional customs, and ancient liberties were being crushed by absolutism. The main struggles were in the south, where the peasants were best organized. Elsewhere, smaller bands looted and burned convents and other soft targets. Müntzer hung a white banner with a rainbow on it in his church at Mühlhausen as a sign of the elect's covenant with God.

It was a matter of faith that the elect should have no truck with compassion. In fact, it was their duty to act as God's butchers, for "a godless man has no right to live if he hinders the godly." They were the midwives of the millennium, whose birth God had ordained to be bloody. "Now go at them, and at them, and at them!" Müntzer urged his flock. "It is time. The scoundrels are as dispirited as dogs. . . . Take no notice of the lamentations of the godless! They will beg you in such a friendly way, and whine and cry like children. Don't be moved to pity. . . ."

Landgrave Philip of Hesse marched into Thuringia and struck towards Mühlhausen. Some eight thousand peasants assembled in a camp at Frankenhausen and asked Müntzer to save them. He arrived in the camp on May 11 with three hundred supporters. The next day he wrote a letter to Count Ernst of Mansfeld claiming, with the supernatural confidence of the elect, that his enemies would be "torn out and destroyed" because this was God's intention. "You have undertaken to destroy the Christians," he warned the count. "Tell me, you miserable, shabby bag of worms, who has made you a ruler of the people whom God has redeemed with his precious blood? . . . The eternal, living God has commanded that you be pushed from your chair with the power that is given us. You are unprofitable to Christendom. You are a pernicious sweeping-brush of the friends of God. . . ." He signed the letter: "Thomas Müntzer with the sword of Gideon."[18]

If these seem the rantings of a lunatic, it should be noted that the other side—made up of eminently sane and indeed relatively tolerant princes—responded in kind. They, too, claimed to be acting directly for God. "As those whom God has given the sword," they replied, "we are here assembled to punish you as blasphemers of God." They were careful to accuse Müntzer not of temporal revolt, but of being the "perverter of the Gospel" who was proceeding, not against themselves, but "against our Redeemer Jesus Christ with murder, fire and other disrespect of God . . ." They offered—"out of Christian love"—to spare the peasants provided that "you turn over to us alive the false prophet Thomas Müntzer and his associates . . ."[19] Müntzer spoke of a victory ordained by God and promised that he "would catch all the bullets in his coat sleeves"* and a rainbow appeared and seemed proof of a coming miracle. He was not handed over.

Philip of Hesse had artillery pieces and two thousand cavalry on a strategic hilltop. The peasants were in a divine coma as the guns opened fire and the cavalry advanced. A chronicler recorded that they sang "Now We Pray the Holy Spirit." They neither resisted nor fled, but stood still "as if they were insane." Some five thousand were slaughtered for the loss of a half dozen princes' men. After the battle, the latter broke into the village, beheading some three hundred men they found there. Müntzer hid himself in the attic of a house near the gate. At length he was identified. Shortly before his death he signed a confession and recantation. He said that he had entered into "wicked and wanton insurrection" and that he had preached "folly and errors"; he now wished to die "as a true and reconciled member of [the] Church, asking it . . . to pray to God for him and to forgive him."[20] This saved him from being burned and meant that his wife and child received his belongings. He was beheaded in the camp of the princes on May 27, 1525, and his head was put on a lance and "placed in a field as a memorial."

"keep watch over the Lives of everyone . . .":

Calvin and the Puritans

The word "Protestant" was coined in 1529. It was used to describe the five Lutheran princes and fourteen cities that signed a "Protestatio" opposing the Catholic majority at the Diet of Speyer in Germany. The Catholics voted to end the toleration of Lutherans in their territories, but the Protestants refused to accept a decision that touched upon "God's honour and salvation and the eternal life of our souls." The term was well chosen. Protestants had other common characteristics—justification by faith, the spiritual involvement of the laity—but protest was fundamental.

All Protestants claimed to draw their faith from the Bible, but it did not unite them. Scriptural debates combined with individual jealousies to divide them, and their protests were aimed as eagerly at each other as at Catholics. Luther's old colleague Andreas Carlstadt was an example. Carlstadt had presided at Luther's doctoral graduation at Wittenberg. The two men had taught together at the university, and Carlstadt had supported the assault on the papacy and suffered excommunication in 1520. He led, and Luther followed, on several issues. It was he, not Luther, who had first celebrated the Eucharist in the vernacular and without vestments at Christmas, 1521; Luther did not abandon his Augustinian habit until 1525. Carlstadt married in 1522, three years before Luther was wed to Katherine von Bora, a former Cistercian nun. Luther's hostility to his radical ideas drove Carlstadt from Wittenberg to become a preacher at Orlamünde, where he refused to baptize infants and said that the Eucharist was no more than a memorial of Christ's Passion. In 1529 he fled to Switzerland with Luther's taunts of "lunatic" ringing in his ears.

The same year, an attempt was made to reconcile Luther with the second great reformer, the Swiss Huldrych Zwingli, at a meeting in Marburg. "I think God has blinded their eyes," Luther wrote contemptuously of the Swiss, refusing

Zwingli a fraternal embrace at the end of their colloquy. For his part, Zwingli complained that the Lutherans "glided around in all sorts of escapes and subterfuges" while their leader "made utterly foolish statements."[1]

The two men were born, and were married, within a few months of each other; they were German speakers, and were ordained as Catholic priests; they rounded on the old Church independently, but for the same reasons; both were powerful and commanding figures, and each believed that he could "interpret the entire Gospel . . . according to divine truth and not human vanity." The words were Zwingli's, but Luther made the same claim, and in that individual certainty—and in individual style, Zwingli cool and radical, Luther zealous and profound—the seeds of their rift were sown.

As a young chaplain, Zwingli had served with Swiss mercenaries in Italy. He "preached frequently in the army camp," acquiring a distaste for foreign intervention that underpinned the desire for self-reliance that marked many Protestant congregations. His early heroes were humanists; "I can glory in nothing less than having seen Erasmus," he wrote after seeing the great man in 1516. A spell in the major pilgrimage center of Einsiedeln, with its multiple relics and indulgence-selling, turned him against Catholic superstition and idolatry. He preached against abuse and vice in others, but his defense of his own morality had the high-handed self-righteousness of the Protestant pastor-prig of future carica-

VENITE AD ME·QVI   IESVS · MAT · XI ·   LABORATIS · & EGO REFICIĀ VOS

HVLDRICVS·ZVINGLIVS·

ANNO ÆTATIS·44·

· B ·

Huldrych Zwingli, seen here, was elected minister of the Great Minster in Zurich in 1518. He rejected the authority of bishops as well as the pope. Relics and images were stripped from churches and organs were dismantled. Worship was compulsory, and the times of sermons were coordinated so that none could avoid them. Heretics were drowned. Zwingli was killed fighting a Catholic force in 1531.

ture. The citizens of Zurich, an imperial free city, were seeking to elect a people's priest for the Great Minster in 1518. Zwingli's robust support of local political rights made him an attractive candidate, but doubts arose due to his excessive love of music and his affair with a barber's daughter in Einsiedeln. "The girl was a 'virgin' during the day and a 'woman' at night," he wrote in angry disdain to the election committee. "She had affairs with many men, finally with me. . . . If she claims that I caused her pregnancy, I will not deny it. I have long ago confessed my guilt to my Highest God. . . . Some have laid my musical inclinations against me. What shameful and foolish jackasses they are! I play for myself and delight in the beautiful harmony of melodies. . . ." He added that he was now studying the Greek and Latin philosophers "day and night," and that this unremitting toil "tames and perhaps extinguishes unchaste desires."[2]

Zwingli was duly elected. He began his work on New Year's Day, 1519, preaching on the books of the Bible, starting with Matthew and the life of Jesus and working his way through Acts and the Pauline Epistles. Politics were mixed with violent denunciations of superstition, purgatory, the invocation of saints, and vice. He urged the city government to maintain law and justice, and to protect widows and orphans. Zwingli also called on the people to retain Swiss freedoms and he rebuked them for their idleness, gluttony, rich clothing, and suppression of the poor. Some of his congregation were eager to hear him and praised God, but others, a chronicler noted, "gave bad names to Zwingli as one who would lead Zurich to great suffering." Drunks mobbed his house and "threw stones, broke windows, shouted, scolded and raged . . ."[3]

A plague struck Zurich in the summer of 1519. More than fifteen hundred people died, including Zwingli's younger brother Andreas. Zwingli was obliged by his contract of employment not to leave the city in time of widespread death; he caught the plague in August, and not until November was he able to write to a friend, "I am doing fine. Yesterday I finally removed the last patch from my pestilential boil." He composed a triumphal Song of Pestilence:

> The illness grows.
> Pain and fear seize
> My soul and body. Come to me then! . . .
> Recovered, Lord God, recovered!
> I think, I am
> Already being restored.[4]

Zwingli maintained a ferocious schedule—his sixteen-hour day interrupted only by hurried meals and two short walks—but his ponderings did not lead to a formal break with Rome until 1522. On Ash Wednesday he was present when a

Zurich printer ate two pork sausages. Zwingli did not touch the "forbidden fruit" himself, but he supported the fast-breaker and published his first reforming treatise, "Concerning Freedom and the Choice of Food." "The general gathering of Christians may accept for themselves fasts and abstinence from food, but not set these up as a common and everlasting law," he wrote. "I leave to each free judgment. . . ." He was secretly married later in the year to Anna Meyer, who was to bear him four children.

The arguments stirred by the people's priest needed resolution. The city council called for a disputation in January 1523 to define Zurich's religious position. Zwingli outlined his views in sixty-seven conclusions. He was irritated by suggestions that he had borrowed them from Luther. "Even if one never read about Luther and is faithful solely to the Word of God," he complained, "he would yet be scolded to be a 'Lutheran' . . . Luther's writings helped me little. . . . Who called me to proclaim the Gospel? Was it Luther?" The conclusions had at least a Lutheran ring to them, however, as they proclaimed justification by faith, and they rejected good works as being, in themselves, "neither right nor good." The Catholic bishop denied that the city had any authority in matters of faith and morals; and the city claimed the right to repudiate any Church authority it pleased, and to determine its own faith. No Catholic attended to defend the Roman dogma, and Zwingli, sitting at a table with copies of the Bible in Latin, Greek, and Hebrew in front of him, was unopposed.

Reforms introduced after a second disputation the following October went far beyond Luther. The authority of bishops as well as the pope was rejected. Relics and images were stripped from Zurich's churches and sold off or smashed; all decorations were stripped from altars; organs were dismantled and, though Zwingli was a fine musician, hymns were banned and only the singing of metrical psalms was allowed. Ministers wore ordinary clothes and faced the congregation: after a sermon, scripture reading, and prayer, the Communion bread was carried on large wooden platters to the silent congregation. Worship was daily, the liturgy plain, the sermons long; church attendance declined. People "spend the time of the sermon voluptuously in inns," the city council complained. "[S]ome of them even ridicule and abusively insult the Word of God and its proclaimers. . . . Everybody is to be obediently present at the third ringing of the bells. Nobody is to evade this."

Many did. A year later, men and women were found idly wandering on the bridges, along the moats, and down alleys at sermon-time. To prevent them claiming that they had already heard a sermon, the preachers in all the churches began to speak at the same time. Heretics were uncovered; unlike Luther, Zwingli believed that magistrates could intervene in religious affairs, and accepted that the city council could impose the death sentence on the unorthodox. Felix Mantz, a young Anabaptist, was led to the fish market in January 1527 and taken onto a boat. His hands were bound, and, as he "sang with a clear voice '*In manus tuas, domine, commendo spiritum meum,'*" the executioner pushed him into the waters of the lake. The Catholic cantons resented Zwingli's efforts to lead Switzerland; Luther opposed efforts to form a Protestant alliance to counter growing Catholic pressure.

The ill will each side bore to the other came to a head over Communion. It was, perhaps, inevitable; the act of Communion is a central mystery of the faith, and any change in its doctrine touches upon the divine presence of Christ. One set of variants concerned the sacraments of bread and wine. For more than a millennium it had been the normal custom to receive Communion in both kinds. There were exceptions; during the Roman persecutions in North Africa and Egypt it had been common for the laity to take consecrated bread home with them for private Communion.[5] The *intinctio panis* was also used, in which the bread is dipped into the wine rather than being taken separately; in the East it remains standard practice to immerse the Host, the bread, in the chalice and administer it with a Communion spoon. From the thirteenth century such intinction was forbidden in the West* and the taking of wine was restricted to the clergy. A doctrine of concomitance stating that the body and blood of Christ are present in both wine and bread was used to justify denial of the chalice to the laity. Hus had insisted that the laity should have both wine and bread; on this, Zwingli and Luther agreed.

Both, too, rejected the Catholic doctrine of transubstantiation. Catholics believed that the bread and wine became the body and blood of Christ after consecration, and that only their "accidents"—their color, taste, and texture—remained. Luther amended this to consubstantiation, in which bread and wine, and body and blood, coexist in union; he compared this with an iron thrust into a fire, where fire and metal are joined in the red-hot iron, but each continues as a substance. Zwingli denied the bodily presence of Christ at Communion. He drew this from the Dutch physician Cornelius Hoen, who argued that the word "is" in Jesus' phrase "This is my body" in reality meant "signifies." "I found the precious pearl," Zwingli wrote; "the 'is' of the words of institution must be understood as 'means.'" He believed that the sacraments remained bread and wine, and that Christ was present purely spiritually in the heart of the faithful. "The mass is not a sacrifice," he wrote, "but is a remembrance of the sacrifice and assurance of the salvation which Christ has given us. . . ."[6]

The Marburg colloquy between the two sides was arranged in October 1529. Zwingli made a circuitous journey, for he was a marked man, writing

*Communion by intinction reappeared in some Anglican churches in the 1980s, in response to health fears over AIDS.

back to Zurich for fresh funds to buy a horse, and asking that his wife—"I left her under the pretence of going to Basle to attend to business"—should be kept in ignorance of his mission. Each man was supported by a tolerant and diplomatic follower, Johannes Oecolampadius for Zwingli, and the conciliatory Philip Melanchthon for Luther. Three days of argument merely hardened positions.

It was, as in so much else, possible to quote the Bible from either side of the divide. Oecolampadius cited Jesus: "I am the living bread which came down out of heaven; if any man eat of this bread, he shall live for ever: yea and the bread which I will give is my flesh, for the life of the world." This, he argued, was purely symbolic since Jesus had added: "It is the spirit that quickeneth; the flesh profiteth nothing: the words that I have spoken unto you are spirit, and are life" (John 6:63). The communicant does not partake of Christ's body in the bread, but shares in his spirit.

"It is up to you to prove that the body of Christ is not here, when the Word says, 'This is my body!'" Luther retorted, "I do not want to hear reason. . . . God is above all mathematics. The words of God are to be adored and observed with awe. God commands: 'Take, eat; this is my body.'" Luther wrote "This is my body" with chalk on the table in front of him.

"Christ is risen and is sitting at the right hand of the Father; consequently he is not in the bread," Oecolampadius replied. "The holy Scriptures use figures of speech, metaphors, metonymies, and the like, where the words mean something else than they say. Thus it is possible that the words 'This is my body' are figurative speech, as we find in some other passages: . . . 'I am the vine', 'The rock is Christ'. . . ."

"I do not deny that there are many metaphors in the holy Scriptures," said Luther. "But you must prove that here 'This is my body' is a metaphor. . . ."

"You consider it faith that Christ is in the bread. It is an opinion and not faith."

"Again and again the body of Christ is eaten, for he himself commands us so," Luther replied. "If he ordered me to eat manure, I would do it, since I would altogether know that it would be my salvation. Let not the servant brood over the will of his Master. We have to close our eyes."

"But where is it written that we must walk with closed eyes through Scripture, Dr. Luther?" asked Oecolampadius.

"Even if we debate for a hundred years, we are not going to prove anything," said Luther. "Explain the text and I am satisfied. He who spoke the words of John 6 also spoke the words 'This is my body.'" When he was asked if he recognized the others as his brothers, Luther shouted: "Your spirit and our spirit do not go together. . . . For there cannot be the same spirit if one side simply believes the words of Christ and the other side reprimands, attacks, denies and blasphemes this faith. . . ."[7]

These were not petty squabbles. Lutherans, and Catholics, believed in the presence of Christ at the moment of Communion; but to Zwinglians it was a simple act of remembrance. The bitterness revealed at Marburg was catastrophic to Zwingli personally. It also confirmed that Protestants were not the united force of Catholic nightmare. They split, and split easily; it was possible to deal with them separately. On his return to Zurich, Zwingli was dangerously isolated. He could expect no Lutheran support. Many citizens were alienated by religious intrusion into their private lives and by the tensions with the five Swiss cantons that had remained Catholic. Zwingli offered to resign. When this was refused, he decided on confrontation.

A blockade was imposed on supplies of salt, iron, steel, and wine to the Catholic cantons. It was thought unchristian—Paul had written: "If your enemy hungers, feed him. . . ."—and it produced a furious response. On October 11, 1531, a "vagabond" came into the city and said that the cantons were marching against it. A force of men and artillery was hastily prepared. Zwingli, in the helmet and armor of a fighting man, rode out with them. The vagabond was sent ahead to reconnoiter; unsurprisingly, he was a spy who promptly rejoined the enemy and "revealed everything about us." The canton forces attacked from woods where they were hiding. The farmers protecting the Zurich guns fled, and the Catholics captured sixteen cannon and the Protestant banners; there was "fierce and obstinate fighting, finally, with table knives, biting and scratching." Zwingli and a dozen other preachers were killed. Zwingli's body was cut into four pieces and burned. Three days later, people were claiming to have parts of his heart and were selling them as relics. The Protestant advance in Switzerland was halted. A pattern was created; the confederation divided into two armed camps of religion.

❖   A FEW MONTHS later the north German city of Münster began its transformation from a respectable Protestant trading center into a New Jerusalem where murder and polygamy flourished. At the extremes, the Reformation freed passions that drove men toward insanity.

Münster was the largest of the German clerical states, with powerful merchant guilds and a strong town council. Commercial self-interest made Lutheranism attractive; the Catholic prince-bishop was an unordained aristocrat who taxed the laity hard. Crop failures and a tripling of the price of rye followed an outbreak of plague in 1529. The following year a special tax was levied to pay for an army to fight the Turkish advance in Hungary. Tensions grew when the pulpit of the large church of St. Lambert was given to Bernt Rothmann in 1532. The gifted and free-speaking son of a blacksmith, Rothmann had been educated by the Brethren of the Common Life and was a Catholic chaplain before becoming a Lutheran. The bishop forbade him to preach, but he won the backing of the town council, led by a cloth merchant named Bernt Knipperdollinck. The city was declared Lutheran, and Catholic priests were expelled. In 1533 the bishop was obliged to recognize Münster as a Lutheran city.

So, quietly, Münster might have transferred its loyalty. But 1533 was the fifteenth centenary of the death of Jesus, and followers of Melchior Hoffman were roaming Germany in search of a safe haven in which to see through the Last Judgment. A former leather-dresser, Hoffman had been a Lutheran lay preacher before joining the Anabaptists. He believed that the Second Coming was imminent and took himself to Strasbourg to await it. Here he begged city officials "to be put in the tower so that he will see neither sun nor moon until God will have mercy upon him and bring the matter to a conclusion." Four months later he warned his jailers that "they should know that he was the prophet Elijah, who will precede the Last Judgment. God had sent him to us, but we did not want to know. He is the last one. God would not send any more." A year later he urged the city to lay in stocks of food in anticipation of God's arrival. In the fifth year of his imprisonment, officials noted that "both his face and legs were greatly swollen. He requests that my lords should let him out for a month until he feels better, then he will gladly go back." It was resolved to "let him out of the hole. He is to be carefully guarded, however." He was returned to the hole after a month, and died in it in the tenth year of his voluntary captivity.

Hoffman mislocated events in choosing Strasbourg. Some of his supporters settled in Münster, and their ideas rapidly captivated Rothmann and the city's poor. In sermons and pamphlets, Rothmann preached for a return to the communal world of the first Christians. The town's wealthy bankers and merchants were urged to give up luxury and vanities, renounce usury, and give to the poor. Some did so, and this remarkable news attracted criminals and fugitives like hungry bears to honey. "And so they came," a Catholic carpenter in the city wrote wearily, "the Dutch and Frisians and scoundrels from all parts, who had never settled anywhere . . ."[8]

Lutherans and Catholics joined forces against the inrush, but at the beginning of 1534, two Anabaptist apostles entered the city to a "contagion of enthusiasm."[9] The Anabaptist Jan Matthys sent them from Holland. Where Hoffman was content to await the millennium in the peace of his prison cell, Matthys believed that the ungodly could be cast out only by blood. He dispatched his followers in pairs, telling them that the Holy Spirit had descended upon them as on the apostles at Pentecost, and instructing them to gain a core of converts in each town they visited before moving on to the next. They found Münster fertile soil, and within a week they claimed to have rebaptized 1,400 of the 10,000 souls in the city, including Rothmann and Knipperdollinck, key targets.

One of the apostles was a handsome twenty-five year old, blond, bearded, and large-eyed, known as Jan van Leiden. The bastard son of a Dutch magistrate and a German serf woman, he was schooled at Leiden and apprenticed to a tailor. He was restless, and his real passion was writing and acting in plays. He spent four years in England and then tailored in Flanders before returning to Leiden and marrying the ex-wife of a sailor. He began trading on his own account, traveling as far as Lisbon before his business collapsed and he was ruined. At All Saints' in 1533, Matthys "came to his house, instructed him in the Scriptures, and rebaptized him," and ordered him to go to Münster. He abandoned his wife and arrived in the city the week after Epiphany in January 1534. The cloth merchant Knipperdollinck was besotted with him; on February 8 the two ran berserk in the streets, calling on all to repent of their sins. A group of Anabaptists occupied the town hall and the marketplace, and many of the better-off Lutherans fled the city with their possessions. Appeals, signed "Emmanuel," were sent to sympathizers urging them to come to the city, bringing lances and firearms with them. The incomers gave the Anabaptists a majority in the town council elections on February 23. Knipperdollinck was appointed *burgomeister*.

It was proclaimed that the rest of the world was to be destroyed before the coming Easter. The city entered a frenzy. The convents were emptied; "they pushed their weapons, halberds, lances and spears into the gate," a nun recalled, "they entered our church, where they took the ornaments, first the three gilded silver chalices . . ."[10] Some nuns joined the rebaptized women who threw themselves to the ground in fits and visions. Matthys now arrived from Holland. Tall, spare-framed, and black-bearded, he spurred on the armed bands as they emptied the city of misbelievers on the morning of February 27, yelling, "Get out, you godless ones, and never come back. . . . ,"[11] driving them penniless into the snow and sleet of the fields. The remaining Catholics and Lutherans submitted to mass rebaptism in the marketplace. By March 3 only the children of God were left in the city.

The mass expulsions brought an armed response from the bishop of Münster. Earthworks were thrown up around the city in a siege by a hastily raised mercenary army. Anabaptists in the diocese, and in the neighboring duchy of Cleves and archbishopric of Cologne, were sentenced to death. As the siege progressed, "countless men and women in the towns were beheaded, drowned, burnt or broken on the wheel."[12] Terror and prophecy were used to stiffen resistance within the city. Matthys publicly stabbed and then shot a blacksmith who criticized him; he had recent converts imprisoned in a church, and forced them to crawl on their knees to beg him to intercede with God to spare them. It was decreed that all wealth should be held in common; "it is God's will that we should bring our money, silver and gold together."[13] In mid-March, Matthys banned all books but the Bible. Other works, privately owned or from the fine cathedral library, were thrown on a bonfire in the cathedral square; the city lost contact with all lore and learning save that which the prophets took from the Scriptures to suit their convenience.

At a wedding party at the end of March, Matthys had a vision. He was sitting jovially waiting for the meat to be served when, "overcome by the Anabaptist spirit," he clapped his hands, nodded his head, and "groaned greatly as if he were about to die." He awoke with a sigh: "Oh, dear Father, not as I will, but as thou wilt." With that, he left; God had told him that he would be able to drive off the besieging army the next morning. He duly sallied out with a few men and was swiftly killed. The bishop's soldiers "cut off his head, tore his body into a hundred pieces, which they drew around." The head was put on a stick and held high in the air; the watchers in the city declined the invitation to collect it. Jan van Leiden assured the people that they had no reason to be dismayed at their prophet's death; "God will raise up someone else, who shall be higher and greater than Jan Matthys was."[14] He was referring to himself.

His performance was an enthralling act of theater, or madness, or spiritual sincerity; perhaps it was all three, for it was powerful enough to hold a large town in a religious trance. The Easter, 1534 deadline passed without incident. In early May, Leiden ran naked through the streets and then lapsed into a silent ecstasy that lasted for three days. When he recovered his voice, he said that God had revealed to him that the city must base itself on ancient Israel. He appointed himself as supreme prophet with twelve elders beneath him. The citizens were known as Israelites; each of them was to be "industrious in his vocation and fear God and his ordained government." All meals were eaten communally under the command of "food-masters." Knipperdollinck, who was appointed "swordbearer" or executioner, dispatched those who hid food or buried money.

Leiden declared that it was God's will that his people should inhabit the earth, and polygamy was sanctioned in order to meet God's call to "increase and multiply." Leiden was already married to Knipperdollinck's daughter as well as to the woman he had abandoned in Holland. He now married Matthys's attractive young widow Divara, a disillusioned citizen wrote, and "continued to take more wives until he had finally had fifteen. In similar fashion all the Dutchmen, Frisians and Anabaptists had additional wives. Indeed, they compelled their first wives to go and obtain second wives for them. The devil laughed hard about this. . . ."[15] A law was passed that all younger women should marry, on pain of death. There was resistance to this edict, but the rebels were defeated and fifty were put to death.

At the beginning of September, in a ceremony in the main square, a goldsmith named Dusentschur declared that God had revealed to him that Leiden was to become the king of the world, inheriting the throne of his forefather David with dominion over all others as the Messiah of the Last Days. Leiden was anointed as King of New Jerusalem. He fell on the ground in humility, but recovered soon enough to warn any opponents that they would be destroyed. "I shall still reign, despite you, not only over this town but over the whole world," he said, "for the Father will have it so, and my kingdom which begins now shall endure and know no downfall. . . ."[16] To celebrate the accession, gold and silver coins were minted with the millenary inscription: "The Word has become Flesh and dwells in us." The new state acquired an emblem, a globe pierced by two swords beneath a cross and the inscription "One King of Righteousness over All." A golden globe was hung on a chain around the king's neck, and others were embroidered in cloth on the sleeves of his attendants. His chief wife, Divara, was proclaimed queen and, dressed in finery, held court in a mansion near the cathedral. A throne was installed in the marketplace above the benches of royal counselors; the king paraded to it on horseback, accompanied by a throng of courtiers. Two page boys flanked the throne, one holding a copy of the Old Testament as evidence of the king's lineage from David, and the other a drawn sword.

It fell to Rothmann as royal preacher to justify the kingdom. He wrote two pamphlets in October and December, *Restitution* and *Bericht von der Wrake,* the *Announcement of Vengeance.* He divided history into three ages. The first was the age of sin, which lasted until the Flood; the second, enduring until the present, was the time of persecution and the Cross; and the third, already underway at Münster, was the era of vengeance and the triumph of the Saints. Christ had tried to redeem the world, Rothmann wrote, but had been thwarted by the Catholic Church, which held Christians in a Babylonian captivity for fourteen centuries. The time of desolation was now ending. The prophecies of the Old Testament were being fulfilled, and Christ had chosen Leiden as the new David to create his kingdom in Münster and to send forth the Saints to expand it until they filled the world with "one sheepfold, one flock, one king," purifying by the sword. "The glory of the saints is to wreak vengeance," Rothmann wrote. "Revenge without mercy must be taken of all who are not marked with the Sign."[17] The sign was the king's emblem of the globe and swords, and only when those who wore it had finished their grisly task would Christ return for the Day of Judgment and the Saints inherit the earth.

Leiden played on his people's emotions with skill. The Trumpet of the Lord, blown in fact by the goldsmith Dusentschur, was sounded each fortnight to summon the Israelites to Mount Zion, the renamed cathedral square. A royal banquet followed with the loaves and wine of Communion, the king marking the end of the celebration by sending to the prison for a captured bishop's man and beheading him. Gold and silver were smuggled out of the city in attempts to hire mercenaries from as far as Switzerland; they were to be paid four gilders monthly and "free plundering." Rothmann's leaflets were taken to Holland and Frisia, calling for the common people to rise and relieve the pressure on Münster. They had some effect. A force of Anabaptists one thousand strong was assembled in Groningen under a prophet who called himself Christ, but it was scattered by the duke of Gelderland before it could march. A group that seized a monastery in western Frisia was dislodged with prolonged cannon fire; other rebels in Amsterdam took the city hall before they were killed.

Deeply disturbed at the spread of the heresy, the rulers of the states of the Upper and Lower Rhine met at Koblenz and agreed to supply the bishop of Münster with enough men and money to tighten the siege. Continuous trenches and lines of infantry sealed the saints and their propaganda within the city from January 1535. A spy named Hans Nagel surrendered to Leiden on the pretext that he had fled from the bishop's camp for fear of being punished for falling asleep on watch. Nagel was first flung into the "heathen tower" where non-Anabaptists were held. When he agreed to be rebaptized, he was released and given the brown and black velvet jacket of the king's servants. He reported that Leiden rode about the city wearing a gold crown on a fallow horse covered with black-green velvet. "In all respects he behaved like a king," Nagel reported after he escaped. "He showed little confidence towards his subjects and through his public and secret informers he kept them from entering into secret arrangements . . . all gatherings were forbidden."[18] The king had fourteen wives by now and had recently fathered a daughter. Meat was scarce for all but the court; almost all the cats had been eaten and no more than three or four dogs survived, but there was still bread and beer.

The king prophesied that the people would be saved before Easter 1535. If this did not happen, he said that they should burn him on the market square. When Good Friday passed with no end to the city's desperation, Leiden explained that he had spoken only of spiritual salvation. By May, hunger was raging and bodies were thrown into communal graves. Leiden said that the Father would convert the cobblestones into bread rather than see his children starve; those who believed him howled in desolation when they remained stones. Two prisoners taken by the bishop's forces reported that they had scraped the white off the walls of houses and mixed it with water to give to their children; "men, women and children look pale like bleached cloth, their bodies are bloated and they have huge stomachs and legs. . . ."[19] In the past few days the king had personally beheaded four men for talking of desertion. Mice were being roasted in pans.

Entertainments—dancing, running races, plays and parodies of the Mass performed in the cathedral—were devised by the king for his starving subjects.

Their numbers were estimated at 1,300 men and 6,000 women, not counting the children. The king gave permission for any to leave the madhouse that wished to do so, but only two hundred went. Perhaps the remainder believed his threat that the reward for desertion was eternal damnation, or perhaps they were too weakened to think or to act. Certainly the bishop's treatment of the refugees was little kinder than the king's. All the able-bodied men were slaughtered on the spot, while the old, the diseased, and the women and children were kept in the no man's land between the forces for five weeks, sleeping in the open, scratching for grass and plants, and begging the mercenaries to kill them. Those left in the dying city remained defiant. They wrote an open letter to the bishop's forces, saying that "we are resolved to uphold the truth which by God's grace is with us undismayedly until death." They affirmed that the millennium was at hand. "How else would the fourth beast," they wrote, "the fourth monarchy of earth, which is the Roman Empire, trample on the saints of God, as is presently taking place?" They included a chapter reference, Daniel 2, and predicted that the kingdom of the world would soon be turned over to themselves, the "saints of the Most High."

Discipline was enforced by twelve "rulers" whom Leiden appointed to control twelve sections of the city, particularly around the gates. Each ruler had several officers and soldiers, and the rulers were forbidden to talk to each other without the knowledge of the king. Two men escaped from the city in darkness, however, and informed the besieging forces of weak points in the defenses. On the night of June 24, 1535, the bishop's forces broke into the city and the emaciated defenders were overwhelmed. Two hundred surviving Anabaptists laid down their weapons and fled to their houses, but they were tracked down and killed over the following days. Rothmann is thought to have died fighting; Queen Divara was beheaded after refusing to recant.

Three were kept alive for the moment: the king, Knipperdollinck, and a man named Krechting. Leiden was led about on a chain and exhibited in towns and villages for some time, as a warning of the perils of Anabaptism. In January 1536 the three were brought back to Münster. Leiden agreed to confess his sins to a priest and asked for the bishop's chaplain, who reported that he had "confessed openly that even if he were executed ten times, he had deserved it," but that he could not be brought to see his errors on baptism and the nature of Christ. Knipperdollinck and Krechting refused to see a priest and said that they had done nothing but seek the glory of God and his salvation. They were executed on the morrow of St. Agnes Day, January 29. They died well, a witness grudgingly admitted, adding that Satan gave courage to those he entangled in his snares. "Father, into thy hands do I commend my spirit," the king said; he remained silent as he was tortured to death with glowing tongs and fire "under the applause and pleasure of the priests." Knipperdollinck was silent throughout his torture;

The body of Jan van Leiden is hoisted to the steeple of St. Lambert's Church in Münster in January 1536 as a perpetual memorial "to warn and terrify restless spirits." Münster was a large and prosperous city when it was entered by a group of Anabaptists seeking a haven in which to await the Last Judgment. Leiden, a bankrupt tailor, proclaimed the city to be the Kingdom of the Saints and himself its king, while the expelled bishop of Münster laid siege outside the walls. "I shall reign over the whole world," Leiden told his starving subjects before the city fell and his pitiful experiment collapsed, "for the Father will have it so, and my kingdom shall know no downfall."

Krechting did no more than murmur twice "Oh, Father, oh, Father." As to the onlookers, for many "there could be nothing more pleasant than this sight" of burning men.

The corpses were put into three iron cages and hoisted high on the steeple of St. Lambert's Church as a perpetual memorial "to warn and terrify restless spir-its"[20] lest they rise again.*

---

*They did, if briefly. In 1567 a cobbler named Jan Willemsen declared a New Jerusalem in Westphalia and at-tracted a core of three hundred saints; they lived by plundering priests and nobles, and practiced polygamy—Willemsen had twenty-one wives—and reprinted *Rothmann's Restitution* to justify their outrages. Willemsen was captured and burned at Cleves in 1580, and violent Anabaptism perished with him. The spirit of peaceful Anabaptism persists to this day. After his biblical studies, Menno Simons joined the Anabaptists to lead "the poor straying sheep" in their post-Münster persecution. He condemned violence and preached the "narrow path of purity," maintaining adult baptism and the symbolism of the sacraments. His followers called themselves Mennonites in his honor; within a century they had flourishing communities in the Netherlands and Germany. They were deeply to influence the English Baptists and Quakers; at the start of the third millennium they num-ber almost a million.

A group of Austrian Anabaptists, led by Jakob Hutter until his death in 1536, settled in Moravia. Hutterite settlements were based on common ownership of property. When they founded a community, a chronicler recorded, a coat was first spread on the ground, and "everybody laid down his possessions, voluntarily and uncoerced, so that the needy might be supported according to the teaching of the prophets and the apostles." Children were brought up communally. A sect of Swiss Brethren, descended from a group who introduced believers' baptism near Zurich in 1525, survived in the mountains around Bern. Protestant and Catholic persecuted them alike with impunity, for they believed in nonresistance; however, they did not accept the Hutterites' community of possessions. Many Hutterites later emigrated to North America. The iron cages still hang from the steeple at Münster; other than that, the saints have disappeared without a trace.

❧ AN ALTOGETHER SANER figure directed the next attempt to impose a theocratic regime on a city, at Geneva. John Calvin was twenty-six when Münster fell in 1535, a Frenchman of precocious brilliance who was toiling to complete *The Institutes of the Christian Religion,* the most significant and lucid text of the Reformation. He completed the great trinity of reformers. The movement had matured; Luther and Zwingli had done much of the theological pioneering. On a personal level, too, barriers had gone. It had taken two years for Zwingli to dare to celebrate his marriage in public; in marrying a former nun, Luther had broken a taboo that stretched back fourteen centuries. Without trace of scandal, Calvin married a girl with an entirely freshly minted background, the widow of an Anabaptist. He was able to build on the work of his predecessors. Zwingli had sought to reform Protestantism, stripping it of the Roman richness in liturgy and music that Luther had allowed to survive; Calvin guided this puritan instinct into a defined and consciously Reformed church.

A lawyer's orderly mind drove his zeal and moral fervor. As a twelve year old he was destined for the Church and received the tonsure, but his father, a financial administrator whose practical bent he inherited, noted that the law "commonly raised those who followed it to wealth" and sent him to get a legal training at Orléans. He had a religious experience—he wrote that "God by a sudden conversion subdued and brought my mind to a teachable frame," extricating him from the "abyss" of popish superstitions—and he immersed himself in theology as well as in his other studies. His moralizing was already evident, his follower and biographer Theodore Beza noting that he was "a strict censor of everything vicious in his companions," and Calvin's intensity attracted those whom it did not repel.

At twenty-six, John Calvin, pale and dark, with a keen temper and a sparkling self-confidence, wrote *The Institutes,* his great handbook of Protestant theology. The young Frenchman drew heavily on Luther, but he added clarity and logic and system to the doctrine. He created a theocracy at Geneva that directed the affairs of the city and of the individual citizens. Calvin brought a joyless edge to Protestant morality, banning popular songs and dancing. "They have always feared me more than they loved me," he admitted of his flock.

"All who had any desire after purer doctrine were continually coming to me to learn," Calvin remarked with telltale confidence, "although I was yet but a mere novice and tyro."[21] His first volume was a commentary on Seneca; the moral gravity of the Roman philosopher was "obviously in accordance with [his own] disposition,"[22] and they shared a cool and lucid style. The excitement of Bible-based thinking was winning a Protestant following in France, and in Paris where Calvin continued his studies, until royal toleration was withdrawn. On the night of October 18, 1534, Lutheran hotheads plastered violently anti-Catholic posters on street walls in Paris and Orléans. One was pinned to the king's bedroom door in the castle of Amboise; in fury, Francis I led a procession to the cathedral at Notre Dame to pray that France should be rid of Protestant poison. Thirty-five Lutherans were burned; Calvin fled Paris for Basel.

Here, not yet twenty-seven, pale and dark, with eyes that were to "sparkle to the moment of his death . . . and a keen temper," he wrote his great handbook of Protestant theology. *The Institutes* drew heavily on Luther, but its clarity and logic gave it a grace that was lacking in more combative Lutheran texts. Calvin dedicated it to Francis I in the hope of defending Protestant principles and regaining toleration. It failed in that, but it was widely translated, and expanded, and it gave him fame. He traveled back to France secretly in 1536, selling the family estate and settling his affairs, intending to lead a scholar's quiet life in exile. Passing through Geneva, he was persuaded by the reformer Guillaume Farel to stay in the city. His early attempts to organize reform in the city were too radical for many to stomach. Calvin detested disorder; he wished to impose uniformity through a compulsory confession of faith, and he was prepared to use excommunication as a means of enforcing civic discipline. He and Farel were expelled to Strasbourg.

A Catholic attempt to win back Geneva failed. In September 1541 the city council asked Calvin to return, and within three months it had adopted his *Ecclesiastical Ordinances*. These were the instruments through which he strove to create a theocratic regime in which the Reformed church claimed authority over civic life and personal behavior as well as faith. Attempts to control popular morals had been made before, by bishops' courts and city councils, but Calvin far exceeded these in the detail of his discipline and intrusion into private life.

The only church offices that survived were those that Calvin claimed had been instituted by Christ, "that is to say," the Geneva regulations stipulated, "first pastors, then teachers, after which elders, and in the fourth place, deacons." The pastors were obliged to meet weekly to study the Scriptures and to preach five sermons a week. Lying, slander, indiscretion, and avarice among them were dealt with by "fraternal admonitions"; but drunkenness, lewdness, blasphemy, and "dancing and like dissolute behaviour" counted as "intolerable crimes" for which they were expelled. To ensure that their parishioners remained true to the faith, pastors paid an annual visit to each household. Deacons were charged to "take watch and ward of the sick and administer the pittance for the poor." No one was allowed to remain sick in bed for longer than three days without notifying a deacon, lest they die "without admonition or instruction in doctrine." It was the duty of elders to spy constantly upon the congregations. They were to "keep watch over the lives of everyone, to admonish in love those whom they see erring and leading disorderly lives and, whenever necessary, to report them to the body which will be designated to make fraternal correction. . . ." This body was the consistory. It was composed of the pastors and twelve elders. Each was responsible, in an echo of Münster, for a section of the city. The consistory acted both as prosecutor and judge. Its members met each Thursday to consider individual lapses in faith and morals.

An extraordinary range of offenses merited punishment. Reverting towards popery was one: a goldsmith made a chalice, a woman knelt at the grave of her husband and cried "*Requiescat in Pace,*" another was found to possess a copy of the lives of the saints, a barber gave the tonsure to a priest. It was an offense to possess a rosary, to go on pilgrimage, to observe a papal fast, to attend mass. A woman named Lucresse Curtet was asked why she had sent money to monks outside

Geneva to have masses said. "She replied that her father and mother have brought her up to obey a different law to the one now in force here," the consistory minutes record. "Asked if she had not fasted, she replied that she fasted when it pleased her. . . . Decision that she be sent to some minister of her choice every sermon day and that the Lord's Supper be withheld from her." She was fortunate. When Jean Ballard insisted that he would follow "the holy mother Church universal in which I believe," he and his family were banished from the city. Old country habits died as hard as popery; a woman was punished for trying to cure her husband by tying a walnut with a spider inside it around his neck. The churches were kept locked except during services, "so that no one may enter at other times from superstitious motives." Men were punished for complaining that the arrival of French refugees was pushing up the cost of living. This was a sensitive matter, for Calvin himself was a foreigner; none of the thirteen pastors in the city in 1546 was Geneva-born, and much of his support came from fellow refugees.

Slashed breeches were banned, lest immoral fashion breed immorality, for "by the loopholes of the breeches, they wish to bring in all manner of disorders." A young schoolteacher fled when he was denounced for saying that the Song of Solomon was a simple love poem. A group of distinguished citizens was imprisoned for holding a dance in a private house; Calvin was so shocked by this that he said he would discover the truth "even at the cost of my life." Cardplaying was prohibited. Faced with ruin, a manufacturer of toys and playing cards named Ameaux complained that Calvin was misguided. At Calvin's insistence, Ameaux was forced to walk through the city dressed only in a shirt, carrying a taper, pleading aloud for God's mercy. Those who invited another to have a drink were fined three sous; drunkards were imprisoned for a third offense; taverns were closed at sermon time; the singing of indecent songs brought an automatic spell in prison.

Commercial purity was enforced. In a sermon, Calvin urged his audience to listen to what the "papists" were saying: "Oh those Genevans, they say they are better than anyone else just because they want to make the whole world better. But look at how they live. You will find their shops are as full of trickery and theft as before . . . watch closely . . . the really well-respected people will be the worst con-men of the lot!"[23] Merchants who shortchanged and underweighted, a doctor who fleeced his patients, a tailor who overcharged a visiting Englishman, were brought before the consistory. When the first dentist arrived at Geneva, Calvin is said to have personally questioned him before deciding that he was reputable enough to be allowed to pull teeth.[24]

❖ MUCH WAS MADE of such Protestant morality. In essence it was no more intense than that of a legion of Catholic ascetics, and when applied with too much rigor, notably at Geneva, it stirred up the same resentments as Savonarola had in Florence. Popular resistance was led by a group known as Libertins. They ruined Calvin's efforts to ban all but biblical first names, to march harlots through the streets in dunces' caps, and to enforce weekly attendance at Communion. Dogs were named after him, rude notes were left in his pulpit, noisy ball games played outside the church where he was preaching. Nevertheless, Protestants acquired some aura of godliness in the popular mind. Whether they practiced it more than Catholics is unverifiable, of course, but the emphasis they placed on individual conscience and proper behavior, and their distaste for public displays of wealth, at least inclined them towards sobriety. They certainly spoke of it more, and the times were propitious.

The arrival of syphilis* was supplying new and urgent evidence that lust and depravity are punishable in this world as well as the next. The disease had begun its lethal European progress after Columbus's crews carried it back across the Atlantic. It was highly virulent, forming contagious chancres in the groin and weeping pustules on the body, and attacking the central nervous system. In its sixteenth-century form, before it calmed into a three-stage disease that deformed and sterilized before it killed, death was rapid and painful. The Spanish called it the "serpent of Hispaniola"; it was the "Neapolitan disease" to the French, the "French disease" to most of Europe, and the "Christian disease" to the Turks. It was seen as a punishment from God, afflicting the mighty—Julius II and Ivan the Terrible, a pope and a czar—as much as the humble. Handshaking replaced kissing, and wigs came into fashion as those who were treated with mercury lost their hair. Licentious bathhouses were closed, and prostitutes were seen as a biblical curse.

Propagandists lost no opportunity to associate the papacy with the new disease. A woodcut by Mathias Gerung in about 1545 showed the pope as the Whore of Babylon astride the seven-headed beast of the Apocalypse. Luther told his students that "the evil spirit sent whores here" and he called them "dreadful, scabby, stinking, loathsome and syphilitic." They were worse than poisoners, he added, for "such a syphilitic whore can give her disease to ten, twenty, thirty, a hundred and more good people." He did not suggest that the customer might disease the girl, only the reverse. Protestants pressured city officials to close public brothels, some of which were owned by city councils and employed salaried civic officials as brothel-keepers. Catholics often regarded whorehouses as sewers which kept the rest of society clean and protected the virtue of respectable women; a Dominican monk, asked for advice by the town council at Cracow, rec-

---

*It acquired this name after an Italian wrote a poem in 1530 about a shepherd named Syphilis who suffered from it.

ommended setting up a civic brothel as "the lesser evil."[25] Filth, Calvin thought, was everywhere in Geneva. "When adultery, drunkenness, loose-living, and all kinds of evil are allowed then all we can do is admit that everything is lost, ruined," he wrote. "No matter where you look all you can see is blasphemy, scandal, ruin. . . ."

On sex within marriage, however, Protestant doctrine was less puritanical than Catholic. The Protestant calendar had no "holy times" which should be kept chaste. No confessors probed the secrets of the marital bed. It was held that forced continence was unnatural, and that a fruitful woman was "healthier, cleaner and happier." Pastors were strongly encouraged to marry; the contrast between their wedded legality and the Catholic priest with his concubine and bastard children was living testimony to Protestant respectability. Calvin was devoted to his own wife and wrote movingly of being "bereaved of the best companion of my life" when she died. Luther held that God created marriage as a "hospital" for lust; married sex is no more sinful than any other human activity, even if its purpose is pleasure, for "this plighted troth permits even more occasion than is necessary for the begetting of children." Indeed, he wrote to a friend congratulating him on getting married: "On the evening of the day when, according to my reckoning, you receive this letter, I shall also make love to my wife and so feel close to you."

The ideal was the consciously biblical family, obedient, orderly, and patriarchal. Duties were divided between husband and wife. The husband must "provide lodging and food for his dear wife and children through his labour," a Calvinist text on the Christian household stated, while she must be "a pious respectable house-mother and leave nothing undone of what she has to do in the house." There was not the slightest doubt of who should dominate. In his highly influential *Small Catechism,* Luther wrote of a household whose servants "are obedient to them that are your masters," whose children "obey your parents in the Lord, for this is right," and whose wives "submit yourselves unto your own husband as unto the Lord." He told a pastor whose wife refused to move to a new parish with him that he had "allowed her to despise and trample underfoot that authority of the husband, which is the glory of God . . . See to it, that you act the man."

Women were believed to be oversexed, best restrained by dull clothing, no cosmetics, and seclusion. "A woman does not have complete mastery over herself," Luther claimed. "God created her body that she should be with a man and bear and raise children. The words of Genesis clearly state this, and the members of her body sufficiently show that God himself formed her for this purpose." He held that men have broad shoulders and narrow hips, and "accordingly they possess intelligence." Women, by contrast, have narrow shoulders and broad hips. "Women ought to stay at home," he divined from this. "The way they were created indicates this, for they have broad hips and a wide fundament to sit upon."[26] Refusal to have sex with a husband was grounds for divorce. "Here it is time for the husband to say 'if you will not, another will; the maid will come if the wife will not,'" Luther maintained.[27] The dangers of childbearing did not concern him: "If women grow weary or even die while bearing children, that does no harm. Let them bear children to death, that's what they're there for."[28]

In refining and extending this Protestant morality, Calvin brought it a joyless edge. "Who loves not wine, woman and song," a Lutheran couplet ran, "Remains a fool his whole life long." That sentiment was anathema to the Calvinist, and so was Luther's lusty advice to "be a sinner and sin strongly, but believe and rejoice in Christ even more strongly." His paraphrase of Psalm 46—"God is our refuge and strength"—gave Protestants their greatest hymn, and Lutheran parishes had cantors, organists, choir schools, and instrumentalists, and the first congregational hymnbooks. The music of Geneva was sterile. Calvin banned "Popish polyphony"; the Geneva psalter had no more than metrical unisons, and the man who made the metrical translations, the poet Clément Marot, left the city after the consistory accused a man of playing backgammon with him. Calvin tried to ban all popular songs. The attempt was futile, and he wearily recognized his failure to eradicate human pleasures. "They have always feared me more than they loved me," he recognized of the people at Basel, and in Geneva he railed against the city council for backsliding. "They enthusiastically outlawed filthy songs," he preached. "Then, they said the new laws did not include nasty and disgusting songs about sex. They can be sung quite legally. . . . They are all just outright whores. I mean all of them when I say whores—the men and women who go round making God look foolish."[29]

In one area he did succeed, however, and it became a significant part of the Protestant image. Together with the pious and industrious family, Calvinists were seen as pioneers of a new and thriving business ethic. Making sharp practice a religious offense was one element; the other was the acceptance of usury. There was a biblical basis to Catholic unease over charging interest on loans. "If you lend money to any of my people with thee that is poor," Exodus states, "thou shalt not be to him as a creditor; neither shall ye lay upon him usury" (Exod. 22:25). The Church itself had lent money in the early centuries, but the Third Lateran Council of 1179 had formally condemned Christian usury. Catholic doctrine regarded money purely as a means of exchange rather than as a creative force. This concept of "barren" money dated back to Aristotle and was to be restated by the pope as late as 1745.[30] Luther condemned usury as "the greatest misfortune in Germany."[31] Referring to a family of Augsburg bankers, he said that a "bridle should be put in the mouth of the Fuggers and such companies who make from twenty to one hundred per cent on their money annually."

Genevans were permitted to charge interest to wealthy debtors, however. As well as pricing and general trading conditions, the consistory discussed the bank rate and the interest on war loans. Calvin embraced business, and by imposing a moral code on it he gave the pursuit of profit an honorable and spiritual framework. The Calvinist in his countinghouse was to become a powerful symbol as the sect spread to the mercantile and financial centers of the coming centuries, London, Edinburgh, Amsterdam. In truth, Venice, Genoa, and Florence had already spawned bankers and traders without the least hindrance from their Catholic faith; risk capital had been raised for the great Catholic voyages of exploration to the Indies and the New World. But the Protestant burghers of Northern Europe enjoyed a sense of religious and social inclusion in their business affairs; they felt that their ethics predestined them to success.

PREDESTINATION SUPPOSES THAT, by divine decree, certain people are led to eternal salvation. Its wholehearted embrace by Calvin revived one of the most powerful and troubling concepts in Christianity. Calvin preached that his followers were "strangers among sinners," an elite and embattled minority of the elect. "The citizens of Heaven have no love for the world, nor for the things which are of the World," he taught. "They cry with the prophet: 'Vanity of vanity, all is vanity and the devouring of the Spirit.'"

The origins to which he returned are as old as Moses. The Old Testament refers to a Book of Life in which God lists the names of those to be saved; those who are erased from it are condemned to Death. Moses pleaded with God to "blot me, I pray thee, out of thy book which thou hast written" (Exod. 32:32) if the sins of his people were not forgiven. Jesus continued in the Mosaic tradition, telling the disciples to "rejoice that your names are written in heaven" (Luke 10:20). The Christian variant of an elect, infallibly chosen by divine grace, and as infallibly saved, was elaborated by Paul—"And we know that to them that love God all things work together for good, even to them that are called according to his purpose. For whom he foreknew, he also foreordained to be conformed to the image of his Son, that he might be the firstborn among many brethren. And whom he foreordained, them he also called: and whom he called, them he also justified: and whom he justified, them he also glorified" (Rom. 8:28–30)—and developed in the Western Church by Augustine. The Eastern Orthodox were little troubled by predestination; they contented themselves that God merely knew in advance who was worthy and would be saved. Augustine, in condemning the Pelagian view that man can help save himself through his own efforts and that every Christian can and should achieve perfection by keeping the commandments of God, drew on Paul to proclaim that salvation is a divine gift. For reasons unknowable to the human mind, God predestines some to salvation and others to their own damnation.

Unnerving questions flow from this act of divine choice. Was Christ crucified for the elect alone? Does God not will the salvation of all His creatures? "Many are called, but few are chosen" (Matt. 22:14), Jesus said. Are the elect drawn only from those of true faith; and, if so, which faith is true? Catholics in general shared the moderate stance proposed by Thomas Aquinas. In order to reconcile the universality of redemption with Augustine's selection of the few, Aquinas suggested that God predestined the saved on the principle that the love of God is the cause of the goodness of things, and allowed the unworthy to be lost. The freedom of the human will and the divine desire that "all men should be saved" were central to Catholic doctrine. In the ninth century, however, the Saxon monk and poet Gottschalk had gone beyond Augustine in formalizing a double predestination, in which some are predestined to blessedness and others to eternal fire.

For his pains, Gottschalk had been condemned at a synod in 849, deprived of his orders, beaten, and sentenced to perpetual imprisonment. Beliefs are less easily locked away. Almost seven hundred years after Gottschalk, Luther and Calvin returned to the double predestination of the saved and the damned. They had incentives to do so. Their followers were a minority, vulnerable to blood and terror. To grant them membership of the elect, and the certainty that their enemies would be blotted out from God's book, was to offer them a divine consolation for fear and hardship. Like Gottschalk, both men denied that Christ had died for all.

This was predestination in its rawest form, and it proved too strong for Lutherans to stomach. In his insistence that both the elect and the reprobate are predestined by divine sovereignty, without reference to personal merits or vices, Luther outpaced the majority in his church. He was accused of spreading antinomianism, the idea that Christians are freed by grace from the necessity of following any moral laws. Moderate Philippists, led by Philip Melanchthon, accepted the absolute depravity of man after the Fall, and the absence of human merit and free will in the justification of man; but they stressed that Christians cannot rely on salvation purely through predestination, and must act justly. This was formally accepted as doctrine in the Formula of Concord in 1577, the final classic Lutheran formula of faith.

Calvinists, by contrast, were more rigorous than their founder. Belief in election was central to Calvin's doctrine of a God of absolute sovereignty, in whose true Church salvation lay. All men were sinners to him, therefore the elect were graced beyond their merit, whilst the nonelect received their just desserts. He did not, however, claim predestination to be anything other than an unfathomable mystery. "We assert that by an eternal and immutable counsel," he said, "God hath once for all determined both whom He would admit to salvation and whom He would admit to destruction." The physician Hieronymus Bolsec argued that this conspired to "make God a tyrant or an idol as pagans made Jupiter"; he was condemned to perpetual exile, but he escaped with his life.* Theodore Beza, Calvin's successor as head of the Geneva Church, was fiercer. He argued that God had predestined the Fall† as a part of his eternal plan, and that he had decreed the election or damnation of individuals before Adam. Beza thus denied that God's saving will extended to humanity in general. Christ's atoning death was offered for the elect alone; the rest of humanity—which hard-liners took to include all Catholics and indeed non-Calvinists—was doomed. "The Lord gave and the Lord hath taken away," the damned must cry with Job; "blessed be the name of the Lord."

A split developed between rigorists and the followers of Jacobus Arminius, a former student of Beza. In a formal remonstrance, Arminians denied the mainstream doctrine that Christ had died only for the elect, that the grace enjoyed by the elect was irresistible and unfailing, and that predestination was decreed either before or after the Fall. The revolt against Spanish rule in the Netherlands gave the dispute a political edge as the Remonstrants were suspected of favoring the pro-Spanish party in their struggle against the Calvinist Prince of Orange. A synod reconfirmed the rigid principles of unconditional election and irresistible grace. Remonstrant clergy were deprived of their livings; the eminent jurist Hugo Grotius was imprisoned for life, but escaped in a box of books to become the father of international law; the elderly advocate of Holland, J van Oldenbarnevelt, was beheaded for high treason.‡

---

*Bolsec took his revenge by writing a *History of the Life of Jean Calvin.* In it, he said that most of the heresies ever invented had been stowed away in Geneva, and described his subject as "ambitious, presumptuous, arrogant, cruel, malicious, vindictive and, above all, ignorant."

†This is known as "supralapsarianism"; more moderate Calvinists supplanted this with "sublapsarianism," which held that the election or nonelection of individuals by God came after rather than before the Fall. Sublapsarian teaching was set out at the Synod of Dort in 1618.

‡The liberal and rigorous wings of Calvinism were to have a profound effect on Methodism, where Wesleyans continued the Arminian tradition against Whitefield's Calvinistic Methodism.

THE EXECUTION OF opponents passed seamlessly from Catholicism to Calvinism. A handbill addressed to Calvin was posted in Geneva in 1547. "You puffed up hypocrite!" it read. "It seems to me that you will soon curse the hour in which you threw off your cowl. Long enough I reprimanded that the devil and all his cursed godless priests have come to damn us. Patience is now over; vengeance is near. . . ." Suspicion over who made this insult to the elect of God fell on one Jacques Gruet. The handbill was not in Gruet's handwriting, Calvin admitted, "but when his papers were examined, much was found of no less importance." Gruet had written an election appeal, arguing that none should be punished unless they actually endangered the commonwealth of Geneva. In some of Gruet's letters, to Calvin's disgust, "I was personally mentioned."[32] In addition to the catchall charge of blasphemy, it was also found that Gruet had "insulted, threatened and slandered the servants of God" and had thus "committed the crime of lèse-majesté requiring bodily punishment." Gruet was condemned to be taken to the village of Champel and "there have your body attached to a stake and burned to ashes and so you shall finish your days . . ."

No less than the Catholics they despised for the same reason, Calvinists held their leader in an awe so profound that they burned those who crossed him. The physician Michael Servetus, who held pope and pastor to be equally fallible, was in peril from both. He was a man of brilliant curiosity, noted for his skill in dissection, his theories on the pulmonary circulation of the blood, and his work on digestion and the medicinal properties of syrups. His scientific researches were combined with a fatal interest in theology; he believed that the divine spirit exists in the blood, transmitted from the liver to the heart and from the arteries to the veins. After studying at Montpellier and Paris, Servetus was appointed physician to the archbishop of Vienna in 1542. Outwardly, he was a conforming Catholic, while in private, disillusioned by witnessing the adulation of the pope on a visit to Bologna, he pursued his religious speculations. He rejected the concept of the Trinity, dismissing those who believed in it as "trinitaires." He was deeply devoted both to Christ and the Scriptures, studying them in Greek and Hebrew, and he noted that neither made mention of it.

He corresponded with Calvin, sending him a manuscript of his work *Christianismi Restitutio* in the mistaken belief that he was a soulmate. The work denied the Trinity and the eternity of the Son, claiming that Jesus' existence was limited to his earthly life. This was heresy to Protestant and Catholic alike. Calvin replied to Servetus in mild enough terms, signing the letter "your servant and hearty friend" with a postscript: "I beseech our good Lord to have you in his keeping."[33] Another letter he wrote the same day was in a different vein. "Servetus lately wrote to me, and coupled with his letter a long volume of his delirious fancies,"

Calvin noted. "He takes it upon him to come hither, if it be agreeable to me. But I am unwilling to pledge my word for his safety, for if he shall come, I shall never permit him to depart alive. . . ."[34]

Publishers at Basle refused to publish an anonymous edition of *Christianismi Restitutio* at Calvin's insistence. An edition of one thousand copies was secretly printed at Vienna and sent to Lyons and Frankfurt for the Easter market in 1553. The inquisitor general at Lyons, Matthieu Ory, took up the case on March 12. Calvin collaborated with Ory, supplying him with examples of Servetus's handwriting and correspondence as evidence of his authorship. Servetus was arrested and interrogated by Ory at Lyons, but he escaped from prison early one morning after asking to walk in the exercise yard still wearing his nightgown and cap. On Saturday, August 6, sentenced to death in absentia, he rode into Louyset, a village on the French frontier. He sold his horse and walked to Geneva the next day. He put up at the Rose hostelry and asked for a boat to take him to Zurich, where he thought he would be safe among the Zwinglians. No boat was available until Monday. Since Sunday church attendance was compulsory in Geneva, he attended an afternoon service, where he was recognized, denounced, and arrested.

His interrogation and trial lasted from August 14 to October 26. He had little hope of survival. Calvin described him as a "monster" whose thoughts were a "rhapsody patched up from the impious ravings of all ages." He was not allowed an advocate, though he was a stranger and was ignorant of Geneva law, and he complained from his cell that "the lice eat me alive . . . my clothes are torn and I have nothing for a change, neither jacket nor shirt. . . ." His crime was denying the tri-personality of the Godhead, and it was in the name of the Trinity that Servetus, a man who had written with passion that the use of force was wrong even in the defense of Christian truth, was condemned to be burned alive. He refused to recant.

Calvin would have preferred beheading, but he displayed no other compassion to a prisoner whose love for Christ was quite equal to his own. Indeed, Calvin's main concern was for the pain such wretches caused to his own tender feelings. How hard it was to be God's advocate! "I always rather desired that they might live in prosperity, and continued safe and untouched," he wrote of his victims, "which would have been the case had they not been altogether incorrigible. . . . I experienced excruciating pain from the malignity of those who ceased not to assail myself and my ministry with their envenomed calumnies."[35] In fact, much of Calvin's suffering was physical—"a feeble and spare body, inclining to consumption," his biographer and disciple Theodore Beza wrote, "taking no food until supper . . . he became afflicted with ulcerated haemorrhoids and discharged considerable quantities of blood"[36]—and Servetus's skills as a physician might have eased his ailments. He attributed his exhaustion and lack of repose to those heretics who assailed his beliefs, however, rather than to his own ill-temper and his hemorrhoids. "At length matters came to such a state," he wrote, "that an end could be put to their machinations in no other way than cutting them off by an ignominious death; which was indeed a painful and pitiful spectacle to me . . ." It was as if Calvin were the martyr rather than the unfortunate Servetus, who was duly burned at Champel on October 27, 1553. As he walked to the stake, Servetus prayed that God would forgive his accusers.

Posters were found on the corpses of other victims :

Wanderer, reflect on the evil accomplished by Calvin
Who, deprived of L and V, presents himself as a second CAIN
Take out one L, which so imprudently flies
Take out one open V; by all the evil of Calvin,
You know his violent rage.
Knowing him, you judge him Cain.

Such revulsion did not inhibit Calvinists. They believed that they were carrying out God's purpose, and the discipline and savage austerity of Geneva attracted religious wanderers from across Europe.

"So many from all countries come hither, as it were in a sanctuary, not to gather riches, but to live in poverty," the Englishman John Bale wrote around 1556. "Is it not wonderful that Spaniards, Italians, Scots, Englishmen, Frenchmen, Germans, disagreeing in manners, speech and apparel, sheep and wolves, bulls and bears, being coupled only with the yoke of Christ, should live so lovingly and friendly. . . ." Almost five thousand arrived in the city over that decade. Many were skilled artisans, who founded watchmaking businesses and printing shops, while others taught at the university and academy. Protestant tracts flooded across the border, so that "nothing in Europe was safe from the fiery brand which set everything in flames"[37]; ministers who had trained at the Geneva academy under Theodore Beza spread Calvin's ideas at great speed. The English exile William Whittingham printed an English New Testament in the city in 1557. This "Geneva Bible" was the first to be divided into verses and was used in England for the next century. John Knox returned to his native Scotland to proclaim Geneva to be "the most perfect school of Christ that ever was in the earth since the days of the apostles." Nowhere else, he said, were manners and religion "so sincerely reformed."

Not all were pleased, of course. The Venetian ambassador wrote in 1561 of his alarm at the way the "contagion" was sweeping France. Not a single province remained uncontaminated; "in three fourths of the kingdom," he said, "assemblies are held . . . according to the rites and uses of Geneva"; every class was affected, and "even bishops and many of the principal prelates." He found Calvin to be a figure of extraordinary authority, rising above all others by his mode of life and his doctrines. "I foresee a manifest and certain division in the kingdom, and civil war as a consequence."

Calvin gave his last sermon on February 6, 1564. He was a dying man; "raising his eyes towards heaven," Beza recollected, "he would say 'O Lord, how long.'"[38] He dictated his last will and testament in April. He immodestly thanked God for making him a "partaker in the doctrine of salvation" and for deigning to "use my assistance in preaching and promulgating the truth of His Gospel," and begged that he might be allowed to stand at the judgment seat "under the shadow of Christ." He died on May 27, 1564. His epitaph was *Soli deo gloria,* "To God alone the glory."

The ambassador's prediction was wholly accurate. French Calvinists, known as Huguenots,* made rapid gains in the south and west and in the cities. They had won a degree of toleration at a colloquy at Poissy in 1561, but tensions were already evident. When the Calvinists had arrived, a cardinal hissed "Here come the Geneva dogs," and Beza retorted that the Lord's flock "needs faithful sheepdogs to drive off wolves." Within six months, forty-eight members of a Huguenot congregation were slaughtered in Champagne by Catholic ultras. Political intrigue, dynastic ambition, and desire for plunder fueled religious war. In the Netherlands, Calvinism surged among the burghers of Amsterdam, Rotterdam, and Leyden. There, too, it fused with politics and nationalism in bloody revolt against Spanish and Catholic domination. In Germany, a third element was thrust into the struggle between Catholics and Lutherans. Gore, not glory, was Calvin's immediate legacy.

---

*The word is probably derived from the German *Eidgenossen,* used of the Swiss "confederates," which was Gallicized in Geneva as *Eigenotz.*[39]

CHAPTER XIX

"The prince's wrath means death":

English Speakers

The last Catholic monarch of England, Queen Mary, died in 1558. This was the gravest of Catholic losses. The rupture with Rome, born of the lusts and marital urges of Henry VIII, transformed England into the greatest Protestant power. It was largely through its empire that Protestant sects—Anglicans and Episcopalians, Presbyterians, Baptists, Congregationalists, Quakers, and Methodists—came to be spread across North America, the West Indies, Oceania, Australasia, and large parts of Africa. Early attempts to kill off Protestantism, by execution and by invasion, produced ingrained hostility and persecution of Catholics. To this day no Catholic can be regent, lord chancellor, keeper of the great seal, or king or queen of England. Yet English coins still bear the proud letters FD next to the head of the Protestant monarch. They stand for *Fidei Defensor,* "defender of the faith," a title awarded to Henry VIII by the Medici pope, Leo X, in 1520.

Such ambivalence was at the heart of the English Reformation. Its theology was foggy, and no single strain dominated its brutal flux of beheadings, burnings, confiscations, and revolts. In terms of high politics, however, it was based on the new realities expressed in two Latin tags. The principle of *cuius regio, eius religio,** "in a ruler's territory, the ruler's religion," gave decisive importance to Henry's individual belief and self-interest, and to those of his son and two daughters when they ruled in their turn. This was underpinned by the physical danger of crossing them: *Indignatio principis mors est,* "the prince's wrath means death."[1] Monarchs,

---

*The principle was formally laid down at the religious settlement in the Holy Roman Empire of Germany at the Peace of Augsburg in 1555. Under this compromise between the Catholic emperor and his Lutheran electors, the existence of both faiths (but not of Calvinism) was recognized, with the proviso that the subjects of each German state should follow the religion of their ruler.

flush with the power of emerging nation-states, could exact greater influence over the local church from the papacy. The French crown did so by the concordat of 1516, which gave it the right to nominate major benefices in France; the papacy had also conceded control of the local inquisition to the Spanish crown. The reformers, in their root and branch attack on the Church, offered much more. The ruler replaced the pope as the moral and spiritual focus of the nation. The English monarch would become head of an English Church.

Reform began with a failed marriage. Henry VIII came to the throne in 1509 at the age of seventeen. Seven weeks later he married Catherine of Aragon, the widow of his elder brother, and daughter of Ferdinand and Isabella of Spain. A special papal dispensation was granted since marriage to a dead brother's wife was usually barred. Catholic reformers had high hopes for the young king. Intelligent and energetic, he was said to be the handsomest potentate in Christendom, with a fair and bright complexion, auburn hair combed straight, and "a round face, so very beautiful that it would become a pretty woman." Henry was pious and orthodox, hearing Mass three times a day when he hunted, and five times when he did not. In 1521 he wrote a defense of the Catholic doctrine of the seven sacraments* against the "pest of Martin Luther's heresy," urging all of Christ's servants to "rise against this common enemy of the faith." Luther countered with a diatribe against "mad giants" who attacked him without grasping his arguments. "Ye teach that faith alone without good works sufficeth," Henry retorted, adding that this "is far from the mind of St. Paul which teacheth us a 'faith worketh by love' . . ."[2] As his parents-in-law had been awarded the title of "Catholic monarchs" by the pope for their work in Spain, so this loyalty earned young Henry his FD.

By 1525 he had tired of Catherine. She had undergone six pregnancies, but three children were stillborn and only the future Queen Mary survived infancy. Her failure to produce a male heir was dynastic anathema. Henry demanded an annulment of the marriage from the pope. He claimed that it was "directly against God's law and precept" for them to be married, on the basis of a passage in Leviticus: "And if a man shall take his brother's wife, it is impurity: he hath uncovered his brother's nakedness; they shall be childless" (Lev. 20:21). The Bible was as ambivalent as ever, however, and a verse in Deuteronomy claimed quite the opposite: "If brethren dwell together, and one of them die, and have no son, the wife of the dead shall not marry without unto a stranger: her husband's brother shall go in unto her, and take her to wife. . . ." (Deut. 25:5). Rome was

---

*Catholics had recognized seven sacraments since the twelfth century: baptism, confirmation, Eucharist, penance, extreme unction, ordination, and matrimony. The Eastern Church also generally accepts seven. Most reformed churches accept only two, baptism and the Eucharist.

Henry VIII came to the English throne in 1509 and married his dead brother's widow, Catherine of Aragon. She failed to produce a male heir. From 1526 he was so in love with Anne Boleyn, an ambassador reported, "that God alone can abate his madness." For six years he sought and failed to get the pope to annul the marriage. Henry then broke off relations with Rome and proclaimed himself supreme head of the English Church. The first Protestant great power now emerged.

sacked by the imperial armies of Charles V in 1527. Charles, Holy Roman Emperor* and king of Spain, was Catherine's nephew. He had no wish to see his aunt humiliated and used his power over the papacy to insure that Clement VII, another Medici pope, delayed any decision on the annulment.

Financial pressures also drove Henry. "If my head should win him a castle in France," his friend and future lord chancellor Thomas More remarked, "it should not fail to go."[3] His attempts to hold a balance between France and Spain on the Continent were ruinously expensive. The Church was the wealthiest institution in England as well as a block to the annulment. It was tempting to plunder it, especially since the English had a strong anticlerical streak. A "Supplication of the Beggars" written by Simon Fish in 1528 and addressed to the king detailed the growing tributes that the "ravenous wolves" of the Church exacted from the people. Fish claimed that the Church owned a third of the land in England outright. It took a tenth of crops, livestock, and other farm produce in tithes. "Yea, and they look so narrowly upon their profits," Fish wrote of the clergy, "that the poor wives

*Although the title of Holy Roman Emperor continued to be held by successive Habsburg rulers, none was crowned in Italy after Charles V in 1529. In effect, the "empire" was already reduced to Germany and soon meant little more than the Habsburg hereditary lands centered on Austria. The title was finally abolished by Napoleon in 1806.

must be accountable to them of every tenth egg or else she gets not her rites at Easter, shall be taken as an heretic . . ." Masses and dirges had to be paid out of the estates of the dead, "else they will accuse the dead's friends and executors of heresy . . ." More money was demanded for hearing confessions, for indulgences, for "hallowing of churches, altars, super-altars, chapels and bells . . ." Fish calculated that the Church received "43 thousand pounds and £333 6s 8d sterling" a year, of which four hundred years before they had not had a penny.

A useful precedent served to prevent the outflow of funds to Rome. Writs of *praemunire facias*, "see that thou warn," had been used since 1351 to summons persons who appealed to papal authority in order to bypass English courts. Cardinal Wolsey, Henry's chancellor and papal legate, fell foul of *praemunire* after failing to obtain the annulment. Henry had Wolsey charged with high treason on grounds of his subservience to the foreign jurisdiction of the pope. In 1531 the whole body of the English clergy was found guilty of the same crime. They were fined 118,840 pounds and were obliged to recognize the king as "protector and supreme head of the church and clergy of England." In the "Submission of the Clergy" in 1532, they promised to enact nothing to which the king did not assent; in return, he granted them his pardon, "having always had a tender eye with mercy and pity and compassion towards his said spiritual subjects." The same year, the king undertook as "the duty of a good Christian prince" to repress annates, or "first fruits," the one year's income from benefices paid to the pope, in order to prevent the "impoverishment" caused by the "great and inestimable sums of money that have been daily conveyed out of this realm" to Rome.

Henry's desire to be rid of his wife quickened when he fell in love with Anne Boleyn. She was an unlikely femme fatale, or so the Venetian ambassador thought, a woman of "middling stature, swarthy complexion, long neck, wide mouth, bosom not much raised, and in fact has nothing but the King's great appetite, and her eyes, which are black and beautiful . . ."[4] A way out of the stalemate was suggested by Thomas Cranmer, a Cambridge theologian. Cranmer was sympathetic to the king's marital affairs. He had lost his fellowship at Jesus College upon marrying "Black Joan," a Cambridge tavern keeper, regaining it and taking holy orders on her death; he later married the niece of a Lutheran church leader at Nuremberg, bringing her back to England in secret. Cranmer recommended that the leading universities and divines of Europe should examine the legality of the marriage; if they resolved that it was unlawful, it must be declared null. The pope's dispensation would be irrelevant since he could not derogate from the law of God.

The king was much pleased by this novel scheme. Convocations of doctors and bachelors of divinity were held at Oxford and Cambridge, and concluded that "the marriage of the brother's wife was contrary both to the laws of God and

ANNA DE BOULEN

To Catholics, Anne Boleyn was the "English Messalina" and a "jezebel and a sorceress." Protestants hailed her as the "chief, first and only cause of banishing the beast of Rome with all his beggarly baggage." Her refusal to sleep with Henry VIII unless he married her—"I would rather lose my life than my honesty, which will be the greatest and best part of the dowry I shall have to bring to my husband"—precipitated the historic English rupture with Rome. Ultimately she paid with her head.

nature." It was more difficult to win over Continental divines. The Venetians remained neutral. At the Sorbonne, after three weeks of reflection, a majority decided that "the king's marriage was lawful, and the pope could not dispense with it." Luther was consulted. Although he agreed that a dispensation from "the Roman Pope" was not necessary, he ruled that, even if Henry had sinned by marrying his dead brother's wife, it would be "a far greater and heavier sin to throw her off now that he has really taken her and to rend the bond of marriage in so cruel a manner . . ."

Henry married Anne Boleyn in secret in January 1533. In February, supreme jurisdiction in all ecclesiastical appeals—including matrimony, divorce, and church taxes, the areas of most interest to Henry—was placed in the king's hands. Appeals and interventions to "the see of Rome, or any other foreign courts and potentates of the world" were banned. Cranmer was consecrated archbishop of Canterbury. He presided over an ecclesiastical court in May that pronounced Catherine's marriage to be null and void; the only bishop to refuse to accept the verdict, John Fisher, was imprisoned. The marriage to Anne Boleyn was validated. It was Cranmer's unpleasant task to inform Catherine that she was no longer queen. She refused to accept it, he wrote, "saying that inasmuch as her cause was before the Pope she would have no other judge; and therefore would not take me for her judge." The new queen was crowned by Cranmer on June 1, 1533, Whitsunday morning, in the great church at Westminster, clad in silver tissue, sitting on a chair of cloth of gold carried between two mules under a canopy of cloth of silver, her hair spilling over her shoulders. In September she gave birth to a daughter, Elizabeth. Cranmer stood as godfather. Henry was excommunicated.

It was, of course, claimed that God smiled on the historic break with the papacy. The evidence of divine favor was said to be "so fair weather with plenty of corn and cattle," the birth of a healthy child, the peace and friendship sought by foreign princes, and the "purity of the air and the freedom from pestilence . . ."[5] No reference was made to religious doctrine; this was not Germany. The break point was Henry's claim to supremacy over both clergy and laity, exploited by his skillful and ruthless secretary of state, Thomas Cromwell. Cranmer accepted the king's authority, "of very right and by God's law," to be "next immediately to God." An Act of Supremacy of November 1534 declared that the king and his successors "shall be taken, accepted and reputed the only supreme head on earth of the Church of England, called Anglicana Ecclesia . . ."[6]

Papal loyalists were brought to trial. John Fisher was sent to the Tower of London; as he languished, his prospect of survival dimmed further when the pope sent him a cardinal's hat. He was joined in the Tower by another of the great figures of English humanism, Sir Thomas More, the former lord chancellor and a ruthless persecutor of Tyndale, whose house at Chelsea Erasmus described as "Plato's academy revived again," a student of astronomy, geometry, and wildlife, and the author of *Utopia,* a description of an island paradise where freedom of religion, universal education, and equality flourish. More was tender to his family if not to heretics—Erasmus thought no man living was so affectionate to children, and he "loveth his old wife as if she were a girl of fifteen"—but he refused her pleas to recant and thus release himself from the Tower. "Is not this house as nigh heaven as mine own?" he said. During the months of interrogation, More wrote on Christ's Passion and a *Dialoge of Comfort agaynst Trybulacion* in his cell. He was convicted of denying the royal supremacy, probably on perjured evidence. Fisher was beheaded on June 22, 1535. More followed a fortnight later.* "I pray you, Master Lieutenant, see me safe up," he said as he climbed to the scaffold, "and for my coming down let me shift for myself." His body was buried in St. Peter's in the Tower, and his head was parboiled and exhibited on London Bridge.

*Both Fisher and More were canonized four centuries later, in 1935.

❖ IT WAS EASY enough to kill "papists" as "traitors." It was more difficult to tamper with Catholicism. Henry's argument was with the pope, but in terms of doctrine he was deeply conservative and orthodox. A priest told Cranmer proudly that he never failed to "speak effectually against the usurped power of the Bishop of Rome and . . . his cardinals and his cloistered hypocrites" when he entered the pulpit. He added, however, that his declarations were confirmed "by the sayings of More and other papists themselves." This was indeed the royal position. Henry despised Lutheranism and was reluctant to allow the new church a new doctrine.

The dissolution of the monasteries followed a survey of Church wealth, the *Valor ecclesiasticus,* carried out in 1535. The excuse was the "manifest sin, vicious, cardinal and abominable living" of the monks, canons, and nuns; booty was the prime mover. "King Henry's sole concern was the income of the Church," the Lutheran envoy Myconius reported back to Germany. "He stripped the gold and silver from the tombs of the saints . . . and robbed the Church of its estates. That was the Gospel that Henry wanted."[7] At Glastonbury Abbey the king's commissioners found three hundred pounds in cash and "a fair chalice of gold and divers other parcels of plate" which the abbot had tried to conceal; he was "but a very weak man and sickly," but they made a note of his "cankered and traitorous heart." Royal officials arrived at another monastery, a chronicler recorded, and turned the abbot, his convent, and the household weeping out of the doors. Animals, corn, implements, and hay were sold off "good cheap" to all who came. When they found the doors open, the locks and shackles broken, the crowds went into the monastery "and took what they found—filched it away." Some took the service books from the chapel, and the glass from the windows, and broke into tombs looking for spoils. "What tearing up of lead there was and plucking up of boards and throwing down of spars," the writer grieved, "and all things of Christ either spoiled, carped away, or defaced to the uttermost."[8]

The south was generally quiescent, although women at Exeter attacked workmen as they demolished a local priory. Popular revulsion in the north started in Lincolnshire and spread rapidly through Yorkshire. The rebels marched under a banner of the five wounds of Christ and called their rising the Pilgrimage of Grace. Henry promised to compromise and offered pardons to persuade them to disperse. He then had the leaders executed.

His intimates had equally little reason to trust him. In 1536, Anne Boleyn and her brother and several attendants were executed on trumped-up charges of treasonable adultery. Before the end of the month, Henry married Jane Seymour, who died the next year shortly after bearing him a son, Edward. Cromwell cajoled Henry into marrying Anne of Cleves on the basis of a flattering portrait by Holbein. When he saw her in the flesh, the king complained that "you have sent me a Flanders mare"; he married her with distaste before sending her back. Cromwell did not long survive this disaster. On the day of his secretary of state's execution, Henry married Catherine Seymour, the niece of the duke of Norfolk; she was pretty, vivacious, indiscreet, and unfaithful, having an affair with her cousin Thomas Culpepper. "I die a queen," she said at her execution, "but I would rather have died a wife of Culpepper." His last bride, Catherine Parr, outlived him. "Divorced, beheaded, died," generations of schoolboys chanted of the marital follies that helped change a nation's faith, "divorced, beheaded, survived."

❖   THERE WERE NO such religious extravagances. True, some Catholic images were destroyed. The most famous was the shrine of Thomas Becket at Canterbury, one of the leading pilgrimage sites in Christendom, but its significance was political, for Becket had been martyred for resisting the will of the Crown. "Our king had destroyed the Pope," the reformer John Hooper commented, "but not Popery."[9] It was a shrewd remark, and one Hooper was well able to judge. A violent and long-lasting malice against the person of the pope permeated Protestantism in Britain. An act of 1536 accused the pope of having "seduced and conveyed" loving and obedient subjects with "dreams, vanities and fantasies" into superstition and godlessness; the pope damaged souls, bodies, and goods by his "infinite abomination" and the "crafty colouring of his deceits." Overwhelmed and fatigued by his mischiefs, the realm was "forced of necessity for the common weal" to exclude him. Papists faced execution and forfeiture of their estates if they persisted in dealing with this devil; so, too, in a catchall warning, did "their abiders, assistants, comforters, abettors, procurers, maintainers, factors, counsellors, concealers and every one of them."

This was not a theological tract; it was the law of the land. It elevated popehating into a patriotic duty; but it was, as Hooper noted, very far from removing popery in the doctrinal sense of Catholicism. Hooper was a thoroughgoing Protestant, a former Cistercian monk who had been converted by reading Zwingli. He wisely fled from England to the safety of Zurich in 1539 rather than incur royal wrath for his radical ideas. Henry imposed the Religion Act in that year. Known as "the Whip with Six Strings," it contained six articles of faith specifically intended to prevent the spread of Reformed doctrines and practices. The Catholic position was defended in all key areas but papal supremacy. Transubstantiation was maintained and the sacrament was said to be "the natural body and blood of our Saviour Jesus Christ, and after the consecration there remaineth no substance of bread or wine." Communion in one kind was upheld;

so was the celibacy of priests, and the "law of God" was invoked to bar their marriage. Monastic vows were also permitted, although there were few places left in which to practice them. Private masses, so disliked by Luther and Calvin, were "admitted in this the King's English Church." Auricular confession, another Protestant bugbear, was found "expedient and necessary to be retained and continued."[10]

A minority of bishops objected. Hugh Latimer thought himself "as obstinate a papist as any in England" when he was a young Cambridge fellow, but later he "began to smell the Word of God." He preferred to resign his see at Worcester and be sent to the Tower rather than compromise his Protestant views on the Eucharist. Cranmer, his marriage now unlawful, sent his wife back to Germany. Like the Catholic martyrs before them, some Protestants were willing to die for their faith. Anne Askew, a young Reformer devoted to Bible study, was racked in the Tower and burned. Most, however, were reassured by the continuation of traditional beliefs. "The people," an observer wrote, "show great joy at the king's declaration touching the Sacrament, being much more inclined to the old religion than the new opinions."[11] The only change of theological importance was the provision of English Bibles in each parish; even here, it was laid down that the book was not to be read in "high and loud Voices" or during services.

Henry died in January 1547, ulcerated and swollen, his girth measuring fifty-four inches. The political tensions surrounding the succession were so great that the death was concealed for three days. He had been sudden and violent in his passions, the Protestant John Foxe noted, and hesitated at nothing by which he could gratify his lust or his revenge. In matters of religion, Foxe added, Henry's severities "made both sides write with great sharpness against him."[12] His children themselves represented those two sides of the great divide that he had opened up, and failed to bridge. Mary, the elder, was Catholic; her nine-year-old half brother Edward was brought up under the Protestant influence of his uncle, the duke of Somerset; Elizabeth, Anne Boleyn's daughter, was raised a Protestant.

❖ THE BOY WAS the heir, crowned as Edward VI. The reformers now moved boldly to eradicate popery. Conservative bishops were detained and replaced by radicals. Latimer went back to his see at Worcester, while clerical wives returned to their husbands. When Hooper came back to England to become bishop of Gloucester, it was said that he "seemed to have brought all Switzerland with him." Chantries, where priests had said Mass for the dead for centuries, were dissolved. The blessing of candles, ashes, and palms at Candlemas, Ash Wednesday, and Palm Sunday was banned. Bishop Bonner held up a wooden model with joints that he moved to turn its head and bless the congregation, to mock the reverence that Catholics paid to images; boys "broke up the idols in pieces"[13] with the bishop's approval. The insides of churches were coated with white lime. Wooden tables replaced stone altars.

An Act of Uniformity prescribed the Book of Common Prayer, largely written by Cranmer in 1549 and revised three years later, and prohibited all other forms of worship. The revised prayer book excluded all prayers for the dead, abolished ritual vestments in favor of a plain surplice, and omitted all references to "mass" and "altar." The Black Rubric, an appended note, made it plain that kneeling at Communion did not imply any adoration of the sacrament. Leaders of a rising in the West Country called the new book "a Christmas game" and demanded the return of the Latin Mass, Communion in one kind, the adoration of the sacrament, and of ashes and palms.

The country had little time to adapt to Protestant rigor before it was gone. Edward, the "sacred imp," died in 1553. His half sister succeeded him. Mary had remained a loyal Catholic during her unhappy childhood, regarded as her father's bastard, humiliated by being driven away from court, bravely refusing to abandon the use of the old Catholic liturgy in her household. "Her soul was God's," she had told Edward's council, "and her faith she would not change." Immediately after she arrived in London, the Venetian ambassador wrote with approval, "she had the mass performed, and the first Parliament restored all the ancient ceremonies and the doctrine of the sacrament." Her subjects were bade to leave "those new-found devilish terms of papist or heretic and such like" and were forbidden to read false books "touching the high points and mysteries of Christian religion" produced by printers and stationers with "an evil zeal for lucre."[14]

Englishmen, the ambassador believed, "would be full as zealous followers of the Mohammedan or Jewish religions did the king profess either of them," their main inclinations being to "licentiousness and profit." But, he felt, it was too much to hope that the Church should recover its lands and possessions—"almost impossible by reason of the endless law-suits that would ensue"—and the ambassador noted that the queen's character, rash, disdainful, and parsimonious, did not endear her to her subjects.[15] Neither did her marriage to Philip II of Spain. He gave her little affection—"the queen is small and rather flabby rather than fat," one of his courtiers remarked, "a perfect saint and dresses badly"—and the Spanish alliance was deeply unpopular. It triggered an unsuccessful conspiracy against her. Although no evidence of complicity could be found, she sent her Protestant half sister Elizabeth to the Tower. The first Protestant to go to the stake was a London preacher, John Rogers, in February 1555. He died, the French ambassador wrote, with "such composure that it might have been a wedding." Such courage was noted; the epithet "Bloody Mary" was in the making. Her impetuousness was ill advised. "Haste in religious matters ought to be avoided," the ambassador of the Holy Roman Empire wrote to her absent husband. "Cruel punishments are not the best way."

❖ MARTYRDOM PROVED THE ruination of Roman Catholicism in England, a horror that all Protestants could nurture in common. The Book of Martyrs, a work of racy propaganda in which John Foxe recorded Protestant deaths, was to become a second Bible in English homes. Those who were attempting to restore the old religion, however, had good reason to see themselves as victims of the new. On November 20, 1554, Cardinal Reginald Pole sailed to pealing bells and artillery salvos from Calais for Dover aboard the royal yacht. He rode to Canterbury with a cavalcade of five hundred horses, entering the city by torchlight in the evening. Here he was presented with letters certifying the repeal of all laws passed against him under the two previous reigns. In London, he formally absolved Parliament from schism with Rome; on December 2 the clergy of the ancient convocations of York and Canterbury knelt before him to receive his absolution "for all their perjuries, schisms and heresies." In January 1555 the pope's supremacy was restored by act of Parliament.

Pole was fortunate to be alive to see England apparently reconciled to Rome. He had been on the Continent since 1536; here, he was declared a traitor as a cardinal and papal legate, and was beset by English spies and would-be assassins, traveling in disguise with few attendants. In England, his brother was executed. His mother, Margaret, countess of Salisbury, godmother and governess to the young Mary, was arrested on suspicion of sending clandestine messages to her traitor-son abroad. The countess remained silent under interrogation, but a search of her house was said to have disclosed papal bulls and an incriminating white silk tunic. It was innocently embroidered on the front with the arms of England, three lions surrounded by a wreath of pansies and marigolds, but on its back it bore the badge of the five wounds of Christ carried by the insurgents of the Pilgrimage of Grace. Falsely convicted of treason, the countess had walked boldly from her cell to be decapitated in the grounds of the Tower of London, asking bystanders to pray for her goddaughter Mary, "to whom she desired to be specially commended."[16] "I am now the son of a martyr," Cardinal Pole said. "This is the king's reward for her care of his daughter's education." He then added calmly: "Let us be of good cheer. We now have one more patron in heaven."

The countess had been mother to Pole, godmother to Mary; both were marked by Protestant cruelty. What they did now was no worse in spiritual terms, unless a burning is counted less godly than a beheading; a merely technical point, for all sides were agreed that it was fitting and Christian to execute heretics. Neither, in human terms, were their victims more distinguished, or the loss more grievous, than More or Fisher or the countess. The distinction is in the historic aftershock. In providing Anglicans with martyrs, the Catholic queen and her cardinal supplied them with the seed of their new Church.

John Hooper, the reformer who in 1536 had complained at the failure to destroy popery, was the first to die. "He has in times past preached and taught the most pestilent heresies," Mary's order stated, "and hath refused mercy. He shall be put to execution in the said city of Gloucester for the example and terror of such as he there seduced and mistaught." He was burned on February 9, 1555. The following month the bishop of St. Davids, Robert Ferrar, was burned in the marketplace at Carmarthen. Attempts were made to prevent the condemned from preaching to bystanders. Hooper's executioner was required to ensure that his victim "be neither, at the time of his execution, nor in going to the place thereof, suffered to speak at large, but thither to be led quietly and in silence . . ."[17]

This was not possible with three more famous men, Thomas Cranmer, Nicholas Ridley, and Hugh Latimer, respectively archbishop of Canterbury, and bishops of London and Worcester, who were lodged in Bocardo, the common jail of Oxford. They had been accused of heresy at disputations in front of a large audience of university divines; cries of "*Vicit veritas!*" had announced the victory of Catholic truth and their condemnation. Latimer publicly refused to submit to Catholic teachings on the real presence and the sacrifice of the Mass; his final words as he was led to the stake on October 16, 1555, with the bishop of London entered Protestant legend. "Be of good comfort, Master Ridley, and play the man," he said. "We shall this day light such a candle by God's grace in England, as I trust shall never be put out."

Cranmer witnessed the martyrdoms from prison. He had himself condoned burnings as archbishop; he was fearful, and a follower rather than a leader—"Do my lord of Canterbury a shrewd turn, and he is your friend for ever," Shakespeare later wrote of him. It was thought safe to make him a spectacle. He was condemned by a papal commission in February 1556, and then publicly degraded outside of Christ Church, Oxford. Cranmer was clothed in canvas replicas of the vestments of subdeacon, deacon, priest, bishop, and archbishop; a mitre and a pall of canvas were put on his head, and then each layer of clothing was stripped from him in turn. A barber shaved his head while the new bishop of London scraped the skin off the tips of the fingers he had used in anointing. He was then delivered to the secular power for execution.

Cranmer signed seven forms of recantation, each more humiliating to him than the last. He appears to have done so voluntarily, for there is no evidence that he was tortured or offered a pardon. He repudiated Luther and Zwingli, acknowledged papal supremacy and the existence of purgatory, promised faithful obedience to the queen and her Spanish husband, and urged all fellow heretics to return to the unity of the Church. He asked Pole for a few days' stay of execution so that he might make his repentance more public, and this was granted. The day set for Cranmer's execution at Oxford, March 21, 1556, was wet. To avoid the rain, the sermon that was to have been preached at the stake was delivered in St. Mary's Church instead. Cranmer was put on a platform opposite the pulpit. He knelt and prayed fervently, weeping and moving the audience to tears. He was then allowed to address the people. He asked them to pray for him as "a wretched caitiff and miserable sinner," and, as in his recantations, he declared his belief in every article of the Catholic faith. Then, to the mounting horror of the Spanish friars who attended him, he recanted his recantations. "And now I come to the great things which so much troubleth my conscience, more than anything that ever I did or said in my whole life, and that is the setting abroad of writings contrary to the truth, which now here I renounce and refuse, as things written in my hand contrary to the truth which I thought in my heart, and written for fear of death, and to save my life," he said. "And that is, all such bills and papers which I have written or signed with my hand since my degradation, wherein I have written many things untrue. And forasmuch as my hand offended, writing contrary to my heart, my hand shall first be punished therefor; for, may I come to the fire, it shall be first burned. And as for the Pope, I refuse him as Christ's enemy and Antichrist, with all his false doctrine."[18]

Cranmer then walked briskly from the church to the place of execution, his head shaven, his beard "long, white and thick," a man "sore broken in studies," but "with a cheerful countenance and willing mind." He pulled off his clothes and was chained upright to the stake in his shirt. The Spanish friars urged him to revert to his former recantation, but he refused. "Let us go from him," they said; "we ought not be nigh to him, for the devil is with him." The wood was kindled. Cranmer thrust his right hand into the flame, and held it there so that it was "seen of every man sensibly burning." He cried out in a loud voice: "This hand hath offended." As soon as the fire got up, he was very soon dead, "never stirring or crying all the while."

The following day, Pole was consecrated archbishop of Canterbury in Cranmer's place. The Oxford burnings fouled the new appointment. Those with worldly reasons for resisting the return to the old religion, beneficiaries from the seizure of Church land and property, secular officeholders, nationalists who resented the Spanish alliance, now had martyrs to give their self-interest an air of idealism. Catholics were themselves disturbed. "His patience in the torment, his courage in dying," a Catholic eyewitness of Cranmer's execution admitted, "I could worthily have . . . matched with the fame of any father of ancient time; but seeing that not the death, but the cause and quarrel thereof, commendeth the sufferer, I cannot

L. Receiue my spirit.

Frier Iohn.

"This hath offended!" Thomas Cranmer said as he was burned at Oxford in 1556. "Oh this unworthy hand!" With that, he thrust the hand with which he had signed recantations into the flames, so that it was the first to burn. Cranmer was the most distinguished of the Protestants to be burned in the reign of Henry VIII's daughter by Catherine of Aragon, the Catholic Queen Mary. When she was succeeded by her half sister, Anne Boleyn's Protestant daughter Queen Elizabeth, Catholics went to the fire.

but much dispraise his obstinate stubbornness and sturdiness in dying, specially in so evil a cause."[19]

Prosperous Protestants with good contacts abroad, merchants and university men, retreated to the Continent. Married priests sent away their wives. Others went to mass, but avoided Catholic practice, looking away at the elevation of the Host and not kissing the pyx, the vessel in which the Host was kept. "You are in the confines of Babylon," the Reform divine John Philpot warned his sister, "where you are in danger to drink of the whore's cup, unless you be vigilant in prayer."[20] Those who maintained their purity were burned, as Philpot was himself. "You have the Word," the Catholic dean of Westminster bragged to Protestants, "and we have the sword."

Papal politics now reduced the Catholic cause to near farce. Paul IV, the obsessive heretic-hunter elected pope in 1555 at the age of seventy-nine, had long believed Pole to be a secret Lutheran. He also nourished a deep loathing for the

Spanish crown, which ruled his home city of Naples. The papacy was thus pitted against the leading Catholic power of the day, and by extension against Mary. Paul branded her as the "wife of a schismatic," for her unhappy marriage to Philip II of Spain, and revoked Pole's legatine authority. To make matters worse, Mary declared war against France in June 1557 in the defense of her husband's Spanish interests. Calais, an English outpost in France for more than two hundred years, fell early the next year. To this humiliation was added a phantom pregnancy, and illness. On November 17, after telling her ladies that she had seen "many little children like angels, playing before her," she died. Twelve hours later Pole was also dead.

❧ "IT IS THE Lord's doing, and it is marvellous in our eyes," Elizabeth said on hearing of her half sister's death. Elizabeth was a survivor in matters personal, political, and religious; under Mary, as she was to remind her Parliament, "I stood in danger of my life, my sister was so incensed against me." Protestant tutors had brought her up; Catholics regarded her as a bastard, the offspring of an illegal marriage, and she had no reason to wish them well. Necessity made Elizabeth a mistress of dissimulation. "She is too clever to get herself caught," the imperial ambassador remarked when she was questioned in the Tower over her alleged links to Protestant conspirators.

The *via media,* the "middle way" in religion, came to her naturally. "Her figure and face are very handsome, and such an air of dignified majesty pervades all her actions that no one can fail to suppose she is a queen," the Venetian ambassador commented, adding the significant rider that "her manners are very modest and affable." Catholics and puritans alike were hostile—the great English Methodist John Wesley was later to describe her as being as "just and merciful as Nero and as good a Christian as Mahomet"—and her religious strength lay in being the reverse of Mary. She was not devout, she did not marry, and she was patient and cautious.

In her first Parliament of 1559, she took back the supreme governorship of the Church and restored an amended prayer book that made some concessions to Catholics. The prayer in the litany for deliverance "from the tyranny of the Bishop of Rome and his detestable enormities" was dropped. Her Injunctions to the clergy gave the visual impression of puritanism. They were instructed to "take away, utterly extinct, and destroy all shrines, coverings of shrines, all tables, candlesticks, trindals, and rolls of wax, pictures, paintings, and all other monuments of feigned miracles, pilgrimages, idolatry and superstition, so that there remain no memory of the same in walls, glass windows. . . ." But she had a crucifix in her own chapel, considered prohibiting clerical marriage, and favored traditional vestments.

The Thirty-nine Articles of 1563 (but not approved in their final form until 1571) that defined Anglican doctrine "for the avoiding of diversities of opinions" were deliberately vague and ambiguous. Article 6 declared that "Holy Scripture containeth all things necessary to salvation," a phrase with which all could agree; on transubstantiation, the formula was so broad that it covered both the belief in the purely symbolic nature of the sacrament and in the actual Presence of the body and blood of Christ. It was not until 1570 that Elizabeth was excommunicated and Catholic plots against her began in earnest.

❧ IN SCOTLAND THE Protestant movement was fitful in its early stages, inhibited by isolation and a low literacy rate. The protomartyr was Patrick Hamilton. As a thirteen year old he had been made titular abbot of Farne; as a young man he visited Wittenberg, meeting and admiring Luther. He was arrested on his return to Scotland in 1527; he refused to recant and was burned the following year. Heretical books were smuggled in by sea and across the English border. The catalyst for revolt was the condemnation of an itinerant Protestant preacher, George Wishart, in front of the cardinal archbishop of St. Andrews, David Beaton, in 1546. As he waited for death, Wishart urged the audience: "I beseech you, brethren and sisters, to exhort your Prelates to the learning of the word of God, that they at the last may be ashamed to do evil, and learn to do good; and if they will not convert themselves from their wicked error, there shall hastily come upon them the wrath of God, which they shall not eschew." He kissed the hangman's cheek: "Lo! Here is a token that I forgive thee. My heart, do thine office."[21]

A group of young reformers, including a former Catholic priest named John Knox, determined to avenge him. Beaton's residence in the castle of St. Andrews was being modernized, and the drawbridge was lowered to bring in supplies of lime and stone. Six conspirators disguised as workmen crossed it and tracked down Beaton, who locked himself in his apartment. They cried "fire, fire" and sent for hot coals to smoke him out. He opened the door: "I am a priest; I am a priest; ye will not slay me." One of them, James Melville, said: "Repent thee of thy former wicked life, but especially of the shedding of the blood of that notable instrument of God, Master George Wishart, which albeit the flame of fire consumed before men, yet cries it a vengeance upon thee, and we from God are sent to revenge it. . . ." He struck him through with his sword, and the cardinal expired, saying, "Fye, fye; all is gone. . . ."[22]

Knox joined the conspirators in the castle and was taken prisoner when French forces were called in to suppress the rebellion. He spent eighteen months rowing in chains in a French galley named after the Virgin. On his release he became a chaplain to Edward VI in England, fleeing to the Continent at Mary's accession. He found his way to Geneva and was deeply influenced by Calvin. Scottish Protestants banded together in December 1557 to subscribe to a covenant: "We, perceiving how Satan in his members, the Antichrists of our time, cruelly doth rage . . . ought, according to our bounden duty, to strive in our Master's cause, even unto death, being certain of victory in him. . . ."[23] With Elizabeth's accession, many Scottish Protestants returned from exile. Appeals were made for Knox to join them; Calvin said that Knox should go lest he be "rebellious unto his God, and unmerciful to his country."[24] On his way he wrote to Scots that they should be prepared "to hazard your lives (be it against kings or emperors) . . ."

Within a month of his return to Scotland, Knox was preaching at Perth and St. Andrews. Other congregations signed fresh covenants, and a group of noblemen pledged themselves at Leith to work for the reform of the Church. In 1560 a Protestant "confession of faith" was put before the Scottish Parliament. It was a Calvinist manifesto. It described the "pestiferous errors" of the "Roman Kirk" as "the doctrine of Transubstantiation; of the Adoration of Christ his body under the form of bread; of the merits of Works, and Justification they allege comes thereby; together with the doctrine of Papistical Indulgences, Purgatory, Pilgrimage and Praying to Saints departed . . ." Protestant members asked Parliament that such "doctrine and idolatry" be "abolished by Act of this present Parliament, and punishment appointed for the transgressors." They insisted, too, that the "Roman harlot and her sworn vassals" be abolished, together with a clergy "living in whoredom, adultery, deflowering virgins, corrupting matrons, and doing all abominations, without fear of punishment."[25]

This was more extreme than any English declaration, as Knox himself was the fiery puritan preacher made flesh. Sir Peter Young, tutor to the future Protestant monarch James VI, wrote to Theodore Beza in Geneva, describing Knox as "grave and stern . . . in anger his very frown became imperious . . . the eyes were dark-blue, keen and animated . . . his beard black, flecked with grey, thick, and falling down a hand and a half long . . ."[26] Nonetheless, Knox triumphed. He noted that only three temporal lords voted against, condemning the Confession on the grounds that they would believe as their fathers had believed. "The Bishops (papistical, we mean) spake nothing," Knox wrote. "The rest of the whole three Estates by their public votes affirmed the doctrine. . . ."[27] The Confession was accepted. Papal jurisdiction in Scotland was outlawed and the celebration of the mass became an idolatry.

It was the last great Protestant victory in Europe.

ROMAN SOLDIERS:

Counter-Reformation

Many who remained loyal to the old Church sought to rescue it from sloth and immorality. Their efforts helped the Counter-Reformation, the conscious attempt to choke Protestant advance through censorship, inquisition, and the military leagues of Catholic powers. But the movement predated Luther, whom it greatly influenced, and it was more than a defensive reflex. Catholic idealism had two strands, devotion, and the desire to purify the priesthood. John Colet, the dean of St. Paul's in London, had preached a sermon in 1512 identifying the ailments of churchmen. Their worldliness, he said, made them "the servants rather of men than of God"; they suffered from a "pride of life" in which "they run, yea, almost out of breath, from one benefice to another," and they sought pleasure and "carnal concupiscence."[1] The remedy lay in a renewed sense of spirituality, and of toil among the sick and suffering.

Vigorous new orders were founded. Their members worked in remote villages, and in prison cells and hospitals, like the first Franciscans. They educated illiterate country priests and set an example to cynical city clerics. The Oratory of Divine Love, a small group of clergy and laity who met for prayer and meditation, and to discuss how best to revive love and charity in the Church, appeared at Rome in 1517, the year of Luther's *Theses*. The Theatines, distinguished by their white socks, were founded in 1524 to pit themselves against "the corruption of manners and souls, which had spread far and wide among the Christian people."[2] They were admired for their poverty and charity, and were forbidden to own property or to beg. Four years later the Capuchin order was conceived to return to Franciscan ideals of simplicity and contemplation. Their preachers, bearded beneath a pointed cowl, or capuche, rejected the comfortable houses and splendid churches of the established Franciscans. Instead they built small communities of mud and wattle huts deep in the countryside, tending to the poor and sick, and evangelizing. The Barnabites, founded at Milan in 1530, preached the Pauline Epistles with zeal and flair. A Venetian nobleman and former soldier, Jerome Emiliani, set up the Somaschi to work among the dispossessed, caring for orphans, lepers, and prostitutes.

Philip Neri, the "apostle of Rome," was the son of a wealthy Tuscan family. He gave up a career in trade and went to Rome in 1533, living in a bare room on bread, olives, and apples. By day he preached in slums and taverns and worked for the relief of the sick, raising money for a new hospital, where cardinals joined him in washing the feet of patients in a display of humility. At night he prayed in the catacomb of San Sebastiano on the Appian Way. "O God," he pleaded, "why have you given us but one heart to love you, and this so little and so narrow?" In response, Neri is said to have experienced a rapture in which divine love so dilated his breast that the "gristle which joined the fourth and fifth ribs on the left side was broken," thus allowing the heart to be enlarged.[3] He tended pilgrims whose numbers—145,000 in the Jubilee year of 1575—showed that pilgrimage continued to give Catholics a comfort that Protestants denied to their followers. Neri's foundation, the Congregation of the Oratory, grew from the meetings he held in the oratory at San Girolamo. Its members, secular priests living in the community without vows, spread rapidly through Italy, Spain, southern Germany, and Poland. Members of the French Oratory went to the backcountry, attracting the peasants with Savonarola-like "joy-fires," where luxuries and erotic pamphlets were burned and hymns were sung to popular tunes. They never stayed in a parish for less than six weeks; "otherwise," the missioner John Eudes wrote, "you conceal the wickedness but do not cure it."[4]

It was the duty of Oratorians to lead men to God and teach the ignorant. Neri found this was best done through using drama and music in services. The oratorio grew out of the *laudi spirituali* sung in Oratorian devotions, biblical stories set to music with soloists, chorus, and organ. These religious operas, fulfilling Pope Nicholas's plea for a Catholicism that appealed to the senses, satisfied the ear in the same way that the baroque churches of the Counter-Reformation, with their painted domes, cherubs, gold leaf, statues, and richly vestured priests, excited the eye. In Protestant countries, organs were often sold off to taverns or broken up; at Worcester Cathedral the pipes were used to make metal plates and the case became a bedstead, while congregations were led by parish clerks in unaccompanied singing that the dramatist Thomas Shadwell sadly described as "a company of peasants praising God with doleful untuneable hoarse voices."[5] At St. Peter's in Rome, Giovanni Palestrina wrote hymns, motets, and more than ninety masses of unconstrained beauty. The composer Girolamo Frescobaldi, who was appointed organist of the great church, had audiences of thirty thousand for his recitals.

Beggared by gambling debts, working as an ass driver and laborer for the Capuchins, the former soldier Camillo de Lellis was guided by Neri into founding his own congregation of Camillians. Camillo suffered from running sores on his legs, and the Camillians took a vow of perpetual service to the sick, in particular those stricken with plague. At Naples, Camillians risked their lives to board plague ships that lay offshore and comfort the crews. Violent epidemics ravaged Rome in the 1570s, carrying off Palestrina's wife and three sons. Camillo built a hospital where those with infectious diseases were isolated in well-lit and airy wards, and fed on special diets; when he was crippled by kidney stones, he crawled on his knees from patient to patient. Particular care was given to the spiritual comfort of the dying, and his order became known as the "Fathers of a Good Death" or the "Agonizantes." Camillo became the patron saint of nurses.

Two years of slavery in North Africa inspired Vincent de Paul, born in the Landes of western France in 1581, who was a shepherd boy before being ordained a priest. Sailing from Marseilles to Narbonne, he was captured by Barbary pirates and brought to Tunis, where he was given slave clothes of loose breeches and a linen jerkin, paraded around the city, and sold to a Moslem. On his master's death, he was resold to a Christian renegade who had fled from Savoy to Tunisia and who used him to till the fields on a mountain farm. Vincent persuaded the man to return to his faith, and the two crossed the Mediterranean in a small boat and landed safely on the French coast. Vincent became chaplain to the French galley slaves, easing their hardships and setting up a hospital for them at Marseilles. He was given charge of the Visitation Order in Paris, whose sisters were charged with works of mercy and nursing the sick. The order was founded in 1610 by Francis de Sales, the bishop of Geneva, who won back many Calvinists to Catholicism on dangerous missions in the Chablais, and whose *Introduction to the Devout Life* was written for the laity, explaining meditation to ordinary men and women with skill and a sweet charm that influenced Protestants as well as Catholics. Vincent founded the Lazarists to train priests and carry out missions to country people; he opened homes for foundlings, and helped establish the Sisters of Charity. This was the first congregation of women who were not enclosed and who took no final vows; they were dedicated to the care of the sick and the poor.

✤ MYSTICISM COMBINED WITH the new orders in Spain. The word "mystics" was first applied to individuals in the sixteenth century who, like Bernard and Hildegard before them sought a mystic union at the *apex affectivae,* the "peak of emotions." The Church played no part in this individual search for personal experience of God or Christ, and it was often hostile to the *illuminati* who sought it. "Prayer is rising above oneself and all created things, uniting oneself with God and submerging oneself in this sea of infinite sweetness and love," wrote Luis of Granada.[6] He was suspected of heresy and his writings were banned. His mentor, John of Avila, the "apostle of Andalucia," founded more than a dozen schools for the laity and two for the clergy, but was still imprisoned for a year.

The same doubts were cast on Teresa of Ávila, a mystic noblewoman who entered a Carmelite monastery in 1535. Her order bitterly opposed her when she established Carmelite houses of primitive rule, where nuns and friars lived in strict austerity. Her writings on the soul's progress from the quiet of contemplation to the height of ecstatic visions had a compelling tenderness and passion. "A beginner in prayer," Teresa wrote, "must look on himself as one setting out to make a garden for his Lord's pleasure, on most unfruitful soil which abounds in weeds. . . ." From this humble start, the believer reached the ecstasy of "mystical marriage" in which she described a seraphim with a spear tipped with fire penetrating to her heart and innermost being. She wrote of the soul as the "interior castle," with God as its keeper, and life as a movement from its outer rooms to the divine lightness at its center. Often ill, mortifying her flesh—"Alas, O Lord, to what a state Thou dost bring those who love thee!"—she labored to maintain her discalced* convents. When she wrote her *Life,* dashed off at rapid pace, almost unpunctuated and uninhibited, the Inquisition seized the manuscript until Philip II ordered it to be returned to her. With her devoted follower, John of the Cross, she revitalized Spanish spiritual life. John was a poet of lyrical power who wrote *Noche oscura del alma, The Dark Night of the Soul,* with a yearning for Christ so strong that life becomes death:

> This life I live in vital strength
> Is loss of life unless I win You;
> And thus to die I shall continue
> Until in You I live at length . . .
> This life I do not want, for I
> am dying that I do not die.

The same streak of mystic practicality—visions, and the power to organize a movement—ran through Ignatius Loyola, founder of the Society of Jesus. The youngest of thirteen children of an old Basque family, he was born between 1491

---

*The word means "unshod." Early Egyptian monks went barefoot in response to Jesus' command: "No wallet for your journey, neither two coats, nor shoes, nor staff . . ." (Matt. 10:10). St. Francis of Assisi introduced the rule into the West; by the time of Teresa of Ávila, discalced monks and nuns wore sandals but obeyed rigorous rules.

and 1493 in the castle of Loyola near the Pyrenees. His elder brothers were killed fighting: one against the Turks in Hungary, two near Naples, a fourth in the Indies. Orphaned at fourteen, he was sent as a page to the court of the treasurer of the kingdom of Castile. By his own admission he was "given over to the vanities of the world" until he was twenty-five, to the martial arts, and to "a burning and vain desire to win renown." Ignatius was nominally a cleric but carried arms, and wore an open cape and long hair with no sign of a tonsure. He was briefly imprisoned for a crime described as "very serious, having been carried out at night, with deliberate intent and premeditation." Like Camillo he was a gambler, seducer, and brawler. On Easter Monday, May 20, 1521, Ignatius was leading resistance to a French attack on Pamplona when a cannonball fractured his right leg.

The leg had to be broken and reset twice, and he limped for the rest of his life. He asked for books while convalescing in the family castle, and was given *Vita Christi,* a popular meditation on the life of Christ by the fourteenth-century German monk Ludolph the Carthusian, and the *Golden Legend,* tales and legends of saints' lives compiled by James of Voragine, a thirteenth-century Dominican. Ignatius copied out passages and underwent a conversion. At the end of February 1522 he rode off from Loyola on a mule, determined to travel to Jerusalem as a beggar. He spent three days confessing his sins at the abbey of Montserrat and identified a single passion within himself: "To serve our Lord." He wrote of it in his famous Prayer for Generosity:

> Teach us, good Lord,
> To serve thee as thou deserveth;
> To give and not to count the cost;
> To fight and not to heed the wounds;
> To toil and not to seek for rest;
> To labour and not ask for any reward
> Save that of knowing that we do Thy will.

Ignatius stayed for many months with the Dominicans at Manresa, still in Spain, starving himself and subjecting himself to harsh penance, wearing an iron girdle and a hair shirt, ill, his hair and nails filthy and long, an *illuminati* on the verge of suicide in the darkness that preceded the "naked love of God." On a riverbank he had a vision. "He understood and knew many things," his *Autobiography* says, "things spiritual as well as things of faith and the profane sciences; and this happened with such a great flash of illumination that all these things appeared new to him."[7] Ignatius wrote down the fruits of his meditations at Manresa and structured them into his *Spiritual Exercises,* a program of prayer of compelling insight. He sailed from Barcelona in February 1523, arriving at Jerusalem, escorted by Turks, on September 4.

On his return to Barcelona, Ignatius enrolled at the University of Alcalá and formed a small group of young men known as the Gray Habits. The Inquisition was suspicious of such cliques, and he was interrogated and forbidden to discuss theology in public. In 1528 he went to Paris to prepare himself to be "useful to souls," living in an almshouse and begging for food. He shared a room with a nobleman from Navarre, Francisco de Jassu y Xavier. He gradually won over a few fellow students, and his roommate. "I have heard our great moulder of men say that the toughest clay he had ever worked on was that of young Francis Xavier in the early days," his secretary Juan de Polanco wrote later. The seven companions went to mass together on Sundays at the Carthusian monastery. In August 1534 they assembled in the crypt of the chapel of St. Denis on the slopes of Montmartre to make a vow binding themselves to "poverty, chastity and obedience for ever . . . to teaching the young and the poor . . . I promise a special obedience to the Supreme Pontiff for the missions he will entrust me with."[8]

The pope was in need of such spirited and obedient young servants. The university at Paris was a breeding ground for Protestants as well as these loyalists; John Calvin, whose studies there overlapped with Ignatius, was about to publish his *Institutes*. In November 1538, Ignatius and ten companions were received by Paul III at Rome. "Seeing that there was no leader among them, nor any superior other than Jesus Christ," Ignatius recalled, "it seemed appropriate to call themselves the Society of Jesus. . . ." The first task of the Jesuits, as they were soon known, was teaching the catechism to children in Rome. Ignatius wrote a mission statement. "In faithful obedience to our Holy Father Paul III and his successors," it stated, "in such a way that, whatever His Holiness commands us to do for the good of souls and the propagation of the faith, we are to carry out immediately without procrastination or excuse, and as far as it is in our power, whether he sends us among the Turks, to the New World, among the Lutherans or anyone else, be they believers or infidels." Paul signed a papal bull approving the order in 1540.

❖   THE PAPACY HAD been slow to come to grips with reform. It had crises other than Protestantism to distract it. In the crucial year of 1527, with Luther making rapid gains in Germany and Henry VIII becoming restless in England, a rabble of Spanish soldiers and German mercenaries had broken into Rome and plundered the city. They were in the service of Charles V, the most devout of Catholics, who was squeezing the papal states between his territories in Lombardy and Naples. None of the troops had been paid for months, and many of the

Germans were Lutherans who delighted in taunting the pope and his priests. They dressed themselves in cardinals' robes, stabled their horses in St. Peter's and the Sistine Chapel, drank from chalices, stole jewels from shrines and ripped them from the covers of Bibles, tossed the bones of saints to dogs, and wrote Luther's name on paintings. Cardinal Giovanni del Monte, a future pope, was taken hostage and hung up by his hair until his ransom was paid. The reigning pope, Clement VII, fled to the Castel Sant' Angelo, a purple robe tossed over his telltale white robes.

Benvenuto Cellini, sculptor, goldsmith, and autobiographer, served as a gunner in the papal defense force. He killed the imperial commander, the constable of Bourbon, with his arquebus, or so he claimed; he wrote of a fellow gunner staring from the battlements to where his house was being sacked and his wife and daughters raped, not shooting for fear of hitting them, while "I continued firing, with an accompaniment of blessings and cheers from a number of cardinals. . . ."[9] Clement recognized a Spanish officer and Cellini aimed at the man, the shot striking his sword and cutting him in two. Clement was "astonished and delighted." When Cellini asked him for absolution, the pope made a great sign of the cross above his head and "forgave me all the homicides I had ever committed and all those I ever would commit in the service of the Apostolic Church . . ."

Looting and arson continued for eight days. The pope's ransom was set at four hundred thousand ducats. Clement summoned Cellini to a locked room in the castle and ordered him to remove the gold settings from tiaras and a great mass of jewels from the apostolic camera. Cellini wrapped the jewels in pieces of paper and sewed them into the linings of the pope's vestments. He then built a small brick furnace and melted down the gold. It weighed about two hundred pounds. With it, "harassed from within and without, completely in despair," Clement was able to buy peace. In due course he settled with Charles. He crowned him Holy Roman Emperor at Bologna in 1530, the last time a pope was ever to do so, and Rome and the papal states were restored to him. The city was beggared, however; half its population had fled, and the shock of its ruination shamed Catholics, for, as Erasmus wrote, it was "not only the fortress of the Christian religion and the kindly mother of literary talent, but . . . indeed the common mother of all peoples."[10]

Papal reform began in earnest with Clement's successor. Paul III was an unlikely source. He was known as "Cardinal Petticoat," the brother of a papal concubine, a flagrant nepotist, and the father of three sons and a daughter. He built a palace of extravagant magnificence for himself on the Via Giulia, commissioning Michelangelo to complete it when he was elected pope in 1534. Bullfights and horse races were staged in the Roman streets, and he entertained his sons and their wives at Vatican banquets. He patronized Cellini to design his coins, rewarding him by giving him a papal "safe conduct" after the hot-blooded gold-smith murdered a rival with a dagger. "Men like Benvenuto, who are unique as far as their art is concerned," Cellini quoted the pope, "are not to be subjected to the law."[11] Paul believed in astrology. This heavily bearded and lusty old man, however, was courageous and shrewd.

He regenerated the Sacred College of Cardinals by slashing its inflated budget and choosing its members well. Gasparo Contarini was one such member, a layman who had undergone a mystical experience in 1511 that made him put his trust in Christ rather than Church traditions. It was similar to Luther's later experience, and it left Contarini with a sympathy for Protestants and a desire for reconciliation with them. Paul persuaded Reginald Pole to become a cardinal during his Continental exile. The Englishman was reluctant, aware of the danger to his family and friends at home, but Paul insisted, sending his barber to Pole's rooms to shave his crown. Giampietro Carafa was a third member of the Sacred College, a Neapolitan aristocrat who had renounced his bishoprics to help to found the Theatines, and had served as a devout and austere papal nuncio in England, Flanders, and Spain.

A group of nine cardinals under Contarini was set up as a papal reform commission in 1536. It was independent of the Curia, whose functionaries remained a byword for corruption and office selling. The indefatigable Cellini had maneuvered himself a position as a mace-bearer for 200 crowns a year; he had his eye on a post in the Piombo, the newly created lead seal department that paid 800 crowns a year, but the pope complained that if he obtained it he would "spend all day scratching your belly, lose all your marvellous skill, and get me blamed for it."[12] The commission reported to Paul in 1537. Little was spared. The papacy, the cardinals, and the hierarchy were held responsible for the abuses that had spawned Protestantism. The papal office was criticized as oversecular and lacking spirituality; high offices were open to bribery; benefices were traded like cattle; Church law was evaded by clergy and laity alike; the country clergy were ignorant and illiterate. All but the most rigorous religious orders should be abolished, and novices removed from lax houses immediately; Rome swarmed with prostitutes, who should be removed; the taking of money for spiritual favors was sinful. The Curia tried to have the report blocked. A copy leaked out, however, and reached Luther, who published a German translation as gleeful evidence of Catholic decadence.

Paul nonetheless allowed Contarini to pursue reunion with the Protestants. Contarini, Pole, and other *Spirituali* sympathized with justification by faith—Pole said that "heretics are not heretics in everything"—and a working outline was drawn up in secret negotiations for a conference to be held at Ratisbon (Regensburg) in 1541. Luther's old adversary Johann Eck was a Catholic participant, with the moderate Philip Melanchthon on the other side. Contarini directed the Catholic negotiators as papal legate. The talks foundered in the divide over papal authority and the sacraments. A dream of reconciliation persisted, at least among moderates. Although Catholics pursued "gross and grievous abomination," the English divine Richard Hooker wrote, "yet touching those main parts of Christian truth wherein they constantly still persist, we gladly acknowledge them to be of the family of Jesus Christ."[13] The Catholic George Cassander, who had many Protestant friends in Cologne, arrived at a formula on which he hoped all could agree: "In essentials, unity; in inessentials, liberty; in everything, charity." An experiment was made in Sweden, where the Protestant king John III had studied under Cassander and was married to a Catholic. In 1571 a large range of Catholic practices were permitted; Latin psalms and prayers, confession, veneration of saints, monastic life. Within six years the king was taking Communion in the Catholic rite, and had deposed the bishop of Linkeoping for calling the pope the Antichrist. The king still supported both sacraments for the laity, however, and Swedish liturgy and the marriage of clergy. The pope refused to allow these concessions, and Sweden returned to standard Lutheranism.

The differences with Protestants were unbridgeable. Calvin said that he could find only "traces" of Christianity in the Roman Church and rejected it root and branch, while Catholic rigorists believed that salvation was impossible outside it. Among them was Cardinal Carafa, who thought Contarini's conciliations were heresy. "What remedy must be devised for this evil?" Paul asked him after the failure at Ratisbon had strengthened the hard-line position. The medieval Inquisition had been moribund for well over a century. Carafa said that it should be revived, to "suppress and uproot error, permitting no trace to remain."[14]

Internal reform continued. In 1545, Paul called a council at Trent, a small town to the south of the Brenner Pass over the Alps. The council sat until 1563 and was perhaps the most significant held since Nicaea in 325. Any lingering ideas of compromise were killed off; the few Protestants who attended held only informal talks and were soon gone. Traditional doctrine was examined in the light of Protestant criticism and was upheld in all major areas. Transubstantiation, justification by faith and works, the seven sacraments, celibacy of the clergy, the existence of purgatory, and the legality of indulgences were reaffirmed. The Latin Vulgate was declared sacred and canonical. Religious truth was restated to be present in Catholic tradition as well as in the Bible, and the Church retained its formal monopoly on the interpretation of the Scriptures. Papal power was enhanced by giving the pope the authority to enforce conciliar decrees, and the clergy was bound to him by oaths of loyalty. Seminaries were established to train boys and young men to the priesthood; bishops and clergy were obliged to preach; the liturgy was reformed, and the Tridentine Mass became a global standard.

The clarification and renewal in Catholic doctrine was matched by a new moral severity. It was hardy enough to weather Paul's successor, Julius III, a pope noted mainly for his obsessions with onion-eating and his teenage monkey-keeper, Innocenzo, whom he made a cardinal. Michelangelo continued to labor on the great dome of St. Peter's, 370 feet high, the symbol of Catholic spirit, an offering to God by a man who waived all fees and wrote that:

> My soul turns to that love divine
> which, to enfold us, opens its arms on the cross.

Julius protected and encouraged Ignatius Loyola's infant Jesuits as they grew into a formidable force. Their *Constitutions* demanded that they travel "wherever there is hope of giving greater service to God." Obedience to the pope was unlimited, for the Jesuit was to be led "like a corpse which lets itself be taken anywhere and be treated as anyone wants, or like an old man's stick, which is used anywhere and for anything required by the hand holding it." The discipline was military. "I have never left the army," Ignatius said, "I have only been seconded for the service of God," and he wrote in his *Spiritual Exercises* that: "We ought always to be ready to believe that what seems to us white is black if the hierarchical Church so defines it." Physical hardiness was encouraged. Ignatius turned against the extreme mortification and contemplation he had practiced as a youth. His Christian soldiers had to be fit enough to wage their campaigns. He said that it was better to "find God in everything" than to spend days in prayer; he added that "fasting and abstinence prevents the stomach from behaving normally and even from digesting a little meat. . . ."

Jesuits undertook missions abroad from the outset. When Ignatius was elected the first general of the order, Francis Xavier had left a sealed letter with his vote, for he was sailing on the galleon *Santiago* for the Indies. In Europe, Jesuits founded orphanages and houses for reformed prostitutes, and above all, they educated and evangelized. "Give me a boy at the age of seven," Ignatius said, "and he will be mine for ever." The first Jesuit college at Messina was followed by the Roman College, the forerunner of the present Gregoranium. Soon to attract two thousand students, a simple inscription defined its purpose: "School for grammar, the humanities and Christian doctrine; non-paying." Under Julius, the Germanicum was founded as a Jesuit-staffed college to train priests to win back Germany for Catholicism. Jesuits were already identified as a lethal enemy by German Protestants, who dubbed them the pope's "black horsemen." In the streets of Augsburg young Lutheran boys ran after them shouting *Jesuswider!*—

The Jesuit Francis Xavier sailed for India in 1541 with nothing but a few books and some coarse clothes. He baptized tens of thousands in India and Ceylon before founding a mission in Japan that endured for a century. He died on an island off Canton in 1552 before his mission to China got under way. Handsome and breezy, he laughed when he was advised to travel with a servant as befitted the dignity of a papal nuncio. "Sir, it was that dignity that reduced the Church of Rome to its present state," he replied. "The best way of acquiring real dignity is to wash one's own underwear."

"Antijesus!" When Julius died in 1555, the original ten companions had grown to a thousand, scattered from Brazil and Mexico to the Congo, India, and Japan, with spearheads of Catholic recovery in Europe.

Soon to die himself, Ignatius "trembled in every bone" when Giampietro Carafa was elected pope as Paul IV. Reformers might praise Paul for obliging 113 bishops living in Rome to return to their sees, retaining only a dozen to help with administration, but there was little else to cheer. The new pope was seventy-nine, narrow in mind and morality, suspicious, and bleak. He indeed mistrusted the Jesuits, referring to Ignatius's "tyranny" and fearing that a "Satan" would one day arise from their ranks. He despised the Spanish, and he thought it simple heresy that a Catholic ruler should agree to the Peace of Augsburg, which ended religious war in Germany in 1555 at the cost of recognizing Lutheran states. He hunted the *Spirituali* with grim tenacity. Cardinal Morone, an admired liberal who had attended Ratisbon, was imprisoned in the Castel Sant' Angelo, accused of heresy on the veneration of saints and relics. Paul fretted over married men singing in the Sistine choir, lest they contaminate the chaste purity of the papal chapel. Jews were pursued with the same vigor as Protestants and Catholics suspected of immorality. In 1556 he decreed that Jews in Rome must wear yellow hats and live in a walled section of the city that had only a single exit. This Roman ghetto was to survive until 1870.

A Roman *Index of Prohibited Books* was introduced the following year. It was a savage weapon. The Koran was placed on the list. Twelve thousand volumes from the great Hebrew school at Cremona were ceremoniously burned. The Jesuits were not opposed to censorship as such—Ignatius had written that "all heretical books found in bookshops and private homes must be burnt or cast out"[15]—but even they were appalled to find that Erasmus's grammatical textbooks, which they used in their colleges, were included in the list. To prevent immoral thoughts he had the painter Daniel of Voltera—thereafter known as "the trouserer"—cover some of the nakedness in the Sistine Chapel. Paul was affectionate only to his nephews, making one a cardinal and the other a duke; they manipulated him to slake their greed, and when their corruption was exposed in 1559, it broke him. Mobs ran gleeful riot in Rome when he died, smashing his statues and freeing his prisoners from their cells.

The "inquisitor general of Christendom" appointed by Paul, Michele Ghislieri, became pope in 1565 as Pius V. He was a fellow ascetic, a friar of skin and bone who wore coarse cloth beneath his robes and lived largely on broth and shellfish. New seminaries were built, twenty in Italy alone, and the Jesuits stepped up training for work in England, Scotland, Ireland, and Germany. The Congregation for the Conversion of the Infidels, soon famous as the Propaganda, was founded in 1568 for missions further afield. Pius claimed that prayers and fasting, and tears and the Bible, were the weapons of the Church. Nonetheless, he encouraged the slaughter of Huguenot prisoners and sent a consecrated hat and sword to the duke of Alva in gratitude for his bloody campaign against Dutch Calvinists.

In Rome, however, Pius behaved as Calvin had in Geneva. Savage penalties were exacted for simony, blasphemy, sodomy, and concubinage. Officials in the Curia who had bought their office were dismissed, even though they faced beggary: "It is always better to die of hunger," Pius told them, "than to lose one's soul." Prostitutes were ordered to marry, enter the Convent of the Penitents, or leave the city; the edict was not fully enforced, but those who did not flee were confined to a walled-in quarter and obliged to listen to special sermons. Householders were forbidden to frequent taverns; decrees limited dowries, the use of carriages, and extravagant dress and banquets; shop signs with paintings of the saints were torn down. Physicians were not allowed to visit the sick for more than three days without getting a certificate to confirm that the patient had confessed to a priest. Pius banned the public from viewing the nude classical statues in the gallery of the Belvedere. He prohibited bullfights and said that no matador killed in one could have a Christian burial; Spanish bishops refused to uphold the ban. Formal confessional boxes were built in churches, and the simple cabinets in which the consecrated Host had been kept were replaced by elaborate tabernacles.

His protégé Felice Peretti, like him a former shepherd and friar, became pope as Sixtus V in 1585. He lived in the Vatican "as if still in his cell."[16] Foul-tempered, violent, and pious, he had shadowy visions of a world free of Turks and Protestants, offering money to help the Armada sail against England, talking of papal armies and fleets that would break the Huguenots in France and recapture Jerusalem from the infidels. At home he was ruthless and efficient. He destroyed the brigands who preyed on pilgrims; there were said to be more heads displayed on spikes on the Ponte Sant'Angelo than melons in the Roman markets. He executed clergy who broke their vows of chastity and attempted to impose the death penalty for adultery. The great obelisk from Nero's Circus was moved by a gang of eight hundred men with forty horses to its present site in the center of St. Peter's Square. Grand new roads were built to make it easier to visit the seven city basilicas on the popular pilgrimage revived by Philip Neri, and during Lent, Sixtus went himself to hold a service in a different church each day. The marshes were drained and the aqueducts restored to bring Rome pure water as it once again became the greatest city of the Western world.

THERE WAS NOW a Third Rome. Ivan III, the grand duke of Russia, had married Sophia, the niece of the last Roman emperor of Constantinople, whose symbol of the doubleheaded black eagle he adopted. He claimed to be "ruler of all the Russias" and to have inherited the Byzantine mantle as defender of the Orthodox Church. Before his death in 1505 a bitter dispute had broken out over monastic property. The "Possessors," monks led by Joseph of Volokolamsk, held that the Church needed wealth and the protection of the state to discharge its duty to provide schools, orphanages, and relief for the poor. Joseph welcomed gifts of money and land, and founded city monasteries to educate "learned monks" for Church offices subservient to the government. "Non-Possessors" under the mystic Nil Sorsky wanted to practice a faith of austere contemplation free of interference from worldly rule. Sorsky founded forest hermitages where startsy, spiritual elders, lived on roots and berries or wandered on long pilgrimages with a staff and a bag holding a few scraps of bread.

Ivan supported Joseph against Sorsky's primitive monks, and a Russian Church emerged that was bound closely to the state. By 1510 churchmen were accepting that the Russian ruler "is on earth the sole Emperor of the Christians, the leader of the Apostolic Church which stands no longer in Rome or in Constantinople, but in the blessed city of Moscow." Two Romes had fallen, Constantinople to Moslems, Rome to Catholics, and "the third, our Moscow, yet standeth, and a fourth there shall never be. . . ."

Far to the south and west Moslems were again advancing. Sultan Suleiman, "the Magnificent" to awestruck Europeans, "the Lawgiver" to his own people, became Ottoman emperor in 1520. Over the next decade he took Rhodes from the Knights Hospitallers of St. John, Orthodox Belgrade, and Catholic Croatia; after the Battle of Mohacs, the Catholic south and center of Hungary fell under Turkish rule. Although Luther wrote a pamphlet entitled *On the War against the Turks,* urging Christian solidarity, Protestants made little attempt to help Catholics stem Suleiman's drive to the west. Columns of smoke from burning villages were rising "like a forest from horizon to horizon" as the Turks advanced on Vienna in September 1529.[17] Churches tolled "Turk-bells" in warning. The first Turkish horsemen reached the walls of the city on September 23, raising pikes impaled with Austrian heads on them. The defenders were outnumbered by at least ten to one. But they were well commanded, by the veteran soldier Count Nicholas von Salm, who had a perfect view of enemy movements from the top of the spire of St. Stephen's Church. The Austrians burned the suburbs to deny the Turks shelter, and their resistance was stiffened by stories of atrocity brought in by refugees. On the morning of October 12, breaches were blown in the walls near the Carinthian Gate. Throughout the day Turkish beys and pashas were seen from the spire as they beat their men forward with the flats of their swords, "crying loudly to heaven and each other of the greatness of God and the glory of Islam."[18] The exhausted Viennese thought themselves done for, but that night Suleiman wrote in his diary: "Council is held in the Vizier's tent of all the beys of Rumelia [Rumelia corresponds roughly to modern Bulgaria]; the cold and lack of food, making themselves felt more and more, the decision is made to retreat. . . ."[19]

Two days later the watchmen on the walls saw flames shoot up as the Turks fired their tents and slaughtered their prisoners, male and female, save those young enough to fetch a good price as slaves. Suleiman fell back, prey to hunger, cold, and imperial cavalrymen. Men, horses, and camels were swept away in flooded rivers or collapsed in snowdrifts. In their spite, the Moslems left a trail of arson and atrocity in Christian villages that created so deep a revulsion that parsons in distant England prayed each Good Friday for more than a century that "all Jews, Turks, Infidels and Hereticks" should be punished as murderers of Christ and haters of God.[20]

Vienna, at least, was saved. Catholic Hungarians were not rid of Turkish rule for 150 years. The Orthodox waited much longer, the Greeks until 1829, and the Serbs, Bulgarians, and Bosnians until 1878. The Orthodox in Macedonia were ruled by Moslems until 1912. They survived at Turkish tolerance, most but the Albanians clinging to their faith despite heavy taxes and restrictions. The Greek

Orthodox Church stagnated, largely severed from the rest of Christendom, its processions and public ceremonies banned. Russia was the only great independent Orthodox nation.

The first ruler to adopt the formal title of czar (or "Caesar") was Ivan IV in 1547. Ivan earned his soubriquet of "the Terrible" through the mass executions and demented cruelty that alternated with his vision and statecraft. When the head of the Russian Church denounced the killings in a sermon, he was arrested, taken to a provincial monastery, and strangled. Ivan was otherwise generous to the Church, ceding it vast estates in return for its servility. Fitful attempts were made to improve education; a Church printing press was opened in Moscow in 1553, though hardly a score of books had been published by the end of the century.[21] The czar was a Christian champion against the Tatars. Kazan was stormed in 1552 and the Moslem khan taken prisoner; four years later Astrakhan was annexed. Basil's Cathedral, its swirling domes topped with onion cupolas, was built on Red Square to commemorate the Christian victories.

Both Lutherans and Catholics took Orthodox soundings. A Lutheran translated the Augsburg Confession into Greek, and a copy was sent to Jeremiah II, patriarch of Constantinople, in the hope of a doctrinal accord. Jeremiah replied that truth would be better served if Protestants accepted Orthodox teaching.

St. Basil's Cathedral was built on Red Square in Moscow to celebrate Christian victories against the Moslems at Kazan in 1552 and Astrakhan four years later. The Russian czar now claimed to be "on earth the sole emperor of the Christians, the leader of the Apostolic Church which stands no longer in Rome or in Constantinople, but in the blessed city of Moscow." Two Romes had fallen, Constantinople to Islam, Rome to Catholicism, but "the third, our Moscow, yet standeth, and a fourth there shall never be."

When Ivan captured Kochenhausen in Livonia in 1577 he chatted amicably with a Protestant pastor until Luther was compared to St. Paul, at which point he whipped him: "To the devil with thee and thy Luther!" Catholic advances were also rejected. Ivan appealed to the pope to mediate when he became hard pressed by Swedes and Poles in Livonia. He received the papal nuncio, the Jesuit Antonio Possevino, in the Kremlin but showed more interest in the pope's lifestyle than his doctrines. Ivan's son Theodor fulfilled Russian dynastic and religious ambitions in 1589, when the impoverished Orthodox patriarch Jeremiah II visited Moscow to beg for alms. Responding to a shower of generosity, he agreed to consecrate the czar's placeman as the first patriarch of Moscow, with precedence over Jerusalem. Here, at least, was a glimmer of light for Rome. The new patriarch claimed authority over the Orthodox across the frontier in Poland-Lithuania. Alarmed, and anxious for Catholic protection, the majority of their bishops founded the Greek Catholic Church of the Slavic Rite, the Uniate communion, at the Union of Brest in 1596. They kept their Orthodox ritual and married clergy but accepted the supremacy of the pope. The historic cathedral of St. Sophia in Kiev and most of the churches of White Russia and the Ukraine became Uniate. It was a slight the Russians did not forget when they became a great power. In the monastery at Zagorsk, a tablet included Catholics among the perils to the Russian soul: "Typhus—Tatars—Poles: Three Plagues."[22] For the moment the surviving bastion of Orthodoxy was dark, feud-ridden, backward, entering a time of troubles. It was a Third Rome in name alone.

"MEN IN ROME," the Venetian ambassador Tiepolo reported of the First, "have become a great deal better—or at least they have put on the appearance of being so."[23] So did the clergy. The Roman Church administered fewer European souls at the end of the sixteenth century than it had at its start, but it did so with greater zeal and spirit.

Charles Borromeo, a nephew of Pius IV, was a clergyman at twelve and an archbishop when still a minor. He became cardinal archbishop of Milan at twenty-two, devoting himself to hunting and clothing his retinue of 150 in black velvet. All of a sudden, he undertook Loyola's *Spiritual Exercises* and resigned his sinecures. He scourged himself with spikes, ate bread and water one day a week, tended to the sick in the great Milan plague of 1576, and preached sermons. By Borromeo's death, the teaching society he founded, the Oblates of St. Ambrose, controlled 740 schools. Here was a cardinal who was a moral match for any Protestant minister. Francis Borgia was the great-grandson of Rodrigo Borgia, the infamous Alexander VI, and descended from a Spanish bishop on his mother's side. As a young man Francis was viceroy of Catalonia and duke of Gandia. In

1546, on the death of his wife, he took a secret vow to join the Jesuits when he had discharged his family and state duties. Publicly a Jesuit from 1550, he worked his passage from a humble post in the Basque country to general of the order, inaugurating the Jesuit missions to the Americas.

A sea change had taken place over the generations. Catholic engines—*Index,* Inquisition, Propaganda, the Society of Jesus—were in place, and with the men and women to fuel them.

"ART THOU BECOME QUITE OTHER THAN THYSELF, SO CRUEL?":

The Spanish Inquisition

Censorship was not new—the first list of works that the faithful were forbidden to read was attributed to Innocent I, an early fifth-century pope of stern morality—but material printed in the safe havens now scattered across Europe, where heretic writers survived and published, vastly increased the scale of its operations. The *Tridentine Index* of 1565 followed Paul IV's list. This banned almost three-quarters of the books printed in Europe. The only category to be given a clean bill of spiritual health were Catholic devotional books, and the only Bible permitted to the faithful was the Latin Vulgate. In 1571 a Congregation of the Index was established to control and update the list. It worked alongside the Propaganda, the department charged with converting the heathen and heretics.

Canon law required the imprimatur, "let it be published," to be printed in a permitted book, and sometimes the words *nihil obstat,* "nothing prohibits," were included with the names of the censors. The *Index* was not suspended until 1966, when it contained about four thousand titles. Calvin had set an ominous precedent in executing Servetus, and Protestant censors were often as heavy-handed as Catholics. In Elizabethan England, book printing was restricted to London and to the university towns of Oxford and Cambridge. All books of Scripture needed a government license before publication; the master of the revels licensed plays. Extremist puritan works as well as Catholic devotional literature were banned. When tracts attacking Anglican bishops were printed on a secret press in 1588, under the pseudonym Martin Marprelate, the puritan writer John Penry was arrested and hanged on the most slender evidence that he was responsible. The poet John Milton, who ran afoul of the censors over a treatise on divorce, complained that who kills a man, kills a reasonable creature, but "he who destroys a good book, kills reason itself, kills the image of God, as it were in the eye."[1] It was not until 1695 that English authors were freed from prepublication inspection, although they could still be prosecuted later.

Both camps may have prevented the casual reader from tasting forbidden ideas; but banning a title encouraged the curious to obtain a copy, and censorship depended on the rigor with which it was enforced. The book trade was highly profitable, smugglers easily crossed frontiers, and their customers naturally resented searches and seizures. At Florence, Cosimo de' Medici's secretary estimated that more than one hundred thousand ducats worth of books would have to be seized if the index was followed. The index included scientific and artistic subjects—Rabelais's masterpieces *Pantagruel* and *Gargautua* were early victims, though the satirist was a faithful Catholic and a friend and physician to cardinals—and a blanket ban was imposed on all titles issued by any publisher who had previously printed a heretical work. Cosimo compromised with a token public book-burning of a small number of books on "religion or sacred things, or magic, spells, geomancy, chiromancy, astrology and other similar matters."[2]

Authors traveled to avoid the censor. The French lawyer Jean Crespin fled to Geneva to write and publish his highly influential Huguenot martyrology; the Englishman John Foxe wrote his *Book of Martyrs* at Basel. Protestant publishers in England avoided problems in editions of Catholic books by simple word changes, replacing "priest" with "minister", "saint" with "holy and ancient father," and St. Francis of Assisi with "a certain holy man." "Shall not the corn be reaped because there is cockle in the field?" a Protestant said of the Catholic author he was translating. "Shall not the rose be plucked because it grows on the briar?"[3] Isaac Basire, a Protestant divine and traveler, sent his fiancée a copy of de Sales's *Introduction to the Devout Life,* marking passages where caution was needed with a cross—"else, all is safe." For his part, the great Jesuit scholar St. Robert Bellarmine thought the index ridiculous; he kept a portrait of the Calvinist divine William Whitaker in his library, pointing it out to visitors as "the most learned heretic I have ever read."

Where censorship was fiercely imposed, however, learning was stifled. Foreign ships arriving in Spanish ports were searched for books that appeared on the Spanish index, itself more far-reaching than the Roman index. Agents were maintained in French cities near the border to spy on book smugglers. The agent in Montpellier in 1566, Hernando de Ayala, reported that he had ingratiated himself with local Protestants so as to learn "if they ship books to Spain or know of heretics there." Ayala boasted of using "a thousand deceptions" to gather information; "I pretended to be a heretic myself," he wrote, "and a bookseller and a merchant volunteered to bring books secretly to Barcelona . . ." He bought several works by Calvin and Theodore Beza from a sympathetic merchant; he learned the names of all his friends in Spain, and forwarded them to the Inquisition. All books printed since 1515 without details of author or publisher, and all pictures and illustrations hostile to Catholicism, were banned. Thousands of volumes, including unique works of Moorish culture, were burned in public squares. Erasmus had praised learning in Spain early in the century as being in "so flourishing a condition as to excite the admiration of, and serve as a model to, the most cultivated nations of Europe."[4] Every word he wrote was eventually included in the index; a string of Erasmist professors were arrested as liberalism at the new Alcalá University was ruined. "We live in such difficult times that it is dangerous either to speak or to be silent," the great humanist Juan Luis Vives protested to Erasmus in 1534.[5]

The fear of contamination by foreign ideas was so strong that, in 1559, Philip II ordered all Spaniards studying or teaching abroad to return within four months; the exceptions were those studying at four named colleges in Italy. Spain became isolated from new Bible scholarship. Martin Martinez de Cantalapiedra, professor of Hebrew at Salamanca, was imprisoned for translating Bible texts into the vernacular. "I have laboured to interpret scriptures before the whole world," he told his inquisitors in 1577, "but my only reward has been the destruction of my life, my honour, my health and my possessions." More damaging, the country was partly severed from the knowledge of great contemporary scientists and thinkers. A century later, the monk Benito Jerónimo Feíjoo, teacher of theology at Oviedo—"I speak as a Newtonian"—spoke of a censor "who is a devotee of antiquity and who, thunderbolt in hand, threatens any book that says anything of the infinite amount we are ignorant of in Spain."[6] While abroad there was startling progress in physics, anatomy, botany, geography, and natural history, Feíjoo said, "We break each other's heads and drown our halls with howls over whether Being is univocal or analogical."

❖ THE GRADUAL EVOLUTION of the alchemist, astrologer, and magician into the empirical scientist was perhaps the most profound event in Europe since the adoption of Christianity itself. The early development of disciplines such as mathematics, optics, and physics was fueled by the desire to acquire and interpret astronomical data. Here it entered into a religious preserve, for the heavens and the earth were the supreme handiwork of God, who was believed to have created the earth as the immobile center of the universe. This was held to be a divine truth. Did not Psalms say that the Lord "laid the foundation of the earth, that it should not be moved for ever"? (Ps. 104:5).

Mikolaj Kopernik, or Copernicus, a canon of the cathedral city of Frauenburg in Polish Prussia, was the first to contradict the Scriptures. Observing the skies from the tower of his church, he proved by experiment and measurement that the sun, and not the earth, lies at the center of the solar system. This was the only logical solution to the mathematical coherence between the period of planetary orbit and distance from the sun. Copernicus's great work *De revolutionibus orbium coelestium, Of the Revolution of Celestial Spheres,* was published in 1543 shortly before his death. It destroyed at a stroke the Aristotelian—and Christian—concept of the universe. He dedicated the book to Pope Paul III, but its impact was reduced because a fearful editor suppressed Copernicus's introduction. In it, Copernicus attacked those who used Scripture to censure him. "The sun also ariseth," they quoted, "and the sun goeth down, and hasteth to his place where he ariseth" (Eccles. 1:5). Copernicus pointed out that this was no longer valid.

His theory lay dormant until the Florentine Galileo Galilei took advantage of the new telescope to reinforce Copernican theory. "In my studies of astronomy and philosophy I hold this opinion about the universe, that the Sun remains fixed in the center of the circle of heavenly bodies, without changing its place; and the Earth, turning upon itself, moves round the Sun," he wrote in 1615.[7] He said that the Bible was not a scientific manual, and quoted Augustine's advice that none should read the scriptures to learn facts about the natural world that were not re-

The title page of Galileo's *Dialogi de systemate mundi,* published at Leyden because it was banned in Italy. Rome responded to the Protestant challenge with a *Congregation of the Index* that established a list of banned books. Galileo was perhaps its most distinguished victim. When he pursued his forbidden Copernican belief that "the Earth, turning upon itself, moves round the Sun," he was summoned by the Inquisition, condemned to abjure his scientific heresies, and sentenced to indefinite imprisonment. Deaf and half-blind, he continued his researches under house arrest.

lated to salvation. When the Book of Joshua* reported the universe as standing still, Galileo said, the text was figurative and not literal. "The eyes of an idiot perceive little by beholding the external appearance of a human body," he remarked, "as compared with the wonderful contrivances which a careful and practiced anatomist or philosopher discovers."[8]

In 1616, Copernicus's *De revolutionibus* was put on the *Index*. It was joined by the *Lettera,* a treatise by Paolo Foscarini, which argued that Copernican theory was intellectually plausible and theologically respectable. Protestant publishers printed both banned books in Amsterdam and London. Galileo was warned that Joshua had clearly described a geocentric universe, and that this was a declaration of the Holy Spirit. Galileo agreed not to continue with condemned doctrines. Cardinal Bellarmine wrote that the plain meaning of biblical text could only be reinterpreted when a scientific conclusion was demonstrated beyond doubt, and was not merely probable, and he confirmed the Catholic view that any natural assertion declared by the Holy Spirit was an article of faith. Galileo did not remain silent, however. *"Eppur si muove!"* he is said to have declared; "But it does move!" In 1632 he returned to the Copernican system in his *Dialogo.* He was summoned by the Inquisition, condemned to abjure his scientific heresies, and sentenced to indefinite imprisonment. Deaf and half-blind, he continued his researches under house arrest. Protestants made much of his treatment—the poet Milton visited Italy in 1638 and wrote of Galileo "grown old as a prisoner of the Inquisition for thinking in Astronomy other than the Dominican licensers thought"—and he himself naturally resented that only Protestant publishers were free to print his work. His final treatise *Dimostrazioni Matematiche,* an exposition of mechanics, was smuggled out of his house in Italy by a member of the Dutch Elsevier printing dynasty and published in Leiden. Galileo complained that he was not able to get a single copy of it, although he knew that it was "circulated through all the northern countries."[9]

Thus a giant of discovery—of lunar mountains and the four moons of Jupiter, the law that all falling bodies descend with equal velocity, the illumination of the moon by reflection, the parabolic path of projectiles, the existence of solar spots, and the rotation of the sun—was dealt with by the Church. As he remarked himself, the "Book of Nature" was by no means open to all to read, cler-

---

*The passage is in Joshua 10:12–14:

> Sun, stand thou still upon Gibeon;
> And, Moon, in the valley of Aijalon
> And the sun stood still, and the moon stayed . . .
> And the sun stayed in the midst of heaven, and lasted not to go down about a whole day. And there was no day like that before it, or after it. . . .

ics included. "Philosophy is written in this grand book, the universe which stands continually open to our gaze," he wrote. "But the book cannot be understood unless one first learns to comprehend the language and read the letters in which it is composed. It is written in the language of mathematics." It was only in 1992 that a papal commission appointed by Pope John Paul II to investigate the "Galileo affair" concluded, after eleven years of investigation, that Galileo's judges were guilty of "subjective error."

It was almost a rite of passage for the scientists who were uncovering the secrets of the material world to move on to speculation concerning the nature of the Creator. Catholicism inhibited genius other than Galileo's. René Descartes was serving with Catholic armies in Bavaria in 1619 when he had an intellectual vision of a new philosophical system modeled on mathematics. The "stove-heated room" in which he was meditating was as significant as Isaac Newton's apple tree, for his rationalist doctrines deeply affected Western thought. Descartes used a method of systematic doubt—"rejecting everything in which one can imagine the least doubt"—to create a system of certainty whose first indisputable truth was his famous phrase *"cogito ergo sum,"* "I think, therefore I am." He remained a Catholic all his life, arguing that the idea of God that he found in himself was proof of the existence of God, who embraces absolute perfection. Had he not derived his existence from God, he said, the idea of God would not have been present in him. Nevertheless, Descartes suppressed his treatise on physics, *Le Monde,* when he heard of Galileo's condemnation by the Inquisition; his concept of the dualism of matter and spirit, in which the mind is wholly distinct from the mechanical body, was rejected by the Church, and he spent twenty-one years in exile in Protestant Holland.

His compatriot Blaise Pascal developed the theory of mathematical probability and integral calculus, and his discovery that the height of columns of mercury decreases with altitude led to the barometer and the hydraulic press. He invented the first calculating machine when still a teenager, but rejected the idea that God was the mere master clockmaker of a mechanistic universe. "I cannot forgive Descartes; in all his philosophy he did his best to dispense with God," he wrote, "but he could not avoid making Him set the world in motion with a flip of His thumb; after that he had no more use for God." In Pascal's intense and spiritual theology, "the heart has its reasons which reason does not know."[10] He had what he called his "first conversion" when he fell in with Jansenists as a young man. These were followers of Cornelius Jansen, the bishop of Ypres, whose massive work *Augustinus* repudiated the traditional Catholic dogma of the freedom of the will and maintained that good works without faith were unavailing. Jansen also stressed the need for grace and spiritual rebirth. These views came close to Protestant theology; although Jansen never vacillated in his support for Rome, his teaching was condemned in a papal bull. The movement centered on the convent of Port-Royal. Its abbess, Angélique Arnaud, had accepted its relaxed rule when she was appointed at the age of eleven, but from her mid-teens insisted on rigorous silence and abstinence. Her brother Antoine Arnaud followed her in emphasizing discipline, arguing in his book *De la frequente Communion* that days of penance were necessary before Communion. He mistrusted the Jesuits and held up parish priests as the true successors to the apostles and the primitive church. The book caused outrage, notably among the Jesuits, and Arnaud was censured, degraded, and driven from public life in Paris, eventually seeking refuge in Belgium.

Pascal tried to save him. The scientist had his "definitive conversion" alone in his room on November 22, 1654, when he discovered the "God of Abraham, the God of Isaac, the God of Jacob, and not of the philosophers and men of science." Pascal wrote down a "Mémorial" of the experience—in disjointed and awestruck phrases in contrast to the incisive and flowing prose of his published work—and sewed it into his clothes. He believed man to be suspended between greatness and squalor. Only faith can free him from this state; man must make a decision, a "wager," for or against God. "Man is a reed, the feeblest thing in nature," he wrote, "but he is a thinking reed."[11] Two years later, abandoning mathematics, Pascal began writing his famous pamphlets, the *Lettres provinciales,* pillorying the Jesuits for their casuistry and jargon, claiming that they "have allowed Catholics to practice idolatry itself," and bombarding them with satire and barbs of brilliant perception. His *Lettres* were put on the *Index* in 1657.

Protestant theology was more sympathetic to science, tending to believe it to be a glory and not a hindrance to religion. Francis Bacon fathered scientific method through induction based on scrupulous experimentation; he died in 1626 from a cold caught while stuffing a fowl with snow to observe the effect of low temperature on the preservation of flesh. Bacon opposed the notion that knowledge could be deduced from axioms accepted by the Church. "If a man will begin with certainties, he shall end in doubts," he wrote; "but if he will be content to begin with doubts, he shall end in certainties."[12] He argued that scientific research was complementary to the study of the Bible—the "scientist became the priest of God's Book of Nature"[13]—and compatible with theology, since knowledge was a rich storehouse "for the glory of the Creator and the relief of man's estate." Bacon wrote prayers and verse translation of the psalms. A little philosophy inclines Man to atheism, he thought; "but depth in Philosophy bringeth Menn's Minds about to Religion."[14]

Speculation did not invariably meet with a Protestant welcome. In Holland the philosopher Benedictus Spinoza moved on from optics and astronomy to advocate a critical approach to biblical sources. Spinoza argued that freedom of thought and scientific speculation were consistent with the true significance of the Bible, which lay in its morality. He saw God as all-embracing, an infinite substance that is *causa sui,* having within itself the reasons for its existence. The human mind is a part of the divine intellect—"We feel and know that we are eternal"—which must practice reason and toleration in order to achieve its highest goal, the loving contemplation of God. For his pains, the Jewish community in Amsterdam expelled Spinoza for heresy, and Protestants regarded him as a pantheist. His anonymous work *Tractatus Theologico-Politicus* was briefly banned.

Protestants also stubbornly rejected the new calendar that Catholic countries had followed since 1582. They claimed it to be inaccurate, though it was not, and their real reluctance was that a pope, Gregory XIII, had introduced it. The Swiss were the first Protestants to adopt it, in 1700; the English grudgingly followed in 1753, while the Eastern Orthodox ignored it until the twentieth century. In general, though, Protestant scientists saw no friction between their religion and the workings of God's universe that they were measuring and explaining. John Wilkins was the first secretary of the Royal Society in England, the most important and freethinking scientific foundation of the seventeenth century, but he was also the bishop of Chester. His musings on space travel supposed a wholly Christian universe in which planets other than the Earth might support life. "The inhabitants of other worlds," he wrote in *The Discovery of a World of the Moon* in 1638, "are redeemed by the same means as we are, by the blood of Christ."[15] Robert Boyle, physicist, chemist, forerunner of modern atomic physics in his advocacy of an atomic or corpuscular theory of matter, and the originator of Boyle's law of gases, was a profoundly godly man. He worked for the evangelization of the East Indies, published translations of the Bible at his own expense, and endowed the enduring *Boyle Lectures* on Christianity. Impressed by the famous clock at Strasbourg, Boyle saw a rational universe whose phenomena were open to mechanical explanation.

Isaac Newton, whose laws of motion and gravity defined the working of the universe for more than two centuries, did not feel himself threatened by Scripture as Galileo had, nor by God or Nature, which he described as "very consonant and conformable with herself."[16] He wrote extensive biblical commentaries, and his observations on the Prophecy of Daniel and the Apocalypse of St. John reflected his millenarian speculations. His concept of a universe of perfect order acknowledged God as the Supreme Being of absolute omnipotence and authority over the material world and the human soul alike.

Catholics were not deprived of scientific advance by Counter-Reformation censorship, of course; the Paris Academy of Science played an equivalent role to the Royal Society. Nevertheless, the Royal Society had fewer constraints; it was able, for example, to translate and publish the *Saggi,* or collected papers, of an

Italian counterpart, the Accademia del Cimento of Florence, long before Italian publication was permitted. Protestant printers specialized in titles that were on the index, and had them smuggled to Catholic countries. "Priests, monks, prelates even, vie with each other in buying up copies of the *Dialogue* on the black market," an observer wrote of Galileo's banned work. "The black market price of the book rises from the original half-scudo to four and six scudi all over Italy."[17] Newton found his way onto the *Index*. It is unlikely that his writings on God— or those of the great German polymath Gottfried Leibniz, with his vision of a world made up of indivisible and isolated "monads" of being, of which the highest is God—would have been tolerated under a strict Catholic regime.

❖ WHERE CENSORSHIP FAILED to prevent spiritual infection, the Inquisition strove to cure. Paul III founded the Holy Office of the Roman Congregation and Universal Inquisition through a bull of 1542, which remodeled the defunct medieval Inquisition. Six cardinals were appointed as inquisitors-general, to whom all baptized Christians were subject, at least in theory. Among them was Cardinal Carafa, who was so eager to proceed that he bought a house at his own expense, and equipped it with offices and dungeons, without waiting for a grant from the papal treasury. The rules he set were rigorous. The fourth stated that: "No man is to lower himself by showing toleration towards any sort of heretic, least of all a Calvinist."[18]

To the Protestant John Foxe, the Inquisition was a "dreadful engine of tyranny" that might "at any time be introduced into a country where the Catholics have the ascendancy." In fact, Catholics in general disliked the papal Inquisition and kept it at bay. Attempts to extend it to the Netherlands, France, and the Austrian Habsburg lands were rejected. Even in Italy its authority was fitful outside the papal states and much resented within them.

Carafa's primary target was a small but influential group of Italians who had converted to Protestantism. He made strenuous efforts in 1542 to capture two of them, the former Capuchin Bernardino Ochino, a man so eloquent that his preaching was said to be "enough to make the stones weep,"[19] and the Augustinian Peter Martyr Vermigli. Both escaped to Switzerland and then to England, where Vermigli became professor of theology at Oxford. Carafa was able to have the body of Vermigli's wife disinterred from her tomb at Oxford during Mary's reign, but he failed to lay a hand on either man.

After Carafa's election as Pope Paul IV in 1555, he briefly terrorized Rome. "Even if my own father were a heretic, I would gather the wood to burn him," he wrote. His hunts destroyed any latent Protestant tendency in the papal states. He even brought his own cardinals in front of the Inquisition and imprisoned one of them, the distinguished Giovanni Morone. After Paul IV's death, Morone was released and the Inquisition moderated. Its one notable success was double-edged. It pursued Giordano Bruno, a Dominican philosopher who had fled from Naples in 1576, for seventeen years before seizing him in Venice and transporting him to Rome. When Bruno was burned on the Campo dei Fiori, his fate outraged Venetians and later became a focal point for Italian anticlericalism. Many Italians felt that the Inquisition was simply a device to extort money from Jews and devoid of religious principle. "In Spain it is held in great horror to be descended from a heretic or a Jew," the Spanish ambassador at Rome reported in 1652, "but here they laugh at these matters, and at us, because we concern ourselves with them."[20]

❧ THE SPANISH INQUISITION was a different beast. It was older, dating from 1478, before Protestants yet existed, and longer-lasting, surviving until 1834;* the crown, not the papacy, controlled it; and it was as much racial as religious. The vast majority of its victims were of Jewish and Moorish blood.

It was founded as the Christian *Reconquista* reached its climax with the capture of Granada. As the invasion of the last Moslem enclave began, the "Catholic monarchs"—the title awarded by the pope to Ferdinand and Isabella, pious both—fretted over the loyalty of the *conversos,* the Jews and Moors who had converted to Christianity. The royal couple had already formed a *santa hermandad,* a "holy brotherhood" of militia, to suppress banditry, and now they sought a religious equivalent to rout out those who still practiced Islam and Judaism in secret. Sixtus IV signed a bull granting them permission to establish an Inquisition, with the powers of appointment and dismissal of inquisitors vested in the crown.

The three great religions had cohabited uneasily since the Moslem invasion of 711. The Moors had alternated between toleration and pogrom when they were in the ascendant. Large-scale massacres of Jews had taken place in Granada in 1066. The arrival of the fierce Almoravides from North Africa a century later had "presaged horror, pillage, destruction and slavery" for Christians. These periods of forced conversion, when "many by denying Christ threw themselves into the abyss," were an exception; but the cult of martyrs—among them Leocritia, a Spanish Perpetua, a convert "begotten of the filth of the Moslems and born from the womb of wolves" who "secretly blossomed in her adopted faith as a sweet

---

*Its officials were pensioned off that year, and its properties sold. A schoolmaster named Cayetano Ripoll was the last person to be executed for heresy in Spain. He was a Deist who was denounced for refusing to take his pupils to mass and for substituting "Praise be to God" for "Ave Maria" in prayers at school. He was sentenced to hanging and burning in July 1826; the burning was symbolic, however; a barrel with flames painted on it was placed beneath the gibbet from which he was hanged.

odour," and who died with her friend Eulogius after their hiding place was betrayed—kept memories alive. As the Christians slowly regained territory, they also blended cruelty with tolerance. St. Ferdinand, the king of Castile in the mid-thirteenth century, prided himself as the "king of the three religions." An edict of the Council of Arles in 1235, ordering all Jews to wear a round yellow badge four fingers in circumference above the heart, was never enforced in Spain. A papal Inquisition set up by Dominicans at Aragon in 1238 was soon inactive, and Castile never had one. Yet zealots at Valencia in 1412 forbade Jews and Moors to drink, bathe, or talk with Christians, and excluded them from many trades. "They compelled us to grow our beards and wear our hair long," a victim complained. "Unshaven, we appeared like mourners."[21] Many thousands were converted as New Christians by the Dominican preacher St. Vincent Ferrer.

Practicing Jews were not marginalized, as elsewhere in Europe, and often prospered: "The most learned, most distinguished Jews that there have been in all the realms of the dispersion," Rabbi Mosé Arragel said of them. "They are distinguished in four ways, in lineage, in wealth, in virtues, in sciences."[22] Jewish *conversos* married into the most powerful families in Spain. A genealogy drawn up by an early Inquisition assessor, the *Libro Verde de Aragon*, showed a majority of nobles to have Jewish blood; the stain on their treasured *limpieza de sangre*—purity of blood—was such that the book was later banned and burned. Half of the senior officeholders in the kingdom had *converso* blood. They included bishops, cardinals, abbots, royal secretaries, and chancellors, and the first two inquisitor-generals, Tomás Torquemada and Diego Deza.

As a Dominican prior, Torquemada had founded the great monastery of St. Thomas Aquinas at Ávila and enforced a statute of *limpieza* that excluded monks who were not Old Christians. As an inquisitor he perfected the interrogations and tortures that flushed out Judaizers. He did this despite having Jewish blood; or, perhaps, because of it. The notorious anti-Jewish polemic *Hebraeomastix* was the work of the former rabbi Jehoshua Ha-Lorqui, who changed his name to Jeronimo de Santa Fe. The cynical thought such intensity of faith to be the mark of *conversos* anxious to prove their new credentials.

❦ OPERATIONS BEGAN IN Seville in the summer of 1480. The Inquisition had no powers over practicing Jews and Moslems, a problem that would be dealt with by expulsion. Its authority was over the baptized; these it so terrified that four thousand *converso* households fled the city. Isabella was warned that commerce was being ruined; "setting little importance on the decline in her revenue, and prizing highly the *limpieza* of her lands," a chronicler recorded, "she said that the essential thing was to cleanse the country of the sin of heresy. . . ."[23] A group of wealthy *conversos* met in the church of San Salvador to discuss what action to take. They were led by Diego de Susán, a banker with a fortune estimated at ten million marevedis. "If they come to take us," they allegedly said of the inquisitors, "we, together with armed men and the people will rise up and slay them and so be revenged on our enemies." Susán's beautiful daughter Susanna betrayed the plot to her Old Christian lover. All were arrested.

They were dealt with at the first auto-da-fé of the Spanish Inquisition at Seville on February 6, 1481. Six were burned at the stake that day; a few days later four of Seville's richest and most prominent men, including Susán and the leading lawyer and magistrate Juan Fernandez Abolasia, were burned together with "many other leading and very rich citizens."[24] Susanna, seeing the results of her disloyalty, is said to have entered a convent before taking to the streets and dying of shame.

The pope feared that uncontrollable forces had been let loose. Sixtus IV complained in a bull in 1482 that the Inquisition was "moved not by zeal for the faith and the salvation of souls but by lust for wealth," and that the arrests of many faithful Christians on the flawed evidence of enemies and rivals acted "to the peril of souls, setting a pernicious example, and causing disgust to many." He ordered that the names and testimony of accusers must be given to the accused, who were to be allowed counsel to represent them. It was the only attempt to provide suspects with a fair trial, and it did not last. Within three weeks King Frederick wrote to the pope to claim that the concessions had been won "through the persistent and cunning persuasion of the said *conversos,*" adding that, "I intend never to let them take effect." Sixtus gave way and the bull was suspended. A further seven hundred *converso* burnings followed over the next eight years at Seville. More inquisitors were recruited, and, like Torquemada, all were Dominican friars. In 1483 he was appointed inquisitor-general of Catalonia, completing the unification of the Holy Office.

A murder now gave the Inquisition a priceless gift, a martyr of its own. On the night of September 15, 1485, the inquisitor Pedro Arbués knelt before the high altar of Saragossa Cathedral. He had been warned that wealthy *conversos* were plotting to kill him, and he wore a coat of mail beneath his gown and a steel cap on his head. Eight assassins, hired for six hundred gold florins, entered by the chapel door and stabbed him in the neck. He lingered for a day, and died. A terrible revenge was had at successive autos-da-fé held in the city over the period of a year. One of the murderers had his hands cut off; he was then taken to the marketplace, beheaded, and quartered, the pieces of his body being suspended in the street. Another committed suicide in his cell the night before his ordeal, swallowing the glass from a broken lamp; the sentence was carried out on his corpse. Members of the leading *converso* families—the royal treasurers Gabriel Sanchez and Sancho de Paternoy, the knight Luis de Santangel—were beheaded and burned. Arbués was hailed as *el santo martyr* and a feast day was assigned to his memory.

Partial expulsions of practicing Jews began amid the continuing terrorization of *conversos*. At Toledo in 1486, 750 alleged Judaizers were spared death after repenting, but were paraded through the city. "The women were together in a group," a chronicler recorded, "their heads uncovered and their faces bare, unshod like the men and with candles . . . they suffered greatly from the great number of spectators (since a great many people from outlying districts had come to see them), they went along howling loudly and weeping and tearing out their hair. . . ." In 1491 at La Guardia in Toledo, six Jews and *conversos* were accused of crucifying an infant and cutting out its heart as part of a satanic conspiracy to destroy the Christian faith. They confessed under torture and were burned, although no child was reported to be missing, and no body was found where the burial had supposedly taken place.*

On the second day of 1492, Granada capitulated. The fall of the great Islamic city was witnessed by Christopher Columbus, who was seeking royal patronage for his voyage into the Atlantic. All Spain was now under control of the Catholic monarchs, and they set about ridding it of non-Christians. On March 31, Jews were ordered to convert within four months or leave. Some 50,000 were baptized while the remainder, the Sephardim, perhaps as many as 400,000, went into exile. The Turkish sultan sent ships to take some to Smyrna and Constantinople; others crossed the straits to North Africa or fled to Portugal. They were not allowed to take gold or silver with them; houses were sold for an ass or mule, vineyards for linen cloth. "Some of them the Turks killed to take out the gold which they had swallowed to hide," a rabbi wrote of the catastrophe; "some of them hunger and the plague consumed and some were cast naked by the captains on the isles of the sea; and some were sold for men-servants and maid-servants in Genoa and its villages, and some were cast into the sea."[25] Many eventually returned to accept baptism into the faith that had ruined them. "In this way was fulfilled the prophecy of David in the psalm," a curate wrote, "which is: 'They shall return at evening, and shall suffer hunger like dogs, and shall prowl round the city.' Thus they were converted at a late hour and by force and after great suffering."

---

*Such stories were common. A claim of ritual murder was made against Jews at Norwich in England in 1144; they were said to have killed a small boy who became known as "St. William." The same was said in 1255 of "Hugh of Lincoln," another "martyred" boy who was given the status of a saint. Chaucer used a similar legend in his epic *Canterbury Tales;* as late as 1905, Christian mobs in Russia were using tales of slaughtered infants as an excuse for pogroms. The papacy rejected them as fictions from at least 1247; in 1759, Jews appealed to Cardinal Ganganelli, later Pope Clement XIV, to investigate them. He reported that there was no evidence that any such ritual murders had taken place at any date.

Moors were treated with gentleness and toleration by the first archbishop of liberated Granada. From 1499, however, the future grand inquisitor Francisco Ximinez de Cisneros directed a campaign of coercion against them. Ximinez was a man of austere brilliance. As a strict Franciscan friar his self-denial attracted such crowds of penitents that he took solitary refuge as an anchorite. He founded the University of Alcalá with his own funds, encouraging scholars from across Europe to teach, and overseeing the production of the great Polyglot Bible, in which the Hebrew, Greek, and Chaldean texts were printed in columns next to the Latin Vulgate. This did not prevent him from making bonfires of Moorish books; his Christian passion was pitiless. Moslems rose in revolt at Granada. After the city was subdued, the survivors were hunted down in the mountains. On February 2, 1502, Isabella ordered the baptism or expulsion of Moslems remaining in Castile. Some went to North Africa or joined the Barbary pirates; most chose to convert. Christian landlords in Aragon opposed this so as to protect their supply of cheap labor; *"mientras más Moros más ganancia,"* the saying went; "more Moors, more profit."[26] In 1520 the Moors of Valencia rose against their lords. Five years later the young Charles V, Holy Roman Emperor and king of Spain, ordered that Spanish Moslems would be tolerated only as slaves. They presented themselves in thousands to be converted to a religion that they did not "love, believe, understand or intend to practice."[27]

Assaults were made on the Moslems' rites, customs, clothes, and language. The final expulsion of all Moors was announced in April 1609. Perhaps 275,000 of the remaining 300,000 were driven from Spain, and Valencia alone lost a quarter of its population. Cardinal Richelieu thought it the most barbarous act in human history. Regrets in Spain were economic, not moral. Wheat and sugarcane production collapsed, and Christian landlords who lived from Morisco rents were left penniless. The nobility complained that Valencia would be ruined, for the Moriscos had done all the work. "Who will make our shoes for us?" cried the saintly archbishop of Valencia, Juan de Ribera. The great dramatist Lope de Vega took holy orders and died a poor man after giving his large earnings to charity; but he was an officer of the Inquisition, and wrote of the pride of blood untainted by Jewish or Moorish admixture. Cervantes was maimed by a gunshot wound to the hand fighting the Turks at Lepanto, and Moslem pirates had carried him into slavery for five years. In his rambling masterpiece *Don Quixote*, Cervantes had a Moor praise the king for his heroic decision "to expel poisonous fruit from Spain; now clean and free of the fears in which our numbers held her . . ."[28]

❖ NONE OF THIS was unique to Spain. The shadow of anti-Semitism had stalked the faith from birth, drawing inspiration from the crucifixion and John's gospel. "Ye are of your father the devil, and the lusts of your father it is your will to do," Jesus had told those Jews who did not love him. "He was a murderer from the beginning, and stood not in truth . . . for he is a liar" (John 8:44). Expulsions and forced conversions had a long and ignoble history. The baptism of all Jews had been decreed, though ineffectually, in Spain itself in 613 and in France and the Byzantine Empire nineteen years later. The first Jewish ghettos were found in Italian cities in the eleventh century and spread to cities with large Jewish communities—Prague, Frankfurt, Venice; enclosed behind gates and walls, the Jews were generally forbidden to leave their ghettos at night or on Christian holy days. The Roman ghetto was set up by Paul IV himself. Wholesale expulsions—involving, in Sicily at least, Moslems—had followed the massacres of the crusading era. All Jews were given three months to leave England in 1290, and were beaten and robbed as they left; they did not reappear in any numbers until 1650. French Jews were banished in 1394. Protestants proved to be unkindly—Jews were often forced to listen to sermons in church in Lutheran states, and they were still barred from sitting in the British Parliament two decades after the Catholic emancipation of 1829—and pogroms infected Orthodox Russia.

It was in scale and persistence that the Spanish malice distinguished itself. Torquemada's system was controlled by the inquisitor-general in a council, the Suprema. Each tribunal—permanent in the big cities, itinerant in country districts—had two inquisitors, an assessor, a constable, and a prosecutor. This team was protected by "Familiars," lay servants of the Holy Office who volunteered to carry arms in its defense. Familiars formed their own *hermandad,* the Congregation of St. Peter Martyr. These gangs were large—1,215 strong in Saragossa, 905 in Barcelona—and they harbored informers, thieves, and blackmailers.

Before an arrest was made, evidence was given to *calificadores,* theologians who decided if heresy was involved. Tips on how to recognize Judaizers were published. People who put clean sheets on their beds on Friday nights, and burned no candles that evening; who purified their meat by bleeding it in water, or cut the throats of cattle and fowl; who circumcised their children; who recited the psalms without the *Gloria Patri*—all were suspect. So indeed was anyone who "on his deathbed turns to the wall to die"; it might be too late to deal with him, but if his family washed the body with hot water, they too were liable for interrogation. A woman in the Canaries was identified as a potential heretic for smiling when she heard the Virgin Mary's name. Not to eat pork aroused suspicions of Judaizing; by contrast, an eighty year old who ate bacon on a fast day was accused of behaving "after the manner of the sect of Luther."

No reason was given for an arrest, only a demand to confess. Arrest was followed by the immediate seizure of possessions. Every item in the house—pots, spoons, rags—was noted in presence of a notary and sold at public auction. Inquisition salaries and expenses were met by fines and confiscations. Any residue supposedly went to the crown; in practice, it was often taken by the Inquisition, and Torquemada used money collected from repentant heretics to build his magnificent monastery at Ávila. Ancient castles with dungeons served as Inquisition prisons: in Córdoba the Alcazár, the Triana in Seville, the Alfería in Saragossa. A typical cell measured twelve feet by eight feet with a wood frame bed, a straw mattress, a water jug and chamber pot, and a candle. John Hill, an English sailor captured in Las Palmas, slept on a stone floor with fleas, all but naked, and was fed bread and water, and often chained.

Torture was permitted according to "the conscience and will of the appointed judges." It was not formally banned by the papacy until 1816. Three principal methods were employed during interrogations. In the *garrucha,* the "pulley," the victim was hung by the wrists from a pulley fixed to the ceiling. Heavy weights were attached to the feet. The body was slowly raised and then loosed with a jerk, so that the arms and legs were dislocated. The victim of the *toca* was tied to a rack while water from a jar was poured slowly down the throat through a *toca,* or linen cloth. Most common was the *potro,* in which cords were passed round the victim's body and limbs as he—or she, for women of seventy and older are recorded as being subjected to the *potro,* and a girl of thirteen overcame it at Valencia in 1607 without confessing—lay on the rack. The executioner tightened the cords, each turn biting into the flesh.

Torturers were usually public executioners working for the secular courts. Sessions were supervised by inquisitors, a representative of the local bishop, and a secretary who kept detailed records of what was said and done. A minority, perhaps a third, underwent physical torture. It was often possible to obtain a confession by taking the accused to the torture chamber and placing them in *conspectu tormentorum,* in sight of the pulleys and racks. Confessions made under torture were not legally valid, as they were obtained by force. The victim was required to ratify his confession the following day. A legal trick was used to get around the rule that a victim could only be tortured once. The end of an individual session was classified as a "suspension"; if the victim refused to ratify the confession, the torture was "continued." A person could also be tortured *in caput alienum,* to "confess to the heresies of others."

No formal trials were held. Instead there was a process of audiences and interrogations that could last many years. Convictions were not automatic, as they had been in the medieval Inquisition. Of 1,227 cases in Toledo over a thirty-five-year period from 1575, 51 of the accused were acquitted, 207 were reconciled to the Church and fined, 56 were merely reprimanded, and a further 104 cases were suspended. The remainder suffered varying fates. In the largest category, 186 were forced to wear the *sanbenito,* a coarse yellow robe with one or two diagonal crosses on it, for periods varying from a few months to life. The *sanbenitos* were then hung in their local church *ad perpetuam rei memoriam,* as "perpetual memory of the infamy of heretics and their descendants." A lesser number, 167, were exiled from their locality, and 133 were scourged, stripped to the waist, seated on an ass, and whipped through the streets by the executioner. Teenage girls and grandmothers were humiliated in this manner. Prison awaited 175 of the guilty; pressure on cell space meant that "perpetual" imprisonment rarely lasted more than three years, and an "irremissible" sentence was usually for eight years. A further 91 were sent to the galleys to provide the fleet with free oar-power. Multiple sentences were also imposed; the unfortunate Francisco de Alarcón received five years' banishment, five years in the galleys, two hundred lashes, and a fine from the Granada Inquisition.

Unrepentant and relapsed heretics were burned, fifteen at Toledo in person and a further eighteen in effigy, since they had fled or already died. In legal terms they were "relaxed"; the Inquisition was forbidden to have blood on its hands, and it "relaxed" its grasp on them in handing them to the secular authorities. Sentences were considered a penance; the public spectacle at which they were carried out was an auto-da-fé, an "act of faith," held in a religious atmosphere of piety.

These were as popular as Roman games and as elaborately staged. A great auto at Madrid on June 30, 1680, was announced a month in advance by a procession of Familiars and notaries. Balconies fifty feet high, at a level with the scaffold, were erected in the Plaza Mayor for the royal family, the *suprema* of the Inquisition, and the nobility. On the evening of June 29 a procession of grandees, Familiars, and Dominicans was led to the square by one hundred coal merchants, who had provided the charcoal and wood for the burnings. They carried the standard of the Inquisition and a green cross hung with black crepe. The Dominicans passed the night in prayer and psalm-singing. Mass was celebrated at daybreak. At 7 A.M. the king and queen, and the queen mother, took their places. An hour later thirty men arrived carrying life-size pasteboard images of condemned heretics who had escaped or died in prison; the bones of the latter were carried in wooden trunks. The nineteen people who were to be "relaxed" had ropes round their necks and torches in their hands; five or six of them were gagged to prevent them from mouthing blasphemies, and each was accompanied by two Familiars and four or five monks who were "preparing them for death as they went along." The *sanbenitos* of the condemned had flames and devils painted on them. They passed beneath the king's balcony followed by the mounted officers of the *suprema* and the grand inquisitor in a purple habit. Mass was again celebrated. At noon the sentences were read out. The condemned were handed to the secular officers and led off on asses to be executed.

Those who were to be "relaxed" were told of their fate the night before exe-

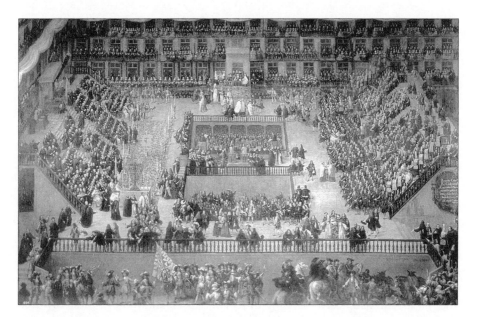

The great auto-da-fé, or "act of faith," held in the Plaza Mayor in Madrid on June 30, 1680. The burnings of heretics in Spain were great public and social events, carried out in an atmosphere of religious piety. A procession of grandees, Dominican friars, and the coal merchants who provided the wood and charcoal, was held the evening before the executions. Mass was celebrated at daybreak, and the king and queen took their places. The nineteen people to be burned were led with ropes round their necks and torches in their hands, followed by the grand inquisitor in a purple habit. At noon their sentences were proclaimed and they were handed to the civil power to be burned.

cution, to give them time to prepare their souls. If they repented, they were strangled when the flames were lit as a sign of mercy. An inquisitor of Logroño left an account of the spiritual joy caused by a Judaizer who was reconciled on the scaffold. A lighted torch was held in front of the man to remind him of his fate. "With perfect serenity," the inquisitor wrote, "he said 'I will convert myself to the faith of Jesus Christ,' words which he had not been heard to utter before. This overjoyed all the religious who began to embrace him with tenderness and give infinite thanks to God for having opened to them a door for his conversion. . . ." When the prisoner saw the executioner, who "put his head out from behind the stake," he asked him why he had called him a dog. The executioner said it was because he had denied the faith of Christ; but now that he had confessed, why, they were brothers, and the executioner sank to his knees to beg the prisoner for pardon. The inquisitor was eager that the moment of the soul's conversion should not be lost. "I went round casually behind the stake to where the executioner was," he wrote, "and gave him the order to strangle him immediately because it was very important not to delay. This he did with great expedition." It was only when he was certain that the prisoner was dead that the inquisitor ordered the executioner to set fire to the brushwood and charcoal.[29]

❖ BIGAMISTS, BLASPHEMERS, USURERS, and homosexuals were also burned; the inquisitors did not confine their attentions purely to *conversos*. The Old Testament had said that "if a man lie with mankind . . . they shall surely be put to death" (Lev. 20:13); Paul wrote of the "vile passions" in which "men, leaving the natural use of the women, burned in their lust one toward another . . . they which practice such things are worthy of death" (Rom. 1:26–32). Homosexuals in medieval Spain had been castrated and stoned to death. The Inquisition at Aragon burned them if they were over twenty-five; younger men were whipped and sent to the galleys, with leniency shown to the clergy.

Protestants were burned out of Spain before they had a toehold. Up to 1558 the Inquisition had dealt with only thirty-nine cases, and most of these involved no more than passing remarks that inquisitors imagined were Lutheran. Two small Protestant groups existed, at Seville and at Valladolid. The Seville group was estimated to number 127. It was led by a former confessor to Emperor Charles V, and included the prior and monks from the Jeronimite monastery of San Isidro and nuns from the convent of Santa Paula. The 55 Valladolid Protestants included Alcalá graduates and a former royal chaplain, Dr. Augustin Cazalla.

A nobleman of distinguished family, Don Juan Ponce de Leon, was arrested in October 1557. He confessed to the Seville Inquisition that he had bought Lutheran literature from Germany through a book smuggler. The books were brought by a messenger who hid them in a field; Don Juan paid the man twenty ducats and went out with a mule, put the books in baskets, and brought them to his house. He distributed them to "trustworthy people" whom he met with over meals of pigeon to discuss the "damned and devilish sect" of Luther. He admitted that he was "involved in great error and heresy . . . that there was no purgatory, that the Inquisitors were antichristian, that one should not believe or obey the Pope."[30] Further arrests followed in Seville and Valladolid.

The Inquisition informed Charles V that former royal chaplains were among the Protestants and that "more are daily being discovered." Charles demanded "a quick remedy and exemplary punishment" lest Protestants divide Spain as they had the Holy Roman Empire. The first Protestant auto-da-fé was held at Valladolid in May 1559. Fourteen were burned, including a brother and sister. Only one died unrepentant; Augustin Cazalla blessed the Holy Office and wept for his sins. A further twenty-six Protestants were condemned four months later. The Valladolid group ceased to exist. Special seating was erected on the square of San

Francisco for the Seville auto in September of the same year. The crowd was so great that it was impossible to find a lodging in the city, so some people took up their positions three days in advance. A guard of more than two hundred armed men—"a pleasure to behold," an observer noted, "well-dressed and decorated"[31]—was selected to march the penitents with drums and flags from the castle to the square. At four in the morning, fifty priests arrived with the cross of St. Ann, followed by monks, magistrates, and, finally, the inquisitors with their banner. Don Juan's confession was heard by a priest. At the stake, repentant, he urged the twenty who died with him to convert themselves back to the holy faith; "he died with many tears of remorse over his sins." The prior of San Isidro and four of his priests were kept back for a second Seville auto-da-fé; for good measure, the prior of the Jeronimite monastery at Toledo was accused of ridiculing the sacraments—"Up, little Peter," he was said to mock when he elevated the Host, "and let the people look at you"—and burned at the gates of his monastery.

Native Protestants were extinguished by such means. Those who now fell into Inquisition hands were almost all foreign sailors and traders. The English mariner William Brook and ship's master Nicholas Burton were among the first of this unhappy new breed; they shared the Seville flames at Christmas, 1560, and Burton's cargo, valued at fifty thousand pounds, was seized to swell the coffers of his tormentors. Fifty-one alleged Lutherans were burned in person or in effigy at Barcelona between 1552 and 1578; all were French, as were the eight who died in Valencia in the last half of the century.

Heresy was a betrayal of baptism; foreign Protestants were held to be legally baptized, even though by heretical priests, and could thus be treated in the same fashion as Spaniards. The Inquisition was, nevertheless, sensitive to the needs of commerce. Foreign travelers were generally secure provided that they watched their tongues, carried no Protestant Bibles or texts, and "gave no scandal to others." The Canary Islands were a major port of call for English ships in the wine trade and on the long voyage to the Indies and South America. Some fifteen hundred English and Dutch residents lived profitably if nervously on Tenerife. At least forty-four English sailors were imprisoned by the local Inquisition between 1574 and 1624. Only one, George Caspar of London, was relaxed.

Cases like these, if rare, produced an understandable and bitter revulsion outside Spain. There is a particular horror to the deaths of men who, like alien creatures falling to earth, found themselves in a strange land where the innocence of their infant baptism became a death warrant. Meticulous accounts of their torture remain. Sixty-eight English seamen, abandoned on the Mexican coast during Sir John Hawkins's disastrous expedition of 1567, were racked for three months with the persistent question on the sacraments: were they "the very true and perfect body and blood of our Saviour Christ, Yea or Nay?" Those from whom a "nay" was extracted were burned as Lutheran heretics, while those able to persist with "yea" were scourged and sent to the galleys.[32] The sailor Jacob Petersen from Dunkirk, age twenty, was examined by the tribunal of the Canaries in November 1597. He was stripped, bound, and given three turns of the cord. "On being given these he said first: 'Oh God!' and then, 'There's no mercy.' After the turns he was admonished, and he said 'I don't know what to say, oh dear God!' Then three more turns of the cord were ordered to be given, and after two of them he said: 'Oh God, oh God, there's no mercy, oh God help me, help me!' After three more turns he confessed."[33]

How could such unspeakable pain be inflicted in the name of a faith that adored the Lamb? Civil justice, it is true, was also cruel. Blinding, mutilation, tearing with hot pincers, burning alive, and breaking on the wheel were among the punishments included in the Carolina, the 1530 criminal code of the emperor Charles V. In England, poisoners were boiled to death in cauldrons of oil; the penalty for high treason was hanging, drawing, and quartering. Men were burned to death or hung by their feet between two starving dogs for coining in France; when Henry II was dying in 1559, struck in the eye by a splinter from a lance, four criminals were beheaded so that surgeons could experiment fruitlessly with their eyes.

Civil practice, and the scriptural excuses first used in the medieval Inquisition, and now dusted off once more, provides only a slender explanation. A part of the answer lies, not in the Bible, perhaps, but in Dostoyevsky. In an extraordinary passage in *The Brothers Karamazov,* the Russian novelist suggested that inquisitors would gladly have burned Christ himself, believing that in making mankind free to believe—"ye shall know the truth, and the truth shall make you free" (John 8:32)—Christ had erected a great and inhumane obstacle to happiness. In the novel, Christ walks through the cathedral at Seville after an auto-da-fé in which one hundred heretics have been burned. The people recognize him,—"It's Him, it's Him," they repeat—and children strew flowers in his path. A little girl lies dead in an open coffin. In compassion, Christ whispers *"Talitha cumi,"* "Damsel arise," and she sits up and smiles, and the wreath of white roses lying beside her becomes a bouquet. The Cardinal Grand Inquisitor watches—an old man of almost ninety, in a coarse monk's habit, Torquemada-like, tall, with a withered face and sunken eyes that retain a "fiery, spark-like gleam"—and orders his guards to arrest Christ. The worshipers let Christ be taken prisoner; they bow their heads to the Inquisitor as he blesses them and hurries wordlessly on his way.

Christ is held in a dank cell in the Ecclesiastical Court. Night falls; the air reeks of lemon and laurel; the Grand Inquisitor enters the prison with a lamp in his hand. He forbids Christ to speak—"I know only too well what you would say. And you have no right to add anything to what was said by you in former times"—and he blames him for offering people a freedom when he was last on earth with which their ill-disciplined and corrupt souls cannot cope. "For fifteen centuries we have struggled with that freedom," the Inquisitor says, "but now it is over, and over for good. . . . people have brought us their freedom and have laid it humbly at our feet. . . . For only now has it become possible to think for the first time about people's happiness. Man is constituted as a mutineer; can mutineers ever be happy? You were given warnings, you had plenty of warnings and instructions, but you did not obey them, you rejected the only path by which people could have been made happy. . . ." Fortunately, the Inquisitor adds, "When you left you handed over the task to us. You gave your promise, you sealed it with your word. . . ." He remonstrates with Christ: "Why have you come to get in our way now? And why do you gaze at me so silently and sincerely with those meek eyes of yours? I do not want your love, because I myself do not love you. . . ." The Inquisitor says that he is one of those "who have corrected your great deed. . . . For if ever was one who deserved our bonfire more than anyone else, it is you. Tomorrow I am going to burn you." Christ quietly kisses the Inquisitor's bloodless lips; the old man shudders and briefly relents; he opens the prison door and releases Christ into the town's dark streets and squares, saying: "Go and do not come back . . . ever . . . ever!" The kiss burns within the Inquisitor's heart, but he remains with his old ideas.

Dostoyevsky was Russian Orthodox and had a deep contempt for Western Christians. He attributed the Inquisitor's rejection of Christ to Rome's claim to be the sole interpreter of faith; since the Catholic Church is the repository of Christian truth, it no longer has need of Christ.

But the Inquisitor is a universal figure, Protestant as much as Catholic. He believes in a "weak, eternally depraved and eternally dishonourable human race" whom he must protect with his strength, as Luther did. As Calvin cursed heretics for obliging him to burn them, so the Inquisitor feels himself among the "martyrs who have taken upon themselves the curse of the knowledge of good and evil." The Inquisitor tells Christ that he is one of those whose flocks "consider us gods because we, in standing at their head, have consented to endure freedom and rule over them . . . but we say that we are obedient to you and that we rule in your name . . ."[34]

That chilling self-portrait applies to the great Calvinist Theodore Beza as well as Torquemada. Beza's 1554 tract "Whether Heretics should be Punished by the Civil Magistrate?" argued that it was misguided for Christians to be lenient simply because Christ was gentle and turned the other cheek. He said that "true charity" lay in defending the flock against the wolf. It was the duty of the magistrate to protect his people against crime. Heresy was a crime, and must be punished as such. Beza allowed that some decent men believed that it was wrong to execute a heretic because it left no chance for penitence. But heresy was as grave an offense as others for which the death penalty was accepted; indeed, Beza argued, it was worse than murder, for that destroyed bodies, where the heretic assassinated souls and God's majesty.

A moving response was made by Sebastian Castellio, himself suspected of heresy by Calvinists and Catholics alike. In his response to Beza—"Whether Heretics Are to be Persecuted?"—he wrote of the necessity for Christians to imitate Christ. "O Christ, creator and king of the world, dost thou see?" he asked. "Art thou become quite other than thyself, so cruel . . . ? When thou didst live upon earth, none was more gentle, more merciful, more patient of wrong. . . . Men scourged thee, spat upon thee, mocked thee, crowned thee with thorns, crucified thee among thieves and thou didst pray for them who did this wrong. Art thou now so changed? If thou, O Christ, has commanded these executions and tortures, what hast thou left for the devil to do?"[35] Were not Christ and his apostles killed as heretics? What was heresy, when there were so many Christian doctrines in the world?

"I have carefully examined what the word *heretic* means," he wrote, "and I cannot make it seem more than this, a heretic is a man with whom you disagree."

CHAPTER XXII

"RATHER A COUNTRY RUINED THAN A COUNTRY DAMNED . . .":

The Wars of Religion

T he misery inflicted on so-called heretics in Spain, being part of the deliberate and long-term policy of the most powerful monarchs in Christendom, has a chilling quality of precision to it. In simple numerical terms, however, the perhaps twenty-five thousand victims of the Inquisition bear no comparison to the eight million or more who died in the swill of religious wars that devastated other parts of Europe. The passions turned against Jews and Moors in Spain were unleashed elsewhere on fellow Christians, and provided spiritual justification for the personal, dynastic, and national ambitions that ravaged the worst affected regions with the haphazard ferocity of the Black Death.

In France, the years between 1562 and 1598 were stained by massacres, deceptions, murders, and eight wars. The immediate crisis was dynastic. In 1560 the crown passed to Charles IX, the ten-year-old son of Catherine de' Medici. Two powerful factions of nobles opposed each other under the cloak of religion. A Catholic party, headed by Francis, duke of Guise, and his brother, Cardinal Charles of Guise, was pitted against Bourbons sympathetic to Calvinist Huguenots. The latter were led in name by Antoine de Bourbon, the king of Navarre, and in practice by the prince of Condé and Admiral Coligny. With the French crown weakened by the boy king and the regency of his foreign mother, political tension was inevitable. Religion simply swelled its scope and fanned its atrocities.

Calvinism spread rapidly over the French border from Geneva. The process was recorded in the small town of Castres in the Languedoc.[1] Some townsfolk traveled to Geneva in 1559 to buy Bibles and Calvinist works, and to ask for a pastor. They chose a man named Geoffrey Brun, who was brought to Castres under cover of night and lodged in a house where he held secret services. The congregation grew rapidly; by 1561, Brun had collected two more pastors from Geneva, and an old schoolhouse was used for public preaching. The town's magistrates were converted. Protestant prisoners were released by force from the jail and the town declared itself Huguenot. This pattern—secret meetings in private houses, barns, and fields, protected by armed men, followed by the seizure of churches as confidence grew—was followed across France. At Rouen, seven thousand Huguenots met to sing psalms in the market square, listening to a preacher under the watchful eyes of five hundred men armed with arquebuses. Admiral Coligny estimated in 1561 that France had 2,150 Protestant congregations.

Some six hundred Huguenots were holding a service in a barn at Vassy in the Champagne country on Sunday, March 1, 1562. The duke of Guise was on his way to Paris with a group of armed retainers when they halted at a nearby monastery to hear mass. A skirmish broke out in which at least forty-eight Protestants were killed. The spark spread fire. In the nervous city of Toulouse, where Protestant students had taunted Catholics with psalm-singing, three thousand Huguenots were slaughtered. Huguenot mobs responded by attacking Catholic churches, destroying stained glass and statues; at Caen the tomb of William the Conqueror was smashed, and in Montauban a choir of children chanted the Ten Commandments as a pile of carvings and other idols was burned. Priests and pastors were murdered, churches looted, towns sacked. The religious fanatics on both sides, and the bands of mercenaries, were uncontrollable. A Huguenot at Orléans murdered the duke of Guise in 1562; his son Henry, known like his father as "le Balafré," "the scarred," took charge of the Catholic League, seeking vengeance and the throne. Condé was taken prisoner by the Catholics and shot. But for the fighting, the Venetian ambassador wrote in 1569, "France would now be Huguenot, because the people were rapidly changing their faith and the ministers were much respected and exercised authority among them. But when they passed from words to weapons, and began to rob, destroy and kill, the people began to say: 'What kind of religion is this?'"[2]

Catherine plotted to assassinate Coligny, but when that failed, she instigated the great massacre of Huguenots in Paris on August 23, 1572, the eve of St. Bartholomew Day. As many as ten thousand Protestants were slaughtered in Paris and other large cities, Coligny among them. When he heard the news, the pope celebrated a Te Deum and Philip II of Spain, supporting the Catholic cause, "began to laugh."

Faith no longer played much part in events. Realists wearied by war, dubbed *politiques,* cared more for Machiavelli than the Bible. "Take out of the Catholic army all the soldiers whose motive is not pure zeal for religion or patriotism or loyalty to the sovereign," the essayist Michel Montaigne wrote, "and you would not be left with enough men to form a company." Catherine's third son aligned himself with Guise when he came to the French throne in 1574 as Henry III, but he then turned on his scarred ally, having him assassinated in 1588. A year later Henry was himself murdered by a Catholic monk enraged by his treachery. The heir presumptive to the throne, Henry of Navarre, had drunk Protestantism with his Huguenot mother's milk, or so he often said. He'd been spared in the St. Bartholomew Day massacre only by professing himself a Catholic, but he had reverted to Calvinism.

The Catholic clergy now refused to anoint Henry—a relapsed heretic—king. His personal chaplain urged him to remain Protestant; can it be, he asked, "that the greatest captain in the world has become so cowardly as to go to mass for fear of men?"[3] He accepted, however, the *politique* advice of his great future minister, the duke of Sully; while Sully himself remained a Huguenot, he recommended that Henry convert on the grounds that a man might find salvation in either religion. In 1593, Henry took an oath on the Gospels to renounce heresy and to live and die a Catholic. He was crowned Henry IV at Chartres before entering his capital in triumph. *"Paris vaut bien une messe,"* he is said to have remarked. "Paris is well worth a mass."

The king was bound by Pope Clement VIII to hear mass daily, to recite the litanies and the rosary, and to bring up his heir in the Church of Rome. Catholicism was recognized as the established religion of France, but Protestantism survived. Henry did not forget his Huguenot roots. In the Edict of Nantes in 1598, he attempted a brave experiment in religious cohabitation. Protestants were granted liberty of conscience throughout France; they could set up their own schools; all offices of state were open to them, and special courts were created to sit in cases that involved them. No other state in Europe but Poland offered such toleration. The pope thought it "the most cursed edict that I could imagine . . . whereby liberty of conscience is granted to everyone, which is the worst thing in the world"; he felt it made him the "laughing stock of the world."[4] Henry himself was fatally stabbed in 1610 by a Catholic fanatic, François Ravaillac, a bankrupt who had joined the Feuillants, a rigorous order of reformed Cistercians. The Edict survived until 1685, however, at which point it was revoked by Louis XIV under the influence of his mistress and second wife, Madame de Maintenon, the granddaughter of a distinguished Huguenot soldier and scholar who had converted to Catholicism in her teens. Thousands of Huguenots converted in the Dragonnades, the persecution that followed the revocation, so called because of the dragoon cavalrymen who were billeted on Huguenot families to the financial ruin of those who refused Catholicism; many fled to Geneva, Prussia, England, and the Netherlands, and from there sailed for South Africa and America.

❖ AN AUSTERE FIGURE, kneeling for hours before statues of the saints in the Escorial, his monastery-palace on a dusty plateau outside Madrid, Philip II was the only Catholic with a realistic dream of undermining Protestantism in Europe, as Judaism and Islam were destroyed in Spain. He inherited his father's possessions in Naples, Sicily, Sardinia, Milan, the Low Countries, and the New World, adding Portugal and its empire to them. He had, too, his father's melancholy, and shared his conviction that it was his Christian duty pitilessly to repress both heretics and rebels.

The Low Countries bore the brunt of his piety. A patchwork of provinces, part feudal and part mercantile, they were acquired by the Habsburgs through marriage and placed under Spanish rule in 1551. Their prosperous cities controlled a large slice of European trade and the taxes extracted from them were several times more valuable to the Spanish crown than the bullion of the Indies. The French-speaking and predominantly Catholic Walloons of the south were divided by religion as well as language from the increasingly Calvinist Dutch speakers of Holland, Zeeland, and Utrecht in the north. Philip intended to unite them in a single Spanish and Catholic state, nominating their bishops and introducing the Inquisition to enforce royal control.

Merchants and skilled tradesmen predominated among Protestant converts. A list of early heretic suspects in Bruges showed a cabinetmaker, a ribbon weaver, a miller, a shingler, and a shoemaker, who met to read the Bible and discuss the Scriptures. A fish seller in Ghent, Roelandt van Loo, petitioning Philip II for pardon, described the informal way in which souls were won over. A local butcher asked him to go for a walk with him; he was led to a grain field where he found a dozen young men and women. One of them preached that "everyone should beware of evil and improve his life and that all drunkards and adulterers would not enter the kingdom of God." A girl gave everyone a handful of black cherries, and the little group dispersed. Roelandt was contacted again at his shop and agreed to let his house be used for meetings. Eight or nine people came, some of whom he recognized; a fat man preached "evil unseemly sermons." Roelandt claimed that he never had bad feelings "toward our Mother, the Holy Church." He was pardoned, presumably because he gave the names of those who did harbor such evil thoughts. Those who were less forthcoming, such as Hans van der Broucke, a young linen weaver arrested at Bruges, were strangled at the stake and burned. Protestant congregations nonetheless continued to worship in fields, as in France, often with armed guards, sending to Geneva for pastors. A congregation at Tournai numbered twenty thousand, a third of them armed; the preacher had a mounted escort of a hundred men.[5]

In August 1566 a mob broke up a procession carrying a statue of the Virgin around Antwerp, and rioting spread through the cities. Stained glass was smashed, missals ripped, monasteries plundered; images were desecrated with blood and beer, and letters of indulgence used as lavatory paper. Philip introduced martial law, but on December 1, 1566, a Calvinist synod at Antwerp authorized armed resistance. For the Catholics, too, the war was a crusade. The duke of Alva, Philip's military commander and regent, fought with a crucifix over his armor; at his side, the archbishop of Cologne rode with pistols in his holsters.

Alva set up a *Bloedraad,* a "blood council," to terrorize the rebels. The counts of Egmont and Horn were beheaded on the great square of Brussels, and their severed heads were sent to Madrid in a box. Resistance was organized by the prince of Orange, William the Silent, one of the richest men in Europe, once a Catholic and raised at the imperial court, but converted to rebellion and Protestantism by Spanish excesses. Atrocities were commonplace. At Naarden in 1572, Spanish troops killed deaf-mutes and the inmates of the local hospital; at Zutphen they drove naked men, women, and children into the icebound river. At Leiden in 1574 the dikes and river defenses were opened to wash away the Spanish besiegers and allow a Protestant flotilla to sail almost to the walls to relieve the starving townsfolk. Rotterdam was sacked during a Spanish advance, and the town of Oudewater was set on fire by its Calvinist defenders lest it fall into enemy hands. In the "Spanish fury" at Antwerp in 1576, unpaid and mutinous soldiers flayed men alive and stretched their skins over regimental drums. "A stage of horror," a contemporary wrote, "the corpses of men and horses in mountainous heaps . . . the streets dyed with their mingled blood."[6]

The Calvinists took as their motto *"God behoed ons,"* "God will provide for us." They saw in their survival evidence of their election to divine favor. "Oh Lord, when all was ill with us," Adrian Valerius wrote in his history of events, "You brought us dry-footed even as the people of yore, with Moses and with Joshua, were brought to their Promised Land."[7] Pastors compared Philip with the king of Assyria and William the Silent with the godly captain of Judah. Alva held the south, but in the north the Dutch defeated the greatest military power of the age. In 1584, the year that William was assassinated at Delft, the northern United Provinces formally renounced their allegiance to Philip and Spain.

Fighting continued fitfully, but, as 150,000 refugees settled in the Protestant provinces, the Low Countries were permanently divided into a Catholic south, the origin of modern Belgium, and the Dutch republic in the north, a haven for dissidents, philosophers, and painters, its Calvinist burghers rich, adventurous, self-ruling, and with the self-confidence of the elect. Calvinist rigorists rejected the gentler precepts of Jacobus Arminius—that Christ died for all, that grace can be lost, that good works play a part in salvation—at the Synod of Dort in 1618. Arminian clergymen were deprived of their livings and expelled. The synod asserted that mankind is utterly depraved and that Christ died only for the chosen, whose election is unconditional and for whom grace is irresistible.

Philip failed, too, in England. He had been married to one queen of England, Mary, and he offered himself to the young Elizabeth. She refused him, and his plotting and planned invasion inspired in part the long and bitter English prejudice against Catholics. Thousands remained faithful to the old religion in England: in Lancashire and Durham, the northern hills, and the Midlands; so did families in Wales, and in remote Highland glens, and on the Scottish islands, and the majority of the Irish. Their courage through the generations has a quality both dogged and noble; elsewhere in northern Europe, in the Scottish lowlands and Scandinavia, Catholic practice was all but obliterated.

The law required attendance at Protestant churches in England from 1559 on penalty of a fine. A ruling from Rome forbade this. Those who obeyed the papal ruling were known as "recusants"; the many who did attend, unable to pay the fine or finding the Anglican liturgy to retain a comfortingly Catholic ring, were called "church papists." The safety of both groups was jeopardized after Mary Queen of Scots, a dynastic rival to Elizabeth, fled to England in 1568. She gave focus to Catholic hopes and plots; she told the Spanish ambassador that she would be queen of England and have the Mass restored within three months if Spain would help her. The earls of Northumberland and Westmoreland led a northern rising in November 1569, marching beneath the Catholic banner of the Five Wounds of Christ, with twelve thousand crowns of cash from Pope Pius V and a promise of aid from Spain. They desecrated the holy table in Durham cathedral, tore the English Bible in shreds, and celebrated the mass. After initial success the rebellion was suppressed; Northumberland was executed with many others while Westmoreland fled to continue his plotting as a pensioner in Spain.

The pope did not realize the extent of the collapse. On February 25, 1570, Pius V published *Regnans in Excelsis,* a bull excommunicating Elizabeth. It followed a formal trial of the queen at Rome, in which English exiles had testified to her heresies. The bull branded her as alien to the Body of Christ, a heretic, and usurper. It absolved her subjects of their allegiance and bade them disobey her laws. Copies were smuggled into England by a chaplain at the Spanish embassy; a Catholic gentleman named Fenton paid with his life for pinning one to the gate of the bishop of London's palace. The bull was wildly intemperate; in making it impossible to serve both Crown and pope, it stained generations of English Catholics as potential traitors.

Fear of Spanish invasion, papal subsidies to Irish rebels, and the plots cascading around the queen of Scots kept popular mistrust of Catholics at a high pitch.

In 1571 the Italian banker Roberto Ridolfi was found to be conspiring with the Catholic duke of Norfolk, the Spanish ambassador, and the pope to plan Mary's escape from house arrest. Norfolk lost his head, though Ridolfi escaped. The Parliament of that year made it treasonable to be reconciled or to reconcile another to Rome, thus exposing recusant priests to the death penalty. By now an English college had been founded at Douai in the Spanish Netherlands by William Allen, a former Oxford fellow, to train Catholic priests for missions to England. Its first martyr was Cuthbert Mayne, who had become a secret Catholic as a student at Oxford. Ordained priest at Douai, he was sent on the English mission in 1576, becoming chaplain to a family of recusant landowners in Cornwall. He passed himself off as their steward, but suspicions were aroused and he was arrested. Mayne was charged with administering the Lord's Supper in a "papalistic manner," possessing a copy of a papal bull, and wearing an Agnus Dei, a wax medallion with the figure of the Lamb. He was executed on November 29, 1577.

The first Jesuit to die was Edmund Campion, who had been at Oxford with Mayne. A fine orator, he had welcomed the queen when she visited the university; he was ordained an Anglican deacon before going to Douai and converting. He was chosen for the initial Jesuit mission to England. "It is a venture which only the wisdom of God can bring to good and to His wisdom we lovingly resign ourselves," he wrote before he sailed in 1580. "But in any case I will go over and take part in the fight though I die for it. It often happens that the front rank of a conquering army is knocked over."[8] Safely across the Channel, Campion preached in London and Lancashire, lodging in the houses of recusants. He was recklessly brave, buoyed up by the enthusiasm he found; the emphasis on the sacrament in Catholicism gave the priest bold enough to administer it a special place in the hearts of his congregation. "I ride about some piece of the country every day," Campion wrote happily. "The harvest is wonderful great. On horseback, I meditate my sermon; when I come to the house I polish it. . . . In the morning after Mass, I preach; they hear with exceeding greediness and very often receive the sacrament."[9] Nevertheless, Campion knew he might end on the scaffold and wrote a note to the priest-hunters warning them "that we have made a league— all the Jesuits in the world . . . —cheerfully to carry the cross you shall lay upon us." He was seized in 1581 and brought to London by horse, his arms pinioned and a sign pinned to his hat: "Edmund Campion. Seditious Jesuit." He was offered his life if he returned to the Church of England. Refusing, he was racked and executed at Tyburn on December 1. "The expense is reckoned, the enterprise is begun; it is of God, it cannot be withstood," he had written before he died. "So the faith was planted: so it must be restored."[10]

Two years later a list of conspirators and notes on potential invasion ports for a Spanish force were found in the possession of another Catholic, Francis

Throckmorton. He confessed under torture that he was a go-between for Mary and Mendoza, the Spanish ambassador. Throckmorton was executed and Mendoza was expelled. He threatened to return with an army. As the threat of Spanish invasion mounted, Jesuits and seminary priests were ordered to leave the realm within forty days on penalty of death. Women now joined the victims. Margaret Clitherow, the convert daughter of a sheriff at York, was charged with harboring priests; to protect her children she refused to plead and was crushed to death. A Catholic plot to assassinate Elizabeth was infiltrated by government agents, who read notes passed from Mary to the French ambassador in a beer barrel. After years of prevarication, Elizabeth signed Mary's death warrant in 1587. "I forgive you with all my heart," Mary told her executioners; "for now, I hope, you shall make an end of all my troubles."[11] The Spanish invasion fleet sailed from Corunna in July 1588 with seventeen thousand troops aboard, and 180 monks and friars to restore the Mass and bring the Inquisition to England.

Had Philip conquered England, Protestantism would have been hard pressed to survive. The king was confident enough to agree with the pope to appoint William Allen as archbishop of Canterbury after the expected Catholic victory, though the financial strains of the Netherlands campaign bankrupted the crown three times, and the phrase *poner una pica en Flandres*—"putting a pikeman in Flanders"[12]—had become an idiom for a lost cause. Allen wrote a violent tract denouncing Elizabeth as a bastard, and a papal secretary wrote that the queen had caused so much injury to the Catholic faith that "whosoever sends her out of the world, with the pious intention of doing God service, not only does not sin but gains merit."[13] Elizabeth prayed for a "famous victory over those enemies of my God, of my Kingdom and of my People." Success was duly delivered, at a cost of some eleven thousand Spanish lives. Deteriorating weather prevented the Armada from collecting invasion troops from the Spanish Netherlands, a body of seven hundred English exiles among them. Protestants interpreted the gales that dispersed the Spanish fleet into the North Sea and drove its ships onto the rocky coasts of Hebrides and western Ireland as evidence of God's favor.

Sporadic executions of Catholics continued. The Jesuit Robert Southwell survived for six years on the English mission, disguised and hiding in London and Catholic country houses until he was betrayed in 1592. During his imprisonment he wrote a collection of poems, including "The Burning Babe," greatly popular with Protestants and Catholics alike:

> As I in hoary winter's night stood shivering in the snow,
> Surprised I was with sudden heat which made my heart to glow;
> And lifting up a fearful eye to view what fire was near,
> A pretty babe all burning bright did in the air appear . . .

He was hung, drawn, and quartered for treason in 1595. To the condemned, treason was no more than a legal fig leaf for persecution. "My Lord, I die only for religion," a recusant named Ingram told a court at Durham in 1594. "Thou art impudent," the judge told him; "the law tellest thee that thou diest for high treason." "There is no Christian law in the world, that can make the saying and sacrifice of the mass treason," Ingram responded.[14] An account by the Jesuit John Gerard of his torture in the Tower of London in April 1597 differs little from the interrogations of Protestant seamen by the Inquisition that so enraged the English: he was escorted to a dark chamber "in a kind of solemn procession the attendants walking ahead with lighted candles," his wrists were put into iron gauntlets, and, to cries to confess, he was suspended until he became unconscious, thanking God "for this most merciful thought, that the utmost and worst they can do is to kill you, and you have often wanted to give your life for your Lord God."[15]

By Elizabeth's death in 1603, 123 priests had been executed in England during her reign, together with about sixty men and women who had harbored them. It was known that 8,750 English recusants were paying a huge fine of twenty pounds a month. The number of Catholic believers was certainly much higher; perhaps one hundred thousand attended Anglican services occasionally to avoid being fined, and as many as 360 priests may have been practicing discreetly, sometimes concealed in priest-holes in the country houses of great Catholic families.

Prejudice was hardened by a near-successful attempt by Catholic hotheads to blow up the king and Parliament. James VI of Scotland, son of the ill-fated Mary, Queen of Scots, succeeded to the English throne in 1603 as James I under the new title of king of Great Britain. A devout if conservative Protestant, he was nonetheless tolerant of his Catholic subjects. His desire to relax the penal laws against them was thwarted by Parliament. Guy Fawkes, a Yorkshireman who was recruited while serving with the Spanish armies in the Netherlands, described in his confession how he and six others plotted in despair "against His Maiestie for reliefe of the Catholic cause." They determined to explode a huge mine beneath the government as it sat in Parliament, "which place wee made a choice of because Religion having been unjustly suppressed there, it was fittest that iustice and punishment should be executed there." They toiled for months to dig a sa beneath the thick foundations of the building, but then discovered that a coal cellar running beneath it was empty. They rented it and bought "twentie Barrels of Powder . . . and covered the same with Billets and Faggots."[16] Fawkes was to light the fuse on November 5, 1605, as the king and the Lords and Commons assembled for the opening of the new parliamentary session. The plot was betrayed and Fawkes was caught red-handed, tortured, tried, and hanged. The superior of the Jesuit mission to England, Henry Garnet—even though his knowledge of the

THE POWDER PLOT

Guy Fawkes and his fellow conspirators plotted "against His Maiestie for reliefe of the Catholic cause" in London in 1605. They decided to blow up Parliament on November 5, 1605, "which place we made a choice of because Religion having been unjustly suppressed there, it was fittest that iustice and punishment should be executed there." The plot was betrayed and Fawkes was caught red-handed, tortured, tried, and hanged. Services of thanksgiving, with fiery anti-Catholic sermons, were held each November 5 in Anglican churches for the next 250 years.

conspiracy may have been purely under the seal of confession,* which required him to remain silent—was also executed. Annual services of thanksgiving for the discovery of the plot were held each November 5 in Anglican churches until 1859, often accompanied by fiery anti-Catholic sermons. Firework celebrations in which effigies of Guy Fawkes are burned on bonfires continue to this day.

PROTESTANTS ALSO HAD religious motives that set them against the Crown and one another. Puritans despised a Church whose parsons wore surplices, that bade their congregation kneel for the sacraments, and accepted the su-

---

*The seal of confession is an absolute obligation—covering any eavesdropper or onlooker as well as the confessor—not to reveal anything said by a penitent using the sacrament of penance. It covers all sins, venial or mortal, and permits no exceptions, whether for reason of life or death, or Church or state.

premacy of the Crown and the authority of bishops. Presbyterians followed Calvin in demanding a Church governed by its ministers and elders in a four-tier polity, which rose from the kirk session of the minister and elders elected by an individual church, through the local presbytery and regional synod to the general assembly. Made up of ministers and elders elected by the presbyteries, and presided over by an elected moderator, this assembly was the Church's highest court of appeal.

This system was supposedly a return to the time of the apostles, in which the Crown played no part. In Scotland, where Presbyterians were in the majority, the moderator Andrew Melville addressed King James as "God's sillie vassal," declaring that he was no more than a subject of "Christ Jesus the King and His Kingdom the Kirk."[17] Puritans in England were a minority, but a troublesome one nonetheless. On James's journey south from Scotland to accept the English throne, they presented him with a petition objecting to "human rites and ceremonies" which included the marriage ring, bowing at the name of Jesus, the use of the cross in baptism, and the profanation of the Lord's Day by amusements. Congregationalists went further than Presbyterians in rejecting any form of Church authority beyond the individual and self-governing congregation. They believed Christ to be the sole head of the Church, in which all believers are "priests unto God" with the right to independence.

To the Crown this was political and spiritual anathema. James believed in the divine right of kings to rule Church as well as country. The monarchy, he told Parliament, "is the supremest thing upon the earth; for kings are not only God's lieutenants upon earth and sit on God's throne, but even by God himself they are called Gods." Although it was not theologically necessary for a Protestant monarch to control his Church through bishops—Lutheran princes in Germany achieved this through "superintendents"—the episcopalian system was the most practical means of maintaining royal control. Bishops were not elected, like puritan ministers; the Crown appointed them. "No bishops, no king," James famously declared. When the disrespectful Melville was lured to London, he was thrown in the Tower.

Early dissent centered among students and teachers at Cambridge. In 1581, Robert Browne, a wealthy puritan, set up independent congregations in East Anglia, each of which elected and deposed its own ministers. He held that the Kingdom of God was "not to be begun by whole parishes, but rather of the worthiest, were they never so few";[18] these congregations were responsible to none but God and themselves. Browne was briefly imprisoned and then fled to Holland with his flock. Another Cambridge divine, Thomas Cartwright, was deprived of his professorship for denouncing the surplice and Church government; he, too, left to become minister to exiled English congregations in Holland. The anonymous

tracts published under the pseudonym Martin Marprelate and attacking the episcopal hierarchy provoked the trial and execution of three separatist leaders in
1593 for "writing with malicious intent."

Small congregations joined the exodus to Holland, each with its own idio-
syncrasies. Some had elaborate rituals of foot-washing; others revived the ancient
agape love feast, or, holding all set forms of worship to be heretical, filled their
services with prophesyings and inspired commentaries. The Cambridge fellow
John Smyth earned the title of "Self-Baptist" because he insisted on baptising
himself, there being no priest or pastor pure enough to do so. He led a colony of
exiles to Amsterdam in 1608, where he established the first Baptist Church. After
his death in 1612, followers led by Thomas Helwys returned to London, where
he founded the first General Baptist congregation. Helwys was from Notting-
hamshire, and it was from that county that John Robinson led his congregation
to Leiden in Holland when forced out of England in 1608. It was Robinson who
encouraged the Leiden group in 1620 to charter a small ship of 180 tons, the
Mayflower, in the belief that, though Luther and Calvin "were precious shining
lights in their times, yet God had not revealed his whole will to them," and that,
in their American emigration, they might find "truth and light" as well as freedom from persecution.

❖   OTHER ENGLISH SOULS thought puritanism had exceeded itself. The
High Church tradition stressed that Anglicanism was a branch of Catholicism
whose roots stretched back before the Reformation. The Elizabethan divine
Richard Hooker had attacked the narrow puritan attitude that what was not in
the Scriptures was unlawful; he wrote of a natural law that embraced beauty and
the senses, and whose "seat is the bosom of God, her voice the harmony of the
world."[19] Anglican poet-clergymen mistrusted the separateness of puritans, their
sense of the elect and the excluded. "No man is an Island, entire of itself; every
man is a piece of the Continent," wrote John Donne, the dean of St. Paul's and
himself a former Catholic. "Any man's death diminishes me, because I am involved in Mankind; And therefore never send to know for whom the bells tolls;
it tolls for thee."[20] They supported king and bishops. "Twixt kings and tyrants
there's this difference known," the royalist parson Robert Herrick avowed; "Kings
seek their subjects' good: tyrants their own."[21]

Puritan influence was held to have made English churches alien and melan-
cholic. In many places they were the only public buildings and had been used for
gossip, horse-trading, promenading, and schooling; Church ales, powerful brews
used to raise money for church repairs, were sold in churchyards, and traders ped-
dled their wares in church porches. The puritanical faction, led by Archbishop

Grindal of York, had ordered a stop to this in 1571. Beadles were appointed to walk around the congregation with sticks to enforce reverent behavior and to wake up those who fell asleep during sermons of such interminable length that hourglasses were used to time them, the manufacturers often erring in favor of the congregation and using only fifty minutes' worth of sand.[22]

Sunday had been a day of sport as well as prayer, with hunting, hawking, hare coursing and fishing; bowls and dice were played, bears and bulls baited, plays performed, and feasts celebrated. Puritans demanded the suppression of such pleasures in a Sabbath devoted to sobriety and worship. From late Elizabethan times, tavern keepers lost their licenses if they sold drink during the hours of divine service. Acts of Parliament forbade anyone to meet for sport outside their own parish. Old habits died hard. People continued to cross themselves as they entered church and to bow to an altar that was now no more than a holy table, its importance replaced by the increasingly elaborate pulpit. Palm Sunday processions were banned, but boys still collected willows on that day. The assault on amusement was so deeply resented that James I issued a *Book of Sports* in 1617 defining the "lawful recreations," including archery and dancing, that all could indulge in after Sunday service. Its publication was bitterly opposed by puritans; the lawyer William Prynne, undaunted by having had both ears cut off for writing a thousand-page denunciation of women actresses and the theater that was felt to slight the queen, was then imprisoned for a furious critique of the *Book of Sports.*

Ill-feeling increased with the succession of Charles I in 1625. His queen, Henrietta Maria, was the daughter of Henry IV of France and a Catholic; it was a condition of the marriage that the penal laws against Catholics be suspended and the queen be allowed to practice her religion. To the suspicion this caused was added fury when Charles favored the "Arminians," as high churchmen were known for their anti-Calvinism. The most prominent of these was William Laud, who had provoked puritans to near-riot when he moved the Communion table to the east end of the choir at Gloucester cathedral. In 1633, Charles appointed him archbishop of Canterbury. Laud, like Pope Nicholas, believed in things that appealed to the eye. Paintings, stained glass, crosses, and crucifixes reappeared; statues were gilded and organs were returned or repaired; the holy table was raised again on steps, replacing the pulpit as a focal point, and once more called an altar; lecturers appointed to preach by puritan town corporations and parishes were suppressed; clergymen were ordered to wear the surplice and clean linen, to bow at the holy name, and to use a prayerbook that many held to be as cryptopapist as Laud and the king. Laud was no admirer of the pope—he recorded in his diary that he would not reconcile "till Rome were other than it is"—but his attempts to enforce uniformity and crush dissent were bitterly resented. Puritans acquired martyrs: the earless, popular, and half-deranged Prynne; John Lilburne, flogged and pilloried for writing illegal anti-episcopal pamphlets; John Bastwick, a Presbyterian who was pilloried and had his ears cropped for writing that the Church was "as full of fleas as a dog."

Laud was undone by the Scots and the king's wish to impose a uniform prayerbook on both parts of the kingdom. In 1637, without reference to the Presbyterian general assembly, Charles issued a royal proclamation at every market cross that a modified Anglican liturgy and prayerbook was to be the only accepted form of worship in Scotland. He personally ordered the new liturgy to be used at St. Giles's Cathedral in Edinburgh on July 23, 1637. A stool was hurled at the bishop during the service and rioting broke out. Presbyterians signed a covenant, swearing to defend the kirk from the king and his bishops; claiming the loyalty of all true Scots against the English, they established their own parliament. In August 1640 an army of covenanters crossed the Tweed and invaded England.

THE CIVIL WAR that followed was partly religious, partly constitutional. It was sparked by Scottish Presbyterians and enflamed by Irish Catholics, and it pitted parliamentarians against royalists, and evangelicals against Anglicans. Puritan republicans won the war, but lost the peace to constitutional monarchists.

Rebellion broke out in Ireland in 1641. With the Jesuits active, and reports of the massacre of Protestant settlers, religious panic and fear of Catholic reconquest added to the existing crises of Church government, parliamentary rights, and taxation. An army had to be raised to put down the rebels, but Parliament did not trust the king to command it. A grand remonstrance was passed, criticizing the king's "popish advisors" and demanding that he should only use such counselors as Parliament "may have cause to confide in." In place of puritans, Archbishop Laud was now imprisoned in the Tower of London—"the sty of all Pestilential faith," he was called—and eventually convicted on vague charges of "popery" under a parliamentary bill of attainder.

Iconoclasts raged through churches and chapels, a throwback to eighth-century Byzantium, smashing the images and pictures that Laud had encouraged. The puritan William Dowling proudly noted his jaunts through the flatlands of East Anglia, hammer and axe in hand. His work began in the college chapels at Cambridge in December 1643. At Peterhouse, he noted, "we pulled down two mighty great angells, with wings, and divers other angells, and the 4 Evengelists, and Peter, with his keyes on the chapell floor, and about a hundred chirubims."[23] The fellows at Pembroke claimed that laymen like Dowling had no right to interfere in Church business. "I cited Calvin," Dowling wrote, telling them that "the people had to doe as well as the clergie." An exchange of Bible quotations followed. The fellows used Deuteronomy—"make you a graven image in the form of any figure, the likeness of male or female"—to defend their paintings. "I deny'd it, and turned to Exod[us]," Dowling noted. He then got to work. "We broake and pulled down 80 superstitious pictures." He and his posse moved on to other colleges. To a good puritan, it was popish for a man to bare his head in church, and to worship at an altar raised above steps. At Queens' College, Dowling recorded, "none of the Fellowes would put on their hats all the time they were in ther chappell, and we digged up ther steps for 3 howers, and broake downe 10 or 12 apostles, and saints pictures in ther hall." At Jesus, they "brake downe of superstitious, of saints and angells, 120 at the least"; at Clare the tally was "3 cherebims, 12 apostles, and 6 of the Fathers in the windowes, and a crosse," and at King's, "one thousand superstitious pictures, the ladder of Christ, and theves to upon, many crosses, and Jesus writ on them . . ." After cutting his swath through the city, Dowling moved on to the villages of south Cambridgeshire. In one three-week period he stripped an average of five churches a day of their ornaments and leveled their altar steps, working a five-day week, Tuesday to Saturday. Thus was the English Church deprived of its medieval legacy.

The royalist armies did well enough in the early fighting against such fanaticism. The tide turned when Parliament signed a Solemn League and Covenant

Puritan soldiers pulled down the cross at Cheapside in London in 1643. They returned a few days later to burn the *Book of Sports*, which defined the "lawful recreations," including dancing and archery, that could be practiced after Sunday service. All amusements were banned on the Sabbath. Tens of thousands of statues and paintings were destroyed or whitewashed by Puritan iconoclasts. "We broake and pulled down 80 superstitious pictures," one wrote of a day's work in Cambridge in 1643, "two mighty great angells, and the 4 Evangelists, and Peter, with his keyes, and about a hundred chirubims . . ."

with the Scots in 1643, undertaking to uphold Presbyterian Church government and to introduce it in England. With twenty thousand Scots fighting alongside the parliamentarians, the royalists were badly beaten at Marston Moor in 1644. A professional New Model Army was raised by Oliver Cromwell, who emerged as the leader of the Independents, demanding religious freedom and the continuation of the war against a peace party of Presbyterian parliamentarians. "God hath taken away your eldest son by a cannon shot," Cromwell wrote to his brother-in-law after Marston Moor. "One thing lay upon his spirit . . . that God had not suffered him to be any more the executioner of His enemies." In 1645 he annihilated Charles's forces at Naseby. The king surrendered to the Scots the following year. He was handed to Parliament, abducted by the army, and executed on January 30, 1649.

Cromwell was one of the regicides who signed the death warrant. He did not appear remarkable. A contemporary found him "in a plain-cloth suit, which seemed to have been made by an ill country tailor; his linen plain and not very clean . . . a speck or two of blood on his collar . . . his countenance swollen and reddish, his voice sharp and untunable, and his eloquence full of fervour . . ."[24] But he was a unique phenomenon; a religiously inspired private citizen who had executed his lawful sovereign and now took it upon himself to rule a great European state. He did so in the conviction that the nation should be ruled by the godly in the way that God willed.

He watered seeds of hatreds in Ireland that still exist. He landed on the island in 1649 and marched on Drogheda, north of Dublin at the mouth of the river Boyne, where Protestant royalists and Irish Catholics defied him. "I forbade [my men] to spare any that were in arms in the Town: and, I think, that night they put to the sword about 2000 men," he wrote. When the last bastion fell, "their officers were knocked on the head; and every tenth man of the soldiers killed; and the rest shipped for Barbadoes. I am persuaded that this is a righteous judgment of God upon these barbarous wretches. . . . It is good that God alone have all the glory. . . ." His Irish settlement established a brutal peace. It "excepted from pardon of life and estate"—that is, it prescribed death and the seizure of goods—for any who had taken part in or abetted rebellion and other crimes in Ireland since 1641; it specifically condemned to death "all and every Jesuit priest, and other person or persons who have received orders from the Pope or See of Rome"; and it sentenced all Irish officers of the rank of colonel and above to be banished at the pleasure of the English Parliament. The rank and file were to forfeit two-thirds of their possessions.[25]

In England, Cromwell experimented with a form of government that would accord with the paths laid down by God. He and the army council appointed an assembly to draft a godly constitution. It was dubbed "Barebone's Parliament" in deference to one of its members, Praise-God Barebone, a leather-seller and lay preacher. This reflected Cromwell's sympathy with fellow radicals who believed that God's will should be followed as much in affairs of state as in private life. They existed in plentiful confusion, and they were often at each other's throats.

One group, for example, the Diggers, held that God had made the earth as a common treasury for all to share. They asserted the people's right to common land, and a group of them began digging up the commons on St. George's Hill in Surrey in 1649. Locals angry with the newcomers destroyed their crops and cabins. Gerard Winstanley wrote their manifestos. To him, God was "the great creator Reason." The ownership of property and mastery over common people resulted from the Fall, he said, and covetousness had overcome righteousness; the millennium would arrive when the land reverted to common ownership and all lived as equals. Fifth Monarchy men believed that the pope, the Antichrist, had usurped the Fourth Monarchy of Daniel's dream, the Roman Empire. They expected the Fifth Monarchy, of Christ, imminently; they believed that the regicides had started the downfall of the Antichrist, and they considered themselves to be saints who would shortly inherit the earth. It was their purpose to destroy all remnants of "carnal" rule in England. One told Cromwell to his face that he "tooke the Crowne off from the head of Christe, and put it on his owne." Their risings were put down.

Another fringe group, Ranters, believed God to be present in all creatures, especially in themselves; since all God's creations are good, they held themselves to be sin-free. They scandalized puritans with their carefree smoking, drinking, swearing, and fornication. Muggletonians followed the London tailor Ludowicke Muggleton and his cousin John Reeve. The pair claimed to receive divine revelations telling them, among other things, that reason was created by the devil, that Elijah had been left in command of heaven during the incarnation, that there was no Trinity, and that only preachers with short hair spoke the truth. Muggleton was convicted of blasphemy, but the sect maintained a reading room in London into the nineteenth century. In Derby, another visionary, Richard Sale, walked through the streets barefoot and in sackcloth, with rank weeds in his left hand and sweet flowers in his right. At Furness a tailor called James Milner fasted for fourteen days in November 1652 and announced that on December 2 a sheep would be lowered from heaven in a sheet to mark the first day of creation. Adamites, a throwback to old Bohemia, worshiped in the nude. The dissatisfied and eccentric were often lumped together as Seekers. Their origins went back to Bartholomew Legate, a puritan preacher burned at Smithfield in 1612 for heresy; he believed that there had been no true church since the victory of the Antichrist, but that God would at length send prophets to found a new church.

Quakers were followers of George Fox, a weaver's son from Leicestershire who began to wander the Midlands villages in 1643 in search of truth. He had no time for churches, dismissing them as "steeplehouses," nor for educated churchmen, since "the Lord opened unto me that being bred at Oxford or Cambridge was not enough to fit and qualify men to be ministers of Christ." Instead he sought what he called the "inner light" of the living Christ that speaks directly to the soul. He rallied a band of followers, all of whom rejected hierarchy and liturgy, and held that Christ's teaching was within each believer. They first called themselves "Children of Light" and then "Friends of Truth." A judge dubbed them Quakers, after Fox had told him that he should tremble at the Word of the Lord, and the public felt it suited the ecstatic shudderings that came on them when they experienced the Light. At their meetings, the Friends waited silently for the Lord to inspire one of them, man or woman, to minister and to speak.

They seemed militant and deranged. They refused to pay tithes, rudely addressed strangers with the informal "thou," and refused to doff their hats to their social betters. A judge sentencing Fox at the Launceston Assizes in 1656 asked what scriptural authority he had for keeping his hat on. Fox retorted that the judge could read in the Book of Daniel that "the three children were cast into the fiery furnace by Nebuchadnezzar's command, with their coats, their hose and their hats on." Fox was duly jailed. His follower James Nayler was arrested while on his way to visit Fox. Nayler was credited with raising a woman from the dead, and a group of Ranters was convinced that he was Christ. When he was released he rode into Bristol on a horse in the driving rain, while his devotees strew their garments in his way and chanted "Holy, holy, holy." Nayler was severely punished for blasphemy; Fox himself was imprisoned eight times. He was a man of forceful character and spirit, however, a tireless traveler who was to visit the West Indies and America. By 1660 the Quakers were perhaps forty thousand strong; they were becoming pacifist and beginning to earn their reputation as that "sedate, sober, silent, serious, sad-coloured sect."[26]

Varied congregations of eccentric independents worshiped in some of the greatest churches in Christendom. Fifth Monarchy men met in a corner of St. Paul's in London, and in Exeter cathedral a brick wall was built to divide Presbyterians on one side from the Independents on the other.[27] Barebone's Parliament brought little but near-anarchy, and at the end of 1653, Cromwell took formal power as lord protector. A written constitution, the Instrument of Government, established Cromwell as lord protector and guaranteed that "such as profess faith in God by Jesus Christ (though differing in judgment from the doctrine, worship or discipline publicly held forth) shall not be restrained from but shall be protected in, the profession of the faith and the exercise of their religion . . . provided this liberty shall not be extended to Popery . . ."[28] In practice, "prayerbook Anglicans" who followed the old liturgy were excluded from toleration, as were Catholics and Quakers.

Public revulsion with extremism was slowly transformed into powerful nostalgia for the departed monarchy. "I secure myself," Brian Duppa, the High Church bishop of Salisbury said, "as the tortoise doth, by not going out of my shell." In Cromwell's last days it was clear that the country was being run, not by the godly, but by cynical careerists and army officers more interested in money than morals. In 1658, Cromwell died and was replaced as lord protector by his son. Richard Cromwell inherited colossal accumulated debts, a slump deepened by war with Spain, and a nation yearning for stability, low taxes, and an end to religious adventure. Charles II was bloodlessly restored to his father's throne, Oliver Cromwell's body was exhumed and hung from the gallows, and the High Churchmen emerged from beneath their shells.

IT HAD SEEMED in the 1560s that all Germany, including the great Catholic states of the south, would slip into Protestantism. Austrian priests openly administered the sacraments in both kinds, dropped prayers for the dead, and married their concubines; Albert, the devout duke of Bavaria, feared that his territories would no longer be Rome's unless the chalice and clerical marriage were tolerated. The Jesuits, branching out from the University of Ingolstadt, played a crucial part in defending the old religion. Peter Canisius preached against Protestantism throughout the south, founding Jesuit colleges at Augsburg, Munich, and Innsbruck, and working to spread Jesuit influence in Prague and Poland. His *Catechism,* a clear and powerful defense of Catholicism in questions and answers easily understood by lay readers, ran to 130 editions as the Jesuits won back some of the intellectual high ground.

The city of Graz was said to have only twenty Catholic communicants in 1570. The Habsburg archduke Charles founded a Jesuit college in 1573, and forbade citizens from attending Protestants schools. His son, Ferdinand, Jesuit-educated and later Holy Roman Emperor, is said to have vowed that "I would rather rule a country ruined than a country damned." In 1598 he expelled all Protestant pastors and schoolmasters from Graz and closed their churches and chapels. The number of Jesuits almost tripled to thirteen thousand during the thirty years when Claudio Aquaviva was their general. He sharpened the quality of their teaching with a basic program, the Ratio Studiorum, in which pupils were prepared in the humanities, philosophy, and science. Musical drama was used to stimulate young minds and teach moral values. "The quickest way to a good education is to consult the Jesuits," the scientist and Anglican Francis Bacon admitted. "Their schools have never been bettered." Enemies, who dubbed

Aquaviva "the Black Pope," acknowledged his impact; the first of many forgeries claiming to be instructions for a worldwide Jesuit conspiracy, the Monita Secreta, was published in Cracow.

Further north, the Rhineland was prevented from becoming a total loss. The prince-archbishop of Cologne, Gebhard Truchsess, was expelled by Spanish and Bavarian troops when he declared that he wanted to marry a nun, become a Protestant, and secularize his see. In Paderborn the Catholic prince-bishop imprisoned priests in his diocese who administered Communion in both kinds in 1596. When angry local people drove off his cattle and horses in protest, he ordered them to accept the Mass or go into exile, and founded a Jesuit college.

Fissures opened up in the Peace of Augsburg. As a compromise between Lutherans and Catholics, the settlement had made no mention of Calvinists. They had no legal status but they existed, in increasing numbers, they were provocative, and they included princes. The elector of the Palatinate advertised his conversion to Calvinism by tearing the Host into pieces and sneering, "What a fine God you are! You think you are stronger than I? We shall see!"[29] Lutherans were as shocked as Catholics. No legal provision was made, either, for a prince-bishop to declare himself Protestant. A so-called "ecclesiastical reservation" declared that any who did so thereby lost his office, but Protestants had not accepted this. Cologne was saved by imported troops, but Catholicism lost the great sees of Magdeburg, Bremen, and Halberstadt.

What little balance existed between emperor, electors, dukes, and free cities was under continuous strain. No consensus was reached even on the calendar; Protestants refused to accept the Gregorian dating and remained ten days ahead of Catholic states. In 1607, Maximilian, the Jesuit-educated duke of Bavaria, annexed the free city of Donauwörth and replaced its pastors with Jesuits after its Protestant majority had attacked a Benedictine procession. The following year, the Protestant states formed a defensive Evangelical Union. Maximilian created a Catholic League in response. Cross-tensions revealed an infinite capacity for Christian self-destruction. The Lutherans of Saxony did not join the Union, through dislike of Calvinists; the French, though Catholic, supported it, driven by fear of the Habsburg dynasty, whose rule surrounded them from the Low Countries and Burgundy to northern Italy and Spain. Suspicion of the Jesuits was rife among Catholic orders; a Dominican said that he crossed himself every time he saw one, and the Capuchins nurtured a particular dislike for them. The Capuchin Armand Richelieu was consecrated in the year that Donauwörth was forcibly Catholicized. As future chief minister of France, he happily allied himself with German Protestant princes against their Jesuit-schooled enemies.

Protestant merchants were seized and burned in the Black Forest. Lutherans beat Calvinists in the alleys of Berlin. Catholic priests in Bavaria carried pistols for self-defense; in Dresden a mob broke up the funeral cortege of a Catholic and tore the corpse into pieces; a Protestant pastor and a Catholic priest attacked each other in the street in Frankfurt am Main. In Styria, Jesuits in plain clothes sat with Calvinist congregations and tore the prayerbooks from their hands, proffering them breviaries. The currency was debased, and the great banking house of Fugger in Augsburg collapsed. An English traveler found that the houses of the least significant nobles were guarded by "hungry halberdiers and reverent musty bill-men with a brace or two of hot shots so that their palaces are more like prisons."[30] Everyone awaited trouble. The explosion was expected in 1621, when the Spanish truce with the Dutch expired.

Catastrophe came early, and with a violence that engulfed Central Europe for thirty years. In May 1618, Protestant noblemen mobbed into the Hradcany Castle in Prague to break up a meeting of the Habsburg commissioners. They seized two hard-line Catholic counselors, Jaroslav Martinitz and William Slavata, and

In May 1618, Protestant noblemen hurled two Catholic counselors sixty feet from a window of the Hradcany Castle in Prague. A dunghill broke their fall and both survived. In the war that followed, Catholic and Protestant armies marauded from the Baltic to Bosnia for thirty years. The religious loyalties of Europe were defined at the Peace of Westphalia in 1648, but at grotesque cost. The population of the German empire is believed to have fallen from 21 million to less than 13.5 million. The survivors, Protestant and Catholic alike, harbored a humiliation that may have played its part in the fury of their later nationalism.

deliberately aped the defenestrations that had started the Hussite wars two centuries before. As he was flung sixty feet from a high window, Martinitz called "Jesu Maria! Help!" The mob kicked at the bloodied fingers of Slavata as he hung from the sill—"we'll see if your Mary can help you"—until he let go. A dung heap broke their fall and both men survived. "By God, his Mary has helped," a rebel said.[31] The Protestants led Bohemia in revolt, expelled the Jesuits, and raided as far as Vienna. Challenging the balance of religious power in Europe, they deposed the Habsburg Ferdinand as king of Bohemia, replacing him with Frederick V, the Elector Palatine, whose court at Heidelberg was a center of Calvinist thought.

Lutherans thought it an act of Calvinist folly. They stood aside as imperial troops under Count Tilly crushed the Bohemians at the great battle of White Mountain in 1620; the Catholic battle cry was "St. Mary!," and a church of St. Mary of the Victory was built at Rome in gratitude to her. Frederick was nicknamed the "winter king," for his rule in Prague lasted but one catastrophic season; Bohemia, a Hussite and Protestant heartland, was Catholicized and Germanized. Jesuits took over Prague University. Protestants lost their rights and thirty thousand families were expelled. Frederick's lands in the Palatinate were overrun by Catholic troops and given to Maximilian of Bavaria; Heidelberg was sacked, its wealth of manuscripts and books taken to the Vatican. In the Valtellina, the isolated valley through which convoys of Habsburg troops and supplies crossed the Alps on their way from Spanish Italy to the upper reaches of the Rhine and Inn and on to Austria and the Netherlands, local Catholics supported by Spaniards from Milan slaughtered every Protestant neighbor they could lay hands on.

The Valtellina was to change hands five times as a plague of armies roamed Europe. They fought and looted from the Baltic to Transylvania and Bosnia, as first Protestant Denmark and Sweden, and then Catholic France intervened to counter Habsburg victories. Italian and Swiss mercenaries changed paymasters as they pleased, and though there was a corps of English Protestant volunteers, men of religious conviction were rare. Gustavus Adolphus, the "lion of the North" and king of Sweden, wearing the buff coat and beaver hat of a common soldier, immensely strong beneath a skin as pale as a girl's, thought God had called him as the savior of Protestants. He enlisted men of all religions, but his army's formal creed was Lutheran, prayers were said daily in camp, and standing orders forbade attacks on hospitals, churches, and schools or those who worked in them. His brilliant crusade took him to Augsburg and Munich, but ended in furious battle at Lützen near Leipzig, his heart brought back to Stockholm in his bloody silk shirt.

He issued pocket hymnbooks to all of his men, but the most common refrain in soldiers' songs spoke of a sword to till the land and plunder for a harvest. Sol-

diers of fortune predominated: the Jesuit-educated Tilly, disgraced by the atrocities committed by his Croat and Walloon mercenaries at Magdeburg, killed by
the Swedes on the Lech; Count Mansfeld, a freebooting Catholic turned Protestant, dead near Sarajevo; Albrecht Wallenstein, born Protestant but brought up
by Jesuits, self-declared "generalissimo of the Baltic and Ocean Seas," intriguing
with Protestants and Catholics alike to become master of Germany, murdered by
Irish and Scottish officers in his retinue.

"I hear nothing but lamentations nor see any variety but of dead bodies," the
Englishman Sir Thomas Rose wrote from Danzig in 1629. "In 80 English miles,
not a house to sleep in, no inhabitants save a few poor women and children . . ."[32]
Far to the south, Tyroleans were grinding beanstalks and acorns for bread, and
cats and rats were sold in the market at Worms. Hans Grimmelshausen, who
served with the Catholic forces, described the fate of the common people abandoned to lawless troopers in his novel *Simplicissimus.* He wrote of soldiers thrusting peasants' thumbs into their pistols as a form of thumbscrew, of cords
tightened round heads until eyes began to start from the face, of the sport where
prisoners were tied in rows behind each other, and soldiers took bets on how
many bodies a gunshot would pierce. The Protestant forces of Bernhard of Saxe-
Weimar burned every village they passed through as a matter of policy; priests
were tied to wagons and made to crawl on all fours until they dropped. Bavarian
Catholics under Johann Weert set the town of Calw on fire and then stood outside the walls, shooting those who tried to escape.

Germany was ruined and in shock when a halt was called. The Peace of
Westphalia in 1648 accepted the old Augsburg formula of *cuius regio eius religio,*
extending this to include Calvinists as well as Lutherans and Catholics. The ecclesiastical lands held by Protestants in 1624 remained Protestant; Switzerland
and the Protestant Netherlands were recognized as states; Catholics gained Bohemia, and their control of Austria and south Germany was confirmed. France
gained Alsace, and the benefit of a Germany in which the emperor was much
weakened against the princes.

The religious lines of modern Europe were settled, but it was scant reward for
a surfeit of misery. For thirty years, unprovisioned armies had used Germany to
slake their thirsts, for women, wine, food, horses, carts, plate, and gold. "The
German Empire, including Alsace but excluding the Netherlands and Bohemia,
probably numbered about 21 million in 1618," the historian C. V. Wedgwood
wrote, "and rather less than 13.5 million in 1648."[33] The population of Marburg,
eleven times occupied, was halved; the citizens of Augsburg, 48,000 in 1620,
were reduced to 21,000; Osterburg and Werben lost two-thirds of their people; a
quarter of Berliners were lost. Two hundred ships were based at ports in East
Friesland in 1621, but by the end of the war only ten remained. Large tracts of

land were abandoned, without people, cattle, or shelter, and thriving cities like Magdeburg were reduced to weed-infested rubble. The mouths of the great rivers, the Rhine, Elbe, and Oder, were held by the Dutch, Danes, and Swedes; the middle reaches of the Rhine were controlled by the French. The survivors, Protestant and Catholic alike, harbored a humiliation that may have played its part in the fury of their later nationalism.

Extremists on both sides despised the peace. "They have sacrificed us," John Comenius, a rector and educator grieving for his looted library, wrote to his Protestant friends from Polish exile. "I conjure you by the wounds of Christ that you do not forsake us who are persecuted for the sake of Christ." Pope Innocent X, who thought the settlement too favorable to the Protestant cause, denounced it in his brief *Zelus domus Dei* of 1650 as "null, void, iniquitous, unjust, damnable, reprobate, inane and devoid of meaning for all time."[34] The same might be said of Europe's wars of religion themselves.

CHAPTER XXIII

GOD'S CHARNEL HOUSE:

The Witch-Finders

There is, as we have seen, some very dangerous ammunition in the Bible for those who care to look. A smattering of biblical references—notably the brief injunction in Exodus that "Thou shalt not suffer a witch* to live" (Exod. 22)—was used to justify the outburst of witch-hunting that disfigured the faith in Europe for two centuries after 1484. At its last gasp, in 1692, the frenzy crossed the Atlantic to its most familiar manifestation—the witch trials at Salem. New England saw no more than forty victims of the terror, however, whereas estimates of those hanged, drowned, or burned alive in Europe number to above a hundred thousand.

Age, status, and sex were no protection. In general, women—particularly unmarried or widowed women—were most vulnerable; in some regions midwives and innkeepers were at special risk, but the finger could point almost at will. The victims of Philipp von Ehrenburg, the witch-finding bishop of Würzburg, included Catholic priests, young mothers, wealthy merchants, seven and eight year olds convicted of having sex with demons, and his own nephew. At one of the burnings he held between 1627 and 1629, the eleven adult victims were outnumbered by six small girls and eleven boys.[1]

Protestants were quite as ferocious as Catholics; devout Lutheran pastors, along with bishops acting at papal prompting, made the terror ecumenical. Other than that, it had few rules or limits. Some witch-finders "swam the witch" to es-

*Witch comes from the Old English words *wicca* (pronounced witcha and meaning male witch), and *wicce* (a female witch, pronounced witcheh), and from the verb *wiccian,* meaning to cast a spell. Sorcerer is from the Latin *sortiarius,* or "diviner," via the French *sorcier.* Magician is from the Greek *mageia,* via the Latin *magia* and French *magique.* The Greek *magos*—from which the Magi who came to pay homage to the infant Jesus is derived—meant a "wise man" and was originally used of the Zoroastrian priests who accompanied the army of Xerxes into Greece.

Swimming a witch in a mill race in a 1613 engraving entitled *Witches Apprehended, Examined and Executed*. If the witch swam, she was guilty. If she sank, she was innocent. A brief injunction in Exodus—"Thou shalt not suffer a witch to live"—fueled a hysteria that disfigured the faith across Europe for two centuries after 1484.

tablish guilt,* trussing the accused and submerging her in a pond on a ducking stool. If she sank, it was a sign that God's water accepted her, and she was rescued as an innocent; if, as was more likely, she floated, she was put to death. In Germany witches were examined for boils or growths from which demons might suckle, the so-called "witch's teat," or for any blemish—a scar, a mole, a discoloration—with which the devil had identified them as his own; this was the "mark of the beast" which the Book of Revelation claimed was received by devil worshipers (Rev. 19:20). In Scotland it was believed that such marks were invisible, and the accused were pricked with needles to see if their skin had an area of in-

---

*This was a survival of the medieval "trial by ordeal" in which the "judgment of God" could also be established by the test of fire or duel. Its use by Crusaders in Jerusalem was witnessed by the astonished Moslem chronicler and diplomat Usamah Ibn Munqidh in 1140. A large cask was filled with water, and a young Crusader who was "the object of suspicion" was pinioned, suspended from a rope by his shoulder blades, and plunged into the cask. If he was innocent, Usamah was told, he would sink into the water and be pulled out; if guilty, it would be impossible for him to sink. "When he was thrown into the cask," Usamah reported, "the unfortunate man made every effort to descend to the bottom, but he could not manage it, and thus had to submit to the rigours of their law, may God's curse be upon them!" He was then blinded by a red-hot silver awl."[2]

sensitivity that might conceal one. Some who were young or frail were weighed against the Bible; those who were lighter than the Holy Book were condemned.

The fever might rage in one town or county but not in its neighbor; as its virulence died out in one country, it attacked another. In the Jura in the borderlands of France and Switzerland, torture was rarely used, accusations had to be made in public, and little credence was given to evidence from children. Not far away, in Trier in 1589, a magistrate and university rector named Dietrich Flade was held to be too scrupulous and lenient. A boy accused him of plotting to poison the archbishop; an old woman under sentence of death was rewarded with the mercy of strangulation before burning for naming Flade as a witch. The magistrate was arrested, tortured, and confessed to having intercourse with the devil and magically transforming mud into a plague of slugs that had eaten the harvest. He, too, named accomplices to merit strangulation, thus providing his torturers with a fresh supply of victims. The frenzy spread as far north as Sweden, but it was worst in Germany and the Alps, and grave in Scotland. Spain and Portugal were all but immune to it; yet the Spanish Inquisition, pallid by comparison, has left a more indelible mark on history.

Common to all is the witch-finders' claim to act in the name of Christ, and their piety. No appeal could be made to the tormentor's own faith; "the more seemingly devout the bishop, the more likely he was to sponsor the brutal intimidation. . . ."[3] One of the most thorough was Johann von Dorheim, a contemporary and colleague of Ehrenburg, and the Catholic prince-bishop of Bamberg in

A witch in chains at the Witches' House in Bamberg. Johann von Dorheim, the Catholic prince-bishop of Bamberg, built a special house without windows to conceal the cells and chambers that lay within it. He equipped it with thumbscrews, leg vices, scalding lime baths, and prayer stools furnished with sharp pegs. Crucifixes and biblical texts hung on the walls, for the victims suffered in the name of Christ. Between 1623 and 1633 the bishop caused at least six hundred alleged witches to be tortured and sent for burning from this place.

Germany. He constructed a special witch-house in the town, a building with a high and handsome facade whose lack of windows concealed the cells and chambers that lay within. He equipped it with thumbscrews, leg vices, scalding lime baths, and prayer stools furnished with sharp pegs. Crucifixes and biblical texts hung on the walls, for this was God's charnel house. Between 1623 and 1633 the bishop caused at least six hundred alleged witches to be tortured and sent for burning from this place.

Among them was a respectable citizen of the town named Johannes Junius. On July 24, 1628, he persuaded a venal or sympathetic jailer to smuggle a letter out of the witch-house to his much-loved daughter Veronica. Prosecutors and observers wrote many meticulous records of trials and interrogations, happy that their part in God's work should be recorded. The Junius letter is one of the few firsthand accounts to be written by a victim. "Innocent have I come into prison, innocent have I been tortured, innocent must I die," he began, "for whoever comes into the witch prison must . . . be tortured until he invents something out of his head."[4] He was interrogated by two of the bishop's clergy, a Dr. Braun and a Dr. Kötzendörffer, and by two other divines he did not know. Junius maintained his innocence while the divines reminded him of the physical consequences of this stubbornness. "And then came also—God in highest heaven have mercy—the executioner," he continued, "and put the thumb-screws on me, both hands bound together, so that the blood ran out at the nails and everywhere, so that for four weeks I could not use my hands, as you can see from the writing."

He was then placed in the strappado, a device in which his arms were strapped behind his back, heavy weights were attached to his legs, and he was hoisted into the air on a pulley and dropped to dislocate his shoulders. "Eight times I was drawn up in the strappado," he wrote, "so that I thought heaven and earth were at an end . . . And so I made my confession . . . but it was all a lie." Junius was told to identify those who had taken part in the sabbats, the witch-meetings he had invented to prevent the pain. He said he did not recognize any, but his torturers told him to think of all those he knew who lived in the town—"take one street after another; begin at the market, go out on one street and back on the next." They started with the main street of the town. "I knew nobody," Junius continued. "Had to name eight persons there . . ." When finally he refused to name any more, the executioner stripped him and shaved him all over to find the devil's mark, which he identified as a bluish patch on the skin. The torture was resumed to reveal the specific crimes that the now-confirmed witch had committed. Junius said that he had wanted to kill his children, but instead had killed a horse. He was not believed and was drawn up in the strappado once more. Only when he said that he had desecrated a sacred wafer was he left in peace until his burning. "Dear child, keep this letter secret . . . else I shall be tortured most piteously and the jailers will be beheaded," he ended. "Good night, for your father Johannes Junius will never see you more."

❧ FUNDAMENTAL TO THE witch-hunt is, of course, the Christian concept of the powers of darkness, and the difficulty of reconciling the existence of evil with faith in a single, all-powerful, and benevolent God. The many ancients who worshiped divinities in which both good and evil are united had no such problem; the Mexican god Quetzalcoatl, for example, embraces life and death, love and destruction. Zoroaster preached a religion—it survives among the Parsees of India today—that has two distinct and warring spirits. Ormuzd is the spirit of light and life, and the creator of all that is pure and truthful; his antithesis, Ahriman, is filth, darkness, and death; and the battle between them is for the soul of man. Other groups we have met, such as the Cathars, shared this dual concept. It influenced Hebrew thought and persisted in Satan, the powerful but noncreator spirit of evil in Orthodox Christianity.

The word *satan* itself is Hebrew, meaning "adversary" or "obstructor"; its alternative, devil, comes from the Greek *diabolos,* originally meaning "slanderer." In the Old Testament, "the *satan*" is used in the early books to describe an actual enemy in battle or the angel in good standing with God who investigates earthly matters on his behalf. In Chronicles the article is dropped and it becomes a proper name—"And Satan stood up against Israel" (1 Chron. 21:1)—replacing earlier use of "the anger of the Lord" (2 Sam. 24:1). In the New Testament it is used for the archenemy of God who takes Jesus to the mountaintop to tempt him with "all the kingdoms of the world, and the glory of them" (Matt. 4:8), and who is rebuked: "Get thee hence, Satan" (Matt. 4:10). His existence on earth is explained as the result of "war in heaven" in which Michael and his angels defeat the dragon, and "the old serpent, he that is called the Devil and Satan, the deceiver of the whole world; he was cast down to the earth, and his angels were cast down with him" (Rev. 12:7–9). Satan's standing as the leader of the fallen angels was confirmed by Jesus himself: "I beheld Satan fallen as lightning from heaven" (Luke 14:18).

A biblical backdrop was thus provided for the witch trials. The Bible identified Satan, or "Beelzebub the prince of the devils," as the leader of the forces of darkness. Witches were identified as his human followers. Passages in the Old Testament condemn the *yidd oni* or *kashaph*—a medium or wizard—who has and consults an *ob,* a Hebrew word translated as a "familiar spirit." Necromancy, the conjuring up of the spirits of the dead, was punishable by death under the law of Moses. "And the soul that turneth after such as have familiar spirits, to go whoring after them," God told Moses of those who listened to mediums, "I will even set my face against that soul, and will cut him off from among his people" (Lev. 20:6). The punishment for those "that hath a familiar spirit" was specific: "they shall stone them with stones; their blood shall be upon them" (Lev. 20:27). Both men and women are referred to as mediums, but a passage in Samuel could be made to suggest that most were women. Faced by the Philistine host, and God's refusal to predict the outcome of battle, Saul demanded of his servants: "Seek me a woman that hath a familiar spirit, that I may go to her, and inquire of her." "Behold," his servants replied, "there is a woman that hath a familiar spirit at Endor" (1 Sam. 28:7). Thus was created the "witch of Endor" upon whom the witch-finders elaborated.

The fate of Bar-Jesus provided a bridgehead into the New Testament. When St. Paul visited Paphos in Cyprus, Bar-Jesus, "a certain sorcerer, a false prophet" employed by the Roman proconsul, denounced Paul's preaching because he feared it would undermine his own lucrative business. Paul cursed him and struck him temporarily blind: "O full of all subtlety and mischief, thou child of the Devil, thou enemy of all righteousness . . . the hand of the Lord is upon thee, and thou shalt be blind, not seeing the sun for a season" (Acts 13:6–12). A Christian precedent for severe punishment was thus established.*

Another case in Acts was significant. Simon Magus was a well-established magician in Samaria—"they gave heed to him, because that of long time he had amazed them with his sorceries" (Acts 8:9–24)—who also saw Christians as formidable professional rivals. Watching St. Peter at work, he noted that those upon whom the apostle laid his hands appeared to receive the Holy Ghost. He was so impressed by this apparent trade secret that he offered to buy it. "Give me also this power," he asked, "that on whomsoever I lay my hands, he may receive the Holy Spirit." He got short shrift—"Thy silver perish with thee," Peter told him—but the incident gave biblical warning of the mutual rivalry between magic and the faith. Christianity claimed miracles, but such wonders were also the stock-in-trade of the sorcerer.

At witch trials it was common for the prosecutor to concede—indeed, to

---

*The Book of Revelation went further. In the apocalyptic struggle between good and evil, the heaven opens to reveal "a white horse, and he that sat thereon, called Faithful and True . . . arrayed in a garment sprinkled with blood" who leads the armies of heaven, also on white horses and clothed in white and pure linen. He fights the "beast, and the kings of the earth, and their armies." The beast, and the "false prophet that wrought signs in his sight" are captured, together with "them that had received the mark of the beast." Beast and false prophet are "cast alive into the lake of fire that burneth with brimstone." Their followers are killed with the sword that comes from the mouth of Faithful and True, "and all the birds were filled with their flesh" (Rev. 19:11–21).

base his case on—the fact that the accused had performed miracles, if perverted ones. Walpurga Hausmannin, for example, a village midwife burned at Dillingen in Germany in 1587, was credited with: having sex with the devil, flying at night on a pitchfork, keeping a familiar spirit named Federlin as a lover, conjuring up hailstorms to damage crops, and killing Christian women and infants at the childbirths she attended by rubbing a magic potion on them. As Simon Magus had "amazed with his sorceries," so it was important to demonstrate that the pitiful midwife had done likewise.

✤ THERE IS A gap of fifteen hundred years between the blinding of Bar-Jesus and the burning of Walpurga Hausmannin. For most of that time, magic and sorcery were relatively minor sins for which punishment was rare and usually restricted to penance. The early Christians lived in a pagan world in which their beliefs seemed foreign and where they themselves were martyred for their "evil superstition." They were in no position to persecute others, and it was largely from their own observation of pagan myths and practice that they slowly fleshed out the scant biblical references to sorcerers. The Bible has no physical descriptions of old crones, no mention of broomsticks or turning into toads; but other writings did.

The Greeks and Romans were familiar with *daimones,* demons, and witchlike creatures. Harpies, vile birds with the faces of old hags, befouled the earth with stench and filth to create famine; the Canidia and Sagana, pallid and hideous, robed in rotting shrouds, met at night to dismember black lambs with taloned hands. Writing at the time of Christ's birth, Ovid described how Medea, the great witch-goddess of the ancients, prayed to the darkness before committing evil: "O night, most faithful guardian of my secrets, and golden stars, who, with the moon, succeed the brightness of the day . . ."[5] Apuleius wrote in the second century of the belief in "abominable women" who gnawed "bits of flesh off dead men's faces for use in their magical concoctions"[6] and who could change their shape at will, turning into "birds or dogs or mice, or even flies." Women worshipers of Dionysius were said to attend nocturnal orgies in caves and grottoes, led by the god in the form of a horned and hairy goat. The goddess Hecate appeared at crossroads on moonlit nights attended by ghosts and the howling dogs of hell; black puppies and she-lambs were sacrificed to her. The images were long-lasting; the rites of the Dionysiacs correspond to the witches' sabbat, while a witness at the trial of the alleged witch Susanna Martin at Salem in Massachusetts in 1692 told the court of a "black puppy, as black as a coal" that flew at him and "would have tore his throat out" until, "naming the name of Jesus Christ, it vanished away at once."[7]

Augustine argued that pagan magic and rites were invented by the devil, and so the deities of the Roman pantheon were transformed from the false gods of mere superstition into actual demons and servants of Satan. The idea of the bargain with the devil reached its height in the legend of Faust, the Renaissance magician who sold his soul for wisdom and pleasure; but it dated back to a sixth-century tale of a priest named Theophilus who gained advancement in the Church by swearing to Satan that he would renounce Christ. Paul the Deacon, a cleric at the court of Charlemagne, translated the story two centuries later. Medieval psalters were illustrated with pictures of Theophilus kneeling in front of the devil, horned and tailed, holding a written contract in his hand. Satan began to take physical shape. A monk of Cluny described him as being like "a small black Ethiopian horribly deformed, with horns coming out of his ears and fire from his mouth as if he were about to eat the flesh of a very sick monk."[8]

Rustics, reported Martin of Braga, a sixth-century Spanish bishop, in his work *De Correctione Rusticorum,* burned candles at trees, springs, and crossroads; they put wine and fruit on a log over the fire; and hung up laurels, and saw devilish auguries in "little birds and sneezing and many other things."[9] The bishop noted that they "apply the very names of demons to each day and speak of the days of Mars, Mercury, Jove, Venus and Saturn," holding weddings on Fridays, the day of Venus, and avoiding travel if they saw ill omens. He was particularly irate with those who celebrated the New Year with the pagan Roman festival of the Kalends of January. Isidore of Seville wrote of *arioli,* magicians or soothsayers, "so called because they offer impious prayer at the altars or *aras* of idols, and offer deadly sacrifices, and accept instructions from the swarms of demons."[10]

As Christianity spread northward it encountered fresh beliefs. The Norsemen, for example, raised evil spirits and placed horse's heads with open mouths on poles in front of an enemy to destroy his protection. They believed that sorcery was carried out at night by *völvas,* witches who rode to *trolla-things,* or spirit meetings, aboard boars, wolves, or fence rails. Teuton sorcerers used figures of wax or dough to harm their enemies, drowning the likeness in water, stabbing it with needles, or burning it in a fire. The witches of Shakespeare's *Macbeth* had their origins in Anglo-Saxon England. Sorcerers mixed dog urine and mouse blood as a potion against warts. A mixture of ale hassock, lupine, carrot, fennel, radish, betony, water-agrimony, rue, wormwood, cat's mint, elecampe, enchante's nightshade, and wild teasel was concocted as an antidote to madness. A dozen masses were sung over the drink, and the patient then swallowed it. Even in a region as apparently Christian as ninth-century Lombardy, St. Barbato found people who worshiped a snake and a sacred tree; clerics complained that many came to church not to pray, but to dance and sing "and do other such pagan things."

THE OFFICIAL REACTION of the Church was restrained. Martin of Braga merely warned the faithful not to break their pact with God by slipping back into pagan habits. The bishops who assembled under Isidore at Toledo in 633 forbade anyone in clerical orders to consult *arioli,* but laid down no penalty for laymen and women who did so. The Synod of Rome in 743 banned the old practice of leaving gifts and drink for local spirits. A "List of Superstitions" the following year prohibited making animal sacrifices to the saints. Candidates for baptism were required to "renounce all the works of the demon, and all his words, and Thor, and Odin, and Saxnot, and all evil beings that are like them."[11] The spirits of the north—fairies, trolls, leprechauns, dwarves, mischievous or malign, some with names like Robin Goodfellow, Rumpelstiltskin—were slowly added to the list.

The punishments recommended in Penitentials, the penalty scales drawn up for the guidance of priests, were not severe and largely aimed at old wives' remedies. The Penitential of Theodore in about A.D. 600 advised that any woman who "puts her daughter upon a roof or into an oven for the cure of a fever, she shall do penance for seven years." The confessional of Egbert in the mid-eighth century stated: "If a woman works sorcery and enchantment and [uses] magic philters, she shall fast for twelve months. . . . If she kills anyone by her philters, she shall fast for seven years."[12]

Neither did the Church yet admit to the physical reality of witchcraft. "Some wicked women are perverted by the Devil and led astray by illusions and fantasies induced by demons," the Canon Episcopi of c. 900 stated, "so that they believe that they ride out at night on beasts with Diana, the pagan goddess, and a horde of women. They believe that in the silence of the night they cross huge distances. They say that they obey Diana's commands and on certain nights are called out in her service. . . . Many other people also believe this to be true, although it is a pagan error to believe that any other divinity exists than the one God." Satan had the power to transform himself into an angel of light, the Canon Episcopi continued, enslaving the mind of a miserable woman, showing her deluded mind strange things and leading it on weird but fictional journeys. "It is only the mind that does this," it stressed, "but faithless people believe that these things happen to the body as well."[13]

By this definition, Pope Innocent VIII and Martin Luther alike were "faithless"; witchcraft slowly shifted from a sickness of the imagination into the concrete manifestation of evil in which they both believed. The first burning took place at Orléans in 1022. The suspects were accused of holding nocturnal orgies in pits and abandoned buildings, desecrating the crucifix and denying Christ, chanting by torchlight until demons appeared, and then throwing themselves on each other; the children who were supposedly thus conceived were burned alive eight days after birth and the ashes were used in a parody of Holy Communion. The trial was immensely popular. It was presided over by King Robert II in the episcopal palace while great crowds gathered outside, and attempts were made to lynch the accused before they were condemned.

The basic charge at Orléans, however, was heresy. Witchcraft was not as yet a capital crime in itself. Those who made it one relied on a single sentence in the 105 verses that make up the Book of the Covenant, the diverse laws that follow the revelation of the Ten Commandments to Moses on Mount Sinai. Most refer to practical moral and legal issues, of slavery, injury to persons and property, and the protection of the weak. The guiding principles are fairness and reciprocity; in context, the famous passage "life for life, eye for eye, tooth for tooth . . ." (Exod. 21:23–24) reflects not bloodlust but the desire to restrict the right of revenge, in which the punishment must not exceed the crime. The witchcraft sentence is preceded by commonsense rulings on farming and marriage issues: if a man's cattle stray into another's field, he must make restitution; if a man "entice a virgin that is not betrothed, and lie with her, he must surely pay a dowry for her to be his wife" (Exod. 22:16). The powerless must not be abused: "And a stranger shalt thou not wrong. . . . Ye shall not afflict any widow, or fatherless child" (Exod. 22:21–22).

Into these humane rulings is injected the line that reads, in the Latin Vulgate Bible, *Maleficos non patieris vivere*. *Maleficium* originally meant "wrongdoing" in the broadest sense, and *maleficos* could refer to any evildoers. It became specifically linked to sorcery, however, as did the *maleficus* or *malefica* who practiced it. The English translators of the King James Bible rendered the line as: "Thou shalt not suffer a witch to live." A similar process was applied to the woman of Endor whom Saul consulted. A *ba'alath ob* in the original Hebrew, or "mistress of a talisman," she became a *mulierem habentem pythonem* in the Latin, a "woman possessing an oracular spirit." In the King James Version, as the frenzy unfolded, she became the "witch" of Endor.

The verse that immediately follows in Exodus was also to have a fateful resonance. "Whosoever lieth with a beast," it says, "shall surely be put to death." It was already established, as the word of God, that a witch should be executed. A witch charged with bestiality was in double jeopardy; and many were so charged, with having sex or kissing the buttocks of the goat-horned devil, with keeping cats, toads, and ferrets as lovers, with suckling the devil's creatures through their witches' teats. The medieval mind had already imagined such beasts in paintings, as it had visualized the devil himself; it also had a vivid sense of the hell from which they sprang. The Inquisition had weakened inhibitions against the use of torture. Hell was seen as a place where, the preacher Richard Alkerton warned in 1406, the accused are "boiled in fire and brimstone without end. Venomous worms . . . shall gnaw all their members unceasingly . . . [T]hey that tormenteth you shall never be weary neither die." To torture witches was merely to anticipate their eternal fate by the few weeks that remained to them on earth.

❖ IN 1424 A man was charged with turning himself into a mouse at Rome. His fate was not recorded, but it is a first blow against the old consensus that sorcery was a matter of imagination and not fact. The trial of Gilles de Rais, marshal of France, in 1440, sensationally combined the growing European interest in alchemy with heresy, necromancy, and mass murder. A renowned soldier who had fought the English at Orléans beside Joan of Arc, he squandered his lands on an extravagant court and on necromancers. He sought to redeem his fortune through alchemy; the rediscovery of Greek science through translations from Arabic had kindled interest in chemistry and experiments in transmuting base metals—copper, tin, lead, and iron—into gold and silver. Gilles failed to find the "philosopher's stone," the chemical elixir it was hoped would achieve this. His own secret—the murdered children, mainly boys, whom his servants kidnapped and he tortured to death—was discovered. He was charged with heresy and murder. His trial was the most notorious of the century and helped give alchemy—a blend of chemistry, astrology, magic, and the occult whose practitioners searched for the elixir of life and the philosopher's stone that would create gold from the humblest metal, and who experimented with magic potions and salves, and concoctions of sulphur, arsenic, and mercury—a notoriety that witch-hunters seized on eagerly. Gilles* was hanged in October 1440.

The appointment of Heinrich Krämer, known as Institoris, as inquisitor in Germany in 1474 was a catalyst. Institoris was so venal and corrupt that he was condemned by his order, the Dominicans, for embezzlement, but his zeal to uncover witches caught the ear of the pope and the mood of the public. At Institoris's prompting, Innocent VIII condemned witchcraft in the bull *Summis Desiderantes* of December 5, 1484. "It has lately come to our ears," the pope declared of the reports from Germany, "that many people of both sexes . . . have abandoned themselves to devils . . . and by their incantations, spells, conjurations, and other accursed charms . . . have slain infants yet in the mother's womb, as also the offspring of cattle, and have blasted the produce of the earth, the grapes of the vine, the fruits of trees."[14] The pontiff warned that, at "the instigation of the Enemy of Mankind," these wretches who blasphemously rejected the Faith did not shrink from perpetrating the "foulest abominations and the filthiest excesses . . ." Sor-

---

*Bluebeard, the monster in Charles Perrault's famous seventeenth-century tale, who murders his wives and hides their bodies in a locked room, was based on Gilles de Rais.

cery now completed its transfer from the imagination to the real. Crop failure, flood, pestilence, or the death of livestock could be blamed on a neighbor or enemy; and the death of a child in the womb on the midwife. Accidents and acts of God could with papal blessing be seen as the acts of a human devil.

The bull was reprinted as the preface to *Malleus Maleficarum,* the *Hammer of Witches,* the handbook to witchcraft that Institoris wrote with his Dominican colleague James Sprenger, the "apostle of the rosary," in 1486. The book established standard accusations—the renunciation of Christianity and devotion to evil, the sacrifice of children, orgies, flights through the air, and magical potions—and became the classic work of demonology. The book, among the most popular in Europe, was reprinted in fourteen editions by 1520. The techniques and personnel of the Inquisition were at hand and adaptable. Guilt was assumed. The interest in examination lay in establishing detail, not innocence: the wording of the spell, the nature of the potion, the form of the orgy.

Protestants, as they emerged during the Reformation, were not subject to the papal bull. Despite this, and their professed desire to return to the apostolic age when such cruelty was the mark of the pagan, they tortured with the same gusto as Catholics. Martin Luther regarded witches as part of the army that the devil was rallying against God; he advised that they be burned as heretics on the grounds that they had entered into pacts with a devil whose powers were actual and physical. "The Devil makes ceaseless attempts on our lives and discharges his anger by causing accidents and bodily hurt," he wrote in 1529. "In several cases he has broken a person's neck or made him lose his reason. At other times he has drowned people. . . ."[15]

The majority of victims were women. They accounted for 82 percent in a group of 1,288 executions recorded in the area of southwestern Germany around Baden-Baden. The ratio varied; the witch-hunts in the region lasted for more than a century—the first in the group was at Wiesensteig in 1562 and the last at Calw in 1684—and the number of men and children who were burned rose with time, but males remained in a minority. Spinsters, living alone without the legal protection of a husband, were easy prey. In the sixteenth century the proportion of women remaining single rose from 5 percent to 15 or 20 percent. Widows were equally defenseless; Thomas Schreiber, a Swabian innkeeper, wrote to his wife shortly before he was burned at Mergentheim, urging her to remarry "on account of the children, for widows and orphans are despised and pushed down in this vile world."[16] *Malleus Maleficarum* claimed that: "No one does more harm to the Catholic faith than midwives," on the grounds that they killed stillborn babies to send them directly to Satan. Midwives suffered terribly, but so, too, could any woman. In 1586, the archbishop of Tières had 118 women, and two men, burned for casting spells that prolonged the winter.

Misogyny was part of the age and Institoris encouraged it. "What else is woman but a foe to friendship, an inescapable punishment, a necessary evil, a natural temptation, a desirable calamity, a domestic danger, a delectable detriment, an evil of nature, painted in fair colours?" he wrote in *Malleus Maleficarum.* He listed a string of reasons why women were more likely to become witches than men; they have "slippery tongues, and are unable to conceal from their fellow-women those things which by evil arts they know"; they are "intellectually like children" with "weak memories"; a woman "is more carnal than a man . . . she is an imperfect animal, she always deceives . . . a wicked woman is by her nature quicker to waver in her faith. . . ." In short, the master witch-hunter wrote of his prey: "She is a liar by nature. . . . Let us also consider her gait, posture and habit, in which is vanity of vanities."[17]

Among men, prominent townsfolk—"magistrates, teachers, innkeepers, wealthy merchants"[18]—were vulnerable. Those who denounced them may have been motivated by jealousy or because they owed them money. An entire family might be suspect. In Mergentheim almost half of those burned were related to each other, and eight members of the Weit family were tried and burned between November 1628 and June 1630. Aristocrats appear to have been almost immune; only one case is known in Swabia, that of the knight Hans Ritter von Gnötzheim, executed in 1591 for practicing *unchristliche Zauberei,* "unchristian magic." There are no known cases of victims among the Jews of the region; traditional hatreds may have been sated by bloody pogroms in the previous century, or, as is more likely, it was felt that only the baptized could commit the heresy of witchcraft.

❖ THAT REMNANTS OF paganism survived—*la vecchia religione* in Italy, "the old religion" in Britain—is not in doubt. Benvenuto Cellini, the soldier-goldsmith, recorded an episode of necromancy in Rome in 1528 in his autobiography. He met a Sicilian priest, an educated man with good Latin and Greek, and remarked that he had always wanted to see something of necromancy. The priest told him that he would need "a brave soul and strong resolution." The headstrong Cellini rose to the challenge and they met by darkness in the Colosseum with a necromancer from Pistoia, who was supplied with perfumes and fire, and a twelve-year-old virgin boy, one of Cellini's shopboys. The priest drew a circle on the ground, and they stepped within it, protected against demons by a pentacle the priest gave to Cellini. The necromancer began to "make his terrible incantations, naming by name a whole host of major demons and commanding them by the virtue and power of the uncreated, living and eternal God, in Hebrew, as well as in Latin and Greek."

The Colosseum filled with shapes; the boy cried that "a million tremendously fierce looking men . . . and four enormous giants" were threatening them. The necromancer himself "was trembling with fear . . . pleading with them softly and gently to go away." The air was sweet with perfume and crackled with the fires they had lit. The shopboy cried that fiery demons were rushing towards them. Cellini tried to reassure him that "these creatures are only our slaves; all you can see is only smoke and shadow." When a foul-smelling mixture was poured on the flames, the demons appeared to retreat. Nonetheless, Cellini's frightened little party huddled under their pentacle within the safety of the circle until matins were rung at daybreak.[19]

The Church had adapted the old fertility rites, which pagans had held four times a year, into "holy days." In a rite the Anglo-Saxons called "need-fire," bonfires had been lit on October 31 to restore power to the waning sun. When November 1 became the Christian All Saints' or All Hallows' Day, the fire festival on its eve became Halloween. The Christian feast of Candlemas replaced another fire festival; the pagan celebration of the return of spring on April 30 was the saint's day of the Anglo-Saxon missionary St. Walpurga, and became known as Walpurgisnight. The feast of the nativity of St. John the Baptist coincided with the midsummer solstice; again, bonfires were lit amid dancing and celebration.

In remote districts the Christian veneer may have been thin. Country lore was rich in hobgoblins, imps, fairies, pixies, and elves. Animal "familiars" were held to be able to divine the future. The Romans had used birds to discover such auguries, and the habit persisted. In France the familiar was usually a toad—pelicans were also held to have such powers—while in England dogs and cats were consulted. The witches' coven, numbering thirteen members, was described early in the fourteenth century in the work *Handlying Synne,* in which a priest's daughter and twelve "fools" dance in the churchyard. A more sinister tone was given to the coven in the trial of Gilles de Rais, where he and his associates numbered thirteen in their murderous rites. Strange potions were concocted by old countrywomen as remedies for ailments. The muttered curse, and the pin stuck into a wax image, was a way for the weak to avenge the misdeeds of the strong.

The detailed crimes for which many were burned, however, went far beyond the scope of ancient rural customs; they involved black miracles, transmutations into cats and toads, night-flights on broomsticks, suckling demons from a wart. They were imaginary; the philosopher Thomas Hobbes, as the tide began to turn in the mid-seventeenth century, described them as "but idols or phantasms of the brain."

It was precisely those who had enough leisure to use their brains, the educated elite, who were most convinced that the ravings were real. "Many deny witches at all, or, if there be any, they can do no harm," noted the writer Robert Burton, himself a clergyman, in 1621, "but on the contrary are most lawyers, divines, physicians, philosophers."[19] Europe's leading witch-hunter, the Protestant Dr. Benedict Carpzov, was a professor at Leipzig and the son and brother of the most celebrated jurists in Saxony; he took the sacrament every week and had read the Bible fifty-three times before his death in 1666. Learned books and treatises were also written about witchcraft: a huge encyclopaedia of witchcraft by the Jesuit Martin del Rio; Carpzov's own *Practica rerum criminalium* on the conduct of trials; and the *Daemonologie* written by James VI of Scotland in 1597.

James was fascinated by the case of the North Berwick witches in 1590. The employer of a young maid named Gilly Duncan tortured her to discover whether her healing powers, for which she was locally famous, came from the devil. Having extracted a confession, he handed her over for trial. The threat of further torture extracted the names of many accomplices in and around Edinburgh. James VI personally examined one of the accused, Agnes Sampson. This elderly and reputable lady refused to confess; she was thus stripped, shaved, and searched for the devil's mark. A witch's bridle, in which metal prongs were forced into the mouth to press against the tongue and the cheeks, was used to fasten her to the wall of her cell. She, too, confessed. Men and women had sailed in sieves to North Berwick on Halloween, she said, where they went into a church lit by black candles and worshiped the devil, kissing his buttocks. They plotted to kill the king, using magic to raise a storm to sink his ship when he sailed to Denmark; if that failed, Agnes would use toad's blood to work magic against him. Agnes and several others went to the stake; the horrified king helped carry the mania south when he added the English throne, as James I, to his Scottish realm. The translators of the King James Bible of 1611 rendered most references to sorcerers as "wizards," but at the king's insistence, they translated the fateful sentence in Exodus as "witch."

Calmer souls wrote against witch-hunts. In his treatise *On Magic* in 1563, the German Johann Weyer suggested that witches were harmless victims of mental disorders; while the Englishman Reginald Scot wrote in his *Discoverie of Witchcraft* in 1584 that, since God himself had ceased performing miracles after the age of the apostles, as Protestants believed, it was unlikely that he would tolerate the devil continuing the practice. Scot, who had witnessed fraudulent accusations in Kent villages, said that all witches fell into one of four categories. Some were falsely accused innocents. Others were semilunatics whose confessions of pacts with the devil were mere delusions. Then there were genuinely evil people, who indeed harmed their neighbors, but by poison and not by supernatural means. Finally there were the "cozeners and impostors" who gulled simple villagers with false cures and fortune-telling.[20] Scot was in favor of punishing the charlatans; but he despaired at the burning of old women for crimes that were impossible to commit. Both Weyer and Scot were castigated in James's *Dae-*

monologie, in which the king argued that those who are not of God's elect are "given over in the handes of the Devill that enemie, to beare his Image"; since these practiced the "grossest impietie," all good Christians should seek them out and destroy them.

The interrogators were men of education and often of the cloth; so were some of their victims. In 1630 at Loudun, the mother superior and nuns of the Ursuline convent claimed that they were being bewitched by their confessor, Father Urbain Grandier. They feigned hysterical convulsions, accused Grandier of gross indecencies, and forged the signatures of Satan, Beelzebub, Lucifer, and Leviathan on a pact that he had supposedly made with the powers of darkness. Grandier was interrogated by a rival cleric named Laubardement but refused to name accomplices, for he had none. He was thus tortured. His legs were bound between two planks, which were then hammered to break the bones. Some nuns publicly admitted their inventions; but Father Grandier was condemned to death without mercy of strangulation, and a treatise he had written on the celibacy of priests was ordered to be burned with him. He remained silent until he was taken on a handcart to the place of execution in front of the church of St. Pierre du Marché. Laubardement ordered him out of the cart; he collapsed on his shattered legs and waited patiently to be carried to the stake. The executioner placed him in an iron girdle and turned him to face away from the church. He tried to address the large crowd. The monks threw holy water in his face and one of them embraced him to silence him. "Behold a kiss of Judas," he said. The crowd called for him to be mercifully strangled, but the monks set fire to the pile. *"Deus meus, ad te vigilo, miserere mei, Deus,"* he cried as he burned. "My God, I have faith in thee, pity me, O God!"[21]

Other nuns, however, degenerated into real madness after his death; one "fell to the ground, blaspheming, in convulsions, lifting up her petticoats and chemise, displaying her privy parts without any shame, and uttering filthy words . . ." while others "struck their chests and backs with their heads, as if they had their necks broken . . . their faces became so frightful one could not bear to look at them; their eyes remained open without winking. . . ."[22]

FOR ALL ITS apparent associations with the Inquisition, witch hysteria was relatively subdued in Spain. The early symptoms were severe, with the tribunal at Calahorra burning thirty suspected *Xorguinas,* or witches, in 1507. The *suprema,* the governing council of the Inquisition, soon insisted that all its tribunals show restraint. A woman named Joana Izquierda was accused of taking part in the ritual murder of children by sixteen witnesses in 1591. She herself confessed this to the Toledo tribunal, which disbelieved her and ordered her to be merely scourged. After six witches were burned in Navarre in 1611, the *suprema* appointed the inquisitor Alonso de Salazar to visit the district with an edict of grace. He reported that he had reconciled 1,802 self-confessed sinners, 1,384 of them children under the age of fourteen, and "several old and even senile, over the age of 70 or 80." They confessed to murder, witch-sabbaths, and having sex with devils. "I have not found even indications from which to infer that a single act of witchcraft has really occurred," Salazar reported. "Three-quarters and more have accused themselves and their accomplices falsely. . . . There is no need of fresh edicts . . . but rather, in the diseased state of the public mind, every agitation of the matter is harmful and increases the evil. I deduce that . . . there were neither witches nor bewitched until they were talked and written about."[23] The Inquisition took Salazar's humane and commonsense view to heart, and it ordered skepticism, caution, and leniency to be applied to all investigations.

The infection spread, however, to countries in which the Inquisition had made little impact and which were now Protestant. At Mobra in Sweden in 1669 and 1670, hundreds of children were said to have been fetched at night "from their lodgings, to a diabolical rendezvous, at a place they called Blockula [Blakulla], where the monsters that so spirited them, tempted them all manner of

Witches, complete with broomsticks, as seen by Goya. Ancient rural customs and medicines had been tolerated by the Church for centuries. The practices invented during the witch frenzy went far beyond this. They involved black miracles, transmutations into cats and toads, night-flights on broomsticks, suckling demons from a wart. The philosopher Thomas Hobbes, as the tide began to turn in the mid-seventeenth century, described them as "but idols or phantasms of the brain."

ways to associate with them." Persons of quality who could afford it sent their children to other counties. The king of Sweden appointed commissioners who took evidence from the inhabitants on August 13, 1670. They were told how the devil "had been seen to go in a visible shape through the county, and appeared daily to the people; how he wrought upon the poorer sort, by presenting them with meat and drink, and this way allured them to himself. . . ." Distraught parents begged the commissioners to "root out this hellish crew"; they claimed that the abduction of children by the devil in the nearby county of Elfdale had ceased after a bout of witch-burning.

All the people of the town, three thousand of them, were summoned to judgment. Seventy adults were condemned to death. Of these, twenty-three confessed their crimes; the rest, "one pretending she was with child, and the others denying," were also sent to be executed at Fabluna. Fifteen children who confessed to being "engaged in this witchery" were also executed. Thirty-six others aged between nine and sixteen were adjudged less guilty and flogged once a week for a year. The mass execution took place on August 25, less than two weeks after the arrival of the commissioners, a memorable event, "the day being bright and glorious, and the sun shining, and some thousands of people being present at the spectacle."[24]

The tortures in Puritan Scotland were particularly notorious. "Thrusting of pins into the flesh, and keeping the accused from sleep, were the ordinary treatment of a Witch," wrote the eminent lawyer Hugo Arnott. "But if the prisoner was endued with uncommon fortitude, other methods were used to extort confession. The boots, the caspie-claws and the pilnie winks, engines for torturing the legs, the arms and the fingers, were applied to either sex. . . . Nay, death itself did not screen the remains of these miserable persons from the malice of their persecutors. If an unfortunate woman, trembling at a citation for Witchcraft, ended her suffering by her own hand, she was dragged from her house at a horse's tail, and buried under the gallows. . . ."[25] When a woman named Alison Balfour was accused under King James, her arms were kept for forty-eight hours in the caspie-claw pincers; her husband was put in heavy irons; her son was strapped into the boots and given fifty-seven strokes; and her little daughter, aged about seven, had her fingers crushed in the pilnie winks while she was forced to look on. Naturally, she confessed; but publicly, at her execution, she declared that the confession had been extorted by torture.[26]

As in Sweden, children were accusers. Christian Shaw, the eleven-year-old daughter of the laird of Bagarran in Renfrewshire, noticed a housemaid named Katherine Campbell steal and drink some milk. She told her mother; the angry maid told the child: "The Devil harle [haul] your soul through hell." Several witnesses heard this and gave the date as August 17, 1696. Within a few weeks

Christian developed fits, complained of violent pains throughout her body, and said that Katie Campbell was cutting her side. She was taken to see a doctor and an apothecary in Glasgow. The fits continued; they may have been epileptic, for she had to be constrained from swallowing her tongue. She began producing odd objects—parcels of hair, wildfowl feathers, ribbons, a nut gall, hay mixed with dung—from her mouth as she lay in bed, apparently by magic. In Christian's lucid moments she took to reading the Bible to the maid. "Thy master the Devil deceives thee; thou shalt find it to thy smart, except thou repent before thou die," she told Katie. "There is no repentance to be had after death. I'll let thee see, Katie, there is no repentance in hell." She read Katie Luke's chapter 16 to confirm it.

Christian could not be parted from her Bible, and any attempt to remove it was met by "horrid screeches and outcries." After these outbursts she "fell a singing, leaping and dancing for a long time, laughing with a loud voice, tearing down the hangings of the bed, and pulling off her head-cloaths and neck-cloaths." Christian had such force and strength that her father and the minister, who had come to pray with her, could not restrain her. When she quieted down, she spoke to the minister of "witches inclosing her in a ring and singing and dancing about her." When she read the Scriptures now, the family friend said, or answered any of the catechisms held out to her, she "was suddenly struck dumb, and lay as one stiff dead, her mouth opened to such a wideness that her jaw appeared to be out of joint, and anon would clap together again with incredible force. The same happened to her shoulder blade, her elbow and wrists. . . ."

Christian turned against the minister on January 22, 1697. "She continued some space after the minister began to pray," the friend reported, "singing, and making hideous noise, fetching furious blows with her fist, and kicks with her feet at the minister, calling him a dog. . . ." When Christian recovered, she said that she was "forced to do it by the hellish crew about her," whom she had begun to name. They included the maid Katie and her great aunt Margaret, a local girl of seventeen called Elizabeth Anderson, an unnamed Highlander, a fourteen-year-old beggar boy, James Lindsay, and his younger brother Thomas, a smith named John Reid, and the chief witch, Margaret Lang.

In his confession the smith John Reid said that he met regularly with the devil and the others. They "consulted Christian's death, either by worrying or drowning her in the well"; the devil assured them that "they should neither be heard, nor confess." To warn them of special meetings, there "appeared a black dog with a chain about his neck, who tinkling it, they were to follow." Reid was found hanged by his own neckcloth in his cell, but his body did not escape the flames, being burned together with the cart that carried it in a field outside Renfrew.

"Lord help the poor daft child, and rebuke the Devil," one of the condemned remarked.

An inspection of Christian's two rooms was made many years later. They were in the upper part of the large house, separated by a partition of paneled oak. Her bedroom still had her richly carved bedstead, bearing the date 1672; the walls of the other room were hung with fading tapestries. It was found that a slanting hole had been made in the partition, concealed by a tapestry, about an inch and a half in diameter, emerging immediately behind the head of her bed. There, perhaps, the tortured little girl hid the hair, the feathers, and stones that she then so miraculously disgorged from her mouth.

England prided itself on its Protestantism and its freedoms, and nursed a particular contempt for the Inquisition. Torture in witchcraft cases was forbidden. Nevertheless, the death penalty for witches, enchanters, and sorcerers was introduced in 1563 under Elizabeth I, a woman not given to flights of fancy. Witches were prosecuted under civil law, not ecclesiastical, and for this reason they were hanged rather than burned. Familiars were commonly talked of in country districts: they were given nicknames—Vinegar Tom, Pyewacket, Tibb, Grizel Greediguts. Once the innocent "little people" of folklore, who often came in pairs, Jack and Jill, Sack and Sugar, they were transformed into demons by a host of pamphlets. These explained the "manner of their divelish practices" and illustrated them—their "fourmes are herein truelye proportioned"—as toads, cats, lapdogs, black hares, ferrets, and horned dogs.

The first major trial was at Chelmsford, the county town of Essex, in 1566. Elizabeth Francis confessed that her grandmother had taught her to renounce God and had given her a white spotted cat called Sathan, the devil in feline form, which she fed with her own blood and which spoke with her. The cat promised her a man called Andrew Byles; although Byles made her pregnant, he refused to marry her, and the cat taught her to abort her unborn child. She later married and had a daughter, who became so irritating that the cat killed her. Elizabeth then gave the cat to Agnes Waterhouse in return for a cake; Agnes changed the cat into a toad, which helped her drown cows, kill geese, and spoil butter. Both women were found to have blemishes on their bodies, through which they fed Sathan. Agnes was hanged the same year; Elizabeth followed after a second conviction some years later.

Puritan Essex was again the focal point at the peak of the English witch craze, during the Civil War tensions of the 1640s. A failed lawyer named Matthew Hopkins set himself up as the "Witch Finder Generall." Although Hopkins maintained the English tradition of Familiars, and his victims confessed to keeping them in the form of dogs, cats, moles, and squirrels, he relied heavily on the Continental imports of night meetings, broomsticks, and pacts and sex with the devil. He began his work in Chelmsford, and then appointed assistants to help his search throughout southern England. Hopkins caused "more people to be hanged in two years than had been hanged on the previous century"[27]—among them an elderly pastor condemned for sinking a ship by magic, the judges making no effort to confirm whether a ship had indeed been lost that day—until the extent of his fraud became obvious. He was forced to retire in 1646; the next year Hopkins was dead.

✤ FROM ENGLAND, WITCH-FINDING emigrated to the American colonies, though with a time lag. The first witch was hanged in Connecticut in 1647. The Salem trial took place after the frenzy in the mother country had abated. It began after two girls, aged nine and eleven, began playing with magic to identify who they would marry when they grew up. Experimenting with the supernatural frightened them, and the girls began to suffer nervous fits. The father of one of them, Samuel Parris, was the Salem Village minister. He called in a physician who, finding no physical reason for their behavior, told Parris that a witch might have cast a spell on them. Suggestion proved powerful. Other girls and young women began to show similar traits; one hurled a Bible across the room, a sign of the devil to a pious community, and another pulled burning embers from the fire and dashed about shouting gibberish.

Interrogated by adults, the girls named three women who had bewitched them, the elderly Sarah Goode and Sarah Osborne, and a Barbadian slave named Tituba. The first two maintained their innocence, but Tituba confessed to dealing with the devil, a "thing all over hairy, all the face hairy, and a long nose."[28] Those who confessed were spared. This may account for the vivid details that now emerged of witches who took black Communion bread, suckled Familiars with their blood, and afflicted the girls with convulsions, all at the behest of a devil who appeared at their rites in the form of a black man. The girls' fits grew worse; they saw evil spirits, and toothmarks appeared on their arms. A fourth witch, Martha Cory, was named. She was interrogated in the village meeting-house; when she wrung her hands, the bewitched girls shouted that they were being pinched, and when she bit her lip they said they could feel teeth biting into their flesh.

Fear spread through the colony and was encouraged by its leading theologian, Cotton Mather. His father, Increase Mather, was the president of Harvard; Cotton, also a Harvard man, had succeeded his father as Nonconformist pastor at the Second Church, Boston. Among the many books he published was *Memorable Providences relating to Witchcraft and Possessions;* this had appeared in 1685 and did much to fan the New England witch craze.

The title page from Cotton Mather's *Tryals of Several Witches,* published "by the Special Command of his Excellency the Governeur of the Province of the Massachusetts Bay in New-England" in 1693. A witch was hanged in Connecticut in 1647, but mass witch-hunting was largely restricted to the Salem outbreak. It was encouraged by Mather, the colony's leading theologian and son of the president of Harvard. "We have now, with horror, seen the discovery of a great witchcraft!" he wrote. "An army of devils is horribly broken in. . . ."

The Wonders of the Invisible World:

Being an Account of the

T R Y A L S

OF

Several Witches,

Lately Executed in

N E W - E N G L A N D :

And of several remarkable Curiosities therein Occurring

Together with,

I. Observations upon the Nature, the Number, and the Operations of the Devils.

II. A short Narrative of a late outrage committed by a knot of Witches in *Swede-Land,* very much resembling, and so far explaining, that under which *New-England* has laboured.

III. Some Councels directing a due Improvement of the Terrible things lately done by the unusual and amazing Range of *Evil-Spirits* in *New-England.*

IV. A brief Discourse upon those *Temptations* which are the more ordinary Devices of Satan.

By *COTTON MATHER.*

Published by the Special Command of his EXCELLENCY the Governour of the Province of the *Massachusetts-Bay* in *New-England.*

Printed first, at *Boston* in *New-England;* and Reprinted at *London,* for *John Dunton,* at the *Raven* in the *Poultry.* 1693.

He took a close and personal interest in the Salem events. "We have now, with horror, seen the discovery of a great witchcraft!" he wrote. "An army of devils is horribly broken in upon the place which is the centre, and after a sort, the first-born of our English settlements: and the houses of the good people there, are filled with the doleful shrieks of their children and servants, tormented by invisible hands, with tortures altogether preternatural. . . ."[29] He compared witchcraft to treason; both crimes were worthy of death, for, though they are "very much transacted upon the stage of imagination," the "effects are dreadfully real." "Our neighbours of Salem Village are blown up, after a sort, with an internal gunpowder," he wrote in May 1692, shortly before the hangings began. "The train is laid in the laws of the kingdom of darkness limited by God himself."[30]

Mather was present at the trial of the Reverend George Burroughs, like him a Harvard graduate. Burroughs had been pastor at Salem Village from 1680 to 1683; he had long since moved to a church in Maine when he was named in a Salem confession. He was arrested and brought to Salem for trial in early August

1692. Mather wrote up the notes of his fellow pastor's trial for the governor of the colony, though he could not bring himself to spell out the accused's name, referring to him only as "B." or "G.B." Burroughs was charged by eight of the "Confessing Witches" with being "an Head Actor at some of their Hellish Randezvouzes and one who had the promise of being a King in Satans Kingdom." The trial was held amid open hysteria by the witnesses; "they would for a long time be taken with fitts"; when they "cry'd out of G.B. biting them, the print of the Teeth would be seen on the Flesh of the Complainers . . . just such a sett of Teeth as G.B.'s . . . which could be distinguished from those of some others mens."

One witness was "cast into Horror at the Ghosts of B's two deceased wives then appearing before him, and crying for Vengeance against him," while others testified that the pastor had "Seduc'd and Compell'd them into the snares of Witchcraft" by promising them fine cloth, and that he had them brought "Poppets," little effigies, and "thorns to stick into those Poppets, for the afflicting of other people." In short, Burroughs had cunningly exhorted them to "bewitch all Salem-Village, but to be sure to do it Gradually, if they would prevail in what they did."[31] The old pastor, Cotton Mather wrote gleefully, was "cast into very great confusion"; well he might, for he had been brought back from Maine to a madhouse in which his appeal to the feelings of his fellow Christians—he recited the Lord's Prayer to them fervently and faultlessly—made no impression. He was hanged on August 19.

An angry confusion was shown by another of the accused, Susanna Martin, when she was asked the unanswerable. She had a cast in her eye which witnesses claimed struck them to the ground, whether she looked at them or not.

"Pray what ails these people?" the magistrate asked her.

"I don't know."

"But what do you think ails them?"

"I don't desire to spend my judgment upon it," she said with contempt.

"Don't you think they are bewitch'd?"

"No, I do not think they are."

"Tell us your thoughts about them then."

"No, my thoughts are my own, when they are in," she said defiantly, "But when they're out, they are another's. . . ."

A witness, John Allen, claimed that Susanna Martin had become angry when his oxen proved too weak to cart a load of staves for her. She said that his oxen would do him no more service. "Dost thou threaten me, thou old Witch?" he shouted at her. "I'll throw thee into the brook." She was too quick for him and escaped over a bridge. When he put out the oxen to graze, they ran into the mouth of the Merimack River and drowned in the sea. A farmer named John

Atkinson then testified that he had exchanged a cow with Susanna's son against her wishes; the cow broke all the ropes used to halter it and caused such trouble that he "could ascribe to no cause but Witchcraft."

For this, she was hanged. The last execution took place on September 22 while the "bewitched" girls taunted the victims as they waited on the scaffold. By then nineteen had been hanged, and churchmen at last took a stand. Increase Mather, more liberal than his son, preached a sermon in colonial Cambridge stating that "it were better that ten suspected witches should escape, than that one innocent person should be condemned."[32] His *Cases of Conscience*, written at the request of the New England ministers in 1693, condemned the acceptance of the intangible and unverifiable claims by witnesses that they had seen specters and spirits; Cotton Mather came to agree with his father.

❖ AS IT BECAME intellectually disreputable, the craze passed. The case of the nuns of Loudon was widely debated in France; they were dismissed by lawyers, theologians, and physicians alike to be frauds. Cyrano de Bergerac, duelist, wit, dramatist, and possessor of the redoubtable nose, wrote a "Letter against Witches" in 1654 that ridiculed belief in witchcraft with his usual scathing vigor. A Black Mass scandal broke out in 1680; priests were accused of invoking parodies of the Mass over the bodies of naked girls, desecrating the sacraments, and dealing in aphrodisiacs and poisons. Louis XIV wanted no fresh hysteria and ordered the investigations closed.

The damage caused by the witch craze in Germany was so grave that a commission sitting at Calw in 1683 suggested that it might be the work of the devil, so effectively had it turned Christians against each other. The Bible had been used by witch-hunters; it was now cited by those who thought them evil. Francis Hutchinson, an Anglican divine, wrote a "Historical Essay concerning Witchcraft" in 1718. It used weighty argument to "confute the vulgar Errors," and its frontispiece quoted Timothy in the New Testament to remind the reader to "refuse profane and old Wives Fables, and exercise thyself unto godliness" (1 Tim. 4:7).

The last person to be hanged for witchcraft in England was Alice Molland at Exeter in 1684. Attacks on witches continued, in the countryside if not the towns. In 1751, Hertfordshire villagers threw an elderly couple suspected of witchcraft into a stretch of water and beat them to death when they floated. This was condoned by neither Church nor state; the mob leader was convicted and hanged for murder. The Scots continued to execute until 1727; nine years later, all previous legislation in Britain was repealed by a statute which barred any prosecutions for "witchcraft, sorcery, inchantment [*sic*] or conjuration." In France the last victims were prosecuted and executed in 1745, in Germany in 1775, in Spain in 1781; the last executions in Protestant Switzerland were in 1782 and in Catholic Poland in 1793.

What was done in the name of Christ, for so long and in so many places, lingers in the record of a trial at Kalisz in Poland. An accused woman, "shaved above and below," anointed with holy oil, was bound hand and foot and suspended from the ceiling, lest she summon the devil to her aid by touching the ground. She would confess nothing beyond bathing sick people with herbs. "Racked, she said she was innocent, God knows," the report continued. "Burned with candles, she said nothing, only that she was innocent. Lowered, she said that she was innocent to Almighty God in the Trinity. Repositioned, and again burned with candles, she said Ach! Ach! Ach! for God's sake, she did go with Dorota and the miller's wife. . . ."[33]

Why did the witch craze happen? It has been suggested that it stemmed from the tensions of the Reformation, but it spread on both sides of the new divide; that alchemy heightened suspicions of magic, but alchemists were not singled out; that it was a by-product of the Inquisition, but England had had no Inquisition; that witch-hunters were rural brutes, but they were supported by some of the most learned and sophisticated Christian men of the day. The printing press no doubt helped spread it; so did a low opinion of women. But they did not create it. More than anything it was a reprise of the ancient obsession with heresy. It was a part of the faith; it was this that, in the words of nineteenth-century historians of Scottish witch trials, Mitchell and Dickie, make the events "so far unsatisfactory as to make the reader disgusted with the religion he ought to adore."[34]

If the Americas were barely touched by this outburst, the faith brought them other ordeals in plenty.

"I THE VOICE OF CHRIST IN THE DESERT OF THIS ISLAND":

The Americas

Spanish captain named Juan de Ayora landed on the coast of Central America in 1514. He carried with him an official statement that officers were under standing orders to read out to each new group of Indians they encountered. It had been drawn up in response to Indian rebellions on the island of San Juan Bautista, modern Puerto Rico, and was issued to subsequent expeditions. It provided the religious and juridical justification for the colossal enterprise of Christian empire in which the natives were about to be engulfed.

The proclamation was made in Spanish, without interpreters, to people confronted for the first time with horses, cannon, and armored white men. Ayora frequently read it from so far away that "even if they knew the language, they could not have heard it."[1] Sometimes the Indians were already in chains and "immediately carried away prisoners, the Spanish not failing to use the stick on those who did not go fast enough."[2] When the Indians learned to flee, it was read out to empty villages.

It was called the *Requerimiento,* or "requirement." Ayora began by reading its brief account of the creation and the unity of mankind under a single God— "The Lord Our God, Living and Eternal, created Heaven and Earth, and one man and one woman, of whom you and I, and all the men of the world, were and are descendants"—and its explanation of the supreme authority of the bishop of Rome. It said that God had placed mankind under the care of one called Saint Peter, and that through him the pope had become "prince, lord, and master of all peoples of the world." In turn, the pope had granted the "islands and terra firma of the Ocean sea" to the monarchs of Spain.

"I beg and require of you to recognize the Church as lady and superior of the universe and to acknowledge the Supreme Pontiff, called pope, in her name, and the king and queen . . . as lords and superiors," Ayora continued, pointing to the friars in his party, "and consent to have these religious fathers declare and preach these things to you." If they did so, the captain said, then those who were over them—"their Highnesses and I"—would treat them with love and charity.

Ayora then advised his listeners of the fate that awaited those who failed to commit themselves there and then to this strange new faith and its alien kings and popes. "I certify to you that, with the help of God," he said, "we shall enter powerfully into your country and shall make war against you in all ways and manners that we can, and shall subject you to the yoke and obedience of the Church and of their Highnesses. We shall take you and your wives and children, and shall make slaves of them, and . . . we shall take your goods and shall do you all the mischief and damage that we can. . . ."[3]

At this, Ayora asked the secretary who accompanied his expedition to witness that the Indians had been *requeridos,* "requested to submit." "And then the captain would declare them slaves and at a loss of all their possessions since they seemed not to want to obey the *Requerimiento,* which [he] read to them in Spanish, which neither the chief nor the Indians could understand," the scholar Alonso de Zuaco recorded. "And in this fashion [Ayora's men] used to come to the villages at night and there steal from them, send dogs to attack them, burn them, and carry them off as slaves."[4]

Many miles to the northeast, the *Requerimiento* was being proclaimed on the coast of Florida by the explorer Juan Ponce de León. His legal contract with the Spanish crown obliged him to read it "once, twice, thrice" to the chiefs and Indians. If they accepted it, the contract required Ponce to "give them the best treatment you can and endeavor to convert them to Our Holy Catholic Faith"; if they did not, he was free under Spanish law to do with them as he willed.[5] Four years later, in Mexico, the *Requerimiento* provided the authority for Hernando Cortés to destroy Aztec rule; Charles V sent a copy to Francisco Pizarro in 1533 as the legal breastplate for his conquest of the Incas of Peru.

Thus, less gently than the Moslem soldiers who had brought Islam to the Christians of the Middle East nine hundred years before, Christians took the gospel to the Indians of the Americas.

❖ THE PROCESS BY which Christendom was to circle the earth had begun with the crews of Portuguese caravels working their way down the coasts of West Africa. It was in part a response to Moslem control of the trade routes from the Indies; in part, it reflected European energy and curiosity and seamanship, but its declared purpose was evangelizing. The Portuguese gave their light and beamy vessels fine Christian names—*Bom Jesus, São Antonio, Nossa Senhora de la Conçe-*

icão—and sewed the cross on their lateen sails. A series of papal bulls, the first in 1436, gave them title of ownership over newly found lands, power to enslave the natives, and a commission to propagate the faith.

Missionaries were sent from Lisbon after the Portuguese reached the ancient kingdom of the Congo in 1482. The king was baptized, and his son and heir Affonso became a committed Christian. He read volumes of theology and built churches in his capital, 150 miles up the Congo River, renaming it São Salvador. Schools were opened to teach Portuguese and educate the young Congolese princes in Catholicism. Affonso gave his counselors titles of dukes, marquesses, and counts. He sent his son Henry to Lisbon, where he was consecrated as bishop of Utica, or Carthage, the see being expanded to include the Congo. Pope Leo X, in his declaration *Exponi Nobis,* permitted other Christian natives—he referred to "Ethiopians, Indians and Africans" who reached the required educational and moral standards—to become priests and monks.

After his landfall in the Bahamas in 1492, Christopher Columbus declared his own sense of mission. He had high hopes that the natives were "very ripe to be converted to our Holy Catholic Faith," and that this was better done "by love than by coercion." He noted that the Indians "are very credulous and cognizant that there is a God in the sky . . . and any prayer that we tell them they repeat and make the sign of the cross."[6] The crosses he erected at the entrance to harbors might act as navigation marks and signs of Spanish sovereignty, but Columbus insisted that they were "principally for a token of Jesus Christ Our Lord and the honor of Christianity."

Papal sanction for exploration was extended to the Spanish. In 1493, Alexander VI granted to Spain—*donamus, concedimus et assignamus,* "we give, grant and assign"—all the mainlands and isles discovered or to be discovered west of the Azores, and Portugal the lands to the east. He did so as *Vicarius Christi* and *Dominus totius orbis,* the "legate of the absolute and universal will of the Son of God."[7] The line, running from the "Arctic pole, namely the north, to the Antarctic pole, namely the south"[8] was moved farther west to a line 270 leagues west of the Cape Verde Islands in 1494, enabling the Portuguese to claim Brazil when Pedro Cabral discovered it six years later.

No mention was made of empire. The only motive specified in Alexander's bull was that the Christian religion "may in all places be exalted, amplified, and enlarged, whereby the health of souls may be procured, and the barbarous nations subdued and brought to the faith." It bound the monarchs "by the bowels of the mercy of our Lord Jesus Christ" to send to the newly discovered lands "honest, virtuous and learned men who fear God and are able to instruct the inhabitants in the Catholic faith." For their part, the monarchs confirmed that "in all matters it is meet that their principal concern be for the service of God, Our Lord. . . ."[9] Some fine-tuning was given to the donation by Palacios Rubios, the Spanish court jurist and probable author of the *Requerimiento*. "All power and jurisdiction were canceled by the coming of Christ," he wrote [in his treatise *Of the Isles of the Ocean Sea*]. The authority given by the Father to the Son having devolved on the pope, the gift of the New World to the Spanish crown was binding upon "the entire world and all men, including infidels."

It was, of course, easy to mock this extravagant claim. "I would be pleased to see the clause in Adam's testament that excludes me from a share in the globe," Francis I of France retorted, while Elizabeth of England remarked that she did not recognize any papal prerogative in the division of the world. An Indian reaction was witnessed by Martin Fernandez de Encisco when he read the *Requerimiento* to the Indians of Cénu through an interpreter. The chiefs agreed that it "seemed fine" that there should be one God who was lord of all; but as to the pope donating their land to the Spanish king, they said that the "pope must have been drunk when he did that because what he gave was not his to give, and the king . . . must have been crazy because he asked for what belonged to others." They suggested that the king should visit them, so that they could "hang his head from a stick as they had hung other heads belonging to their enemies."[10]

The belief that Christian conquest was sanctified—and indeed demanded—by the expansion of the faith was nonetheless firmly implanted. The Indians were in no position to relieve the king of Spain of his head; rival European powers soon adopted the formula of cross and colony for themselves. By 1584 the Protestant clergyman and geographer Richard Hakluyt was urging the English to seize their own slice of the New World; to do so would be the "most godly and Christian work [that] may be perfourmed, of inlarginge the glorious gospell of Christe. . . . for the salvation of those poore people which have sitten so longe in darkness." Hakluyt noted that the Spanish and Portuguese, though mired in Catholic "superstition" and motivated by "filthie lucre and vaine ostentation," had already established more than a dozen transatlantic bishoprics and hundreds of churches. It was the duty of the English to bring the natives to "our true and syncere Relligion" and thus transport them "from the depe pit of hell to the highest heavens."[11] Like the Spaniards, however, the English adventurers whom Hakluyt inspired* were more interested in lucre than in promoting the "swete and lively liquor" of the gospel.

---

*Notably the half brothers Humphrey Gilbert and Walter Raleigh, whose abortive attempts to colonize Virginia, Roanoke Island off North Carolina, and Newfoundland were the first stirrings of English empire.

❖ THEREIN LAY THE rub. Columbus wrote that his objectives were "to gain to Our Holy Faith multitudes of people, and to Spain great riches and immense dominions." The salvation of souls could not be reconciled with the temptations of treasure. The empire attracted few of the God-fearing men for whom the pope had appealed. Instead it became the refuge and haven of "all the poor devils of Spain," the great novelist Miguel de Cervantes wrote, the sanctuary of the bankrupt, the safeguard of murderers, the way out for gamblers, the promised land for ladies of easy virtue. Christianity provided a cloak for their cruelty. They made much of their duty to destroy the ungodly, and an air of sanctity attached itself to their slave hunts and massacres. "Who can deny that the use of gunpowder against the pagans is the burning of incense to our Lord?" the inspector general of gold mines on Hispaniola, Gonzalo Oviedo y Valdés, commented with acid contempt for his fellow conquistadors.

The edifice of native coercion rested on the faith. The crown authorized the enslavement of the Carib Indians on the grounds that they were cannibals and thus denied God. It was permissible to kidnap them from one island and take them to another where their labor was needed because, Queen Isabella wrote in 1503, "being utilized by Christians, they can be more quickly converted to our faith."[12] This gave free license for colonists to mount raids against any natives whom they accused of cannibalism or resistance to Christianity. It made no difference whether the charges were true or not; the inhabitants of poor islands were simply labeled Caribs so that they could be captured and shipped to the mines and plantations of Hispaniola and Cuba.

In theory, peaceful Indians who accepted the *Requerimiento* could not be enslaved. A forced labor system, the *encomienda,* or "assignment," was introduced in 1513 to circumvent this legal technicality. Individual Spaniards were allocated native communities to do whatever labor was required; in return, the master was responsible for catechizing his Indians. The Old Testament was cited by court theologians as justification; if a city sued for peace, Deuteronomy stated, "then it shall be, that all people that is found therein shall become tributary unto thee, and shall serve thee" (Deut. 20:11). The system was criticized as making a mockery of piety and charity during a bitter debate in Spain in the 1540s, but Dominican friars in the New World argued that religion would collapse without such exploitation. "The perpetuity of the faith and Christian religion of the natives of this land depends on the perpetuity of the Spaniards there," they insisted. "And because in this land there cannot be perpetuity without rich men, nor rich men . . . without the service of Indians . . . it follows clearly, that it is necessary for the service of God and the perpetuity of the land, and the stability of the faith of the natives, that the Spanish have assigned [*encomendados*] towns." The Indi-

Dominicans baptize Indians in Mexico. One father wrote of baptizing 14,000 with a companion in a single day. Bishop John de Zumárraga declared that his Franciscans alone had converted 1.5 million in the seven years since they had landed in Mexico. "Formerly, in their infidelity, they were accustomed to sacrificing as many as twenty thousand human hearts," he wrote in 1531; "now they offer themselves not to evil spirits but to God. . . ."

ans themselves were supposedly beneficiaries, since contact with whites enabled them to be "taught good behavior and customs and our Christian faith . . ."[13]

What was done to the Indians was therefore done to them in the name of the Church. That does not mean, of course, that the Church directly controlled events. The papacy had little influence. In 1508, Julius II issued a bull establishing the *Patronato* in which the Spanish crown was granted the right to name bishops and other priests in the Americas. Successive popes were aware of dreadful happenings. Leo X said of the Indies in 1516 that "not only the Christian religion but nature herself cries out against a state of slavery." Paul III decreed in 1537 that "all Indians are truly men, not only capable of understanding the Catholic faith, but . . . exceedingly desirous to receive it." In the bull *Veritas Ipsa* he proclaimed the abolition of slavery and the right of existing slaves to free themselves. Indians were not to be denied their freedom or property, regardless of whether they remained pagans, on pain of excommunication.

The mission was, however, effectively out of papal hands. Liberal popes were ignored, and those missionaries courageous enough to campaign against atrocities risked the wrath of their superiors, the Inquisition, and the settlers. When Bartolomé de Las Casas, a Dominican known as the "apostle of the Indies" for his pity and conscience, wrote the first narrative of "very terrible and savage events . . . committed by Spanish soldiers and settlers in the Indies," copies were burned and the book was put on the *Index*.[14]

✣ IT WAS CLEAR to Columbus by 1505 that the earthly Paradise he had so recently discovered was becoming a very Hell. Sick and conscience-stricken, he admitted that six in seven of the Indians to whom he had brought the cross on the great island of Hispaniola (now shared by Haiti and the Dominican Republic) had been "butchered, beaten, starved and ill-treated to death" digging the mines for gold, or forced to work on sugar plantations "as beasts usually do."[15] His brother, Admiral Diego Colon, was authorized to kidnap Lucayans from the Bahamas and ship them to Hispaniola to make up the shortage.

They too perished, with consequences that flowed to the other side of the Atlantic. Diego Colon wrote to King Ferdinand at the end of 1509 complaining that Indian slaves were expensive, their price having gone up from 50 to 150 gold pesos, and that it was beyond the strength of the survivors "to break the rocks in which the gold is found." On January 22, 1510, the king gave permission for fifty black slaves—"the best and strongest available"[16]—to be sent out to the island as replacements. Bought by Portuguese slavers from African chiefs and resold in Seville, they were the first of the estimated eleven million slaves[17] to be shipped to the New World over the next 380 years. It was reported in 1511 that one black slave did as much work as four Indians; the Africans were hardier, more tolerant of disease, and worked better with horses. High Indian mortality was no longer a concern; West Africa acted as a great reservoir of labor to make up for the loss of Indians.

The first known sermon against the cruel treatment of Indians was given by a Dominican friar, Antonio de Montesinos, in Santo Domingo on Hispaniola on November 30, 1511. His congregation included Diego Colon. "I have come here to declare it unto you, I the voice of Christ in the desert of this island," he said. "This voice says that you are living in deadly sin for the atrocities you tyrannically impose on these innocent people. Tell me what right you have to enslave them? . . . How can you . . . not care to feed or cure them, and work them to death to satisfy your greed? . . . Are they not human beings? Have they no rational soul? Are you not obliged to love them as you love yourselves?"[18] Las Casas also tried to breathe humanity into the settlers. He himself had been a planter with an *encomienda* before a religious experience led to his ordination. Las Casas freed his Indians and began to take notes of their exploitation. He wrote of squalid huts, rotting food, and masters who called them "no sweeter name than dogs"; of women who had just given birth carrying heavy loads and being forced to abandon their infants at the roadside. Fierce hounds tracked down those who fled to the mountains, trained "to tear them in pieces at the first view, and in the space that one may say a Credo, assail and devour an Indian as if it had been a Swine." When Las Casas remonstrated with the settlers, they were astonished; they found the notion that it was a sin to use Indians to be as "incredible as saying man could not use domestic animals."[19]

Las Casas was to spend fifty years working for the Indian cause, but he and Montesinos were exceptions. Priests often shared the general contempt for Indians. "They are more given to sodomy than any other nation," another Dominican, Tomás Ortiz wrote. "There is no justice among them. . . . They are stupid and silly. They are brutal. . . . Punishments have no effect on them." He added that God had never created "a race more full of vice and composed without the least admixture of kindness and culture."[20] Las Casas sailed to Spain to arrange for a commission of inquiry to be set up for the Indies, but the calamitous decline in population continued.

Friars reported in 1517 that the Indians were still being treated "like dung on the ground that is stepped on" and that disease had become rampant. A smallpox epidemic at Christmas in 1518 killed perhaps a third of the surviving Hispaniolan natives. Other fathers visiting the island in 1519 wrote to the pope that he should know that, though there had been hundreds of thousands of natives when the Christians had come to Hispaniola, "we found so few that it is like the leftover remains on the tree branches after the harvest."[21]

THAT YEAR HERNANDO Cortés landed in Mexico. The natives of the islands were already ravaged beyond recovery. In 1570, 127 of them remained in Hispaniola, and they were also on the edge of extinction in Cuba, Jamaica, and Puerto Rico. The mainland was now to bear the brunt of assault on a yet wider scale. Cortés was a brilliant exponent of the savage calling of the conquistador. His virtues, and vices, may seem to be purely martial. Few commanders have ever achieved so much with so little. He subdued the Aztec empire with 550 men, seventeen horses, and ten cannon; his flair, his cruel courage in riding his luck and momentum to the breaking point, and his profound grasp of Aztec psychological inhibitions, compensated for the grotesque inferiority in numbers.

Cortés thought of himself principally as a crusader for Christ, however, and—at least in his reports and writings—claimed to draw his strength and inspiration from his faith. Before laying siege to the Aztec capital, he told his men that bringing the natives to Christ "is my principal motive in undertaking this war and any other one I should undertake."[22] A contemporary described Cortés as a "new Moses," a spiritual figure leading the Aztecs from "idolatry, vice and sin" into the bosom of the Church.[23] "Although as a man he was a sinner," wrote one who knew him well in Mexico, the Franciscan monk Motolinia, "he displayed the faith and works of a good Christian. . . . He confessed with many tears, communed with great devotion. He made great restitution and gave much alms. God visited him with great affliction, trials, and illnesses to purge his sin and cleanse his soul: I believe that he is a son of salvation. . . ."

Born into a noble family at Medellín in Spain in 1485, admirers noted that the great pagan temple Cortés was to destroy in Mexico City had been dedicated with the sacrifice of "eighty thousand human lives" on the very day of his birth.[24] Abandoning his law studies, Cortés sailed to seek adventure in Hispaniola in 1504. He took part in the conquest of Cuba with Diego Velázquez de Cuellar, who commissioned him to lead a small expedition to Mexico.

After landing on the mainland in March 1519, the party was attacked by the Indians of Tabasco, killing eight hundred for the loss of thirty wounded. As in the Crusades four hundred years before, legend soon attributed the victory to the miraculous intervention of James, patron saint of Spain, mounted on a ghostly gray charger. "Perhaps, on account of my sins, I was not considered worthy of the good fortune to behold him," the soldier and historian of the conquest, Bernal Díaz del Castillo, who was at the battle, wrote sarcastically.[25] The Indians had not seen muskets, crossbows, or horses of flesh and blood before, and shock played a decisive part in the campaign. The defeated chiefs sent gold trinkets in homage, and twenty women. The expedition's priest, the Franciscan Bartolomé de Olmedo, instructed the women briefly, told them that they "should now adore Christ our Lord," and baptized them. They were the first converts of New Spain. One of them, Doña Marina, by whom Cortés later had a son, became an interpreter.

Cortés assembled the chiefs and read them the *Requerimiento*. A final sentence was added to make it clear that recalcitrants were responsible for their own fate. "And furthermore," Cortés advised them, "I protest that the damage and death which you shall suffer thereby shall be your own fault."[26] He said that they must no longer sacrifice to idols, and presented them with a cross and a statue of the Virgin to put in their place. A village named Vera Cruz, True Cross, was founded. On Easter Day an altar was set up and mass was celebrated in front of the assembled Indians.

Word of the arrival of the white men reached the emperor Montezuma II in the Aztec capital at Tenochtitlán, the future Mexico City. He sent messengers

An Aztec manuscript shows the Spanish advancing on horseback while an Indian is hanged from a tree. "We should realize the truth," the missionary Bartolomé de Las Casas wrote in 1552, "that in forty years some twelve millions of souls . . . have died unjustly and tyrannically at the hands of Christians." He said that the conquistadors sometimes hanged their victims in two rows of six with a single gibbet at the end, "in honor and worship of our Savior and his Twelve Apostles."

to find their identity and purpose, and they returned with gifts from Cortés, a string of pearls, and a brightly polished helmet. This last gift proved to be priceless, for it resembled the helmet that adorned the head of the war god Huitzilpochtli, and it gave the rough and mortal Christian adventurers entry into Aztec religion.

The Aztecs had settled on a marshy island in the brackish lake of Tezcoco in 1325. This settlement of Tenochtitlán was their base for annual campaigns to subjugate neighbors and acquire captives for sacrifice. The first conquests outside the valley of Mexico began under the first Montezuma in 1440, who drove south towards Yucatán and Guatemala. Montezuma II was elected emperor in 1502. He was an accomplished warrior and administrator, enlarging the empire with expeditions that penetrated as far as Nicaragua and Honduras. Tenochititlán had grown into an elaborate city of pyramid temples, palaces, gardens, and one hundred thousand people.

They worshiped many deities.[27] Some were of charm and sweetness: the twins Xochipilli and Xochiquetzal, god and goddess of flowers and love, surrounded by musicians and laughter; Chalchiutlicue, goddess of running water, protector of newborn children and the chaste. The most powerful, however, were dark and vengeful, assuaged by human sacrifices, and often adopted, as the Romans had, from conquered peoples. The helmeted Huitzilpochtli, the "hummingbird of the south," had feathers fastened to his left leg and carried a snake made of fire; human sacrifices were made to him to insure victory in war and to protect Aztecs on their journeys. The most terrible cult was of Tlaloc, "pulp of the earth," the god of mountains, rain, and springs. He was painted black, with a garland of white feathers and the mask of a two-headed snake. At the festival in his honor, priests took children and infants at the breast from their mothers. Spectators rejoiced if they cried before they were sacrificed, for it meant plentiful rains. After the killings, the children were cooked and eaten.

Tezcatlipoca, "Smoking Mirror," was the god of the sun, appearing as a flying shadow or as a jaguar, represented in carvings with a bear's face and brilliant eyes, with bells on his ankles. He wandered by night in a veil of ashes, carrying his head in his hand. The fearful died of their terror if they saw him at night; the brave captured him and demanded wealth and power as ransom to release him before dawn. Blood sacrifices were paid to him. A handsome captive was chosen to personify Tezcatlipoca each year. The lad was taught to sing and play the lute, to wear flowers, and smoke tobacco; he was richly dressed and eight pages waited on him. Twenty days before his death, four girls were given to him to act as his goddesses. Festivals and dances were held until the day when he was slain on the last terrace of his temple. A priest opened his chest with an obsidian knife and tore out the beating heart as an offering to the sun.

Tezcatlipoca's sworn enemy was the Spaniards' trump. Quetzalcoatl, the "snake-bird," was the god of the conquered Toltec, the master of life, creator, patron of the arts and smelting, and god of wind. Tezcatlipoca had driven him into exile; he had burned his palaces of silver and shells and set sail on the Eastern Sea preceded by his attendants, whom he transformed into birds of brilliant plumage. He had vowed to return to rule over his people. Sentries were posted on the eastern shore to peer over the waters into the rising sun for the reappearance of the god, who was portrayed as a white-haired old man with a long beard. The watchers reported that the Spaniards were heavily bearded, with bright breastplates and helmets, and had come on their fabulous vessels with their strange horses from the east. Quetzalcoatl had redeemed his vow, or so it seemed. Montezuma sent Cortés the god's emblems, a snake mask encrusted with turquoises and a feather cloak.

Aware that he and his men were thought of as *teules,* or "god-men," Cortés quickly subdued the Sempoalla people near Vera Cruz. A veteran named Heredia of Boscay was selected to accompany the small party, for he resembled Quetzalcoatl; "the malignancy of his features, his huge beard, his half-mangled countenance, his squinting eyes, and his lame leg constitute him the most fitting purpose for this object," Cortés said, "besides which he is a musketeer."[28]

The Sempoalla did not resist and were at once introduced to the religion of their new masters. Cortés destroyed the idols in their temple; as these were smashed with axes, the Indians "set up a miserable howl, covered their faces and begged forgiveness of their idols, as they could not protect them against the *teules.*"[29] The Sempoalla priests were summoned to bury the remains, their black cloaks and hoods clogged together with the blood of past sacrifices, smelling of sulphur and putrid flesh. The temple was cleansed and plastered and an altar was set up beneath a cotton cloth. The Indians were ordered to bring fresh branches and flowers to strew around it and their priests, hair shorn and bloodsoaked clothes replaced with white cassocks, were charged with renewing them. They were taught to make candles and ordered to keep them burning at the front of the altar at all times. A cross was set up and Father Olmedo said mass in front of the chiefs. Eight women were given to the Spaniards. They were baptized "after an edifying discourse." The niece of the principal chief was presented to Cortés; although he received her "with every appearance of delight," Diaz del Castillo recorded that she was a "very ugly woman" and that Cortés passed her on to one of his officers.

A long march through hostile country was needed to reach Tenochtitlán. Cortés first burned his ships, lest his men dream of returning to Cuba. "The aid of Jesus Christ our Lord only can bring us victorious," Cortés told them. They evangelized as they went. "Doña Marina [the interpreter] told the people a good deal about our Holy Religion and how we were subjects of the emperor Don Carlos who had sent us to bring them back from kidnapping and from sacrificing human beings," Diaz del Castillo recollected. "We erected a cross in every township and explained its significance to the inhabitants, and what reverence was due it."[30] Before fighting a key battle against the fierce Tlaxcalans, they spent the night in prayer and confession. After the victory, Cortés bade the natives to abolish their sacrifices and other abominations, and to adore and believe "in Him whom we believe, who is the only true God." The Tlaxcalans became loyal allies and provided him with native troops.

As they advanced on the capital, the great buildings that rose from the waters of the lake seemed an "enchanting vision" to the Spaniards. In Tenochtitlán they were lodged in palaces of magnificent stone, cedar, and other sweet-smelling woods, with courtyards covered with awnings of woven cotton. A straight causeway led to the city, whose lime-painted towers shimmered above the lake, which filled with canoes as the Indians came to gaze in wonder at the mounted men. Montezuma came out of the city in a litter on November 8, 1519 to meet them, Cortés wrote, with his brother and a retinue of "two hundred chiefs, all barefooted and dressed in a kind of livery, very rich . . ."[31] The emperor descended from his litter and stood beneath a canopy of green feathers decorated with gold work, silver, and pearls; the soles of his sandals were made of gold and the upper parts were decorated with precious stones. His subjects kept their eyes reverently downcast. Cortés dismounted and bowed to the emperor, wishing him good health through Doña Marina, and presented him with a necklace of glass beads dipped in musk.

Vast numbers of men, women, and children filled the streets, balconies, and canals to gaze at the four hundred white men. Diaz del Castillo was aware of his vulnerability. "I am daily more sensible of the great mercy of our Lord Jesus Christ," he wrote, "that He lent us sufficient strength and courage to enter this city."[32] The Spaniards were led to luxurious apartments where matting beds with canopies over them had been prepared; they were given a sumptuous dinner, and Montezuma hung a rich necklace of golden crabs around Cortés's neck. They slept with their artillery close at hand and posted mounted sentries.

Cortés visited the emperor in his palace the next day. He spoke to him of Christ; how the cross was the emblem of the salvation of the human race, that "by him heaven, earth, sea and every living creature was formed," and that nothing existed but by his divine will. He explained that his own emperor, aggrieved that so many souls should be sent to the everlasting fires of hell by false idols, had sent him to put an end to such misery. He added that his emperor would soon send priests of great piety and virtue to "explain these things more fully."[33] Weeping, Montezuma accepted Cortés as the envoy of Quetzalcoatl. He said that the Aztecs knew from the chronicles of their forefathers that their lands had once belonged to a different race, whose lord had brought the Aztecs here and who would himself return. "According to the direction from which you say you come, which is where the sun rises," he told Cortés, "and from what you tell us of your great lord or king who has sent you here, we believe and hold for certain that he is our rightful sovereign."[34]

The hearts of three human victims sacrificed a short time before were still burning in the temple of Huitzilpochtli when Cortés was taken to visit it. The walls were smeared with blood, and the stench was "worse than a Spanish slaughterhouse." The Spaniards made a point of saying mass in public, kneeling before an altar. "It was our Christian duty that Montezuma and his grandees might notice it and become accustomed to these holy things by seeing us kneel before them," Diaz del Castillo wrote, "particularly when we repeated the Ave Maria."[35]

Cortés warned that his soldiers would kill the Aztec priests if the Virgin and the cross did not replace the idols. He had the principal idols "overturned from their seats and rolled down the stairs," he reported to Charles V; the temples were cleansed, for they were full of the blood from sacrifices, and he "set up images of our Lady and other saints in them, which grieved Montezuma and the natives not a little."[36]

This caused great fury among the people, who said that the great gods would remain only if the Spaniards were slaughtered. An Aztec force attacked the men Cortés had left to guard Vera Cruz. The head of one of them was sent back to the capital, undermining the myth of Spanish immortality. Cortés seized Montezuma and forced him to surrender the warriors who had fought at Vera Cruz, and had them burned alive in front of the palace gates. The emperor was chained, and Cortés obliged him to ransom himself with gold and jewels. A Spanish force had been sent from Cuba by Velázquez with orders to replace Cortés as commander. Cortés hurried to challenge it, leaving two hundred men in Tenochtitlán under Pedro de Alvarado. The cruelties imposed by Alvarado led to a rising in the city in June 1520. Cortés returned after winning over the Velázquez group, with a force of 1,300 men and 96 horses, supported by Tlaxcalans. They were set upon as they entered the city. Montezuma fell victim to the wrath of his own people, killed as he went onto the roof of his palace to order them to surrender. Cortés barely managed to cut his way free on the *noche triste,* the "night of sorrow," losing the whole of his rear guard as he retreated for the coast. After six days of heavy fighting, he defeated the Aztecs in a decisive battle on the plain of Otumba on July 7, 1520. Only 440 men and twenty horses survived to fall back into friendly Tlaxcala territory; the number of musketeers was reduced from eighty to seven.

Cortés returned to lay siege to Tenochtitlán, taking with him reinforcements, Tlaxcalans and boats to navigate the lake, and a banner with a Latin inscription. *Amici sequamur crucem; si nos fidem habuerimus, in hoc signo vincemus,* it read, redolent of that seen by Constantine twelve hundred years before: "Friends, let us follow the cross, and if we have faith, in this sign we shall be victorious."[37] The Aztecs fought stubbornly and the city was captured slowly, quarter by quarter. The Spaniards were close enough to see their captured comrades being sacrificed on the altar of Huitzilpochtli to the beat of drums. The Aztec priests placed too much confidence in the god of war, declaring that Huitzilpochtli would deliver the city from the Spaniards in ten days. When this failed to happen, the defenders lost heart and the city fell to Cortés on August 31, 1521.

Cortés razed the temples and much of Tenochtitlán, rebuilding it in Spanish style as Mexico City. The "wicked and rebellious," he wrote, were to be "punished and chastized as enemies of Our Holy Catholic Faith"; this would impress those who were "reluctant in receiving knowledge of the truth."[38] He welcomed the first group of Franciscans sent out to evangelize, "kneeling on the ground in front of one after the other"; he told the Indians to revere and esteem them as "guides of your souls, messengers of the great God."[39]

Mexico was won for Christ, or so it seemed. The missionaries worked eagerly among the conquered peoples, organizing the young under "captains" who led them to services. One father, Pedro de Gante, wrote of baptizing fourteen thousand with a companion in a single day. Bishop John de Zumárraga of Mexico declared that his Franciscans alone had converted 1.5 million in the seven years since they had landed in Mexico. He had himself supervised the destruction of five hundred temples and twenty-six thousand idols; in many places churches had been built and the cross raised up. "Formerly, in their infidelity, they were accustomed to sacrificing as many as twenty thousand human hearts," he wrote in 1531; "now they offer themselves not to evil spirits but to God. . . ."[40]

THE CONQUEST OF another empire, of the Incas, was begun the following year. Here, too, human sacrifice provided justification and rich gold and silver mines a motive. The Inca believed themselves to be descended from Inti, the sun god, his face a disc of gold surrounded by rays and flames, his name so sacred that none but the Inca themselves could utter it. His worship required human victims; so did that of Viracocha, the god of rain who lived in Lake Titicaca, the fire god Pachacamac, and Catequil, god of thunder and lightning. Children died

Indi Hispanis aurum sitientibus, aurum lique- XX.
factum infundunt.

South American Indians, angered by the Spanish lust for treasure, pour molten gold down the throats of their prisoners. Another is cut in pieces, his leg prepared for grilling. Theologians felt that the human sacrifices and cannibalism carried out by Indians, and the fact that missionaries accompanied every expedition, justified the conquests. However, the treatment of the natives and their forced conversion to Christianity was held by Francisco de Vitoria, theologian and a founder of international law, to "far exceed what is allowed by human and divine law."

in honor of Supai, the god of death.[41] The Inca lands, Peru, Ecuador, and parts of modern Bolivia and Chile, were laced with temples to the sun and with fortress-sanctuaries, most famously Machu Picchu, hanging fifteen hundred feet above the gorge of the Urubamba.

Francisco Pizarro sailed south for Peru from Panama with 183 men and 37 horses, beginning his march inland in May 1532. Tension among the Incas made his timing fortuitous. That year Atahualpa, ruler of the northern half of the Inca empire, centered in Quito, had seized the southern half that his brother had governed from Cuzco. Reaching Cajamarca in November, Pizarro captured Atahualpa by treachery. He extorted a colossal ransom from his captive, and then, using the powers granted him by the *Requerimiento,* had the last Inca ruler strangled for treason in 1533.

The conquistadors were besieged by an Indian revolt in Cuzco and newly founded Lima, and fell out among themselves. Pizarro was murdered and his half brother Gonzalo beheaded, but ultimately the Inca were broken and the cross was planted. By the mid-sixteenth century there were eight dioceses in the Caribbean islands, eight in Mexico, and three in South America. Almost a thousand Franciscans, Dominicans, and Augustinians were working to save souls.

❖   IN HIS WILL, Cortés made provision for five thousand masses to be said on successive days after his burial. A thousand were for the souls in purgatory, and two thousand for those who had lost their lives in serving him and the conquest of New Spain. The final two thousand were "for the souls of all those toward whom I have obligations of which I am ignorant or forgetful."

The last category might, perhaps, be taken to include those Indians of the American mainland who suffered the same fate as those on the islands. The population of Mexico when Cortés landed in 1519 has been estimated at 25 million. By 1600 it had fallen to one million. The estimated 32 million of preconquest Peru had declined to five million by 1548.[42]

Las Casas had no doubt what was to blame; for forty years human predators had torn the Indians to pieces. "We should realize the truth," he wrote, "that in forty years some twelve millions of souls of men, women and children have died unjustly and tyrannically at the hands of Christians."[43] He described Spaniards placing bets on slicing off heads or cutting bodies in half with a single blow, seizing infants from their mothers' breasts and dashing them against cliffs; men "mocking and laughing" as they threw their victims into rivers. He saw them cut off the noses, hands, and ears of Indians without provocation "merely because it pleased them to do so"; they broiled chiefs on gridirons because they failed to produce enough gold. Sometimes, he said, the Spaniards hanged their victims in two rows of six on gibbets with a single gallows at the end "in honor and worship of our Savior and his Twelve Apostles, as they used to speak"; he recorded that when a woman hanged herself from a beam rather than be taken, and dogs attacked her child, her tormentors attended to the religious niceties, for "before the creature expired a friar baptized it." Contemporary woodcuts showed the Spaniards looking like fashion-plate demons in ruffs, high hats, and puffed breeches with pits of impaled bodies before them, while offshore their ships lay at anchor, the symbol with their muskets and horses and mastiffs of Christian mastery. Las Casas thought that the Spaniards were "not just cruel but extraordinarily cruel" because this prevented the Indians from "daring to think of themselves as human beings or having a minute to think at all."

❖ INITIALLY THE PORTUGUESE in Brazil made less impact. There were fewer of them; the population of the motherland was no more than 1.5 million. Only the *degredados,* criminals, exiles, and malcontents, were under pressure to emigrate. Brazil's forests and swamps were difficult to penetrate. Many of the fourteen captaincies into which the country was divided by royal gift were Portuguese only in name. The Spaniards were able to use existing roads and buildings, as their monarch had succeeded to the thrones wrested from the last Aztec and Inca emperors. Brazil's Tupi Indians were in the stone age and had no such assets, no laws or administration; they had only bows and wooden axes to defend themselves. The captain of Pernambuco, Duarte Coehlo, referred to them as "this poison." The leader of the first Jesuits to land at Bahia in 1549, Manuel de Nobrega, said that his ideal was to "make savages unto men, and men unto Christians"[44] but he compared them in their existing state to pigs and dogs, and thought that forced settlement offered the only hope of making the second generation of converts better than the first.

Peaceful Indians were given the legal status of minors, who in principle were to be protected by the crown and evangelized; "just wars" and enslavement awaited the bellicose. The first settlers dealt mainly in brazilwood and dyewood. The development of plantations and sugar mills intensified the demand for labor. The natives' cannibalism provided an excuse for enslaving them. The bishop of Bahia, Dom Pedro Fernandes Sardinha, was shipwrecked on the Brazilian coast while returning to Lisbon in 1556. He and his companions were seized by Caete Indians, killed, and eaten. The governor, Mem de Sá declared war in vengeance for the martyr. Caetes were put in the mouths of cannon and blown to pieces; de Sá burned sixty villages on the coast, the flames from the palm thatch of the *malocas* visible well out to sea, while the inhabitants were driven off to the plantations. A smallpox epidemic in 1562 was followed by drought; Indians were reported to be selling themselves to settlers in return for food and shelter. The natives' primitive culture on the coast collapsed; as black slaves were shipped in from Africa, the native remnant was absorbed into the underclass of *mameluco* half-castes or fled to the backlands.

Licenses were given to settlers to send *bandeirantes,* organized slaving expeditions, to the interior. Cannibal tribes often had stocks of prisoners, held in anticipation of eating them; the *mamelucos* traded these with the chiefs for fishhooks and metal axes. They seduced others with tales of the abundance of fish and shellfish on the coast, or gave them gifts of clothes and tools. "With these tricks," Father Vicente de Salvador reported in the 1570s, "they wiped out whole villages." When they got within sight of the coast, families were separated, and individuals were given to the *mameluco* captains, and to the expedition outfitters and the officials who had issued licenses, and "all made use of them on their plantations, or else sold them . . ." They were branded on the face at the first fault. "Preachers banged their pulpits over the matter," Salvador wrote, "but they were preaching in the desert. . . ."[45]

❖   DISEASE WAS A greater killer than inhumanity, however. Smallpox arrived with the conquistadors, the first great epidemic breaking out in Mexico in 1520. Waves of smallpox, tuberculosis, measles, and influenza, to which they had no immunity, are thought to have carried off between one-third and one-half of the Brazilian Indians in the century after 1562. A mortal melancholy, called *banzo* by the Portuguese,[46] was another. An observer (Juan Bautista Pomar) in 1682 concluded that the Mexicans had so little resistance to disease due to an "affliction and fatigue of their spirits because they had lost the liberty God had given them, for Spaniards treat them worse than slaves."[47] An inquiry carried out in Lima and Quito between 1582 and 1586 reported that the Indians themselves gave "freedom" as a reason for their decline; they were in a state of shock at the destruction of their familiar world.

Missionary reports from the Americas horrified liberal churchmen in Europe. The Dominican Francisco de Vitoria, professor of theology at Salamanca and a founder of international law, argued that the papal donation and the *Requerimiento* were sinful and illegal. He said that the pope had no temporal power over natives to "donate" them to a different nation. Neither could anyone be compelled to become Christian; he quoted Thomas Aquinas—"the act of faith is proper to the will"—as evidence that conversion must be voluntary. It was quite absurd to claim that, if the Church allowed barbarians to reject the reign of Christ with impunity, they were nonetheless obliged to subject themselves to Christ's Vicar on pain of war and slavery. The use of force was legitimate only against an aggressor nation, Vitoria maintained. Although cannibalism and resistance to missionaries might give the Spanish some justification for their invasions, they had "far exceeded what is allowed by human and divine law."[48] As to the colonists giving "religious examples of living" to the natives, he pointed out that news of their "many scandals, cruel crimes and profanities" had reached as far as Salamanca.

Another theologian, Matías de Paz, thought that conquest was legitimate only if "inspired by the zeal of the faith." If it resulted from a "whim for domination or for desire to gain riches" it was invalidated. Paz conceded that, since Christ was the true monarch of the whole world from the beginning of his Nativity, the pope "has the right, founded on St. Peter's faith, to dominate the entire earth." Christians were obliged to convert natives, he agreed, since salvation was impossible outside the Church. Nonetheless, he bitterly condemned those who enslaved Indians. "Neither Christ nor the pope wished such evils," he wrote, adding that countless numbers had died who "if left free or not subjected to slavery, would now adore Christ." Ximinez de Cisneros, the austere inquisitor-general, reacting to reports from Hispaniola in 1516, ordered an experiment in which Indians were resettled in segregated villages under their own chiefs, tilling their own fields to produce food for the colonists, with a routine of Christian prayers to assimilate them into the faith. The scheme failed.

Soul-searching over the Christian issues of empire, and the separate horrors of African slavery, was more intense in Spain during the sixteenth century than in any other nation, Catholic or Protestant, for two hundred years. The Church in the New World, however, and its influence over converts, was spread thin; and settlers objected, sometimes violently, to its attempts to aid the natives. It was common for two or three friars to have charge over one hundred thousand souls, and rivalry between the orders prevented other friars from offering help. "Nearly all the people die without confession or other sacrament than baptism," the archbishop of Mexico complained in 1556.[49] He found that little fruit had come from the gospel; those few who knew the articles of faith said them "like parrots" without knowing what they meant. The bishops did not know the native tongues and used untrustworthy half-castes as interpreters, the friar Juan de San Ramón observed; the state of Christian teaching was so low, and so little respected, as "to make a Catholic weep."[50] The Council of Lima prevented Peruvians from receiving the Eucharist, on grounds of the shallowness of their faith; the Council of Mexico barred Indians and the growing number of half-castes—mestizos and mulattoes of mixed Spanish-Indian and Spanish-African blood—from the priesthood.

The energetic Bishop Zumárraga had founded a college at Tlateloleo in 1536 to train native priests. He was gratified by the Indian ability to learn Latin but soon found that the "best students are more inclined to marriage than to conti-nence"[51] and the college failed. Pope Gregory XIII was aware that the acute short-age of locally born priests threatened to reduce the faith to mere lip service. In a bull of 1576 he permitted the ordination of half-castes and illegitimates, provided that they knew Indian languages and were of good character. The Spanish crown used its control of the Church to crush this initiative, which settlers feared would undermine white prestige. Philip II wrote to the bishop of Lima in 1578 forbid-ding him from conferring Holy Orders on any mestizo, claiming that none were qualified for such a dignity. The College of Cardinals at Rome condemned the continued exclusion of Indians and mestizos in 1631. No notice was taken in the field. The ban was not lifted in Peru until 1772; the first three Indian priests were ordained in 1794. The first native Mexican to be priested was probably Nicolas de Puerto, who became bishop of Oaxaca in 1679.

In Brazil, *mamelucos* were barred from entering the priesthood and from holding government posts; they were excluded from some religious schools, since whites did not want their children to sit with half-castes, "most of who are of vile and obscure origin." The Carmelites at Olinda rejected any aspirant of Brazilian birth, whether white or not, and accepted only those born and bred in Portugal during the monastery's 145 years of existence. Of eighty-nine Carmelites in reli-gious houses in Amazonia, only eight worked with the Indians. The crown spent twenty-six times more on building the cathedral at Salvador than on missions to the interior.

Awe and grandeur served to bolster ill-understood belief. In Mexico, great baroque churches were built whose carvings blended Aztec skulls, masks, macaws, and monkeys with saints and angels in lavish elaboration; the Peruvian carvings of the crucified Christ, with their traceries of thorns and piercings, mir-rored the passion of the Indians as they labored to produce the quinto silver tax in ever deeper mines, on ranches and plantations, and in mills.

This quality of pain and sadness marked the first saint of the Americas, the "Rose of Lima," Isabel de Santa Maria de Flores y del Oliva. Born at Lima in 1586, her father was ruined by speculation in the mines, and she sold flowers as a child to help her parents. At nineteen she joined the Third Order of St. Dominic. She inflicted extreme penance upon herself in order to make reparation for the sins and cruelties of the age and the place. To make herself repulsive to suitors, she cut her cheeks and rubbed pepper into the wounds to cause inflammation and pus; when complimented on her smooth hands, she soaked them in lime. She scourged herself daily and fasted to emaciation, chewing bitter herbs to blister her gums. Her home was a garden hut, her mattress a pile of bricks; she wore gloves filled with nettles, a hair shirt, and a skullcap with spikes inside in imitation of the crown of thorns. As she walked through the Lima streets, mocked and desolate, she dragged a crucifix behind her. She was thirty-one when she died, and it was apt that she should become the patroness of South America, for she shared the Indian sense of suffering that suffused their faith.

Perhaps the greatest kindness that could be done to Indians, however, was to remove them from the proximity of whites. This the Jesuits attempted among the Guarani of Paraguay.

❖

❖

❖

CHAPTER XXV

"A DESERT-DWELLER IN PURSUIT OF WILD BEASTS":

The Jesuits in Paraguay

A great experiment in isolating Indians from the ravages of *encomienda*—the "measure devised by Pharaoh for oppressing the people of Israel"[1]—was undertaken by the Jesuits among the Guarani. It centered on the Jesuit province of Paraguay, established in 1607.* Jesuits were transferred to this wild region of forest, rivers, and scrub from Peru. "Spaniards have not penetrated this area," Father Antonio Ruiz de Montoya wrote proudly. "It was conquered by the Gospel alone."[2] The Guarani had lived in isolated clumps of a few huts scattered in clearings and along the banks of streams. The Jesuits gathered them into large settlements, or "reductions," where they lived as families and were taught the faith. The first reduction was built at San Ignacio Guazú, south of Asunción, in 1609.

The Jesuits went on missions in pairs, carrying no more than a breviary and crucifix, supported by twenty or thirty converted Indians with axes to hack their way through the scrub. They traversed swamps and quagmires, and "dens where wild beasts or savage men may be lurking"; they ate roots and berries and what fish and game they could catch. The Indians they contacted were offered a settled and secure life in the reductions. These were built in the colonial style, with a grid system of streets of neat houses running at right angles from a central square, with a church, schoolrooms, and the priests' quarters. Trenches and earthworks served for defense. The Indians grew their own food crops, maize, sweet potatoes, cassava, and worked in communal fields to raise cash crops of cotton, tobacco, and maté, the valuable green tea of Paraguay. It was fine ranching country, and the reductions had large herds of cattle.

At San Ignacio adults were instructed in groups of 150 men and women.

*This included territories surrounding modern Paraguay now in Argentina, Brazil, and Uruguay.

The catechism was explained to children on Sundays and feast days. Two hours were devoted to reading and writing each afternoon. "There are still many non-Christians in this town," Father Roque Gonzalez noted in 1613, "but among the 120 adults baptized this year were several elderly witch-doctors."[3] The Jesuits did not insist on conversion. The prime aim was to prevent the "spiritual and temporal ruin" that accompanied forced labor on settler estates, leaving the Indians as "vagabonds in strange lands and byways." White settlers and slavers were bitterly hostile. "They have such hatred for Indians and for us," Gonzalez wrote. They accused the Jesuits of exploiting the Indians for their own profit. Montoya wrote of Jesuit fathers without a shirt on their back who disguised their penury with a bit of linen round their neck, sleeping on cowhides; he said that to place Indians in the power of whites would "furnish them a knife for butchering the sheep of Jesus Christ in a slaughterhouse."[4]

Slavers from São Paulo mounted *malocas,* raids to carry off Indians in chains. To the beat of drums and in military order, the *paulistas* burst into the mission of San Antonio, slashing the Indians with cutlasses when they sought shelter in the church. Some of the marauders asked the fathers for confession while others were despoiling the altar and searching the priests' rooms, finding nothing but ragged shirts and torn cotton cassocks. An Indian was shot dead in the arms of Father Simón Masseta. When the *paulistas* left, they set the mission on fire, and many sick and wounded were lost to the flames. Father Simón followed his abducted congregation on the long march to São Paulo, finding abandoned Indians to baptize and confess. When he reached the town, the people whistled and mocked him, and he was arrested.

Apostate Indians were used against the Jesuits. Father Roque established several reductions in the east of the province, in modern Uruguay. At a place called Caró, or the "house of wasps" on the Piratini River, he won over the local chief and built a church. A ceremony was held in November 1628 to dedicate the new town. A maverick led an attack as the bell began to ring for the festival. Roque was clubbed to death; as he tried to drag himself into the church—repeating "Sons, why are you killing me?"—his companion Father Alonso was also martyred. The church was burned and the Indians used the bell to make arrowheads. The bellies of the dead Jesuits were found to have been ripped open; "according to their fantastic custom," Montoya explained, "unless the killer opens the dead man's belly, he himself will swell up and die."[5] At Villaroyon, a group of Indians that had been taught by Father Cristóbal de Mendoza "re-enacted the mockery of the Jews" on him when they captured him. They knocked out his teeth with a sword; when he told them that he longed to wash their souls "in the pure water of baptism," they cut off his lips, ears, and nose. Then, to cries of "Let us see if his soul dies now," they flayed his chest and belly and pierced his heart with arrows before flinging his corpse into a stream.

Montoya felt himself "a desert-dweller in pursuit of wild beasts." Eleven of the thirteen reductions he and his companions had toiled to build were abandoned after repeated slaver attacks. The Jesuits led the Indians on an epic evacuation to the west, rafting down the Paraná River to the precipitous Guairá Falls, climbing down the almost sheer rock face to the rapids below, where they built new rafts to found new reductions beyond the reach of white marauders. Militias were formed for defense. Skilled Jesuits, many of them German, taught the Guarani handicrafts and raised them to a basic literacy. Metalwork, locks, clocks, and guns were made along with fine musical instruments and furniture. San Ignacio Miní, an enormous baroque church built of red sandstone, 230 feet long and 75 feet wide with walls seven feet thick, was adorned with elaborate bas-relief sculptures carved by Guarani artists. The mission was famous for the quality of its choirs and its trumpets and violins.

There were usually two Jesuits on each reduction. One traveled the district visiting the sick, saying mass in remote chapels, and persuading those still in the

A Jesuit is depicted in marquetry by a Chaco Indian at a mission in Paraguay. "Spaniards have not penetrated this area," a Jesuit wrote proudly. "It was conquered by the Gospel alone." The Indians were gathered into large settlements, or "reductions," where they were educated and taught music and crafts. The first was built near Asunción in 1609. The aim was to avoid the "spiritual and temporal ruin" that colonizers brought with them. In 1767 the Jesuits were ordered to surrender all their possessions and lands and leave the Spanish Empire. The Indians of Paraguay were abandoned to the settlers and to catastrophe.

forest to join the new community. The other, so Father Antonio Sepp claimed in a letter to his family, did the work of seven or eight priests in Europe. He rose before dawn for his own private devotions in the church and then heard confessions and celebrated mass. After instructing children in the catechism, he visited the sick. "I give them holy communion and extreme unction, and, if it is not too late, prescribe medicines," he wrote. "I have daily burials. After the sick, I visit the offices; first the school, where the boys are instructed in reading and writing and the girls in spinning and needlework. I also visit my musicians, singers, trumpets, haut-boys, etc. On certain days I instruct some Indians in dancing. . . . After that, I go among the workmen, to the brickmakers and tilemakers, the bakers, smiths, joiners, carpenters, painters, and above all the butchers who kill fifteen or sixteen oxen a day." All this was done before 9 A.M.[6]

The reductions were useful to the Spanish crown. They protected the frontier against the Portuguese in Brazil, with the Indians permitted to bear arms, and rich taxes were raised from their thriving trade in maté. A royal governor wrote to Madrid that "everywhere I meet missioners or traces of their good works,"[7] and he also said that countless families heard mass and confessed only when Jesuits passed their homes. By 1750 more than 150,000 Indians were living in thirty missions.

❖   TRAGEDY BEGAN THAT year. By a boundary treaty signed in Madrid, Portugal gave up its claims to the region of La Plata around Buenos Aires. In return, the Spanish ceded the rich pastureland on the eastern bank of the Uruguay River to Portuguese Brazil. A clause in the treaty obliged the Jesuits to leave with all their movable property, taking the thirty thousand Indians in the seven affected reductions with them. Their churches, buildings, and land were granted to the Portuguese.

The Spaniards in Buenos Aires, jealous of mission success in the maté trade, refused to help. Jesuits who tried to sail to alert their order in Rome were turned back at Rio. They appealed to Madrid, on the basis of a contract of conscience existing between the king and his loyal Indian subjects. The theological faculty at the University of Córdoba in central Argentina pointed out that innocent subjects could not be dispossessed without adequate compensation. A father estimated the combined value of seven missions at sixteen million pesos; the crown offered a flat four thousand pesos to each. As Indian anger rose, the Córdoba faculty wrote to the Jesuit general in Rome, Ignacio Visconti, warning that it was unsafe to obey a human directive that was in plain contradiction to the laws of nature, God, and the Church.

Visconti ordered the Jesuits under pain of mortal sin not to impede the evacuations; on the contrary, they were to use every effort to oblige the Indians to leave "without resistance, contradiction or excuse." He named a Jesuit from Andalucia, Luis Altamiro, the "worst type of court priest . . . appointed by a weak General to please the King"[8] as visitor plenipotentiary to South America. The Indians protested to the viceroy that "seven innocent and most loyal populations are condemned to all evils . . . with danger of temporal death and ruin to their souls." Public prayers were said in the great squares of the missions. Parties were sent out to search for new sites, but found that the alternatives were exposed to hostile Indians, or rocky, or infested with ants, or waterless. When the time for migration came, the Indians refused to go or slipped away from the columns of march and returned.

They nursed a special hatred for Altamiro. "They believed he was a Portuguese and threatened to throw him into the Uruguay," reported one Jesuit. "Terrified at the report that the Indians were approaching . . . he consulted his safety by flying in the night, and soon after I found him in Santa Fe, out of danger."[9] Altamiro ordered the Jesuits to subdue the Indians by denying them the mass and sacraments; the mission churches were to be closed and the chalices destroyed lest they fall into "profane hands." As to the Jesuits themselves, they were to leave immediately for Buenos Aires, taking only their breviaries with them. All of them refused and resigned.

The Guarani prepared for war. Scrap metal was turned into arrowheads; women selected stones for slings and practiced shooting, saying they would die with their husbands. As Altamiro closed their churches, they built their own chapels in honor of Our Lady and the Angels, patrons of the Guarani army. Banners were woven and inscribed *Quis et Deus,* processions of penitents organized, special litanies composed and sung. Toward the end of 1755 a combined force of almost three thousand Portuguese and Spaniards was raised to drive the Indians from the reductions. The Guarani were led by a chief named Sepé—"active and courageous," a Jesuit wrote of him, "but as ignorant of military tactics as I am of black magic"—and fashioned cannon out of bamboo cane reinforced with rawhide.

A decisive battle was fought on a ridge above the Yacui River near the mission of San Miguel. The Indians dug trenches and raised ramparts as they had been taught in the missions. The whites attacked to the sound of drumrolls. "The artillery shot first, the enemy fell into disorder . . . the cavalry on both right and left wrought fearful destruction," wrote a Spaniard. "The infantry . . . rushed some caves and a small wood into which some four hundred Indians had fled."[10] The slaughter lasted seventy-five minutes; the greater part of the fifteen-hundred-strong Guarani army was killed, and the trenches they had dug served as their burial pits. The whites lost three Spaniards and two Portuguese killed. The spoil included eight homemade cannons, two standards, a few firearms, four statues of the saints, and many musical instruments.

Spanish cavalrymen were astonished when they saw the magnificent church and buildings of San Miguel through a telescope. The governor of Montevideo, Joachim de la Viana, thought "our people in Madrid are out of their senses to deliver up to the Portuguese this town which is second to none in Paraguay."[11] When the allies entered the town on May 17, 1756, it was deserted. Its seven thousand Indians had fled to the woods, giving the treasures from their church to a venerated hermit who lived on the banks of the Piratini River. By the end of May all seven missions had been occupied. The troops were impressed by the faith of the Indians. "The spiritual organization of the pueblos is very edifying, especially in these days of preparation for Corpus Christi," a captain of dragoons wrote in his diary on June 17, 1756. "The church functions have been splendid, Vespers, the offices, and procession. . . . [T]he musical corps has played and dances have been performed with great precision." Nonetheless, those who did not flee were shipped across the Uruguay.

In far distant Madrid, the Spanish changed their minds and rescinded the boundary treaty in 1761. The Portuguese withdrew under Spanish pressure. The Indians stealthily returned to the missions. The cattle had been driven off, the fields were overrun with brambles and insects, and their homes were either burned or dilapidated; they found "the dens of jaguars and the holes of serpents"[12] in them. The Jesuits sought out their abandoned flocks and brought fourteen thousand of them back to the missions. Sixteen thousand had been lost.

✤ BOTH SIDES USED the Jesuits as scapegoats for the failure of the treaty. The chief minister of Portugal, the marquis of Pombal, was anticlerical, and as a key supporter of secular education he had a particular mistrust of Jesuits. He expelled them from Portugal and wrote a hostile tract, *A Short Account of the Jesuit Republic,* to extend his attack abroad. Partly based on his brother's experiences in Paraguay, Pombal's work was translated and circulated throughout Europe as part of a well-orchestrated campaign of vilification aimed at Catholic kings and the pope.

It accused the Jesuits of rebellion to protect their "empire" and riches. They were soon said to be working secret gold mines on the missions, and to have proclaimed the Guarani chief Nicolás Neenguirú as "king of Paraguay." While "every mouth and press in Europe" spread this myth, the Jesuit padre Dobrizhoffer complained, "I saw this famous Nicolas, with naked feet and garments after the Indian fashion, sometimes driving the cattle before the shambles, sometimes chopping wood in the market place; and . . . I could hardly refrain from laughter."[13] Pamphleteers in Europe also claimed that a Jesuit, the Bohemian Tado

Enis, was commander of the Guarani army. So persistent were these tales of a bloodsoaked fiend in holy garb that Enis was summoned to explain himself to a tribunal in Paraguay. His diary showed that he had refused to accompany the Indians except as chaplain and physician to the wounded, and so he was cleared of any crime.

Others wished the Jesuits harm. They fed on disputes over Jesuit education, on the rites they used in China, their freedoms from episcopal rule, and their close links to the pope, and on the jealousy of other orders. A scandal broke out in Martinique, where a Jesuit father, Lavalette, was heavily involved in plantations and shipping. Two ships he had sent to carry sugar and coffee to France were intercepted and seized by the British, forcing Lavalette's businesses into bankruptcy. The creditors turned to French Jesuits to repay his colossal debt of three million livres. They refused to pay and appealed to the Parlement of Paris. After a stormy anticlerical debate in August 1762, the Parlement held them responsible for the debt. It ordered the Society's property to be sequestered, and said that Jesuits who refused to take an oath of loyalty to the king should be expelled. They were accused of conspiring, "by all means, direct and indirect, covert and overt," to seize power. The pope, Clement XIII, was Jesuit-educated and refused to change the constitution of the Society to permit the oath to be taken. *"Sint ut sunt aut non sint,"* he famously declared: "Let them be as they are, or not be at all."[14] When Louis XV declared at the end of 1764 that the Society in France had ceased to exist, Clement could do no more than reply with a bull warmly praising Jesuit courage and good works.

Rioting broke out in Madrid in 1766 and was cynically blamed on Jesuit intrigue. The chief minister, the count of Aranda, told Charles II that they were plotting to overthrow him. The king was persuaded to take brutal action. He ordered "the expulsion from all my dominions of the religious of the company of Jesus, priests as well as lay brothers and novices" and the sequestration of their property.[15] All five thousand Jesuits were to be deported from Spain and the empire. All lands, goods, chattels, buildings, and livestock were to be surrendered. The only compensation was a pension of one hundred pesos a year; enough, as one said, "to clothe a man if he did not eat, and to feed him if he did not wear clothes."[16] Even that pittance was to be withdrawn if any Jesuit conspired to disturb the peace. No one was to produce any pamphlet, book, or picture dealing with the expulsion.

The sanction was published in the Prado palace on April 2, 1767, to the accompaniment of trumpets and drums and the voice of the public crier. The king gave no reason. "The just and grave motives which forced me to this measure, despite the pain it causes," the sanction stated, "remain hidden in my royal person." Sealed letters were sent to the governors of every province of the empire, with the date and hour when they were to be opened written on them. They instructed the governors to surround Jesuit houses with troops, and to force the inmates into transports without delay or explanation. The fathers were to be taken to depots and then shipped to Europe. Their houses were to be searched, all documents seized, all property confiscated.

The first expulsion took place in Buenos Aires at 2:30 A.M. on July 3, 1767. Had the Jesuits raised the Indians to revolt in this wild country of marsh and forest and rivers, the Spanish would have been hard pressed. Aranda knew they would not. "Naturally," he wrote to a colleague, "the Jesuits will accept the decree with resignation and will not give any reason for the royal displeasure to manifest itself further."[17] They had to steel themselves to reject the heartrending pleas of their Indians, and to abandon them to the savagery of estate owners and slavers; but the pope dared not fly in the face of the Spanish crown, and their discipline held. When their provincial was shown the royal decree, he bowed his head before it in homage; the lawyer who delivered it to him broke down in tears at his humility. The commissioner responsible for the expulsions, Marquis Francisco de Paula Bucareli, added a fresh humiliation. He ordered the missioners to promise the Indians that they would come to no harm, lest they decided to rebel. "You will first have to give them some sort of explanation which will make them calm and patient," he instructed the missioners at Belen de los Ulbayas. It was as well; at a mission near Santa Fe, the resident father said that his Indians would have left the town "in a heap of ruins" had he not pacified them.

Bucareli insisted that every Jesuit, "however old, infirm or moribund," be removed at once.[18] Thus Father Chomé was carried in a hammock by two of his Chiquitos Indians for six hundred miles across the eastern Andes, not being allowed to rest even when passing through the town of Cochabamba. He was seventy; he died in a mountain village. The works and dictionary he had written in the Chiquitos dialects perished with him. Father Messnar, seventy-seven, was taken for 320 miles from the San Ignacio mission to Santa Cruz de Sierra, his feet bloodied with sores; he was lodged in a slum for several months while snow remained on the Cordillera, dying on muleback in the spring. Forty Jesuits who had sailed from Cádiz had a terrible journey of six months before reaching Montevideo. The expulsion order was read to them as they disembarked; they were crammed in a hovel and then shipped back to Europe having hardly been ashore. The novices in training were given the choice of returning to their homes in Spain rather than following the "old men" into exile. They remained faithful, receiving such ovations from onlookers as they were taken to Buenos Aires that they were transferred to prison secretly and at night.

The fathers were forbidden to say mass or receive Communion. A group from Tarija were constantly strip-searched for riches and documents during their forced ride to the coast. They were not allowed to carry any change of clothing. When one of their number died and was given the Last Sacraments and buried, the conductor of the prisoners was severely reprimanded for lack of discipline. By September 1767, 224 Jesuits of the Paraguay region were gathered at the port of Ensenada near Buenos Aires. Five ships took them to Spain, journeys of from four to five months. Cádiz was reached in February and March of 1768; four months of close imprisonment followed.

They were then shipped out of Spain to the papal states without the Spanish crown seeking permission or even informing the pope. Clement declined to receive them. "If they are good men, the King has no right to banish them," the cardinal-secretary Torrigiani commented. "If they are criminals, he has no right to commit to the Holy Father their punishment or imprisonment."[19] Harried from Rome, they were carried to Corsica—though it was French and not Spanish—and abandoned to the kindness of the inhabitants there. When the French in turn expelled them, they wandered to Faenza. They were joined there by thirty-five novices who had been held for eighteen months at Jérez de la Frontera in southern Spain while attempts were made to break their vocation. Nine succumbed. The others were exiled and found their way to Faenza. "May God preserve us all in this sweet Society!" one of them wrote to a friend. "If at present we cannot do much, at least we can endure much, and that is better. . . ." He closed with St. Paul: *"Quia non sunt condignae passiones hujus temporis ad futuram gloriam quae revelabitur in nobis."*[20] "The sufferings of this time are not worthy of the glory that shall be revealed in us."

The whites they had left behind felt an emptiness. Within a year of the expulsions, the bishop of Buenos Aires was begging for replacements from other orders. "This city," he wrote, "so full of vices, and those increasing daily, and at the same time so void of spiritual workers, is also in extreme necessity. . . . Many die without the last Sacraments."[21] Of the Indians the bishop knew nothing. The forest and bush reclaimed the missions; the choirs and musicians were scattered, the craftsmen and sculptors lost their skills. The Jesuits had protected their Indians, but had ordained no native priests nor equipped them to withstand the brutalities of colonial life that overwhelmed them. Only two traces of the great experiment survived; sandstone ruins, and the Guarani language. The fathers had not taught them Spanish, the better to isolate them from the white world. Paraguay became the only country in South America where an Indian tongue, Guarani, is the national language.

❖ FIVE THOUSAND MILES to the northeast the same end game was being played out. The Jesuits had also established missions in California, Arizona, and

Texas. They were pioneers, soldiers following them to build presidios, or block-houses, to hold the new frontier line. Father Eusebio Kino, an Austrian from the Tyrol, spent twenty-four years from 1687 working among the Pima in Arizona. He learned the Pima language, studying their beliefs—according to their mythology the world had been created by an Earth Magician dancing on a cake of dust—and breeding cattle to feed them. "Exploring lands, converting souls, such are the virtues of Father Kino," the Pima said of him. "Frequent is his prayer; he is without bad habits. He neither smokes nor uses snuff. He sleeps in no bed; he drinks no wine."

Captain Juan Mateo Manje, who accompanied Kino on nine arduous journeys to contact the Indians, confirmed his godliness. Kino used no wine except in the celebration of Mass; he had no bed beyond saddle blankets for a mattress and two rough quilts for cover. He refused bleached clothing and wore rough underclothes, "because he gave away everything as alms to the Indians. He was kind to all and harsh in disciplining himself." His temperament was fiery, but he had such self-control that he would embrace those who insulted him, saying "In your goodness, you must be my dearest master, even if you do not so desire."[22] Manje knew him to spend whole nights in his little chapel without sleeping, and sometimes he scourged himself.

In his terrible bouts of fever, Kino touched no food or drink for six days at a time, only getting up to say mass. He died of exhaustion in 1711. His deathbed was two sheepskins and a packsaddle for a pillow; he had no change of clothing. Kino was said to have converted some thirty thousand Indians; their descendants still pray in the great mission of San Xavier del Bac that he founded at Tucson. Jesuits entered Baja California in 1697, setting up a mission at Loreto and working the silver mines at La Paz. By 1767 they had sixteen missions among the Indians.

They too were driven into exile. Troops broke into the Jesuit houses in the California settlements in the early hours of June 26, 1767, and ordered the priests to assemble in the chapels. The royal decree sentencing them to perpetual exile was read out to them in the midst of profound silence. They were not allowed to return to their rooms. They were taken away in carriages the same day; they could take nothing but their breviaries with them, but onlookers flung them purses with gold and silver as tokens of affection. In the California and Arizona missions the Indians wept as seventy years of teaching and comfort was wiped out in a morning. Those who were still learning their catechism cried out, "pleading for baptism," the mission father Benno Ducrue recalled, "as they returned to the wilderness from which they had emerged." Ducrue himself had spent twenty years trying to secure for them "not only the bread of eternal life but also bodily food and clothing."[23] The vast province of California, extending for sixteen hun-

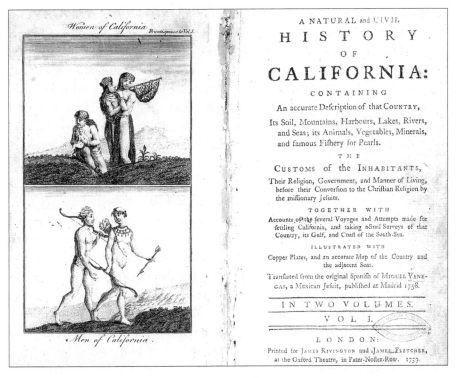

The Jesuit Miguel Venegas wrote *A Natural and Civil History of California* in 1758, with engravings of natives. The Jesuits were expelled from their missions in California and Arizona in a single day in 1767. Indians who were still learning their catechism cried out, "pleading for baptism," a mission father recalled, "as they returned to the wilderness from which they had emerged." The vast province of California, extending for sixteen hundred miles, was emptied of any priest but the governor's chaplain.

dred miles, was emptied of any priest but the governor's chaplain, an old man who knew no native language.

At the coast, as the Jesuits waited to be rowed out to the ship offshore, some soldiers knelt on the sand to kiss their hands and feet, and others knelt with their arms outstretched in the form of the cross, pleading for pardon. The governor wept for pity. On the ship, the sailors were ordered to climb the mast and shout out *"Viva el rey!"* To Ducrue, this false suggestion that the Jesuits had taught the Indians to acknowledge no king but the missionaries was an added insult; had not "our Father Treasurer in the name of all the missionaries yearly sworn allegiance to the King?"[24]

The results were not as catastrophic as in Paraguay. The Jesuit missions were run by Dominicans from 1772, while Franciscans moved deeper into Alta California. Juniper Serra, a Spanish Franciscan who took his name from the holy fool in *The Little Flowers of St. Francis,* founded the first of the twenty-one new missions that underpinned the vast province. He set up the mission of San Diego, named for a Franciscan lay brother, in 1769. San Francisco Bay was discovered the same year; there, too, and at San Jose, Los Angeles, Santa Cruz, and Santa Barbara, Serra planted his missions. They flourished, keeping great herds of cattle for tallow and hides, producing wine and brandy, employing Indians to grow oranges and wheat, and to make soap and mission furniture. In their turn, in 1823 the Franciscans were expelled by the Mexican government, but indelible traces of the religious foundation of California have been left in the names of its great cities.

The European monarchies were not finished with the Jesuits. In 1769 the ambassadors of Spain, Naples, and France demanded that the pope irrevocably destroy the Society. The misery of his position is thought to have hastened Clement XIII's death the same year. The Spanish cardinals who took part in the angry conclave to find a successor admitted that they had come "not to elect a Pope but to do away with the Society." The new pope, Clement XIV, gave way in July 1773. As he signed the brief *Dominus ac Redemptor* that dissolved the Jesuits, he is said to have sighed: "I acted under constraint." The brief was the work of the Spanish ambassador Joseph Moniño; it was first printed on a secret press at the Spanish embassy. The last general of the Society, Lorenzo Ricci, was flung into prison.

That the hardiest of Catholic orders was not totally obliterated was through the grace of a Lutheran king and an Orthodox empress. Poland, partitioned between Frederick II of Prussia and Catherine of Russia, had twenty-four hundred Jesuits in 1773. The rulers opposed the dissolution; indeed, a novitiate was opened in Belorussia, and the Jesuits in Russia were allowed to hold a general congregation. In Protestant England, too, the government ignored the brief; Catholic bishops there were inhibited by antipapal legislation from enforcing it, and the Jesuits were able to found their famous school at Stonyhurst Hall in Lancashire. In 1792, Ferdinand, the duke of Parma, asked for Jesuits from Russia, and three were sent to him. A semiclandestine novitiate was opened near Parma seven years later. Recovery came with Pius VII. Returning to Rome in August 1814 after his imprisonment by Napoleon, he went to the Jesuit church of Gesù with all the cardinals who were in the city and celebrated mass. In the chapel of Marian congregations he was awaited by more than a hundred former Jesuits bowed with age. His secretary read out the bull *Sollicitudo omnium Ecclesiarum,* and the Jesuits were restored.

CHAPTER XXVI

"The Attractive African Meteor":

The Slave Trade

Across the Atlantic, the Christian king of the Congo, Affonso, complained in 1526 of the "many traders in all parts of the kingdom. They bring ruin. . . . Every day people are kidnapped and enslaved, even members of the King's family." Parts of his territory were becoming depopulated barely sixteen years after the first consignment of fifty black slaves had been shipped from Spain to Hispaniola. A thriving and direct trade from the river mouths of West Africa across the "middle passage" of the Atlantic to the New World had already been spawned. Africans proved an ideal labor force for the mines, plantations, factories, and mills of the Americas. Only in the high copper and silver mines of Peru, where the altitude and cold were unsuited to blacks, were Indians used for preference.

Affonso's misgivings were temporary and not based on his faith. He objected to the kidnapping of his own subjects, but was eager to capture and trade other Africans. When slaves were taken from higher up the Congo River, he was happy to tax the slavers and deal on his own account at São Salvador, his capital. "No king in all these parts esteems Portuguese goods as much as we do," he wrote to Lisbon in 1540. "We favor the trade, sustain it, open . . . roads, and markets where the pieces are traded."[1] The word "pieces" meant "pieces of Indies," or prime slaves with no faults. Other African chiefs sold slaves over the coming centuries for horses, bolts of cloth, firearms, gunpowder, brandy, cutlasses, brass pots and pans, cowry shells brought by European captains from the Indian Ocean, and other products that the slaves themselves had produced in the Americas such as gold, copper bars, sugar, rum, and molasses-dipped tobacco.

The same absence of moral and religious scruple was shown by Affonso's fellow monarchs in Europe, and by churches of all denominations. Lutherans, Anglicans, Quakers, and Huguenots were to sell slaves to one another, and to

Catholics; the most minor of imperial powers, Denmark and Sweden, competed with the Portuguese, Spanish, English, and French giants for their share of the trade; Jesuit, Franciscan, Dominican, and Carmelite missionaries, who often decried the enslavement of Indians, were nonetheless owners of black slaves.

Where formal theology was used to justify the Christian conquest of the New World, faith provided the merest fig leaf for the enslavement and transport of Africans. Biblical texts were used to show that the slavery of Africans was divinely ordained because their color was the mark of the murderer Cain—"and the Lord appointed a sign for Cain" (Gen. 4:15)—or of descendants of Ham, cursed and turned black by Noah when he saw him naked and drunk, fit only to be "servants of servants" (Gen. 9:25). A Dominican friar at Lima, Fray Francisco de la Cruz, claimed that an angel had revealed to him that "the blacks are justly captives by reason of the sins of their forefathers, and that because of that sin God gave them their color."[2] Planters made sure that Anglican priests in Barbados and the Carolinas neither opposed slavery nor missionized their slaves.[3]

Baptism was held to be slavery's blessing. Portuguese captains were required by King Manuel the Fortunate in the early sixteenth century to baptize their slaves, unless they were unwilling, as some Moslems were; Manuel also arranged for slaves in Portugal to receive Communion in a Lisbon church. In a bull of 1513, Pope Leo X permitted captains to baptize dying slaves at sea. It was later common for slaves to be baptized before leaving Africa, and this became a requirement of the Spanish and Portuguese crown in 1607. Little attempt was made to provide any explanation of the faith into which the slaves were being inducted. In the big slaving center of Luanda in Angola they were led into one of the town's six churches or massed in the main square. A slave catechist told them in their own language that they were to become Christian. A priest then went among them, giving each a Christian name, sprinkling salt on their tongues, and then holy water. "Consider that you are now children of Christ," he would tell them. "You are going to set off for Portuguese territory, where you will learn matters of the Faith. Never think of your place of origin. Do not eat dogs, nor rats, nor horses. Be content."[4] Since it was against ecclesiastical law to baptize adults who had not been instructed in the faith, slaves were supposed to be initiated into Christianity on the long Atlantic crossing. Indeed, Philip III of Spain, who was also king of Portugal as Philip II, ordered that all slave ships should carry a priest to minister to its human cargo; a shortage of priests rendered this pious thought largely worthless.

It was argued by Catholics and Protestants alike that slaves benefited from their removal from the savageries of Africa. The sixteenth-century Jesuit Luis de Molina condoned the trade on the grounds that the slaves' spirits gained from the conversion to Christianity, and their bodies from the higher material standards of

America, where conditions were "much better than what they had when they went about naked and had to content themselves with a miserable existence."[5] Another Spaniard, Carlos Esteban Deive, said, "The slave's body was chained so that, as recompense, his soul could be saved." The great Jesuit preacher António Vieira, a tireless supporter of Amazonian Indians, held that Brazil was a mere Purgatory for blacks—and one in which baptism gave their souls an eventual hope of heaven—compared with the hell of Africa. The American clergyman Cotton Mather, observer of the Salem witch trials and minister at the Second Church in Boston, thought that slaves in New England "lived better than they would have done as free men in Africa." Joseph Hawkins, a slave captain from Charleston, South Carolina, who brought slaves from Africa in 1793, was "fully convinced that the removal of these poor wretches, even to the slavery of the West Indies, would be an act of humanity, rather than one exposed to censure . . . The slaves I had purchased were young men, many of them being eager to escape from their bondage in Ebo. . . ."[6]

Cruelty in Africa itself was partly a result of the slave trade. As the Dominican Tomás de Mercado wrote in 1569, the high prices that Europeans paid for black slaves encouraged African rulers to mount frequent raids to obtain captives, and even gave fathers an incentive to sell their children. Little of the missionary zeal found in the Americas was visible in Africa. After King Affonso's death in 1543, the promising experiments in Christian education were abandoned. The Portuguese governor of São Tomé, the island where slaves were held in barracoons before being loaded for the Atlantic crossing, pressured the few priests in the Congo to ignore the natives on the grounds that conversion and education would render them unfit for slavery. A charter was given to Paulo Dias de Novais, grandson of the discoverer of the Cape of Good Hope, to colonize Angola in 1571. Plans were made to import Portuguese settlers in the hope that they would exploit its minerals and farm its rich soil, and so help to convert and civilize its people. The easy profits of slaving destroyed the scheme, and the *lançados,* Portuguese adventurers, employed fierce Jaga cannibals to carry out raids for captives. "Here one finds all the slaves which one might want and they cost practically nothing," the Jesuit Frei Garcia Simaes wrote from Luanda in 1576. "With the exception of the leaders, almost all the natives here either are born in slavery or are reduced to that condition without the least pretext. . . . After his victories the king gives entire villages over to his subalterns, with the right either to kill or sell the inhabitants."[7] The demand was tremendous. An epidemic of dysentery combined with influenza to wreak the same carnage among Brazilian Indians in the 1560s as smallpox had in Mexico and the Indies. "The expenditure in human life here in Bahia in these past twenty years is a thing hard to believe," a Jesuit wrote in 1583, "for no one could believe that so great a supply could be exhausted, much less in so short a time." By the end of the century the coastal population in distant Angola had so declined that slave traders had to travel three months into the interior to find markets.

Italian Capuchins working in Angola and the Congo showed what might have been achieved. In the area between the Bengo and Loge Rivers, chiefs were baptized into the faith and Portuguese was widely spoken; some mulattoes were ordained and Bantu venerated the Capuchins, the only missionaries to work far into the interior. The Capuchins complained that the bishop and clergy of Luanda were deeply involved in slaving, and recommended that the Angolan clergy should be trained in Lisbon, where they would be far from the venality and immorality of Africa and its white scoundrels and ex-convicts. In the main, as Manuel Severim de Faria admitted of Angola in 1625, the Portuguese had brought nothing but fighting; "very little has been done for the conversion of the inhabitants of that great province, the majority of whom are in the same state as when we first entered therein," he added ruefully, "and are more scandalized by our weapons than edified by our religion."[8] He wrote shortly after the mass executions of chiefs suspected of plotting against Portuguese rule, which "left all the heathen of these kingdoms frightened and terrorized, since it is only by force and fear that we can maintain our position over these indomitable heathen."[9]

Matters changed little when other Europeans—French, English, Dutch, Germans, Swedes, and Danes—established their own forts and trading settlements in West Africa. The Christians kept to the coast and river mouths, rarely venturing inland, awaiting the caravans of slaves and ivory that shuffled in chains from the darkness of the interior. Missionary efforts and conversions were limited to the areas immediately around the coastal strongholds. Indeed, the Protestants made matters worse; where the Portuguese banned trading in firearms and the export of paper, for African literacy was not encouraged, the Dutch and particularly the English were eager to trade guns for slaves, and it was estimated that 150,000 guns were sent to West Africa in 1765 from gunsmiths in Birmingham alone. Local chiefs often used the guns, of course, to obtain more slaves.

Moslems had been dealing in black slaves since the Islamic conquests, and it was a sad fact that a slave generally fared better under a Moslem master than a Christian. Slaves were spared the terrible journey across the Atlantic; the labor was usually less arduous than in the mines and plantations of the Americas; household slaves were treated as family members and had an accepted place in society; and an ambitious slave could advance in civil government or as a soldier. A Moslem slave could have his own slaves. Castration was a particular hazard; those who survived the operation, however, found soft billets guarding the harems and households of the Ottomans and the North African kingdoms.

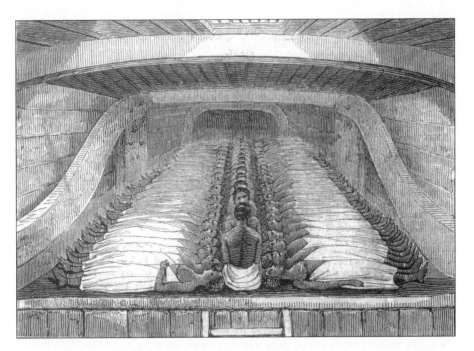

The stowage of slaves belowdecks on a slave ship plying the Middle Passage from Africa. By the 1730s, John Wesley and George Whitefield, founders of Methodism, were condemning slave owning as a grave sin that scotched Christ's call for spiritual rebirth. Congregationalists argued that slavery violated America's covenant with God. "I will not turn away the punishment thereof," preached Samuel Hopkins, capturing the visions of the prophets, "because they have sold the righteous for silver, and the needy for a pair of shoes."

❧   SLAVERY ROUSED LITTLE initial indignation among Christians because it was a tradition and a commonplace. Black slaves had been taken to North Africa and the eastern Mediterranean from the time of ancient Egypt. In antiquity they came primarily from Ethiopia, and all black slaves were known as "Ethiops" well into the fifteenth century. The first Christians had accepted slavery as an economic and social fact of life, and it had continued to thrive after the fall of the Roman Empire. St. Isidore, the pious and charitable bishop of Seville from A.D. 600, was typical in thinking it to be God's will. "Because of the sin of the first man," he wrote, "the penalty of servitude was imposed by God on the human race; to those unsuitable for liberty, he has mercifully accorded servitude."[10] There were flourishing slave markets at Arles, Lyons, and Verdun under Charlemagne. The Church had some misgivings, notably against the enslavement of Christians, but this did not prevent Christians from trafficking in pagans from the Slav territories, at least until they were converted; merchants in the eastern borderlands of Germany drove columns of slaves to the markets of the Mediterranean. Some

Europeans were exchanged for Africans; there were black slaves in Renaissance Italy, and a religious brotherhood known as "los Negritos" was founded in Seville in the late fourteenth century by a benign archbishop.

True, slavery had disappeared from northern Europe during the Middle Ages. Many English slaves were freed after the Norman conquest of 1066, and by 1200 slavery had given way entirely to serfdom. The Church frowned on the en-slavement of Christians, and cart-horses, wheeled plows, and watermills made slave labor less of an economic necessity. Constant raiding between Christians and Moslems, however, had kept it very much alive in the Mediterranean. The trade was predominantly Moslem. Although the Koran recognized the freeing of a slave to be a noble act, Islam did not query the morality of slave-owning. The great Arab historian Ibn-Khaldun believed that it was through slavery that some of the strongest Moslems, such as the Turks, learned "the glory and the blessing and [were] exposed to divine providence."[11] After the Moorish conquest of Spain it was said that thirty thousand Christian slaves were sent to Damascus alone; Suleiman carried off many Austrians as he retreated from Vienna in 1529.

For the first two centuries of the Christian trade in black African slaves, it was common for white Christians themselves to be enslaved by Moslems. St. Vincent de Paul, captured by Barbary pirates, was one of many to suffer such a fate. The Englishman William Atkins described in 1622 how he had been seized by a Moorish captain while a lad. At Salé on the Atlantic coast of North Africa near modern Rabat, he found himself with eight hundred other Christian slaves, Spanish, French, Portuguese, Italian, Irish, Flemish. He wrote of how a French-man who tried to escape was recaptured by his Moslem master, who "first cut off his ears, then slit his nose . . . and lastly drove him naked, thus disfigured, through the streets, for a warning to other slaves not to try to escape."[12] By 1626 more than fifteen hundred English captives alone were held as slaves at Salé.

In Daniel Defoe's great novel, published in 1720, Robinson Crusoe sailed twice from England to Africa in the slave trade before being captured by Moor-ish pirates off Salé in the 1650s, and finding himself transformed from "a mer-chant into a miserable slave" for two years. After he made his escape to Brazil, Crusoe told his fellow merchants of "the manner of trading with the negroes [in Guinea], and how easy it was to purchase upon the coast, for trifles, such as beads, toys, knives, scissars, hatchets, bits of glass, and the like, not only gold dust, Guinea grains, elephants' teeth, &c., negroes, for the service of the Brasils, in great numbers."[13] It was, perhaps, fitting that the ex-slave should have been shipwrecked on his desert island on his subsequent voyage from Brazil to obtain slaves in Africa; but Defoe—and, by extension, Robinson Crusoe himself—was a man of some conscience, a nonconformist, who nonetheless shared the prejudice of the age that the enslavement of blacks, and indeed of whites captured by

Moslems, was natural whereas the degradation of American Indians was unchristian.

Defoe had Crusoe condemn "the conduct of the Spaniards in all their barbarities practis'd in America, where they destroy'd millions of these [Indians], who, however they were idolaters and barbarians, and had several bloody and barbarous rites in their customs, such as sacrificing human bodies to their idols, were yet, as to the Spaniards, very innocent people . . ." He said that "the very name of a Spaniard is reckon'd to be frightful and terrible to all people of humanity, or of Christian compassion. . . ."[14] Crusoe decided not to attack the Indian savages when they came to his island; this was partly because he was outnumbered, but "religion joyn's in with this prudential, and I was convinc'd now in many ways, that I was perfectly out of my duty when I was laying all my bloody schemes for the destruction of innocent creatures, I mean innocent as to me. As to the crimes they were guilty of towards one another, I had nothing to do with them; they were national, and I ought to leave them to the justice of God, who is the governour of nations. . . ."[15]

Yet trafficking in Africans made no impact on Defoe, while Spanish and Portuguese priests were the first to condemn it; and they proved swifter to do so than Protestant clergy would when their countries became involved.* The Dominican theologian Fray Domingo de Soto wrote in 1557 that it was wrong to keep a man in slavery who had been born free, or who had been captured by fraud or violence, even if he was legally bought in a market. The archbishop of Mexico, Alonso de Montúfar, wrote to Philip II a few years later ridiculing the accepted wisdom that distinguished between black and Indian slavery. "We do not know of any just cause why the negroes should be captives any more than the Indians," he argued, "because we are told that they receive the gospel in good will and do not make war on Christians."

Tomás de Mercado described slave ships in 1569 so overcrowded that the smell alone was lethal; he wrote of one on which 129 slaves had died during their first night aboard. He said that all those engaged in the trade risked mortal sin, and he advised them to discuss this with their confessors. Writing four years later, Bartolomé Frías de Albornoz, the first professor of civil law in New Spain, wrote in his book *Arte de los contratos* that it was indeed doubtful whether any captive from war could be legally enslaved. He said that it was a nonsense to pretend that Africans benefited from living as slaves in the Americas, and that the faith could justify kidnap and transportation. He thought it obvious that Christian clergy were too lazy to go to Africa and do their evangelizing there. A Portuguese sea

---

*As early as 1462, Pope Pius II had warned the Portuguese in Guinea that they would be severely punished if they enslaved Christian converts.

captain, Fernão de Oliveira, accused his colleagues of "buying and selling of peaceable freemen as one buys and sells animals" in the spirit of "a slaughterhouse butcher." When he arrived in Brazil in 1580, the Jesuit Fray Miguel Garcia was disgusted to find that the Society of Jesus owned African slaves, and refused to hear the confession of slaveholders. The Portuguese archbishop of the Cape Verde Islands, a major slaving depot, tried to end the traffic and suggested that the blacks should be baptized and then set free.

A figure of noble compassion, the Spanish Jesuit Fray Pedro Claver called himself "the slave of the Negroes." He cared for them at Cartagena de Indias, founded on the Colombian coast as the main slave port for the Spanish empire in the 1530s. Conditions were shocking. Another Jesuit described going into a patio in the town and finding two dead slaves, "stark naked, lying on the bare ground as if they had been beasts, face up, their mouths open and full of flies,"[16] ignored as though they were pieces of scrap paper. By 1616, when Claver began his ministry, ten thousand blacks a year were passing through Cartagena. He went out to the ships as they arrived, entering the slave holds, and "not only brought the captives spiritual comfort but bandaged their wounds and sores"[17] assuring them that their new owners would not boil them down for oil. He carried the sick out on his shoulders. Many had already been baptized on the Gold and Slave Coasts; realizing the superficial nature of African baptisms, priests in America often rechristened slaves upon their arrival and gave them medallions to put around their necks. Claver may have baptized one hundred thousand slaves during his four decades of ministry. Once ashore, he brought them medicine, brandy, lemons, and tobacco in the yards where they were kept until sold. Each spring he toured the plantations and mines. At his death, Indians and blacks held their own mass for him and attributed miracles to him. It was said that when a Spanish grandee struck a slave girl, spilling and breaking the eggs from her basket, Claver touched the broken shells with his staff and made them whole again. When he was canonized, it was as the "saint of the black slaves."

❖ BUT PEOPLE LIKE Claver did not have the power to instigate abolition; the Inquisition condemned Albornoz's book, and Jesuits who complained too openly of slavery were returned to Europe. Protestants showed some early contempt for slavery as a Catholic vice. The Englishman Richard Jobson, visiting the Gambia in the 1600s, told an African merchant who offered him slaves that "we were a people who did not deal in such commodities, neither did we buy or sell one another, or any that had our own shapes." Attitudes changed once the northern Europeans entered the trade. By 1642 the Huguenot synod at Rouen was criticizing the "over-scrupulous persons who thought it unlawful for Protestant merchants to deal in slaves."[18] There is no record of any preacher who, in any sermon, "whether in the cathedral of Saint-André in Bordeaux, or in a Presbyterian meeting-house in Liverpool,"[19] condemned the trade in black slaves.

Quakers became prominent in the trade, with families such as the Wantons, Richardsons, Claypoles, and Framptons sailing from Newport, Rhode Island, and carrying slaves from the West Indies to their own city of Philadelphia. Pennsylvania started to import slaves within three years of its foundation, when 150 Africans were brought in to clear trees and build houses. A ship belonging to the sect, named the *Society* after the Society of Friends, was active; her captain, Thomas Monk, loaded 250 slaves in Africa in 1700 and lost all but twenty-two of them on the return voyage. In England the Quaker gunmaking family of Farmer, and Glaton of Birmingham, which exported thousands of firearms to Africa, financed the slaver *Perseverance* to carry more than five hundred slaves to the West Indies.

Those who objected to the slave trade were considered eccentrics. William Edmundson, a friend of George Fox, the founder of the Society of Friends, wrote from Philadelphia to fellow Quakers describing slavery as an "oppression of the mind" that was incompatible with Christianity. The father of the colony, Roger Williams, retorted that Edmundson was "nothing but a bundle of ignorance and boisterousness." Benjamin Lay, a hunchback originally from Colchester in England who settled in Abington near Philadelphia, campaigned for abolition after seeing a naked slave hanging dead in front of a Quaker house as a warning to runaways. Lay dressed in homemade cloth to avoid using slave-made material and broke coffee cups to discourage the use of sugar. He once lay at the door of the Quaker meetinghouse with one leg bare and half buried in snow: "Ah, you pretend compassion for me, but you do not feel for the poor slaves in your fields who go all winter half-clad." He also filled a sheep's bladder with blood and plunged a sword into it at a Quaker meeting: "Thus shall God shed the blood of those persons who enslave their fellow-creatures." He was ignored. A group of Baptists who wrote home to England to ask how they should treat a brother member of the Church who had castrated his slave received the irritated advice not to risk dissension over "light or indifferent causes."[20]

Concern gradually crept forward, although it was inspired as much by fears of slave revolt as by Christian humanity. "They import so many negroes hither," Colonel William Byrd wrote from his estate near Jamestown in Virginia in 1736, "that I fear this colony will sometime be confirmed by the name of New Guinea." English Protestants by now dominated the traffic, which they called "the attractive African meteor." It largely financed the fine stone houses and elaborate docks of Liverpool. The first recorded slave ship was the *Liverpool Merchant,* which carried 220 slaves to Barbados in 1700. By the middle of the century the city was the largest slave port in Europe, with upwards of thirty-three ships a year sailing for Africa, picking up slaves on the coasts of Sierra Leone, Gabon, and the Cameroons, and selling them in Havana and Cartagena de Indias. The slave trader Foster Cunliffe sent out four or more ships a year; he was three times mayor of the city, a philanthropist who supported schools and infirmaries, described in his church memorial as "a Christian devout and exemplary."

Repeated horrors appalled enlightened opinion. The Dutch ship *Leuden* was stranded by gales on rocks off the coast of Surinam; the crew closed the hatches of the slave decks and escaped with fourteen slaves who had been helping them, leaving 702 others to drown. The Danish vessel *Kron-Printzen* foundered in a storm with the loss of 820 slaves. "Suddenly, the weather closes in," a captain wrote of a storm. "It is then that the din from the slaves, chained to one another, becomes horrible. The clanking of the irons, the moans, the weeping, the cries, the waves breaking over one side of the ship and then the other . . . Many slaves break their legs and their arms, while others die of suffocation."

In 1729 the ship's surgeon, Dr. Thomas Aubrey, recollected that the captain on his ship *Peterborough* had asked, "What the devil makes these plaguey toads die so fast?" Aubrey thought the answer was "inhumanity, barbarity and the greatest of cruelty"; he advised slavers to be as careful of their charges as they would be of white men. "For, though they are heathens," he said, "yet they have a rational soul as well as us; and God knows whether it may not be more tolerable for them in the latter day [of Judgment] than for many who profess to be Christians."[21] The Scottish poet James Thomson, who was given the sinecure of surveyor-general of the Leeward Islands, wrote in his much-read collection *The Seasons* of a shark following a slave ship:

> Lured by the scent
> Of steaming crowds, of rank disease, and death,
> Behold! he, rushing, cuts the briny flood,
> Swift as the gale can bear the ship along . . .

John Newton, later to become vicar of St. Mary's Woolnoth, was captain of the British slave ship *Duke of Argylle* when he wrote his hymn "How Sweet the Name of Jesus Sounds." He admitted that he knew "no method of getting money, not even that of robbing for it upon the highway, which has so direct a tendency to efface the moral sense"[22]; nevertheless, only poor health drove him away from the sea. He read prayers twice a day to his crews, taught himself Latin, read Erasmus, Livy, and Virgil aboard ship, and wrote to his wife of "innumerable dangers and difficulties which, without a superior protection, no man could es-

John Newton was the captain of a British slave ship when he wrote his famous hymn, "How Sweet the Name of Jesus Sounds." He read prayers to his crew twice a day, attributed his survival of a slave rebellion to "the Divine Assistance," and became an Anglican vicar when ill health forced him to retire from the sea. If crews were cruel, he thought it was because "there is no trade in which the seamen are treated with so little humanity."

cape or surmount . . ."[23] He attributed his survival of a slave rebellion on the ship to "the Divine Assistance."

If crews were cruel, it was, Newton thought, because "there is no trade in which seamen are treated with so little humanity." They suffered terribly. "They lie on deck and they die on deck," a former cabin boy on a slaver, James Morley, told a House of Commons inquiry. When he once accidentally broke the captain's glass, "I . . . was tied up to the tiller in the cabin by my hands, and then flogged with the cat, and kept hanging there some time." Deaths were rarely less than a fifth of the crew on each voyage; the *Marie-Gabrielle* of Nantes lost thirty-one sailors out of thirty-nine. On Dutch ships an average of about 18 percent of crews died on each voyage, compared with 12 percent of the slaves. The crews were aboard longer than the slaves, of course; as Newton recorded, the trade "gradually brings a numbness upon the heart and renders those who are engaged in it too indifferent to the sufferings of their fellow-creatures."

By the 1730s, John Wesley and George Whitefield, founders of Methodism, were condemning slave owning as a grave sin that scotched Christ's call for spiritual rebirth—"Verily, verily, I say unto thee, except a man be born anew, he cannot see the Kingdom of God" (John 3:3)—and urged slave owners to go out into the world to preach the gospel. Wesley, who had witnessed slavery firsthand while in Georgia, wrote a popular and influential attack, *Thoughts upon Slavery*. "Do you never feel another's pain?" he wrote of slave captains. "When you saw the flowing eyes, the heaving breasts, or the bleeding sides or tortured limbs of your fellow beings, were you a stone or a brute?" The great appeal of Methodism gave weight to his writing and his conviction that the Holy Spirit would move all true Christians to free their slaves and evangelize them. Congregationalists argued that slavery violated America's covenant with God. "I will not turn away the punishment thereof," preached Samuel Hopkins, capturing the visions of the prophets, "because they have sold the righteous for silver, and the needy for a pair of shoes" (Amos 2:6).

The annual meeting of the Society of Friends in Philadelphia in 1754 took a concrete step toward banning the trade. An open letter was published, referring to Quaker "uneasiness and disunity with the importation and purchasing of negro and other slaves," and stating that "to live in ease and plenty by the toil of those whom violence and cruelty have put in our power" was contrary to Christianity and common justice. John Woolman, a tailor from New Jersey, visited prominent Quaker slaveholders to convince them of the "inconsistency of holding slaves." He wrote powerfully of Christ's warnings against laying up treasures on earth and of the evil of doing violence to strangers: "I was a stranger, and ye took me not in; naked, and ye clothed me not; sick and in prison, and ye visited me not. . . ." (Matt. 24:43). Woolman's Philadelphia friend Anthony Benezet argued that it was extraordinary for the English, a nation "looked upon as generous and humane," to indulge in such oppression and cruelty. In 1758, Philadelphia Quakers agreed with Woolman that no one could keep a slave without risking damnation. English Quakers meeting in London the same year condemned the "iniquitous practice of dealing in negro and other slaves" and threatened to exclude any who did so from positions of authority in the Society. In 1767, Quaker pressure resulted in the first bill against the slave trade being introduced into a legislature, the House of Representatives of Massachusetts. The bill failed, but a substantial duty was placed on the imports of slaves. Maryland put a prohibitive duty of eight pounds a head in 1771. The Rhode Island Assembly banned imports outright and stated that any slave brought in would be freed, although it was too weak to prevent slavers from continuing to operate in Newport.

The American Revolution delayed matters, and it discredited Quakers since they had refused to bear arms against the British. The slavery debate reopened after the war was won. Pennsylvania abolished slavery in 1780 for future generations, although no serving slaves were freed until they reached the age of twenty-eight. Between 1780 and 1804, gradual or qualified acts of emancipation were enacted in New York, New Jersey, and Rhode Island. Upper and Lower Canada, still British, followed suit, although these areas had few slaves. Connecticut abolished the trade in 1788 after pressure from the theologian Jonathan Edwards Jr., the pastor of the White Haven Church at New Haven. Three states,

North and South Carolina and Georgia, continued to regard the trade as legal, however. A bill stating that it would be illegal to bring into the United States any "negro, mulatto or person of colour, as a slave" after January 1, 1808, was passed by the Senate and the House of Representatives, and signed by President Jefferson on March 2, 1807. With the southern states continuing to hold slaves, it was a partial victory.

A sad experiment in returning slaves to Africa was attempted by English idealists. Slaves who had fought for the British in the War of Independence and had been freed and settled in Nova Scotia, a place whose cold climate did not suit them, inspired the "Sierra Leone plan." The London government was persuaded to grant twelve pounds per African for the cost of transporting 290 freed black men and 41 black women to West Africa. A tract of country ten miles by twenty, between the famous slaving rivers Sherbro and Sierra Leone, was bought for sixty pounds from a local chief known as "Tom." The philanthropist Granville Sharp was confident that the community would prosper. Malaria, drink, war with local Africans, rain, and idleness ruined his high-minded ideal. Settlers deserted; some went to work for nearby slave dealers. "I could not have conceived that men who were well aware of the wickedness of slave dealing, and had themselves been sufferers," Sharp wrote in horror from London, "should become so basely depraved as to yield themselves instruments to promote, and extend, the same detestable oppression over their brethren." He was particularly hurt that one Henry Demane, a slave Sharp had rescued from slavery by sending a writ of habeas corpus to a vessel already under sail from Portsmouth to Jamaica, had set himself up as a slave merchant. "King Tom's" successor, King Jemmy, then gave the remaining settlers three days to leave their town, and burned it down. A further attempt was made, and over a thousand blacks from Nova Scotia were settled at Freetown in Sierra Leone; it, too, failed.*

As the world's greatest naval power, the English journey from slaving to abolition was critical. The campaign had an emblem, a medallion by the great potter Josiah Wedgwood, showing a chained Negro on bended knee above the legend, "Am I not a man and a brother?" It had, too, lines by the evangelical poet William Cowper, addressed to the slave trader:

Canst thou, and honour'd with a Christian name,
Buy what is woman-born, and feel no shame?

---

*The United States established its own equivalent of Sierra Leone. A "colonization programme" under the auspices of Henry Clay, then speaker of the House of Representatives, was formed in 1816. In 1820, eighty-six black ex-slaves on the brig *Elizabeth* landed at Sherbro Island sixty miles south of Sierra Leone with the Reverend Samuel Bacon as the government agent. A colony was eventually established in 1823 on the mainland and named Liberia.

Trade in the blood of innocence, and plead
Expediency as a warrant for the deed . . . ?

A young Cambridge graduate, Thomas Clarkson, dropping the idea of a
Church career, helped found the Committee for Effecting the Abolition of the
Slave Trade in London in 1787. He was supported by William Wilberforce, a
brilliant and equally young politician blessed with a fine voice—"the nightingale
of the House of Commons"—and a conviction strengthened by a religious conversion he had undergone on a Continental holiday.

They faced considerable political opposition. Having lost the American
colonies, the British had no wish to offend the powerful West Indian planters
with abolition. The trade was thus separated from the institution. "Slavery itself,
odious as it is," Charles James Fox, gambler, hard drinker, and generous liberal,
told the House of Commons during a debate in 1806, "is not nearly [so] bad a
thing as the slave trade." The latter was made illegal from May 1, 1807. A British
West Africa Squadron was dispatched almost immediately to prevent slaving on
a three-thousand-mile stretch of coast. The perplexed king of the Ashanti on the
Gold Coast asked a British official why Christians no longer wanted to buy slaves.
Was not their God the same as the Moslems', who continued to buy, kidnap, and
sell slaves as they always had? From 1807 to 1870, British ships remained on station off West Africa, intercepting slavers and freeing their cargoes.

❧   THE BRITISH ABOLISHED slavery throughout their possessions in 1833.
The cotton gin made matters more difficult in the United States. In 1792 its cotton exports were an insignificant 138,328 pounds. By 1800, Eli Whitney's invention had increased the figure to 17.7 million pounds; by 1820 it had reached
35 million. With it came a vast new demand for slaves, particularly skilled female
slaves, in the cotton-growing states. Illegal slaving continued through Texas—
Spanish, Mexican, and then independent, until 1846—and at ports in South
Carolina and Spanish Florida.

Southern evangelicals, both Methodist and Calvinist, constructed new biblical arguments to justify Christian slaveholding on the thriving plantations. "A
Scriptural View of Slavery," a sermon of 1856 by Thornton Stringfellow, a Virginia Baptist, held that God sanctioned slavery through Noah and the slave sons
of Ham, the flight of the servant Hagar—"And the angel of the Lord said unto
her, Return to thy mistress and submit thyself under her hands" (Gen. 16:9)—
and the selling of Joseph. He also argued that slavery was in Mosaic Law: "Thou
shalt not covet thy neighbour's . . . manservant, nor his maidservant . . ." (Exod.
20:17), and that Jesus and the apostles recognized slavery as a "lawful institution

among men"; he also quoted St. Paul: "Servants, be obedient unto them that according to the flesh are your masters, with fear and trembling. . . ." (Eph. 6:5). Evangelical abolitionists replied with writings such as Angelina Grimke's *Appeal to the Christian Women of the South* of 1836, in which she said that Hebrew slavery was different in nature and substance from the American and thus she could not justify this newer type. She said that in Mosaic Law, slavery was more limited than in the American chattel slave system, and that Jewish slaves had legal protections lacking in American law: "If thou buy an Hebrew servant, six years he shall serve, and in the seventh he shall go free for nothing" (Exod. 21:2).

Slaves and free blacks in the antebellum period had their own radical vision of evangelical Christianity; they compared themselves with Israelite captives in Egypt, and proclaimed the triumphant Exodus as the destiny of slaves on earth. This inspired some leaders—Gabriel Prosser, Denmark Vesey, and Nat Turner, all Methodists—to lead slave rebellions in the name of God. David Walker's *Appeal to the Coloured Citizens of the World* in 1829 damned slaveholders for not observing the Christian mandate of peace—"The word which he sent unto the children of Israel, preaching good tidings of peace by Jesus Christ" (Acts 10:36)—and called down on them the judgment of the returning Christ: "He that is unrighteous, let him do that unrighteousness still: and he that is filthy, let him be made filthy still. . . . Behold, I come quickly; and my reward is with me, to render to each man according as his work is" (Rev. 22:11–12). Disputes over slavery brought southern and northern Presbyterians, Methodists, and Baptists to schism by 1845, and encouraged the fratricidal Civil War that finally resolved the crisis.

In August 1860 the slave ship *Erie* captained by Nathaniel Gordon was detained by the U.S. Navy ship *Jacinto* after loading nine hundred slaves aboard in the Congo bound for Cuba. The slaves were taken to Liberia, and Gordon was sent to New York for trial. Gordon claimed that he had sold the *Erie* to a Spaniard before the slaves were aboard and that he was merely a passenger. Several seamen gave evidence that Gordon had offered them a dollar a head for each slave safely landed in Cuba. "Do not imagine that because others shared in the guilt of this enterprise, yours is thereby diminished," Judge William Shipman told him as he sentenced him to be hanged. "But remember the awful admonition of your Bible: 'Though hand join in hand, the wicked shall not go unpunished.' " Gordon tried to kill himself with strychnine, but he was hanged in public on February 21, 1862, the "first, and only, North American to be executed for slave trading."[24]

In France, Diderot's great *Encyclopédie* published in 1765 described the slave trade as, "This purchase [of slaves] is a business which violates religion, morality, natural law, and all human rights." Any slave entering France who was baptized was automatically freed. Napoleon revived slavery in 1804, and then abolished it during his "hundred days" in 1815 at the urging of antislaving minister Benjamin Constant.

A law of 1870 in Spain allowed for the liberty of children born to slave families, and for all slaves over age sixty-five. Slaves who fought for Spain in the war against Cuban nationalists were also proclaimed free, but there were still two hundred thousand Cuban slaves at the end of the war. "I will say that we have had 19 centuries of Christianity, and still there are slaves. They only exist in the Catholic countries of Brazil and Spain. . . . Nineteen centuries of Christianity and there are still slaves among Catholic peoples! One century of revolution, and there are no slaves among revolutionary peoples," the great liberal orator Emilio Castelar said as the law was passed. Slavery was not abolished in Puerto Rico until 1873, and in Cuba until 1886.

There were still 1.5 million slaves in Brazil, for the most part on coffee plantations. In 1871, Emperor Dom Pedro took the initiative for *o lei do ventre livre,* under which children born to slave mothers were declared free. State-owned slaves were liberated at once. The final end to slavery in the Americas came in 1890, when the abolitionist minister Rui Barbosa in 1890 issued his famous order for papers in the Ministry of the Treasury relating to slavery and the slave trade to be burned.

Black Africans continued to be enslaved. David Livingstone told audiences in London in 1857 that the European slave trade might be dying, but that of the Arabs in East Africa was growing. At Ségou on the upper Niger, an ancient slaving city 350 miles southwest of Timbuktu, a Frenchman wrote in 1883 of carnage, desolation, and growing slavery. But that was Moslem business. After four hundred years, Christian consciences were clear.

"rock, rock, oh when will thou open, rock?":

Eastern Missions

T he Christians of St. Thomas knew nothing of heresy and the Inquisition when they welcomed Vasco da Gama to the Malabar Coast of
India in 1498. Their Christian community, on a strip of pepper-
producing land between inland mountains and the sea, was among
the oldest on earth. They dated their faith back to a mission made
by the apostle Thomas, and a shrine marked the spot near Madras where they believed he had been martyred. Syrian pepper merchants certainly evangelized the
coast at an early date, and Eusebius recorded that the Alexandrine scholar Pantaenus had preached the gospel "to the heathen in the East . . . as far as India" before his death in about A.D. 190.[1] Their liturgy was in Syriac, and their bishops
had come from the Assyrian Church of the East at Baghdad.

They had been dimly aware that there were other Christians farther to the
west, in Europe, for Dominican friars and an Italian merchant-adventurer had
visited them in the fourteenth century. Vasco da Gama's arrival with a fleet of
sturdy ships suggested that these were powerful men. The Indians thought it a
miracle, and they gave him the symbol of the Christian kingdom they wished to
establish for themselves, a scepter made of a red rod with silver decorations and
three silver bells on top, to take as a gift to his king in Lisbon. The Portuguese had
come as conquerors, however, and the Indians were vulnerable to their newfound
brothers in Christ in a manner alien and inconceivable to them.

The infidels among whom they lived, Moslems and Hindus, were unbaptized and thus beyond the remit of the Inquisition. As Christians, they enjoyed
no such immunity. In time, they became subject to the Catholic bishop of Goa,
Alexis de Menezis. To this former Augustinian hermit, the ancient Malabar faith
was a heretical throwback to the fifth-century Nestorian doctrine of the two Persons, one human and one divine, in the Incarnate Christ. He used the Inquisition

An auto-da-fé is held by the Portuguese Inquisition in Goa. A Christian community had survived on the Malabar Coast of India at least since the fifth century, and conceivably since the first. They had welcomed the first Portuguese explorers as their brothers in Christ. They became subject to the Catholic bishop of Goa, however, who denounced their ancient faith as heresy. He used the Inquisition to purify it.

to purify it. At the Synod of Diamper in 1599, Nestorian errors were denounced, clerical celibacy enforced, the Inquisition and papal supremacy recognized, and the old books and records of Malabar burned. Those who refused were tortured. Loyalists fled inland to mountain fastnesses to continue their rites. They later contacted the Coptic patriarch of Alexandria and, in response to their pleas, he ordained a Syrian priest named Atallah as bishop of India. The seaports were closely guarded; Jesuits seized Atallah when he landed and sent him to Goa. Here he was tried by the Inquisition for heresy and burned. His followers marched to an ancient cross in Cochin; grasping a rope tied to it as a symbol of their sacred vow, they swore "a solemn oath to cast off the Roman yoke, to expel the Jesuits, and to seek a bishop from one of the churches of the East."[2]

The Malabar Christians had yearned for their own kingdom. In its place, the white Christians they had received with such rapture brought them schism, the Inquisition, and the stake, burning them and their precious records for beliefs they thought had been implanted in them by an apostle, and which they had pursued in peaceful innocence for the better part of fifteen hundred years.

✤ MALABAR WAS ALREADY evangelized, and thus exceptional. Elsewhere in the East, long-established faiths, Buddhism, Hinduism, Islam, resisted the sea-borne missionaries. After its capture by Affonso d'Albuquerque, Goa became the main base for the Estado da India, the name the Portuguese gave to all their possessions and trading posts from the Cape of Good Hope and the east coast of Africa to Japan. Early tolerance gave way to the destruction of Hindu and Buddhist temples, the expulsion of holy men, and the banning of traditional marriage and funeral rites as the local population was intimidated into conversion.

This cruelty had a lasting effect in Goa. A friar noted of the converts many years later that they still despised the Portuguese, "not out of hatred to our religion, for by the mercy of God they have become very good Christians, but withal they still have a certain antipathy to us, as is frequently seen." As in Brazil, the power and status that poor whites acquired merely by stepping ashore encouraged greed and vice. The governor in the late 1540s, Dom João de Castro, thought there was a net loss to the faith in India, for "more souls are lost among the Portuguese who come out than are saved among the heathen who are converted by the preachers."

The first Jesuits found that many Indians wished to be baptized, but their motives were hardly reassuring. "I ask them why they want to become Christians," the Jesuit Nicolas Lancilotto wrote to Ignatius Loyola in 1550. "Some reply because the lord of the land tyrannizes and oppresses them, and others reply that they must become Christian because they have nothing to eat." The Portuguese did not catechize or indoctrinate, Lancilotto complained; for fifty years they had conquered and enslaved, and the Indians had converted through fear or for hope of money, or "for other disgusting reasons which I need not mention."

Goa's control over the missionaries in East Africa was nominal. The first Portuguese arrived in Mozambique wishing to break into the gold, ivory, and slave trade of the Arab and Swahili coastal settlements. They were permitted to enslave Moslems because, royal instructions to the viceroy Francisco de Almeida stated, "They are the enemies of our Holy Catholic Faith and we have continual war with them." At the end of the sixteenth century, Fray João dos Santos reported from the Querimba Islands that there were still converts who remembered the "cruelty with which they used the natives who did not want peace and friendship with them, and whom they punished so severely." Dos Santos tried to stamp out Moslem practices among his parishioners, damning the "pernicious practice" of Moslem women visiting Christian women on Sundays and saints' days, when they "sang, danced and feasted together as if they were all Moslems." Dos Santos's successors were less rigorous, and the Inquisition at Goa denounced the "rites, ceremonies and superstitious abuses" that grew up there. Fray João de Menezes ignored all orders from Goa—including several to return—and ran the islands as a personal fief. He traded contraband and sired numerous sons. Fray Pedro da Trinidada, his colleague on the mainland, though apparently celibate, owned great estates and traded slaves and ivory with chiefs as far inland as Mashonaland. Both these friars maintained personal armies of freemen and slaves.

Purer souls were attracted to the East, of course. Francis Xavier sailed from Lisbon on the first Jesuit mission to India aboard the big galleon *Santiago* in 1541. He took nothing with him but a few books and some coarse clothing. A courtier advised him to take a servant, since it was beneath the dignity of a papal nuncio to do his own washing. "Sir, it was that dignity that reduced the Church of Rome to its present state," Xavier replied. "The best way of acquiring real dignity is to wash one's own underwear." He was a handsome and breezy soul, and he set about his mission with gusto after landing at Goa after a long passage the following year.

Xavier baptized entire communities of Parava fisherfolk during his three years on the Coromandel Coast. He evangelized alone and without an interpreter; his methods seemed superficial, but his enthusiasm was catching, and his converts persisted with their new faith. "You can imagine the exhortations I am able to make, since they do not understand me and I understand them even less," he wrote. "I baptize the newborn who are brought to me; for that, there is absolutely no need of an interpreter." Xavier arrived at a very rough translation of basic prayers in Tamil, which he taught local boys to learn by heart and to teach the adults. On Sundays he assembled all the people of a village. "I give out the First Commandment, which they repeat, and then . . . we recite the Pater Noster together . . . and an Ave Maria, and proceed in the same manner through each of the remaining nine Commandments," he wrote.[3] He was soon restlessly on the move, to Japan and greater targets than simple fishermen. By the end of the century, however, Christianity was firmly embedded among the Paravas. They were gathered into sixteen large villages, each with a Jesuit resident; no Parava catamaran sailed on Sundays, and part of each Friday's catch had to be given to the Church.

The Jesuits had brief hopes of converting the Moguls, the masters of northern India who had swept down from the crags and valleys of Afghanistan in 1526. The emperor Akbar the Great, who came to the throne thirty years later, was a ruler of genius. He took Bengal, Kashmir, Sind, and Kandahar, controlling India to an extent unmatched until the British raj. Liberal and sympathetic, he abolished slavery, permitted widows to remarry, and restricted polygamy. The Moguls were Moslem, but Akbar had a lively interest in all religions, and constructed the Ubadat Khana as a meeting place for scholars and theologians. He was developing his own concepts in the Din Illahi, the "divine faith," and invited the Jesuits to come to his court from Goa. The potential prize, the conversion of the grandest ruler in the East, was tremendous. Father Rudolf Aquaviva arrived at Akbar's court in 1580. The emperor enjoyed Jesuit company, and two further missions were sent. The emperor proved too wedded to his Din Illahi, though he borrowed Christian baptism for it; after his death in 1605, Jesuits continued to reside at the Mogul court for almost two hundred years, but their influence was slight.

Brahmans, the priestly caste of Hinduism, enjoyed a deep social and religious influence. Roberto de Nobili, a young Jesuit recently arrived in India, believed that a missionary might acquire the same prestige and credibility by adopting Brahman customs and etiquette. He dressed in the saffron robe of the Brahman ascetic, with shaven head and earrings, and wore a white veil on his shoulders with a cord around his neck, the sign of the Brahman and rajah castes, from which he hung a small cross. Eating a vegetarian diet of rice and herbs, he lived in a turf hut and was recognized by the Brahmans themselves as a holy man. His Brahman converts continued to wear the sacred thread and celebrate Hindu feasts. De Nobili respected Hindu taboos on caste. He allowed no outcaste to touch him and, when administering the sacrament to a convert of lower caste, offered the Host at the end of a short stick. Pandarams or go-betweens were allowed to mix with the lower castes, and de Nobili created Catholic pandarams so as to reach the poor. He allowed a Brahman flavor to remain in worship; gradually, he wrote, "we cut out these superstitious ceremonies and replace them with Christian prayers." De Nobili's mission was thriving—one of his pandarams baptized twenty-five hundred converts in three years—but fellow Europeans were scandalized. De Nobili was brought before the court of the archbishop of Goa in 1618, appearing in his Brahman dress. The "case of the Malabar rites" was referred to Rome, but for the moment at least the pope refused to condemn him.

A Protestant chaplain accompanied the ambassador of the British East India Company to the Mogul court in 1616. The English and Dutch clergy ministered almost entirely to their own merchants and traders, however, and the trading companies were often hostile to missionaries, fearing that interference with Indian beliefs would be harmful to commerce. A Bengali boy was brought to England in 1614 and baptized as Peter with the curiously non-Protestant surname of Pope. No other baptism of an Indian into the Church of England was recorded throughout the century,[4] and it was two hundred years before the first Anglican bishop in India was appointed at Calcutta. The first Protestant missionaries to India were German pietists serving Frederick IV, the Danish king. Pietism was a semimystical Lutheranism, and the aim of its adherents was to reach a state of true piety through penance, grace, and spiritual rebirth. Its followers met in devotional circles for prayers and Bible reading, and many pietists had a strong sense of the imminence of Christ's Second Coming, believing that an outpouring of the Spirit on Jews and heathens would precede it. This stirred a missionary zeal, and the interest of Frederick, who wished to evangelize the Indians in the small Danish enclave of Tranquebar on the Coromandel Coast.

A young pietist, Bartholomäus Ziegenbalg, arrived in Tranquebar in 1705. His methods remain a basis for Protestant missions. He rejected mass conversions, aiming to instill personal conviction in the individual, a more arduous but deeper process; he studied Indian religions in detail in order to have a better grasp of local beliefs. He held that all Christians must be able to read the Word of God, and in their own language, so he opened a school to encourage literacy. Unlike Xavier, he learned the difficult nuances of classical Tamil, and he had translated the New Testament and the Old as far as the Book of Ruth when he died. At Ziegenbalg's death in 1719, the Tranquebar Christians numbered only 350. His work had lasting quality, however. The first Indian pastor, named Aaron, was ordained in 1733; a Hindu convert, he already had fifteen years of experience as a catechist, and he and other carefully chosen pastors proved to be loyal and effective. As English influence grew, the Tranquebar missionaries were financed by the Anglican Society for Promoting Christian Knowledge to evangelize and serve the British communities elsewhere in India. The most remarkable of these was Christian Friedrich Schwartz, who became chaplain to the East India Company, and *Diwan,* or chief minister, to the rajah of Tanjore, creating a Church of the English Rite, though he was a German and was never ordained an Anglican. The first English missionary did not arrive until 1793, aboard a Danish ship, since the company banned missionaries from sailing on East Indiamen.

❖ XAVIER AND OTHERS set their eyes farther east, sailing from Goa for Japan, a place of which they knew little beyond the hearsay Marco Polo had picked up in China more than two hundred years before. It was, Polo wrote with some accuracy, a great island "towards the East in the high seas" whose people were "civilized and well-favored . . . idolaters and dependent on nobody." Gilding the lily, he had gone on to claim that the pavements of its great Palace "are entirely of gold, in plates like slabs of stone . . ." The first Europeans to see the mysterious land were Portuguese sailors, driven far off course by violent storms in 1542. Six years later Xavier met a renegade in Goa named Yajiro who had fled from Japan after killing a man. Yajiro said that, if Xavier succeeded in answering the innumerable questions which he would be asked, and if he were observed to live in perfect harmony with his beliefs over several months, then "the king, the

Ceremony of TREADING on the CRUCIFIX, and other IMAGES, at the beginning of the Year, in Nagasaki, the Imperial City of Japan.

Suspects tread on crucifixes at Nagasaki in Japan to prove that they are not Christians. Between 1614 and 1646, 4,045 proven martyrdoms took place in Japan. A group of seventy at Yedo was crucified upside-down on the beach at low water, to drown as the tide came in. The country was closed to all foreigners, traders as well as priests, in 1638. A group of Jesuits who landed secretly in 1648 were uncovered and tortured to death.

nobility and all other people of discretion would become Christians, for the Japanese are entirely guided by the law of reason."[5]

Xavier landed at Kagoshima, Yajiro's hometown, in August 1549. He was fortunate. Japan was temporarily open to foreigners; central rule had collapsed, and some 250 daimyos, or local lords, disputed regional power between themselves. They were eager to trade, particularly for cannon and guns. In the winter of 1550–51, Xavier was able to trek for six hundred miles on foot to visit the Mikado, bringing him gifts of a clock, an arquebus, glass decanters, and some mirrors. Xavier was charmed and impressed; he thought that "we will never find among heathens another race equal to the Japanese," finding them "men of honor to a marvel," intelligent, eager for knowledge, and "very fond of hearing about the things of God." They were not a blank page, like the simple fishermen of southern India; Christianity had to coexist with their existing civilization, and there was no question of attempting mass conversions. Xavier concentrated on the daimyos in creating three small groups of converts during his twenty-seven months in Japan.*

The first daimyo to be baptized was Omura Sumitada in 1563. His subjects followed his lead, and by 1575 the majority of the fifty thousand people in his region were Christian. Although they thought of their visitors as barbarians, the Japanese were fascinated by European mechanical skills and ordnance. Non-Christian nobles tolerated the Jesuits, who organized a Portuguese trade through Macao. The "visitor" responsible for the eastern missions, Alessandro Valignano, went over the head of the local "superior" to insist that they wear silk, since cotton was the mark of the poor. Valignano sent four young nobles from Kyushu with a Jesuit tutor on the hazardous journey to Europe, where Philip II and Pope Gregory XIII received them. A seminary was opened to train Japanese for the priesthood. There were more than 200,000 baptized converts and 240 churches by 1587.

That year, however, Hideyoshi, the powerful regent who was reimposing centralized control, ordered the expulsion of all foreigners. The edict was specifically aimed at removing the "devilish" influence of the padres. It was only fitfully enforced, but the arrival of Dutch and Spanish ships heightened suspicions of European motives. The Spanish, sailing from the Philippines, came with Franciscans and Dominicans and claimed that Japan lay under their influence under the 1493 papal division. The pilot of a Spanish galleon wrecked on the Japanese coast in 1596 revealed the extent of Spanish conquests in the Americas and the use made of missionaries in converting the natives. Japanese fears that priests were the reconnaissance arm of an invasion had some basis. A fanciful evangelistic plan for the invasion of China had been mooted by the Jesuit Alonso Sánchez, and the bishop of Manila had told Philip II that: "Not even Julius Caesar nor Alexander the Great ever had such an opportunity as this; and on the spiritual plane, nothing greater was ever projected since the time of the apostles."[6] In 1596, twenty-six Japanese converts were crucified at Nagasaki, the main Christian town, on suspicion of treason. Tensions continued among the Europeans. When the English pilot Will Adams arrived in the port of Bungo in 1600, jealous Portuguese traders had him flung in prison. He earned his release by building two fine ships for Ieyasu, the first of the Tokugawa shoguns who were to be the effective rulers of Japan for the next 250 years. Adams was released with the rank of samurai and, "living like unto a lordship in England," warned his shogun patron of Catholic machinations. Nonetheless, the first Japanese Jesuits were ordained in 1601.

---

*One of the greatest of Christian missionaries, to whom the Jesuits attributed seven hundred thousand conversions, he returned to Goa in January 1552 after leaving Japan. He then sailed for China, but fell ill and died in December on the miserable island of Sancian, modern Changchuan, south of Canton. His body was brought back to Goa and enshrined in the Church of the Good Jesus.

The fury broke in 1614. Ieyasu ruled that the "Kirishitan band" of foreigners had come not only to trade, but also with priests "longing to spread an evil law, to overthrow true doctrine, so that they may . . . obtain possession of the land."[7] This was the "germ of a great disaster," Ieyasu said, and it was to be crushed by banishment of all priests and the banning of Christianity. It was almost impossible for a European to remain in the country undetected, but twenty-seven Jesuits, fifteen friars, and five secular clergy disguised themselves and remained to suffer with their converts. The first to be discovered, a Jesuit and a Dominican at Omura, were beheaded; the remainder were usually burned alive, taken to their martyrdom with bits in their mouths to prevent them from preaching.

As to the Japanese Christians, they were slowly boiled in cauldrons, hung upside down over pits of excrement to bleed to death from head wounds, or, as happened to a group of seventy at Yedo, crucified upside down on the beach at low water to drown as the tide came in. Between 1614 and 1646, 4,045 proven martyrdoms took place. Apostasy was encouraged. After a peasant rebellion in Shimabara, only those captives who declared themselves Christian were executed. From 1623, as in the Roman Empire, magistrates in many districts insisted that everyone produce a paper each year to certify membership of a Buddhist sect. Suspects were obliged to soil a likeness of Christ or the Virgin with their feet. The

It was ruled in 1614 that the "Kirishitan band" of foreigners in Japan had come not only to trade, but also with priests "longing to spread an evil law, to overthrow true doctrine, so that they may . . . obtain possession of the land." This was said to be the "germ of a great disaster," and was to be crushed by banishment of all priests and the banning of Christianity. Those who remained in the country were crucified when they were discovered. Twenty-three were martyred on September 10, 1622.

country was closed to all foreigners, traders as well as priests, in 1638. A group of Jesuits who landed secretly in 1648 was uncovered and tortured to death. Persecution was not relaxed; its intent was to eradicate the religion in its entirety, and 486 Japanese Christians were executed or died in prison at Bungo between 1660 and 1691, long after the first wave.

Yet, when Commodore Perry and his black ships reopened Japan to foreigners two centuries later, there were still Christians in Japan. Some women warily approached a Catholic missionary, Father Petitjean, when he was allowed to enter Japan in 1859. They asked him questions about the Virgin and the "king of the doctrine," the pope. In Nagasaki and Okuma and the Goto Islands, secret communities had kept the faith, each led by two men, one a baptizer, the other saying prayers on Sundays and consoling the dying. There were at least twenty thousand of them; many, having declared themselves, were deported until granted liberty of worship in 1890.

❧ "ROCK, ROCK," VALIGNANO exclaimed as he gazed at the immensity of China from Macao in 1579, "oh when will thou open, rock?" Christians had been in China until the coming of the Ming dynasty had destroyed them two hundred years before; a brilliant Ming emperor, Wan-li, remained in power in Peking. Francis Xavier had died of fever on an island in the estuary of the Canton River in 1552, waiting for permission to land on the mainland that had not come. Since then the Portuguese had established a trading post on the desolate estuary islands and the small promontory of Macao; their ships moored off during the three-month trading season, and in 1583, Matteo Ricci was allowed to live in the provincial capital of Chao-ch'ing.

Ricci, a thirty-one-year-old Italian Jesuit, was a skilled mathematician and linguist. He anticipated de Nobili by transforming himself, as best he could, into a Mandarin-speaking Chinese. He wore a dark red silk gown with pale blue embroidered lapels, and a red sash and embroidered silk shoes; he plaited his hair and learned the elaborate flatteries that marked the etiquette of the Middle Kingdom. He petitioned the imperial court for authority to visit Peking, writing that he desired to "live out my life as one of your Majesty's subjects"; he promised to share his knowledge of geography, geometry, and arithmetic, adding humbly that his methods were "entirely in keeping with ancient Chinese methods."[8] He arrived in the capital in January 1601.

Wan-li took a liking to the Jesuit. Ricci presented the emperor with a clock that chimed the hours and drew a map of the world for him, with China in its center and scriptural texts in the blank spaces; in return he was allowed to build a church and a Jesuit house within the "pink walls" of the compound for high officials. His reputation among learned Chinese increased when he persuaded Rome to send the astronomer Sebastiano de Ursis to Peking to set about reforming the calendar. Ricci claimed to have converted two thousand Chinese in a letter written to Aquaviva, the Jesuit general, in 1605; of these, three hundred were in Peking, "literate and good Christians." Progress was slow, he admitted; the "time in which we live in China is not one of harvest," but he was gaining local novices to carry on the work, and three of his converts founded important new missions, Paul Hsu in Shanghai, Michael Yang in Chekiang, and Leo Li in Hangchow.

Ricci wrote an introduction to *Catholicism, A True Doctrine of the Lord of Heaven,* which was translated from Chinese into Manchurian, Korean, and Japanese. He kept as close to Chinese thought as possible; "we neither speak nor eat nor drink nor live except in the Chinese manner," he told Aquaviva.[9] He used the Confucian term *t'ien chu,* "lord of heaven," for God, and accepted that Christians could follow rites held in honor of Confucius and their ancestors since these had no purpose beyond thanking Confucius for "the excellence of his doctrine" and were required by imperial law. At Ricci's death in 1610 the emperor provided an honored funeral for him.

Jesuit scientific skills served the Chinese well. The Chinese calendar needed accurate astronomy to divine lucky and unlucky days. In 1622 the great German astronomer and Jesuit Johann Adam Schall arrived in Peking. He predicted eclipses in 1623 and 1624 where Chinese experts had failed. Christian prestige soared; some called it the "religion of the great Schall." He was appointed director of the imperial observatory and minister of state of the board of mathematics. His ancestors were ennobled and he was given the title of "master of the mysteries of heaven." A purist might doubt that a Jesuit should be a state minister responsible for good or ill fortune; but the Jesuit calendar, refined by Schall's Flemish colleague Ferdinand Verbiest, remained in use well into the twentieth century. The Jesuits survived the fall of Peking to the Manchu dynasty in 1644, and by 1650 there were Christian congregations in the major cities. The number of converts was put as high as 150,000, although this figure is likely to include the many children who were baptized at death.[10] Quick-tempered, active, writing copiously on Chinese arithmetic and geometry, building a cannon foundry, Schall stirred jealousies and in 1664 was condemned to death for allegedly preparing an invasion of China. An earthquake, a fire in the imperial palace, and the appearance of a comet were taken to be signs of heavenly disapproval of his sentence. Schall was reprieved, dying a natural death the following year, but his five Chinese assistants were executed, and the thirty-five foreign priests in the country were taken to Canton to await expulsion.

Four Jesuits were allowed to remain at Peking. Ferdinand Verbiest struck up

a close friendship with the young emperor K'ang-hsi based on their mutual interests in science and astronomy. Verbiest was appointed to Schall's old position
at the board of mathematics, and he perfected the foundry, dedicating the cannon in stole and surplice with the name of a Christian saint engraved on each.
"The Europeans are very quiet; they do not excite any disturbances," the grateful
K'ang-hsi ruled. "We decide therefore that all temples dedicated to the Lord of
heaven . . . ought to be preserved, and that it may be permitted to all who wish
to worship this God to enter these temples, offer him incense and perform the
ceremonies practiced by the Christians."[11] Franciscans and Dominicans were also
active in China. Among their converts was a young peasant, Lô, who was raised
to the priesthood after studying in Manila, taking a European name as Gregorio
Lopéz. In 1674 he was appointed bishop and vicar apostolic for northern China,
the first Chinese Catholic bishop, and the last until the twentieth century.

Lô's elevation brought to a head the fractiousness that haunted even the most
remote Christian outposts. The faith had disappeared without trace from China
before; a Jesuit searching for remnants of the Franciscan's fourteenth-century
mission reported that "during these thirty years we have gone about all China . . .
without having been able to obtain our purpose in the least. . . ."[12] Its tenuous
reestablishment was threatened once more. In 1615, Pope Paul V had granted a
number of "permissions" on Chinese liturgy at Jesuit request. Mass could be said
with the head covered, and in Chinese, and the Bible could be translated into
Mandarin. The Jesuits had broadened this to allow converts to continue with the
cult of Confucius and their ancestors; as well as *t'ien chu* for "lord of heaven,"
Ricci had accepted that the word *sheng*, or "holy," was a term of veneration that
could be used of Confucius. These "Chinese rites" shocked Dominicans and
Franciscans. They argued that *t'ien* meant the physical heavens or "sky" in Chinese, and that the Jesuits were promoting a pagan God; Blaise Pascal, seeing a
stick with which to beat the Jesuits, said that they "have allowed Catholics to
practice idolatry itself." Papal reactions to this, and to de Nobili's Malabar rites in
India, were confused. In 1645, Innocent X condemned Confucian ceremonies,
but in 1656, Alexander VII, who supported the Jesuits against Pascal's Jansenists,
ruled that the rites were inoffensive. In 1669, Clement IX condemned them
afresh.

Under the original permission, Lô continued to use Chinese in the liturgy.
The three Chinese he ordained as priests, however, either under pressure or because they wished to save face by not appearing ignorant, said mass in Latin. Father Philipucci, who assisted at a mass said by one of them in 1688, noted the
disastrous effects. "He sweated, was in agony of mind, and those present were
equally put out and irritated," he wrote. "God knows how many faults and mis-
takes he made, all hot and bothered as he was, reciting parrot-like what he could

not understand."[13] Candidates for the priesthood were now sent to a seminary at Ayuthia in Siam, which served Vietnamese, Koreans, Japanese, Burmese, and Indians as well as Chinese. They were instructed in Latin, the only common language, but one they did not share with their congregations, for whom the Latin liturgy was meaningless. A convert did not have to understand every word of his new religion. Islam managed well enough despite the Arabic language and script of the Koran. Its expansion was spontaneous, however, in the sense that it had no corps of professional missionaries and no central command; it traveled light, where the Christian evangelist was freighted with theological dispute and the distant demands of Rome.

The use of *t'ien* and the honoring of ancestors were forbidden by the all-China vicar apostolic, Lô's superior, in 1693. The Jesuits responded by asking K'ang-hsi to comment on the offending rites. The emperor wrote a kindly statement, confirming that Confucius was not praised as a god but as a wise philosopher, that the respects paid to ancestors were no more than affectionate remembrances of the departed and their lives, and that sacrifices to *t'ien* were made not to the visible sky but to the Supreme Lord.[14] The Jesuits sent the statement to Rome. It was rejected. Clement XI condemned the veneration of Confucius and the placing of offerings on the graves of ancestors in a decree in November 1704. The pope sent a special legate to the East to enforce it, Charles Maillard de Tournon, a tactless and sickly young aristocrat. He arrived in Peking in December 1705 to the anger of the emperor who, though fond enough of the respectful Jesuits at his court, was outraged that an obscure foreign dignitary such as the pope should claim sovereignty over his Christian subjects and seek to treat him as an equal.

Expelling Tournon to lick his wounds in Macao, the emperor issued a counter-edict in 1706. All missionaries who wished to remain in China were ordered to report to Peking. Those who swore to accept the rules laid down by Ricci on Chinese rites were issued with a *p'iao,* an imperial document entitling them to toleration. Recalcitrants were deported. Four bishops and scores of missionaries took the oath. From Macao, Tournon declared that all who accepted the *p'iao* were excommunicated; a later papal bull laid down that the permissions won by Ricci must be treated "as though they had never existed" and condemned them as "detestable" and "superstitious."

The Church went into free fall. The emperor Yung Chêng declared in 1724 that he was prepared to tolerate the missionaries at court in Peking—"they are useful for the calendar" he noted—but not in the provinces, where they attracted the "ignorant" to churches where "men and women assemble together indiscriminately." They were to be sent to Macao and their churches closed. "How can one write in the overpowering sadness of this hour?" Father de Mailla grieved from

Peking in 1724. "The thing we feared all these years has at last come upon us. Our holy religion has been entirely banished from this land . . . the churches have been demolished, or put to profane uses; edicts are published commanding the Christians, under threats of rigorous punishment, to renounce their faith, and forbidding anyone to embrace it. . . ."[15] Only in Peking did churches remain open, while the remaining fathers endeavored to stay in favor by advising on the calendar and diplomacy. It was recorded in 1743 that forty thousand Christians were still in the city, and a thousand baptisms were performed that year. Secret evangelism continued in the provinces, made more dangerous by a decree of the emperor Ch'ien Lung in 1746 that approved the decapitation of Christians "persisting in their errors"; but, in round terms, the mission to China had foundered.

VIETNAM GAVE THE measure of what individual courage and clarity could achieve. The formidable Jesuit Alexander de Rhodes, finding Japan closed to missionaries when he arrived in Macao in 1623, sailed west for southern Vietnam instead. Like Ricci, he sought to adapt the Church to Vietnamese life and culture. A linguist of genius, he mastered Vietnamese and succeeded in writing the popular language in the Latin alphabet reinforced with five signs. His method was adopted, and remains, as the national script. His frequent expulsions—from Cochin China in the south, Tonkin in the north, and then from Sinoa, modern Hue in central Annam—convinced him of the need to form a "company of catechists" to keep the faith in being when priests were imprisoned or deported.

This lay brotherhood lived in community and took three vows: to remain celibate, to pay alms and gifts into a common pool, and to obey the superior appointed by the missionary. Rhodes taught them basic medicine as a way of gaining public trust, and the fortitude to persist and evangelize despite the area's lack of priests. His own expulsion in 1645 was, to say the least, definitive; the decree stated that the captain of any ship that brought Rhodes back to Vietnam would be decapitated, and two of his catechists were executed as proof of the ruler's earnest. Yet Christianity spread with formidable speed. By 1658, a year in which only two priests were in Vietnam, and being hunted at that, it was claimed that there were three hundred thousand Christian Vietnamese. No doubt this was exaggerated; but the first Vietnamese priests were ordained ten years later, and despite constant persecution that accounted for many thousands of lives, the true number of Christians climbed well above the quarter million mark in the next century.

Empire and conquest made it physically easier to spread the faith, of course; the native peoples were in no position to expel missionaries and were liable to harsh punishment if they harmed them. The Eastern rulers were rightly suspicious that a colonizing army might follow the cross; French missionaries encouraged Paris to intervene against the persecution of Vietnamese Christians, and in 1884 this culminated in the country becoming a French colony with local society dominated by the Catholics of Tonkin. The early Protestant missions beyond India were equally based on empire. Between 1619 and 1658 the Dutch took Malacca, Ambon, Java, and Ceylon, founding Batavia and hanging in its new church the bells stolen by Dutch raiders from the Catholic cathedral in Puerto Rico. Ministers were trained in Leyden for service in the Dutch East India Company. Their first duty was to provide for Dutch employees, but they also received a cash bonus for each native they baptized. The numbers were impressive since local Christians were given political and trading privileges. By 1700 the Dutch were claiming to have 100,000 Christians on Java and 40,000 in Ambon. Not one in ten ever attended Communion,[16] however, and although the New Testament was translated into Malay in 1668, the first in any Southeast Asian language, only a handful of the ministers in the Dutch territories could speak it. Conversion was shallow. Ministers were sent to Taiwan after the island was partially wrestled from the Spanish in 1624, and a church was established. It evaporated when Chinese pirates expelled the Dutch in 1661.

The rapid and almost total conversion of the Philippines was undertaken by friars with colonial experience in Mexico. Priests sailing with the explorer Ferdinand Magellan in 1521 carried out the first baptisms on Cebu; the archipelago was conquered by Spain in 1565. Augustinian friars arrived with the conquerors, to be joined by Franciscans, Dominicans, and Jesuits. Islam was not firmly rooted enough to withstand a mission financed and controlled by the Spanish crown, although small groups of Moslems persisted in the south. In 1585, four hundred thousand converts were claimed, and by 1620 the figure had climbed to two million. The Filipinos had a flamboyance to their faith. When news came to Manila of the beatification of Loyola in 1609, a lifesize and jeweled statue of him was placed above the high altar of the Jesuit church, and fireworks burst from the tower while figures staggered into the square below, halt, maimed, and blind until they cried the saint's name and leapt to their feet in a sword dance. At Easter, crowds of flagellants competed in penitence,* and in celebration of the faith's one unalloyed triumph in the East.

---

*Despite such enthusiasm, native priests remained sharply inferior to the rich Spanish clergy, and the first Filipino bishop, in a country of sixty dioceses, was not appointed until 1905, after control had been ceded by Spain to the United States.

CHAPTER XXVIII

"The Lord make it Like new engLand":

Protestant America

The settlement of North America was a reward for Pentecost, for the wild dynamic of the faith, for its splits and persecutions. To those untouched by the Holy Spirit it was a desperate place, a "wildernesse among savages and wild beasts" an English pamphleteer wrote in 1633, so bleak that, when offered transportation or the rope, "divers malefactors have chosen to be hanged than go to Virginia."[1] It had no instantly exploitable assets, no sugarcane, spices, sandalwood, or gemstones; its gold lay three thousand miles and 250 years beyond the grasp of those who first sought it on the eastern seaboard. Few found fortune, and some were ruined; the rich idealist William Penn was flung into the Fleet Street debtors' prison in 1708 for his American debts and died in penury and self-pity.

The passage from England could take three months if the winds were unfavorable and seldom lasted less than seven weeks. It was all "smells, fumes, horror, vomiting," an emigrant wrote of a crossing from Cowes for Philadelphia, "fever, dysentery, headaches, constipation, boils, scurvy, cancer, mouth-rot and similar afflictions." Young children were at particular risk; thirty-two of them perished among the five hundred passengers on his ship, and their bodies were thrown overboard to "be devoured by the predatory fish of the ocean." A pregnant woman who died in labor during a storm was pushed out through a porthole because she was far back in the stern and could not be brought on deck.

Yet respectable men chose to inflict upon themselves and their wives and children a fate that criminals turned down at gallows-point. A divine compulsion drove them to transplant their faith to a place where it could flourish and remain pure, isolated from the taunts and persecutions of the established churches in their native lands. America was their Jerusalem, and their pilgrimage to it through the storms and terrors of the North Atlantic had echoes of the Cru-

John Winthrop was a man of parts in England, a Cambridge-educated lawyer, from a family of prosperous Suffolk clothiers. He abandoned this to sail on the *Arbella* to become the governor of the tiny Bay Colony of no more than 700 souls. He helped organize the United Provinces of New England in 1643. "We shall find the God of Israel is among us," he said proudly after the foundation of Boston, "that man shall say of succeeding plantations: the Lord make it like New England."

sades.* To the Massachusetts settler Edward Johnson, America was the place where "the Lord will create a new Heaven, and a new Earth, new Churches and a new Commonwealth."[2] John Winthrop was a man of parts in England, Cambridge-educated, a lawyer, a member of a prosperous family of Suffolk clothiers. All this he happily abandoned in 1630 to become governor of the tiny Bay Colony of no more than seven hundred like-minded souls. "We shall find the God of Israel is among us," he said proudly after the foundation of Boston, "that man shall say of succeeding plantations: the Lord make it like New England."[3]

They were to come, sometimes as complete congregations, from almost all of Europe's whirligig of sects, each convinced that its variant was the true faith: English Quakers and recusants, Salzburg Lutherans, German Baptists, French Huguenots, Irish Catholics, Moravian Brethren, Russian Old Believers, Swiss Amish. The process continued into the twentieth century, but its pattern was established by the *Mayflower* group of 1620 and confirmed by the Bay colonists a decade later.

A background of active European persecution was common; the *Mayflower* settlers were liable to imprisonment as separatists from the Church of England who refused to conform to the Book of Common Prayer. Typical, too, was a sense

---

*The "pilgrim fathers" derive from the use of "pilgrims" by John Winthrop to describe the early settlers. He did so with reference to a passage in Hebrews: "These all died in faith, not having received the promises, but having seen them and greeted them from afar, and having confessed that they were strangers and pilgrims on the earth" (Heb. 11:13).

of furious urgency, of a "reformation without tarrying for any" which flowed from a desire to protect the young. The heads of the *Mayflower* families had first fled to Leyden in Holland. Here they saw their children tempted from puritanism by the "great licentiousness of the youth of that countrie," their pastors explained, some becoming soldiers and sailors, others "tending to dissolutnes and the danger of their soules." However dangerous it might be to expose children to the ocean and the unknown, if it were not done, then "their posteritie would be in danger to degenerate and be corrupted," a fate far worse.⁴ Winthrop also feared that the young, "even the best witts and of faierest hopes," were being "perverted, corrupted and utterlie overthrowne" by the state of religion in England. The faithful, he thought, had "noe place lefte to flie into but the wildernesse."⁵

Emigration was an act of faith in itself. "We veryly beleeve and trust the Lord is with us," the Leyden pastors wrote, "and that he will graciously prosper our indeavours according to the simplicitie of our harts therin."⁶ Winthrop thought it evident that the Bay Colony was God's "great worke in hand" because he "hath stirred up to encourage his servants to this Plantation." Such confidence in the divine purpose was a necessity, to pit against the enormity of the undertaking, and it was the mark of the religious emigrant.

So, of course, was the search for freedom of conscience. Those on the *Mayflower* "desired to injoye the ordinances of God in their puritie, and the libertie of the gospell with them" far from the prisons of England.⁷ But they did not necessarily wish to see this toleration extended to others. In his list of the motivations of the Bay Colony Protestants, Winthrop gave pride of place to the desire "to raise a Bulworke against the kingdome of Ante-Christ which the Jesuites labour to reare up in those parts."⁸

Such loathing did not prevent Catholics from becoming in time the largest single denomination in America; and the fact that the settlers hailed from many different traditions lies at the heart of American Christianity. No established Church dominated it in colonial days. At independence, the Constitution declared that "no religious test shall ever be required as a qualification to any office or public trust in the United States." The First Amendment of 1791 added that "Congress shall make no law respecting an establishment of religion, or prohibiting the free exercise thereof." The separation of Church and state was a revolutionary departure from European practice; for an overwhelmingly Christian country not to proclaim its faith was unique.

MANY EARLY SETTLERS regarded such a laissez-faire attitude toward religion as damnable and dangerous. The Word of God, so the colony of New Haven affirmed, was "the onely rule to be attended unto in ordering the affayres of government."⁹ Anglicans and Congregationalists argued over the interpretation of God's will, but both agreed that they should be governed by it and reacted violently to those who insisted on toleration and individual choice.

A mother and midwife, Anne Hutchinson, was accused of "troubling the peace" of Massachusetts by exalting direct contact with the Holy Spirit as a truth above that of the Bible, and denying that good works are a sign of salvation. The governor, Sir Henry Vane, who strongly disliked the Calvinist system of state-enforced discipline, tried to defend her and clashed so bitterly that he was forced to resign and return to England. Winthrop was reelected governor, and Anne Hutchinson was tried in front of him in 1637.

She was asked how she knew that it was the Spirit that spoke to her. "How did Abraham know that it was God that bid him offer his son?" she responded. "By an immediate voice," the court officer replied. "So to me by an immediate revelation," she said. "You have power over my body but the Lord Jesus hath power over my body and soul; and assure yourselves . . . if you go on in this course, you will bring a curse upon you and your posterity, and the mouth of the Lord hath spoken it." She was found guilty and excommunicated. Eventually she and several of her children were slain by Indians on Long Island, but she found immediate sanctuary with the remarkable Roger Williams.

The poet Milton, who knew him well, admired Williams as a champion of liberty; the Boston clergyman Cotton Mather thought he had "a windmill in his head." Williams had taken Holy Orders on graduating from Cambridge before becoming disillusioned by Anglicanism and sailing to New England in 1630. He soon ran afoul of the congregation at Boston, since it refused to make public penance for being in communion with a Church of England he now felt to be impure; moving to Salem, he was expelled for denying magistrates the right to punish Sabbath-breakers. He took shelter with the Indians of Rhode Island, where he bought land and founded the city of Providence in 1636 as a haven for free spirits. Freshly convinced by the doctrine of adult baptism—he later became a Seeker, rejecting all formal creeds—he set up the first Baptist church in America in 1639. Williams returned briefly to England, publishing a stout attack on *The Bloody Tenent of Persecution;* in 1644 he obtained a charter for his new colony with the help of his friend Henry Vane.*

Williams furiously defended religious liberty in his colony for almost half a century. The Bay colonists strongly disapproved of Baptists, arresting and publicly whipping one in 1651. Williams dispatched an impassioned letter to the

---

*Vane was a leading figure in the English Civil War on the parliamentary side. He fell out with Oliver Cromwell, regarding him as a dictator and traitor to republican principles. Although he was not a regicide, he was executed on Tower Hill in London after the restoration of the monarchy.

governor, John Endicott, to remind him that conscience—"a persuasion fixed in the mind and heart of man, which enforceth him to judge (as Paul said of himself a persecutor) and to do so and so with respect to God"[10]—was the most noble of all liberties.

Williams's concern for the vulnerable extended to Jews and Quakers. Dutch Jews, some doubtless the descendants of Spanish expulsees, arrived on Manhattan Island to trade in 1654. Others followed the next spring, and members of the congregation of the Dutch Reformed minister Johannes Megapolensis muttered that they would soon build a synagogue. "They have no other God than the unrighteous Mammon, and no other aim than to get possession of Christian property," Megapolensis said, adding that the Jews wept and moaned and falsely claimed poverty while begging Christians for charity. He wrote to Holland asking that these "godless rascals" be sent away. Manhattan already had enough Papists, Mennonites, and Lutherans among its Dutch Calvinists, he said, to say nothing of English Puritans, Atheists, and other "servants of Baal." To allow the "obstinate and immovable" Jews to remain would "create a still greater confusion."[11]

Rhode Island offered Jews a sanctuary of last resort. Williams also welcomed Quakers when they first appeared in America in 1656. He did not share their beliefs—with typical aplomb, he recorded his dispute with them in a work entitled *George Fox digged out of his Burrowes*—because, although conscience may be false and deluded, "yet it is not by any arguments or torments easily removed." On this point, at least, he and the Quaker William Penn were at one. Penn described liberty of conscience as "a free and open profession and exercise" of duty to God. He complained that Quakers "above every tribe of men are most maliciously represented, bitterly envied, and furiously impugned by many of the scribes and phariseehs of our time."

Quakers touched a raw spot in New England's disciplined piety. They had "no ministry, no sacraments, no liturgy, no structure, no weapons; yet they confidently asserted that they and their precepts would soon take over the world."[12] Mary Dyer had fled Massachusetts for Rhode Island at the same time as Anne Hutchinson; she lived with her husband William at Newport before traveling to England. Here she heard George Fox preach and returned to America as a Quaker in 1657. The Boston clergy and magistrates tried to silence her "Enthusiastick" preaching; she was expelled from the colony and warned to stay away on pain of death. "In my coming to Boston," she told the Massachusetts general court on returning in May 1660, "I am therein clear, and justified by the Lord, in whose Will I came, who will require my Blood of you . . . who have made a Law to take away the Lives of the Innocent Servants of God . . . who are called by you, *Cursed Quakers,* altho' I say, and am a living Witness for them and the Lord, that he hath Blessed them, and sent them unto you. . . ."[13] Her husband's plea to Endicott still tears the heart—"O, do not deprive me of her, but I pray give her me once again & I shall be so much obliged forever"[14]—but Mary Dyer was correct in her prediction that the governor "will not Repent, that you were kept from shedding Blood, tho' it were from a woman."[15] She was hanged.

AMERICA WAS TOO vast, however, too unpopulated, its colonies too isolated and individual, to keep such undesirables at bay. Puritans predominated in New England and Anglicans in Virginia; but the Anglicans had no bishop to give them focus, although they constantly pleaded for one, and the Congregationalists by definition had no national authority. By 1646, eighteen languages could be heard along the banks of the Hudson alone[16]; it was already too late to impose an orthodoxy. As Williams had carved Rhode Island as a refuge, so William Penn founded a colony for Quakers.

Penn was the son of the English admiral who had captured Jamaica from the Dutch, an island with a trade then more valuable than all the American colonies combined. As a radical young student in 1661, Penn had been sent down from Oxford for refusing to conform to the restored Anglican Church. He served briefly in the navy against the Dutch and studied law in London before his father sent him to manage his Irish estates. He attended Quaker meetings in Cork and was imprisoned for his adherence to the sect. On his return to England he attacked the orthodox doctrines of the Trinity in his work *The Sandy Foundations Shaken* and was thrown into the Tower of London. Here he wrote a classic outline of Quaker practice—"No pain, no palm; no thorns, no throne; no gall, no glory; no cross, no crown"—and a self-vindication, *Innocency with her Open Face.* His father's friendship with the future James II secured his release, although he had further spells in prison for his preaching, in which he extolled religious tolerance and Quaker truths. His father had a large claim on the Crown, for the conquest of Jamaica, and Penn was granted territory in America in settlement of the debt, to be called "Pensilvania" in honor of the old admiral.

He sailed for the Delaware with his band of Quakers in 1682. On arrival, he named Philadelphia for the "brotherly love" that he vowed to extend to all in his holy experiment. "That there is such a thing as conscience, and the liberty of it, in reference to faith and worship towards God," he wrote, "must not be denied." The great majority of the 250,000 whites in the American colonies at this date were British Protestants; Penn, in inviting European sects, began to change the balance. He encouraged Lutherans fleeing from persecution in the Palatinate to settle in the colony; by the 1750s some 50,000 Germans were in Pennsylvania and almost 200,000 in the colonies as a whole, with strong contingents in New York and New Jersey.

More exotic sects flowed in. Parties of Mennonites, Anabaptist survivors, arrived in Pennsylvania from 1683. Dunkers were a sect of German Baptists formed by Alexander Mack, who rejected infant baptism and the Old Testament, professing no covenant but the New. Their name came from the total triple immersion of their baptism. The movement spread rapidly in Germany, Switzerland, and Holland from 1708; the persecution that followed their refusal to bear arms or take oaths led to waves of emigration to America in the decade after 1719.*

Moravians were descendants of the Bohemian Brethren, who dated from the Hussite tensions of the fifteenth century. They had been organized into a church by Lukáš of Prague before his death in 1528, rejecting oaths and military service, stressing purity and discipline, and trying to realize the ideals of the Sermon on the Mount through poverty and simplicity. Moravians retained the celibacy of the clergy and the public and private confession of sins, but held to Communion in both kinds and justification by faith; they were thus open to persecution by Protestants and Catholics alike. The sect was centered in Moravia in the sixteenth century. Exiled after the Catholic victory in the Battle of White Mountain in 1620, they made their way to America. New York would not tolerate the Moravians on the grounds that their preaching might "seduce the Indians from their fidelity to his Majesty." After a transit in Georgia, they settled largely in Pennsylvania, at Nazareth and later Bethlehem.

In 1731, in another typical example, the Catholic archbishop of Salzburg expelled all the Austrian Lutherans in the city. English Protestants came to their aid and arranged for them to take passage from Dover to Savannah in 1734. They sailed "in God's name" on January 8, the journal edited by Pastor Urlsperger recorded, "praising Him diligently" for the fair southeasterly wind that sped them down the Channel. On January 10, as they passed into the Atlantic, they gathered on the top deck to consider the wonders of God's ocean and sing "Wondrous King." Five days later they met severe headwinds and Urlsperger reminded his congregation of St. Paul's advice to his exhausted crew as the tempest drove them towards the rocks: "Be of good cheer; for there shall be no loss of any man's life among you, but of the ship" (Acts 27:22). God heard the Salzburgers' prayers, or so they believed, for the wind turned favorable at nightfall.

A panic broke out on January 28 as the vessel filled with the smell of steam and fire. Some crewmen thought that the powder magazine had caught fire, and

---

*They divided in the 1880s and remain in groups. The majority are known as the Church of the Brethren; one liberal wing is called the Brethren Church of Ashland, Ohio, and another the Grace Brethren, while the ultraconservative are referred to as Old German Baptist Brethren. A group in Canada that originated from an awakening in Lancaster County in Pennsylvania in the eighteenth century is known as the Brethren in Christ.[17]

the captain led a rush to the bows; all thought their last hour had come. It transpired that the smell came from broth spilled into the galley fire by a cabin boy preparing the captain's dinner. Urlsperger called them together to sing a hymn of thanks and to read them Psalm 13: "I have trusted in thy mercy; my heart shall rejoice in thy salvation" (Ps. 13:5). The Salzburgers had pocket prayerbooks and continually gave thanks for easterly winds. On Sundays there was much "reading of the Bible and other useful books, even by the sailors." A violent storm shook the ship forty days out, and they sang: "Put your ways in the hands of God."

Land was sighted at sunrise fifty-four days out from Dover. The hymn "Lord God we praise thee" was sung, and then Psalm 66: "We went through fire and through water: but thou broughtest us out into a wealthy place. . . ." (Ps. 66:12). They attributed the foul winds that blew them back into the Atlantic the next day to God "giving us time to drive out false gods and to truly purify our hearts before landing." On March 10 they were again lying off the Georgia shore on a calm sea with the birds singing sweetly; but they grounded on a sandbank and, despite dumping drinking water overboard to lighten ship, would have remained stuck fast "if God had not sent an unusually high tide." They moored in the Savannah River, which they found "even wider than the Rhine" and full of fish and oysters. On March 14 they gave thanks in a nearby church; it had only a roof and walls, with no windows or choir, but it suited them very well.[18] They in turn were followed by Schwenkfelders, descendants of followers of the sixteenth-century German nobleman and mystic Caspar Schwenkfeld, who believed in the deification of Christ's humanity and who arrived at Philadelphia in 1734.

If they found toleration, however, it did not imply Protestant harmony. Pastor Henry Muhlenberg at Upper Providence, between Philadelphia and Reading, struggled to keep the peace between Lutherans, Anglicans, and Baptists, preaching in Dutch, English, and German. Typical of his problems was an Englishwoman, baptized a Presbyterian at the age of nine, who wished to be rebaptized as a Baptist. Her German Lutheran husband said that she would no longer be the woman he married if she did so, and that he would divorce her. Muhlenberg struggled to persuade her that it would cause grave offense if she persisted, since it would suggest that Presbyterian baptism was invalid.

The Anglican Evan Evans complained bitterly to London that Pennsylvania had no ecclesiastical jurisdiction or laws; the inhabitants refused to submit to any form of "Church Discipline, and men Commit Adultery, and Polygamy, Incest and A Thousand other Crimes."[19] Another wrote of perpetual squabbling between the people and their ministers, "whom they change much oftener than they renew their cloaths."[20] The Society for Promoting of Christian Knowledge and the Society for the Propagation of the Gospel were founded by Anglicans in 1698 and 1701 respectively to support missionary work in the American colonies and the West Indies. Although the Anglicans worked among Indians, blacks, and unchurched colonists, Congregationalists in New England and New York treated them as unwanted rivals.

"Unchristian broils" between Anglicans and dissenters in North Carolina were so rife that the Quaker John Archdale feared lest the colony become "a Prey of the Wolves and Bears, Indians and Foreign Enemies." He held the Church of England responsible for "over-toping its power with too great a Severity."[21] Many French Huguenots had emigrated to South Carolina after religious toleration was withdrawn by Louis XIV in 1685. They, too, clashed with the Anglicans, their minister John Lapierre protesting to the bishop of London in 1726 that the Anglican minister in Charleston was an "open adversary" who bombarded him with "canons and rubricks" and accused him of insolence.

✤ CATHOLICS CAME, TOO. The oldest Christian settlement in North America was founded by the Spanish at St. Augustine in 1566, and the first party of English Catholic colonists had sailed into Chesapeake Bay aboard two ships in March 1634. It was a body of water whose beauty was excelled only by the Potomac River, wrote Andrew White, the Jesuit priest to the expedition; by comparison, the Thames he had left behind in England was "a mere rivulet." The dinghy capsized as they rowed ashore and most of White's linen clothes floated away, "no small loss in these parts"; but he was charmed by the cedar and sassafras trees, flowers, herbs, and walnuts. On the day of the Annunciation of the Virgin Mary, White celebrated mass and noted that "this had never been done before in this part of the world." After the sacrifice had been completed, they erected a great cross they had hewn out of a tree, "humbly reciting, on our bended knees, the litanies of the Sacred Cross . . ."[22]

It might seem an act of generosity for Protestant England to allow even one of the thirteen British colonies in North America to be founded by Catholics; if so, the charity was carefully disguised. A Catholic nobleman, Lord Baltimore, conceived the colony and his son Cecilius acted as its proprietor. A pamphlet written in 1633 for Baltimore reassured Protestant readers that, in accepting banishment from their own pleasant and native country, the Catholics were sailing "from one persecution to a worse." As to the loss of Catholics from the motherland, it was a blessing. Even if all of them were to emigrate, the pamphlet said, the number of declared Catholic recusants was not so great as to make "any sensible diminution" in the population of England, and "their profession in Religion would make them lesse missed here . . ."[23]

Loyalty to Rome was equated with treason in the English mind, and this suspicion crossed the Atlantic. It was feared that "the said Roman Catholiques will bring in the Spaniards or some other foreign enemy to suppress the Protestants in those parts." Baltimore's propagandist pointed out, however, that Maryland was a hundred miles from the Virginia Protestants and five hundred from New England. It would be many years before the Maryland planters would have the leisure to indulge in any such designs.

Far from scheming with the French and Spanish, in fact, the new colonists invited Protestants to settle in Maryland. They passed an Act of Toleration in 1649 guaranteeing Protestants religious liberty. Father White wrote that the astonished Indians had thought the pioneers' ships to be canoes as large as islands, carrying as many white men "as there were trees in the woods"; in fact, the inflow of Catholics from England was too small for them to maintain a majority in Maryland. When Maryland became a royal colony toward the end of the century, Anglican clergy campaigned with the help of Governor Francis Nicholson of Virginia for the Church of England to displace Catholicism "before we be overrun withe enthusiasm, idolatry, and atheism." They appealed to the bishop of London in 1694 for help against the "popish priests" in Maryland who had "perverted divers idle people from the Protestant Religion." They warned that "great numbers of Irish Papists [are] brought continually into this province, and many Irish Priests [are] suspected to be coming incog. among us as having no better place of refuge in the King's Dominions upon their being banished from Ireland"; they said that Quakers and Catholics "are jointly bent against our Church, and daily endeavour to draw people to their parties."[24] When the Protestants gained control of the colony, they offered no reciprocal toleration to the descendants of its Catholic founders, and the landmarks that Father White had named for the saints were changed, St. Gregory's promontory becoming Smith Point, and Point Lookout replacing St. Michael's headland.

Catholics were not welcomed elsewhere. The government of Virginia, for example, was confirming standard practice when it formally declared in 1641 that "no popish recusant" who strayed into the colony could hold office as a "secretary, counsellor, register, commissioner, surveyor or sheriff, or any other public place, but be utterly disabled for the same."[25] Any Catholic who was unmasked was to be dismissed of his office and fined one thousand pounds of tobacco. Any "popish priest" who landed in Virginia was to leave within five days, provided wind and weather did not force his ship to remain in harbor.

The tolerance given to the Dutch Reformed Church after the English takeover of New York in 1664 did not extend to Catholics. An act of 1700 complained of Jesuit priests and missionaries in remote parts of New York province, who by "wicked and Subtle Insinuations Industriously Labour to Debauch Seduce and w'thdraw the Indians from their due obedience." They, and any priest who celebrated Mass or used "any Romish Ceremonies" in the city or countryside, were given three months to leave New York. Any who failed to do so faced "perpetual Imprisonm't" as an "incendiary and . . . an Enemy to the true Christian Religion"; if he escaped and was recaptured he would suffer the death sentence. The penalty for aiding and abetting a Catholic priest was a large fine of two hundred pounds and humiliation "by being Set in ye pillory on three Severall dayes." As in Virginia, deference was paid to the perils of the sea. The act did not apply to clergy "who shall happen to be Shipwrackt, or thro' other adversity shall be cast on shoure." Provided that they declared themselves immediately to the governor or a justice of the peace, they could remain until a suitable ship was found for them.

Catholics were to benefit hugely from the liberties that followed the American Revolution; the vast influx of Irish and then Italian immigrants transformed the importance of the denomination. But the colonies had few Catholics indeed at the time of independence. John Carroll, Jesuit-trained and named vicar apostolic for the United States in 1784, provided an account of the condition of his flock at the request of the Vatican the following year. He found there to be 15,800 Roman Catholics in Maryland, some 6,000 of them children or black slaves. Pennsylvania had 7,000, almost all of them white. Nineteen priests served them in Maryland and five in Pennsylvania; of this handful, two were over seventy and three others nearly so. No more than 200 Catholics lived in Virginia, visited four or five times a year by a priest. "In the State of New York, I hear there are at least 1,500," Carroll wrote. "Would that some spiritual succour could be afforded them! They have recently, at their own expense, sent for a Franciscan Father from Ireland. . . ." There were others, too, scattered in other states, "utterly deprived of all religious ministry," and French-speaking former Canadians in the territory bordering the Mississippi were served by a single French-speaking German priest; but these were tiny numbers to put against a total population of some three million souls.

Carroll was concerned that Catholic morality would be undermined by its exposure to loose-living Protestants. The now wealthy descendants of the Maryland pioneers were "reasonably pious, if lacking fervour." The others, and particularly the growing number of immigrants from Ireland and elsewhere, had picked up the bad habits of Protestant America. The young of both sexes mingled more freely than was compatible with chastity; they were too fond of dancing and other amusements, and the girls especially had "an incredible eagerness . . . for reading love stories which are brought over in great quantities from Europe."[26]

SPORADIC WARS AND revolts did much to bedevil Protestant missionary efforts among the Indians. The English Crown made little attempt to justify colonization by official missionary zeal. The charter granted to the Massachusetts Bay Company by Charles I in 1629 merely expressed the hope that the people from England "may be so religiously, peaceably and civilly governed" that their good life and orderly conversation "may win and incite the natives of the country to the knowledge of the only true God and Saviour of mankind."[27]

Pocahontas, the noble and Christian princess of the Tidewater tribes of New England, inspired much verse and sentimentality, but her life was brief. An English expedition to colonize Virginia landed at Jamestown in 1606. Among its members was Captain John Smith, a soldier of fortune who had escaped after being taken prisoner and sold into slavery by the Turks while campaigning in Hungary. While hunting outside Jamestown, Smith was captured by Indians under the chief Powhatan. He was saved from death by the pleadings of the chief's eleven-year-old daughter, Pocahontas. Smith's own tact and sympathy toward Indians, a legacy perhaps of his experience as a slave, and Powhatan's magnanimity to the white intruders, may also have played a part. Smith was elected president of the colony on his release.

Pocahontas was cajoled into visiting Jamestown in 1612. She met the settler John Rolfe. Their marriage scandalized the whites, although her father gave it his blessing, and it helped preserve a tense peace with the Indians. Rolfe complained to the governor of Virginia that other settlers, judging him by "the base rule of

Pocahontas, savior of the adventurer Captain John Smith, was the best-known Christian convert in New England. The settler John Rolfe married her in Jamestown in 1613, "for the honour of our countrie, for the glory of God, for my owne salvation, and for the converting to the true knowledge of God and Jesus Christ, an unbeleeving creature, namely Pokahuntas." She sailed to England in 1616, where she was received by royalty and much praised for her charm. She died of smallpox as she prepared to return.

their own filthiness," accused him of taking her to satisfy his lust. He explained that he had married "for the good of this plantation, for the honour of our countrie, for the glory of God, for my owne salvation, and for the converting to the true knowledge of God and Jesus Christ, an unbeleeving creature, namely Pokahuntas."[28] Pocahontas was converted and given the Christian name of Rebecca at her baptism, and she bore Rolfe a son. The couple sailed to England in 1616, where she was received by royalty and much praised for her charm. She was aboard a ship off the Kent coast preparing to return to Jamestown in 1617 when she died of smallpox, one of countless Indians to succumb to the disease; she was twenty-two. Her father died the following year and he was succeeded by his brother, Opechancanough, who found white encroachment intolerable. The Virginia settlements were attacked by a confederacy of Indians in 1622 and Rolfe was killed. White reprisals and crop raiding followed. Opechancanough led fresh assaults in 1644; by then in his nineties, he was captured and killed, and the confederacy was obliterated. Survivors had little interest in evangelizing Indians; the settler Thomas Shepherd wrote of the defeat of the Pequots as "divine slaughter by the hand of the English."[29]

A mission station for "praying Indians" on Martha's Vineyard, an island off the Massachusetts coast, was founded in the 1640s by Thomas Mayhew. His work was continued by his grandson, Experience Mayhew. On the mainland, John Eliot, the Puritan minister at Roxbury, translated the New Testament into the Algonquin language. He evangelized among them, going into their wigwams, reading them biblical texts and preaching to them, "catechising their children, who were soon brought to answer him some short questions, whereupon he gave each of them an apple or a cake." Sometimes a crowd of two hundred Indians came to hear him, growing "very inquisitive after knowledge both in things divine and also human . . ." He gathered them into "praying towns," settlements where he gave them a basic education and taught them trades. He sent several to Harvard to train as pastors. By 1675 more than twenty evangelists were working in fourteen "praying towns" and there were some four thousand Christian Indians.

The Wampanoags and other tribes butchered through Massachusetts and Rhode Island in King Philip's War in 1675. Eliot wrote to the New England Company in London that his work "is, as it were, dead, but not buried"; he had managed to evacuate about 350 Indians to "a bleake bare Island . . . where they suffer hunger & cold," but a group had been surprised by a war party as they prepared to go to the island and were carried away captive, "more than an hundred, & sundary of them right Godly, both men and women . . ."[30] Whites were slaughtered, too, and long-lasting fears and suspicions were born. Mary Rowlandson, a minister's wife, described how a war party broke into Lancaster, Massachusetts, with muskets, hatchets, and flaming brands of flax and hemp. "Some in our house were fighting for their lives," she wrote, "others wallowing in their blood, the house on fire above our heads . . . There were 12 killed, some shot, some stabbed with their spears, some knocked down with their hatchets. . . . It is a solemn sight to see so many Christians lying in their own blood, some here, some there, like a company of sheep torn by wolves. All of them stripped naked by a company of hell-hounds, roaring, singing, ranting and insulting. . . ." One of her children died of wounds and she herself was held captive for four months before being ransomed. She found comfort in a verse from Hebrews—"for whom the Lord loveth, he chasteneth, and scourgeth every son whom he receiveth" (Heb. 12:6)—and thought it good that she had been afflicted, for "the Lord hath shown me the vanity of these outward things."[31] Cotton Mather, the Boston minister, referred to Indians as "the veriest Ruines of Mankind."[32]

William Penn was full of goodwill to Indians. He wrote them a letter from London in October 1681 before sailing for the Delaware. In it, he grandly told

William Penn negotiates with Indians after sailing for the Delaware with his band of Quakers in 1682. He named Philadelphia for the "brotherly love" that he vowed to extend to all in his holy experiment. "That there is such a thing as conscience, and the liberty of it, in reference to faith and worship towards God," he wrote, "must not be denied." Most of the 250,000 whites then in the American colonies were British Protestants. Penn began to change the balance by encouraging German Lutherans fleeing from persecution to settle in the colony. By the 1750s there were some 50,000 Germans in Pennsylvania.

them that God "hath been pleased to make me concerned in your part of the world," and that the king of England "hath given me a great province therein," signing himself "your loving Friend" and assuring them that he desired to enjoy the land "with your love and consent, that we may always live together as neighbours and friends." He said that he was well aware of the "unkindness and injustice" with which his fellow Englishmen had treated them, and that the resulting bloodshed and "grudgings and animosities" had made God angry. He hastened to add that "I am not such a man."

Penn's attitude and Quaker pacifism outraged frontiersmen during the French and Indian Wars of the mid-eighteenth century. A group of frontiersmen murdered twenty Conestoga Indians and marched into Philadelphia in 1764 to kill other Indians being held in the city barracks. The Quakers armed themselves to fight them; astonished children ran after a supposed pacifist, crying, "Look, look, a Quaker carrying a musket on his shoulder!" The frontiersmen said that the Quakers had not fired a shot against the French and Indians, but were now prepared "to put on horns of iron like Zedekiah"* against their suffering fellow colonists, whom the Quakers damned "as nothing but a mixed crowd of Germans and Scotch-Irishmen" and cared not whether they lived or died. The frontiersmen were impressed by this show of force, however; they said that they had only intended to "escort" the Indians out of the barracks, and provided that these "Bethlehem Indians" were being guarded by the king's soldiers, and not by Quakers, they would leave them be.[33]

❖ IT WAS, IRONICALLY, the Jesuits whom Winthrop and his Protestant pioneers so loathed who showed most humanity and compassion to the Indians. Cod had first lured the French to the Grand Banks off the coast of Newfoundland. Samuel de Champlain then explored the eastern coast and the mouth of the St. Lawrence, founding Quebec in 1612. Fur tempted the French further along the St. Lawrence to the Great Lakes. Priests, particularly Jesuits, were key frontiersmen, serving as explorers, mapmakers, guides, translators, missionaries, and martyrs. To the bitterness of the winters and the isolation of vast distance was added the ferocity of the natives whom they sought to convert. A pioneer Jesuit, Father Pierre Baird, arrived in Samuel Champlain's colony of Acadie, now Nova Scotia, in 1611. He described the Indians as "savage, haunting the woods, ignorant, lawless and rude"; they were wanderers, attached to no place and no person, "treacherous, cruel in their revenge," wife-beaters who boasted of killing French

*"And Zedekiah the son of Chenaanah made him horns of iron, and said, Thus saith the Lord, With these shalt thou push the Syrians, until they be consumed" (1 Kings 22:11).

fishermen on the coast. Baird hoped nonetheless that "with the help of divine mercy, they could be brought to Catholicism."[34]

Epic journeys were involved. A Jesuit, Joseph le Caron, left Quebec in 1615 with a young Huron named Hinonskwen whom he had befriended when the Indian came to the town to barter furs. The pair set out on the St. Lawrence in a canoe, with an altar stone for saying mass, vestments, and trade goods—combs, little bells, fishhooks, needles and thread. They paddled past the site where Montreal would later stand and into the Ottawa River; from there, they passed the French River for Lake Huron. Seven hundred miles from Quebec, the priest was allotted a wigwam, eight feet by four. Here he labored to compile a dictionary of Huron-Iroquois, a language of totally alien structure in which nouns, adjectives, and pronouns were conjugated with the verb, and with nine tribal variants of the Amen.

"The low roof prevents you from standing up, so that . . . you have to adopt the usual posture of the savages, lying or sitting on the floor," le Caron wrote of his workplace. "This prison has four discomforts: cold, heat, smoke and dogs. . . . The smoke nearly killed me, and made me shed tears all the time, although I had neither grief nor sadness in my heart. My eyes burned like fire and distilled drops like alembic. I repeated the psalms of my breviary as best I could, and waited until the pain might relax a little to recite the lessons; but when I came to read them, they seemed written in letters of fire or of scarlet."[35] Le Caron made candles from rolls of bark, but they burned too quickly. He lived on sagamity, a porridge of crushed Indian corn, boiled peas, wild onions, and the fruit of the askutasquash. When ill, he drank the juice of the maple tree.

His dictionary was used by Jean de Brébeuf, one of the Jesuits who followed le Caron to the Hurons. He wrote in 1636 to warn those of a sentimental mind that they would find no romance in the missionary calling. They would find mosquitoes, sandflies, cramped bark canoes, rapids, and hunger on their way to join him; and when they arrived, Brébeuf could offer them no more than a hut and a skin to serve as a bed, and a winter of "excessive cold, smoke, and the annoyance of the Savages . . ." He gave them other practical advice: to bring along a tinderbox and a burning mirror in order to light the Hurons' pipes for their evening smoke, a service that won their hearts; to tuck up the gown when getting into a canoe, and to avoid bringing sand and water into it; to eat the dirty and half-cooked food without showing revulsion; above all, to "have sincere affection for the Savages . . . as ransomed by the blood of the son of God."[36]

Patience, and courage, was essential. In his first two years Brébeuf made only two Huron converts; after seven years he had no more than sixty. "One has to accept the fact that although one may have been a great teacher and theologian in France," he wrote, "here one is a mere schoolboy, and—O Lord!—what teachers one has!" Danger from other tribes was constant. Isaac Jogues, the Jesuit who set up the Sault Ste. Marie mission station, was ambushed by Mohawks while traveling with Hurons to Quebec in 1642. The Mohawks and other Iroquois thought that their fortunes in war improved in proportion to their cruelty, and Jogues was exposed to the full force of this wretched belief. "They burnt one of my fingers and crushed another with their teeth," he reported, "and they dislocated those that had already been crushed by breaking the nerves."[37]

He was taken prisoner into upstate New York and his captors showed him off to Johannes Megapolensis, the Dutch Reformed minister at Fort Orange, now Albany. The Dutchman did not approve of the Jesuit's attempts to convert the Huron to "popery"; he referred to the Mohawks as "our Indians" and was ambivalent over their war with "the Canadian or French Indians." But he pitied the savagery done to Jogues—his left thumb and several fingers on both hands had been cut off, and the nails of the remaining fingers had been chewed off—and the Mohawks told him that they intended to burn their prisoner since they were at war with the French. Megapolensis offered to protect the Jesuit if he could escape, which he did. After concealing him for six weeks, the Dutchman wrote, "We sent him to the Manhattans and thence to England and France."[38] Jogues bravely returned in 1644 to find fresh warfare between Hurons and Iroquois. He took part in peace talks at Trois-Rivières and fell again into Mohawk hands. Holding him guilty for the year's bad harvest, they chopped him to shreds with a tomahawk. The Mohawks proudly presented Megapolensis with the dead man's missal and breviary.

The Jesuits refused to abandon the Hurons, even though their St. Ignatius and St. Louis missions were overrun by Iroquois. Brébeuf was seized in the latter in March 1649. An assistant who found his body and that of his colleague Gabriel Lalement, recorded their terrible ordeal. "The flesh had been hacked from Fr Brebeuf's legs, thighs and arms," he wrote. "I saw and touched a great many blisters in several places on his body; from the boiling water that those barbarians had poured over him in mockery of Holy Baptism. I saw and touched the wounds made from a belt of bark filled with pitch and resin which burnt all his body. I saw and touched the burns from a 'necklace' of hatchets that they had put on his shoulders and stomach. I saw and touched both his lips that they had cut off because he was still talking of God while they were making him suffer, I saw and touched the hole those barbarians had made in him to tear out his heart."[39] In June 1650 the surviving Jesuits set off with three hundred Hurons for Quebec. The remnants of the Huron Nation were settled on the Île d'Orléans in the safety of the St. Lawrence River.

Persevering, the Jesuit Jacques Marquette brought the faith to the Ottawa Indians around Lake Superior and then joined the expedition in 1673 that discovered and explored the Mississippi and, along the great river, the heartland of mid-America. New France was proclaimed on June 4, 1671, at Sault Ste. Marie, itself founded as a mission station by a Jesuit martyr; Indians from fourteen Nations were invited to the ceremony, in which a vast arc of territory from Hudson's Bay to the Gulf of Mexico was claimed by the French crown with the motive of "subjecting these nations to Jesus Christ's dominion." The Jesuit Claude Jean Allouez spoke in front of the twin symbols of colonial Christianity, a cross and a cedar pole to which were attached the armorial bearings of the king of France. He urged the Indians to look at the cross where Christ, the "master of our lives, of Heaven, of Earth and of Hell," had chosen to be fastened and die in atonement for human sins; then he told them to look at the other post, of Louis XIV, "the Captain of the greatest Captains [who] has not his equal in the world."

In 1763 the Jesuits in New France shared the fate of their colleagues in Paraguay and Arizona. The council of New Orleans decreed that the Jesuits in the colony were hostile to royal authority, had failed to take care of their missions, and thought only of the value of their estates. All their property, a few books and clothes apart, was seized and sold at auction. Their chapel ornaments and sacred vessels in Louisiana were given to the Capuchins, and in Illinois to the royal procurator. The chapels themselves were to be demolished. The Jesuits were ordered to return to France on the first available ship; before sailing, they were not to keep each other's company. François Watrin, a Jesuit with thirty years' experience in Louisiana, complained bitterly at the falsehoods. The judgment of the council was made, not by experts, but by "elderly shopkeepers, physicians and officers of troops," he wrote; and the Jesuit conscience was free from stain by the calumnies invented against them.[40] What Indian torture could not do was achieved by Christian jealousy.

French Canada was seized physically by the British, but it did not lose its soul. The British had learned from their own troublesome colonials to leave religion well alone, and the Quebec Act of 1774 guaranteed freedom of exercise to Catholics and replaced the Anglican oath of supremacy with a simple oath of loyalty, permitting Catholics who took it to remain in public office. French Canadians remained loyal through the Revolutionary War; they "might not love their new masters, but they had no intention of changing them for New England Yankees."[41] The British did not allow priests to be recruited from France, however; and, since only British subjects were allowed to hold property, the large tracts of land belonging to orders in France were transferred to their Canadian colleagues, severing another link with Paris. The old seignurial class lost prestige after the conquest; Protestant English-speakers arrived in Montreal, with a large postwar influx of loyalists, and took control of business and politics. The Catholic clergy maintained French Canadian unity, and the language and culture as well as the religion remained solidly entrenched.

❖ AMERICAN PROTESTANTS HAD no such sense of isolation to bolster their faith. Once off the boat, piety might pall over the generations. In the Puritan states, some congregations dwindled so badly as people declined to affirm the onerous Covenant that a Half-Way Covenant was recognized. Those who took it were allowed to exercise their citizenship, although they could not receive the sacraments or have any say in religious affairs.

A moral malaise in the South was recorded by Charles Woodmason, an itinerant Anglican preacher who traveled the South Carolina backcountry west of the tidewater lands. He claimed that Sunday assemblies had degenerated into "Rendezvous of Idlers, under the Mask of Devotion"; the young went to make assignations and their elders for liquor. He wrote of a plague of "Riots, Frolics, Races, Games, Cards, Dice, Dances"; many traveled outside the colony to be married to conceal the fact that they already had children, and Woodmason estimated that "around nine tenths labour under a filthy Distemper" as the result of their fornications. The magistrates turned a blind eye to promiscuity, since it "contributes to multiply subjects for the King in the frontier country."

Revivalism, or the Great Awakening, was a response to this loss of faith. Jonathan Edwards, the movement's first great figure, described a "Spiritual and Divine Light" shining into the soul which imparted an immediate sense of the excellence of God and Christ and a conviction of the truth which is revealed in the Word of God. His preaching aimed to stir a "sense of the loveliness of God's holiness . . . There is a difference between having a rational judgment that honey is sweet, and having a sense of its sweetness." Since the light was "immediately let into the mind by God," no subtle train of reasoning was necessary; the Awakening was a mass happening, which any American, even of "mean capacities and advantages," was capable of grasping. Edwards encouraged families to come to his meetings, for "babes are as capable of knowing these things as the wise and prudent"; he was pleased at displays of emotion, often weeping with the "joy of the light" himself, for he held that Awakening changed the nature of the soul and assimilated it to the divine."[42] To some he seemed a charlatan, and the huckster-preacher indeed became an American phenomenon; but he had a brilliant intellect and sincerity as well as insight into the American mind. He was minister at the Congregationalist Church in Northampton, Massachusetts, for many years; when patricians engineered his dismissal for overzealotry in 1750, he served as a missionary to the Housatonnuck Indians at Stockbridge. Shortly before his death he became president of the new College of New Jersey, later renowned as Princeton.

His friend George Whitefield followed the Methodist John Wesley from England to Georgia in 1738 and was appointed minister at Savannah. Although

Whitefield went back to England, he made seven evangelistic visits to America and died near Boston in 1770. He preached at a frenetic pace. On October 12, 1740, a crowd of twenty thousand came to Boston Common to hear him, "a sight," he claimed immodestly but truthfully, "perhaps never seen before in America." Whitefield spoke almost until dusk fell and many were moved to tears; it was said that he could make hard men weep merely by pronouncing the word "Mesopotamia." The following Sunday, he was in Northampton, lodging with Jonathan Edwards. He preached in the morning, with Edwards in tears throughout; "The people were equally affected," he wrote, "and in the afternoon the power increased yet more." By November 9, Whitefield was in Philadelphia, and several thousand came to listen to him in a new hall whose roof was not yet in place. He urged them to "go to the grammar school of faith and repentance" and to spurn "Christless talkers."[43]

Staider souls found these naked emotions to be obscene, a mass hysteria that ill-served true religion. Timothy Cutler, the Anglican rector of Boston, grudgingly admitted that Whitefield had phenomenal pulling power; "the Awakener" preached twice a day, in conventicles, commons, and open spaces, and he was thronged "seldom by less than Thousands 2, 5, 8, and at his Farewell, by not less than 20,000." Whitefield raised large sums of money, it was true, including three hundred pounds for an orphanage in Georgia; but people spoke of nothing else, and to criticize him was "neither credible nor scarce safe." He aroused "Fury and Ferment," Cutler found, with "hideous Yellings, and shameful Revels" and, as he passed through a district, "Enthusiasm has swelled to much higher degrees of Madness."[44]

The "new light" revivalists were frequently at odds with "old light" conservatives, who looked upon their antics with cool disdain. In Philadelphia, William Smith, an Anglican reverend, described Whitefield as whipping up "an instantaneous sort of conversion the signs of which were Falling into Fits, Faintings, etc. etc." and that the born-again "mistake their own Enthusiasm for the inward Operations of the holy Spirit." He said that the "new light" took men from plow to pulpit in a few months, with no higher qualification than to "cant out a few unintelligible sounds . . ."

That was cruel, for the Awakening counted among its lasting achievements the foundation of the College of New Jersey, to become Princeton. Religion inspired the foundation of all of America's colonial colleges. Harvard had been created by Puritans in 1636, and its town was named after Cambridge, the English university that had succored so many Protestant radicals. The college laws left no doubt about its divine purpose. "Every one shall consider the mayne end of his life and studyes," they read, "to know God and Jesus Christ which is Eternal life." Students and their teachers were required to read the

Scriptures twice a day, to eschew all profanities, to learn with reverence and love, and "carefully to retaine God and his truth in their minds . . ."[45]

Anglicans were primarily responsible for the College of William and Mary in 1693. Its purpose was to educate Virginian youth to "learning and good Morals" and to supply Church of England ministers. It was also hoped that the "Indians of America should be instructed in the Christian Religion," and that, after being prepared by the divinity school, they would preach to others in their native tongue.[46] Dartmouth was originally founded in Lebanon, Connecticut, for the same purpose by the "new light" supporter Eleazar Wheelock in 1754. He called it "the Indian Charity School," and described it as "a feeble attempt to save the swarms of Indian Natives in this land, from final and eternal ruin," which he thought to be their unavoidable fate unless God mercifully intervened. When Dartmouth was moved to New Hampshire in 1769, it was opened to whites, who soon heavily outnumbered the Indians.

At Congregationalist Yale, the rules of 1754 laid down that "all Scholars shall Live Religious, Godly & Blameless Lives," diligently reading the Scriptures as the fountain of light and truth; they added that they should "constantly attend upon all Duties of Religion in both Publick and Secret." Baptists were prime movers in establishing Brown, or the college of Rhode Island, but its charter in 1764 opened it to all as a "liberal and catholic institution" whose members need pass no religious tests and who "shall forever enjoy full, free, absolute and uninterrupted liberty of conscience."[47] Plans to make the future Columbia University in New York exclusively Anglican failed; the Presbyterian lawyer William Livingston said that New Yorkers had never accepted the Church of England as their official church and that they were "warm in the Negative" to the proposal. Rutgers, at first known as Queen's College, was established with the help of funds raised in 1766 by the Dutch Reformed Church in Holland.

❖ NEW SECTS WERE still arriving on the boats from Europe as America entered revolution. An Englishwoman named Ann Lee led a band of six men and two women who came from Lancashire to Albany, New York, in 1774. Known as Shakers,* they believed that "Mother Ann" was the "female principle in Christ" through whom the Second Coming would be fulfilled. Their name came from the movements they made as they sought spiritual exaltation in their meetings;

---

*The sect may have been inspired by the Camisards, French Protestant ultras who practiced inspired prophesyings; after a failed revolt against the French crown in 1705, in which forty thousand died, some of the survivors fled to England, where they were known as the "French prophets," and gathered some devotees. Strange indeed was the journey from Louis XIV's France to revolutionary Albany.

New sects constantly landed in America on the boats from Europe. The Shakers arrived in Albany, New York, from the north of England in 1774. Their name came from their search for spiritual exaltation by "dancing, singing, leaping, clapping their hands . . . turning around on their heels with astonishing swiftness, to show, as they say, the power of God." Their everyday behavior was as modest as their meetings were exotic. Simplicity was praised, in dress and in the home, and Shaker design and furniture had a plain and lasting beauty.

"dancing, singing, leaping, clapping their hands . . . turning around on their heels with astonishing swiftness, to show, as they say, the power of God," an observer wrote, "and shuddering not unlike that of a person in a strong fit of the ague."[48] America proved fertile and revivalists were recruited; after Mother Ann's death in 1784, Shaker communities were tightly organized by Joseph Meacham and Lucy Wright. Everyday behavior was as modest as their meetings were exotic, and celibacy was held to lead to a holy life; all goods were held in common; nonessential contact with the outside world was limited; tobacco and alcohol were shunned, and herbal medicine and spiritual healing practiced. Simplicity was praised, in dress and in the home, and Shaker design and furniture had a plain and lasting beauty.

American Methodism, previously an offshoot of the Wesleyan societies within the Church of England, declared its own independence at the "Christmas conference" in Baltimore in 1784. "We rode to Baltimore, where we met a few preachers," wrote Francis Asbury of his journey with Thomas Coke, John Wesley's personal representative. "It was agreed to form ourselves into an Episcopal Church, and to have superintendents, elders and deacons. When the conference was seated, Dr. Coke and myself were unanimously elected to the superintendence. . . ." Coke, in his capacity as an Oxford graduate and presbyter of the Church of England, ordained Asbury a deacon on Christmas Day, an elder on Boxing Day, and a superintendent on December 27. Twelve elders were elected for the United States, two for Nova Scotia and one for Antigua. "We were in great haste," Asbury said, "and did much business in a little time." So simple was it to import a sect; within a few years, the Methodist circuit rider, with his message of the attainability of sinless perfection, and his fund of "pathetic stories . . . calculated to effect the tender passions," was sweeping through the southern states.

Religion little motivated or affected the war. The Quakers took no part, "persuaded in their consciences to love their enemies, and not to resist Evil." This was equated with support for the Crown, and they were held in contempt for some years. Mennonites explained to the Pennsylvania Assembly in 1775 that they could not assist in anything that hurt men's lives; "we beg the patience of all those who believe we err on this point," they added tactfully. The Schwenkfelders declared themselves willing to pay heavy fines rather than kill their fellow men.

Many northern Anglicans were among the loyalists who streamed north to Canada. In New York the Anglican rector of Trinity Church, Charles Inglis, despised the "unnatural Rebellion" and complained of clergy "treated with Brutal Violence . . . carried prisoners by armed Mobs . . . flung in jails." Some simply shut up their churches for the duration; they were under oath to pray for the king, but feared the reaction this would provoke. In the southern colonies, where they were most numerous, the Anglicans as a whole did not oppose the revolution. Inglis noted that some of the clergy prayed for "the Commonwealth" rather than the king; "for my part," he wrote icily, "I never expected much Good of those clergy."[49]

Prorevolutionary Baptist preachers made much of a verse from Isaiah: "Loose the bands of wickedness, undo the heavy burdens, let the oppressed go free, that ye break every yoke. . . ." (Isa. 58:6). A minister recently arrived from England, John Allen, delivered the most famous sermon of the war at Boston. "Liberty, My Lord, is the native right of the Americans," he said, dedicating his warning to Lord Dartmouth, the British colonial secretary; "it is the blood-brought treasure of their Forefathers; and they have the same essential right to their native laws as they have to the air they breathe, or to the light of the morning when the sun rises. . . . O America! America, let it never be said that you have deserted the Grand Cause, and submitted to English ministerial tyranny. . . ."[50] No doubt the rebels were stirred by such oratory, but it was scarcely decisive.

With victory, the sheer number of sects made it difficult for the new nation to establish a new Church, even had it wished to do so. New York State alone had eleven different denominations; they were, it is true, overwhelmingly Protestant—244 Protestant congregations were counted in the 1790s against one Catholic*—but there was no prospect of accord being reached between them. A single Jewish congregation apart, however, all were Christian. It seemed entirely natural to Patrick Henry, four times governor of Virginia, the most influential of the states, that if America could not choose a church it should at least declare its religion. He and others tried repeatedly to have Virginia pass a bill that would declare "that the Christian Religion shall in all times coming be deemed and held to be the established Religion of this Commonwealth . . ."

Powerful attacks were made by Thomas Jefferson and James Madison. Both men were Deists, an extension of the "universalism" in which some Americans had come to reject sectarian exclusivity as counter to God's benevolence. The Boston theologian Charles Chauncy argued that God was too infinitely good for it to be possible that he would abandon souls because of the congregation from which they came; man would universally be saved, he wrote, in a work entitled *The Salvation of All Men, the Grand Thing aimed at in the Scheme of God.* Deism went beyond this to reject all institutional religion. It had a short lifespan—it had no priests or dogma and, being opposed to all churches on principle, naturally had none of its own to sustain it—but it intervened at the critical moment when the Constitution of the infant republic was forged.

Thomas Paine, son of a Quaker, a corset-maker, sailor, and exciseman in England, American revolutionary philosopher and journalist after his emigration to Philadelphia in 1774, and French revolutionary after 1789, wrote a thundering attack on accepted religion in *The Age of Reason.* He explained Deist principles in their bluntest form. "I totally disbelieve that the Almighty ever did communicate anything to man, by any mode of speech, in any language, or by any kind of vision, or appearance, or by any means which our senses are capable of receiving," he wrote in *The Age of Reason,* "otherwise than by the universal display of himself in the works of creation, and by the repugnance we feel in ourselves to bad actions, and disposition to good ones."[52]

Paine went too far for his admirers. He added that it would be better to have a thousand devils roaming the land than to have one such "impostor and monster" as Moses, Joshua, and the prophets coming with "the pretended word of

---

*The Congregational clergyman Jedidiah Morse, in his *American Geography,* found English Presbyterians to dominate with 87 congregations, followed by 66 Dutch Reform congregations, several of them German-speaking; the Baptists had 30; Episcopalians, despite their Anglican connections, still mustered 26, the Quakers 20, and German Lutherans 12. There were two Moravian congregations, and one apiece for Methodists, Catholics, and Jews. Morse said Shaker strength was "unknown"; he said that they had increased to a "considerable number" but were now fast declining.[51]

God in his mouth." He said that the Bible taught nothing but rapine, cruelty, and murder, and that the New Testament would have its readers believe "that the Almighty committed debauchery with a woman engaged to be married; and the belief of this debauchery is called faith."[53] This was taken for atheism, and George Washington and other old friends disowned him. Paine died, alone and impoverished, on the farm at New Rochelle given to him by the once-grateful state of New York.

But the essence of his philosophy—"as to religion, I hold it to be the indispensable duty of government to protect all conscientious professors thereof, and I know of no other business which government hath to do therewith"[54]—was a foundation stone of the United States. Madison insisted that "the Religion of every man must be left to the conviction and conscience of every man; and it is the right of every man to exercise it as these may dictate. . . ." Any attempt to establish Christianity would defeat the American tradition, established by Williams in Rhode Island, of "offering an Asylum to the persecuted and oppressed of every Nation and Religion."

Jefferson, replying to a letter from his fellow Deist, John Adams, accepted that "if the sublime doctrines of philanthropism and deism taught us by Jesus of Nazareth in which we all agree, constitute true religion, then, without it, this would be as you say, something not fit to be named, even indeed a Hell." But in his Bill for Establishing Religious Freedom, which, with the Declaration of Independence, he said was the work for which he wished to be remembered, he insisted that: "Almighty God hath created the mind free. . . . [N]o man shall be compelled to frequent or support any religious worship, place, or ministry whatsoever, nor shall be enforced, restrained, molested, or burthened in his body or goods, nor shall otherwise suffer, on account of his religious opinions or belief. . . ."[55]

In America, at least, the faith was freed from test acts, penal codes, oaths of supremacy, autos-da-fé, inquisitions, and other instruments of state repression.

CHAPTER XXIX

"Τhe melαncholy wastes of woe":

Revolutions

The French Revolution, unlike the American, had seemed a mortal foe to the faith. At the height of the Jacobin terror, an effort was made to dechristianize the nation. The Christian year was abolished on October 5, 1793; time was no longer measured from the birth of Christ, but from the declaration of the French Republic, so that 1793 became Year One.* Sundays and saints' days disappeared; the poet Fabre d'Églantine, who renamed the months, said proudly that the new calendar no longer commemorated "some skeletons found in the catacombs of Rome." Christian festivals and holidays were to be replaced by five days dedicated to virtue, genius, labor, opinion, and rewards.

Church land and property had already been expropriated, monastic vows dissolved, and a Constitutional Church proclaimed whose priests were obliged to swear an oath of loyalty reducing them to state functionaries. Jacobin fanatics were now set on removing Christ and indeed God from religion. "It is time, since we have arrived at the summit of the principles of a great revolution," the fiery dechristianizer Jacques Thuriot de la Rozière said three days after the calendar was voted, "to reveal the truth about all types of religion. All religions are but conventions. Legislators make them to suit the people they govern. . . . It is the moral order of the Republic, of the Revolution, that we must preach now. . . ."[1] A few weeks later the bishop of Paris, Jean Baptiste Gobel, was forced to announce that "there should be no other public cult than liberty and holy equality"; his public resignation was followed by that of a Protestant pastor, who declared

---

*Although the new calendar became law in October 1793, it was regarded as beginning on September 22, 1792, the day of the proclamation of the French Republic. Year One thus ran from September 1792 to September 1793.

that "the same destiny awaited every virtuous man whether he adores the God of Geneva, Rome, Mahomet or Confucius."[2]

A festival was held at Notre Dame to celebrate the triumph of Reason over Religion on November 10, 1793. The ancient cathedral was decked out with a pyramid of linen and papier-mâché at the end of the nave alongside busts of Voltaire and Rousseau, erected in honor of Philosophy. At the climax of the ceremony an actress from the Paris Opéra, the *image fidèle de la beauté,* carrying a pike and dressed in a long white robe with a blue mantle and a red Phrygian bonnet on her head, emerged from the pyramid and was solemnly enthroned as the Goddess of Reason; the cathedral itself was rebaptized the Temple of Reason. "Here," a visitor to Paris observed, "there are people of repulsive appearance saying that the existence of God was a hoary superstition, that Hell was a myth, and man a being without a soul. . . ."[3]

In Lyons on the same day, an ass was paraded, dressed in the robes and mitre of the bishop, with a Bible and a missal tied to its tail, followed by cartloads of church vessels. These were then smashed while a Jacobin drank from a chalice to mock the liturgy: "Verily I say to you, my brothers, this is the blood of kings, the true substance of republican communion, take and drink this precious substance."[4] A fête de Raison was held in the Cathedral of Saint-Jean a few weeks later, where republicans bowed to a statue of Liberty and sang the antihymn "Reason as the Supreme Being." Elsewhere, dechristianizers smashed altars, burned hymnals, mutilated images of the saints, paraded crucifixes upside down for passersby to spit on, and pressured priests to resign. "I am a priest, a curé, that is to say a charlatan," a country clergyman from the Seine-et-Marne confessed; "up to now a charlatan in good faith, for I have deceived no-one but myself." A former Oratorian priest, Joseph Fouché, stripped cemeteries of crosses and other symbols and posted on the gates his dictum: "Death is but an eternal sleep." In the Vendée, after the counterrevolutionary Grand Royal and Catholic Army was crushed, priests were condemned to "vertical deportations" in the river Loire; they were trussed up in barges which were then holed below the waterline and sunk.

Yet the blood and bombast soon failed. The Jacobin leader himself, Maximilien Robespierre, thought the festivals of Reason to be "ridiculous farces" put on by "men without honor or religion."[5] Before his fall, he called for God to be recognized as the Supreme Being in a new state religion. Voltaire and Rousseau, the departed philosophers with whose reputations the revolutionaries made such play, were no atheists, but Deists. Rousseau had affirmed a belief in God, the soul, and future life. His description of a "civic religion" in which the just State forbids all priestly bigotry and privilege ran parallel to a "natural religion" in which the individual maintains a personal relationship with God. Voltaire

The Christian year was abolished in France on October 5, 1793. The revolutionaries measured time from the declaration of the French Republic, 1793 becoming Year One. Sundays and Saints' Days were abandoned so that the new calendar no longer commemorated "some skeletons found in the catacombs of Rome." The cathedral of Notre Dame in Paris was rebaptized the Temple of Reason. But Maximilien Robespierre, the Jacobin leader sketched here, himself recognized that the attempt to eradicate Christianity led to "ridiculous farces." He called for God to be recognized as the Supreme Being in a new state religion.

was violently opposed to Catholicism—*"Écrasez l'infâme,"* he had said, the infamy to be crushed being the Church—because of its superstitions and deceit, but he thought existence would be a dark anarchy without belief in God and immortality. "If God did not exist, it would be necessary to invent Him," he wrote.[6]

The murderous excesses of the Jacobins made his point. By Year Two, 1794, they were themselves being guillotined; seven years later Napoleon signed a concordat with the pope that formally restored the Church in France. "Of all the religions that have ever existed, the Christian religion is the most poetical, the most favorable to freedom, art and letters, and the modern world owes all to it, from agriculture to the abstract sciences," the writer and statesman Chateaubriand wrote in celebration in his *Génie du christianisme* in 1802. Postrevolutionary France was more pious and fervent than ever.

❖   THE INDUSTRIAL REVOLUTION proved more dangerous than the French. In 1844, the year that the Young Men's Christian Association—the famous "Y"—was founded in London, Friedrich Engels was writing about conditions in the slums of Manchester, where his father owned a textile factory. The YMCA was created by George Williams, a rich draper who devoted his spare time to temperance work and lay preaching; his purpose was to provide hostels and Christian companionship for the young in industrial cities where foul lodgings and alienation from religion were commonplace. Reformers were talking of an "English slavery" in mills and factories, and Williams saw the slums as a threat to social order as well as to individual salvation; a grateful government recognized this and awarded him a knighthood.

Engels's ambitions were wholly opposite, and the Communist Komsomol youth movement that later represented their fulfillment reserved a special loathing for the YMCA. He was the devoted soulmate of Karl Marx, and the two were creating from the misery of the Industrial Revolution an ideology that posed an extreme danger to the faith. Marx claimed religion to be "the opium of the people," but Marxism was to develop into a narcotic of its own, replete with chants, banners, show trials, a Propaganda, an inquisition, and a granite shrine in Moscow's Red Square where the mummified remains of its first practitioner were venerated by millions of pilgrims; and Communism, though it drew brilliantly on religious techniques, was the very anathema of religion. It denied that spirituality played any valid part in a world dominated by the material; God and Christ were denied by nothing as abstract or genteel as Reason, but by the march of history towards the dictatorship of the proletariat.

Industry was spawning cities, and the proletariat, at a titanic pace and scale. Chicago, little more than a village in prerailway 1831, had more than three hundred thousand people by the fire of 1871. In England, Engels described the working districts of Manchester, whose population increased tenfold over the century.*

Tanneries, bone mills, and gasworks lined the banks of the river Irk in Manchester; the stream was choked with blackish green slime and refuse, and the bubbles of miasmatic gas that rose from it fouled the air on the bridge forty feet above its stagnant pools. The yards of the houses that rose on the left bank were piled with dirt and offal; the buildings were packed closely together, all black, smoky, crumbling, and ancient, with panes and window-frames broken. Behind them were rows of mills and barracks-like factories. Landlords thought nothing of renting cellars on the quayside, Engels wrote, even though they were two feet below the low water level of the Irk and were slick with damp. Pigs rooted through the offal heaps in the alleys or were imprisoned in small pigpens no filthier than the lodgings of the human helots of industrial society. The huts along the embankment of the Liverpool to Leeds railway line had earthen floors, and the doorless

---

*In 1819 mounted militia of the local yeomanry had killed or wounded four hundred while breaking up a radical reform meeting in Manchester. Dubbed the "Peterloo massacre," the measures taken by the government showed the fear of godless revolution even in stable England. The laws against blasphemous libel were tightened, all meetings of more than fifty people were banned, and duty on newspapers and cheap pamphlets was raised to put them beyond slender pockets.

privies were thick with pools of urine and excrement. In the background lay the places of final degradation, the pauper burial-grounds, where the parish was obliged to deposit the penniless dead, and the workhouse, where it dumped the living, which stood "like a citadel . . . on the hilltop," looking down with menace from behind its high walls and parapets to the working people's quarter below.[7]

It was so noisy in the Lancashire textile mills that the weavers had to learn to lip read; molten metal spilled on flesh in the iron foundries, and in the Glasgow shipyards, men tied themselves to the scaffolding with ropes when gales whipped in. Miners in the faulted, thin seams of South Wales and Durham worked lying on their sides, in a slurry of water and dust, instantly recognized by the blue scars where coal dust had filled a wound. "Apart from musclepower, nothing significant is required—neither literacy, skill nor even quickwittedness," an observer wrote. "To carry iron, to load and unload wagons, to fetch and carry all kinds of heavy weights, to dig and prop up pits, these are some of the tasks of the labourer. But his chief task is to survive on a pittance. . . ."

None of this was specifically British—the writer above was describing the laborers of St. Petersburg in Russia. But nineteenth-century industrialization was Christian, at least in the geographic sense that it took place almost exclusively in Christian countries. In America, John Lancaster Spalding, the Catholic bishop of Peoria, Illinois, noted another "great evil that afflicts a manufacturing population." It was, he wrote, the "breaking down of family life . . . Now, the poor in our great cities have no homes. Lodging houses where people eat and sleep are not homes. Hired rooms which are changed from year to year, and often from month to month, are not homes."[8] Moral degradation accompanies great physical wretchedness, he said, and it was thus the duty of the Church to deal with the poverty and want that were destroying spirituality. "It keeps its electrical engines immaculate in burnished cleanliness," the Baptist Walter Rauschenbusch wrote of American industry, "and lets its human dynamos sicken in dirt . . ."

❖ "HUMANITARIAN" WAS THEN a term of contempt, an equivalent to the modern "do-gooder." Lord Shaftesbury, an evangelical and one of the greatest reformers of the age, caught the essence of this new breed: "I must ever be groping where there is most mischief."[9]

Such men and women, often laypeople, driven by the Bible to meddle in the affairs of others, were often heartily disliked. Jonas Hanway campaigned to help the "climbing boys," used by chimney sweeps to scour the sooty recesses of chimneys, and for orphans abandoned to the untender mercy of the parish. He established the Magdalen Hospital for penitent prostitutes and started a Marine Society to start lads out on careers in the navy; curiously, Hanway also crusaded against the "pernicious" effects of drinking tea. His reward was to be dubbed "the greatest bore in British history"; the historian Carlyle described Hanway as "dull and worthy," the twin adjectives so often used to damn reformers.

Their politics and their views of fellow Christians differed wildly. Granville Sharp, the antislavery campaigner and creator of Sierra Leone, so despised non-Anglicans that he founded a Protestant Union to fight Catholic Emancipation, and a Society for the Conversion of the Jews. Shaftesbury saw through the Ten Hour Act, limiting the working day; his 1842 Mines Act barred women and boys under thirteen from working underground in the coal pits. Shaftesbury did much for public hygiene and farm laborers, and helped Florence Nightingale with her plans for army welfare; and he trained destitute children in "Shaftesbury homes" that he maintained at his own expense. All this Shaftesbury did in the face of ferocious opposition from his fellow aristocrats and the new breed of coal mine owners and manufacturers. Yet he was a high Tory, and a seventh earl, who deeply mistrusted popular democracy. He saw no reason why Christians should focus on the niceties of the spirit while abandoning materialism to dangerous radicals. "The same God who made the soul made the body also," Shaftesbury said. "Our bodies, the temples of the Holy Ghost, ought not to be corrupted by preventable disease, degraded by avoidable filth, and disabled for his service by unnecessary suffering."[10]

Others, like Charles Kingsley, author of the bestselling children's book *The Water Babies,* with its "loveliest fairy in the world . . . Mrs Doasyouwould-bedoneby," were Christian Socialists. They worried about the alienation of working people from the faith. Kingsley said that the Bible was used like a policeman's handbook, "an opium-dose for keeping beasts of burden patient while they are being overloaded."[11] Unlike Shaftesbury, they believed that Christ's teaching led to socialism; the idea of communal property was, of course, as old as the earliest desert monks. They formed workers' cooperatives and encouraged adult education in workingmen's colleges. Primitive Methodists* held American-style camp meetings lasting several days under canvas for miners and farm workers, and were close to the trade union movement. The leader of the Durham miners, John Wilson, was converted at a meeting—"all was joy even while the tears were chasing

---

*The Primitive Methodists were expelled from the Wesleyan Conference in 1811 because these meetings, introduced by the American Lorenzo Dow, were held to be "highly improper and likely to be of considerable mischief." Methodists, themselves a splinter from Anglicanism, proved to be one of the most fissiparous of sects. They divided into Wesleyan and Calvinistic Methodists, Methodist New Connection, Wesleyan Methodist Reformers, Bible Christians, and Wesleyan Methodist Association as well as Primitive Methodists; an 1851 religious census also identified the Wesleyan Christian Union, Benevolent Methodists, and Temperance Methodists.

down my cheeks. . . . I began seriously to consider how I could be useful in life"[12]—and went on to become a Member of Parliament.

All saw reform as a blend of evangelism, conscience, and social safety valve. The first prison reformer, John Howard, was an evangelical independent who was moved by the terrible conditions in the Bedford County jail when he became high sheriff in 1773. The jailers were unpaid; they lived off fees extorted from prisoners, and those who were acquitted were not freed until they paid. Howard recommended that jailers should be paid official salaries, an idea so radical that his fellow magistrates rejected it. Howard devoted the rest of his life to visiting prisons throughout Britain and Europe, evangelizing and pressing for change; he died of typhus contracted in a Russian prison.

The Quaker Elizabeth Fry continued Howard's work, with Bible readings among women convicts. In 1817 she formed an Association for the Improvement of the Female Prisoners at London's Newgate Jail; it provided clothing and education, and introduced them to the Scriptures so that they might learn "those habits of order, sobriety and industry which may render them docile and peaceable in prison, and respectable when they leave it."[13] Her piety may sound patronizing, but it was wholly practical; women prisoners were not segregated, being preyed on by male convicts and jailers alike, and the government cared little about moral and physical degradation until shamed into making improvements by the evidence that Fry gave to a parliamentary commission in 1818. She visited every convict ship that was preparing to transport women prisoners to Australia. Fry strove, too, to redefine punishment, whose purpose she said was not "revenge, but to lessen crime and reform the criminal"; as to the death penalty, it "hardens the hearts of men, and makes the loss of life appear light to them . . ." The Bible condones capital punishment, a fact that has inhibited Christian campaigns against it, and it was not effectively abolished in Britain until 1965. Elizabeth Fry nonetheless helped to change perceptions. Executions had long been a popular and public blood sport in which large crowds flocked to see a hanging, after which, in a practice dating back to 1306, the corpse might then be gibbeted, and left swinging in iron hoops at a prominent place. The last gibbeting in London took place in 1832, and executions were carried out privately in prisons from 1868, the same year that transportation of convicts out of the country was abolished.*

The Sunday school was the earliest of the great institutions founded by such reformers. Its originator was a layman, like the YMCA's Williams, and his ideas also spread rapidly to America. The first school was formed at Gloucester in En-

---

*After 210,000 men and women convicts had been exiled, the first 50,000 to the American colonies and the remainder to Australia.

Teachers and pupils at a Sunday School in 1858. A newspaper owner at Gloucester in England founded the first school in 1780, to instruct poor children in reading and the catechism. The schools spread rapidly to America. They were followed by Ragged Schools, that fed and sometimes clothed their pupils, children's homes, mission tents, soup kitchens, and rescue homes for fallen women, as part of a great explosion of Christian charity in response to the hardships in industrial cities.

gland in 1780* when the newspaper owner Richard Raikes engaged four women to instruct the children of the town's poor in reading and the catechism. He was opposed by Sabbatarians, and by conservatives who worried lest popular education lead to revolution; but children as young as ten worked six days a week, with only Sundays free, and Raikes saw the schools as a civilizing counterbalance for families torn from villages to city slums. He promoted his experiment in his paper, the *Gloucester Journal,* and founded a Sunday School Union. The early emphasis was on literacy, and adults as well as children were encouraged to attend; as educational standards improved, religious teaching became more important. Within a century, half the children in England were learning the rudiments of their faith in Sunday schools.

---

*Education had been synonymous with religion in Western Christendom, of course, at least since Charlemagne. In 789 the first Holy Roman Emperor had ordered that "there may be schools for reading-boys; let them learn psalms, notes, chants and grammar, in every monastery and bishop's house."[14] He founded a palace school teaching the seven liberal arts—the trivium of grammar, rhetoric, and dialectic, and the quadrivium of music, arithmetic, geometry, and astronomy—and the children of plebeians as well as nobles attended it. Cathedral and monastic schools followed; universities—in America and Europe—were invariably religiously inspired. Rich donors in England had founded charity schools for the poor since Elizabethan times; from 1699 the new Society for Promoting Christian Knowledge had established "Catechetical schools" to teach seven to eleven year olds. Unlike Sunday schools, however, these taught full-time and had no place for working children.

A policeman's torch illuminates sleeping children and huddled women at night in a London slum. Physical wretchedness was believed to cause moral degradation, and many nineteenth-century Christians thought it their duty to allay the poverty that destroyed spirituality. They were called "humanitarians," then a term of contempt. Lord Shaftesbury, an evangelical and one of the greatest reformers of the age, caught the essence of this new breed: "I must ever be groping where there is most mischief."

For the destitute, starvelings, and strays, children so weak with hunger that they had to be fed before they could be taught, a Portsmouth cobbler named John Pounds pioneered the Ragged Schools, to "chase away ignorance, to relieve distress, and to teach the Gospel." The schools were free; they fed their children soup, a little meat, bread, and cheese, and sometimes clothed and shod them. "Kindness, Christian love to the children," a supporter wrote, "and teaching them their duty to their neighbours and to their God, and making the Bible the theme of all our instruction . . ."[15] The Ragged School Union was formed in 1844, and most cities and large towns had at least one. A strong practical streak was mixed with charity; shoeblack brigades were set up so that the children got into the habit of earning their own money, and later schemes encouraged them to emigrate to the colonies. Thomas Barnado, a young Irish doctor who abandoned plans to become a medical missionary to China while working in the slums of London's East End, founded Dr. Barnado's Homes to care for sick and destitute children. By his death in 1905, Barnado had taken 59,384 children out of the gutter and helped perhaps half a million, also sending many to new lives in Canada.

Sentimentality, of course, ensured sympathy for slum children; but the needs of adults were often as pressing. The "severely workful" city of Coketown, in

Dickens's novel *Hard Times,* was transformed into a "pious warehouse of red brick" by its abundance of chapels. Baptist tabernacles, Primitive Methodist bethels, and others met the needs of the "chapel working class," the respectable poor. The Wesleyan revival was the "antidote to Jacobinism," the historian Elie Halévy wrote of nineteenth-century England; the evangelical movement stripped the working elite of revolutionary ardor and gave them purpose and piety.[16] But beneath them was what William Booth described as the "submerged tenth," to whose redemption he devoted his life; "denizens of Darkest England . . . sodden with drink, steeped in vice, eaten by every social and physical malady." Booth was born in the mean streets of Nottingham and was apprenticed to a pawnbroker as a boy. After a religious experience when he was fifteen, he became a Methodist and a revivalist preacher among the shipyards and foundries of Tyneside. In 1855 he married Catherine Mumford, a preacher as formidable as himself, who shared his energetic compassion for the lost and desperate souls beyond the reach of the conventional church. The Booths opened a mission tent in 1865 at Whitechapel in London's East End.

From these foul alleys, where Jack the Ripper dumped his victims, Booth created the Salvation Army in 1878. He ran it with immense flair. With its military-style uniforms, corps, citadels, and bands, and its lively magazine *The War Cry,* it was both an entertainment and a moral force whose evangelical purpose was plain:

> The Army is coming—amen, amen!
> To conquer this city for Jesus—amen!

The use of military ranks gave it an air of crusade, and discipline, for Booth was not simply a leader but a "general" with a "chief of staff"; and the rawest recruit, he said, realized that "every soldier is in some degree an officer, charged with the responsibility of so many of his townsfolk." In its early stages it needed this esprit de corps. Its officers were frequently imprisoned for preaching in the open air and its campaigns against sweated labor and the demon drink brought it powerful enemies. "Mrs W. of Haggerston slum. Heavy drinker, wrecked home, husband a drunkard, place dirty and filthy, terribly poor," an early case note ran. "Saved now over two years. Home A.l, plenty of employment at cane-chair bottoming; husband now saved also."[17] Brewers, their profits threatened by such championing of teetotalism, paid ruffians to join a "skeleton army" that mocked and frequently beat up Salvationists. In 1882, 642 Salvation Army officers were assaulted in Britain, women among them, and sixty buildings were damaged.

By then, however, the Army had already spread to America, Australia, and Continental Europe. Its emphasis had switched from personal evangelism to "so-

William Booth, who founded the Salvation Army in 1878, tours through Scotland. He and his equally energetic wife devoted themselves to what they called the "submerged tenth" who lived in the slums, "sodden with drink, steeped in vice, eaten by every social and physical malady." He ran the Army with a showman's flair. It became a formidable moral force in the British Empire, Europe, and the United States, where its "Hallelujah lasses," armed with no more than a bonnet and a smile, prided themselves on being able to evangelize in the roughest taverns.

cial salvation." It provided shelters for the homeless and rescue homes for fallen women. Its cheap food depots and soup kitchens distributed cent-meals; it had secondhand clothes stores, employment bureaus, penny ice wagons, slum posts for meetings, dispensaries for free medicines. Officers went prison-visiting and kept in touch with released prisoners. They organized summer outings and worked in missing friends and inquiry departments, and provided Christmas and Thanksgiving dinners. "You get a bigger bit of meat on your plate than you ever seen before," a boy said to explain Christmas and the birth of Christ. "When He dies," he added of Easter, "you get a bun." Salvage brigades collected household and office waste. In traversing the "melancholy wastes of woe," root principles were found. Above all, the founder's son-in-law, Frederick Booth-Tucker wrote, "The poor were to be treated with love, and not with suspicion or contempt." They were not "one seething cauldron of dirt, rags, hunger, hypocrisy and misery"; the experienced officer saw "castes as separate as the Hindus," and was careful to respect their sensitivities.

America had not less than three million members of the "submerged classes," Booth-Tucker calculated on a visit in 1900, including "the criminal, the vicious and the purely pauper." This godless multitude drifted past the doors of evangelical meetings, he said, and to reach them they had to be followed to their haunts and hiding places. A "Hallelujah lass" armed with no more than a bonnet and a smile could go into the roughest bars and taverns. "If there is a fight, we make straight for the center of it," said one well-bred girl. "Even if they are inflamed with drink or are using knives and revolvers, they never touch us. The people would almost tear them to pieces if they did."[18] Thousands who never entered a church went to their meetings, possessed by "a strange fascination drawing them away from the glittering allurements of the saloons and dives and low music halls."

Grateful governments saw this as an antidote to rioting and unrest; Booth was invited to coronations and opened the U.S. Senate with a prayer.

IN AMERICA, black slaves were more likely to revolt than white proletarians. Their evangelization was largely due to their own efforts. The secretary of the Society for the Propagation of the Gospel, David Humphreys, had complained as early as 1730 that the Society had performed badly in converting slaves, even though most "are very capable of receiving Instruction." Some hundreds had been baptized and admitted to Communion and lived "very orderly lives"; but this was nothing in respect to the many thousands "uninstructed, unconverted, living, dying, utter Pagans." Blacks and whites generally attended the same services, although the blacks usually sat in the gallery and a different chalice was used at Communion for each race.

Slaveholders were often reluctant to have their slaves evangelized. A former Kentucky slave, Henry Bibb, recalled that a poor white girl, Miss Davis, offered to teach a Sabbath school for them. "I had some very serious religious impressions," he wrote, "and there was quite a number of slaves . . . who felt very desirous to be taught to read the Bible." She provided books, but "news soon got to our owners that she was teaching us to read. . . . Patrols were appointed to go and break it up the next Sabbath. For slaves this was called an incendiary movement."[19] Bibb said that slaveholders encouraged the blacks to spend their Sundays gambling and drinking in the woods; they gave them whiskey to see them dance, sing, and play the banjo, and wrestle and box, and thus deny them moral instruction. Slaves had no reason to trust Christianity, Bibb said, because it was preached as a pro-slavery doctrine; and yet many did. A Scot who visited South Carolina in 1840, William Thomson, watched a river baptism of eighteen slaves in Beaufort. The banks were crowded with several hundred black faces, and only a few whites; after the ceremony, held by a white Baptist minister, Thomson attended a church service where the membership included some twelve hundred blacks, mainly slaves from nearby cotton plantations. He found them "the most serious and attentive congregation I have ever seen"; they sang beautifully—they had no hymnbooks, "for it is contrary to the law to teach a negro to read or write," and the pastor gave out the hymn two lines at a time—and Thomson's only regret was that the minister never turned his eye to the galleries where they were sitting, though they paid great attention to the service.[20] Baptists and Methodists licensed blacks as preachers. Daniel Payne, a black ordained as a Lutheran minister, later becoming a Methodist bishop, was present when some of these "exhorters" converted destitute white farmers near Charleston; but white patrols "scented their track and put them to the chase . . . and the poor whites [were] constrained to go without the preaching of the gospel."[21]

A former slave, Richard Allen, was the pioneer of the blacks' own churches. He determined to build one in Philadelphia in 1787. "As I was the first proposer of the African Church, I put the first spade in the ground to dig a cellar for the same," he wrote. "This was the first African Church or meetinghouse in the United States of America."[22] He felt that Methodism was the natural denomination to associate with; he found that "the plain and simple gospel suits best for any people, for the unlearned can understand, and the learned are sure to understand . . . and the reason that the Methodist is so successful in the awakening and conversion of coloured people [is] the plain language and having a good discipline." By 1794, Philadelphia had two black churches, the Bethel African Methodist and the St. Thomas African Episcopal, led by Absalom Jones.

In 1816, Allen founded the African Methodist Episcopal Church and was elected its first bishop. It became the major denomination as the black churches rapidly expanded; as the only institutions under black control, they led efforts for education, self-help, temperance, and abolition. Delegates to the first National Negro Convention in 1830 met under the presidency of Bishop Allen. Women were in a clear majority in church membership, holding home prayer meetings and strongly influencing missionary and Sunday school work, although the clergy were all men. Most black churches were Protestant, since blacks had little contact with Catholics outside Maryland and Louisiana; two religious orders for black women were established in Baltimore and New Orleans, the Oblate Sisters of Providence in 1829, and the Holy Family of Sisters in 1842. The first black American priest, James Augustine Healy, was ordained in 1854.

Religion played as small a part in the Civil War as it had in the War of Independence. The Southern and Northern churches had divided on the slavery issue well before the fighting began. The Southern Methodists declared themselves independent in 1845, the same year that the Southern Baptist Convention was organized. There was an air of sadness but inevitability. Northern Methodists held slavery to be "contrary to the laws of God, man and nature," while in the South some 25,000 Methodist laymen and 1,200 clergy were slave owners. "The separation has taken place," a Southern Baptist wrote simply. "Posterity will judge of the matter, and lay the responsibility where it ought to be laid." The Presbyterians divided in 1857, and by then the debate had hardened opinions. "The Southern slave-holder is now satisfied, as never before, that the relation of master and slave is sanctioned by the Bible," Frederick Ross, pastor of the Presbyterian Church in Huntsville, Alabama, wrote to a northern ex-colleague. Catholics had no formal schism; but, where Northerners were abolitionist, the bishop of South Carolina, John England, maintained that neither natural law nor papal decree precluded Southern Catholics from being slave owners. He did not deny that slavery had its evils, but it also insured that the slave had "food, raiment, and dwelling . . . it relieves him from the apprehensions of neglect in sickness, from all solicitude for the support of his family, and in return, all that is required is fidelity and moderate labour."[23] The escaped Maryland slave Frederick Douglass spoke powerfully against such sentiments. "It is because I love this religion," he told a packed meeting in London in 1846, "that I hate the slave-holding, the women-whipping, the mind-darkening, the soul-destroying religion that exists in the southern states of America." Sojourner Truth, born a slave in Ulster County, New York, preached across the North against slavery and for woman suffrage; her vivid speaking drew large crowds.

At the outbreak of war in 1861, ministers on both sides encouraged the young to enlist. Northern chaplains were paid one hundred dollars a month by Congress; Leonidas Polk, the bishop of Louisiana, became a Confederate major general, commanding a corps at Shiloh before being killed on Pine Mountain. Each side's army naturally claimed divine favor. In her "Battle Hymn of the Republic" in 1861, Julia Ward Howe explained that God is "trampling out a vintage where the grapes of wrath were stored." "Lay thou their legions low, roll back the ruthless foe," the Confederates countered; "Let the proud spoiler know, God's on our side."

After emancipation in 1865, northern missionaries streamed South to organize churches among former slaves. With the demise of Reconstruction, race relations worsened and some blacks considered emigrating to Africa. The American Colonization Society, founded in 1817, had already sent some six thousand free blacks to Liberia, on the lines of the British experiment in Sierra Leone; that had been at white instigation, but the African Methodist Episcopalian bishop Henry McNeal Turner now promoted the idea, to little effect. As rural blacks moved north they started new urban churches in rented shop fronts. There was a huge increase in black church members after 1865. By the end of the century they numbered 2.7 million; the greatest increase was in Baptists, who united to form the National Baptist Convention in 1895. Where there had been almost no black Baptist churches in the South, by 1890 there were almost twelve thousand church organizations, most with a Sunday school; forty schools and colleges, and as many newspapers, also catered to blacks. "We had no personal property, scarcely so much as a 'vine and fig tree' under which to worship God," wrote the black Baptist E. M. Brawley in 1890. "Now our total wealth is estimated to be many millions."[24]

✤ IN TIME, in 1918 in Oklahoma, a Native American Church was chartered. Its purpose appeared conventional enough; it was to foster the worship of a Heavenly Father amid "the several Tribes throughout the United States" and to "promote morality, sobriety, industry, charity and right living . . ."[25] The Indians were a wounded people, however, pursued by the ruthless doctrine of Manifest Destiny. To some whites this was a simple matter of a superior civilization and race; General James Carleton, who fought the Apache and Navaho along the Pecos River in the 1860s, said that it was "their destiny, as it had been of their brethren, tribe after tribe, away back toward the rising of the sun, to give way to the insatiable progress of our race . . ."[26] Others hinted that God had a hand in the sweep of his Christian people to the West. "The Indians must stand aside or be overwhelmed by the ever advancing . . . tide of emigration," frontiersmen in Cheyenne declared. "The same inscrutable Arbiter that decreed the downfall of Rome has pronounced the doom of extinction upon the red men of America."[27]

A missionary effort was mounted, though it did not compare with the earlier toil of the Jesuits in Arizona and California. The Presbyterian Narcissa Whitman trekked with her husband from the East Coast to the Oregon Territory in 1836 at the age of twenty-eight. She worked among the Cayuse, Nez Percé, and Flathead Indians. The mission was a farmstead, a T-shaped single-story log house with barns and fences. She felt herself "so widely separated from kindred souls, alone, in the thick darkness of heathenism"; the mission was on the lands of Old Chief Umtippe of the Cayuses, "a savage creature in his day . . . full of all manner of hypocracy deceit and guile . . ." The Indians had been taught tunes and prayers by a Catholic trader, and family evenings were hard for them "when we spend considerable time in teaching them to sing. About 12 or 14 boys come regularly every night & are delighted with it." She found that singing was the way to their hearts; "while I was at Vancouver one Indian woman came a great distance with her daughter as she said to hear me sing with the children."[28] As white settlement increased, with land-hungry ranchers and miners, so did Indian resentment. In 1847 the mission was attacked by a war party of Cayuse. Narcissa Whitman and her husband and twelve other whites at the mission were killed.

An occasional missionary won Indian confidence. In 1864, with violent hostility between whites and Indians in the Dakota Territory, and the bitterly resented confinement of Indians to reservations, the Jesuit Pierre Jean de Smet was asked to restore peace. He was known to the Sioux as Black-robe for the cassock he wore, and they loved him; the general commanding the U.S. Army in Dakota wrote that the Jesuit "alone of the entire white race could penetrate to these cruel savages and return safe and sound." De Smet rode seven hundred miles at the age of sixty-three to the Yellowstone River to meet Sitting Bull and other Sioux chiefs. Sitting Bull slept beside him, lest one of the three thousand Indians in the camp should wish to avenge the death of a kinsman killed by whites; he "declared that he had been the most mortal enemy of the whites . . . but now that Black-robe had come to utter words of peace, he renounced warfare. . . ." De Smet died in 1873; three years later Sitting Bull led the Sioux in the massacre of George Custer and his cavalrymen at the Little Big Horn in 1876.

Sitting Bull was killed during the suppression of "ghost dancing." This was the Indian response to their immolation on the reserves, and its visions—the Messiah, apocalypse, the Second Coming, the Kingdom of Heaven on earth, Resurrection—were poignant evidence of how much of Christianity they had absorbed. In October 1890, Kicking Bear, a Minneconjou from the Cheyenne River agency, told Sitting Bull about the Messiah of the Paiutes of Nevada. Kicking Bear was told that Christ had returned to earth. He was at Walker Lake when the Messiah appeared. To Kicking Bear's surprise, for he had assumed that Christ was as white as the missionaries, he looked like an Indian. "I will teach you how to dance a dance, and I want you to dance it," the Christ said, and he sang as they danced the "dance of ghosts" until late at night.[29] The next morning Kicking Bear went up to the Messiah to see if he bore the marks of crucifixion, which missionaries had mentioned. There was a scar on his wrist and one on his face; his feet were in moccasins and could not be seen. For a day the Christ spoke to the Indians. He told them that God had sent him to earth to teach, but white men had scarred him and abused him, and he had returned to heaven. Now he had returned, as an Indian, and all would be restored as it had been. The next spring, new soil would cover the earth with sweet grass and trees, and bury all the white men, and great herds of buffalo and horses would come. The Indians who danced the "ghost dance" would be swept into the air and suspended while the wave of new earth was passing, and they would then alight among the ghosts of their ancestors in a world in which only Indians would exist. As Kicking Bear rode back to Dakota, the Christ flew above him, teaching him songs for the dance and telling him to ready his people; after the winter the Christ would bring the ghosts of their ancestors to meet them in the new resurrection.

The phenomenon spread through Dakota, Arizona, and Nevada. Sitting Bull was skeptical, but his Dakota Sioux were fearful that they would miss the resurrection, and he did not prevent them from joining the ghost dance. Kicking Bear assured him that even bullets could harm no Indian wearing a "ghost shirt" painted with sacred symbols; and the Messiah had preached calm and love. "You must not hurt anybody or do harm to anyone," he said. "You must not fight. Do right always."[30] By mid-November, ghost dancing dominated the Sioux reservations; groups wearing ghost shirts danced from dawn until after nightfall and were told that if attempts were made to stop them, the soldiers and their horses would sink into the earth. "Indians are dancing in the snow and are wild and crazy," an agent telegraphed Washington. "We need protection and we need it now. The leaders should be arrested and confined at some military post until the matter is quieted. . . ."[31] An experienced former agent thought that there was certain to be trouble if troops were used; recognizing the ghost dance as a Christian cult, he pointed out that the U.S. Army was not used against Seventh-Day Adventists when they prepared for the Second Coming of their Savior. Nonetheless, Indian police were sent to arrest Sitting Bull in his cabin on December 15. There was a scuffle; he was shot dead.

No retribution followed his killing, for the Indians believed that he would return with their ancestors in the spring, as the whites disappeared. The War Department nonetheless ordered the arrest of Big Foot, the Minneconjou Sioux chief. He was surrounded along with 350 of his people by cavalry near Wounded Knee Creek on December 28. Firing broke out the following morning; the ghost shirts were ineffective and 153 Indians are known to have been killed. A survivor, Black Elk, recollected dressing in his sacred shirt when he heard sounds of gunfire at the creek. He had made it himself, and "no one was to wear it but me." It had a spotted eagle on the back and the daybreak star on the left shoulder; across the breast ran a flaming rainbow, with eagle feathers at the shoulder and red streaks of lightning; he painted his face red "and in my hair I put one eagle figure for the One Above." He had no gun, "only the sacred bow I had seen in my great vision." He attributed his life to the ghost shirt, for he heard bullets all around him; but most were killed. During the day the sun shone; but when the massacre was over and the soldiers withdrew, the snow came and "drifted deep in the crooked gulch, and it was one long grave of butchered women and children and babies . . ."[32] Wagons of wounded Sioux were brought to the post at Pine Ridge. The barracks were crowded with soldiers, and the ghost dancers were left in the freezing open until the Episcopal mission was opened, and they were carried into the church.

When, at length, the Native American Church was chartered, it had no membership rolls or written theology. It combined Christian teaching with the belief that the peyote button, a cactus growth that contains the hallucinatory drug peyote, embodies the Holy Spirit. When taken as a sacrament at nightlong ceremonies, peyote was held to place the worshiper in direct contact with God. In this way, Indians from Arizona to Saskatchewan sought to come to terms with the faith of their conquerors.

"AMERICAN ZION":

Mormons

1 n novelty, at least, the nineteenth was the American century. The country had been an importer of European sects; it now became the flamboyant exporter of its own creations. New sects had long been a natural phenomenon of the faith, of course, a reprise that flowed from interpretations of a Bible whose contents had been fixed in A.D. 382. In Europe, German scholars spent decades meticulously establishing that Moses could not have written the Pentateuch, the five "Books of Moses";* but the validity of the Scriptures was not questioned. In upstate New York, however, an entire new book was added to the Bible. This was startling indeed, evidence that something distinctly American was now entering the faith.

The man to whom this Book of Mormon was revealed paid for the discovery with his life at the hands of a lynch mob. His movement, the Church of Jesus Christ of Latter-Day Saints, came perilously close to sharing the fate of the slaughtered saints of Münster, with whom they enjoyed a taste for polygamy; yet his followers now number eight million worldwide, and out of the wastes of the Far West have created a city of enviable order and prosperity, Salt Lake City. Their variant of the faith may be divine or fraudulent; undeniably, it has proved hardy and transplantable.

---

*Tradition accorded authorship of Genesis, Exodus, Leviticus, Numbers, and Deuteronomy to Moses himself. The scholar Richard Simon had been expelled from the French Oratory in 1678 for claiming that varieties in styles and accounts made this impossible. Johann Gottfried, professor of philosophy at Göttingen a century later, studied biblical books and contemporary Semitic writing and concluded that Genesis and other Old Testament books had been frequently reedited and were thus of composite authorship. Another German scholar, Julius Wellhausen, concluded that the Pentateuch, though drawing on sources dating back to the ninth century B.C., was not finalized until about 400 B.C. It remained hazardous to criticize too freely—clergymen-scholars in England complained of an "abominable system of terrorism" that threatened them with deprivation of their livings for querying the divine inspiration of the Scriptures—but it was slowly accepted by scholars that Moses was not as prolific a wordsmith as had been thought.

A bookplate in a biography showing Joseph Smith, founder of the Mormon Church, as "The American Mahomet." He fascinated his contemporaries. Mormon recruits were gathered from distant Britain, where he earned a grudging respect from reviewers. The *Edinburgh Witness* described the book as "one of the most painfully interesting volumes that ever issued from the press." The *Kent Herald* found that Smith, "whether a great impostor or a great visionary, or perhaps both," was one of the most remarkable figures in modern history.

Joseph Smith Jr. was born to a poor Vermont farmer in 1805, moving as a child to Manchester, New York, a hilly area in Ontario County known as "the burned-over district" for the strength of its revivalist passions. The Smiths were a striking family. Joseph Jr. and his brothers were powerfully built six-footers, self-confident and religious. Their maternal grandfather had written a narrative of his life, with an account of his conversion and with hymns he had composed, which their mother Lucy read to them. Young Joseph was torn by the "war of words and tumult of opinions" between the local Baptist and Methodist preachers. He did not know where to turn, he wrote, until he read a sentence in the Epistle of James: "If any of you lack wisdom, let him ask of God. . . ." (James 1:5). On a spring day in 1820 he walked into the woodland and knelt and prayed to God for enlightenment. His first vision followed; speechlessness, thick darkness, terror, a pillar of light, two personages of brightness and glory beyond description, and the one pointing to the other: "This is my Beloved Son, Hear Him." Joseph asked which of all the sects he should join. "I was answered that I must join none of them," Joseph wrote, "for they were all wrong." The personage who spoke to him told him that their professors were all corrupt, that "they draw near to me with their lips, but their hearts are far from me; they teach for doctrines the commandments of men. . . ."[1]

No comfort could be drawn from the knowledge that all existing Christian sects were wrong, of course. Further visions were needed to establish what was right. On a fall night in 1823, Joseph was praying for forgiveness for his sins and follies while the others slept, when the farm cabin was lit with a brilliance that outshone sunlight. A figure appeared in a loose robe of exquisite whiteness. "His hands were naked, and his arms also, a little above the wrist" Joseph wrote; "his whole person was glorious beyond description, and his countenance truly like lightning."[2] This vision identified himself as Moroni, the son of the prophet Mormon. He told young Smith that God had a mission for him so remarkable that his name would be "had for good and evil among all nations, kindreds and tongues." Moroni explained that Smith would be shown a book containing the "fullness of the everlasting Gospel" as delivered by the Savior to the ancient inhabitants of America. This "Book of Mormon" was written on gold plates, and the key to its translation lay in "two stones in silver bows" fastened to a breastplate which was deposited with it. Moroni then quoted prophecies familiar to young Joseph from revivalists preaching on the Second Coming, from Acts, Malachi, and Joel: "The sun shall be turned into darkness, and the moon into blood, before the great and terrible day of the Lord come" (Joel 2:31). The American farm boy was to prepare himself for the return of Christ.

A further vision revealed that the plates were hidden beneath a stone on a hillside three miles southeast of the Smith farm and a few hundred feet from the main road between Palmyra and Canandaigua. Smith lifted the stone with a crowbar and touched the plates; the angel reappeared and rebuked him, saying to him that the time for translating them had not yet come. When Smith told the family, his mother Lucy recalled, they all gave "the most profound attention to a boy, eighteen years of age, who had never read the Bible through in his life . . . The sweetest union and happiness pervaded our house, and tranquility reigned in our midst."[3] The golden plates were never displayed, although three witnesses testified that they had seen them; from them, and with the help of the stones in the silver bows, Smith translated the Book of Mormon. It told the history of two Hebrew peoples who had emigrated to ancient America, where the sinful Lamanites had eventually exterminated the virtuous and industrious Nephites. Its style, and its moral cycle of virtue leading to pride, sin, chastisement, and repentance, had the ring of the Old Testament. Smith added that Christ had visited America after his death and Resurrection, thus giving Christian roots and intimacy to a landmass still alien and foreboding.

to Carthage, where he was lodged in the visitors' room of the jail pending the trial. A mob of about two hundred men, their faces smeared with lampblack, assaulted the jail on the afternoon of June 27, 1844. The Carthage militiamen let themselves be led away. The front door of the jail was forced. Shots were fired into the room where the Mormons were held. Smith's brother Hyrum was killed first; as the prophet tried to leap from the window, he was struck by shots fired from inside and outside the building. His body fell from the windowsill onto the path outside. The remains of the two martyrs were brought back to Nauvoo the following afternoon, "amid the most solemn lamentations and wailings that ever ascended into the ears of the Lord of Hosts." More than twenty-five thousand of the prophet's followers filed past as the bodies lay in state; the bodies were buried secretly in the basement of an unfinished building, and coffins filled with sand were at the funeral lest their enemies steal their remains. Smith was thirty-nine. He had often told Brigham Young that he did not expect to reach forty. "You do not know me," he had said to followers a few months before his death. "You never knew my heart. No man knows my history. I cannot tell it. . . . If I had not experienced what I have, I could not believe it myself."[13]

❖   THE MORMONS SPLIT, with the majority following Brigham Young. Hostility in Illinois continued. In October 1845, Young was driven to a desperate measure. He announced the exodus of the saints "from these United States to a far distant region of the west, where bigotry, intolerance and insatiable oppression lose their power over them." This gamble beyond the known frontier was "the word and will of the Lord, given through President Brigham Young." Those who might think that the divine authority had not passed from Adam, Abraham, Moses, Jesus, and the martyred Joseph Smith to Brigham Young were tartly warned that "if any man shall seek to build himself up, and seeketh not my counsel, he shall have no power, and his folly shall be made manifest."[14]

Preparations were meticulous, for these were self-reliant and hardy people. Each wagon was to take five adults, with three yokes of oxen, and at least two cows and a bull. It was to be loaded with one thousand pounds of flour, a bushel of beans, one hundred pounds of sugar, dried apples, pumpkins, peaches, and beef, a pound of cayenne and two pounds of black pepper, salt, a rifle per man with powder and lead, salt, tent and furniture, saws, nails, cooking utensils, seed, iron and steel, and trade goods for Indians. Though Mormons were famously abstemious, each wagon was loaded with coffee and tea and every second wagon with a five-gallon keg of alcohol. Each company of wagons had a seine net, and pulley blocks, rope, and ferryboats for river crossings.

A young lawyer from Pennsylvania wrote of Nauvoo shortly after the Mormons abandoned it. He saw on the left bank of the Mississippi "a large and gay city which shone brightly . . . Its houses were all new, mostly of a cheerful red brick with pretty garden plots around them—and a splendid marble building with gilded cupola rose above them all with the dignity of proud beauty. As I drew near I was surprised to see in this new city no sign of life. . . ." All he found were degraded drunks, vomiting and drinking heavily in the deserted Mormon Temple, heavily armed with rifles, pistols, knives, and cannon "marked as property of the U.S." As the last Mormon refugees watched from the Iowa shore, these marauders set the temple aflame and its walls were toppled with dynamite.

The Mississippi was still frozen when the first companies crossed it and drove their wagons through the snows and rains of Iowa, sowing crops and leaving shelters behind them for those who followed. The vanguard reached the Missouri in June and camped on the lands of the Potawatomi Indians. They were on the frontier. With a picked company of 143 men, three women, and two children, Brigham Young set off beyond it into the great plains between the Missouri and the Rockies in April 1847. He left messages for the family group that followed the pioneers, urging them to keep a sharp lookout for "buffalo, Indians and bears," and told them to accept accidents and deaths "patiently and cheerfully, and murmur not for Christ's sake."[15] He favored the Salt Lake valley over the valley of the Utah Lake forty miles to the south because he had heard that the nearby Indians were less warlike. The valley was sighted on July 24, 1847, Brigham Young lying feverish on a bed in a wagon. It stretched for a dozen miles to the crusty whiteness of the lake, with a river soon named the Jordan. This was Mexican territory when the trek began, and it was not formally ceded to the United States for another year; the gentile settlements were a thousand miles back to the east, and California lay seven hundred miles across the deserts and mountains of the western emptiness. "Give us ten years in this place," Brigham Young said, "and we'll ask no odds of Uncle Sam and the devil."[16]

A seemingly biblical plague of crickets "as large as small mice" attacked the first crops; the sky then darkened with great flocks of gulls, which fell on the insects, consuming them with such ferocity that the birds disgorged those they could not digest and continued their feasting until the pests were destroyed. It was thought a miracle. The winter of 1848–49 was severe; the mountain valleys were closed by heavy snowfalls and many families were still camped in wagons and tents. They ate the bitter roots of the sego lily; an inventory in February showed that corn reserves had fallen to twelve ounces a day for each person until the next harvest could be reaped at the beginning of July.

The first news of a gold strike east of San Francisco was published in the *California Star,* a newspaper set up by a group of Mormons who were working on the coast. It set off the greatest gold rush in American history. Salt Lake City lay on the direct route from the East to the gold fields, and the gold seekers who sluiced along it traded horses, mules, wagons, and supplies with the Mormons. Young assured Mormons who caught the gold fever that "those who stop here and are faithful to God and His people will make more money . . . than those who run after the god of this world." The Mormons' growing prosperity proved him right. President Taylor refused the Mormons' petition for Utah statehood—when Young heard of his death, he told his people "Zachary Taylor is dead and gone to hell, and I am glad of it"—but Congress appointed Young governor of Utah Territory in 1850, a huge area that included Nevada and parts of modern Colorado and Wyoming. The eastern immigrants were swelled by several thousand European converts. The English traveler Richard Burton saw a train of twenty-four wagons "slowly wending its way to the promised land"; it was escorted by a nephew of Brigham Young, a man with yellow hair and beard, an intelligent face, and "a six shooter by his right and a bowknife by his left side." Burton noted that " 'British English' was written in capital letters upon the white eyelashes and tow-coloured curls of the children." An early traveler in Utah found a "strange, harsh, hardy, severe-looking people," the men tanned and muscular mountaineers, the young girls looking as "retiring backwoods children ordinarily do," dressed cleanly in simple stuffs.[17] The Indians were friendly. Some joined the church, perhaps impressed by Mormon claims to knowledge of their ancestors; Young stressed that they "are the seed of God, and God is ever their God," adding with typical practicality that it was cheaper to clothe and feed them than to fight them.

Young had furious outbursts of patriarchal anger, but observers agreed that it was tempered by a firm grasp of reality. His motto was "Men not books—deeds not words"; he warned prospective immigrants that their ability to build a house, irrigate land, and raise crops would be tested as severely as their faith. Mormon services were taken by laymen, since there was no professional clergy; sermons dealt more often with the problems of child-rearing and bread-baking than with heaven. Burton found Young to have the air of "a gentleman farmer in New England. . . . he converses with ease and correctness, has neither snuffle nor pompousness."* A reporter who saw him in Navajo country, where Mormons had discovered iron ore, noticed that people spoke to him on any subject "from the fluxing of an ore to the advantages of a Navajo bit . . . I noticed that he never seemed uninterested, but gave unforced attention to the person addressing him,

---

*Burton's interest in adventure and erotica may have heightened his sympathy for the pioneering and polygamous Young. The Englishman discovered Lake Tanganyika, and entered Mecca disguised as a Pathan pilgrim; he also translated the *Kama Sutra* and *The Perfumed Garden,* publishing them privately to avoid prosecution and making a fortune from them. His longsuffering (and only) wife burned the manuscript of his last work, *The Scented Garden Men's Hearts to Gladden,* lest it compromise his reputation.

which suggested a mind free from care."[18] The Mormons were fine farmers, with great skills in irrigation, and road and bridge builders of note; they carried through a one-hundred-mile contract for the new Union Pacific Railroad and produced able mining engineers. Settlements had choirs and bands, and Salt Lake City a philharmonic society; a French visitor in 1856 thought the music was "very good, and better than one meets with in most provincial towns in Europe."

The twin problems of polygamy and politicians in Washington remained. There was no disguising Brigham Young's marital affairs. He had the largest family in the territory, and probably in America. In 1843, for example, he married Harriet Cook and Augusta Adams, the first age nineteen, the second forty-two, the same age as himself. He also married four of Joseph Smith's widows. Young himself put the number of his children at forty-seven, educating them in his own schoolhouse, and the number of wives was probably half that. He had three houses in the center of Salt Lake City—the White House, the Beehive House, and the Lion House; he also had farms and cottages near the city and a winter

Mormon prisoners in the Utah State Penitentiary. The first antipolygamy bill was passed in Washington in 1862. It made marriage to more than one woman a crime and was specifically aimed at Mormons like these, for it applied only in territories like Utah, and not in the States. In 1890 the Supreme Court ruled the antipolygamy laws to be constitutional. The Mormon Church no longer solemnized plural marriages, and Utah was admitted into the union in 1896. Individuals continued to be convicted of polygamy, however, most recently in 2001.

house in St. George, where the desert climate suited him. Young kept a wife in each property, sending her supplies from his bakery and his gardens, orchards, and mills. He also owned sawmills, a hotel, and a lake shipping company. At the theater he had built, he sat in a rocking chair in the center of the box reserved for him, with several of his wives and children.

Officials sent out from Washington to govern the Mormons and administer the law complained that the task was impossible. A federal judge complained that a crowd had broken into his office and burned federal court records along with his personal papers. Polygamy was becoming an international embarrassment—European newspapers were full of it—and American pride smarted at the defiance of the self-declared Nation of Israel. In 1857, President Buchanan ordered a force of U.S. troops to prepare to enter the territory to restore U.S. authority and install a non-Mormon governor. "Good God! I have wives enough to whip out the United States, for they will whip themselves," a hothead preached, cursing "the President of the United States . . . and all his coadjutors in his cursed deeds in the name of Jesus Christ and by the authority of the Holy Priesthood, and all Israel shall say amen."[19]

A battle hymn was prepared:

Up, awake, ye defenders of Zion,
The foe's at the door of your homes
Let each heart be the heart of a lion
Unyielding and proud as he roams.
Remember the wrongs of Missouri
Forget not the fate of Nauvoo
When the God-hating foe is before you
Stand firm and be faithful and true."[20]

The Mormons' Nauvoo Legion of some two thousand men was put on a war footing. Franklin D. Richards, the brigadier general commanding, reminded them of past atrocities. "We have experienced the repeated desolation of our homes," he wrote. "Our women have been ravished. Our prophets and brethren have been imprisoned and murdered. . . . You are required to hold your Regiments in readiness to march at the shortest possible notice. . . ."[21] No one was to dispose of "a Kernel of grain to any Gentile merchant or temporary sojourner."

Relations with the territory's Indians were necessarily good; in the southern part of the territory around Cedar City, whites were outnumbered by four to one, and isolated Mormon farms were vulnerable to war parties. Friendship had been fostered by teaching the Indians farming and cattle raising, and the Indians distinguished between Mormons and other whites whom they called "Mericats," interlopers whom they plundered without qualms when the opportunity arose. In the anticipated war with federal troops, the Indians were seen as allies and "the battle-ax of the Lord"; Brigham Young gave instructions that "they must learn that they have either got to help us or the United States will kill us both."[22]

An emigrant wagon train making for California entered a territory shrill with apocalypse in the late summer of 1857. It halted in Cedar City to buy supplies. A man riding a large gray mare wanted a gallon of whiskey; when no one would sell to him, an eyewitness said, he "swore at us all, said that he had the gun that had killed Old Joe Smith, and that his company would go on to California and get an army and come back and wipe out every ———— Mormon."[23] Among those thus insulting the dead prophet were Missourians. Memories of the killings of 1838 were still fresh, and it was a part of Mormon faith to importune the Lord to avenge the blood of their martyrs. "The Missourians drove us out to starve," Isaac C. Haight, president of the Cedar City Mormons, told a crowd. "When we pled for mercy, Hawn's Mill was our answer, and when we asked for bread they gave us a stone. . . . The Gentiles will not leave us alone. They have followed us and hounded us. . . . God being my helper I will give the last ounce of strength and if need be my last drop of blood in defence of Zion."[24] When the wagon train moved on to Mountain Meadows, the last settlement and source of supply on the road, the Mormons refused to trade with them.

Responsibility for what followed has never been fully established. The wagon train was well outfitted and had some 350 head of cattle. The Indians attacked it, but were beaten back with some loss of life. They sent for John D. Lee, a major in the Nauvoo Legion. He found them, he said in his confessions, "in a frenzy of excitement. They threatened to kill me unless I agreed to lead them against the emigrants . . . unless they could kill all the Mericats they would declare war against the Mormons and kill everyone in the settlements."[25] Another Mormon major, John M. Higbee, described the consequences. "The valey was strewn with carkuses of catle and horses which the Indians had shot down," he wrote later. "Indians were painted like devils . . . & Howling with rage over some of their braves being wounded . . . The Savages came to Lee and said if he and the Mormons did not help them to kill the Merry Cats they would join the Soldiers and fight the Mormons. . . . J. D. Lee being a Major in the Nauvoo Legion said we dare not make war with Indians. . . . Lee said those that are too big Cowards to help the Indians can Shoot in the air then Squat down So Indians can rush Past them and finish up their Savage work. . . . Some Guns were fired and the Men Squated down and Indians . . . jumped out of the Brush, and rushed like a Howling tornado past us. And the Hideous Deamon like yells of the Savages as they thirsting for blood rushed Past to Slay their helpless Victims. . . ."[26]

After not more than thirty minutes, all the 120 men, women, and children in the wagon train were dead. Their bodies were looted for watches, knives, money, and valuables; the Indians ransacked the wagons and scattered the feathers from pillows "like gleeful, mischievous chldren." The wagons and what was left of their loads were taken to Cedar City, stored in the tithing office, and later sold at auction.

❧   IT IS, PERHAPS, a political miracle that this scene of biblical horror—saints and their savage allies putting gentiles to the rifle and the axe in the name of the Lord—did not lead to the federal armageddon of the Mormons. A wave of revulsion swept the country. President Buchanan prepared to use force to bring Zion to heel, appointing Albert Cumming as governor in place of Brigham Young. A force of fifteen hundred troops under Colonel Albert Johnston was ordered into the territory in the autumn of 1857. He was shut out of Salt Lake Valley by winter snows and a blocking force of Mormons.

By the spring, anger was dissipating. Cumming entered Salt Lake City and was received with great goodwill. The Civil War submerged interest in Utah. Colonel Johnston became a Confederate general and was killed at Shiloh. Lincoln compared the Mormons to a log he had come across when clearing farmland in Illinois. "It was too hard to split, too wet to burn and too heavy to move, so we ploughed round it," he said. "Tell Brigham Young that if he will let me alone, I will let him alone."[27] The Mormon did so, building temples, tabernacles, schools, and mercantile and industrial projects, and sending missionaries to the far corners of the globe.

Polygamy remained an irritant. The first antipolygamy bill, passed in 1862, made marriage to more than one woman a crime; it was specifically aimed at Mormons, for it applied only in the territories and not in the states. The Mormons evaded it by maintaining that they were not legally married to their wives under United States law. Young certainly took no notice; the following year, at age sixty-two, he married a twenty-five year old, and, two years later, a twenty-one year old by whom he became a father in his seventieth year. When his last wife, Ann Eliza Webb, sued him for divorce on the grounds of neglect, cruelty, and desertion, she stated that he had assets of $8 million and an income of $40,000 a month; he claimed a fortune of not more than $600,000 and an income of $6,000 a month.* He maintained that since he was not legally married to her, he could not be divorced, a legal argument that won the day. Ann Eliza

---

*She exaggerated, although Mormons proved to be shrewd businesspeople. The actual figure at his death was $2.5 million.

joined the gentile crusade against the Mormons, publishing a book called *Wife No. 19.*

Young was a national figure, renowned from coast to coast. When Phineas T. Barnum visited Salt Lake City in 1870, the great showman told Brigham Young that he could guarantee him earnings of $200,000 a year if he would allow himself to be exhibited in New York, "for," Barnum said, "I consider you to be the best show in America." Brigham Young died seven years later. Polygamy did not long outlive him. A vigorous federal "crusade" was mounted against those who practiced it. Polygamists claimed that the new laws infringed on their religious liberty and thus were illegal. In 1890 the Supreme Court ruled the antipolygamy laws to be constitutional. The Mormon Church withdrew from further solemnization of plural marriages. Polygamists received presidential pardons on condition of future obedience. In 1896, Utah was admitted into the union.

❖ OTHER AMERICANS HAD millenary visions. The Millerites were followers of William Miller, a Baptist farmer and preacher from Dresden in the religious breeding ground of upstate New York. He believed that the Second Coming or Advent would take place within a year of March 21, 1843. Taking the words of Daniel 8:14—"And he said unto me, Unto two thousand and three hundred evenings and mornings, then shall the sanctuary be cleaned"—to mean years rather than days, he calculated that the cataclysm would take place in 1843. "Let us begin where the angel told us, from the going forth of the decree to build the walls of Jerusalem in troublous times, 457 years before Christ; take 457 from 2300, and it will leave AD 1843...."[28] Some fifty thousand followers sold their property and went to hilltops to await Advent, inspired by Miller's hugely popular newspaper, the *Midnight Cry.* The rival *New York Tribune* published an extra edition in 1843 to explain that Miller had got his mathematics wrong.

When Christ failed to appear, Adventists suffered "the Great Disappointment"; many had sold their assets and houses in anticipation. Ellen White, a Millerite who married an Adventist minister, gathered a group of those who still clung to the prophecy of Advent. White explained that Christ had entered the heavenly sanctuary in 1843, as a prelude to his reappearance to establish the New Jerusalem on earth. This was confirmed by the "two thousand visions and prophetic dreams" that she had experienced. White established the Seventh-Day Adventist Church in 1863; she is still looked upon as the "spirit of prophecy" and, through her many writings—her book, *Steps to Christ* has sold more than twenty million copies—dominates the movement still. White's followers cling fiercely to the Bible, believing it to contain the unerring rule of faith. They observe the Sabbath from sunset on Friday to sunset on Saturday, practice adult Baptism by total immersion, and continue to believe that the Second Coming is imminent, although they have set no date for it. They are otherwise puritanical Protestants, believing in the Trinity and in salvation through faith alone.

Seventh-Day Adventists' strict temperance—no alcohol or tobacco, and abstinence from coffee, tea, and meat recommended—is based on the belief that the body is the temple of the Holy Spirit. Their first overseas mission was to Southampton, England, in 1878. Several million now follow Ellen White's teachings worldwide, including all the inhabitants of Pitcairn Island in the Pacific, descendants of Christian Fletcher and the mutineers on the *Bounty*. Founded in the old witch-hunting town of Salem, Massachusetts in 1860, the Advent Christian Church preaches "conditional immortality" in which the dead remain unconscious until the Second Coming heralds the resurrection. Members of the Church of God (Abrahamic Faith) also believe the dead to be merely asleep, with the righteous waiting to reawake with the return of Christ. Adventists have a missionary zeal that has taken them far from their American roots. The thirty thousand American and Canadian members of the Advent Christian Church support missions in Japan, the Philippines, India, Mexico, and Malaysia.

❖ KINGDOM HALLS AND the familiar door-to-door missions of Jehovah's Witnesses, with their eagerly proffered copies of *The Watchtower* and *Awake!* magazines, are the creation of another American Adventist. Charles Taze Russell worked in his father's Pennsylvania drapery business before becoming convinced that Christ had returned invisibly to earth in 1874. Christ was actively preparing the Kingdom of God, so Russell claimed, which would follow the Battle of Armageddon. "The full end of the times of the Gentiles, i.e. the full end of their lease of dominion, will be reached in AD 1914," he wrote, "and that date will be the farthest limit of the rule of imperfect men."[29] His mathematics differed from Miller, who had taken 2,300 years as his base. Russell calculated the "time of the Gentiles" to be 2,520 years from 606 B.C., the date he gave for the removal of the crown from Zedekiah, the last king of Judah.* He formed his sect as the Zion's Watch Tower Bible and Tract Society in 1881, and his followers were known as Bible Students. They were baptized with total immersion, studied the Bible in their own translations, refused blood transfusions, and paid no respect to symbols of nationhood; they did not vote, salute flags, do military service, or accept allegiance to a government. They were also required to warn as many people as pos-

---

*Modern scholarship puts the date when Zedekiah was captured by Nebuchadnezzar's Babylonians near Jericho as 586 B.C. On that basis, the world should have ended in 1936.

Charles Taze Russell worked in his father's Pennsylvania drapery business before becoming convinced that Christ had returned to earth in 1874. "The full end of the times of the Gentiles," he wrote, "will be reached in A.D. 1914, and that date will be the farthest limit of the rule of imperfect men." His Jehovah's Witnesses were baptized with total immersion, refused blood transfusions, and paid no respect to symbols of nationhood. Although the world did not end as he predicted, there are now some five million Witnesses across the world.

sible about the coming "end time" to enable them to survive a First Judgment, Christ's millennial reign on earth, and a Second Judgment.

Russell set his survival rate pitilessly low. He preached that only a "small flock" of 144,000 people chosen from the entirety of human existence—"and there were sealed an hundred and forty four thousand of all the tribes of the children of Israel" (Rev. 7:4)—will qualify for eternal life in heaven. "Goats" by the billion will be flung into dishonored graves; they include all who have offended Witnesses, the leaders of other churches—"Pious frauds," he said, "called preachers or clergymen"—and Charles Darwin and the evolutionists, those who salute flags or urge blood transfusions or celebrate Christmas and, particularly, ex-Witnesses. The number of believers continued to grow despite the world not ending in 1914, for Christ's invisible reign as king was held to have begun. Russell traveled a million miles and delivered thirty thousand sermons before dying on a railway train in Pampa, Texas, in 1916. His last wish was to be wrapped "in a Roman toga," and his companions did the best they could with sheets from a Pullman coach. His successor, "Judge" Rutherford, a Missouri lawyer, was imprisoned in 1918 for inciting disloyalty and refusal of duty in the American armed forces; nonetheless, Witnesses already numbered in the millions.

Spiritualism dates back to biblical times. Its condemnation in Deuteronomy—"there shall not be found with thee . . . a charmer, or a consulter with a familiar spirit, or a wizard, or a necromancer" (Deut. 18:10–11)—and by the Church in general did not prevent its reappearance in modern form in upstate New York in 1848. A young girl named Margaret Fox heard what were known as the "Rochester knockings," after her hometown. Her mother described these as a rapping that the girl could conjure up, "not very loud, yet it produced a jarring of the bedsteads and chairs, that could be felt by placing our hands on the chair, or while we were in bed. . . . I asked the ages of my different children successively, and it gave a number of raps, corresponding to the ages. . . . Many were called in that night, who were out fishing in the creek, and they all heard the same noise." Mrs. Fox added that she was "very sorry that there has been so much excitement about it." As an adult, however, her daughter made a business of her rappings; she "conducted séances, made converts, and annoyed sceptics."[30] It became fashionable to make apparent contact with the souls of the dead through mediums and table-turning, rapping, automatic writing, and other devices. A Society for Psychical Research was founded in Britain in 1882 to study the phenomenon scientifically; most mediums have transpired to be frauds, but a number of inexplicable cases persist.

Another American woman, Mary Baker Eddy, founded her own church and a newspaper of international standing, the *Christian Science Monitor*. She had a sickly childhood in New Hampshire. Her ailments lingered and she turned to a mesmerist to relieve them, but suffered a relapse. Recovering from a severe fall in 1866, she claimed to have undergone a healing while reading the passage in Matthew's gospel where Jesus tells the man sick of the palsy to arise. She believed that she had found in the Bible the spiritual law and science underlying the healing work of Jesus, which was not a miraculous intervention in nature but the operation of God's power, and that this healing was open to all those who accepted his teaching. Nothing is truly real that does not reflect the nature of God, she said; evil and sickness are "unreal" and are destroyed, not by medical treatment, but by the patient's awareness of God's power and love. "God's ways are not ours," she told an audience at Chicago. "His pity is expressed in modes above the human. His chastisements are the manifestations of Love. The sympathy of His eternal Mind is fully expressed in Divine Science, which blots out all our iniquities and heals all our diseases. Human pity often brings pain. Science supports harmony, denies suffering, and destroys it with the sympathy of Truth. Whatever seems material, seems thus only to the material senses, and is but the subjective state of mortal and material thought."[31]

Her thoughts were laid out in her book *Science and Health* in 1875; it had a huge success, and four years later, with her third husband, Asa G. Eddy, she founded the Church of Christ, Scientist in Boston. She had been brought up as a Congregationalist, and the church structure she laid down in her *Manual of The Mother Church* was largely run by its congregations, administered by a board of five directors who appoint their successors. Services were simple and austere; on Sundays there were readings from the Bible and *Science and Health,* hymns, the Lord's Prayer, and silent prayer; members gave accounts of healings at midweek meetings.

By Eddy's death in 1910 there were more than a thousand churches in America, and others were spreading through Protestant Europe. It was only in charities that the transatlantic flow was reversed, and in the great voids of Christendom—Africa, the East, the Pacific—that Old World missionaries competed with the zeal of the New.

❖

❖

❖

"Drawing the eye-tooth of the tiger":

Missions

Christian conquest underpinned the century's colossal missionary enterprises. In 1810 the Baptist William Carey wrote of the "Pleasing Dream" of holding a general missionary conference at which every country on earth would be represented. "Expect great things from God," Carey said, "and attempt great things for God." He practiced his motto with the indefatigable piety of his age and calling. As a young shoemaker in the English Midlands, he cobbled at night while running a school and teaching himself Latin, Greek, and Hebrew by day. The Baptist Missionary Society was founded at his pleading in 1792; a year later, Carey sailed to India as its first missionary. Here he ran an indigo factory while evangelizing and translating the New Testament into Bengali; when a Christian college was opened at Calcutta, Carey became a professor there and translated parts of the Bible into a further twenty-four languages and dialects. He was shocked by suttee, the ancient Hindu custom in which Indian widows were burned on their husbands' funeral pyres, and achieved its abolition.

As Carey wrote, a few missionaries were working in China, India, and the East Indies, with a handful in the Pacific and none in Japan, Korea, or the vast interior of Africa. A century later, however, the first World Missionary Conference* was held at Edinburgh, and his vision was within a whisker of reality. Most denominations now had missions, and often the smallest, such as the puritanical Plymouth Brethren, made the greatest proportional effort. They were active

---

*About 1,200 delegates representing 160 missionary boards and societies took part in it. The slogan of the chairman, the American Methodist John Raleigh Mott, was: "the evangelization of the world in this generation." With the Bible translated into all the main living languages, universities producing a stream of well-educated and well-funded missionaries, and Christian kings and presidents ruling four-fifths of the land surface of the planet, Mott's ambition was less boastful than might seem.

William Carey is seen in Calcutta with
his pundit, who advised him on his
translations of the Bible. Carey was
awash with the tireless piety of his age
and calling. The Baptist Missionary
Society was founded at his prompting
in 1792, and he sailed for India as its
first missionary the next year. He ran
an indigo factory, helped build a Christian college, evangelized, translated the
Bible into Bengali and several dialects,
and achieved the abolition of suttee,
the Hindu custom of burning widows
on their husbands' funeral pyres.

around the globe. Bishop Archibald Fleming, "Archie of the Arctic," was spending his first winter in an igloo at Kinguckjuak, amid the acrid smoke of blubber
lamps, spared from starvation only when a wind shift enabled the Inuit to find
walrus, feeling "an at-one-ness we had not known before." Six thousand miles to
the south, amid the Lenguas of the Chaco, the solitary missionary W. Barbrooke
Grub rejoiced that a "chaotic mass of savage heathenism" was now so peaceful
that "anyone can wander alone and unharmed . . . over a district larger than Ireland."[1] Missionaries were absent only from Afghanistan, Tibet, and Nepal, and
parts of Arabia.

Much of this mirrored the headlong expansion of Western power, a fact that
some ascribed to divine will. "I should consider myself worse than despicable," a
Methodist missionary in West Africa, Dennis Kemp, observed, "if I failed to declare my firm conviction that the British Army and Navy are today used by God
for the accomplishment of His purpose."[2]

The British, seemingly in retreat at the start of the nineteenth century after
the loss of the American colonies, ruled a quarter of the planet's people and its
land surface by 1900. Their empire was so vast that the compilers of the Colonial
Office List, which tabulated British territories, wearied of their task, signing it
off: "And countless other smaller possessions and nearly all the rocks and isolated

islands of the ocean." Administrators were often hostile to missionaries, even though men like David Livingstone first explored areas of Africa and the Pacific; but they could not keep them out. France had carved out four million square miles of territory, much of it in the Moslem world, and Germany had large swaths of East and West Africa. Indeed, almost the whole of Africa was ruled by Christian powers, and the notable exception, Ethiopia, was itself Christian, while in Southeast Asia only Thailand retained its independence.

The doctrine of the White Man's Burden* mingled with Manifest Destiny to justify the new wave of Christian expansion. Scientific and technological superiority gave the West the means of mastery: steamships, railroads, Maxim guns. The bringing of the Bible, schools, sanitation, hospitals—many missionaries were medically trained—supplied moral purpose. Livingstone opened Central Africa to colonization as well as to Christ; A. J. Beveridge, a U.S. senator, justified the American annexation of the Philippines as "the mission of our race, trustees under God, of the civilization of the world."[4] French missionaries in Tahiti complained that their British counterparts "appear to have undertaken to invade all the islands of the Pacific Ocean . . ."[5] It was easy to mock the missionary, sweating beneath the palms in his stovepipe hat and black frock coat, grimly caging the natives like captured birds of paradise, ripping away at their simple pleasures and replacing them with Bible-reading and a sense of sin. A joylessness is caught in the popular hymn for foreign missions that Reginald Heber wrote before exchanging his Shropshire parsonage for the bishopric of Calcutta:

> What though the spicy breezes
> Blow soft o'er Ceylon's isle.
> Though every prospect pleases
> And only man is vile . . .

Many missionaries were fundamentalists who thought all native religions were idolatry, so they often had little sympathy for local customs, imposing European dress and morals, and stripping old and deep roots from their converts.

Yet there is a nobility to missionaries' lonely lives and sometimes terrible deaths. They were buried alive, and roasted and eaten; of nine Basel missionaries landed on the African Gold Coast in 1828, all but one died of disease within six

---

*"If there is in the British race, as I think there is, a special aptitude for taking up the white man's burden," wrote J. E. C. Welldon, "it may be ascribed, above all other causes, to the spirit of organized games."[3] Welldon was headmaster of Harrow, one of the British public schools that supplied many of the proconsuls of missions and empire, and his praise of sports—the world's first soccer, tennis, and golf championships were all nineteenth-century British creations—reflects the evangelical culture of "muscular Christianity" which held the health of the spirit to be nurtured by a healthy body. He later became bishop of Calcutta.

months. Allen Gardiner, a former Royal Navy commander, went with six companions to Tierra del Fuego in 1850. A ship with provisions failed to arrive, and the party died of starvation on the shore. Gardiner's diary was found; though weak, he wrote, "We feel and know that God is here. I am, beyond the power of expression, happy."[6] Father Damien of the Picpus Society was sent along at his own request to the leper colony at Molokai in the Hawaiian Islands; he tended to six hundred lepers, dressing their wounds, building houses, digging their graves, and when he caught the disease, he continued to nurse them until he himself became helpless and died.

Missionaries were persistent. The Scot Alexander Duff was twice shipwrecked on his way to India; once there, he made thirty-three converts in eighteen years. American missionaries in Thailand had translated the New Testament by 1843, but it took a further sixteen years for them to win their first Thai convert. Francis McDougall was sent out to the headhunting Dyaks of Borneo in 1847. Five of his children were lost to disease; in a letter to *The Times,* he ascribed his own survival in encounters with pirates to "my double-barrelled Terry's breechloader which proved the most deadly weapon from its true shooting and certainty of rapidity of fire."* After four years McDougall was ministering to five converts.

No doubt some converts saw baptism in terms of colonial favors, better jobs, housing, and schooling, or, in the case of Moslem horse thieves in Central Asia, lighter sentences from Orthodox magistrates; others were faithful to death. In Madagascar, Queen Ranavalona told her soldiers to "seize every Christian they could find, and without trial bind them hand and foot, dig a pit on the spot, and then pour boiling water on them and bury them." In 1849, eighteen Christians were killed, fourteen hurled over cliffs and the others burned alive. "They prayed as long as they had life," an eyewitness reported. "Then they died, but softly. Indeed, gentle was the going forth of their life, and astonished were all the people around them that beheld the burning of them."[7] After the death of the ferocious queen in 1861, converts who had refused to apostatize, men and women, came out of the forests where they had been held. They "reappeared as if they had risen from the dead"; some bore the deep scars of chains and fetters, and others were worn to skeletons who could scarcely walk, but they sang the pilgrim song: "When the Lord turned against the captivity of Zion, we were like them that dream."[8]

---

*This public revelation of his unmissionary relish for a fight earned McDougall a gentle admonition from his bishop in London, who suggested that "when next you get into a similar encounter, you must get your wife to write about it." In fact, missionaries were by no means all prim and docile. Tribal chiefs threatened to kill the Methodist George Brown on New Britain, an island west of Papua, in 1875. Brown armed himself with two fowling pieces and a revolver, and a posse of Fijian converts, and attacked and defeated them.

Missionaries stimulated interest in distant continents among Europeans and Americans with piteous tales of cannibalism, slavery, and nakedness. The "missionary box" for donations became part of the table furniture in many homes. They were filled by worthy women like Mrs. Jellyby, in Dickens's *Bleak House,* who "could see nothing nearer than Africa," and who abandoned her family duties in favor of the mission station of "Borrioboola-Gha" on the banks of the Niger. Single women served as both Protestant and Catholic missionaries from midcentury, but by its end women greatly outnumbered men, and there were forty-four thousand Catholic nuns alone working in mission territories. If they had little direct power in the colonies, whose administrators often found them bothersome, the grandest imperialist did well to bear their influence in mind. "I have to think of the howling Societies at home who have sympathy with all black men," General Sir Garnet Wolseley, the British commander in chief in South Africa wrote in 1879, reluctantly abandoning a plan to have Swazi tribesmen kill rebellious Zulus, "whilst they care nothing for the miseries inflicted on their own kith and kin who have the misfortune to be located near these interesting niggers."[9]

❖ THE NEW WAVE of Protestant missions began in Britain with successors to the Society for the Promoting of Christian Knowledge and the Society for the Propagation of the Gospel. The Methodist venture of 1786 was followed by a flood of missionary societies—the London, the Church, the British, and Foreign Bible, the South American, Melanesian, and Central African; donations to the Church Missionary Society, for example, increased thirty-eight-fold in the three decades from 1813. The Basel Mission followed the Berlin Society of 1824 a year later, and others joined apace—Danish, Swedish, French, and Norwegian—until almost every European country had a mission. The American Bible Society began in 1816 by sending Bibles to the frontier settlers, and by the end of the century the American Board of Commissioners and other missionaries were as familiar abroad as the British. Catholic foreign missions revived powerfully, with new orders, Marists, Holy Ghost Fathers, and White Fathers; the congregation of the Society of the Divine Word was active in Argentina, West Africa, Papua New Guinea, and Japan.

Steam power and the vast resources of empire provided the Christian soldier and missionary with global reach. The career of General "Chinese" Gordon, mystic and martial, gives individual flesh to the nineteenth-century phenomenon. As Islam weakened, the young Gordon surveyed the new frontier between Russia and Turkey in 1857. Three years later he captured Peking from a rebel force as China was opened up to missionaries. Returning to England, he used a routine posting to relieve the needs of the poor, visiting the sick, teaching, and clothing orphans and strays. In 1873 he was in Egypt, vowing to suppress the slave trade through control of the territories of the equatorial Nile. Gordon established forts along the river and had steamers assembled above the rapids, navigating the waters of Lake Albert. He was appointed governor of the Sudan in 1877; his bailiwick ran from the Second Cataract of the Nile to the Great Lakes, and from the Red Sea to the headwaters of the streams that fall into Lake Chad. For three years, wracked with fever, plagued by enemies, he explored the vast flatlands to the west of the Nile basin. In 1880 he resigned due to ill-health, spending the next two years visiting China and India and proposing land law reform in Ireland. He spent most of 1883 in Palestine, in contemplation and strengthening his faith. The following year, Muhammad Ahmad, a Moslem revivalist known as the Mahdi to his Dervish followers, declared holy war in the Sudan. Gordon returned to relieve garrisons under threat there. A month after he arrived in Khartoum it was besieged by the Mahdi. A relief column arrived outside Khartoum in January 1885, more than six months after the siege had begun. Gordon had been murdered on the steps of the palace in Khartoum two days earlier.

The historic victories of Islam were reversed as European powers preyed on Turkish weakness. The great bulk of the Ottoman subjects in southeastern Europe had remained Christian; only in Albania, Bosnia, and parts of Bulgaria had significant numbers embraced their rulers' faith. The Turks were tolerant in matters of religion and culture, much more so than Catholic Crusaders had proved; political dissidence was another matter, and savage reprisals created spasms of righteous revulsion in Christian capitals, running most deeply among the Orthodox in St. Petersburg. Bishop Germanos proclaimed a Greek rising in 1821 at the monastery of Aghia Lavra in the Peloponnese. Within fifteen months the Greeks had captured Missolonghi, Athens, and Thebes; the Turks responded by hanging the Patriarch Gregorios in Constantinople. The poet Byron joined the insurgents in 1823, dying of marsh fever at Missolonghi the following year, his masterpiece *Don Juan* unfinished:

> The mountains look on Marathon
> And Marathon looks on the sea:
> And musing there an hour alone,
> I dream'd that Greece might still be free.

An army under the son of the pasha of Egypt was sent to crush the revolt in 1825. The largely Sudanese force burned and plundered for two years. The British, incensed by reports of Greek Christians sold as slaves in Cairo, joined with France and Russia to force concessions from the Turks. They annihilated the Turco-

Egyptian fleet at Navarino Bay in 1827 and Greece was freed after almost four hundred years of Turkish rule.

Others—Romanians, Bulgarians, Serbs, Macedonians—waited longer. Their liberation was primarily a matter of their own nationalisms and the intervention of the great European powers; but religion was inseparable from their sense of identity, and Ottoman reprisals, such as the Bulgarian Horror of 1876 in which 20,000 Christian peasants were slaughtered after the murder of 136 Turkish officials, provided a moral cloak for outside intervention. By 1913, Turkey's presence in Europe was reduced to a narrow strip, albeit containing Constantinople. The whole of the southern Mediterranean fell to the European powers. France occupied Algeria, birthplace of Augustine, from which Christians had wholly disappeared after the Moslem conquest twelve hundred years before, in 1830. Tunis and Morocco, from which Moslems had sailed to conquer Spain, and whose corsairs had enslaved thousands of Christians, were divided between France and Spain. The British occupied Egypt in 1881, and the Italians conquered Libya in 1911.

Only in Central Asia, however, where the Russians mounted great spring campaigns against the descendants of the Golden Horde, the troops marching barefoot across the steppe to the sound of kettledrums, were there large numbers of Moslem apostates. The "apostle of the Kalmucks," Michael Jakovlevich Glucharev, worked amid the valleys and dark lakes of the Altai Plateau; many Chuvashes and Tartars converted, and some Turkomen after the emir of Bokhara became a dependent of the Christian czar in the 1880s. By the end of the century the Russians were in the Pamirs, on the borders of China and Afghanistan. But the conversions were often superficial. A monk traveling in Siberia asked an old Buriat why he was not baptized. "I haven't stolen a horse," he replied. "Why in the world would I want to be baptized?"[10] It transpired that every rogue, swindler, and horse thief in the district asked for baptism, since magistrates passed lighter sentences on Christians, and missionaries, anxious to boost their conversion statistics, were happy to oblige.

Missionaries had some success in the East Indies, modern Indonesia. The Portuguese planted the faith firmly in their colony on Timor, the site of Christian and Moslem violence at the end of the twentieth century. Freelance preachers were in the vanguard in the Dutch islands. Johannes Emde, a German with the pietist's regard for inner experience and personal commitment, became fascinated by Java because he was told that the island had no winter. This contradicted Genesis—"while the earth remaineth . . . cold and heat, and summer and winter . . . shall not cease" (Gen. 8:22)—and Emde sailed off to look for himself. He set himself up as a watchmaker in Surabaya, married a Javanese girl, and in 1843 brought thirty-five Moslems he had converted in local villages to a Dutch minister for baptism. Planters and others founded Christian communities in East Java.

Sulawesi (Celebes) and Sumatra were less Moslem dominated, and progress was easier. Two American missionaries, Samuel Munson and Henry Lyman, were killed and eaten by Batak cannibals in the wilds of upland Sumatra in 1834; the number of Christian Sumatrans was put at 52 in 1866, but several chiefs then converted, and the figure had climbed to 103,000 by the end of the century.

Elsewhere, however, Moslems were generally impervious to Christianity. "I am not reaping the harvest; I scarcely claim to be sowing the seed; I am hardly ploughing the soil; but I am gathering the stones," the Irish missionary Robert Bruce wrote from Isfahan in Iran. "That, too, is missionary work; let it be supported by loving sympathy and fervent prayer."[11] He created a tiny community; ninety years later, in 1961, the first Iranian bishop of the Anglican Church, Hassan Barnabas Dehqani-Tafti, was consecrated. Across the Persian Gulf, the Anglican Thomas French began work in Muscat in 1891, and was followed by Americans. In its first fifty years the Church in Arabia won five converts. The White Fathers, in their white cassocks and mantles, were bound by solemn oath for lifelong work in the African missions. Their founder, Cardinal Lavigerie, the great archbishop of Algiers, was the friend and champion of slaves. It was largely through his pressure that an international agreement for abolition was finally signed in 1892. Lavigerie persisted in his evangelism despite the massacre of missionaries by Tuaregs, yet he knew his task was near hopeless, at least with North Africa Moslems. "I claim the right to love you as my children," he told them, "even though you do not recognise me as your father."

❖ CAREY, THE FIRST English missionary in India, landed there in 1793. He sailed on a Danish ship, however, and at first worked in the Danish territory of Serampore. The East India Company, the British monopoly that controlled large parts of the subcontinent, banned missions until 1813. The American Congregationalist John Scudder who then arrived in Bombay was followed by other Americans, Presbyterians in the Punjab and Baptists working among the headhunting Nagas in northeast Assam, by Germans and Swiss of the Basel and Leipzig missions among the destitute of the west coast, and the south by Danes and Swedes. The Norwegian Lars Olsen Skefsrund, atoning for a wasted youth, founded his own mission among the Santali aborigines, writing a classic grammar of their language and mustering 15,000 converts. Hinduism and Islam were difficult to crack, however; by 1851, only 91,000 in a population of 150 million were claimed as Christian, though 339 missionaries were working among them.

Even when British rule replaced that of the East India Company after the Indian Mutiny of 1857, the government retained a wary neutrality toward religion. Most converts were low-caste, or outcastes—the poor of the Telegu-speaking areas of Madras, Bihari tribes, polyandrous Todas from the Nilgiri hills whose women had several husbands, sweepers, workers in the tanning trade. A few of the Moslem and Hindu elite converted: the Brahman Marayan Vaman Tilak, a poet and hymn writer, hostile until an Englishman gave him a New Testament to read on a train, and a believer before he had reached the end of Matthew, chapter 5; Ramabai, daughter of a Brahman scholar, working among famine orphans and young and neglected widows who under Hindu law cannot remarry. The Jesuits built different entrances to their churches, and separated the castes by low walls; the British, although building many churches for their own soldiers, engineers, planters, and civil servants, and establishing bishoprics in Madras, Bombay, and Calcutta, were uneasy about sharing their faith with their subjects. At the end of the century, Americans alone outnumbered British missionaries.

In Burma the pioneer was another American, the Baptist Adoniram Judson, who said that winning a convert was "like drawing the eye-tooth of a live tiger." He translated the Bible into Burmese, the rite of passage for so many first-comers, but had little success in the towns. The Karen tribespeople in the hills welcomed him, however. Illiterate, despised by the more sophisticated Burmese, they had a tradition of a creator God and believed that they had fallen from favor to servility because they had lost a sacred book. Judson had such a book, and he preached the mercy of Christ with conviction. By 1851 there were ten thousand Baptists among the Karen.

❖ CHINA WAS THOUGHT the glittering prize. The first Protestant missionary to China, Robert Morrison, arrived at Canton on an American ship in 1807. He worked for twelve years to translate the Bible; it was illegal for foreigners to be taught Chinese, and so he studied silently and furtively. "To acquire the Chinese," his colleague William Milne wrote, "is a work for men with bodies of brass, lungs of steel, heads of oak, hands of spring steel, eyes of eagles, hearts of apostles, memories of angels, lives of Methuselah."[12] It took Morrison seven years to win his first Protestant convert, Tsae A-ko, whom he baptized at "a spring of water issuing from the foot of a lofty hill by the seaside, away from human observation." He had greater success among the overseas Chinese. In 1818, Morrison founded an Anglo-Chinese college at Malacca, which taught English and Western science, to reflect Morrison's hope that "the light of science and revelation will, by means of this institution, peacefully and gradually shed their luster on the eastern limit of Asia and the islands of the rising sun."

Gunboats proved more effective in gaining influence. The British wished to open China to the opium trade as well as to Christ; the ruthless application of sea power forced the Chinese to cede Hong Kong to Britain as a colony, and to open five "treaty ports" to foreigners, including Shanghai and Canton. The classic colonial trinity unrolled: God, government, and—in case these failed—force. Force was the priority; the first great British building in Hong Kong was Flagstaff House, the seat of the commander of British forces, but it was followed immediately by the airy Anglican Cathedral of St. John, at whose altar the taipans, the great merchants of the China trade, might, if they were so minded, beg God to pity the opium addicts from whom they extracted their fortunes. The bishopric of Victoria in Hong Kong was founded in 1849. Within a few years Hong Kong had become a base for Methodists and Presbyterians, Baptists and Episcopalians, and missionaries from the American Board.

Education and medicine were mission planks. Many missionaries studied medicine, founding hospitals and medical schools. The University of Calcutta, and the American University of Beirut, originally the Syrian Protestant College, are among their many surviving creations. In Hong Kong, St. Paul's College was founded to train Chinese ministers; in Shanghai, the first American bishop, William J. Boone, ordained his first deacon in 1851. Some hoped that Chinese converts would evangelize deep into the still forbidden interior of China. Karl Gützlaff used Swiss and German funds to employ dozens of Hong Kong Chinese, who wrote graphic reports of journeying into all of China's eighteen provinces, distributing Bibles and forming small congregations; but most of these "evangelists" were opium addicts or criminals, and few bothered to leave the colony before squandering their money.

The strange rebellion of T'ai P'ing—meaning "great peace"—was Christian-inspired. Its leader, Hung Hsiu-ch'uan, became interested in Christian books he received from Liang Fah, the first Chinese pastor of the Protestant missions, whom Robert Morrison had ordained. In 1843, Hung made lengthy visits to Issachar Roberts, an American Baptist missionary; he did not go through with baptism, although he was prepared for it and himself baptized his followers. His followers called themselves the Worshippers of Shang Ti, the true God, and they formed the liberation army of T'ai P'ing, dedicated to the destruction of idols, the abolition of opium, and the overthrow of Manchu domination. The rebels stormed Nanking in 1853, proclaiming the dynasty of T'ai P'ing, with Hung as T'ai P'ing Wang, the king of the great peace. His followers accepted the Ten Commandments—extending the seventh to condemn opium—observed the Sabbath, and practiced baptism. Their liturgy was Christian-based:

> Praise God, the heavenly and holy Father,
> Praise Jesus, the holy Lord and Savior of the World.
> Praise the Holy Spirit, the sacred Spiritual Force
> Praise the Three Persons United, the one true Lord.

Missionaries hoped that the movement would open China to the faith. They were welcomed to Hung's headquarters. "I fully believe that God is uprooting idolatry in this land through the insurgents," Griffith John, of the London Missionary Society, wrote in 1860, "and that he will by means of them, in connection with the foreign missionary, plant Christianity in its stead."[13] Ironically, the fervently Christian General Gordon earned his "Chinese" sobriquet in crushing the rebellion.

James Hudson Taylor, a medical man who arrived in 1853, carried the faith into the heart of China. His interdenominational China Inland Mission became the largest mission in the world. It accepted any committed Christian and was directed in China; its missionaries wore Chinese dress and lived closely with the Chinese. By 1896 more than fifteen hundred foreign missionaries and their families were living in five hundred stations in China; 641 Chinese missionaries, ex-drug addicts among them, were working up to the borders of Tibet. That year, however, the Dowager Empress, the "old Buddha," openly sympathized with the violent antiwestern movement I Ho Chu'an, the Righteous Harmony Fists, or Boxers.

A cry of *mieh yang*—"destroy the foreigner"—was roused. On June 24, 1900, an imperial decree ordering the killing of all foreigners was issued in Peking. The foreign legations in Peking were besieged for fifty-five days; 135 adults and 53 children from Protestant missionary families were killed in the cities while others fled for the coast. Among Chinese victims, those among the half million Catholic converts suffered worst. The carnage was brief, and by August a six-nation foreign force had taken Peking.

China, humiliated, was open to foreign influence. "Not since the days of the Reformation, not indeed since Pentecost," Bishop Bashford of North China declared in 1910, "has so great an opportunity confronted the Christian Church."[14] He seemed right. Protestant missionaries alone numbered 5,462, and converts were multiplying. Revolution swept away the emperor, and a republic was declared.

Its provisional president, Sun Yat-sen, was a Christian (the son of a Christian farmer in Canton) educated by missionaries in Honolulu. He was married to the daughter of Charles Jones Soong, a merchant who had converted to Methodism while studying at Vanderbilt University and who had founded the YMCA in Shanghai after setting up as a Bible publisher and salesman. Sun Yat-sen was asked what had made the revolution successful. "Christianity more than any other single cause," he replied. "Along with its ideals of religious freedom, it brings a knowledge of Western political freedom, and along with these it inculcates everywhere a doctrine of universal love and peace. These ideals appeal to the Chinese; they largely caused the Revolution, and they largely determined its peaceful character."[15]

✤ THE FIRST KOREAN Christians were prisoners captured during the Japanese invasions of Korea in 1592–98 who converted to Catholicism. The faith then died out, to be revived in 1777 by a group of scholars who came across Matteo Ricci's treatises in Chinese, especially his *True Principles Concerning God*. They sent one of their number, Yi Seng Hung, to Peking in 1783 where he was baptized as Peter. He baptized other converts on his return; these in turn organized their own Korean Church with a bishop and priests, celebrating mass and hearing confessions in the Catholic manner.

In 1794 a Chinese priest, James Ti-yu, was sent to care for them. To his astonishment he found four thousand self-made Christians who accepted his ministry. Korea's Confucian rulers were hostile to foreign religion, and he was put to death in 1803. Three European priests of the Société des Missions Etrangères de Paris smuggled themselves into Korea in 1836, but were detected and executed after three years. Catholicism continued in secret in Korea until a further persecution in 1866. Two bishops, seven priests, and at least two thousand lay Catholics were martyred.* Catholicism was permanently weakened. The first Korean Protestants were baptized by Scottish missionaries in Manchuria in 1876. Large numbers of American Presbyterians and Methodists entered Korea from 1884, founding dozens of schools, colleges, and hospitals; the Underwood and Appenzeller families served the Korean churches for many years. Presbyterians baptized their first converts in 1886. By 1910 they had thirty thousand communicants and claimed many more believers.

Similar persecution in Indochina was used as a pretext for colonization there. The emperor Minh-Mang ruled in 1833 that any subject who entered a church "adhering to these abominable customs" was to be killed. The first European martyr, Father Isidor Gagelin, was strangled a few months later; nine others followed him. Minh-Mang sent crucifixes to provincial governors in 1836, ordering them to be placed on the ground at the entry to towns. "Those who refuse to trample the cross underfoot," he ruled, "are to be beaten without mercy, tortured and put to death."[16] The emperor Tu-Duc started a fresh campaign; the vicar apostolic of Tonkin, Monsignor Retord, died of privation, and other priests fled to the central mountains. Napoleon III cited 115 martyred priests—and a claimed Catholic congregation of three hundred thousand—as justification for sending an expedition to occupy Cochin China in 1862. The French occupied the whole peninsula, Vietnam, Laos, Cambodia, in 1885.

A high-minded Episcopalian, Townsend Harris, was the first American resi-

---

*On his visit to South Korea in 1984, 103 Korean martyrs were canonized by John Paul II.

dent allowed into Japan, in 1854. The Christian services he held in his residence at Edo (Tokyo) were the first to pass unpunished for two hundred years, though it was confirmed that Japanese Christians had survived underground when the Catholic missionary Father Petitjean arrived four years later. It was still illegal for Japanese to go abroad, but a young convert, Shimeta Niishima, escaped in 1864 through the northern port of Hakodate and studied at Andover Theological Seminary. Baptized Joseph Neesima, he was ordained and accepted by the American Board as a missionary. He returned to Kyoto, not far from the imperial palace, and established what was to become Doshisha University. Two hundred students were baptized there in 1884; other early converts were made at a school founded by the West Point graduate Captain L. L. James at Kumamoto in western Japan. The "Sapporo band" arose among students converted by Dr. W. S. Clark of Massachusetts, who taught in the new agricultural college in the Hokkaido city. One of them, Uchimuru, formed the Mukyokai, a "non-Church" movement which had no structure and no guide beyond the Bible. "The truly Christian temple has God's earth for a floor, and his sky for a ceiling," Uchimuru explained; "its altar is the heart of the believer; its law is God's Word, and his Holy Spirit is its only pastor."[17] He was a fiery preacher and drew crowds of a thousand to his Bible lectures in Tokyo.

Russia lay across the Sea of Japan and to the north in the Kurile Islands. The Orthodox missionary John Veniaminov had reached the Aleutians in 1824 after a fourteen-month journey from Irkutsk in Siberia. Three years later he crossed the Bering Sea to the American mainland at Nushagak, establishing a base on the island of Sitka. From 1850 he was the archbishop of a vast Orthodox diocese running from Yakutsk to the Aleutians, Kuriles, and Kamchatka, and including Alaska and the northern California coast to Fort Ross. In 1861, six years before Alaska was sold to the United States, the Russian American colonies had seven churches and thirty-five chapels; a visitor found the Aleuts to be "intensely pious, greeting you with a prayer, and bidding you farewell with a blessing."

Veniaminov helped found the Orthodox Missionary Society in 1870. Ivan Kasatkin, known as Nikolai, at first carried out secret baptisms in Japan, but later moved to Tokyo and built a splendid cathedral. The Russo-Japanese War did not affect his growing congregation. At Nikolai's death in 1912, he had created a church with 33,000 members in more than two hundred congregations, with three dozen Japanese Orthodox priests and a seminary. Henry St. George Tucker, the presiding bishop of the American Episcopalian Church, thought Nikolai the "outstanding Christian missionary" of the age. The total number of Christians in Japan may have reached 250,000. At the Three Religions Conference held by the government in 1912, Christianity was recognized with Shinto and Buddhism as one of the religions of Japan. The government wanted it to "step out of the narrow circles within which it is confined, and endeavor to conform to the national polity . . ."

✤ THE MISSION DRIVE in the Pacific was supported from Australia and New Zealand, where white settlers outnumbered the natives. The Australian aboriginal religion was too closely tied to the land and their ancestors for Christianity to make headway, despite Protestant missions and the efforts of Spanish Benedictines in western Australia. Anglican chaplains ministered to the early white convicts, who were obliged to attend Anglican services, although many were Irish rebels and Catholics. They were sometimes served by convict priests and then by missionary priests; the Benedictine scholar monk J. B. Polding became Australia's first Catholic bishop in 1835, a year before the consecration of an Anglican bishop. As in Britain itself, Anglican claims to the status of the established Church raised tensions among Presbyterians as well as Catholics; South Australia was founded as a separate colony in 1836 to encourage the free settlement of dissenters, including the Lutheran refugees from Germany who built the region's wine industry.

The first Christian service in New Zealand was held at Rangihoua on the Bay of Islands on Christmas Day, 1814, by Samuel Marsden. He had sailed to New South Wales in 1794 to become Anglican chaplain at Sydney; he was a fine sheep farmer who took the first consignment of Australian wool to England in 1807, but he was known as "the Flogging Parson" for his harshness to Irish prisoners. The first Maori baptism took place a decade later. French Marists were also converting Maoris, but the Treaty of Waitangi which the Maori chiefs signed in 1840 made New Zealand a British colony. The first Anglican bishop, George Augustus Selwyn, was the epitome of the "muscular Christian," an athlete who had rowed for Cambridge in the first university boat race in 1829 and a man of deep earnestness who had mastered Maori on the boat out from England. Although even the agnostic Charles Darwin approved of the mission work—"five years ago nothing but the fern flourished here," he wrote on visiting the Church Missionary Society station at Waimate; "the lesson of the missionary is the enchanter's wand"—fighting plagued it. A group of Maoris apostatized during the wars with the British and created a new cult that blended old beliefs with Christianity. The archangel Gabriel was said to have appeared while Maoris were celebrating the death of a Captain Lloyd by drinking blood from his penis. The angel promised to expel the English from the land provided that the Maoris carried the captain's pickled head with them, for through it they would be able to contact Jehovah. The movement was called the Hau-Hau after its war cry. When the rebellion was put down, Bishop Selwyn commented sadly that it "is simply an expression of an utter loss of faith in everything that is English, clergy and all alike."[18]

Cannibalism was an occupational hazard in the South Pacific, as the first expedition of the London Missionary Society reported in 1796. It was found that once the king was converted, his subjects would rapidly follow, but before this was achieved the missionary stood a fair chance of being killed and eaten. Of the pioneer party of ten missionaries who landed on Tonga, three were murdered, one "went native," and the other six were picked up by a ship and returned to Australia. John Thomas, a former blacksmith from Worcester, persevered; in 1830 he baptized Taufaahua, king of the island of Haabai, who took the name George. By 1839, George was king of the whole Tonga group and the islands were Christian.

On Tahiti, King Pomare was a "resolute idolater and cannibal" engaged in subduing the island. The missionaries supplied him with ammunition in order to curry favor with him; they helped his son Pomare II in his war, and, duly grateful, he was baptized in front of four thousand subjects in 1819 in a church he had built himself. Whether he was a true convert is doubtful; Herman Melville described him as a "sad debauchee and a drunkard, and even charged with unnatural crimes"; he ensured that his people followed him into the faith by executing the recalcitrant.[19] The missionaries' regime was pious and worthy; but set against

A missionary in the Mariana Islands of the South Pacific. Victorian missionaries were later criticized as joyless bigots, but there was a nobility to their lonely lives and often terrible deaths. Pioneer missionaries were killed and eaten in Tonga, the Solomons, and New Hebrides. Eighty were lost to disease or murder in the first fifty years in New Guinea. Of nine missionaries who landed in West Africa in 1828, all but one was dead in six months. "We feel and know that God is here," a British missionary wrote as he was dying of starvation in Tierra del Fuego in 1850. "I am, beyond all power of expression, happy."

the anchorage at Papeete, a "vortex of iniquity, the Sodom of the Pacific" where their writ did not run and American whalers were free to trade liquor for the favors of local girls, it was joyless. Sunday observance and church attendance were compulsory, while dancing, strong drink, and promiscuity were banned. Catholic missionaries were less puritanical than Protestants, and the islanders may have been relieved when the French took control in 1843.

The Congregationalist John Williams, sent out by the London Missionary Society to the Society Islands that bore its name, traveled so extensively by small boat and canoe that by 1834 he reported that "no group of islands, nor single island of importance, within 2000 miles of Tahiti has been left unvisited." He left converts as teachers on the major islands, including eight Tahitians on Samoa, and when French missionaries later arrived they found a Christian community of two thousand on the island. In 1834, Williams returned to England to oversee the printing of the New Testament in Raratongan, and raised four thousand pounds to build a mission ship. In 1838 he sailed in her to the Solomons and New Hebrides; he was clubbed and speared to death by the natives of Erromanga and eaten at a feast. Erromanga produced five missionary martyrs and was not fully evangelized until the twentieth century.

Fiji was "dark and brutal." The first task of a Methodist who arrived in 1835 was to gather and bury the heads, hands, and feet of eighty victims who had been cooked and partially eaten. Twenty years later, after the chief Thakombau had been baptized, missionaries reported that the island was wholly Christian. Peter Chanel, a Catholic Marist, landed on the dangerous island of Futuna in 1837. Four years later he had progressed enough to baptize the chief's son; the father had his warriors dismember Chanel with axes, but within a few months the son had helped convert the island.

John Coleridge Patteson, the son of a judge, his mother a niece of the poet Samuel Taylor Coleridge, spent sixteen years as a missionary in the New Hebrides and the Solomon and Loyalty Islands. He founded a college on Norfolk Island for training Melanesian boys and cruised the islands on the missionary ship *Southern Cross,* learning the languages and trying to protect his flock against "blackbirders," white traders who kidnapped islanders and sent them to the Queensland plantations as indentured laborers. In 1871 he landed alone on Nukapu in the Santa Cruz group. Patteson was set upon and killed, and his body was put in a canoe to drift back to his ship; five wounds were made in the breast, and a palm branch with five knots was placed on it. It was later found that he had been murdered in revenge for islanders killed by blackbirders.

The mountains of New Guinea rise to nineteen thousand feet, a place of deep, wild valleys and stone-age cannibalism. Eighty missionaries were lost there in fifty years; the Utrecht Missionary Society made twenty converts in a quarter century, for those who became Christians were expelled from their tribes. Land for the Anglican cathedral was bought for 112 pounds of tobacco, ten tomahawks, a bundle of knives, beads, pipes, and a bolt of red cloth. The missionary-explorer James Chalmers spent ten years with the isolated people of the Fly River before he was clubbed to death and eaten. By the end of the century, though the great island had been colonized by both the British and the Germans, many of its tribes had still not been contacted.

❧ "IN THE EIGHTEENTH century Europe stole the African from Africa," the black American Baptist C. S. Morris complained after a visit in 1899. "In the nineteenth, she is stealing Africa from the African."[20] No place on earth needed Christ more, he said; robbed, sucked dry like an orange, its soul fettered, it had been turned into a slave pen and a rum shop, still in pagan darkness or washed over by the "red deluge of Mohammedanism." On the day of judgment, Morris predicted, "what an awful many-sided charge the vast cloud of African witnesses will have against the civilized world. . . ."

Missionary work was at least a partial atonement. At the start of the century the faith existed only in African coastal pockets, where it had been planted by the Portuguese and Dutch. The Jesuit Gonçalo da Silveira had penetrated inland as far as modern Zimbabwe; he was martyred there in 1561 and, although the mission was sustained by Dominicans for a century, it died out. Capuchin missions in Nigeria also faded. A Catholic presence was maintained by the Portuguese in Angola and Mozambique. At Cape Town the Dutch had opened churches, since they established the city as a victualling station in 1652. When the British took over the colony in 1795 there was a white population of twenty-one thousand most of whom were Boers, the descendants of Dutch, Flemish, and Huguenots who had been in Africa for so long that they described themselves as Afrikaners.

A former Dutch cavalry officer and profligate, Johannes Vanderkamp, was the pioneer missionary at the Cape. He underwent a religious conversion after watching helplessly as his wife and children drowned in a boating accident. Arriving at the Cape in 1799, Vanderkamp established a settlement for Hottentots at Bethlesdorp; he taught them to read and write, and, at age fifty-six, married a seventeen-year-old slave girl. This outraged the Boers, who were already smarting under British rule, for they were a hardy and independent people, sustained at the tip of Africa by a sense of divine destiny, austere and deeply pious, with a racial pride affronted by Vanderkamp taking a Hottentot wife. They thought no better of John Philip, an Englishman of the London Missionary Society who championed native rights—"in the course of a century and a half," he wrote back to London, "the Hottentots have been despoiled of their lands, robbed or cajoled out of their flocks and herds, and . . . reduced to personal servitude"[21]—and made his mission a sanctuary for Hottentots who did not want to work on Boer farms.

A large group of Boers, determined to break free of British influence, moved out of Cape Colony in wagon trains in 1836. The Great Trek took them northward to found the independent Boer republics of the Transvaal and Orange Free State. They compared this hazardous journey with the flight of the Israelites into the Promised Land; patriarchal, bearded, and Bible-reading, many were members of an evangelical sect, the Doppers, so puritanical that hymn-singing was considered a sin. This feeling of mission, and the raw edge of their self-exile from the tender pleasantries of the Cape into the wilderness of the bush, created the Hervormde Kerk, a harsher variant of the Dutch Reformed Church. The Hervormde Kerk became the established church in the Boer republics. Hostile to other Protestants and to any mingling between Boers and natives, in 1858 it declared that "this nation will not have any equality of blacks with whites not in Church not in state."[22] Some argued that Noah's "curse on Ham" applied to blacks, others that the cultural gulf between the races was too wide to bridge. From 1881 blacks were expected to worship separately, and apartness—apartheid—was given a religious as well as a social basis.

Missionaries continued to irritate the Boers. Robert Moffat, a Scot who had been a gardener, used his skills to create thriving farmland at Kuruman in Bechuanaland by diverting river water through canals. He built a church and translated the Bible into Sechwana. Another young Scot, David Livingstone, came to Moffat's mission station when he arrived in Africa; later, he married Moffat's daughter Mary. Livingstone moved on to build his own mission at Kolenbeng. In 1852 the Boers burned it down. They accused Livingstone of being a gun-runner; and the missionary had indeed given some arms to the Bechuana chief Sechele for defense against the Boers and for hunting.

Livingstone, born to a poor Lanarkshire family, had worked in a cotton factory from the age of ten to twenty-four. His missionary sense was aroused by reading a tract by Karl Gützlaff, the man defrauded in Hong Kong; he studied medicine in London before sailing to join Moffat in Africa. The Boers ruined his attempts to plant native missionaries in the Transvaal, and he set out on an epic journey in 1852 to "try to make an open path for commerce and Christianity." He did this to explore possible trade routes and potential British colonies, convinced that trade was the only way to stop Africans from selling each other into slavery, and that they would be improved "by a long continued discipline and contact with superior races by commerce." He discovered the Victoria Falls on the Zambezi;* from six miles away, he wrote, he could see the spray, "a dense white cloud with two bright rainbows upon it . . . from this rushed up a great jet of vapour 200 or 300 feet high; there condensing, it changed its hue to that of dark smoke." He was lionized on his return to England, awarded gold medals and honorary degrees. His plea for volunteers during a speech at Cambridge led to the founding of the Universities' Mission to Central Africa. Basing itself in Zanzibar, the holding point for slaves being shipped to Arabia, the mission pressured the sultan into abolishing the trade in 1873. An Anglican cathedral was built on the old slave market, its altar sited where the whipping post had been.

In March 1866, Livingstone sailed from Zanzibar to explore the watersheds of Central Africa and the sources of the Nile. Sick, exhausted, he pushed west to the river Lualaba, thinking it might be the Nile, though it transpired to be the Congo. No word was had of him. In October 1869 the *New York Herald* sent a terse instruction to its foreign correspondent Henry Stanley: "Find Livingstone." Stanley caught up with him in November 1871, at Ujiji in Tanganyika. Livingstone complained that people thought of a missionary as a "dumpy sort of man with a Bible under his arm" clad in black. Stanley found he was "pale, wearied, had a grey beard, wore a bluish cap with a faded gold band round it, had on a red-sleeved waistcoat, and a pair of red trousers . . ." He was not a gifted evangelist, and made few converts. He had, however, a dedication so ruthless and self-possessed that an admirer thought him "a more dangerous enemy than a useful friend."

"I will place no value on anything I have or may possess, except in relation to the kingdom of Christ," Livingstone wrote; and he felt that all he did, shooting a buffalo for his men or taking an astronomical observation, was in the service of Christ. His faith consumed him. His wife Mary, exposed to heat, malaria, child-bearing, and squalor, died in 1862. Though worn through with fatigue, Livingstone did not return with Stanley's well-equipped expedition to the coast; the two explored Lake Tanganyika together, and then Stanley returned on his own to write his bestseller, *How I Found Livingstone*. "All I can say in my loneliness is, may Heaven's rich blessing come down on everyone—American, English or Turk—who will help to heal the open sore of the world," he wrote, as he contin-

---

*Mount Kenya and Kilimanjaro, Africa's great volcanic peaks, were also discovered by a missionary-explorer, Johann Krapf, who was a pioneer in Aden, Zanzibar, and Mombasa. Krapf's observation that the mountains were snowcapped, though close to the equator, was ridiculed at first. He translated the New Testament into Swahili; when his wife died in Kenya in 1844, he wrote to the Christian Missionary Society: "Tell our friends that in a lonely grave on the African coast rests a member of the mission. This is a sign that they have begun the struggle in this part of the world, and since the victories of the Church lead over the graves of many of her members, they may be more convinced that the hour is approaching when you will be called to convert Africa. . . ."[23]

ued his quest to "open a highway for the progress of the Gospel in the interior of Africa." He died in Old Chitambo, now in Zambia, in 1873, where his faithful people embalmed his body and carried it to the coast.

Stanley came back to Africa in 1873, crossing the continent from east to west. He became friendly with King Mutesa in Uganda, who said that he would welcome Christian missionaries as a counterweight to Islam. Stanley's reports inspired an eccentric millionaire to finance a Church Missionary Society mission to Lake Victoria. Here it clashed with French White Fathers, who won the king's favor by giving him some grand French uniforms; the British Protestants responded by telling the king that their Catholic rivals worshiped a woman called Mary. Empire was at stake; the British, French, and Germans all had an eye on East Africa. Mutesa died in 1884 and was succeeded by his eighteen-year-old son Mwanga, who had been taught by both Protestants and Catholics but leaned toward Islam. Mwanga had a taste for sodomy. One of his page boys refused him; the boy was under tuition by a Protestant catechist, and Mwanga turned on Christian boys. The first three martyrs were roasted over a slow fire; the killings culminated in the burning on a single pyre of thirty-two young men in the summer of 1886. The Anglican bishop James Hannington was speared to death on his arrival. Mwanga was overthrown, and then restored; Christians fought Moslems, and Protestants burnt down the Catholic cathedral in Kampala.

The British soldier Frederick Lugard was sent by the Imperial British East Africa Company to forestall a German annexation. He had the Maxim gun and a small army, and could thus impose, though personally a free thinker, a religious settlement. He allocated six provinces to Protestants, six to Catholics, and three to Moslems. In the interests of the Church, the Church Missionary Society urged the British government to intervene; in 1895, Kenya and Uganda became part of the British Empire. A British MP (member of Parliament) noted acidly that he did not think it the business of government "to prevent these Protestant missionaries from cutting the throats of Roman Catholic missionaries," or vice versa. Ugandans were not so cynical. They took to Christianity with such a will that by 1911 it was found that 282,000 out of a population of 660,000 had been baptized; but Moslem resentment at the arrival of Christianity on the southern flank of Islam was to flare into violence later in the century. In the Sudan, too, where missionaries had great success with the Dinka and Shilluk, and in Nigeria, northern Moslems were to fight savage wars against the Christian converts in the south.

Congo, site of Affonso's remarkable sixteenth-century Christian kingdom, was a heart of darkness. Stanley had opened it, and Leopold II, king of the Belgians, had employed him to carve out a vast and personal Central African fiefdom, the Congo Independent State. Leopold ran it as a private monopoly, its rubber and ivory exploited, its natives forbidden to leave their villages without a permit, a place of cruelty and forced labor. Missionaries did what they could. English Baptists arrived on the upper Congo in 1884, building stations every hundred miles along its banks; American Presbyterians were active in Katanga, and the White Fathers in the east. "Many a little Protestant Pope in the lonely bush is forced by his self-imposed isolation to be prophet, priest and king rolled into one—really a very big duck, in his own private pond," a Plymouth Brother, Dan Crawford, wrote. "Quite seriously, he is forced to be a bit of a policeman, muddled up in matters not even remotely in his sphere. . . ."[24] After a white officer killed the local chief in Katanga Msiri, Crawford became Konga Vantu, the "gatherer of the people," and founded the new Christian city of Luanza on the north shore of Lake Mweru. Missionaries helped to heighten international revulsion at abuses in the Congo, and Belgium annexed the territory as a regular colony in 1908.

Unhappy attempts were made to keep the Sierra Leone experiment alive in West Africa. By 1846, fifty thousand former slaves had been brought in. They were thought to speak 117 different tribal languages; an Africanized English was the only common tongue. "A confused mass, destitute of the slightest feeling of community," the German Gustav Warneck reported, "who lived in a state of constant conflict among themselves, and were dull, lazy, and in the last degrees unchaste."[25] The Church Missionary Society founded a college at Fourah Bay with the aim of encouraging a native church. Its first student was Samuel Adjai Crowther, who had been rescued from a slave ship by a British man-of-war; from 1857 he led the Niger mission with an all-African staff, translating the Bible into Yoruba. Crowther became the first African Anglican bishop in 1864, but his mission was effectively taken over by whites.

Africans could create their own cults, however, and with as much vigor as whites. William Wadé Harris was born in about 1860 among the Glebo people of Liberia. His childhood was Methodist; he voyaged abroad as a seaman, and at about age twenty he had a conversion experience, joining the American Episcopal Church and training as a catechist and schoolmaster. In 1910, while in prison for political activity, he began to see himself as a prophet of the last times. In seventeen months from 1913 to 1915, "Prophet Harris" preached across the Ivory Coast through to Axim on the Gold Coast, modern Ghana, proclaiming the coming judgment of Christ, calling on all to abandon traditional fetishes and to worship God alone. In the Ivory Coast, where the faith had made little impact, he baptized not fewer than one hundred thousand people. The French authorities, alarmed by his charisma, expelled him. Harris was striking, tall, clothed in white with a white cloth round his head and wearing a black stole; "in his right hand a high cross and on his belt a calabash, containing dried seeds," a Frenchman observed, "which he shakes to keep rhythm for his hymns."[26] He appeared with an escort of woman singers and engaged in trials of strength with medicine men, fetishists, and diviners. He encouraged converts to attend churches, where they existed, and appointed local leaders of "Harrist churches" where they did not. Though he died paralyzed and in poverty in 1929, the charismatic churches he pioneered were to gain millions of converts as sub-Saharan Africa confirmed itself in the faith.

❖

❖

❖

CHAPTER XXXII

The Descent of Man:

Darwin

F ar from its new frontiers, the faith struggled with the old issues of scientific discovery and the powers of the papacy. The naturalist Charles Darwin claimed that mankind was not descended from Adam, but had evolved from a "hairy quadruped, furnished with a tail and pointed ears, probably arboreal in its habits," the progenitor of the orangutan, chimpanzee, and gorilla.[1] Eleven years later, in 1879, the pope was declared to be infallible. Both assumptions had their subtleties, of course, but the principles were easily grasped and the clashes were fiery.

Scientists had known long before Darwin that Genesis bore no relation to the actual timetable and manner of creation. The Danish palaeontologist Niels Steno had written a treatise on the antiquity of fossils in 1669; since then, scientific geologists had been at odds with the "diluvians," who attributed geological strata to the results of the Flood. The first scientific computation of the age of the earth, published in 1778 by the Jesuit-trained naturalist Georges-Louis Buffon, had put it at seventy-five thousand years, far beyond biblical parameters; and the great mathematician and astronomer Pierre Laplace had presented his nebular hypothesis of planetary origins in 1796, ascribing the origins of the universe to an expanding cloud of gas. As to the origin of man, another Frenchman, Jean Baptiste Lamarck, had concluded in his *Philosophie Zoologique* in 1809 that acquired characteristics could be inherited by future generations. Lamarck broke the old notion of immutable species; he died blind and poor two years before Darwin sailed on HMS *Beagle* in 1831 for South America and the Galapagos Islands.

Darwin's great work, *The Origin of the Species by Means of Natural Selection,* published in 1859, was an immediate scientific and religious sensation. It argued that all living species of plants and animals, including man, had evolved through natural selection, in which those best adapted to circumstance and competition survive and propagate. A famous meeting of the British Association for the Advancement of Science was held at Oxford a year later. Samuel Wilberforce, the bishop of Oxford, known as "Soapy Sam" and fiercely against evolution, battled with the palaeontologist Professor T. H. Huxley, known as "Darwin's bulldog." Wilberforce asked Huxley whether he "claimed his descent from a monkey through his grandfather or his grandmother?" Huxley whispered that "the Lord hath delivered him into mine hands" and rose. Given the choice between an ape as an ancestor and a man who used his influence to ridicule a grave scientific discussion, he retorted, "I unhesitatingly affirm my preference for the ape."[2] There was uproar; a woman fainted.

Passions ran highest in America. A paper at the Oxford meeting was written by John W. Draper, son of an English Methodist minister who became professor of chemistry at the University of New York. Draper saw a direct conflict between science and religion, with "the expansive force of the human intellect on one side, and the compression arising from traditional faith and human interests on the other." He agreed that the "tranquillity of society" depended on the stability of its religious convictions; but where faith was unchangeable and stationary, science was progressive by its nature, and the divergence between them could no longer be concealed. Draper felt that the civilization had left the old religious track upon which it had voyaged for so long, and that with science "a new departure, on an unknown sea, has been taken." He claimed that "ecclesiastical spirit no longer inspires the policy of the world" and that the only souvenirs of faith's crusading vigor were the marble effigies of knights "reposing in the silent crypts of churches."[3]

Charles Darwin in a watercolor of 1840. His great work, *The Origin of the Species by Means of Natural Selection,* was an immediate scientific and religious sensation. In it, he claimed that mankind was not descended from Adam, but had evolved from a "hairy quadruped furnished with a tail and pointed ears." Christian opponents of evolution in America called it "an idea filled with the chatter of apes, and the hiss of serpents, and the croak of frogs" that was "infidel and atheistic and absurd." The battle continued until the famous "monkey trial" in Tennessee in 1925.

John Wesley Powell, the geologist who surveyed the Colorado River from 1868, dismissed religion as the "hashish of mystery" compared with the pure water of scientific truth.

Religion fought back. American revivalism remained a powerful force. Charles Finney had created new techniques; "protracted meetings" where all non-religious activity ceased over several days, the "anxious bench" where sinners meditated, public prayer for named individuals. He and his wife held meetings at the Park Street Church in Boston that spilled onto the sidewalks. Crowds in New York were so dense that "brethren" were asked to abide by a five-minute rule, which allowed individuals no more than two prayers or exhortations, to give all a chance to be heard. Finney claimed to have made fifty thousand conversions in a week; Dwight Moody, whose fiery preaching was backed by the songs and organ playing of Ira Sankey, succeeded him from the 1860s. Entertainment was a part of religion, and the antievolutionists fought with panache.

From the pulpit of Brooklyn's Free Tabernacle, T. DeWitt Talmage lacerated Darwinism as a "stenchful and damnable doctrine." Evolution—"an idea filled with the chatter of apes, and the hiss of serpents, and the croak of frogs"—was not simply "infidel and atheistic and absurd"; it also depraved, for if anything "will make a man bestial in his habits it is the idea that he was descended from the beast."[4] Cardinal James Gibbon of Baltimore argued that God "is the Author of all scientific truth." He said that it was the responsibility of the Catholic Church to stand up to all "false pretensions of science." If any scientist opposed the unity of the human species, he wrote, or the immortality of the soul, then when the Church "sees him raise his profane hands and attempt to touch the temple of faith, she cries out, 'Thus far shalt thou go and no farther!'"[5] In 1896, John Zahm, a Holy Cross priest and professor of physics at Notre Dame, argued that there was no danger to the faith or to the Bible in evolution; Catholic dogma "would remain absolutely intact and unchanged" even if Darwin were proved entirely correct. Zahm's work was put on the *Index* in 1898 and withdrawn from circulation.

Protestant resistance proved more stubborn than Catholic. The arguments had a last-ditch and beleaguered quality, perhaps reflecting concern at the threat posed by the huge increase in non-Protestant immigration. The American Society to Promote the Principles of the Protestant Reformation was founded in 1840. Its members were committed to "maintain and perpetuate the genuine truths of Protestantism unadulterated" at a time when "the influence of Romanism is rapidly extending throughout this Republic, endangering the peace and freedom of our country."[6] Samuel Morse, inventor of the electric telegraph and the Morse code, listed "facts" to prove that Catholicism, "opposed in its very nature to Democratic Republicanism," was working to place American liberty in the hands of foreign powers. He claimed that the despotic states of Europe were sending money and Jesuit agents into the U.S.; that these "Priest-police" swayed elections, since politicians curried favor with them; and that Irish Catholics in particular were forming armed bands, among them the O'Connell Guards, "a military corps of Irishmen in New York." His list concluded that: "It is a fact, that the greater part of foreigners in our population is composed of Roman Catholics." He wrote this in 1835; if it were not true then, it very soon was.[7]*

The first prominent clergyman publicly to support evolution was the Presbyterian James McCosh, the president of Princeton. He did so, he wrote, because he knew Darwin to be a most careful observer, that "there was great truth in the theory, and that there was nothing atheistic in it if properly understood." By 1888 he was congratulating himself that "intelligent Christians are coming round gradually to the views which I have had the courage to publish." He was premature. Fundamentalists continued to denounce Darwin and Modernists, and the famous "monkey trial" did not take place until 1925.

A young biology teacher in Dayton, Tennessee, John Thomas Scopes, was charged that year with teaching evolution in defiance of a state law. The case pitted the outstanding Chicago trial lawyer Clarence Darrow, for Scopes, against William Jennings Bryan, three times a presidential candidate, for the prosecution. Darrow said that the case was "as brazen and as bold an attempt to destroy learning as was ever made in the Middle Ages, and the only difference is that we have not provided that they shall be burned at the stake."[9] Bryan asked whether the time had come when a minority could take charge of a state like Tennessee, and compel the majority to pay their teachers "while they take religion out of the heart of the children . . ." In his summation, Bryan described science as "intelligence not consecrated by love," an evil genius which threatened to wreck civilization and which could be contained only by "the moral code of the meek and lowly Nazarene." He compared the case with the crucifixion. "A bloody, brutal doctrine—evolution—demands, as the rabble did 1900 years ago, that He be crucified," he said. "That cannot be the answer of this jury, representing a Christian State and sworn to uphold the laws of Tennessee."[10] The jury duly found Scopes guilty; he was fined one hundred dollars, but the Tennessee Supreme Court overturned the conviction on a technicality.

---

*The 1890 federal census asked questions on religious membership for the first time. The data on the largest denominational families showed there to be 8 million Catholic communicants, compared with 5.4 million Methodists, 4 million Baptists, 1.4 million Presbyterians, and a similar number of Lutherans. None of the other nine major denominations reached the million mark, although Disciples of Christ came close, and Episcopalians and Congregationalists topped the 500,000 mark; the number of Jews was put at 139,000, little more than Quakers, and substantially less than the 234,000 Mormons.[8]

❖ THE PAPACY WAS the the oldest office of significance in the world, and popes seemed at times to be on the verge of extinction. Napoleon came close to putting paid to them, but they were hardy and still able to evolve. Pius VII had been humiliated in 1804, compelled to travel to Paris to consecrate Napoleon as emperor. French troops occupied Rome and in May 1809 annexed the papal states. The following month, Pius excommunicated the "robbers of Peter's patrimony"; he did not name them, but Napoleon was clearly the robber chief. The pope was kept a prisoner in the Quirinal Palace for his impudence, and then padlocked in a carriage and exiled to Savona; from there he was escorted to Fontainebleau in the clothes of a common priest, with his white satin slippers darkened with ink, to sign a concordat that stripped him of his temporal power.* Without it, he was "reduced to saying his prayers and mending his linen."[11] After Napoleon's defeat at Waterloo, Pius regained full control of the papal states; that, however, exposed the papacy to the growing Italian desire for a unified state free from foreign rule. A secret revolutionary society, the Carbonari, or "charcoal burners," grew rapidly. It was dedicated to independence and had a virulent anti-clerical element.

A revolt broke out in the papal states in 1831. The pope, Gregory XVI, called in Austrian troops to repress it. His dislike of anything modern extended to railways, which he said were "infernal machines"; he warned his bishops to beware of "impostors and propagators of new ideas." These included the eloquent French priest and writer Félicité de Lamennais, once hostile to toleration and individualism but later a champion of liberty, whose journal *L'Avenir* proclaimed "God and freedom" on its masthead and campaigned for a "Free Church in a Free State." Lamennais hoped that the pope would lead this crusade, but instead Gregory lambasted those who "agitate against and upset the right of rulers" for their "detestable and insolent malice," and condemned *L'Avenir*. Nationalists in Rome were imprisoned or fled into exile to stir antipapal feelings. Gregory was succeeded by Pius IX, elected in 1846 at the unusually young age of fifty-five.

Pius was at first a reformer—Gregory had complained that "even his cats are liberals"—and wildly popular. He amnestied political prisoners and lifted the restrictions that had pinned Roman Jews into their ghettoes for three hundred years, allowed railways to be built, and proposed a government of two chambers for the papal states, one nominated by the pope and the other elected by the people. A revolutionary fever spread through Europe in 1848. In Rome, nationalists seeking to overthrow Austrian rule looked to Pius to lead reunification with the patriots Giuseppe Mazzini and Giuseppe Garibaldi, and Victor Emmanuel II,

---

*Pius later repudiated it, saying that he had signed from "human frailty, being only dust and ashes."

king of Sardinia and Piedmont. The pope declared in April that he would not wage war against Catholic Austria, and he bade Italians to remain faithful to their princes. The Romans turned on him; in November his prime minister was murdered on the steps of the chancellery, and two days later Pius fled from the mob dressed as an ordinary priest and hid in Neapolitan territory. Mazzini and Garibaldi declared a republic in Rome; from his refuge in Gaeta, Pius called on the Catholic powers to restore him. French troops occupied Rome in July 1849 and Pius returned to the surly city nine months later, implacably opposed to reform.

The nationalist cause passed to Victor Emmanuel, whose anticlerical government suppressed convents and monasteries in Piedmont. French bayonets protected Pius in Rome, but in 1860 a popular vote incorporated the Legations and the Marches of Ancona into Victor Emmanuel's kingdom, and the papal states shrank in size by two-thirds. Pius refused to accept the losses, and an international brigade was recruited from devout Catholics to defend them. Pius blessed his doomed volunteers at the Campo di Annibale before they marched off to be slaughtered.

The papal wounds won it the sympathy of the faithful. In England a romantic revival of interest in the medieval Church, and in the High Church ideals of the seventeenth century, fueled the so-called Oxford Movement. This stressed the continuity of the Church of England as a branch of the Catholic Church and as a part of the apostolic succession. Monastic orders were revived, and a richer ceremonial found a place for incense and ornate vestments that Low Churchmen thought to be papist aberrations. John Henry Newman, an Oxford don and clergyman, wrote a tract claiming that the Anglican Thirty-nine Articles of faith was Catholic in spirit, and that, though they might criticize papal supremacy, they did not clash with Catholic doctrine. Most who followed the Oxford Movement remained Anglicans, but Newman was received into the Catholic Church in 1845. Another convert was Henry Manning, also a former Oxford don and Anglican archdeacon, and the future cardinal archbishop of Westminster.

At the requiem mass for the Irish volunteers beyond Rome in 1860, Manning described them as martyrs for divine order. The pope's temporal power was the sign of the "sovereignty of the kingdom of God upon earth"; the papal states were the "only spot of ground on which the Vicar of Christ can set the sole of his foot in freedom," and this was why "they who would drive the Incarnation off the face of the earth hover about it to wrest it from his hands."[12] Manning was part of an ardent and fresh Ultramontanism, the reaction to liberalism that favored absolute papal authority at the expense of national or diocesan influence. Pius IX issued a *Syllabus Errorum* listing eighty modern and liberal errors in 1864. It condemned "all socialist, communist, secret, bible-reading, and clerico-liberal societies"; it denied that national churches could be freed from papal control or that kings and princes could be exempted from the laws of the Church, but accepted that it was impermissible "to rebel against legitimate princes." Its eightieth and final thesis said that it was an error to claim that "the Roman Pontiff can and ought to reconcile and adjust himself with 'progress,' 'liberalism' and 'modern civilization.'"[13] Popes had always claimed to pursue eternal values rather than whims of the moment, of course, and Pius was restating an ancient principle; but it was awkwardly done, for it appeared to divorce the Church from the modern world, and it aroused a firestorm of liberal protest.

Pius brought a surge of energy. He created more than 200 new bishoprics and apostolic vicariates, many in the United States; in three years from 1862 he approved 74 new congregations for women, so that France alone had 127,000 women religious, as against 30,200 men. But dogma damaged relations with the Uniates, the Eastern Rite Catholic churches in Ukraine, India, and the Middle East. They had a married clergy, elected their own bishops, used the Byzantine liturgy, held their own synods, and differed from the Orthodox only in recognizing papal authority. The Ultramontanes identified Catholicism with *Romanitas,* involving a single liturgy, canon law, and authority. Latin missionaries were encouraged to wean Uniate congregations away from Eastern rites, to press against married clergy, and to encourage the election of pro-Latin bishops. An attempt was made to impose the Gregorian calendar on the Melchite Church of Syria, driving some into communion with the Orthodox. In 1867, Pius issued the bull *Reversurus,* rebuking the Eastern Rite churches for their schismatic tendencies. Manning thought all this was to show "the beauty of inflexibility," but others thought it smacked of absolutism at a time when religious toleration was spreading in Europe. Discrimination against Catholics in Britain had been largely dismantled in 1829, and in Prussia and the Netherlands shortly afterward; most Catholic states reciprocated, with religious toleration guaranteed in Austria-Hungary in 1867. Russia was the exception; it was czarist policy to hound Polish Catholics, suppressing them with great brutality after a rising in 1830, and to badger Uniates into abandoning Rome and uniting with the Russian Orthodox Church.

A great revival in the cult of Mary accompanied the defiance of the embattled pope. Catherine Labouré experienced a vision of the Virgin crowned with stars; this became the basis of the "miraculous medal" which bore the legend "O Mary Conceived without Original Sin, Pray for us who have recourse to thee."[14] In 1846, two shepherd children at La Salette in Savoy had a vision of a beautiful weeping lady, who lamented the desecration of Sunday, swearing, and blasphemy and drunkenness. Pilgrimages to the "holy mountain of La Salette" had a mass popularity seldom seen since medieval times. Then, between

Crowds gather to watch fourteen-year-old Bernadette Soubirous experience a vision of the Virgin Mary in the grotto of Massabielle at Lourdes in 1858. The spring in the grotto is thought to have miraculous powers of healing. A church was built over the grotto, and beside it the splendid Church of the Rosary. Five million people visit Lourdes each year, evidence that Christian belief in miracles and faith-healing remains strong.

February and July 1858, came the eighteen Marian visions of an asthmatic and rake-thin peasant girl at the grotto of Massabielle at Lourdes in the French Pyrenees.

Bernadette Soubirous was fourteen when she saw a girl of infinite beauty, dressed in white with a blue sash and golden roses round her feet, borne by a rush of wind; the girl told Bernadette that she was *immaculada concepciou,* the Immaculate Conception, and urged her to pray, and to drink from a spring of water that began to flow from the rock. Locals who mocked the miller's daughter and her apparition or trampled the roses near the grotto fell sick or suffered ill fortune, whereas the water from the spring was found to heal. Bernadette was scrutinized carefully by the Church, and so harassed by visitors that she sought refuge in a convent at Nevers, but the sincerity of her ecstasies and long vigils was not dented. A great basilica was built above the grotto in 1862, and a book describing the first miraculous cures sold eight hundred thousand copies as Lourdes became the great center of Christian faith-healing. Other miracles of healing and prophecy were reported after the death of the "Little Flower of Lisieux," Thérèse Martin, who had entered a Carmelite convent at fifteen, hoping to be sent to China as a missionary, but she had a series of hemorrhages and was dead of consumption in nine years. Her superiors had asked her to write her autobiography, *History of a Soul,* in which millions of readers saw the sanctity of the suffering faithful. *Je vais tomber un torrent de roses,* she wrote; the miracles were seen as fulfilling the promise. The cult of the Sacred Heart of Jesus was also greatly promoted; it had a political context—in the Vendée rising in France in the 1790s, the doomed monarchists had carried the symbol on their banners as evidence of their devotion—and the great Sacré Coeur basilica was built in the 1870s to tower high above Paris in Montmartre in passionate disdain for the secularization of the city beneath it.

Pius attributed his own recovery from epilepsy to the Virgin; he also defined Mary's Immaculate Conception as part of Catholic doctrine. This was contentious, but so was the matter of his own infallibility.

A decade after the Oxford debate on evolution, on July 18, 1870, a day of savage Roman heat and rain, the Vatican Council gathered to approve the decree of papal infallibility. A storm had threatened all morning, and it burst with violence as the cardinals struggled through it to take their places, a loud clap of thunder following as each confirmed his presence. The tempest reached its height as the result of the voting was taken to the pope, the *London Times* correspondent recorded; "the darkness was so thick that a huge taper was necessarily brought and placed by his side as he read the words *'Nosque, sacro approbante Concilio, illa, ut lecta sunt, definimus et apostolica auctoritate confirmamus.'* "Lightning again flickered round the hall as the Te Deum and the Benediction followed; "the entire crowd fell on their knees, and the Pope blessed them in those clear sweet tones distinguishable among a thousand."[15] Manning, a zealot for infallibility, wrote tartly that "critics saw in the thunderstorm an articulate voice of divine indignation against the definition. They forget Sinai and the Ten Commandments!"

Cardinal Guidi, archbishop of Bologna, insisted that infallibility did not apply to the pope himself, but only to his teaching. Since papal teaching reflected consultation with other bishops, Guidi suggested that the decree should state that "the counsel of the bishops manifesting the tradition of the churches" assists the pope. Enraged by this slight, Pius accused Guidi of treachery. Guidi said he had done no more than maintain that bishops are witnesses to the tradition. "Witnesses of tradition?" the pope said. "*La tradizione son' io.* I am the tradition."[16] In that, to Protestants and not a few Catholics, lay the stupendous arrogance of infallibility; but to supporters it was a distillation of Catholic devotion and discipline.

Infallibility was, in fact, hedged. It applies only when the pope speaks ex cathedra in defining a doctrine concerning faith and morals that is binding on the whole Church, and that reflects his office of teacher and pastor to all Christians. Then, and only then, is the pope possessed of "that infallibility which the Divine Redeemer wished his Church to be endowed." The daily round of papal comments and teaching are not infallible; that divine status is reached only when his words are ex cathedra. When they are, however, his statements are deemed to be irreformable "of themselves"—*ex sese*—and, indeed, only one papal statement since 1870 has formally been identified as infallible, the definition of the Assumption in 1950.*

The vote was 533 for, with two against; 57 others left Rome the day before to avoid embarrassment. Bishop Fitzgerald of Little Rock, Arkansas, who opposed it, knelt at the pope's feet when the result was declared and cried out, *"Modo credo, sancte pater"; "*Now I believe, Holy Father."[17]

The following day the Franco-Prussian War broke out, and the council was prorogued indefinitely. Napoleon III withdrew his troops from Rome to send them to the front, leaving the pope defenseless. King Victor Emmanuel invaded the papal states within a month; on September 19, 1870, Pius locked himself into the Vatican, instructing his troops to put up at least a show of resistance to the royal troops, as proof that he had not surrendered the city. Rome fell on September 20 and was declared capital of a united Italy within a year. The Law of Guarantees was passed in November 1870. The pope was granted the honors and immunities of a sovereign, including the Swiss Guard and a postal and telegraph service. He had exclusive use of the Vatican, the Lateran, and the summer residence at Castel Gandolfo, and he was awarded 3.5 million lire a year as compensation for his lost territories.

Pius refused to accept the Law, or the money; he withheld the customary *Urbi et Orbi* blessing of the city and the world as a reminder that he was the "prisoner of the Vatican." Catholics were banned from voting or standing in Italian elections until after the First World War. Fifteen hundred years of papal rule in Rome was at an end.

⚜ PIUS NEVER SET foot outside the Vatican again; he died in 1878 after the longest pontificate in history. His final years saw the ominous development of Kulturkampf, a "culture struggle" between Church and state for the soul of the nation. It was inspired by Bismarck, the German chancellor, who saw the Vatican as an alien power within the heart of the German empire. He first suppressed the Catholic department of the Prussian ministry of public worship, and in 1872 he appointed Adalbert Falk as minister with the task of breaking Catholic influence, particularly in education. Catholic schools and seminaries were brought under state control. Ordinands had to pass through a state gymnasium and take a state examination.

Religious orders were forbidden to teach; the Jesuits, and then all religious

---

*The doctrine that the Virgin, having completed her earthly life, was assumed into heavenly glory in body and in soul. Pius XII defined it after repeated demands, together with a new Mass for the Feast, in the bull *Munificentissimus Deus.*

orders, were expelled. Five Franciscan sisters were drowned aboard the *Deutsch-land* as it was wrecked while taking them into exile, a tragedy remembered by the English poet Gerard Manley Hopkins, himself a Catholic convert from Oxford:

> Sister, a sister calling
> A master, her master and mine!—
> And the inboard seas run swirling and hawling . . .

More than a thousand "recalcitrant priests" were imprisoned or exiled, including bishops and cardinals. A supreme ecclesiastical court was established whose members were appointed by the emperor. By 1876 all the sees in Prussia were vacant and more than a million Catholics had no access to the sacraments.

Pius denounced the Kulturkampf laws and excommunicated the few clergy who submitted to them. Bismarck retorted that, "We will not go to Canossa." The German embassy at the Vatican was withdrawn. Catholic diehards reveled in the drama. "Society is a sewer—it will perish—with the debris of the Vatican God will stone the human race," Louis Viuellot wrote.[18] Persecution played its usual role in strengthening the Church; resistance mounted, and after Pius's death, Bismarck thought it wise to reach a concordat with Leo XIII, his successor. By 1887 most anti-Catholic laws had been rescinded; for his part, Leo defused the reactionary ferocity of the Syllabus by warming to liberalism, democracy, and freedom of conscience in the *Encyclical Libertas* the following year. The Jesuits were not allowed to return to Germany, however, a compliment to their skills in instilling ideology, and a warning that the modern state wished to preserve this for itself.

Another ill omen lay in the German philosopher, or prophet, Friedrich Nietzsche, son of a Lutheran pastor from Prussia. Nietzsche wrote in aphorisms that outraged and fascinated; he described the philosopher as a "stick of dynamite" and he turned on Christianity with biblical rage. "Christianity resolved to find that the world was bad and ugly," he wrote, "and has made it bad and ugly." He despised modern man as a sickly and weak creature. "Many, too many, are born, and they hang on their branches much too long," he said. Man was something that is to be surpassed.

"I teach you Superman," he wrote, a magnified man, freed of scruple, pitiless, a perfection of mental and physical strength, suffused with the will to conquer and to rule. Life is the will to power by this *Übermensch*, the culmination of evolution. There had been gleams of this new creature in the past, in Cesare Borgia and Napoleon, and in the pursuit of power. But a true Superman could not exist until the inhibitions of Christianity—with its pity and compassion and morality, the values of the weak and disinherited—had been swept away. "I call Christianity the one great curse, the one enormous and innermost perversion, the one great instinct of revenge, for which no means are too venomous, too underhand, too underground and too petty," he wrote in *The Antichrist.* "I call it the one immortal blemish of mankind."

In *The Will to Power,* he called for a "declaration of war by higher men on the masses . . . The great majority of men have no right to existence." Nietzsche's visions were tortured and high-strung; his health was shattered, probably by syphilis, and he suffered psychosomatic agonies in which he found the thought of suicide provided "a calm passage across many a night." He dreamed of a "transvaluation of all values," where the "blond beast, hungry for plunder and victory" would prevail, and religion, a "world of pure fiction," would end.

"God is dead," he rejoiced, adding a brief rider that "there will perhaps be caves, for ages yet, in which his shadow will be shown." He himself died, demented, in 1900, but his *Übermensch* was not long in coming.

❖

❖

❖

CHAPTER XXXIII

"The Godless Rulers of Darkness":

Totalitarians

The greatest modern attempt to put God to death and raise a Superman-dictator in his place was made in Russia, a nation that seemed ill-suited for the experiment. Before 1917 its people sometimes spoke of it as "Holyrussia" in a single word; since St. Vladimir, and the intervening centuries of Mongol Moslem domination, the faith had become an inseparable part of nationhood.* Its soul remained so stamped with piety that a Western ambassador found all Russians to share "a haunting obsession of the invisible and the life beyond . . ."

A "red corner" graced the meanest hovels. "Red" in its prerevolutionary sense was synonymous with "beauty," and the family icon was kept in this space, a likeness of the Virgin or a saint in a cheap metal frame with a candle beneath it. The icon comforted the sick, blessed the marriage bed, guarded infants, and followed the dead to the cemetery. During the Napoleonic campaigns a Swiss had noted that almost every dying Russian soldier "clutched at the image of the patron saint he wore about his neck, and pressed it to his lips before drawing his last breath." Faith permeated the Russian landscape. Onion domes of village churches pierced the infinite horizons of the plains, swelling like sails in the monotony of an ocean. In Moscow, the city of "forty times forty churches," the golden cupolas suspended above the green roofs reminded a visitor of brilliant treetops in an autumnal forest. The Church was Russian and Orthodox, and an intensity lay in both adjectives, for it was inward looking, untouched by the Reformation, and hostile to Western influence; a military attaché thought that the "almost incredi-

---

*The campaigns against the descendants of the Golden Horde were still fresh. The Russians occupied Samarkand, the old capital of the Mongol empire, in 1868; the drive into Central Asia was completed in the Pamirs in 1895.

ble" amount of time the Russian army devoted to religious ceremonials had "not much to do with morals, but a great deal to do with hatred of foreigners."[1]

The Orthodox Church was indispensable to ordinary life. It was impossible to exist without it, at least in a bureaucratic sense, since it alone registered births, marriages, and deaths. Its courts dealt with cases of adultery, divorce, and obscenity as well as heresy, and its schools provided basic education. It was served by 51,000 village priests in rough boots and threadbare cassocks, as poor as their flocks, distinguished by their unkempt and uncut beards and hair. The cells and dormitories of more than a thousand convents and monasteries sheltered 94,600 monks and nuns. Tens of thousands of *strannik,* "wanderers," roamed the empire in sandals made of bark, with a pilgrim staff and a cross and scraps of food in a burlap sack, chanting *Kyrie eleison, Kyrie eleison,* "Lord have mercy," to the rhythm of their feet as they plodded between holy sites. Penitents wore chains on their legs or went barefoot in winter, rejoicing in the flecks of blood they left in the snow. Peasants fed and lodged them in haylofts and barns, and in return, the *strannik* would say prayers for them at the next shrine he came to, or give them holy water. "Politicals," the intellectuals exiled from western Russian cities to Siberia for political crimes, were astonished at the kindness and sympathy shown them by the roughest villagers; the peasants remembered the robbers next to the crucified Christ, and they thought with pity of prisoners as *neshastnye,* "unfortunates."

Holy men known as starets, or elders, many of them former wanderers, lived in huts in forest glades or in cells in hermitages. They prayed and meditated, and mortified their flesh, sleeping on the bare ground and eating little; pious Russians fasted on Wednesdays, the day of Judas's treachery, as well as Fridays. Pilgrims visited them to tell of their sins and sufferings and ask for spiritual advice. Ambriose, a starets in the famous hermitage of Optima Pustyn, was sought out by "plebeians and the most nobly born," grand dukes, peasant women, and Guards officers as well as Fyodor Dostoyevsky and Leo Tolstoy. "The elder takes your soul and your will into his soul and will," Dostoyevsky wrote, "and you surrender your will and give it to him in complete obedience, with complete self-abnegation." It was a pact in which the binder and bound were linked in perpetual confession; the person bound received "a total freedom, that is, freedom from himself . . ."[2] Czar Nicholas and Alexandra had such a starets, Grigory Rasputin, and Dostoyevsky's description captures the awe and devotion which the last empress so recklessly expended on the dissolute Siberian holy man.

The czar was the absolute master of the Church, with spiritual as well as temporal authority. Nicholas controlled the Holy Synod and vetted all senior appointments. Priests swore an oath of loyalty to him which obliged them to override the secrecy of the confessional and to report any parishioner with dissident political views. He did not salute his troops. They knelt, and he blessed them. The empire was vast, however, with more than a hundred nationalities; fewer than half were Great Russians. The millions of Catholics in Russian Poland and Lithuania, and the Lutherans in Finland and the Baltic states, looked west and saw Orthodoxy as backward; Uniates in the Ukraine and Byelorussia, and Georgians and Armenians also resented czardom's pro-Orthodox prejudices. Seventh-Day Adventists had arrived in 1883 and were making converts among the ethnic Germans of the Crimea. Baptists were active in the Caucasus, and in the Ukraine where they were known as Stundists after the *Bibelstunden* or "Bible hour" of German Protestant settlers. The Englishman Lord Radstock introduced the preaching of the Plymouth Brethren to St. Petersburg; followers were called Pashkovites after their leading light, Colonel A. V. Pashkov. He held a conference of Baptists, Stundists, and his own followers in the capital in 1884; Pashkov's aim was to merge the three evangelical streams into a single movement, but police broke up the conference and deported delegates.

The Moslems in the Caucasus and Central Asia feared Russian immigration and control. Christians released their tensions in sporadic pogroms against the Jews. In the great Kiev pogrom of 1905, the banker Alexander Gunzburg shouted at the mob, "Have you no fear of Christ?" In reply they beat him with blows "so powerful that my head was almost driven into my shoulders." The painter Marc Chagall recalled the panic that overwhelmed him as he passed butcher's windows, where calves lay alive amid the butcher's axes and hatchets while gangs with knives roamed the streets looking for Jews. Theoretically penned up in the Pale of Settlement, in eastern Poland, Lithuania, the Ukraine, and Bessarabia, restricted in their right to travel, to study at university, and to hold public office, a million and a quarter emigrated in the years before the Great War, mainly to the United States and Britain. "A third will emigrate," the czar's tutor and adviser, Constantine Pobedonostsev, said of the Jews, "a third will convert to Christianity, and a third will die out."

Orthodoxy had its own schisms and sects. It had split in 1666 when the Patriarch Nikon reformed the liturgy to bring it back in line with Greek practice. The differences were arcane and largely numerical: the Russian cross had eight points to the Greek four; the Greek *Iissous* for Jesus had two "i"s, and the Russian one; the Greeks extended three fingers to make the sign of the cross against the Russians' two. Those who refused to accept this, thinking that the change of liturgy marked the start of the rule of the Antichrist, called themselves Old Believers. Anathemas were imposed on them in 1667, not to be lifted until 1971, and they were dubbed *raskolniks* or "schismatics." They were violently persecuted; their leader Archpriest Avvakum was deported to Siberia and burned in 1682, thus becoming their saint and martyr. Peter the Great's attempts to westernize

Russia, also thought to be the work of the Antichrist, swelled their numbers in the early eighteenth century.

No bishop quit the reformed Church to join the *raskolniks,* thus preventing them from ordaining priests by traditional rites. A "priested" group created its own clergy regardless of this inhibition; the "unpriested" denied that a priesthood was necessary and did without. Many fled to Siberia and prospered. Their services, slow and melancholy, the men bearded, the women in black or white veils, candles reflecting walls entirely covered with icons, the choirs intoning "Heavenly King, Comforter, Spirit of Truth," had a medieval intensity. They were respected for their sobriety, hard work, and financial acumen; they included many merchants, in heavy coats of antique cut and top hats, their wives in ornate brocades. Persecutions continued fitfully. In the 1880s an Orthodox bishop, Methodius, who had given the sacraments to a *raskolnik,* was transported to Siberia in irons, and then, manacled to a horse, was ordered to ride for seven hundred miles to his place of exile. He died, aged seventy-eight, on the track. The first Russian census was held in 1898. The people of one unpriested *raskolnik* village, thinking this the snare of the Antichrist, dug four tunnels when they heard of it; as the census takers approached, they held their own burial service and jumped singing into the tunnels, dying of suffocation. The elder of another community decapitated his flock and cut his own throat rather than submit. The census put their number at 2.25 million. The true figure may have been more than 15 million.

Communities of *skoptsy,* "eunuchs," believed sexual abstinence to be a prerequisite for entry into Paradise. They based this on a passage from Matthew's gospel. "For there are some eunuchs, which were so born from their mother's womb; and there are some eunuchs, which were made eunuchs of men; and there be eunuchs, which have made themselves eunuchs for the kingdom of heaven's sake," Jesus said. "He that is able to receive it, let him receive it" (Matt. 19:12). The *skoptsy* maintained that the first apostles were castrates who had undergone baptism by fire. They cut off their own testicles to achieve a similar state of grace, destroying the infected tissue in the wound with a branding iron; some strove for perfect purity by having the penis itself hacked off. The head of the Okhrana, the czarist secret police, General Vassilyev, took a professional interest in the activities of the sects. He noted that the dancing and revelries that followed a *skoptsy* castration "continues until those taking part are in a condition of absolute frenzy." It might seem like religious insanity, he wrote, "but the amazing fact is that this body counts many adherents not merely among peasants, but among townspeople, the merchant class and even officials."[3] Police who raided the house of a rich merchant in Tambov Province found a colony of forty *skoptsy,* flabby men with womanly hips. The *skoptsy* were hard workers and their villages were prosperous and without crime. A visitor was unnerved by their appearance, however. None was under forty, they were sallow and beardless, and they spoke in high-pitched voices.[4]

The *khlysts,* "whips," occupied the other extreme of the sexual spectrum. Danilo Filipov, an army deserter from Kostroma, had founded the cult in the seventh century. He held there to be no barrier between the human and the divine; a man could be reborn as God if he mortified the flesh and denied desire. He proclaimed himself to be a living God, and his follower Ivan Suslov to be his Christ. Filipov was exiled to Siberia. Suslov was crucified on the Kremlin wall in Moscow. *Khlyst* legend claimed that he rose from the dead to preach and was again tortured, flayed, and crucified; believers wrapped him in a shroud, which turned into a second skin, and he rose from the dead once more before ascending to heaven in 1718 at the age of a hundred. Filipov had added two new commandments to the Mosaic ten; *khlysts* were not to drink alcohol or marry. If they were already married, he ordered them to abandon their wives and call their children "sins"; they could then take "spiritual wives" but sex was forbidden.

If a man could be divine, however, it followed that he could be beyond sin. A *khlyst* named Radaev taught his disciples that chastity was no more than the sin of pride. The sexual urge, he said, expressed the will to God and should thus be released in rituals. "Arks" or groups were established under a "pilot" or "Christ" who appointed women as Blessed Mothers, angels, and prophetesses. The pilot admonished his followers to lead blameless lives between rituals. These began with singing and drumming in air heated with bonfires. The celebrants wore white or black robes of calico, "tunics of fervor" which commemorated the robe worn by Ivan Suslov during his crucifixion. As the tempo of the drumming increased, the members of the ark danced themselves into a state of *radenie,* "frenzy," in which they cried out in tongues—they called it the "language of Jerusalem"—as the Holy Spirit possessed them. The head of the czar's secret service, General Alexander Spiridovich, described how the *khlysts* then knelt in front of the pilot and the Blessed Mother to be whipped before forming a moving circle and turning the rods on themselves while chanting:

> I whip. I whip. I search for Christ.
> Come down to us, Christ, from the seventh heaven,
> Come with us Christ, into the sacred circle,
> Come down to us
> Holy Spirit of the Lord.

After this came the "fervour of David." As they approached hysteria, the pilot took a woman and "all surrendered to debauchery, without regard to age or parentage." *Khlysts* were secretive since they were liable to a long prison term if they were detected, and a figure of 120,000 adherents given in 1896 was no doubt an exaggeration; but Spiridovich, a sober and professional policeman, estimated that they had arks in at least thirty Russian provinces.

"Stranglers," *dushtels,* practiced a form of euthanasia, cutting short the pain of the terminally ill by choking them from "motives of human pity and retrospective pity for Christ and His Calvary." In another extreme of sacrifice, a peasant, transported to Siberia for killing his wife and children under the inspiration of Abraham's slaying of Isaac, nailed his feet and left hand to a cross before driving his right hand back onto a nail placed in the crosspiece. He was discovered wearing a crown of thorns, declaring that he was dying for the sins of the world.

Other sectarians were gentler. Communities of *dukhobors,* "spirit warriors," known as Siberian Quakers, believed in inner inspiration as the only source of faith. The sect is thought to have arisen among peasants around Kharkov about 1740. They believed God to be present in all human beings, who are thus equal; ownership was sinful, and they lived in communes. They rejected all priestly rituals, hierarchies, dogma, and the Bible. They held that Christ was merely one of a succession of inspired figures, among whom they counted their own leaders. Their pacifism and communal life attracted Tolstoy. In his later years the novelist renounced his property and lived as a poor peasant under his wife's roof. He, too, denied the divinity of Christ, and thought the worship of Jesus to be blasphemy, believing the essence of the faith to be nonresistance to evil, the suppression of anger, and unreserved love for one's enemies. Tolstoy took up the *dukhobor* cause in 1895, when they stripped naked rather than be enlisted in the army; he defended them in his last great novel, *Resurrection,* and helped them emigrate to Cyprus and Canada.* The Orthodox Church excommunicated Tolstoy himself in 1901.

Molokans, "milk drinkers," vegetarians who lived in Galilean simplicity, were also linked to the troublesome writer. They were "in permanent and stubborn conflict with the authorities," General Vassilyev wrote. "Their views were closely related to the views of Leo Tolstoy, and exercised a strong influence on him." *Dyrniks,* "holers," prayed looking upwards to the sky through a hole in the roof of their cabins, *Kamenshchiks* defied the sins of the world in remote mountain fastnesses. *Bezpopovts* thought that the world would soon end, so corrupted was it by the priesthood. They knelt for hours, their mouths opened to the rainy sky to receive drops of blessing that they believed were distilled in heaven. Worshipers of the Holy Spirit breathed deeply as they prayed, hoping to swallow the Third Person of the Trinity; a famous portrait painter, Borovikovsky, collapsed after

---

Dukhobor refusal to register births, deaths, marriages, and land ownership soon vexed Canadian officials.

overbreathing during a prayer session, and members of the sect claimed that he had died of a surfeit of the Holy Ghost.

✤ RUSSIAN AUTOCRACY—the czar's state and the czar's Church—was shattered by World War I. Though the casualties at the front were huge,* the collapse was internal. Overwhelmed by fatigue, defeat, scandal, corruption, food lines, and its subjects' furious sense of its degeneration, the three-hundred-year-old Romanov dynasty was swept away in a few days of February 1917 by a mutiny in the Petrograd† garrison. The Church, intimately entwined with the fallen monarchy, did not escape the humiliation. Its most powerful figure, Metropolitan Pitirim of Petrograd, had been suspected of stealing church plate and treasures from his palace while bishop of Kursk, in collusion with a young deacon with whom he had "relations disapproved of by both the church and the law." His name had been put forward by Rasputin, who openly boasted that "I begat Pitirim"; when the czar appointed him, the procurator of the Holy Synod resigned in protest and was replaced by another Rasputin nominee, Rayev, "old and completely insignificant, with a wig, and very comical." One of the first acts of the new provisional government that emerged from the February Revolution was to appoint a commission to examine Rasputin's involvement with the Church and the autocracy.

The government did not survive long enough for the inquiry to be completed. Eight months later, in what came to be called Red October 1917, Lenin staged his coup d'état and the Bolsheviks seized power. Thus the Communist policy of "scientific atheism" was introduced to the world's largest country.

Orthodoxy was identified with the old regime from the outset. Lenin called its priests "gendarmes in cassocks" and equated them with hangmen as agents of autocracy; while the hangman had dealt with popular resistance by force, he said, the priest was used to "sweeten and embellish the lot of the oppressed by empty promises of a heavenly kingdom." Other sects, and the large Moslem community, were less harshly treated at first. Their time would come, however, for, as Lenin

---

*The cumulative losses have never been calculated. "In the Great War ledger, the page on which the Russian losses were written has been torn out," the German commander Paul Hindenburg wrote after the war. "No one knows the figure. Five millions or eight millions? We too have no idea." A reason that the czarist troops did not crack at the front, the British military observer Alfred Knox thought, was because "religion is a power in the Russian army. . . . Officers crowd round, with serious bearded faces in the little dug-out to tell of the power of prayer." After inflicting 80 percent casualties on Russian infantry attacking them during the Easter offensive in 1916, the Germans were astonished to hear the survivors singing the Easter hymn, "Christ is risen from the dead, conquering death by death."

†The Russified name for the capital; it had replaced the German-sounding St. Petersburg at the start of the war.

wrote, the Communist Party could not remain indifferent to "ignorance or obscurantism in the shape of religious beliefs"; its writ ran to the innermost parts of the soul. The Lenin Rooms in workplaces, the chant of the International, red flags, the volumes of Marxist-Leninist philosophy, Chekhist secret policemen; these were respectively their chapels, hymns, crosses, dogma, and inquisitors. When Lenin died he was deified in his granite mausoleum on Red Square, and Stalin projected himself as Lenin's Christ, of whom mystic panegyrics were composed:

> Thou bright sun of the nations
> The unthinking sun of our times,
> And more than the sun, for the sun has no wisdom.

Shrewd observers realized very quickly what was a foot. "Lenin is like a prophet of Israel, and what he preaches is a lay religion," the philosopher Miguel de Unamuno wrote in 1920. "Materialistic, if you like . . . but a religion. Atheistic, undoubtedly, but a religion."[5] The brilliant economist John Maynard Keynes, visiting Russia four years later, wrote, "I feel confident of one conclusion, that if communism achieves a certain success, it will achieve it not as an improved economic theory but as a religion." Christianity was a rival bidder for the human spirit, and a natural enemy to Soviet Communism.

Church and state were swiftly separated. A decree in January 1918 declared that "every citizen may confess any religion or no religion at all." It went on, however to ban religious teaching in all schools, colleges, and universities. All church buildings were taken by the state, although the authorities could allow buildings to be used for worship "by special decision." Church and monastic land was nationalized. No compensation was offered for confiscated assets. Only civic marriage and divorce were recognized. Under the new constitution, the clergy—together with capitalists, criminals, and imbeciles—were deprived of the right to vote or to hold state offices. In practice this denied the clergy the right to food rations and their children to education. At a stroke the Orthodox Church was stripped of its legal privileges, its land, and its source of income; in response, the patriarch, Metropolitan Tikhon excommunicated the "godless rulers of darkness." The civil war that broke out in 1918 deflected Bolshevik interest away from the Church, although the ex-czar and his family, still symbols of Orthodoxy, were murdered.

Calculated persecution returned after the Bolshevik victory in 1921. Lenin sanctioned terror as a form of pesticide to be used on people whom he dehumanized as "harmful insects . . . scoundrel fleas . . . bedbugs"; Leon Trotsky, too, found "nothing immoral" in the proletariat "finishing off" the bourgeoisie and its clergy. Valuables and consecrated articles were stripped from churches, many of which were closed. Emigrés estimated that 1,200 priests and 28 bishops had been killed by 1923,[6] and thousands of others, with monks and nuns, were deported. In 1922, Tikhon was imprisoned. A "Renovationist Church" quiescent to the regime was encouraged. Weary from interrogation, worried lest the new church supersede his own, Tikhon agreed to cooperate. His release and temporary Orthodox survival were bought by a well-publicized apology. "Raised in a monarchical society and until my imprisonment exposed to the influence of anti-Soviet circles," he wrote, "I succumbed to negative attitude towards Soviet Power. I disavow definitely and clearly any connection with counter-revolution. . . ."[7] "Holyrussia" disappeared; the country was renamed the Soviet Union, and St. Petersburg became Leningrad.

On Easter Day, 1925, the foundation congress of the League of the Militant Godless was held. Its duty was to eradicate religion through propaganda, pressure, and ridicule. Tikhon died the same year. The election of a successor was forbidden. Metropolitan Sergey, who took over the tasks but not the title of the patriarch, was arrested. After two years of captivity he was released and issued a pastoral letter: "We want to remain Orthodox believers and also want to recognize the Soviet Union as our earthly fatherland." Metropolitan Joseph of Leningrad thought this craven; he and others were imprisoned, and a number were executed.

A survey of Russian peasants in the mid-1920s suggested that 55 percent of them remained active Christian worshipers.[8] The Red worker and the Communist intellectual were city phenomena, while the villages remained, as the poet Alexander Blok had found, full of "twisted, unhappy and browbeaten people with ideas from before the Flood, people who have forgotten even themselves." They mocked Bolshevik agitators as *belorucha,* "white hands," urban types untouched by rural toil. "Your nails are very long," one young militant was greeted in a village. "You're not the Antichrist, are you?" With that, he was attacked to see "if he didn't have a tail or whether he was covered in hair." Such people did not take kindly to state control, or the compulsory collectivization of their land and the destruction of the Church. Joseph Stalin imposed these measures on them in 1930.

AS A BOY in Russian Georgia, his hardworking mother had destined Stalin for the priesthood. She took in washing to send her son to a church school in Gori, and then to the theological seminary at Tiflis, the Georgian capital. Each day started with an Orthodox service at seven; classes were led by monks, and the gates were locked at five. "Shut up within barrack walls we felt like prisoners, innocent of any crime, who were forced to spend a long time in jail," a fellow pupil wrote. Stalin already had revolutionary leanings, and he was frequently punished for reading books condemned by the monks. A note from the school principal survives: "Confine him to the punishment cell for a prolonged period. I have already warned him once about an unsanctioned book, *Ninety-three* by Victor Hugo." He was expelled in 1899, ostensibly for failing to sit exams, but more probably on suspicion of political disloyalty. He was to show no further interest in religion, except to inflict on believers a censorship and punishments incomparably more savage than any he had suffered in the seminary.

His subsequent career as oil field agitator, terrorist, convict, and Siberian exile had led him to the Bolshevik central committee, and after Lenin's death in 1924 to eventual leadership of the Party; his atheist credentials were impeccable, but he retained an instinctive grasp of the uses of liturgy and faith. It was Stalin who had urged the preparation of Lenin's tomb in Red Square, who called on the Party to collect Lenin relics, and who composed the Communist catechism: "In leaving us, Comrade Lenin ordained us to hold high and keep pure the great title of Member of the Party. We vow to thee, Comrade Lenin, that we shall honorably fulfill this thy commandment. . . . In leaving us, Comrade Lenin ordained us to guard and strengthen the dictatorship of the proletariat. We vow to thee, Comrade Lenin, that we shall honorably fulfill this thy commandment. . . ."[9]

The method that Stalin used to force the peasantry onto collective farms was terror-famine, and the result was a holocaust. Boris Pasternak, who made a trip to gather material on collectivization, found himself dumb with horror. "What I saw could not be expressed in words. . . . There was such inhuman, unimaginable misery, such a terrible disaster, that it began to seem almost abstract, it would not fit within the bounds of consciousness." Grain was confiscated from starving families to gain hard currency for Stalin's industrialization program. In 1933, 1.7 million tons of grain were sold on international markets at knockdown, depression prices. A social class, of kulak peasants, a definition broad enough to include families that owned a single cow, was entirely liquidated in some areas of the Ukraine. An American labor organizer, Fred Beal, made a random visit to a village two hours by train from Kharkov. He found a single living person, a woman who had gone mad; "in the houses there were only corpses," he wrote. It is probable that fourteen million peasants died, although no accurate estimate can be made for, as the future Soviet leader Nikita Khrushchev was to explain, "no one was keeping count."

Communist activists led the grain searches, shot hoarders, and herded families onto deportation transports as a matter of dogma; they were pitiless, for dogma demanded "no concessions to rightist-deviationist attitudes" and "no pacifism." "We were realizing historical necessity," the activist Lev Kopolev wrote. "We were obtaining grain for the socialist fatherland. . . . I saw women and children with distended bellies, turning blue. And corpses—corpses in ragged sheepskin coats and cheap felt boots; corpses in peasant huts, in the melting snow of old Vologda, under the bridges of Kharkov . . . I saw all this and did not go out of my mind or commit suicide. . . . I believed because I wanted to believe."[10]

Terror, and scientific atheism, was also applied to the Church. Stalin introduced a Law of Religious Associations in 1929 that banned churches from all work with children and young people. Churches were not allowed to organize reading rooms, libraries, excursions, children's playgrounds, sewing groups, or Bible readings; they could not sponsor sanatoria or medical care; their priests were forbidden to take part in any activity outside the immediate neighborhood of the "prayer building," the new name for "church." An attempt was made to extinguish religion as a whole. The fury fell most harshly on the Orthodox clergy, but thousands of other Christian priests, Baptists, Jehovah's Witnesses, Catholics, and mullahs and rabbis, who had partly escaped earlier measures, were also persecuted. Churchmen were like chickens in a shed, an Orthodox priest observed, from which the cook seizes victims in turn, "one today and one tomorrow, but not all the chickens at once."[11] Some were shot, though most of those arrested suffered a lingering death in the work camps of Siberia and the Arctic. Others lived on the run. When the last church in a town was closed, a sympathizer wrote, the churchmen went from place to place, teaching "in the stables, in the forests and under the open sky in the field. They look pale and miserable, and their clothing is often torn. A few crumbs of bread are their only nourishment. In their little sack they carry a Bible, their most precious possession. They are warmly received by the people, but woe to them if they fall into the hands of the stool-pigeons of the police."[12]

Membership in the League of the Militant Godless reached five million by 1935. Children between eight and fourteen were enrolled in Groups of Godless Youth before graduating to Komsomol, the League of Communist Youth. Prizes were offered for the best "godless hymns" and to children who denounced their parents for voicing anti-Party sentiments. Universities established chairs of Atheism. Antireligious museums were set up in former churches, with exhibits of the art treasures that "parasite" priests had bought with money stolen from the poor; caravans went on tours of the villages to show films exposing the "wickedness" and "stupidity" of believers. Only one in forty churches survived; the others were smashed to rubble or turned into warehouses, offices, and museums. The Cathedral of Christ the Savior in Moscow was destroyed with dynamite, though care was taken to do so in the dead of night. A Palace of Soviets topped by a huge statue of Lenin was to be built in its place, but the site had weak foundations and it was used for a giant open-air swimming pool instead. No churches or meeting places were permitted in the new industrial cities. The huge steel complex at Magnitogorsk had 250,000 workers; John Scott, an American volunteer who helped build it, thought it was probably the only place of such size on earth that had no building devoted to a religion.

The effect was much as it had been during the Roman persecutions sixteen hundred years before. The faith went underground. Bishops and priests were ordained in secret and worshiped in houses, apartments, and sheds; fathers took the role of priests in family worship. In the 1937 census, 57 percent of the population revealed that they were still believers[13] although the true figure was almost certainly higher. A priest did not stop being a priest merely because he was deprived of his church and congregation, Yemelian Yaroslavsky, chairman of the Militant Godless, complained at a conference in Moscow in 1939. "He travels round with his primitive tools in the villages, performs religious rites, reads prayers, baptizes children," he warned. "Such wandering priests are at times more dangerous than those who carry out their work at a designated place of residence."[14]

In statistical terms the Godless looked to have won. There were 163 Orthodox bishops in 1914, and by 1939 only four survived in freedom; of the old body of 51,105 clergy, the number still in their parishes was in the hundreds. Sects such as the Dukhobors and the Moloknas seemed to have disappeared without a trace. But they had not. "Religion is like a nail," Yaroslavsky wearily admitted. "The harder you strike it, the deeper it goes." The religious lay low and waited for a respite. It came in 1941, and from a strange source, a man in his own way as godless as Stalin, Adolf Hitler.

HITLER HAD BEEN an insignificant prisoner in a Bavarian jail when Stalin was writing his Oath to Lenin in 1924, but he learned much from the Communist dictatorship to the East. Fascism and communism, the two great godless creeds of the century, had mutually exclusive ends in mind. Nazi hatreds were ethnically rather than class-inspired, though the death camps in which they were played out differed little save in their exposure to the outside world;* Jews, gypsies, and Slavs replaced kulaks and the bourgeoisie, and the supposed beneficiar-

*The Nazi concentration camps were, of course, overrun by Russian, American, and British troops in 1944 and 1945, and the evidence of genocide and overwhelming bestiality was filmed and photographed. The camps of the Soviet gulag lay in Siberia and the Arctic; though in existence for much longer than the German camps, they were beyond the reach of independent witnesses and remained so until they were dismantled. Soviet propaganda and Western fellow-travelers largely concealed the 1930s starvation in the Ukraine, much closer to the West. When the French prime minister Edouard Herriot visited a collective farm near Kiev, the buildings were decorated with furniture from a local theater, and the peasants were given special rations. The playwright George Bernard Shaw was given a chauffeur-driven tour in 1932, when the famine and the arrests of priests were at their height. "I did not see a single undernourished person in Russia, young or old," he wrote on his return. "Were they padded? Were their hollow cheeks distended by pieces of india-rubber inside?" He also assured the *London Times* that "there is more freedom of religion in the Soviet Union than in England"; the Moscow correspondent of the *New York Times*, Walter Duranty, told his readers that "any report of a famine in Russia is today an exaggeration or malignant propaganda."

ies of Nazism were Aryans rather than the proletariat. Means were another matter. In his assault on the spirit and the intellect, his skills in adapting ritual to serve his own egocentric paganism, his dehumanizing of opponents, and in his contempt for religion, Hitler was quite the match for Stalin.

As a six year old, Hitler served briefly as a choirboy and acolyte at the Benedictine monastery at Lambach in Austria; he said later that he had the opportunity "to intoxicate myself with the solemn splendor of church festivals."[15] Any residual Catholicism had disappeared by the time he began to expound his philosophy as a thirty-year-old ex-soldier in Munich in 1919. Such religious feelings as he had were *völkisch,* a word crammed with a racial mysticism and a violent, bittersweet atavism that the rustic English "folkish" cannot translate. A *völkisch* faith, consciously Aryan and anti-Semitic, had been put forward by the theologian Paul de Lagarde in an essay on the German state and religion in 1873. He claimed that "Christianity, namely Catholicism and Protestantism, is a distortion of the Bible." De Lagarde blamed this on St. Paul, who had Judaized Christianity: "The whole Jewish view of history has been foisted on us by him."[16]

Crude religious books of this sort circulated in prewar Vienna as the morose young Hitler drifted through the city, selling sketches and beating carpets. One popular title was "Forward to Christ! Away with Paul! German Religion!" The book claimed that "the poisoner Paul and his Volk" were the archenemies of Jesus and that they had to be "removed from the entrance to the kingdom of God" before "a true German church can open its doors." The difficulty of Jesus being Jewish was solved by making him an Aryan. The *völkisch* writer Theodor Fritsch accomplished this by proving philologically, to his own satisfaction at least, that the Galileans were in fact Gauls, and that the Gauls were Germans. He thus demonstrated "how from Germanic blood could emerge a religious genius" whose "great idealism is Germanically related to us." It was, Fritsch wrote, impossible for Jesus to be Jewish: "The unfathomable opposition between Christian and Jewish doctrine precludes any racial kinship."[17]

These hatreds were the sum total of Hitler's Christianity. He claimed to see in Christ a mirror of himself, as a brave and persecuted struggler against the Jews. He laid out his philosophy in a speech in the Bürgerbräukeller in Munich on April 12, 1922. During the speech he savaged a recent statement by Count Lerchenfeld, the minister-president of Bavaria, in which the count had said that, "as a human being and a Christian," he could not be anti-Semitic. "My Christian feeling points me to my Lord and Savior as a fighter," Hitler said, to prolonged applause. "It points me towards the man who, once lonely and surrounded by only a few followers, recognized these Jews and called for battle against them, and who, as true God, was not only the greatest as a *sufferer* but also the greatest as a *warrior*. . . . I read the page which declares to us how the Lord finally rose up and seized the whip to drive the usurers, the brood of serpents and vipers, from the Temple. Today, two thousand years later, I am deeply moved to perceive his tremendous struggle against the Jewish poison." Hitler than made a direct comparison between himself and Christ. "Two thousand years ago, a man was also denounced by the same race," he said. "The man was dragged before the court and it was also said of him, 'He stirred up the people.' So he too had been a 'rabble rouser'! And against whom? Against 'God,' they cried. Yes, indeed he roused the rabble against the 'God' of the Jews, for this 'God is gold.' "[18]

Hitler drew on the work of his friend Dietrich Eckart, a Munich religious writer. At the time of his death in 1923, Eckart was writing a dialogue entitled, "Bolshevism from Moses to Lenin. A conversation between Adolf Hitler and Myself." It portrayed Jews as the bane of history from Moses to Lenin, while an Aryan Christ with "flashing eyes in the midst of the creeping Jewish rabble" lashed them with sermons whose "words fall like whiplashes: 'Your father is the devil.' "[19] Hitler's thoughts were identical and they remained with him until the end. In November 1944, Martin Bormann, the Nazi *Reichsminister,* recorded Hitler as saying that Jesus had fought "against the depraved materialism of his time and thus against the Jews," and that it was "St. Paul who had first falsified the Christian idea in a subtle way."[20]

In *Mein Kampf,* the political testament he dictated in prison in 1924, Hitler claimed that he was "acting in accordance with the will of the almighty Creator: by defending myself against the Jews, I am fighting for the work of the Lord."[21] He described Judaism, Christianity, and Bolshevism as interlinked evils. He said that the Jews had been expelled from ancient Egypt because they had stirred up the rabble with humanitarian phrases—"just as they do here"—and from this it followed that Moses was the first leader of Bolshevism.[22] Conscience was a "Jewish invention, a blemish like circumcision."[23] Paul had invented Christianity in order to undermine the Roman Empire, just as Lenin was using Marxism to bring down the modern system.

The anti-Semitism on which Hitler throve, as well as inflation, unemployment, and revanchism, partly resulted from Germany's defeat in World War I. Jews had lived in one German territory or another since the earliest medieval times; the country was too fragmented to allow for the mass expulsions that had taken place in England, France, and Spain. The atrocities of the Crusades (see chapter XI) and the peasants' wars showed that Jews did not enjoy any special protection, but their presence was commonplace, and their numbers had increased with Prussia's part in the partition of Poland in the late eighteenth century. The Prussian government had slowly emancipated them. At the outbreak of the war they were debarred only from the officer corps, the higher civil service, and the judiciary; during it, they became eligible for army commissions. The

Kaiserreich had collapsed with the abdication of the emperor and Germany's defeat of November 1918.

The postwar Weimar Republic that replaced it was tolerant, much more so than many of its citizens and its priests and pastors. Protestantism had been close to a state religion in the vanished *Kaiserreich,* but republican Weimar appeared godless and unpatriotic, and some Protestants stressed their abiding Germanness and their loyalty to the *Volk.* "The Church must have eyes and words for the threat that Jewry poses to German folkdom," a theologian told the 1927 German Evangelical Congress. "Service to the Fatherland is divine service."[24] The Lutheran bishop of Kurmark, Dibelius, wrote that, "One cannot fail to appreciate that Jewry plays a leading role among all the disruptive phenomena of modern civilization."[25] Catholics, too, were often hostile to Weimar liberalism and suspicious of Jewish influence in the years before Hitler came to power. In 1930 the vicar-general of Mainz stated that, although it was wrong for Christians to hate other races, he concurred with Hitler's criticisms of Jewish influence in the press, theater, and literature.

Hitler, however, shunned religious Nazis. Dr. Artur Dinter, a former science teacher and dramatist, proposed starting a German national church. He said that the church must reach the spiritual and moral heights "which shine upon us from the teaching of the greatest antisemitist and anti-materialist of all time, the Hero of Nazareth"; by including materialism, Dinter demonized Communists as well as Jews. The aim of the proposed church was to "lay the axe to the spiritual roots of Judaism in the Christian church."[26] Dinter was a veteran Nazi, holding party card number 5 and acting as party *gauleiter* (administrator) in Thuringia. He was dismissed in September 1927, supposedly on grounds of "executive stress," but in fact because Hitler had decided to distance the party from religion. Dinter nonetheless founded the *Geistchristliche Religionsgemeinschaft,* a Christian association that attacked the "Jewish-Roman" and "Jewish-Protestant churches." Hitler wrote to him to say that there was no time to complete a religious reformation. Dinter was expelled from the party and his number 5 card was stamped "never to be readmitted." Hitler vowed to keep the Nazis out of all religious issues "for all time to come."[27]

In the Reichstag (legislative) election of September 1930 the Nazis increased their share of the vote from 2.6 percent to 18.3 percent, while the Communists also surged forward. The Nazi vote was predominantly Protestant. Germany had retained religious divisions dating back to the Reformation. In twenty-five of the thirty-five Reichstag electoral districts, Protestants or Catholics had majorities of 70 percent and more. The Nazis won over 20 percent of the vote in Lutheran areas such as Pomerania, Liegnitz, and Schleswig-Holstein. That fell to 14 percent in Catholic-dominated regions like Cologne-Aachen, Koblenz-Trier, and Lower

Bavaria. The reasons were not sectarian. The Center Party, with a Catholic ideology, attracted much of the Catholic vote. No such religiously-based party catered to Protestants. Large numbers of them voted Socialist, but only the Nazis appealed to those with right-wing or nationalist views.

Jewish businesses were boycotted in April 1933 immediately after the Nazi seizure of power, but Hitler was careful to express some support for the churches in the early months. He told his propaganda minister Joseph Goebbels that the best technique for dealing with them was to "hold back for the present and coolly strangle any attempts at impudence or interference in the affairs of state. . . . He [Hitler] views Christianity as a symptom of decay. Rightly so. It is a branch of the Jewish race. . . ."[28] He was contemptuous of Protestants, finding them weak and malleable, but he was wary of Catholicism. "They are insignificant little people, submissive as dogs, and they sweat with embarrassment when you talk to them," he said of the Lutheran clergy. "They have neither a religion they can take seriously nor a great position to defend like Rome."[29]

The Vatican was ambivalent to fascism in its early stages. Pius XI had been pope since 1922, the year when Benito Mussolini had marched on Rome with his Blackshirts and established the first fascist dictatorship. Pius was a mountaineer, a scholar of medieval handwriting, a decisive, genial man nonetheless capable of disciplinarian rages. He disliked racism in all its forms. At his accession, no missionary diocese had an indigenous bishop. In 1926, Pius consecrated the first six Chinese bishops in St. Peter's, and the first Japanese as bishop of Nagasaki; by his death in 1939 the Church had forty such bishops, and the number of locally born mission priests had tripled to seven thousand. He dealt severely with Action Française, an extreme right-wing movement led by the royalist and anti-Semitic Charles Maurras, which had a large following among French Catholics. All its members were excommunicated in 1927. French Holy Ghost Fathers sympathetic to Maurras objected to this, among them the rector of the French seminary in Rome. Pius sent for the superior of the order and told him to get rid of the rector. "Yes, Holy Father, I'll see what can be done," the superior said. "I didn't say, see what you can do," Pius retorted angrily. "I said fire him."[30]

Pius was more circumspect with Mussolini, concluding a concordat with him in 1929. After much hard bargaining, the pope won independence for his own tiny sovereign state, Vatican City, together with its post office and radio station, and the extraterritorial dependencies of Castel Gandolfo and the Lateran. It was a shadow of the lost papal states, perhaps, but Pius also won recognition of canon law alongside Italian state law, financial compensation of 1,750 million lire, and agreement that Catholic doctrine could be taught and the crucifix displayed in state schools. Vatican support for the centrist Catholic Partido Popolare was withdrawn as part of the arrangement. Pius spoke of Mussolini as "a man sent by Providence"; the priest and leader of the Partido Popolare resigned in disgust and went into self-exile in London. Pius was rapidly disillusioned himself, particularly when Mussolini—"youth shall be ours"[31]—insisted on suppressing the Catholic scout movement. In June 1931 the pope denounced the regime in the encyclical *Non Abbiamo Bisogno* describing fascism as idolatry and "pagan worship of the state," and singled out the fascist loyalty oath as contrary to the law of God.

Nonetheless, Hitler was also able to sign a concordat with the Vatican in 1933. Cardinal Eugenio Pacelli, the Vatican secretary of state and future Pius XII, who had been nuncio in Munich in the 1920s, negotiated it. Pacelli admired Germany and its culture, though he had few illusions that he was now dealing with anti-Christian racists. The Church retained autonomy in the German see and a narrow control over education and its institutions in exchange for diplomatic recognition of the regime. As in Italy, a Catholic political party, the Center Party, was sacrificed to the deal; its leader, Monsignor Ludwig Kaas, was summoned to Rome to become keeper of the building works at St. Peter's.

In response, the Nazis required all parents to enroll their children in religious instruction classes; praising Hitler for his "solemnity," Cardinal Hauber said that "the Chancellor, there is no doubt, lives in a state of belief in God."[32] Seven Catholic feast days were recognized as legal holidays. Party members who were lapsed church members rejoined on the orders of their superiors, and the Storm Troopers were ordered to attend services en masse. Until 1936 the German army insisted that every soldier had to belong to one of the two official Christian denominations, Catholic and Evangelical, and maintained a full complement of regimental chaplains. Churchgoers saddened that Hitler himself refused to go to church prayed for the remission of his sins. "The aims of the Reich government have long been those of the Catholic Church," Bishop Bürger declared.[33]

A new "German Christian" movement was formed among Protestants. Its leading light was Ludwig Müller; he had met Hitler while serving as an army chaplain and advised him on church affairs. The German Christians won a large majority in the Church elections of July 1933, with backing from Hitler and the Storm Troopers, and Müller was elected as *Reichsbischof* of the German Evangelical Church. Extremists called for the Old Testament to be eliminated entirely, as Marcion had pleaded eighteen hundred years before, and to excise everything Jewish or "servile" from the New; they wanted to scrap "the scapegoat and inferiority theology of Rabbi Paul," as they mockingly dubbed the saint, and to abandon Augustine for his "Jewish" sense of sin. The Evangelical Church of Saxony replaced the Hebrew "Amen" and "Hallelujah" with "May God grant it" and "Praise be the Lord"; Abraham's sacrifice of Isaac was stripped from the syllabus in Schleswig-Holstein.[34] At a mass meeting in the Sports Palace in Berlin in November 1933, held to honor the Aryanized "Christ the Hero," the delegates agreed to adopt the "Aryan paragraph," which excluded Jews from official posts, for the Church. The *Judenmission* for the conversion of Jews was supported by a wide range of evangelicals; the German Christians denied that Jews, as a "separate race," could become Christians even through baptism. Such virulent extremism alienated many Protestants. The same month a Pastor's Emergency League was founded by the Lutheran pastor Martin Niemöller to organize an anticollaboration Confessing Church.

Reichsbischof Müller handed the Protestant youth movement, Evangelisches Jugendwerk, to the Hitler Youth leader Baldur von Schirach in December 1933. The deal was done over dinner at the Esplanade Hotel in Berlin, to the accompaniment of a popular violinist. "Bishop Müller told me that Protestant youth had given him total control," Schirach recalled, "and that he now wanted to transfer all Protestant boys and girls under the age of eighteen to the Hitler Youth. We would soon reach agreement on the details. . . ."[35] There were protests— "Church dies at hand of bishop, ashamed and sad for such a church" one telegram read—but Protestant youth was effectively suborned.

The fiercest resistance came from Jehovah's Witnesses. Responding to attacks by police and Storm Troopers on their meetings, their leader, Brother Rutherford, sent a personal letter to Hitler by registered post in October 1934. It was read out to Witnesses at meetings in each German city where they had groups. Rutherford told Hitler that his suppression of Witnesses was "contrary to God's law and in violation of our rights." God commanded them to bear witness, Rutherford wrote; "therefore this letter is to advise you that at any cost we will obey God's commandments, will meet together for the study of his Word, and will worship and serve him as he has commanded. If your government or officers do violence to us because we are obeying God, then our blood will be upon you and you will answer to Almighty God. . . ."[36] Many Witnesses paid for this extraordinary courage with their lives.

Assaults on Christianity grew with Nazi confidence. Attendance at school prayers was made optional, and religion was dropped from school-leaving examinations. Priests were then forbidden to teach religious classes. In 1935 the Gestapo arrested seven hundred Protestant pastors for condemning Nazi neopaganism from the pulpit. Clergy in Württemberg were punished for "violating the moral instincts of the German race" by referring to Abraham, Joseph, and David in their teaching. Karl Barth, a leading Protestant theologian and member of the Confessing Church, declared that it was no longer possible for a Christian to remain neutral in the face of Nazism and refused to take an oath of loyalty to the Führer. He was dismissed from his chair at Bonn; as a Swiss citizen he could not be arrested, and he left Germany for Basle. Here he wrote that, in man's wickedness, the primary sin is man's endeavor to make himself rather than God the center of the world, a sin writ monstrously large in Hitler.

The young head of the Confessing Church's seminary at Finkenwalde in Pomerania, Dietrich Bonhoeffer, warned that, in fighting injustice, the church might find itself called "not only to help the victims who have fallen under the wheels, but to fall into the spokes itself."[37] In September 1935, less than a fortnight after the Nuremberg Laws had eliminated all remaining civil rights for Jews, the leaders of the Confessing Church convened in the Berlin suburb of Steglitz. A Berlin deaconess, Marga Meusel, condemned those who saw Jewish persecution as reflecting the divine will. "Since when has the evildoer the right to portray his evil deeds as the will of God?" she asked. Most delegates wanted to avoid the Jewish question entirely; some even proposed a resolution supporting the right of the state to regulate Jewish affairs. The synod finally passed a statement supporting the baptism of Jews; Bonhoeffer thought it totally inadequate. Within two years the Gestapo declared the education of candidates for the Confessing ministry to be illegal, closed Bonhoeffer's seminary at Finkenwalde, and arrested twenty-seven of his former students; Martin Niemöller was sent to a concentration camp, refusing offers of release in return for collaboration.

A sustained assault against Catholic monasteries and convents began in 1936. Charges ranging from illegal currency dealing to sexual offenses were brought against monks and nuns, amid glaring publicity. Monks who nursed crippled patients and were obliged to hold their penises while they urinated were accused of homosexuality. At one mass trial in Koblenz, 267 Franciscans were charged with abusing children in their care. It was claimed that the archbishop of Baden had a Jewish mistress, and that Jews financed the Vatican. Protestant and Catholic youth groups, and the Scouts, were suppressed in favor of the Hitler Youth. Membership in the movement became compulsory for all boys and girls from age ten to eighteen in 1936. The song they sang at Nuremberg party rallies left no doubt of their indoctrination:

No evil priest can prevent us from feeling
    that we are the children of Hitler.
We follow not Christ, but Horst Wessel.
Away with incense and holy water.
    The Church can hang for all we care.
The Swastika brings salvation on earth.

The rallies were themselves a pinnacle of Nazism, in which Nuremberg became the "Rome of a new paganism," with their eagles, loudspeakers, organs, and prayers that matched those sung of Lenin:

> Führer my Führer
> Thou hast rescued Germany from deepest distress
> I thank thee for my daily bread
> Abide thou long with me, forsake me not
> Führer my Führer, my faith and light.

A favorite Storm Trooper song had the refrain: "Hang the Jews and put the priests up against the wall."[38] Ceremonial book burnings were held by university staff to celebrate the defeat of the intellect; the rector of Göttingen said he was "proud of the new appellation—barbarians," and his colleague, the theologian Professor Hirsch, said that Hitler was "an instrument of the Creator of all things."[39]

An effort to separate believers from the churches was made by the Nazi-backed German Faith Movement. Its members were called *Gottgläubige,* "God-believers," although it was a mere pastiche of paganism in which God was replaced by Nazi theatricality and a labored respect for the ancients. "The Führer is a man totally attuned to antiquity," Goebbels claimed. "What a difference between the benevolent smiling Zeus and the pain-wracked crucified Christ . . . between a gloomy cathedral and a light, airy, ancient temple . . ."[40] Its main purpose was to dechristianize rituals and festivals.

At weddings, bride and groom were blessed by "Mother Earth, Father Sky and all the beneficent powers of the air," while passages from Nordic sagas were read; wedding announcements reported that the bridal couple had married "in the belief in the Divine Revelation of our nation through Adolf Hitler." At "christenings" the infant was carried by its father on a Teutonic shield, wrapped in a blanket decorated with oak leaves and swastikas; the parents placed their hands on the child and pronounced its name, which was written on the first page of its "book of life."[41] The swastika itself was taken from the symbol found on Germanic runic stones; in terms of Teutonic myths, Hitler passed muster as Woden, the god who lets slip the furies of the world, and his death in the ruins of Berlin matched the epic catastrophe of the Götterdämmerung, the twilight of the gods in which the vault of the heavens is cracked as the deities butcher one another and the earth becomes a furnace. Christmas—the word itself was censored during the war and replaced by "yuletide"—was replaced by a festival of the winter solstice celebrated on December 21. Carols and nativity plays were banned from schools in 1938. It proved impossible to abolish the cross. An order to remove all crucifixes from classrooms in 1937 created such an uproar that it was rescinded. This did not prevent the Faith Movement's journal *Sigrune* from describing Jesus as "a cowardly Jewish lout who . . . insulted the majesty of death in an obscene manner."[42]

Pius was increasingly hostile to the Nazis, shouting at the German ambassador that if it came to another Kulturkampf for the very survival of Christianity, the Church would triumph again.[43] Between 1933 and 1936 the Vatican sent three dozen formal protests to Berlin complaining of blatant breaches of the concordat. Cardinal Faulhaber, the archbishop of Munich, was commissioned to write an encyclical that was smuggled into Germany and read from pulpits on Palm Sunday, 1937. Titled *Mit Brennender Sorge,* "With Burning Anxiety," it denounced the "idolatrous cult" which was replacing belief in the true God with the "myth of race and blood," contrasting this with the Christian teaching that there is a home "for all peoples and all nations." Five days later the encyclical *Divini Redemptoris* denounced Communism as well, saying that it was "intrinsically hostile in any form whatever."

Hitler visited Mussolini in Rome in May 1938. Pius took himself off to Castel Gandolfo, explaining to pilgrims that he could not bear to "see raised in Rome another cross which is not the cross of Christ." In September the pope declared to pilgrims that the canon of the Mass spoke of Abraham as "our father in faith," and that no Christian could be anti-Semitic, because "spiritually we are all Semites." The nationwide German pogrom of *Kristallnacht* took place on the night of November 9–10. Four hundred synagogues and thousands of Jewish homes and shops were burned, and twenty thousand Jews were arrested. Dietrich Bonhoeffer wrote the date in his Bible next to Psalm 74: "They said in their heart, let us make havoc of them altogether; they have burned up all the synagogues in the land . . . How long, O God, shall the adversary reproach?" (Ps. 74:8–10). Bishop Martin Sasse of Thuringia, however, a leading Protestant who published a collection of Martin Luther's anti-Semitic writings, noted with approval in the book's foreword that, "On November 10, 1938, on Luther's birthday, the synagogues are burning," adding that the Germans should mark the words "of the greatest antisemite of his time, the warner of his people against the Jews."[44] In Rome, Pius XI worked on an encyclical, *Humani generis unitas,* in which he was expected to proclaim the unity of humanity and to condemn Nazi racism. He died before it was ready for publication, on February 19, 1939. "At last the stubborn old man is dead," said Mussolini.[45]

THE CATHOLIC VIEW of the relative evils of fascism and communism was colored by the early clash between the two in Spain.

A Republican victory in the Spanish elections of 1931 had obliged the king, Alfonso XIII, to go into exile. Manuel Azaña, a future president of the new Republic and a devout anticlerical, declared that Spain had "ceased to be Catholic." He exaggerated. The country had 20,000 monks, three times as many nuns, and 31,000 priests. It was true, however, that the Church was deeply illib-

684 / THE FAITH

eral and unpopular. "What kind of sin is committed by one who votes for a liberal candidate?" had been a question published in the catechism of 1927. The answer was, "Generally a mortal one."[46] Liberals resented its great estates and its rich holdings in banks, tramways, property, and utilities. A triumvirate of priest, landowner, and army officer blocked progress and entrenched poverty in much of the country.

The Spanish primate, Cardinal Segura, attacked atheism in a violent pastoral letter. It urged Catholics not to remain "quiet and idle" in the face of republicanism, but to "fight like intrepid warriors prepared to succumb gloriously." On May 10, a few days after this verbal onslaught, a rumor flew round Madrid that a group of pro-monarchist officers had killed a taxi driver who had shouted *Viva la Republica!* A mob burned the Jesuit church in the Calle de la Flor in central Madrid, chalking a slogan on its blackened walls: "The Justice of the People on Thieves." Several other churches and convents were destroyed in the capital, and the fires spread to Andalusia. Azaña declared that he would prefer all the churches of Spain to be burned than for a single Republican to be harmed.

All religious orders were obliged to register with the justice ministry under the new republican constitution. Orders that required an addition to the standard canonical vows were to be dissolved; this was a means of expelling the Jesuits, since they took a special vow of loyalty to the pope. Every "public manifestation of religion," including Easter and Christmas processions, had to be officially licensed. Divorce was permitted in cases of mutual disagreement, in defiance of Catholic practice. Religious education was ended. Augustinian and Jesuit schools were closed before any state-run replacements were ready. Even some liberals were appalled, but Azaña thundered, "Do not tell me that this is contrary to freedom. It is a matter of public health."

Increasingly polarized, Spain lurched through five years of strikes, political murders, shootings between fascist Falange *pistoleros* and Anarchists, church burnings, bombings, Catalonian and Basque separatism, and peasant invasions of estates. Elections in February 1936 were won by the Popular Front, an uneasy and anticlerical coalition of socialists, republicans, communists, and Catalans. Azaña was elected president in May. Communists predicted the liquidation of the "capitalist and bourgeois classes"; a socialist deputy called for "waves of blood that turn the seas red."[47] By June there had been 269 political murders and 160 church burnings since the elections. In July, General Francisco Franco flew from his command in the Canaries to Spanish Morocco, and landed troops in Spain, vowing to save it from Red revolution. The republican government defeated the army garrisons in Madrid and Barcelona, and held the great mass of the country; but Franco's army rebels had enclaves from which to expand, in the northwest and Burgos, along the Portuguese border, and in the south around Seville. Franco

A church in Barcelona burned by communists at the outbreak of the Spanish Civil War in July 1936. The left-wing republicans had an unprecedented hatred of religion and all its works. They killed almost eight thousand religious people, including twelve bishops and many novices and nuns, before their defeat in 1939. Catholics described the war as "a furious battle between Christian civilization and the most cruel Paganism that has ever darkened the world."

was supported by the Nazis and the Italian fascists; the aircraft of the German Condor Legion gave him air superiority. Communist International Brigades were raised for the republican cause, and Moscow provided tanks, munitions, and advisers.

"At no time in the history of Europe or even perhaps of the world," the great historian of the civil war, Hugh Thomas, wrote, "has so passionate a hatred of religion and all its works been shown."[48] The original army rising was an affair of generals, in which the Church had taken no part. Indiscriminate church burnings and priest-killings broke out immediately, however; when the left-wing parties took control of Madrid on the night of July 19, 1936, they set fifty churches on fire.

Both communists and anarchists harbored a special dislike for the Church—the old anarchist hero Mikhail Bakunin had said that the new world would be won only when "the last king is strangled with the guts of the last priest"—but atrocities were general. Priests who were thought to have slighted the working class, by wearing a dirty collar to the funeral of the poor and a clean one for the rich, for example, were often killed; those who survived were not allowed to practice or wear the cassock. The parish priest of Navalmorales told militiamen that he wished to suffer for Christ. They told him that indeed he would as they stripped and scourged him, fastened him to a beam and gave him vinegar and a crown of thorns. "Blaspheme and we will forgive you," they said. "It is I who forgive and bless you," he said. After discussing crucifixion, they shot him; his last request was to face them so that he could die blessing them.[49] The bishop of Jaén was killed by a specially invited militiawoman, La Pecosa, "the Freckled," before a tumultuous crowd of twenty thousand on swampy ground near Madrid; the bishops of Guadix and Almería were forced to wash the deck of their prison ship before being murdered near Malaga. Rosaries were forced into priests' ears until the tympanum was perforated. In Barcelona the bodies of nineteen Salesian nuns were dug up and exhibited. No one said "adios" in republican-held areas, only "salud." A man named Fernández de Dios asked the justice minister if he could change his name to Bakunin; a ministry official replied that "the change of name appears justified by its notoriety."[50]

A paler version of Spanish-speaking anticlericalism had followed the Mexican revolution of 1910. It was fueled by the same feeling that the poor were exploited by an alliance of churchmen and landowners. The Church was barred from owning land, its schools were closed, religious orders were suppressed, and the number of priests was regulated. The presidency of Plutarco Calles, a fanatic anti-Catholic, had led in 1926 to a rebellion by the *Cristeros,* named for the crosses at their neck and their war cry of *Viva Cristo Rey!* Pius XI condemned Mexican action in 1932; the government responded by expelling the apostolic delegate and decreeing that socialism, Marxism, atheism, and sex education be taught in schools. Some three hundred Catholic priests were martyred between 1926 and 1935.

The murders in Spain were on a wholly different scale. Republicans killed 7,937 religious people, including twelve bishops, 249 novices, 283 nuns, 2,494 monks, and 5,255 priests, before their defeat in 1939. It is true that the overall casualties in the war were immense, with estimates running between four hundred thousand and one million; true, too, that massacres were carried out by both sides, or, in Barcelona, by communists and anarchists on their fellow leftists. The clergy nonetheless suffered with a particular virulence, which their adoption of the nationalist cause only partly explains.

Archbishops, canons, and priests called on the Virgin to protect nationalist troops; some priests fought with them, and one in Estremadura had four militiamen buried alive. Cardinal Ilundaín attended mass with the nationalist general Queipo de Llano, while an honor guard of Falangists attended the effigy of the Virgin. Priests from republican zones who had fled to Paris prayed daily to the Virgin for a Spain "vilified, outraged, befouled by criminal Bolshevism, deprived by Jewish Marxism and scorned by savage Communists," concluding their devotions with the cry of *Viva Cristo Rey!* Few churchmen condemned the nationalist slaughter of leftists and trade unionists. The Church merely insisted that all those executed should have the opportunity for confession, and derived satisfaction from the large number who exercised it. "Only ten percent of these dear children refused the last sacraments before being dispatched by our good officers," a "venerable Brother" at Majorca recorded."[51] Many republicans remained Catholics; Moorish troops of the Army of Africa, Moslems all, were used against them with no sense of irony.

The Vatican recognized the nationalist authorities as the legitimate government in August 1937 and sent a nuncio to their headquarters in Burgos. Theological blessing had been given to the war the month before, when the Spanish hierarchy, led by Cardinal Gomá, archbishop of Toledo, issued a joint letter to the "Bishops of the Whole World." It said that they had not wanted an "armed plebiscite" in Spain, but thousands of Christians had "taken up arms on their responsibility to save the principles of religion." It claimed that, although the enemy was inspired by the "doctrines of demons," most were reconciled to God before their execution, citing figures of 98 percent in Majorca and 80 percent elsewhere. It was not signed by the bishop of Vitoria, whose dioceses included the antinationalist Basque provinces. Almost all the Basque priests supported their flocks; when Guernica was terror-bombed by German aircraft on a market day in 1937, a priest, his face blackened, his clothes in tatters, pointed to the flames and whispered "aviones . . . bombas . . . mucho, mucho," in horror. The Basques were admitted to be "the most Christian people in Spain" and their suffering earned much sympathy. The eminent French Catholic writers François Mauriac and Jacques Maritain issued a pro-Basque manifesto and stressed that those who killed the poor, the "people of Christ," in the name of religion, were as evil as those who murdered priests through hatred of religion. They were accused of being Chrétiens Rouges for their pains.

Catholicism did not give the fascists carte blanche. The fiery Cardinal Segura, who returned to Spain from republican exile as archbishop of Seville, denounced the Falange as irreligious and deplored Nazi influence. Cardinal Gomá criticized "exaggerated nationalism" in his Lenten pastoral letter. The archbishop of Westminster expressed the standard view, however, when he described the war as "a furious battle between Christian civilisation and the most cruel Paganism that has ever darkened the world." Catholics were naturally glad to have won it.

❖ "NOTHING IS LOST by peace: everything may be lost by war." Thus in August 1939 the new pope, Pius XII, made a forlorn plea to prevent a struggle that, as it escalated, would be the darkest yet visited on the world. Religion was peripheral to it. There was perhaps a religious element to the Nazi holocaust of the

Eugenio Pacelli in 1939, a few months before he became Pope Pius XII. He had spent most of his life as a diplomat. His suspicion of communists, acquired in Munich in 1919, was deepened by the anticlerical atrocities in the Spanish Civil War. Having promoted the 1933 concordat with the Nazis, he believed it was possible to negotiate with fascists. His instincts, at a time of total war, were for compromise. His near-silence over the Holocaust was politically understandable, and morally indefensible.

Jews, although its basis was atheistic racism; likewise, the "emperor-worship" of the Japanese reflected much nationalism and little theology, and the softened stance Stalin offered to Soviet Christians and Moslems during the war was a matter of strategy and not belief. Winston Churchill, certain though he was that the West was fighting to defend Christian civilization, cheerfully admitted that, if Hitler had invaded Hell, "I would make at least a favourable reference to the Devil in the House of Commons." The two devils started the war by signing the mutual Nazi-Soviet pact; when they fell out in June 1941, and Hitler invaded the Soviet Union, Churchill indeed allied himself with Stalin.

It is the ease with which the faith was made irrelevant that scars it. The British and Americans, whose forces were overwhelmingly Christian, at least in the sense that they identified themselves as such on their dog tags, had little with which to reproach themselves. They liberated half of devastated Europe, and its survivors. The campaigns were often described as a "crusade" against Nazism, but it cannot be said that it was a consciously Christian crusade. In Britain, church attendance increased when the Germans began their blitz of cities in 1940, and remained high in 1941, but dropped as soon as the bombers departed. Those who had faith before the war found it deepened, the survey Mass Opinion reported, and in those who had little it was weakened.

The one significant moral debate centered on the bombing of civilian targets in Germany. Raids of intense ferocity, with a thousand aircraft involved, were made indiscriminate by their lack of accuracy. Air Marshal "Bomber" Harris, who led RAF Bomber Command, vowed to bomb Berlin "until the heart of Nazi Germany ceases to beat." George Bell, the Anglican bishop of Chichester, retorted that civilians had become a target and that "to justify methods inhumane in themselves smacks of the Nazi philosophy that might is right."[52] The bishop saw a principal goal of the war to be "the recovery of Christendom. We want to see Europe as Christendom." At its end, he warned that no nation, no church, and no individual were guiltless. "Without repentance, and without forgiveness," he said, "there can be no regeneration."[53] Bell was an isolated figure, however. Though Harris was denied the peerage that would normally have honored him and the crews who flew for him, scapegoats for an uneasy national conscience, there was little public debate. The bombings of Hiroshima and Nagasaki, too, stirred few consciences at a time when evidence of Japanese atrocities was mounting.

In Germany's churches there were instances of resistance to the Nazis, and of outright collaboration with them, but for the most part there was silence. In March 1941, Archbishop Grober of Freiburg in a pastoral letter blamed the Jews for the death of Christ and spoke of their self-imposed curse.[54] When the Soviet Union was invaded in June, Archbishop Jäger condemned the Russians for their hostility to God and hatred of Christ, and spoke of them as "a people who had almost degenerated into animals."[55] Others denied Communion to conscientious objectors. The 1939 Conference of Lutheran Leaders had declared that "the Evangelical Church holds the State in reverence as an Order set up by God, and requires from its members loyal service within that Order, and instructs them to apply themselves with full devotion to the furthering of . . . the constructive work of the Führer."[56] The declaration was not rescinded. In December 1941, when troops returning from the front had made the killing of Jews in Russia well known enough for the minister of the American Church in Berlin to be aware of them, Evangelical Church leaders in seven German states issued a collective statement declaring that the Jews were "born enemies of the world and Germany" incapable of being saved even by baptism. The church leaders urged that "the severest measures against the Jews be adopted and that they be banished from German lands."[57]

Yet Cardinal Galen publicly decried the secret euthanasia program from the pulpit of St. Lambert's Church in Münster and cried, "Woe unto the German people when not only can innocents be killed, but their slayers remain unpunished!"[58] Priests who distributed copies of the sermon among troops were shot, but the outcry was strong enough to suspend the program; when an attempt was made to restart it, Church officials refused to fill in questionnaires on the health of inmates in their asylums. Galen and Bishop Frings of Cologne condemned the killing of hostages and unarmed prisoners of war in pastoral letters. Dietrich Bonhoeffer helped smuggle Jews out to Switzerland. He was arrested in April 1943 and charged with conspiring to rescue Jews and to keep Confessing Church pastors out of the military. He was hanged with other anti-Hitler conspirators in Flossenbürg concentration camp on April 9, 1945, three weeks before the end of the war. "This is the end, for me the beginning of life," Bonhoeffer wrote in a final message to his friend George Bell.

"Are we still of any use?" Bonhoeffer had written in December 1942. Christians have been "silent witnesses of evil deeds," he said. "We have learnt the arts of equivocation and pretence . . . intolerable conflicts have worn us down and even made us cynical."[59] The churches still functioned and performed their patriotic duties. As Bonhoeffer was asking his unanswerable question, a chaplain was celebrating Christmas Communion in the ruins of Stalingrad. The altar was an ammunition box. "Yesterday the box still held anti-aircraft shells," the chaplain wrote. "Today my hand spread over it the field-gray tunic of a comrade whose eyes I closed last Friday in this very room. I read my boys the Christmas story according to the gospel of Luke. The men sat on footstools and looked up to me from large eyes in their starved faces. . . ." But the regime was reducing the faith to invisibility. Almost all the Catholic press disappeared, with paper shortage as a pretext; shortage of metal was used as an excuse to melt down church bells. Crucifixes were removed from hospital wards. Mention of religion was banned in the new evacuation schools where children from bombed-out cities were sent. The unspeakable sufferings of Russian prisoners, four-fifths of whom died in some camps, passed unnoticed. A Protestant pastor, Heinrich Grüber, head of a bureau set up by the Protestant Church to help Jewish converts to Christianity, was imprisoned for protesting the deportations of Jews. A hospital chaplain, Walter Höchstädter, wrote that Germany had sunk back into the Middle Ages—the Nazi era "instead of indulging in an orgy of crazed witch-hunting, feasts itself in an orgy of maniacal Jew-hatred."[60]—and sent copies of his tract to soldiers at the front. A single Protestant bishop, Theophil Wurm, protested at the killings of Jews in a confidential letter to Hitler. Such individual acts were rare, and the genocide of the Jews attracted a single public protest from a Christian body, a declaration by the consistory of the Confessing Church of the old Prussian Union, read out from pulpits in 1943.[61]

The pope made no outright, named denunciation of the Nazis. It is, barely, understandable; whether it is excusable is another question. By instinct and by training, Eugenio Pacelli avoided confrontation. He had been a priest for forty years when he became pope as Pius XII in 1939, and he had spent thirty-eight of them as a diplomat in the papal secretariat of state. As apostolic nuncio to Bavaria, he was threatened by armed communists during the brief Munich rising in 1919, and retained a deep suspicion of all hues of Red. The following year he became nuncio in Berlin, where he was doyen of the diplomatic corps; he negotiated concordats with Bavaria and Prussia, and promoted the 1933 concordat with the Nazis. To this intricacy of mind, which polished and minutely weighed each phrase, was added a stifling awe of office. At night Pius descended into the Vatican crypt to pray among the tombs of his predecessors, and he required his staff to kneel when they answered the telephone from his apartment.[62]

From the start of the war, Communist as well as Nazi atrocities were on his agenda. Under the terms of a secret protocol to their pact with the Germans, the Soviets seized the eastern part of Poland and the Baltic states. They at once set about destroying the Church. Catholic priests in Poland and Lithuania were shot or deported; some fifteen thousand Polish officers were rounded up and taken to the Soviet Union, where they were murdered at Katyn in 1940. It was not until September 1941 that all Jews in the Third Reich were ordered to wear the yellow star, and October before the first deportations to the East from Berlin began. It was rational for the Vatican to believe before then that communism was the greater of two evils. Afterward, as the outline of the Jewish genocide became clear, the pope had to bear Catholic vulnerability in mind. A fifth of the Polish population was killed during the war; out of a total of 3,646 Catholic priests sent to concentration camps, 2,647 died. The Germans proposed to exempt converted Jews from deportation from Amsterdam when the Dutch bishops threatened to protest; when the bishops refused to be silent, the Gestapo arrested forty thousand, including non-Aryan Christians such as the Carmelite nun Edith Stein.

Pius ordered the religious houses in Rome to be opened to Jews, and five thousand were sheltered there and in the Vatican itself. In his Christmas address in 1942 he declared that a return to a society under the rule of God was a debt owed to the dead, to their widows and orphans, and to "the hundreds of thousands of innocent people put to death or doomed to slow extinction, sometimes merely because of their race or their descent."[63] The innocents numbered in the tens of millions, however, an estimated 5.85 million of them Jews, and the reference was oblique, failing to denounce the Nazis by name; as a response to a holocaust it rings pitifully meek. Mussolini certainly thought so. "The vicar of God, who is the representative on earth of the master of the universe, should never speak: he should remain in the clouds," he sneered. "It is a pile of platitudes which the parish priest of Predappio"—the Duce's native village—"would declaim with more talent."

One of the war's sad Christian by-products confirmed that commitment to a political cause could cohabit with an outspoken moral sense even in a Nazi puppet state. Croatia gained quasi-independence after the German invasion of Yugoslavia in 1941. The nationalist archbishop of Zagreb, Aloysius Stepinac, welcomed the Germans with a Te Deum and ordered it to be sung in all parishes on subsequent anniversaries. The Croat Ustasi, a fascist terror group under the puppet head of state Ante Pavelić, settled old ethnic scores by murdering some three hundred thousand of the Orthodox Serbian minority, including 128 Orthodox priests and three bishops, and burned three hundred Orthodox churches. Several atrocities were directed by Catholic military chaplains, and some Franciscans were implicated in them. Panegyrics in praise of Pavelić were written by Archbishop Sarić of Sarajevo.

Stepinac condemned the terror from the pulpit. He denounced the killings of Serbs, the forced conversions to Catholicism, the deportation of Jews and gypsies, the shooting of hostages. He hid Jews in the roof of his palace, a castle above Zagreb, and refused to force converts to wear yellow stars in church. Marshal Tito's communist partisans shot Croatian Catholic priests as a matter of policy as they advanced at the end of the war; the twenty-eight friars in a Franciscan house were slaughtered, and some four hundred priests who surrendered to the British after retreating over the northern border with the Ustasi were returned to Tito and shot without trial. Archbishop Sarić reached safety in Switzerland. Stepinac remained with his people. The new regime shut all Catholic newspapers, confiscated Church property, expelled monks and nuns, and banned the crucifix and religious teaching from schools. Slogans urging "Death to Priests!" were ubiquitous; a mob smashed the venerated image of Our Lady of Marija Bistrica, and sermons were recorded by police. Stepinac condemned those actions in a pastoral letter read from pulpits in September 1945. By the end of the month he was tried at Zagreb on collaboration charges. He told the court, "I did everything according to the Catholic moral law."[64] He was sentenced to sixteen years' hard labor. Created a cardinal in 1952, he died under house arrest eight years later.

In their advance into the Soviet Union in 1941, the Germans had also been welcomed by pealing church bells and flower-strewing girls in national dress in the Baltic states. In the Ukraine, country women brought them gifts of salt and bread, kissing the black Maltese crosses on the sides of their tanks. It was very soon clear, however, that the Germans had not come as brothers in Christ to liberate the faithful from scientific atheism, but as slavemakers. The Orthodox Church gave immediate spiritual and moral blessing to the war effort. Vast numbers of Russians had remained believers and patriots, and communists could no longer afford the luxury of persecuting them. In 1943, Metropolitan Sergey was received by Stalin in the Kremlin and elected patriarch of Moscow by a synod of bishops. The patriarchate, which had been a log cabin on an unpaved street in the Moscow outskirts, was moved into the grand surroundings of the former German embassy. A government-sponsored Council for the Affairs of the Orthodox Church was established. Churches reopened, bishops and priests emerged from hiding and from prison, and relics were restored to shrines. The Godless Militants ceased operations. Military units were again blessed by priests, and the Church raised enough money to equip an armored division. Russian Christians ended the war largely free from persecution and abuse. It was not to last.

CHAPTER XXXIV

"I have a dream":

Liberation Theology

Aburning question of the faith—the point at which compromise with a brutal regime becomes collaboration—did not vanish with Hitler. It spread.

One of Alexander Solzhenitsyn's earliest childhood memories was of church. "There were lots of people, candles, vestments . . . the service was brusquely interrupted," he wrote. "I saw, filing arrogantly down the central aisle of the nave, the sugar-loaf 'Budenny' hats of Soviet soldiers."[1] As an adult rich in qualities detestable to the state, this uncowed, cantankerous, majestic gulag survivor was deported to the West. Shortly afterward, Patriarch Pimen of Moscow addressed a pastoral letter in 1975 to Orthodox émigrés, appealing to them to foster a love of the church in their children and to set them a personal example.

Solzhenitsyn was stung that the patriarch should reprimand émigrés while remaining silent about affairs at home. He wrote his own Lenten Letter to Pimen. The Russian Church, he said, had sold itself to the state—"a church dictatorially ruled by atheists is a sight not seen in two thousand years"—and had thus forfeited the right to propagate the faith. He added that Russians had been deprived of all beauty, faith, and transcendence; their churches were despoiled or closed. Under Communism, priests were powerless in their own parishes and had to seek permission to visit the sick or attend a ceremony. He said there was no argument that the arrangement with an atheist state offered preservation. "Preservation for whom? Certainly not for Christ. Preservation by what means? Falsehood? But after falsehood, what sort of hands should perform the Eucharist?"[2]

A leading Christian dissident, Father Sergei Zheludkov of Pskov, publisher of an underground religious samizdat, retorted that it was impossible for the Orthodox Church in the Soviet Union to become an island of freedom in a sea of unfreedom. "What would you have us do? Insist on all or nothing?" he asked.[3]

❖ OUTSIDE THE SOVIET zone of Germany the defeated fascists were spared such a dilemma. Religion joined American and British aid and influence in restoring free societies. The first postwar governments in West Germany and Italy described themselves as Christian as well as democratic. Konrad Adenauer, who was to become Hitler's successor as chancellor, founded the Christian Democratic Union in 1945. The council of the Evangelical Church made a self-indictment of its wartime record the same year: "We accuse ourselves of not having made our avowal more completely, not having prayed more faithfully, not having believed more joyfully and not having loved more ardently."[4] A communist electoral victory was a real danger in Italy, where fifty-two priests were murdered in the Emilia between 1944 and 1946. The Vatican responded by helping to fund the Christian Democrat Party. In 1949, suggesting that he was more concerned with the faith than the democracy, Pius XII threatened to excommunicate anyone who joined the communists. The divinity of Christ could be queried with impunity, Monsignor Alfredo Ottaviani, the head of the Holy Office, remarked, but "if, in the remotest village in Sicily, you vote communist, your excommunication will arrive the next day."[5]

A servile national church, Nippon Kirisuto Kyodin, the Church of Christ in Japan, had been created at the start of the Pacific war. Missionaries had been expelled or killed in occupied territories. In Korea the churches went underground. In Papua New Guinea, Anglican priests had stayed on when the Japanese invaded. "God expects this of us," their bishop, Philip Strong, had written. "We could never hold up our faces again if, for our own safety, we all forsook Him and fled, when the shadow of the Passion began to gather around Him in His spiritual and mystical body, the Church in Papua."[6] Within a few weeks the Japanese had murdered eight missionaries. The American supremo in Japan, Douglas MacArthur, asked for a thousand missionaries when he took up his post after the Allied victory. The atomic bombing of Nagasaki, the most Christian city in Japan, gave this a sad poignancy, but the appeal was answered. Four thousand Protestant missionaries were working in Japan in 1963; by 1980 there were almost a million Japanese Protestants, and 750,000 Catholics. Christians in South Korea, who had come out of hiding at the end of the war, numbered more than a quarter of the population by then. The first two presidents of South Korea were prominent Christians, and liberal Protestants helped make the religion a focal point for democracy and opposition after the military takeover of 1961.

❖ IN COMMUNIST NORTH Korea, however, Christians remained hunted; ten of their leaders were executed in 1957. Christians in China, too, were exposed to a new onslaught by the victory of Mao Zedong's communists in 1949. The faith was doubly vulnerable because of its links with the defeated Nationalists and with foreign "imperialists." Chiang Kai-shek had been baptized in 1931, and several of his cabinet ministers were also Christians by the time of the final collapse. There were, too, four thousand Protestants missionaries and 5,682 non-Chinese Catholic priests and nuns in the new People's Republic.

The communist style was soon set. "Our god is none other than the masses of the Chinese people," Mao declared. Children were taught to sing, "Don't worship heaven, don't worship earth, only worship the labor of the masses."[7] Document 19 of the Chinese Communist Party stated that "in human history, religion will ultimately disappear" and insisted that all religious organizations must obey the party leadership. The Three Self Patriotic Movement or TSPM was imposed on the churches in 1950.

The TSPM's name came from self-government, self-support, and self-propagation; but far from implying independence, "self" was synonymous with "Chinese" and strict control by the regime. Foreign elements were purged. The first chairman of the TSPM, the Protestant Y. T. Wu, told an official Christian conference at Peking in 1954 that he realized the use that imperialism was making of the faith only after the Communist takeover. Before, he said, he had thought of Hudson Taylor, the great nineteenth-century figure of the China Inland Mission as "a warm-hearted evangelistic 'missionary.'" Now, it was proven that Taylor "spoke greedily of the mineral resources of China" which he wanted to use to "make western nations rich." Wu said that for more than a century, foreigners had "misinterpreted the Scriptures, perverted Christian doctrine, nurtured unspeakable renegades within the Church . . . and made Chinese Christians unconsciously breathe in the poison of imperialistic thought.[8]

By the time Wu spoke, all but sixty-one of the foreign priests in China had been expelled; of the remnant, 21 were in prison, as were more than four hundred Chinese priests.* All Christian schools, universities, and hospitals were taken over by the government. The TSPM was used for naked anti-American propaganda. During the Korean War it acquired the prefix "China Christian Oppose-American Help-Korea," and "denunciation" meetings were held—228 in 133 cities in 1951 alone according to Wu—to condemn America and bless the "religious toleration" of the regime. Warnings were issued that foreign Christians were active in Hong Kong and Japan, from where they "try to spy on the Chinese church, and send out false reports about our religious liberty, and still hope to find stooges among us . . ."[9]

Many boycotted TSPM churches and worshiped at home and in secret.

*The longest-lasting foreign missionary was Helen Willis of the Plymouth Brethren, who was expelled in 1959.

TSPM clerics insisted that unauthorized "worship-halls" and "family meetings" must cease at once. Warnings and threats made little impact. In Hopeh Province, Catholics went underground, praying in some two hundred secret dugouts. Resistance centered on Shanghai, home of 150,000 Catholics led by Bishop Ignatius Gong Pinmei. Gong was arrested in 1955, and the regime set up a puppet Catholic Patriotic Association. The archbishop of Shenyang (Mukden), his spirit broken by his own imprisonment, headed this. He declared that the Chinese Church "must rid itself completely of all control by the Holy See." He entered schism with Rome by ordaining "patriotic" bishops in defiance of its orders.

Bishops and priests who remained faithful to the Vatican were imprisoned, some for decades. Dominic Tang, bishop of Canton, was arrested in 1958. He suffered beriberi, living on a bowl and a half of rice a day. His interrogations lasted days at a time, he was put to work pasting cardboard boxes together, and, in his twenty-two years in a cell, he was not allowed to receive one letter from his family. "In the prison, I always asked God to grant me grace to progress in virtues, for example humility and obedience," he wrote. "Every day I sang in a soft voice 'Jesus I live for you, Jesus I die for you . . .' This hymn was taught to me by a Protestant prisoner who lived in my cell."[10] Though the visible TSPM churches were dying out, a Chinese writer reported in the *Hong Kong Standard* in 1962, the "invisible, formless, non-political and true ones are growing in numbers in Shanghai, Nanking, Beijing and elsewhere." He said that covert Christians "have won many who have found God a great help in time of trouble . . ." Their meetings were short, he wrote, because if two or more people were found praying together they faced charges as counterrevolutionaries and prison sentences.

The Chinese were instructed to destroy the "Four Olds"—old ideas, culture, customs, and habits—by the Communist Party plenum in August 1966. It was made clear that this included Christianity on August 22, when posters appeared on the former YMCA building in Beijing. They contained the creed of the Red Guards, the spearheads of Mao's Cultural Revolution. "There is no God," they proclaimed. "There is no Spirit. There is no Jesus, there is no Mary, and there is no Joseph. How can adults believe these things? . . . Like Islam and Catholicism, Protestantism is a reactionary feudal ideology, with foreign origin and contacts. We are atheists, we believe only in Mao Zedong. We call on all people to burn Bibles, destroy images and disperse religious associations."[11] As the Red Guards were let loose in the city, the *South China Morning Post* ran a headline: "Christianity in Shanghai comes to an end."

The obituary was premature. Chinese continued to pray illegally in private houses, fields, and caves despite every attempt to destroy their faith. Red Guards ransacked the houses of Christians who refused to confess their errors at public meetings; they burned their Bibles and hymnbooks and forced them to eat the

"Our god is none other than the masses of the Chinese people," Mao Zedong said on winning power in China in 1949. Christians were persecuted and missionaries expelled. In 1966, Mao set loose young Red Guards in the Cultural Revolution. Christianity was a target. "There is no God," Red Guard posters in the YMCA in Beijing proclaimed. "There is no Jesus, there is no Mary, and there is no Joseph. . . ." But Mao failed to expunge the faith. Even in solitary confinement, a young Christian from Guangdong converted another prisoner through a hole he had made in his cell wall. "Eventually he wanted to believe in Christ," he wrote. "So I dipped my chopsticks in the remaining water I had used to brush my teeth, and baptized him on the forehead through the hole."

ashes, cut their hair off, put placards on them, and made them collect sewage. They sent them to labor camps. "Hell on earth, a camp for killing," wrote Wang Xiaoling, arrested as a youth leader of the Legion of Mary in Shanghai. "Every night we could hear the piteous cries of those in solitary confinement, the moaning of those who had been tortured, the slogan-shouting of those butchers of the 'criticism-struggle' meetings, the jangling of chains and fetters. . . . 'Lord, how will you protect your little lamb?'" While fashionable students in the West proudly waved Mao's *Little Red Book* in Vietnam protest marches, a young Catholic from Guangdong Province in solitary confinement converted another prisoner through a hole he had made in his cell wall. "Eventually he wanted to believe in Christ," he wrote. "So I dipped my chopsticks in the remaining water I had used to brush my teeth, and baptized him on the forehead through the hole."[12]

❖ A NEW POLICY followed Mao's death in 1976. "World religions" with scriptures, such as Christianity, Islam, and Buddhism, were to be allowed "freedom of religious belief"; this was not extended to "feudal superstitions" such as wizardry and fortune-telling. It was the barest toleration; believers were still sub-ject to party "propaganda and education" until they "extricate themselves from this kind of mental shackle." The TSPM was resurrected to ensure that "govern-ment organs strengthen the control of religious bodies."[13] Itinerant evangelism, exorcism, and faith healing, approaches to youngsters under eighteen, and preach-ing by non-TSPM-ordained priests were banned. Bibles and Christian literature were, and remain, available only to state-registered churches.

Mao's failure to deal with the faith was soon clear. At least 6,375 churches were opened up under the official China Christian Council. In 1984, Bishop Ding, the head of the TSPM's Protestant wing, declared in 1984 that the number of Protestant Christians had multiplied more than four times since 1949, from 700,000 to three million; by 1987 he had increased the figure to four million. But the number of "house churches" was in the tens of thousands, and the num-ber of non-TSPM Christians were estimated at more than 50 million.

The regime was so concerned about the explosion of interest that it coined the phrase "Christianity fever" and stepped up the arrests and torture of evangel-ists. The result was as predictable as it had been under Diocletian. "Recently the gospel here has been greatly promoted because ten brothers and sisters were im-prisoned, beaten and bound," a letter writer from Fangcheng in Henan noted in 1982:

> They regarded their sufferings for the Lord as more precious than the treasures of Egypt. They started to preach the gospel in the poorest and most barren regions. . . . They preached with tears streaming down, causing the passersby and street sellers, Christians and non-Christians, to stand still and listen. Even fortune-tellers were moved by the Holy Spirit and burst out crying. . . . The authorities laid hands on them, dragging them away one by one, binding them with ropes, and beating them with electric shock poles. . . . When the brothers and sisters in that region saw them bound and forced to kneel on the ground for more than three days, without food or water, and beaten with sticks until their faces were covered with blood, and their hands made black by the ropes—but still praying, singing and praising the Lord, then they wished to share their persecution, be bound with them and cast into prison. So in this area recently the flame of the gospel has spread everywhere. There had never been a revival here before, but through this persecution this place has truly received the seeds of life.[14]

Restrictions were further tightened in 1989. The TSPM banned any refer-ence in sermons to "negative themes" or to politics, justice, education, or marriage; the aim of all preaching was to lead the congregation to "love country, love religion." Any "twisting of the Scriptures, spreading rumors to deceive the masses, proclaiming nonsense to please the public, healing and exorcism, and 'dancing in the spirit'" was forbidden on pain of disqualification from "sacred work."[15] The "dancing" ban referred to evangelizing Pentecostals and charismatics.

A house-church leader from the remote Shaanxi Province in North China said that one hundred from his group were in prison. He welcomed it. "Some were thrown into manure pits, others were beaten with electric stun-batons, some were beaten so they could not stand, and could only crawl to the toilet," he wrote. "But our 500 to 600 full-time Christian workers and 50,000 to 60,000 believers will have to stand on their own feet now."[16] Entire villages in Shaanxi were reported to be turning Christian, and others in Henan and Anhui.

Throughout the 1990s the Public Security raided house churches. The leader of a large underground evangelical church, Peter Xu Yongza of the New Birth Church, was arrested in March 1997 for violating laws governing "social organizations." Han Wenzao, president of the state-approved Christian Council of China, denied that Xu's arrest was persecution on the grounds that Xu's beliefs were not Christian and that his preaching on the Last Judgment led people "to do no normal work but cry collectively every day."[17] News reports in Hong Kong suggest that Xu's church, based in the central Chinese city of Zhengzhou, has several million followers.

Hundreds of evangelists and house church leaders are known to be still serving sentences of up to thirty years in reeducation camps. It is illegal for Chinese Christians to speak to foreigners without official permission, and it is impossible to know their numbers. Estimates, however, range from 50 to as high as 100 million.

PERSECUTION AND THE persistence of faith helped undo Communism in Eastern Europe. In 1980, striking Polish shipyard workers in Gdansk knelt in prayer and outlined the democratic demands of their Solidarity movement. The broadcast of mass every Sunday on radio and television was one of them. Solidarity was in part inspired by the visit of John Paul II the year before; at Czestochowa, 3.5 million came to see him, the largest human gathering recorded. A young priest, Jerzy Popieluszko, won a congregation of several thousand for his pro-Solidarity sermons. His house was trashed, and explosives and pamphlets inciting armed rebellion were planted in it by the secret police. In July 1984 he was arrested for denouncing Communist repression of the Church. He was released after a month, returning to the pulpit to demand that the government enter into true talks with Solidarity. Seven weeks later he was thrown into the trunk of a car

The young Polish priest Jerzy Popieluszko is seen before a mass in 1984, the year he was murdered. His sermons supporting the Solidarity freedom movement won him a large congregation, and the enmity of the Communist secret police. Security police abducted him and his body was dumped in a reservoir. His killing exposed the desperation of a failing regime.

by three security police and abducted and killed. His bound and beaten body was found in a reservoir.

The Communist Party in Poland did not recover. Like the other regimes imposed on Eastern Europe by the victorious Red Army after 1945, it had already been rendered morally moribund by the methods of its arrival, through rigged elections, intimidations, and imprisonments, and by their continuation. Hitler had closed Catholic schools, universities, and seminaries in Poland and murdered a third of the clergy. The incoming Communists assumed it would be simple to complete his work. Two thousand Polish priests were in prison by 1954; religious education was banned in elementary schools, and the property of religious orders was seized. The primate, Cardinal Stefan Wyszynski, was arrested and held incommunicado in a monastery. Yet the Polish Church of 1980 had almost twice as many priests in 1980 as it had in 1937, 20,234 against 11,239. Its young were resistant to scientific atheism. A poll of teenagers by Lublin University in 1979 found that 87 percent claimed to be religious, that 72 percent worshiped regularly, and that almost as many went to confession.

In the other Iron Curtain countries, too, Communist academics found dispiriting evidence in the 1980s of the failure to eradicate the faith. The Institute of

Scientific Atheism in Czechoslovakia in 1984 found that 30 percent of Czechs and 51 percent of Slovaks were willing to identify themselves as Christians.[18] Slovakia had been nominally independent during the war, although under Nazi control. Its president, Monsignor Josef Tiso, was a prewar leader of a Catholic Slovak party that had demanded Slovak autonomy from the Czechs. Tiso remained a monsignor as well as president throughout the war. In August 1944 he had asked the Germans for help when Slovak army units mutinied in favor of the advancing Russians; despite the atrocities that marked the suppression of the revolt, Tiso had celebrated a mass of thanksgiving and decorated SS officers. He fled to Austria in April 1945; the Americans handed him to the new Slovak regime and he was brought to Bratislava in chains. Pictures of Tiso making the Nazi salute and having tea with Goebbels were produced at his trial. Just before he was hanged in April 1947, he told the ministering priest that he died a martyr in defense of Christian civilization against Communism. Many Slovaks agreed with that and felt they had fared better with Tiso than they would have without him; the Czechs did not, and the tensions symbolized by the executed monsignor played their part in the eventual breakup of the Czechoslovak federation.

In Bulgaria the Academy of Sciences reported that although two-thirds of adults claimed to have no religion, fourth-fifths of them had church funerals and half of all babies were baptized in church. In Hungary, Cardinal Jozsef Mindszenty had been sentenced to life imprisonment on trumped-up charges of spying in 1948; during the 1956 uprising he was freed, but sought sanctuary in the American embassy when Soviet tanks took Budapest. He remained there for eleven years until, politically embarrassing to Washington and the Vatican, he was moved to Vienna and deprived of his Hungarian see. He remained a hero to young Hungarians. In 1987 more than a third of them were attending church each Sunday, a figure by then beyond the dreams of Western European churchmen, and a fifth of them had a personal copy of the Bible.

SOME SECTS IN Russia survived by disappearing into the vastness. A group of Baptists originally exiled to Siberia in 1907 by the czar had settled near Achinsk, and lived through the First World War, the revolution, and the civil war without being molested. Their luck ran out during Stalin's drive to collectivize agriculture in 1930; their prayer house was turned into a clubhouse and agitators lectured them on the evils of religion. The community of almost two hundred men, women, and children decided to retreat into the deep forest with their livestock and tools. They marched for ten days and built a new settlement on a meadow by a riverbank; they fashioned thread out of hair and needles from bone, sewed clothes from hides, and used resin for lamps. They enjoyed almost total isolation for more than twenty years, not even knowing that the Second World War had taken place.

One day in the winter of 1951, however, their dogs started to bark louder than usual. A week later, when they were in their prayer house, the dogs started barking again. "Some people came rushing in so scared they couldn't say anything: all they could do was point out the door," their leader Nikifor recollected. "Outside was a detachment of soldiers on skis. . . . One of the soldiers came up to us and asked who was our leader. I told him that we didn't have a leader, that we were all equal, that our only leader was God. When I said this, one of the soldiers laughed. . . ."[19] The Baptists were interrogated for three weeks, accused of contacting American spies by a nonexistent radio, led to Achinsk, and sentenced to twenty-five years' hard labor. All the children were taken away to special camps.

Father Simon, head of the Old Believers, with his congregation from the Russian village of Lugovaya in 1996, having survived centuries of persecution by the czars and the Bolsheviks. The Molokan milk-drinking sect was thought to have become extinct in the Stalinist terror of the 1930s. In 1952 it was found that more than 10,000 Molokans had survived in Transcaucasia and Central Asia. The pacifist "True and Free Adventists," too, reappeared from the dead in the 1950s. Mennonite history in Russia was thought to be finished. But American and Canadian Mennonites visiting in 1956 were astonished to find at least 50,000 living in small groups in Central Asia, the Urals, and Siberia. Women often conducted services because male ministers had been killed. Christian sects die hard.

The Molokan milk-drinking sect was thought to have become extinct in the Stalinist terror of the 1930s. In 1952, two of their number appeared at a church peace conference in Zagorsk and reported that more than 10,000 Molokans had survived in Transcaucasia and Central Asia. The pacifist True and Free Adventists, too, reappeared from the dead in the 1950s. Officials put their number at 26,000, mainly in the Ukraine and in Estonia and Latvia, but the actual figure was much higher. Their leader, Vladimir Shelkov, spent twenty-three years in prison and the camps for his faith; he received his last sentence, five years in a strict regime camp, in March 1979 when he was eighty-three. He died in the camp the following January. Mennonites had been scheduled for resettlement in the East in 1941, since they were German speakers, but German troops overran their settlements before this was complete. Some 35,000 fled with the retreating Nazis three years later; six thousand managed to get themselves to South America, but most of the others were repatriated to the Soviet Union and were shot or died in the camps. The Mennonite history in Russia seemed finished; yet American and Canadian Mennonites visiting the Soviet Union in 1956 were astonished to find at least 50,000 living in small groups in Central Asia, the Urals, and Siberia. Women often conducted services because male ministers had been killed.

A new sect arrived with returning prisoners of war, converts made by German Jehovah's Witnesses who were fellow inmates in Nazi concentration camps. In the Soviet mind this tainted them with fascism. In mass arrests at the beginning of 1951, seven thousand Witnesses were transported to Arctic and Siberian camps; here they converted fellow *zeks,* who in turn made door-to-door calls on their release, making the Soviet branch of the Witnesses one of the strongest in the world.

The uneasy wartime concordat between the Orthodox Church and the state, never accepted by members of the breakaway True Orthodox Church, who preferred the camps to compromise, broke down in 1959. Nikita Khrushchev treated the Church as a "survival of capitalism." An infant would be baptized only with the signed agreement of both parents; since this had to be lodged with the authorities, the parents ran the risk of being dismissed from work. Children from sectarian, particularly Baptist, families were taken from them and sent to atheistic boarding schools. Monks and nuns were drafted into factories. KGB (secret police) agents reported on sermons, and controversial priests were sent to mental hospitals or dismissed to live as beggars. Half of the twenty thousand churches open at the end of the war were closed, together with five of the eight seminaries, and 37 of the 67 surviving monasteries and convents.

When Archbishop Yermogen of Kaluga forbade the closure of churches and the burning of icons and Bibles in his diocese, he was dismissed and sent to a remote monastery. Another archbishop, Methodius of Omsk, is believed to have been murdered. The Moscow priest Gleb Yakunin was dismissed from the priesthood for accusing Patriarch Alexey of violating the apostolic command by "compromising with the world." Yakunin formed a nonpolitical Christian Committee and was sentenced to five years' prison and five years' internal exile for "anti-Soviet agitation and propaganda." He told the court, "I thank God for this test that he has sent me. I consider it a great honor and, as a Christian, accept it gladly."[20] Vladimir Osopov was given eight years for floating the idea of Christians as a "loyal opposition" to the regime.

The disintegration of Soviet Communism was internal; under Mikhail Gorbachev, amid the near ruin of the economy, defeat in Afghanistan, and unsustainable military spending, the party lost the will to repress. The Church was not a dissenting power, as in Poland. It had, however, more than merely survived the years since Lenin; almost two-thirds of Russians still considered themselves believers.

❖ RELIGION WAS A KEY in the great American moral issue of civil rights. The many black churches helped to preserve black hopes, for they provided dignity, an identity with the suffering Christ, and a promise of freedom. Martin Luther King Jr., an orator and organizer of unbreakable spirit, led the struggle. The son of a Baptist pastor, King set up the first black ministry at Montgomery, Alabama, in 1955. That year Rosa Parks was arrested for refusing to move to the black section (the rear) of a racially-segregated bus in Montgomery, and the new pastor found himself leading the resulting bus riders' boycott. He held that strong, constant, and peaceful resistance was the only effective way of forcing whites to confront the issue. "We shall match your capacity to inflict suffering with our capacity to endure suffering," he told white opponents. "We will meet your physical force with soul force. Do to us what you will, and we shall continue to love you. . . ."[21]

He founded the Southern Christian Leadership Conference in 1957, which organized civil rights protests throughout the Southern states. It was a dangerous calling. King was arrested, writing from a Birmingham, Alabama, jail that, as Paul had left Tarsus to carry word of Christ to the far corners, "so I am compelled to carry the gospel of freedom beyond on my own home town." His marchers were attacked by men and police dogs and beaten. After one such assault the Unitarian minister James Reeb died in Selma. King remained steadfast in his nonviolence, and in the "dream" he expressed in his famous speech in Washington in 1963: "I have a dream that one day on the red hills of Georgia the sons of former slaves and the sons of former slave owners will be able to sit down together at the

Dr. Martin Luther King leads a civil rights march to the Capitol building in Montgomery, Alabama, in 1965. The son of a Baptist pastor, he held that whites would only confront segregation if faced by constant and peaceful resistance. "We shall match your capacity to inflict suffering with our capacity to endure suffering," he said. "Do to us what you will, and we shall continue to love you. . . ." His murder polarized the civil rights movement. Black churches grew at a spectacular rate, but some rejected Christianity root and branch as a white conspiracy.

table of brotherhood. . . ." King was assassinated by a white gunman in Memphis, Tennessee, in 1968.

His murder polarized the civil rights movement. Black churches continued to grow at a spectacular rate, with the Church of God in Christ achieving annual gains of two hundred thousand members and six hundred new congregations. Some blacks, however, rejected Christianity root and branch as a white conspiracy. A "Black Manifesto" of 1969 demanded five hundred million dollars from the "racist white Christian churches and the Jewish synagogues" in reparations to blacks for being enslaved by "the military machinery and the Christian Church working hand in hand."[22] Malcolm X, himself the son of a Baptist minister, preached a Black Muslim creed that claimed that white slave masters had concealed the superiority of the black man by "injecting" him with Christianity. "This 'Negro' was taught to worship an alien God having the same blond hair, pale skin and blue eyes as the slave master," he wrote. "This religion taught the 'Negro' that black was a curse. . . . The white man's Christian religion further deceived and brainwashed this 'Negro' to always turn the other cheek, and grin, and scrape . . . and to sing, and to pray . . ."[23] After a visit to Mecca in 1964, Malcolm X fell out with other Black Muslims and was murdered during a rally in Harlem the following year.

Others remained Christian because they saw it as the faith of the oppressed. James Cone, professor of theology at Union Theological Seminary in New York, argued that white theology gives religious sanction to the genocide of Indians and black enslavement by "the devil white man." True Christianity, he said, is a "theology of liberation" which is "identified unreservedly with those who are humiliated and abused." The God who reveals himself in Christ and in the Exodus narrative is the God of those who labor and are heavy laden; and "the Christ event in 20th century America is a black event, an event of liberation taking place in the black community."[24]

❖ WHITE THEOLOGY WAS indeed used to buttress apartheid in South Africa. The Afrikaners were the "white tribe of Africa," identifying themselves with their land by name. They were an embattled people, outnumbered by blacks, mindful of their brave and bitter struggle against British imperial might at the turn of the century, resentful of the English-speaking whites who dominated finance and the mines. Vulnerable and defiant—"we are standing like Luther at the time of the Reformation," the archsegregationist Hendrik Verwoed said, "with the back against the wall"—they drew sustenance from religion.

The architect of apartheid, Dr. Daniel Malan, was a *predikant* of the Dutch Reformed Church before becoming prime minister in 1948. He justified white supremacy on the grounds that Afrikanerdom "is not the work of man but the creation of God."[25] The Hervormde Kerk declared in 1960 that apartheid provided "the only just solution of our racial problems." Its moderator, C. B. Brink, claimed that the Afrikaner had to love himself, "that which he had become through the grace of God," in order to remain faithful to his "divine calling"; it was necessary for him to separate himself from other races in order to be able to love his neighbor and "to be a blessing to the millions of non-Whites."[26]

Anglican churchmen rejected this ideology. Trevor Huddlestone, an Anglican missionary who became parish priest of Sophiastown, a Johannesburg slum, was banned from South Africa after preaching the universal brotherhood of man. Opinion overseas was first stirred in 1956 by his book *Naught for Your Comfort.* The following year the archbishop of Cape Town condemned new legislation that restricted black participation in public worship. "We should ourselves be unable to obey it," he said, "or to counsel our clergy and people to do so." Nelson Mandela, imprisoned for life in 1964, remained the great symbol of black resistance, but Desmond Tutu, the first black bishop of Johannesburg, mirrored the role of Martin Luther King. He, too, preached for peaceful reconciliation of white and black, and was awarded the Nobel Peace Prize; he led the South African Council of Churches, organized demonstrations, and called for international sanctions. These pressures aided the gradual dismantling of apartheid, culminating in a black government under Mandela in 1994.

Oppression in Latin America raised acute problems. Corrupt and brutal regimes were met by violent campaigns in a string of countries. Liberation theology inspired some priests to side with the guerrillas. American Maryknoll fathers expelled from Guatemala in 1967 for contacting guerrillas said that their faith demanded that they stop the "dehumanizing" of peasants. "The top 2 percent is bleeding the masses white and will not give up their power peacefully," they said. "It must be taken from them. It is they who are provoking the violence, not the poor."[27] A guerilla in a Guatemalan camp stressed that "all these comrades of Indian origin that you see here are Catholic, fervently Catholic."

A young Colombian priest, Camilo Torres, was killed fighting with guerrillas. He traveled villages and shantytowns as the cardinal archbishop's representative for agrarian reform, and became convinced that the Church should share the poverty of its flock. He called publicly for Church property to be expropriated and for Colombia to be freed from "American imperialism." Cardinal Concha Córdoba said that this was irreconcilable with Catholic doctrine, and Torres was reduced to the laity. Torres produced his own newspaper advocating revolution. He wrote that loving one's neighbor was the basis of Catholicism; revolution was the only way to create a government that would clothe the naked and educate the ignorant. "That is why the Revolution is not only allowed to Christians," he said, "but is obligatory. . . ." As a Christian and a priest, he added, he could not be anticommunist; "although they may not know it, many communists are true Christians. . . . I am ready to fight with them for common aims."[28]

Torres took to the mountains in January 1966. The Colombian army issued a press release stating that it was aware that the "ex-priest Camilo Torres" had joined a guerrilla unit and that it would track him down. It took a month. On February 15 he was shot and mortally wounded in an ambush by an army patrol. Six other priests died with guerrilla forces, although many revolutionaries were anticlerical. Fidel Castro ordered the expulsion of Spanish and foreign priests from Cuba, and confiscated their property. Only eighty priests were left to minister to six million Cubans. In Peru the violently anti-Church MIR group proclaimed their rejection of "the pseudo-Christians and the archbishop and primate," accusing him of putting the Church "at the service of the oligarchy and its lackeys."

Bishops were divided over liberation theology. Peruvian prelates, fearing

Marxism, jointly condemned it as a perversion. The theologian Gustavo Gutiérrez, like Torres a former student among radical Catholics at Louvain, was dubbed
the "Red priest" for challenging violence against the poor in his influential book
A Theology of Liberation. But nine Latin American bishops, urged on by the outspoken bishop of Recife, Dom Helder Camara, defined revolution in sympathetic terms a year after Torres's death as "a breach with a system which no more
guarantees the common good . . ." The Sandinista revolution in Nicaragua drew
heavily on liberation ideas, and five Catholic priests served in the Sandinista cabinet. Bishop Proano of Riobamba in Ecuador was fearless in defending Indian
rights; a synod of seventeen Latin American bishops was arrested at his house in
1976 and deported. It was typical of Rome's ambivalence that a conservative
canon lawyer was appointed to succeed Camara. John Paul II, with his Polish
background, was suspicious of any hint of Marxism; when Evaristo Arns, the
archbishop of São Paulo, was felt to have strayed too far in his demands for the
poor, his diocese was subdivided without his agreement, and conservative and
hostile bishops were appointed to five new suffragan sees.

Liberal churchmen frequently ran afoul of the regimes. The Argentine Juan
Perón, though his wife Evita was projected as a sort of secular Virgin Mary, had
ordered crucifixes removed from public buildings and banned religious teaching
in schools when he seized power in 1943. Priests who protested were arrested,
and mobs burned several churches and the episcopal palace in Buenos Aires. Between 1964 and 1978, 260 foreign missionaries were expelled by Latin American
states; thirty-five bishops were arrested, two were killed, and two disappeared. As
for priests, 455 were arrested and 41 killed. Many of the expelled missionaries
were *evangelicos* from Protestant sects, often Americans, who made striking progress
in city slums. Chile, once all-Catholic, numbered 1.25 million *evangelicos* by
1980; Seventh-Day Adventists worked in Bolivia, and Pentecostals were among
the Indians of Guatemala.

The most striking martyr was nonetheless a Catholic. The military had welcomed Oscar Romero's appointment in 1977 as archbishop of El Salvador. He
was a spiritual and conservative man who was thought unlikely to be a trouble-
maker. Amid murders by death squads, and police and army killings of peasants,
he changed. Early in 1980 he denounced government brutality in passionate sermons broadcast by Catholic radio across the country. In February he wrote to
President Carter condemning American military aid to the regime, and he called
for land reform, reminding the rich that "Christ made himself poor to save us."
He received death threats. A bomb destroyed the Catholic radio station, YSAX; a
cab driver who saw the archbishop at a red light gave him his takings and drove
off, crying, "For the radio!" Worshipers bought tape recorders to his sermons at
the Sacred Heart Basilica so they could take his words back to their communities,

and a Costa Rican shortwave radio station broadcast them across Central America. Nicaragua offered Romero a safe have but he refused. He made his retreat for the first week of Lent in a house in the hills above San Salvador. "Archbishop Romero foresaw his very probable and imminent death," his confessor recalled. "He felt terror at it, as Jesus did in the garden. But he did not for that leave his post and his duty, ready to drink the chalice that the Father might give him to drink."[29] The following week, security forces and right-wing terrorists murdered seventy people. They included a democratic politician and his Danish wife, found dumped on a roadside after their arrest. Their bodies were in the basilica when Romero gave his Sunday address, warning of the systematic militarization of the country. On March 9 he said a mass for a Christian Democrat leader who had been murdered by a death squad. The following morning workmen found a suitcase with enough dynamite in it to destroy the basilica and its occupants.

Sixty people were killed in bombings and shootings on March 17. YSAX was back on the air to carry the archbishop's Sunday sermon on March 23. Romero spoke of the sorrow of crime and the disgrace of violence, and made a direct appeal to the troops, national guards, and police who were responsible for much of it. "You kill your own *campesino* brothers and sisters," he told them. "The law of God must prevail that says, Thou shalt not kill! No soldier is obliged to obey an order against the law of God. No one has to fulfill an immoral law. It is time to . . . obey your consciences rather than the orders of sin. . . . In the name of God, and in the name of this suffering people whose laments rise to heaven each day more tumultuous, I beg you, I ask you, I order you in the name of God: Stop the repression!"[30] It was a definite stand against state coercion and brutality, of the sort so lacking in wartime Europe; it was also undeniably political, for Romero spoke of "liberation," of land distribution, and of finding a "political organization fitted to the common good." To his enemies, of course, his sermon was an incitement to mutiny and an act of treason.

He made his confession the following morning. "I want to be clean in the presence of the Lord," he told the confessor. He worked in his office and then had lunch on the seashore with a priest of Opus Dei. In the afternoon he saw a doctor about a slight ear infection. At 6 P.M. he was due at the mass for the mother of a friend, whose moderate newspaper *El Independiente* had been bombed a few days before. An announcement stating that Romero would say the mass was published in the press. Friends were fearful; for several months the Vatican had been warning him of the dangers that he was running, and the papal nuncio had urged him to quieten his preaching. The mass was celebrated in the oratory of the Divine Providence Hospital. In his homily, Romero told the congregation that "whoever out of love for Christ gives himself to the service of others will live, like the grain of wheat that dies, but only apparently dies. . . ." As he

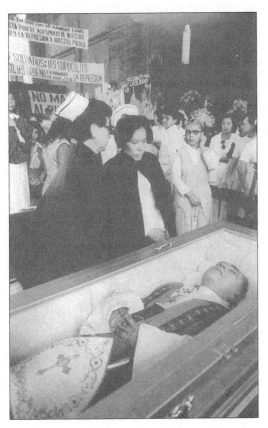

Archbishop Oscar Romero lies in his coffin before his funeral mass in San Salvador in 1980. A gunman shot him as he was conducting a service, in order to silence Romero's denunciations of repression and persecution. Gunmen also fired on the funeral crowds. An archbishop who defied rulers in the twentieth century was as vulnerable as Thomas à Becket, slain in his cathedral at Canterbury in the twelfth.

finished, standing at the altar, he was killed by a single bullet from a high velocity rifle.

A vast crowd gathered in front of the cathedral for the funeral mass on Palm Sunday. The pope's representative, Cardinal Corripio, was preaching his homily when a bomb exploded in the plaza. The scene was "too grotesque, too horrible to be reality," an Irish eyewitness wrote. "The corner of the square was ablaze and, as shots began to ring out, 100,000 people stampeded . . . the children and many poor, overweight women were being crushed against the bars."[31] Forty died, some shot, most suffocated. Romero's body was hastily buried in the tomb prepared in the east transept. Like his last mass in the hospital oratory, Romero's funeral mass was not completed.

chARISMA

The problems of churches in the affluent West were increasingly those of the self-indulgent societies they served: divorce, promiscuity, drugs, pornography, crime, and the abasement of the spiritual to the material. The illegitimacy rate in Britain was 3 percent before the First World War; at the end of the Second, the figure had crept up to 5 percent. By 2000, 41 percent of British babies were born to unmarried parents. The descriptions "husband" and "wife" were disappearing from official forms, replaced by "partner." The rise in the divorce rate was more rapid still. One marriage in a hundred had foundered before 1939; by 1989, half of British marriages were ending in divorce. These figures were not merely high by historic standards; they were staggeringly so, and the moral decay they reflect in terms of the past is too complete to be wished away on the contraceptive pill, the glamour of sex and drugs and rock and roll, or the cults of money, megastars, and instant gratification. The religious instinct in society is giving way.

Apathy is the mortal peril to the faith in Western Europe. For the first time in twelve hundred years, Britain has ceased to be a majority Christian county. By 2000, only one in ten of the population had attended any service other than a funeral or a wedding. Missionaries from Zambia and Brazil are now working among the godless in the cities of England, an astounding role reversal for a country that had for so long evangelized others. The archbishop of Westminster, Cardinal Cormac Murphy-O'Connor, said in 2001 that Christianity in Britain "has almost been vanquished." "London is today's field of mission," says Glaucos Soares de Lima, the Anglican Primate of Brazil. "It is so secular, we have to send people there for their salvation." The United Society for the Propagation of the Gospel, the missionary wing of the Church of England established in 1701 "to convert the heathen of all races," also works in England. A Zambian, Francis Makombwe, is a missionary in London's Waterloo district; the archdeacon of Croydon is from Uganda; and the vicar of West Dulwich is from Ghana. For the first time in four hundred years, too, England was no longer predominantly Anglican; Catholics outnumbered practicing members of the Church of England. It is debatable whether France is still predominantly Christian; the number of Catholic ordinations collapsed from a thousand in 1950 to less than a hundred in 1990, and by 1994 only 9 percent of the population were regular churchgoers.

The very landscapes of the First World War had seemed a denial of the divine. "This country stinks of corruption," Oliver Lyttleton, a British Guards officer wrote from Flanders. "As far as the eye can reach is that brown and torn sea of desolation and every yard is a grave, some marked with rifles others with crosses, some with white skulls, some with beckoning hands. But everything is dead: the trees, the fields, the corn, the church . . . it is all dead and God has utterly forsaken it." It bred an alienation from faith. "Personally, I held it my one true form of courage," an infantryman noted, "that I never once called on God for help."

Atheism was encouraged, too, by the fashionable theories of Sigmund Freud, founder of psychoanalysis. Freud described religion as "the universal obsessional neurosis of humanity." He held God to be a concept created by the mind to ease the stresses of guilt and pain. The human father figure is externalized into a divinity who offers life and security, and who also disciplines and sets rules. God is the father who smiled at the child in the cradle, who, "now magnified to infinity, smiles down upon us from heaven." Thus faith became no more than a desire to win control of the sensory world through the "wish-world" of the mind. C. S. Lewis, writer and Oxford professor, and his hugely popular *Screwtape Letters,* upheld traditional Christianity. "God whispers to us in our pleasures," he wrote, "speaks in our conscience, but shouts in our pains: it is his megaphone to rouse a deaf world."[1] On a more abstract basis, the Protestant theologian Paul Tillich countered Freud's atheism by attempting to relate depth-psychology and modern secular thought to Christian culture. He explained faith as an "ultimate concern," which must be located in God, and which transcends finite existence; the nonbeliever may believe that he has rejected God, when he has merely failed to encounter him. Despite such efforts by theologians, however, Christianity in Western Europe has not recovered its nineteenth-century self-confidence.

Americans, however, maintained their enthusiasm and revivals. The revivalist Billy Sunday and others in the Baptist-led Anti-Saloon League, supported by many Protestant pastors and some Catholics, attacked the "hell-soaked liquor business" to such effect in the early 1900s that the ill-fated Prohibition Amendment was passed in 1917. Politicians took notice, for their career might rest on the answer to the question: "Will you vote dry?"

Similar idealism made the new Pentecostal churches a force. They originated in the Holiness movement of mid-nineteenth-century America. Phoebe Palmer, a Methodist lay leader, taught that Wesley's desire for Christian perfection remained attainable, and that perfection in love is a divine blessing that does away with sinful desire. The concept of perfection remained as easy to mock as it had been with the Cathars; but, to its devotees, it offered more than mere salvation, for they believed that they could so grow in God's grace as to become holy or sanctified in themselves. Holiness was described by the Methodist De Witt Clinton Huntington, a Vermont pastor and professor, as a "state of unreserved consecration of the being to God, secured through the constant revelation of Christ to the soul of the believer by the Holy Spirit." The divinely-strengthened soul reaches a state, Huntington emphasized, in which "the believer *does not commit sin*."[2] Holiness camp meetings and an Association for the Promotion of Holiness based in Vineland, New Jersey, spread the movement. Tensions between Holiness leaders and Methodist bishops led to the creation of separate Holiness denominations, such as the 1881 Church of God, of Anderson, Indiana, and the largest, the Church of the Nazarene, of 1908. These were among the first churches to admit women to the ministry.

Pentecostalism was spun off from Holiness. It was more radical, and its congregations believed that they could receive the same gifts from the Spirit as the first Christians—powers to speak in tongues, of prophecy, healing, and exorcism. The initiate receives a "baptism of the Holy Spirit" in place of sacramental baptism by water. It is seen as the direct work of Christ—"I baptized you with water," John the Baptist had said of Jesus, "but he shall baptize you with the Holy Spirit" (Mark 1:8)—and its sign is glossolalia, speaking in tongues. A revival that began in Azusa Street in Los Angeles in 1906 had a strong apocalyptic strain, and the many visitors to Azusa Street, some from Europe and Latin America, were urged to preach it round the world "before the end came." Pentecostalism spread rapidly among poor whites and blacks in the Southern states. Its appeal was dynamic, for it promised ecstasies of the spirit and contact with the divine. Worship was uninhibited, with a powerful sense of congregation, where all could sing and clap to powerful rhythms, and a freedom from hierarchy and dry liturgy. Faith is "turned loose" and pent-up emotions are poured into belief in deliverance.

Elder C. H. Mason, founder of the Church of God in Christ, the largest and earliest black group, stressed its identity with the earliest stirrings of the faith. At Pentecost, he said, at Caesarea and at Ephesus, the Holy Spirit had fallen on those who heard the word and had given them new tongues and gifts. "And these signs shall follow those that believe," he quoted Jesus. "In my name shall they cast out devils; they shall speak with new tongues." It is as true now as then, Mason preached, that the glory of the son is revealed with immense power to the believer who is baptized with the Holy Spirit; "he will glorify Christ, he will show us the things of Christ." The core of Pentecostalism lies in the passages "concerning spiritual gifts" in Paul's first Epistle to the Corinthians, where God promises "miracles, then gifts of healings, helps, governments, diversities of tongues" (1 Cor. 12:28). The groanings and cries of the believer might be unintelligible, but this was of no consequence, for "he that speaketh in an unknown tongue speaketh not unto men, but unto God: for no man understandeth him; howbeit in the spirit he speaketh mysteries" (1 Cor. 14:2). The belief is shot through with immediacy. "Christ is coming soon again to the earth," Mason taught. "Prepare to meet your God in his glory."[3]

The movement is not a denomination in itself. Its followers are largely orthodox in belief; the significant exceptions are the "Jesus Only" churches, the United Pentecostal Church being the largest, which regard the godhead as a single entity and baptize in the name of Jesus alone. The charismatic element in Pentecostalism, of ecstatic personal experience and spontaneity, has been adopted by otherwise mainstream Protestants and Catholics, and has so swept developing countries that it now influences a quarter of Christendom's two billion souls. Rich whites no longer leave its flamboyances to the poor. In 1960, at St. Mark's Episcopal Church in Van Nuys, California, the well-heeled congregation of Rector Dennis Bennett experienced a baptism of the Spirit accompanied by speaking in tongues. The bishop of Los Angels frowned on the outbreak of glossolalia and banned it. Bennett moved to the diocese of Seattle and founded another thriving congregation. Catholic disapproval did not prevent a charismatic conference from taking place at the Catholic University of Notre Dame.

❖   A BLEND OF Pentecostalism, old-fashioned morality, conservative politics, and the power of radio and television created a new revivalism in America on a scale that influenced presidential elections. Before World War II, Charles Coughlin, a Catholic priest from Detroit, had achieved radio audiences of ten million; in 1980, one "tele-evangelist" alone, Jerry Falwell, was reaching fifty million viewers.

Billy Graham, the postwar pioneer, was a Southern Baptist evangelist from North Carolina. He made his first great preaching crusade in Los Angeles in 1949 and followed it with missions to every continent. His message was simple, he said, and could easily be encapsulated: "Christ died for our sins according to the Scriptures; . . . was buried, and . . . rose again on the third day, according to the Scriptures" (1 Cor. 15:3–4). This terse proclamation, Graham found, "stretches over the broad frame of man's basic need. It declares that man is a sinner, that Christ is the only Savior, that Christ lives evermore and the Scriptures are trustworthy. . . ."[4] He had no qualms about exploiting new media to the full or in acting as a counselor to politicians such as Richard Nixon. He preached with a

The evangelist Billy Graham, Bible thrust out before him, applied techniques as ancient and effective as the faith itself. They can adapt to television and radio, and Graham used them on every continent. His message, he said, could easily be encapsulated: "Christ died for our sins according to the Scriptures; . . . was buried, and . . . rose again on the third day, according to the Scriptures." This proclamation, Graham found, "stretches over the broad frame of man's basic need. It declares that man is a sinner, that Christ is the only Savior, that Christ lives evermore and the Scriptures are trustworthy. . . ."

success that left him "bewildered, challenged and humbled." His converts are said to number in the millions, and his striking decency lent a moral aura to younger and more politicized evangelists that they did not always deserve.

Healing was another strand in Pentecostal and revivalist services. The teleevangelist Oral Roberts dated his mission from a healing revival he attended in Ada, Oklahoma, in 1935. He was taken to the meeting lying on a mattress in the backseat of a car, bedbound with tuberculosis in both lungs. The line of the sick waiting to be anointed by the healer, Brother George Muncie, was long; it was past midnight before Roberts was touched with hands and with oil on his forehead. "I believed God!" Roberts said. "Every ache and pain disappeared. The glory rushed into my soul . . . I was lost in the sheer ecstasy of divine deliverance . . . I was leaping and shouting and running on the long platform. I was healed! Faith had wrought it!" From then on, Roberts claimed, "through my right hand I feel the healing virtue of the Son of God." At his healing sessions he touched the sick and adjured the afflictions to come out of them in the name of Jesus Christ. "I feel the pressure of the disease rising to meet my right hand," he said, and as the divine surges into the person, "the deaf ears are opened, the cancers wither and die and pass from the body, demons come out and humanity is set free. . . ."[5]

Hollywood directors had already mined the Bible for film epics, such as Cecil B. de Mille's *Ten Commandments*. Television proved as dynamic as the printing press. A belting, crusading style delivered immense congregations at a profit, and the modest cost of producing programs was covered several times over by donations. "Tear 'em up," the Southern Baptist revivalist James Robison said of his technique. "I'd have truck drivers push back their beer and start crying and say 'tell me more.'"

The growth of these "electronic churches" was extraordinary. By 1980 an estimated 130 million Americans were watching a religious program each week, about 47 percent of the population. Thirty TV stations and sixty-six cable systems offered only religious programming; so did fourteen hundred radio stations. Annual revenue from radio and television evangelism was estimated at one billion dollars that year. Oral Roberts had a weekly television program and a radio station, and his sixty-million-dollar-a-year income helped provide for the thirty-eight hundred students at Oral Roberts University in Tulsa. Pat Robertson, founder of the Christian Broadcasting Network, a charismatic Baptist and son of a Virginia senator, was taking in $58 million; his one-time employee Jim Bakker earned $51 million after starting his own Christian network, his two-hour show bringing support from 700,000 contributors. Bakker was later alleged to have defrauded his followers out of $158 million.[6] Robison's ministry employed 125 people and was budgeting $15 million a year for primetime television specials.[7]

The American elite paid little attention to this phenomenon until 1979, when Jerry Falwell founded Moral Majority Inc. Falwell, a former high school football player and engineering student, created a thriving congregation in an abandoned pop factory at Lynchburg, Virginia. His fiery preaching brought average Sunday attendances of four thousand. Television multiplied his audience more than ten thousand times. His *Old-Time Gospel Hour* was carried by 324 stations, generating an income of a million dollars a week and enabling him to employ 950 people and support his Liberty Baptist College, where seven thousand students were trained in his brand of fundamentalism.

Falwell's Moral Majority was a focal point for the religious right, regardless of denomination. Revivalism had long had a conservative strain. Bob Jones University in Greensboro, South Carolina, whose revivalist founder had once posed himself the question "Is Segregation Scriptural?" and answered it in the affirmative, had been producing rigidly right-wing preachers for three decades. The Moral Majority, however, was seized on by the news media and had an immediate impact on politicians and voters. Its claims that it helped Ronald Reagan win the 1980 presidential election appear justified; it certainly transformed state elections, particularly in the South, where Alabama elected its first Republican senator in a century. The Moral Majority had a burning panoply of fears, of the growth in pornography, drug use, divorce, and promiscuity, of abortion, feminism, gay rights, and AIDS, which some saw as divine retribution for homosexuals.

Two decisions by the Supreme Court fueled particular religious outrage. In 1962, in *Engel v Vitale,* it ruled that the daily recital of prayers in public schools was unconstitutional. Robison claimed that this had incited "plagues" such as "escalation of crime, disintegration of families, racial conflict, teenage pregnancies and venereal disease."[8] In *Roe v Wade* eleven years later, the Court declared that the state had no right to prevent a woman from having an abortion in the first three months of pregnancy. "The laws of the land," as the theologian James Burtchaell wrote in the "pro-life" cause, "ought not allow the unborn to be put to death for our convenience."[9]

As the influence of the Moral Majority slowly waned and allegations of fraud and sexual scandal ruffled the rise of the tele-evangelist, the running was taken up by more extreme groups. Operation Rescue militants demonstrated outside abortion clinics, citing the Book of Proverbs: "Rescue those who are being taken away to death; hold back those who are stumbling to the slaughter." A member of the pro-life Rescue American group shot dead a doctor at a clinic in Pensacola, Florida, in 1993; he regarded the Bible as a legal document in his defense.[10]

The wilder charismatics seem merely eccentric. The Holy Spirit manifested itself to followers of the "Toronto Blessing" movement, which originated in the Vineyard Church at Toronto airport in 1994, in "barking, laughing, embracing and collapsing in convulsions."[11] A sinister force found refuge, however, in a handful of charismatic prophets.

The Reverend James Jones, a Midwesterner with a background in the evangelical Disciples of Christ, founded the People's Temple church and gathered a congregation among the poor in rural northern California. He spoke of leading them to a Promised Land where he would free them of hurt and oppression. More than nine hundred followed him from California to a jungle encampment in Guyana, without telephones or exit roads, which he called Jonestown. He confiscated their passports and money and posted armed guards around the camp to prevent escape; mail was censored, and his followers were forbidden to talk to outsiders. As relatives demanded an investigation, Jones warned that "we are devoted to a decision that it is better even to die than to be constantly harassed from one continent to the next." In November 1978, Jones precipitated his church's Armageddon; he and all but a few of his followers killed themselves by drinking Kool-Aid laced with poison. Another "messiah," David Koresh, formed the breakaway Branch Davidian sect of the Seventh-Day Adventists at Waco in Texas in 1993. He called his community Mount Carmel and preached the imminence of the Last Judgment. Fires and shooting broke out after government agencies surrounded the buildings, and 53 adults and 21 children died. Such sects are only nominally Christian, of course, but they do demonstrate that Christianity remains as vulnerable to cults now as it was in the sixteenth-century Kingdom of the Saints at Münster.

❖ ANCIENT MARCIONITES and a few other sects apart, only men had been ordained by the churches. To priest a woman was held to flout the Bible; the Old Testament priesthood was a male preserve, the apostles were men, and God was the Father and Christ the Son. Yet women outnumbered men among worshipers in most denominations, and had long done so; there were more nuns than monks, and women were a majority in many missions. After the pope, Mother Teresa, the sparrow-thin Albanian working in the slums of Calcutta, was perhaps the best-known Christian on earth. The order she founded, the Missionaries of Charity, which cared for children, the homeless and incurables, had 1,700 sisters and 300 brothers.

Not enough men were coming forward to fill the priesthood, Catholic and Protestant; women were eager candidates. Feminism gave the issue added bite, and it was not as new as it seemed. The American suffragette Elizabeth Cady Stanton, who insisted on dropping the word "obey" at her marriage in 1840, had produced *The Women's Bible* in 1895 to show that the Church presented women as inferior to men. The pioneer feminists, such as Stanton's fellow American Susan B. Anthony, a champion of women's rights, were often steeped in Christianity. In England, Josephine Butler, the great Victorian campaigner for exploited women, described her life in her autobiography as "a Great Crusade." Deeply devout, married to the canon of Winchester, Butler campaigned successfully against licensed brothels and secured the repeal of the Contagious Diseases Act, which had made women in seaports and garrison towns liable to compulsory examination for venereal disease. She also succeeded in having the age of consent raised to sixteen, to prevent girls of twelve and thirteen from being sold into prostitution, and wrote widely on women's education. Elizabeth Blackwell, the English-born first woman doctor in the United States, and Elizabeth Garrett Anderson, the first woman doctor and town mayor in England, both came from highly Christian backgrounds; so did the founders of the first women's colleges at Cambridge, Sarah Emily Davis of Girton College, and the suffragette Dame Millicent Fawcett of Newnham.

Governments and equal rights became involved in the priestess issue. Danish Lutherans had elected a woman as a pastor in 1946; when bishops proved reluctant to ordain her, the Danish government ruled that a woman could indeed be elected a pastor if so ordained. In 1967 the Swedish government, and then the Norwegian, introduced legislation to permit woman priests despite objections by church assemblies.

An Anglican council meeting in Kenya in 1971 recommended, against the advice of the archbishop of Canterbury, that any province wishing to ordain women should be free to do so. Two were ordained in Hong Kong the following year.* American bishops of the Episcopal Church agreed that women might be ordained, although bishops should not act independently. Three retired American bishops, and one from Costa Rica, nonetheless independently ordained eleven women in Philadelphia in 1974. The issue, including that of woman bishops, was bitterly contested by the provinces of the Anglican Communion at the Lambeth Conference of 1988. Barbara Harris was consecrated the next year in Boston as the first woman bishop of the Episcopal Church in America, soon followed by the first woman diocesan bishop in New Zealand. This was a red rag both to Anglo-Catholics and hard-line Evangelicals; when the Anglican synod voted in 1992 to ordain women in England, some left the Church.

Homosexuality has been equally divisive for Protestants. The Old Testament provides condemnations in plenty. "There shall be no harlot of the daughters of Israel," the Book of Deuteronomy states, "neither shall there be a sodomite of the sons of Israel" (Deut. 23:17). Transvestism is especially condemned: "A woman shall not wear that which pertaineth unto a man, neither shall a man put on a woman's garment: for whosoever doeth these things is an abomination unto the Lord thy God" (Deut. 22:5). The biblical sanctions appeared so clear that, although attacks on basic gay rights were largely the preserve of fundamentalists, many of otherwise moderate conscience found the ordination of gay priests to be theologically and morally indefensible. Early warnings by American tele-evangelists that the door was being opened to gay church marriages were largely mocked. By 2000, however, an Anglican priest who was to undergo a surgical sex change did not find it necessary to resign, while the leader of the extreme gay rights group Outrage! "outed" priests whom he said were closet homosexuals, and interrupted the archbishop of Canterbury in the pulpit to denounce church "homophobia." In America, a retired bishop of Iowa was charged in 1996 with violating Episcopal Church doctrine by ordaining a homosexual. He was acquitted, implying that such ordinations were feasible, a development that traditionalist bishops attempted to block.

It is the fact that modern morality is defined by governments, often responding to lobby groups and electoral pressure, that intensifies the difficulties for national Protestant churches in the West. The rules on abortion, gay rights, equal rights, the limits of what is permissible and what is illegal in pornography, are es-

---

*Florence Li Tim Oi had become the first Anglican woman to be ordained, also in Hong Kong, in 1944. This was due to pastoral urgency in wartime, and the bishop of Hong Kong's action was later repudiated.[12]

tablished by politicians and interpreted in lay courts. Priests can object, but they no longer set the moral agenda. In America, this is offset by their access to television and the media; as with the Moral Majority, they can become a formidable lobby in their own right. Religious broadcasting in Europe has no such clout, and mainstream congregations are aging and falling in numbers.

Catholicism, international in its nature, is less inhibited by individual governments and the mood of the moment. It maintains formal diplomatic relations with a majority of the world's states, and it is older than any of them. It has trimmed its essential doctrines little to suit the age; its members were in no doubt of where it stood, much though they might object to the stance.

Pius XII warned against applying modern criticism to the study of theology in the encyclical *Humani generis* in 1951. He declared the bodily Assumption of the Virgin to be an article of faith, although this had no biblical basis, and his invocation of papal infallibility was provocative even for the Orthodox, who agreed with the doctrine but rejected his unilateral right to define it. He canonized Pius X, the archenemy of modernism, and sent his embalmed body on a tour of Italy. He suppressed the Worker Priests, a French movement that, accepting that parts of urban France were so dechristianized that they needed evangelizing as badly as pagans, sent priests to work in factories and the docks. Pius thought it smacked of Marxism. At the end of his life he was isolated, guarded by a nun-housekeeper, injected with "living cell therapy" and other quack remedies, subject to uncontrollable hiccups. At his funeral in 1958, his coffin was poorly embalmed and exploded.

His successor, John XXIII, was seventy-six, the son of a peasant, expected neither to live long nor do much. He was warmhearted and good humored, and a duster of cobwebs. He threw out Pius's Cold War rhetoric, received Khrushchev's daughter and son-in-law, and declared that war in an atomic age was no longer a "fit instrument with which to repair the violation of justice." He sought *aggiornamento,* a "bringing up to date" of the Church, and called an ecumenical council of the whole Church.

This vast gathering, the Second Vatican Council, opened on October 11, 1962. It met fully the plea of the dying Nicholas V five hundred years before for "something that appeals to the eye." The high command of the Church flowed across St. Peter's Square as though in answer to Stalin's mocking question, "How many divisions has the pope?" Bishops in rows of six, 3,281 strong, in white damask copes and mitres, the uniformity relieved at points with the black cassock, full beard, and round headdress of an oriental, and the bulbous gold crown of a bishop of Byzantine rite; Swiss guards in blue and orange with iron breastplates; papal gendarmes with black top boots and busbies; the scarlet ranks of cardinals; and finally, undulating gently on the shoulder-borne *sedia gestatoria,* the pope himself, smiling and quietly weeping.

In his sermon, John said that he disagreed with the "prophets of doom" who told him that the modern world was full of prevarication and ruin. The Church must "bring herself up to date where required" and look to the present and the new while never departing from the "sacred patrimony" of the past. John died the following June, before the council had got into its stride, but it retained his liberal outlook and openness, covered by television and radio. The most visible change was in the liturgy. The Latin Tridentine Mass was replaced after almost five hundred years, to give congregations a clearer understanding of the service. The canon of the Mass was said in the vernacular, although many found the language graceless and pedestrian; the altar now faced the people; and in some circumstances, Communion could be in two kinds. Those who had found comfort in the timeless mysteries of the Latin Mass shared their grievance with Protestant traditionalists, who felt assaulted by New Bibles and the rendering of ancient liturgies into updated language that lacked the cadence of the old.

A sense of Christendom was renewed. The Decree on the Church, *Lumen Gentium,* stated that the Church of Christ "subsisted in" rather than "was" the Roman Catholic Church. This was not a nuance; it did not deny a place in Christ's Church to other churches, and it set the primacy of the pope amid the shared responsibility of all bishops. *Gaudium et Spes,* the Pastoral Constitution of the Church in the Modern World, said that the religious pilgrimage towards "the heavenly city" involved a greater effort to work with all men to create a more human world. The decree of Ecumenism broke sharply with Pius XI's 1928 encyclical *Mortalium Animos* that had mocked "pan-Christians consumed by the zeal to unite Churches" and said that God's revealed truth could not be negotiated.[13] Unity was now to be a central aim of the Church. Pardon was humbly begged of God "and of our separated brethren" for the past sins of Catholics against them. The decree on other religions denied that the Jews were responsible for the death of Christ, and admitted and deplored Catholic persecution of the Jews.

The council's most bitterly argued act was the Declaration on Religious Liberty. It was guided by John Courtney Murray, a Jesuit professor from Maryland, and reflected the American emphasis on individual freedom. It declared that "the human person has a right to religious freedom." No one was to be coerced "by any human power" and no one was to be restrained from "acting in accordance with his own beliefs, whether privately or publicly, alone or in association with others, within due limits."[14] This was indeed revolutionary. The desire to coerce heretics had been indulged in by the early Church, formally so since Constantine the Great. Pope after pope had denied liberty; at best, they tolerated the nonorthodox. Italian and Spanish bishops fought fiercely against the declaration. Marcel Lefebvre, former archbishop of Dakar, would have none of it or of the new liturgy. He formed the "Priestly Confraternity of Pius X"; in the spirit of that antimodernist pope, Lefebvre set himself up in Switzerland, ordaining priests in defiance of Rome before being formally excommunicated in 1988.* The decree was strongly pressed by the American bishops, however, and the conservative archbishop of Cracow, Karol Wojtyla, the future John Paul II, gave it key support as a valuable prop against communism.

At Jerusalem in 1964, as he strove to give substance to ecumenism, Paul VI met the Greek patriarch Athenagaros. The mutual excommunication of the Eastern and Western Churches, almost a millennium old, was lifted the following year. Paul welcomed the archbishop of Canterbury on a formal visit to Rome in 1966. He spoke of the Anglican as a "sister church" and gave the archbishop his own episcopal ring. He became the first pope to visit Africa. He sold the papal tiara and gave the money to the poor; he introduced compulsory retirement for bishops, though not the pope, at age seventy-five and decreed that octogenarian cardinals could no longer vote in papal elections.

THOUSANDS OF PRIESTS were quitting their posts to marry, however; nuns abandoned the veil and religious vocations tumbled. Millions of Catholics were flouting Church teaching on premarital sex, contraception, and abortion. "I was solitary before, but now my solitariness becomes complete and awesome," Paul noted a few weeks after becoming pope. "Jesus was alone on the cross. . . . My solitude will grow."[15] He did indeed seem adrift in a rising social storm. Christians of all persuasions had been putting personal pleasure ahead of religious principle since time immemorial, of course; but society had accepted that this was at least technically sinful, and the sinners were usually loath to make public protest.

This was no longer true. Paul ran into new attitudes head-on over contraception. He removed the issue from the council and referred it to an advisory body of theologians, doctors, and married couples. They recommended that traditional teaching, which tolerated only natural methods, be modified to permit artificial birth control in some circumstances. It was expected that he would accept this, but he could not bring himself to do so. In *Humanae Vitae* on July 29, 1968, Paul reaffirmed the historic view that all forms of artificial birth control were "absolutely prohibited."

Priests were well aware that the ban was the most troubling aspect of Catholic

*The author was present at the Latin ceremony, held in the open in a Swiss cow pasture, where Lefebvre brought John Paul II's excommunication upon himself. As he laid his hands on the kneeling rebels to ordain them, thunder growled through the mountains; reporters awaited a flash of divine lightning, but none came.

dogma for many of their parishioners, and huge numbers flouted it. Sales of con-
traceptives were as high in many Catholic countries as in Protestant; and, in the
hungry slums and shanties of Latin America and Africa, overpopulation itself
menaced the quality of marginal lives. Shocked theologians at the Catholic University of America issued a declaration the next day stating that the encyclical betrayed a "narrow" notion of papal authority; that the "special witness of many
Catholic couples is neglected"; and that it was "insensitive to the witness of many
men of good will." They concluded that spouses could responsibly decide according to their own conscience that artificial contraception was permissible,
"and indeed necessary," to preserve the values of marriage.[16] Paul was certain that
he was right, but the fury of protests and resignations that followed unnerved
him. He wrote no further encyclicals, and in his last ten years he felt isolated and
little loved. His successor, John Paul, was found dead of a coronary embolism in
the papal apartments a month after his election in 1978. Murder was rumored,
amid a fraud and financial scandal at the Vatican Bank, although not a scrap of
evidence supported it.

Karol Wojtyla, the Pole who became John Paul II, was the first non-Italian
pope since 1522 and the first Slav ever; at fifty-eight he was the youngest since

Pope John Paul II on his triumphant visit to Poland in 1979. At Czestochowa, 3.5 million came
to see him, the largest human gathering ever recorded. His success was a measure of the
Communist failure to expunge Christianity. A poll of Polish teenagers found that 87 percent
claimed to be religious, and that 72 percent worshiped regularly. In Russia, too, and in China,
persecution increased devotion to the faith, a phenomenon first noticed by a Roman governor,
Pliny the Younger, in A.D. 112.

1846. The son of an army officer, who had labored in a quarry and a chemical plant under the communists, John Paul was a mountaineer, skier, philosopher, linguist, and poet. He was personally charismatic. His overseas visits, sheltered in a "popemobile" after an assassination attempt in 1981, attracted colossal crowds from Latin America to Africa; half the population of Ireland came to see him. He was deeply concerned with the "Church of silence" under communist rule; he thought little better of capitalism, and in his *Sollicitudo Rei Socialis* in 1987 attacked both and called for "preferential love for the poor."

He was, however, deeply conservative. He campaigned ferociously against birth control and abortion, treating them as a single evil. His contempt for abortion permeated his encyclical *Evangelium Vitae,* which called for a new culture of love and respect for life, and excoriated the "culture of death" which had brought abortion to materialistic societies. On the ancient issue of clerical celibacy, given fresh impetus by resignations and vacancies, he was unbending. Alarmed at radical opinions among the Jesuits, he chose a seventy-nine-year-old and half-blind conservative as his candidate for the generalship of the order. Though he at length conceded a free election, his point was made. John Paul chose the Bavarian cardinal Joseph Ratzinger to be head of the Doctrines of the Faith, the new name for the Holy Office, or Inquisition. Ratzinger had been marked by the sixties student riots and promiscuity in Germany. The questioning of Catholic doctrine was anathema to him; liberal theologians were silenced, and the radical Hans Küng, professor at Tübingen, had his license to teach as a Catholic withdrawn. Ratzinger had as little time for homosexuality, which he said in 1986 implied a "strong tendency towards an intrinsic moral evil."[17]

The encyclical *Veritatis splendor* in 1993 complained of "an overall and systematic calling into question of traditional moral doctrine," and restated the ban on artificial contraception and opposition to homosexuality, premarital sex, and abortion. Good intentions, it said, might diminish the evil but could not remove it. As to woman priests, John Paul was equally inflexible. He stated in his apostolic letter "Ordinatio Sacerdotalis" of 1995 that only men could be priested, since Christ had chosen only men as apostles: "All doubt to be removed . . . the Church has no authority whatsoever to confer priestly ordination to women."

❖ THESE THOUGHTS WERE binding on almost one billion Catholics. Two millennia after Calvary, Christians numbered some two billion souls, close to a third of humanity.[18] They were in a majority in Latin and North America, Africa, the Caribbean, Europe and Eurasia, and the Pacific. Only in Asia and in the old heartlands of the Middle East were they a small minority. Catholics accounted for almost 17 percent of the world population, Protestants for 10, the Orthodox for

4 percent. Gains were highest among Pentecostals and Charismatics.[19] It was reported that 1.5 million people joined a March for Jesus in São Paulo in Brazil in March 1997; that evangelicals make up 15 percent of the Mexican population; and that there are thirty thousand Evangelical churches in the Philippines.

Christianity had not originated as a European faith, and at some time in the late 1960s it ceased to be predominantly Western. In 1960 about 58 percent of professing Christians lived in Europe, North America, and the Pacific. This had fallen to 38 percent by 1990. It is continuing to fall due to vigorous expansion in Africa, Latin America, and Asia; in all these places the churches abound with teenagers, an endangered species at services in Europe. A majority of the world's 73 million Anglicans now live in the developing world.

The independent churches of Africa expanded at extraordinary speed; by 1946 it was estimated that there were thirteen hundred of them. In the Congo, Simon Kimbangu, a young Baptist catechist, after a healing experience founded a church that became so popular that alarmed Belgian colonial officials jailed him for life in 1921; the church survives and today claims more than four million Kimbanguists in Zaire. The Aladura or "praying movement" in Nigeria began with evangelists prescribing rainwater to the victims of an influenza epidemic; it developed into the Church of the Lord and spread across the continent. The Zulu prophet Isaiah Shembe created his own church. The Balokale—the "saved ones"—flourished in East Africa.

Evangelical groups—an array of them, India Evangelical Team, Filadelphia Fellowship, Rajastan Bible Institute, Friends Missionary Prayer Band—claim to have founded more than fifty-five hundred churches and preaching stations in North India since 1975. "World Reach," the missionary branch of the Christian Broadcasting Network of Virginia Beach, and Newlife Fellowship Churches, a network of twelve hundred house churches in Bombay, are cooperating in a plan to reach five hundred million people through "evangelistic direct mail." The Delhi pastor K. Y. Geevarghese says that his movement has planted hundreds of churches in Rajastan and Haryana. "Jesus' power is again and again demonstrated," he claims, "and we regularly experience healings, deliverance from demons and people being raised from the dead."[20]

In Bihar, at the village level, the evangelists must cope with jealous spell-casters. "They call up demonic powers but the demons return to tell them: 'We can do nothing against them, as they are surrounded by angels and fire,'" an evangelist reported. As the spell-casters spoke with the evangelists, "the conviction of God fell on all four and they were converted and delivered from evil. The whole village followed, amazed at God's power."[21] Claims of miracles abound. A six-year-old boy who drowned in Gujurat was to be buried the same day when members of the Indian Pentecostal Church prayed in Jesus' name and placed Bibles on his body. "Then the child opened his eyes, alive," Parthing Matchar, the father, said. "We could find no words to express our feelings as we experienced God's power raising the dead as he did in Acts."[22] In Bihar, as a man consumed with leprosy went to throw himself under a train, a man in a white robe walked with him for a while. When the man in white vanished, the leprosy was gone. "That man is now winning whole villages for Christ," evangelists claim.

�֍   IT IS EASY, of course, to mock such stories as imaginary or fraudulent. Nonetheless, many tens of thousands of Christian converts are being made every day. If the process seems biblical, with miracles declared and witch doctors outsmarted in Pauline fashion, that is because they are taking place in villages and *favelas* whose poverty and backwardness are biblical.

The continuity with the past is an essence. Christianity has, in recent times, survived the rise of Positivism, Marxism, Fascism; "true religion is slow in growth and, when once planted, is difficult of dislodgment," John Henry Newman observed, "but its intellectual counterfeit has no root in itself; it springs up suddenly, it suddenly withers."[23] It has kept its belief in miracles and faith healing. In cynical Europe, five million pilgrims visit Lourdes each year. Like their medieval predecessors, they have turned the shrine into an industry, spending three hundred million dollars on food, hotels, and keepsakes. In 1999, six cases were authenticated as "legitimate" miracles.*

Persecution continues apace in China. The government reacted furiously to the pope's decision to canonize 120 Catholic martyrs on October 1, 2000, China's National Day. Most of the martyrs had been killed by the Boxers in 1900; to the Communist regime the Boxers were patriotic heroes, while the new Catholic saints were described by Beijing as "notorious criminals" and "rapists." A fierce campaign was mounted against Catholics in Wenzhou, in the eastern province of Zhejiang. Wenzhou, a place of sweatshops, shoe factories, and pirate goods, has foreign trading links and has long been a Christian center. Priests and bishops, including an eighty-one-year-old bishop, Lin Xili, were thought to have been arrested. Catholic and Protestant churches together with Buddhist and Taoist temples were dynamited as part of the atheist assault.[25]

Violent tremors continue to shake the borderlands of Christendom with Is-

---

*A herniated disc, two ovarian tumors, breast cancer, deafness, and a skin lesion. The conditions for proclaiming miracles had been set down by Pope Benedict XIV in his *De Servorum Dei Beatificatione et Beatorum Canonizatione*. The original disease has to be incapacitating, with a precise diagnosis; psychiatric conditions are excluded as too uncertain. The cure should be sudden, instantaneous, and without convalescence; recovery must be permanent and restore normal functions to the patient. Although experts examine each case, the decision to declare a miracle is left to the bishop of the patient's diocese.[24]

lam. In Africa, a civil war with attendant horrors of starvation resulted from the attempt by Christian southerners to break away from Moslem-dominated northern Nigeria; they failed to create an independent state of Biafra, but the hundreds of deaths that followed the imposition of Islamic Shar'ia law in Kaduna early in 2000 showed that communal tensions had crossed into the new millennium. The Anglican archbishop of Uganda was martyred during Idi Amin's reign of terror, though the dictator's savagery was personal and little motivated by Islam; to the north, fighting between Christian Ethiopians and Moslem Eritreans, and the continuing struggle by southern Sudanese Christians against Khartoum's large Moslem army, had at least some religious undercurrent.

The nuances of faith and politics in Israel and Lebanon, the Middle East's seismic zone, are too subtle to be glibly unwound; Christians in southern Lebanon allied themselves with the Israelis, for example, while Palestinian Christians led anti-Israeli terror groups, but the pictures of the Virgin that Maronite militiamen taped to their gun butts, and the Islamic fundamentalism of other private armies of Lebanon, indicated the religious roots of the crisis. In Cyprus, Christians and Moslems are separated by a "green line" manned by United Nations troops after centuries of uneasy cohabitation ended in killings and an invasion of Turkish paratroopers. The collapse of Communism in the Balkans reawoke religious bigotries and "ethnic cleansing" involving Moslems and Orthodox and Catholics; if the Serb atrocities against Kosovar Moslems at the close of the twentieth century were secular in inspiration, the context had distinct fourteenth-century echoes: in the intervening years it had often been the Moslems who were the aggressors. In Kosovo, Moslems protected by NATO troops from Christian countries turned against their Christian neighbors. Fighting across the religious divide continued in the new century in Chechnya, where rebels saw themselves as reviving Moslem resistance to Russia. Tens of thousands died when Moslem gunmen terrorized Christians who had voted for independence in East Timor, and other Christians were killed in atrocity and counteratrocity in Indonesia's Molucca Islands and in the Philippines.

The first war of the twenty-first century, as President Bush described the murderous assault on New York and Washington in September 2001, was a new phenomenon in its method and scale, and in its eruption in the heart of an overwhelmingly Christian nation far from the troubled frontiers of Islam and Christendom. But it had other, older echoes of ancient fanaticism we have met before, of jihad and Crusade, in Jerusalem, Alexandria, and Constantinople, in medieval Spain and at the gates of Renaissance Vienna. Islam has retained a powerful and cohesive sense of itself that Christendom has largely lost, but which it must now, in response to the taunts of "infidel," justly seek to reestablish.

There is a deeply troubling irony that the Pakistani Christians massacred at

prayer at St. Dominic's Church in Bahawalpur in October 2001 came from an Anglican community converted by British missionaries 140 years ago. Most Hindus were murdered or driven out of Pakistan at the time of partition in 1947. The Christians who survive have the courage to face Pakistan's 1985 Blasphemy Act, so vicious that Bishop John Joseph, the Catholic bishop of Faisalabad, committed suicide on the steps of the Sahiwal Sessions Court in 1998 after a young Christian was sentenced to death.

Yet in Britain itself, for so long a bastion of missionary zeal, the faith has been so abandoned that mosque-going Moslems are expected to outnumber church-going Anglicans by 2013. Though Britain is nominally overwhelmingly Christian, the number of Anglicans attending Sunday services is falling below the one million mark, whilst practicing Moslems—many of them Pakistanis—approach the 750,000 level.[26] In Western Europe, at least, Christians seem not only to have abandoned their persecuted brothers in Asia and Africa, but to have abandoned their very selves.

Within the faith itself, the Catholic declaration *Dominus Jesus* of the summer of 2000 shows that the Reformation is still a scourge that raises welts on Christian flesh. The document said that Protestant communities are "not Churches in the proper sense"; the umbilical cord with Christ and St. Peter having been broken, they "have not preserved the valid Episcopate." Ecumenical goodwill has not salved a hurt of almost five hundred years' duration. Christianity's self-inflicted wounds still fester.

At its heart remains the Son of God who is also the resurrected Son of Man. It is a faith exposed to the inconstancies and energies of mankind. Any may be touched by the divine, by grace, and the Holy Spirit, and its history continues to be shot through with those who so claim, and with their vanities, feuds, inspirations, beauties, and catastrophes. Its consolations and compassion are its own.

❖

❖

❖

NOTES

Chapter I. The Cross

1. William K. Klingaman, *The First Century,* New York, 1991, p. 200.
2. Tertullian, *Apologeticum,* xxi., Trans. ANCL (Ante Nicene Christian Library), Edinburgh, 1868–70.
3. Josephus BJ cf. Flavius Josephus, *Jewish War,* trans. G. A. Williamson, London, 1959. i.4.6.
4. *The Eerdmans Bible Dictionary,* Grand Rapids, 1987, p. 246.

Chapter II. Paul

1. *Oxford Companion to the Bible,* New York, Oxford, 1993, p. 40.i.
2. Eerdmans, *Oxford Dictionary of the Christian Church* (*ODCC*), Oxford, 1997.
3. Epistulae as Lucilium cxx. cf. *Seneca,* M. T. Griffin, Oxford, 1976.
4. *Encyclopaedia Britannica,* 14th Edtn, London & New York, 1932, p. 430, col. 2.
5. *Oxford Companion to the Bible,* p. 815.
6. cf. *Oxford Companion to the Bible,* p. 26, col. i.
7. 1 *Apologia* 14 qu C. C. Martindale, *St. Justin the Martyr,* London, 1921, p. 37.
8. Eusebius, *The History of the Church,* trans. G. A. Williamson, London, 1965, III, 5.
9. Eamon Duffy, *Saints and Sinners,* Yale, 1997, p. 51.
10. Flavius Josephus, *Jewish War,* trans. G. A. Williamson, VI, 2, 9, London, 1959.
11. Ibid., VI, 8, 4–5.

Chapter III. Early Writing and Worship

1. *Oxford Companion to the Bible* (*OCB*), p. 122.
2. Justin, *Apologies I* 65–66, English translation in ANCL, 1867.
3. *The Times,* August 12, 1999, p. 20.
4. Eusebius III 24.
5. Eusebius II 15.
6. Eusebius III 39.15.
7. Robert J. Miller, ed., *The Complete Gospels,* Calif., 1992, p. 371. *Infancy Gospel of Thomas* v 1–4.
8. Ibid., p. 393. *Infancy James* v 20.2.
9. Eusebius II 7.
10. John Malalas, *Chronography,* x.
11. Tertullian, *Apologeticum,* xxi.
12. *Gospel of Peter,* p. 403 v 4.
13. Correspondence with Trajan, F. S. Hardy, 1889. cf. J. Stevenson, ed., *A New Eusebius,* London, 1957.
14. 1 *Apologia* 14 qu C. C. Martindale, *St. Justin the Martyr,* London, 1921, p. 37.

15. Tim Dowley, ed., *The History of Christianity,* Batavia 116., 1990 edtn, p. 115.

16. Tertullian, *Apologeticum* 39.

17. Justin, *Apologies* 1 65–66.

18. H. Chadwick, *The Early Church,* London, 1967, pp. 262–64.

19. Chadwick, p. 275.

20. Chadwick, p. 54.

21. Vivian Green, *A New History of Christianity,* Stroud, UK, 1996, p. 13.

22. *Oxford Companion to the Bible,* p. 817.

23. Hugh Thomas, *The Slave Trade,* London, 1998 edtn, p. 25.

24. Philem 16. cf. J. Knox, *Philemon among the Letters of Paul,* Chicago, 1935.

25. Thomas, p. 31.

26. Chadwick, p. 49.

27. Robin Lane Fox, *Pagans and Christians,* London, 1988, p. 505.

28. Chadwick, p. 47.

29. Lane Fox, p. 501.

30. *Ancient Christian Writers* No. 13, *Tertullian on Marriage and Remarriage,* trans. W. P. Le Saint, Westminster, Md., 1951, p. 70.

31. Tertullian, *Apologetica,* 37; Chadwick, p. 65.

32. Lane Fox, pp. 269–70.

Chapter IV. The Blood of Martyrs

1. *The Fathers of the Church. Tertullian: Disciplinary, Moral, and Ascetic Works,* trans. R. Arbesmann, E. J. Daly, E. A. Quinn, New York, 1959, pp. 294–95.

2. *Tertullian,* ibid.

3. Passio SS Perpetuae et Felicitatis, *ODCC.*

4. H. Musurillo, *The Acts of the Christian Martyrs,* Oxford, 1972, pp. 106–31.

5. Eusebius VIII, 12.

6. Gregory of Tours.

7. Eusebius VIII, 12.

8. Ibid. VIII, 8.

9. Bishop Possidius, *Life of St. Augustine,* in *The Western Fathers,* F. R. Hoare, London, 1954, p. 236.

10. Eusebius VIII, 11.

11. Tacitus, *Annals,* C. D. Fisher, Oxford, 1906. 15:44.

12. Green, p. 23.

13. Tr. 110, Dialogue with Trypho. qu C. C. Martindale, *St. Justin the Martyr,* London, 1921, p. 40.

14. Justin 1, *Apologia* 17, Martindale, p. 38.

15. *The Ecclesiastical History and the Martyrs of Palestine,* trans. H. J. Lawlor and J. E. L. Oulton, London, 1927, vol. i, p. 123.

16. John McManners, ed., *Oxford Illustrated History of Christianity,* Oxford, 1990, p. 42.

17. Eusebius VI, 42.2.

18. Musurillo, pp. 47–53.

19. Musurillo, "The Acts of the Scillitan Martyrs," in *The Acts of the Christian Martyrs,* pp. 86–89.

20. Norman Davies, *Europe,* London, 1997, p. 180.

21. E. R. Hardy, ed., *Faithful Witnesses: Records of Early Christian Martyrs,* London, 1965, pp. 55–64.

22. Green, p. 18.

23. Eusebius VIII, 8.

24. Lane Fox, p. 421.

25. Musurillo, pp. xv–xvi.

26. Wordsworth, Michael, 48.

27. Martyrium Polycarpi XVII.3.

28. Duffy, p. 30.
29. *Oxford Illustrated History of Christianity,* p. 79.
30. Ibid., p. 78.
31. H. Chadwick, *Priscillian of Avila: The Occult and the Charismatic in the Early Church,* Oxford, 1976, p. 8.
32. V. Burrus, *The Making of a Heretic: Gender, Authority, and the Priscillianist Controversy,* London, 1995, pp. 26–27.
33. Burrus, p. 33.
34. *Fathers of the Church,* vol. 7, *Sulpicius Severus: Writings,* trans. B. M. Peebles, New York, 1949, p. 254.
35. Chadwick, *Priscillian of Avila,* p. 86.
36. Trans. Peebles, p. 253.
37. Trans. Peebles, pp. 253–54.

Chapter V. Constantine
1. Eusebius IX 5.1.
2. Ibid. IX 5.2.
3. Ibid. IX 8.
4. Ibid. IX 8.
5. Lactantius, *On the Death of the Persecutors* 44, 1–11, ed. Jacques Moreau, Paris, 1954, pp. 126–28, trans. John W. Eadie, in *The Conversion of Constantine,* ed. J. W. Eadie, New York, 1971, pp. 11–12.
6. Eusebius IX 9.9.
7. Ibid. X 5.1–11.
8. Ibid. X 7.2.
9. Ibid. X 8.11.
10. Lane Fox, p. 653.
11. Eusebius X 9.5.
12. Davies, p. 206.
13. Ibid., p. 208.
14. Lane Fox, p. 653.
15. Ibid., p. 666.
16. Eusebius X 6.
17. Dowley, p. 143.
18. Eusebius X 5.22.
19. Ibid. X 5.22.
20. Eusebius, *Vita Constantini* 3.15.
21. Lane Fox, p. 656.
22. Eusebius, *Vita Constantini.*
23. Richard Fletcher, *The Conversion of Europe,* London, 1998, p. 23.
24. Fletcher, p. 24.
25. Lane Fox, p. 310.
26. *Butler's Lives* i, p. 112 et seq.
27. Ibid.
28. *Res Gestae* XXVII iii 12–15; B. J. Kidd, ed., *Documents Illustrative of the History of the Church,* London, 1938, no. 94, p. 123.
29. P. R. Coleman Norton, *Roman State and Christian Church,* vol. 1, London, 1966, pp. 318–19.
30. *The Fathers of the Church,* vol. 26, *St. Ambrose: Letters,* trans. M. M. Beyerka, Washington, 1954.
31. Kidd, vol. II, p. 100.
32. Lane Fox, p. 667.

33. Ibid., p. 587.
34. Charles Freeman, *History Today* 51, no. 1, p. 12.
35. Res Gestae XXVII iii 12–15; Kidd, no. 94, p. 123.
36. St. Ambrose qu Butler iii, p. 189.
37. *Encyclopaedia Britannica,* XVII 926.i.
38. Dowley, pp. 146–47.
39. *St. Ambrose: Letters,* p. 24.

Chapter VI. Heretics

1. Eusebius X 5.
2. "Letter to the Church at Smyrna," in J. B. Lightfoot, *The Apostolic Fathers,* 1885, 8.2.
3. CIC can. 751.
4. "Letter to the Church at Tralles," 9.
5. "Letter to the Church at Smyrna," 3.
6. "Letter to the Church at Magnesia," 10.
7. "Letter to the Church at Philadelphia," 8.
8. "Letter to the Church at Tralles," 5.
9. Lane Fox, p. 332.
10. "Letter to the Church at Smyrna," 6.
11. Excerpta ex Theodoto: ("Excerpt of Letter to Theodoret"). 78.2.
12. *Encyclopaedia Britannica* XXII, 952.i.
13. Leo Ep XV to Turubius, Bishop of Astorga and Metropolitan of Gallaecia, in Kidd, vol. II, pp. 314–19.
14. R. E. Heine, *The Montanist Oracles and Testimonia,* Macon, Ga., 1989, p. 3.
15. Eusebius, Bishop of Caesarea, *The Ecclesiastical History of the Martyrs of Palestine,* c. 260–c. 340, trans. H. J. Lawler & J. E. L. Oulton, London, 1927, vol. 1, v. 16.7.
16. Ibid., v. 16.19.
17. Heine, p. 5, from *Epiphanius Panarion* or *Refutation of All the Heresies,* 49.1.
18. *Documents Illustrative of the History of the Church,* vol. 1, ed. B. J. Kidd, London, 1938, no. 100, Tertullian, *De anima* c. 208–11 c.ix.
19. Kidd, op cit, no. 119, *Hippolytus Refutatio omnium haeresium* VII 35 c. AD235.
20. Kidd, no. 120, *Hippolytus Refutatio omnium haeresium* ix.12.
21. Eusebius, *Martyrs of Palestine,* VI 43.i.
22. *The Fathers of the Church,* vol. 51, *St. Cyprian: Letters,* trans. R. B. Donna, Washington, 1964, Letter No. 52, Cyprian to Cornelius, p. 128.
23. *Encyclopaedia Britannica* VI 659.i.
24. Leo ep XV to Turubius, Kidd vol. II, pp. 314–19.

Chapter VII. Monks

1. St. Jerome, *The Life of St. Paul the First Hermit,* from *The Desert Fathers,* trans. from Latin and intro. by H. Waddell, London, 1936, p. 48.
2. Athanasius, *The Life of Antony,* trans. and intro. by R. C. Gregg, London, 1980, p. 31.2.
3. Ibid., p. 36.7.
4. Ibid., p. 99.94.
5. Waddell, p. 91.
6. Ibid., p. 138.
7. Gregg, p. 64.44.
8. Pachomian Koinonia, vol. I, *The Life of St. Pachomius and His Disciples,* trans. Armand Veilleux, Kalamazoo, Mich., 1980, p. 39.

9. Ibid., pp. 45–46.

10. Armand Veilleux, *The Rules of St. Pachomius,* Kalamazoo, Mich., 1980–82, vol. II, pp. 141–67.

11. Veilleux III, p. 37.

12. *Palladius: The Lausiac History,* trans. R. T. Meyer, Westminster, Md., 1965, p. 94.

13. Veilleux III, p. 14.

14. Ibid., II, p. 142.

15. Ibid., II, pp. 166–67.

16. *Oxford Companion to the Bible,* pp. 817–18.

17. *The Fathers of the Church,* vol. 22, *On St. Basil the Great,* trans. L. P. McCauley, new trans., Washington, 1951, pp. 78–79.

18. *The Fathers of the Church,* vol. 13, *St. Basil: Letters,* trans. A. C. Way, pp. 46–48.

19. *Fathers,* vol. 22, pp. 80–81.

20. Daniel J. Boorstin, *The Discoverers,* New York, 1985, p. 492.

21. Anon., *The History of the Monks of Egypt,* in *Oxford Illustrated History of Christianity,* p. 130.

22. *Lives of the Monks of Palestine, Cyril of Scythopolis,* trans. R. M. Price, Kalamazoo, Mich., 1991, p. 57.

23. *Oxford Illustrated History of Christianity,* p. 135.

24. Ibid.

25. *A History of the Monks of Syria, Theodoret of Cyrrhus, 393–466,* trans. R. M. Price, Kalamazoo, Mich., 1985, p. 7.

26. *A Select Library of Nicene and Post-Nicene Fathers of the Christian Church,* vol. III, Oxford, 1982, from *The Ecclesiastical History of Theodoret,* trans. B. Jackson, pp. 114–15.

27. Ibid.

28. Ibid., and *The Imperial Church from Constantine to the Early Middle Ages,* K. Baus, H.-G. Beck, G. Ewig, H. J. Vogt, trans. A. Biggs, London, 1980, pp. 371–72.

29. qu *Les Saints Stylites,* H. Delehaye, Brussels, 1923, p. 174, from *Georgs der Araber-Bischofs Gedichte und Briefe,* p. 5.

30. qu ibid., p. 174.

31. Ibid., p. 176.

Chapter VIII. Augustine

1. Augustine, *Confessions,* trans. H. Chadwick, Oxford, 1992, III i (1).

2. *Lives of the Fathers, The Life of St. Augustine,* F. W. Farrar, Edinburgh, 1889, and London, 1993, p. 180.

3. *Confessions* III iv (7)–III iv (8), pp. 38–39.

4. Ibid. III iv (8), p. 40.

5. Ibid. IX i.

6. Ibid. IX x (25).

7. Ibid., fn p. 174.

8. Ibid. X xxvii (38), p. 201.

9. *The Western Fathers,* trans. and ed. F. R. Hoare, London, 1954, pp. 202–3.

10. Ibid., p. 229.

11. Ibid.

12. *Victor of Vita, History of the Vandal Persecution,* trans. J. Moorhead, Liverpool, 1992. *Translated Texts for Historians,* vol. 10, p. I.4.

13. Hoare, p. 232.

14. Ibid., p. 233.

15. Ibid., p. 239.

16. Ibid., p. 242.

17. Ibid., p. 236.

18. Ibid., p. 237.

19. *History of the Vandal Persecution,* p. 91, III.67.

Chapter IX. The Islamic Invasions

1. *The History of Al-Tabari,* vol. 13, trans. G. H. A. Juynboll, Albany, 1989, pp. 163–65.

2. *Chronique de Seert* II, p. 261; cf. L. E. Browne, *The Eclipse of Christianity in Asia,* Cambridge, 1933, p. 41.

3. *Chronique de Michel le Syrien* II, pp. 412–13.

4. Gibbon, *Decline and Fall,* Everyman's Library, ch. 50, v. 207.

5. Butler IV, p. 198, col. 2.

6. Ibid., p. 199, col. 1.

7. Yemen, p. 72.

8. A. S. Atiya, *A History of Eastern Christianity,* London, 1968, p. 259.

9. *Encyclopaedia Britannica* XV, p. 649.

10. qu Atiya, p. 148.

11. Kitab al-kharaj, p. 79; cf. L. E. Browne, p. 29.

12. Davies, p. 245.

13. F. E. Peters, *Jerusalem,* Princeton, 1985, p. 170.

14. Ibid., pp. 170–73.

15. Ibid. from Conybeare, 1910, 506:513.

16. Browne, p. 34.

17. Koran Sura V-85.

18. II 214–15; viii 39–42.

19. Abu Yusuf, p. 171; cf. Browne, p. 31.

20. Al-Baladhuri, cf. Browne, p. 132.

21. Assemani III pt. II xcvi.

22. J. Coubage, *Christians and Jews under Islam,* trans J. Mabro, London, 1997, p. 9.

23. Browne, p. 33.

24. Ibid.

25. Atiya, p. 270.

26. Abdul-Hasan Ali bin al-Shabushti (died 998), *The Book of Monasteries,* ed. Gurgis 'Awivad, Baghdad, 1951.

27. *Al-Tabari,* vol. 12, trans. J. Friedman, Albany, 1992, p. 175.

28. Ibid., p. 175.

29. Ibid.

30. *Chronique de Michel le Syrien* II, p. 412.

31. qu Peters, p. 175.

32. Conybeare, 1910, 506:513.

33. *Ya'quibi History* II 167.

34. *Bishop John of Nikiu,* cxix. 12.

35. Atiya, p. 226.

36. Qaduma d. 948, *The Cambridge Medieval History,* vol. 4, *The Byzantine Empire,* ed. J. M. Hussey, Cambridge, 1966, p. 697.

37. Atiya, p. 77.

38. qu Atiya, p. 77.

39. *The Chronicle of John, Bishop of Nikiu,* trans. R. H. Charles, Oxford, 1916, cxv.9.

40. Ibid., cxi.10.

41. Ibid., cxi.12.

42. Ibid., cxi.14.

43. Atiya, p. 80.
44. *Chronicle of John, Bishop of Nikiu,* cxii.4.
45. *Al-Tabari,* vol. XIII, p. 164.
46. Ibid., cxii.10.
47. *Al-Tabari,* p. 170.
48. Ibid., p. 168.
49. *Chronicle of John, Bishop of Nikiu,* cxxiii.10.
50. Ibid., cxxi.10–11.
51. Ibid., cxiii.2.
52. Ibid., cxiii.6.
53. Ibid., cxix.4.
54. Ibid., cxx.6.
55. Ibid., cxx.4.
56. *Al-Tabari,* p. 164.
57. *Chronicle of John, Bishop of Nikiu,* cxx.17.
58. *Al-Tabari,* p. 167.
59. Ibid., p. 173.
60. Ibid., p. 173.
61. *Chronicle of John, Bishop of Nikiu,* cxx.30.
62. Ibid., cxxiii.7.
63. Browne, p. 42.
64. Atiya, p. 84.
65. Coubage, p. 32.
66. *Church History,* vol. 19, 1960, pp. 379–97.
67. Ibn 'Abd al Hakam, *Conquete de l'Afrique du Nord et de l'Espagne,* trans. A. Gateau, Alger, 1948, pp. 61 et seq.
68. Ibid., p. 63.
69. *Al-Tabari,* vol. 18, trans. M. G. Morony, Albany, 1987, pp. 102–3.
70. Gateau, p. 73.
71. *Al-Tabari,* vol. 13, p. 175.
72. Gateau, p. 79.
73. Ibid.
74. *The Chronicle of Theophanes anni mundi 6095–6305 (602–813 A.D),* trans. H. Turtledove, Philadelphia, 1982, p. 68.
75. Theophanes, p. 68.
76. qu from Alfonso X, A. G. Chejne, *Muslim Spain,* Minneapolis, 1974, p. 126.
77. *The Chronicle of 754 (Anonymous Continuation of the Chronicle of John of Biclaro)* in *Conquerors and Chroniclers of Early Medieval Spain,* trans. and intro. by K. B. Wolf, Liverpool, 1990, p. 132.
78. *The Fourth Book of the Chronicle of Fredegor with its Continuations,* trans. J. M. Wallace-Hadrill, London, 1960, p. 90.
79. Ibid., p. 91.
80. Coubage, p. 39.
81. Richard Hall, *Emperor of the Monsoon,* London, 1998, p. 246.
82. Atiya, p. 261.
83. C. Carey-Elwes, *China and the Cross,* London, 1957, p. 24.
84. Ibid., p. 54.
85. A. C. Moule, *Christians in China Before the Year 1550,* London, 1930, p. 111.
86. Ibid., pp. 172–73.
87. Carey-Elwes, p. 60.

Chapter X. The Pagan Conversions

1. Duffy, p. 48.
2. Ibid., p. 38.
3. Richard Fletcher, *The Conversion of Europe,* London, 1998, p. 112.
4. Duffy, p. 50.
5. Ibid., p. 51.
6. Judith Herrin, *The Formation of Christendom,* London, 1987, p. 240.
7. Fletcher, p. 104.
8. Ibid., p. 113.
9. Ibid., p. 111.
10. Duffy, p. 56.
11. Fletcher, p. 49, from Gregory of Tours.
12. Bede, *A History of the English Church and People,* trans. Leo Shirley-Price, London, 1955 i. 30, pp. 86–87.
13. Fletcher, p. 118.
14. Ibid., p. 85.
15. L. M. Bitel, *Saints: Monastic Settlement in Early Ireland,* Cork, 1990, p. 102.
16. *Adomnán's Life of Columba,* ed. and trans. A. O. and M. O. Anderson, Oxford, 1991, p. 7.
17. J. Ryan, *Irish Monasticism,* Dublin, 1931, p. 241.
18. J. Marsden, *Sea Road of the Saints,* Edinburgh, 1995, p. 17.
19. *Adomnán* p. 15 i.i.
20. Ibid., pp. 16–17.
21. Bitel, p. 226.
22. Fletcher, p. 206, from Willibald's *Life of Boniface.*
23. *ODCC,* p. 290.
24. *Epistolae Kaorilini Aevi* qu Dowley, p. 239.
25. Fletcher, p. 214.
26. Ibid., p. 373.
27. Ibid., p. 391.
28. Ibid., p. 153.
29. Davies, p. 325.
30. Fletcher, p. 385.
31. Ibid., p. 413.
32. *ODCC,* p. 821.
33. Duffy, p. 82.
34. Davies, p. 249.
35. Peter de Rosa, *Vicars of Christ,* London, 1989, p. 68.
36. Ibid., p. 71.
37. Ibid., p. 76.
38. W. E. H. Lecky, *History of European Morals,* 2 vols., London, 1911.
39. De Rosa, p. 86.
40. Fletcher, p. 439.
41. Ibid.
42. Fletcher, p. 488.
43. Ibid., p. 501.
44. Ibid., p. 502.
45. Ibid., p. 505.

Chapter XI. Crusades

1. Fulcher of Chartres, *A History of the Expedition to Jerusalem, 1095–1127*, book 1, chapter 3, trans. Rita Ryan, Tennessee, 1969.
2. Baldric of Bourgueil in *Historia Jerosolimitana;* Guibert of Nogent in *Historia quae dicitur Gesta Dei per Francos;* Robert the Monk in *Historia Heirosolymitana* in *RHC Occ,* vol. 3, pp. 727–29.
3. Matthew of Edessa, p. 37.
4. Nicephorous Bryennius.
5. Fulcher.
6. Fulcher of Chartres, *Historia Hierosolymitana,* ed. H. Hagenmeyer, Heidelberg, 1913.
7. Anon., *Gesta Francorum,* ed. R. Hill, London, 1962.
8. R. W. Southern, *The Making of the Middle Ages,* London, 1953, p. 34.
9. Elizabeth Hallam, ed., *Chronicles of the Crusades,* London, 1989, p. 25.
10. Michael Cerularius, Letter to Peter of Antioch.
11. *The Alexiad of Anna Comnena,* Book X, trans. E. R. A. Sewter, 1969.
12. Runciman, *A History of the Crusades,* i, p. 101.
13. Amatus of Montecassino, *History of the Normans.*
14. cf. Barbara Tuchman, *A Distant Mirror,* London, 1995 edition, p. 34.
15. Hallam, p. 13.
16. Lambert of Hersfeld, *Chronicon, MGH SRG,* 1895.
17. Ibid.
18. Geoffrey of Malaterra, *Sicilian History,* ed. E. Pontieri, Bologna, 1927–28, ii iv qu p. 51, col. 1.
19. qu Amin Maalouf, *The Crusades through Arab Eyes,* p. 205.
20. Guibert of Nogent, *Historia Hierosolymitana* in *RHC OCC* iv cf. Régine Pernoud, *The Crusades,* trans. Enid McLeod, London, 1962, p. 27.
21. Ibid., p. 27.
22. Ibid., p. 28.
23. Robert the Monk, *Historia Hierosolymitana.*
24. Ibid., p. 28.
25. Salomon Bar Simeon qu Pernoud, p. 30.
26. Guibert, ibid., p. 31.
27. Bishop Lietbert of Cambrai, *Chronicon S Andrei Cameracensis,* 29–31.
28. *The Alexiad of Anna Comnena,* book 10, trans. E. R. A. Sewter, Penguin, 1969, p. 309.
29. *Gesta Francorum* qu p. 34.
30. Comnena, p. 312.
31. B. Guérard, ed., *Cartulaire de l'Abbaye de Saint-Victor de Marseille,* vol. 1. Paris, 1857, p. 167.
32. H. Hagenmeyer, ed., *Die Kreuzzegsbriefe aus den Jahren, 1088–1100,* Innsbruck, 1901.
33. *Anna Comnena,* p. 422.
34. Maalouf, p. 39.
35. *Anna Comnena* qu Pernoud p. 51.
36. Richard the Pilgrim, *Chanson d'Antioche,* 76.
37. *Gesta Francorum,* 74.
38. *Miscellanea Historica Alberti di Meyer,* trans. from Armenian into Latin by Father Peeters.
39. Guibert of Nogent, *Historia Hierosolymitana* qu Hallam p. 85.
40. Fulcher of Chartres, 85.
41. Radulph of Caen, Hallam, p. 89.
42. *Gesta Francorum,* Pernoud, p. 90.
43. *Gesta Francorum.*
44. *Die Kreuzzusgbriefe* op cit, p. 93.

Chapter XII. The Laws of War

1. *The Damascene Chronicler Sibt Ibn Al-Jawzi* qu Maalouf, p. ii.
2. Siberry, p. 30.
3. Augustine, reply to Faustus the Manichaean at xxii, 73–79.
4. Ibid., 73–79.
5. *Confessions* 12.25.
6. Ep ad Marcellinus, 138.
7. *Civitatis Dei,* book 19, 21.
8. *Decretals: Decreti secunda pars cause* XXIII Quest. I, c. 6.
9. Quest IV, c. 48.
10. Quest V, c. 46.
11. Quest III, c. 5.
12. Quest VIII, c. 28.
13. Quest I, c. 7.
14. Quest VIII, c. 6.
15. Maalouf, p. 69.
16. Steven Runciman, *A History of the Crusades,* vol. 2, London, 1990 edition, p. 465.
17. Pernoud, p. 105.
18. *Gesta Francorum,* Pernoud, p. 99.
19. Imad el-Din, *Crusades,* trans. A. Ereira and T. Jones, London, 1996, p. 63.
20. Trans. Ryan, p. 271.
21. Desmond Seward, *The Monks of War,* London, 1995 edition, p. 32.
22. *De laude novae militiae* iii, 4 in S. Bernardi, *Opera,* ed. J. Leclerq and H. M. Rochais, 3 vols., Rome, 1963, p. 217, trans. Kendar, p. 61.
23. *Bull Quantum praedecessores Eugenius* III.
24. John of Joinville, 158–59.
25. Jacques of Vitry, Pernoud, p. 223.
26. *Scripita Leonis, Rufini et Angeli sociorum S Francisci,* ed. and trans. Rosalind B. Brooke, Oxford, 1970, pp. 214–15. St. Francis was referring to Charlemagne and his generals.
27. Charles Panati, *Sacred Origins of Profound Things,* London, 1997, p. 235.
28. Louise and Jonathan Riley-Smith, *The Crusades: Idea and Reality, 1095–1274* (1981).
29. Siberry, p. 208.
30. Benjamin Z. Kedar, *Crusade and Mission,* Princeton, 1984, pp. 106–7.
31. Ibid., pp. 104–5.
32. *The Alexiad of Anna Comnena,* book 10, trans. E. R. A. Sewter, 1969.
33. *De expugnatione Lyxbonensis,* ed. C. W. David, New York, 1936, pp. 184–85.
34. Kedar, p. 52.
35. Ibid., p. 43.
36. *Eudes of Deuil,* Kedar, p. 66.
37. *The Travels of Ibn Jubayr,* trans. R. J. C. Broadhurst, London, 1952, p. 323.
38. Albert of Aachen, see vi, 5, p. 469 et seq in *RHC HOCC* 4:295.
39. Kedar, p. 90.
40. J. Kritzek, *Peter the Venerable and Islam,* Princeton, 1964, p. 231.
41. Maalouf, p. 131.
42. St. Bernard of Clairvaux, *Epistolae MPL* vol. clxxxii Runciman i, p. 254.
43. *Annales Herbipolenses Wurzburg,* annals in *MGH SS* xvi Hallam, p. 137.
44. Imad ad-Din al-Isfahani.
45. Imad ad-Din al-Isfahani.
46. *Itinerarium regis Ricardi,* ed. W. Stubbs, London, 1964. qu Hallam, p. 160.
47. *Itinerarium regis Ricardi,* qu Hallam, p. 156.

48. *Annales Herbipolenses* 3 *MGH SS* xvi.
49. Austorc d'Aurillac, *Ai! Dieus per qu'as facha STT* i, iii qu p. 194.
50. Elizabeth Siberry, *Criticism of Crusading, 1095–1274,* Oxford, 1985, p. 121.
51. Ibid., pp. 128–29.
52. Matthew Paris CM v 524.
53. Caesar of Heisterbach, *Dialogus Miracolorum* i, 70–72.
54. Siberry, p. 163.
55. Lecky.
56. Villehardouin, p. 50.
57. Ibid., p. 59.
58. Runciman III, p. 121.
59. Villehardouin, p. 83.
60. Ibid., p. 92.
61. *Crusades,* p. 167.
62. Innocent III PL XXXV qu pp. 173–74.
63. *Chronica Regine Coloniensis Continuatio prima 1213;* cf J. A. Brundage, *The Crusades: A Documentary Survey,* Milwaukee, 1962, p. 213.
64. *Chronica Majora Matthew Paris;* cf L. and J. Riley-Smith, *The Crusades: Idea and Reality,* p. 141.
65. Brundage, p. 213.
66. Ibid.
67. *Annales Marbacenses MGH SS* XVII p. 172 qu pp. 332–33.
68. *Annales Placentini Guelfi ad ann. 1212 MGH SS* XVII p. 426.
69. *Annales Alberti Abbatis Stadiensis MGH SS* XVI p. 355 cf p. 335.
70. *Sigeberti Gemblacensis Chronica MGH SS* VI p. 467.
71. *Chronica Albrici Monachi Trium Fontium MGH SS* XXII pp. 893–94.
72. Estoire d'Eracles.
73. *Guilhelm Figueira poem D'un sirventes far STT* III, vii qu p. 174.
74. Pernoud, p. 280.
75. Hallam, p. 280.
76. Pernoud, p. 259.
77. Niccolo Barbaro qu Hallam pp. 316–17.
78. Doukas, *Decline and Fall of Byzantium,* trans. H. J. Magoulias, Detroit, 1975, p. 218, para. 18.
79. *The Fall of the Byzantine Empire: A Chronicle by George Sphrantzes, 1401–1477,* trans. M. Philippides, Amherst, 1980, pp. 124–25.

Chapter XIII. Manifestations of the Spirit

1. G. K. Chesterton, *Father Brown Stories: The Hammer of God,* London, 1994 edition, p. 130.
2. Jean Gimpel, *The Cathedral Builders,* London, 1983, p. 14.
3. Ibid., p. 34.
4. Ibid., p. 48.
5. Dowley, p. 313.
6. *De diligendo Deo* c. 10.
7. Marina Warner, *Alone of All Her Sex,* London, 2000, p. 128.
8. Trans. Christopher Page, *Hyperion Notes,* pp. 8–10.
9. *Meister Eckhart: Treatises and Sermons,* trans. James M. Clark and John Skinner, London, 1994 edition, pp. 136–37.
10. Ibid., pp. 48–49.
11. Davies, pp. 279–80.
12. Tuchman, *A Distant Mirror,* p. 31.
13. Ibid., p. 32.

14. Green, p. 83.

15. G. Appleton, ed., *The Oxford Book of Prayer,* Oxford, 1985, no. 217.

16. *Butler's Lives* iii, p. 132.

17. Ibid. iii, p. 145.

18. De Rosa, p. 228.

19. Lord Acton, *Essays in the Liberal Interpretation of History,* London, 1967 edition.

20. Dowley, p. 327.

21. Emmanuel Le Roy Ladurie, *Montaillou,* London, 1980 edition, p. 81.

22. Ibid., p. 123.

23. De Rosa, p. 223.

24. Ibid., p. 224.

25. Ladurie, p. 13.

26. Ibid., p. 297.

27. Ibid., p. 224.

28. Gregor PP I Homil. in Evangel. XL 8.

29. *Annales Alberti Abbatis Stadensis ad ann 1212 MGH SS* xvi, p. 355 qu *A History of the Crusades,* ed. Robert Lee Wolff and Harry W. Hazard, Philadelphia, 1962, vol. 2, p. 328.

30. Matthew Paris, *Chronica Majora,* vol. 246.

31. Philip Ziegler, *Black Death,* London, 1969, p. 17.

32. Norman Cohn, *The Pursuit of the Millennium,* London, 1970, p. 127.

33. Ziegler, p. 41.

34. Ibid., pp. 18–19.

35. Ibid., p. 20.

36. Ibid., p. 39.

37. Tuchman, *A Distant Mirror,* p. 109.

38. Cohn, p. 136.

39. De Smet, *Brevi Chronicum Clerici Anonymi,* vol. 2, p. 17 qu Ziegler, p. 67.

40. Cohn, p. 139.

Chapter XIV. Early Reformers

1. H. E. Winn, ed., "Sermons Ye Fourthe Sondai aftir Estir," in *Wycliff: Select English Writings,* Oxford, 1929, p. 4.

2. Ibid., p. 3.

3. Ibid., p. 4.

4. Ibid., p. 3.

5. "Pardoner's Prologue," *Canterbury Tales,* 500–503.

6. "Pardoner's Prologue," lines 5–125, and 594.

7. "Pardoner's Prologue," 165–206.

8. D. Fountain, *John Wycliffe: The Dawn of the Reformation,* Southampton, 1984, p. 18.

9. G. Mollat, *The Popes at Avignon, 1305–1378,* trans. J. Love, London, 1963, p. 67.

10. Ibid., p. xx.

11. H. G. Beck et al., *History of the Church,* vol. 4, *High Middle Ages to the Eve of the Reformation,* London, 1980, p. 338.

12. Ibid., p. 343.

13. Petrarch, *Liber Sine Nomine,* trans. N. P. Zacour as *Book without a Name,* Toronto, 1973, p. 74.

14. Ibid., p. 88.

15. Mollat, p. 249.

16. *I, Catherine: Selected Writings of St. Catherine of Siena,* ed. and trans. K. Foster and H. J. Ronayne, London, 1980, p. 109.

17. J. H. Dahmus, *The Prosecution of John Wycliff,* New Haven, 1952, p. 46.

18. Ibid., p. 48.

19. De Rosa, p. 124.

20. *Wyclif, De Potestate Papae: Documents in Renaissance and Reformation History,* ed. D. Webster and L. Green, Melbourne, 1960, p. 138.

21. Green, p. 107.

22. Robert Mannyng in *Handlyng Synne* c. 1303 qu Green, p. 107.

23. Fountain, p. 37.

24. Dahmus, pp. 93–95.

25. Fountain, p. 40.

26. Ibid., pp. 23–26.

27. T. Arnold, ed., *Select English Works of John Wyclif,* Oxford, 1871, iii 98–99.

28. Fountain, p. 45.

29. A. Hudson, ed., *Selections from English Wycliffite Writings,* Cambridge, 1978, p. 10.

30. Green, p. 96.

31. Ibid., p. 96.

32. J. Gairdner, *Lollardy and the Reformation in England,* London, 1908, vol. 1, p. 48.

33. H. S. Cronin, "The Twelve Conclusions of the Lollards," *English Historical Review* 22, 1907 qu Davies, p. 405.

34. *Oxford Dictionary at the Christian Church,* p. 464, col. ii. The act's Latin title was *De Haeretico Comburendo.*

35. Gairdner, vol. 1, p. 51.

36. Ibid., p. 52.

37. Bale, op cit 87.

38. Gairdner, vol. 1, p. 73.

39. Ibid., vol. 1, p. 78.

40. H. Christmas, ed., *Select Works of John Bale, Bishop of Ossory, 1495–1563,* Cambridge, 1849, p. 42.

41. M. Aston, *Lollards and Reformers,* London, 1984, p. 21.

42. Ibid., p. 25.

43. Christmas, p. 56.

44. M. Spinka, *John Hus,* Princeton, 1968, p. 59.

45. G. R. Elton, ed., *Renaissance and Reformation,* New York, 1976, p. 14.

46. Ibid., pp. 138–40.

47. De Rosa, p. 128.

48. Spinka, p. 178.

49. "Chronicle of Ulrich Richental," *The Council of Constance: The Unification of the Church,* trans. L. R. Loomis, ed. J. Hine Mundy and K. M. Woody, New York and London, 1961, pp. 129 et seq.

50. Ibid.

51. The legate was named Palec. Spinka, p. 241.

52. *The Times,* August 12, 1999, p. 20.

53. Loomis, p. 469.

54. Loomis, p. 130.

55. *Oxford Dictionary of the Christian Church,* p. 404, col. i.

56. *Decline and Fall.*

57. *The Trial of Hus, in 2 Letters by a Member of the Council, Fra Poggius to Leonhard Nikolai,* ed. B. von Berchem, New York, 1930, pp. 43–49, p. 44.

58. Ibid., p. 59.

59. Ibid., p. 59.
60. Peter of Mladonovice, *An Account of the Trial and Condemnation of Master John Hus in Constance from John Huss at the Council of Constance,* trans. and ed. M. Spinka, New York, 1965, p. 225.
61. Peter, in Spinka, pp. 230–31.
62. Richental, p. 132.
63. Ibid., p. 133.
64. Peter, in Spinka, p. 232.
65. Ibid., 233. Richental says that he "started to preach in German, but Duke Louis would not permit that and ordered them to burn him."
66. Ibid., p. 165.
67. Ibid., pp. 233–34.
68. Inferno III.
69. *Paradiso* xxvii 22–27.
70. Eileen Gardner, ed., "Tundale's Vision," in *Visions of Heaven and Hell before Dante,* New York, 1989; pp. 149–95.
71. *Paradiso,* 3.
72. Spinka. p. 234.
73. Cohn, p. 216.
74. Ibid., p. 218.

Chapter XV. Papal Attitudes

1. Lisa Jardine, *Wordly Goods,* London, 1966, p. 248.
2. L. Pastor, *History of the Popes from the Close of the Middle Ages,* vol. 2, London, 1912, p. 166 qu Duffy, p. 139.
3. Duffy, p. 133.
4. Jardine, p. 365.
5. Petrarch, *Secretum Meum,* in H. Baron, *Petrarch's Secretum: Its Making and Meaning,* Cambridge, Mass., 1985.
6. Niccolo Machiavelli, *The Prince,* trans. George Bull, London, 1995 edition, p. 38.
7. Ibid., p. 58.
8. Jardine, "History of Mehmed the Conqueror by Kritovoulos of Imbros," in *Worldly Goods,* pp. 72–73.
9. *Decretals Ad Conditorem Canonum of 1322* and *Cum Inter Nonnullos 1323.*
10. "The Talks of Instruction," in *Meister Eckhart,* trans. James M. Clark and John Skinner, London, 1994 edition, xx. p. 74.
11. Thomas à Kempis, *Imitation of Christ,* trans. L. Sherey-Price, London, 1952, I.i.
12. W. G. Naphy, ed. and trans., *Documents on the Continental Reformation,* Basingstoke, 1996, p. 7.
13. Cohn, p. 229.
14. Roberto Ridolfi, *Life of G. Savonarola,* trans. C. Grayson, London, 1959, p. 20.
15. O. Ferrara, *The Borgia Pope: Alexander VI,* trans. F. J. Sheed, London, 1942, p. 236.
16. M. de la Bedoyere, *The Meddlesome Friar,* London, 1957, pp. 60–61.
17. Ibid., p. 86.
18. Ibid., p. 90.
19. P. van Passen, *A Crown of Fire: The Life and Times of Girolamo Savonarola,* London, 1961, p. 110.
20. De la Bedoyere, p. 101.
21. Van Passen, p. 112.
22. *The Prince,* pp. 19–20.
23. *The Praise of Folly,* trans. Hoyt Hopewell Hudson, Princeton, 1941, pp. 56–98, K. H. Donnenfeldt, in *The Church of the Renaissance and Reformation,* St. Louis, Mo., 1970, p. 124.

24. *Daily Telegraph,* January 9, 1999, p. 22.

25. Erasmus to Marcus Laurinus, written April 1518. Naphy, p. 10.

26. September 13, 1520. *Opus Epistolarum Des. Erasmi* IV, 345. qu Hillerbrand, p. 424.

Chapter XVI. Printing and Protestants

1. Jardine, p. 160.

2. Jerome, p. 166.

3. *The Prince,* p. 54.

4. Ibid., p. 81.

5. De Rosa, p. 155.

6. J. A. Froud, *Life and Letters of Erasmus,* London, 1895, p. 158.

7. Duffy, p. 148.

8. De Rosa, p. 138.

9. Duffy, p. 150.

10. Green, p. 119.

11. Naphy, p. 11.

12. Frederick Mecum in Naphy, p. 12.

13. Friedrich Myconius, *Historia reformationis,* p. 14 qu Hillerbrand, p 43.

14. J. Hillerbrand, ed. and trans., *The Protestant Reformation,* London, 1968, p. 23.

15. Ibid., p. 28.

16. *Acta Augustana 1518,* p. 63.

17. Chadwick.

18. Ibid., p. 56.

Chapter XVII. The Bible as Lethal Weapon

1. *Oxford Companion to the Bible,* p. 80.

2. Menno Simons, *The Complete Writings,* Scottsdale, 1956, pp. 668–72.

3. *Oxford Dictionary of the Christian Church,* p. 1070.

4. Narrative of William Maldon, Harleian MS 590, folio 77. qu Hillerbrand, pp. 336–37.

5. To Count Ernst of Mansfeld, in Hillerbrand, p. 225.

6. *A supplicacyion for the Beggars de Rosa,* pp. 140–41.

7. A. G. Dickens, *The English Reformation,* London, 1989, p. 84.

8. Martin Luther, "Friendly Admonition to Peace, 1525," *Works of Martin Luther: The Philadelphia Edition,* vol. 4, Philadelphia, 1931, pp. 219–44.

9. Duffy, p. 137.

10. Luther, *Philadelphia Edition.*

11. *The Cambridge Modern History,* vol. 2, *The Reformation,* ed. A. W. Ward, G. W. Prother, & S. Leathes, Cambridge, 1904, chapter 6 by A. F. Pollard, p. 191.

12. Luther, "Friendly Admonition to Peace," *Philadelphia Edition,* vol. 4.

13. All above are ibid.

14. *The Prague Manifesto,* in Hillerbrand, pp. 223–24.

15. Green, p. 154.

16. Otto Brandt, pp. 38–39, in Hillerbrand, pp. 222–23.

17. Cohn, p. 239.

18. May 12, 1525, to Count Ernst of Mansfeld, in Hillerbrand, p. 225.

19. Response of the Rulers, May 15, 1525, Hillerbrand, p. 226.

20. Ibid., p. 227.

Chapter XVIII. Calvin and the Puritans

1. Hillerbrand, pp. 162–63.
2. *Zwinglis Samtliche Werke* VII 110ff, Hillerbrand, pp. 116–17.
3. Heinrich Bullinger, *Reformationsgeschichte* I 12.
4. Hillerbrand, pp. 121–22.
5. *ODCC*, p. 386, col. ii.
6. Conclusion XVIII *Samtliche Werke* I 458–61, Hillerbrand, pp. 132–33.
7. Walther Kohler, *Das Marburger Religionsgesprach*, pp. 6–37.
8. Cohn, p. 259.
9. Ibid., p. 260.
10. *Chronik des Schwesterhauses Marienthal*, pp. 430–32, Hillerbrand p. 254.
11. Cohn, p. 262.
12. Ibid., p. 267.
13. *Meister Heinrich Greshek's Bericht*, pp. 32–33, Hillerbrand, p. 257.
14. Ibid., p. 256.
15. Ibid., p. 259.
16. Cohn, p. 272.
17. Ibid.
18. *Neue Zeitung*, in Hillerbrand, pp. 261–62.
19. May 21, 1535, letter, Justinian von Holtzhausen, in Hillerbrand, p. 262.
20. *Corvinus Epistola* in Hillerbrand, p. 266.
21. Commentaries, Psalms, pp. xl–xli.
22. Beza, p. lxi.
23. Naphy, pp. 53–54.
24. Chadwick, p. 86.
25. "Luther: Lyndal Roper," *History Today* (December 1983): p. 33.
26. Ibid., p. 34.
27. Ibid., p. 37.
28. Ibid., p. 37.
29. Naphy, *Calvin Documents*, pp. 53–54.
30. By Benedict XIV in his pronouncement Vix pervenit.
31. "Address to the Christian Nobility of the German Nation on the Improvement of the Christian Estate."
32. Hillerbrand, p. 200.
33. Ibid., p. 202.
34. Ibid., p. 203.
35. Commentaries, Psalms, in Hillerbrand, p. 197.
36. Beza, *Life of Calvin*, cxx–cxxxi.
37. Green, p. 136.
38. Beza, *Life of Calvin*, cxx–cxxi.
39. *Oxford Dictionary of the Christian Church*, p. 801, col. i.

Chapter XIX. English Speakers

1. Green, p. 146.
2. *The Answer of King Henry VIII . . . unto the letter of Martin Luther*, Hillerbrand, pp. 408–9.
3. *Dictionary of National Biography (Oxford)*, XIII, p. 883.
4. Venetian calendar IV, p. 365.
5. Hillerbrand, p. 323.
6. Gee and Hardy, pp. 243–44.

7. Chadwick, Owen, *The Reformation,* London, 1964, pp. 384–85.

8. Ellis qu Hillerbrand, p. 340.

9. Green, p. 146.

10. Gee and Hardy, pp. 303–36.

11. Green, p. 145.

12. John Foxe, *Book of Martyrs,* pp. 250–51.

13. Green, p. 147.

14. Gee and Hardy, pp. 373–75.

15. Ellis, *Original Letters, Second Series* II, 263ff.

16. *Dictionary of National Biography,* XVI, p. 29, col. ii.

17. *Goldsmid Collection of Documents* II, 16 qu Hillerbrand, p. 352.

18. *Dictionary of National Biography,* V, p. 21 et seq.

19. Harleian MS. 422, Hillerbrand, p. 354.

20. Green, p. 148.

21. John Knox, *History of the Reformation* II qu Hillerbrand, pp. 358–59.

22. Knox, *History of the Reformation* I, pp. 76–78.

23. Ibid., pp. 136–37.

24. Ibid., p. 132f.

25. Ibid., pp. 336–37.

26. Sir Peter Young to Theodore Beza, November 13, 1579, John Knox, Hume Brown, Edinburgh, 1895, II 322f.

27. Knox, *History of the Reformation* I, pp. 338f.

Chapter XX. Counter-Reformation

1. The Sermon of Doctor Colet, made to the Convocation at St. Paul's, pp. 293–97.

2. Green, p. 162.

3. Butler ii, p. 218.

4. Green, p. 175.

5. Chadwick, p. 439.

6. Green, p. 171.

7. Page 37.

8. Page 41.

9. Benvenuto Cellini, *Autobiography,* trans. George Bull, London, 1956, pp. 75–79.

10. Duffy, p. 159.

11. Cellini, *Autobiography,* p. 136.

12. Ibid., pp. 106–7.

13. Chadwick, p. 371.

14. Duffy, p. 164.

15. *Jesuits,* p. 55.

16. Duffy, p. 170.

17. Suleiman the Magnificent, *A Bridge,* Frogmore, St. Albans, Herts., 1984, p. 115.

18. Ibid., p. 118.

19. Ibid., p. 118.

20. Ibid., p. 120.

21. George Vernadsky, *Russia,* 4th ed., New Haven, 1954, p. 109.

22. Davies, p. 505.

23. Chadwick, pp. 283–84.

Chapter XXI. The Spanish Inquisition

1. Milton, *Areopagitica.*
2. Jardine, p. 173.
3. Chadwick, p. 374.
4. Henry Kamen, *The Spanish Inquisition,* London, 1965, p. 68.
5. Ibid., p. 75.
6. Ibid., p. 251.
7. Letter to the grand duchess Cristina di Lorena.
8. Elizabeth L. Eisenstein, *The Printing Revolution in Early Modern Europe,* Cambridge, 1983, p. 237.
9. Ibid., pp. 253–54.
10. *Pénsees* IV 277.
11. *Pénsees* VI 347.
12. *Advancement of Learning.*
13. Davies, p. 509.
14. Essays 16, "Atheism."
15. Davies, p. 509.
16. *Opticks* Bk. 3.
17. Eisenstein, p. 250, quoting Giorgio de Santillana.
18. Chadwick, p. 270.
19. *ODCC,* p. 1172.
20. Page 293.
21. Kamen, p. 19.
22. Ibid., p. 13.
23. Ibid., p. 36.
24. *Relacion Historica de la Juderia de Sevilla,* Seville, 1849 qu Kamen, p. 37.
25. Kamen, p. 16.
26. Ibid., p. 106.
27. Ibid., p. 25.
28. *Quixote,* book 2, chap. 58.
29. *La Inquisición de Logroño y un Judaizante Quemado en 1719 Fidel Fita Boletin de la Real Academia de la Historia* XLV, 1904, pp. 457–59 qu Kamen, pp. 193–94.
30. Madrid, Bibl. Nac. qu Hillerbrand, p. 468.
31. Hillerbrand, p. 468.
32. Miles Phillips, *Principal Voyages,* R. Hakluyt.
33. Kamen, pp. 175–76.
34. Fyodor Dostoyevsky, *The Brothers Karamazov,* trans. David McDuff, London, 1993, pp. 283–84.
35. Chadwick, pp. 401–2.

Chapter XXII. The Wars of Religion

1. Chadwick, pp. 156–57.
2. Ibid., p. 163.
3. Ibid., p. 165.
4. Ibid., p. 167.
5. Ibid., p. 169.
6. Pieter Hooft qu Simon Schama, *The Embarrassment of Riches,* London, 1991, p. 86.
7. Schama, p. 98.
8. Alain Woodrow, *The Jesuits,* London, 1995, pp. 106–7.
9. Ibid.
10. Ibid., p. 103.

11. Robert Wynfielde, *Original Letters Illustrative of English History,* ed. H. T. Ellis, London, 1825.

12. Davies, p. 534.

13. Chadwick, p. 288.

14. Ibid., p. 289.

15. John Gerard: *The Autobiography of an Elizabethan,* trans. Philip Caraman, London, 1951.

16. *King's Book,* 1605.

17. Green, p. 192.

18. *ODCC,* p. 399, col. i.

19. *Laws of Ecclesiastical Polity* 1.16.

20. *Devotions* 17.

21. Hesperides.

22. Chadwick.

23. *The Journal of William Dowling: Iconoclasm in East Anglia during the English Civil War.* www.williamdowling.org.

24. Sir Philip Warwick.

25. S. R. Gardiner, ed., *Constitutional Documents of the Puritan Revolution,* Oxford, 1889, pp. 397–98.

26. Thomas Hood.

27. Chadwick, p. 239.

28. December 16, 1653, Gardiner, p. 416.

29. C. V. Wedgwood, *The Thirty Years War,* London, 1992 edition, p. 42.

30. Ibid., p. 49.

31. Ibid., p. 79.

32. Ibid., p. 256.

33. Ibid., p. 516.

34. Davies, p. 568.

Chapter XXIII. The Witch-Finders

1. H. C. Erik Midelfort, *Witch-Hunting in Southwestern Germany, 1562–1684,* Stanford, 1972, pp. 179–90.

2. Maalouf, p. 131; see Usama Ibn Munqidh, *Autobiography: An Arab and Syrian Gentleman of the Crusades,* ed. and trans. P. Hitti, New York, 1929.

3. Green, p. 185.

4. George Lincoln Burr, ed., *The Witch Persecution at Bamberg, from Translations and Reprints from Original Sources of European History,* University of Pennsylvania, vol. 3, pp. 23–28.

5. Ovid, *Metamorphoses* vii, lines 192–93. See also Julio Caro Baroja, *The World of the Witches,* trans. Nigel Glendinning, London, 1964.

6. Apuleius, *The Golden Ass,* trans. Robert Graves, London, 1950, pp. 63–71.

7. J. Mitchell and J. Dickie Paisley, *The Philosophy of Witchcraft,* 1839, p. 210.

8. Green, p. 115.

9. Fletcher, *The Conversion of Europe,* op cit, p. 54.

10. Ibid., p. 54.

11. Jeffrey B. Russell, *A History of Witchcraft, Sorcerers, Heretics, and Pagans,* London, 1981, p. 53.

12. Russell, p. 45.

13. Ibid., pp. 53–54.

14. Green, p. 115.

15. Green, p. 115.

16. Midelfort, *Witch-Hunting,* pp. 179–90.

17. *Malleus Maleficarum,* trans. Montague Summers, London, 1928, pp. 43–46.

18. Midelfort.

19. qu Thomas op cit.

20. Keith Thomas, *Religion and the Decline of Magic,* London, 1971, see chapter 18.

21. Mitchell and Dickie Paisley, p. 188.

22. Russell Hope Robbins, *Encyclopaedia of Witchcraft and Demonology,* New York, 1959, pp. 312–17.

23. Kamen, pp. 207–8.

24. Mitchell and Dickie Paisley, pp. 215–29.

25. Ibid., pp. 156–57.

26. Records of Justiciary, June 4, 1596, cf Mitchell and Dickie Paisley, p. 156fn.

27. Russell, pp. 97–98.

28. Paul Boyer and Stephen Nissenbaum, *Salem Possessed: The Social Origins of Witchcraft,* Cambridge, Mass., 1974, p. 3.

29. Mitchell and Dickie Paisley, p. 204.

30. E. S. Gaustad, *Documentary History of Religion in America,* Grand Rapids, 1982, vol. 1, p. 139; cf Kenneth Silverman, ed., *Selected Letters of Cotton Mather,* Baton Rouge, 1971, pp. 36–43.

31. Gaustad, pp. 136–38.

32. Boyer and Nissenbaum, p. 10.

33. qu Davies, p. 567.

34. Mitchell and Dickie Paisley, p. 188fn.

Chapter XXIV. The Americas

1. L. N. Rivera, *A Violent Evangelism: The Political and Religious Conquest of the Americas,* Louisville, Ky., 1992, p. 33.

2. D. E. Stannard, *American Holocaust: The Conquest of the New World,* London, 1992, p. 66.

3. Ibid., p. 66.

4. Rivera, p. 37.

5. D. B. Quinn, ed., *New American World,* New York, 1979, I 238–39 qu Gaustad, *Documentary History,* pp. 63–64.

6. S. E. Morison, trans. and ed., *Journals and Other Documents on the Life and Voyages of Christopher Columbus,* New York, 1963, p. 92.

7. Rivera, p. 26.

8. Gaustad, pp. 22–24.

9. In their instructions to Columbus for his second voyage. Morison, pp. 203–4.

10. Rivera, p. 36.

11. "Discourse of Western Planting, Richard Hakluyt the Younger," in Gaustad, *Documentary History,* vol. 1, pp. 53–54.

12. Rivera, pp. 99–106.

13. Ibid., p. 125.

14. Kamen, *Spanish Inquisition,* p. 103.

15. D. M. Traboulay, *Columbus and Las Casas: The Conquest and Christianization of America, 1492–1566,* Lanham, Md., 1994, pp. vii–ix.

16. Hugh Thomas, *The Slave Trade,* London, 1997, p. 92.

17. Ibid., p. 805.

18. Traboulay, pp. 45–47.

19. Ibid., p. 49.

20. Stannard, p. 217.

21. Rivera, p. 178.

22. Ibid., p. 48.

23. Geronimo de Mendieta, *Historia Eclesiastica Indiana* III, pp. 174–75.

24. Ibid.

25. *Historia de la conquista de la Nueva España.*

26. González Dávila, *Teatro Eclesiástico,* trans. in C. S. Braden, *Religious Aspects of the Conquest of Mexico,* Durham, N.C., 1930, pp. 126–27.

27. Max Fauconnet, *Mythology of Mexico, New Larousse Encyclopedia of Mythology,* London, 1968, pp. 436–39.

28. del Castillo I, p. 94 qu Braden, *Religious Aspects,* pp. 91–92.

29. Ibid., I p. 121.

30. Ibid., p. 139.

31. MacNutt, *Letters of Cortes to Charles V,* I p. 233, in Braden, p. 106.

32. del Castillo, I p. 220.

33. Ibid., pp. 225–26.

34. MacNutt, I pp. 234–35.

35. Ibid., I p. 242.

36. Ibid., I pp. 260–62.

37. Rivera, p. 58.

38. MacNutt, I pp. 164–65.

39. Mendieta, *Historia Eclesiastica,* III pp. 211–12.

40. Braden, p. 223.

41. Fauconnet, pp. 442–44.

42. Traboulay, pp. 56 et seq.

43. Las Casas, *Very Brief Relation of the Destruction of the Indies, in Traboulay,* pp. 173–74.

44. C. R. Boxer, *Race Relations in the Portuguese Colonial Empire, 1415–1825,* Oxford, 1963, p. 88.

45. H. B. Johnson, *Cambridge History of Latin America,* p. 275.

46. Thomas, p. 420.

47. Traboulay, p. 57.

48. *Oxford Illustrated History of Christianity,* p. 308.

49. Braden, p. 248.

50. Ibid., p. 250.

51. Neill, p. 149.

Chapter XXV. The Jesuits in Paraguay

1. Father Antonio Ruiz de Montoya, *The Spiritual Conquest by the Religious of the Society of Jesus in the Provinces of Paraguay, Paraná, Uruguay and Tapé, 1639,* trans. C. J. McNaspy SJ, J. P. Leonard SJ, and M. E. Palmer, St. Louis, Mo., 1993, p. 133.

2. Ibid., p. 38.

3. C. J. McNaspy SJ, *Conquistador without a Sword: The Life of Roque Gonzalez SJ,* Chicago, 1984, p. 95.

4. Montoya, p. 134.

5. Ibid., p. 173.

6. P. Caraman, *The Lost Paradise: An Account of the Jesuits in Paraguay, 1607–1768,* London, 1975, p. 140.

7. G. O'Neill, *Golden Years on the Paraguay: A History of the Jesuit Missions from 1600 to 1767,* London, 1934, p. 159.

8. Caraman, p. 243.

9. Ibid., p. 245.

10. Ibid., p 249.

11. Ibid., p. 250.

12. Ibid., p. 252.

13. Ibid., p. 254.

14. *OCDD,* p. 363.

15. W. E. Shiels SJ, *King and Church: The Rise and Fall of the Patronato Real,* Chicago, 1961, p. 248.

16. O'Neill, p. 262.
17. Ibid., p. 252.
18. Ibid., p. 257.
19. Ibid., p. 261.
20. Ibid., p. 266.
21. Ibid., p. 267.
22. E. J. Burrus SJ, *Kino and Manje: Explorers of Sonora and Arizona,* St. Louis, Mo., 1971, pp. 13–15.
23. *Ducrue's Account of the Expulsion of the Jesuits from Lower California,* trans. and ed. E. J. Burns SJ, St. Louis, Mo., 1957, p. 50.
24. Page 74.

Chapter XXVI. The Slave Trade

1. Thomas, op cit, p. 110.
2. Thomas, p. 147.
3. *Oxford Comp. Bible,* p. 701.
4. Thomas, p. 396.
5. Traboulay, p. 58.
6. Thomas, p. 306.
7. Ibid., p. 132.
8. Boxer, p. 177.
9. Ibid.
10. Thomas, p. 24.
11. Ibid., p. 37.
12. Ibid., p. 180.
13. Daniel Defoe, *Robinson Crusoe,* London, 1994, p. 32.
14. Ibid., pp. 139–40.
15. Ibid., pp. 140–41.
16. Thomas, p. 434.
17. Ibid., p. 433.
18. Ibid., p. 450.
19. Ibid., p. 449.
20. Ibid., p. 457.
21. Ibid., pp. 452–53.
22. Ibid., p. 307.
23. Ibid.
24. Ibid., p. 774.

Chapter XXVII. Eastern Missions

1. Eusebius, *Hist. Eccl.* V x.
2. A. S. Atiya, *A History of Eastern Christianity,* London, 1968, pp. 359–70.
3. Neill, p. 128.
4. Ibid., p. 198.
5. Ibid., p. 132.
6. Chadwick. p. 34.
7. Neill, p. 137.
8. Alain Woodrow, *The Jesuits,* London, 1995, p. 72.
9. C. Cary-Elwes, *China and the Cross,* London, 1957, p. 94.
10. Neill, p. 160fn.
11. Cary-Elwes, p. 122.

12. Ibid., p. 71.
13. Ibid., p. 136.
14. Neill, p. 163.
15. Cary-Elwes, p. 162.
16. Neill, p. 191.

Chapter XXVIII. Protestant America

1. Gaustad, *Documentary History* I pp. 110–11.
2. Green, p. 220.
3. Ibid.
4. William T. Davis, ed., *Bradford's History of Plymouth Plantation*, New York, 1920, pp. 44–46.
5. Gaustad, p. 105.
6. *Bradford's History*, p. 54.
7. Ibid., p. 44.
8. Gaustad, p. 105.
9. Green, p. 220.
10. Perry Miller, *Roger Williams: His Contribution to the American Tradition*, Cleveland, 1953, pp. 161–64.
11. Ecclesiastical Records, State of New York, Albany, 1901, 335–36, qu Gaustad, p. 87.
12. Gaustad, p. 117.
13. Horatio Rogers, *Mary Dyer of Rhode Island*, Providence, 1895, pp. 84–86.
14. Ibid., p. 134.
15. Ibid., p. 135.
16. Gerald R. Cragg, *Christianity in the Age of Reason*, London, 1990 edition, p. 174.
17. *Oxford Dictionary of the Christian Church*, p. 1646.
18. *Detailed Reports on the Salzburger Emigrants Who Settled in America*, Athens, Ga., 1968, qu Gaustad, pp. 162–67.
19. Gaustad, p. 158.
20. Ibid., p. 180.
21. Ibid., p. 182.
22. Page 114.
23. Pages 110–11.
24. W. S. Perry, ed., *Historical Collections Relating to the American Colonial Church*, New York, 1969, IV pp. 8–13, qu pp. 145–47.
25. Page 96.
26. Peter Guilday, *The Life and Times of John Carroll*, Westminster, Md., pp. 225–27.
27. Tim Dowley, ed., *The History of Christianity*, Batavia, Ill., 1990 edition, p. 477.
28. Leon G. Tyler, ed., *Narratives of Early Virginia, 1606–1625*, New York, 1907, pp. 240–44.
29. Green, p. 220.
30. *Some Correspondence between the Governors and Treasurers of the New England Company*, London, 1895, pp. 52–54, qu pp. 122–23.
31. Richard Slotkin and J. K. Folsom, *So Dreadful a Judgment*, Middletown, 1978, pp. 323–25.
32. Green, p. 220.
33. Page 178.
34. D. B. Quinn, ed., *New American World*, New York, 1979, IV pp. 392–94.
35. Aloysius Roche, *Christians Courageous*, London, 1955, p. 123.
36. R. G. Thwaite, ed., *Jesuit Relations and Allied Documents, Cleveland, 1896–1901*, qu Gaustad, pp. 75–77.
37. Woodrow, *The Jesuits*.
38. *Narratives of New Netherlands, 1609–1664*, New York, 1909, pp. 403–4.

39. R. Latourelle, Jean de Brébeuf in *Dictionnaire Biographique du Canada* 1, p. 217, qu Woodrow, p. 82.
40. Gaustad, pp. 171–73.
41. Cragg, *Christianity,* p. 187.
42. Gaustad, p. 220.
43. *George Whitefield's Journals,* London, 1960, pp. 472–91.
44. Gaustad, pp. 199–200.
45. Ibid., pp. 201–2.
46. Ibid., pp. 202–3.
47. Ibid., p. 210.
48. Jedidiah Morse qu Gaustad, p. 308.
49. J. W. Lydekker, ed., *The Life and Letters of Charles Inglis,* London, 1936, pp. 157–60.
50. Roger Burns, ed., *Am I Not a Man and a Brother,* New York, 1977, pp. 259–60.
51. Gaustad, p. 308.
52. Moncure D. Conway, ed., *The Writings of Thomas Paine,* New York, 1967, IV pp. 183–84.
53. Ibid.
54. *Common Sense,* chapter 4.
55. Julian P. Boyd, ed., *The Papers of Thomas Jefferson,* Princeton, 1950, II pp. 545–47.

Chapter XXIX. Revolutions

1. Simon Schama, *Citizens,* London, 1989, p. 776.
2. Ibid., p. 778.
3. Green, p. 187.
4. Schama, p. 779.
5. Ibid., p. 778.
6. Épîtres.
7. Friedrich Engels, *The Condition of the Working Class in England,* London, 1845.
8. Gaustad, II p. 108.
9. *Diary,* 1847.
10. Dowley, p. 524.
11. *Letters to the Chartists* 2.
12. Dowley, p. 524.
13. *Oxford Dictionary of the Christian Church,* p. 645.
14. *Oxford Dictionary of the Christian Church,* p. 290.
15. Dowley, p. 528.
16. E. Halévy, *A History of the English People in the Nineteenth Century,* 6 vols., London, 1924–34, vol. 1, pp. 371–77.
17. Dowley, p. 524.
18. Gaustad, II p. 184.
19. Willie Lee Rose, *A Documentary History of Slavery in America,* New York, 1976, pp. 458–59, qu Gaustad, pp. 467–68.
20. Rose, pp. 463–65, qu Gaustad, p. 468.
21. Gaustad, p. 471.
22. Gaustad, I p. 301.
23. Ibid., p. 488.
24. Ibid., II p. 29.
25. Ibid., II p. 527.
26. Dee Brown, *Bury My Heart at Wounded Knee,* p. 27.
27. Ibid., pp. 152–53.
28. C. M. Drury, ed., *First White Women over the Rockies,* Glendale, Calif., 1963, I pp. 123–26.

29. Brown, p. 342.
30. Ibid., p. 343.
31. Ibid., p. 344.
32. John G. Neihardt, ed., *Black Elk Speaks,* New York, 1932.

Chapter XXX. Mormons
1. B. H. Roberts, ed., *History of the Church of Jesus Christ of Latter-Day Saints,* Salt Lake City, 1964 edition, I pp. 4–6.
2. Richard L. Bushman, *Joseph Smith and the Beginnings of Mormonism,* New York, 1984, p. 61.
3. Ibid., p. 64.
4. Ray B. West Jr., *Kingdom of the Saints,* New York, 1958, pp. 16–17.
5. Ibid., p. 82.
6. J. B. Turner, *The Rise, Progress, and Causes of Mormonism,* New York, 1842, p. 52.
7. Ibid., p, 65.
8. West, p. 50.
9. Ibid., p. 41.
10. *Deseret News Extra,* September 14, 1852, qu Gaustad, pp. 355–56.
11. Frank J. Cannon and George L. Knapp, *Brigham Young and His Mormon Empire,* New York, 1913, p. 91.
12. Capital letters in original; West, p. 137.
13. Ibid., p. 137.
14. Ibid., pp. 121–25.
15. Ibid., p. 185.
16. Ibid., p. 191.
17. Ibid., p. 205.
18. Ibid., p. 212.
19. Juanita Brooks, *The Mountain Meadows Massacre,* Oklahoma, 1962, p. 19.
20. Ibid., p. 29.
21. Ibid., p. 20.
22. Ibid., p. 41.
23. Ibid., p. 56.
24. Ibid., p. 52.
25. Ibid., p. 78.
26. Ibid., p. 90.
27. West, p. 283.
28. William Miller, *Evidence from Scripture and History of the Second Coming of Christ about the Year 1843,* Boston, 1841, p. 54.
29. "The Time is at Hand," *Studies in Scripture,* series 2, Brooklyn, 1889, p. 76, qu Gaustad, p. 292.
30. Gaustad, p. 377.
31. Ibid., p. 246.

Chapter XXXI. Missions
1. Neill, p. 330.
2. Green, p. 312.
3. Lawrence James, *Rise and Fall of the British Empire,* London, 1994, p. 201.
4. James, p. 207.
5. Green, p. 264.
6. Neill, p. 271.
7. Ibid., p. 269.
8. Ibid., p. 270.

9. James, p. 194.
10. Neill, p. 378.
11. Ibid., p. 311.
12. Ibid., p. 238.
13. Ibid., p. 244.
14. Green, p. 320.
15. Latourette, p. 610.
16. Neill, p. 350.
17. Ibid., p. 279.
18. Green, p. 275.
19. Ibid., p. 264.
20. Gaustad, II p. 170.
21. Green, p. 268.
22. Ibid., p. 269.
23. Neill, p. 268.
24. Ibid., p. 321.
25. Ibid., p. 259.
26. W. J. Platt, *An African Prophet,* 1934.

Chapter XXXII. Darwin

1. Davies, p. 792.
2. Green, p. 231.
3. John W. Draper, *History of the Conflict of Religion and Science,* New York, 1889, pp. v–viii.
4. T. DeWitt Talmage, *Live Coals: "The Missing Link,"* New York, 1885, pp. 271–75, qu Gaustad, pp. 332–34.
5. James Cardinal Gibbons, *Our Christian Heritage,* Baltimore, 1889, p. 301 et seq.
6. Ray Allen Billington, *The Protestant Crusade, 1800–1860,* New York, 1938, p. 437.
7. Gaustad, pp. 460–61.
8. Gaustad, II p. 92.
9. Leslie Allen, ed., *Bryan and Darrow at Dayton,* New York, 1925, p. 16, qu Gaustad, p. 348.
10. Gaustad, p. 355. Bryan died before making his summation, but his wife released a copy of it.
11. Duffy, p. 214.
12. Ibid., p. 255.
13. *ODCC,* p. 1565.
14. Duffy, p. 226.
15. Green, p. 232. The *Times* corespondent was Thomas Mozley.
16. Duffy, p. 231.
17. Ibid., p. 232.
18. Duffy, p. 234.

Chapter XXXIII. Totalitarians

1. *Claws of the Bear,* p. 9.
2. *The Brothers Karamazov.*
3. A. T. Vassilyev, *The Ochrana,* Philadelphia, 1930.
4. Benson Bobrick, *East of the Sun,* London, 1992, p. 327.
5. Hugh Thomas, *An Unfinished History of the World,* London, 1981, p. 630.
6. Trevor Beeson, *Discretion and Valour,* London, 1982, p. 37.
7. Ibid., p. 61.
8. Robert Service, *A History of Twentieth-Century Russia,* London, 1997, p. 135.
9. *Claws,* p. 58.

10. *Russian Century,* p. 119.
11. Beeson, p. 64.
12. Ibid., p. 66.
13. Service, p. 250.
14. Beeson, p. 66.
15. Joachim C. Fest, *Hitler,* London, 1982, p. 17.
16. Klaus Scholder, *The Churches and the Third Reich,* trans. John Bowden, London, 1987, p. 82.
17. Scholder, p. 83.
18. Ibid., p. 86.
19. Ibid., p. 90.
20. Ibid.
21. *Mein Kampf,* London, 1972.
22. Fest, 211.
23. Alan Bullock, *Parallel Lives,* London, 1998, p. 418.
24. Richard Grunberger, *A Social History of the Third Reich,* London, 1991 edition, p. 550.
25. Ibid., p. 551.
26. Scholder, p. 95.
27. Ibid., p. 96.
28. Michael Stürmer, *The German Century,* London, 1999, p. 158.
29. Bullock, p. 418.
30. Duffy, p. 257.
31. Ibid., p. 258.
32. Grunberger, p. 120.
33. Ibid., p. 553.
34. Ibid., p. 554.
35. Ibid., pp. 576–77.
36. Gaustad, II pp. 176–77.
37. www.ushmm.org/bonhoeffer
38. Grunberger, p. 557.
39. Ibid., pp. 390–91.
40. Stürmer, p. 158.
41. Grunberger, p. 561.
42. Ibid., p. 563.
43. Duffy, p. 260.
44. Daniel Jonah Goldhagen, *Hitler's Willing Executioners,* London, 1997, p. 111.
45. Duffy, p. 261.
46. Hugh Thomas, *The Spanish Civil War,* London, 1961, p. 34.
47. Ibid., p. 107.
48. Ibid., p. 175.
49. Ibid., p. 173.
50. Ibid., p. 175.
51. Ibid., p. 166.
52. *The British Century,* p. 194.
53. Davies, p. 923.
54. Green, p. 297.
55. Grunberger, p. 566.
56. Green, p. 304.
57. Goldhagen, p. 112.
58. Grunberger, p. 568.
59. www.ushmm.org/bonhoeffer

60. Goldhagen, p. 431.
61. Grunberger, p. 570.
62. Duffy, p. 263.
63. Ibid., p. 264.
64. Chadwick, p. 66.

Chapter XXXIV. Liberation Theology

1. Michael Scammell, *Solzhenitsyn*, London, 1986, p. 42.
2. Beeson. *Discretion and Valour*, p. 77.
3. Scammell, pp. 764–69.
4. Stürmer, p. 221.
5. Duffy, p. 266.
6. Neill, p. 435.
7. D. Adeney, *China: The Church's Long March*, Eastbourne, 1988, p. 116.
8. W. C. Merwin and F. P. Jones, *Documents of the Three-Self Movement*, National Council of the Churches of Christ in the USA, New York, 1963, pp. 85–86.
9. Ibid., p. 91.
10. T. Lambert, *The Resurrection of the Chinese Church*, London, 1991, p. 179.
11. Ibid., p. 11.
12. Ibid., pp. 177–78.
13. Ibid., pp. 35–36.
14. Ibid., pp. 164–65.
15. Adeney, p. 237.
16. Lambert, p. 172.
17. P. F. Lawler, ed., *The Catholic World Report* 7, no. 9 (October 1997), San Francisco.
18. Owen Chadwick, *The Christian Church in the Cold War*, London, 1982, p. 81.
19. Bobrick, p. 448.
20. Beeson, p. 86.
21. Dowley, p. 606.
22. Gaustad, II pp. 498–99.
23. *The Autobiography of Malcolm X*, New York, 1964, pp. 163–64.
24. J. H. Cone, *A Black Theology of Liberation*, Philadelphia, 1970, pp. 17–24.
25. Green, p. 378.
26. Ibid.
27. Richard Gott, *Revolutionary Movements in Latin America*, London, 1997, p. 89.
28. Ibid., p. 212,
29. J. R. Brockman, *The World Remains: A Life of Oscar Romero*, Maryknoll, 1982, p. 211.
30. Ibid., p. 217.
31. D. Keogh, *Romero: El Salvador's Martyr*, Dublin, 1981, p. 110.

Chapter XXXV. Charisma

1. *The Problem of Pain.*
2. D. W. C. Huntington, *Sin and Holiness, or What It Is to Be Holy*, Cincinnati, 1898, pp. 152–58.
3. *History and Formative Years of the Church of God in Christ*, Memphis, 1969, pp. 37–39, qu Gaustad, II pp. 301–3.
4. *Christian Century* (February 17, 1960): pp. 186–89, qu Gaustad, II p. 513.
5. Oral Roberts, *If You Need HEALING Do These Things*, Tulsa, 1954, pp. 35–38, qu Gaustad, II pp. 304–5.
6. Green, p. 371.
7. D. E. Harrell Jr., *Occasional Papers*, Collegeville, Minn., 1981, pp. 3–7, qu Gaustad, II pp. 540–42.

8. Harrell qu Gaustad, II p. 544.

9. Gaustad, II p. 585.

10. Green, p. 368.

11. Ibid., p. 367.

12. Ibid., p. 347.

13. Duffy, p. 262.

14. *Declaration on Religious Freedom,* December 7, 1965.

15. Duffy, p. 279.

16. *Dissent I and For the Church: Theologians and Humanae Vitae,* New York, 1969, pp. 24–26.

17. Green, p. 390.

18. P. Brierley and V. Hissock, eds., *UK Christian Handbook,* London, 1993, p. 26.

19. Patrick Johnstone, *Operation World,* Carlisle, 1995, pp. 21–27.

20. *DAWN Fridayfax* 1997, no. 43.

21. Jesus Fellowship UK.

22. K. Y. Geevarghese, IPC-WCR.

23. H. Newman, *The Idea of a University,* London, 1853, qu Paul Johnson, *A History of the Modern World,* London, 1984, p. 699.

24. *The Economist* (April 22, 2000). Bernadette herself was canonized in 1933.

25. www.cardinalkungfoundation.org Joseph Kung, head of the American-based Cardinal Kung Foundation, which monitors the underground Catholic Church in China, which has not registered with the State Administration for Religious Affairs.

26. Christian Research, *Sunday Telegraph,* October 28, 2001.

select bibliography

Adeney, D. *China: The Church's Long March,* Eastbourne, 1988.

Adomnán's Life of Columba, ed. and trans. A. O. and M. O. Anderson, Oxford, 1991.

Allen, Leslie, ed., *Bryan and Darrow at Dayton,* New York, 1925.

Al-Tabari, History of, Vol. 12, trans. J. Friedman, Albany, 1992.

Al-Tabari, History of, Vol. 13, trans. G. H. A. Juynboll, Albany, 1989.

Al-Tabari, History of, Vol. 18, trans. M. G. Morony, Albany, 1987.

Ancient Christian Writers No. 13. *Tertullian on Marriage and Remarriage,* trans. W. P. Le Saint, Westminster, Md., 1951.

Anonymous. *Gesta Francorum,* ed. R. Hill, London, 1962.

Apuleius. *The Golden Ass,* trans. Robert Graves, London, 1950.

Aston, M. *Lollards and Reformers,* London, 1984.

Athanasius. *The Life of Antony,* trans. and intro. by R. C. Gregg, London.

Atiya, A.S. *A History of Eastern Christianity,* London, 1968.

Autobiography of Malcolm X, New York, 1964.

Baldric of Bourgueil in *Historia Jerosolimitana,* in *RHC Occ,* Vol. 3.

Baroja, Julio Caro. *The World of the Witches,* trans. Nigel Glendinning, London, 1964.

Beck, H. G., and K. Baus, G. Ewig, H. J. Vogt. *History of the Church,* trans. A. Biggs, London, 1980.

Bede. *A History of the English Church and People,* trans. Leo Shirley-Price, London, 1955.

Bedoyere, M. de la. *The Meddlesome Friar,* London, 1957.

Beeson, Trevor. *Discretion and Valour,* London, 1982.

Billington, Ray Allen. *The Protestant Crusade, 1800–1860,* New York, 1938.

Bishop Lietbert of Cambrai, *Chronicon S Andrei Cameracensis.*

Bitel, L. M. *Saints: Monastic Settlement in Early Ireland,* Cork, 1990.

Bobrick, Benson. *East of the Sun,* London, 1992.

Boorstin, Daniel. *The Discoverers,* New York, 1985.

Boxer, C. R. *Race Relations in the Portuguese Colonial Empire, 1415–1825,* Oxford, 1963.

Boyd, Julian P., ed., *The Papers of Thomas Jefferson,* Princeton, 1950.

Boyer, Paul, and Stephen Nissenbaum. *Salem Possessed: The Social Origins of Witchcraft,* Cambridge, Mass., 1974.

Braden, C. S., trans.; González Dávila, *Teatro Eclesiástico,* in Braden, *Religious Aspects of the Conquest of Mexico,* Durham N.C., 1930.

Bradford's History of Plymouth Plantation, ed. William T. Davis, New York, 1920.

Bridge, A. *Suleiman the Magnificent,* St. Albans, 1984.

Brierley, P., and V. Hissock, eds., *UK Christian Handbook,* London, 1993.

Brockman, J. R. *The World Remains: A Life of Oscar Romero,* Maryknoll, 1982.

Brooks, Juanita. *The Mountain Meadows Massacre,* Oklahoma, 1962.

Browne, L. E. *The Eclipse of Christianity in Asia,* Cambridge, 1933.

Brundage, J. A. *The Crusades: A Documentary Survey,* Milwaukee, 1962.

Bullock, Alan. *Parallel Lives,* London, 1998.

Burns, Roger, ed., *Am I Not a Man and a Brother,* New York, 1977.

Burr, George Lincoln, ed., *The Witch Persecution at Bamberg, from Translations and Reprints from Original Sources of European History,* University of Pennsylvania, Vol. 3.

Burrus, E. J., SJ. *Kino and Manje: Explorers of Sonora and Arizona,* St. Louis, Mo., 1971.

Burrus, V. *The Making of a Heretic: Gender, Authority, and the Priscillianist Controversy,* London, 1995.

Bushman, Richard. *Joseph Smith and the Beginnings of Mormonism,* New York, 1984.

Butterfield, H. *Chrisitanity and History,* London, 1949.

Cambridge Modern History, The; Vol. 2, *The Reformation,* ed. A. W. Ward, G. W. Prother, & S. Leathes, Cambridge, 1904, chapter 6 by A. F. Pollard.

Cannon, Frank J., and George L. Knapp. *Brigham Young and His Mormon Empire,* New York, 1913.

Caraman, P. *The Lost Paradise: An Account of the Jesuits in Paraguay, 1607–1768,* London, 1975.

Carey-Elwes, C. *China and the Cross,* London, 1957.

Cartulaire de l'Abbaye de Saint-Victor de Marseille, ed. B. Guérard, Vol. 1, Paris, 1857.

Cellini, Benvenuto. *Autobiography,* trans. George Bull, London, 1956.

Chadwick, H., trans., Augustine, *Confessions,* Oxford, 1992.

———. *The Early Church,* London, 1967.

———. *Priscillian of Avila: The Occult and the Charismatic in the Early Church,* Oxford, 1976.

Chadwick, Owen. *The Reformation,* London, 1964.

———. *The Christian Church in the Cold War,* London, 1982.

Chesterton, G. K. *Father Brown Stories: The Hammer of God,* London, 1994 edition.

Chronicle of 754 (Anonymous Continuation of the Chronicle of John of Biclaro) in *Conquerors and Chroniclers of Early Medieval Spain,* trans. and intro. by K. B. Wolf, Liverpool, 1990.

Chronicle of John, Bishop of Nikiu, trans. R. H. Charles, Oxford, 1916.

Chronicle of Theophanes anni mundi 6095–6305 (602–813 A.D.) trans. H. Turtledove, Philadelphia, 1982.

Cohn, Norman. *The Pursuit of the Millennium,* London, 1970.

Comnena, Anna. *Alexiad of Anna Comnena,* Book 10, trans. E. R. A. Sewter, London, 1969.

Cone, J. H. *A Black Theology of Liberation,* Philadelphia, 1970.

Conway, Moncure D., ed., *The Writings of Thomas Paine,* New York, 1967.

Coubage, J. *Christians and Jews under Islam,* trans. J. Mabro, London, 1997.

Cragg, Gerald. *Christianity in the Age of Reason,* London, 1990 edition.

Cronin, H. S. "The Twelve Conclusions of the Lollards," *English Historical Review* 22 (1907).

Dahmus, J. H. *The Prosecution of John Wycliff,* New Haven, 1952.

Davies, J. G., ed., *A Dictionary of Liturgy and Worship,* London, 1986 edition.

Davies, Norman, *Europe,* London, 1997.

Declaration on Religious Freedom, December 7, 1965.

Decretals: Decreti secunda pars cause XXIII, Quest. 1.

De expugnatione Lyxbonensis, ed. C. W. David, New York, 1936.

Defoe, Daniel. *Robinson Crusoe,* London, 1994.

De laude novae militiae iii, 4 in S. Bernard, *Opera,* ed. J. Leclerq and H. M. Rochais, 3 vols., Rome, 1963.

Delehaye, H. *Les Saints Stylites,* Brussels, 1923, from Georgs des Araber-Bischofs *Gedichte und Briefe.*

De Rosa, Peter, *Vicars of Christ,* London, 1989.

Detailed Reports on the Salzburger Emigrants Who Settled in America, Athens, Ga., 1968.

Dickens, A. G. *The English Reformation,* London, 1989.

Die Kreuzzegsbriefe aus den Jahren 1088–1100, ed. H. Hagenmeyer, Innsbruck, 1901.

Dissent I and For the Church: Theologians and Humanae Vitae, New York, 1969.

Dostoyevsky, Fyodor. *The Brothers Karamazov,* trans. David McDuff, London, 1993.

Doukas. *Decline and Fall of Byzantium.* trans. H. J. Magoulias, Detroit, 1975.

Dowley, Tim, ed., *The History of Christianity,* Batavia, Ill., 1990 edition.

Dowling, William. *The Journal of William Dowling: Iconoclasm in East Anglia during the English Civil War.* www.williamdowling.org

Draper, John. *History of the Conflict of Religion and Science,* New York, 1889.

Drury, C. M., ed., *First White Women over the Rockies,* Glendale, Calif., 1963.

Duffy, Eamon. *Saints and Sinners,* Yale, 1997.

Ecclesiastical Records, State of New York, Albany, 1901.

Eerdmans Bible Dictionary, Grand Rapids, 1987.

Eisenstein, Elizabeth. *The Printing Revolution in Early Modern Europe,* Cambridge, 1983.

Engels, Friedrich. *The Condition of the Working Class in England,* London, 1845.

Eusebius, Bishop of Caesarea c. 260–c. 340, *Ecclesiastical History of the Martyrs of Palestine,* trans. H. J. Lawler & J. E. L. Oulton, London, 1927, Vol. 1.

———. *The History of the Church,* trans. G. A. Williamson, London, 1965.

Fall of the Byzantine Empire: A Chronicle by George Sphrantzes, 1401–1477, trans. M. Philippides, Amherst, 1980.

Farrar, F. W. *Lives of the Fathers, The Life of St. Augustine,* Edinburgh, 1889, and London, 1993.

Fathers of the Church, Vol. 7. *Sulpicius Severus: Writings,* trans. B. M. Peebles, New York, 1949.

Fathers of the Church, Vol. 13. *St. Basil: Letters,* trans. A. C. Way.

Fathers of the Church, Vol. 22. *On St. Basil the Great,* trans. L. P. McCauley, new trans., Washington, 1951.

Fathers of the Church, Vol. 26. *St. Ambrose: Letters,* trans. M. M. Beyerka, Washington, 1954.

Fathers of the Church, Vol. 51. *St. Cyprian: Letters,* trans. R. B. Donna, Washington, 1964, Letter No. 52, Cyprian to Cornelius.

Fathers of the Church. Tertullian: Disciplinary, Moral, and Ascetic Works, trans. R. Arbesmann, E. J. Daly, E. A. Quinn, New York, 1959.

Fauconnet, Max. *Mythology of Mexico, New Larousse Encyclopedia of Mythology,* London, 1968.

Ferrara, O. *The Borgia Pope: Alexander VI,* trans. F. J. Sheed, London, 1942.

Fest, Joachim. *Hitler,* London. 1982.

Fletcher, Richard. *The Conversion of Europe,* London, 1998.

Fountain, D. *John Wycliffe: The Dawn of the Reformation,* Southampton, 1984.

Fourth Book of the Chronicle of Fredegor with its Continuations, trans. J. M. Wallace-Hadrill, London, 1960.

Froud, J. A. *Life and Letters,* London, 1895.

Fulcher of Chartres. *Historia Hierosolymitana,* ed. H. Hagenmeyer, Heidelberg, 1913.

———. *A History of the Expedition to Jerusalem, 1095–1127,* Book 1, trans. Rita Ryan, Tennessee, 1969.

Gairdner, J. *Lollardy and the Reformation in England,* London, 1908, Vol. 1.

Gardiner, S. R., ed., *Constitutional Documents of the Puritan Revolution,* Oxford, 1889.

Gardner, Eileen, ed., *Visions of Heaven and Hell,* New York, 1989.

Gaustad, E. S. *Documentary History of Religion in America,* Grand Rapids, 1982.

Geoffrey of Malaterrea. *Sicilian History,* ed. E. Pontieri, Bologna, 1927–28.

Gerard, John. *John Gerard: The Autobiography of an Elizabethan,* trans. Philip Caraman, London, 1951.

Gibbon. *Decline and Fall,* Everyman's Library.

Gibbons, James Cardinal. *Our Christian Heritage,* Baltimore, 1889.

Gimpel, Jean. *The Cathedral Builders,* London, 1983.

Goldhagen, Daniel Jonah. *Hitler's Willing Executioners,* London, 1997.

Gott, Richard. *Revolutionary Movements in Latin America,* London, 1997.

Green, Vivian. *A New History of Christianity,* Stroud, UK, 1996.

Grunberger, Richard. *A Social History of the Third Reich,* London, 1991 edition.

Guibert of Nogent in *Historia quae dicitur Gesta Dei per Francos,* in *RHC Occ,* Vol. 3.

Guilday, Peter. *The Life and Times of John Carroll,* Westminster, Md.

Halévy, E. *A History of the English People in the Nineteenth Century,* 6 vols., London, 1924–34.

Hallam, Elizabeth, ed., *Chronicles of the Crusades,* London, 1989.

Hardy, E. R., ed., *Faithful Witnesses: Records of Early Christian Martyrs,* London, 1965.

Harrell Jr., D. E. *Occasional Papers,* Collegeville, Minn., 1981.

Heine, R. E. *The Montanist Oracles and Testimonia,* Macon, Ga., 1989.

Herrin, Judith. *The Formation of Christendom,* London, 1987.

Hillerbrand, Hans J., ed., *The Protestant Reformation,* London, 1968.

Historical Collections Relating to the American Colonial Church, ed. W. S. Perry, New York, 1969.

History and Formative Years of the Church of God in Christ, Memphis, 1969.

History of the Crusades, ed. Robert Lee Wolff and Harry W. Hazard, Philadelphia, 1962, Vol. 2.

Hoare, F. R. Bishop Possidius, *Life of St. Augustine,* in *The Western Fathers,* London, 1954.

Huntington, D. W. C. *Sin and Holiness, or What It Is to Be Holy,* Cincinnati, 1898.

Hussey, J. M., ed., *The Cambridge Medieval History,* Vol. 4, *The Byzantine Empire,* Cambridge, 1966.

Ibn 'Abd al Hakam. *Conquete de l'Afrique du Nord et de l'Espagne,* trans. A. Gateau, Alger, 1948.

I, Catherine: Selected Writings of St. Catherine of Siena, ed. and trans. K. Foster and H. J. Ronayne, London, 1980.

Itinerarium regis Ricardi, ed. W. Stubbs, London, 1864.

James, Lawrence. *Rise and Fall of the British Empire,* London, 1994.

Jardine, Lisa. *Worldly Goods,* London, 1966.

Johnson, H. B., *Cambridge History of Latin America.*

Johnson, Paul. *A History of the Modern World,* London, 1984.

Johnstone, Patrick. *Operation World,* Carlisle, 1995.

Jones, Tony, and Alan Erena, *Crusades,* London, 1994.

Josephus, Flavius, *Jewish War,* trans. G. A. Williamson, London, 1959.

Journals and Other Documents on the Life and Voyages of Christopher Columbus, trans. and ed. S. E. Morison, New York, 1963.

Kamen, Henry. *The Spanish Inquisition,* London, 1965.

Kedar, Benjamin. *Crusade and Mission,* Princeton, 1984.

Keogh, D. *Romero: El Salvador's Martyr,* Dublin, 1981.

Kidd, B. J., ed., Leo Ep xv to Turubius, Bishop of Astorga and Metropolitan of Gallaecia. *Documents Illustrative of the History of the Church,* Vol. 2, London, 1938.

King's Book, 1605.

Knox, J. *Philemon among the Letters of Paul,* Chicago, 1935.

Kritzek, J. *Peter the Venerable and Islam,* Princeton, 1964.

Ladurie, Emanuel Le Roy. *Montaillou,* London, 1980.

La Inquisición de Logroño y un Judaizante Quemado en 1719, Fidel Fita Boletin de la Real Academia de la Historia XLV, 1904.

Lambert of Hersfeld. *Chronicon, MGH SRG,* London, 1895.

Lambert, T. *The Resurrection of the Chinese Church,* London, 1991.

Lane Fox, Robin. *Pagans and Christians,* London, 1988.

Latourette, K. S. *A History of the Expansion of Christianity,* 7 vols., London, 1947.

Lawler, P. F., ed., *The Catholic World Report* 7, no. 9 (October 1997).

Lea, H. C. *A History of the Inquisition in Spain,* 4 vols., London, 1906–7.

———. *A History of the Inquisition of the Middle Ages,* 3 vols., London, 1888.

Lecky, W. E. H. *History of European Morals,* 2 vols., London, 1911.

Loomis, L. R., trans., *Chronicle of Ulrich Richental,* in *The Council of Constance: The Unification of the Church,* ed. J. Hine Mundy and K. M. Woody, New York and London, 1961.

Lord Acton. *Essays in the Liberal Interpretation of History,* London, 1967 edition.

Luther, Martin. *Works of Martin Luther: The Philadelphia Edition,* Vol. 4, Philadelphia, 1931, "Friendly Admonition to Peace 1525."

Lydekker J. W., ed., *The Life and Letters of Charles Inglis,* London, 1936.

Maalouff, Amin. *The Crusades through Arab Eyes,* London, 1984.

Machiavelli, Niccolo. *The Prince,* trans. George Bull, London, 1995 edition.

Malalas, John. *Chronography.*

Malleus Maleficarum, trans. Montague Summers, London, 1928.

Marsden, J. *Sea Road of the Saints,* Edinburgh, 1995.

Martindale, C. C. *St. Justin the Martyr,* London, 1921.

McNaspy, C. J., SJ. *Conquistador without a Sword: The Life of Roque Gonzalez SJ,* Chicago, 1984.

Mein Kampf, London, 1972.

Meister Eckhart: Treatises and Sermons, trans. James M. Clark and John Skinner, London, 1994 edition.

Menno Simons: The Complete Writings, Scottsdale, 1956.

Merwin, W. C., and F. P. Jones. *Documents of the Three-Self Movement,* National Council of the Churches of Christ in the USA, New York, 1963.

Meyer, R. T., trans., *Palladius: The Lausiac History,* Westminster, Md., 1965.

Midelfort, H. C. Erik. *Witch-Hunting in Southwestern Germany, 1562–1684,* Stanford, 1972.

Miller, Perry. *Roger Williams: His Contribution to the American Tradition,* Cleveland, 1953.

Miller, Robert J., ed., *The Complete Gospels,* Calif., 1992.

Miller, William. *Evidence from Scripture and History of the Second Coming of Christ about the Year 1843,* Boston, 1841.

Mitchell, J., and J. Dickie Paisley. *The Philosophy of Witchcraft,* 1839.

Mollat, G. *The Popes at Avignon, 1305–1378,* trans. J. Love, London, 1963.

Montoya, Father Antonio Ruiz de. *The Spiritual Conquest by the Religious of the Society of Jesus in the Provinces of Paraguay, Paraná, Uruguay, and Tapé, 1639,* trans. C. J. McNaspy SJ, J. P. Leonard SJ, and M. E. Palmer, St. Louis, Mo., 1993.

Moreau, Jacques, ed., *Lactantius, On the Death of the Persecutors* 44, 1–11, Paris, 1954, trans. John W. Eadie, in *The Conversion of Constantine,* ed. J. W. Eadie, New York, 1971.

Morison, S. E., trans. and ed., *Journals and Other Documents of the Life and Voyages of Christopher Columbus,* New York, 1963.

Moule, A. C. *Christians in China Before the Year 1550,* London, 1930.

Moynahan, Brian *Claws of the Bear,* London, 1989, *The British Century,* 1997.

Musurillo, H. *The Acts of the Christian Martyrs,* Oxford, 1972.

Naphy, W. E., ed. and trans., *Documents on the Continental Reformation,* Basingstoke, 1996.

Narratives of New Netherlands, 1609–1664, New York, 1909.

Neihardt, John G., ed., *Black Elk Speaks,* New York, 1932.

Newman, H. *The Idea of a University,* London, 1853.

Norton, P. R. Coleman. *Roman State and Christian Church,* Vol. 1, London, 1966.

O'Neill, G. *Golden Years on the Paraguay: A History of the Jesuit Missions from 1600 to 1767,* London, 1934.

Oxford Book of Prayer, ed. G. Appleton, Oxford, 1985.

Oxford Companion to the Bible, New York & Oxford, 1993.

Oxford Dictionary of the Christian Church (ODCC), 1998 edition.

Panati, Charles. *Sacred Origins of Profound Things,* London, 1997.

Pastor, L. *History of the Popes from the Close of the Middle Ages,* Vol. 2, London, 1912.

Pernoud, Régine. *The Crusades,* trans. Enid McLeod, London, 1962.

Peter of Mladonovice. *An Account of the Trial and Condemnation of Master John Hus in Constance from John Huss at the Council of Constance,* trans. and ed. M. Spinka, New York, 1965.

Peters, F. E. *Jerusalem,* Princeton, 1985.

Petrarch. *Liber Sine Nomine,* trans. N. P. Zacour as *Book without a Name,* Toronto, 1973.

Platt, W. J. *An African Prophet,* 1934.

Praise of Folly, trans. Hoyt Hopewell Hudson, Princeton, 1941, in K. H. Donnenfeldt, *The Church of the Renaissance and Reformation,* St. Louis, Mo., 1970.

Price, R. M., trans., *Lives of the Monks of Palestine,* Kalamazoo, Mich., 1991.

Quinn, D. B., ed., *New American World,* New York, 1979.

Relación Historica de la Juderia de Sevilla, Seville, 1849.

Renaissance and Reformation, ed. G. R. Elton, New York, 1976.

Ridolfi, Roberto. *Life of G. Savonarola,* trans. C. Grayson, London, 1959.

Riley-Smith, Louise and Jonathan. *The Crusades: Idea and Reality, 1095–1274* (1981).

Rivera. L. N. *A Violent Evangelism: The Political and Religious Conquest of the Americas,* Louisville, Ky., 1992.

Robbins, Russell Hope, *Encyclopaedia of Witchcraft and Demonology,* New York, 1959.

Robert the Monk in *Historia Hierosolymitana* in *RHC Occ,* Vol. 3.

Roberts, B. H., ed., *History of the Church of Jesus Christ of Latter-Day Saints,* Salt Lake City, 1964.

Roberts, Oral. *If You Need HEALING Do These Things,* Tulsa, 1954.

Roche, Aloysius. *Christians Courageous,* London, 1955.

Rogers, Horatio. *Mary Dyer of Rhode Island,* Providence, 1895.

Rose, Willie. *A Documentary History of Slavery in America,* New York, 1976.

Runciman, Steven. *A History of the Crusades,* Vol. 2, London, 1990 edition.

Russell, Jeffrey. *A History of Witchcraft, Sorcerers, Heretics, and Pagans,* London, 1981.

Ryan, J. *Irish Monasticism,* Dublin, 1931.

Scammell, Michael. *Solzhenitsyn,* London, 1986.

Schama, Simon. *Citizens,* London, 1989.

——. *The Embarrassment of Riches,* London, 1991.

Scholder, Klaus. *The Churches and the Third Reich,* trans. John Bowden, London, 1987.

Scripta Leonis, *Rufini et Angeli sociorum S Francisci,* ed. and trans. Rosalind B. Brooke, Oxford, 1970.

Select Library of Nicene and Post-Nicene Fathers of the Christian Church, Vol. 3, Oxford, 1982, from *The Ecclesiastical History of Theodoret,* trans. B. Jackson.

Seneca, M. T. Griffin, Oxford, 1976.

Service, Robert. *A History of Twentieth-Century Russia,* London, 1997.

Seward, Desmond. *The Monks of War,* London, 1995 edition.

Shiels, W. E., SJ. *King and Church: The Rise and Fall of the Patronato Real,* Chicago, 1961.

Siberry, Elizabeth. *Criticism of Crusading, 1095–1274,* Oxford, 1985.

Silverman, Kenneth, ed., *Selected Letters of Cotton Mather,* Baton Rouge, 1971.

Slotkin, Richard, and J. K. Folsom. *So Dreadfull a Judgment,* Middletown, 1978.

Some Correspondence between the Governors and Treasurers of the New England Company, London, 1895.

Southern R. W. *The Making of the Middle Ages,* London, 1953.

——. *Western Society and the Church of the Middle Ages,* London, 1970.

Spinka, M. *John Hus,* Princeton, 1968.

Stannard, D. E. *American Holocaust: The Conquest of the New World,* London, 1992.

St. Jerome. *The Life of St. Paul the First Hermit, from The Desert Fathers,* trans. from Latin and intro. by H. Waddell, London, 1936.

Studies in Scripture, Series II, "The Time is at Hand," Brooklyn, 1889.

Stürmer, Michael. *The German Century,* London, 1999.

Suleiman the Magnificent. *A Bridge,* Frogmore, St. Albans, Herts., 1984.

Talmage, T. De Witt. *Live Coals: "The Missing Link,"* New York, 1885.

Thomas à Kempis. *Imitation of Christ,* trans. L. Sherey-Price, London, 1952.

Thomas, Hugh. *The Slave Trade,* London, 1998 edition.

———. *The Spanish Civil War,* London, 1961.

———. *An Unfinished History of the World,* London. 1981.

Thomas, Keith. *Religion and the Decline of Magic,* London, 1971.

Thwaite, R. G., ed., *Jesuit Relations and Allied Documents,* Cleveland, 1896–1901.

Traboulay, D. M. *Columbus and Las Casas: The Conquest and Christianization of America, 1492–1566,* Lanham, Md., 1994.

Travels of Ibn Jubayr, trans. R. J. C. Broadhurst, London, 1952.

Trial of Hus, in 2 Letters by a Member of the Council, Fra Poggius to Leonhard Nikolai, ed. B. von Berchem, New York, 1930.

Tuchman, Barbara. *A Distant Mirror,* London, 1995 edition.

Turner, J. B. *The Rise, Progress, and Causes of Mormonism,* New York, 1842.

Tyler, Leon G., ed., *Narratives of Early Virginia, 1606–1625,* New York, 1907.

Usama Ibn Munqidh. *Autobiography: An Arab and Syrian Gentleman of the Crusades,* ed. and trans. P. Hitti, New York, 1929.

Van Passen, P. *A Crown of Fire: The Life and Times of Girolamo Savonarola,* London, 1961.

Vassilyev, A. T. *The Ochrana,* Philadelphia, 1930.

Veilleux, Armand, trans., *Pachomian Koinonia,* Vol. 1., *The Life of St. Pachomius and His Disciples,* Kalamazoo, Mich., 1980.

Vernadsky, George. *Russia,* 4th ed., New Haven, 1954.

Victor of Vita. *History of the Vandal Persecution,* trans. J. Moorhead, Liverpool, 1992. *Translated Texts for Historians,* Vol. 10.

Vision of Heaven and Hell before Dante, ed. Eileen Gardner, New York, 1989.

Warner, Marina. *Alone of All Her Sex,* London, 2000.

Wedgwood, C. V. *The Thirty Years War,* London, 1992 edition.

West Jr., Ray. *Kingdom of the Saints,* New York, 1958.

Whitefield, George. *George Whitefield's Journals,* London, 1960.

Woodrow, Alain. *The Jesuits,* London, 1995.

Works of John Bale, Bishop of Ossory, 1495–1563, ed. H. Christmas, Cambridge, 1849.

Wyclif, De Potestate Papae, Documents in Renaissance and Reformation History, ed. D. Webster and L. Green, Melbourne, 1960.

Wycliffe, John. *Select English Works of John Wyclif,* ed. T. Arnold, Oxford, 1871.

———. *Selections from English Wycliffite Writings,* ed. A. Hudson, Cambridge, 1978.

———. *Wyclif: Select English Writings,* ed. H. E. Winn, Oxford, 1929.

Wynfielde, Robert. *Original Letters Illustrative of English History,* ed. H. T. Ellis, London, 1825.

Ziegler, Philip. *Black Death,* London, 1969.

PICTURE CREDITS

INDEX

Abercius, 67

Abgar II, 67

Abolition, 545, 548, 550, 551, 552, 606, 636

Abortion, 717, 718, 720, 725

Abraha, 160

Abraham, 26, 34, 104, 160, 161, 175*f,*
    616, 668, 683; Apocalypse of, 47

Achard of Montmerle, 232

Acre, 247, 250, 253, 254, 262

Acton, Lord, 279

Adalbert, 220

Adam, 34, 57, 138, 149

Adam-Moses, 322

Adam of Perseigne, 240, 247

Adamites, 322

Adams, John, 592

Adams, Will, 560

Adenauer, Konrad, 695

Adhemer, 215

Adolas, 143

Adolphus, Gustavus, 476

Adso, 215

Advent Christian Church, 625

Aelfric, 304*f*

Aetius, Flavius, 154

Affonso, 506, 537, 539, 648

Africa, x, 33*f,* 57, 60, 78, 157, 631, 633,
    726; Augustine and, 148; barbarian
    invasions in, 152–53, 155; Islamic
    invasion in North, 182–86; missionaries
    from, 712; missionaries to, 539, 540,
    633, 645–50; slaves from, 539–40, *541,*
    546, 550 (*See also* Slaves, African); slaves
    returned to, 549, 606, 649

African Methodist Episcopal Church, 605,
    606

Africanus, Julius, 104

Afrikaners, 645, 707

Agape love feast, 466

Agatha, St., 290

Agathonice, 84

Agnes, St., 196, 271

"Agonistici," 148

Agonizantes, 417

Agrippina, 37, 38

Aidan, 202

Akbar the Great, 556–57

Aladura, 726

Alans, 150, 152–53

Alaric, 150–51

Alban, 196

Albania, 428

Albany, 588*f, 589*

Alberic of Tusculum, 213–14

Albert of Aachen, 250

Albert of Aix, 234

Albert of Bavaria, 473

Albert of Brandenburg, 346, 347, 350

Albigensians, 277, 281, 283

Albornoz, Bartolomé Frías de, 543, 544

Alchemy, 489, 503

Alcuin, 203–4

Aleander, Girolamo, 352, 353

Aleuts, 641

Alexander III, Pope, 85*f,* 278

Alexander the Great, 7, 14, 25, 30, 102

Alexander V, Pope, 309, 310

Alexander VI, Pope, 335–37, 338, 430, 506

Alexander VII, Pope, 564

Alexandra (Russia), 664

Alexandria, 3, 12, 56, 57, 65, 66–67, 102, 107, 108, 121; Islam and, 156, 157, *170*, 177, 178–79; torture in, 71, *82*

Alexey, Patriarch, 705

Alexius, 256, 257

Alexius Comnenus, 222, 223, 231, 234, 237

Alexius IV, 257

Alexius Murzuphlus, 257–58

Alfonsi, Pedro, 251

Alfonso XIII (Spain), 683

Alfred (England), 206, 304*f*

Algeria, 182, 186, 226*f*

Alkerton, Richard, 488

All Saints' (Hallows) Day, 492

"Alleluia," 59

Allen, John, 590

Allen, Richard, 605

Allen, William, 461, 462

Allouez, Claude Jean, 585

Almeida, Francisco de, 555

Almoravid, 226*f*

Alopen, 189

Altamiro, Luis, 529

Alva, 459

Alvarado, Pedro de, 517

Alvares, Francisco, 187

Amandus, 206–7

Ambon, 567

Ambriose, 664

Ambrose, St., 86, 105, 108, 109, 146, 147, 430

Americas, 504–24

Amiens, 265, 266, 268

Amin, Idi, 728

Amish, 569

Anabaptists, 355–56, 357, 360, 373–74, 377–84, 383*f*; in Colonial America, 574

Anastasius, 108–9, 125

Anathema, 37, 64, 248, 665

Anatolia, 212, 223

Anderson, Elizabeth Garrett, 719

Andrew, St., 235

Angles, 154, 196, 198

Anglicans, 374*f*, 398, 466–73, 538, 558, 636, 642, 645, 647, 648, 656, 689, 695, 712, 720, 730; apartheid and, 707; in Britain today, 730; Catholics and, 464, 656, 723; in Colonial America, 573, 575–76, 587, 588, 590; slavery and, 537. *See also* Church of England

Anglo-Saxons, 196, 206, 304*f*, 486, 492

Angola, 539, 540

Ann, St., 451

Anna Comnena, 231, 232, 233, 248

Anno Domini, 1–2

Anomoeans, 123

Anseau, 244*f*

Anselm of Lucca, 241*f*

Anskar, St., 209

Anthony, Susan B., 719

Anthony of Lorraine, 365

Anti-Semitism, 445–46, 675–83

Anticaesar, 218

Antichrist, 72, 215, 665, 666, 671; "ambassadors of," 215; Frederick II as, 261; pope as, 298, 307, 310, 352, 410, 423

Antinomianism, 392–93

Antioch, 25, 27, 32, 45, 66, 103, 120, 125, 125*f*; in Crusades, 234, *235*, 236, 262; Islam and, 157, 169, *170*; torture in, 71, *82*

Antiochus IV, 46, 73

Antipope, 117, 213, 218, 326, 363*f*

Antony of Egypt, St., 129, *129*, 134, 200*f*

Antony of Padua, 247*f*

Apartheid, 707–8

Apex mentis, 270

Apocalypse/Revelation, 46–47, 47, 49, 50*f*, 72, 206, 207, 321, *358*, 439, 484*f*

Apocrypha, 19, 25*f*, 36, 48–49, 354*f*

Apollinaris, 124

Apostasy, 117, 164, 166, 176, 182, 186, 561; by popes, 213

Apostles, 3, 18–23, 22–23, 25, 47, 111*f*; Epistle of the, 50*f*

Apostolic Church, *429*

Appenzeller family, 640

Apuleius, 485

Aquaviva, Claudio, 473–74

Aquaviva, Rudolf, 557, 563

Aquinas, Thomas, St., 243*f*, 287, 318, 521

Arab Christians, 166–67, 251

Arab Moslems, 77, 552; as "Ishmaelites," 157, 158, 175; as Jewish converts, 159; worshipping with Christians, 159. *See also* Islam; Moslems

Arabia, 67, 70, 157, 159, 166–67, 636

Arabic, 157, 167

Arbués, Pedro, St., 443–44

Archdale, John, 576

Arctic, 630, 674*f,* 704

Argentina, 525*f,* 528, 709

Arians /Arianism, 121–22, *125,* 135, 150, 153, 182, 186*f;* Berbers as, 183; Lombard, 193, 194, 195; split in, 123; Visigoths as, 197; *vs.* Imperial Catholicism, 153–55

Aristides, 54–55

Aristotle, 29, 390, 435

Arius, 99, 121, 122

Ark of the covenant, 6–7

Arles, Council of, 196, 442

Armada, 427, 462

Armenia, 66, 127, 167, 243, 244, 280, 325, 665; in Crusades, 234; Islam and, 165, 223; Moslem armies and, 157

Arminians, 460, 467

Arminius, Jacobus, 393, 459

Arnald-Amalric, 283

Arnaud, Angélique and Antoine, 438

Arnold of Brescia, 279

Arnoldists, 279

Arnott, Hugo, 496

Arns, Evaristo, 709

Arnulf, 215, 243

Arundel, Thomas, 305, 306, 307, 308

Asbury, Francis, 590

Asceticon, 135

Ascetics, 129, 139

Ashanti, 550

Asia, x, 150, 189, 632, 635

Asia minor, 67, 72, 223

Askew, Anne, 406

Asklepius, 40

Assemblies of God, 33*f*

Atahualpa, 519

Atallah, 554

Athanasius, 107, 121–22, 152

Athenagoras, 36, 59, 723

Atkins, William, 542

Attila the Hun, *151,* 154

Aubrey, Thomas, 546

Aubrey of Trois-Fontaines, 260, 261

Augsburg Confession, 429

Augustine, St., 57, 72, 144–55, *146,* 182, 241–42; before conversion, 119; Crusades and, 225; Ethelbert and, 197, 198; Galileo and, 435; Gregory the Great and, 196–97; Luther and, 348, 349, 350; Nazis and, 679; predestination and, 391, 392; slavery and, 61

Augustinians, 144, 347, 440, 519, 553, 567, 684

Augustus, 4, 100*f,* 105, 203

Austorc d'Aurillac, 254

Australia, 642, 643

Austria, 428, 477, 655–56

Auto-da-fé, 448, *449,* 450, *554*

Avignon, 298–301, 310, 326, *355*

Avvakum, Archpriest, 665

Ayala, Hernando de, 433–34

Ayora, Juan de, 504–5

Azaña, Manuel, 683–84

Aztecs, 505, 511–18, *513,* 520

Babel, tower of, 128

Babuni, 281

Bacon, Francis, 438, 473

Bacon, Samuel, 549*f*

Baghdad, 167, 243, 553

Bahawalpur, 730

Bahira, Sergius, 160

Baird, Pierre, 582–83

Bakker, Jim, 717

Bakunin, Mikhail, 685

Baldric of Bourgueil, 222*f,* 223*f*

Baldwin II, 259

Baldwin (Jerusalem), 244

Baldwin of Boulogne, 234

Baldwin of Bourg, 250

Baldwin (Romania), 259

Bale, John, 396

Balfour, Alison, 496

Balkans, 210, 728

Ballard, Jean, 387

Balokale, 726

Baltic States, 665, 691, 692

Baltimore, Lord, 576–77

Bamberg, 227, *481*

Bantu, 540

Baptism, 27, 35, 55, 56, 149; adult, 356, 357, 383*f,* 384, 571; in early church, 40, 52, 55–56, 57; heresy and, 451; of Holy Spirit, 714; infant, 40, 57, 225, 357; of Jesus, 29, 58; Moslem requests for, 250; slaves and, 538

Baptists, 40*f,* 398, 466, 597, 605, 629, 645, 654*f,* 713, 715, 717, 726; African Americans as, 606–7, 705, *706;* Anabaptists and, 383*f;* charismatic, 717; in Colonial America, 569, 571, 574, 575, 588, 590; in England, 602; as missionaries, 636, 637, 638, 649; in Russia/ Soviet Union, 665, 673, 702–3, 704; slavery and, 545, 550, 551, 604–5

Baradeus, Jacob, 127

Barbarians, 150–55, *151,* 182, 191, 192, 196, 199, 258; as Christian converts, 157, 180

Barbaro, Niccolo, 264

Barbarossa, Frederick, 254

Barbato, St., 486

Barbosa, Rui, 552

Barca, 175, 182

Barebone's Parliament, 470–71, 472

Barnabites, 416

Barnabus, 25, 50*f*

Barnado, Thomas, 601

Barnum, Phineas T., 624

Baronius, Cesare, 213

Barqa, 182

Barth, Karl, 680

Baruch, 47

Basil II (Byzantine Empire), 209

Basil the Great, St., 123, 134–36, 226

Basil the Macedonian, 212

Basiliscus (emperor), 142

Basire, Isaac, 433

Basle, Council of, 344

Basques, 207*f,* 687

Bastwick, John, 468

Bavaria, 208, 473, 474, 476, 675

Baybars, 187, 261

Beal, Fred, 672

Beaton, David, 413

Beauvais, 265, *266*

Becket, Thomas à, 247*f,* 296, 405

Bede, St., 197, 198, 202

Bedouin nomads, 160, 162

Beguines, 330

Beirut, 244, 245, 262

Belgium, 649

Belgrade, 230–31, 428

Bélibaste, Bernard, 284

Belisarius, 182, 191

Bell, George, 689, 690

Bellarmine, Roberto, St., 349, 433, 436

Bellini, Gentile, 329

Belorussia, 536

Benedict IX, Pope, 213, 214, 216

Benedict XII, Pope, 284

Benedict XIII, Pope, 309, 312*f,* 314

Benedict XIV, Pope, 727*f*

Benedictines, 642, 675

Benefictus, 310

Benezet, Anthony, 548

Benjamin I, 174, 181

Bennett, Dennis, 715

Bennett, John Cook, 615–16

Berbers, 183, 184, 185

Bergerac, Cyrano de, 502

Bernadette, St., 658, *658*

Bernard of Clairvaux, St., 220, 245, 246, 252–53, 267–68, 319

Bertha (queen), 197–98

Bethlehem, 2, 16; Islam and, 169

Beveridge, A.J., 631

Beza, Theodore, 384, 393, 395, 396, 397, 413, 434, 453–54

Biafra, 728

Bibb, Henry, 604

Bible, 359–60, 455; American Standard, 358*f;* Anabaptists and, 379; apocrypha of, 19, 25*f,* 36, 48–49, 354*f;* ban on, 327; Boyle and, 439; burning alive for selling, *355;* Calvin and, 385; canon of, 19, 47, 50–51; Carey and, 629, *630;* in China, 699; English, 304–5, 341, 357*f;* 358*f,* 406; Erasmus and, 338–39, *339;* feminism and, 719; Geneva, 396; Great, 357*f;* Hollywood and, 716–17; Hus and, 309; King James, 354*f,* 488, 493; Latin Vulgate, 68, 145, 304, 341,

349, 423, 432, 488; Lollards and, 306; Luther and, *349*, 353, 354–55, 358; Newton's commentaries on, 439; Old Latin, 67, 145; Polyglot, 445; printed, 325, 340–41; Protestants and, 370, 406; in Renaissance, 354; Revised, 358*f*; Roman Catholic *vs.* Protestant, 354*f*; Savonarola and, 335; slavery and, 60–62, 538, 550–51; social reform and, 597; translations of, 109, 207, 303–4, 354–55, 359–60, 434, 564, 567, 580, 632, 637, 644, 646, 647*f*, 649; Tyndale and, 357–58; witchhunts and, 502; as Word of God, 247, 248, 248*f*, 558, 570; Wycliffe and, 295–96, 303–4, 304; Zwingli and, 372

"Bible hour," 665

"Bible men," 295, 305

Bible scholarship, 434, 610, 625*f*

Bigamists, 450

Bishops, 85*f*, 111, 194, 218, 298, 338, 465, 564, 567*f*, 638, 642, 657, 708; black, 605, 649; Constantine and, 98–99, 101, 102, 104; in early church, 36, 41, 60, 62–65, 65; friars and, 275; liberation theology and, 708–9; as martyrs, *70*, 70–71, 154, 709–11, *711;* Orthodox *vs.* Roman Catholic, 225; Peter as first, 41; at Second Vatican Council, 721, 722–23; women as, 134, 720

Bismarck, 660, 661

Black Death, 290–93, 455

"Black Manifesto," 706

Black Muslims, 706–7

"Black Pope," 474

"Black-robe," 607–8

Black Rubric, 407

Blackfriars, 303

Blackshirts, 679

Blackwell, Elizabeth, 719

Blanche of Castile, 288

Blasphemy, 110, 450, 471, 472, 730

Blessed Juliana, 303

Blok, Alexander, 671

"Blood council," 459

"Bloody Mary," 407

Bob Jones University, 717

Bobbio, 202

Boccaccio, Giovanni, 291

Boers, 645–46

Bogomil, 280–81

Bohemia, 207, 308–11, 320–22, 476, 477

Bohemond of Antioch, 250

Bohemond of Taranto, 224, 232, 235, 236

Böhm, Hans, 332–34

Boleyn, Anne, 401–3, *402*, 404, 406

Bolivia, 709

Bolsec, Hieronymus, 393

Bonaventura, St., 270, 275

Bonfire of Vanities, *334*, 337

Bonhoeffer, Dietrich, 681, 683, 691

Boniface of Crediton, 202, 203, 242

Boniface VIII, Pope, 319, 327*f*

Book burning, 426, 433, 434

Book of Common Prayer, 407, 569

Book of Martyrs, 408, 433

Book of Sports, 467

Book of the Covenant, 488

Boone, William J., 638

Booth, William, 602, *603*

Booth-Tucker, Frederick, 603–4

Borgia family, 335, 336, 339, 342, 430–31

Borman, Martin, 676

Borneo, 632

Borovikovsky, 668

Borromeo, Charles, 430

Bosnia, 281, 325, 428

Botticelli, Sandro, 328, 335

Bourbon, Antoine de, 455

Bourbons, 455

Boxers, 639, 727

Boyle, Robert, 439

Bramante, 329, 336

Branch Davidians, 718

Brawley, E. M., 607

Brazil, 506, 520–21, 523, 525*f*, 528, 539, 552, 726

Brébeuf, Jean de, 583, 584

Bremen, 220

Brethren churches, 574, 574*f*; Moravian, 569, 574; Plymouth, 629, 649, 665, 696*f*; Swiss, 384

Brethren of the Common Life, 330, 331, 377

Bridget, St., 300

Brink, C. B., 707
Britain, 196, 197, 712–13, 730
British East African Company, 648
British East India Company, 557, 558, 636
British missionaries, 629–50 *passim,* 730
British social reform, 595–603
Britons, 154, 201, 631*f*
Brook, William, 451
Brothers of the Sword, 220
Brown, George, 632*f*
Brown University, 588
Browne, Robert, 465
Bruce, Robert, 636
Brun, Geoffrey, 455–56
Brunhilde, 195, 196
Bruno, Giordano, 441
Bruno, St., 270
Bryan, William Jennings, 654
Bubonic plague, 288–89, *291,* 291–92,
    292
Bucareli, Francisco de, 532
Buchanan, James, 621, 623
Buddhists, 555, 561
Bulgaria, 212, 263, 280–81, 428, 635,
    702
Bulgars, 207, 208
Bultsu, 208
Burchard, 336
Burgundians, 154
Burma, 637
Burton, Nicholas, 451
Burton, Richard, 619
Burton, Robert, 492
Bush, George W., 728
Butler, Josephine, 719
Byrd, William, 545
Byron, Lord, 634
Byzantines, 156, 163, 167, 168, 173,
    176–88, 191, 213, 223, 280, 657;
    Crusaders and, 226, 234, 257, 259;
    description of Christian, 225
Byzantium, 174–75, 208, 209, 212, 213,
    281

Cabral, Pedro, 506
Cadaveric Synod, 214
Cadwallon, 201

Caecilian, 98
Caesarea, 172
"Caesaropapism," 213
Caetes, 520
Cairo, 178, 243; Old, 174
Cajetan, Cardinal, 350
Caleb (Aksum), 160
Caligula, 37–38, 49
Calles, Plutarco, 686
Callistus, St., Pope, 53, 117
Callistus III, 335
Calvin, John, 384–97, *385,* 406, 423, 434,
    453, 466; Knox and, 413; Loyola and,
    420; predestination and, 391–93;
    Presbyterians and, 465; Puritans and,
    468; Servetus and, 394–95, 396, 432
Calvinism, 398*f,* 457, 476
Calvinistic Methodism, 393*f,* 598*f*
Calvinists, 459–60, 474, 477, 550; Armini-
    ans *vs.,* 467; business ethics and,
    390–91; as Catholic converts, 417;
    Dutch, 458; French, 397; Huguenot,
    455–56, 457; Jesuits and, 475; Luther-
    ans *vs.,* 390, 474, 476; persecution and,
    394, 395, 426, 440
Camara, Dom Helder, 709
Camillians, 417
Camillo, St., 417
Camisards, 589*f*
Campbell, Katherine (Katie), 496–97
Campion, Edmund, 461
Canada, 585, 625
Canisius, Peter, 473
Canossa, 218, 226
Canterbury, 197, 198, 405, 408, 720, 723
Canute (Denmark), 209–10
Capek, John, 321
Capital punishment, 599
Capuchins, 415–16, 417, 440, 474, 540,
    585, 645
Carafa, Giampietro, 422, 423, 425, 440
Carbonari, 655
Carcassone, 283, 284
"Cardinal Petticoat," 421
Cardinals, 217, 301, 309, 319, 344; in
    Counter-Reformation, 422–23; in
    Inquisition, 440–41
Carey, William, 629–30, *630,* 636

Caribs, 508

Carleton, James, 607

Carlstadt, Andreas, 352, 366, 370

Carlyle, Thomas, 598

Carmelites, 188, 523, 538, 658, 691

Carpzov, Benedict, 493

Carroll, John, 578

Carter, Jimmy, 709

Carthage, 65–66, 89, 183, 506; Augustine at, 145; Council at, 50, 62; Cyprian at, 182; fall of, 154, 185, 186

Cartwright, Thomas, 465

Casimir, 365

Caspar, George, 451

Cassander, George, 423

Cassian, John, 136

Castelar, Emilio, 552

Castellio, Sebastian, 454

Castile, 442, 445

Castro, Dom Joáo de, 555

Castro, Fidel, 708

Catacombs, 53, 104

Catechumens, 56–57, 103

Cathari, 117–18

Cathars, 254, 277, 278, 280–85

"Cathedral crusades," 268

Cathedrals, 265–69, 266; ornaments in, 267, 328

Catherine de Médicis, 455, 457

Catherine de Ricci, St., 338

Catherine of Aragon, 399–403

Catherine of Siena, 300, 301

Catherine II, the Great (Russia), 536

Catholic League, 456, 474

Catholic University of America, 724

Catholicism: Calvinist converts to, 417; Crusades and, 225; Imperial, 183; modern criticism and, 721–22; Protestant converts to, 461

Catholics, 477, 690; Anglicans and, 656, 723; anti-Semitism and, 677, 683; Arians vs., 153–55; charismatic, 715; in China, 727; Civil War and, 606; in Colonial America, 569, 570, 576–78; Darwin and, 653; Hitler and, 678–79, 681, 701; liberation theology and, 708–9; as missionaries, 633, 640, 644, 645, 709–10; Nestorians vs., 190;

persecution and (See Martyrs; Persecution); in Poland, 700–701; prostitution and, 388–89, 424, 426; Protestants vs., 388–89, 398, 456–78, 475, 598, 648, 653–54, 730; reconciliation of Protestants with, 422–23; Roman and Maronite, 245; slavery and, 538, 552, 606; in Soviet Union, 673; statistics on, 725; Turks' attack on, 428–29; unity of Western and Eastern, 324–25; Zwinglians and, 376

Caxton, William, 341

Cazalla, Augustin, 450

Celestine, Pope, 126

Celestine II, Pope, 250

Celibacy, 19, 36–37, 63, 212, 216, 218, 305, 313, 406, 423, 554, 725; Luther on, 352

Cellini, Benvenuto, 421–22, 491–92

Celsus, 59

Celts, 196, 202, 202f

Cenaculum, 104

Censorship/banning, 426, 432–40, 436

Cerinthus, 111f

Cerularius, Michael, 212, 225

Cervantes, Miguel de, 445, 508

Ceylon, 425

Chacos, 527

Chagall, Marc, 665

Chalcedon, 169, 173–74; Council of, 127, 169

Chalmers, James, 645

Champlain, Samuel de, 582–83

Chanel, Peter, 644

Charisma, 34

Charismatics, 33, 715, 718, 726; in China, 700

Charlemagne, 186, 203–4, 218, 277, 362f, 486, 541, 600f

Charles I (England), 467–68, 470

Charles II (England), 473, 531

Charles IX (France), 455

Charles ("Martellus" and "the Hammer"), 186

Charles of Durazzo, 301

Charles the Bald, 204

Charles the Great, 203

Charles V (Holy Roman Empire and Spain), 329, 351–52, 400, 420, 421, 445, 450, 505, 517; civil law under, 452

Charles VIII (France), 335

Chartres, 265, 269

Chateaubriand, 595

Chaucer, Geoffrey, 296–97, 444*f*

Chauncy, Charles, 591

Chi-Rho, *54, 92*

Chiang Kai-shek, 696

Chiesa evangelica Valdese, 280

Child labor, 598, 600

Chile, 709

China, 67, 190, 562–66, 633, 634, 637–39;
Nestorians in, ix, x, 166, 189–90;
persecution in, 190, 695–700, 727

Chomé, Father, 532

Chosroes, 163–64

Chrestus, 98–99

Christian art, ix, 1, 53, 104, 188, 258; Julius
II and, 342; popes and, 328, 329, 336,
426; Savonarola and, 335

Christian Democratic Party, 695, 710

Christian literature: Catholic *vs.* Protestant,
432–33, 436; in China, 699; early
printed, 340–41, *345;* by Luther, 350,
352, 364–65; poetry in, 271–72, 330;
in Russia, 429

Christian music, ix, 58, 194, 203, 271, 275;
Catholic *vs.* Protestant, 416; Gregorian
chant, *193,* 194; Lutheran *vs.* Calvinist,
390; of Oratorians, 416; Zwingli and,
372, 373

Christian Scientists, 627–28

Christian Socialists, 598

Christianity: architecture and, 265–69, *266,*
328, 329; catastrophes of, ix–x; criticism of, 59, 85, 107; cults in (*See*
Cults); early beliefs of, 19; education
and, 203–4, 424, 473, 600*f,* 637, 638,
644, 645; first universal creed of, 122;
Gentile converts to, 26–27, 28; as
global enterprise, ix; Greco-Roman
influence on, 29–30; Hitler's view of,
678; hospitals and, ix, 245*f,* 417, 597,
638; as the "Luminous Religion," 189;
moral code of, 52–53; politics and, 598,
695, 721; science and, 434–40, 637,
651–62; "sect" in, 110*f* (*See also* Protestantism, sects of); social reform and,
595–609; universities and, ix, 30, 277,

587–88, 638, 641; vengeance in, 72,
220; violence and, 247, 248; war and,
222, 225, 227–28, 240–42, 246, 247

"Christianity fever," 699

Christians: first, 19–21; and Law of Moses,
26–27; as martyrs (*See* Martyrs); non-
Catholic, 225, 243; "of St. John," 115;
Old, 442, 443; persecution of and by
(*See* Persecution); statistics on, 725–26;
as term, 19, 25; worshipping with
Moslems, 159

Christmas, 58, 94, 114

Christology, 34, 119–20, 125*f,* 126, 127,
157, 164, 182–83; Moslems and, 164,
176; of Nestorius, 125, 126; Nicene
creed and, 123. *See also* Jesus Christ,
nature of

Christopher, St., 85*f*

Chrysostom, St. John, 61, 103, 108, 138,
152

Church: black, 706, 707, 714; buildings of,
68, 265–69, *266* (*See also* Cathedrals);
"catholic," 111; Decree on the, 722;
"electronic," 717; in homes, 40–41,
697–98, 699, 700; as term, 32; wealth
of, 109, 327

Church of Christ in Japan, 695

Church of England, 403, 461, 557, 569,
588, 590. *See also* Anglicans

Church of God (Abrahamic Faith), 625

Church of God in Christ, 33*f,* 706, 714

Church of God (of Anderson, Indiana), 714

Church of Rome, 19, 36–37, 57, 63, 64;
Celtic Church and, 202*f;* Constantinople *vs.,* 208; Scandinavians and, 209–10

"Church of the East," 126

Church of the Lord, 726

Church of the Nazarene, 714

Church of the Pantocrator, 259

Church reform, 295–323, 330–53, 655–56;
Bible and, *355* (*See also* Hus, John;
Wycliffe, John); church ornaments and,
267; by Gregory VII, 218–19; of
Protestantism, 384. *See also* Counter-
Reformation; Reformation

Churchill, Winston, 688

Chuvashes, 635

Cicero, 145

Circumcellions, 148

Circumcision, 26–27, 187

Cisneros, Ximinez de, 522

Cistercians, 245, 248, 255, 267, 282, 283, 286; reformed, 457

Claesz, Jan, 355–56

Clairvaux, 268

Clare, St., 274

Clark, W. S., 641

Clarkson, Thomas, 550

Claudius, 38, 49

Claver, Pedro, 544

Cleanthes, 29*f*

Clement, 56, 64, 65, 79

Clement IX, Pope, 564

Clement V, Pope, 190, 286, 298, 299

Clement VI, Pope, 291, 293

Clement VII, Pope, 41, 301, 364, 400

Clement VIII, Pope, 56*f,* 457

Clement XI, Pope, 565

Clement XIII, Pope, 531, 536

Clement XIV, Pope, 444*f,* 536

Cleopatra, 3

"Clergy" (as term), 275*f*

Clermont, *223,* 224, 228, 239, 243

Clitherow, Margaret, 462

Clotilda, 195

Clovis, 195

Cluny, 216, 232, 248*f,* 251

Cochlaeus, Johannes, 354–55, 357

Coehlo, Duarte, 520

Coke, Thomas, 590

Colet, John, 415

Coligny, Gaspard II de, 455, 456

College of New Jersey, 587

College of William and Mary, 588

Coloman (king), 230

Colombia, 708

Colon, Diego, 510

Columba, 201

Columbanus, 202

Columbia University, 588

Columbus, Christopher, 445, 506, 508, *510*

Comenius, John, 478

Communalism, 321–22, 377, 384

Communion, 39, 117; AIDS and, 374*f;* excommunication and, 37*f;* Henry VIII and, 405–6; Host in, 374; infant bap-tism and, 40*f;* Luther on, 352, 374, 375–76; misunderstanding of, 51; modern changes in, 722; in Orthodox Church, 225; during Roman persecu-tions, 374; silverware for, 134; *utraquism* in, 321; Zwingli on, 374, 375, 376. *See also* Eucharist/Mass; Lord's Supper

Communism, x, 596, 669–74, 683, 694, 723, 727, 728; in China, 696; libera-tion theology and, 708; in Mexico, 686; in Poland, 700–701; in Soviet Union, 704–5; in Spain, 684–85

Concomitance, 303, 374

Condé, prince of, 455

Cone, James, 707

Confessing Church, 680–81, 691

Confession, 57, 313, 427; defined, 464*f;* Henry VIII and, 406; under torture, 447

Confirmation, 40*f*

Confiteor, 224

Confucius, 563, 564, 565, 640

Congo, 540, 648–49, 726

Congregation of the Index, 435

Congregation of the Oratory, 416

Congregationalists, 398, 465, 636, 654*f;* in Colonial America, 573, 576, 586, 588; as missionaries, 644; slavery and, *541,* 548

Conrad III (Germany), 252

Conrad of Marbug, 285–86

Conrad of Masovia, 220

Constance, Council of, 310, 311, 312, 317, 318, 351

Constans II, 158

Constantine Copronymus, 211

Constantine of Mananali, 114–15, 280

Constantine the African, 249

Constantine the Great, 76, 84, 89–109, *91,* 122, 163, 201, 722; Donation of, 217, 362

Constantine XI Paleologus, 263

Constantinople, 95, 96, 102, 125, 192, 193, 203, 208, 210, 212, 217, 324–25, 328–29, 429, 634, 635; barbarians and, 150; Byzantine prophecy about, 262–63; council at, 123, 124*f,* 127; in

Constantinople (*continued*)
    Crusades, 231, 232–33, 257, 259,
        262–64; Islam and, 157, 158, *170,* 173,
        177, 178, 180; monasteries in, 137,
        138; monks' riots in, 211; Ottoman
        Turks in, 263; university at, 212
Constantius, 106, 108, 123
Consubstantiation, 374
Contarini, Gaspara, 422, 423
Contraception, 723–24, 725
Convent of the Penitents, 426
Convents, 264, 335; first, 134, 137
Conversion: "definitive," 438; as term, 198*f;*
        by word of God, 247, 248, 248*f*
Convocation, 305
Copernicus, 434–35, 436
Coptic Christians, 31, 65–67, 127, 243,
        554; Moslem armies and, 157, 170,
        173–82; Pilate and, 49; *vs.* Melchite,
        173–74
Córdoba, Concha, 708
Cordoba caliphate, 226
Corinthian church, 32–33, 39, 40–41
Cornelius, Pope, 117
Corpus Iuris Canonici, 242
Corripio, Cardinal, 711
Cortés, Hernando, 505, 511–17, 519
Cossa, Baldassare, 309
Coughlin, Charles, 715
Counter-Reformation, 415, 422–23, 439–40
Courtenay, 303
Cowper, William, 549
Cranach, Lucas, 352
Cranmer, Thomas, 401–7, 409–10, *411*
Crawford, Dan, 649
Crescenti family, 214
Crespin, Jean, 433
Crispus, 94
Cristeros, 686
Croatia/Croats, 207, 428, 477, 692
Cromwell, Oliver, 470–71, 472–73, 571*f*
Cromwell, Richard, 473
Cromwell, Thomas, 403, 404, 405
Cross, 53, 165, 187, 261, 284–85; crucifix
        vs., 210; in Crusades, 224, 229, 252,
        253, 260; "first war of the," 164; Greek
        vs. Russian, 665; hatred of, 281; Irish
        High, 200*f;* "True," 164, 244, 244*f;*

253, 346; variants of, 14*f;* visions of,
        91, 92, 104–5
Cross-Bearers, 292
Crowther, Samuel Adjai, 649
Crucifixion, 97; of Christ, 1, 2, 15–16, 104,
        654; described, 14; of Jews, 14, 42; of
        Peter, 41, 50; in Russia, 667
"Crusade tithe," 299
Crusaders, 187, 247, 255, 288; description
        of, 232–33; in Europe, 219–20;
        Moslem view of, 251–52; profits of,
        232*f*
Crusades (Holy Land), 222–39, *256,* 345,
        728; cannibalism in, 234; as Catholic
        vs. Christian, 225; children in, 237,
        259–61; condemnation of, 247–48,
        254; final one, 264; first, *223,* 248;
        fourth, 255–56, *256,* 283; Jerusalem in,
        228, 237–39; justification for, 243–44,
        247; Orthodox Church and, 226, *256,*
        257, 258–59; peasants in, 228–29;
        reasons for, 227–28; second, 253, 255;
        taxes and, 254–55, *256;* third, 254
Cruz, Francisco de la, 538
Cuba, 551, 552
Cults, 719; of martyrs, 72, 85; moon,
        188–89; in Russia, 665–69, 704; of
        Virgin Mary, 48–49, 60, 126, 292,
        657–58
Curia, 299, 301, 344, 345, 422, 426
Cutler, Timothy, 587
Cyprian, St., 53, 67, 76, 77, 117, 118, 182
"Cyprian saints," 615
Cyprus, 262, 728
Cyril of Alexandria, 125–26, 182*f*
Cyril the Barefoot, 281
Cyrillic alphabet, 207, 209
Cyrus of Alexandria, 174–79, 181
Czechs, 207, 309, 318, 702

Da Gama, Christofe, 188
Da Gama, Vasco, 553
Dalmatia, 194
Damascus, 24, *24,* 168
Damasus, Pope, 50, 86, 100, 101, 102
Damien, Father, 632
Daniel of Voltera, 426

Danishmend, 243

Dante, 272, 298, 318–19, 320, 327f

Dark Ages, 155, 207f

Darrow, Clarence, 654

Dartmouth, 588

Darwin, Charles, 642, 651–62, *652*

David (king of Georgia), 244f

David (king of Nubia), 187

David (of Bible), 242

David of Thessalonica, 143

Davis, Sarah Emily, 719

Day of Atonement, 58

De Cernay, Vaux, 283

De Lagarde, Paul, 675

De Montfort, Simon, 283

De Nobili, Roberto, 557, 562, 564

De Sá, Mem, 520

DeSales, Francis, 417, 433

DeSmet, Pierre-Jean, 288, 607–8

Deaconesses, 51, 54, 60

Deacons, 37, 41, 53, 56, 62, 63, 386

Dead Sea, 36, 47

Deborah, 321

Decius, 73, 77, 117, 129

Declaration on Religious Liberty, 722

Decretals, 217–18, 249, 330; Luther and, 351

Decretum Gratiani, 242

Defoe, Daniel, 542–43

Deists, 441f, 591, 592

Deive, Carlos Esteban, 539

Demons, 130, 138, 192, 201, 486, 490–92, 498

Denis, St., 267, 269, 346

Denmark/Danes, 206, 209, 210, 558, 636, 719; as crusaders, 220; slavery and, 546

Dervish, 634

Descartes, René, 437

Devotio Moderna, 330

Diamper, Synod of, 554

Dias de Novais, Paulo, 539

Diáz del Castillo, Bernal, 512, 515, 516

Dickens, Charles, 602, 633

Dictatus Papae, 217, 226

Diggers, 471

Dinter, Artur, 677

Diocletian, 29, 75, 76, 82, 84, 90, 92f, 318

Dionysius Exiguus, 1

Dionysius the Areopagite, 270

Dioscorus, 126, 127

Disciples, 1, 6, 9–10, 16, 18–23

Disciples of Christ, 654f

"Divine right of kings," 97, 465

Divorce, 360, 390, 432, 684, 712

Dobrizhoffer, 530

Docetism, 113f

Döllinger, Johann, 214f

Dom Pedro (Brazil), 552

Dome of the Rock, 171, *172,* 238

Domentianus, 177

Dominic de Guzman, 272, 276–77

Dominicans, 144, 224, 243f, 247, 272, 334, 338, 338f, 419; in Africa, 645; in Americas, 509, 510–11, 511, 519, 523, 535; in China, 564; Hus and, 311; in Inquisition, 277, 278–85, 442, 443, 448, 489, 490; in Japan, 560; Jesuits and, 474; in Philippines, 567; slaves and, 538, 539; in St. Thomas, 553

Domitian, 47, 59–60, 75

Domitilla, Flavia, 53

Donatists, 98, 148, 152, 182

Donne, John, 466

Doppers, 646

Dorheim, Johann von, 227f, 481–82

Dort, Synod of, 392f, 460

Dos Santos, Joáo, 555

Dostoyevsky, Fyodor, 452, 664

Douglass, Frederick, 606

Dow, Lorenzo, 598f

Dowling, William, 468–69

Dragonnades, 457

Draper, John W., 652

Druids, 200

"Drummer," 332–34, 363–64

Ducrue, Benno, 534–35

Duff, Alexander, 632

Dukhobors, 668

Duncan, Gilly, 493

Duppa, Brian, 473

Dura-Europos, 68, 102

Durand of Le Puy, 288

Duranty, Walter, 674f

Dürer, Albrecht, 358, *358*

Dutch, 540, 546, 547, 557, 567, 645–46

Dutch East India Company, 567

Dutch Reformed Church, 572, 577, 588, 646, 707
Dyer, Mary, 572–73

East Indies, 636–37
Easter, 165, 202f, 669f; in early church, 57
Easter Monday, 165
Easter Synod, 216
Eastern church, 58, 111f, 124f, 226, 318, 657; canon law of, 225; Inquisition and, 553–54; predestination and, 391–92; Western vs., 259, 324–25, 723. See also Orthodox Church
Eastern religions, 28–29
Eastern Rite Catholic Church, 657
Ebionites, 27
Eck, Johann, 350–51, 422–23
Eckart, Dietrich, 676
Eckhart, Meister, 272, 330
Ecuador, 709
Ecumenism, 99, 721, 722, 723, 730
Eddy, Mary Baker, 627–28
Edessa, 31, 67, 74, 105, 127, 234, 244, 252; fall of, 165
Edmundson, William, 545
Edward VI (England), 406–7, 414
Edwards, Jonathan, 586, 587
Edwards, Jonathan, Jr., 548
Edwin, 198
Egypt, 66, 129, 130–31, 137, 200f, 634; Islam and, 164, 170, 173. See also Coptic Christians
Ehrenburg, Philipp von, 479
El Cid, 226
El Salvador, 709–10
"Elect," 110, 118–19, 280, 281, 392; Müntzer and, 366–67. See also Predestination
Elias of Cortona, 274
Eliot, John, 580
Elizabeth I (England), 357f, 403, 406, 412–13, 460, 498, 507; excommunication of, 460; plot to assassinate, 462; sent to Tower, 407
Elizabeth of Hungary, St., 285–86
Elvira, Council at, 37
Emde, Johannes, 635
Emich of Leisingen, 229, 230

Emiliani, Jerome, 416
Engels, Friedrich, 595, 596
England, 199, 202, 206, 209, 358, 396, 460–73, 712; censorship in, 432–33; Jesuits in, 536; martyrdom in, 408; Reformation in, 398–99; slavery and, 540, 549–50; social reform in, 595–602; witch-hunts in, 492, 498–99, 502
England, John, 606
Enoch, 47
Eon d'Etoile, 287
Ephesian Church, 46, 66
Ephesus, council at, 126
Epictetus, 29–30
Epiphany, 58; on the Nile, 181
Episcopalians, 398, 638, 640, 649, 654f; charismatic, 715; homosexuality and, 720; women's ordination and, 720
Epistle of Barnabas, 50f
Epistle of the Apostles, 50f
Erasmus, 338–39, 340, 341, 343, 349, 403, 421, 426, 434; proverbs of, 338; Zwingli and, 371
Erigena, John Scotus, 270
Erik, St., 210
Erik (Jutland), 209
Eritreans, 728
Esdras, 47
Esquiline Hill, 103
Essenes, 36
Estonians, 220
Ethelbert, 197–98
Ethiopia, 13, 67, 187–90, 541, 631, 728
Ethiopic Church, 44, 354f
"Ethnic cleansing," 728
Eucharist/Mass, 39, 40, 207, 303, 352; baptism and, 40; under Constantine, 98; deacons and, 62; Gospels and, 44f; Henry VIII and, 406; heresy and, 110f, 114; Host in, 303, 305, 309f, 411, 427, 451; Hus and, 311; as idolatry, 413; martyrs and, 70; in Reformation, 356–57; transubstantiation and, 302–3, 313, 374, 405, 413, 423; unleavened bread in, 212, 225, 324; in vernacular, 352, 376, 722. See also Communion; Lord's Supper
Eudes, John, 416

Eugenius III, Pope, 252
Eulogius, 442
Eunuchs, 213, 666–67
Europe, x, 206, 221, 434–35, 477, 540;
    apathy in, 712–13; Catholicism in,
    210, 460; pagans in, 219; Protestantism
    in, 458, 460
Eusebius, 42, 45, 66, 77, 80, 81, 105, 110,
    366, 553; Constantine and, 92, 93, 94,
    95, 97, 99, 100; on martyrdom, *70,* 71,
    72
Euthanasia, 666, 689
Euthymius, 137
Eutyches, 126, 127
Evangelicals, 551, 695, 720, 726; in Ar-
    gentina, 709; in China, 700
Evangelism, 209, 629–40, 715–16; in China,
    699, 700; in Colonial America,
    586–87; in Counter-Reformation, 416;
    in England, 602; Jesuits as, 424; Puri-
    tan, 580; St. Patrick and, 199–200,
    200; slaves and, 604, 605; social reform
    and, 598, 599; television, 715, 716–17,
    720; in United States, 653
Evans, Evan, 575
Evanson, Edward, 46
Eve, 35
Excommunicanus, 278
Excommunication, 37*f,* 111; Decretals and,
    217–18; of each other by Orthodox and
    Roman churches, 225–26, 723; of
    emperors, 218, 219; of heretics, 87; for
    nonpayment of *servitia,* 299; of pope,
    212, 218, 225, 261, 301; regarding
    relics, 85; for sexual sins, 65; of Theo-
    dosius, 109
Exile, 211, 215, 219, 437, 444
Exorcism, 57

Fabian, Pope, 63, 75
Faisalabad, 730
"Faith, the," 55
Falk, Adalbert, 660
Falwell, Jerry, 715, 717
Farel, Guillaume, 386
Faria, Manuel Severim de, 540
Fascism, 674–93, 695, 727

Faulhaber, Cardinal, 683
Faust, 486
Fawcett, Dame Millicent, 719
Fawkes, Guy, 463–64, *464*
Fazzan, 183, 184
Feast of Candlemas, 492
Feast of Corpus Christi, 303
Feast of Orthodoxy, 211
Feast of St. George the Martyr, 181
Feast of the Purification, 215
Feíjoo, Benito Jerónimo, 434
Felicitas, 69
Felix V, 326
Feminism, 719
Ferdinand, Duke of Parma, 536
Ferdinand, St., 442
Ferdinand (Bohemia), 476
Ferdinand (Castile and Leon), 226
Ferdinand (Spain), 329, 399, 441, 510
Fernandez Abolasia, Juan, 443
Fernandez de Enciso, Martin, 507
Ferrar, Robert, 409
Ferreus, Hugh, 260, 261
Festival of St. Cecilia, 192
Feuillants, 457
Fifth Monarchy, 471, 472
Figueira, Guilhelm, 261
Filipov, Danilo, 667
Finland, 220, 665
Finney, Charles, 653
Fish, sign of, 53, *54*
Fish, Simon, 361, 400–401
Fisher, John, 338, 402, 403
Flade, Dietrich, 481
Flagellation, *289,* 289–90, 292–94, 301, 567
Flanders, 462, 713
Fleming, Archibald, 630
Flemish, 236, 238, 258, 645
Fleury, 215
Florence, 334, 335, 337; Council of, 124*f*
Floretum, 305
Florus, Gessius, 42
Folkhyrd, Quentin, 309
Foot-washing, 466
Formosus, Pope, 214
Foscarini, Paolo, 436
Fournier, Jacques, 284, 285
Fox, Charles James, 550

Fox, George, 471–72, 545, 572
Fox, Margaret, 627
Foxe, John, 406, 408, 433, 440
Française, Action, 678
France, 206, 215, 399, 417, 477, 567, 721;
 Americas and, 536; Calvinist
 Huguenots in, 455–57; crusaders from,
 224, 229, 257*f*, 288; flagellation in,
 292; Jesuits in, 474, 531; missionaries
 from, 631; papacy in, 298–99; slavery
 and, 551–52; witch-hunts in, 481,
 487–88, 489, 492, 502
Francis, Elizabeth, 498
Francis I (France), 343, 385, 507
Francis of Assisi, 272–76, *273*, 418*f*, 433,
 536; Moslems and, 246–47, 274
Franciscans, 190, 247*f*, 272, 274, 276, 290,
 415, 445, 661, 692; in Americas, *509*,
 512, 518, 519, 535, 536; in China,
 564; Hitler and, 681; in Japan, 560; in
 Philippines, 567; slaves and, 538; split
 in, 329–30, 363*f*
Franco, Francisco, 684–85
Franco-Prussian War, 660
Frankfurt Book Fair, 340
Franks, 154, 186, 194, 195, 203, 228,
 232–33, 236, 237, 253, 258, 262
Frederick II (Holy Roman Empire), 261,
 288, 293–94, 443
Frederick II (Prussia), 536
Frederick IV (Denmark), 557–58
Frederick the Wise, 347, 351
Frederick V (Bohemia), 476
Freemason, 268*f*
French, Thomas, 636
"French prophets," 588*f*
French Revolution, 593–95
Frescobaldi, Girolamo, 416
Freud, Sigmund, 713
Friars, 275. *See also* Augustinians; Domini-
 cans; Franciscans
Fridays, no meat on, 227
Frings, Bishop, 690
Frisians, 202, 203, 379
Fritsch, Theodor, 675
Froben, Johann, 352
Fry, Elizabeth, 599

Fulcher of Chartres, 222*f*, 231, 234, 239,
 244, 252
Fundamentalists, 631, 654, 720, 728
Fust, Johann, 340, 341

Gabriel, 160
Gagelin, Isidor, 640
Gaiseric, 153, 154
Galen, Clemens August von, 689–90
Galerius, 90, 91
Galileo, 435–36, *437*, 439, 440
Gallen, St., 202
Gallic Christians, 87–88
Gallus, 106
Gamaliel, 24
Gambia, 544
Ganganelli, Cardinal, 444*f*
Gangra, Council at, 62
Garcia, Miguel, 544
"Garden Tomb," 15*f*
Gardiner, Allen, 632
Garibaldi, Giuseppe, 655, 656
Garnet, Henry, 463–64
Gaucelm de Beziers, Raimon, 255
Gaul, 150, 154, 186, 194, 195, 196, 202
Gebel-Tarik, 185
Gelasius, Pope, 134
Gelimer, 182
Geneva, 386–91, 396, 455, 456
Gentiles, 26–27, 28
George (bishop), 142
George (king of Nubia), 187
George (king of Tonga), 643
George the Martyr, St., 181
Georgian church, 66, 243, 665
"German Christian" movement, 679–80
German Evangelical Church, 679
German Faith Movement, 682
Germanic barbarians, 150, 196
Germanicus, 37
Germanus I, 211
Germany, 202–3, 208, 218, 255, 473–78;
 crusaders from, 230, 232, 252–53, 260;
 flagellation in, 290, 292; Jesuits in,
 424–25, 473–75; Jews in, 293; Luther
 and, 351; pilgrims from, 227; Weimar

Republic of, 677; witch-hunts in, 481–83, 502

Gerung, Mathias, 388

Ghislieri, Michele, 426

"Ghost dancing," 608–9

Gibbon, Edward, 214, 312

Gibbon, James, 653

Gilbert, Humphrey, 507*f*

Gilbraltar, 185

Gilles de Rais, 489, 492

Giustinianni, Giovanni, 263

Glossolalia, 33*f,* 714, 715

Glucharev, Michael Jakovlevich, 635

Gnostic texts, 50*f,* 113–14, 115, 118

Gnötzheim, Hans, Ritter von, 491

Goa, 553–54, *554,* 555, 557

Gobel, Jean Baptiste, 593–94

God: belief in single, 17, 29*f;* dualism of, 50*f;* names for, 17*f*

"God-bearer," 125, *125*

Goebbels, Joseph, 678, 682, 702

Golden Horde, 635, 663*f*

Gomá, Cardinal, 687

Gong Pinmei, Ignatius, 697

Gonzalez, Roque, 526

Gorbachev, Mikhail, 705

Gordon, "Chinese," 633–34, 639

Gordon, Nathaniel, 551

Gospel of Peter, 49

Gospel of the Hebrews, 50*f*

Gospels, 30, 44–46; Eucharist and, 44*f;* "infancy," 48; Mary in various, 48–49; nameless characters in, 50; orthodox *vs.* apocryphal, 19, 47; read in early church, 50–51

Goths, 150, 154, 191–92

Gottfried, Johann, 610*f*

Gottschalk, 219, 392

Graham, Billy, 715–16, *716*

Granada, *441,* 445, 448

Grandier, Urbain, 494

Gratian, 242, 249

Gray Habits, 420

Great Awakening, 586–87

Great Bible, 357*f*

Great Persecution, 72, 76, 84, 91, 98

Great Schism, 301, 309–10, 324

Greece, 634

Greek Catholic Church of the Slavic Rite, 430

Greek Orthodox Church, 13, 66, 111*f,* 212, 243, 634; culture and, 213; on Holy Spirit, 124*f;* Pilate and, 49; Turks and, 428–29. *See also* Eastern church; Orthodox Church

Gregorian calendar, 439, 474, 657

Gregorian chant, *193,* 194

Gregorios, 634

Gregory I, Pope, 249

Gregory IX, Pope, 250, 261, 278, 286*f*

Gregory of Nazianzus, 123, 124

Gregory of Nyssa, 123

Gregory the Great, Pope, 191, 192–99, *193,* 287; Anglo-Saxons and, 196, 198–99; Brunhilde and, 196; missionary work of, 196–97, 210; on torture, 286

Gregory VI, Pope, 216, 217

Gregory VII, Pope, 210, 217–19, 226

Gregory VIII, Pope, 253

Gregory XI, Pope, 300

Gregory XII, Pope, 309, 314

Gregory XIII, Pope, 439, 523, 560

Gregory XVI, Pope, 655

Grimke, Angelina, 551

Grimmelshausen, Hans, 477

Grindal of York, 467

Groote, Gert, 330

Grotius, Hugo, 393

Grub, W. Barbrooke, 630

Grüber, Heinrich, 690

Gruet, Jacques, 394

Guarani, 524, 525–36

Guatemala, 708, 709

Guernica, 687

Guibert of Nogent, 222*f,* 228, 229, 236

Guidi, Cardinal, 659

Guiscard, Robert, 226–27

Guise, 455, 456, 457

Gunszburg, Alexander, 665

Gunther, 227

Gutenberg, Johannes, 340–41

Guthrun, 206

Gutiérrez, Gustavo, 709

Gützlaff, Karl, 638, 646

Guy of Bré, 243

Habsburgs, 400*f*, 458, 473, 475, 476

Hadrian, 77, 196

Hadrian IV, Pope, 249*f*

Hadrian VI, Pope, 344

Haec Sancta, 312

Hakluyt, Richard, 507

Halévy, Elie, 602

Halloween, 492, 493

Hamilton, Patrick, 413

Hannington, James, 648

Hanway, Jonas, 597–98

Harald Bluetooth (Denmark), 209

Harris, Barbara, 720

Harris, Air Marshal "Bomber," 689

Harris, Townsend, 640–41

Harris, William Wadé, 649–50

Harvard, 587–88

Hau-Hau, 643

Hausmannin, Walpurga, 485

Hawaiian Islands, 632

Hawkins, John, 451

Hawkins, Joseph, 539

Healing, 22, 34, 716, 726, 727

Healy, James Augustine, 605

Heathens, 196, 202. *See also* Pagans

Heber, Reginald, 631

Heidelberg, 476

Helena (mother of Constantine), 104–5

Heliodorus, 139

Hell, 37, 83–84, 318–20, 319–20, 488–89

Hellenism, 106–7

Hellenist Jews, 22, 23

Helwys, Thomas, 466

Henry II (France), 452

Henry III (England), 255, 457

Henry III (Holy Roman Empire), 216

Henry IV (France), 457, 467

Henry IV (Holy Roman Empire), 218, 226

Henry of Navarre, 457

Henry V (England), 306, 307, 311

Henry VI (Holy Roman Empire), 254

Henry VIII (England) , 357*f*, 359, 398–405, *400*

Heraclius, 163, 164, 168–69, 173–74, 175, 177, 181

Heresy, 99*f*; about Trinity, 119–24; act passed against, 305; baptism and, 451; blasphemy and, 110; definition of, 278;

first widespread, 111–12; formal *vs.* material, 110*f*; Gnostic, 50*f*; Hippolytus and, 116, 117; Hus and, 313, 314, *316*; Luther and, 350–51; Manichaean, 118–19; Orthodox Church view of, 212; penalty for, 86–88; poverty doctrine as, 330; Queen Elizabeth charged with, 460; regarding Mary, 49; Savonarola and, 337; schisms and, 110*f*, 182; witchcraft as, 488, 491, 503; Wycliffe charged with, 295, 303. *See also* Apostasy

Heretics, 110–28, 408, 425; As "ambassadors of Antichrist," 215; Arabs and, 159; Arians and, 71, 155; Beza on, 453–54; burning alive of, 306–8, 316, 317, 330, 334, 382, 448 (*See also* Martyrs); Castellio on, 454; Crusades and, 229, 254; Dominic and, 276–77; Inquisition and (*See* Inquisition); Judas and, *10*; Nestorians as, 158; non-Catholic Christian, 225; popes as, 309; Second Vatican Council and, 722–23; writers as, 432; Zwingli and, 373–74

Hermits, 129, *130*, 130–31, 131, 138, 228, 553, 664; flagellation by, 289–90; of Karoulia, 213; women as, 134

Herod, 2

Herod Antipas, 5, 12

Herod the Great, 3, 5, 6, 47

Herrick, Robert, 466

Herriot, Edouard, 674*f*

Hervormde Kerk, 646

Hieria, Synod at, 211

Higbee, John M., 622

Higges, Eleanor, 305

Hilarion, 137

Hilary, St., 152, 186*f*

Hildebrand, Pope, 216, 217

Hildegard of Bingen, 271–72

Hill, John, 447

Hindenburg, Paul, 669*f*

Hindus, 553, 555, 557, 558, 629, 636, 637, 730

Hippo, *151*, 152, 154

Hippodrome, 123

Hippolytus, 56, 57, 59, 62, 116, 117, 302–3

Hitler, Adolf, 674–83, 688, 695, 701

Hobbes, Thomas, 492

Höchstädter, Walter, 690

Hoen, Cornelius, 374

Hoffman, Melchior, 376–77

Holiness Movement, 713–14

Holland, 465–66, 570

"Holy days," 492

"Holy fools," 287

Holy Ghost Fathers, 633, 678

Holy Lance, 235, 236

Holy Land, 104, 215, 244; first English
    pilgrim to, 203; Templars and, 245–46

Holy Roman Emperor, 203*f,* 215, 216, 218,
    254, 400*f*

Holy Week, 58

Homoeans, 123

Homosexuality, 65, 681, 717, 720, 725;
    Bible and, 450; Inquisition and, 450

Hong Kong, 637–38, 646, 696, 700, 720,
    720*f*

Honnecourt, Villard de, 269

Honorius, 152

Hooker, Richard, 423, 466

Hooper, John, 405, 406, 409

Hopkins, Gerard Manley, 661

Hopkins, Matthew, 498–99

Hopkins, Samuel, *541*

Horne, Thomas, 354*f*

Hosius, 99, 108

Hospitals, ix, 245*f,* 417, 597, 638

Hottentots, 645

Howard, John, 599

Howe, Julia Ward, 606

Hradcany Castle, *475*

Hübmaier, Balthasar, 287

Huddlestone, Trevor, 707

Hugh de Payens, 245

Hugh of Cluny, 232

Hugo, Victor, 672

Hugo (of Edessa), 252

Huguenots, 397, 426, 427, 433, 455–56,
    457, 645; in Colonial America, 569,
    576; slavery and, 537, 544–45

Hum, 281

Humanism, 325

Humanists, 352, 353, 371, 434

Humbert, Cardinal, 225

Humphreys, David, 604

Hung Hsiu-ch'an, 638–39

Hungary, 210, 220, 230, 288, 292, 428, 702

Huns, 150

Huntington, De Witt Clinton, 714

Hus, John, 308–9, 310–18, *316,* 325;
    Luther and, 350–51, 352

Hussites, 321, 351, 476

Hutchinson, Anne, 571

Hutten, Ulrich von, 352

Hutter, Jakob, 384

Hutterites, 384

Huxley, T. H., 652

Hypatia, 108

Iamblichus, 106

Iberia, 182–86, 226*f,* 248

Iconoclasts, 211, 468–69, *469*

Icons/images, 19, 191, 213, 263, 666; in
    Crusades, 258; in Ethiopian Church,
    187; of Justinian, 191; Protestants and,
    211–12, 407; in Russia, 209, 663; of
    Virgin Mary, *125;* "war of the icons"
    and, 210–11

Idolatry, 197, 210–11, 438

Ignatius Loyola, 418–20, 424, 430, 555, 567

Ignatius of Antioch, 32, 52, 64, 71, 425;
    heresy and, 114; on nature of Christ,
    124; orthodoxy established by, 111–12

Illuminated manuscripts, 134, 136, 307, 308

Illuminati, 417

Imitation of Christ, 330–31

Incas, 505, 518–20

Independents, 472–73

Index of Prohibited Books, 426, 431, 433,
    440, 510, 653

India, ix, 67, 553–58, 629–36, *632,* 636–37;
    Carey in, 629–30, *630,* 636; evangeli-
    cals in, 726–27; Gordon in, 634; St.
    Thomas and, 31; Xavier and, *425*

Indian Mutiny, 636

Indians (East), 553–58; converts in, 555

Indians (of Americas) , 504–24, *509, 518,*
    577, 709; Jesuits and, 524, 525–36,
    527, 535; protest about cruelty to,
    510–11; religion of, 513, 514, 518–19;
    slavery of, 509, 510, 522, 526, 537,
    538, 543

Indians (of North America), 578–82, 607–8; Anglicans and, 588; Catholics and, 577; "ghost dancing" of, 608–9; Jesuits and, 582–85, 607–8; Mormons and, 619, 621–23; Penn, William, and, *581,* 581–82; Williams, Roger, and, 571

Indochina, 640

Indonesia, 33*f,* 635, 728

Indulgences, 268, 309, 312, 313, 413; Luther and, 344, 349–50; printing of, 341; purgatory and, 318; Zwingli and, 371

Industrial Revolution, 595–97

Inge, 210

Inglis, Charles, 590

Ingram, 463

Innocent I, Pope, 432

Innocent III, Pope, 249, 255, 259, 260, 274, 280; Cathars, 278, 280, 282–83

Innocent IV, Pope, 278–79

Innocent VIII, Pope, 345, 487, 489–90

Innocent X, Pope, 478, 564

Inquisition: castles used in, 447; medieval, 277–88, 294, 423, 489–90; new name for, 725; protests against, 279, 287; Roman, 431, 434, 440–41; Seville, 450–51; Spanish (*See* Spanish Inquisition); Valladolid, 450

Institoris, 489, 490, 491

Iran, 115, 636

Iraq, 115, 165, 166, 167

Ireland, 200–203, 468, 470, 634

Irena, 211

Irenaeus, 55, 63, 67; heresy and, 114, 116

Irish, 196, 200–203, 319, 654; Antichrist beliefs among, 215; Patrick, St., and, 199–200

Irish Church, 67*f*

Irish Litany of Saints, 200*f*

Isaac Angelus, 256, 257

Isaac (Cistercian), 248

Isabel, St., 523–24

Isabella (Spain), 329, 399, 441, 508

Isidore of Seville, St., 86, 195, 486, 487, 541

Islam, ix, x, 555; in Africa, 728; in Bosnia, 281; converts to, 162, 176, 185; Crusaders' lack of interest in, 251; "five pillars of," 162; jihad in, 165–67, 252,

728; militancy of, 170; moral force in, 169; Orthodox Church and, 212; as rival to Christianity, 158, 161–62; Spanish Inquisition and, 441. *See also* Arab Moslems; Moslems

Islamic invasions, 156–90, 428–29; in African and Iberian regions, 182–90; 'Abd ar-Rahman in, 186; Copts in, 173–82; fall of Jerusalem in, 168–73; Grän "the Left-Handed" in, 187–88; ibn Tumart in, 186; jihad in, 165–67; Kahina and, 184–85; 'Amr ibn al-As in, 173–80, 181; Nubians in, 186–90; in Socotra, 188–89; Uqba ibn Nafi al-Fihra in, 183–85; Waddan and, 183; welcomed by some, 157

Israel, 728

Italy, 191, 193–94, 218, 290, 440, 441, 542; crusaders from, 224, 260

Ivan III, 427

Ivan the Terrible (IV), 388, 429–30

Ivo of Chartres, 241*f*

Izquierda, Joana, 494

Jacobins, 593–95, 602

Jacobites, 127, 169, 243, 244

Jacques of Vitry, 247, 250, 275

Jaga, 539

Jaime I of Aragon, 248

James, L. L., 641

James, St., 36, 41, 46, 48, 512; Book of, 48, 361; Protevangelium of, 48

James I (England), 463, 465, 467, 493

James II (England), 573

James of Voragine, 419

James VI (Scotland), 413, 463, 493

Jannaeus, Alexander, 14

Jansen, Cornelius, 437–38

Jansenists, 437, 564

Janszoon, Laurens, 346*f*

Japan, 558–62, 641–42, 688, 689, 695, 696

Java, 567, 635

Jefferson, Thomas, 549, 591, 592

Jehovah's Witnesses, 625–26, 673, 680, 704

Jeremiah II, 429, 430

Jerome, St., 36, 68, 85, 100–101, 105, 109, 123, 130, 145, 349

Jerome of Prague, 312, 317

Jeronimite monastery, 450, 451

Jeronimo de Santa Fe, 442

Jerusalem, 4, 5, 26–27; beliefs about, 229; in
Crusades, 228, 237–39, 245, 253–59,
261–62; fall of, 168–73, *170;* pilgrims
to, 227; siege of, 42–43, 163–64; Stations of the Cross in, 276*f;* temple in,
6–7, 8–9, 45, 46

Jesuit Antonio Possevino, 430

Jesuits, 424, 426, 430, 433, 468–77, 654,
660, 661, 722; in Africa, 645; in Americas, 520, 524, 525–36, *527, 535,*
607–8; Arnaud and, 438; calendar of,
563; in China, 189, 562–66; in Colonial America, 577, 578, 582–85; founding of, 420; in India, 554, 555–57, 637;
in Japan, *559,* 559–62; Pascal and, 438;
Paul IV and, 425; persecution of, 461,
463, 470; slavery and, 538, 539, 544; in
Spain, 684; witchcraft and, 493

Jesus Christ, x, 2–17, 26, 46, 47–49, 69,
270, 271; Americans' belief about, x;
baptism of, 5, 58; and "baptism of Holy
Spirit," 714; birth of, 1–2, 4, 16, 111;
in Book of Mormon, 612; in *The
Brothers Karamazov,* 452–53; crucifixion
of, 1, 2, 15–16, 104; divinity of, 121,
124; Hitler and, 675–76, 682; Hus
compared to, 317; as Messiah, x, 2,
4–5; name of, 4*f;* nature of, 19, 34,
110, 119–20, 124–25, 126, 173 (*See
also* Christology); Nazis and, 682;
personal faith in, 295, 353; prayer
taught by, 2, 3 (*See also* Lord's Prayer);
predictions by, 8–9, 45; prophecies
fulfilled by, *x,* 4–5, 6, 15, 16; "Q" and,
33*f;* resurrection of, 3, 17–18, 34–35,
46, 48, 57–58; as Son of God, x, 2, 11,
55, 183, 730; vision of, 608; war and,
241; women and, 18, 35, 45

Jesus Movement, 330

"Jesus Only" churches, 715

Jews, 7, 17, 21, 31, 35; Arabs as converted,
159; Bonhoeffer and, 690; census on,
654*f;* as "Christ-killers," 293; and
Christian martyrs, 74; in Colonial
America, 572; as converts, 442; crucifixion of, 14, 42; Crusaders compared
to Old Testament, 246; Crusades and,
229–30, 239, 676; as early Christians,
26–28; hatred of, 49, 690 (*See also*
Anti-Semitism); Hellenist, 22, 23; in
medieval Inquisition, 285; Messiah of,
4, 17; Moslems and, 161, 163, 166;
Nazis and, 674–75, 677–83, 690–91,
692; Orthodox, 5, 22, 23; persecution
of, 13, 73, 108, 225*f,* 229–30, 242,
249, 285, 292–93, 425–26, 442, 446,
449, 665, 675–83, 689, 722 (*See also*
Nazis); Protestants and, 598; in Roman
Empire, 25, 42–43, 47; in Russia, 665;
Second Vatican Council and, 722; in
Spanish Inquisition, 441, 442, 444,
448–50, 455; Spinoza and, 439; witch
hunters and, 491

Joachim of Fiore, 251, 329–30

Joan, Pope, 214

Joanna of Naples, 298, 301

Job, Book of, 193

Jobson, Richard, 544

Jogaila, 221

Jogues, Isaac, 583–84

Johannes, 185

John, Griffith, 639

John, St., 45, 46, 47, 72, 72*f,* 152, 439

John III (Sweden), 423

John Mark, 45*f,* 60

John of Avila, 418

John of Barca, 175

John of Damascus, St., 211

John of Marga, 189

John of Monte Corvino, 190

John of Nikiuu, 175, 176, 177, 181

John of the Cross, 418

John Paul, Pope, 724

John Paul II, Pope, 437, 640*f,* 700, 709,
723–25, *724*

John the Baptist, 5, 8, 40, 241, 492

John Tzimisces, Emperor, 280

John VIII, Pope, 213

John X, Pope, 214

John XI, Pope, 85*f,* 214

John XII, Pope, 214

John XV, Pope, 215

John XVI, Pope, 213

John XXII, Pope, 298, 310–13, 317, 330, 363*f*
John XXIII, Pope, 312*f*, 721–22
Johnston, Albert, 623
Jones, Absalom, 605
Jones, James, 718
Joseph, John, 730
Joseph, Metropolitan, 671
Joseph of Arimathea, 16, 104
Joseph of Volokolamsk, 427
Josephus, 42, 43, 47
Jubilee, 327, 416
Judaism, 111–12; conversion to, 306
Judas Iscariot, 9, 10, *10,* 18, 46*f,* 47, 319, 664
Jude, St., 31, 46
Judson, Adoniram, 637
Julian of Norwich, 271
Julian "the Apostate," 105–6
Julius II, Pope, 329, 341–43, *342,* 388, 509
Julius III, Pope, 424
Junius, Johannes, 482–83
Justin Martyr, 39, 44*f,* 53–56, 74–77, 78
Justinian, 182, 183, 191, 192
Jutes, 154
Jutland, 209
Juvenal, 79

Kaas, Ludwig, 679
Kalmucks, 635
Kanis, Peter, 322
Katherine, St., 305
Kemp, Dennis, 630
Kempis, Thomas á, 330–31
Kent, 197
Kestutis, Grand Duke, 221
Keynes, John Maynard, 670
Khartoum, 728
Khlysts, 667–68
Kicking Bear, 608
Kiev, 208–9, 665
Kimbangu, Simon, 726
King, Martin Luther, Jr., 705–6, *706,* 708
King Philip's War, 580–81
Kingsley, Charles, 598
Kino, Eusebio, 534
"Kirishitan band," 561, *561*

Knighton, Henry, 304
Knights Hospitallers, 428
Knights Templars, 245, 247, 248, 261, 262, 286
Knipperdollinck, Bernt, 376–77, 379, 382
Knox, Alfred, 669*f*
Knox, John, 396, 412–13
Konga Vantu, 649
Kopolev, Lev, 672
Koran, 19, 158, 160, 161, 162, 181, 426, 542; Abraham in, 161; on Christianity, 164; translation into Latin of, 251
Korea, 640, 695–96
Korean War, 696
Koresh, David, 718
Kosovar Moslems, 728
Krak des Chevaliers, *233*
Krämer, Heinrich, 489
Krapt, Johann, 647*f*
Khrushchev, Nikita, 672, 704, 721
Kublai Khan, 189–90
Kudugers, 281
Kulturkampf, 660–61, 683
Küng, Hans, 725
Kurds, 167

La Pecosa, 686
Labouré, Catherine, 657
Lactantius, 92
Lake Constance, 202
Lalement, Gabriel, 584
Lalibela, 187
Lamberts, Lucas, 355–56
Lamennais, Félicité de, 655
Lancilotto, Nicolas, 555
Langland, William, 290
Langres, 216
Languedoc, 254, 281, 282, 455
Laodicean Church, 124
Laon, 269
Lapierre, John, 576
Lapps, 221
Las Casas, Bartolomé de, 510–11, *513,* 519–20
Last Supper, 20
Lateran, St. John, 102–3
Lateran Council, Fifth, 343

Lateran Council, Fourth, 302

Lateran Council, Third, 254, 390

Latimer, Hugh, 406, 409

Latin, 67–68, 243, 303, 304; in China, 564–65; decline of, 325; replacing Greek, 182

Latin America, 33f, 708–11

Latin Mass, 207, 328, 722

Latin Rule of Benedict, 136

Latins (vs. Eastern Catholics), 244–45, 248

Latrocinium, 126, 127

Latzenborck, Lord Henry, 310, 311

Laud, William, 467–68

Lausanne, 269

Lavalette, 531

Lavigerie, Cardinal, 636

Lay, Benjamin, 545

Lazarists, 417

LeCaron, Joseph, 583

LePuy, 236, 237, 288

Leander, 197

Lebanon, 728

Lee, Ann, 588–89

Lee, John D., 622

Lefebvre, Marcel, 722–23

Leibniz, Gottfried, *440*

Leiden, Jan van, 378, 379–83, *383*

Lenin, Vladimir, 669–70, 672, 674, 676, 681

Lent, 57, 227

Leo III, "the Isaurian," 210, 211

Leo IV, Pope, 242

Leo IX, Pope, 216–17

Leo the Great, Pope, 62, 114, 119, 120–21, 126, 127, *151,* 154

Leo V, "the Armenian," 211

Leo X, Pope, 343–45, 363, 364, 398, 506, 509, 538; Luther and, 350, 352–53, 361

Leo XIII, Pope, 661

Leocritia, 441–42

Leontius (emperor), 185

Leopold II (Belgium), 648

Lepers, 135–36, 727; Damien and, 632; Francis of Assisi and, 273, 274; in Inquisition, 285

Lewis, C. S., 713

Li Tim Oi, Florence, 720f

Liberation theology, 707–10

Liberia, 549f, 551, 606, 649

Libertins, 388

Libya, 182, 183, 186

Licinius, 93, 94–95

Lilburne, John, 468

Lima, Council of, 522

Lin Xili, 727

Lisbon, 248, 506

"List of Superstitions," 487

Litanies, 457

Lithuania, 220–21, 665, 691

"Little Flower of Lisieus," 658

Liutprand, 214

Livingston, William, 588

Livingstone, David, 552, 631, 646–48

Livonia, 220, 430

Llano, Queipo de, 686

Ló, 564–65

Lollards, 304–7, 308, 340; Hus and, 309, 311

Lombards, 193, 194, 195, 362f

Lombardy, 486

London, 595–96, 599, *601*

Lopéz, Gregorio, 564

Lord's Prayer, 40, 115, 132. *See also* "Our Father" (Paternoster)

Lord's Supper, 39, 55–56, 103. *See also* Communion; Eucharist/Mass

Louis, Duke, 315, 316, 317, 318

Louis, St., 346

Louis VII (France), 250, 251, 252, 254

Louis IX (France), 288

Louis XIV (France), 457, 502, 576, 585

Louis XV (France), 531

Lourdes, 658, *658,* 727

Low Countries, 458, 459–60

Lucas of Tuy, 287

Lucian of Samosata, 63

Luciferians, 286

Lucius III, 278

Ludolph the Carthusian, 419

Lugard, Frederick, 648

Luis of Granada, 418

Luke, St., 45, 345

Luther, Martin, 339, 344, 347–53, *349,* 358, 361, 363–68, 384, 385, 388, 399, 406,

Luther, Martin (*continued*)
413, 453, 466, 707; anti-Semitism of,
683; apocalyptic risings and, *358;*
Carlstadt and, 352, 366, 376; Counter-
Reformation and, 415, 422; on predestination, 392; on Turks, 428; on usury,
390–91; on witches, 487, 490; on
women, 389–90; Zwingli and, 370–71,
373–76
Lutheranism, 359; Henry VIII and, 404;
Pietist, 557–58; in Sweden, 423
Lutherans, 370, 376, 377, 429–30, 477,
654*f;* Calvinists *vs.,* 390, 474, 476;
Catholics *vs.,* 377, 398*f,* 420, 421, 424,
476; in Colonial America, 569,
573–75, 575; Hitler and, 678, 689;
Jews and, 446, 677; persecution of, 385,
446, 450, 451; slaves and, 537, 605;
women's ordination by, 719
Luxembourg, 202
Luxor, 108
Lyman, Henry, 636
Lyttleton, Oliver, 713

MacArthur, Douglas, 695
Maccabean wars, 73
Maccabees, Book of, 246
Macedonia, 263, 428, 635; torture in, 70,
82
Machiavelli, 218, 328, 337, 341–42, 456
Machu Picchu, 519
Mack, Alexander, 574
Macrufius, St., 137
Madison, James, 591, 592
Magdalen Hospital, 597
Magellan, Ferdinand, 567
Magi, 479*f*
Magyars, 205, 207–8, 215
Mahdi, 634
Mainz, 230, 325, 332
Malabar, 31, 188, 553–57, *554,* 564
Malan, Daniel, 707
Malcolm X, 706–7
Malleus Maleficarum and, 490–91
Manchester, 595, 596–97
Manciano, Girolamo, 336
Mandaeans, 115

Mandela, Nelson, 707, 708
Mani, 118–19, 145, 280
Manichaeans, 118–19, 145–46, 148
"Manifest Destiny," 607, 631
Manje, Juan Mateo, 534
Manning, Henry, 656, 657, 659
Mansfeld, Count, 477
Mantz, Felix, 373–74
Manuel Comnenus, 248*f*
Manuel the Fortunate, 538
Mao Zedong, 696–97, *698, 699*
Map, Walter, 247–48
Marcellinus, 71, 89, 101
Marcellus, 76, 122–23
Marcellus II, 79
March for Jesus, 726
Marcian (emperor), 141
Marcion, 112–15, 280, 679
Marcionites, 28, 113–15, 719
Marco Polo, 188, 189, 558
Marcus of Arethusa, *70*
Margaret of Salisbury, 408
Marine Society, 598
Marists, 633, 642, 644
Maritain, Jacques, 687
Mark, Republic of St., 67*f*
Mark, St., 31, 45, 66–67
Maronites, 66, 245, 728
Marot, Clément, 390
Marozia, 214
Marprelate, Martin, 466
Marquette, Jacques, 584–85
Marriage, 65, 86, 313, 724; "Forbidden
days" in, 227; Orthodox *vs.* Roman
Catholics on, 225; Protestants *vs.*
Catholics on, 389
Marsden, Samuel, 642
Marsiglio of Padua, 363
Marston Moor, 470
Martin del Rio, 493
Martin I, Pope, 158–59, 191
Martin of Braga, 486, 487
Martin of Paris, Abbot, 258–59
Martin of Tours, 87–88
Martinez de Cantalapiedra, Martin, 434
Martinitz, Jaroslav, 475–76
Martyrs, ix, x, 23, 36, 69–88, *70,* 70–71, 73,
92*f,* 154, 211; in Africa, 57, 648; asce-

tics *vs.*, 129; in China, 698, 727; Christian *vs.* Moslem, 171; Crusaders as, 247; cults of, 72, 85; in England, 408, 409; Henry VIII and, 406; in Indochina, 640; Irish, 656; in Islamic invasions, 170–71; in Japan, *559,* 561, *561;* Korean, 640; in Latin America, 709–10; in Mexico, 686; missionaries as, 631–32, 695; popes as, 71, 76, 158–59; in Roman games, *74,* 79–81, 85; in Russia, 665–67; in South Pacific, 643–45; in Spain, 686; Tertullian on, x, 69, 71, *74. See also* Persecution

Marx, Karl, 596

Marxism, 670, 686, 709, 721

Mary, Queen of Scots, 460–61, 462, 463

Mary (England), 357*f,* 398, 399, 406–12

Mary Magdalene, St., 16, 17, 47, 346

Mary (mother of James), 16, 17

Mary (mother of Jesus), 15, 48, 125. *See also* Virgin Mary

Mary (mother of John Mark), 60

Maryknoll fathers, 708

Masada, 47

Mason, C. H., 714, 715

Masonic lodge, 268*f*

Masseta, Simón, 526

Mater Dolorosa, 292

Mather, Cotton, 499–502, *500,* 539, 571, 581

Mather, Increase, 499, 502

Matilda of Tuscany, 218

Matthew, St., 45

Matthys, Jan, 377–79

Maundy Thursday, 58

Mauriac, François, 687

Maurice (emperor), 193, 194

Maurras, Charles, 678

Maxentius, 91, 92

Maximian, 67, 76, 91

Maximilian, 474, 476

Maximilla, 115–16

Maximus of Smyrna, 106, 107

Mayflower, 466, 569–70

Mayhew, Thomas, 580

Mayne, Cuthbert, 461

Mazzini, Giuseppe, 655, 656

McCosh, James, 654

McDougall, Francis, 632

Meacham, Joseph, 589

Mecklenburg Appeal, 219

Medici family, 335, 336, 343, 364, 400, 433, 455

Medina, 166

Megapolensis, Johannes, 572, 584

Mehmed, 263

Mehmed II, 328–29

Melanchthon, Philip, 356, 375, 393, 423

Melchite church, 66, 173–74, 657

Melitius, 89

Melito, 57

Melville, Andrew, 465

Melville, Herman, 643

Menas, 174

Mendoza, Cristóbal de, 526–27

Menezes, Joáo de, 555–56

Menezis, Alexis de, 553–54

Mennonites, 357*f,* 383*f,* 574, 590, 704

Mercado, Tomás de, 539, 543

Mesopotamia, 165, 166, 253

Messalians, 138–39

Messalina, 38

Messiah, 4, 17; Jesus Christ as, x, 2, 4–5; Mahdi-, 186; of the Paiutes, 608–9

Messnar, Father, 532

Mestizos, 522–23

Methodism: Calvinism and, 393*f;* in Colonial America, 589–90; slavery and, *541,* 548; splits of, 598*f*

Methodists, 398, 602, 629*f,* 630, 632*f,* 633, 654*f;* Holiness movement of, 714; as missionaries, 638, 640, 644; Primitive, 598*f,* 602; slavery and, 550, 551, 605; Southern *vs.* Northern, 605

Methodius (brother of Cyril), 207

Methodius (of Constantinople), 211

Methodius of Omsk, 705

Methodius (Orthodox bishop), 666

Meusel, Marga, 681

Mexico, 511–18, 523, 536, 686; Council of, 522

Michael III, 211, 212

Michael the Syrian, 169

Michelangelo, 329, 343, 421, 424

"Middle Kingdom," 204

Miller, William, 624

Millerites, 624

Milner, James, 471

Miltitz, Charles von, 350

Milton, John, 432–33, 436, 571

Milvian Bridge, 92, 102

Mindszenty, Jozsef, 702

Mirabel of Sicily, 260–61

Miracles, 22, 34, 45, 140, 184, 201, 202, 235, 237, 247*f*, 292, 544, 727; Gregory the Great and, 192; in India, 726–27; in "infancy gospels," 48; by Jesus Christ, 3, 5, 6; at Lourdes, 658

Missionaries, 199, 200, 629–40; cannibalism and, 643, 645; to Central Asia, 635; of Dark Ages, 207*f*; to East, 553–67; to East Indies, 635–37; Gregory the Great and, 196–97, 210; as martyrs, 631–32, 695; Nestorian, 127; slaves and, 538; to South Pacific, 642–45, *643;* to southern states, 606. *See also specific countries*

Mladonovice, Peter, 314*f,* 317, 320

Moffat, Robert, 646

Moguls, 556–57, *557*

Molina, Luis de, 538

Molokans, 668–69, 704

Monarchians, 119–20, 123

Monasteries, 200–203, 275; Augustinian, 144, 148; at Ávila, 447; Benedictine, 136; Carmelite, 418; in China, 189; of Cluny, 216; coenobitic *vs.* idiorhythmic, 212–13; Columbanus and, 202; contemplation in, 137–38; in Egypt, 180; founded by Amandus, 207*f;* of Fritzlar, 202; of Fulda, 202; of Gallen, St., 202; Gregory, Pope, and, 192; Henry VIII and, 404; Islam and, 180, 181; of La Verne, 270; Lindisfarne, 204, 205; Matins in, 135*f;* of Monte Cassino, 249; at Mount Athos, 212–13; mysticism and, 270; of Our Lady, 66*f;* of Pachomius, 131–34; of San Marco, 334; of St. Bernard, 268; of St. Matthew, 167; of St. Thomas Aquinas, 442; Vikings and, 204, *205;* for women, 134

Mongols, ix, 167, 190, 263, 663*f*

Moniño, Joseph, 536

Monita Secreta, 474

Monk, Thomas, 545

Monks, 129–43, 188, 211, 219, 220, 656; Basil the Great and, 134–36; Carthusian, 270; as cathedral builders, 268; in China, 189; discalced, 418*f;* in Egypt, 180; Erasmus and, 338; "hammer of the," 211; Hitler and, 681; Ionian, 201, 202, 204, 205, 206; in Ireland, 200–201, 202, 319; as martyrs, 211, 219; riots of, 211; Savonarola and, 335; in Soviet Union, 704. *See also specific orders*

Monophysites, 127

Monothelitism, 127, 173

Montaigne, Michel, 456

Montanus, 115–16, 117

Monte, Giovanni del, 421

Montesinos, Antonio de, 510, 511

Montezuma, 513, 516, 517

Montezuma II, 512–13

Montier-en-Der, 215

Montoyo, Antonio Ruiz de, 525, 526, 527

Montúfar, Alonso de, 543

Moody, Dwight, 653

Moon cult, 188–89

Moors, 183, 185, 226, 434, 542, 687; in Inquisition, 441, 442, 445, 455

Moral Majority, 717, 721

Moravia, 207, 208, 310, 384

More, Thomas, 400, 403, 404

Mormons, 19, 610–24, *614,* 654*f;* imprisonment of, *620;* split in, 617

Morocco, 167, 182, 186, 226*f*

Morone, Giovanni, 425, 441

Morris, C. S., 645

Morrison, Robert, 637, 638

Morse, Jedidiah, 591*f*

Morse, Samuel, 653

Moscow, *429,* 596, 663; as "Third Rome," 325, 427–28

Moses, 7, 112, 241, 327*f,* 328, 391, 676; Books of, 610; Crusades and, 225; early Christians and Law of, 26–27; statue of, 343

Moslems, 687; in Africa, 648; as apostates, 635; in Britain, 730; as converts, 162, 248–50, 445, 635, 636, 637; Crusades and, 222, 237, 238, 239, 243, 245, 246–47; Francis of Assisi and, 246–47,

274; Gordon and, 634; in India, 553; Jacques of Vitry and, 247; Kosovar, 728; in modern times, 728; Orthodox Christians and, 248; Ottoman Turks as, 428–29 (*See also* Ottoman Turks); persecution and (*See* Persecution); Russia and, 665, 669–70; slavery and, 207, 445, 538, 540, 542, 550, 552, 555; in Spanish Inquisition, 442, 446; Sunni *vs.* Shiite, 161–62, 243; Westerners as viewed by, 251–52; worshipping with Christians, 159

Motolinia, 512

Mott, John Raleigh, 629*f*

Mount Athos, 212

Mount of Olives, 6, 9, 10, 62, 105

Mount Sion, Cathedral on, 163

Mount Tabor, 321

Mozambique, 555

Muggleton, Ludowicke, 471

Muhammad, 19, 118, 156–62, 183, 248, 319

Muhammad II, 324*f*

Muhlenbuerg, Henry, 575

Müller, Ludwig, 679, 680

Mumford, Catherine, 602

Muncie, George, 716

Munson, Samuel, 636

Münster, 376–84, 719

Müntzer, Thomas, 359–60, 366–69

Muratorian Canon, 51

Murphy-O'Connor, Cormac, 712

Murray, John Courtney, 722

Musa, 185–86

Mussolini, Benito, 678–79, 683, 691

Mutesa, 648

Mwanga, 648

Myconius, 404

Mystics, 83, 114, 139, 148, 159, 160, 269–94, 300, 338, 366, 427, 575, 633; in Counter-Reformation, 417–18; as heretics, 86–88; nuns as, 270–72

Nagel, Hans, 381

Nantes, Edict of, 457

Napoleon (Bonaparte), 203*f,* 400*f,* 536, 551–52, 595, 655

Napoleon III, 640, 660

Native American Church, 607, 609. *See also* Indians (of North America)

Nayler, James, 472

Nazis, 674–75, 677–83, 688–93, 702, 704; denunciation of, 690–91, 692

Nebuchadnezzar, 174

Neenguirú, Nicolas, 530

Neesima, Joseph, 641

Neoplatonism, 106, 108

Neri, Philip, 416, 417, 427

Nero, ix, *38,* 38–39, 41, 42, 50, 73, 427; as Antichrist, 72; Pilate and, 49

Nestorians, 66, 126, 127, 158, 165–66, 167, 553; Catholics *vs.,* 190; in China, ix

Nestorius, 125, *125,* 126

Netherlands, *289,* 397, 461, 462, 477

Netter, Thomas, 305, 311

New Church of Justinian, 163

New Jerusalem, 376, 383*f*

New Orleans, Council of, 585

New Testament, 25, 44, 47, 107, 637; canonical *vs.* apocryphal books of, 19, 47, 50–51

New Zealand, 642–43, 720

Newman, John Henry, 656, 727

Newton, Isaac, 434, 437, 439, 440

Newton, John, 546–47, *547*

Nicaea, 233–34

Nicaea, Council of, 57*f,* 63*f,* 99, 110, 121, 211

Nicaragua, 709, 710

Nicene creed, 122, 123, 128, 212, 324

Nicephorus I, 167

Nicholas I, Pope, 286

Nicholas II, Pope, 217

Nicholas II, czar (Russia), 664–65

Nicholas the Great, Pope, 212, 213

Nicholas V, Pope, 324–27, 328, 329, 349, 363*f,* 721

Nicholson, Francis, 577

Nicodemus, 16

Niemöller, Martin, 680, 681

Nietzsche, Friedrich, 661–62

Nigeria, 645, 726, 728

Nightingale, Florence, 598

Niklashausen, 331–32, 333, 363–64

Nikolai (Ivan Kasatkin), 641

Nikon, Patriarch, 665

Nixon, Richard, 715

Noah, 227, 646

Nobrega, Manuel de, 520

Norfolk, 461

Normandy, 206

Normans, 186, 218–19, 232, 235, 542

Norsemen, 486

Northumbria, 198, 202*f,* 203

Norway, 209, 210, 636, 719

Notre Dame (France), 244*f,* 265, 594, 595

Notre Dame University, 715

Novatian, 117

Nubians, 67, 186–87

Nuns, 144, 211, 270–72, 330, 418, 418*f,* 633, 661; Anabaptists and, 378; black Americans as, 605; during Crusades, 258, 264; Nazis and, 681, 691; witch-hunts and, 494

Oak of Thor, 202

Ochino, Bernardino, 440

Ockham, William, 363, 363*f*

Oecolampadius, Johannes, 375

Olaf Haraldsson, St., 210

Olaf Skötkonung, 210

Old Believers, 569, 665, 703

Old Cairo, 174

Old Testament, 19, 30, 107, 183; Crusaders and, 245–46; rejection of, 28, 112, 115, 119, 280, 574, 679

Oldcastle, John, 306–8

Oldenbarnevelt, J. van, 393

Oliveira, Fernão de, 544

Omar, 166, 167, *170,* 170–78, 171, 179

Omar II, 166

Orange, Prince of, 393, 459

Oratorians, 416

Oratory of Divine Love, 415

Ordination, 666, 713; in early church, 41; of homosexuals, 720; of women, 719–20

Origen, 46, 56, 64, 66, 100*f,* 104

Original Sin, 34, 57, 149; Virgin Mary and, 211

Orphanages, 424, 597

Orsini, Pietro, 312*f*

Orthodox Church, 111*f,* 725; emperors and, 213; Ivan III and, 427–28; Ivan the Terrible (IV) and, 429–30; Moslems and, 248; Paulicians and, 280; plundered in Crusades, *256,* 257, 258–59; Protestants and, 429–30; Roman *vs.,* 208, 210, 212–13, 225–26, 243–44, 259, 324–25, 430, 453; sects of, 665–69; in Serbia, 692; Turks and, 428–29; union of Roman and, 324–25; *vs.* Uniates, 657. *See also* Eastern church; Greek Orthodox Church; Russian Orthodox Church

Orthodoxy, 126, 127; Feast of, 211; heresy *vs.,* 99*f,* 110–12; Nestorius and, 125

Ory, Matthieu, 395

Osopov, Vladimir, 705

Ostian Way, 103

Ostrogoths, 150

Oswald (king), 201, 202

Ottaviani, Alfredo, 695

Otto I (Holy Roman Empire and Germany), 208, 215

Otto of Constance, 311

Ottoman Turks, 167, 263, 281, 428–29, 540, 634, 635

"Our Father" (Paternoster), 40, 281, 284, 303. *See also* Lord's Prayer

Outremer, 244, 249–50, 251, 261

Ovid, 485

Oxford Movement, 656

Pacelli, Eugenio, 679, *688, 690*

Pachomius, 131–34, 136

Pacific Islands, 631, 642, *643*

Paganism, in Nazism, 682, 687

Pagans, 28, 30, 34, 52, 64–65, 158, 159, 219, 492; as Christian converts, 54, 183, 191–221; Islam and, 163; reaction to Christian martyrs, 69–70, 74, *74,* 75; as term, 28*f;* witchcraft and, 485–86, 491–92

Paine, Thomas, 591–92

Pakistani Christians, 728, 730

Palaeomon, 131

Palestine, 168, 172, 220, 634, 728

Palestrina, Giovanni, 416

Palladius, St., 137, 200

Pallium, 196

Palm Sunday, 58, 467

Palmer, Phoebe, 713–14

Pantaenus, 553

Papias, 45

Papua New Guinea, 695

Papylus, 84

Paraguay, 524, 525–36

Paravas, 556

Parfaits, 282–84

Paris, Matthew, 255, 274, 288

Parma, 536

Parris, Samuel, 499

Parthenon, 108

Parthians, 7, 11

Pascal, Blaise, 437, 438, 564

Paschal II, Pope, 249*f*

Pashkov, A. V., 665

Pashkovites, 665

Passover, 7, 9, 12, 15, 57–58

Pasternak, Boris, 672

Patarene, 281

Patrick, St., *199,* 199–200

Patripassians, 120

Patteson, John Coleridge, 644

Paul, St., 21, 23–45, *24,* 24–28, 30–37, *38,*
    41, 53, 200; Acts of, 25*f;* burial site of,
    42; Constantine compared to, 89, 90,
    91; Epistles/letters of, 25, 44, 46, 277,
    416; Hitler and, 676, 679; mysticism
    and, 269, 270; Pentecostals and, 715;
    relics and, 327, 345; shrine of, 86,
    103

Paul III, Pope, 420, 421–22, 435, 440, 509

Paul IV, Pope, 411–12, 424, 432, 440–41,
    446

Paul of Samosata, 120–21

Paul of Thebes, 129, 130

Paul the Deacon, 486

Paul V, Pope, 564

Paul VI, Pope, 85*f,* 723, 724

Paulicians, 280

Paulinus, 198

Pavelić, Ante, 692

Payne, Daniel, 605

Paz, Matias de, 522

Peace of Augsburg, 398*f,* 425, 474

Peace of Westphalia, 477–78

Peking, 190

Pelagius, 149, 192, 392

Penda of Mercia, 198, 201

Penitentials, 487

Penn, William, 568, 572, 573, *581,* 581–82

Penry, John, 432

Pentateuch, 610

Pentecost, 20, *20,* 21, 33, 48, 58, 128

Pentecostalism, 33, 335

Pentecostals, 709, 713–14, 716, 726; in
    China, 700; in India, 726

"People of the Book," 164, 173

Pepin the Short, 362*f*

Peretti, Felice, 427

Perón, Juan and Evita, 709

Perpetua, 69, 82, 83, 157

Perpignan, synod at, 309

Perrault, Charles, 489*f*

Perry, Matthew, 562

Persecution: by Catholics, 397, 407–8, 426,
    427, 476, 574, 665–66, 692; of
    Catholics, 386–89, 394, 403, 408–9,
    425, 461–64, 577–78, 657, 665–66,
    685–86, 692, 697, 698, 704–5; in
    China, 190, 696–700, 727; of Chris-
    tians by other Christians, 105, 159,
    243–44, 258–59, 305, 379, 386–87,
    403, 407–8; of early Christians, ix, 9,
    23, 24*f, 32, 38,* 41, 51–54, 65, 69–71,
    70, 72, 76, 374, 485; of Jews, 13, 73,
    108, 225*f,* 229–30, 242, 249, 285,
    425–26, 442, 446, 665, 674–83, 722;
    of Mormons, 617, 620–23; by
    Moslems, 156, 163–64, 166, 167,
    171–72, 178, 181, 222, 225*f;* of
    Moslems, 240, 242, 249; of Protestants,
    407, 408, 425, 440, 450, 458, 476,
    574; in Soviet Union, 673–74, 704–5;
    in Vietnam, 566–67. *See also* Martyrs

Persians, 31, 126, 163–64, 168

Peru, 519–23, 525, 537, 708–9

Perugino, Pietro, 328

Peter, St., 10, 11, 19, 20, 22, 27, 32, 36, *38,*
    42*f;* 45, 46, 49, 53, 225, *326,* 327;
    burial site of, 42; crucifixion of, 41; as
    first bishop, 41, 63–64; legends about,
    50; Revelation of, 50; shrine of, 86

Peter, Young, 413

Peter Bartholomew, 235–36

Peter Martyr, St., 440

Peter of Alexandria, 89

Peter of Castelnau, 282, 283

Peter of Verona, 286

Peter the Great, 665

Peter the Hermit ("Little Peter"), 228, 229, 230, 231

Peter the Venerable, 251

"Peterloo massacre," 596*f*

Peterson, Jacob, 452

Petitjean, Father, 641

Petrarch, 299–300, 328

Petrucci, Cardinal, 344

Pharisees, 5, 6, 14, 26

Phileas, 84

Philip, John, 645

Philip II (Portugal), 538, 560

Philip II (Spain) , 407, 412, 418, 434, 456, 458–60, 462, 523

Philip III (Spain), 538

Philip of Hesse, 368, 369

Philip V (France), 293

Philippines, 289, 567, 631, 726, 728

Philippists, 393

Philo, 12, 13

Philpot, John, 411

Photius, 212

Picardy, and *Pikarti,* 321

Pico della Mirandola, 335

Picts, 196, 201

Piedmont, 280

Pietism, 557–58

Pilate, Pontius, 11–13, 16, 37, 47, 110; Acts of, 49, 50; Duke Louis compared to, 317; legends about, 49; Memoranda of, 89

Pilgrimages, 104–5, 140, 163, 413, 427, 657; of Arabs, 160; in Counter-Reformation, 416; Crusades and, 229; French, 215; Jubilee and, 327; to monasteries, 137; "of Grace," 404, 408; as penance, 227; to Wilsnack, 309

"Pilgrims" (as term), 569*f*

Pima, 534

Pimen, Patriarch, 694

Pisa, Council of, 309, 314

Pitirim, Metropolitan, 669

Pius II, Pope, 264, 335–36, 344, 543*f*

Pius IV, Pope, 430

Pius V, Pope, 426–27, 460

Pius VII, Pope, 536, 655

Pius IX, Pope, 655–57, 659, 660–61

Pius X, Pope, 721, 723

Pius XI, Pope, 678–79, 683, 686, 722

Pius XII, Pope, 660*f,* 687–88, *688,* 690–91, 695, 721

Pizarro, Francisco, 505, 519

Plato, 29, 59, 106, 112*f,* 113, 403

Platonism, 146

Pliny the Younger, 51–53, 54, 82, 320

Plotinus, 146

Plymouth Brethren, 629, 649, 665, 696*f*

Pobedonostsev, Constantine, 665

Pocahontas, *579,* 579–80

Polanco, Juan de, 420

Poland, 207, 210, 220, 221, 457, 503, 665, 676, 691; Jesuits in, 473, 536; John Paul II in, *724;* Solidarity movement in, 700–701

Polding, J. B., 642

Pole, Reginald, 408–9, 410–12, 422

Polk, Leonidas, 606

Polycarp, 50, 60, 80–81, 82, 113; cult of, 85

Polygamy, 360, 376, 379, 383*f,* 610, 615, 616, 620, 621, 623–24, *624*

Pomare (Tahiti), 643

Pompey, 3, 11

Ponce de Leon, Don Juan, 450, 451

Ponce de Leon, Juan, 505

Pontus, Evragius, 71, 137

"Poor Clares," 274

Popes/papacy, 19, 97, 328–29, 655–61; Americas and, 505–10, *521,* 536; anti-, 117, 213, 218, 326, 363*f;* as Antichrist, 298, 307, 310, 352, 410, 423; Augustine and, 50; authority of, 423; under Constantine, 101–2; depravity of, 213–14; early, 67; Erasmus and, 338; in France, 298–99; friars and, 275; Great Schism and, 301, 309–10; Henry III and, 216, 420; Henry VIII and, 399–405; Hus and, 309, 310, 325; icons and, 210–11; infallibility of, 192, 313, 651, 659–60, 721; Kempis and, 331; Latin replacing Greek with, 182; loss of prestige of, 191–92; Luther and,

344, 350, 352, 361–62, 420; as martyrs, 71, 76, 158–59; Michelangelo's
view of, 343; Oldcastle and, 307; Orthodox church and, 213; powers of,
217, 312; protestantism and, 405;
protests against, 279–80, 363; rejection
of, 359; Savonarola and, 335, 337;
"she-", 214; spending by, 299–300;
syphilis and, 388; as term, 63; traitor,
71; Wycliffe and, 296, 298, 300–304,
302, 310, 325
Popieluszko, Jerzy, 700–701, *701*
Poplicani, 281
Popolare, Partido, 678–79
Porcus, William, 260, 261
Porette, Margaret, 330
Portuguese, 150, 187, 188, 481, 635; in
Africa, 540; in Americas, 505–6, 507,
520–21, 528, 529, 530; in Malabar,
553–54, *554,* 555; slavery and, 538,
543*f,* 544
Positivism, 727
"Possessors" *vs.* "Non-Possessors," 427
Pothinus, 67
Pounds, John, 601
Poverty (as virtue), 329–30, 363*f*
Prague, 207, 220, 230, 309, 310, 312,
321–22, 366–67, *475,* 476; Jesuits in,
473
"Praying movement," 726
Predestination, 19, 34, 110, 149–50, 391–93
Presbyterians, 398, 465, 468, 472, 654,
654*f;* Civil War and, 605–6; in Colo-
nial America, 575; as missionaries, 636,
638, 640, 649; Native Americans and,
607; slavery and, 551
Presbyters, 36, 41, 60, 62, 63, 111
Prester John, 189
Priests: American Indians and, 511; celibacy
of (*See* Celibacy); under Constantine,
98, 100; as Crusaders, 258–59; in early
church, 62–63; first black American,
605; homosexuals as, 720; Orthodox *vs.*
Roman Catholic, 225, 243; seminaries
for, 423, 426; war and, 243; women as,
719, 720
Prignano, Bartolomeo, 301
Printing press, 325, 340–41, 503

Prisca, 115–16
Priscillian, 86–88
Prison reform, 599
Proano, Bishop, 709
Prohibition Amendment, 713
Propaganda, the, 426, 431, 432
Prophetesses, 115–16, 321
Prosser, Gabriel, 551
Prostitutes, 388–89, 424, 426, 597, 719
Protestantism, 398, 406; business ethic in,
39091; Calvin and, 385–86, 388;
converts to, 458; on marriage, 389;
papacy *vs.,* 405; science and, 438; sects
of, 398, 591, 654*f*
Protestants: anti-Semitism of, 677; Bay
Colony, 569–70, 579; census on, 654*f;*
charismatic, 715; Darwin and, 653–54;
Hitler and, 678–80; in India, 557–58;
Jews and, 446; liberal, 695; as missionaries, 557–58, 567, 633–50, 642, 644,
709; in North America, 568–92; Oldcastle and Elizabethan, 308; persecution
and (*See* Martyrs; Persecution) ; reconciliation of Catholics with, 422–23;
relics and, 211–12, 286*f,* 311*f;* slavery
and, 538, 540, 544–45; Spinoza and,
439; splits among, 370, 376; statistics
on, 725–26; as term, 370; at University
of Paris, 420; at Wilsnack, 309*f. See also*
Catholics, Protestants *vs.*
Prudentius, Aurelius, 109
Prussians, 220, 676
Prynne, William, 467, 468
Ptolemaic empire, 7
Ptolemy, 327
Puerto, Nicolas de, 523
Purgatory, 305, 318, 361, 413; in Dante,
319
Puritanism, 117, 570; among Boers, 646; of
Calvin, 384; in early church, 65; of
Savonarola, 335
Puritans: in Colonial America, 573, 586–87;
in England, 432, 461, 464–68, *469,*
498–99

"Q," 33*f,* 45*f*
Qalawun, 262

Quakers, 359, 383*f,* 398, 577, 582, 590, 654*f;* in Colonial America, 569, 572–73, 576; in England, 471–72, 473; prison reform by, 599; Siberian, 668; slavery and, 537, 545, 548

Quartodecimans, 58

Quelle, 33*f,* 45*f*

Quetzalcoatl, 514–15, 516

Qumran, 36

Rabelais, François, *433*

Racism, 706; of Nazis, 678, 683, 688

Radbertus, Paschasius, 302

Radstock, Lord, 665

Ragged Schools, 601

Raikes, Richard, 600

Raleigh, Walter, 507*f*

Ramabai, 637

Ramses III, 108

Ranavalona, 632

Ranters, 471, 472

Raphael, 329, 342, 343

Raskolniks, 665–66

Rasputin, Grigory, 664, 669

Ratzinger, Joseph, 725

Rauschenbusch, Walter, 597,

Ravaillac, François, 457

Ravenna, 191, 194, 214, 218

Raymond IV of Toulouse, 282, 283

Raymond of Penyaforte, 248

Raymond of Saint-Gilles, 243

Raymond of Toulouse, 236, 238, *238,* 239

Raymond of Tripoli, 253

Reagan, Ronald, 717

Recantation, 284, 294, 306, 317, 324, 369, 409–10; recanting of, 410

Reccared, 195

Reconquista, 186, 226*f,* 249, 441

Reconstruction, 606

Recusants, 460, 461, 463, 569, 576

Reeb, James, 705

Reeve, John, 471

Reformation, 356, 366, 382–83, 384, 730; Counter-, 415, 422–23, 439–40; in England, 398–99; extremes of, 376; priests during, 356–57; Waldensians and, 280; witch-hunts and, 490, 503

Regula Magistri, 136*f*

Reid, John, 497

Relics, 85–86, 105, 164, 181, 192, 196, 286*f,* 305, 327, 347, 376; Black Death and, 290; Crusades and, 231, *235,* 236, 259; of flagellants, 292; Protestants and, 211–12, 286*f,* 311*f;* rejection of, 371, 373; scandal of, 345–46; trade in, 211

Religious right, 717

Remonstrants, 393

Renaissance, 325, 329, 334, 339; Bible and, 354; slavery in, 542

Requerimiento, 504–5, 507, 508, 512, 519; protest against, 521

Revivals, 33, 586–87, 602, 653, 713–17

Rheims, 216, 265, 269; Synod of, 215

Rhodes, Alexander de, 566

Ribera, Juan de, 445

Ricci, Lorenzo, 536

Ricci, Matteo, 562–63, 564, 565, 640

Richard the Lionheart (England), 254

Richards, Franklin D., 621

Richelieu, Cardinal, 445, 474

Richental, Ulrich, 310–11, 312, 314*f,* 315, 316

Ridley, Nicholas, 409

Ridolfi, Roberto, 461

Ripoll, Cayetano, 441*f*

"Robber council," 126

Robert II (France), 488

Robert le Bougre, 285

Robert the Monk, 222*f*

Roberts, Issachar, 638

Roberts, Oral, 716, 717

Robertson, Pat, 717

Robespierre, Maximilien, 594, *595*

Robinson, John, 466

Robison, James, 717, 718

Rock of Tarik, 185

Roderick, 185–86

Roger, 228, 249

Rogers, John, 407

Rolfe, John, 579–80

Roman Catholic Church: union of Orthodox Church and, 324–25; *vs.* Orthodox Church (*See* Orthodox Church, Roman *vs.*). *See also* Catholics; Church of Rome

Roman Empire, 7, 30–32, 37–38, 127; Christian converts in, 59; fall of, 150–51; games of, 73, *74,* 79–81, 151; Islam and, 162–64; Jews in, 11, 25, 42–43, 47; religion of, 17, 28, 75, 83*f,* 107–8; women in, 35

Romania, 259, 635

Rome, ix, 3–4, 192–93, 194, 427; church of (*See* Church of Rome); Eastern religions in, 28–29; Jews in, 446; plundering of, 420–21; return of papacy to, 300; Synod of, 487

Romero, Oscar, 709–11, *711*

Roncalli, Angelo, 312*f*

Rosary, 457, 490, 686

Rose, Thomas, 477

"Rose of Lima," 523–24

Ross, Frederick, 606

Rothmann, Bernt, 377, 380, 381, 382, 383*f*

Rousseau, Jean-Jacques, 594

Royal Society, 439–40

Rubios, Palacios, 507

Rule of Truth, 55

Runkelers, 281

Rus, 208–9

Russell, Charles Taze, 625–26, *626*

Russia, 210, 427–28, 641, 663–74; cults in, 665–69, 704; czars of, 213, 325, 429, 657, 664–65, 669; emigrants from, 659; Jesuits in, 536; Jews in, 444*f,* 446; missionaries from, 635; Moslems in, 728

Russian Orthodox Church, 427–28, 429, 453, 657, 663–64, 692; Communists and, 669–74, 694; Jews and, 446; missionaries from, 641; schisms in, 665–69, 704; sects of, 703–4; Solzhenitsyn and, 694; Tolstoy and, 668

Rutgers, 588

Sabas, St., 164

Sabbath, 39; Puritan, 467; Saturday, 187

Sabbatical, 327*f*

Sabellius, 119–20

Sacraments, 110, 399*f,* 423, 461; Henry VIII and, 406; heresy and, 114; Lollards and, 305; torture and, 451–52

Sacred College, 344, 422

Sacred Heart of Jesus, 658–59

Sadducees, 5, 7–8, 9, 20

Saints: in Americas, 523–24; Gregory, Pope, and, 192; images of (*See* Icons/images); martyrs as, 85; "of the black slaves," 544; patron, 104, 274*f,* 417, 512, 524, 663; praying to, 413; relics of (*See* Relics); veneration of, 85–86

St. Bartholomew Day massacre, 456, 457

St. Basil's Cathedral, 429, *429*

St. Denis Cathedral, 267, 269

St. Lambert's Church, 383, *383*

St. Peter's Basilica, 42*f,* 103, 190, 326, 342–43; funding of new, 344, 346–47

St. Sophia's Basilica, 257, 258, 263; changed to mosque, 264, 328

Saladin, 187, 228, 253–54, 255

Salazar, Alonso de, 495

Sale, Richard, 471

Salm, Nicholas von, 428

Salvador, Vicente de, 521

Salvation Army, 602–3

Salzburg, 207, 569, 574

Sampson, Agnes, 493

San Ramón, Juan de, 522

San Sebastiano, 86

Sánchez, Alonso, 560

Sanhedrin, 11, 12, 23, 317

Santiago, Military Order of, 250

"Sapporo band," 641

Saracens, 186, 247, 250, 262; as term, 169*f*

Saragossa Synod, 87

Sasse, Martin, 683

Satan/devil, 37, 83*f,* 84, *146,* 152, 286, 483–84, 486, 487, 494, 498, 502; heresy and, 287; Manichaean beliefs about, 118, 119; Paul's doctrine on, 64; pope as, 284, 285

Saturninus, 65, 78, 82

Saturus, 83

Sauma, 190

Savonarola, Girolamo, *334,* 334–38

Savoy, 292

Sawtrey, William, 306

Saxons, 154, 196, 198, 203, 220

Saxony, 208, 346, 474, 493, 679

Scandinavians, 204–6, 209–10, 220, 460

Schall, Johann Adam, 563, 564
Schirach, Baldur von, 680
Schmid, Konrad, 292–94
Schola Cantorum, 194
Scholarius, George, 324f
School prayer, 718
Schreiber, Thomas, 490
Schwartz, Friedrich, 558
Schwenkfeld, Caspar, 575, 590
Scintilla, 270
Scopes, John Thomas, 654
Scot, Reginald, 493
Scotland, 196, 308, 396, 413, 460, 465;
    missionaries from, 640, 646; Salvation
    Army in, *603;* witch-hunts in, 480–81,
    496–97, 502, 503
Scots, 201, 229, 468–70
Scudder, John, 636
Second Coming, 22, 47
Second Vatican Council, 721–22
Seekers, 471, 571
Segura, Cardinal, 687
Sejanus, Lucius, 13
Seleucid empire, 7, 14, 46, 73, 246
Self-Baptist, 466
Self-castration, 66, 213
Seljuk Turks, 222–24, 231, 233–34, 243
Selwyn, George Augustus, 642, 643
Seneca, 29, 79, 385
Sepp, Antonio, 528
Serapis, temple of, 108
Serbia/Serbs, 207, 263, 325, 428, 635, 692,
    728
Sergey, Metropolitan, 671, 692
Sergius, church of St., 66f
Sergius III, Pope, 214
Sergius IV, Pope, 225f
Serra, Juniper, 535–36
Servetus, Michael, 394–95, 396, 432
Seventh-Day Adventists, 39f, 609, 624–25,
    665, 710, 718
Severus, Septimius, 65, 69
Severus, Sulpicius, 87
Seville, 197, 226f, 542
Sex, 35–36, 725
Seymour, Jane, 404
Shadwell, Thomas, 416
Shaftesbury, Lord, 597, 598

Shakers, 588–89, *589*
Shakespeare, William, 306, 409, 486
Shang Ti, 638
Sharp, Granville, 549, 598
Shaw, Christian, 496–98
Shaw, George Bernard, 674f
Sheba, Queen of, 159–60
Shelkov, Vladimir, 704
Shembe, Isaiah, 726
Shepherd, Thomas, 580
Shepherd of Hermas, 50f
Shipman, William, 551
Siberia, 189, 207, 635, 664, 666, 674f, 704
Siberian Quakers, 668
Sicily, 186, 194, 226–27, 228, 290–91, 446,
    695; Moslem converts in, 249
Sierra Leone, 549, 598, 606, 649
Sigfrid, St., 210
Sigismund (Holy Roman Empire), 310, 311,
    320, 321, 323
Silveira, Gonçalo da, 645
Silverius, Pope, 191–92
Silvester III, Pope, 215
Simaes, Frei Garcia, 539
Simeon the Stylite, 139–42, *141*
Simon, Father (Russia), *703*
Simon, Richard, 610f
Simons, Menno, 356–57, 361, 383f
Simony, 216, 298, 313, 344
Siricius, 102
Sisters of Charity, 417
Sistine Chapel, *326,* 327, 329, 343, 421;
    Paul IV and, 425, 426
Sitting Bull, 608, 609
Sixtus II, Pope, 76
Sixtus IV, Pope, 329, 341, 345, 441, 443
Sixtus V, Pope, 427
Skefsrund, Lars Olsen, 636
Skoptsy, 666–67
Slavata, William, 475–76
Slave ships, 545–47, 551
Slaves, 202, *541;* African, 510, 521, 537–52,
    541, 543, 544, 551, 552, 604–6,
    646–47; Angle, 196; under Charle-
    magne, 204; under Constantine, 97;
    cotton gin and, 550; Cuban, 552; in
    early church, 60–62; emancipation of,
    548; Indian, 509, 510, 522, 526, 537,

538, 543; Lavigerie and, 636; Moslem, 445, 538, 540, 542, 555; in North Africa, 183–84; papal bulls regarding, 509; returned to Africa, 549, 606, 649; in Scandinavia, 209; Slavs as, 207; white Christian, 542

Slavs, 206–8, 219, 281, 541

Slovaks, 702

Smith, John, 579–80

Smith, Joseph, 19, *611,* 611–17, 620

Smith, William, 587

Smyth, John, 466

Social reform, 595–609

Socialism, 686

Society of Jesus, 418, 420, 431

Society of the Divine Word, 633

Socotra, 188–89

Socrates, 29

Sojourner Truth, 606

Solinus, 200

Solomon, 6, 159–60

Solomon's Temple, 6, 171, *238, 239*

Solzhenitsyn, Alexander, 694

Somaschi, 416

Song of Songs/Solomon, 183, 270, 387

Soong, Charles Jones, 639

Sophia, St., 114, 212

Sophronius, 169–73

Sorcery, 189

Sorsky, Nil, 427–28

Soto, Domingo de, 543

Southwell, Robert, 462–63

Soviet Union, 671, 691, 692–93, 694, 704

Spain, 157, 185, 186, 195, 197, 226, 250, 399, 417–18, 458–59, 460, *685;* Americas and, 506–22, 528–33, 536; censorship in, 434, 440; fascism/communism in, 683–87; Japan and, 560; Philippines and, 567; slavery and, 538, 552; Suevi in, 150; witch-hunts in, 481, 494, 502

Spalding, John Lancaster, 597

"Spanish fury," 459

Spanish Inquisition, 441–54, *449,* 455, 462, 481, 494–95, 498, 503; in Malabar, 553–54, *554;* principal tortures in, 447–48

Spanish Netherlands, 461, 462

Spartacus, 14

"Speaking with tongues," 33, 667, 714

Sphrantzes, George, 263

Spinoza, Benedictus, 438–39

Spiridovich, Alexander, 667–68

Spiritualism, 626–27

Spirituals, 329–30

Sprenger, James, 490

Stalin, Joseph, x, 670–73, 674, 688, 692, 702, 721

Stanley, Henry, 647–48, 648

Stanton, Elizabeth Cady, 719

Stations of the Cross, 276

Stein, Edith, 691

Stephanus, Robert, 360

Stephen, St. (in Book of Acts), 22–23, 73, 247

Stephen, St. (István), 208

Stephen II, Pope, 362f

Stephen of Blois, 232f

Stephen VI, Pope, 214

Stephen VII, Pope, 214f

Stephen VIII, Pope, 213

Stepinac, Aloysius, 692

Stigmata, 275

Stoicism, 29–30, 79, 137

Storch, Niklas, 366

Strasbourg, 377; cathedral at, 265, 292

Stringfellow, Thornton, 550

Strong, Philip, 695

Stundists, 665

Stylites, 140–41

Sublapsarianism, 393f

Sudanese Christians, 728

Suetonius, 39

Suevi, 150

Suger of St. Denis, 269

Suleiman, 428, 542

Sully, 457

Sun Yat-sen, 639

Sunday, 305, 467

Sunday, Billy, 713

Sunday school, 599–600, *600*

Supralapsarianism, 393f

Susán, Diego de, 443

Susanna, 443

Suslov, Ivan, 667

Swabia, 218, 490, 491

Sweden, 209, 210, 220, 423, 476, 636, 719; witch-hunts in, 481, 495–96
"Sweyn the Sacrificer," 210
Switzerland, 67, 477; witch-hunts in, 481, 503; Zwingli and, 370–76, *371*
Sylvester I, Pope, 121, 362
Syphilis, 388
Syrian Christians, 138, 157, 158, 172, 245, 657
Syrian Jacobites, 127. *See also* Jacobites

Taborites, 321–23, 366
Tacitus, ix, 28, 38, 73, 206, 248
Tafurs, 236
T'ai P'ing, 638
Taiwan, 567
Talmage, T. DeWitt, 653
Tamerlane, 167, 189, 263
Tancred, 237, 238, 239
Tang, Dominic, 697
Tarik, 185
Tartars, 189, 635
Tatian, 64–65, 304
Taufaahua, 643
Taylor, James Hudson, 639, 696
Taylor, Zachary, 619
Tebaldeschi, 300–301
Telemachus, 84–85
Television, 716–17, 721
Ten Commandments, 40, 456
Teresa, Mother, 719
Teresa of Ávila, 272, 418
Tertullian, x, 25f, 29, 49, 55, 64, 65, 70, 116, 119, 124, 152, 182; on martyrs, x, 69, 71, *74;* on women, 36, 60
Tetzel, Johann, 346–47, 349
Teutonic Order, 220, 321
Teutons, 202, 204–6, 486; Hitler and, 682
Thaddeus, 31
Thailand, 631, 632
Thaumaturgus, Gregory, 77
Theban Legion, 67
Theodora, 191, 214, 280
Theodore of Mopsuestia, 125f, 182–83
Theodoret, 138–39, 140, 141–42, 182f
Theodosius, 107–8, 109, 123, 126
Theophanes, 185

Theophilus, 486
Theophlyacts, 214
"Theotokos," 125, *125,* 126, 182f
Thérèse, St., 658
Thessaly, 263
Thomas, Hugh, 685
Thomas, John, 643
Thomas, St. ("doubting"), 31, 48, 188, 346, 553
Thomson, James, 546
Thomson, William, 604–5
Thoros, 234
Thrace, 280
"Three Chapters," 182, 192
Three Self Patriotic Movement (TSPM), 696–97, 699
Throckmorton, Francis, 461–62
Thuringia, 295, 368, 677, 683
Ti-yu, James, 640
Tiberius, 4, 8, 11, 13, 37
Tiepolo, 430
Tikhon, Metropolitan, 670, 671
Tilak, Marayan Vaman, 637
Tillich, Paul, 713
Tilly, Count, 476, 477
Timothy (Nestorian), 189
Tiridates, 90
Tiso, Josef, 702
Titian, 336
Tito, Marshal, 692
Titus (Roman Empire), 42–43, 45
Toledo, 186, 226, 249, 293, 444, 447, 487, 687; Council of, 249
Tolstoy, Leo, 664, 668
Torquemada, Tomás, 442, 443, 446, 447
Torres, Camilo, 708, 709
Torture: denounced, 286; of early Christians, *70,* 70–71, 77–85, *82;* in papal bull, 278–79; principal methods of, 447–48; sacraments and, 451–52. *See also* Martyrs; Persecution
Toulouse, 277, 282, 456
Tournai, 292
Tournon, Charles Maillard de, 565
Tours, 203–4
Tower of David, 238
"Tradition, the," 55
Trajan, 174

Tranquebar, 558

Transubstantiation, 302–3, 313, 374, 405, 413, 423

Trapezuntius, 325, 327

Treaty of Lausanne, 324

Trent, Council of, 354f, 423–24

Tridentine Index, 432

Trier, 227

Trinidada, Pedro da, 556

Tripoli, 244, 245, 247, 253, 262

Trotsky, Leon, 670–71

Truchsess, Gehard, 474

True and Free Adventists, 704

True Orthodox Church, 704

Tsai-tsung, 189

Tucker, Henry St. George, 641

Tunisia, 182, 186

Tunstall, Cuthbert, 357f

Tupis, 520

Turkestan, 150, 189

Turkopoles, 250

Turks, 57f, 190, 324, 329; Crusades and, 222–24, 231, 233–34, *234,* 236, 243, 252; missionaries and, 634–35. *See also* Ottoman Turks

Turner, Henry McNeal, 606

Turner, J. B., 614

Turner, Nat, 551

Tutu, Desmond, 708

Tyndale, William, 357–58, 403

Tyre, 262

Tzimisces, John, 280

Uchimuru, 641

Uganda, 648, 728

Ulrich, 85f

Ultramontanism, 656, 657

Unamuno, Miguel de, 670

Underwood family, 640

Uniates, 430, 657, 665

Union of Brest, 430

Unitarians, 705; on Trinity, *120,* 121

United Pentecostal Church, 715

United States: civil rights in, 705–6; civil war, 605–6; colonial era, 568–592; constitution of, 591–92; Darwinism denounced in, 653–54; denominations in, 654f; missionaries from, 631–40 *passim;* Moral Majority in, 717–18; new sects in, 610–28; revivalism in, 715–17; Salvation Army in, 604; slaves in, 549f, 604–6; states in (including colonial era): Alabama, 606, 717; Alaska, 641; Arizona, 533–34, 608, 609; California, 533–36, 618, 641, 714, 718; Connecticut, 588; Dakotas, 607, 608; Florida, 505, 718; Georgia, 575; Illinois, 596, 597, 614–17; Kentucky, 604; Louisiana, 605, 606; Maryland, 576–78, 589, 606, 722; Massachusetts, 548, 569, 571, 579, 580, 586, 589, 625; Missouri, 613; Nevada, 608; New Hampshire, 627; New Jersey, 548, 586, 587; New York, 548, 588, 590, 591, 611, 624, 627; North Carolina, 549; Ohio, 613; Oklahoma, 607, 716; Oregon, 607; Pennsylvania, 545, 548, 573–75, 581, 590, 605, 625; Rhode Island, 545, 548, 572, 580, 588; South Carolina, 549, 586, 604, 717; Tennessee, 654; Texas, 533, 626, 718; Utah, 618–23; Virginia, 545, 550, 568, 577, 579, 588, 591, 717; war of independence, 590–91; witch-hunts in, 499–502

Urban II, Pope, 222–28, *223,* 239, 244, 249f

Urban V, Pope, 299

Urban VI, Pope, 301

Ursinus, 101–2

Ursis, Sebastiano de, 563

Ursulines, 494

Uruguay, 525f

Usamah ibn Munqidh, 251–52

Usury, 390–91, 450

Uthman, 167

Utraquism/Utraquists, 321, 322, 323

Valdemar the Victorious (Denmark), 220

Valdes, Peter (Waldo), 279–80

Valencia, 248, 336, 442, 451; Moors of, 445

Valens, 150

Valentinian, 100, 101

Valentinian II, 102, 145, 151

Valentinian III, 154
Valentinus, 114
Valerian, 75, 76, 77
Valerius, Adrian, 459
Valignano, Alessandro, 560, 562
Valla, Lorenzo, 362
Valtellina, 476
Vandals, 150, *151,* 152–53, 154, 182, 183, 191
Vanderkamp, Johannes, 645
Vane, Henry, 571
Vanozza, Rosa, 336
Varro, Marcus Terentius, 75*f*
Vassilyev, General, 666
Vatican, 326, 476, 660; communism and, 683, *688,* 691, 695; fascism and, 678–79, *688,* 691
Vatican Bank, 724
Vatican Council, 192, 659
Vatican Hill, 42, 103
Vatican Library, 325
Vega, Lope de, 445
Veláquez de Cuellar, Diego, 512, 517
Venefas, Miguel, *535*
Veniaminov, John, 641
Verbiest, Ferdinand, 563–64
Vercelli, Battista de, 344
Verdun, 204
Vermigli, Peter Martyr, 440
Veronica, St., 296, 327
Verwoed, Hendrik, 707
Vesey, Denmark, 551
Vespasian, 42
Viana, Joachim de la, 530
Vicenzo, Padre, 188–89
Victor Emmanuel II, 655–56, 660
Victor of Vita, St., 155, 182, 232
Vieira, António, 539
Vietnam, 566–67, 698
Vigilius, Pope, 182–83, 191, 192
Vikings, 204–6, *205,* 209
Viilehardouin, 257, 258
Vincent de Paul, 417, 542
Vincent Ferrer, St., 301, 442
Virgil, 318, 319
Virgilius, 207
Virgin Mary, 103, 126, 182*f,* 709, 728; adoration/veneration of, 19, 125, *125;*
Annunciation of, 126, 576; in apocryphal gospels, 47, 48–49; Assumption of, 48, 49, 211, 660, 721; cult of, 48–49, 60, 126, 292, 657–58; in Dante, 319; flagellants and, 292; icons and, 210, 211; Immaculate Conception of, 110, 211, 658, 659; as "Mother of God," 125, 126; in Nicene creed, 123; as perpetual virgin, 36, 48; visions of, 288, 332, 657, 658, *658*
Virgin of the Sorrows, 292
Visconti, Ignacio, 528–29
Visigoths, 150, 154, 185, 195, 197
Vitoria, Francisco de, 243*f,* *518,* 521–22
Viuellot, Louis, 661
Vives, Juan Luis, 434
Vladimir, St., 208–9, 663
Vogelweide, Walther von der, 255
Voltaire, 594–95

Waddan, 183
Walburga, 203
Waldensians, 279–80
Walker, David, 551
Wallenstine, Albrecht, 477
Walloons, 458, 477
Walpurga, St., 492
Walpurgisnight, 492
Walter the Penniless (Sans-Avoir), 229
Warneck, Gustav, 649
Washington, George, 592
Waterhouse, Agnes, 498
Watrin, François, 585
Wedgwood, C. V., 477
Wedgwood, Josiah, 549
Weert, Johann, 477
Welldon, J. E. C., 631*f*
Wellhausen, Julius, 610*f*
Wenceslas (Bohemia), 320–21
Wends, 219–20
Wenzao, Han, 700
Wenzhou, 727
Wesley, John, 412, *541,* 547, 586–87, 590, 714
Wesleyan revival, 602
Wesleyans, 393*f,* 598*f*